Introduction to Forensic and Criminal Psychology

Visit the *Introduction to Forensic and Criminal Psychology*, fourth edition Companion Website at **www.pearsoned.co.uk/howitt** to find valuable **student** learning material including:

- Multiple choice questions to test your learning
- Essay questions to give you further practice at exam-style questions
- Guidance on answering essay questions, to help you maximise your marks
- Annotated further reading to help you explore topics in more depth
- Information about becoming a forensic psychologist to help you plan for the future
- Audio interviews with researchers in the field to help you keep up to date with topics of interest
- Annotated links to other useful websites
- Interactive online flashcards that allow the reader to check definitions against the key terms during revision
- An online glossary to explain key terms

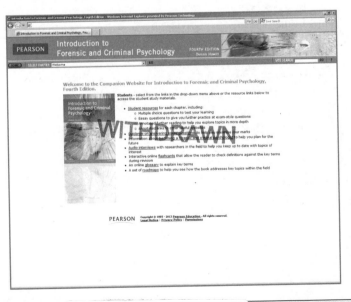

Introduction to Forensic and Criminal Psychology

4th Edition

Dennis Howitt Loughborough University

PEARSON

Harlow, England • London • New York • Boston • San Francisco • Toronto • Sydney • Auckland • Singapore • Hong Kong
Tokyo • Seoul • Taipei • New Delhi • Cape Town • São Paulo • Mexico City • Madrid • Amsterdam • Munich • Paris • Milan

Pearson Education Limited
Edinburgh Gate
Harlow
Essex CM20 2JE
England

and associated Companies throughout the world

Visit us on the World Wide Web at:
www.pearson.com/uk

First published 2002
Second edition published 2006
Third edition published 2009
Fourth edition published 2011

© Pearson Education Limited 2012

ISBN 978-0-273-73621-9

British Library Cataloguing-in-Publication Data
A catalogue record for this book is available from the British Library

Library of Congress Cataloging-in-Publication Data
Howitt, Dennis.
   Introduction to forensic and criminal psychology / Dennis Howitt. – 4th ed.
    p. cm.
   Includes bibliographical references and indexes.
   ISBN 978-0-273-73621-9 (pbk.)
   1. Criminal psychology.   2. Forensic psychology.   I. Title.
   HV6080.H69 2012
   364.3–dc23

                      2011038645

10 9 8 7 6 5 4 3 2 1
15 14 13 12 11

Typeset in 9.5/12pt Minion by 35
Printed by Ashford Colour Press Ltd., Gosport

To the continued memory of Professor Marie Jahoda who died in 2001. I have a big personal debt. Not only did she let me study on the psychology degree course she had set up at Brunel University, but she showed me that some things in life are worth getting angry about.

Brief contents

Contents

Contents

Contents

Supporting resources

Visit **www.pearsoned.co.uk/howitt** to find valuable online resources

Companion Website for students

- Multiple choice questions to test your learning
- Essay questions to give you further practice at exam-style questions
- Guidance on answering essay questions to help you maximise your marks
- Annotated further reading to help you explore topics in more depth
- Information about becoming a forensic psychologist to help you plan for the future
- Audio interviews with researchers in the field to help you keep up to date with topics of interest
- Annotated links to other useful websites
- Interactive online flashcards that allow the reader to check definitions against the key terms during revision
- An online glossary to explain key terms

Also: The Companion Website provides the following features:

- Search tool to help locate specific items of content
- E-mail results and profile tools to send results of quizzes to instructors
- Online help and support to assist with website usage and troubleshooting

For more information please contact your local Pearson Education sales representative or visit **www.pearsoned.co.uk/howitt**

List of figures, tables and boxes

Figures

Tables

Boxes

Guided tour

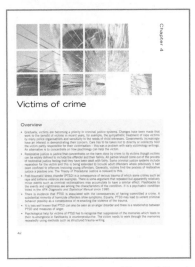

The **overview** gives an outline of the topics discussed in the chapter.

Key concept boxes highlight important terms and concepts introduced in the text.

Controversy boxes focus on issues that are sensitive or controversial, and the debate surrounding them.

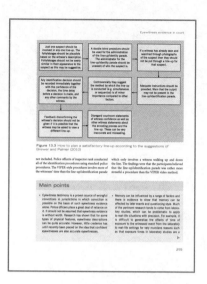

Examples of **Forensic psychology in action** offer a chance to find out about forensic and criminal psychology in the real world.

Main points at the end of each chapter provide a recap of the topics discussed.

Further reading suggests sources of more information on the topics discussed. Additional suggestions are provided on the website accompanying the book.

Guided tour of the website

Introduction to Forensic and Criminal Psychology is accompanied by an interactive website, where you can learn more about the topics, test your knowledge and find links to other interesting sites.

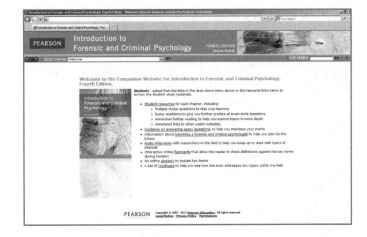

Listen to **audio interviews** with researchers in the field and find out more about topics of interest.

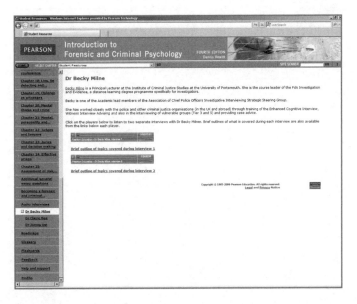

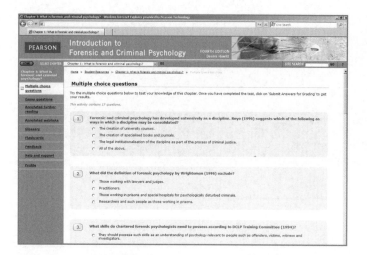

Test yourself and prepare for exams with each chapter's **essay questions** and **multiple choice questions**.

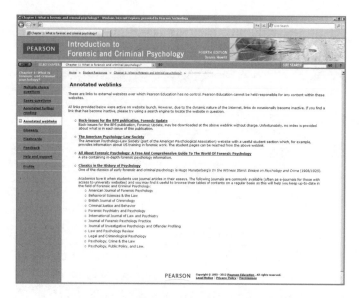

Find links to additional reading and websites on relevant topics with the suggested **weblinks**.

Preface

Revising *Introduction to Forensic and Criminal Psychology* for its 4th edition seems very different from the previous editions. The last decade has seen tremendous advances in the field – there have been massive changes and, suddenly, the underlying confidence in the theory, research and practice that many of us had has been rewarded. To be sure, this is partly the consequence of the general good health and vigour of the parent discipline of psychology but there is more to it than that. Forensic and Criminal Psychology is a hybrid field which prospers from the fact that it is a synthesis of the theoretical, practical and the empirical in a way which until now has been rare in the history of psychology. Probably the biggest disappointment is that Forensic and Criminal Psychology has not developed as strongly as a joint venture of the disciplines of psychology and the law as one might have hoped. The engaging interaction between psychologists and lawyers has been replaced by psychologists being much more sophisticated about the law than they ever were. Maybe this is just a different way of achieving the same end. Certainly, forensic and criminal psychologists need a strong understanding of the law to make their research and other work fully effective.

The task of writing this textbook has changed markedly over the four editions. The very first edition preceded the rapid growth in the teaching of Forensic and Criminal Psychology. It was a tentative venture in that some felt that there was not a clear need at the time for a textbook. Forensic and Criminal Psychology was not being extensively taught around the year 2000. But the first edition was perfectly on time and coincided with

the start of the rapid growth of teaching in the field. In a sense, the first edition had nothing to copy from. There were good books on psychology and criminal behaviour but forensic psychology was more than this and, to an extent, different from this. It was about psychology working for all aspects of the criminal justice system. So the first edition was my attempt to define what was good and stimulating about the field. Ideas for chapters came from conference symposiums, books, and what was being published in journals on forensic and criminal psychology. Inevitably there was an imbalance since significant topics had been paid little attention by researchers and practitioners did not always define what was important in their work clearly enough. So it was a struggle, at times, to fill some of the chapters. Gradually this has changed. The rise in teaching and the growth of research tend to go closely together. As an increasing amount of good research has been carried out in the field, the range and interest of material available to teach students has become greater.

It is important to ask just what should be in a textbook of this sort. I am not thinking about topics here but what it is about the content of forensic and criminal psychology which beginners should know about. It would be a hopelessly ambitious task for a textbook to review all research in the field. There is not enough space and it would be indigestible to students. So although you will find a lot of empirical research discussed in this book and usually in substantially more detail than is typically the case, empirical research is not the primary focus. When choosing material for inclusion there are obviously things that everyone working in the field of

Forensic and Criminal Psychology knows about and which should be included. However, some research is based on such especially good, interesting ideas that it warranted inclusion irrespective of its impact on research and theory in general. Thus the first criterion for inclusion is the basic matter of a darned good idea. The second criterion is theory. Ideas which stimulate theory tend to integrate empirical studies because of this impact on theory. For this reason, one of my aims for the 4th edition has been to promote theory in Forensic and Criminal Psychology as a more systematic enterprise than was possible for earlier editions. This is possible simply because the field has increasingly accepted theory development as one of its primary tasks. In order to make the theory accessible, a number of pedagogic features have been added which make clearer the essential elements of particular theories.

As well as introducing new material in this latest edition, it has become increasingly necessary to rewrite what has been written in earlier editions. A decade is a long time in research and 'facts' which seemed incontrovertible in earlier editions now can seem to be rather short-sighted and inadequately based. That the police are no good at spotting a liar is a good example. Research is beginning to turn this on its head – at least in some circumstances. So the eagle-eyed may spot some reformulation taking place in this edition. Another slightly frustrating matter for the textbook writer is that developments in Forensic and Criminal Psychology do not occur steadily on all fronts. Some topics which were hot when the earlier editions were produced are now somewhat moribund with little by way of new ideas emerging. This is absolutely typical of all fields of psychology but that is no comfort. One consequence of this is that some chapters in the 4th edition are stuffed with new material whereas one or two chapters are relatively little changed. There has been, however, no wholesale deletion of material from earlier editions. Indeed, very little of what appeared in earlier editions does not appear in this new edition. Sometimes it has been moved around a little, sometimes a new emphasis has been added to it on the basis of recent developments, and sometimes it has been possible to understand things better as more research has become available. Of course, I have updated statistical data as far as possible where necessary. Unfortunately, it is not possible to do so for every candidate for updating since the up-to-date material may not be available. A good example of this is the monetary cost of crimes like murder and rape where updated estimates have not been published.

There are new chapters but these are where the old chapters were getting rather too big for their boots and needed dividing. In particular, the topic of lies and their detection has developed radically in recent years and needed space to expand. So it now has a chapter to itself. The polygraph and Statement Validity Analysis, as formal techniques for identifying a lack of truthfulness have, consequently, been given their own chapter. The material on treatments for offenders has previously been located in a number of other chapters but good research and theory in this area has grown remarkably in recent years and so a chapter on the treatment of sex offenders and violent offenders has been created. Finally, I have always considered the coverage of courts of law somewhat difficult because of the lack of good research and theory in this area. In particular, the heavy and almost exclusive reliance on laboratory data was not in keeping with this book. The last few years have changed things somewhat. There is increasingly available convincing research into law courts and the activities of judges, lawyers and juries. Furthermore, there seems to have been a shift towards developing theories in the field of forensic and criminal psychology. As a consequence, for the 4th edition a significant amount of high quality new material was available for inclusion. This would not fit into one chapter, so the coverage of courts of law has been expanded into two chapters, the first concentrating on judges and lawyers and the second on juries. This split is primarily for convenience since theory, especially, does not neatly divide in this way.

All of this has meant that the individual chapters have become lengthier. This has encouraged me to increase the variety of pedagogics included in the text. Having a table, diagram or figure to refer to can ease the task of the reader considerably – and that of the author. The 4th edition should have more visual impact as a consequence of this change. Once again, my priority was theory, so many of the new tables, figures and diagrams are designed to make it easier to absorb the essential elements of the key theories discussed in the text. But this is not to the exclusion of empirical research and tables, figures and diagrams have provided for some of this. These changes ensure that this 4th edition is a substantial update both pedagogically and in terms of new material.

All of this is very different from the situation when I was a student. My first real contact with the criminal justice system was the six months I spent at Wakefield

Prison, in Yorkshire, living at the Staff College across the way. My strongest recollection of this period was the emerging realisation that, for the most part, the men there seemed like ordinary men despite the fact that they were incestuous fathers or killers or had committed some other unfathomable crime. Nobody at university, staff or student, shared my interest in the field of crime and I had no idea of how my fumbling research interest could be turned into good psychology. Sex offenders fascinated me and I tried to research incestuous fathers but this was not a serious topic for research in the prevailing ethos of those days. A few years on and the sexual abuse of children became a massive area for research in several disciplines. Perhaps I could have been responsible for that but I was not. The boat was missed. Others, a little later, had much better ideas of what were the important things to think about, research and practise. But the field of Forensic and Criminal Psychology has, nevertheless, been a stimulus to my own work and its massive development over the last few years a delight to watch. Psychology students today who study Forensic and Criminal Psychology are exposed to the power of research and theory in creating understanding of one of the fundamental institutions of the state – the criminal justice system.

This 4th edition of this textbook has the following features:

- It is comprehensive and attempts to cover the major aspects of the field. As a consequence, it is modular in structure and virtually every chapter is useful in its own right. Where other pertinent material is to be found elsewhere in the text, cross-referencing has been employed.

- The text uses an extensive range of pedagogic techniques – most notably boxes that deal with significant additional issues such as controversies in the field and issues of practical concern to forensic practitioners. Each chapter begins with a summary and tables and diagrams are used extensively to facilitate understanding of important theory, concepts and research. Recommendations for additional reading are provided including the Internet.

- The text is truly international in nature. Forensic and Criminal Psychology has developed in many different parts of the world and research reflects this. At the same time, the law and legal systems are very different in different parts of the world. A good textbook needs to reflect this and encourage the reader to consider the law as a socially contextualised institution. For that reason, almost without exception I have indicated the location of research and the locally specific importance of some issues. To my mind this makes Forensic and Criminal Psychology even more exciting. So you will not find this text dominated by American research. Instead it reflects the true situation in which major contributions are made in many different parts of the world.

- I have attempted to have a wide perspective. Forensic and Criminal Psychology is a very broad topic and involves researchers with very different perspectives – clinical, developmental, cognitive, social and biological perspectives are all clearly represented in the field. Furthermore, there are other disciplines which can contribute a great deal, Criminology in particular. It is truly impossible to demarcate the dividing line between Psychology and Criminology. Indeed, to do so would be counterproductive. So I have freely taken from outside of Psychology where I believe it to be essential.

- Practitioner issues have been incorporated throughout the book. However, this is a textbook which, hopefully, will encourage readers to develop their interest in the field further. It is not the intention to produce a manual of good practice. Practitioner issues are part of the maturity of psychology as a discipline and, with this in mind, my preference has been to opt for real-life situations as far as possible though not to the exclusion of other key, laboratory-based research.

A book with such a wide agenda as this cannot truly be held to be the work of any one individual. So, although they may not realise it, I have a great debt to many forensic and criminal psychologists whose work I know and admire. These are individuals whose writings I greatly respect and trust so I have felt free to rely on much of what they have written and said. The list is so long now that individuals are best not named since the risk of inadvertently overlooking people who have greatly influenced my thinking is too great. Nevertheless, I think they know who they are.

Finally, anyone wishing to explore the possibility of becoming a forensic and criminal psychologist is advised to use the WWW to search for up-to-date information. The *American Psychology and Law Society* (American Psychological Association) and the *Division of Forensic Psychology* (British Psychological Society) are good starting places for these countries and provide appropriate search terms. Elsewhere search for the national psychological association or governing body.

Acknowledgements

Author's acknowledgements

A book is not the work of a solitary author working alone in a cold, dusty attic. It is a collective enterprise involving a great variety of skills. This book is no exception. Probably the most influential person is the Editor who is at every stage of the planning, writing and production. Janey Webb is a remarkable person who gets her way in the most charming fashion in order to make the book far better than the author ever contemplated. Her accomplice – I can think of no better word – has been Jane Lawes. Despite this, working with them is great fun.

In terms of the production, I am indebted to Lauren Hayward, Desk Editor, at Pearson Education. She is the latest in a long line of superwomen who can do things never even dreamed of by mere mortals such as authors. Again with abundant charm – or is it merely indefatigable patience. I am expecting weekly miracles as the time of publication approaches. Others who make a big contribution to the production are the text designer, Kevin Ancient, who makes the book readable and the cover designer, Carol Abbott, who makes sure that the book will attract attention. The copy editor turns the scruffy manuscript into the text design. This time this was down to Mary Dalton who, also did the preliminary proof reading so amazingly well that the number of queries that I had to answer must be in the Guinness Book of Records. Jonathan Price also did a brilliant job of the final proof reading but with no chance of the British record let alone the World record because of this.

The web-site is crucial to this book but those responsible can be easily be forgotten. Hayley McCarthy was in charge of the Web Site production and Kerry Sheldon, once again, did a fantastic job of writing materials.

Reviewers contribute greatly to the quality of a textbook like this. Fleetingly what they have got to say about the book will always be dismissed as garbage by the proud author but, then, a moment of reflection on what they have got to say transforms the book in important ways into something which has maximum usefulness in teaching and meets the needs of students closely. This edition continues the tradition of thanking the reviewers for their all-important work. This list follows.

Dennis Howitt

Reviewers

We would like to thank the following reviewers:

Dr John Bogue, National University of Ireland, Galway
Dr Erica Bowen, Coventry University
Professor Pär Anders Granhag, University of Gothenburg, Sweden
Dr David Heathcote, Bournemouth University
Dr Mary Morris, Charles Darwin University, Australia
Associate Professor Stephen Moston, University of Canberra, Australia
Rita Santos, Royal Holloway, University of London
Dave Walsh, School of Law and Criminology, University of Derby
Dr Dave Williams, University of Hertfordshire

Publisher's acknowledgements

We are grateful to the following for permission to reproduce copyright material:

Figures

Figures 2.1 and 2.2 adapted from Home Office Statistical Bulletin, *Crime in England and Wales 2009/10. Findings from the British Crime Survey and police recorded crime* (Flatley, J., Kershaw, C., Smith, K., Chaplin, R. and Moon, D. (Eds) 2010), http://www.nationalarchives.gov.uk/doc/open-government-licence/; Figure 3.1 after *Psychology and Crime: Myths and Reality*, Harlow: Longman (Ainsworth, P.B. 2000) Copyright © Pearson Education Ltd. 2000; Figure 3.3 adapted from Fear of crime and criminal victimization, *The British Journal of Criminology*, 38 (3), pp. 473–84 (Winkel, F.W. 1998), by permission of Oxford University Press; Figure 5.3 from H.J. Eysenck in Fagin's kitchen: the return to biological theory in 20th-century criminology, *History of the Human Sciences*, 19, pp. 37–56 (Rafter, N.H. 2006), Copyright © 2006 by Sage Publications, reprinted by permission of SAGE Publications and the author; Figure 6.3 from The development of children's orientations toward a moral order: I. Sequence in the development of moral thought, *Vita Humana*, 6, pp. 11–33 (Kohlberg, L. 1963), S. Karger AG, Basel; Figure 6.4 from Physically aggressive boys from ages 6 to 12: family background, parenting behavior, and prediction of delinquency, *Journal of Consulting and Clinical Psychology*, 62 (5), pp. 104–52 (Haapasalo, J. and Tremblay, R.E. 1994), Copyright © American Psychological Association,

reprinted with permission; Figure 7.3 from The statistical association between drug misuse and crime: A meta-analysis, *Aggression and Violent Behavior*, 13 (2), pp. 107–18 (Bennett, T., Holloway, K. and Farrington, D. 2008), Copyright © 2008 with permission from Elsevier; Figure 8.3 from Multiple murder: a review, *The British Journal of Criminology*, 34 (1), pp. 1–14 (Gresswell, D.M. and Hollin, C.R. 1994), by permission of Oxford University Press; Figure 12.1 from Differentiation of international terrorism: attack as threat, means, and violence, *Journal of Investigative Psychology and Offender Profiling*, 4, pp. 131–45 (Yokota, K., Watanabe, K., Wachi, T., Hoshino, A., Sato, A. and Fujita, G. 2007), © John Wiley and Sons 2007; Figure 12.2 adapted from Life story accounts of left wing terrorists in India, *Journal of Investigative Psychology and Offender Profiling*, 2, pp. 69–86 (Sarangi, S. and Alison, L. 2005), © John Wiley and Sons 2005; Figure 12.3 from Role playing: applications in hostage and crisis negotiations skills training, *Behaviour Modification*, 32 (2), pp. 248–63 (Van Hasselt, V.B., Romano, S.J. and Vecchi, G.M. 2008), Copyright © 2008 by Sage Publications, reprinted by permission of SAGE Publications; Figure 12.4 from Introducing the four-phase model of hostage negotiation, *Journal of Police Crisis Negotiations*, 9 (2), pp. 119–33 (Madrigal, D.O., Bowman, D.R. and McClain, B.U. 2009), reprinted by permission of the publisher (Taylor & Francis Group, http://www.informaworld.com) and the authors; Figure 13.3 from Eyewitness identification tests, *Legal and Criminological Psychology*, 15, pp. 77–96 (Brewer, N. and Palmer, M.A. 2010), © John Wiley and Sons 2010; Figure 15.6 from What works in offender profiling? A comparison of typological, thematic, and multivariate models, *Behavioral Sciences and the Law*, 27, pp. 507–29 (Goodwill, A.M., Alison, L.J. and Beech, A.R. 2009), © John Wiley and Sons 2009; Figure 15.9 from When is profiling possible? Offense planning and aggression as moderators in predicting offender age from victim age in stranger rape, *Behavioral Sciences and the Law*, 25, pp. 823–40 (Goodwill, A.M. and Alison, L.J. 2007), © John Wiley and Sons 2007; Figure 17.4 from Custodial interrogation: What are the background factors associated with claims of false confession to police?, *Journal of Forensic Psychiatry and Psychology*, 18 (2), pp. 266–75 (Gudjonsson, G.H., Sigurdsson, J.F., Asgeirsdottir, B.B. and Sigfusdottir, I.D. 2007), reprinted by permission of the publisher (Taylor & Francis Group, http://www.informaworld.com) and the authors; Figure 20.1 after Forensic interviews of children in A. Memon and R. Bull (Eds), *Handbook of the Psychology of Interviewing*, pp. 253–77 (Lamb, M.E., Sternberg, K.J. and Orbach, Y. 1999), Chichester: Wiley. Copyright © John Wiley & Sons 1999, reproduced with permission of John Wiley & Sons Ltd.; Figure 20.4 from Post-event information affects children's autobiographical memory after one year, *Law and Human Behaviour*, 33 (4), pp. 344–55 (London, K., Bruck, M. and Melnyk, L. 2009), Copyright © 2008, American Psychology-Law Society/Division 41 of the American Psychological Association, with kind permission from Springer Science + Business Media and the authors; Figure 23.5 from Dangerous decisions: a theoretical framework for understanding how judges assess credibility in the courtroom, *Legal and Criminological Psychology*, 14, pp. 119–34 (Porter, S. and ten Brinke, L. 2009), Figure 1, p. 126, © John Wiley and Sons 2009; Figure 24.2 from Juror selection: a comparison of two methods in several criminal cases, *Journal of Applied Social Psychology*, 10 (1), pp. 86–99 (Horowitz, I.A. 1980), © John Wiley and Sons 1980.

Tables

Table 2.1 from *Technical Report on Revised Population Estimates and NLSY79 Analysis Tables for the Pew Public Safety and Mobility Project*, Harvard University (Pettit, B., Sykes, B. and Western, B. 2009), reproduced with permission of the authors; Table 14.1 adapted from *Profiling Violent Crimes: An Investigative Tool*, Thousand Oaks, CA: Sage (Holmes, R.M. and Holmes, S.T. 1996) Copyright © 1996, reproduced with permission of Sage Publications Inc. Books in the format textbook via Copyright Clearance Center; Table 25.1 after Crime treatment in Europe: a final view of the century and future perspectives In J. McGuire (Ed.), *Offender Rehabilitation and Treatment: Effective Programmes and Policies to Reduce Re-Offending*, pp. 131–41 (Redondo, S., Sanchez-Meca, J. and Garrido, V. 2002), Chichester: Wiley. Copyright © John Wiley & Sons 2002, reproduced with permission of John Wiley & Sons Ltd.

Text

Extract on page 357 from Statement validity analysis of 'The Jim Ragsdale story': implications for the Roswell incident, *Journal of Scientific Exploration*, 12 (1), pp. 57–71 (Houran, J. and Porter, S. 1998), published by the Society for Scientific Exploration, www.scientificexploration.org, reprinted with permission.

In some instances we have been unable to trace the owners of copyright material, and we would appreciate any information that would enable us to do so.

Chapter 1

What is forensic and criminal psychology?

Overview

- Forensic psychology is psychology applied to the work in law courts. However, the term is currently used rather more generally than this. Criminal psychology is the psychology of criminal behaviour.

- The term *forensic psychology* can be focused narrowly on the work of the relatively small number of psychological practitioners who work directly in law courts. A wider definition is employed in this book. This embraces the activities of all psychologists whose work is related to the criminal justice system including psychologists working in the prison system. Hence the phrase *forensic and criminal psychology* is used to encompass the very wide field of psychology applied to the law.

- Psychology and the law are very different disciplines although both involve understanding human nature. Their ways of understanding are not the same and sometimes they are incompatible. Even when the lawyers and psychologists use identical words, they may intend very different meanings.

- There are many practitioner-researchers in forensic and criminal psychology. Practitioners who are both skilled researchers and skilled practitioners can add a great deal to the development of such an applied discipline. Training in forensic psychology includes both knowledge and practice-based elements.

- Crucial changes in the criminal justice system over the centuries have gradually led to the demand for psychological expertise within the system. Most forensic and criminal psychology is very recent and mainly confined to the past 30 to 40 years or so. Academically, forensic and criminal psychology is nearly as old as modern psychology itself. It was being practised and researched shortly after Wundt set up his psychological laboratory in Leipzig in the 1870s – an event which itself is often lauded as the symbolic founding of modern psychology. However, interest in the field was at best spasmodic and minimal until the late twentieth century when growth became rapid and it continues to accelerate.

- Forensic and criminal psychology developed differently in different regions of the world. Nevertheless, it now constitutes an important branch of modern psychology which benefits greatly from its inter-national nature. Furthermore, it unites psychologists from a variety of fields of psychology though, increasingly, it can be regarded as a specialism in its own right.

Introduction

The definition of *forensic and criminal psychology* is not unproblematic. Forensic psychology literally is psychology to do with courts of law. The words *forensic* and *forum* have the same Latin origins. A forum is merely a room for public debate, hence the word *forensic*. Criminal psychology is mainly to do with psychological aspects of criminal behaviour and includes issues such as the origins and development of criminality. The difficulties in the definition of the field are largely to do with how precisely boundaries are to be drawn and just how broadly or narrowly the terms should be applied. Modern law deals with an incredible variety of aspects of life, and so psychology, when applied to the legal system, is potentially boundless in its compass. Few, if any, aspects of life are unaffected by the law, including:

- where we live;
- where we are educated;
- by whom we are educated;
- who may work;
- when we can work;
- what we may do at work;
- how we get to work;
- when we may retire;
- what happens to us when we die.

Legislation covers many of these as well as the practice of psychology itself. Increasingly, the work of psychologists in general is subject to laws as are many of the vocations that students trained in psychology enter. A very good example is social work in its many forms, which substantially deals with prime matters of government legislation including children and the family. Other examples include education, mental health, health and advertising, all of which are closely governed by law. Furthermore, all sorts of psychologists may provide expert evidence on virtually any matter to courts of law. So precisely who should be designated a forensic and criminal psychologist? Many psychologists work primarily in the criminal justice system (i.e. police, criminal courts and prisons). Should they all be classified together as forensic psychologists, for example?

Things have changed over the years in terms of how forensic psychology has been defined though, recently, a consensus is increasingly apparent. Twenty-five years or so ago when the field was beginning to expand around the 1990s, some influential psychologists defined forensic psychology in terms of the professional activities of practitioners working primarily in law courts. Gudjonsson and Haward (1998) are a good example of proponents of such a viewpoint when they defined *forensic psychology* as:

> . . . that branch of applied psychology which is concerned with the collection, examination and presentation of evidence for judicial purposes. (p. 1)

The key elements in this definition would seem to be 'evidence' and 'judicial'. While they may not actually intend this, Gudjonsson and Haward seem to be referring to legal evidence for the use of lawyers and judges. This clearly sets limits to the meaning that they wish to apply to the phrase 'judicial purposes' also. Definitions exist for a reason and they achieve particular ends. In this case the purpose is to limit the field of forensic psychology to those working in close collaboration with officials of the court. The following is essentially similar and from much the same period of time:

> [forensic psychology is] the provision of psychological information for the purpose of facilitating a legal decision.
>
> (Blackburn, 1996: 7)

Both are relatively narrow and specific definitions which are not in keeping with more recent approaches. What the above definitions exclude is as important as what they include. The main omission is the work of psychologists in settings such as prisons and special hospitals for psychologically disturbed criminals. Their activities are clearly relevant to courts of law though such psychologists may only rarely, if ever, work directly in courts. It comes as no surprise, then, to find that in recent years psychologists have tended to broaden their definition of the term forensic psychologist. For example, the British Psychological Society extends the definition to include much of the criminal justice system beyond courts of law:

> Forensic Psychology is devoted to psychological aspects of legal processes in courts. The term is also often used to refer to investigative and criminological psychology: applying psychological theory to criminal investigations, understanding psychological problems associated with criminal behaviour and the treatment of criminals. (British Psychological Society, What is Forensic Psychology? http://www.bps.org.uk/careers/society_qual/forensic_qual.cfm. Accessed 4 September 2010)

In much the same way but more succinctly, the Australian Psychological Society defines forensic psychology such that it also includes aspects of psychology beyond the courts – for example the areas of prison and other forms of correction, the police, and so forth:

> Forensic psychology is the branch of psychology that interfaces with the legal and justice systems. (p. 2) (*Australian Psychological Society* http://www.psychology.org.au/community/specialist/forensic/. Accessed 22 April 2011)

Although its language is not quite so direct, the American Psychological Society takes a fairly similar stance:

> Forensic psychology is the professional practice by psychologists within the areas of clinical psychology, counseling psychology, school psychology, or another specialty recognized by the American Psychological Association, when they are engaged as experts and represent themselves as such, in an activity primarily intended to provide professional psychological expertise to the judicial system. (American Psychological Association, Public Description of Forensic Psychology http://www.apa.org/ed/graduate/specialize/forensic.aspx. Accessed 4 September 2010)

In contrast, Wrightsman (2001) defined forensic psychology in much broader terms. He regarded forensic psychology as:

> . . . any application of psychological knowledge or methods to a task faced by the legal system.

Nevertheless this is quite a wide definition since Wrightsman lists some of the types of psychology he includes as follows:

- A *clinical psychologist* in private practice. This psychologist works as a consultant to police departments.
- A *mediator psychologist* employed by a law firm to mediate between parties in an attempt to resolve legal disputes.
- A *social psychologist* dealing with civil cases such as commercial litigation. The psychologist conducted surveys of role-playing 'jurors' in order to assess what might work in a real trial.
- A *counselling psychologist* who works on the assessment of potentially violent behaviours for the US secret service. For example, threats of violence are often made to the national leaders – which ones are to be taken seriously?

- A *correctional psychologist* who assesses the competence of prisoners to stand trial and makes suggestions about possible treatments for particular offenders.

Whether by intention or oversight, it is notable that all of the above examples are of *practitioners* rather than researchers. They may do research, but it is not the primary focus of their work. The examples Wrightsman gives seem very unrepresentative of the majority of psychologists who describe themselves as forensic psychologists. The problem is that Wrightsman's basic definition of forensic psychology may be adequate, but his list needs to be extended. In other parts of the world, psychologists working in the prison service, teaching and working in university departments, working in the mental health field and elsewhere all claim at least some identity with forensic psychology.

We are probably past the stage where it could be suggested that there is a substantial lack of consensus over the definition of forensic psychology (e.g. McGuire, 1997). Stanik (1992) considered that the use of the term 'forensic' was disorderly and described the situation as 'chaos'. Forensic psychology has become much more structured and defined in recent years. A key to making progress in defining forensic psychology is to differentiate between defining the *field of forensic psychology* and identifying *who should be entitled to call themselves forensic psychologists*. The first (what is forensic psychology?) is essentially addressed by all of the definitions discussed so far. The question of who is qualified to call themselves a forensic psychologist has been approached in a different way. The issue becomes that of identifying the nature of the skills and knowledge required by anyone working in the field, apart from a basic training in psychology itself. In the United Kingdom, it has been suggested that forensic psychologists (i.e. all chartered forensic psychologists) should possess the following knowledge and skills (DCLP Training Committee, 1994). The list probably would be much the same elsewhere in the world, though the precise mix of skills varies with the area of practice within the field:

- Understanding the conceptual basis of their work context in terms of:
  - the psychology relevant to the study of criminal behaviour;
  - the legal framework including the law and structure of the criminal justice system, for example, of the country in which they practise.

- An understanding of the achievements and potential achievements of the application of psychology to:
  - criminal investigation processes;
  - legal processes;
  - custodial processes;
  - treatment processes (for both offenders and victims).
- A sufficiently detailed understanding of the psychology relevant to the following individuals, including adults and children where appropriate:
  - offenders (whether or not mentally disordered);
  - victims;
  - witnesses;
  - investigators.
- An understanding of the practical aspects of forensic psychology in terms of the following:
  - different demands for assessment;
  - processes of investigation, prosecution and defence;
  - decision making in respect of innocence, guilt, sentencing, custody, treatment and rehabilitation;
  - approaches to assessment;
  - professional criteria for report production and giving of testimony.
- This is combined with an additional requirement of having had extensive practical experience in at least one area of forensic psychology (pp. 7–8).

This comprehensive list defines the skills and knowledge base of practitioners in the discipline. It also indicates that no matter the exact specialism of the forensic psychologist, he or she has a more comprehensive education in their field than the minimum needed to function on a day-to-day basis.

Defining *criminal psychology* tends to be less controversial. This is partly because it is not a title that is claimed by any significantly large or influential group of psychologists. Like forensic psychology, criminal psychology may be defined relatively narrowly or somewhat broadly. The narrow definition would merely suggest that it concerns all aspects of the psychology of the criminal. A difficulty with this is that it seems to concentrate solely on the offender. Does it or should it also include psychological aspects of the wider experience of the criminal, for example, in courts of law or prison? Criminality, as we shall see, is not a characteristic of individuals that can be separated meaningfully from the social context of crime and the criminal justice system. Thus the field of criminal psychology must be defined in terms of knowledge and skills which substantially overlap those of the

forensic psychologist described above. Indeed, one might suggest that the main difference between the two is that forensic psychology may involve the civil law as well as the criminal law. The use of the phrase 'forensic and criminal psychology' in this book acknowledges problems in the definition of both *forensic* and *criminal psychology*. There is no intention to suggest that the two things effectively are different. Forensic psychology and criminal psychology are to be regarded as inseparable rather than a marriage of two distinct aspects of psychology.

Other terms sometimes used for this field of psychology include *psychology and the law* and *legal psychology*. These more clearly hint of an interface between the two disciplines and practices – psychology and the law. Again, there is some merit in a designation of this sort. In particular, it stresses the two disciplines in combination. The implication is that both lawyers and psychologists may be interested in similar issues but from their differing perspectives. Contributions from both lawyers and psychologists are important in the field's development. While the terms suggest that researchers/practitioners should be knowledgeable about both psychology and the law, this is also a weakness. Very few researchers/ practitioners are trained in both disciplines. The club has a minuscule membership. In recent years there has been a movement to define investigative psychology as a somewhat wider block of forensic psychology. So topics such as eyewitness testimony and deception detection are included with the more statistical forms of profiling (Granhag and Vrij, 2010). Whether or not this term gains wider prominence is for the future to decide.

Forensic and criminal psychology may also be understood in terms of the organisational infrastructure that supports it. For example, it is not possible to define the discipline of medicine without reference to the medical associations that promote and organise it. Some individuals have 'permission' or a licence to practise medicine, others do not. The institutional basis of forensic and criminal psychology varies from country to country. It is mainly associated with the professional associations of psychologists such as the American Psychological Association, the Australian Psychological Society and the British Psychological Society.

The relationship between psychology and the law has not and is not without its difficulties. Both psychologists and lawyers may have problems when engaging with each other's discipline. Psychology is not a compact discipline united by a single theory or approach – it is a broad church which psychologists themselves often find lacking in coherence. Clifford (1995) suggested that lawyers should be excused for regarding psychology as a 'bewildering confederacy' (p. 26). Eastman (2000) wrote of the two disciplines as if they were different countries – Legaland and Mentaland. These differ, like countries do, in terms of their culture, language, history and terrain. When the inhabitants of these two lands mix together things are difficult because they have big differences of purpose. Nevertheless, there are times when the people of Legaland need the help of people from Mentaland but Legaland language is confusing to the people of Mentaland – and vice versa. Legaland people are often more powerful and make it extremely obvious that in their view the ideas of Mentaland are secondary to those of Legaland. So, according to them, it is the people of Mentaland who need to make it abundantly clear that Mentaland ideas are subservient to those of Legaland and that Mentaland people will have to adjust their language. Mentaland people also sometimes need the people of Legaland to give them the authority for things they do. For example, social and public policy legislation may need to be tested by Legaland, then interpreted for the people of Mentaland. In this way the people of Mentaland obtain extra tools to get on with their job.

BOX 1.1 Forensic psychology in action

The expert witness

Given that psychologists are experts in many different aspects of human nature and behaviour, it is not surprising that their knowledge is frequently applicable in court. The extent of their involvement is dependent on a number of factors. According to Groscup *et al.* (2002), a quarter of expert witnesses in American criminal appeal hearings were from the social and behavioural sciences. Different legal jurisdictions have different requirements of expert witnesses and certain expert evidence may not be admissible in all legal systems. An expert witness differs from any other witness in court since they are allowed to express opinions rather than simply report facts. The opinions of forensic and criminal psychologists will normally be supported by scientific evidence and they will be required to establish their scientific credentials. The expert witness should not offer evidence outside the terms of their expertise. These matters are normally determined at the stage of the *voir dire* (usually described as a trial within a trial but essentially a preliminary review of matters related to the trial such as jurors and evidence, before the trial proper begins) in the Anglo-American system. Different legal jurisdictions vary in terms of how the expert witness is employed. In the Anglo-American system, the adversarial system, this is normally the decision of the prosecution or the defence. Inquisitorial legal systems such as those common in Continental Europe (Stephenson, 1992) are likely to use experts employed by the court itself (Nijboer, 1995) and, furthermore, they will be regarded much as any other witness. Guidelines for expert witnesses are available (e.g. British Psychological Society, 2010).

The *Daubert* decision currently influences which 'experts' may be allowed to give evidence in American courts. The Daubert case was about a child, Jason Daubert, who was born with missing fingers and bones. His mother had taken an anti-morningsickness drug and sued the manufacturers. 'Rules' designed to exclude 'junk' science were formulated. What is interesting is that the decision formulated what should be regarded as proper scientific methodology. That is, it should be based on the testing of hypotheses which are refutable. Furthermore, in assessing the admissibility of the expert evidence, attention should be paid to issues such as whether the research had been subject to review by others working in the field (Ainsworth, 1998). Perry (1997) lists Daubert criteria as including:

- whether the technique or theory is verifiable;
- whether the technique or theory is generally accepted within the scientific community;
- what the likelihood of error in the research study is.

▶

BOX 1.1 (continued)

This obviously causes problems for expertise that is not part of this model of science: for example, therapists giving evidence on the false memory syndrome in which there is a fierce debate between practitioners and academics (see Box 16.1).

In England and Wales, the main guidelines according to Nijboer (1995) are as follows:

- Matters that the judge believes are within the capacity of the ordinary person – the juror – in terms of their knowledge and experience are not for comment by the expert witness.
- The expert witness cannot give evidence that 'usurps' the role of the judge and jury in connection with the principal issue with which the trial is concerned.
- Expert opinion is confined to matters that are admissible evidence.

A survey of American lawyers (including judges) investigated how mental health experts were selected to give evidence (Mossman and Kapp, 1998). Their academic writings and national reputation were rarely criteria – nor was the fee that they asked. Apart from knowledge in a specific area, the key criteria for selection were their communicative ability and local reputation. There may be reason to be concerned about the value of some expert testimony since there are many examples of what might be described as pseudo-science. Coles and Veiel (2001) took issue with the willingness of psychologist expert witnesses to reduce complex matters to fixed characteristics of the individual. So the idea of fitness to plead is regarded in the thinking of some psychologists as a characteristic of some individuals – that is, it is a characteristic of their personality. But the legal definition of fitness to plead (see Chapter 21) concerns whether an individual has the intellectual resources to contribute effectively to their own defence. Naturally, this means that fitness to plead evaluations need to take into account the complexity of the trial in question. Someone may be perfectly fit to plead where the trial is simple but unfit to plead in a complex trial. Furthermore, they may appear competent in one area but not in another area. An individual may be perfectly capable of communicating with their lawyer but unable to understand the purpose of the trial.

Researcher-practitioners

The concept of the 'scientist-practitioner' originated in the late 1940s among clinical psychologists seeking to improve both research and practice. Some argue that the synergy resulting from combining research and practice has not been achieved (Douglas, Cox and Webster, 1999) though this may be disputed on the basis of the extensive research contributed currently by forensic psychology practitioners. Historically and traditionally in psychology, researchers and practitioners were seen as at odds with each other – each side being dismissive of the contribution of the other. Academics criticised practitioners for their lack of knowledge of the pertinent research; practitioners criticised academics for their ignorance of clinical needs and practices. Such views seem increasingly old-fashioned and inaccurate from a modern perspective. More and more, employers of forensic and criminal psychologists require that practitioners should partake fully in a research-led discipline. Practitioners do not just apply psychological knowledge, they create it. Appropriately for an applied discipline such as forensic and criminal psychology, the usual and preferred term is researcher-practitioners rather than scientist-practitioners. The latter reflects a view of psychology which many practitioners have difficulty relating to. For some, the purpose of psychology is not to develop scientific laws of human behaviour but to ground the discipline in social reality through the effective use of empirical research. There is another phrase – evidence-based practice – which is increasingly used to describe an ideal relationship between practitioners in any discipline and research in that discipline. It means that practice should be based on what research has shown to be effective.

So in forensic and criminal psychology, the division between researcher and practitioner is breached. It is a generally accepted principle that training in both research and practice is crucial to effective practice. Practitioners who understand research methods well are much more likely to be able to employ the findings of other researchers into their therapies, assessments and when giving their

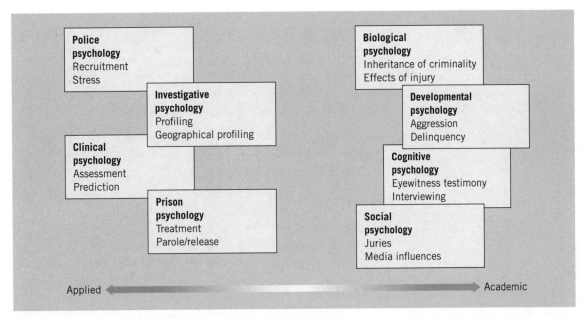

Figure 1.1 Major components of forensic psychology

professional advice to clients and colleagues. Furthermore, practitioners are usually in a good position to know what sorts of research are needed by them compared with academics whose knowledge of practitioner requirements cannot be so direct. Indeed, academic researchers may have academic and theoretical priorities that are different from those of practitioners. There is nothing wrong with this. Many academic psychologists make important contributions despite lacking the practical experience and training of practitioners. The roles of the academic researcher and the researcher-practitioner are overlapping but distinct though the contributions of both of are equal value.

Figure 1.1 illustrates some of the major components of forensic and criminal psychology. Notice how widely they are drawn from the discipline of psychology. Also note the underlying dimension of applied research/practice versus the academic. The distinction is not rigid but nevertheless must be considered as an essential component of the structure of the field (e.g. BPS, 2007/8; 2011).

History of forensic and criminal psychology

Histories are written from the viewpoint of the teller. American and European academics may give rather different versions of forensic and criminal psychology's history – each offering accounts that stress the contribution of their traditions to the discipline. The history as written by a psychiatrist will be different from that of a psychologist since it may ignore the contribution, for example, of cognitive psychology. And the history written by a lawyer would be different from all of these. Nevertheless, it is possible to identify some key elements in the history of forensic and criminal psychology which are shown in Figure 1.2.

Changes in the law

A number of crucial developments in the law that occurred centuries before psychology was founded were vital to the development of forensic and criminal psychology. In medieval times, Bartholomaeus Anglicus, a professor of theology in France, published *De Proprietatibus Rerum* in 1230. This contained descriptions of a wide variety of conditions such as *melancholie*. In England and Wales, legal categories classifying the mentally disordered first appeared in the *Statutes at Large* in 1324. These distinguished between lunatics and idiots. In both cases the property belonging to the individual could be transferred to the Crown or some entrusted person. The difference was that the idiot lost his or her property forever but the lunatic might have their property returned when they recovered from

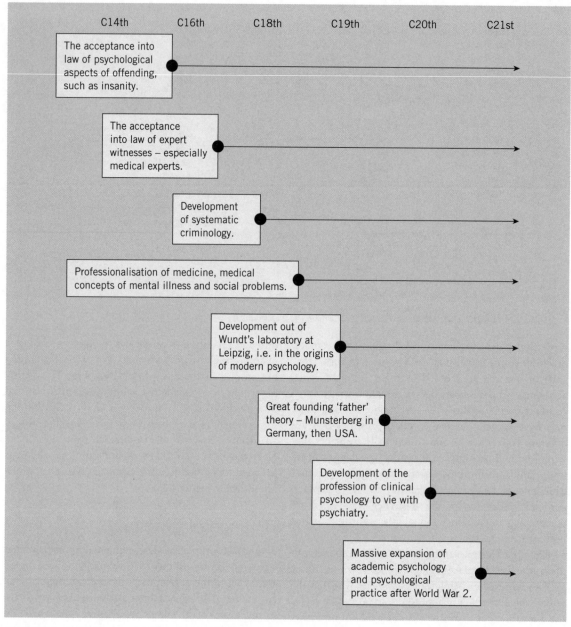

Figure 1.2 Different components in the historical origins of forensic and criminal psychology

their lunacy. Thus the law enshrined the possibility that some mental disorders were temporary or curable. Legal changes allowing the detention of dangerous lunatics emerged at about the middle of the eighteenth century. Such persons could be held in workhouses or prisons or madhouses. By the end of the nineteenth century legal categories such as idiot, insane, lunatic and person of unsound mind were well entrenched (Forrester, Ozdural, Muthukumaraswamy and Carroll, 2008). Other notable points are:

- Madness was not always an issue in law although it was a consideration as long ago as Roman times. Before the thirteenth century, in English law, the doing of something evil was sufficient to establish the individual liable for that evil. The offender's mental condition was simply irrelevant to sentencing (Eigen, 2004). The first English trial in which the accused was acquitted on the basis of insanity occurred as early as 1505. However, not until the eighteenth century did courts begin to develop criteria to assess insanity. The criterion developed at this time essentially held that insane persons are equivalent to wild beasts – which, of course, are not capable of committing crime. Such a definition was a difficult one to meet but nevertheless required no degree of psychiatric knowledge to apply – ordinary members of the jury could identify such an extreme case as this. So expert advice from the medical profession, such as it would have been at this time, was not needed. Insanity became an important issue in the nineteenth century when deluded reasoning became part of the legal test of insanity. Such a definition required the advice of experts much more than the wild beast criterion had. Expert witnesses were required with increasing frequency and, as a consequence, lawyers became increasingly concerned that evidence of experts might replace the jury in deciding the verdict.

- The issue of competence to stand trial (see Chapter 22) is a development originating in eighteenth-century English common law (i.e. law not laid down by statutes but essentially by tradition). The crucial concept was the idea that the defendant must be competent at certain minimal levels in order to have a fair trial (Roesch, Ogloff and Golding, 1993). Although competence is a legal matter and one to be defined by the courts and not psychologists or psychiatrists, the emergence of the expert witness encouraged the eventual use of medical and other practitioners to comment on the mental state of the defendant. As might be expected, even these key changes had their roots in earlier times. For example, the notion that some individuals were unfit because of their limited intellectual ability had actually entered the legal consideration of cases much earlier, in fourteenth-century England.

Links with the parent discipline

It is not possible to separate developments in forensic and criminal psychology from developments in psychology in general. To fully study the history of forensic and criminal psychology one needs to understand the changes that occurred in psychology in general. The following illustrate this:

- The study of memory has been common in psychology since the pioneering work of Ebbinghaus. Obviously, the psychology of memory is very relevant to eyewitness testimony. Not until the 1960s and later did psychologists properly begin to address the important issue of memory for real events. This set the scene for expansion of research into eyewitness testimony beginning in the 1970s.

- The new emphasis in social psychology on group dynamics in the 1960s was associated with a rise in interest in research on the dynamics of decision making in juries.

- Many of the psychological assessment techniques, tests and measurements used, particularly, in assessment of offenders for forensic purposes have their origins in other fields of psychology. Their availability to forensic and criminal psychologists is contingent on developments in academic, educational and clinical psychology in particular.

Social change

Both the law and psychology are responsive to changes in society in general. Here are a few examples that illustrate this:

- Child sexual abuse: although nowadays concern about child sexual abuse (and rape and domestic violence for that matter) is extensive and ingrained, this has not always been the case despite the fact that in 1911, the Belgian J. Varendonk had given expert opinion in a sexual abuse trial. The massive social impact of feminism during the 1960s and 1970s brought concern about a number of issues. Among them was child sexual abuse, which was found to be more common than had been thought. This interest brought to forensic and criminal psychology a need to understand and deal better with matters such as the effects of child sexual abuse, the treatment of abusers and the ability of children to give evidence in court. The history of the radical change in the way in which professionals regard child sexual abuse victims makes fascinating reading (e.g. Myers *et al.*, 1999). Dominant themes in early writings on sexual abuse contrast markedly with modern thinking. For example, a century or so ago children were regarded as being the instigators of their own victimisation, their mothers were held to blame for the fate of the children and sexual abuse was construed as rare. This does not mean that prosecutions for sexual offences against children were unknown. In the United States at least, they increased steadily during the twentieth century, although Myers *et al.* describe the rates as modest by modern standards. It is worth noting that other countries may experience apparently different patterns. For example, Sjogren (2000) claims that the rates of child sexual abuse in Sweden were as high in the 1950s and 1960s, before concern about sexual abuse rose due to American influences, as they were in the 1990s.

- Government policy: the work of forensic and criminal psychologists is materially shaped by government policy on any number of matters. For instance, government policy on the treatment of offenders (say to increase the numbers going to prison and the length of their sentences) is critical. Similarly, the issue of the provision of psychiatric/psychological care (say increasing the numbers managed within the community) profoundly changes the nature of the work of practitioners. Furthermore, changes in research priorities may well be contingent on such developments as researchers often tend to look for funding where there is political interest and governments fund research into changes they are planning.

We can now turn from the broad societal and legal framework in which forensic and criminal psychology developed to consider some of the key events in the history of research and theory in forensic and criminal psychology.

Early work in the disciplines of criminology, sociology and psychiatry

The intellectual origins of forensic and criminal psychology are to be found in related disciplines, especially criminology, sociology and psychology. Indeed, some of the earliest criminological contributions seem unquestionably psychological in nature. There are a number of aspects to consider:

- One could regard the work of the Italian Cesare de Beccaria in the later 1700s as a contender for the first example of forensic and criminal psychology. Beccaria regarded humans as possessing free will. This was subject to the principles of pleasure and pain. This is an 'economic' model in which we are seen to evaluate the costs and benefits (pleasures and pains) of our actions prior to engaging in them, such as when we decide to commit a crime. He believed that punishment for criminal behaviour was not desirable in itself. It was important, though, to deter people from crime. Thus punishments need to be proportionate or commensurate with the crime – and inflicted as a means of deterrence. It is argued by some that De Baccaria's ideas led directly to the abandonment of barbaric torture of prisoners in a number of European countries (McGuire, 2000).

- The publication of the first official crime statistics was a crucial development that occurred in France in 1827. Statistical data allowed the development of investigations into the geographical distribution or organisation of crime. This continues in criminology today and geographical profiling of crime is important in areas of forensic and criminal psychology. The Frenchman André-Michel Guerry and the Belgian Adolphe Quetelet began the tradition of crime statistics. Modern computer applications have refined this approach enormously. It is now possible to study databases specifying the geographical locations of crime down to the household level.

- The idea of the biological roots of crime was an important late nineteenth-century idea in the work of the Italian doctor Cesare Lombroso. He took groups of hardened criminals and carried out what might be called an anthropological study of their features. He compared the criminals' features with those of soldiers on whom he practised his medicine. Lombroso believed that certain structural anomalies of the skull were commoner among criminals. These abnormalities, he said, were indications that criminals represented an earlier stage of evolution of humanity than the rest of society had achieved. According to Lombroso, criminal characteristics include a lack of skull-space for brain tissue, pronounced structural differences between the two sides of the skull, ears that stick out, a bent or flat nose, colour blindness, left-handedness and a lack of muscular strength. The differences could be even more specific since different characteristics distinguished murderers from sex offenders. Murderers' eyes are bloodshot, cold and glassy, whereas the eyes of sex offenders glint. Lombroso is largely remembered for being wrong and few give his ideas any credence. For example, Lombroso's findings could not be replicated just a few years later in Britain by Charles Goring. Harrower (1998) argues that the observation that some criminals are mentally deficient is indirect support for Lombroso's point of view. Her idea is that in Lombroso's time biological defects including mental deficiency were seen as linked, though Goring's evidence was that criminals had low intelligence, not that they showed the cranial characteristics Lombroso claimed. Just to confirm how wrong the theory was, Lombroso claimed that it could be used even to explain the lack of criminality in women. It was not that women are socially more evolved than men. Quite the reverse. They were so backward in terms of human development that they had not evolved to the stage at which it was possible to be criminal!

European psychology's early contribution to forensic and criminal psychology

One of the earliest concepts related to forensic and criminal psychology was that of *kleptomania*. The term appears in modern dictionaries and has some popular currency today among the general public. Mathey, in 1816, coined the term *klopemania*, which means 'stealing insanity', whereas Marc, in 1840, used the term *kleptomania*, which means exactly the same thing (Fullerton and Punj, 2004). The main characteristics of kleptomania for these early physicians were as follows:

- Impulses to steal things of negligible value.
- Economic necessity was not a reason.
- The theft was accompanied by an elated state of exhilaration together with relief from feelings of tension.
- Kleptomaniacs tend to be women.

Perhaps not surprisingly, given its emergence at a time of great economic growth in terms of industrialisation and commerce, the concept was popular throughout the nineteenth and twentieth centuries. Its explanation though was difficult since kleptomania was not fuelled by economic necessity – the things stolen were of little economic worth – and frequently the thief would not even unwrap the item or use it. The motive was sexual according to some and the psychoanalytical psychiatrist Wilhelm Stekel held it to be a suppressed sexual desire (Stekel, 1911). Women, it was argued, suffered from penis envy (envy at not possessing a penis) so might seek to replace their missing penis through symbolic objects that they stole (Fenichel, 1933). Kleptomania is not an outmoded concept in the sense that it is a diagnostic category in the American Psychiatric Association's current *Diagnostic and Statistical Manual of Mental Disorders* (DSM-IV). See Box 21.1.

Early interest in lie detection through hidden emotions (an idea which relates directly to the modern work discussed in Chapters 18 and 19) can be found in the writings of Charles Darwin (1872) who suggested that an angry person can control their body movements but not the muscles of the face which are not under wilful control. These ideas reflect very much the approach to the detection of lies through facial expression offered by Paul Eckman in his theory (see Chapter 18). Anyone wishing to find further British roots of Forensic and Criminal Psychology could draw on the fact that in Sir Francis Galton, Darwin's cousin, tried to find a word association test that would serve as a procedure for lie detection. In this, the truth assessor would say a word such as 'thief' and study the response from the 'suspect' (Matte, 2002).

More directly important, the development of modern psychology at the University of Leipzig in the late nineteenth century quickly led to an interest in forensic issues. Generally speaking, it is accepted that the origins of modern psychology lie in the establishment of the psychological laboratory at this university in 1875. This was part of the legacy of Wilhelm Wundt to psychology. It was a number of his students, colleagues and co-workers who took the initial steps in developing forensic and criminal psychology, though there were other influences:

- Albert Von Schrenk-Nortzing (*c.* 1897): in 1896, Von Schrenk-Nortzing appeared at a Leipzig court in a role that some might describe as the first true forensic psychologist. His was early testimony into the effects of the media on matters relevant to the courtroom. He argued that witnesses at a murder trial confused their actual memories of events with the pre-trial publicity given to the event in the media. They were not able to distinguish between what they had witnessed and what they had read in the newspapers. Von Schrenk-Nortzing described this memory effect as 'retroactive memory falsification'. Related issues continue to be studied although the researchers do not necessarily concur with Von Schrenk-Nortzing – for example, Roberts and Blades (1995) asked whether children confuse television and real-life events. Their answer was that children as young as 4 years are good at identifying the source of their memories correctly. Significantly, at the lower age studied they can be confused by the way they are questioned into making errors.

- J.M. Cattell (*c.* 1895) investigated using the techniques of laboratory experiments into human memory on the quality of eyewitness testimony. He was an American who returned to the United States and studied forensic issues after studying in Wundt's laboratory. His research included situational influences on eyewitness accuracy as well as the issue of whether some individuals tend to be resistant to error and outside influences. Binet, the originator of intelligence testing, in France, replicated Cattell's work. He focused particularly on the question of the amenability of testimony to outside suggestion in interrogations. In Germany, at about the same time, William Stern conducted research on similar themes to those of Cattell in relation to both adults and children.

- Sigmund Freud did not write about legal matters although his ideas about human nature so profoundly affected the legal system that he was given an honorary doctorate in law from an American university. Nevertheless, a number of the psychoanalytically influenced followers of the psychodynamic psychology of Sigmund Freud made contributions to the field. For example, in 1929, Theodor Reik wrote about the compulsion to confess; Erich Fromm, in 1931, discussed the psychological diagnosis of fact (Jakob, 1992). Also in Germany, around 1905, C.G. Jung experimented with using word association to test a criminal suspect – that is, the characteristics of the delay of responding to different words with another word. Emotional stimulus words tend to produce greater delay.

- Udo Undeutsch in 1953 presented arguments to a German Psychological Association meeting that moved the issue of testimony to the question of the veracity of a statement rather than the credibility of the witness.

American roots of forensic and criminal psychology

The timescale is short between the German origins of forensic and criminal psychology and its beginning to appear in the United States. This is because a significant number of early American psychologists actually trained at Wundt's laboratory and either returned home or emigrated to the United States as academic positions became available. Thus early work in the United States involved both American researchers as well as European émigrés:

- L.W. Stern (*c.* 1910) continued the tradition of testimony research in the United States. Among his achievements was the introduction of realism to the study of testimony in that he introduced staged events into lectures such as a student brandishing a revolver which was witnessed by the class of students! Stern in 1903/4 was the first to distinguish between two kinds of interview called *Bericht* and *Verhö* (Myklebust and Bjøorklund, 2006). *Bericht* allowed the interviewee to give their account as a free narrative by the use of open questions. In the *Verhö* approach the interviewees answered a set of pre-set questions which are known as closed questions. Generally modern research suggests that open questions lead to longer responses and greater accuracy.

- Hugo Munsterberg was the first major and one of the most resolute applied psychologists. He was another of Wundt's students and he developed a lifelong interest in forensic issues. While still in Europe, he worked in support of Flemish weavers who were being sued by a customer. They were accused of supplying material of a different colour shade from that ordered. They disputed this. Munsterberg, with the help of the great physiologist of the visual system, Helmholtz, showed that the apparent difference in colour was a function of the different lighting conditions involved. The shades were *not* different. After migrating to the United States, he found that the adversarial Anglo-American system of law was not so sympathetic to hearing psychological opinion as the European system had been. His interests were wide in the field of applied psychology (Howitt, 1992) and included jury decision making as well as eyewitness testimony in the domain of forensic psychology.

- William Marston was one of Munsterberg's students. Under another name, he was the creator and cartoonist for the comic strip character Wonder Woman. He essentially developed the lie detector test (polygraphy) in 1915. His prototype of polygraphy was known as the 'systolic blood pressure deception test' and employed repeated blood pressure measurement during questioning. He claimed that changes in systolic blood pressure are indicative of lying (Grubin and Madsen, 2005). Furthermore, Marston was the first psychologist to be appointed in an American university as a professor of legal psychology (Bartol and Bartol, 1999). Importantly, Marston was an expert witness in the *Frye vs. the United States* case in 1923. In this, the Federal Court of Appeals laid down the principle that procedures, assessments and technique used in evidence should normally be well regarded in their field.

- Karle Marbe (*c.* 1911) testified in court that human reaction time latencies were such that an engine driver had no chance of stopping his train in time to prevent a crash. This was possibly the first psychological testimony at a civil rather than criminal trial. Less praiseworthy, Marbe also argued in court that the alleged victims of child sexual abuse made unreliable witnesses against their teacher. Society has changed a great deal since that time in terms of its attitudes to children. In 1911, Marbe was also the first psychologist to testify in a civil trial.

- Louis Thurstone (1922) published the findings of a study of the intelligence of police officers in the United States. It was found that, in general, junior officers tended to be more intelligent than older ones. Thurstone suggested that the brighter officers tend to leave the force for more rewarding and stimulating work, leaving the less intelligent to be promoted within the police force. This, effectively, was the start of the study of police psychology.

The modern development of forensic and criminal psychology

The development of psychologists' involvement as expert witnesses in American courts was an important determinant of the growth of forensic psychology. Although psychologists could serve as expert witnesses, the general principle was that they should do so in circumstances where they were not stepping into the area of expertise of members of the medical profession. However, eventually it was established that an individual's knowledge of the topic in question was the determining standard for an expert witnesses (*The People v. Hawthorne, 1940*). This meant that the mere possession of a medical profession was not a sufficient criterion for an expert witness. As empirically based psychology developed the judicial system gradually became more prepared to employ the services of psychologists in courts of law. However, their lack of medical qualifications was sometimes a stumbling block. Eventually, in 1962, in *Jenkins v. United States* the ruling emerged that psychologists could act as expert witnesses on the matter of mental illness when the crime was committed. The ruling essentially said that expertise on mental disease was not the sole province of medics. The consequence was the increased acceptance of psychologists on a wide range of legal matters by American courts.

So, for a number of reasons, psychologists made very slow headway in the journey into the courtroom. As we have seen, an important factor was the reluctance of courts to accept the evidence of psychologists equally with that of psychiatrists where these overlapped (Bartol and Bartol, 1999). Another factor was that key disciplines in the development of forensic and criminal psychology did not grow significantly until the second half of the twentieth century. This is especially true of social psychology and clinical psychology. Hall (2007) refers to the situation in the United Kingdom for psychology as being 'bleak' in these early years owing to the small numbers of psychologists that were working in academic contexts. In this sort of setting, it was probably inevitable that the development of clinical psychology was slow in the United Kingdom. Things were different in the United States where the returning veterans from World War Two led to the more rapid development of clinical psychology. Nevertheless, from about the 1970s onwards psychologists were increasingly, but in small numbers, turning their attention to matters of relevance to criminal psychology. In the United Kingdom, for example, Lionel Haward of the University of Surrey was beginning to speak of forensic psychologists and the work that they were doing to help, especially defence lawyers. As an illustration of this, Haward carried out a study into the adequacy of a police officer's claim in court that the officer had recorded the licence plate of a motor cycle travelling at speed. A hundred trained observers tried to replicate this but none of them could identify licence numbers in such circumstances (Smith, 1977).

Although, for example, Hans Eysenck was proposing his general theory of crime in the 1960s (see Chapter 5), by the 1970s others were making important contributions. For example, Ray Bull was beginning to apply social psychological principles to the work of police officers (e.g. Bull and Reid, 1975) and Philip Sealy was applying social psychology to the jury (e.g. Sealy and Cornish, 1973).

Forensic and criminal psychology has different historical antecedents in different countries. This is particularly the case in terms of the institutional basis of forensic and criminal psychology internationally. The institutional basis of the discipline is not the same in all countries. For example, although universities may provide the training in the legal area of psychology in Western Europe, the training is more likely to be in non-university settings in other countries. To illustrate how the origins of forensic and criminal psychology may be different in different countries, we can consider the example of Spain. The first textbook on legal psychology (or judicial, which may be preferred by some to the term forensic psychology) was written by a Spanish psychiatrist in 1932 (Royo, 1996). The author left Spain along with many other intellectuals because of the Spanish Civil War. It was not until 1971, when the Barcelona College of Barristers created a Department of Sociology and Legal Psychology, that the field was reopened. The first international meeting on Legal Psychology in Spain was held in 1976. While the specific details differ from country to country (see accounts of the development of the discipline in Hungary in Szegedi, 1998; in Portugal in Goncalves, 1998), generally speaking it would be common experience in different countries that forensic and criminal psychology, despite early interest, was in the doldrums until the 1970s (cf. Wrightsman, 2001), certainly in the United States and Western Europe. It should also be noted that the pattern of the steady expansion of forensic and criminal psychology since that time is not characteristic of all nations, especially those in Eastern Europe (Kury, 1998). In recent years, forensic and criminal psychology has developed extensively as

a discipline as well as in its institutional base. As with many academic and practical fields, this has involved the establishment of specialist journals in which to publish research and ideas, organisations devoted to psychology (e.g. the American Psychology and Law Society and the European Association for Psychology and Law), and national and international conferences devoted to the general field and specialist topics. Royo (1996) suggests that there are four basic ways in which a discipline may be consolidated. These are the formation of associations, the creation of specialised books and journals, the legal institutionalisation of the discipline as part of the process of criminal justice and the creation of university courses devoted to the subject. All of these may be recognised as characteristic of forensic and criminal psychology in many countries. There has been a general interest in integrating lawyers and psychologists in a variety of ways. An obvious example is joint conferences involving legal experts as well as psychologists specialising in the field.

The field of forensic and criminal psychology is not now fixed with its foci, boundaries and future clearly defined. It is an evolving field that will inevitably change:

- Developments in both the law and psychology will ensure that new issues become incorporated into the field. For example, the development of the concept of stalking and its first incorporation into law in California in 1990 (Emerson, Ferris and Gardner, 1998) led to considerable psychological and psychiatric effort to understand stalking behaviour.

- Increased employment of psychologists as personnel within different components of the criminal justice system will bring its own developments. So too will increases in private practice in the field. For example, a broadening of the role of psychology in police organisations – such as recruitment of officers – will bring a shift of interest in that direction in the field.

- Increasing numbers of students training in the field will ensure a fuller professionalisation of work and practice.

Main points

- The sub-discipline of forensic and criminal psychology deals with aspects of psychology relevant to the criminal justice system though, taken literally, the term *forensic psychology* refers to psychology in the context of law courts. The wider definition of the field underlies the selection of material in this book. As a consequence of the broad definition, the field unites psychologists from a wide variety of academic and practitioner backgrounds.

- Forensic and criminal psychology began to become important in the 1980s and increasingly so afterwards. The history of the field can be taken back many centuries to the times when issues such as diminished responsibility and fitness to stand trial were first developed in the legal system and so the demand for expert help from outside of the court itself. There was a period of interest in the field during the early years of academic psychology around 1900. However, for most of the twentieth century there was very little interest in the field.

- Forensic and criminal psychology has developed an appropriate infrastructure to ensure the continued development of the field. This includes specialist international organisations and journals in which the latest research is published.

Further reading

Histories of Forensic and Criminal Psychology are few in number. The following is reasonably thorough but hopefully a more comprehensive discussion will be published before too long covering all aspects of the field:

Bartol, C.R. and Bartol, A.M. (2005) 'History of forensic psychology' in I.B. Weiner and A.K. Hess (eds), *Handbook of Forensic Psychology* (4th edn) Chichester: Wiley (pp. 1–27).

The following are some reasonably accessible texts in the field of forensic and criminal psychology though their coverage is narrow compared to the above text:

Adler, J. and Gray, J.M. (eds) (2010) *Forensic Psychology: Concepts, Debates and Practice* (2nd edn) Cullompton: Willan Publishing.

Bull, R., Bilby, C. and Cooke, C. (2009) *Criminal Psychology* Oxford: Oneworld Publications.

Davies, G.M. and Beech, A.R. (eds) (2011) *Forensic Psychology* (2nd edn) Chichester: Wiley.

For a website containing forensic psychology information in depth please try:

All About Forensic Psychology. A Free And Comprehensive Guide To The World Of Forensic Psychology. http://www.all-about-forensic-psychology.com/index.html

One of the classics of early forensic and criminal psychology is Hugo Munsterberg's On the Witness Stand: Essays on Psychology and Crime (1908/1925). This can be found in full at: http://psychclassics.yorku.ca/Munster/Witness/index.htm

Visit our website at www.pearsoned.co.uk/howitt for self-test and essay questions, annotated further reading, audio interviews with researchers in the field, weblinks and more information on becoming a forensic psychologist.

Chapter 2

The social context of crime

Overview

- There are many sources of information about crime in society. For example, the mass media are full of crime and criminal justice system news. Governments publish crime statistics regularly and these are frequently presented as news items. For many of us, family, friends and acquaintances provide further information. Personal experience as a victim of crime or even a perpetrator can also contribute to our knowledge and beliefs. Nevertheless, misconceptions about crime and criminals are common.

- Crime statistics provide some insight into levels of crime, though they have their shortcomings. Crime trends can change rapidly for a number of reasons and so forensic and criminal psychologists should keep up to date. The Internet is a ready and reliable resource for information on the most recent crime trends for many countries such as the United States and the United Kingdom.

- Criminal and crime statistics are based on data collected from a range of different sources. Sometimes information collated by the police will be used but there are also statistics, for example, by surveying the general public. Different types of statistical information may superficially appear incompatible because of the different types of data involved. Each method of data collection has its own advantages and disadvantages which need to be taken into account when assessing their implications. The various approaches should be regarded as complementary and any differences in what the different approaches indicate are not so much problems as part of the challenge of making sense of crime in society.

- Crime statistics have to be interpreted and different researchers will interpret them differently. Consequently, there are alternative interpretations possible for crime statistics depending on one's viewpoint.

- A great amount of research has demonstrated that criminal behaviour is quite common – sufficiently so that it might be described as normal. Of course, relatively trivial incidents of stealing form the bulk of this criminal activity. Nevertheless, there is evidence that half of men and nearly a third of women admit to committing at least one crime such as burglary, theft, criminal damage, robbery, assault or selling drugs at some stage in their lives.

- International comparisons tend to suggest considerable variation in levels of crime in different nations. However, international trends in crime statistics do not indicate that levels of crime invariably increase over time. For some crimes (homicide is a good example), the trends are downwards or flattening out in some countries traditionally believed to be violent.

- The great variety of criminal justice systems in the world poses a challenge to forensic and criminal psychology. Justice is administered differently and is based on different principles in different parts of the world. Even where the systems are closely related (e.g. the United Kingdom and the United States) there may be crucial differences in certain respects. So avoid the assumption that the principles of forensic and criminal psychology are universally applicable.

Introduction

Our ideas about the world of crime come from a variety of sources. Personal experience clearly must play some part but imagery of crime and the criminal justice system is everywhere. For example, Howitt (1998c) found that the largest proportions of UK media news stories concerned crime and the criminal justice system. Characteristically, almost by definition, the news is about relatively unusual, new or sensational events. As such, it is not intended to be indicative of the mundane reality of most crime. Studies demonstrating a lack of correspondence between the reality of crime and the contents of newspapers go back many years (Croll, 1974; Davies, 1952; Roshier, 1971, 1973). Property crimes such as theft are grossly under-represented in newspapers, yet these are the very crimes that the general public is most likely to experience. Similarly, violent crime including homicide is disproportionately over-reported (Chermak, 1995). The situation is more extreme for movies and television. These are replete with cops and crime. In other words, to the extent that the media determine people's perceptions of crime, the risk is that they receive a rather distorted view.

It cannot be stressed too much the extent to which most crime is relatively petty and mundane. The emphasis of forensic psychology on the extreme and dramatic forms of crime stands in contrast with the patterns of crime as we experience them in our communities. One way of quantifying the types of crime experienced by the public are victim surveys in which criminal victimisation in the last year is recorded. Victimisation studies of this sort are increasingly employed as a way of accessing the social reality of crime in a less 'distorted' way than, for example, crimes reported by the general public to the police would be. Crimes reported to the police can consist only of the crimes which a victim decides to tell the police about. Victim studies are not without their own

biases since they can be affected by memory and they do not include crimes against businesses or crimes for which there is no clear victim. The British Crime Survey is a good example of such a survey. Flatley, Kershaw, Smith, Chaplin and Moon (2010) report findings from the survey conducted in 2009/10 involving nearly 45,000 participants as well as the corresponding figures for crimes recorded by the police. They estimate, based on these interviews, that 9,600,000 crimes are committed annually. The breakdown for the different types of crime can be seen in Figure 2.1. Overwhelmingly, crimes against property are the largest categories. The exception to this is the 'All violence' category. Some categories are missing including sexual crimes since they are not included in the main survey.

For crimes recorded by the police, the pattern is much the same except that more categories appear in the categorisation scheme used. (There is no universal, standard categorisation scheme for crime.) Indeed, based on police reports, the number of crimes in the UK was 4,300,000 – half of the crimes estimated from the British Crime Survey. It is noteworthy that if the violence categories are combined (violence against the person and robbery), the figure for violent crime is 22 per cent of crimes recorded by the police. If we combine the crimes involving property (including, theft, burglary and vandalism), the figure for property crimes is 66 per cent of all crimes recorded by the police. Drug offences and sexual offences are not found in the victim survey data for various reasons. Drugs offences may be regarded as victimless crimes and, as a consequence, are recorded in a separate part of the national survey in which crimes committed may be reported. Sexual offences are part of the victim survey coding but did not contribute significantly to the figures. The important lesson is that crime statistics are socially created and not laid down in tablets of stone.

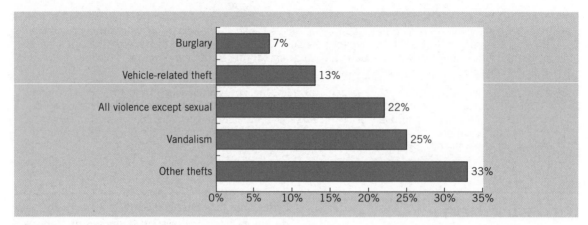

Figure 2.1 Proportions of different types of crime victim found in the British Crime Survey

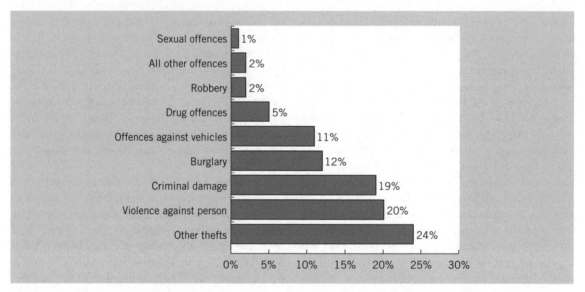

Figure 2.2 Proportions of different types of crime found in police recorded crime in the UK

The important points emerging from all this are (a) the confirmation that the vast majority of crime by whatever measure is theft and other property crimes and (b) that different ways of assessing crime rates to some extent can give different outcomes. We will discuss this further in the next section.

The extent of crime

Specifying the reality of crime is not simple. There is no single reality to be described. There are very basic questions

such as at what point do events begin to be construed as a crime. What is it about a set of circumstances which results in an eyewitness labelling events as a crime? This is an important question because it is known that eyewitnesses are responsible for bringing violent crimes to the attention of the authorities. The US Bureau of Justice Statistics (2003) indicates that 27 per cent of known violent crimes are reported by eyewitnesses. In their research into bystanders' reactions to crimes, Langsdale and Greenberg (2006) showed participants a video of a conversation between a man and a woman lasting just 10 seconds before the man either walked or ran away or

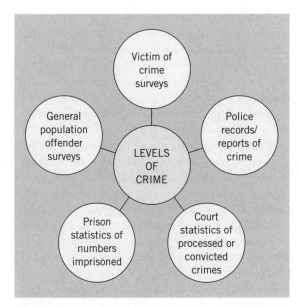

Figure 2.3 Different ways of estimating levels of crime

another version in which there was a 30-second delay. If the man ran away after 10 seconds then the witness was more likely to perceive the events as a robbery than if it took 30 seconds before he ran away or if he walked away, irrespective of the amount of time involved. In real-life situations, this may be the difference between a crime being reported to the police or not. Interpretative processes like this underlie criminal statistics and may occur at various stages in the data collation process.

Among the various sources of information about the extent of crime are the following:

- Surveys of the *general public's experience of crime* in, say, a particular year. These are usually known as victim or victimisation surveys. Basically, members of the public are interviewed about their experience of crime in the previous year. These have their difficulties. They are subject to problems of recall and accuracy over the period in question. Not surprisingly, such surveys tend to produce the highest estimates of the rates of crime and victimisation. Crimes for which the victim is corporate (a big company) or for which there is no obvious victim (such as vandalism in the public park) are likely to be omitted from the data collected. Furthermore, they may include events that may well not lead to a conviction by a court of law.

- Aggregate data of *crimes recorded by/reported to the police*. These are affected by reporting biases. For

example, some victims may decide not to go to the police. The police may decide that certain events are best ignored and no attempt made at arrest (e.g. racist chants at a football match). The police may choose to see the events as not being a crime for some reason. How the police classify events as crimes or not crimes and particular types of crime may affect the overall pattern. Crimes recorded by the police are not the same as crimes reported to the police. When a victim reports a crime, the police may decide that it is not appropriate to record it as a crime.

- *Court statistics* that codify the numbers and types of offences being processed in a given year and the outcomes in terms of sentencing of these different cases. The obvious biases here are in terms of the factors that lead to prosecution as opposed to no charge.

- *Prison statistics* provide breakdowns of the numbers in prison at any one time, their offence categories, their sentence and so forth. Biases here may be due to sentencing policies at the time. For example, a concerted clampdown on burglary may lead to an increase in the numbers of burglars in prison.

- *General population offender surveys* have recently been developed in which members of a random sample of households are interviewed about the crimes they have committed ever in their lives and/or recently, say, in the previous year. This is likely to include at least some crimes that would be ignored by the police and other components of the criminal justice system as being too trivial to warrant prosecution. Furthermore, there is probably a bias against the more serious crimes since those who have committed the more serious crimes may well have been arrested, prosecuted and sent to prison, so that they are excluded from such surveys.

For obvious reasons, the rates of crime that would be estimated from these different statistics vary. One would rightly expect that surveys of victims produce substantially higher levels of crime in general than any of the other statistical indices. A number of matters warrant consideration:

- None of the statistics is simply wrong. They each provide different perspectives on criminal activity.

- Each of the statistics has its own value and may be more useful for a particular purpose than others. Even though, say, crimes recorded by the police may be just a small fraction of crimes committed, they may still be very useful for examining changes in crime rates over time. This is especially true if the biases in reporting crimes to the police remain relatively constant over time. Unfortunately, this is difficult to ascertain. So, for example, if we find more cases of child sexual abuse in the 1990s than in the 1960s, is this due to higher levels of sexual abuse? The data are equally consistent with there being an increased awareness in the danger of abuse which makes people more vigilant and more prepared to report crimes. It may also reflect an increase due to retrospective prosecutions of previously unreported abuse that happened many years earlier.

- Care is always needed in terms of the interpretation of any of these statistics. For example, legal and other changes may result in crimes being classified differently at different points in time. A change in the definition of rape to include, say, male rape may produce an increase in the number of rapes. While it is common practice for statisticians to signal changes in the basis on which the statistics are compiled, it is much more difficult to adjust previous years on the basis of such information unless the compilers do so. This is not simply a matter of governments manipulating crime statistics for their own political advantage, it reflects the changing nature of the law and the fact that what is criminal changes over time.

In short, while some will point to the inadequacies of crime statistics as fatal flaws in those statistics, it is better to regard crime statistics as being of limited usefulness in limited circumstances. This makes them very similar to much of the data that psychologists collect. That they are the result of a complex social process makes their understanding all the more important; it is not an excuse for dismissing them as worthless. Often the problem is not the nature of the data but how they should be interpreted. The more familiar one is with a variety of different sorts of crime statistics and just how particular crime statistics are compiled, then the more adequate one's interpretations are likely to be.

Because there are broad changes in crime over time and considerable international variation in its levels, crime statistics go out of date rapidly. Increasingly, extensive information about crime statistics is published on the Internet by governments and other organisations. Obviously, Internet addresses can change overnight, but good search engines readily find suitable sites. Useful search terms are crime statistics and criminal statistics. This material is probably as up to date as any publicly

available since it is far quicker to update web material than books or pamphlets. As with any material on the Internet, one should always carefully assess the adequacy of its source and try to anticipate the sort of spin that may be put on what the statistics mean or just what statistics are presented. This applies to all sources of information, it is not simply a consideration when using the Internet as a source.

The term *crime index* is commonly used in relation to criminal statistics. This is merely a composite measure of the number of crimes based, usually, on the more serious types. US sources will be referring to a composite of murder and non-negligent manslaughter, forcible rape, robbery and aggravated assault (these are the contribution of violent crimes) and burglary, larceny theft, motor-vehicle theft and arson (the property offences included). Other countries may have their own variants on this, more appropriate to the major crime categories in those countries. These indices provide a very broad picture of crime trends. The sub-components of the index may actually be showing rather different trends. For example, rape may be increasing but since motor-vehicle theft is decreasing much faster, the overall trend is downward.

The extent of criminality

One of the classic ideas of criminology and sociology is that of white-collar or middle-class crime. This is not just about the extent to which white-collar workers are punished for matters such as fraud and embezzlement, for instance, although the prosecution of these may be difficult. It is also about activities such as 'borrowing' stationery from the office or using the office telephone for private calls. These activities are ones that would be regarded as criminal from other perspectives. Generally, those who engage in them regard these activities as acceptable, if not normal. Tax evasion, for some people, is seen as almost morally justified and hence not truly a crime.

The extent of criminality in the population is remarkably high. Even if we take the stringent criterion of imprisonment, in the United States the chance of a person going to prison during their lifetime is estimated at nearly 7 per cent according to estimates (Bureau of Justice, 2004). The odds are much worse for some groups, which may reflect biases in the criminal justice system:

Table 2.1 Generational and racial trends in the likelihood of imprisonment in the USA by the age of 30–34 years

	All white	All black	White high school dropouts	Black high school dropouts
1945–9 Cohort	1%	10%	4%	15%
1975–9 Cohort	5%	27%	28%	68%

Source: Pettit, Sykes and Western (2009)

- The figure is 11 per cent for men but only 2 per cent for women.

- A black person has a 19 per cent chance compared with 3 per cent for white people.

- The figure for black men is 32 per cent as opposed to 6 per cent for white men. That is, nearly one in three black men will spend time in prison!

- Over 64 per cent of jailed persons were of racial or ethnic minority origin in 2001.

More recently, Western and Pettit (2010) have pointed out that the risk of being imprisoned in the USA is affected by both generational factors, racial factors and school dropout. They compared men born in the 1940s (1945–9) with men born in the 1970s (1975–9). The key variable was whether the men had received a prison sentence by the time they were 30 years of age (i.e. 30–34 years). Table 2.1 clearly demonstrates that the younger generation had a much greater risk of imprisonment than the older one by substantial margins. It is also clear from the table that black men were substantially more likely to serve a prison term than white men. Furthermore, dropping out from high school led to a greater likelihood of imprisonment. Putting all of these factors together, two-thirds of black high school dropouts in the younger generation received prison sentences compared to less than a third of white high school dropouts.

The extent of potential criminality can also be seen from other studies of youngsters. For example, Wilson (1980) took samples of 10- to 17-year-olds living in deprived housing estates in inner city or suburban settings. Evidence concerning their criminality was obtained directly from police records of convictions and cautions:

- Twenty per cent of the boys had a record of crime. Theft and burglary were the commonest offences.

- This should be contrasted with their self-reported misbehaviours. Crime is much more common in terms of self-reported offences rather than criminal convictions – over 40 per cent had shoplifted, 67 per cent had drawn graffiti in the street and so forth.

The British Crime and Justice Survey (Budd, Sharp and Mayhew, 2005) extended our knowledge of self-reported rates of crime. A national sample of the general household population in the age range of 10 to 65 years were asked in detail about the offences of burglary, vehicle-related thefts, other thefts, criminal damage, robbery, assaults and selling drugs. Over 50 per cent of men and 30 per cent of women had committed at least one of these core crimes in their lives. Given that other types of offences such as sexual ones were omitted from the survey, it is likely that the figure for people who had ever committed a serious offence could be higher. Of course, some of these crimes were not very serious since they involved property of low value or involved assaults that did not lead to injury. About 20 per cent of the population had committed a serious offence at some stage and this usually involved assault with injury. The survey also assessed the numbers who had committed an offence in the last year. These figures are naturally smaller than the equivalent lifetime percentages. Six per cent of people had committed a property crime in the last year and 5 per cent had committed a violent offence. For juvenile offenders the majority of offences were violent in nature though generally these did not involve injury. For people above the age of 25 years, the majority of offences were to do with property. Drug offences were commoner than property offences and much more common than violent offences in the 18- to 25-year-old age group.

There is a further approach that warrants attention in this context: that is, the field of experiments into honesty/dishonesty carried out by psychologists. Carefully staged situations, of a variety of sorts, have been contrived in order to investigate dishonesty. The origins of this were in the classic studies of Hartshorne and May (1928) who investigated aspects of dishonesty such as lying, cheating and stealing in pubescent children. Among their measures was the failure or not of children to return a coin they had been given. This and later research is reviewed in Farrington (1979). A range of other ways of assessing stealing has been developed. For example, some researchers have deliberately 'lost' money in the street to see whether the finder attempts to return the cash or merely just keeps it. Farrington and Kidd (1977) lost envelopes in the street containing varying amounts of money:

- With no money enclosed, 95 per cent of the envelopes were returned to the address in the enclosed letter.

- With £1 in cash enclosed, 75 per cent were returned.

- With £5 in cash enclosed, then 55 per cent were returned.

This is a notably high rate of dishonesty given that, in the United Kingdom, to keep money knowing that one is depriving its rightful owner of it constitutes theft. Many of these studies were carried out to investigate the effects of different environmental circumstances on the rates of honesty. They also indicate the baseline rates of dishonest behaviour in fairly general samples of the population. None of this should be too surprising given what we know about the illegal downloading of music from the Internet (music piracy). Wingrove, Korpas and Weisz (2011) showed that young people's attitudes to illegally downloading were very different from their attitudes to stealing a CD from a music shop – despite the fact that the illegal download and the CD might contain exactly the same music tracks. This goes some way to understanding why so many disregard the law on piracy.

Of course, there is an important implication for forensic and criminal psychology in all of this. That is, in many ways the study of criminal behaviour is the study of the behaviour of normal people – a high proportion admit to having committed some sort of crime in their lives no matter how trivial. That does not imply that there are no abnormal psychological features in any criminal, merely that much crime has to be explained in terms of normal behaviour.

Crime rates compared internationally

The International Crime Victimisation Survey (2001) revealed a great deal about the relative rates of crime in countries in different parts of the world. The international survey included Australia, Austria, Belgium, Canada, England and Wales, Finland, France, Germany (the West prior to reunification), Italy, Malta, the Netherlands, New Zealand, Northern Ireland, Norway, Scotland, Spain, Sweden, Switzerland and the United States. The crimes surveyed ranged from property offences against cars, such as theft of the car, damage to the car and theft from the car, on the less serious side, to sexual offences and assault and threat. To survey national populations in such diverse locations is, manifestly, logistically complex. Indeed, sampling in economically developing countries was very much confined to cities as a consequence. The surveys were not all conducted at exactly the same time in the different nations, so it is really only possible to describe the data as being collected in the 1990s. Since forensic and criminal psychologists are most likely to work in developed nations, the data for industrialised countries are the most pertinent. It should be stressed that this was a victimisation survey, not a collation of, for example, crimes known to the police. So the information was obtained directly from the public, thus avoiding the sorts of reporting bias that can affect the numbers of crimes known to the police. Of course, surveys of the public are subject to all of the potential biases of any survey (refusals to take part, for instance). Nevertheless, victim surveys generally indicate greater rates of victimisation than do the number of crimes known to the police. How much the two are truly different is difficult to assess as this particular survey reported prevalence rates as opposed to incidence rates. The meanings of prevalence and incidence are as follows:

- Prevalence rates are simply the percentage of people who report having been a victim of crime or a particular sort of crime in the previous year. If they have been robbed twice, for example, this is not recorded in prevalence figures. The choice is between having been victimised or having not been victimised. They give the probability of being a victim in a given year; multi-crime victims are treated in the same way as single-crime victims.

- Incidence rates reflect the frequency of being victimised and, as such, would be better estimates of the numbers of crimes committed annually. So one could not multiply the prevalence rate by the size of the population to obtain the number of crimes committed in a particular country in a given year.

Internationally there is considerable variation in the likelihood of victimisation and, for some countries, noticeable variation over time. Overall, the chances of victimisation were the highest in England and Wales of the countries surveyed. The prevalence rate was almost 31 per cent for victimisation for any sort of crime. Other countries had rates of 25 per cent or so. For example, the figure for the United States in the 1990s was 24 per cent. In general, Belgium and Northern Ireland had the lowest victimisation rates.

For certain types of offence, it is not common practice to report the crime to the police. Assault has reporting rates of 38 per cent in England and Wales and 45 per cent in the United States. Sexual offences are less likely to be reported. The figures are 20 per cent for England and Wales and 28 per cent for the United States. There is a lot of international variation in reporting sexual offences. For example, the rate is 5 per cent in Spain and 43 per cent in Northern Ireland. Reporting rates found from victim surveys allow the 'true' rate of crime to be assessed from known numbers of crimes reported to the police. Thus, for example, the true rate of rape in England and Wales should be multiplied by approximately five (i.e. victim surveys suggest that just over 20 per cent of rapes are reported) in order to correct for the low reporting rate.

Rates of reporting are highest for burglary in virtually all countries. The reason is probably the insurer's requirement that the crime is reported to the police if an insurance payment is to be made. Chapter 4 discusses, in part, the psychology of reporting crime. The international survey has been updated in recent years though things have not changed substantially for the most part. Table 2.2 gives a few comparisons between England and Wales, the United States, Australia and Canada based on the most recent available figures (van Dijk, van Kestern and Smit, 2007). Despite there being substantial differences between the USA and England and Wales in terms of perceptions of the relative levels of crime, the victim data suggest relatively little difference in general. It should also be noted that according to crime report figures, there were major reductions in levels of violent crime in the United States in the 1990s (Bureau of Justice, 2001a). The trend continues to be downwards (Bureau of Justice Statistics, 2011).

Figures suggest that, in a lifetime, the vast majority of North Americans become victims of an index crime recorded by the police – 83 per cent will be victimised by violence in this way and 99 per cent by theft. Criminality may be common; victimisation is a virtual certainty (Bureau of Justice, 2001a). For every 1,000 Americans from 12 years of age and above there are 11 simple assaults, 3 aggravated assaults, 2 robberies and 1 rape or other form of sexual assault (Bureau of Justice, 2011) each year. Based on the British Crime Survey of 2009/10, 22 per cent of the population had been the victim of any sort as of violence that year (Flatley et al., 2010). The British Crime Survey of 2000 (Home Office, 2001) found that 59 per cent had at some time in their life been the victim of a crime reported to the police. In contrast, only 10 per cent had been in court as a person accused of a crime. In other words, in terms of experiences of crime, the victim role is the commonest despite the centrality of the offender in forensic and criminal psychology.

There have been other attempts to compare crime rates internationally. One of the most recent involved a cross-national comparison of eight countries – England and Wales, Scotland, Canada, United States, Australia, the Netherlands, Sweden and Switzerland (Farrington, Langan and Tonry, 2004). As with other studies, there are difficulties involved in making statistical comparisons among different countries. For example, in some European countries burglary and vehicle theft are not distinguished in the legal code from other types of theft. This meant that the rates of burglary and vehicle theft in these countries had to be estimated from general theft data. The period studied was the two decades between 1980 and 2000. One of the startling features of the data is that different countries may show exactly the opposite trend rates of particular crimes. In some countries, the rates

Table 2.2 Prevalence rates for England and Wales, the United States, Australia and Canada in 2003/4				
	England and Wales	**United States**	**Australia**	**Canada**
Sexual crime against women	0.9%	1.4%	–	0.8%
Assault and threat	5.8%	5.3%	3.8%	3.0%
Burglary	3.5%	2.5%	2.5%	2.0%

of recorded burglary per 1,000 population increased over time (e.g. Australia and the Netherlands); in other countries the rates of recorded burglary decreased over time (United States). Some countries have several times the rate of recorded burglaries of other countries. Australia had the highest rate overall and Switzerland the lowest rate. Rates can change dramatically within a country over time. So the United States had far higher rates of robbery than England and Wales in the 1980s but at the end of the study period, rates in the two countries were virtually identical. Rates in the United States had declined markedly and rates in the United Kingdom had increased markedly.

Statistics may rapidly go out of date as will a psychologist's knowledge of them. Furthermore, what may be true of one type of crime (e.g. homicide) may not be true of other types of violent crime. Blackburn (1995b) was almost certainly correct at the time to point out national differences in terms of violent crimes, especially. He suggested that the United States was a nation especially prone to such crime. The variation is remarkable, as Blackburn suggests, but crime statistics are not necessarily stable even over a relatively short period of time. He argues that different homicide rates may be due to socio-cultural factors: but just what socio-cultural factors could be responsible for rapidly changing homicide rates? Changes in crime policy may produce changes in policing, sentencing and punishment that result in a quick reduction in crime statistics. Governments make claims about the efficacy of their criminal justice policy based on declining rates of certain crimes.

To be precise, for the United States the statistical evidence is that homicide, adjusted for the size of the population, has become less frequent in recent years. By 1999 it was at a low level equivalent to the figures for the latter part of the 1960s – in 1999 the rate was 6 homicides for every 100,000 people in the population. This is substantially less than the rate of 10 homicides per 100,000 in 1980 – the United States' peak homicide year for the latter part of the twentieth century (Fox and Zawitz, 2004). Homicide rates in the United States have been more or less constant since 1999. The US homicide rates remained stable at about 6 per 100,000 inhabitants between 1998 and 2007. These figures are lower than for the 1980s and 1990s in general. The figure for 1980 was 10, for example (US Census Bureau, 2011).

According to important international comparative data (Farrington et al., 2004), homicide has also tended to decline since 1980 in some countries included in the survey. In Australia, the homicide rate is about 2 homicides but has declined slightly; in Canada the rate has dropped from 3 to 2 per 100,000 of population. The Netherlands' homicide rate stayed remarkably constant over the period at 1. The UK figures have increased slightly over time but still are currently approximately 1.5 per 100,000 in the population. Other data (Barclay, Tavares and Siddique, 2001) show that the United States' homicide rates, although two or three times the rate for Western European countries, are comparatively low. For example, Finland has a homicide rate of 12, Russia a rate of 21 and South Africa a rate of 56 – nearly ten times the rate in the United States. National rates tend to disguise the fact that some areas within a country may have disproportionately high homicide rates. For example, the rate for Washington, DC, in the United States was virtually the same as the massive South African one at 51 per 100,000.

It cannot be emphasised too much that, even for a so-called (or possibly mislabelled) violent society such as the United States, the crimes recorded by the police are overwhelmingly property crimes. In 1999, larceny theft was 60 per cent, burglary 18 per cent and motor-vehicle theft 10 per cent of crimes. Violent crimes appear next in the list with aggravated assault at 8 per cent of crimes, robbery at 3 per cent, rape at less than 1 per cent and murder at 1 recorded crime in 1,000 crimes (Bureau of Justice, 2001a). Furthermore, great care should be taken over whether homicide rates truly reflect the violent nature of different countries. If we compare the rate of assault for England and Wales with that of the United States, it would appear that England and Wales is proportionately more violent. In 1999, the rate of serious assaults per 100,000 population in England and Wales was 1,395 based on victim surveys and 415 based on serious assaults recorded by the police. For the United States, the serious assault rate was 669 according to victim surveys and 336 based on those recorded by the police (Farrington et al., 2004). These rates paint a different picture of violent crime from that painted by homicide rates.

Conservative and radical interpretations

No matter how carefully obtained, criminal statistics are subject to interpretation. For any set of figures there are several equally viable interpretations. Crime statistics are aggregates of many distinct happenings and, by and large, we have little knowledge of the detail. For example, the US data on felony convictions in state and federal courts for 1994 (Bureau of Justice, 2001c) reveal that drug trafficking accounted for 20 per cent of convictions and drug possession for 12 per cent of convictions. That is, combined, the drugs offences are responsible for nearly a third of convictions. What does one conclude from these figures? One interpretation is that drugs offences are such a major crime problem that more should be done to arrest and punish offenders. This would probably imply a need for greater police activity, which ought to result in even more convictions. An alternative, more radical, view would be to point out that such high figures reflect the failure of policy on drugs to make significant inroads in reducing drug use. The country might be better off decriminalising drugs or some such strategy. The savings to the criminal justice system would be enormous simply in terms of time and money. Naturally, each of these positions can be criticised with further arguments. Nevertheless, the basic point should be clear – crime statistics do not carry with them implicit meanings: interpretation has to be imposed.

Take another example: black people are over-represented in both the homicide perpetrator and victim figures in the United States. In terms of rates standardised by population size, a black person has six times the risk of being a victim compared to a white person, and is eight times more likely to be a perpetrator (Fox and Zawitz, 2004). While some authors (Rushton, 1990) might interpret this as indicative of racial differences in the inheritance of criminal tendencies, for others they reflect the huge social inequalities experienced by black communities and biases in policing (e.g. Howitt and Owusu-Bempah, 1994; Stark, 1993). Of course, some explanations become more and less viable when other statistical information is incorporated. For example, the United States has achieved substantial reductions in violence between intimates (partners, spouses, etc.) which cannot possibly be accounted for by changes in the gene pool (e.g. Bureau of Justice, 2001d).

International variations in justice systems

Whatever the means by which crime rates are assessed, the socio-legal contexts in which forensic and criminal psychologists operate differ in many other respects. The variability in criminal justice systems, broadly defined, is immense. This is not generally problematic as most will work solely within one criminal justice system. Nevertheless, it is important to understand that a given system is just one of many possibilities. Furthermore, each criminal justice system has many components of which practitioners need to be aware. By way of illustration, Table 2.3 gives some information from three criminal justice systems – Japan, France, and England and Wales (other parts of Britain have different systems). The data are taken from an international compendium of information about criminal justice systems around the world (International Crime Victimisation Survey, 2001). Despite the data being supplied by specialist researchers, certain information is unavailable from particular countries. A few areas of comparison have been taken to illustrate the similarities and diversities in countries both near together and far apart. The following points are fairly self-evident and are mostly illustrated in Table 2.3:

- *The legal system*: France has an inquisitorial legal system in which judges or magistrates seek to obtain the truth about a particular case from various sources. In other words, they have a leading role in determining what evidence and expert advice is needed. In England and Wales (and other countries such as Canada, the United States and Australia, which derive their legal systems from Britain), the adversarial system is adopted: that is, the prosecution and defence are adversaries who battle to convince the judge or jury that theirs is the winning argument. Their success is then judged, often by a jury. The different systems vary in terms of the sorts of evidence that may be admitted as valid and the need to consider the fitness of the accused to stand trial. Japan basically moved from one system to another.

- *Jury system*: some legal systems do not use juries but rely on judges and magistrates to decide issues of guilt. Other systems use juries but there can be substantial differences in the sizes of the jury used or the rules used for determining the verdict of the jury. In some systems, it is possible for the judge to take part with the jury in determining guilt (see Chapter 23).

- *The age of criminal responsibility*: this is twice as old in Japan (20 years) as in England and Wales (10 years). Of course, there may be provision for treating young people separately, such as juvenile courts and

Table 2.3 Some international comparisons of criminal justice systems

ASPECT	JAPAN	FRANCE	ENGLAND AND WALES
LEGAL SYSTEM	Influenced historically by French and German systems but more adversarial in recent times	Inquisitorial system – essentially the judge seeks the facts of the case from a variety of sources	Adversarial system based on cases put forward by prosecution and defence
JURY SYSTEM	Not in use in fact despite being available	Not used	Jury system for more serious crimes
AGE OF CRIMINAL RESPONSIBILITY	20 years of age	18 years of age	10 years of age but special provision up to 18 years
CRIMINAL STATISTICS: ASSAULTS AND THREATS IN ONE YEAR – VICTIM SURVEY**	0.6%	2.1%	5.6%
CRIMINAL STATISTICS: SEXUAL OFFENCES IN ONE YEAR – VICTIM SURVEY**	0.8%	0.3%	0.9%
CRIMINAL STATISTICS: ROBBERY IN YEAR – VICTIM SURVEY	0.2%	0.8%	1.4%
POLICE SYSTEM	Two-layered structure: (1) the national police and (2) the prefecture police	Four police divisions: (1) Four police divisions***	No national police force – separate forces at local level. Some smaller forces such as railway police
PRISON*	59/100,000	96/100,000	152/100,000
CIVIL CASES	–	A court can hear both civil and criminal cases	Separate systems for civil and criminal cases

Source: *Kings College London, Department of Law (2010)
**van Dijk, van Kesteren and Smit (2007)
***(1) General Information (2) City Police – city law enforcement (3) Judiciary Police and (4) Territory Surveillance – state security

other institutions, which reduce the apparent huge differences between the various countries. It may be helpful to note that Heilbrun *et al.* (1997) suggest that in most parts of the United States the trend is to allow younger people to be tried in adult courts. They report that in the majority of jurisdictions, 14-year-olds can now be tried in criminal courts. This touches on fundamental beliefs about the nature of crime and how it is dealt with. This is discussed more fully in Chapter 3.

- *Crime statistics*: while, as we have seen, the figures vary among nations, it is equally important to note that crime classifications in different countries may not be the same. In other words, direct comparisons may be impossible. It is also notable that actual numbers of certain crimes such as murder and rape are probably rather lower than most people believe them to be. More recent data from international victim surveys have been added in the table.

- *Police system*: there are a number of differences among police organisations across nations. One particularly obvious dimension is the extent to which police organisations are national or local. Often there is a mixture of the two, but sometimes, as in the case of England and Wales, there are numerous small forces covering areas of just a few million people. The more small units there are then the greater the communication problems and, consequently, the greater the need for provision to ensure good inter-force communications.

- *Prison*: different nations differ substantially in their prison populations. This may be indicative of different base levels of crime, but it may also reflect profound differences in penal policies.

- *Civil cases*: civil law deals with legal cases that are about private rights rather than the public concern of crime. Criminal penalties (such as prison) do not apply in civil cases where financial payments to the aggrieved party are the means of righting wrongs. In some jurisdictions, they are dealt with by the same courts, whereas in other jurisdictions there is a totally separate civil law court system. Civil courts may sometimes deal with criminal matters (e.g. civil actions have been brought against alleged criminals but these do not result in criminal penalties).

It is a substantial task to become sufficiently familiar with the legal system of any country to practise as a forensic and criminal psychologist. The international nature of research in the field should encourage researchers to develop a knowledge of these different systems of justice. If nothing else, such knowledge will help one to understand why certain sorts of research will be of interest in only some countries. Jury research may be relevant in the United States, Australia, Canada and the United Kingdom, but of much less interest to forensic and criminal psychologists from much of mainland Europe, for example. Some issues such as inquisitorial versus adversarial systems have been fairly extensively researched (e.g. Stephenson, 1992).

Main points

- It is important for forensic and criminal psychologists to be familiar with trends in crime as reported in crime statistics and from surveys of the general population. A degree of sophistication is necessary in their interpretation since each source has its own particular characteristics. Crime rates obtained from victim surveys are different from those obtained by collating the number of crimes recorded by the police. Court statistics and prison statistics give us different sorts of information. It is unwise to regard the characteristics of different statistics as flaws.

- Quite high proportions of the general population are known to have been involved as a victim and a perpetrator of crime at some stage in their lives. Experimental studies have shown that various forms of dishonesty are very common. Of course, the precise figures will depend on quite how crime is defined. Clearly, the number of persistent offenders is a much lower figure.

- International comparisons reveal many differences between the criminal justice systems in different parts of the world. So research that is important in one country may have no bearing on what happens in another country. Similarly, crime statistics vary internationally in important ways. England and Wales seem to have disproportionately high rates of victimisation.

Further reading

The following will help you understand the problematic nature of crime statistics:

Coleman, C. (1996) *Understanding Crime Data: Haunted by the Dark Figure* Buckingham: Open University Press.

Green, S., Johnson, H. and Young, P. (2009) *Understanding Crime and Criminal Justice Data* Buckingham: Open University Press.

Crime statistics are to be found in many locations on the Web. These provide much more up-to-date information than is possible in most books.

The UK Home Office has Research Development Statistics at http://www.homeoffice.gov.uk/rds/index.html

European Sourcebook of Crime and Criminal Justice Statistics: http://www.europeansourcebook.org/

US Bureau of Justice, Bureau of Justice Statistics: http://www.ojp.gov/bjs/

Visit our website at www.pearsoned.co.uk/howitt for self-test and essay questions, annotated further reading, audio interviews with researchers in the field, weblinks and more information on becoming a forensic psychologist.

Chapter 3

Crime and the public

Overview

- What is a crime is defined in terms of a complex social process. Each stage of the process requires detailed examination in order that we obtain a full understanding of the nature of crime. Identical events may be classified as crime or otherwise depending on circumstances. The decision to report events to the police as crimes is just one important aspect of this. Other factors are also influential. Government policy on crime is a delicate political issue that can be sensitive to public opinion, for example, such that certain crimes may be targeted for police attention.

- There is evidence that the public appear to have a tough-minded attitude towards crime. This may influence the way in which criminal justice is administered, perhaps by influencing politicians to be more tough-minded on crime themselves.

- The public's knowledge about aggregate rates of crime and trends in criminal statistics tends to be poor and generally inaccurate. This is partly because it is difficult to think statistically in terms of percentages and probabilities.

- Moral panics are essentially an overreaction against some event (such as a crime) that has been perceived as a threat or a risk to society's major values. The alarm generated may lead to demands that action should be taken against the source of the threat. The strength of feeling tends to be self-nurturing such that the panic escalates.

- The media and personal experience form the basis of the public's knowledge about crime. The links between the two are far from simple and not apparent in all research. There is often little or no relationship between an individual's risk of victimisation and their level of fear of crime. This is the fear–victimisation paradox. Understanding the psychological processes involved in the fear of crime seems to improve predictions about media influences on the individual and the consequences of victimisation.

- Theories about the origins of the fear of crime suggest that: (1) the distorted image of crime portrayed by the media affects heavy television viewers disproportionately (cultivation theory); (2) any source of information may provide the individual with a particularly vivid but negative impression of a particular crime or a particular sort of crime such that the individual responds to similar situations to the vivid imagery with fear (availability heuristic); and (3) fear of crime is the consequence of the independent influences of beliefs about the negative consequences of being victimised and the subjective risk of being victimised (cognitive theory).

Introduction

Crime does not just involve the criminals. It is the result of a complex social process, which operates at virtually every conceivable level of social and psychological analysis. So the nature of the task facing forensic and criminal psychologists cannot be fully appreciated without understanding the social context of crime. According to Ainsworth (2000a), the path from the commission of a crime to the punishment of an offender is a long, complex and tortuous one (p. 15). Crime is not simply (or even) the product of the mind of the criminal, it is a social product. The following are just some of the things which need to be taken into account:

- what laws apply;
- what the set of circumstances surrounding the events is;
- what the public thinks about crime;
- what the victim thinks about crime;
- what the ethos of the policing system is;
- what the system for dealing with psychiatric cases is;
- who decides whom to prosecute;
- the rules governing court procedure;
- the skills of the lawyer;
- the characteristics of the judge;
- what the jurors have read in the newspapers about the case or any one of a number of other aspects of the crime, the criminal and the criminal justice system. Each is essential and, in some circumstances, any may become crucial.

There is a very real sense in which a crime is committed only once a court hearing has determined that one has occurred. The reason is that very much the same events can be seen quite differently according to the prevailing circumstances. If a person takes a few coins from a colleague's desk at work to pay for a lunchtime sandwich, fails to tell the colleague that the money has been taken, and then fails to pay it back, has a crime been committed? Was it really the intent to deprive the colleague of the coins? If so, then surely this is a crime? What if the colleague fails to notice that the money is missing? Would this mean a crime had not taken place? What if the colleague realises the money is missing but the boss does not want the police informed? Does this mean that a crime has not taken place? What if the police decide that the sum of money involved is very small anyway and suggest to the owner of the money that perhaps they may have forgotten they had spent it? Does this mean that a crime has not taken place? What if the police (or other body) decide that there is little point in prosecuting in this case because the colleague was taking antidepressant drugs at the time and these were having unfortunate side effects on his memory and behaviour? Does this mean that a crime has not taken place? What if the colleague is prosecuted but the case is discharged because of irregularities in the way in which the police obtained a confession? Does this mean that a crime has not been committed? Finally, the colleague pleads guilty and is convicted by the court of stealing the money, then fined. Does that mean that a crime has been committed?

At each of these stages, a crime may or may not have been committed. The process of defining a crime is not just complex but will have a multiplicity of perspectives. Crime is a category, which is the result of a process involving different individuals, different institutions and different settings. From one perspective a crime may have been committed, from another a crime may not have been committed. All of these things are dependent on the jurisdiction involved since the practice of the law varies. The thief who is so mentally impaired that he/she does not know that he/she is committing a crime may be not guilty of theft in the eyes of the court. The driver who inadvertently drives over the speed limit because his/her speedometer is faulty, in law may well be committing a crime even though he/she had not intended to, simply because this is a strict (i.e. absolute liability) offence. Once in a while, there may be behaviours that would seem to be criminal but against which there is no law (for example, it is only in recent years that an offence of grooming a child for sexual purposes has been created in the United Kingdom despite its being a matter of concern for many years). Legal processes are social in nature and cannot be understood simply through knowledge of what the relevant law is.

Figure 3.1 shows something of the complexity of the processes involved. A number of issues should be considered:

- The figure suggests a relatively closed criminal justice system but this is an incomplete picture. It is a more open system than this implies.
- Legislation is the result of a political process that may involve interest groups pressuring the government,

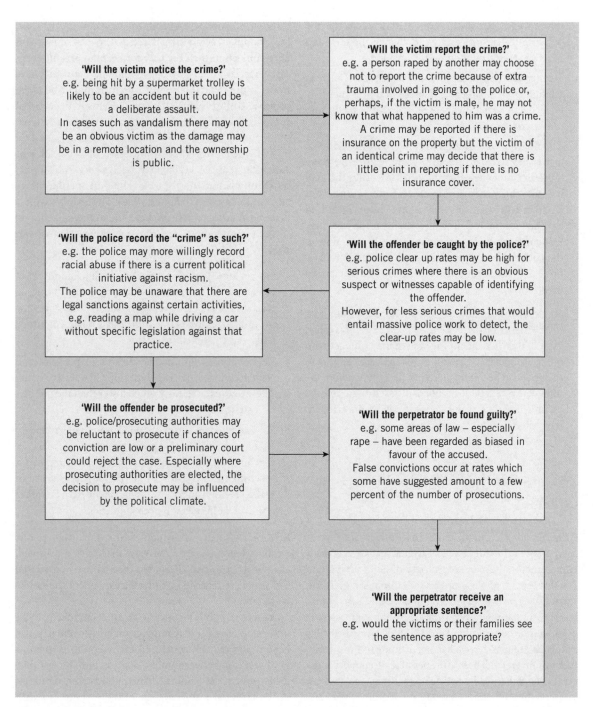

Figure 3.1 Stages in the process of crime described by Ainsworth

Source: After *Psychology and Crime: Myths and reality*, Harlow: Longman (Ainsworth, P.B. 2000) Copyright © Pearson Education Ltd. 2000

for example. An illustration of this would be the pressure of feminist groups to change the laws and practices concerning domestic violence.

- Furthermore, some actions by the police – such as attempts to control private sexual practices that may be illegal in a technical sense – may bring media and public condemnation.

- The figure would seem to indicate that the criminal law is the recourse for the victim. However, there are other remedies available such as using the civil law to achieve compensation. Private prosecutions of homicide suspects who have been acquitted by the criminal courts are an example of this. Standards of evidence are slightly less exacting in the civil law and the penalties are also less serious – financial costs rather than imprisonment being involved.

- Single arrows operating in just one direction join the elements of the system in Figure 3.1. In reality, each of the elements of the system may interact with other elements. For example, if rape cases appear to the public to be failing to lead to the conviction of the offender in sufficient numbers of cases, there may be an unwillingness of the victim to report the crime to the police.

Attitudes towards crime

Crime is an issue with the public in a multiplicity of ways. It is part of the broader political agenda that attracts many commentators from a wide variety of party affiliations. For that reason, public attitudes may impinge on government policy on crime. For example, research in Canada has shown that the public supports trying youngsters in the same courts as adults (Sprott, 1998). Those believing in this also tend to have a harsher attitude to the punishment of juveniles. These attitudes at least support if not create the situation in which increasingly the separate youth system of justice is being eroded in Canada and the United States. It is not easy to identify the precise influence of public opinion on the criminal justice system. It is clearly present in particularly dramatic cases such as the Moors Murderers (Ian Brady and Myra Hindley) in the United Kingdom. The influence stretches from prosecution and sentencing to the eventual

disposal of offenders back into the community. Take, for example, recidivism. If recidivism was infrequent after conviction then the case for keeping prison terms, say, short would be stronger and, perhaps, attitudes towards the rehabilitation of offenders might be more positive. Unfortunately, the public seems to believe that recidivism is rife and almost the norm for many types of offence.

Evidence for this comes from a study of a range of individuals in Spain and Canada who have good educational backgrounds and, mostly, a close interest in criminology (Redondo, Luque and Funes, 1996). The Spanish sample believed that for a first offender the average likelihood of their reoffending for drug trafficking offences was high:

- On average, they thought that the likelihood of re-offending was 61 per cent within five years. The figure reached 100 per cent average prediction of reoffending for multi-recidivists (i.e. individuals having offended and been convicted many times).

- This contrasts with actual rates of 11 per cent and 44 per cent for the two types of offender in Spain. These figures are clearly much lower than the public's expectations.

- Similar findings were obtained for sexual offences. Recidivism estimates ranged from 31 per cent to 54 per cent in both the Canadian and Spanish samples for first offenders, recidivists and multi-recidivists. In reality, recidivism for sex offences tended to be rather low in sex offenders in both countries.

In other words, it would seem that the public strongly tends towards the view that once a criminal, always a criminal. Perhaps that is why custodial sentences are regarded by many members of the public favourably.

Thus the public's concern about crime needs to be understood since it may impinge on how criminal justice is administered. Of course, in many countries there is no direct link between public opinion and the criminal justice system (few countries have publicly elected officials in the criminal justice system of the sort employed in the United States). Understanding public attitudes, for example, may be very relevant to recommendations about the disposal of sex offenders once their prison sentence has been completed. Public demonstrations against their release into the community have been seen in a number of countries.

Box 3.1 Key concept

Moral panics

The concept of moral panic had its origin in Stanley Cohen's study of the phenomenon of youth crime in Britain in the 1960s (Cohen, 1972, 1980). At the time, the two opposing teen gangs – Mods versus Rockers – came to the attention of the media and the public. Clashes between the two, often at seaside towns at weekends and holiday times, was reported in terms that, to Cohen at least, seemed out of proportion to the scale of the actual phenomenon. There was a sense of outrage and distress, fuelled by the media, which led for calls for action against such youth crime. Furthermore, there was a process of escalation in which the media overstated the situation and attributed to Mods and Rockers much more threat than existed in real life but, at the same time, the Mods and Rockers were attracted by the publicity and excitement that it brought. So there was a sort of spiral which fed public opinion.

A little later, Hall *et al.* (1978) applied the concept to an analysis of those street crimes commonly called mugging. Once again, the perceived threat was greater than the evidence of the real-life phenomenon. Nevertheless, the public feeling was that something had to be done about mugging. This encouraged police activity in the community which, again, could not be justified by the more objective evidence.

The term *moral panic* has commonly been used to describe the circumstances in which demands for new legislation or other forms of legal action are intense. So, for example, the term has been used to describe situations in which there is a high level of demand that action is taken against a particular form of crime or criminal: for example, legislation to deal with child sexual abuse protests against paedophiles living in the community and so forth. While it may be true that emotions are intense in such cases, the term *moral panic* is merely descriptive of the events rather than an explanation of why interest was at such levels. Hall *et al.* (1978) suggested that moral panics tend to occur when two ideologies are in conflict. For example, the emergence of the Mods and Rockers may have been the result of traditional moral values held by adults and emerging youth cultures with different ideas about the freedom and appropriate lifestyle of young people. It is the conflict between these two ideological positions that results in the moral panic.

Knowledge of crime

There is plenty of evidence that the public's perceptions of rates of crime are rather inaccurate no matter how measured. For example, Ainsworth and Moss (2000) surveyed students at a British university. Not only would we expect students to be more knowledgeable than the general population, but the fact that they had enrolled on an undergraduate module on crime and deviance would suggest that these should be among the most sophisticated about the topic. The students were asked a number of questions and provided with a range of answers:

1   How many crimes were recorded by the (England and Wales) police per year in the 1990s?

    3 million

    5 million

    8 million

    12 million

Only about a quarter correctly chose 5 million. There was a tendency to overestimation. (The new correct figure for 2009/10 is 4,300,000.)

2   What proportion of officially recorded crimes do crimes of violence make up?

    5%   10%   20%   30%   40%   50%

Again, about a quarter chose the correct answer, 10 per cent. About a half said more than the true figure. (The new correct figure for 2009/10 is 20 per cent.)

3   What percentage of crimes result in someone being convicted and sentenced in court?

    2%   5%   10%   20%   30%   40%

Only 1 in 10 chose the first option of 2 per cent of crimes. In other words, the vast majority failed to appreciate what a low figure it is. (This remains the correct answer.)

Without going into other examples of the public's imprecise knowledge of crime, it is clear that it is futile, possibly unrealistic, to expect the public to have an accurate perception of the nature and extent of crime. Some researchers suggest that such aggregate, statistical or actuarial estimates are not realistic expectations of the general public's thinking styles (Howitt, 1992, 1998b). To be able to answer such questions accurately would require an awareness that is possibly not easily achieved. After all, criminologists, sociologists and psychologists would have to obtain the answers to the questions from rather 'dry' official statistics on crime. Perhaps more important is the public's general perception of the extent to which society might be becoming increasingly criminal and risky (Docherty, 1990).

The nature of the fear of crime

The general public demonstrates its fear of criminal victimisation in any number of different ways. Table 3.1 illustrates some of these indicators. The fear that one's home is likely to be burgled is rife in England and Wales, Ireland and Australia, for example. The belief that one is particularly unsafe in the street after dark is common among the public everywhere but especially in England and Wales and Scotland. Practical defences against crime such as installing a burglar alarm into one's home are especially common in England and Wales but more so in Ireland. Just what is the fear of crime? It is important to stress that fear of crime is an important political concept as it is something that governments may actively influence. The less fear of crime, in a sense, the better job the government is doing.

In 1977, a survey showed that two-thirds of Polish citizens were not afraid of crime in the slightest (Szumski,

1993). Another quarter said that they were rarely afraid of crime. Overwhelmingly there was little fear of crime in Poland at that time. A few years later, in 1988, 60 per cent of Polish people regarded Poland as a safe country. Interestingly, the crimes regarded as the most dangerous to society were profiteering, bribery and corruption, appropriation of public property and theft of private property, and abuse of power by persons holding executive office. At this time Poland was still a communist state. Violent crime was scarcely referred to as problematic in any way. Although Polish people at the time perceived their country as safe, surveys in Western nations provided evidence that high levels of fear of crime are common. In Poland, the police gathered crime statistics not in terms of offences known to them but as offences confirmed by the police. Thus the discretion of the police to define a notifiable offence was central to the nature of crime statistics. Crime statistics provided propaganda to shape public attitudes in line with the political ideology of the powerful communist elite. A declining threat of crime was held to indicate progress in building a socialist society. If crime increased then the state would claim that criminal activity was causing the deteriorating economic outlook. Similarly, increasing crime figures justified amendment to legislation, resulting in even more repressive social policies. Szumski argues that the figures were essentially manipulated. Eventually, as crime rates increased, detection rates fell dramatically since the numbers of crimes had been held at unrealistically low levels because of the recording process involved. Fear of crime, it would seem, is not an objective response to the reality of crime. Neither is it a totally irrational thing.

Surveys of the public's fear of crime are now regularly conducted. One of the most useful of these is that of the British Crime Survey, which regularly asks a

Table 3.1 Some international comparisons for indicators of fear of crime

Indicator of fear	England and Wales	Scotland	Ireland	Australia	Canada	USA
Burglary of house likely or very likely in coming year	35%*	21%	33%	36%	25%	16%
Feel unsafe or very unsafe in street after dark	32%	30%	27%	19%	17%	19%
% homes with a burglar alarm system	42%	33%	49%	27%	28%	28%

*Figures taken from van Dijk, van Kesteren and Smit (2007)

random sample of the public about a range of crime-related matters, including their fear of crime (Allen, 2004). Although those who were very worried about crime have tended to decline in number over the years 1998 to 2003, quite sizeable proportions of the population claim to be very worried about certain types of crime. Twenty-one per cent were very worried about violent crime in 2003 and 15 per cent were very worried about burglary. However, to put this in context, very nearly three-quarters of the people surveyed did not have a high level of worry about either violent crime or burglary. Some sectors of society are more fearful of crime than others. Women were disproportionately more worried about burglary and violent crime than men. Those over 75 years of age tended to be the least worried about these crimes (this is an unusual finding as generally fear of crime studies suggest that older people have greater fear). People who reported that their general health was poorer tended to be more likely to be worried about crime – those with poor health were nearly twice as likely to report being very worried about burglary than those in good health. Professionals were the least likely to be worried about crime and people living in the most deprived areas tended to be the most worried about crime. People who believed that crime rates had increased in the previous two years were more likely to have high levels of worry about crime.

Traditionally, increasing levels of crime have been regarded as a clear sign of the disintegration of society – that people cannot be trusted any more and that neighbours no longer care. There is a belief that once upon a time doors did not have to be locked for fear of burglars. Whether or not there was such a golden age free from crime has little relevance to modern experience. The fear of crime touches people emotionally in all sorts of unexpected ways. There is little that is common sense or predictable in the fear of crime – the research findings tend to be complex and, superficially at least, a little inconsistent. Some things have been established with some certainty. Most important among these is that the fear of crime has no clear and invariant relationship to the statistical risk of being a victim of crime.

There are three main ways in which our levels of fear of crime might be influenced:

- Our direct knowledge about crimes in the immediate community and beyond. This includes personally being victimised, members of our family being victimised, seeing others being victimised and gossip about crimes in the local neighbourhood.

- The mass media contain a lot of crime news. Our beliefs about crime may be affected by these sources. A number of difficulties are involved when considering this possible connection:

  - media crime news is massively selective in favour of the more serious and sensational crimes (Marsh, 1991; Schlesinger, Tumber and Murdock, 1991);
  - generally speaking, it is difficult to find a correspondence between the newspaper an individual chooses and their perceptions of levels of crime;
  - people tend to read little of the crime news available to them (Graber, 1980) so it is somewhat unpredictable what information they become aware of.

- Aspects of our personality and social characteristics may make us more or less afraid of crime. For example, Bazargan (1994) found that fear of victimisation at home related to factors such as feeling lonely, having poorer educational standards and believing that one lives among neighbours who are not trustworthy and lack vigilance when it comes to crime.

Examples of the mismatch between fear of crime and the objective risk of being victimised are easy to find. Asked about the risk of violence and their personal fear of it, the elderly tend to report the highest levels (Bazargan, 1994). Yet when we look to see who is statistically the most likely to be the victim of violence the victims turn out to be much the same group as their victimisers for the most part: that is, males in their late adolescent and early adult years – the very group who in some surveys claim to be the least bothered by the risk of being victimised. Clark (2004) describes this as the fear–victimisation paradox, which refers to the often unpredictable relationship between reported fear of crime and personal victimisation.

Women seem to have higher levels of fear of crime than males. Feminists have claimed that women are discouraged from being independent through being inculcated with a fear of an unpredictable attack by a stranger (Walter, 1996). Put another way, this is a means of keeping women in their place. Women tend to fear the sorts of crime that could be perpetrated against them by strangers in public places (Stanko, 1995; Voumvakis and Ericson, 1982). The following should be considered:

- Men are actually most at risk of attack in public places and of attack by a person whom they do not know.

- Women are most at risk from the physical violence of people whom they know. There is also a substantial likelihood that they will be sexually attacked by persons who are relatively close. Date and marital rape are neither rare nor trivial matters (Ainsworth, 2000a; US Department of Commerce, Economics and Statistics Information, 1996).

- Finally, even in the area of child abuse, the public's perceptions and the reality differ. If asked 'what is the most dangerous (risky) stage of life in terms of homicide victimisation?' the temptation is to say childhood. This is not correct except for the first year or so of life when the risk is high. Generally, though, the factual reply ought to be adulthood, especially young adulthood (Howitt, 1992).

Farrall and Gadd (2004) query the extent to which fear of crime is a significant feature of most people's lives. It is a different thing to suggest that many people have a fear of being a crime victim than to suggest that people frequently have fears about crime – that is, regularly feeling anxious about possible victimisation. So surveys have suggested that as many as 25 per cent of people are very afraid of certain crimes such as burglary and rape. However, just how often do individuals feel very afraid? The researchers asked participants 'In the past year, have you ever felt fearful about the possibility of becoming a victim of crime?' (p. 128). They were also asked the number of times they felt this in the year and how fearful they felt. One-third of participants said that they had felt fearful in the previous year. Nearly 50 per cent said that they had felt fearful between one and four times. Fifteen per cent of the entire sample claimed to have experienced quite high or very high levels of fear. However, only half of these were individuals who had felt afraid five or more times in the year. This is a relatively small percentage who felt high levels of fear more than once every three months or so. In some ways, this puts fear of crime into perspective.

Just what is meant by 'fear' in the fear of crime? Clark (2004) asks whether the fear of crime is actually a crime phobia, which like other phobias would be a debilitating condition that can severely constrain a person's day-to-day activities. So to what extent is fear of crime as measured in surveys akin to other phobias? Clark's approach was to take Australian survey data which contained both fear of crime items and items related to various types of phobia. The first thing to note is that the three phobias that she studied – social phobia, blood-injury phobia and agoraphobia – tended to coexist. Those who had a social phobia were more likely to have the other two phobias and so forth: that is, some individuals are more inclined to phobias than others. If fear of crime is a phobia like these other phobias then one would expect that those with high levels of phobias in general would tend to have the highest levels of fear of crime. This simply was not the case. If anything, there was a slight negative correlation between fear of crime and the other phobias. That is, fear of crime has a slight tendency to be lower in those with greater levels of other phobias. So Clark's conclusion is that fear of crime is not like other phobias. Fear of crime was measured for personal crime (violence), property crime and sexually based crime. The findings for each type of crime followed the general trend. All of this may indicate that fear of crime measures are not pure measures of a basic psychological emotion – fear. According to Clark, there is no evidence available in the vast literature on fear of crime to suggest that fear of crime is dysfunctional or even completely irrational. She suggests that fear serves protective functions and so to reduce the fear may be to encourage the abandonment of protective strategies.

Theories of fear of crime

Whatever measures of the fear of crime actually indicate, concerns about fear of crime need explanation. There are three significant theories that should be considered:

- cultivation theory;
- availability heuristic theory;
- cognitive theory.

Cultivation theory

Cultivation theory (Gerbner, 1972) builds on the assumption that the mass media, and television in particular, are means of cultural transmission. The world of television is believed to be full of crime and violence that fails to capture the essence of crime in reality. For example, crime on television is highly biased towards violent acts perpetrated by strangers. A media researcher and theorist, Gerbner carried out numerous immense analyses of the content of American television. The message obtained from the aggregate classifications of the content of programmes is one of a distorted world of crime (Gerbner,

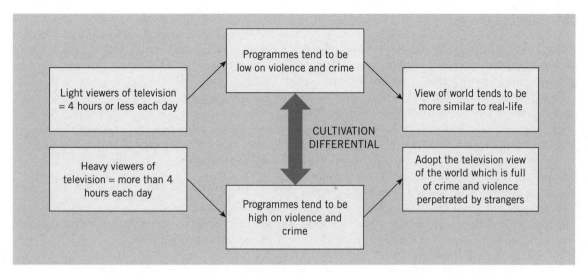

Figure 3.2 Media effects on viewer's worldview according to the cultivation analysis model

1972; Gerbner *et al.*, 1977; Signorielli and Gerbner, 1988). The viewing diet of heavy viewers of television tends to consist disproportionately of this distorted model. Lighter viewers may prefer to watch, say, news programmes in proportionately greater amounts to the rest of television. Hence, the world that the heavy viewer perceives on television is much more distorted than that experienced by the lighter viewer. In other words, there is a difference or differential between the two groups in terms of the potential of the viewing to distort their view of crime (see Figure 3.2). The basic prediction of the model is that the culture of crime cultivated in the heavy viewer will be more like the television view than that inculcated in the lighter viewer. So since the world of television involves attacks by strangers, then the heavy viewer should believe that he or she is at risk from strangers, for example.

The main things to remember concerning the value of the theory are as follows:

- In Gerbner's analyses, there does seem to be a very weak relationship between heavy viewing and having a distorted perception of crime and violence. This relationship is not due to 'third' variables such as social class which may be related to viewing and perceptions of crime and violence. However, even shortly after Gerbner's studies were first published, other researchers were reanalysing the original data. They concluded that when the influence of variables such as type of

neighbourhood and other demographic characteristics of the sample were removed statistically, the relationship between media and fear of crime became negligible or even reversed (Ditton *et al.*, 2004).

- The relationship where it is claimed is very small statistically and dependent on very large samples to achieve statistical significance.

- The relationships may not occur in all communities. For example, the evidence seems to be that the relationship has not been found in the United Kingdom despite a number of studies (e.g. Gunter, 1987). This may reflect a cultural difference, perhaps even a difference in media environments.

Caution must be exercised about these findings. Gerbner's approach is fairly crude in terms of its predictions of effects. Research that predicts subtler relationships between media use and fear of crime may obtain stronger relationships and greater insight into the impact of media coverage on the public. For example, Liska and Baccaglini (1990) examined responses to the questions 'how safe do you feel in your local neighbourhood in the day? at night?' It was possible to predict feeling unsafe in the neighbourhood by reference to the local media coverage. In the communities where people tended to feel unsafe, the local newspapers covered more local crime. The more news about, say, non-local homicides then the less the fear of the neighbourhood.

Availability heuristic theory

Certain sorts of information are more readily available from memory than other sorts of information. This may vary substantially from person to person. Nevertheless, it is important to consider just what happens when approached by a researcher asking about fear of crime in the local neighbourhood. People probably do not spend their days routinely computing risks of being victimised in each location they enter based on statistical knowledge of crime risks. They may feel unsafe in some situations, but this is different. A woman who steps into a car with a man she has only just met at a nightclub may become afraid when she suddenly remembers that a young woman had been found murdered a few miles away having left a nightclub in the same circumstances:

• The *availability heuristic* (Shrum, 1996) suggests that to the extent the media (or any other factor) create a vivid and readily accessible image of crimes in the mind of the individual, this imagery will be rapidly accessed and will partly determine fear of crime.

• Shrum studied the contents of television soap operas over a two-week period. The story lines during this period were reviewed for 'critical portrayals' which are those events that were dominant in the soap episodes. Crime was a major theme and especially rape.

• Consequently, the viewers of the programmes should have rape imagery more readily available. Those who did not watch the programmes might be expected to have less rape imagery available.

• The availability heuristic hypothesis was supported. Viewers were quicker in answering questions such as 'What percentage of women are raped in their lifetime?' This appeared to be a specific effect and not related to the general amount of television the individual watched.

These findings are supported by other research (Vitelli and Endler, 1993). These researchers used a more general measure of the availability heuristic. They based their index on the number of crimes participants knew of through the media, but other information in addition:

• the number of times they had personally been victimised;

• the information they had obtained from other people.

For men, one study showed that the availability of media imagery went together with a lack of a belief that they could cope with victimisation situations. For women, the media were also important. Additionally, higher levels of fear were also associated with their general levels of anxiety.

Cognitive theory

Winkel (1998) points out that much of the research indicates that there are two distinct components of emotional vulnerability:

• The subjective belief about the likelihood or risk of the event.

• The belief about the seriousness of the consequences of experiencing those events.

He suggests that these are much the same dimensions that emerge in the study of the fear of crime. The first element he calls the *subjective victimisation risk* and the second element is the *perceived negative impact* that would result from victimisation. Thus fear might be seen as reflecting the product of risk and seriousness. The implication of this is that increased fear of crime will follow from events such as being a victim or seeing a news programme about a particular crime – that is, if the following apply:

• The event makes the individual aware of there being a risk of victimisation and of the consequences of victimisation (i.e. the priming effect).

• There is an increase in the subjective victimisation risk or the negative impact or both increase as a consequence (i.e. the change effect).

An example may be helpful. An American in, say, Dallas sees on the television news a serious bank robbery in Germany. This probably will not prime that person's awareness of his or her own risk of victimisation. The distant events in Germany will not impact on the viewer's fear of crime. On the other hand, take the case of a woman who sees a television programme about rape. She may discover for the first time the extent of the violence and humiliation that may be associated with rape. This may well increase her fear of victimisation.

An important aspect of Winkel's theory is the relative independence of risk and seriousness in the creation of fear. It is possible to imagine events in which the risk perception increases but the seriousness perception decreases. For example, a household has just been burgled. Members of the household rightly discern that

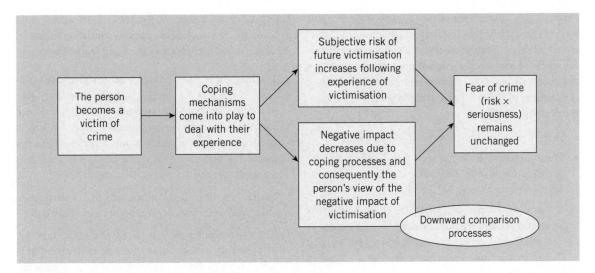

Figure 3.3 Winkel's model of the fear of crime

Source: Winkel, F.W. (1998) 'Fear of crime and criminal victimisation' *British Journal of Criminology* 38, 473–84. Reproduced by permission of Oxford University Press

the risk of their being a victim is higher than they previously thought. However, in their case the burglar simply took some money and did not foul or ransack the place. The householders also find that they were less bothered and disturbed by the burglary than they had previously imagined. In these circumstances, the seriousness perception may move to regarding the crime as less serious. More generally, downward comparison processes may achieve adaptation or coping: that is, the development of the view that one got off lightly compared with what could happen or what has happened to other people. In this theory, fear is hypothesised to be a product of risk × seriousness. So, in some circumstances, although the perception of risk has increased this may be compensated by the reduction in the perception of seriousness. In other words, there is no change in fear of crime. Figure 3.3 presents this schematically as a model. Of course, downward comparison processes may not be possible in all crimes. For example, does the rape victim whose rapist is acquitted in court following a court hearing in which her character is besmirched show such processes?

Winkel (1998) reports empirical evidence in support of the model based on research on a variety of crime victims compared with a control group:

- Over a data collection period of about two years, there was evidence that the subjective victimisation risk perceived by victims converged with that of the non-victim control group.

- If anything, in terms of the negative impact of being victimised, the gap between the victims and the controls increased. Victims saw less of a negative impact from further victimisation than did the control group. This is just what the theory suggests would happen.

Nevertheless, we need to understand better the victims for which these compensatory processes do not appear to work. The evidence that some victims are profoundly affected by their victimisation in terms of stress and distress (Miethe, 1995) suggests that we have much to learn about the public's perceptions of and fears about crime. Predicting who is most at risk of the consequences of victimisation is one important task to be faced (Winkel and Vrij, 1998).

Chapter 4 discusses psychological concepts related to victimisation.

Alternatives to the statistical/actuarial models

One advantage of the availability heuristic hypothesis is that it does not assume that everyone will have the same experiences and imagery of crime, even when it is obtained 'second-hand' through the media. Thus the relative failure of the cultivation approach to gain empirical support does not impinge on the availability heuristic theory. This, in itself, does not mean that the media and personal direct experience factors have no impact on the level of fear experienced in different situations by different individuals. Despite what has already been written, the levels of fear of crime and the asymmetry between statistical risk and fear of crime may be overemphasised (Gilchrist *et al.*, 1998). These authors prefer to interpret the evidence as follows:

- Fear of crime is actually at fairly low levels.
- The differences between men and women are not particularly startling. For example, the British Crime Survey (Home Office, 2001) indicates:
  - burglary: 18 per cent of males claim to be very worried compared with 26 per cent of females;
  - mugging: 12 per cent of males being very worried compared with 26 per cent of females.

Thus the idea of people being confined to their homes through fear of crime is more of a stereotype than a reality. Gilchrist *et al.* studied groups of men and women in Glasgow. They compared groups consisting of fearful men, fearful women, fearless men and fearless women:

- Fearful people irrespective of gender give victimisation of others as a source of fear. They also were apprehensive about the possibility of a serious offence following on from a relatively minor one. A fear of a particular type of assault was not mentioned but the possibility that a weapon might be used was given as a reason for fear.

- Fearless people tended, for example, to feel less vulnerable because they took precautions and could cope.

- There were differences between the sexes in terms of how they talked about the fear of crime. These were smaller, though, than the differences between members of the same sex who were high or low on fear of crime.

Main points

- Although crime has an impact on the public, the public also have an impact on crime either directly or indirectly. Victims of crime may or may not decide to report events as a crime and public opinion may influence government and police policy on crime, for example. All aspects of the process of criminal justice may be influenced by the public although perhaps in rather indirect ways.

- Surveys have demonstrated many aspects of the public's attitudes towards crime and there is at least some evidence that relatively tough attitudes are expressed about the ways in which criminals should be dealt with. However, it would appear that the public have a rather poor understanding of such matters as the extent of crime and trends or patterns in criminal activity.

- The fear of crime is both a researcher's and a policy maker's concept. Surveys of the general public's levels of fear of crime are now regularly conducted on behalf of some governments. The fear of crime is not at similar levels throughout all sectors of society. It has proven notoriously difficult to understand the fear of crime as it does not seem to follow common-sensical patterns. There is little relationship between fear of crime and the objective risk of being a victim. Researchers have questioned whether the fear of crime is as central to most people's lives as some surveys suggest.

Further reading

The relationship of public opinion about crime to the criminal justice system is extensively covered in:

Wood, J. and Gannon, T. (2008) *Public Opinion and Criminal Justice* Cullompton: Willan Publishing.

For a wider perspective of the fear of crime which includes political as well as psychological issues see:

Lee, M. and Farrall, S. (2008) *Fear of Crime: Critical Voices in an Age of Anxiety* London: Routledge Cavendish.

For a more radical account:

Lee, M. (2007) *Inventing Fear of Crime: Criminology and the Politics of Anxiety* Cullompton: Willan Publishing.

Fear of crime is a political issue and the response of the UK government may be found at the following web address: Crime Reduction Toolkits:

http://webarchive.nationalarchives.gov.uk/20100413151441/
http://crimereduction.homeoffice.gov.uk/toolkits/index.htm

Visit our website at www.pearsoned.co.uk/howitt for self-test and essay questions, annotated further reading, audio interviews with researchers in the field, weblinks and more information on becoming a forensic psychologist.

Victims of crime

Overview

- Gradually, victims are becoming a priority in criminal justice systems. Changes have been made that work to the benefit of victims in recent years, for example, the sympathetic treatment of rape victims by many police organisations and sensitivity to the needs of child witnesses. Governments increasingly have an interest in demonstrating their concern. Care has to be taken not to directly or indirectly hold the victim partly responsible for their victimisation – this was a problem with early victimology writings. An alternative is to concentrate on how psychology can help the victim.

- Restorative justice is justice that concentrates on the harm done by crime to its victims though victims can be widely defined to include the offender and their family. All parties should come out of the process of restorative justice feeling that they have been dealt with fairly. Some criminal justice systems include reparation for the victim and this is being extended to include adult offenders where previously it had been confined to offences involving young offenders. Generally, victims find the process of restorative justice a positive one. The Theory of Procedural Justice is relevant to this.

- Post-traumatic stress disorder (PTSD) is a consequence of serious trauma of which some crimes such as rape and extreme violence are examples. There is some argument that repeated but apparently relatively minor events such as criminal victimisations may accumulate to have a similar effect. Flashbacks to the events and nightmares are among the characteristics of the condition. It is a psychiatric condition listed in the *APA Diagnostic and Statistical Manual* since 1980.

- There is evidence that PTSD is associated with the consequences of having committed a crime. A substantial minority of homicide offenders show symptoms. Equally, PTSD may lead to violent criminal behavior possibly as a consequence of re-enacting the violence of the trauma.

- It is less well known that PTSD can also be seen as an anger disorder and there is a relationship between PTSD and measures of anger.

- Psychological help for victims of PTSD has to recognise that suppression of the memories which leads to their re-emergence in flashbacks is counterproductive. The victim needs to work through the memories repeatedly using methods such as structured trauma writing.

- Victims, whether or not severely affected by the experience, have to make decisions about whether or not to report the crime to the police. Usually it is the nature of the crime which determines whether or not it will be reported. It is common for victims to talk with others before deciding to report the crime or not. Often they receive advice about what to do and act in accordance with that advice.
- The decision to report a crime is also dependent on the rewards for reporting and the costs, the tendency of emotionally arousing crimes to be reported more commonly, and the social push from those around the victim to report the crime. However, counterfactual thinking which leads to holding oneself responsible for the crime may have a contribution to make.
- Based on Rational Choice Theory, there is evidence that self protective behaviours may have an impact on the way in which a crime unfolds.

Introduction

The victims of crime should have access to justice and fair treatment in terms of compensation, social assistance and restitution according to The United Nations Declaration of Basic Principles of Justice for Victims of Crime and Abuse of Power of 1985. Until relatively recently, victims of crime had few rights within criminal justice systems. The needs of victims may still appear to be peripheral to the massive effort and resources put into dealing with offenders. Of course, there has been progress in some aspects of the treatment of crime's victims such as allowing vulnerable child witnesses to give evidence through video links. In addition, victims have increasingly been a focus of government policy in many parts of the world. A major stimulus to this was the influence of the feminist movement, which highlighted the plight of victims of domestic violence and rape, for example, and provided support to victims. Government financing for organisations providing victim support has become more commonly available. Schemes providing financial compensation to victims have been established in various countries. The rhetoric used by governments is one of 'balance' in which the rights of the victim are contrasted with those of the perpetrator of the crime. This has enormous popular appeal, of course. Nevertheless, Edwards (2004) argues that this shifts responsibility for crime more towards the community and less on government. This change allows 'good customer relations' to be the criterion of crime policy success rather than reductions in crime figures. Crime is, of course, a political 'hot potato'.

As a branch of the general field of criminology, *victimology* studies the victim–offender interface. In particular, victimology's original focus was on victim characteristics which increased the likelihood of being victimised. This was sometimes criticised as being anti-victim – it could be construed as holding the victim responsible for being a victim. Explanations of crimes such as rape including the suggestion that the victim was 'asking for it' by dressing provocatively are a good example of this. The proper study of victims avoids such an implication by, for example, regarding victimisation as being the consequence of the offender choosing an optimum victim for their offending. In recent years, the term *victimology* has become used in a more general sense to denote the study of the victim in all respects. Consequently, in modern usage the original term *victim* is often replaced by *target*. This has the advantage of emphasising the role of the crimininal's decision-making processes rather than the characteristics of the offender's chosen victim. A number of important findings about the experience of being a victim and the patterns of victimisation have emerged because of this change in conceptualisation. Among the important findings concerning crime, for example, are the following:

- In the UK, about 16 per cent of the population have been subject to a property crime. But this in itself disguises the fact that just 2 per cent of the population are involved in over 40 per cent of property crimes as victims (Farrell and Bouloukos, 2001).

- In industrialised countries, approximately 40 per cent of crimes against individuals and households are repeat victimisations of targets during the same year. The International Crime Victims Survey (van Dijk, van Kesteren and Smit, 2007) suggests, for example, that something like half the incidents of sexual crimes against women will be repeat victimisation of a woman previously victimised in this way. Furthermore, there is a greater incidence of repeat victimisation for personal crimes against an individual than for property crimes.

All of this suggests the important conclusion that crime victimisation follows patterns. These patterns cannot be understood solely on the basis of psychological characteristics of the victim – indeed, much of this research makes no reference to psychological characteristics but uses geography and knowledge of the everyday activities of offenders in the territory that they inhabit and visit. Furthermore, simply because a victim possesses the characteristics which offenders choose to target does not make the victim responsible for this targeting. It is obvious that forensic and criminal psychology need to pay due regard to issues related to victims. Although the more criminological issues are clearly important, this chapter will concentrate on dealing with some of the more patently psychological issues involved such as the psychological consequences of being victimised criminally.

Box 4.1 Key concept

Restorative justice

Victims of crime may exhibit a wide range of responses. In DeValve's (2005) study, victims of crime mentioned the following consequences on themselves:

- afraid of retaliation by the offender 39 per cent
- afraid of the repetition of a similar event 53 per cent
- angry with offender 81 per cent
- anxiety or panic attacks or some other psychological consequence 67 per cent
- blamed themselves for the crime 47 per cent
- felt isolated and alone 53 per cent
- felt unsafe at home 53 per cent
- relationship with partner affected 44 per cent
- time off from work 69 per cent
- wanted revenge 44 per cent
- work affected 61 per cent.

They had various feelings about the offender including:

- wanted the offender committed to prison 56 per cent
- wanted an apology from the offender 33 per cent
- wanted the offender to receive help 31 per cent.

Furthermore, 56 per cent wanted to tell the offender about how the crime had adversely affected them and 47 per cent wanted to understand why the offence happened. Some of these needs are met by the concept and practice of restorative justice.

Although restorative justice programmes have been in existence since the 1970s, the term itself was first used in the 1980s. Restorative justice has emerged as a substantial trend in a number of countries. This is primarily a practice-led activity though some psychological theory is relevant as we shall see. Restorative justice generally refers to processes involving some sort of formal mediation between the offender and the victim. The restorative justice model can be conceived as an alternative approach to the Western, court-based criminal justice system. When laws are broken, there are two notions of justice which help determine responses. These are termed retributive and restorative justice. Retributive justice is about the repair of justice through a one-sidedly imposed punishment by the criminal justice system. Restorative justice, on the other hand, means the repair of justice by the reaffirmation of consensual shared values. A consensus is sought in the areas of the nature of the harm done, the attribution of responsibility, and the values involved (Wenzel, Okimoto, Feather and Platow 2008). According to Wright (2002), there are a number of characteristics of restorative justice:

- Restorative justice concentrates on the harm caused by crime, not the criminal activity in itself.
- All of those who are harmed are the focus, including the offender and the offender's family. Children may be construed as victims of the crime because, say, their father has been sent to prison thus depriving the child of the positive benefits of their father's day-to-day parenting. Visits may be infrequent because of transport difficulties to a prison which may be very distant. Furthermore, the children of offenders may experience social stigma (Philbrick, 2002). The consequences of crime spread very widely. In addition, police officers, for example, may also be victims of the crime because of the trauma that dealing with a distressing crime may cause them.
- Healing and reintegration are the main objectives.
- The ideal outcome from restorative justice includes a satisfied victim and an offender who feels that they have been dealt with fairly. Thus the process of restoration is the focus, not merely financial compensation for the victim.
- The community is involved in the outcome.
- Integration of parts of the system so that victims and offenders, in dialogue with one another, identify the factors that led to the crime (e.g. social and economic pressures). In this way, the process can inform community crime reduction strategies.

The community benefits from restorative justice as well as the victim. Umbreit, Coates and Vos (2001) studied a substantial number of victim–offender mediation programmes in a number of different Western countries. Victims chose to participate for reasons such as understanding why the crime happened and to communicate to the offender just what effect the crime had had on the victim. Other benefits include the opportunity to express their emotions in the presence of the offender, the opportunity to be forgiving and a possibility of peaceful coexistence of the offender and victim in the community. The process of restorative justice may take quite some time. For example, some victims are not open to the idea immediately after being victimised and will not talk about restorative justice procedures until quite some time has elapsed when they may be more receptive. Some victims may never be willing to be involved. Restorative justice is largely administered and organised by mediation services. They work with victims and offenders in order to enable the process to work. This may be difficult because it may be counterproductive to pressurise victims into participating.

Victims sometimes feel that they have undergone secondary victimisation by the insensitive response of the criminal justice system to them. It is undeniable that victims currently receive very little recognition in the criminal justice system. Some countries such as Australia and England and Wales have included reparative procedures into some legislation. Initially, work focused on young offenders (under the age of 18 years) but now it has extended to adult offenders in some countries. The mediation service elicits the victim's proposals for reparation or compensation following an instruction from the court. Wright (2002) suggested that although a criminal act has taken place, the criminal courts may not be the best way of dealing with it, especially in those cases which occur from within a relationship and involve a dispute between two or more parties. In these circumstances such restorative justice procedures as victim–offender mediation may have more to offer the victim with the least risk of further damage to the victim by the criminal justice system.

Direct offender mediation involves direct contact between the victim and the young offender (currently legislation applies to young offenders) in the form of face-to-face meetings which are supervised (mediated) by project staff. The aim is to reach some sort of agreement – possibly including financial reparation. Both the victim and the victimiser may ask questions, express their sentiments and proffer explanations. Failure to achieve a satisfactory agreement may result in an alternative punishment being applied to the offender. In contrast, indirect mediation involves the mediator as a go-between communicating between the victim and the perpetrator offender without a face-to-face meeting being involved. Of course, such procedures are not the only way in which the victim can take control and redress the balance. Victims may also have access to civil-legal procedures

▶

Box 4.1 (continued)

such as suing for compensation or even bringing a private prosecution against the perpetrator of the crime in order to obtain redress.

Wenzel, Tyle, Okimoto, Feather and Platow (2008), provide a social psychological model of restorative justice. They argue that the consensus which is sought in restorative justice programmes attempts to reaffirm the shared and identity-defining values of the community from which the victim and offender come. This concept of community they define widely and it can be a community of the values and identity shared by that particular criminal and that particular victim, for example. The result of the restorative justice process will not always be harmonious. Where identities are not shared in some way by the victim and the offender, the rebalancing following the offending behaviour may result in the desire of the victim to shame and humiliate the offender. The key issue is the extent to which the victim and the offender share at least part of their identities. Restorative justice requires the parties to see themselves in terms of an overriding or superordinate category involving both parties. The victim and offender may share a subgroup identity which itself may contribute to defining the offender as deviant. This can result in punitive responses despite identity sharing. For example, if it transpired during the meetings that both victim and offender had suffered sexual abuse as a child, the victim's strong feelings about not using this as a reason for victimising others may lead to difficulties in conciliation between victim and offender.

The psychological Theory of Procedural Justice (Thibaut and Walker, 1975) was a significant early step towards understanding why victim–offender mediation and similar strategies can be so important and what makes them effective (see Figure 4.1). Although the procedural justice theory accepts that the outcomes of judicial processes are important in achieving a feeling of justice, the procedures involved in the judicial process are more important – especially knowing in advance that the procedures are fair. There are two factors which determine the sense of procedural fairness:

- Process control: This is the extent to which those involved are able to make an input throughout the decision-making process. That is, the degree to which it is possible for them to present information at all stages.

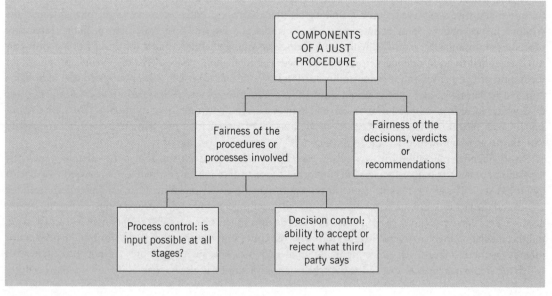

Figure 4.1 Elements of Procedural Justice Theory

- Decision control: The extent to which the parties can control the outcome. To what extent is it possible for the parties involved to be able to accept or reject the decisions and recommendations made by a third party?

However, in Tyler and Lind's (1992) Relational Model of Procedural Justice, three factors are identified which lead to the sense of fairness about the procedures:

- Trust: The belief that the authority (the criminal justice system) is trying to do the right thing.
- Standing: The feeling that one is being treated with dignity and respect in a way which demonstrates the individual's rights. Respect is sometimes referred to as interactional fairness (Van den Bos and Lind, 2002).
- Neutrality: The term describing honesty and lack of prejudice with decisions being factually based.

All of this would imply that the ways in which professionals interact with victims is a crucial aspect of victim-offender mediation.

Many of these principles can be seen to be working in Wemmers and Cyr's (2006b) study of crime victims participating in a victim–offender mediation programme for young offenders. In terms of judgements of procedural justice fairness, 71 per cent of victims felt that the procedures were fair but 26 per cent of victims felt them to be unfair – only a few victims claimed to be neutral about the programme. There were significant relationships between feeling the process was fair and (a) feeling that they were heard, (b) perceiving that they had the ability to express themselves in the procedures, (c) having a good initial impression of the project workers, (d) feeling that they were given the information they desired, (e) faith in the mediator, (f) feeling respectfully treated, and (g) seeing the project worker as neutral. These relationships provide support for procedural justice theory and, more specifically, the concepts of trust, standing and neutrality found in Tyler and Lynd's (1992) theory. In a closely related report, Wemmers and Cyr (2006a) further investigated the experience of the victims who had been invited to join a victim–offender mediation programme. Once again, there was a tendency for victims to polarise towards the extremes and relatively few of them picked neutral points or milder versions of fair and unfair.

Not everyone is convinced that victim–offender mediation is a boon to victims. Pease (2007) complained that 'there is more in the practice of restorative justice for the perpetrator than the victim, and the dangers of railroading well-intentioned and kindly victims into a process that is primarily for the benefit of the offender may, particularly in unskilled hands, become a form of secondary victimization' (p. 607). This view is partly based on the lack of significant instances of reconciliation between victim and offender following mediation (Daly, 2002). Certainly the research discussed above concentrates on the quality of the procedures rather than the success of the outcomes. However, research has begun to emerge in the United Kingdom suggesting that there are reductions in offending associated with restorative justice (Shapland et al., 2008). Over three different research sites, there were reductions in the frequency of reoffending and reconviction. Offenders involved in restorative justice committed a quarter fewer crimes during the follow-up period. This finding involved randomised allocation to restorative justice procedures.

Post-traumatic stress disorder and victims

The characteristics of PTSD

One frequently mentioned consequence of victimisation is the risk of post-traumatic stress disorder (PTSD). Being a victim of crimes such as rape and extreme violence is traumatic for many victims and they may have great difficulty dealing with the psychological consequences of the trauma. Although PTSD is an extremely familiar idea, it is important to be clear as to its major characteristics. None of the characteristics alone defines the condition but collectively they help establish what PTSD is (see Figure 4.2). These characteristics include the following:

- Repeatedly reliving the trauma in the form of being disturbed by intrusive flashbacks of the events during

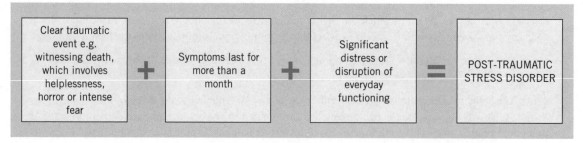

Figure 4.2 Main diagnostic features of PTSD (Post-Traumatic Stress Disorder)

the day. At night, the events may be incorporated in nightmares. Anything that reminds the victim of the distressing incident may be avoided. Things such as the anniversary of the trauma can lead to renewed upset. Because of the intensity of some flashbacks, victims can believe that they are experiencing the events once again. Unlike normal autobiographical memory for life events, which is largely verbally coded and stored, flashbacks are overwhelmingly full of vivid sensory detail such as loud sounds or other images, though they tend to be of a somewhat fragmentary nature (Brewin and Holmes, 2003). Intriguingly, good working memory capacity (which is an individual's ability to 'hold and manipulate' material which is the focus of attention) is associated with the ability to exclude unwanted ideas from intruding into activities. In this way, the intrusions are prevented from adversely affecting performance on the activity. Since flashbacks are also intrusions into thought, it might be expected that those with good working memory capacity should be less affected by flashbacks. It may be relevant, then, that low intelligence, which may be associated with poorer working memory capacity, is a risk factor for PTSD (Brewin, Andrews and Valentine, 2000).

- Profound depression and possible thoughts of suicide.

- Sleep disturbances of all sorts. Some may have difficulty sleeping, some may sleep for abnormally long periods.

- Oversensitivity to noise. Such noises cause a startle response since the fight/flight reflex is heightened.

- Paranoia or fear of others: the victim may feel afraid of the reoccurrence of the traumatic event which causes them to be uncomfortable with people who may be their future victimisers (Broken Spirits Network, 2004).

PTSD is not the inevitable consequence of trauma and trauma may have other adverse consequences other than PTSD including depression, substance misuse and anxiety states. In a forensic setting, PTSD is more likely to be assessed against the psychiatric features of the condition. The diagnostic category of post-traumatic stress disorder was first introduced into the *Diagnostic and Statistical Manual of the American Psychiatric Association* with the release of DSM-III in 1980. The current version of the *Diagnostic and Statistical Manual* (DSM-IV) requires that the following criteria are met in order to apply a diagnosis of PTSD. In many respects, these are more stringent and precise requirements than those we have just described:

- There needs to be a clearly defined traumatic event in which a person experiences or witnesses a death or its threat or a threat to the bodily integrity of themselves or others. The response at the time should involve helplessness and/or horror and/or intense fear.

- There is clinically significant distress or significant impairment in important areas of the individual's functioning socially, at work or other aspects of life.

- The symptoms should be present for at least a month (Grey, 2002). The criteria for PTSD employed by the DSM-IV require that the individual reports, at a minimum, symptoms in the following categories:

  - experiencing/intrusion symptoms (minimum of one) plus
  - avoidance/numbing symptoms (minimum of three) plus
  - hyperarousal symptoms (minimum of two) (Winkel, 2007).

It is the primarily the presence of certain memory phenomena (flashbacks/dissociation) which distinguishes PTSD from other conditions such as depression and anxiety (which may occur in PTSD).

Winkel (2007) suggests that the prevalence of chronic PTSD following crime victimisation is of the order of 10–15 per cent when estimated from studies that include a later follow-up assessment, which indicates the chronic nature of the condition. This can be regarded as a conservative estimate and some studies report higher rates. Of course, from a psychological point of view the precise rates are less important than the fact that significant numbers of victims of crime urgently need help to deal with the emotional and other psychological consequences of their victimisation.

PTSD among offenders

Of course, there is nothing in the nature of PTSD which, in itself, implies that only victims can suffer. Pollock (1999) raises the superficially paradoxical question of whether perpetrators of crime also suffer PTSD. There are two main possibilities why there might be a link between offending and PTSD:

- A person suffering PTSD has a heightened propensity to act violently. Hence the association is that PTSD leads to violence. For example, battlefield trauma leading to PTSD has been implicated in later antisocial behaviour according to Pollock.

- The person who commits a horrific violent act cannot cope with the act and develops PTSD. In this case, we have the reverse association that violent experiences lead to PTSD.

Both may be true, of course. However, Pollock notes research which identified 2 per cent of criminals as having PTSD before committing their crime but 15 per cent showing the symptoms after committing the crime (Collins and Bailey, 1990). This would be consistent with both of the above sequences. Pollock argues that homicide may lead to offender PTSD in circumstances where the offender's beliefs about themselves are undermined by the events of the crime. If the violence was unplanned, for example, then the risk of trauma is heightened because that violence is not seen by the offender as part of their personality or character. A sample of homicide offenders was studied by Pollock of which 42 per cent exhibited the criteria for a PTSD diagnosis. It was found that reactive violence tended to be associated with PTSD – that is, non-goal-directed, unplanned, angry aroused violence typically directed at a known victim considered by the participant to have

contributed to the offence by provocation (p. 193). Typically it was controlled and inhibited offenders who show PTSD and not psychopaths.

There is plenty of evidence of the reverse process – that PTSD can lead to criminal behaviour. This has largely been explored in American war veterans. A study by Begic and Begic (2001) into the violent behaviour of combat veterans showed that over two-thirds had been diagnosed with PTSD. Violent behaviour was virtually universal in those diagnosed with PTSD and three times more common in PTSD sufferers than the others. Not only that, but the annual number of violent acts for the PTSD sufferers was 18 as opposed to 3 for the non-PTSD group. These data seem to imply that being exposed to trauma in itself was not responsible for the violence but that it was the consequence of the PTSD consequent to exposure to trauma. Getting into fights can be a way of living the violence that had traumatised war veterans as in combat addiction. The literature contains graphic instances of the effects of PTSD. Silva *et al.* (2001) give the case of a man who, while experiencing a flashback, saw in the face of his victim the face of the enemy. Such cases as these clearly raise questions about criminal responsibility although PTSD is not a psychosis. (A psychosis means an abnormal condition of the mind. These conditions involve a loosened grip on reality and deficient reality testing. Thinking is impaired because of hallucinations, delusions and similar thought disturbances. Psychotic conditions affect the individual's ability to function effectively in society.) Friel, White and Hull (2008) discuss the issue at length. They point out some similarities of PTSD to automatism in which the offender has no *mens rea* as the offence is committed, for example, while sleepwalking. In England and Wales, the law recognises two forms of automatism. Sane automatism is the consequence of an external cause such as a blow to the head. It regularly results in acquittal. Insane automatism is the consequence of an internal cause such as epilepsy or sleepwalking. It is dealt with in a way similar to the insanity defence (see Chapter 22).

Cognitive and other factors in PTSD

Quite a lot is known about the sorts of factors associated with the trauma or the victim which may lead to PTSD:

- Intense levels of feelings of helplessness, fear or horror at the time of the traumatic event are associated with the likelihood of PTSD six months after the traumatic event. However, PTSD may occur without such high levels of emotion at the time. According to Brewin, Andrews and Rose (2000), 89 per cent of people who went on to have PTSD following a traumatic happening reported such intense responses. However, 44 per cent of those reporting intense levels of these emotions failed to manifest PTSD later. Thus it would appear that about 11 per cent of individuals who experienced traumatic events but did not experience intense levels of helplessness, fear or horror, nevertheless did develop PTSD. However, it is worth noting that the 11 per cent who did not manifest these emotions actually reported high levels of anger or shame.

- PTSD is associated with negative beliefs about the world (including the self and others) following trauma. Victims tend to believe that the trauma has caused a permanent negative change in the individual and their ability to achieve life goals (Brewin and Holmes, 2003). These negative feelings are not necessarily at the time of the trauma but may be a consequence of later appraisal processes.

- The onset of PTSD is more likely in those who demonstrate 'dissociation' during traumatic events (although not those who show dissociation later). Dissociation is when the sense of possessing a single identity which links our life stages together is temporarily disrupted (ibid., 2003).

Situations that threaten an individual's life have a high likelihood of promoting PTSD. Nevertheless, subjective beliefs about the threat to life can be even more influential than the size of the actual threat. Appreciation of the nature of the cognitive processes involved is important to understanding PTSD (ibid., 2003). One important explanation is that the trauma actually destroys core attitudes, beliefs and assumptions about the nature of their world and the victim's ability to cope with it. For example, the belief that other people are benevolent and well-intentioned may be shattered by the traumatic event. Someone who is subject to a malicious attack may find this difficult to reconcile with a sense of community conducive to positive social relationships. Of course, people will naturally try to cope with PTSD themselves. However, research suggests that simply attempting to avoid the disturbing thoughts is counterproductive since it may delay recovery. Social support is important in

recovery though the presence of negativity in the support network is worse than having little or no social support (ibid., 2003).

Theoretical accounts of PTSD clearly have a variety of aspects of memory to explain as disturbing memory phenomena characterise the condition in many sufferers. Among the main theories explaining the condition according to the important review by Brewin and Holmes (2003) are the following:

- *Stress response theory* (Horowitz, 1986): the traumatic event fundamentally disturbs the victim's beliefs about the world, the future and themselves. The new view of the world and the old view are very different. Prior to victimisation, the individual may feel competent and in control of their lives and the situations they face. Following the trauma, the victim may see themselves as vulnerable and driven by external events rather than being personally driven. Traumatic events produce a complex psychological situation in which the victim needs to avoid memories of the traumatic event since those intrusions are distressing; but, in order to deal with the traumatic events, the victim also needs to relive the traumatic events through memory. Flashbacks, intrusions and nightmares provide an opportunity to process the old cognitions of the world alongside those brought about by the trauma. So there is a defensive mechanism (avoiding memories of the trauma) and the healing mechanism (working with the memories) which are fundamentally in opposition to each other.

- *Conditioning theory*: Keane, Zimering and Caddell (1985) suggested that PTSD involved a two-state process along the lines of Mowrer's (1960) two-factor learning theory. The traumatic events naturally produce a fear response, such as when an individual's life is at risk in a hostage situation. At the same time, aspects of the traumatic situation which, in themselves, do not have fear-evoking properties actually are conditioned to be fear arousing by association with the fear response. For example, if the hostage is threatened with death by a man wearing a red hat then a red hat may become capable of evoking fear. Avoiding memories of the event by blocking or suppression merely ensures that the normal processes of deconditioning cannot operate – that is, normally, thinking of red hats would gradually cease to evoke fear. However, avoidance of red hats is rewarding in that it is associated with reductions in fear levels. So avoidance is conditioned. The consequence of this is that the PTSD is maintained and healing cannot take place. Brewin and Holmes (2003) suggest that one of the weaknesses of the theory is that it deals ineffectively with the types of cognitions that are associated with PTSD since it concentrates merely on a simple conditioning process.

- *Dual representation theory* (e.g. Brewin, Dalgleish and Joseph, 1996): this suggests that ordinary memories and traumatic memories are fundamentally different processes. Trauma memories are problematic when they are dissociated from ordinary memories. Recovery from PTSD is partly dependent on transforming the trauma memories into ordinary memories (so-called narrative memory). This alternative memory system is known as 'perceptual memory' and it consists of information that has had little or no conscious processing. Perceptual memories are not verbally coded whereas narrative memories are. There is research which suggests that people fail to actively perceive things in their field of vision that are not expected. This is known as inattentional bias. Despite being unaware of these things they may nevertheless affect the individual. Brewin points out that some trauma victims claim that they have not noticed, say, shots fired at the scene of the trauma. Perceptual memories for highly emotional and important things may be long lasting. Therapeutic improvement will occur when the elements of the traumatic situation are substantially encoded into the narrative memory. Until this stage, stimuli like the red hat will trigger the intense perceptual memory. Once the red hat is more likely to trigger the more reasoned and processed cognitive narrative memory, then the power of the intrusive memories of the trauma is disabled.

Trivial crime and PTSD

So far we have discussed PTSD in terms of the traumatic consequences of very serious criminal acts. However, despite this, is the assumption of seriousness crucial to the development of PTSD necessary? We can readily apply the concept of PTSD to serious criminal acts such as rape or some other serious sexually violent incidents. What of the plight of people who suffer repeated but trivial criminal victimisation? Shaw and Pease (2002) argue

that the police, for example, are not able to deal with the multiple trivial incidents that profoundly impact their victim in the same way as they can deal with the clearly traumatic incident such as rape. Some provisions for the support of rape victims are sophisticated multi-agency initiatives employing carefully trained personnel. There is another reason why the neglect of seemingly trivial incidents is unsatisfactory. It fails to acknowledge that early trivial incidents may well lead to something much more serious. Shaw and Pease give details of an interview with a woman victim who had noted that children and drunkards were often to be seen hanging out around a hostel for the homeless which was close to her home:

> [they] use the wall outside as a toilet . . . the drunks sit at the bottom of the stairs and I'm scared of them throwing bottles through – this is what happened before. I wish someone would move them on. The police know but the CCTV doesn't cover that bit – the station and the alleyway on the back of the shops behind the building. About eight drunks loiter there most nights to drink because there's an old carpet they can sit on. I'd come down the next day and the windows would end up being put through again.
>
> (p. 43)

Her complaint was largely about what might happen to her and the sources of her concern were trivial taken individually. Despite this, events eventually culminated in a situation in which the victim and her property were attacked. According to Shaw and Pease, successive minor incidents may make it increasingly difficult for the victim to cope. Furthermore, if other stress is occurring in the individual's life perhaps, say, as the result of a bereavement then the effects of the repeated trivial victimisations may be worse.

Psychological help for victims

It is inevitable at the moment that the front line psychological support for victims comes largely from friends, family, police officers and others largely untrained in psychology. Even in the medium term, psychological support is often provided by people less than fully trained in psychology such as volunteers and police officers (Winkel and Blaauw, 2001). It is difficult to assess the value of such support. Winkel and Blaauw argue that one common error made by such personnel is to assume that victims compare themselves with someone better off than themselves by deciding that 'I am worse off than . . .'. This is termed an *upward comparison process*. However, victims are much more likely to employ a *downward comparison process* in which they compare themselves with someone who is worse off than themselves.

As already mentioned, one approach to dealing with memories of trauma is through the use of structured trauma writing. This may employ homework exercises as well as one-to-one interactions with support workers. Structured trauma writing provides the victim with the possibility of self-confrontation, self-disclosure and emotional disinhibition, and something called narrativation. By employing self-confrontation the traumatic events are effectively relived and so the intensive traumatic response to those events may become extinguished. Describing the traumatic events in words in a form of self-disclosure is therapeutic. Pennebaker (1995) provided a number of exercises based on the fundamental assumption that when stressful/traumatic experiences are articulated into words, physical and mental health are improved. Thus he claimed that talk about traumatic events may lead to fewer medical problems, better work performance and even better immune functions. In this context, narrativation is the construction of a story or narrative about the distressing and traumatic events.

Winkel and Blaauw (2001) asked a group of people to ventilate their deepest fears and emotions about a traumatic event; another group (downward comparison) was encouraged to write about the ways in which they were doing well in comparison to other groups; and the third group engaged in a rather trivial writing process (about, for example, their plans for the next day). The downward comparison condition was much more effective than the emotional expression condition in terms of clinically significant improvements in terms of intrusion symptoms. Examples of intrusions would include having difficulty sleeping because ideas and thoughts about the traumatic events keep occurring and thinking about the events when one did not mean to. On the other hand, avoidance symptoms were better improved by emotional expression writing. Avoidance symptoms include avoid-

ing letting oneself get upset by thoughts of the events and trying not to talk or think about the events. Stone *et al.* (2000) explored possible therapeutic processes which are involved in the use of structured trauma writing. There was no evidence that improvement was the result of lowered levels of perceived stress, improvement in the quality of sleep, changes in affect or changes in the use of medications.

Post-traumatic anger

It is possible to regard PTSD not simply as an anxiety disorder, as DSM-IV holds it to be, but also as an anger disorder. About 100 years ago, Walter Cannon's classic formulation of people's responses to emergencies (threat) proposed that following the arousal of the sympathetic nervous system to the emergency the individual may exhibit the characteristics of flight (fear) or those of fight (anger). It is readily seen that PTSD has characteristics associated with flight and fear but there is also evidence of a relationship between PTSD and anger. There is a conceptual problem since anger is among the defining symptoms of PTSD according to the DSM. So researchers tackling this question have compared the relationship when anger is included in the possible defining characteristics of PTSD and where anger-related items have been removed (Orth *et al.*, 2008). The correlations tended to be medium in size (of the order 0.4 to 0.5) between PTSD and anger – and it made little difference whether the anger-related items were removed from the measure of PTSD. Meta-analyses (see Box 4.2) have established that the relationship (correlation coefficient) is about 0.5 over numerous studies (Riggs *et al.*, 1992). It is an important question whether therapeutic interventions can actually reduce the anger felt by the crime victim. Winkel (2007) is very dubious that restorative justice interventions (see Box 4.1) which consist of a single meeting can be effective since the evidence is that PTSD needs multiple therapy sessions in general to be effective. Sherman *et al.* (2005), in a meta-analysis, found that compared with conventional justice, those going through restorative justice procedures agreed with significantly fewer items dealing with revenge/anger agreed. Unfortunately, there was no pre-test involved in this study to establish that these groups did not differ prior to treatment. This is an emerging field and a great deal of research is still needed.

Box 4.2 Key concept

Meta-analysis

Meta-analysis is based on statistical techniques. The purpose is to combine and summarise the findings of studies on a particular topic. The quality of the studies on whom the meta-analysis is based is obviously important. In terms of the effectiveness of, say, cognitive behavioural programmes for the treatment of offenders, a researcher would search every possible database for empirical studies of the effectiveness of the treatment in the penal setting. Unpublished research, which may show different trends, is as important as the published research. The researcher needs to define the domain of interest for the analysis. For example, they may confine themselves to studies that use a control group and that measure recidivism in terms of its incidence (whether or not there is any reoffending) versus its prevalence (how often reoffending is done).

The meta-analyst then computes a measure of effect size – this is merely an index of how much effect the cognitive behavioural treatment has on recidivism compared with the untreated control group. Although the original researchers may have expressed this as a difference in means, percentages or any of a range of appropriate indexes, these are converted using simple formulae to a standard effect size index. Although there are a number of effect size indices, the commonest are Cohen's d and the Pearson correlation coefficient. There is a simple relationship between these two and one can easily be converted to the other. Howitt and Cramer (2008) provide a table for doing this. They also recommend the correlation coefficient as the best measure since it is familiar to most psychologists. So the effect size of cognitive behaviour therapy would simply be the correlation between the treatment variable (treated or not treated) and the outcome variable (reoffends within a given time of release versus does not reoffend). If treated is coded 1 and not treated coded 2, and then reoffends is coded 1 and does not reoffend is coded 2, the Pearson correlation between the two variables is the effect size expressed as a correlation coefficient. Some will refer to this as the phi-coefficient.

It is relatively easy to compute a (weighted) average of these effect sizes in order to assess the effects over a range of studies.

Another useful feature of meta-analysis is that it allows the researcher to refine the analysis by examining trends in selected aspects of the data. For example, it would be possible to compare the effect size of cognitive behavioural programmes carried out in the community with those in prison. Any type of difference between studies – the type of sample, the size of sample and so forth – may also correlate with the effect sizes obtained by the researcher.

In recent meta-analytic studies you will find reference to the Collaborative Outcome Data Committee (CODC) study quality guidelines. These were developed by a group of 12 experts in the field to encourage researchers to include studies of a satisfactory quality in their meta-analyses. The guidelines contain 20 items which are structured into seven different categories: (a) administrative control of the independent variable (was it be manipulated), (b) experimenter expectancies, involving the extent to which the researcher has some sort of interest in finding a particular outcome to the study and is aware of the group to which the individual has been assigned and so may inadvertently affect the outcome of the study, (c) adequate sample size, (d) information about attrition – that is, dropout rates from the study, (e) the equivalence of the groups, (f) the outcome variables, and (g) that the correct comparisons are conducted. The studies are categorised on the basis of these into various study quality categories from strong through good through weak to rejected. A strong study might have the following features:

- proper random assignment to experimental and control conditions without any compromise to the randomisation process
- a minimum of five years for the follow-up period in the case of a recidivism study
- less than 20 per cent loss (attrition) of participants
- no pre-existing differences found between the experimental and control conditions.

Victim decision making

Victims are the major gatekeepers in the process that brings a crime into the ambit of the criminal justice system. Three-fifths of crimes in the United States are reported to the police by the victims (Greenberg and Beach, 2001). Other important groups of people responsible for reporting crimes include the police themselves and bystanders who have witnessed a crime. Whether or not a crime gets reported is largely determined by the nature of the offence. The characteristics of the victim are rather less important. Although the seriousness of the crime has an influence on reporting, the perception that there is a benefit to be gained from reporting the crime to the police is more important. Thus the theft of a motor vehicle is highly likely to be reported because it is necessary to do so in order to make an insurance claim. Furthermore, crimes involving violence, especially if they result in injury, have a high likelihood of being reported.

Although there is plenty of evidence from social psychological research, for example, that bystanders may be influenced by the social situation not to intervene (Darley and Latané, 1968), there is limited evidence to suggest that bystanders may influence the process by which a victim decides to report a crime. Experimental research has been carried out in which a bogus crime occurred and a bystander attempts to influence the victim to report the crime. The bystander was influential on the actions of the victim especially when the victim was the sole victim – that is, there was no co-victim (Greenberg and Beach, 2001). Field research indicates further the extent to which victims of crime talk with other people about their victimisation. The precise figures vary somewhat according to the type of crime involved:

- The majority (78 per cent) of victims of sexual assault at a rape crisis centre talked to others about the crime. Of these 76 per cent received advice and 84 per cent of these followed the advice.

- A similar pattern occurred for a sample of burglary, theft and robbery victims who had reported the crime to the police. Sixty-two per cent talked to others before reporting the crime, 58 per cent of these received advice and 95 per cent of these followed the advice.

Of course, these are victims who made the decision eventually to report the crime. It is difficult to generalise from this to victims in general, many of whom decide not to report the crime.

To understand both reporting and non-reporting of crime better, Greenberg and Beach (2001) contacted a sample from the community at random by telephone. Anyone agreeing to take part was asked whether they had been a victim of a crime in the previous 12 months. Those over 18 years of age who had been victims of burglary or theft and were personally responsible for the decision of whether or not to report the crime to the police were interviewed in greater depth. About half had reported the crime to the police. Again, a majority (three-fifths) discussed the crime with others before making the decision of whether or not to report the crime to the police. Family members (60 per cent) and friends (24 per cent) were the major categories of people with whom the events were discussed. Mostly (i.e. in 61 per cent of cases) this social contact was actually present when the crime was discovered. Forty-seven per cent of those who talked about the crime before making the reporting decision had also received advice from that other person. The researchers then studied the relative influence of a number of predictors of reporting or not using logistic regression (see, for example, Howitt and Cramer, 2008, for a readable account of this complex statistical procedure). The most powerful factor in the decision to report the crime to the police (once demographic variables such as age, sex and race had been taken into account) was the type of advice given by those around the victim. So, if the advice was to call the police then this was extremely influential in the sense that the victim would call the police in a high proportion of instances. The type of crime was important since burglaries were much more likely to be reported than theft. The financial loss had a significant but small influence on the willingness to report as did generalised arousal which is a sort of measure of the emotional response the victim had to the crime.

However, it would be wrong to think that this is simply the consequence of social influence. This would be to assume that the victim had no independent view of whether or not to report the crime since the other person may simply agree with what the victim had decided in the first place.

Greenberg and Beach (2004) studied how victims of property crime decide to report the crime to the police. They tested the idea that the decision-making process includes three broad mechanisms:

- *Reward/costs driven* – basically are the gains of going through the reporting process and possibly court appearances as a witness sufficiently warranted by the monetary value of their loss. If the value of the loss is small then victims will be less likely to report the crime to the police. In the study, this was measured on the basis of the amount stolen in dollars.

- *Affect driven* – the arousal of emotion on being victimised may influence reporting in a number of ways. The more emotionally arousing it is then the more their attention will continue to be focused on the crime and the more likely they are to report. Alternatively, a crime that raises fear or anger may arouse patterns of behaviour that involve seeking the protection of the legal system by reporting the matter. Emotional arousal was assessed by asking how they felt immediately after becoming aware of the crime – such as how angry, afraid and upset.

- *Socially driven* – the decision to report the crime is taken under the influence of significant social others who advise or inform the victim about what to do. If the victim had been advised to call the police immediately after the crime had been discovered then the report was classified as socially driven.

A sample of victims of burglary and theft was obtained using random telephone contact methods. Eligible participants had to be 18 years of age, had been a victim of one of a burglary or theft but no other crime, and was the person who took the decision to report the crime to the police or not to do so. It was found that *all* of the above three explanations for reporting the crime to the police were influential in the reporting process. However, they worked independently in that the effect of each type of variable had an influence distinct from other types. There was no interaction between the predictors in the sense that, say, those who were very angry and who had received advice to call the police were not disproportionately more likely to report the crime to the police.

The victims of burglary were more than three times more likely to report the crime irrespective of the dollar value involved than the victims of theft were. Maybe burglary was seen as a more personally invasive crime than theft.

Counterfactual thinking

Another aspect of the thought processes of victims is that of counterfactual thinking. We are all prone to this such as when we imagine different outcomes to an event other than what actually happened. For example, 'If only I had not gone to the bank then I would not have been carrying all the money that was stolen.' Counterfactual thinking may affect our decision whether or not to report a crime because it tends to increase the negative emotion experienced by the victim (Miller, Adya, Chamberlain and Jehle, 2010). The easier it is to complete the 'If only . . .' sentence then the greater the annoyance or anger that we feel about what had happened. But this is turned on ourselves and not the offender. One consequence of not reporting a crime to anyone is that we lose the protection of others such as friends, family, police and mental health workers. Furthermore, because the offender cannot be punished for a crime which is not reported, the victim may be left with feelings of vulnerability and injustice.

If the victim was engaging in their typical routine behaviours when the crime occurred then it is less likely that they will report the crime (see Figure 4.3). In the study by Miller *et al.* (2010), the participants were given one of several different stories in which their handbag or wallet was stolen as they walked home. So (a) in the typical behaviour version the participants were told that

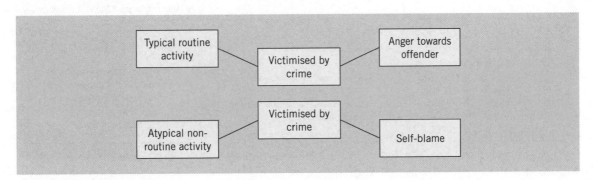

Figure 4.3 Counterfactual thinking and victim self-blame

they had taken their normal route home and (b) in the atypical behaviour version it was explained to them that they took a rather unusual route home. The size of the financial loss is a factor which will increase the likelihood that the crime is reported. This was varied by indicating that a small, medium or substantial amount of money had been taken in the different versions. Both greater financial loss and taking an atypical route home increased the participant's subjective likelihood of reporting the crime. Furthermore, those who lost the most money and took a typical route home were disproportionately more likely to feel angry. However, in this study, it is not accurate to suggest that crime reporting was due to the feelings of anger since typicality versus non-typicality did not predict anger levels though typicality was related to reporting. The researchers argue that there was evidence that these findings were the result of counterfactual thinking because those who took an unusual route home tended to have a stronger belief that the incident was the consequence of luck and that it was preventable.

An important decision to make when being victimised is the question of whether to resist in any way or to be passive. There are a minimum of four different strategies that could be adopted in order to resist a rape or robbery, for example:

- Forceful physical resistance: things such as kicking, punching, scratching, and the use of judo or some other martial art.

- Non-forceful physical resistance: removing the offender's hands, running away or trying to escape, and avoiding contact with the offender.

- Forceful verbal resistance: screaming, shouting, threatening.

- Non-forceful verbal resistance: begging, pleading, crying or reasoning with the attacker.

Clearly the victim undergoing the crime is seeking to force the offender to abandon the crime. So a good measure of the success of the self-protective behaviour is whether the offender abandons the crime before completing it. Of course, what the victim would wish to avoid is personal injury to themselves. Generally these methods are reasonably successful with the exception of non-forceful verbal resistance which does not reduce the likelihood of rape completion. Using forceful methods against a robber seems to increase the risk of violence to oneself.

Why should victim self-protective acts be effective at all? According to Guerette and Santana (2010), Rational Choice Theory (Clark and Cornish, 1985) provides part of the explanation. Criminals engage in decision making in preparation for and during a crime. Different crimes involve different decision-making models and are committed for a particular purpose. Offending is not a random occurrence but is dependent on both the offender and the immediate situation. According to Rational Choice Theory, offenders assess the effort, risk and reward involved in a potential crime so that they can decide whether or

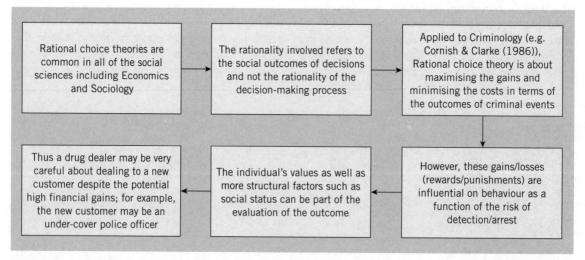

Figure 4.4 Elements of rational choice theory

not to go ahead and commit a particular crime. It is a rational process but limited as such by the quality of information available to the offender concerning when, where and by what methods to commit the crime. The self-protective responses of the victim and other actions may alter their suitability as a target or, of course, risk alerting other people close by who may intervene. The latter are known as guardians in Rational Choice Theory. Where the victim resists the offence the chance that it will be successfully completed is reduced. Quite simply, the relationship between effort and reward is changed by victim resistance. Additionally, where the attack takes place (in a public setting or not) might have an influence since the self-protective behaviour may alert guardians.

Guerette and Satana (2010) used data from the US National Crime Victim Survey for the years 1992 to 2004. Information collected in this was used to assess whether a rape attempt was completed, whether a robbery attempt was completed, and whether the victim was injured. Injuries were further categorised in terms of (a) whether

they occurred before resistance to the crime or (b) whether they occurred during or after resisting the crime. For this study, only crimes involving a single offender were used. The level of resistance was coded on a scale ranging from verbal resistance to physical resistance to physical resistance with a gun or another weapon or an object. Robberies and rapes were completed on just over 60 per cent of occasions each. Only 20 per cent of injuries were received during or after resisting the crime. Robbers used less physical force than rapists but this was because the use of guns was commoner during robberies. This might also explain the finding that more force was used by rape victims than robbery victims. All forms of resistance increased the likelihood that the offender would abandon the crime attempt. The higher the level of resistance used against the offender, the lower chance that the crime would be completed. The situational variables had less effect on the likelihood of the crime being completed though a public location or taking place at night did have some influence.

Main points

- The victims of crime have increasingly been regarded sympathetically as a consequence of a number of changes. The feminist movement, for example, pushed for public awareness of the plight of the victims of crimes such as domestic violence and sexual abuse. It was argued that often the victim was revictimised by the police investigation and the subsequent trial. While elements of this remain, the concept of restorative justice changes the focus of the criminal justice system onto the needs of the victims of crime rather than simply the disposal of the offender through the criminal justice system. It also allows for victims to express their emotions towards their victimiser. A court may seek a victim's proposals for reparation.

- There are many consequences of crime, some of which have been dealt with elsewhere, such as cycles of abuse. Post-traumatic stress disorder is a psychological state in which the victim is unable to deal effectively with their memory of the traumatic events which the criminal subjected them to. By trying to suppress the distressing memories the psychological processes of healing cannot take place. Nevertheless, the memories are still there and burst through into consciousness in the form of nightmares and flashbacks, for example. Treatment involves working through the memories safely. These memories tend to be sensory motor ones rather than narrative ones. Trauma memories are converted to ordinary narrative memories and so can be dealt with by the victim through a normal healing process which was previously unavailable.

- Victims of crime are also the major source of information to the police. The process by which they choose to report the crime or not is therefore of great importance in the criminal justice system. It is clear that this is a social activity since a large proportion of victims of crime talk the crime over with friends, relatives and others, and solicit their advice. The decision to report a crime is influenced by a range of factors including the emotional significance of the crime and the benefits/costs ratio involved in the decision to report the crime.

Further reading

For a wide view of the study of victims see:
Walklate, S. (ed.) (2007) *Handbook of Victims and Victimology* Cullompton: Willan Publishing.

For a popular introduction to post-traumatic stress disorder see:
Goulston, M. (2008) *Post-traumatic Stress Disorder for Dummies* Hoboken, NJ: Wiley Publishing.

A somewhat more demanding but recommended source on post-traumatic stress disorder is:
Brewin, C.R. (2003) *Posttraumatic stress disorder: Malady or Myth?* New Haven, CT: Yale University Press.

Frans Willem Winkel's (2007) publication 'Post traumatic anger: Missing link in the wheel of misfortune' (Tilburg University) may be downloaded at the following link: http://www.tilburguniversity.edu/research/institutes-and-research-groups/intervict/publications/oratiefww.pdf

An American manual for police officers dealing with the immediate needs of victims of crime can be found at: First Response to Victims of Crime (2008) National Sheriffs Association http://www.ovc.gov/publications/infores/pdftxt/FirstResponseGuidebook.pdf

The following provides information about victims' and witnesses' experience within the British criminal justice system:
Moore, L. and Blakeborough, L. (2008) Early findings from WAVES: information and service provision. Ministry of Justice Research Series 11/08 http://www.justice.gov.uk/docs/witness-victims-experience-survey.pdf

---

Visit our website at www.pearsoned.co.uk/howitt for self-test and essay questions, annotated further reading, audio interviews with researchers in the field, weblinks and more information on becoming a forensic psychologist.

Chapter 5

Theories of crime

Overview

- There are many general theories relevant to the study of crime, only a portion of which can be classified as psychology. However, it is important to appreciate that crime can be understood from a variety of perspectives and forensic and criminal psychologists can benefit from insights from other disciplines. Theories dealing with more specific aspects of crime are dealt with as appropriate in other chapters.

- Levels of explanation of crime range from the biological/genetic through to the social and economic. Psychological theories tend to be more limited but nevertheless cover much of that range between the biological and the social. The theories described in this chapter are fairly general theories trying to address the broad range of crime. Any reasonably complete understanding of crime should consider every different level of explanation. Few theories operate at more than one level of analysis.

- Theories of crime may be divided into: (1) societal or macro-level theories; (2) community or locality level theories; (3) group and socialisation influence theories; and (4) individual level theories. Most psychological theories of crime would be classified in the last two categories.

- Few, if any, of the theories compete in the sense that they make different predictions about crime and criminal activity. In other words, it is unlikely that one can reject a theory simply because another theory makes better predictions. Few of the theories have been falsified. Rather, they should be seen as complementing or supplementing each other.

- Among theories described and evaluated are: (1) physiological; (2) genetic; (3) intellectual deficits; (4) psychoanalytic; (5) addiction; (6) biosocial; (7) social learning; and (8) social constructionist approaches.

Introduction

This chapter takes a broad look at the role of theory in forensic and criminal psychology. Along with research, theory is the lifeblood of psychology. While the other chapters in this book are replete with theory, some theory does not fit into these because it is more all-embracing or may represent a perspective which can be applied to crime in general. Theories of crime come in a variety of styles, types and shapes. Crime is of concern to a number of disciplines and it is possible to find economic, geographical, sociological, psychiatric, psychological and biological theories – and ones from other disciplines such as social work may have their own distinctive features. Figure 5.1 illustrates some of the main levels of analysis that may be applied to crime. Indeed, it might be fair to suggest that forensic and criminal psychology has contributed less theory to our understanding of crime than some other disciplines. While there is little space here to explore theories from all of these disciplines, they are very relevant to understanding crime from a wide perspective. Indeed, they are almost essential to anyone working in the field of forensic and criminal psychology wanting a broad perspective on crime. Figure 5.1 explains in some detail the operation of these different levels of explanation. (McGuire (2000) adopts a similar sort of scheme and some of the ideas are borrowed from him.) These are not theories in the sense that research can establish which one is the best empirically. They are alternative perspectives, sometimes on the same matters to do with crime and criminality but, more often, reflecting different aspects.

- *Societal or macro-level theories*: the broadest level of analysis, according to Figure 5.1, comprises the societal or macro-level theories which basically suggest that crime is a consequence of social structure rather than, say, genetic tendencies or psychiatric problems. Marxist conflict theory regards the criminal justice system as a means by which the dominant or privileged classes retain their dominance and privilege. Possibly this is most clearly seen in the way land has become owned whereas once it belonged to nature. More immediately linked to psychology is the feminist analysis that fundamentally assumes that power is gendered in society and that male power is reflected in laws that, for example, have regarded females as the possessions of their fathers and husbands. Another example of a theory that links psychological process to macro-societal changes is the idea that there is a connection between hate crime (e.g. lynchings of black people in post-Depression United States) and prevailing economic conditions such as unemployment. Although early evidence claimed a link, the connection is less than clear or consistent (Green, Glaser and Rich, 1998; Green, Strolovitch and Wong, 1998).

- *Community or locality theories*: crime is not randomly distributed geographically and neither is criminality. Some parts of cities tend to suffer more crime and others (perhaps the same areas) tend to be home to more than their fair share of criminals. If crime is geographically organised, why is this so? The answers vary somewhat but basically the theories suggest that there is either something different about those areas or that different areas provide different opportunities for criminality. In general, crime tends to be committed fairly close to the offender's home base but, often, with a sort of buffer zone just around home where they do not offend. Within that zone they may not offend because the risk of recognition is high. One suggestion is that the social problems of migrants into these 'twilight' areas are particularly great. They are economically deprived, for example, thus heightening the risk that youngsters, in particular, offend.

- *Group and socialisation influence theories*: these are more about direct social influences on criminal behaviour. In a sense they are about the influence of the group

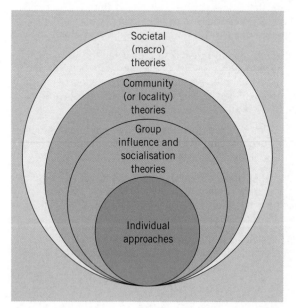

Figure 5.1 How crime can be explained at different levels of analysis

Societal or macro-level theories

††

Marxist conflict theory holds that society has evolved in a state of conflict between competing groups in society over material resources and institutionalised power. The dominant class uses laws to control other groups and maintain its command or hegemony.

Robert Merton's strain theory recognises that society's goals (prosperity, achievement, etc.) are only available to a limited few. The rest can achieve the goals only through deviant means. Some of these deviant forms of adaptation are innovative, as in some gang property crime. Others adapt to the strain by retreating into alcoholism, drug addiction, suicide and vagrancy.

Feminist theory holds that criminality is associated with males. Males seek to maintain power in the gendered social system through the deployment of violence against women and, by extension, children. Male control is through their access to power over social institutions such as the law, though relatively powerless men are inclined to the cruder expressions of power which lead to their imprisonment.

Community or locality theories

†††††††††††   †††††††††††   †††††††††††   †††††††††††

The *Chicago School* of the 1920s held that there are transitional zones of cities that harbour the greatest levels of crime. These were essentially twilight zones that had been deserted by the middle classes which gravitated to the suburbs. Migrants of all sorts would settle in the transitional zones and experience numerous social pathologies. As their affluence grew, these migrant groups would move to the suburbs and cease to be a crime problem.

Differential opportunity theory explains the patterns of crime likely to be exhibited by individuals in terms of the range of crime opportunities close to home. Different individuals display different modes of adjustment or adaptation to their particular social strains.

Group and socialisation influence theories

†††††††††   †

Subcultural delinquency theories: youngsters with problems especially to do with the home and school tend to associate with gangs and other groupings in which they can achieve some status. Through criminal activity, delinquent groups may provide an opportunity to achieve a sense of self-esteem.

Differential association theory: Edwin Sutherland viewed criminal behaviour as learned. The circumstances of an individual's upbringing determine their exposure to crime and pressure to commit crime. This theory claims to apply at different strata of society. The process of learning to be a criminal in middle-class communities may encourage exposure to fraud, tax evasion and similar, more middle-class, crimes.

Lifestyle and routine activities: most crime is trivial and impulsive with an element of opportunism. A mix of motivated offenders inadequately supervised by the community plus the availability of suitable targets for crime are the basic requirements of this theory, formulated by Cohen and Felson (1979).

Individual

†

Personality theories of crimes: Hans Eysenck's biosocial theory is a prime example of this. It emphasises the link between biological factors, personality and crime. Nevertheless, many others have attempted to find the particular patterns of personality associated with either specific crime or crime in general.

Biological theory: Many attempts have been made to identify the particular biological characteristics of offenders – their genetic make-up, brain activity irregularities and hormonal imbalances being typical examples. Evolutionary theories are related to genetic theories but concentrate on just how evolutionary factors lead to the selection of certain genes, including those associated with gender, to be passed on to the next generation (Quinsey, 2002).

Figure 5.2 Levels of explanation of crime

Table 5.1 Some theories of crime and the types of psychology they involve

Theory	Biological	Psychoanalytic	Cognitive	Individual differences	Learning	Social
Neuropsychology	✓	✗	✗	✗	✗	✗
XYY	✓	✗	✗	✗	✗	✗
Intelligence	✓	✗	✓	✓	✗	✗
Bowlby's attachment	✓	✓	✗	✗	✗	✓
Addiction model	✗	✗	✓	✓	✗	✗
Eysenck's biosocial	✓	✗	✗	✓	✓	✓
Learning theory	✗	✗	✗	✗	✓	✓
Social constructionism	✗	✗	✗	✗	✗	✓
Strain theory	✗	✗	✗	✓	✗	✓

(including the family) on criminality. They vary widely but basically they assume that associates may determine whether or not the youngster gets involved in delinquent activities. These approaches are particularly important if they are regarded as a contrast with the purely individual theories that assume that the roots of criminality lie in the individual.

• *Individual approaches*: while no psychologists seriously believe that criminality can be divorced from the social and societal context, some stress the importance of biological and psychological differences as a root cause of criminality. However, distinguishing between the influences of the individual characteristics and more social influences is not at all easy. Generally speaking, it is not possible to identify personality characteristics that are associated with criminality very precisely. Investigations using traditional psychometric measures of personality to try to understand the characteristics of particular offender groups (for example, paedophiles) have not, in general, produced very convincing findings. There are some aspects of personality types that are associated with criminality. Psychopathy and the somewhat similar antisocial personality disorder are among the exceptions.

Concentrating on psychological theories still leaves us with a considerable range of different approaches to deal with. The theories to be outlined are illustrative of psychological approaches. They also constitute a useful body of theory for any forensic and criminal psychologist since they reflect the range of levels of theory from the biological to the social. Since the theories may be associated with more than one level of psychological theorising, Table 5.1 lists the theories and the types of psychology they reflect. The classifications, on occasion, may be disputed, but it can be seen that as we move down the table the analysis tends to be more social. At the start of the table, the theories are much more biological in nature. Also, it should be clear that some theories are practically confined to a particular type of psychology (e.g. the biological only for the first two) but others such as Eysenck's theory, especially, involves several different types of psychology.

One should appreciate that many of the colleagues that a psychologist works with will have been trained in fields which differ quite significantly from that of psychology. The better able a psychologist is to understand the theoretical orientations of these other disciplines, the better will he or she be able to relate effectively with colleagues such as medics, psychiatrists, social workers and the like. The perspective of psychiatrists is much more medicine-based than the typical psychologist's. Social workers probably will have been trained to eschew genetic explanations of criminal behaviour in favour of societal explanations which depend on social structures such as social class.

Neuropsychology of offending

Miller (1999a) argues that biological explanations of crime tend not to be popular among forensic psychologists and criminologists. This is for the obvious reason that there is a vast amount of evidence to suggest important social and psychological causes of crime. There have been numerous attempts to find physiological, anatomical, genetic and similar defects in criminal subgroups such as rapists, child molesters, etc. From time to time biological differences are detected, or so it is claimed, but technical problems make their interpretation difficult. For example, if participants are tested who have lived in a psychiatric or penal institution for a long time, their physiological characteristics may be the result of this long-term institutionalisation rather than the cause of their criminality. A good example of this is the enzyme *serum creatine kinase*, which has been found in higher levels in psychotic patients. Hillbrand *et al.* (1998) studied this in a forensic psychiatric population. It was found that involvement in aggressive incidents was associated with higher levels of the enzyme. Importantly, this was true only of patients on antipsychotic medicine. Those not on such medication showed no such trend. In other words, here is a biochemical difference that is predictive of aggression but only in limited circumstances. So, while it is of interest, this difference does not readily explain aggressive crime in general. Another example is Stalenheim's (1997) study of the extent of psychopathy in a Swedish forensic psychiatric population. He found that the enzyme platelet *monoamine oxidase* was to be found at lower levels in psychopaths but the levels of the enzyme were not correlated with the amount of criminal behaviour exhibited. A further point should be considered. Even if an anomaly is found that is related to crime, there remains the question of why this anomaly should cause crime.

Head injuries can occur in a number of circumstances: road accidents are a significant cause, especially in young men, but Miller (1999a, also see Miller, 1999b) lists assault, falls, sports injuries and injuries at work. Head injuries can be divided into:

- *penetrative head injuries* in which an object penetrates the skull and enters the brain; and
- *closed head injuries* which may involve fractures of the skull. The damage is actually caused by the force of momentum, say, on the head as an accident occurs and its sudden deceleration. Closed head injuries may cause generalised damage to important parts of the brain. The frontal, temporal and occipital lobes seem especially vulnerable.

Head injury may involve unconsciousness lasting for just a few seconds to a much longer term. Memory and attention are among the cognitive functions that suffer long-term impairment. Furthermore, there are personality changes such as loss of ability to plan and to see the likely consequences of one's actions. Lack of tact is another consequence. The effects of brain injury very broadly are predictable from knowledge of the site in the brain where injury has occurred. This is the consequence of the specialisation of different parts of the brain to serve different functions. An apathetic personality may result from damage to the frontal lobe of the brain. Such injuries also cause a tendency to persist with inappropriate courses of action, a degree of irritability and unrealistic/grandiose thoughts. Such individuals show *disinhibition* – a lack of response to the social niceties that makes behaviour acceptable in most people.

Some fairly well-established, pertinent findings include the following, according to Miller:

- Electro-encephalogram readings (EEG) tend to show higher rates of abnormal electrical activity in the brains of aggressive/violent offenders than other offenders and non-offender controls. Abnormal EEG activity is especially likely in the left temporal lobe.

- Positron emission tomography (PET scan) uses radioactive markers injected into the bloodstream to detect differences in blood flow through different areas of the brain. There is some evidence that metabolism of a chemical based on glucose is lower in parts of the brain for some criminals.

- Offender groups seem to have greater rates of head injury in their medical histories. Frequent loss of consciousness is commoner among them – and this can be a sign of brain injury.

- Difficulties around the time of being born and evidence of early brain damage are associated with violent crime. They are known as perinatal complications.

- There are studies of the effects of brain injury on rates of offending after the injury compared with before. When statistical adjustments are made for the decline of offending with age, there is evidence that there is on average a small but consistent increase in offending rates, certainly of less than 5 per cent of the sample.

Methodological difficulties abound in this sort of research:

- Violent people are likely to get into fights and consequently suffer brain damage. So their violence caused the brain damage rather than vice versa. Perinatal studies, for example, somewhat negate this possibility.

- Some of the samples used may be non-representative. Thus murderers on death row might be disproportionately black, poor and of low intelligence and may well suffer from other disadvantages. In essence, they may be on death row because of these handicaps rather than simply because of their crime.

- Pre-injury/post-injury comparison studies tend to use participants who have been on intensive rehabilitation programmes – that is, the most seriously injured – so a misleading picture may emerge.

- The appropriate comparison figures are difficult. Offender groups tend to be working class – the group most likely to suffer head injury. So without carefully matching on social class, the findings may be misleading.

The biological approach is fascinating in its potential but less practical than at first appears. For example, Evans and Claycomb (1998) found an abnormal EEG pattern in violent criminals with a history of violence who denied that they had been involved in a particular act of violence or claimed to have been guided by external forces such as Satan. They demonstrated extremely strong alpha-type brain wave patterns in the frontal part of their brains. While this is clearly of great interest, whether or not such patterns could be used to distinguish genuine cases of 'hearing voices' from those in which the offender feigns psychiatric problems requires much work.

Schiffer *et al.* (2007) provide a recent example of an attempt to locate the origins of paedophilia in abnormalities of the brain structures of such offenders. In comparison with control groups consisting of homosexual and heterosexual men, the paedophiles tended to have less grey matter volume in parts of the brain.

Evaluation of the theory

Pros:

- Knowledge of a biologically based cause of criminality would contribute to better-targeted treatments. Medical treatments rather than psychological therapy might be considered for appropriate cases. Unfortunately, it is very difficult to establish such a relationship for individual cases except where changes have followed accidents, etc.

- The evidence to date suggests that biological factors have some influence on criminality although they are probably restricted to a small proportion of cases. This possibly applies to the notion of the genetic transmission of criminality though evidence on this is also almost always interpretable in terms of environmental influences.

Cons:

- We seem to be a long way from fully understanding any biological basis to criminality, let alone the mechanism by which this possible influence might operate.

- For most forensic and criminal psychologists, whatever the biological basis of crime, biological approaches at the moment do not deal with the immediate task of helping treat criminals through therapy or with the problems of making assessments about individuals and their future behaviours.

Intelligence and crime

It has been a traditional theme that offenders tend to be lacking in intelligence and, consequently, are somewhat under-equipped to cope with their social and work environments. Countless early criminological discussions of offenders would describe them as typically being feeble-minded. Superficially, the idea that low intelligence leads to criminality is compelling. Low intelligence being indicative of poor learning skills might mean that the individual takes senseless risks, lacks the resources to avoid detection, is unlikely to have good earning power in the workplace and so forth. Some of the factors that are known to be associated with criminality are potentially associated with low intelligence. These factors would include school failure, unemployment and similar characteristics. Nevertheless, few criminal and forensic psychologists seem to regard intelligence as a particularly important factor in crime. There are, of course, some offenders of low intelligence but, in general, these appear to be seen as a special case, not the norm.

Relatively recently the argument that poor intelligence is associated in a causal way to any number of social ills has reappeared – poverty, for example, being seen as a result of low intelligence, genetically determined, rather than social factors. More important to the work of forensic and criminal psychologists is the claim that low intelligence is associated with crime. Herrnstein and Murray (1994) essentially argued that cognitively limited individuals are almost invariably likely to experience and to be involved in social ills. Many psychologists reject this point of view on the grounds that intelligence, as measured by IQ (intelligence quotient) tests, is little determined by hereditary factors relative to environmental ones and that it is virtually impossible to separate the inherited from the environmental influence (Kamin, 1977). Is IQ a fixed characteristic largely determined by poor genetic potential? Is it, on the other hand, more or less affected by the quality of life experienced by the individual perhaps from before birth, but certainly in interaction with parents and others in the fastest stages of development in early childhood? This is an argument that became increasingly common in psychology from the 1970s onwards, especially in connection with the view that a person's race is associated with intelligence, so social disadvantage is an almost inevitable consequence of race rather than racism and discrimination. A wide range of authorities has dismissed such a view (Howitt and Owusu-Bempah, 1994). Some would regard positions such as Herrnstein and Murray's as being part of a right-wing political agenda critical of liberal welfare and other service provisions. If social position is fixed biologically through intelligence, then it is a waste of money to try to change things. Of course, forensic and criminal psychology is subject to political influence in many respects (crime is a political issue) so the political implications of the theory in themselves are not a reason for its rejection.

Cullen *et al.* (1997), going beyond general criticisms of the theory, have systematically integrated the research on intelligence and criminality. They reach the conclusion that IQ is only weakly or modestly related to criminality. More importantly, they regard criminality as being largely influenced by identifiable factors other than intelligence. These influential factors are largely amenable to change. If Herrnstein and Murray were right, social welfare policy is misdirected and tougher crime control policies would be a better strategy, Cullen *et al.* suggest. On the other hand, if crime can be affected by welfare provision, then tougher crime control policies are unnecessary and probably counterproductive:

- Cullen *et al.* (1997) reanalysed data crucial to Herrnstein and Murray's point of view. This concerns the relationship between the AFQT (Armed Forces Qualification Test) and various measures of criminality. These measures of criminality included: (a) being in the top 10 per cent on a self-reported crime scale and (b) having been interviewed in a correctional facility. The relationships are only modest at their highest. The correlation would be approximately 0.3 between IQ and ever having been interviewed in a correctional facility. However, this correlation is the one obtained if no attempts are made to adjust for the influence of social class which tends to be associated with both of these variables. If socio-economic status is removed in the analysis, then the correlations become much smaller – at best about 0.15. In contrast, in further analyses, it turns out that criminality is more strongly but inversely related to measures such as being religious, expectations of future work and academic aspirations. These relationships are not supportive of the theory as they suggest environmental influences are stronger. Furthermore, living in urban environments and low social class are implicated in criminality in precisely the ways that those who believe in environmental causes of crime would predict.

- A number of meta-analyses of studies of the relationship between IQ and criminality exist. A meta-analysis is a sort of secondary analysis of several similar studies into a particular topic. So it provides us with understanding of the general trends in the research on related themes (see Box 4.2). At best, adult criminality correlates only 0.1 with IQ although it is closer to 0.2 for juveniles. In comparison, other risk factors correlate with criminality at up to approximately 0.5. In other words, overall, research reveals the importance of environmental influences more than hereditary ones. This is simply because the other risk factors for crime have a much stronger influence than IQ: for example, criminogenic needs such as attitudes, values, beliefs and behaviours like associating with other delinquents.

Quite clearly, intelligence is a relatively minor aspect of criminality compared with many more social factors. The failure of the Herrnstein and Murray thesis to be sustained by the research evidence should be taken by psychologists as indicating the potential for social and psychological interventions to affect criminality.

Nevertheless, researchers continue to address the topic. One recent study (Bartels, Ryan, Urban and Glass, 2010) examined the relationship between estimates of intelligence in different states of the United States of America and crime. With appropriate statistical adjustments having been included, it was found that there was a relationship between the average IQ in a state and murder statistics for aggravated assault and robbery and murder but also property offences such as theft, motor vehicle crimes, and burglary. As ever, the problem is knowing just what these relationships mean.

Evaluation of the theory

Pros:

- If we tease out the biological issue from the ability issue, knowledge that crime is associated to some extent with low ability, low educational achievement and low measured intelligence is useful to psychologists. It suggests that action to alleviate such factors may have a positive contribution to make. This is generally recognised as penal systems frequently offer educational and vocational courses to help remedy such deficits (see Chapter 24). Any assessment of offenders needs to include ability and intelligence testing as this suggests appropriate courses of action.

- We know that crime and criminality are not equally distributed through different levels of social structure. As such, it is attractive to seek simple explanations that justify the status quo. Unfortunately, this quickly turns to a con when it is realised that the case against the theory is strong.

Cons:

- The biological (genetic) approach to social policy generally receives little support from psychologists wherever it appears, though such notions have been disseminated through books and other media to the general public. The idea that social problems are basically intractable offers little for professionals dedicated to reducing criminality. Indeed, it is a good reason for not developing psychological services aimed at offenders as such.

- Even if the theory is regarded as true, it is of little practical value when working with offenders.

Psychoanalysis and crime

Psychoanalysis, especially that closest to Sigmund Freud's original writings, has little to say directly about crime (Valier, 1998). Freud carried out no analyses of criminals and lacked apparent interest in them. He regarded them as manifesting disturbances of the ego that resulted in their incapacity to be honest. Nevertheless Freud had some impact on legal thinking. In 1909 Freud was given an honorary doctorate in law from Clark University, Worcester, Massachusetts. This recognised his impact on legal thinking through ideas of unconscious motivation and the like. A number of Freud's followers dealt with crime issues directly. However, other psychoanalysts such as Bion and Bowlby did attempt to treat criminality (ibid., 1998).

John Bowlby is probably the most famous of the 'neo-psychoanalysts' to modern psychologists. This is largely because of his ideas about early separation of a child from its mother. These were enormously influential in terms of justifying social policy about the employment of mothers in the workforce, which was relatively uncommon at the time. Mothers, he indicated, should not work. The reason was that the separation of the ties between mother and baby destroyed the emotional bond between the two that was essential for the effective social development of the child. It was Bowlby's belief that there is a human predisposition to form attachment to others. The primary care-givers – usually the parents – are a sort of bedrock for future relationships (Bowlby, 1944, 1951, 1973, 1980). Positive, intimate attachments are required for attachment to be satisfactory, otherwise long-term problems may ensue. Once the bonds are broken, the child develops in ways indicative of an inability to form functional social relationships.

One of Bowlby's cases (he was a psychiatrist) was the child he called Derek who had been hospitalised for nearly a year starting before he was one. When he returned to the family he addressed his mother as 'nurse' and lacked affection for any members of the family. The period of separation, in Bowlby's terms, resulted in Derek's inability to form social relationships. Indeed, in his study 'Forty-four juvenile thieves', Bowlby showed the role of maternal separation in the aetiology of a number of delinquents. To stress, this was in terms of the 14 delinquents out of the 44 whom he classified as affectionless characters. Maternal separation was rather rarer in the other delinquents he studied. Valier (1998) writes of the notion of latchkey kid being a popularisation of Bowlby's ideas – for latchkey kid simply read potential delinquent.

Another Freudian influence was the way that psychology until the last third of the twentieth century regarded homosexuality as a clinical deviation rather than a chosen sexuality. Where homosexuality resulted in individuals being in trouble with the law their homosexuality could be treated – that is, they could be diverted back to hetero-sexuality. This is an idea that appears to be singularly old-fashioned in the light of current ideas about homosexuality. Valier quotes East and Huber (1939, p. 93) as saying of a homosexual, 'In treatment every effort was made to release as far as possible his heterosexual drives . . . with treatment, stands an excellent chance of developing his heterosexual possibilities.'

Evaluation of the theory

Pros:

- Some of the ideas, especially those of Bowlby, have been highly influential in directing the attention of researchers from many disciplines towards the impact of early life experiences, especially parenting, on later delinquency and criminality (see Chapter 6).

Cons:

- Few modern psychologists make direct use of Freudian concepts. This is because it is generally considered that when subjected to research, the concepts fail to gain the support of researchers.

- Similarly, the evidence is that, in terms of efficiency and effectiveness, psycho-analytic therapies are not simply extremely time consuming but apparently ineffective.

Addiction to crime

One of the mysteries of criminal behaviour is its persistence in some individuals despite its serious negative consequences. This basic observation has led some (Hodge, McMurran and Hollin, 1997) to propose that crime can have many similarities to behaviours that are classified as addiction. At first, it would seem unlikely that a simple biological explanation of addiction could account for crime – after all, there is no substance that is being introduced to the body, no changes in metabolism or brain activity that have been identified. However, few psychologists specialising in the field of addiction hold resolutely to a purely biological model of addiction. There are a number of socio-psychological explanations to explain at least some aspects of addiction. From this wider viewpoint, addiction is a product of the interaction of personal and environmental factors of which stereotypical biological

addiction is merely a part. One consequence of this is that concepts such as addiction to sex or addiction to gambling began to be seen in a different light. Reasons for considering some crime as an addiction include the following:

- Addiction, substance abuse and alcohol abuse all co-occur frequently in criminal populations. The co-occurrence of addictions may imply that addiction-prone personalities exist or a predisposition explanation of a similar sort. Co-occurrence does not happen with all types of offence. Take, for instance, sex offending. For such crimes, the evidence for co-occurrence is mixed, at best, and fairly weak overall (McGregor and Howells, 1997). However, there is evidence that the risk factors or antecedents or predictors of addictive behaviour are much the same as those for criminality (e.g. school problems, conduct difficulties in childhood, association with delinquent peers).

- Persistence and escalation: despite the well-known tendency for criminal activity to decline with age – to be a product of youth – this is not so for all offenders. For a minority, antisocial behaviour appears more like a lifelong career (see Chapter 6).

- The process of change: successful treatments are much the same for a variety of crimes and a variety of addictions. They tend to adopt a cognitive behavioural model (see Chapter 25). Furthermore, the processes of change in therapy are not dissimilar for substance abuse and crime (McMurran, Hodge and Hollin, 1997).

The disease model of addiction is a familiar concept in terms of alcohol and drugs. It assumes a genetic or biological predisposition for addiction. Problem drinkers, as in the Alcoholics Anonymous formulation, cannot be 'cured' but must always abstain. Use is followed by increased tolerance and more use. Withdrawal leads, in this account, to profound distress and craving. This is a disease that is out of control (e.g. McGregor and Howells, 1997). The model usually includes a component of 'predisposition' as well as increased consumption as a consequence of consumption. The consequences of withdrawal in the disease model are seen as severe but eventually the wanting and craving will decline as the disease disappears.

In contrast, the cognitive behavioural model of addiction concentrates on social-psychological influences that are distinct from biological vulnerability of individuals to drugs (McGregor and Howells, 1997). Learning processes are involved and the expectation of rewards from drug taking is powerful. Indeed, the learnt expectations may be more powerful than the biological properties of the substance. Drug taking is seen as adaptive since it is the individual's way of coping with stresses. It is not assumed in the cognitive behavioural model that sooner or later the 'disease' (the addiction) will become out of control. The notion of craving is replaced by the idea that withdrawal effects must be understood in terms of the user's expectations of the consequences of withdrawal.

Kilpatrick (1997) argued that the characteristics of addiction could be found in persistent joyriders in Ireland. She studied a sample of juvenile offenders incarcerated in a special centre for a variety of car-related offences, including taking and driving away, allowing oneself to be carried in a stolen car, careless driving, reckless driving, theft of goods from a car and so forth. Six common characteristics of addiction can be evaluated using the data collected from the joyriders:

- *Tolerance*: the need for more to produce the same effect. Multiple thefts were the norm, ranging from 50 to indeterminate numbers in the hundreds. Faster and more secure cars were particular targets. Universally, the offenders talked of stealing on demand or when they needed the money.
- *Salience*: the increasing importance of the addiction in the lifestyle. The joyriders frequently seemed to have abandoned their previous interests in activities such as boxing, snooker and video games. Car thefts tended to be episodic – that is, following a drinking session or glue-sniffing episode, the youngsters would steal cars over two or three days, exhaust themselves and take a break to get a decent sleep.
- *Conflict*: increasing awareness of negative consequences. While all of the youngsters were aware of the negative consequences, whether or not this is increasing was difficult to assess. Certainly, over half of them were trying to stop.
- *Withdrawal*: distress after a period of non-engagement. Some had absconded from the school to joyride, and absconding is a very common feature of joyriders at other institutions.
- *Craving*: distress associated with desire to re-engage. Some, but by no means all, had daydreams around the theme of joyriding.
- *Relapse*: reinstatement after decision to stop or reduce. There was some evidence of difficulty in those who were trying to stop but again this was not universal.

Similarly, Kellett and Gross (2006) also found evidence that the talk of young joyriders reflected ideas related to addiction. For example, the researchers regard the following quotation as indicative of the tolerance that can build up which effectively reduces the stimulating effect of a given level of activity: 'if it's getting a wee bit boring you know, just driving about or something, and you see them then you's, come on we'll get a chase, you know.'

Shoplifting and addiction are related. As many as a third of heroin addicts may finance their use through shoplifting. (See Chapter 7 which includes a more detailed discussion of the relationship between drugs and crime.) Among other evidence, McGuire (1997) describes three case studies that he examined for the components of 'addiction'. He found evidence for the following characteristics of addiction in shoplifting:

- *Salience*: the dominance of the addictive behaviour in thoughts, feelings and behaviour.
- *Arousal*: a depressed state may precede shoplifting and there is excitement at the prospect or actuality of shoplifting.
- *Tolerance*: the need for increasing amounts to achieve desired effect.
- *Withdrawal*: there are aversive states of feeling on discontinuation.
- *Relief*: this occurs for aversive feelings when activity is recommenced.
- *Cessation*: leads to a repetition of the activity with complete reinstallation even after a long period of cessation.

The fit of the data to the above cognitive behavioural model to shoplifting of this sort was generally good.

Like other new theories, it may take considerable time before research indicates just how adequate the concepts are.

Evaluation of the theory

Pros:

- The main appeal of the concept of addiction to crime is that it could explain the continued involvement in criminality of those who are otherwise regularly punished for it.
- Criminals tend to be involved in a wide variety of crimes and relatively few are total specialists. Addiction to crime can be applied widely to the offending patterns of criminals.

Cons:

- Without a good deal of research, it is difficult to know whether the concept of addiction to crime explains anything that cannot be explained using other theories. There is a possibility that the theory merely describes features of some deviant behaviour without explaining why the individual is deviant in the first place.

Eysenck's biosocial theory of crime

Hans Eysenck's contribution to understanding crime was largely an extension of his general psychological ideas. His theory might best be described as biosocial since he believed that genetic factors contributed enormously to human behaviour but they have their effects under the influence of environmental or social factors. Genetic variations substantially influence the psychological differences between people that lead to different propensities to crime (and other sorts of behaviour). During his lifetime, Eysenck was a controversial figure who, seemingly, pushed his theory to the limits. He was well known to the general public for his books on self-measurement of intelligence (Eysenck, 1990), smoking and disease (Eysenck, 1980), pornography (Eysenck and Nias, 1978) and racial differences in intelligence (Eysenck, 1973). His views on crime tended to antagonise academic and practitioner colleagues who found his theorising not to follow from the research findings quite so closely as he suggested. Further, his tendency to relate complex social phenomena to fairly gross differences between people was unacceptable to many.

Figure 5.3 gives an overview of Eysenck's theory as it developed during the course of his writings. There are a number of shifts in his stance over the years which are highlighted in this figure.

Genetics

Perhaps the most familiar cautionary tale in this connection is to be found in the difficulties of the *XYY chromosome hypothesis*. The basic genetics of sex is that women have two X chromosomes and men have an X and a Y chromosome in the pair that determines sex. Occasionally, some men are born with two Y chromosomes – that is, XYY rather than XY. This is known as Klinefelter's

syndrome. Since the Y chromosome is what makes males male rather than female, then, speculatively, one might suggest that the XYY male is extra-masculine. Masculinity is associated with aggression, so the XYY male might be more aggressive – they are hyper-masculine after all. So the idea developed that offenders in places such as prison or hospital may well include a big proportion of XYY men (Price *et al.*, 1966). Later research found that they were rare in the general population of men but more common in men involved in crime. The difficulty for the XYY theory was that these men were not particularly involved in violent crime, but only in non-violent crime (Epps, 1995; Witkin, Mednick and Schulsinger, 1976). It is reputed that an American serial killer of at least 13 women, Arthur Shawcross, had this chromosomal pattern. Nevertheless, we can be reasonably confident that, since this pattern has not been shown in other cases, irrespective of what caused Shawcross to kill, the XYY theory does not help us to understand other similar offenders (Coleman and Norris, 2000). Epps (1995) describes a case of an adolescent boy with a very rare XXYY pattern. He was sexually abusive of children. XYY theory is now defunct in the research literature and is discredited among forensic and criminal psychology, though one still finds reference to it (but not its failings) in many psychology textbooks.

Some psychologists accept a possible minor influence of genetics on crime. However, this may have little relevance to the day-to-day activities of forensic and criminal psychologists. For example, just how does genetics help psychologists, say, in therapy with sex offenders? In contrast, genetics is an essential feature of Eysenck's theories. In relation to crime, he was convinced that evidence from the study of twins brought up together and separately supported the hypothesis that there is a substantial inherited component to crime. Twins identical in their genetic make-up (monozygotic twins) tend to be much more similar in terms of whether they grow up to be criminal or not than twins who share only half of their genetic make-up (dizygotic twins) just as any siblings. Thus he cites Cloninger *et al.*'s (1978) finding that there is a correlation of 0.7 between monozygotic twins in terms of their criminality versus non-criminality. This correlation reduces to the much lower figure of 0.4 for dizygotic twins. If everything else were equal, then this suggests that genetics makes a substantial contribution to the criminality of individuals. Unfortunately for Eysenck's argument, as several authors have shown (e.g. Guthrie, 1998; Kamin, 1977), all other things are not equal. Monozygotic twins

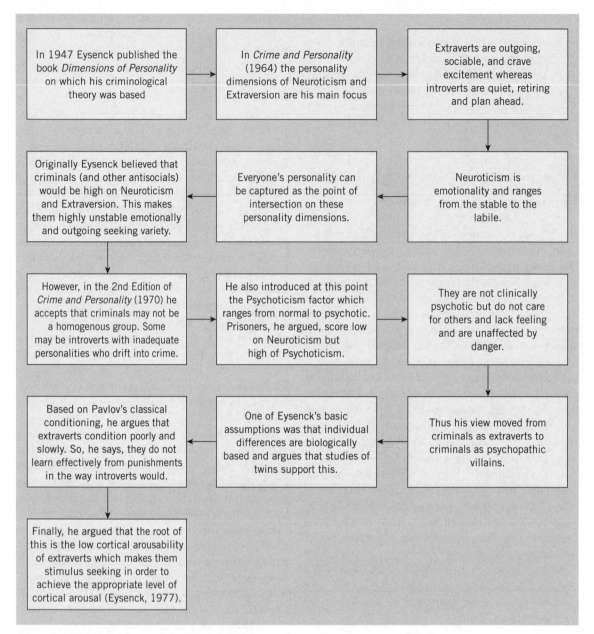

Figure 5.3 Changes and developments in Eysenck's theory of crime as outlined by Rafter (2006)

may be treated much more similarly because they are identical, which might enhance their similarity in terms of eventual criminality. He also placed importance on 'adoption' studies. For example, one study involved over 14,000 adopted individuals (Mednick, Gabrielli and Hutchings, 1994). There was no relationship between the number of criminal convictions the adoptee had and the number of criminal convictions of the adopting parents. However, there was a correlation between the criminal convictions of the adoptee and those of their natural parent. This finding was only true for property crimes such as theft; it was not true for violent crime.

Constitutional factors

Moving beyond the genetic factors, Eysenck, again provocatively, argued that there are physical differences between criminals and non-criminals. The idea that there are morphological characteristics of criminal types was the view advocated by Lombroso (1911). While Eysenck accepted that Lombroso was wrong, he nevertheless was interested in the body types proposed by Sheldon (1940, 1942). Basically, Sheldon's idea was that there are three somatypes or body types:

- *Endomorphs*: people who most characteristically lay on fat especially around the abdomen.
- *Ectomorphs*: people who have an overabundance of sense organs and the nervous system and brain compared to their body mass.
- *Mesomorphs*: people with a preponderance of bones, muscles, connective tissue and heart/blood vessels.

Research by Sheldon (1949) suggested that delinquents compared with college students were very endomorphic and certainly not ectomorphic. Other studies, according to Eysenck, gave similar findings. Crucially, according to Sheldon, the three body types correspond fairly closely to three different personality types:

- *Endomorphs*: relaxed, love of physical comfort, love of eating, sociable, amiable, tolerant and communicate feelings easily (this was called *viscerotonia*).
- *Ectomorphs*: assertive, adventurous, like power and dominance, enjoy risk and taking chances, and ruthlessness (*somatonia*).
- *Mesomorphs*: like privacy and need solitude, are not sociable, are very sensitive to pain and are physiologically over-reactive (*cerebrotonia*).

In other words, body type is related to personality, which itself is related to criminality.

Personality

Eysenck believed that there are three major, largely unrelated, components of personality – *extraversion*, *neuroticism* and *psychoticism*. These dimensions were obtained by the analysis of numerous measures of personality that he developed based on the work of others and his own ideas. The following indicates the characteristics of each of these personality dimensions:

- *Extraversion*: active, assertive, creative, carefree, dominant, lively, sensation-seeking and venturesome.
- *Psychoticism*: aggressive, antisocial, cold, creative, egocentric, impersonal, impulsive, tough-minded and lacking empathy.
- *Neuroticism*: anxious, depressed, emotional, guilt feelings, irrational, low self-esteem, moody, shy and tense.

Which are characteristic of criminals? According to Eysenck, all of them. Criminals should show higher levels of extraversion, psychoticism and neuroticism. He has some evidence to support this.

Environmental influences

Nothing described, so far, explains why genetics may be associated with criminality. Eysenck's argument is that criminal behaviour (and other forms of antisocial behaviour) results from a failure of socialisation to stop immature tendencies in some individuals. These immature tendencies include being concerned solely for oneself and wanting immediate gratification for one's own needs. The process of socialisation is responsible for making individuals more social and thus less criminal:

- Antisocial behaviour of all sorts is punished by significant others in the life of the child, such as parents, siblings, teachers and peers. The process, according to Eysenck, is through classical Pavlovian conditioning – punishment of all sorts acts as an unconditioned stimulus whereas the planning or execution of the behaviour is the conditioned stimulus.

- So socialisation leads to a situation in which even the thought of acting antisocially leads to the unpleasant pain or anxiety of the unconditioned stimulus. To avoid this pain or anxiety, the individual avoids thinking of or engaging in antisocial behaviour.

This argument requires one further step in order to explain criminality. Those low on extraversion (i.e. introverts) tend to learn quickly through conditioning whereas those high on extraversion (extraverts) condition much more slowly. (Conditioning is the process by which associations are learnt between our actions and the consequences of our actions.) There is evidence to support the idea of the slower conditioning of extraverts according to Eysenck. Slow conditioning leads to poorer socialisation and hence to greater criminality. Such an argument also explains why crime is characteristically the activity of younger people – they have not had time to become completely socialised.

So why the association of crime with psychoticism? Eysenck explains this by pointing to the wider evidence that psychosis (i.e. severe mental derangement which may involve a poor grasp of reality or delusions) is associated with crime. Furthermore, the characteristics of psychoticism are patently associated with non-conforming and antisocial activities. And why neuroticism? One thing that may explain their criminality is that their emotionality may make them rather difficult to socialise and condition. Hence, the conditioning process fails for a different reason from that employed for extraversion. The other possibility is that being emotional, volatile or hyperreactive implies that one may well overreact to aversive situations (such as those that are stressful or emotional). If an individual's basic repertoire of responses to situations is antisocial or criminal, then these responses are much more likely in the neurotic individual than in the more stable individual.

From the point of view of forensic and criminal psychology, the question of the scientific adequacy of Eysenck's theory is perhaps not the key issue. Its practicality is much more important, although Eysenck believed that appropriate therapy for offenders is dependent on understanding their personality in relation to the socialisation or conditioning process. For example, younger offenders seem more amenable to treatment than older ones. Things to bear in mind include the following:

- Even if Eysenck is right about the socialisation process, a great deal of research has indicated that problematic childhoods are associated with long-term criminality. Understanding the failures of parenting and so forth may be a more practical way of dealing with criminality.

- Very few of the concerns of forensic psychology are addressed by Eysenck's theory of crime. Why, for example, do some men rape and others abuse children? Knowing that rapists and child molesters are extravert, neurotic and psychotic does not help us to understand their crimes in useful ways.

In the final analysis, Eysenck's theory was conceived to be part of a grand conception of human behaviour which became reduced to just a few key variables. However, it bred research and hostility in roughly equal proportions. Most of us probably gain very little which is of benefit to our understanding of forensic and criminal psychology through exploring Eysenck's theory in depth. It does

warrant some appreciation in so far as it tries to integrate the social with the psychological with the biological. Whether that is a futile exercise compared with the more pressing and immediate tasks of forensic work is another matter. Some issues are still current, such as the relationship between accidents and criminality, which were part of Eysenck's theory since they were both seen as having a similar genesis (Junger, 1994; Junger and Wiegersma, 1995; Junger, Terlouw and Van der Haijden, 1995). Furthermore, the impulsivity of delinquents continues to be actively researched (Ruchkin, Eisemann and Cloninger, 1998). However, researchers seem to prefer a leisure activity/lifestyle explanation of the relationship (Junger, 1994; Junger and Wiegersma, 1995).

Rafter (2006) presents a thorough review of Eysenck and his theory, warts and all, and concludes sometimes in his favour, sometimes against. His contribution to socio-biological approaches to crime are highlighted as being influential on developing that field.

Evaluation of the theory

Pros:

- Eysenck's theory was remarkable in its scope. Like some other theories, it was an account of general criminality although he believed that some patterns of personality might be more common in different sorts of offender. His evidence on this, though, was fairly limited.

- The theory brings together several different levels of theorising.

Cons:

- While other theories described in this chapter lack complete support from research findings, Eysenck's theory has tended to be seen by many psychologists as based on flawed data.

- Although the theory is impressive in that it operates at both the biological and the social levels, in fact the social input is little more than a matter of rewards and punishments. Sociological approaches, for example, have little place in the scheme of things.

Social learning theory

It is widely accepted that children and adults may learn effectively from the actions of another person through a process of imitation. 'Modelling' effects have been a central aspect of social psychological theorising since the early work of Miller and Dollard (1941). They regarded imitation as a form of *vicarious* learning. They extended the notion of learning through conditioning acting directly on the individual to include observing the experiences of other people being rewarded or punished. In other words, Miller and Dollard saw the process of learning being mediated, in part, by the consequences of actions for other people. Much more crucial nowadays is the work of Albert Bandura (Bandura, 1973, 1983). This began in the 1950s and eventually led to his social learning theory. This became a relatively complex theory in its eventual form. His early studies demonstrated that young children imitate the actions of adults, modelling behaviours such as hitting an inflatable clown-doll with a hammer (Bandura and Huston, 1961; Bandura, Ross and Ross, 1963). This is taken as evidence that learning can occur in just a single experience of that behaviour (that is, it is not slowly built up through a process of conditioning).

That learning through modelling can take place is not controversial. What is more of a problem is the usefulness of the theory in explaining the acquisition of antisocial behaviours such as crime and the circumstances in which this behaviour will be reproduced. To suggest that people learn their violent and criminal actions from others is a weak argument. Unless violence and crime are entirely genetically transmitted then inevitably they must be learnt socially in some way. Quite clearly, any explanation of violence and crime in terms of learning is not particularly helpful unless the conditions under which it is learnt can be specified. Violence and crime are not the exclusive means by which goals are achieved. A variety of tactics are involved in achieving goals – working rather than stealing to get a television set being a simple example. As work is a major form of modelled behaviour, how can we explain why there is any crime at all if it is simply through social learning?

Bandura (1977), along with others including, most importantly, Miller and Dollard (1941), recognised that rewards and punishments are involved in the reproduction of modelled behaviour. If a model were rewarded for theft then we would expect that the observer would be more likely to reproduce that behaviour, whereas if the model is punished, for example sent to prison, then we might expect the observer to be less likely to exhibit that behaviour. Bandura developed this aspect of his theory poorly in his later writings according to Bjorkqvist (1997). While this suggests that factors other than observing

crime are needed to explain the involvement of individuals in crime, from the point of view of the forensic and criminal psychologist even this does not take us very far. For example, it suggests that criminal behaviour is essentially goal-directed. This clearly contrasts with some sociological theories of crime, which emphasise the circumstantial/opportunity features of crime.

Evaluation of the theory

Pros:

- The importance of social learning theory lies in its dealing with the learning of complex forms of behaviour holistically rather than as a process of slow conditioning.
- Social learning theory stresses the importance of normal processes in the acquisition of behaviour. Hence there is no need to assume some sort of pathology in those who become criminal.

Cons:

- The theory's weak ability to explain under what circumstances criminal behaviour will or will not be learnt means that it has limited explanatory power.

Strain theories of crime

There have been a number of strain theories to explain criminality. The sociologist Robert K. Merton introduced the concept in the 1960s (e.g. Merton, 1968). His was an account of crime which was (social) structural in nature. The idea was that if normal opportunities to attain goals successfully are in some way blocked, this generated strain or frustration which acted something like a pressure towards criminality. The individual was said to be exhibiting a state of anomie or normlessness. So the desire for monetary success is an American value and (lower economic class) individuals thwarted in this wish because of, say, lack of opportunities in their immediate environment, may turn to crime to achieve that end, albeit illicitly. For example, a lower class parent may be unable or unprepared to provide the economic resources required for schooling to a higher level. The strain that this imposes on the child is then dealt with by illegal means such as drug selling or other forms of crime. There is a singular lack of support for this type of strain theory in the research literature and it is more-or-less merely of historical interest now. Other theorists have suggested that strain is unlikely to operate in this way unless the individual is part of a deviant subculture (Cloward and Ohlin, 1960).

Social-psychological strain theories emerged with relative deprivation theory (Blau and Blau, 1982; Box, 1981). This basically suggests that structural factors which lead to inequality generate feelings of deprivation. The consequence may be aggression or some form of crime. Unlike Merton's earlier sociological theory, the strain (feeling of deprivation) was not measured against some absolute criterion but by reference to a group of individuals. This implies that poor people will not feel deprived if their reference group is other poor people but they will feel deprived if their reference group is better-off friends, for example.

Agnew's General Strain Theory assumes that if people are treated badly (i.e. not as they would wish to be treated) then their consequent upset and distress leads them to respond with deviant behaviours such as aggression or crime. These negative relationships and the attendant emotions are known in the theory as 'strain' (Agnew, 1992). The theory is primarily concerned with young people and strain pressurises young people into delinquency through negative affect such as anger especially. Figure 5.4 illustrates this. Based on psychological theory dealing with stress, Agnew argues that there are two types of strain – objective and subjective strain. This is illustrated in Figure 5.5. Objective strain is strain which people in general would experience given a particular set of circumstances. Examples of this include a lack of food or inadequate shelter. Subjective strain is more particular to the individual. Thus being turned down for a job may

be a major strain for some but inconsequential for others. Personality traits, life circumstances, self-esteem and a range of other factors contribute to subjective strain.

There are three major categories of strain in Agnew's General Strain Theory as can be seen from Figure 5.5. The first category of strain is somewhat like Merton's theory in that it occurs when other people stop or threaten to stop a person from obtaining their positively valued goals. Within this category there are three types of strain: (a) strain as a mismatch between an individual's expectations and their aspirations; (b) strain as a mismatch between their achievements and their expectations; and (c) strain as a mismatch between what would be a fair outcome and the actual outcome. This implies that an individual may have many and varied goals. According to Agnew (2001), the important goals for young people are the status and respect that they have in the eyes of others and autonomy. The second category of strain is the removal or its threat of positive things in the individual's life such as the breakup of a romance. The third category of strain is to subject, or threaten to subject an individual, to negatively valued stimuli such as physical abuse.

The negative emotional or evaluative states created by strain include anger, depression, disappointment and fear. Anger is the most important since it promotes a desire to correct the situation or protect oneself, perhaps through revenge. So, in a sense, delinquency may be seen as a coping strategy. There are four aspects of strain which are likely to increase the likelihood of deviancy as a response in circumstances where:

- the events (strain) are perceived as unjust
- the strain is extreme in magnitude or duration or is very recent

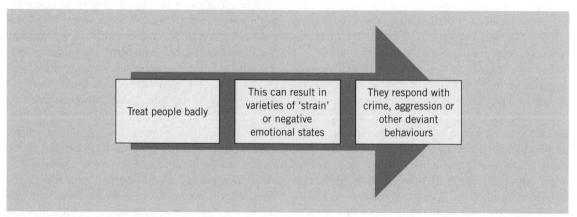

Figure 5.4 Basics of Agnew's Strain Theory

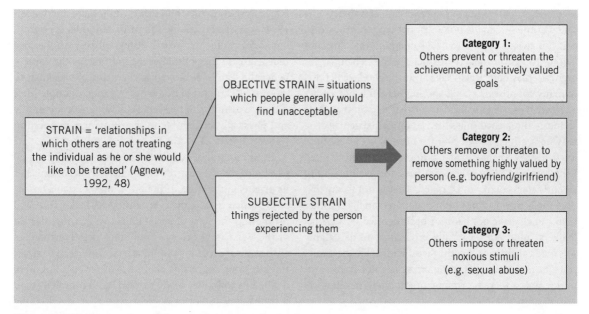

Figure 5.5 Agnew's main categories of strain

- the young person lacks social controls
- there are models for deviant coping strategies.

Not every coping strategy is available equally to every person. Individuals differ in terms of their coping resources. And traits such as self-esteem and intelligence will have their own impact. Similarly, the level of social support available to individuals differs widely. According to Agnew (1997), certain strains are more related to delinquency than others including:

- child abuse and neglect
- failure to obtain goals easily through legitimate means which may be easily achieved through crime
- harsh, erratic parental discipline
- homelessness
- rejection by parents
- unemployment or very poor quality employment.

Evaluation of the theory

Pros:

- According to a major review by Froggio (2007), the last decade or so has produced a substantial number of empirical studies testing key aspects of General Strain Theory. These are detailed in depth in Froggio's report. Generally speaking, the research finds some but not complete support for the theory.
- There is research linking negative life experiences, anger and other negative emotions less strongly so, and delinquency.
- The theory is a fairly encompassing theory to explain deviant behaviour and criminality in particular.
- It is of relevance to forensic and criminal psychology especially as it is a clearly psychological approach to theory. Its level of analysis is largely socio-psychological.

Cons:

- This would appear to be a theory in development and so the strength of all of its principles is not known.

The social construction of crime

It is too easy to regard crime as an immutable thing and to understand the task of forensic and criminal psychologists as being merely to understand what leads some individuals to crime. Crime simply is not a static, universal thing that needs no explanation in itself. There is a very real sense in which crime is made not done. As

McGuire (2000) points out, there are no acts that can be called crime – crime is not a distinct type of behaviour. It is not always a crime to take something that does not belong to one against the owner's wishes (bailiffs, for example, may quite legally take away the goods of debtors in many countries). To kill another person is not always a crime. It may be an accident or that person may have seriously threatened one's life. To take a particular drug may be a crime in one country but not so in another. Even history changes what crimes are. In the United Kingdom and some other countries, for example, until recently men could not be raped. That is not to say that previously men had not been penetrated anally by other men but that the act had not been defined as a crime. Stalkers could not be readily prosecuted until stalking was made an offence in some jurisdictions. Furthermore, since in many jurisdictions a crime has not been committed unless there is criminal intent, then the situation is even more complex.

Social constructionism can be banal as an explanation and as such is weak in terms of explanatory power. It is not helpful to speak of knowledge being socially constructed without knowing by whom it was constructed and what ends it served. Such a weak version of social constructionism largely serves to reaffirm that we live in a social world and this profoundly affects all we think and do. Social constructionism is sometimes offered as an 'antidote' to the positivist view that there are natural and largely immutable laws or principles of human behaviour that psychological research should strive to discover. Anyone entering forensic and criminal psychology with such a view will rapidly be frustrated to find how situationally specific and, sometimes, unreplicable findings in the field can be. Examples of the difficulties caused by this, for example, for expert psychological witnesses, are given in a number of later chapters.

A more powerful version of social constructionism is elite social constructionism (Howitt, 1992). This assumes that knowledge does not just happen in society but effective knowledge is that which is produced, disseminated and advocated by social groups of some status, standing or power. Much of this knowledge can be seen as partisan or in the interests of the group promoting that knowledge. This has profoundly affected the law, of course, and has implications for the study of forensic and criminal psychology. For example, the medical profession, especially during the nineteenth and early twentieth centuries, had an immense influence on the way in which many social issues were construed and dealt with (Haller and Haller, 1974). Characteristically, the medical model for studying social problems such as crime is based on the idea that a disease (or pathological condition) is the cause – hence the search for biological characteristics peculiar to criminals. Thinking about drugs is a good example since users are assumed to be seen as 'flawed' psychologically and physically susceptible to the substances in question (Howitt, 1991a,b).

Even more directly relevant to forensic and criminal psychology is the case of serial killers. This concept has its origins in the work of the FBI training establishment at Quantico in Virginia. According to Jenkins (1994), promoting the idea of serial killers was in the interest of the Behavioral Science Unit since they benefited as an organisation from public interest and fear. Indeed, there is some suggestion that rates of serial killing were defined in ways that made it seem more prevalent than it probably was. For example, statistics on serial killing have been manufactured that include all cases in which someone was murdered but apparently by someone unknown to them. This inevitably results in spuriously high estimates of the amount of serial killing. Other examples of the effective social construction of issues to do with crime include child abuse, domestic violence, sexual abuse, date-rape, marital rape and other issues which have been particular projects of feminist groups. That the way in which we regard crime and criminals is socially constructed does not mean that there are not serious problems such as child abuse to be tackled. In relation to child abuse, the development of public awareness of the problem does not mean that the problem has got worse, merely that the public nowadays regards violence against children in a different light. The involvement of feminists in these issues was essential to create a shift in ideological foundations of the way they are regarded nowadays. However, one should be aware that the domination of such issues by ideas of male power might create a particular focus of interest and cause the neglect of others. For example, physical and sexual abuse by female perpetrators would be minimised by such a feminist viewpoint (e.g. Straus, 1992).

Evaluation of the theory

Pros:

- The theory encourages awareness of the societal processes that change our ideas of crime and criminals.

- Agencies in the criminal justice system may have their own viewpoints and priorities about the ways in which issues are understood.
- The theory should encourage one to explore the origins of new ways of thinking about crime. For example, the idea of a 'war' on drugs powerfully structures the way in which the policing of drugs may operate.

Cons:

- Social constructionism does not explain crime but it does help us to understand why conceptualisations of crime are what they are.
- Its relevance to the day-to-day activities of forensic and criminal psychologists may be a little remote.

Main points

- Crime can be understood at a number of different levels of analysis ranging from biological factors such as genes through to broad sociological and economic theories. Often they can be conceived as alternative conceptualisations of aspects of crime. Theories at all levels should be part of our understanding of forensic and criminal psychology since they all contribute to a full and rounded conceptual base for the advancement of the discipline.

- Many of the theories probably have very little day-to-day utility in the work of forensic and criminal psychologists. For this reason, the later chapters of this book rarely refer back to these theories but tend to employ much more specific and focused theories instead. Understanding something of the various levels of theory will help facilitate the forensic and criminal psychologist's interactions with other professional colleagues such as social workers and psychiatrists who were trained differently from most forensic and criminal psychologists.

- Most forensic and criminal psychologists will move between theoretical perspectives depending on the matter under consideration. This flexibility can only contribute to the value of the discipline of forensic and criminal psychology.

Further reading

For a broad introduction to criminological theory see:
Marsh, I. (2006) *Theories of Crime* London: Taylor & Francis.

For informative and accurate descriptions of many theories of crime and concepts in criminology see:
McLaughlin, E. and Muncie, J. (2005) *The Sage Dictionary of Criminology* (2nd edn) Sage: London.

For introductory material on all sorts of theories from all aspects of criminology including psychology see:
The Criminology Megasite: http://www.drtomoconnor.com/criminology.htm

Visit our website at www.pearsoned.co.uk/howitt for self-test and essay questions, annotated further reading, audio interviews with researchers in the field, weblinks and more information on becoming a forensic psychologist.

Chapter 6

Juvenile offenders and beyond

Overview

- Childhood is the starting point of criminality for many offenders although, of course, some criminal careers begin in adulthood. While delinquent behaviour occurs throughout society, children from some types of family and environment are more at risk of long-term criminality and involvement with the criminal justice system. Childhood conduct disorder, which is a psychiatric condition, seems to share much the same aetiology as delinquency.

- While the risk factors associated with later delinquency and adulthood criminality are well understood, it is a much more formidable task to say precisely what childhood factors actually cause the deviancy.

- Risk factors for delinquency include problematic parenting behaviour such as inconsistency in discipline and harsh and abusive parenting styles, low intelligence in the child and living in violent or disorganised areas.

- Strong evidence is available that early social interventions can have a substantial effect on children who are at risk. Educational programmes provided to very young children at kindergarten or some other form of pre-school are a good example of interventions that have demonstrated positive benefits.

- A high proportion of sex offenders are young people in their late teenage years or earlier. For example, about a third of the rapists of adult women are under the age of 18 years.

- Delinquents tend to justify their actions using less mature levels of moral reasoning than comparable non-delinquent youngsters. It should not, however, be concluded that young offenders are necessarily incapable of moral reasoning.

- Parents who use violent methods of dealing with situations tend to pass the propensity to violence to their children. These cycles of abuse are among the ways in which children are brought up to be delinquent. A number of mechanisms that may underlie cycles of abuse have been proposed including Bowlby's attachment theory, which proposes that the child subjected to violent parenting develops an insecure attachment style which leads to violent methods of dealing with important relationships.

- It is difficult to research the different patterns of criminal careers despite the potential importance of the field. For example, some individuals will offend only during their adolescence, many are spasmodic offenders who offend from time to time more or less throughout their life, though they do little offending in adolescence, and some begin their offending career with any regularity quite late on in life.

Introduction

For many offenders, the roots of criminality are in their childhood. Important differences in the childhoods of criminals may exist even at birth since perinatal factors may be involved in future criminality. Criminality can result from poor parenting, can be learnt from parents and others, can be encouraged by some types of community and can be affected by the greater opportunities for crime available in some types of community. It is more likely to result from all of these things and more. Although many of us do things at some time in our lives that could potentially lead to criminal convictions, a large proportion of convictions accrue to a small number of individuals. Their criminal activity often begins young and continues for much of their lifetime, as we shall see.

Crime runs in families, to a degree. It is concentrated in a small number of families. Over a third of UK prisoners claimed that they had a family member also in prison (Walmsley, Howard and White, 1992). The trend is even higher for juvenile offenders. Farrington, Barnes and Lambert (1996) assessed the prevalence of convictions among males with family members who had been convicted of an offence compared with those with family members who had not been convicted. Fifty-three per cent of those with a convicted family member had a conviction themselves; 24 per cent of those without a convicted family member had a conviction themselves. Most family relationships showed this trend – father, mother, older brother, younger brother and older sister. Only the criminality of the younger sister was not predictive. Genetic factors in the inheritance of criminality or adverse family circumstances may be the reason for these intrafamily trends. In truth, it is impossible to disentangle genetic and environmental factors in these data. Indeed, the strongest relationship between the family and one's own criminality is not explicable on either of these bases. Eighty-three per cent of males had a conviction if their wife had a conviction. Only 35 per cent of men whose wife did not have a conviction herself had a conviction. Wives share neither genetics nor parents with their husband. Thus factors such as early environment and heredity are irrelevant to explaining this finding. The concentration of convictions in certain families is such that 1 per cent of the families were responsible for nearly 20 per cent of the convictions. Half of all convictions were the responsibility of just 6 per cent of families.

The family linkages in criminality are further demonstrated in the study by Putkonen, Ryynänen, Eronen and Tiihonen (2007) in Finland. They were interested in intergenerational factors in repeat homicide offenders. They obtained a small group of these of 35 repeat offenders from a large number of homicide offenders convicted between 1981 and 1993. Criminal and prison records were obtained for their parents and for those of a matched control group. In addition, there were data available concerning the children of the repeat homicide offenders (see Figure 6.1). The likelihood of committing any sort of crime was five times greater for the parents of the homicide recidivists compared to the control group. However, despite there being three times the likelihood of violent offending in the parent generation, it was not statistically significant. The prevalence of persons convicted for any crime was 13 per cent in the parent generation compared to 3 per cent in the controls. Turning to the offspring generation, the prevalence of being convicted of a crime was 36 per cent compared to 3 per cent for the control groups. Furthermore, the likelihood of violent offending was significant for the offspring generation whereas it had not been for the parent generation. In terms of statistical probabilities, this is evidence of intergenerational relationships for both crime in general and violent crime in particular. Nevertheless, the proportions involved suggest very much a minority of the parents and children of repeat homicide offenders show criminal patterns.

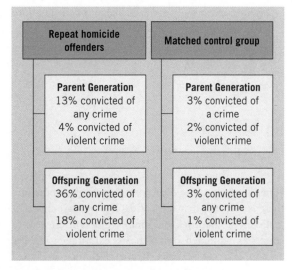

Figure 6.1 Criminal behaviour in the parent and offspring generations of groups of repeat homicide offenders and matched controls

Most young offenders in custody (in the United Kingdom) are convicted for a number of offences. Rarely are young offenders imprisoned for a single offence (Skett and Dalkin, 1999). Young offenders have a varied repertoire of offending behaviour and recidivism rates are high. Seventy-five per cent reoffend within two years of leaving prison. This is important. It suggests not only a broad criminal repertoire for incarcerated young offenders but also that they are highly likely to be quickly reconvicted. Research suggests that for 8–25-year-old males, most offending occurs at about 16–17 years (Farrington, 1990). After this, offending rates tail off to a plateau. Those convicted earliest tend to become the most persistent offenders. Those convicted six or more times are likely to have future convictions in adulthood. Put another way, Farrington (1987) reported that, in London, children rated most troublesome at 8–10 years of age by their peers and teachers amounted to about a fifth of the age cohort. They made up over two-thirds of future chronic/repeated offenders. To illustrate this, Tracy, Wolfgang and Figlio (1990) found that boys with five and more contacts with the criminal justice system made up only 7.5 per cent of the age group. Nevertheless, they were responsible for three-fifths of all recorded offences including homicides, rapes and aggravated assaults.

The data seem to indicate that young offenders may be broadly classified into two groups:

- those with a career of delinquency by the time they become adolescent, which is likely to continue into adult crime; and
- those whose delinquency is temporary and confined to their adolescence.

International comparisons

While juvenile crime is an international phenomenon, there is evidence that rates of delinquency are different in different countries and among different clusters of countries. Although by no means comprehensive, the Second International Self-Report Delinquency Study (Enzmann et al., 2010) involved young people between 12 and 15 years in a total of 31 different countries. The delinquency covered any of the following in the previous year:

- breaking into a building with the intention of stealing
- carrying a knife, chain, or stick (not knife)
- deliberately hurting someone with a stick or knife or beating them up so badly that they had to see a doctor
- purposefully damaging something such as a window, a car, a bus or train seat etc.
- selling a soft or hard drug or acting as an intermediary in such a transaction
- stealing a bicycle, moped or scooter
- stealing a motorcycle or car
- stealing from a shop or department store
- stealing something from a car
- snatching a purse, bag, or something else from somebody
- taking part in a group fight in a public place
- threatening someone with a weapon or violence in order to steal from them.

It needs to be stressed that serious crime rates are low overall compared to delinquency in general. The highest levels of self-reported delinquency were found in the Western/European countries studied as well as for Anglo-Saxon countries (USA, Canada and Ireland for this research). Lower in the hierarchy came Northern European countries, Latin American and Mediterranean countries in that order. The least delinquency was in post-socialist countries. The participants reported the delinquent acts that they had committed in the previous year. Forty per cent of the Irish children admitted at least one delinquent act with only 14 per cent of children in Venezuela doing so. Countries such as the Netherlands and Germany had rates of about 29 per cent. Similar trends were found for serious violent crime and serious property crime – Ireland had the highest rates. The study's conclusions, although based on self-report measures which have their own characteristic distortions, were broadly supported by separate data on victimisation for theft and robbery or extortion.

Criminogenic factors in childhood

Understanding just how some families are more vulnerable to rearing delinquent children is not the simplest of matters. Although one can find a number of studies that demonstrate an association between family characteristics and delinquency, convincing evidence that these are causal relationships is harder to come by. Johnson *et al.* (2004) argue that problematic parenting is an important mediating variable in the intergenerational transmission of aggressive and antisocial behaviour. That is to say, parents who have manifested aggressive and antisocial behaviour have offspring who manifest the same characteristics because these are the consequence of problematic parenting. They studied data from New York State mothers who had been interviewed in 1975 when their children were between the ages of 1 and 10 years. The sample was re-interviewed (obviously with some attrition of sample size). Data collected at various stages could be used to assess the important aspects of parenting behaviour and antisocial and violent behaviour. Official investigation records of arrests and charges during an individual's lifetime provided the key information on the dependent variable of criminal activity. Problematic parenting behaviour had been assessed during interviews at various stages. The sort of behaviours in question were inconsistent enforcement of rules by the mother, use of guilt to control the child's behaviour, arguments between the parents in front of the child, problems in controlling anger with the child and so forth.

Even after controlling variables such as parental education, parental income, offspring age and offspring gender, problematic parental behaviours were found to be commoner in parents who had a history of antisocial behaviour. The next stage was to identify whether problematic parental behaviour was related to the antisocial behaviour and aggressive behaviour of the offspring. The researchers found that these were related just as expected. Statistical analysis revealed that problematic parenting was responsible since there was a relationship between parental antisocial behaviour and offspring aggressive behaviour before but not after poor parenting behaviour was controlled. This means that poor parenting behaviour is the mediating factor in the process. There is plenty of evidence from other countries of the relationship between inadequate patterns of interacting in families and delinquent behaviour. In Spain, Arce *et al.* (2004) found that a measure which asssessed inconsistent, harsh or abusive parenting, parental rejection and coldness, inadequate supervision of the child by its parents, little parental involvement with the child, and lack of affection in the family was associated with greater levels of deviant and antisocial behaviour as well as delinquency.

The major childhood factors associated with future criminality are well known. Some researchers may dispute whether these factors actually *cause* delinquency and adult crime. All researchers accept the utility of these correlates in identifying the sorts of children at most risk of becoming criminal. Several authors have reviewed aspects of this research. Haapasalo and Pokela (1999) concentrated on the longitudinal research (that is, studies involving the assessment of children at different stages of childhood) into the effects of aspects of parenting. These studies go back to the earliest and seminal studies of Glueck and Glueck (1962, 1968) whose work began in the 1950s. The evidence strongly supports the view that the following are antecedents of antisocial and criminal behaviour:

- deviant parental characteristics (criminality, substance abuse, mental problems)
- family disruption (separations, divorce, instability, marital conflict)
- lack of love or rejection
- laxness (poor monitoring, lack of supervision)
- punitive child-rearing practices and attitudes (including corporal punishment, strict discipline, authoritarian attitudes).

However, the list is probably much longer than this.

Of course, parenting style is only one aspect of childhood. Many factors are associated with both delinquency and adult crime (Yoshikawa, 1995), suggesting that the two have similar origins. While the important factors are fairly well agreed by researchers, they vary in nature and are extensive. So delinquency, Yoshikawa argues, is the product of the interaction of a multiplicity of factors occurring in a number of settings. These settings include school, home and the community. The *risk* factors she believes to be involved include:

- history of antisocial behaviour for the child
- low cognitive ability in the child as measured by low IQ or poor educational achievement
- media violence
- neurological and biological factors
- parental substance abuse
- violent or socially disorganised neighbourhoods.

The above are single factors which act independently of each other. There are instances of complex interactions where the presence of two or more factors makes the risk of delinquency much worse than the sum of the separate effects. This 'multiplicative' tendency is illustrated by her next five factors:

- insecure attachment of the child to parent made worse by poor parenting, unplanned birth, life stress and low social support;
- lone parenthood, though probably to do with cases of poor parenting or low socio-economic status;
- parental criminality made worse by early family conflict;
- perinatal difficulties (i.e. around the time of birth) associated with low socio-economic status and the presence of family adversity;
- poor or harsh parenting made worse by marital discord.

There are also instances of buffering effects of second variables which reduce the risk:

- low socio-economic status effects are reduced by good parenting and age-appropriate verbal ability;
- poor or harsh parenting effects are reduced by emotional and community support.

A few factors on the list, such as the effects of media violence, are rather more controversial than she implies (see Chapter 8 for a detailed discussion of media effects on violent crime). Nevertheless, give or take the occasional quibble, the implications of the thrust of the evidence is agreed by most researchers.

Of course, some might argue that the predictive factors are so intertwined that it is impossible to say exactly which factors cause later criminality. For example, conflict between parents and the self-confidence of the mother may be interrelated. If they both tend to occur together, it is difficult to know which is the most important. Furthermore, there are some criticisms of some studies as they are dependent on how offenders remember their early family environment. Such recollections may be inaccurate or self-justificatory. However, there would seem to be enough evidence from studies that do not use such *retrospective* procedures to negate this view. For example, McCord (1979) used information from a study of parenting behaviours obtained from counsellors who had visited families. Thirty years later she collected data on their children's criminal behaviour in the ensuing years. She found that characteristics (as measured between 5 and about 13 years of age) such as the following predicted the child's criminality:

- conflict between the parents
- little or casual supervision of the child
- mother's lack of affection for the child.

Statistically, such parenting variables in combination identified as serious adult criminals about two-thirds of men who had no record of offending as juveniles. Furthermore, if one considers those with juvenile criminal records, the parenting variables indicate which ones go on to have an adult criminal record reasonably well.

Similar trends seem to emerge in countries culturally and geographically very removed from the Western location of the majority of studies. For example, research findings in northern Russia support those from elsewhere quite well. Ruchkin, Eisemann and Hagglof (1998a) studied a group of delinquents of 15 to 18 years of age. These were compared with a similar group of non-offenders. Their delinquency was fairly serious but consisted of repeated thefts in the main. A few were more serious cases such as rape and murder:

- Some types of aggression in the delinquents were best predicted by the father's rejection of the boy.
- In contrast, for the control, non-delinquent group, rejection by the boy's mother was associated with aggression.
- According to information obtained from self-reports, delinquents scored higher than controls on rejection and overprotection by both mother and father (Ruchkin, Eisemann and Hagglof, 1998b).
- Delinquents also claimed to have problems such as bodily complaints, feeling anxious/depression, difficulty in paying attention, feeling withdrawn and a number of others. It is not clear that these problems are the result of parenting styles since there was little relationship between bodily complaints and parenting styles.

Increasingly, information is becoming available concerning the impact of factors such as father absence on the development of children. Families with the father present allow him to be involved with the child as in the form of play, reading bedtime stories, outings and so forth. Unfortunately few studies if any measure such involvement with the child and researchers have tended to concentrate on father present or father absent as a substitute. Sakardi, Kristiansson, Oerklaid and Bremberg (2007) reviewed a total of 24 studies which concerned the impact of fathers (including father substitutes such as stepfathers and live-in partners of the mother). They were interested in studies of a longitudinal nature in which key variables are measured at different points in time. This, of course, is beneficial to assessing causal influences of variables on each other – the researchers were not interested in single-stage cross-sectional or snapshot studies which lacked this temporal dimension. Some of the available studies controlled for social economic status but others did not. Children who engage interactively with their father or a father substitute have fewer behavioural problems if they are boys and fewer psychological problems as young women if they are girls. Among children from low socio-economic status families, the evidence showed that key variables such as criminality and economic disadvantage later in life were also affected positively by father absence. Although these effects happened irrespective of biological links between father and child, biological fathers seem to contribute other more specific things. Having a biological father who does not live with the child but is nevertheless involved with the child has important influences on children from low income families. The behavioural trajectory into adolescent delinquency for children with otherwise inadequate or criminogenic backgrounds is significantly reduced by the involvement of the biological parent with the child. This remained the case irrespective of whether the father lived at home or not.

It is not only natural families that can cause problems. The consequences of fostering and institutional placements on children should not be neglected. While these children are clearly ones most likely to have difficulties, the problems are sometimes worsened by such alternative arrangements. Foster placements as well as institutional care can exacerbate, and sometimes cause, problem behaviour. This, of course, may be one way in which long-term criminal careers are maintained during childhood. D. Browne (1999, 2000), as have others, showed that there is a strong relationship between problem behaviours (such as running away and destructive tantrums) as reported by foster parents and breakdown of the placement. The consequence may well be multiple foster placements for a child with worsening problems.

There is one issue that needs to be addressed before we move on. That is, to what extent do the same factors lead to delinquency in girls as they do in boys? There is substantial evidence to suggest that girls are increasingly to be found participating in delinquent activity. Of course, currently the proportion of girls engaging in delinquent acts is rather lower than that for boys. Zahn (2007) evaluated the many research studies into the correlates of delinquency in girls. In general it was found that the factors involved in the delinquency of boys are also involved in the delinquent activities of girls. One factor – sexual abuse – stands out as being commoner for girls than for boys and there is good evidence that abuse is predictive of delinquency. Intriguingly, the more girls associated with boys the greater their risk of delinquency – this may imply the adverse influence on males.

Continuity of childhood and adult antisocial behaviour

Let us summarise some of the factors associated with youthful and adult criminality (according to Farrington, 1995; Skett and Dalkin, 1999; West, 1982):

- criminal parent or siblings
- large family size
- low family income
- poor accommodation
- poor parenting such as disinterest and inconsistent discipline.

This list is very similar to the factors associated with the aetiology of psychiatric disorders. Not surprisingly, then, researchers have examined more directly the relationship between psychiatric disorder and criminality in childhood. *Childhood conduct disorder* is defined in the *Diagnostic and Statistical Manual of the American Psychiatric Association* (American Psychiatric Association, 1987) as disturbed behaviour in childhood which persists for more than six months (see Box 21.1). The behaviours taken to indicate this disorder are at best antisocial and, in some cases, may be regarded as criminal. Table 6.1 lists some of these criteria. In order for the diagnosis of childhood conduct disorder to be applied, a child must exhibit three or more of the types of behaviour listed in the table. In other words, if not showing a range of criminal activities, they are demonstrating strong antisocial tendencies. Table 6.1 also lists some of the criteria which can be used to identify an individual as suffering from *antisocial personality disorder* (ASPD), which is discussed in Chapters 21, 22

Table 6.1 Diagnostic criteria for childhood conduct disorder and antisocial personality disorder

Childhood conduct disorder: three or more of the following	Antisocial personality disorder: four or more of the following
Animal cruelty	Debts repeatedly defaulted on
Broken into buildings or cars	Drives recklessly or when drunk
Cruelty to people	Employment history unstable
Destroyed property	Impulsive
Destruction of other people's property	Lacks remorse
Fire-setting deliberately	Lies repeatedly
Lies often	Neglects children
Runs away from home overnight more than once	No monogamous 1 year plus relationships
Stolen more than once	Physically fights repeatedly
Truants frequently (the list includes other things)	Steals and vandalises repeatedly

and 27. Basically, it is evidenced by an individual showing a range of criminal and other antisocial characteristics which are grossly at variance with social norms. This adult condition is not completely identical with that for childhood conduct disorder, but there are considerable similarities. Indeed, the individual must have exhibited conduct disorder as a child to be classifiable as having ASPD as an adult. There has been considerable research into the factors associated with childhood conduct disorder and ASPD. The research ranges widely from large-scale demographic studies to investigations of a small number of factors. Nevertheless, there is a degree of consistency in the research findings concerning the two conditions. This led Farrington (1996) to argue that childhood conduct disorder and ASPD share much the same aetiological precursors. These precursors, according to Farrington, include:

- convicted parent
- early school leaving
- harsh or erratic parental discipline
- large family size
- low family income
- low intelligence
- poor housing.

These are factors similar to those that predicted delinquency.

Data from several stages of the *Cambridge Study of Delinquent Development* support the sequential progression of antisocial behaviour. This study was begun in the 1960s by the famous criminologist Donald West, though the psychologist David Farrington became associated with the long-term project a few years later. It was (and is continuing) longitudinal research in which the same group of boys is studied intensively at different points in their lives. Data have been collected, as part of the study, on a large number and variety of factors and characteristics that may be associated with criminal offending. Care has to be taken not to assume that these factors are proven causes of delinquency and adult crime. They may be, but proof in this area is notoriously difficult. While the measures taken in the Cambridge study do not overlap precisely with those in the *Diagnostic Manual*, composite measures from the study are available on variables which strongly reflect childhood conduct disorder and ASPD. Antisocial personality as assessed from data collected at ages 10, 14, 18 and 32 years was explored in terms of possible predictors from the rest of the data. Table 6.2 gives the best predictors out of the vast range of different precursor variables for the variable antisocial personality.

Although it contains merely part of the findings, Table 6.2 reveals important things. Crucially, there is a very strong relationship between having characteristics of antisocial personality at one stage and demonstrating

Table 6.2 Major predictors of antisocial personality at different ages

Age group	Best predictors of antisocial personality
10-year-olds	Poor parental supervision
	Low school attainment at age 10
	Poor child-rearing by parents at age 8
	High neuroticism
14-year-olds	Antisocial personality score at age 10
	Separated from parent at age 10
	Low non-verbal IQ at age 8–10 years
	Many friends at age 8
18-year-olds	Antisocial personality score at age 14 years
	Convicted parent at age 10
	Father not involved at age 12
	Father unemployed when child was 14 years
32-year-olds	Antisocial personality score at age 18 years
	Convicted parent at age 10 years
	Did not stay at school
	Hospitalised for illness at age 18 years

antisocial behaviour at later stages. These later stages include adulthood. Of interest, but less important, is that having fewer friends at age 8 years is negatively related to antisocial personality behaviours: that is, youngsters with few friends tend not to become criminal. Nevertheless, apart from their lack of crimes, Farrington points out that such individuals are somewhat dysfunctional as adults – misfits. Having few friends, though, may protect them from peer group pressure which otherwise might have encouraged them to commit offences.

Convincing as this may be, the Cambridge study covers the later stages of childhood into adulthood. There is good reason to think that problems develop at an even younger age than that. Haapasalo and Tremblay (1994), using kindergarten classes containing children of low socio-economic class in a French school board in Montreal,

explored antisocial behaviour especially aggression. The main features of their study were as follows:

- Kindergarten teachers rated the behaviour of each boy in the study – over 1,000 remained in the longitudinal follow-up. This included aggression such as fights other children, kicks, bites, hits other children, bullies or intimidates other children.

- The children were grouped by fighting patterns:
  - stable high fighters were high fighters in kindergarten and continued to be in at least two subsequent years;
  - high fighters with late onset were not fighters in kindergarten but became so in subsequent years;
  - desisting high fighters: high fighters in kindergarten but declined in next two or three years;
  - variable high fighters: some years were high fighters, other years were not;
  - non-fighters at any time.

- They were assessed on an index of family adversity based on parents' ages at birth of their first-born child, amount of schooling parents had and occupational status.

- The children provided information about the parents' parenting behaviour: do your parents know your whereabouts when you go out? Do your parents know with whom you are spending your time when you go out?

- The measure of punishment was based on such questions as: do your parents punish you by slapping or hitting you? Do your parents punish you by not letting you do things you would like to do?

- Parents' use of rules was assessed by such questions as: is there a rule at home about the time to come home in the evenings? Is there a rule at home about how much time you can spend in front of the TV? And so forth.

Stable fighters – those who remained aggressive at each stage of the study – differed from the other groups in terms of background. They came from the more socially disadvantaged home environments according to the index of family adversity. The boys who were classified as non-fighters tended to be the most carefully supervised by their parents and they received the least punishment of all of the groups. Perhaps the most important finding in the present context was that delinquency scores at early adolescence (ages 11 to 14 years) were higher for the groups who fought most in early childhood than the other groups. That is, the consistently violent boys in early childhood were especially prone to delinquency.

Similar continuities between childhood behaviours and later criminality have been found in very different cultures. Viemero (1996) reports longitudinal data from Finland. Again, there was evidence that later criminal behaviour was commoner among youngsters who were identified as more aggressive in childhood and by higher levels of violence in their favourite television programmes.

Social interventions to reduce delinquency

Is it possible to reduce criminality and future criminality in youngsters through social interventions? Does, for example, providing parents with support to improve their parenting compensate for the effects of a poor home background? Early childhood is not too young for initiatives to be effective ways of reducing delinquency. Yoshikawa (1995) argues that to wait until the children have grown into delinquent adolescents before intervening is a mistake. Not to intervene much younger overlooks the findings from decades of criminological, sociological and psychological research. Yoshikawa analysed the outcome of the 40 existing evaluation studies that met certain criteria. These requirements were as follows:

- The intervention should involve the groups of children most at risk of delinquency/antisocial behaviour. Children with low birth weight and those living in low-income families are examples of this category.

- The intervention should take place between the prenatal stage (i.e. prior to birth) and primary school entry.

- The researchers should study the effects of intervention on juvenile delinquency or the risk factors for long-term juvenile delinquency.

Included were two main sorts of intervention aimed at a variety of factors believed to affect the risk of criminality. These are described below together with the broad trends in the outcomes of these interventions:

- *Educational programmes* focusing on the children involved such provisions as part-time kindergarten

or pre-school of one sort or another. Although not all studies evaluated all possible outcomes, there was consistent evidence that children receiving the educational intervention were cognitively (intellectually) more advanced than those who did not.

- *Parent-focused family support programmes* involved matters such as regular home visits from a professional in childcare. The results of these studies seem a little more varied and with mixed success. Some find improvements in the intellectual functioning of children whose parent receives the intervention but others show little difference. Parenting skills also showed mixed outcomes and there were few differences, if any, between the children in terms of antisocial behaviour.

- *Combined family support and early education*. This group of studies showed the most promising outcomes of all. Cognitive abilities of the children and parenting abilities were all improved. Most significantly in this context, antisocial behaviour (aggressive and delinquent behaviour in the long term) was reduced by this mixed intervention.

To be sure, such interventions were costly but not so costly as delay would be. An economic analysis compared costs of interventions with the cost to society dealing with delinquent children in the criminal justice system. Early intervention programmes were more cost effective in these terms. The economic cost of juvenile crime is massive according to researchers such as Welsh *et al.* (2008). They estimated the economic costs of the self-reported crimes of a cohort of young males in the 7–17 year range in the metropolitan areas of Pittsburgh, USA. The self-reported crimes of these boys were dominated by assaults (69 per cent) followed by larcenies (25 per cent). Virtually no sexual crimes were reported. The estimates of the costs varied, of course, but they ranged from about $90 million to $110 million. This was for 500 boys!

Despite this, it is remarkable that there are very few evaluation studies of interventions with children who currently offend or who are at high risk of offending in the near future (Nee and Ellis, 2005). It is clearly not very practical to try to research the effects of interventions on future delinquent offending because of the long timescale involved. So, instead, Nee and Ellis studied the influence of intervention on the recipient's scores on a powerful risk and needs assessment tool known as the LSI-R. This stands for the Level of Service Inventory –

Revised (Andrews and Bonta, 1995). It measures many of the risk factors which we know are associated with offending. Consequently, it forms a convenient indicator of the success of any treatment programme. About half of the young people were in the age range of 7–12 years of age. Data on police charges were also available. This may be less useful as the police may avoid criminalising such young people if at all possible. The youngsters were overwhelmingly male and they had largely committed offences against property although a small number had supposedly committed sex offences. In some cases, they had referred themselves for help but more usually they had been referred by social workers, their parents and so forth. The programme (The Persistent Young Offender Project) included a range of practices:

- one-to-one mentoring in order to help the youngster reintegrate into the school;
- group work addressing life problem-solving, anger management, victim awareness, interpersonal skills, substance misuse, appropriate sexual behaviour and health;
- self-esteem and social skills building activities such as music, art and drama.

Compared with a similar group with little experience of the programme, the number of police charges for members of the treatment group declined during their time on the programme. Furthermore, risk as assessed by the LSI-R also declined in the treated group. Thus interventions to deal with delinquent behaviour can be effective even with those who are actively delinquent.

It would seem unlikely that just one type of therapeutic intervention is much more effective than any other type. If one considers that interventions may be cognitive behavioural therapy, drug court, family therapy, victim–offender mediation and prison visitations among many others, an important question is just what is it about a treatment(s) which make it effective? To answer this question, Lipsey (2009) carried out a meta-analysis (see Box 4.2) of intervention programmes for young or juvenile offenders. There were no limitations as to the sort of intervention programmes involved. As might be expected, a very large number of research reports were involved giving a total of over 500 samples of young people with the range of 12 to 21 years. Recidivism was an important outcome variable and was standardised for the different studies. The factors which emerged as being important in reducing recidivism were:

- a therapeutic intervention philosophy (programmes strongly based on the concept of discipline were generally much less effective at reducing recidivism)
- higher treatment effectiveness was associated with the involvement of high risk offenders with two or more previous convictions though violent or aggressive youngsters were not likely to benefit in this way
- quality of the intervention.

Few differences existed between the effectiveness of the different types of therapeutic intervention. This was the case when other relevant variables such as study design and methods of measuring recidivism were controlled for. The overall effect size was small but the range of effect sizes was 'enormous' according to the study's author. Some effect sizes were even negative implying that treatment made recidivism worse not better! While it was true that generally the different types of intervention differed by little in their effectiveness, the detail is important. Counselling-based treatments were relatively ineffective whereas behavioural and cognitive-behavioural interventions were somewhat better than the other forms of intervention.

There is a fundamental risk with any treatment programme – that is, they inevitably bring together groups of individuals with problems. The risks are fairly evident if the programme involves youngsters showing criminal tendencies and other forms of antisocial behaviour. The technical medical term for a treatment which has negative consequences is an iatrogenic effect. So bringing together adolescents with the same sorts of problems may, quite simply, reinforce that behavior. Such an effect may also be described as a peer contagion effect in this more specific context. There is quite some evidence according to Cécile and Born (2009) in favour of the idea of an iatrogenic effect of treatment in such studies. Granting that this is the case, then there are some fairly obvious ways of avoiding such iatrogenic effects in treatment programmes. For example, treating a delinquent youngster before their trial may be less damaging than treatment after they have been convicted, which may risk greater iatrogenic effects simply because of the mix of offenders undergoing treatment after conviction. As one of the problems is the influence of delinquent peers then a good treatment programme might involve adults perhaps as leaders of the group or ensuring that there is contact with non-deviant peers or working on good relationships with the family. Generally speaking, the focus ought to be on structuring social interaction during the course of the programme to minimise the opportunities for deviant behaviour to be among the group's activities. All of this is similar to the common argument that prison is undesirable because it reinforces criminality by putting criminals together.

Young sex offenders

For whatever reason, many researchers have ignored juvenile sexual offences. This is a surprise given the intense research activity into child victims of sexual abuse. Young offenders, international statistics show, form a moderate proportion of sex offenders (Langstrom, 1999). His figures for Sweden suggest that, compared with their high levels of offending in general, the sex offending of young persons of 15–20 years is low. Nevertheless, over 10 per cent of rape, child molestation and sexual harassment offences can be attributed to this age group. Children under the age of 15 cannot be criminally prosecuted in Sweden or be subjected to the standard forensic psychiatric evaluation of sanity.

The corresponding figures for other countries, especially the United States and the United Kingdom, seem higher. Note, though, that the age ranges reported are not identical to those used in Sweden. Based on UK Official Criminal Statistics (crimes recorded by the police), sexual offences by offenders under the age of 18 years may include as many as 30 per cent of the rapes of adult women and perhaps up to a half of all sexual offences against children (Langstrom, 1999). British surveys of victims (in which the general public are questioned directly about their experiences of various crimes) suggest that youngsters of less than 18 years carry out over a third of sex crimes against children. Data from the United States indicate that about half of sexual offences against boys and a quarter of sexual offences against girls are committed by young people.

Vitacco et al. (2009) argue that the burgeoning of interest in adolescent sexual offending was fuelled by legislation to protect the public from adolescent sex offenders. In particular, the USA's Sexual Offender and Notification Act of 2006 (also known as the Adam Walsh Act) made provision for including adolescent sex offenders on public registers. According to Vitacco et al., public policy was made before relevant research was carried out which may have had an impact on policy. For example, researchers may doubt the idea that adolescent sex offenders go on to become adult sex offenders. Adolescent sex offenders seem to have much the same risk of reoffending sexually as adolescent offenders in general. Many juvenile sex offenders do not show continuity in their future offending and do not go on to offend sexually after adolescence (Caldwell, 2007). Another common assumption is that treatments for sex offenders have little impact despite the evidence of their effectiveness (see Chapter 26).

One important question is whether the characteristics of childhood that predict general delinquency the same as those that predict sexual delinquency? If they are the same, then this has obvious implications for how young sexual offenders are managed in the criminal justice system as well as for theory. Langstrom (1999) studied 15- to 20-year-olds who had been subject to the *Forensic Psychiatric Examination* over the period 1988–95. These young sexual offenders had extensive previous histories of sexually abusing others. For example, young sexual offenders brought to the attention of the authorities for the first time already had an average of seven victims. Over a quarter of sexual offenders of 12 or more years of age had a previous history of sexually abusive acts. The predictors of sexual offending included:

- early onset of sexually abusive behaviour;
- male victims;
- multiple victims;
- poor social skills.

These are rather different from the factors predictive of non-sexual delinquency discussed earlier. Not surprisingly, then, in Langstrom's study when we exclude sexual recidivism, general reoffending is predicted by some of the factors we are already familiar with:

- early onset (childhood) conduct disorder (DSM-IV);
- previous criminality;
- psychopathy (Psychopathy Checklist–Revised, PCL-R);
- use of death threats/weapons at the time of the index offence (the offence which led to the offender being included in the researcher's sample).

Thus one interpretation of all of this is that the childhood origins of sex offending may be specific ones to that type of offence. But this does not mean that sexually abusive children confine themselves to only that sort of delinquency. In this context, it is important to understand that children as young as ten years of age carry out a sizeable minority of sexually inappropriate acts. Nevertheless, it is not uncommon to find that juveniles who commit sexually harmful acts against others also offend more generally. That is to say, sexually harmful behaviours are not entirely independent of delinquent behaviour in general. Indeed it has been suggested that sexually harmful behaviours may be a marker for (i.e. predictor of) a future more general crime pattern (McCrory, Hickey, Farmer and Vizard, 2008). According to Moffitt (1993) and Moffitt, Caspi, Harrington, and Milne (2002) a group of children can be identified who persistently engage in antisocial behaviours at the different stages of their life history – from their preschool period into adulthood. Deficits in their self-regulatory abilities, cognitive functions and temperament are manifested in various aspects of their life. McCrory *et al.* hypothesised:

- early sexually harmful behaviours which have begun by the age of ten years will predict a general crime offence trajectory into adolescence and adulthood
- sexually harmful behaviours first begun after the age of ten years are *not* predictive of a child's long-term future of general crime.

These hypotheses were supported by the data.

In detail, the study showed that early onset sexual abusers generally had childhoods characterised by a lack of parental supervision and inadequate sexual boundaries in the family. Generally there was evidence that that the early onset of sexually harmful behaviour serves as as a clinical marker of the increased likelihood of future risk of general delinquency. Consequently, any treatments and interventions they receive should not be limited to their sexually abusive behaviours but extend to factors related to delinquency in general. However. there was evidence that the early onset of sexually harmful behaviours was linked to a number of factors:

- a history of educational difficulties
- a more continuous pattern of non-sexual antisocial behaviour over childhood and adolescence
- more serious background issues such as maltreatment, temperament problems, aggression and mental health problems
- higher levels of psychopathy on a standard measure and higher levels of hyperactivity.

The early onset group was less likely to use verbal coercion though they tended to have a rather indiscriminate pattern in terms of the victims chosen and they were more likely to abuse both boys and girls. The late onset group had a preference for children much younger than themselves. There were differences in terms of non-sexual delinquency. For example, physical aggression between the ages of 7 and 10 years was commoner among the early sexually harmful behaviour onset group as was physical cruelty towards animals. Inconsistent and harsh discipline, disruption in terms of the primary care-giver is, and parental mental health problems would appear to be more influential on the early onset sexually abusive children because of their heightened levels of vulnerability in early childhood. Furthermore, educational and personality difficulties restrict these children's opportunities for change. Consequently, the antisocial youngster eventually becomes locked into an adult deviant lifestyle and an antisocial personality. This increases the risk of them developing long-term antisocial characteristics. Thus, early onset sexual abusers may become adults manifesting characteristics such as violence, mental health issues, and psychopathic traits.

Seto and Lalumiere (2010) reviewed explanations of adolescent sex offending in boys and tested them using meta-analysis (see Box 4.2). Figure 6.2 summarises some of the possible explanations. The data came from 59 separate studies which compared male adolescent sex offenders with male adolescent non-sex offenders. A big problem is that adolescent sex offending is treated as homogenous so rapists of adult women are treated as one with child sexual molesters. This issue will always make interpreting research findings more difficult or even impossible. Various theoretically derived variables were coded which dealt with general delinquency risk factors (antisocial tendencies), childhood abuse, cognitive abilities, exposure to violence, family problems, interpersonal problems, psychopathology and sexuality. Adolescent sex offending could not be explained in terms of general antisocial tendencies alone. They had more restricted criminal histories, fewer antisocial peers, and fewer substance abuse issues. However, more specific explanations such as sexual abuse history, exposure to sexual violence, other abuse or neglect, social isolation, early exposure to sex or pornography, atypical sexual interests, anxiety, and low self-esteem were shown empirically to be possible factors in adolescent sexual abuse. The largest effect sizes were for atypical sexual interests, sexual abuse history, criminal history, antisocial associations and substance abuse in that order.

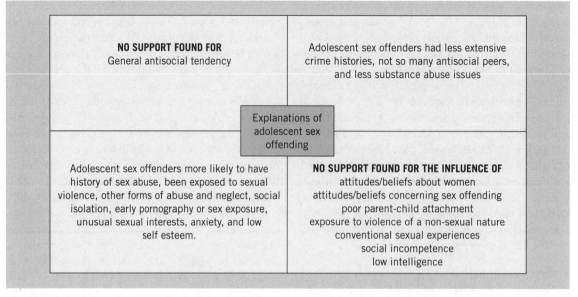

Figure 6.2 Some ways of explaining why some youngsters are sex offenders during adolescence

---

Box 6.1 Key concept

Factors protective from delinquency

Farrington (1998) suggests that there are four major methods of crime prevention:

- Situational prevention which involves targeting the physical environment in which crime takes place so as to make it difficult to commit a crime but at the same time making sure that the risks of getting caught, for example, are maximised.
- The traditional criminal justice approach involving deterrents, incapacitation and rehabilitation. For example, the prison service in the United Kingdom uses a variety of accredited offending behaviour programmes. One targeted specifically at young offenders, given their typical varied offence history, concentrates on factors such as criminal thinking and pro-social interpersonal skills. Activities would include enhancing socio-moral reasoning, attempting impulsivity reduction, challenging pro-offending cognitions and helping tackle substance abuse. Given the aggressiveness common to this age group, anger management courses appear effective at reducing angry events as measured from staff checklists by about a third or more (Ireland, 1999).
- The community prevention interventions which are designed to change social conditions and institutions (e.g. families and parenting as we saw earlier).
- The final category of crime reduction strategy Farrington calls developmental prevention. This involves tackling the risk factors involved in youthful criminality.

In addition, he mentions protective factors. Just what is a protective factor?

One might imagine that if, say, poor parenting is a factor that puts an individual at risk then good parenting is a protective factor for antisocial behaviour in childhood. This would equate protective factors with un-risk factors – that is, the opposite pole of the risk factor. We need to go one stage further. There may be many children whose parents are inadequate and unskilled in various ways. Some of these children will become antisocial, as we know from the research evidence. On the other hand, there will be a proportion of children who grow up in similar circumstances who do not become criminal. This is obvious and a fairly commonsensical notion. Not everyone who smokes gets cancer but smoking is a strong risk factor for cancer. Other factors may protect the individual and make it less likely that they will become ill. Just the same sort of argument may apply to crime. There may be factors which if they co-occur with risk factors will reduce the impact of those risk factors. For example, poor parenting may be a risk factor for antisocial behaviour but some at-risk children may have grandparents close by who take a great interest in the child. Grandparents in these circumstances can be described as a protective factor. This is a made-up illustration, so how can we go about identifying risk factors?

One way of looking at the risk-factor approach is to conceive of it as a deficit model – that is, something is missing in childhood which pushes the young person towards crime. They are, for example, deficient in social skills because of the poor parenting they received. There is a more positive approach that tries to see what it is about some youngsters who are faced with the most unpromising start in life that leaves them capable of resisting the impact of a raft of grave life stressors that turn some youngsters criminal. One exemplary approach is to be found in Bender, Bliesener and Lösel's (1996) study of adolescents in a residential institution. As one might expect, the backgrounds of many of these left much to be desired. The researchers chose to consult with the teams caring for the youngsters in the institutional setting:

- *Protected youngsters*: the carers were asked to identify examples of youngsters whose backgrounds were inadequate, who seemed to be at risk of developing serious problems, and who, in fact, had turned out to be pretty decent young people who were not problems.
- *The risk-succumbing group*: a comparison group was formed from nominations of children who manifested high levels of the risk factors but also exhibited serious behavioural disorders.

These two groups were loaded with similar risk factors (deaths, divorces and separations, parental unemployment and financial problems, marital conflict and drug and alcohol abuse within the family). Nevertheless, the outcomes in their lives were different. What was it about the resilient youngsters that helped prevent them from succumbing to the effects of the risk factors? Things that distinguished the resilient youngsters from the rest (the protective factors) included the following:

- *Personal resources*: resilient youngsters had better technical/spatial intelligence, had flexible temperaments, were approach-oriented, had more positive self-esteem and had active coping styles.
- *Social resources*: the resilient youngsters were more satisfied with social support and experienced the climate of their residential institution as socio-emotionally oriented (openness, autonomy and low conflict).

Using a similar sample of resilients and deviants suffering similar levels of risk factors, Bliesener and Lösel (1992) found an association between intelligence (especially that involving problem solving) and resilience. The resilients seemed to actively 'face-up-to-problems' rather than simply respond passively – they did not see themselves as in some way fatalistically helpless.

Given the involvement of forensic psychology in the aftermath of parental separation and the ensuing divorce, the work of Czerederecka and Jaskiewicz-Obydzinska (1996) is important. While not specifically concerned with criminal behaviour, the research investigated Polish children involved in divorces for signs of emotional or social problems. Children classified as having no disorder were found to have stayed with their mother as the custodial parent but they also had a 'clearly defined' relationship with their father. By this is meant either having regular contact with their father or *no* contact. They also found that the amount of conflict between the parents did not necessarily lead to problems for the child. It was when the child was put into a position in which they were expected to take sides that the problems arose. A child passively observing parental conflict did not appear to be so affected. In other words, despite our expectations about divorce, these effects can be essentially neutralised in some cases by other factors. A good psychological relationship with both parents seems to be the neutralising agent. ▶

Box 6.1 (continued)

In another study, Lösel, Bender and Bliesener (1999) took the issue of protective factors further. There is a rather well-established physiological fact about children and adolescents who manifest strong antisocial behavioural characteristics: their heart rate tends to be slower when they are at rest or relaxing. Fewer heartbeats when inactive in antisocial youngsters may have a number of explanations. Similar effects are found for cardio-vascular, skin electrical activity and cortical responses. According to Lösel *et al.*, in excess of 20 studies have found this resting heart rate phenomenon. Only one study has failed to replicate it. Possibly one could describe having a higher resting heart rate as a protective factor – criminal involvement in adults is inversely related to resting heart rate in childhood. One could speak of the protective effect of higher resting heart rate against criminality in adults, as it is a long-term predictor of lack of involvement. This 'protection' seems to be strongest in non-institutionalised, younger samples from relatively normal family backgrounds. In other words, there is a possibility that the factors responsible for antisocial behaviour in families experiencing deprivation and other strain (i.e. social stress) factors are different from those that lead to antisocial behaviour in more normal families.

Lösel *et al.* (1999), therefore, chose to study a sample of 16-year-old male students in Nuremberg and Erlangen in Germany. Distinct groups were identified on the basis of a number of measures. These groups were: (1) a group of bullies; (2) a group of victims; (3) a group of normal students; and (4) a group of highly socially competent students. Pulse rate was measured at different times – lying down for short periods of relaxation, after an interactive game, after different stages of a role-play of social conflicts. At every occasion at which resting heart rate was measured, the bullies had the lowest heart rate levels and victims of bullying had the highest. The researchers then re-examined their data in an attempt to see for which boys low heart rate was a particular risk factor. It appeared that the difference between bullies and victims was greater for boys from non-stressed family backgrounds. When boys from stressed family backgrounds were considered, heart rate was not particularly predictive of bullying or victimisation.

Specific explanations of antisocial behaviour in childhood

While the broad childhood factors related to delinquent and adult crime are reasonably well established, there are a number of explanations that warrant description.

Moral reasoning development

Kerby and Rae (1998) showed that moral reasoning is quite subtly articulated in young offenders. This is especially the case when the issue of their own personal moral identity is under consideration such as when discussing whether they are good or bad as a person. Young offenders can and do reason morally about a range of issues. Moral reasoning changes and develops during childhood. This is the basis of Kohlberg's theory of moral reasoning (Kohlberg, 1963, 1984). This theory extended Piaget's theory of cognitive stages in thinking (Piaget, 1970). Kohlberg argued that moral reasoning develops in six relatively discrete stages which are grouped into three levels – the pre-conventional, the conventional and the post-conventional. The stages differ – not in terms of what the moral decision is but the reasons for that decision, whatever it is. The basics of Kohlberg's theory are to be found in Figure 6.3. Numerous studies have demonstrated that delinquents tend to reason at lower levels than non-delinquents do – that is, there is a relative delay in moral reasoning development in delinquents compared to controls (Blasi, 1980; Gibbs, 2003; Palmer, 2003). Those youngsters with less developed moral reasoning are more likely to commit crimes. For example, Nelson, Smith and Dodd (1990) carried out a meta-analysis (Box 4.2) of 15 studies. Overall, these studies clearly showed that delinquents operate at a lower stage of moral reasoning development than appropriate comparison groups. A later meta-analysis by Stams,

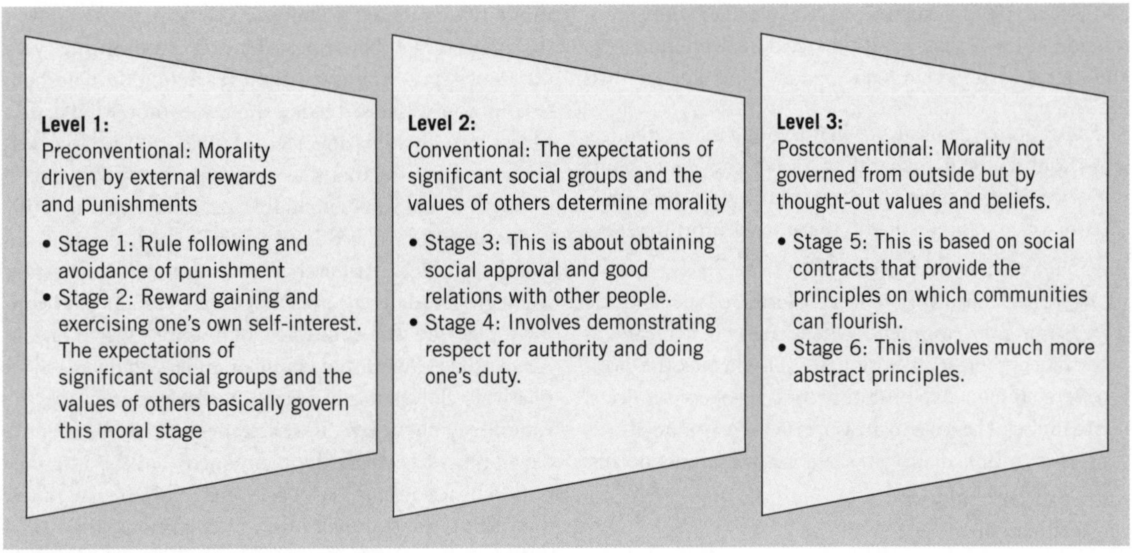

Level 1:
Preconventional: Morality driven by external rewards and punishments

- Stage 1: Rule following and avoidance of punishment
- Stage 2: Reward gaining and exercising one's own self-interest. The expectations of significant social groups and the values of others basically govern this moral stage

Level 2:
Conventional: The expectations of significant social groups and the values of others determine morality

- Stage 3: This is about obtaining social approval and good relations with other people.
- Stage 4: Involves demonstrating respect for authority and doing one's duty.

Level 3:
Postconventional: Morality not governed from outside but by thought-out values and beliefs.

- Stage 5: This is based on social contracts that provide the principles on which communities can flourish.
- Stage 6: This involves much more abstract principles.

Figure 6.3 Kohlberg's Model of Moral Development

Brugman, Dekowic, van Rosmalen, van der Laan and Gibbs (2006) extended that of Nelson *et al.* to include 50 studies. The relationship between moral judgement level and delinquency was a strong one. The relationship was particularly strong where male offender groups, late adolescents, incarcerated, and lower-intelligence delinquents were involved. These conclusions held even where socio-economic status, gender and age as well as other variables were controlled. The authors suggest that that the superficiality and self-centredness associated with lower levels of moral development may become criminogenic in late adolescence.

This seems to make intuitive sense. It suggests poorer (slower) moral reasoning development may be responsible for some delinquency. There are difficulties, however, with the underlying theory that should be considered. For example:

- By virtually any criterion one wishes to mention, boys are substantially more delinquent than girls. This would suggest that girls, generally, ought to be more morally advanced year on year than boys. Remarkably, some research suggests that girls are actually less likely than boys to achieve the highest level of moral development! One possible reason for this may be a bias in the theory which places factors that appear to be female at a lower level (Gilligan, 1982): that is, Level 3 reasoning seems more female in nature. However, these findings of a gender difference are actually excep-

tional. A study by Gregg, Gibbs and Basinger (1994) showed that when age and verbal IQ were controlled for or equated, girls, whether or not delinquent, were at a morally more advanced stage than boys.

- Others have argued that Kohlberg's theory is biased against any group that is collectivist (community) rather than individualist in social orientation (Owusu-Bempah and Howitt, 2000), which implies that immigrant groups in individualistic Western cultures might be regarded as at a lower stage of moral reasoning development if Kohlberg's criteria apply.

- There is an argument in the child development research literature that children actually have far more developed moral thinking than theory had previously allowed (Tisak, 1995). That is to say, even three-year-old children can distinguish between moral behaviour and mere conventions which we follow. Furthermore, the development of moral judgement is not the same irrespective of the domain or matter in question (Turiel, 1983; Turiel and Nucci, 1978). Indeed, researchers have even suggested that early moral thinking is moral thinking rather than pre-moral thinking. All this suggests that the developmental stages approach may be fundamentally incorrect.

Moral reasoning development differences between delinquents and non-delinquents are greatest for issues that are especially relevant to criminal behaviour (Palmer and Hollin, 1998). A survey was conducted of young non-offenders (13–22 years) and convicted male offenders (13 and 21 years) in the United Kingdom. This showed that:

- Self-reported delinquency in the young male offenders was substantially higher than for the non-delinquents (when age and socio-economic status were statistically controlled). Interestingly, there were no differences between male and female non-offenders.

- There were also differences in terms of socio-moral reasoning development. Offenders were typically at Kohlberg's pre-conventional level whereas the non-offenders tended to operate at the level of conventional reasoning. The scale to measure moral reasoning development included questions tapping five distinct norms:
  – contract and truth;
  – affiliation;
  – life;
  – property and law;
  – legal justice.

- For each of these areas, male delinquents were at a lower stage of moral development than other males. Interestingly, non-offending boys tended to be at a lower stage of moral reasoning development than the non-offender females. Delinquent males tended to score at a lower level of development than other males in the following areas:
  – helping your parents;
  – keeping a promise to a child;
  – keeping a promise to a friend;
  – keeping a promise to a stranger;
  – lying even if you do not want to;
  – not taking things that belong to others;
  – obeying the law;
  – saving the life of a friend;
  – sending criminals to jail;
  – telling the truth.

Only on saving the life of a stranger were delinquent males and other males similar. When the moral issue was related to crime, the differential suggesting poorer moral development in delinquents was greatest.

Given that moral reasoning tends to be less well developed on an age-for-age basis in delinquents than in non-delinquent youngsters, why do different youngsters commit different types of crime? Is it possible to link different types of crime to differences in moral reasoning development? According to Chen and Howitt (2007),

moral reasoning development has a fairly limited power to differentiate between offenders committing very different types of crime. Moral reasoning development is commonly assessed using the Socio-moral Reflection Measure (Gibbs, Basinger and Fuller, 1992). However, this measure is actually a composite based on several different moral values including contract, affiliation, life, property and law, and legal justice, which derive from Kohlberg's ideas. Researchers are beginning to question whether these different aspects of moral reasoning development mature at the same rate. For example, Brugman and Aleva (2004) found that young offenders tended to show relatively slower moral reasoning development for the value 'obeying the law'. If we assume that moral reasoning development is partly the consequence of the internalisation of actions (as Piaget accepted in his theory) rather than being the externalisation of cognitions, then such differential development in different areas of moral values is possible. In other words, the different experiences of different types of delinquent may produce differential moral value development.

Chen and Howitt (2007) studied Taiwanese young offenders divided into drug, violent and theft types. Their research question was whether different levels of the development of these different moral values were related to the delinquents' offence types. The research findings provided only limited support for this. Only the moral value 'life' helped differentiate members of the different offence-type groups. This moral value was relatively poorly developed in violent offenders compared with the theft and drug offenders. Using this moral value 'life' together with age was capable of differentiating among drug, violent and theft offenders with an overall accuracy of about 60 per cent. So what is the moral value 'life'? Well, it is measured by the question 'How important is it for a person to live even if that person doesn't want to?' That people who act violently have less well-developed moral reasoning in relation to this seems understandable, although why drug offenders do not share this is less clear. A lot of work remains to be done to understand just how offenders understand their offences and the relevance of moral reasoning development to this.

This is an area where there is some controversy. One fundamental question is quite what criterion of delinquency to apply. The vast majority of studies compare delinquents with non-delinquent controls in terms of arrest or conviction. Tarry and Emler (2007) carried out their research using self-report delinquency measures which are clearly different from arrests or convictions. They found that self-reported delinquency was not related to structural measures of moral reasoning level of the sort discussed above after controls for demographic and other relevant variables had been applied. They also had a measure of attitudes towards authority which may, in part, be based on experience. This did predict self-reported delinquency – the more negative the attitude of the adolescent the more negative their attitudes towards authority. Now this is a radically different way of looking at the issue from the moral reasoning level one. But, of course, there is one thing that stands out as a problem. That is, this study used self-reported delinquency and did not have an arrest or conviction measure. This leaves open the possibility that the means of measuring delinquency is crucial. Tarry and Emler argue strongly for their self-

report approach. Brusten, Stams and Gibbs (2007) question self-report approaches and point to studies which say that they are more problematic than Tarry and Emler suggest. They criticise Tarry and Emler's study for using a sample which was too young to demonstrate moral reasoning development influences which they say only emerge later in adolescence according to research.

Cycles of abuse

The idea of cycles of violence has been part of professional thinking for quite some time. The violence-breeds-violence hypothesis originates in the work of Curtis (1963) who considered that violent social environments create violent youngsters and adults. Figure 6.4 gives an overview of

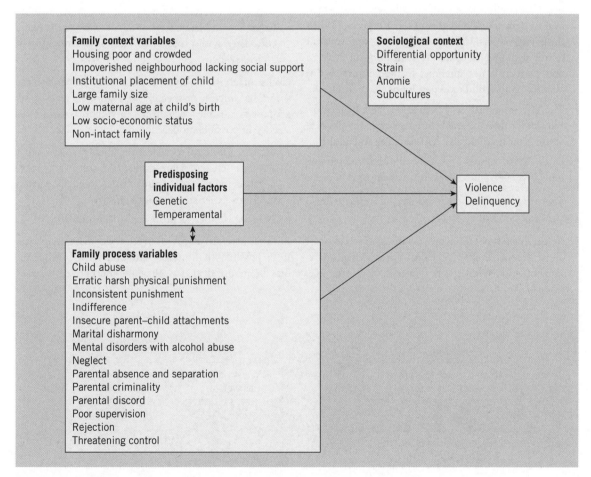

Figure 6.4 Widely established psychological model of aggression according to Haapasalo and Tremblay (1994)

the range of factors that appear to be involved in the development of aggressiveness (Haapasalo and Tremblay, 1994). This illustrates something of the magnitude of the task facing researchers trying to develop integrated approaches to the development of aggressiveness. The links between violence and future violence need separating in order to clarify precisely what researchers have shown. It is abundantly clear that there is some sort of relationship between the two, but it depends on what is meant by a cycle of violence. There are several meanings of the term 'cycle of violence' or 'cycle of abuse':

- The process by which women physically abused by their partners are persuaded back by the man with promises of love and that the episode will not be repeated. Events then build up to another episode of violence. She may leave but returns because she 'loves' her abuser or 'for the sake of the children'. Events then lead to more abuse and greater levels of abuse. While these violent acts are frequently severe and warrant criminal prosecution, this is a meaning of cycle of abuse which is not intended in the context of this chapter on the childhood development of crime.

- The effects of early experience on later behaviour. Put simply, does the child who is subjected to physical abuse grow up to be a violent teenager and adult?

- Does a child who is physically abused by its parents grow up to be a parent who abuses their own children?

There are a number of methodological issues involved in assessing cycles of violence:

- Research tends not to involve the direct observation of abuse. Instead, there may be difficulties with information obtained retrospectively in interviews. For example, parents believed to have abused their children may be asked whether they themselves were physically abused as children. This approach risks self-justificatory replies: that is, 'my excuse for abusing my child is that my parents did it to me.'

- The retrospective nature of many studies means that memory processes may affect recollections.

- There is no standard definition of physical abuse common to all or most studies. As a consequence, it is difficult to know what sorts and degrees of violence are necessary to produce what levels of effects.

- Child abuse is associated with a wide range of family characteristics that may be also harmful to children. It may be impossible to tell whether a particular outcome is directly the consequence of abuse or whether other family characteristics associated with abuse are responsible. This is mainly a problem for those wishing to understand the effects of abuse. For practitioners concerned with problem families, it is something of an irrelevance.

Cycles of abuse involve processes that, generally, are somewhat unclear or speculative. Figure 6.5 gives some proposed plausible mechanisms and Figure 6.6 indicates a range of possible models:

- Model 1 (based on social learning theory) suggests that the experience of aggression may result in its incorporation in one's repertoire of behaviours. Direct and vicarious experience are both effective.

- Model 2 is much as proposed by John Bowlby.

Both of these are discussed in some detail in Chapter 5. It is possible that more than one of the processes may be involved: that is, they are alternative processes

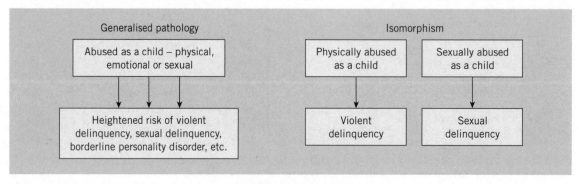

Figure 6.5 Isomorphism versus generalised pathology as a consequence of abuse

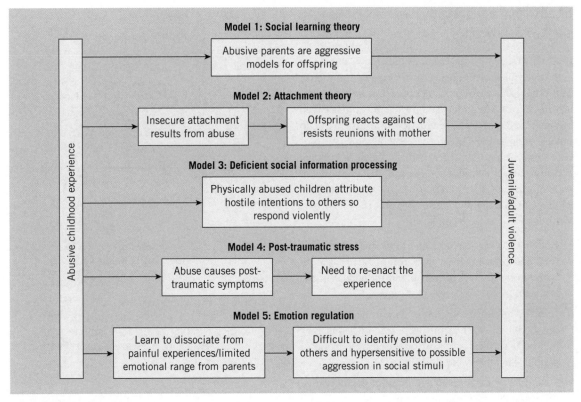

Figure 6.6 Psychological models of the cycle of violence

rather than competing theories. Figure 6.5 brings to our attention the contrast between generalised effects of abuse and specific isomorphic ones. While violence may lead to violence, some researchers believe that the effects of violence are more generally pathogenic than that.

Widom (1989) studied records of a county court in the United Kingdom to find children of 11 years of age or younger who had been subject to child abuse. She then investigated the adult criminal records of these youngsters:

- Twenty-nine per cent of these had later criminal records compared with 21 per cent of controls who had been matched with the research group on variables such as age, class, sex, race and so forth. The findings, using refined statistical techniques, were that there was 1.7 times the risk of getting an adult record if one had been abused as a child. But these are, of course, the extremes of abuse and many offences do not lead to conviction.

- The *isomorphism hypothesis* argues that there is a close relationship between the characteristics of abuse and its effects on the victim (see Chapter 10). In support of this hypothesis, in this study victims of physical abuse had the highest rate of violence offences (16 per cent of sample). This trend was not great. Victims of neglect (at 13 per cent) had similar levels of violent crime. Physical abuse together with neglect victims (7 per cent), sexual and other abuse cases (7 per cent) and sexual abuse (6 per cent) all had lower risk of violent offending in adulthood. Controls who, obviously, had not been abused had a 7 per cent risk of violent crime, which is the same for the latter types of abuse victim. Care is needed in interpreting any such data. Nevertheless, as far as can be seen, physical abuse in childhood does seem to increase the risk of violent offending somewhat compared with the controls. Sexual abuse, for example, is not implicated in violent crime despite the vast range of behaviour problems that have been associated with it in the research literature (Rudo and Powell, 1996).

Bullying and bullying victimisation

Research frequently suggests that bullying is associated with non-violent delinquency (e.g. burglary and theft). This is not just true for bullying's perpetrators but also its victims. It is easy to understand the relationship between bullying and violent delinquency but just why do bullies often engage in non-violent delinquency too? One suggestion is that anger mediates between bullying and non-violent delinquency. Sigfusdottir, Gudjonsson and Sigurdsson (2010) carried out a study of over 7,000 adolescents in Iceland of between 15 and 16 years of age. Various measures were employed:

- Bullying was measured by questions such as whether they had been involved in a group starting a fight with another group or hurting an individual in the last year.

- In order to measure the experience of being a bullying victim, the participants were asked whether they had been attacked and hurt or teased by a group of people when they were alone in the last year.

- Delinquency was measured in terms of the individual reporting that they had stolen things etc.

- Anger was measured by the question whether they wanted to break or damage things.

The relationships between the first three variables above (excluding anger) were analysed using the complex statistical technique known as structural equation modelling (see Howitt and Cramer, 2011 for a discussion). Structural equation modelling attempts to develop 'models' describing the best fitting account of the interrelationships. The procedure allows the researcher to control for other influential variables such as family structure, gender and parental education in this case. Figure 6.7 shows the model linking being victimised by bullying and non-violent delinquency. The arrows indicate the paths between the variables and the numbers indicate the size of the relationship. As can be seen, the pathway through anger shows modest relationships but it is clear that a more direct pathway between victimisation and delinquency which does not involve anger is also important. The model for the effect of bullying behaviour on delinquency is not given here but is very similar. So bullying is a factor in non-violent delinquency for both bullies and their victims. But it is also clear that at least part of this relationship is mediated by anger.

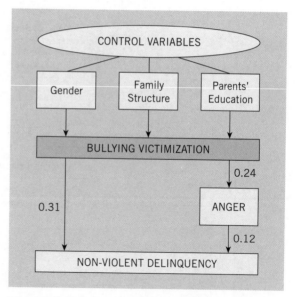

Figure 6.7 How anger partially mediates between being a victim of bullying and non-violent delinquency (based on the work of Sigfusdottir, Gudjonsson and Sigurdsson (2010))

Sigfusdottir, Gudjonsson and Sigurdsson (2010) discuss their findings in terms of Agnew's social-psychological revised general strain theory (see Chapter 4). This theory acknowledges the important role of emotions. Agnew's strain theory argues that adolescents who experience adverse circumstances are pushed towards delinquency because of the negative emotional reactions these experiences produce. The list of negative emotions includes anger, which was the focus of Sigfusdottir et al.'s study. According to Agnew (1992), strain arises in relationships where an individual is not treated in the way they would like to be treated (see Figure 6.8). The underlying idea is that people treated badly behave badly. Bullying and being bullied are both part of the delinquent lifestyle so youngsters experiencing these are more likely to express their negative emotions through delinquency. Victimisation by bullying is an example of Agnew's concept of *strain*. That is, it is likely to cause distress and frustration plus it has a negative impact on mental health. Although the same cannot be said of the bullies themselves, it has to be remembered that bullies tend to come from a stressful background which amounts to a form of strain. They experience low levels of parental warmth and the discipline that they receive tends to be harsh and physical.

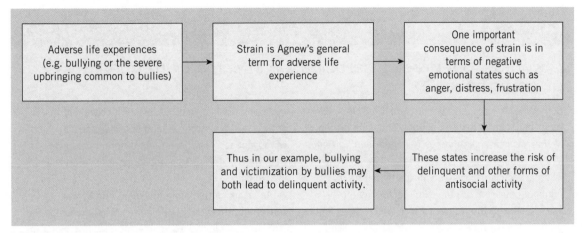

Figure 6.8 Theory Summary: Agnew's Strain Theory applied to bullying and its victims

Given this, it is worth mentioning the work of Karnik and Steiner (2007) who argued that psychology's understanding of the developmental originals of juvenile offending behaviour has advanced significantly. However, it remains the case that much more needs to be known about how interventions may be best targeted in order to reduce delinquent behaviour. They, too, suggest that therapeutic methods need to take much more seriously the role of aggression of juvenile offending.

Lack of parental control

One particularly well-documented research finding is that of birth order effects in the development of delinquency. Many, but not all, studies of delinquency have found that first-born children are less likely to be delinquent than later-born children. Although the research findings in this field may be a consequence of poorly controlled research designs, it would seem better to try to understand why birth order effects may occur. One possibility, of course, is that parents do not and cannot treat all of their offspring in exactly the same way. For example, it would hardly be surprising to find that parents give less time to their younger offspring than the first-born. This might simply be a matter of time resources but other

explanations are possible. It is known from a number of studies that parental control of their offspring has an influence in preventing delinquency. Parental supervision may encourage self-control in their offspring, for example. So if first-born children are more likely to receive parental supervision, it is easy to see that they are less likely to become delinquent and, if they do, are more likely to offend trivially. Furthermore, the more time that a child is being supervised by its parents the less opportunity that peers can influence the child adversely.

Bègue and Roche (2005) tested these ideas on French families. They took large samples of first-born and middle-born male and female adolescents. They measured parental control using a standard measure which concerns things like going out in the evening without their parents, adherence to return-home times fixed by their parents, and failing to tell parents where they were going when they went out. First-born children were more supervised than later-born children according to this measure. Delinquency was measured using a self-report delinquency questionnaire including minor offences such as shoplifting and minor vandalism and serious offences such as arson, violent theft and serious violence. First-born children reported less minor and less serious delinquency than middle-born children. There was evidence that parental supervision had a moderate impact on delinquency.

BOX 6.2 Controversy

Do predictors predict participation in crime or frequency of participation?

Sometimes researchers overlook what, in retrospect, seem important questions about crime. One example of this has been identified by Ramoutar and Farrington (2006). They became interested in understanding whether factors associated with participating in criminal behaviour are the same factors as those associated with the frequency with which the offender participates in crime. Most theories of crime seek to explain why some people become criminal, and scant attention is paid to the frequency with which they carry out criminal acts. Some previous researchers, notably Gottfredson and Hirschi (1986), have promoted the view that different features of a person's criminal career, such as frequency, participation, onset and desisting from crime, are part and parcel of a single propensity to be criminal and that they need not be differentiated. Clearly this is an assumption which has to be tested.

Ramoutar and Farrington systematically looked at factors associated with (a) participating in crime and (b) frequency of participation in serious violence and property crimes. They took several broad categories of explanatory variables which might be associated with crime. These were (a) Bandura's social learning theory and (b) personality theory dimensions such as those proposed by Eysenck (both of these are discussed in Chapter 5) together with (c) labelling theory, which suggests that the adverse reaction of the criminal justice system and other people to an individual's crimes leading to their being defined as deviant

increases the likelihood of further involvement in crime. They developed a total of 24 explanatory variables based on these three different categories. Data were collected from male and female prisoners in Trinidad.

As far as participating in violent crimes was concerned, there were 19 significant relationships for the male sample and 16 significant relationships for the female sample. In terms of participating in property crimes, there was a total of 12 significant relationships for the male sample, for example. However, what was the case for participating in these crimes was not the case for the frequency of participation measures. For violent crime, only seven significant relationships were found for male offenders and only three significant relationships for female offenders. For property crime, there was only one significant relationship between frequency and any of the 24 explanatory variables. In other words, variables that are associated with participation in a type of crime may not be associated with frequency of carrying out that criminal activity.

The conclusion, for the time being at least, is inescapable that important theories of crime may only explain participation in crime rather than the frequency of participation in crime. So there is a case for suggesting that important theories of crime such as social learning and personality explanations need to be re-examined in order to improve their ability to explain frequency of involvement in crime.

Lifespan development and criminal careers

Childhood experiences are important in the development of criminality. However, not all criminals reveal their criminality early in life. To be sure, delinquency is reasonably predictable early in some children's lives. Similarly, antisocial behaviour in the form of juvenile delinquency

is predictive of adult crime. Some of the research discussed earlier is still continuing over 40 years after its initial stages. It is unrealistic, nevertheless, to expect rapid progress in understanding the development of criminal careers given the timescale of such studies. Especially difficult for such studies is the question of whether criminality that develops late in life can be traced back to childhood. Some criminals do not appear to begin to offend until their thirties or even later.

The Berlin Crime Study (Dahle, 1999) took a sample of male adult offenders admitted into the Berlin prison system in early 1976. Not only were detailed histories taken, but also the offenders were followed up for nearly 25 more years through their prison, legal and health records. Property offences and fraud accounted for nearly 60 per cent of the sentences. Robbery and bodily harm accounted for nearly 10 per cent each, whereas sexual offences and homicide were relatively rare. Inexplicably, nearly 17 per cent of the sample died in the study period. The commonest age of death was between 30 and 45 years of age. Something like 30 times as many of the men died then as would be expected from the relevant national statistics. A number of variables were entered into a statistical analysis (cluster analysis). These included age at first offence, age at most recent offence, the number of offences in each four-year period since the age of 14 and the amount of time spent in prison during each of these periods. There appear to be at least five different types of offending career:

- *Adolescence-limited offenders*: this group had reached maximum offending by their early twenties. From then on seriousness and rate of crimes decreased slowly. Early offending was largely associated with peer groups. After this, there is evidence that offending is individual, trivial and drug related. Their childhood featured multiple problems such as unemployment, drinking in parents and so forth. As they got older, despite the peer influence in their early offending, they seemed rather isolated. This group made up about one in six of the sample.

- *Limited serious offenders*: this group was about one in nine of the offenders. They began their delinquency in adolescence but their crimes escalated in seriousness and violence in their twenties. They dropped out of criminality at about age 30. This group was particularly associated with bio-psycho-social risk factors such as pre- and perinatal complications. Although they had good intelligence and concentration, they were school failures when relatively young. Suicide attempts were quite common among them.

- *Persistent serious offenders*: this group was about one in seven of the sample. They had spent a lot of time in prison and very few of them had succeeded in abandoning crime. They reoffended (recidivated) very quickly. Serious violent crime was common among them. Members of this group had accumulated risk factors

across the spectrum of risk factors in childhood. They were also social loners in childhood.

- *Occasional offenders*: this group made up nearly half of the sample. They showed a low level of delinquency during their life though they had little or no adolescent involvement in crime. They were specialists in that they carried out a limited repertoire of crimes. Risk factors in childhood were relatively absent. Nevertheless, in the period leading to their offending, they experienced critical life events such as adultery, debt, bankruptcy and so forth.

- *Late-starting offenders*: these were similar to the occasional offenders and amounted to about one in eight of the sample. They too had a preference for crime specialisation and the crime tended to be fraud or burglary. One suggestion is that they defined themselves as professional criminals and they began offending not because of stressful life events but on the basis of a rational decision to do so.

Quite a lot is known about the development of criminality through the lifestyle according to Farrington (2010). The following summarises some of the major conclusions – facts, if you like – about key features in the development of criminality through the life cycle:

- Offending is most prevalent in the later teenage years – that is amongst 15–19-year-olds.

- However, the peak in the onset of offending is rather younger and involves 9–14-year-olds predominantly.

- The evidence suggests that distance (actively avoiding or rejecting offending) appears to be at its peak among the 20–29-year-old age group.

- Those who begin criminality (delinquency) earlier tend to be those who have the highest rates of offending and the longest criminal careers.

- There is considerable evidence that there is a continuity in offending (and antisocial behaviours in general) through childhood, adolescence and adulthood. That is, there is a tendency for those who commit crimes younger in life to commit them more often later in life. Some care is warranted over this since the prevalence of offending varies quite markedly at different stages in life. It is especially important to note that many of those who offend earlier in life do *not* go on to offend later in life.

- As we saw earlier for younger people, a disproportionately small number of chronic offenders are responsible for a large proportion of all crimes. This applies irrespective of age group.

- As discussed elsewhere, offenders are versatile rather than specialist in that many of them commit a whole variety of different types of crime during their criminal careers.

- Criminal offences are just part of a wider group of antisocial behaviours developmentally. These other behaviours include truancy, sexual promiscuity and reckless driving.

- Younger offenders tend to offend as part of a group or with one or two others. In contrast, adult offenders tend to act on their own in a solitary way.

- The motives for crime tend to be different at different ages. Younger offenders mention a variety of types of explanations for their crime including excitement, revenge and utilitarian functions (e.g. to get money). This contrasts greatly with the reasons for offending mentioned by older offenders for which the utilitarian function of crime is the major motive.

- The sorts of crime committed at different stages in the life cycle tend to be characteristic of that stage. Thus shoplifting tends to start younger in life than burglary, which tends to be committed at a younger age than robbery.

Quite clearly, any account of the development of criminality in childhood and later needs to be capable of explaining each of these facts. This is something of a tough call to address.

The concept of a serious criminality trajectory beginning at a young age and leading to long-term and significant adult criminality is increasingly an aspect of our understanding of criminal behaviour. Associated with this is the idea of a relatively minor or less significant trajectory for antisocial behaviour also beginning in childhood but in which the individual has abandoned delinquency after adolescence. As is not unusual, the research literature is a little ambivalent about this idea and some studies fail to support it. One possible explanation or factor to take into account is that different offences may have different trajectories (Van Lier, Viatro, Edwards, Koot and Tremblay, 2009). So what might be true for one sort of offence may not apply

to other sorts of offence. As an instance, violent behaviour commonly starts in childhood but is declining by adolescence while, in contrast, vandalism and substance abuse are more characteristic of adolescence than of childhood. There is a possibility that certain sorts of antisocial behaviour actually evolve into other sorts. It is known, for example, that a child who demonstrates high levels of violence is likely to commit high levels of other crimes such as theft in the future but such children do not typically demonstrate high violence levels later on in their lives. The study by Van Lier *et al.* into this involved children studying in schools in Quebec, Canada. Each spring, the children completed questionnaires including self-reported delinquent behaviour together with teacher assessments of each child's level of violent behaviour. The researchers used very sophisticated statistical methods which led to the identification of various different crime change trajectories. The crimes studied were drug abuse, physical violence, theft and vandalism. Each of these tends to result in a different shaped trajectory:

- Drug abuse tends to have an early onset in childhood with the trajectory increasing to its highest levels during childhood. However, there is an alternative drug abuse trajectory which begins in adolescence and escalates.

- Physical violence involves the highest levels of offending at each stage in life. It moves to a peak and then declines.

- However, theft and vandalism tended to have generally increasing levels throughout childhood.

In other words, different types of delinquent behaviour seem to have different developmental trajectories.

The origins of criminal behaviour in childhood are a complex matter. Different patterns exist of offending during the lifespan. For the forensic psychologist, it is useful to know that different risk factors are associated with different patterns of offending. Research into this is at such an early stage that caution is appropriate when drawing conclusions. It seems evident, though, that early problem behaviour should not be neglected for two reasons – it is predictive of later, more serious, problems and, if it is acted on, then even simple interventions may be effective at reducing future delinquency.

Main points

- The study of juvenile offending is one of the most thoroughly researched areas of crime. A great deal is known about delinquency, its antecedents and consequences. Not surprisingly, various sorts of deficiencies in the functioning of families have been found to be associated with later delinquency. So deficiencies in parenting (e.g. abusive behaviour leading to cycles of abuse) are closely associated with delinquent and other forms of problematic behaviour in children. Nevertheless, it would be wrong to suggest that all delinquent children are the result of such family inadequacies. Delinquency is the result of many different influences, not all of which are directly to do with the family. Peer pressure to engage in delinquent activity is an obvious example.

- There is very good reason to believe that social interventions in early childhood intended to counteract some of the deficiencies of families known to be associated with delinquency can be very effective. Certain interventions with older children, maybe after they have become delinquent, can also be effective. Especially effective are those programmes which combine early childhood education with direct support for the parents of high-risk children.

- Despite knowing a great deal about the development of delinquent behaviour, there is a gulf between what we know about the risk factors for delinquency and the causes of delinquency. There is strong evidence that violence is transmitted generationally through cycles of abuse but we are less clear about how, say, moral development affects delinquent behaviour. A great deal more needs to be known about the different patterns of criminal careers, some of which begin only in adulthood while others are over by adulthood. The implications of these different patterns are difficult to research (as it is such a long-term project to do so) but it is vital to reject the idea that there is a single, simple pathway from problem home backgrounds to delinquency to adult criminality. Sometimes that is the route but equally there are alternatives.

Further reading

The following contains up-to-date material on the Cambridge Study discussed extensively in:

Piquero, A.R., Farrington, D.P. and Blumstein, A. (2007) *Key Issues in Criminal Career Research: New Analyses of the Cambridge Study in Delinquent Development* Cambridge: Cambridge University Press.

Moral reasoning and criminal behaviour is discussed extensively in the following:

Palmer, E.J. (2003) *Offending Behaviour: Moral Reasoning, Criminal Conduct and the Rehabilitation of Offenders* Cullompton: Willan Publishing.

The following has a range of resources on delinquency and its prevention:

National Centre for State Courts: Juvenile Justice and Delinquency Resource Guide: http://www.ncsc.org/Topics/Children-Families-and-Elders/Juvenile-Justice-and-Delinquency/Resource-Guide.aspx

More accessible material on the Cambridge Study can be found in:

D.P. Farrington, J.W. Coid, L.M. Harnett, D. Jolliffe, N. Soteriou, R.E. Turner and D. West (2006) *Criminal Careers up to Age 50 and Life Success up to Age 48: New Findings From the Cambridge Study*. Home Office Research Study No. 299: http://www.psychblog.co.uk/ForensicPsych/OriginalStudies/16456515851247828851.pdf and http://www.compassunit.com/docs/r281.pdf

Visit our website at www.pearsoned.co.uk/howitt for self-test and essay questions, annotated further reading, audio interviews with researchers in the field, weblinks and more information on becoming a forensic psychologist.

Chapter 7

Theft and other crimes against property

Overview

- Property crime is the most common sort of crime but has been largely neglected in forensic and criminal psychology perhaps because it is so common that it is, in a sense, normal hence needing no special explanation. Two in every five males admit committing a property crime such as theft, burglary and criminal damage at some time in their lives. Mostly the crimes were thefts.

- One of the earliest psychological explanations of crime was the concept of kleptomania. It is an impulse to steal without there being a need for the property or money and is said to be associated with some form of positive emotion when committing the offence. However, researchers have failed to find evidence of kleptomania in shoplifters. For example, substantial numbers of shoplifting offences involve pairs or groups of individuals working together. These could not be explained on the basis of kleptomania.

- Shoplifters tend to give different reasons for shoplifting than non-shoplifters use to explain the crime. Non-shoplifters might suggest that shoplifters cannot afford to pay for the goods whereas shoplifters actually are more likely to say that they do not want to pay. It has been suggested that cultural factors may be involved in shoplifting.

- There is a problem in research on shoplifting because of biases towards targeting those who fit the 'offender profile' or stereotypes about that crime.

- Burglary has a strong connection with drug use. There is a range of explanations of these links such as that drug users may associate with criminals so are more likely to get involved in crime. However, the need for finance seems to be an important motive. There is evidence that property offences are more common when supplies of drugs are scarce and they are more expensive as a consequence. There is also evidence that being on methadone support therapy, which helps heroin addicts come off of the drug, is associated with a reduction in property crime.

- Rational choice theory regards burglars as decision makers and encourages the study of their decision-making processes. In a sense, this makes the study of burglars the study of normal behaviour rather than some sort of psychological abnormality. There is no absolute process that burglars employ since a suitable target household to burgle will be assessed using different criteria in different circumstances. For example, security measures may deter a burglar even though in other respects the house seems to be a better target than the house that is finally targeted.

- Arson is largely committed by youngsters perhaps for reasons of boredom or thrill seeking. There is a psychiatric disorder, pyromania, which is a deep-seated urge to set fires. Not many arsons are committed by pyromaniacs and the figure may be as low as 1 per cent of arsonists who are also pyromaniacs. Less than one in five arsonists suffer from a mental disorder.

Introduction

Historically, forensic and criminal psychology has tended to ignore property crime in favour of sexual and violent crimes against people. Even now, one will not find extensive research on all aspects of this topic from a psychological perspective. Nevertheless, the property crime of theft is so common that it swamps all other forms of crime in terms of incidence but also in terms of its range of victims. Perhaps because of the mundane nature of most property crime, it has not been the focus of concern in the same way that sexual and violent crime have been. McGuire (2004) puts it this way:

> The role of psychological factors in such offences [property crimes], more than any other type of crime, may appear marginal, even irrelevant. On the other hand, if 'crime is normal', then most of psychology, which is about people generally considered 'normal', is potentially relevant to an understanding of it!
>
> (p. 76)

Actually, the situation is more remarkable even than McGuire suggests since the field of forensic and criminal psychology is replete with examples of the successful application of concepts, ideas and theories developed in relation to the psychology of 'normal people'. Good examples of this include work on eyewitness memory which employs normal memory process, work on the jury which emphasises group dynamics familiar from social psychology, and forensic interviewing which focuses on normal cognitive processes. However, McGuire is correct in that the psychology of criminal behaviour has largely stressed clinical aspects rather than, say, social-psychological explanations. This is, of course, partly because clinical approaches to psychology are based on the psychology of abnormal behaviour rather than the

psychology of normal behaviour. Nevertheless, if one wishes to consider the profiling approach of the social psychologist David Canter with the more clinical approach of the FBI profilers (see Chapter 15) then the advantages of the non-clinical research epistemology are almost self-evident.

Most of us have been victims of theft. Most of us have probably taken something that did not belong to us at some time in our lives – keeping change, not going back to the shop when undercharged, taking paper or paper clips from the office to use at home and so forth. Many of us would regard these things as so trivial that we do not see them as criminal in any sense. The normality of property crime is underlined by a survey of households in England and Wales in 2003 (Budd, Sharp and Mayhew, 2005) in which participants were asked about their own offending behaviour. A high proportion of the general population reported committing some sort of property offence (theft, vehicle-related theft, burglary and criminal damage, and robbery):

- Forty per cent of men and 22 per cent of women reported committing a property crime at some time in their lives.

- Overwhelmingly, the property crimes involved were relatively minor ones involving theft (e.g. theft from a person, work, school or a shop). Thirty-five per cent of men and 21 per cent of women reported committing a theft. Eleven per cent of men reported vehicle-related thefts (e.g. theft of a motor vehicle or theft from a motor vehicle) though the corresponding figure for women was only 2 per cent.

- Four per cent of men reported committing burglary in their lifetime but only 1 per cent of women. However, the major category was commercial burglary and not domestic burglary. Only 1 per cent of men reported domestic burglary and a fifth of this number of women did so. However, the major categories of theft were those from work, school and shops.

- Thefts from an individual (as opposed to thefts from work, school or shops) were actually very uncommon. Less than 1 per cent of men and half that percentage of women reported ever committing the crime of theft from a person.

The above figures are rates ever in a person's lifetime. The researchers also collected information on the numbers of people reporting committing a crime in the previous year. These figures are naturally lower. So, in the year before the survey, 8 per cent of men and 4 per cent of women had committed some sort of property offence. As might be expected, some of the sample committed very few offences and others committed many offences. It was found that 82 per cent of the total number of offences reported to the researchers were actually committed by just 2 per cent of the sample (Budd *et al.*, 2005)!

The variety of property crimes makes its explanation difficult. The crimes range from the very serious to the trivial. Furthermore, some property crimes have a component of violence actual or implied – robbery is an example of this. The neglect of property crime in forensic and criminal psychology is all the more surprising given that the concept of kleptomania is about two hundred years old, thus pre-dating most other psychological explanations of crime by many years.

Box 7.1 Key concept

Arson and pyromania

In 2001, according to England and Wales fire service figures, 14,800 out of 69,000 fires in dwellings were malicious; 19,700 out of 43,000 fires in other buildings were malicious; and 79,100 out of 102,100 vehicle fires were malicious. However, many of these would not be recorded by the police as arson since the legal definition of arson states that the firesetter must have acted deliberately and/or recklessly.

The UK government's Crime Reduction Toolkit (Home Office, 2005a) for arson identifies the major categories of motivation for arson and indicates the proportion of arsons that are in each category:

- Youth disorder and nuisance: boredom and thrill seeking may be associated with this – 80 per cent of arsons.
- Malicious: revenge and racism are among the motivations for this – 5 per cent of total.
- Psychological: triggered by a mental illness or suicide attempts – 5 per cent of total.
- Criminal: concealment of another crime is the reason for these or where the perpetrator may profit financially from the fire as in the case of insurance frauds – 4 per cent of total.

Given these figures, it is not surprising to find that male youths under the age of 18 years are about half of the total of individuals either found guilty in court or cautioned by the police for an arson offence. Approximately one third of US juveniles arrested for arson are under fifteen years of age. So young people who fireset tend to begin doing so early in life (Hickle and Roe-Sepowitz, 2010). The proportion of females involved is less than 15 per cent. About 10 per cent suffer from mental illness. Similarly, it is perhaps also not surprising to find that only one arson in six is prosecuted as a danger to life. So, in many ways, the explanations of arson should lean more to explaining delinquent behaviour than the deep psychological motivations of arsonists. Despite females being under-represented among arsonists, researchers have given them some attention. Gannon (2010) in her review of what is distinctive about female arsonists compared to males suggests that the following seem to be differentiating features of female arson offenders:

- Female arsonists are relatively less likely than males to try to watch the consequences of firesetting such as firefighting.
- Female arsonists show a higher prevalence of depression and psychosis.
- Females do not demonstrate sexual fetishism involving fire.

- Females do not typically carry out arson for reasons of profit and the concealment of crimes.
- Sexual abuse is much more prevalent in the childhoods of female arsonists.
- Various forms of attention seeking and cries for help predominate in the motives of female arsonists.

This does not address the important question of the background factors resulting in girls becoming involved in arson. Evidence has begun to accumulate about the sorts of home environment that may contribute to male arson. Some of these are given in Figure 7.1. To what extent do these characteristics reflect those of female arsonists? Hickle and Roe-Sepowitz (2009) carried out a study of juvenile females charged with arson in a southern state of the USA. Generally, the findings replicate those of firesetting boys. Young female arson offenders frequently (70 per cent) came from extremely unstable home environments – often with little or no contact with more of their parents (55 per cent). Behaviour at school and attendance was problematic. Usually their arson offending happened at a time of substantial crisis such as a loved-one's death or parental separation or divorce. Physical, sexual and emotional abuse may also be involved. The commonest location for their offences was at school which accounted for nearly 40 per cent of the arson crimes.

When the girls tried to explain their offending they suggested that their offences were essentially impulsive or accidental rather than planned in origin. Sixty percent of offences were committed with peers. If they offended alone then they tended to demonstrate high levels of home instability and they had poorer school records for attendance. Contact was likely to be highly unsatisfactory for one parent. The girls tend to have anger, upset and suicidal thoughts if they were solo offenders. These factors tended to encourage Hickle and Roe-Sepowitz to regard arson as a signal or warning sign of the high levels of distress being experienced by these girls. Serial arsonists were not common.

One popular view about such fires is that they are caused by individuals who get pleasure out of setting fire to property (Doley, 2003). They might be regarded as pyromaniacs who are driven by deep-seated urges to

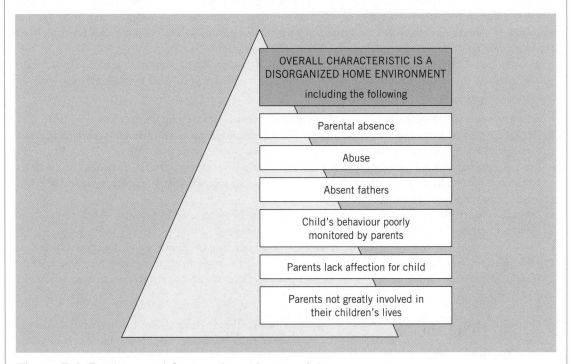

Figure 7.1 Background factors in male arsonists

Box 7.1 (continued)

light fires. So it is believed that flames have an irresistible attraction for them and that they even get sexual satisfaction from their activities. As a consequence, they begin to carry out more and more arson attacks of increasing seriousness purely for reasons of self-gratification. But, of course, pyromania is a psychiatric disorder which is defined in the *Diagnostic and Statistical Manual* of the American Psychiatric Association (see Box 21.1) in the following terms:

- A deliberate, purposeful starting of a fire on two or more occasions.
- There is a state of emotional arousal or an experience of tension before the fire is started.
- The individual has an attraction to, 'a fascination in, or a curiosity about fire and the situational contexts of fire (they might be interested in the consequences of fire or with artifacts used in connection with fires)'.
- The individual will feel 'pleasure, gratification, or relief' when starting fires or in connection with the aftermaths of fires.
- A number of motives are contra-indicative of pyromania – monetary gain, political ideology, concealment of crime and acts of vengeance are excluded. Furthermore, impairments of judgement such as when intoxicated, having limited intellectual ability and suffering dementia are also contra-indicative.
- There should not be a better way of accounting for the fire starting such as indications of conduct disorder, antisocial personality disorder or a manic episode.

Actually, pyromania seems rare among arsonists (Doley, 2003). It is difficult to say precisely what proportion of them are pyromaniacs as the reported figures vary somewhat in the bulk of studies reviewed. Doley found 0 and 1 per cent of arsonists meet the study's criteria for pyromania. However, some studies find much higher percentages. Indeed, mental disorders are uncommon among arsonists as only 17 per cent of those arrested manifest a mental disorder (Almond *et al.*, 2005). Furthermore, the idea that arson or even pyromania is motivated by sexual urges has little force. Lewis and Yarnell (1951) found that out of more than 1,100 arsonists only 3 per cent reported sexual arousal in association with their crime.

Almond *et al.* (2005) investigated Shye's (1985) action system model in relation to arson. Four different 'modes' of arson emerge in the analysis and there is empirical evidence in support stemming from a study of arsonists in a British psychiatric prison:

- *Adaptive mode*: an external event is exploited for some sort of gain. Setting fire to a crime scene to hide evidence of a crime is an example of this. Because of the links of this mode with criminal activity, it includes variables such as more than one offender involved, business, vehicle, force and theft.
- *Expressive mode*: internal psychological factors are expressed against external targets. The choice of the target for the arson would have a symbolic or emotional significance for the arsonist. Variables associated with this include school and civic buildings.
- *Integrative mode*: internal psychological factors are dealt with by using arson as a means of seeking attention. Variables associated with this include self, own home and hospital.
- *Conservative mode*: an external source of frustration has an effect on the individual who responds by setting a fire which restores their sense of well-being. Using fire to exact revenge on another person is an aspect of this. Variables associated with this include victim known, prior threats of violence or arson, arguments and planning.

Shoplifting and kleptomania

It is easy to neglect the extent to which businesses are the victims of property crime compared with individuals.

Perhaps the view that it is worse to steal from a person than a wealthy business is responsible for this. Nevertheless, proportionately, crime against business is more common than crime against individuals. For example, 80 per cent of retailers and 63 per cent of manufacturers in the United Kingdom had experienced crime whereas the corresponding figure for the general population was about 30 per cent in 1999 (Hopkins, 2002). Theft by customers was the most common (47 per cent of retailers reported this), then burglary (24 per cent), then theft from vehicles (23 per cent) and then vandalism (22 per cent). Certain sorts of businesses are more likely to be victims of crime – alcoholic drinks shops and DIY stores were the most likely to be burgled.

The issue of what sort of people commit particular types of crime is an important one in this context. Policing and security work often involves targeting a certain sort of person because it is believed they are more likely to shoplift, for example. This is not the same as offender profiling, discussed in Chapters 14 and 15, where crime scene characteristics are used in an attempt to identify the characteristics of the person who committed that crime. Instead, sometimes police forces use knowledge about the sorts of people arrested for particular types of crime (e.g. shoplifting) in order to target likely shoplifters. In very much the same vein, the police might target Muslims as suspects in terrorism cases. There is a big problem with this sort of targeting. It is appropriate only to the extent that the evidence of a link between a particular type of individual and a particular type of crime is valid. It should not be based simply on prejudice and bias. If arrests for a certain type of crime are systematically biased, targeting simply reproduces that bias and may be considered oppressive by the targeted group.

Shoplifting can be very difficult for security workers to deal with. Shoplifters merge with a large number of shoppers who serve as cover for or to hide the shoplifter. With so many shoppers, how does one choose possible shoplifters for surveillance as they move around the shop? Dabney *et al.* (2006) were not satisfied by previous research which is almost entirely based on official statistics and self-reports of shoplifting. Instead, they believed that the use of strict observational methodologies with strict sampling criteria would be more productive of useful data. So they planned research based on unobtrusive observations in a retail pharmacy/drugstore. The data were collected from high-resolution, closed circuit (CCTV) cameras used for shopper surveillance. The observers were rigorously trained about all aspects of their work.

During the first six months of the research, the observers were required to select every third shopper for observation. In this way, purposeful selection on the basis of characteristics such as race or youthfulness could be avoided. Unfortunately, these exacting standards were expensive both in terms of time and money. Very few

shoplifters were identified in this way. So the sampling protocol was relaxed a little. Instead of every third shopper the new protocol required that every third shopper should be selected if their manner of dress gave them opportunity to conceal shoplifted items. So a person who was wearing tight clothes would be excluded from the sample since such a style of dress would make shoplifting difficult. What appears to be a small change in the sampling method made a big difference to the sort of person who was selected into the sample – the numbers of African American and Hispanic people surveyed increased markedly. So before the change in sampling there was no flexibility and discretion as to who was observed – every third person coming through the door was observed without any deviation. After the sampling method change, the observer had to decide whether a person's clothing was amenable to shoplifting and then select every third such individual. This gave the opportunity for preconceptions about likely shoplifters to have an influence.

Kleptomania

Psychology's neglect of property crime is surprising since one of the earliest 'psychological' (psychiatric) explanations of crime concerned theft. This concept, *kleptomania*, has a two-hundred-year history (see Chapter 1) and remains a psychiatric category in the current edition of the American Psychiatric Association's *Diagnostic and Statistical Manual* (TR) 2000). It is listed as part of the broader category of impulse control disorders. The APA *Diagnostic and Statistical Manual* describes kleptomania as:

> the recurrent failure to resist impulses to steal items even though the items are not needed for personal use or for their monetary value. The individual experiences a rising subjective sense of tension before the theft, and feels pleasure, gratification or relief when committing the theft.

(p. 667)

Since kleptomaniacs are aware that the thefts they commit are both wrong and 'senseless' then the condition is not a psychotic one. Little is known about the extent of kleptomania in the general population. One study of students in the USA suggests that the figure may be 0.4 per cent of the population even though 30 per cent of the students admitted acts of stealing and theft. They simply failed to have the required symptoms for the diagnosis (Odlaugh and Grant, 2010).

There is some modern research into the question of whether kleptomania is a characteristic feature of shoplifting behaviour. Indeed, there are questions about whether kleptomania explains much theft at all. Sarasalo, Bergman and Toth (1997) conducted a study of shoplifters who, literally, had just been apprehended by store security staff. Those who agreed to take part in the study were interviewed in the short period prior to the arrival of the police. The researchers assessed each shoplifter for the presence of four of the main criteria used in the APA *Diagnostic and Statistical Manual* for identifying kleptomania. Kleptomania cannot be diagnosed simply on the basis of a single characteristic but requires the presence of a number of different ones:

- Criterion A is the 'recurrent failure to resist impulses to steal items even though the items are not needed for personal use or for their monetary value' (American Psychiatric Association). A lot of shoplifters (78 per cent) mentioned needing the stolen object; 90 per cent said that the stealing was a sudden impulse; and 56 per cent mentioned that they had had similar impulses in the past.

- Criterion B is 'a subjective sense of tension before the theft'. Over 84 per cent mentioned a sense of thrill before their offence.

- Criterion C is the 'pleasure, gratification, or relief' experienced on carrying out the theft. Only 40 per cent of shoplifters mentioned that they had experienced a feeling of relief or gratification during their offence.

- Criterion D is that the offence is not due to anger or vengeance and is not the consequence of a delusion/hallucination. On average, only 14 per cent of shoplifters agreed that their offence was the consequence of anger or a need for revenge.

According to Sarasalo *et al.*, in order for an individual to be classified as a kleptomaniac, they should meet the above criteria and more. For example, they argue that

34 per cent of the sample were stealing with the assistance of other people so it is difficult to classify them as suffering from kleptomania since kleptomania is a psychological condition of individuals. Of course, it is possible that the co-offenders were also kleptomaniacs but this is not a realistic possibility since very few of the offenders met Criteria A–D above anyway. Of those who acted alone, only a very few (8 per cent) mentioned an inability to resist impulses to steal unneeded items (Criterion A). However, half of this 8 per cent did not experience the rising sense of thrill before committing the crime and the others did not meet Criterion C since they did not feel pleasure, gratification or relief when they committed the theft. In other words, although a number of shoplifters met certain of the criteria, when more than one criterion is used then there is no evidence of kleptomania in the sample. The commonest reason for taking the thing in question was to use it personally (64 per cent) and 12 per cent intended to sell it and 6 per cent intended to give it away or discard it.

Virtually none of the criminals in this sample was in full-time employment. Some were students and others were unemployed. Another remarkable finding was that about a third reported a history of chronic bodily illness (the mean age of the sample was actually quite low). Furthermore, two-thirds of the offenders reported a history of psychiatric disorder.

Not surprisingly, kleptomaniacs can have considerable levels of involvement with the criminal justice system. Grant, Odlaug, Davis and Kim (2009) studied a group of kleptomaniacs attending a clinic seeking treatment. It was found that 27 per cent had never been stopped by a shop security staff member or arrested. Most had been arrested for their offences (68 per cent) but despite this 37 per cent were not convicted. Twenty-one percent had been convicted and incarcerated. Of those with a history of being arrested, 10 per cent had been arrested more than four times. Thus those suffering from kleptomania are at significant risk of being disposed of as criminals in the criminal justice system.

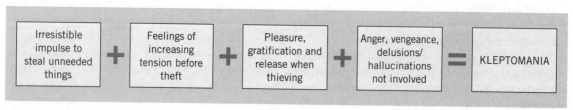

Figure 7.2 DSM criteria for a diagnosis of kleptomania (American Psychiatric Association, 2000)

Culture as an explanation

Kleptomania is a psychiatric classification which strongly hints that offences such as shoplifting are driven by internal psychological states. It is possible to find almost diametrically opposite explanations of shoplifting. One of these identifies cultural variations as a possible influence on patterns of shoplifting. While it is patently obvious that rates of crime vary across cultures, there are questions about how cultural influences impact on the criminal behaviour of individuals. Following many others, Sweeney (2004) argued that key variables identified by cross-cultural psychologists have been shown to be associated with criminal behaviour. She notes that, for example, crime in general and specifically homicide, child abuse, domestic violence against females and rape, together with juvenile delinquency, all seem to be more common in the individualistic cultures that characterise Western countries. They are less of a feature of the collectivist cultures that characterise other parts of the world. Individualism 'is a multi-faceted outlook on life that emphasises, among other things, independence and self-reliance' (p. 62), whereas collectivism 'focuses on duty and obedience' (p. 62). Triandis (1995) claimed another dimension of culture has to be taken into account – he suggests that there is a horizontal/vertical dimension. Consequently, when these two dimensions are used, it is possible to identify cultures that manifest one of four different patterns. These are: (1) horizontal individualism; (2) vertical individualism; (3) horizontal collectivism; and (4) vertical collectivism. Horizontal individualists operate largely as individuals doing 'their own thing' as do vertical individualists – however, vertical individualists are competitive with others whereas horizontal individualists do not have this competitive streak and do not constantly need to be better than others. Horizontal collectivists focus their activities around their group/family but do not feel subordinate to that group, whereas vertical collectivists are willing to defer their personal needs and wishes in favour of the group's needs and wishes.

Sweeney carried out research into shoplifting based on this cross-cultural perspective on a sample of American university students. Three different groups of shoplifters were distinguished: early shoplifters and later shoplifters. These were compared with a group who had never shoplifted. Early shoplifters began offending at the age of about 11 or 12 years or even earlier but never shoplifted after this time. Later shoplifters included anyone who shoplifted at over 12 years of age. Shoplifting had peaked in frequency among this sample at the age of about 13 or 14 years. The explanations they gave for shoplifting were monetary (41 per cent), thrill seeking (21 per cent), peer pressure (18 per cent) and immaturity (14 per cent). Shoplifters were compared with non-shoplifters and actually gave similar reasons why they thought people shoplift. However, there were some differences. Shoplifters, when giving financial reasons for shoplifting, would include words like 'I wanted something and I did not want to pay for it' (p. 64), whereas non-shoplifters would suggest that the shoplifter could not afford to pay. It was uncommon for shoplifters to claim inability to pay rather than not wanting to pay as their financial reason.

The SVS (Schwartz Value Survey) was used to measure individualism–collectivism among the members of the sample. This scale measures a number of pertinent values such as power, achievement, hedonism, stimulation, self-direction, benevolence, tradition, conformity and security. The pattern of values identifying collectivist culture would include conformity, tradition and benevolence. Individualism would be identified by such values as achievement, hedonism and stimulation. There were differences in their values as measured by the SVS. Later shoplifters scored more highly on the power and hedonism values but lower on benevolence and conformity compared with non-shoplifters. Sweeney emphasises that the power value is correlated with vertical individualism, benevolence with horizontal collectivism, and conformity with vertical collectivism. However, care should be taken because this pattern is not simply that vertical individualists are much more likely to shoplift. That is, not all values that are associated with vertical individualism demonstrated a relationship to shoplifting.

One should not assume that shoplifting is necessarily a casual form of criminal activity. Schneider (2005) studied the methods by which persistent offenders who burgle and carry out other forms of theft operate. They were asked about how they disposed of the goods they stole. Thirty-eight per cent gave selling to a handler/fence as their preferred mode of disposal and 24 per cent said sell it to friends. Sixteen per cent had as their first choice using the property themselves. This implies the organised nature of some shoplifting.

It is widely accepted that at least an element of shop stock losses can be attributed to shopworkers rather than shoplifters. But, of course, theft in this context has a wider meaning since it can include things such as fiddling time records and taking information for personal gain. Crime by shopworkers in the United States may involve losses ten times those attributable to street crime. It is possible to find estimates as high as $40 million a year which are attributable to such thefts. Something like a third of employees admit to some form of stealing when questioned (Kulas *et al.*, 2007). A new viewpoint on this sort of crime presents a different perspective on cultural influences on shop crimes.

It is tempting to believe that dissatisfied employees are primarily responsible for these losses at the hands of shopworkers. Although employee dissatisfaction is an antecedent of some theft, there are many dissatisfied employees who do not steal. Consequently, Kulas *et al.* (2007) argue that theft is more likely in organisations where there is a climate or ethos conducive to theft – organisational characteristics conducive to a climate of theft include the ease with which it is possible to steal, perceptions about the amount of workplace theft perpetrated by co-workers, the likelihood that thieves will be caught stealing, perceptions of the amount of theft perpetrated by management, perceived sanctions against those caught thieving, and whether co-workers are permissive about theft.

BOX 7.2 Controversy

The different motives underlying different property crimes

Although there is evidence that many offenders commit a variety of types of crimes, nevertheless some only commit one type of crime or mainly commit one type of crime. That is, although there are specialists in particular crimes, other offenders are generalists. Youngs (2006) argues that research seeking to identify different types of offence specialisms has generally failed to adopt a pertinent psychological theory on which to differentiate different types of offenders. For example, previous research has tended to use legally based crime categories in order to identify specialisms. But legal categories of crime may not correspond to psychological categories of crime as experienced by offenders. There is no reason why crime categories developed for legal purposes should equate to psychological processes especially. Past research effectively identifies that there are specialisms but fails to clarify what the psychological basis of the specialism is.

Youngs proposed that Bandura's social foundations of thought and action (Bandura, 1986) might be an appropriate theoretical framework. Bandura's model assumes that behaviours learnt by vicarious exposure to the behaviours of others are reinforced by different fundamental human motives. In the theory, these are delineated into seven different kinds of incentives including primary incentives, sensory incentives, social incentives, monetary incentives, activity incentives, power/status incentives and self-evaluative incentives. According to Youngs, three of these incentives can be

seen as particularly pertinent to mainstream criminal activity and so it is these that she concentrates on. These are the (a) monetary, (b) power/status and (c) sensory incentives.

The monetary incentive concerns obtaining whatever one desires. This becomes criminal when it involves taking that desired thing from others. So behaviours ranging from forging a cheque to robbing a shopkeeper may have this fundamental incentive. Youngs prefers to describe this as a material incentive as the accumulation of money for its own sake does not reflect the incentive adequately. Items that appear to reflect this material incentive include 'Bought something you know to have been stolen', 'Used fake money in a machine' and 'Broken into a locked car to take something from it'.

The power/status incentive is about achieving control over other people. Societies are structured in terms of status or power hierarchies and it is a fundamental motivation of people in these contexts to elevate themselves higher in the hierarchy. The motivation is not merely to obtain the monetary rewards associated with higher status. This incentive may become criminal when violence or other forms of coercion are used in order to achieve control. Offences associated with this included 'Been involved in gang fights?', 'Beat someone up so badly they probably needed a doctor?', and 'Had sex in a public place?'

Sensory incentives involve the need or desires for novel, pleasurable and stimulating experiences and the avoidance of negative experiences such as boredom. This incentive becomes criminal when the associated activity involves the destruction of property. Items which seem to reflect this include 'Intentionally starting a building on fire?', 'Sniffed glue or other solvents (e.g. Tippex thinner)' and 'Broken into a house, shop, school or other building to break things?'. Thrill-seeking behaviours such as joy riding are also related to this. These different motives might be differentially related to various types of property crime. So shoplifting might frequently have a simple monetary motive, for example.

Crimes which share incentives are more likely to be committed by an offender than those which do not share the same incentive basis. Youngs used data from self-reported offending behaviours from 185 convicted young offenders. A multidimensional scaling analysis of the offence inter-correlations identified three different styles of offending which were similar to Bandura's material, power/status and sensory incentives. These different incentive bases may help us to understand the aetiology of different types of crime and may help to identify crimes which are behaviourally equivalent.

The researchers studied a number of supermarket companies using the Employee Perceptions study which has 74 questions including demographic information, desirable and undesirable employee workplace behaviours including theft, sick leave abuse and so forth. Job satisfaction, as measured in the Kulas *et al.* study, included pay, supervision, co-workers and global satisfaction such as 'All in all, I am satisfied with my present job and I would recommend this job to a friend.' It was found that employee dissatisfaction proceeds to employee theft through the employee's perceptions of the workplace's climate for theft. Dissatisfied workers carry out more thefts than other employees. There was an association between dissatisfaction and theft-permissive work environments which produced higher levels of theft. The implication is that organisations should avoid a permissive attitude towards theft since the organisational climate in this regard forms an explanatory mechanism linking job dissatisfaction with employee theft.

Burglary

Although there have been a number of attempts to identify the major different types of burglar, mostly these have been based on qualitative methods. Vaughn, DeLisi, Beaver and Howard (2008) chose instead a more quantitative approach. A sample of over 450 career criminals provided a wide variety of information. The offenders were interviewed by a researcher working for a bail bond agency so the data, unusually in research, were collected under oath. A range of topics was covered including the offender's employment, residency and criminal history

supplemented by other officially recorded data. Using insights from some of the previous typologies of burglars, fifteen different variables were extracted from the data set including aliases, drug use, length of criminal career, sex offences, tattoos and so forth. The interrelationships between these variables led to four different types of burglar being identified statistically:

- Versatile Burglars: These were characteristically young and had a variety of different types of offences in their criminal history.
- Vagrant Burglars: They had been charged with numerous offences which were primarily a consequence of the vagrant lifestyle that they had adopted. Their offending was primarily for material gain and ensuring survival during the winter months.
- Drug-Oriented Burglars: Their background offence history involved drug possession and trafficking. Their backgrounds often included numerous theft and weapons charges which probably reflects the risks of their drug-user lifestyle. They can be seen as using criminality to meet their financial needs to pay for drugs. Not surprisingly, then, they had a history of charges to do with drug possession and trafficking – they also had numerous theft and weapons charges. They typically tended to use aliases and to be tattooed.
- Sexual Predator Burglars: These showed the indications of involvement in deviant sexual acts. For instance, their criminal histories tended to include rape and prostitution related offences. They were also likely to have convictions for aggravated assault and robbery. This group was the most violent and they had the longest lasting criminal histories which also tended to have an early onset in childhood.

Such a typology is useful especially to the extent that it emphasises the variety of possible motives for burglary which do not all involve financial gain primarily. The identification of a group of drugs-oriented burglary offenders is salient given that there would appear to be a strong connection between drugs use and acquisitive crime which we will go on to discuss below.

Burglary–drugs connection

Of particular importance is the idea that drug use is a stimulus to crime of all sorts and property crime in particular. It is not uncommon for researchers to note that there is a relationship between the use of drugs such as heroin and acquisitive crime. Of course, there are at least three possible bases to this relationship:

- Some researchers argue that users of drugs simply associate with people who are more likely to be criminal anyway and this is the reason for the association.

- Others argue that illegal drugs are expensive to buy in the quantities needed by some users and as a consequence the user finds it difficult to finance their drug use. Illegitimate means of obtaining finance may be resorted to such as theft, robbery, and perhaps sex work (i.e. prostitution) although some users may finance their illicit drugs use entirely from legally obtained funds.

- The relationship between drug use and property crime is the consequence of a third factor which is a common influence on both. For example, it is possible that inadequate parenting in childhood leads separately to criminality and drug use. Thus the association between criminality and drug use is the consequence of this third factor.

It should be obvious that all three above pathways are feasible and that they are not mutually exclusive. A more systematic categorisation of theories linking drugs and crime can be found in Figure 7.3 in which examples of relevant theories are mentioned. This is based on the conceptualisation by Bennett, Holloway and Farrington (2008).

The association between drug use and property crime has been demonstrated frequently. In Australia, for example, it has been found that 70 per cent of heroin users admit committing acquisitive crimes (Degenhardt *et al.*, 2005). Furthermore, it has been estimated that over

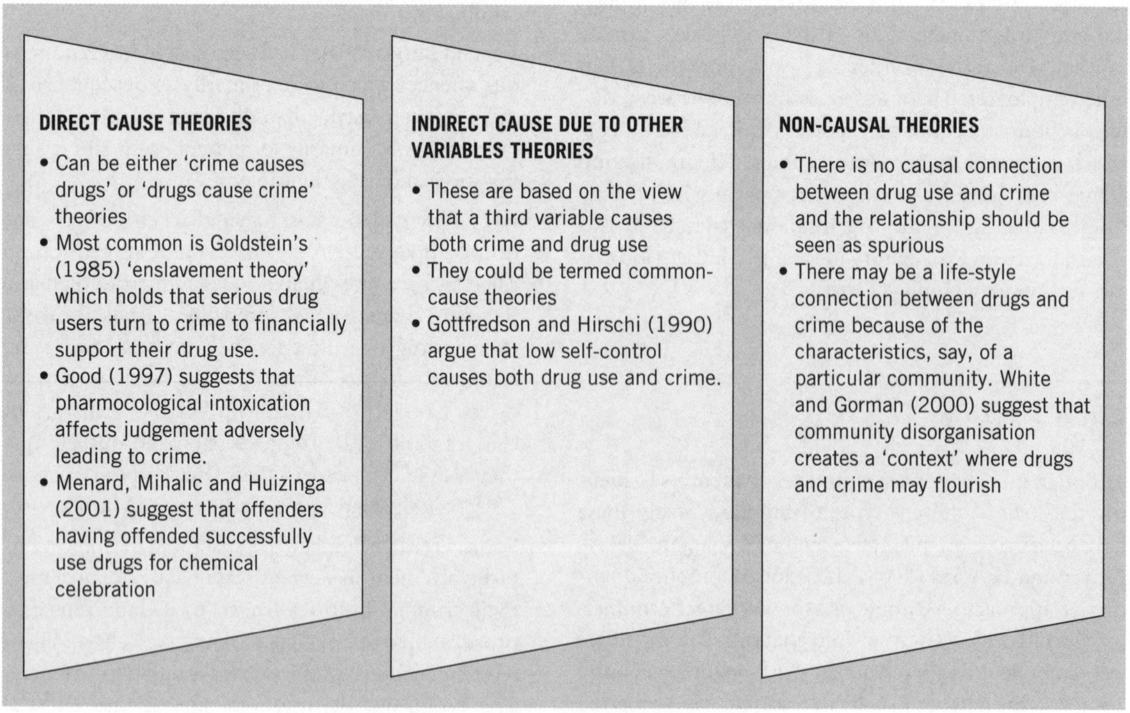

DIRECT CAUSE THEORIES

- Can be either 'crime causes drugs' or 'drugs cause crime' theories
- Most common is Goldstein's (1985) 'enslavement theory' which holds that serious drug users turn to crime to financially support their drug use.
- Good (1997) suggests that pharmocological intoxication affects judgement adversely leading to crime.
- Menard, Mihalic and Huizinga (2001) suggest that offenders having offended successfully use drugs for chemical celebration

INDIRECT CAUSE DUE TO OTHER VARIABLES THEORIES

- These are based on the view that a third variable causes both crime and drug use
- They could be termed common-cause theories
- Gottfredson and Hirschi (1990) argue that low self-control causes both drug use and crime.

NON-CAUSAL THEORIES

- There is no causal connection between drug use and crime and the relationship should be seen as spurious
- There may be a life-style connection between drugs and crime because of the characteristics, say, of a particular community. White and Gorman (2000) suggest that community disorganisation creates a 'context' where drugs and crime may flourish

Figure 7.3 Some of the main theories concerning the drugs–crime relationship according to Bennett, Holloway and Farrington (2008)

half of the crimes committed in the United Kingdom are committed by drug users and that the proportion is much higher for shoplifting (85 per cent) and domestic burglary (80 per cent) (Home Office, 2002). Primarily, users of heroin and crack cocaine are responsible for the cost of drug-related acquisitive crime to the economy. Nevertheless, just 10 per cent of drug users cause half of drug-related crime's costs. However, this begs the question of just what created this trend. One obvious argument is that the cost of drugs determines the need to resort to property crime, which implies that fluctuations in the cost of drugs may be associated with fluctuations in the levels of property crime. Degenhardt *et al.* (2005) took advantage of a sudden change in the availability of heroin in Australia to assess its impact on acquisitive crime among other things. In a market economy, the cost of products (including illegal drugs) is partly determined by the scarcity of the product. So the significance of the 'shortage' of heroin is that one would expect its price to increase as a consequence. Thus, if heroin use causes acquisitive crime because of financial pressures, one would expect that users would need to engage in acquisitive crime more frequently when drugs were in scarce supply. Using a variety of data sources to confirm trends in availability and cost, the researchers were able to show that during the period of scarcity of heroin there were substantial rises in the numbers of property crimes. The crimes that increased included robbery without a weapon, robbery with a weapon other than a firearm, and breaking and entering homes. This seems to indicate the role of financial motives related to the purchase of heroin in property crimes. Certainly, in this study, when supplies began to return to normal, property crime also returned to its previous levels.

Something of the importance of stopping drug use for reducing crime levels is demonstrated by the findings of a study by McIntosh, Bloor and Robertson (2007). This used the data from the Drug Outcome Research in Scotland (DORIS) study – a longitudinal study of over 650 people some of which were in prison seeking treatment for problematic drug use. Mainly they were male. The study design involved each person being interviewed four times over a period of 33 months. The researchers were concerned with data on whether the offender had been involved and/or arrested for an acquisitive crime in the previous three months or since the previous interview:

- About 35 per cent of the participants claimed to have committed an acquisitive crime.

- 25 per cent said that they had been arrested for such a crime.

- Drug users were seven times more likely to have committed an acquisitive crime than those who had been abstinent for three months (excluding marijuana). This was true of both prisoner and non-prisoner participants.

Interestingly, the number of previous drug treatments and a scale measuring perceptions of treatment were not or very weakly associated with crime. The researchers concluded that drug treatment has an indirect effect of reducing crime but this effect is mediated by drug consumption. That is, the treatment's effect on drug use is the most important thing since a reduction in drug consumption is reflected in lower levels of acquisitive crime.

In this context, it is worthwhile noting Parker and Kirby's (1996) study in the United Kingdom on the impact of a methadone support programme on crime rates in a community which they suggest had been going through a heroin epidemic, with consequent elevated levels of property crime. Methadone is a synthetic drug with properties like those of morphine. It is used in programmes that attempt to help people who are withdrawing from heroin, which itself is a semi-synthetic derivative of morphine. Methadone helps the user to deal with heroin withdrawal symptoms such as fever, insomnia and vomiting. It is a dangerous drug in its own right but is used as a means of dealing with the worse evil of heroin addiction. A large sample of addicts undergoing the methadone support programme was compared with a large control group. Self-report questions as well as in-depth interviews were employed. During the period of the study, which reflected a fairly massive methadone support programme, the acquisitive crimes of burglary from a dwelling and theft from a motor vehicle declined 'dramatically' in the areas studied:

- The vast majority reported reductions in their illicit drug usage as a consequence of being on the programme.

- About a fifth claimed to have not used illicit drugs at all as a consequence of being on the programme.

As a result, the treatment sample spent only a fifth of the amount on illicit drugs which the non-treated community control group sample did. The implications of this for the need for property crime are obvious. Those on the support programme claimed to be involved in less crime in keeping with this.

An Australian study into the effectiveness of methadone maintenance treatment found similar evidence of its impact on the amount of property crime (Lind *et al.*, 2005). The researchers used a reoffending database to track the offending of drug users during the periods when they were undergoing methadone treatment compared with those when they were not. They also had a separate database that provided information about periods when the drug users were in custody, which could be used to adjust for the time that the user could potentially commit a crime. In terms of theft offences (defined mainly as robbery, theft and related, burglary and breaking and entering, and fraud and forgery), there seemed to be an impact on the rates of criminal charges. The extent of the impact depended on gender and age group. Expressing the reductions as numbers of charges per hundred drug users:

- men under 30 years of age: a reduction of 8 theft charges;
- women under 30 years of age: a reduction of 20 theft charges;
- men 30 years and over: a reduction of 11 theft charges;
- women 30 years and over: a reduction of 20 theft charges.

So this methadone maintenance treatment seems to be more effective with women than men though the general conclusion is one of its effectiveness in reducing charges of theft.

Of course, methadone is a chemical treatment and not a psychological treatment for drug use. Its importance in this context is that there is clear evidence that making users less dependent on illicit market drugs has the important consequence of crime reduction. The implication is that any treatment which makes individuals less dependent on illicit drugs may result in reductions in crimes against property. A study in the United Kingdom by Gossop *et al.* (2003) partly answers this question. They studied drug users on a variety of drug treatment programmes. These included methadone support programmes of the sort described above but they also included drug dependency units in which drug users, as residents, would undergo some psychiatry-based support programme. Drug dependency units are often housed within psychiatric hospitals and the sort of treatment that would be available would involve multi-disciplinary teams mostly of psychiatrists and nursing staff. The in-patient treatment would last from 2 to 12 weeks. The treatment offered would be some form of detoxification together with psychosocial rehabilitation work. The findings generally confirmed that treatment resulted in lower levels of drug use of various sorts. Furthermore, it was confirmed

that there was a substantial drop in reported crime following the commencement of treatment. Acquisitive crime dropped substantially to just about a quarter of the pre-treatment levels in both the methadone community treated group and the residential drug dependency units. Unfortunately, it is not possible to fully separate the effects of detoxification from the effects of the psychosocial work.

Surprisingly, few attempts have been made to synthesise the sizeable body of research into the relationship between drug misuse and crime. Bennett, Holloway and Farrington (2008) carried out a meta-analysis (Box 4.2) of 30 studies which had investigated this relationship. They took the opportunity of fine-tuning their analysis by looking at the relationship between different types of drugs use and different types of crime. Compared to non-drug users, drug users were three or four times more likely to be involved in crime. The basic relationship was true for the offences of burglary, prostitution, robbery and shoplifting. The increase in offending due to drug use was the greatest for users of crack cocaine (about six times greater) and least for recreational drug users such as marijuana. The increase in offending due to drugs was:

- Amphetamines 2x
- Cocaine 2.5x
- Heroin 3x
- Marijuana 1.5x

One could construe these findings as evidence in support of the idea that the most expensive drugs (crack cocaine, cocaine and heroin) are more strongly related to crime since users are more under pressure when it comes to financing their drug use.

As a coda to this, the case of the impact of alcohol on acquisitive crime is important. There is plenty of data to suggest that offenders often commit their crimes while under the influence of drink. Not unexpectedly, much of this research concentrates on alcohol as a cause of violent crime. To what extent is acquisitive crime used to support problem drinking? Of course, relatively speaking alcohol is much cheaper than illegal drugs in general so the financial pressures on the drinker are probably much less than on the drug user. McMurran and Cusens (2005) studied self-reported data from 126 offenders in British prisons. Some financially motivated crime includes violent offences (e.g. robbery) and so these were studied alongside other forms of acquisitive crime. The researchers found that self-reports of crime were about 80 per cent accurate against what was recorded on official records. The offenders were screened using the Alcohol Use Disorders Identification Test (AUDIT) for hazardous drinking (i.e. high frequency, poorly controlled, and resulting in adverse consequences). Those who had been violent when drinking were higher on this measure than those who were not drunk when they committed a violent crime. Among the important findings concerning the role of alcohol on acquisitive crime were:

- Half of those in prison for acquisitive offences said that they were drunk at the time of the offence and the scores on the hazardous drinking measure were higher when the offender had been drunk when committing their acquisitive offence.

- About one in five indicated that their acquisitive offending was carried out in order to get alcohol.

- Crime in order to finance alcohol consumption characterised only a small numbers of violent and acquisitive criminals. Such crime was more common where the offender scored highly on the measure of hazardous drinking.

A more general view about the relationship between alcohol and acquisitive offending can be found in the work of Felson, Savolainen, Aaltonen and Moustgaard (2008). They acknowledge that there is a strong relationship between alcohol use and criminal behaviour but ask the question of just how much the relationship is causal and just how much is spurious. Their study involved data on over 5,000 participants in the Finnish Self-Reported Delinquency Study of 2004. This study compared the size of the correlations between:

- delinquent behaviour when the offender sober at the time of the offence with their alcohol consumption in general;

- delinquent behaviour irrespective of whether the offender was drunk or sober with their alcohol consumption in general.

If these correlations are the same then quite clearly alcohol consumption cannot be responsible for the criminal behaviour when drunk; if there is a weaker correlation when the offender is sober then this is evidence that alcohol consumption led to criminal behaviour. For every crime-type studied by the researchers, a strong relationship was found between drinking and the amount of crime committed when sober. This clearly indicates that much of the relationship between alcohol use and crime may be spurious (i.e. alcohol use does not cause crime). However, a more detailed analysis was quite revealing. For some crimes of petty theft such as shoplifting and theft from one's home, there was virtually no difference between the total crime relationship whether drunk or sober. For these offences, the alcohol–crime relationship is totally spurious as the relationship was the same when they had been drinking at the time of the offence. On the other hand, for some crimes there was a difference between the sizes of the two relationships. These were crimes such as violence, vandalism and car theft. In these cases, alcohol is having a direct causal effect. These seem to be the sort of crimes which we might expect to be affected most directly by drunkenness.

Burglar decision making

Many studies of burglary are presented as if they were studies of their victims. However, who and whose property is targeted by burglars is more than just a study of the victim, it tells us a lot about the decision-making processes of burglars. Furthermore, these decisions are actually the result of a complex interplay between the burglar and the burgled. For example, a householder who fits burglar alarms has an influence on the burglar's decision whether or not to target that householder's property. The burglar also influences the householder to fit the alarm since other burglaries in the area might motivate the purchase of the burglar alarm. So, in a sense, burglary is an interaction between the burglar and the householder, though this interaction may be very indirect. As a consequence, it is equally possible to argue that studies of who is victimised are equally studies of the decisions made by offenders about where to burgle.

One of the recurrent themes in research on crime is that offenders are in some way driven to crime by some sort of propensity to criminality. This encourages researchers to try to find the distinctive psychological features of offenders such as burglars. In other words, one needs to seek to find the ways in which burglars differ from the rest of the population. One important theory, rational choice theory (Cornish and Clarke, 1986), is built on a different set of assumptions. The theory sees offenders as decision makers who seek to gain advantage for themselves in ways which are rational within the constraints of the information available, the offender's ability to reason, and the amount of time available to make the decision. Decisions that have to be made instantly may not be optimally rational. Although the theory deals with the decision to become criminal in the first place, its most significant contributions have considered the rationality of the decisions made in relation to particular opportunities for crime. The focus is on the crime event, as a consequence, and not on the personality of the offender, for example. However, the theory does accept the role of background factors such as low intelligence or poor upbringing and the role of situational factors such as being drunk, having a row with one's partner, pressure from friends and so forth. Pease (2001) suggests that rational choice theory freed researchers from trying to find the explanation of crime in the pathological character of the offender. The theory pushes researchers more in the direction of questioning offenders about the methods they employ and the precautions they take in the course of their offending. So, in a sense, the big advantage of the theory is that it pushes researchers in a streetwise direction of listening to offenders.

Sometimes it is suggested that rational choice theory works better for property crime than for expressive crime. Certainly, some of the more profitable research has explored the rationality of burglary. According to Nee (2004), interview research with burglars has led to the view that they are far less opportunistic than was once believed. They plan rather than make impulsive choices as to targets. This does not mean that all burglars plan but merely that only a minority work completely haphazardly. Furthermore, burglars largely search out targets. The motivation for burglary was to obtain cash to finance a relatively lavish lifestyle. Nee (2004) carried out a study in Ireland of the motivation and decision making of burglars. Intriguingly, she included a comparison group who were not burglars, which allowed her to investigate whether the decision making of burglars was truly distinctive or simply what anyone would decide in similar circumstances. Rather than have burglars survey actual properties with the researcher, it was decided to simulate vulnerable residential areas by the use of photographs on slides. The participants were shown numerous pictures of five houses. Rather than single factors being decisive in the decision that a particular household would be a good one to burgle, the burglars had patterns of factors which led to the decision to burgle or not. The same combination of cues to decision making would not apply in every circumstance. For example, the least popular target for burglars would have been somewhat easy to enter because it had timber doors and sash windows.

However, it had a scruffy and 'downmarket' appearance and was exposed in that it could easily be observed by people in the street. The burglars, however, may well have seen this house as a better target if it had been next to cheaper housing. The burglars' preferred target house had a mature appearance and looked as if it would be easy to get inside. The house next to it looked as if it might yield more profits, provided a lot of cover for the burglar and was easy to break in at the rear of the property. Despite this, the burglars were deterred by it because it had a number of security measures installed – such as double glazing, a visible burglar alarm box and mortice locks on the doors.

In contrast, when householders assessed the same houses in terms of how desirable they would be to a burglar as a target they seemed to lack an appropriate strategy or plan for making their decision. They did not choose the same target houses as the burglars did. Furthermore, the householders took rather more time over reaching a decision than the burglars did since they explored a greater number of photographs of the properties before selecting what for them appeared to be the best target. They lacked the experience and expertise that burglars possessed.

There are a number of fairly closely related theories that can be applied to burglary. One is routine activity theory. Again, like rational choice theory, this counteracts the idea that research should identify the distinct social and psychological characteristics of criminals which lead to their offending. In routine activity theory the emphasis is on the day-to-day activities of some individuals and the way their daily lives are structured that provides them with opportunities to commit crime. So, to illustrate this, it is useful to note that studies show that low-income households as well as inner-city ones have the greatest risk of burglary. This is simply because they are the ones most likely to be in close proximity to where the burglar lives – that is, are encompassed within the routine ambit of the burglar. Felson (1996) identified three different factors which contributed to property crime:

- motivated offenders need to be around (i.e. proximity to potential offenders);

- there needs to be suitable property available where the burglary could be committed (target attractiveness);

- an absence of guardians of the property capable of protecting the property. The guardians may simply be members of the household or neighbours whose presence is noted. Johnson and Bowers (2004) mention guardianship which includes such things as household composition, house occupancy and having neighbours who watch the dwelling when it is unoccupied. A high proportion of burglars avoid occupied dwellings. That is social guardianship; physical guardianship consists of things such as burglar alarms. Suitable targets for burglary are characterised by: (1) greater value as judged by the burglar (target attractiveness) and (2) absence of physical aspects of the target household which reduce its suitability – these include the visibility of the property (the more obscured from public view then the greater risk of being targeted) and the accessibility of the target.

One attempt to test routine activity theory as applied to property crime studied burglary victimisation across three countries (Tseloni *et al.*, 2004). The areas involved were the Netherlands, United States, and England and Wales. They took the major precepts of routine activity theory and tested whether the predictions of the theory worked in such a wide variety of settings. Tseloni *et al.* coded many variables from crime survey data relating to routine activity theory. These were then correlated with known risks of burglary victimisation. It is important to note that the researchers found that their variables measuring aspects of routine activity theory left a great deal unexplained in burglary rates. That is, a great deal is yet to be found out about why certain households are more likely to be burgled than others. The following are among the general findings:

- The social guardianship variable lone parent (there are fewer adult social guardians) increased the risk of burglary to a similar extent in all three countries.

- Households that had preventative measures against burglary were actually more likely to be burgled than those that did not. This is contrary to expectations. The researchers suggest that the precautions against burglary may have been a consequence of being burgled and that in some of the cases the preventative measures were token efforts which would not deter burglars. The finding should be not taken as indicating that burglars are attracted to houses that take preventative measures.

- Living in inner-city or urbanised areas increased the risk of burglary perhaps due to living closer to where offenders live.

With the above exceptions, it should be stressed, though, that there was a degree of inconsistency as to the factors which related to burglary rates in the different countries. So, taken overall, there is evidence in support of routine activity theory but it is also true to say that the fit of the theory to the data on burglary was far from complete.

In terms of the geography of burglary, there are certain areas that tend to have a high concentration of burglaries and so may attract greater police attention as a consequence. Johnson and Bowers (2004) suggest that a perspective from behavioural ecology, optimal foraging theory, may be of help in understanding burglars' thought processes which lead to such hot spots. The theory suggests that animals when seeking food (and so burglars when seeking money) adopt strategies that keep the rate of rewards to a maximum while at the same time keeping to a minimum the amount of time spent foraging and the risk of being caught by other animals (and so the police in terms of burglary). Thus the strategy of at least some offenders is to keep the rewards of their criminal activity at a high level while minimising the time spent committing the offence (which reduces the risk of being caught). This suggests to Johnson and Bowers (2004) that the burglar would burgle one property then continue to target ones close by if they are unlikely to be observed/overlooked, if there are ready escape routes, and if there is a likelihood of stealing valuable goods. This strategy would eventually be recognised by members of the targeted community or by the police. At this stage, the wise burglar would move on from that area. Put another way, there should be a spate of burglaries in a particular area which is contained within a limited period of time. That is, there will be a hot spot for burglary which lasts for just a short time. This is what Johnson and Bowers' (2004) research showed – hot spots for burglary move dynamically. Hot spots involve potentially lucrative households in an area but the burglars' strategy is to move on to another location when the yields are poor and/or the risk of arrest is high. This may have important practical policing implications. It may be an ineffective strategy for the police to target those areas which have been shown to have high burglary rates one month since the hot spot is likely to have moved. The chances are, however, that the hot spot moves to a nearby area. Hot spots are likely to be found in the most affluent areas, which are not necessarily the areas where burglary is the most frequent. This is not the consequence of certain households being repeatedly targeted since the researchers excluded such repeat victimisations.

A prospective burglar will assess a property in order to decide whether it is occupied or unoccupied. There

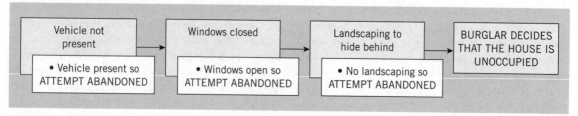

Figure 7.4 The Matching Heuristic Model applied to a burglar's decision-making process

is a general preference among burglars to try to avoid the risk of being disturbed by householders – which increases the likelihood of the offender being arrested. Over three-quarters of the burglars prefered unoccupied homes and check that the property appears empty before breaking in (Nee and Meenaghan, 2006). Of course, their assessment is not always successful and crimes such as rape are not infrequently one consequence. Rational choice theory (Clark and Cornish, 1985) suggests that a number of different sorts of cues are considered when deciding whether to commit a particular crime (see also Chapter 4). According to Snook, Dhami and Kavanagh (2010), the rational choice model proposes that criminals can be regarded as entirely rational decision makers using what is essentially a compensatory process – they attach weights or values to the potential rewards and costs of a particular course of action. For example, the possibility of a large financial gain is considered against the risk of arrest. In other words, the positive and negative prospects of a crime are weighted in terms of their prospect of occurrence and these integrated together when deciding whether or not to offend. That is, the burglar, in this case, makes their decision in terms of the course of action that maximises gains and minimises costs. So if the probability of a large financial gain is big and the probability of being punished by the law is low then this increases the likelihood that the burglary will go ahead.

This approach, however, is not the only way in which offenders might make their decision. An alternative model is that burglars use a non-compensatory strategy or matching heuristic. In this the burglar would examine a number of homes one by one until a home that meets certain requirements sufficiently is found and targeted. Heuristics are step-by-step information processing procedures. So, for example, the process employed by the offender is to use different sorts of information are sequentially. Once a cue supporting a particular decision by the offender is found then the search stops. It is a quick process which relies on a minimal amount of information. Snook *et al.* used the matching-heuristic

developed by Dhami and Ayton (2001). This is used for binary classification tasks such as deciding whether a house is unoccupied or occupied. Imagine that a particular burglar's matching heuristic model is based on using three cues – vehicle absent, windows above ground level closed, and landscaping to hide. Each of these cues is used in turn when making the decision to burgle or abandon the attempt. This is illustrated in Figure 7.4. As can be seen, the burglary attempt will be abandoned at each stage if the cue that the house is unoccupied is missing. Because, for example, if a vehicle is seen on the house drive then a burglar will abandon this particular burglary attempt – this explains why this model requires a minimal amount of information. There is no point in looking for the other cues as an important one is present.

In order to study the processes involved, Snook *et al.* asked convicted burglars to make judgements about whether homes were occupied or not from photographs of each of the properties. The actual occupancy at the time of the photograph was checked and the permission of the householders to use these photographs in the research obtained. The researchers had deliberately included properties which had different sorts of cues to possible occupancy. These clues seem to be ones that burglars themselves identify as being involved in their decision-making processes concerning occupancy:

- attached garage (or none)
- curtains above ground level open (or closed)
- deadbolt present (or none)
- landscaping to hide behind (or none)
- security system visible (or not visible)
- vehicle present on the property (or absent)
- windows above ground level open (or closed).

As they examined the photos, the burglars assessed whether each property was occupied. Then they explained to the researchers just how they had made their decision. Additionally, they rated the importance of a range of cues when making their decisions. The burglars were relatively good at the task since their predictions of whether the house was occupied or not was better than chance levels though not spectacularly so. However, the most important cue to occupancy by far was the presence of a vehicle at the house. With this cue excepted, in general, the cues in the above list had poor ecological validity. That is to say, most of the cues were actually not strong indicators of whether or not the property was truly unoccupied. This, perhaps, emphasises the difficulty of the decision facing the burglar (though, of course, in real life they would be able to use surveillance and other methods which are not possible from photographs alone). The researchers attempted to fit both the more complex rational decision model and the simple heuristic model to their data on how the burglars actually made decisions. Their analysis strongly suggested that the matching heuristic model – the simple model – characterised burglars' thinking better than did a more complex, compensatory model. Basically this means that burglars employ an unsubtle model when making their decisions.

Main points

- Property crime is commonplace and it is probably impossible to find anyone who has not committed some sort of trivial theft at some time in their lives. Perhaps as a consequence, psychologists have not devoted so much activity to researching property crime as a specific topic. Relatively large proportions of the general population admit to committing some sort of property crime at some time in their lives. Mainly these are thefts and the proportions reporting having crimes such as burglary or robbery are much smaller. There is clearly a need to develop psychological approaches to the understanding of property crime much further.

- Psychiatric classifications such as kleptomania and pyromania seem to have little to do with the vast majority of property crimes or firesetting offences against property. Their lack of importance to the majority of crimes contrasts somewhat with the familiarity of these terms among the general public. Some forms of theft such as shoplifting, just like firesetting, are offences overwhelmingly carried out by youngsters. As such they are probably best considered as crimes of delinquency (Chapter 6).

- It is not surprising that financial motives underlie a great proportion of thefts of all sorts. One of the most disturbing property crimes is burglary. There seems to be clear evidence that this sort of crime is partly carried out in relation to the need to finance drug usage. Research has shown that times when heroin becomes expensive because of supply shortages are associated with increases in property crimes such as burglary. Furthermore, methadone treatment (a replacement for heroin to help users come off heroin) is associated with a decrease in the amount of crime carried out by heroin users.

Further reading

There are few in-depth accounts of the psychology of property crime. The following are exceptions:

Canter, D. and Alison, L. (2000) *Profiling Property Crimes* Aldershot: Ashgate.

Mawby, R.I. (ed.) (2007) *Burglary* Aldershot: Ashgate.

Useful material from the Web includes:

Crime Reduction Toolkits: Arson:

http://webarchive.nationalarchives.gov.uk/20100413151441/
http://crimereduction.homeoffice.gov.uk/toolkits/an00.htm

Arson Research Bulletins:

http://www.communities.gov.uk/fire/researchandstatistics/
firesearch/operationalandsocial/socialresearch/
arsonresearchbulletins/

Visit our website at www.pearsoned.co.uk/howitt for self-test and essay questions, annotated further reading, audio interviews with researchers in the field, weblinks and more information on becoming a forensic psychologist.

Chapter 8

Violent offenders

Overview

- Despite the public's belief that violent crime continues to rise, trends in violent crime indicate that the rate may be relatively modest, even assessed over the period since records began a hundred years ago. The most serious violent crime, homicide, has shown quite a small increase over a hundred years of about 300 per cent, which is tiny compared to the growth of reported violent crime against the person.

- Violent crime is economically very costly, just as is property crime. In addition, it has many direct psychological consequences on the victim (see Chapter 4).

- The effects of media violence on violent crime have rarely been seriously considered by forensic and criminal psychologists. Nevertheless, it is a major area of psychological research relevant to criminology. However, few studies concentrate on media influences on actual criminal violence compared with the voluminous literature on media effects in general. Generally speaking, despite laboratory evidence to the contrary, field research is less indicative of an adverse influence of the media on violence.

- Explanations of violent crime, including homicide, may be at various levels of analysis – the sociological, the psychological and the biological, for example. Of course, societal trends in violent crime (e.g. gender differences) need explanation and cannot be effectively dealt with at the level of individual psychology. Most forensic and criminal psychologists would accept that extreme acts of violence are multiply determined. These may be grouped under headings such as predisposing, maintenance and situational/triggering factors.

- Care must be taken to guard against the assumption that there are many extremely violent individuals who will act violently in many situations and against any target of their violence.

- Violence between intimates in the form of domestic violence and stalking is a significant part of violent crime especially as far as gender relationships are concerned. There are many complex forensic issues surrounding both of these types of violence and they make an important case study in the understanding of how crime is gendered.

Introduction

Statistically speaking, the vast majority of crime consists of relatively trivial property offences (Chapters 2 and 7). Nevertheless, violent offences occur frequently according to crime statistics. Violent crime appears to be among the most salient factors in the public's perceptions of crime in general and its levels an indicator of society's malaise. Official crime statistics for the last few decades have generally shown increases in all sorts of crime. Violent crime is no exception to this long-term trend, although it has reversed in some countries in recent years as has that of other crimes. In the United Kingdom, for example, crime in general increased 66-fold during a hundred-year period ending in the year 2000/1. The figures for violent crime reflect a high growth rate of 315 times in the same period. These are recorded crime rates. It is generally held that homicide is one of the most accurately recorded crimes. So changes in homicide rates may be an indicator of the true underlying trend. Other forms of violence may be partly the consequence of the increasing unacceptability of violence which leads to greater levels of reporting. Domestic violence is an example of a violent crime that is likely to have gone unreported to the police or been ignored by them in the past. Nevertheless, it is particularly striking to note the way in which crime statistics escalated markedly in the second half of the twentieth century (Table 8.1).

Care is needed over the interpretation of these increases. According to the Home Office (2005b, 2007, 2010) figures, in England and Wales the trend for homicide is actually quite modest in comparison. For example, in 1900 there were 312 homicides in total, in 1950 there were 346, in 1975 there were 515 and in 2009/10 there were 615. (Notice that the peaking of the homicide statistics for 2002/3 is an artifact of the killings by Dr Harold Shipman in the UK of many of his patients. Although they had taken place in earlier years, they were first recorded during this year.) This is an extremely slow growth rate of less than three times over the century compared with the figures for violence against the person and other crimes. Remember that adjustment is also needed for population growth to obtain a reasonable comparison. So the growth in homicide is less than it appears to be from these figures owing to the increase in population size. Improved medical services saving more lives might have also affected the trend somewhat but this would decrease the levels of apparent violence. Taking all of these things into account, as an indicator of violence, homicide seems not to show the pattern that is generally expected.

Table 8.1 The growth of violent and other crime in the twentieth century

Year	Notifiable crimes recorded by police	Total violence against the person	Homicide recorded crimes
1900	78,000	1,908	312
1925	114,000	1,495	318
1950	479,000	6,249	346
1975	2,106,000	71,002	515
1980	2,688,000	97,246	620
1985	3,612,000	121,731	616
1990	4,544,000	184,665	669
1995	5,100,000	212,588	745
2000/1	5,171,000	600,922	850
2002/3	5,899,000	835,101	1,047
2003/4	6,014,000	967,000	904
2004/5	5,638,000	1,048,000	868
2005/6	5,555,000	1,060,000	764
2006/7	5,428,000	1,046,000	758
2007/8	4,951,000	961,000	774
2008/9	4,703,000	903,000	657
2009/10	4,338,000	871,000	615
2010/11	4,150,000	822,000	642

Statisticians normally distinguish between violent crime and property crime. However, the costs of violent crime are not simply in those of pain and suffering. Violent crime has enormous economic costs. The estimate of these costs needs to include factors such as costs of prosecution, imprisonment, lost earning potential and so forth (Brand and Price, 2001):

- The average cost of a case of violence against the person was £19,000 ($38,000, €24,000).
- Sexual offences also cost £19,000 per case.
- Robberies/muggings cost £4,700 per case.
- Burglary cost £2,300 per case.
- Common assault cost £540 per case.
- Murder costs a colossal £1,100,000 on average.

When reported as total amounts, the figures become even more alarming. Each year, the cost of burglary is £2.7 billion (a billion = 1,000 millions), robbery/mugging £2 billion, common assault £1.7 billion, homicide £1.2 billion, sexual offences £2.5 billion and violence against the person the phenomenal total of £16.8 billion. A similar study (Dubourg, Hamed and Thoms, 2005) suggested that in 2003/4 the cost of the typical sexual offence had risen to £31,438, that of the typical homicide was £1,459,000 and the typical common assault £1,440. Unfortunately there are no more up-to-date figures.

Nevertheless, forensic and criminal psychology concentrates rather more on homicide and violent crimes (including rape and other sexual offences). Comparatively little attention has traditionally been paid to the more frequent property offences. Trivial offences cost nations dearly – even minor violence costs more than extreme acts of violence in total.

The heading of violent offences includes an array of rather different crimes which need disaggregation. Can a bar brawl be explained in the same terms as a serial killing? Intuitively we would say that they are very different. Yet there are a number of matters to consider. One very obvious thing uniting violent crimes (and all forms of crime) is the profound gender difference in terms of involvement with the criminal justice system. Males make up the majority of violent criminals in categories ranging from simple assault to serial killing. Age is an important factor in violent crime. Violent offenders tend to be young. These things need to be taken into account when studying violent crime. Several of the chapters in this book are very relevant to explanations of violent crime:

- The development of violent crime through childhood was discussed in Chapter 6.
- The role of mental illness in the aetiology of violent crime is discussed in Chapter 21.
- Serial killers are a special focus of Chapter 14 on offender profiling.
- Anger management and other therapies for violence are covered in Chapter 26.
- Risk assessment for violent offenders is dealt with in Chapter 27.

Before we move on to examine explanations of violent crime further, it is important to note that much violence is easily explained superficially. The deep and complex psychological motives characteristic of violent offenders as portrayed in the media often give way to more obvious causes. In the United States, substantial numbers of offences are known to be associated with alcohol. Out of the 5 million offenders under various correction agencies, over a third had been drinking alcohol at the time of the offence. The trend is especially clear for violent offences where approximately 40 per cent of those on probation, in local jails and in state prisons had consumed alcohol at the time of the crime. The figure reduces to 20 per cent for those in federal prison for violent crimes.

While there may be a clear association between alcohol and crime in these US figures, this may be somewhat misleading in that it implies that the offenders were drunk rather than that they had merely consumed some alcohol. They may have been drunk, but it is not certain. Figures from a study of arrestees arriving at police stations in London seem to suggest fairly low levels of drunkenness in arrestees (Robertson, Gibb and Pearson, 1995). Even serious violent offences tended to involve drunkenness relatively infrequently. Nevertheless, only 69 per cent of grievous bodily harm cases were free from signs of drunkenness when they arrived. It is known from the British Crime Survey that 44 per cent of victims of violence believed that their assailant was under the influence of alcohol (Smith and Allen, 2004).

According to McMurran, Jinks, Howells and Howard (2011), three distinct types of violence may be identified:

- violence when pursuing material goals,
- violence related to social dominance goals, and
- defensive violence to deal with threat.

This typology was used to classify the violent crimes committed by a sample of young males between 18 and 21 years of age who had committed alcohol-related offences. Many of these young men drank to excessive levels prior to committing their crimes. They were interviewed using semi-structured methods. But in addition various psychological measures of anxiety and anger were employed. Some of the research findings comparing the three types of violence are summarised in Figure 8.1:

- Social dominance: The most frequent form of violence among them was violence in relation to social dominance (62 per cent). This tended to be accompanied by strong anger feelings. There were few expressions of remorse. Social dominance-motivated violence tends to be associated with high levels of both trait anger and trait aggression – that is, they were characteristically angry and aggressive (as opposed to a response to a particular situation).

Violent for gain (62%)

- High aggressive traits
- High on trait anxiety
- High on anger suppression
- Positive effect from offence
- More likely to expect to be aggressive after drink
- Least likely to be a lone offender
- Age first conviction 11 years
- 90% approx. certain to have previous violent conviction

Violent for social dominance (24%)

- High aggressive traits
- Positive effect from offence
- Lower on trait anxiety
- More likely to expect to be aggressive after drink
- Not likely to be a lone offender
- Age first conviction 11 years
- 90% approx. certain to have previous violent conviction

Violent for self-defence (14%)

- Lower aggressive traits
- Lowest trait anxiety
- The most likely to show remorse
- Less likely to expect to be aggressive after drink
- Most likely to be a lone offender
- Age first conviction 12 years
- 90% approx. certain to have previous violent conviction

Figure 8.1 Different characteristics of different types of violent offenders with alcohol-related offences

- Gain or material goals: A further 24 per cent of the violent offences related to alcohol were violent in the course of achieving their material goals. There was evidence that this type of violent offender make efforts to inhibit their anger since a measure of the inward expression of anger was higher on average for them. In this case the violence was typically both brief and severe.

- Self-defence: The remaining 14 per cent of the violent crimes were for reasons of self-defence. These, perhaps not surprisingly, were lower on trait aggression – that is they are not characteristically aggressive. The violence in this case was associated with both fear and anger.

There were no differences between the three types in terms of the amount of alcohol consumed prior to the offence. There were no differences either in terms of the level of violence shown during the offences of the three different types.

Media influences

Forensic and criminal psychologists have traditionally ignored the role of the media in the genesis of crime. One exception is Blackburn (1993). He reviewed the research evidence on media violence and concluded that the violent content of the media was influential on the violence exhibited by the audience. Harrower (1998), again unusually for the field, devoted considerable space to the topic, though her conclusions are largely rhetorical rather than research-based. If one relied solely on general psychology textbooks rather than on forensic texts, there would be no other conclusion but to accept that media violence has a significant effect on societal violence (e.g. Passer and Smith, 2001). However, there have been a number of reviewers who dispute the media violence causes societal violence notion (e.g. Cumberbatch and Howitt, 1989; Fowles, 1999) though this is far from a universal view (K. Browne, 1999; Pennell and Browne, 1998a). This is not to argue that the media have had no impact on society – that would patently be an absurd suggestion. Nevertheless, apart from laboratory experiments, a range of research employing a variety of methods seems to indicate little or no influence of the media on real-life violence (e.g. Howitt, 1998b). The neglect of media influences by criminologists was noted quite a few years ago (Cumberbatch and Howitt, 1989; Howitt and Cumberbatch, 1975). There are a number of reasons why criminologists have tended to ignore the media as a cause of crime:

- Much of the research on media violence effects is based on laboratory experiments that are of little interest to many researchers.

- Explanations of media violence effects have largely been in terms of social influences rather than the clinical perspectives frequently favoured by some forensic and criminal psychologists.

- Research findings in the field appear somewhat chaotic at first, with some studies suggesting effects and others suggesting no effects. Consequently, the complexity of the research is difficult for non-specialists in media research to comprehend.

- Few media researchers have much knowledge of crime. Indeed, the media violence research very rarely involves acts that are likely to be illegal since the 'victim' has agreed to the aggression or it is directed against an inanimate object or it may be verbal aggression.

Research strategies

What is the case for believing that media violence causes violence in society? This can be broken down into several broad research strategies.

Laboratory experiments

There have been numerous laboratory studies of the effects of media violence. This style of research is still current, for example, in relation to video games (e.g. Ballard and Wiest, 1996). Essentially, and usually, the researchers show one group of participants a violent film/video snippet and another a non-violent snippet. Then their aggression levels as measured by an electric shock machine in the fashion of the classic Milgram experiment on obedience (Milgram, 1974) are compared. Alternatively, as in the case of the Bandura studies of social learning through modelling, children watch a model of knocking over and otherwise maltreating a blow-up plastic clown which is regarded as analogous to other forms of violence (Howitt, 1998b):

- It is clear from meta-analysis (Box 4.2) that overwhelmingly the findings of laboratory experiments suggest the strongest effects of media violence of any studies (Hearold, 1986; Paik and Comstock, 1994; Wood, Wong and Chachere, 1991).

- However, a number of studies have failed to reproduce findings using different methods and, in some cases, the effects are so specific that they are likely to apply only in the laboratory setting. For example, in

Berkowitz's famous studies (Berkowitz and Rawlings, 1963; Berkowitz, Corwin and Heironimus, 1963) the aggression effects claimed were very short lived and applied only to the person who had deliberately insulted participants.

- Howitt (1998b) called for the criminological relevance of research to be the basis for deciding whether research on media violence should be taken seriously by forensic and criminal psychologists. Research on 4-year-olds imitating the modelled, seemingly play aggression against a squeaky blow-up plastic clown that cannot be knocked over without it bouncing back up, is hardly the sort of activity that warrants the description criminal (Howitt, 1998b). Ultimately, the concern with media violence is its influence on the development of serious violence in the audience.

Studies of the development of aggression during childhood

We saw in Chapter 6 that there are quite a few studies of the development of delinquency. Rarely in these studies is media violence included in the research. Of course, this may be oversight or deliberate. The exception to this is the work of Leonard Eron. In the early 1960s he published a study into factors associated with aggression in a large sample of youngsters of about eight years of age (Eron, 1963). Peer and teacher ratings of aggression were obtained as well as a range of other measures. The number of hours of television watched each week was one such measure. In addition, the violence level contained in the child's favourite television programmes was assessed. This was based on the nominations *each child's mother* made about their child's favourite television programmes. The amount of television watched did not correlate positively with the aggression exhibited by the youngsters. Indeed, for boys, the less television watched the more aggressive they were – the reverse of the 'media causes violence' hypothesis. Although, maybe, this ought to have been the end of the story, it was not. The reason was that the *mothers' nominations of the boys' favourite television programmes* were more often violent programmes than were those of the non-aggressive boys. Remember that it was not even the claims of the boys themselves. No such relationship was found for girls. This seems, overall, rather weak evidence that television is responsible for violence.

A few years later, with a number of collaborators, finance was obtained to study the youngsters when they had reached their late teens (Eron *et al.*, 1972). This new stage is probably the most famous. It showed that the violent television variable at age 8 years predicted aggression at age 18 years . . . apparently. One major problem was that this measure at age 18 years was actually retrospective. Peers were rating each other as they were quite a few years earlier. In other words, these were ratings of aggression going back close to the time of the original phase of the study. It is hardly surprising that media use at age eight predicted aggression at age 18 years since aggression at age 18 years was simply not what it appeared to be. There were more follow-ups. The final stage studied the same group when they had reached adulthood. It was possible to check the actual crimes and motor traffic offences they had committed. Remarkably, it looked like adult criminality could be predicted from those ratings of favourite television programmes decades earlier. One interpretation of this is that it is an effect of liking violent television that persists into adult behaviour and results in criminal and other antisocial behaviour (e.g. Newson, 1994a,b). There are other possibilities. For example, we saw in Chapter 6 the continuities between childhood antisocial behaviour and adult antisocial behaviour. Perhaps the mothers, when they nominated their son's television viewing favourites, were conscious that sometimes their son was a little wayward in his behaviour. Thus when they answered about television programmes they nominated a violent programme because this fitted with their son's personality; the boy was not asked. Consequently, this adult behaviour was merely a continuation of the difficulties that some mothers recognised in their sons' behaviour and nothing to do with television at all. If it were television that caused their behaviour, would we not expect the problems to be associated with watching more television, not with watching less?

- Milavsky *et al.* (1982), in a major replication in the style of the above study, found little to support the Eron *et al.* data (Eron *et al.*, 1972; Huesmann and Malamuth, 1986; Lefkowitz *et al.*, 1977).

- A later American study by Huesmann and Eron (1986) failed to detect similar effects for boys. This time, quite unlike the original study, some evidence was found that girls' viewing was associated with aggression.

- International studies of the development of aggression supervised by Eron and his co-workers (Wiegman, Kuttschreuter and Barda, 1992) found, at best,

extremely varied results with very little support other than North American research. There were many zero relationships between television viewing indexes and violence in viewers. Indeed, the relationships were very inconsistent even within countries.

Studies of the criminal statistics

While crime statistics can be difficult to interpret (see Chapter 2), they have been used in two ways to study media effects on societal violence:

- Messner (1986) took the crime statistics of different states of the United States and related them to the public's viewing of media violence obtained from surveys of media use. The areas with the greatest amount of public consumption of media violence then should have the greatest levels of societal violence – according to the 'media violence causes violence' hypothesis. Of course, it is essential in such a study to control/adjust for demographic characteristics when making the comparisons. After that was done thoroughly, Messner (1986) found that the *more* television violence watched the *less* the violence in the community. This is the reverse of expectations if the media violence causes violence hypothesis were true.

- Centerwall (1989, 1993) took a different approach. He studied changes in violent crime rates in the United States for the period before the introduction of television to many years after its introduction. Previous research had found no immediate impact of the introduction of television on US violent crime rates (Hennigan *et al.*, 1982). Nevertheless, Centerwall argues that one would not expect effects until several years later when children have grown into adolescents – the time when they are most likely to demonstrate violence. This is a reasonable idea although many other researchers had studied the immediate effects of witnessing media violence and found effects in the laboratory. At first sight, the crime data appear to support this thesis – a rapid rise in societal violence occurred several years after the introduction of television in the United States. In comparison, in South Africa, where television was not introduced until many years later, there was no such rapid rise at that time. Howitt (1998b) applied Centerwall's idea to Great Britain where television was introduced as a mass medium during the 1950s. He found that there was a steady growth in violent crime during the period researched by Centerwall but no rapid rise at the time predicted by Centerwall's argument. In other words, there is no general effect of television violence on violent crime statistics, which casts considerable doubt on Centerwall's interpretation of the US data.

Studies of delinquent offenders

There have been a small number of studies of the media use of delinquent offenders (Hagell and Newburn, 1994; Halloran, Brown and Chaney, 1970; Kruttschnitt, Heath and Ward, 1986). They have generally failed to produce evidence of the influence of media violence on offenders. One study found an association between serious delinquency and television (Browne and Pennell, 1998; Pennell and Browne, 1998b). They took a sample of violent teenage boys in a young offenders' institute for violent offending. The young offenders were compared with appropriate control groups – including a similar group of incarcerated young offenders but *not* convicted of violence and community controls of the same age range, sex and so forth:

- There were differences in the media use of the incarcerated groups and the community groups, such as that the offenders tended to prefer violent videos though they also seemed to like soap operas more.
- There were psychological differences such as the lower level of moral reasoning in offender groups which might have contributed to their offending (see Chapter 6).
- Physical abuse by parents was far commoner in the childhood of the violent sample.
- When experience of childhood abuse was taken into account, any differences between the groups in terms of liking violent videos disappeared. Thus their violence is the result of their abusive childhood and their interest in violent video is a consequence of and not a cause of their violence. Abuse creates violent youngsters who then use media violence more frequently than non-abused youngsters.

Does media violence make violent crime?

The answer to the question of whether media violence causes societal violence must concentrate on the criminologically relevant aspects of aggression – criminal violence. This means that much of the voluminous literature on media violence effects is irrelevant as it does not deal with criminal acts. One should also bear in mind that we know a lot about the development of criminality and criminal violence in particular from longitudinal studies of development from childhood into adulthood (see Chapter 6). It is clear that early experience, especially experience of inadequate parenting broadly defined, leads to problem children, problem teenagers and problem adults. With these matters in consideration, the following seems to be a reasonable assessment of the media violence issue as far as it affects criminal violent acts:

- Virtually no developmental evidence exists concerning the influence of the media on criminality. The studies that deal with the media tend to be associated almost exclusively with the work of Leonard Eron and his co-workers. Despite being frequently cited in the debate on media violence effects, the original findings are inconsistent and apply to boys and only in terms of their mothers' assessments of their favourite television programmes. When the amount of television viewed is considered, the evidence suggests that the more television watched, the less impact it has on aggressive behaviour! Later studies fail to reproduce these findings, or find similar outcomes but for girls and not boys, which is the reverse of the original findings, or produce inconsistent outcomes for different parts of the world. In short, there is less than convincing evidence of the effects of media violence.
- Crime statistics do not show a relationship with the levels of violence viewed in communities – the reverse trend exists in fact. Crime statistics in the United States have been interpreted as demonstrating a delayed effect of the introduction of violent media but this claim has not been substantiated for the United Kingdom.
- Violent delinquents do seem to have a preference for certain sorts of programme including violent video. Despite this, the biggest factor in their violence is their abuse by their parents in childhood. Once this is taken into account, then their media consumption

can be regarded as no different from non-violent controls.

In summary, a forensic and criminal psychologist should exercise great caution before assuming a role of the media in generating violent criminality. Although there have been claims that offenders have been influenced by movies, no court in the United States has accepted such arguments (Lande, 1993). Nevertheless, there have been accusations that movies such as *Child's Play 3* (directed by Jack Bender in 1991) and *Natural Born Killers* (directed by Oliver Stone in 1994) influenced youngsters to kill, the latter in very substantial numbers. However, the evidence in support is weak. For example, whether the culprits actually saw the movie in question is doubtful in some cases and that an accused person attempts to excuse their acts by blaming a movie might be expected. It is not the sort of rigorous evidence that forensic and criminal psychologists normally seek. The inhibition of aggression is socialised from early in childhood, long before the child is capable of giving much attention to television programmes. Failures of parenting at an early age have clearly been shown to be associated with later criminality and violence.

Another, totally independent review of the evidence (Felson, 1996) makes a number of related points. They are worth mentioning as they reinforce some of the comments made above:

- Violent offenders tend to be versatile offenders – they do not confine their activities to violent crime but commit all types of crime. This is somewhat incompatible with the idea that violent offenders have a problem caused by their violence socialisation, either via the media or any other source.

- The contents of the media concerning violence do not appear to give a radically different message about violence than any other source of socialisation. The media give much the same message about when it is appropriate to use violence and when it is not appropriate. The one area where Felson makes an exception is illegitimate violence that is by definition unacceptable. The media show this sort of violence being punished more so than does any other source of socialisation.

Although they were not the first to identify this, Savage and Yancey (2008) express surprise that out of the thousands of studies relating media exposure to aggressive behaviour, very few have studied criminal violence. There are probably far less than 40 such studies even if one is generous with the criteria of what is criminal violence. Savage and Yancey included studies which used measures of exposure to media violence about whose validity they had doubts. For example, they used studies, among others, which employed violence ratings of the individual's favourite programmes even though they say that studies using violence ratings of general viewing would be preferable. For the study they incorporated into their analysis, when they estimated the effect size of studies they found no significant effects of media violence on real criminal violence for studies using female participants or studies combining female and male students. Even for male participants alone, the size of the effect of television violence on real-life criminal violence was tiny at 0.07 which is virtually no effect. Even this, they claim, was a highly biased estimate because some important control variables were missing from some studies.

If that were not enough, Ferguson (2009) launched a technically sophisticated critique of the same body of research which Savage and Yancey had meta-analysed. But he goes further in terms of the forensic implications of the media/violence research debate. He points out that forensic psychologists can (and have been) asked to provide sound information concerning media violence research. He mentions two main contexts for this: as an expert witness, and when speaking to the media or more directly to the public. Ferguson says that the psychological community has failed to properly inform the legal system and the public about the many significant difficulties with media violence effects research. He writes, 'I submit here that psychologists have an ethical responsibility to provide full disclosure of research limitations to the courts and public so that an informed conclusion can be reached' (p. 117). This failure by psychologists has a long history.

Similar arguments have been made about the impact of violent video games on the user's violent behaviour as were made about the effects of media violence. Ferguson, Rueda, Cruz, Ferguson, Fritz and Smith (2008) discuss the issue and mention that meta-analyses (see Box 4.2) of research studies into the effects of violent games on interpersonal violence have found very small effects of about 1–4 per cent of the variance in interpersonal violence being accounted for by playing violent video games. But they say that these are overestimates because unpublished studies tend to have insignificant findings and were excluded from these meta-analyses. When unpublished studies are incorporated then the relationship effectively becomes zero.

Theories of homicide

Societal level theory

There is a tendency to assume that violence can be explained only in terms of the psychology of individuals. Most of us do not murder so there must be something 'odd' about murderers. For most homicides, there is little to implicate psychiatric factors (see also Chapter 21), which indicates that other factors need to be taken into account. This is not to suggest that researchers can ignore psychiatric and other individual factors in violent crime. The evidence that homicide rates tend to increase during a war and show different characteristics from those perpetrated previously shows that broad societal events may significantly affect the criminal acts of individuals (Pozgain, Mandic and Barkic, 1998). Nevertheless, psychiatric factors simply cannot be discounted. For example, Steck (1998) found that spouse murderers in a German sample characteristically had a history more likely to feature a psychologically deviant development, especially involving psychiatric disorder and if they are disengaged socially. Nevertheless, this does not mean that other levels of explanation of extreme violent crime are wrong.

One of the more interesting societal level suggestions is Leyton's (1986) view that multiple murders (i.e. those in which the killer kills more than one individual) may be explained in terms of social structure. A problem in understanding multiple killing (including serial killing) is that the targets of such crimes tend not to be a random sample of potential victims. Instead, victims tend to have particular characteristics. Leyton's key insight was that he realised that multiple killing is not merely a recent phenomenon but one with roots in history. He identified three major periods in which multiple killing was common. Then he realised that these three periods varied markedly in terms of the social characteristics of the killers and the victims. The historical epochs in question are the *pre-industrial period*, the *industrial period* and the *modern period*. The typical killer during these times and the typical victim are given in Figure 8.2.

What appears to be happening, very broadly, is that the killers have been of decreasing social class since the

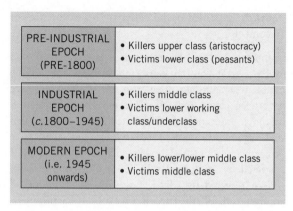

Figure 8.2 Leyton's epochs of murder

pre-industrial period. In contrast, their victims have become of higher social class. In the pre-industrial period the typical multiple murderer was Gilles de Rais, a French nobleman who killed peasant children by the hundred. The typical multiple killer of the industrial period was a middle-class individual who killed housemaids or prostitutes. Finally, in the modern period the multiple killer is largely of a lower social status than the victim. If this is true, then the question is why do these changes occur? Basically, Leyton argued that multiple killings are indicative of *homicidal protest*. This means essentially that at different times in history a (social) class comes under threat from another social class. The general dissatisfaction, concern and anxiety felt by the threatened class becomes expressed by a few of the discontented class through multiple murders of the threatening class. In other words, the murders are symbolic of structural discontent. The epochs differ in the focus of this discontent:

- In the *pre-industrial period* there was challenge to the social order by the peasant classes as well as merchant classes. Revolts and the like illustrate the challenge.
- In the *industrial period*, the middle classes held their position through a 'moral' superiority over the working class. Consequently, the threat to their social position came largely from those in society who most threatened that moral order. Prostitution was by its nature a threat to the family and the patriarchal social organisation of the family. Women who engaged in sexual activity willingly outside marriage would threaten the moral basis of family life. Housemaids, of course, were the lowest level of employment; the sexuality of single women was also a threat. They were also in the sector of employment that somewhat

morally disgraced young women could be encouraged to enter if their chances of marriage had been sullied. Killing such women symbolically reinforced the moral superiority of the middle class. Jack the Ripper would appear to represent this type of killer – if he were a member of the middle class rather than royalty, of course, in the light of some claims about the Ripper's identity.

- In the *modern period*, according to Leyton, the challenge to the social order comes from the changed social order in which rigid class structures have loosened and upward mobility is seen as a realistic ambition of the lower social classes. It is when those who expect to progress feel thwarted that *homicidal protest* comes into play. Hence students may be victims of such protest since they have the privileges that the disaffected feel should have been theirs.

There are a number of problems with this theory. The historical record concerning crime, especially in the pre-industrial period, may be inadequate. Can the findings concerning the modern period be replicated away from the North American context? Grover and Soothill (1999) took Leyton's ideas and attempted to apply them to serial killing in recent British criminal history. A total of 17 serial killers (three or more victims) were found for the period beginning 1960. According to Grover and Soothill, it was clear that the victims were simply not middle-class people as the theory predicts that they should be. They were in fact typical of the weak and powerless groups in society – gay men, women, children, young adults and pensioners. The serial killers included Ian Brady, Myra Hindley and Beverly Allitt who killed children, and Dennis Nilsen, Colin Ireland and Peter Moore who killed gay men. While at least a substantial number of the killers could be described as working class, the data do not support the idea of a class-based homicidal protest. Grover and Soothill suggest that the idea of homicidal protest may be useful if the idea of its basis in social class conflicts is abandoned. It should be replaced by consideration of broader social relations which make certain groups vulnerable.

Psychological disposition theories

There is no easy way of explaining homicide. While it is tempting to regard murderers as exceptionally violent personalities suffering from extremes of psychopathology, this is to ignore the large number of killers who are non-aggressive and not suffering from an identifiable psychopathology. Murderers have been divided into various typologies. After studying murderers in a psychiatric prison hospital, Blackburn (1971) suggested that there are four types of murder:

- depressive
- over-controlled repressors (of aggression)
- paranoid-aggressive
- psychopathic.

This pattern has been found in a non-psychiatric group of offenders so it is not merely the result of the extreme psychiatric difficulties of a selected group of offenders.

Biro, Vuckovic and Duric (1992) carried out a standardised interview with Yugoslavian men convicted of homicide offences. As in the above research, the MMPI (Minnesota Multiphasic Personality Inventory) scores of the men were an important aspect of the categorisation. Four categories were identified:

- Normal profiles (28 per cent).
- Hypersensitive-aggressive (49 per cent): this group consists of people with the characteristics of being easily offended, prone to impulsive aggressive outbursts and intolerant of frustration. They are very rigid, uncooperative and permanently dissatisfied with things.
- Psychopathic (17 per cent): these tend to score highly on emotional instability, impulsivity and immaturity. They tend to have poor control of their aggression.
- Psychotic (5 per cent): these seem to be 'mistakes of the system' since they are individuals who show extreme psychiatric signs and would normally have been confined to a special psychiatric unit. Their crimes appear to be bizarre such as the man who cooked his own child in a pot. These offenders had not been psychiatrically evaluated before being sentenced.

The percentages in each category seem to indicate that only in a large minority of the cases is the issue primarily to do with aggression. A quarter plus show normal profiles overall. The normal personality category seems to act aggressively out of a situational pressure, not because its basic personality structure leads to aggression.

Socio-biological theory

At the opposite pole, there are biologically based ideas about murder, which on the surface would appear to be as different as possible from the societal approaches such as that just described. While it is tempting to believe that there may be some biological factor (e.g. brain dysfunction) in extreme violence such as serial killing, the research evidence in its favour is best described as minimal (Coleman and Norris, 2000). There are two important issues here:

- Research on the biological basis of criminality, and criminal violence in particular, is somewhat rare and patchy in scope. There is a lack of a coherent body of knowledge as a consequence. This situation is no help to forensic and criminal psychologists.

- Biological factors are generally beyond the scope of psychologists to change materially.

The typical biological approach seeks to find the biological 'defects' which result in criminal behaviours.

When one considers the topic of violence, it is tempting to point to the statistics that show that violent crime is an overwhelmingly male activity. This, surely, must be irrefutable evidence of a firm biological basis to violent crime. A little care is needed. Bjorqkvist (1994) argued that men and women do not differ in their aggressiveness. What is different is the way in which it is expressed. Bjorqkvist goes so far as to indicate that the claim that men are the more aggressive is nonsensical. Aggression is largely seen from a male perspective that equates aggression with physical aggression. It is this male perspective that has dominated research on human aggression. If men are the most aggressive, then the fact that same-sex aggression (female vs. female, male vs. male) seems to be more common than cross-sex (male vs. female) is difficult to explain. Bjorqkvist argues that the physically weaker sex, women, is likely to learn different aggressive strategies from those used by the physically stronger sex, men (Bjorkqvist and Niemela, 1992; Bjorkqvist, Osterman and Kaukiainen, 1992). It is inappropriate then to extrapolate from animal studies to human aggression since animal aggression is mostly physical. For adults, the reasonable assumption is that physical aggression is the least common form of aggression.

The putative link between testosterone and aggression is very much a dubious proposition for humans. According to Bjorkqvist, the closer an animal species is to humankind the less is the link between testosterone level and aggressiveness. Injecting testosterone experimentally, which should, if the theory is correct, lead to higher aggression levels, does not have clear-cut results. Sometimes such experiments seem to suggest no link

between the testosterone and aggression. Edwards (1969) and Edwards and Herndon (1970) found that female mice given the male hormone androgen at birth grew up to be more aggressive as adults than non-treated mice. While this appears to support the view that maleness = aggression, perhaps this is not the case. Similar female mice given the female hormone oestrogen at birth also tended to fight rather more than non-treated mice as adults. Bjorkqvist proposed an effect/danger ratio theory for human aggression. This is based on the notion that there is a subjective estimation of the ratio between the effect of the intended strategy (such as physical aggression) divided by the danger involved of such a strategy. This operates in such a way that risk is minimised while the effect of the strategy is maximised. Hence, women have a greater risk if they engage in physical aggression than men so they may prefer other strategies. There is some evidence that aggression in males is expressed directly (perhaps in the form of fighting) whereas aggression in females is expressed indirectly (perhaps in the form of maliciously telling a teacher something).

Bjorkqvist and Niemela (1992) had peers rate Finnish seven-year-olds, indicating what each child did when angry. Direct means were kicks/strikes, swearing, chasing the other child and pushes/shoves. Indirect responses included gossiping, becoming friendly with another child in revenge, suggestions that the other child should be shunned in some way. The study was essentially repeated with a similar sample of 11-year-old and 15-year-old adolescents. At the younger age, it was clear that boys used direct forms of aggression more than did girls. There was no difference in terms of indirect aggression. But during adolescence girls were still using direct aggression less than did boys, whereas they used more indirect forms of aggression. The girls seem to manipulate their friendship networks as a means of effecting some of this indirect aggression. Similar findings were found concerning indirect aggression in females cross-culturally (Osterman, Bjorkqvist and Lagerspetz, 1998). Others have found that relational victimisation of this sort (telling lies about another person so they will be disliked or leaving another person out of social activities when one is angry with them) is more characteristic of girls (Crick and Bigbee, 1998) even at the pre-school age level (Crick, Casas and Mosher, 1997). There is evidence that girls see social aggression as little or no different from physical aggression in terms of its hurtfulness (Galen and Underwood, 1997). Thus if aggression is seen as the intention to hurt or harm another then the use of indirect aggression by females relates more closely to physical aggression. It might be argued that it is physical aggression that is punished in law, not the indirect forms of aggression. This is to ignore, for example, libel and slander laws which are clearly about controlling what might be described as verbal social attacks on individuals. Lindeman, Harakka and Keltikangas-Jarvinen (1997) had Finnish adolescents rate themselves in terms of their strategies in conflict situations. In this context, in late adolescence, the preferred mode for male adolescents was to join in with any verbal aggression. In contrast, girls said that they would adopt a strategy of withdrawal from the situation or used a more social model of response such as 'I would clearly tell the backbiters that their behavior is mean and I would ask them to stop' (p. 343). Of course, some have argued that direct forms of physical aggression are becoming more characteristic of females. Much of the physical aggression between girls concerns their relationships with males and threats to those relationships (Artz, 1998). As such, the aggression is regarded as the right thing to do.

It is worthwhile noting Crick's (1997) findings concerning social-psychological adjustment as assessed through self-ratings and teacher ratings. Gender normative aggression was associated with good adjustment ratings. Boys who engaged in aggression through relationships and girls who were overtly aggressive tended to be less well adjusted. In other words, there is evidence of the deeply seated nature of these gender differences in aggression.

There is a substantially different perspective concerning gender differences in aggression. Daly and Wilson (1988) put forward a socio-biological explanation of homicide. They worked primarily on the basis of the following established socio-biological principles:

- The process of natural selection shaped human nature: that is, random genetic variation produces diversity of offspring and those best fitted to survive tend to pass on their genetic material. While the ideas are essentially those of Charles Darwin, Herbert Spencer's phrase 'survival of the fittest' is the most familiar way to describe it. In this context, survival is survival of the genes or species rather than a particular individual. Fitness really refers to those who are able to transmit their genes – individuals who do not win out in mating may live to an old age, but they have not passed on their genes so they were not fit in terms of the species.

- Daly and Wilson use the term 'adaptively constructed' to describe the way we are – that is, we are what we are because that is what allowed the species to survive. There is a competition in mating whereby the fittest (best genes) tend to be transmitted to the next generation.

- People (as well as other creatures) have evolved such that they spend much of their efforts on the posterity of their genes: that is, sex is not some sort of secondary motivation that comes into play when hunger and thirst, for example, have been satiated. It is much more to the forefront than that.

- Homicide, like any other field of human activity, should show characteristics that reflect in some way the characteristics of how we have been adaptively constructed.

- Daly and Wilson accept that there is cultural variation over and above socio-biological influences on homicide. Some cultures seem to exhibit higher levels of killings than others. Nevertheless, part of the pattern of homicides is socio-biologically determined.

These basic ideas, in themselves, did not take Daly and Wilson far. Something else needs to be considered. They recognised that much of the available statistical evidence was incapable of answering crucial questions about homicide. Furthermore, the available database needed reanalysis to provide helpful answers. To illustrate, in the context of the family, socio-biological thinking would suggest that both parents should have an interest in ensuring that their offspring (their genes) survive. At the same time, Daly and Wilson argue that we are often encouraged to believe that the family is a dangerously violent place in which the offspring are at considerable risk. In other words, rather than preserve their genes, parents may kill their offspring, thus destroying the future potential of their genes. This is certainly the impression created by the research literature on family violence. There is a problem with this. When homicide of children is subdivided into killing by natural biological parents and by step-parents, interesting findings emerge. Put another way, natural parents kill their offspring rather rarely in comparison with step-parents who kill the children of the family relatively frequently. Step-parents are not destroying their own distinctive genes by killing, say, a child fathered by the woman's previous partner.

Another example is their argument concerning intra-sexual homicide – that is, men killing men, women killing women. The genes of men, they argue, are best helped to survive by fertilising as many women as possible. Hence other men are a handicap to genetic survival since they monopolise women. Women help their genes survive best by protecting and nurturing their offspring. Thus Daly and Wilson argue that men should kill men much more frequently than women kill women. The data on homicide suggest that this is the case. Indeed, young men are much more in competition for mating than older men – and crime statistics suggest that young men kill each other much more frequently. There are a number of matters to bear in mind:

- The socio-biological approach, since it attempts to explain society from the point of view of biology, competes with social explanations of the same phenomena. For example, step-parents may murder children of the family more often simply because the stresses in step-parent families are likely to be greater. Furthermore, bonds between step-parents and step-children may have had less opportunity to develop. It is difficult to decide which is the better explanation. Socio-biological approaches tend not to have any verifiable genetic evidence: both they and societal explanations rely on observations of the same social processes.

- Socio-biological approaches to a variety of social phenomena tend to be a little unhelpful because of the assumption that what is genetically fixed becomes incorporated into social structure. Forensic and criminal psychologists are more interested in changing individuals rather than in regarding their criminality, for example, as a built-in feature.

- Whatever the long-term value of Daly and Wilson's approach in helping us to understand homicide, it teaches a valuable lesson about crime statistics: that is, statistical compilations of data may sometimes hide important relationships simply because very different things are classified together in published tables.

The multi-factorial approach

Generally speaking, most forensic and criminal psychologists would take the view that extreme acts of violence, including homicide, have multiple causation. Rarely is a single factor seen as sufficient to explain violent crime. Since extreme violence, such as serial killing, is such a rare phenomenon, it is unlikely that a single factor could be identified which is only associated with serial killing. Extremely violent behaviour may, then, best be understood by the application of the sort of multi-factorial framework suggested by Gresswell and Hollin

(1994, 1997). This is illustrated in Figure 8.3. Basically it involves three levels of factor – *predisposing factors*, *maintenance factors* and *situational/triggering factors*. These three types should be considered as part of the explanation of a homicide. No particular specific factor is assumed to be essential to homicide. Nevertheless, the accumulating pattern of factors when applied to a particular case may help understand that case. It is clear from Figure 8.3 that serial killing is rare because the contributing factors in themselves may not be common and the presence of several of them together may be a rare situation.

Equally, when considering the many frequent minor assaults that pervade the criminal statistics concerning violence, we might look for commonly occurring factors. However, the likely influence of factors acting separately may not be the same as factors acting in combination. For example, Haapasalo (1999) examined intergenerational cycles of physical abuse by taking a Finnish offender sample. He collected a variety of information about physical abuse as well as other matters such as marital conflict and involvement with the child protection services. In a sense, studies such as this are particularly important for forensic and criminal psychologists since they are about their main clientele. Studies involving the general population are less relevant to their work and may show less strong or even dissimilar trends. Following a complex statistical analysis (Lisrel), it became clear that the paths leading to the sons being physically abused in childhood can have unexpected twists. As shown in Figure 8.4, there was clear evidence that the variable *mother physically abused in childhood* leads fairly directly to her son being *physically abused in childhood*. This is probably very much what one might expect on the basis of the assumption that aggression is, in part, socially learnt.

What of the influence of another variable *economic stress* (financial and related difficulties)? We would expect, surely, that the more stress on the mother the more likely she would be to physically abuse her children since stress makes her irritable and moody, among other things. Take a look again at Figure 8.4. Starting with the factor *economic stress*, we can see that it leads to a higher level of *maternal problems*. But the most likely route from there is involvement of the child protection services for some reason. This might include, for example, some sort of respite help for the mother. The path from *maternal problems* to the son being *physically abused in childhood* is the reverse of expectations: that is, the greater the maternal problems the *less* the likelihood that her son

PREDISPOSING FACTORS

1) A failure of normal bonding with parents or other primary care-givers, leading to a lack of similar feelings towards others.
2) Traumatic experiences are not dealt with properly, as a consequence.
3) Fantasies about the traumatic experience may develop and dominate.
4) Through fantasy, feelings of power, which are lacking through poor interpersonal skills and so forth, can be experienced and so the fantasy becomes increasingly rewarding.

MAINTENANCE FACTORS

1) Cognitive inhibitory factors: most children gradually learn not to act aggressively through normal socialisation processes. A child with unsatisfactory bonding and social relationships may fail to learn.
2) Cognitive facilitative processes: the tendency towards fantasy may allow the use of violent fantasy to deal with situations.
3) Operant processes: the feeling of power experienced through fantasy is rewarding, encouraging further fantasy. It also serves to isolate the individual from the bad aspects of life.

SITUATIONAL/TRIGGERING FACTORS

1) These are the factors that encourage the acting out of the fantasy against a real person.
2) Particularly influential may be stressful situations such as financial problems, employment problems and relationship problems.

Figure 8.3 Multi-factorial model of serial killing

Source: Gresswell, D.M. and Hollin, C.R. (1994) 'Multiple Murder: A Review' *British Journal of Criminology* 34, 1–14. Reproduced by permission of Oxford University Press

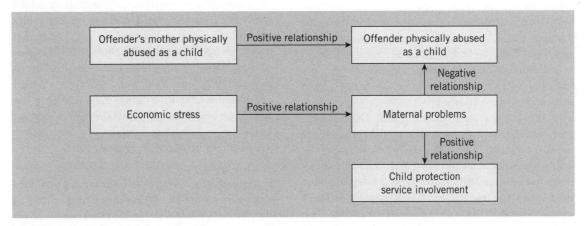

Figure 8.4 The relationship between cycles of abuse and economic stress

would be physically abused in childhood. Whether the mothers regard economic stress as a warning sign that they are not coping cannot be addressed simply from these data. Nevertheless, this is feasible, which may make them more inclined to seek the help of social services. This completely unexpected finding tells us to avoid making simplistic assumptions about how social and psychological factors influence violent behaviour.

Domestic violence: forensic issues

Much of this chapter has dealt with explanations of extreme acts of violence. It is important for a forensic and criminal psychologist to understand the range of theoretical approaches that can be brought to the discipline. At the same time, forensic and criminal psychology is not merely a branch of psychological research and theory, it is also a practical discipline that seeks to help deal with otherwise tricky questions for the criminal justice system. Let us take a particularly difficult issue – that of domestic violence within a family. There are a number of aspects to this. One is that this is the sort of situation with which social workers, the police and sometimes psychologists may have to deal. So what can we say if we know that a man at 25 Beeches Road has split up with his partner? There are children in the household and social workers insist that he lives at another address. He attempts to obtain visitation rights to have the children at his new home at the weekend. The mother objects. Her reason is that he has been violent to her on numerous occasions and that every time there has been a meeting in the past, the children have become distressed. Called in to give advice or even evidence to court, just what practical suggestions might a psychologist make?

Common notions suggest that violence is a trait in some people, and that such people act aggressively in a wide variety of situations. The suggestion is sometimes heard that a particular person has a short fuse, for example: that is, the person is readily provoked to be aggressive. Unfortunately, one cannot rely on folklore as a definitive treatise on human behaviour. Put more formally, the issue is one of the co-occurrence of spousal abuse and physical child abuse – if the one is present, how likely is it that the other is also present? This has been sporadically an issue for research since the 1970s when it was first suggested that if there was spousal abuse in the family the risk of that child being abused was increased. It was not until the 1990s that it became recognised that child abuse and spousal abuse were simply different aspects of family violence (Appel and Holden, 1998). This has clear implications for forensic issues such as whether spouses who batter their partners are fit to be the custodial parent on divorce or separation. According to Appel and Holden, what at first appears to be a relatively simple question becomes a complex one when the research literature is addressed. Issues include the following:

- The criteria employed to decide whether spouse abuse and child abuse had occurred. The mother's report, the father's report, the child's report and professional assessment may all be expected to produce different findings.

- The sorts of act classified as abuse may profoundly influence rates of co-occurrence. For example, if a gentle slap of a child were to be regarded as physical child abuse, then since a gentle slap is a very frequent form of disipline in families, it is extremely likely that a man who has abused his partner will also have abused the child.

- What period of time was covered by the retrospective reports? The greater the time period the greater co-occurrence.

Appel and Holden reviewed studies of different types of sample: community (or non-clinical) samples, samples of battered women and samples of maltreated children. Self-reports, agency records, hospital records and clinical impressions were included. The detail of the outcomes of the studies differed quite widely although it is fair to suggest that, generally, co-occurrence does take place but the magnitude of this varies:

- Most of the work on community samples (i.e. general population samples) has been carried out by Gelles (e.g. Gelles, 1979; Gelles and Cornell, 1985). They use the *Conflict Tactics Scale*, which consists of a list of ways in which conflict between family members has been resolved during the year. Figures on violent means of conflict resolution give a 6 per cent occurrence figure for spousal and child abuse. This increases substantially when the period under consideration is extended. If violent methods of conflict resolution are considered for any time during the relationship (i.e. if violence ever occurred), then the figures increase: 11–21 per cent overlap depending on the study in question (Silvern, Karyl and Landis, 1995).

- Studies using data from battered women showed bigger variation. Overlap between spousal and child abuse varied from 10–100 per cent. The studies using the Conflict Tactics Scale tended to suggest 51–72 per cent overlap between spousal and child abuse. Of course, battered women as a group might be expected to produce more extreme tendencies than those in the general public. For example, the battered women may go to the shelters not for their own safety but for the safety of their child.

- Child abuse reported to the authorities gave figures of co-occurrence varying between 26 per cent and 59 per cent.

In other words, just basing one's assessment of risk to the child on the fact that the spouse claims to have been beaten seems unsatisfactory. The increase of risk is very difficult to know with any precision. Furthermore, we have already seen that the risk of violence by step-parents is greater than the risk from natural parents: that is, there is more to put into the equation than the act of spousal abuse alone.

There are still further considerations. Appel and Holden argue that the structure of violence within families falls into a variety of types which are, at least, theoretically feasible:

- Single perpetrator model: the man beats the woman and the child.

- Sequential perpetrator model: the man beats the woman who then beats the child.

- Dual perpetrator model: the man beats the woman and the woman also beats the child.

- Marital violence model: the woman and man beat each other and both beat the child.

- Family dysfunction model: all three family members beat each other – including the child who beats the adult perpetrators.

There is at least some evidence in favour of each model. Each of them may apply at least in a proportion of cases. So, if we do not understand the family dynamics in more detail, we may make unfounded assumptions. The child may be at risk from the mother as well in some types of family.

Quite clearly, simplistic common-sense assumptions about violence may prove woefully inadequate in the setting of professional forensic and criminal psychology work. Confirmation of this comes from US data on homicide of partners. Estimates suggest that, annually, a minimum of 2.5 million women are battered by their partner/spouse. Twelve hundred are killed annually by their partners/spouses. Thus domestic violence is quite a poor predictor of murderous outcomes given the ratio of abuse to deaths, statistically stated: there is a 2,100 to 1 chance of a death compared with the numbers of battering households. What makes this an even more formidable statistic is that about half of such homicides were not preceded by violence/battering at any stage (Walker and Meloy, 1998). While it is clear that domestic violence is predictive of homicide, at least weakly, just about half of the spousal murders are not associated with abuse. See Chapter 27 on risk assessment for more details.

Domestic violence by women against men

Radical changes in the ways police forces around the world deal with domestic violence have occurred in the past 20 or so years. The police attitude has moved from that of regarding violence within the household as a domestic matter and not normally one for police involvement to one where they are proactive about the issue. This is partly the result of the massive changes in gender relations brought about by feminist activists in the 1970s and 1980s especially. It would seem obvious that most domestic violence is the actions of men against women. Certainly the public seem to believe so. In a study in the United States, Stalans (1996) found that the public estimated that two-thirds of the victims of domestic violence where the police are called out were the woman, 17 per cent thought that the victim was the man and another 17 per cent saw the injuries as being to both. The message is clear from this. Women are overwhelmingly the injured victims of domestic violence.

However, one researcher in particular, Murray Straus, seems to take a different view. Straus was one of the first researchers to carry out major studies into the extent of domestic violence. His work with Gelles (e.g. Gelles and Straus, 1979) was profoundly influential partly because it exposed the extent of the problem. Few would doubt the impact of this work. The method used by these authors was the Conflict Tactics Scale which, as we have seen above, has been extensively used by researchers in the field of family violence (Straus *et al.*, 1996). As we have already seen, the scale does not directly ask about the extent of violence but, instead, how conflicts are resolved within the family. Various means of dealing with conflict are considered ranging from verbal conflict resolution techniques (e.g. 'discussed issues calmly' or 'got someone to help settle things') to minor physical aggression (e.g. threw something, pushed or slapped), to severe physical aggression (e.g. burned, used a knife, or fired a gun).

Straus (1992) argued that one of the aspects of his work that has been neglected was the extent and seriousness of the violence of women against men. Numerous

US family violence surveys, he argues, have demonstrated the extent to which violence by women against men is almost as common as violence by men against women. The concept of 'husband-battering' (Steinmetz, 1977), he suggests, has been ridiculed and not taken seriously. Some have taken issue with Straus on the basis of what the Conflict Tactics Scale measures. For example, the measure may be so general that it fails to differentiate effectively between a woman slapping a man once and a man beating a woman on several occasions. In addition, based simply on the 'act' it is not possible to know the motivation for the violence. For example, if a person slaps another, one cannot assume that it was done as part of an unprovoked attack or in retaliation. However, there have been claims that violence by women is treated more seriously in the legal system than that by men. For example, it has been suggested that homicides of the female partners of men are relatively leniently treated compared with where a woman kills her male partner (Roberts, 1995).

The issues can be regarded as boiling down to the question of whether female domestic violence against men is symmetrical or asymmetrical (Dobash and Dobash, 2004). By this is meant the extent to which violence against men by women has the same damaging consequences as that by men against women. Even if women are as likely to resort to violence as men, does it, for example, lead to the same level of serious injuries? Straus's view, therefore, is an example of the symmetrical argument. Dobash and Dobash, in an attempt to shed light on what they regard as a puzzling issue, studied the reports of men and women involved in court cases involving domestic violence – the men had all been convicted of an assault on their female partner. As one might expect, there was a difference between the reports of men and women concerning issues of domestic violence, so it is difficult to summarise some of the trends exactly. A number of things were clear in terms of violence against partners:

- Women were less likely to have acted violently against their partner in the previous year.

- Men were more likely to have carried out a series of violent acts than were the women.

- Men were much more likely to punch, scratch, slap, kick the body, use objects as a weapon and so forth. In the extreme example, men were about 50 times more likely to choke their partner. There was no category

of violent act in which the rates by women exceeded those by men.

- The injuries sustained by women were much more common – bruises, black eyes, cuts, scratches, split lips, fractured teeth or bones, and unconsciousness.

- Ratings of seriousness of the violence were on average higher for men's violence than for women's violence. Somewhere between a quarter and a half of the ratings for men's violence were in the serious or very serious category whereas only about 1 in 20 of the acts perpetrated by women were placed in these extreme categories.

Although this is rather convincing evidence of the dangerousness of men's domestic violence, it does not mean that we can totally disregard those cases were women are initiating extremely serious acts of violence against their partner. And the issue does not stop there. We can turn to stalking, which frequently follows the break-up of a relationship.

Stalking: what sort of crime?

Stalking may be motivated by a number of different factors and may be of a number of different types. What is important to realise is the extent to which it arises out of intimate relationships and involves people previously close to the victim. The origins of anti-stalking legislation in some ways belie its true nature. Initially, it was the stalking of the famous which provided the impetus for legislation. Among the famous victims of stalking are the British television presenter Jill Dando, actress Brooke Shields who was stalked for 15 years, the actress Jodie Foster – stalked by John Hinckley who shot President Ronald Reagan in the belief that this would gain her attention – David Letterman, Madonna and Rebecca Schaeffer who was killed by her stalker in 1989. Some of these could be described as cases of *erotomania* which is obsessive, excessive, unwanted or delusional love according to Fitzgerald and Seeman (2002). So in these instances, it would seem an appropriate description since the offender suffered from a delusional belief that the celebrity in question was in love with them – examples of this would include the Madonna, David Letterman and the Rebecca Schaeffer examples. Erotomania is defined as a delusional disorder in the *Diagnostic and Statistical Manual* (American Psychiatric Association, 2000). Part of the diagnosis is that there is little or no prior contact between the erotomaniac and their target. While these high-profile examples have been important in developing anti-stalking legislation, they do not define the typical stalking offence or offender. Stalking had not really been established as criminal behaviour until after the Rebecca Schaeffer killing.

Many of the people who become fixated on public figures are severely mentally ill and often this fixation is associated with mental illness (Mullen *et al.*, 2009). For example, Ronald Dixon went to Buckingham Palace and claimed to be King Ronald, the son of Edward VIII and the rightful king of England. He said that he would kill Queen Elizabeth II because she had had him tortured by an electronic crown put into his head which prevented him sleeping. After being legally sectioned to the local mental health services he was eventually discharged. Weeks later he stabbed a mental health worker to death. His response to all questions in court was 'King!'. Relatively little is known about the risk factors for violence perpetrated against important people. James *et al.* (2010) employed what they term 'proxies' for violence against the British Royal Family. By this is meant examples of inappropriate approaches to the Royal Family such as unauthorised entry to royal events by deception. The list of 'proxies' was obtained from the files of the Metropolitan Police Service Royal Protection Unit. Most of the instances were simple approaches in which someone behaved inappropriately at a royal residence or a royal event (58 per cent) and a further 10 per cent included cases were the person had previously communicated, say, by letter to a member of the Royal Family but then approached that royal in person. The more serious approaches tended to be attempts to breach security barriers or cordons. Seven per cent of the total approaches were failed attempts to breach security barriers or cordons and 25 per cent were successful crossings of a barrier or security perimeter (including those involving the use of deception).

Stalking is a form of predatory behaviour that is characterised by repeated patterns of harassment of a particular individual to a degree which may frighten the victim or worse (Sheridan and Davies, 2001). Among the examples of stalking/harassment behaviours that have been described in a number of studies are annoying telephoning, letters, visiting the victim at home, following the victim, verbally threatening violence, physical assaults, gift-giving, visiting the place where the victim works, face-to-face contacts, aggressive letters and property damage.

A number of surveys have demonstrated the extensiveness of stalking behaviour. The precise figures obtained depend somewhat on the style of the survey and the sources of information. One of the better studies is Tjaden and Thoennes' (1998) national violence against women survey. This was basically a telephone survey of a sample of the general population in the United States. It was not restricted to female victims and both men and women were surveyed. For the purposes of this survey, three key characteristics were used to define stalking behaviour:

- The victim is spied on, sent unsolicited letters or receives unwanted telephone calls, finds that someone is standing outside their home and other behaviours of this sort.
- These behaviours had to be carried out by the same person on at least two occasions.
- These incidents had to make the victim either 'very frightened' or fear that they would be the victim of violence.

Of the people in the survey reporting that they had been stalked, 78 per cent of them were women and 22 per cent were men. For the women, overwhelmingly it was men who stalked them – 94 per cent of stalkers of women were men. Most significantly, 48 per cent of the stalkers were intimates of the women in the sense of being a past husband or partner or having had a brief sexual relationship with the stalker. The average stalking continued for 1.8 years. Approximately 1.3 million American women would be stalked annually if we extrapolate from the base rate figures collected in this survey (Tjaden and Thoennes, 2000). The fear of violence is not unrealistic. Meloy (2002) reports a number of studies of interpersonal violence among obsessional followers, stalkers and criminal harassers. The figures vary, of course, but most studies report rates between 30 per cent and 50 per cent. Furthermore, some studies where the victimiser is a former 'intimate' of the victim yield figures of around the 60–90 per cent level.

Roberts (2005) examined stalking by former romantic partners following relationship break-ups. Undergraduate female students completed a self-report questionnaire which showed that a third had been a victim of stalking, a third had suffered harassment and a third experienced neither from their previous partner. The stalking behaviours included unwanted letters, telephone calls and gifts, and violence such as physical violence or destruction of property. Stalking was differentiated from harassment in terms of its involving unwanted attentions on two or more occasions. Those who experienced harassment or stalking were more likely to have been subject to controlling behaviours and denigration during their relationship with the offender. So they were more likely to report that during the relationship they were discouraged from having relationships with others such as friends and relatives, sex was demanded when the woman did not want it, and the partner would humiliate her in front of others. These are behaviours which are commonly reported in surveys of domestic violence. Roberts argues that these findings are in line with the idea that stalking is a variant of domestic violence.

Recent research has addressed the question of what factors predict longer-term or persistent stalking. Persistent stalkers are not generally deterred from their activities by the involvement of the police or other authorities. On the other hand, recurrent stalkers may desist from stalking in these circumstances for some time only to return to stalking at a later time – perhaps with a different victim. McEwan, Mullen and MacKenzie (2009) studied 200 stalkers who had been referred to a community mental health clinic, for example, by a court. About a quarter of the stalkers persisted with their stalking for more than a year. The nature of the prior relationship involved was a major predictor of persistence. Those who stalked prior acquaintances were significantly more persistent than those who had stalked strangers. Persistent stalkers tended to:

- be over the age of 30 years
- be seeking intimacy or were motivated by resentment
- have the symptoms of a psychosis
- send victims unsolicited things through the postal services.

It is a misunderstanding, however, to equate persistence with high risk of violence. They were not more violent.

Nevertheless, it is inevitable that there is concern about the stalkers most likely to carry out the more extreme acts including violence. Recent research suggests that psychopaths who stalk are relatively uncommon among stalkers though their stalking patterns are not typical. A Canadian study by Storey, Hart, Meloy and Reavin (2009) used Hare's Psychopathy Checklist Revised which is a common assessment tool for psychopathy (see Chapters 21, 22, and 27). Actually, only one diagnosable psychopath was found in this study which suggests that there may be only very small prevalence rate of psychopathy among stalkers. The sample was obtained from those attending a forensic psychiatry clinic. Their victims were mostly female with an average age of about 50 years. There was evidence of secondary victimisation of members of the primary victim's family, for example, in about 20 per cent of cases. Evidences of psychopathic symptoms were uncommon among stalkers but where they were found then casual acquaintances rather than close ones were likely to be the target. Psychopathic stalkers tended to have higher levels of some standard risk factors for reoffending. Figure 8.5 summarizes some of the characteristics of psychopathic stalkers.

Different legal jurisdictions have very different approaches to stalking according to Sheridan and Davies (2002) and none of the legal or research definitions effectively distinguishes between the dangerous, predatory stalker and what they term 'the over-attentive suitor'. In US legislation, the fear of physical injury or death

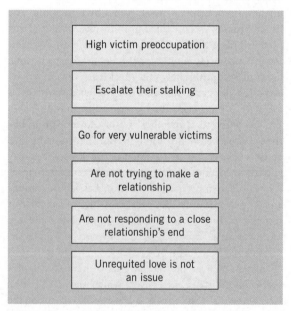

Figure 8.5 Psychopathic stalkers are uncommon but they show some of the characteristics above

is a requirement, whereas in the United Kingdom the requirement is merely a minimum of two acts of harassment. Australian legislation includes the word 'intends' into aspects of the definition, such as intending to cause serious physical harm or intending to cause fear (ibid., 2002). Quite clearly these are very different and give very different powers to the police to intervene at an early stage.

Sheridan and Davies (2001) had participants in a study rate a number of vignettes in terms of stalking. Different participants were given different instructions about the criteria to employ. Three groups had either US, British or Australian legal definitions to work with and another group just based their assessment on their own opinions. Some transcripts seem to exemplify the different penal codes more effectively than others. For example, the following was more likely to be judged stalking according to the US principles:

After our divorce, whenever I saw my ex-husband he would use obscene and threatening language towards me when such was entirely inappropriate (i.e. not during an argument situation). He also threatened to kill me. I also received an obscene threatening telephone call from his girlfriend.

(p. 11)

The following is perhaps even more illustrative since it was regarded as the most like the UK legal definition of stalking but least in keeping with the US definition of stalking:

A chap in the recent past kept turning up at my house uninvited and just walking in. He was sometimes difficult to get rid of. The relationship was flirtatious at first but his behaviour I considered inappropriate and I therefore cooled off a bit in friendliness towards him. He failed to acknowledge or accept this and chose to write weird poetry and one particularly worrying letter to me which was menacing and full of 'magical thinking' abstract type stuff. This behaviour stopped after a few weeks.

(p. 11)

This is another reminder that jurisdictions differ and what is true in one may not apply elsewhere.

Finally, we should not forget the potential of the Internet in relation to many sorts of crimes. The concept of 'cyberstalking' has been mooted, though without a clear distinction being made between cyberspace being used as an extra way of stalking victims and cyberstalking being an entirely new and different form of stalking behaviour. Some of the ways in which the Internet can be used to frighten and harass victims include deluges of unwanted e-mail, ordering goods and services in the name of the victim without the victim's immediate knowledge, posting unpleasant material about the victim, and threatening the victim in some way on the Internet. Alexy et al. (2005) found that cyberstalking tended to be more likely to involve behaviour such as threats to the victim and threats of suicide by the victimiser – and the victims were less likely to contact the police.

Sheridan and Grant (2007) studied victims of four different types of stalking: (1) pure online-only cyberstalking; (2) crossover from cyberstalking to real-life stalking; (3) real-life stalking with crossover to cyberstalking; and (4) pure real-life stalkers. The researchers developed a series of features which identify cyberstalking. These included the fact that the stalking began online first of all and the stalking was solely online for a minimum of four weeks. Most (74 per cent) of those victims who met these criteria of being cyberstalked had originally come into contact with the offender over the Internet. It was found that in terms of the psychological and medical effects of stalking and cyberstalking on the victim, there were no differences that reached statistical significance. In terms of social and economic effects of victimisation then the only significant effect was that the victim, not surprisingly, was more likely to change her e-mail address. Compared with real-life stalking, cyberstalkers were likely to have been former romantic partners and more likely to have been people who had been met on the Internet. Given that the study involved several hundred different variables to assess the differences between stalking and cyberstalking, the main finding was of great similarity between the two.

Main points

- As violent crimes range from the most trivial of assaults to the most disgusting of serial killings, a range of theoretical perspectives are needed in order to begin to explain such crimes. Similarly, given that violent crime has traditionally been found to be commonest among young men, we should not expect to find a single psychological explanation to be sufficient. Nevertheless, there is a great deal to suggest that violence is socially learnt. It has often been claimed that media violence is part of the cause of violence in the young though this has not been a major theme in forensic and criminal psychology or criminology for that matter. Evidence in support of the media causing violence is strongest from laboratory studies and much less a feature of field studies asking the same question. There is virtually no evidence concerning the media and actual acts of criminal violence.

- Homicide might seem to be largely determined by psychological factors but evidence of psychiatric abnormalities in such crimes is generally fairly exceptional. Furthermore, it has been shown that broad societal factors (e.g. periods of wartime) may affect levels of homicide. Leyton (1986) claimed that homicide is related to social structure (social class). Others have provided socio-biological explanations of such phenomena as the different rates of killing of step-children and biological children by their parents.

- There are a number of particularly forensic issues. Psychologists now have methods of helping individuals with their aggression in the form of anger management treatment and, in the prison service, violent offender programmes. Part of the challenge, however, is to identify the future most violent individuals. This is difficult because violence, say in the form of domestic violence, is commonplace. Related to this is stalking, which often is the aftermath of the break-up of an intimate relationship.

Further reading

Recent books on the psychology of violent offending are scarce. Among those that can be recommended are:

Boon, J. and Sheridan, L. (eds) (2002) *Stalking and Psychosexual Obsession: Psychological Perspectives for Prevention, Policing and Treatment* Chichester: Wiley.

Holmes, R.M. and Holmes, S.T. (2009) *Profiling Violent Crimes: An Investigative Tool* (4th edn) Thousand Oaks, CA: Sage.

Kocsis, R. (ed.) (2008) *Serial Murder and the Psychology of Violent Crimes: An International Perspective* New Jersey: Humana Press.

Visit our website at www.pearsoned.co.uk/howitt for self-test and essay questions, annotated further reading, audio interviews with researchers in the field, weblinks and more information on becoming a forensic psychologist.

Chapter 9

Sexual offenders 1: rapists

Overview

- Nowadays, rape tends to be defined in terms of unwanted penetration of the vagina, anus or mouth of another person. Statutory rape is penile penetration of any child below the age of consent to sexual intercourse. The law in some countries has changed markedly under the influence of feminist arguments about the nature of the crime since rape is frequently regarded as a crime of power and control rather than of sexual gratification.

- The frequency of rape is difficult to assess and is surrounded by controversy. It is widely accepted that reported rape does not reflect the true levels of rape and reporting rape to the police may be declining in some countries. In a British survey, approximately 5 per cent of woman claimed to have been raped at some point in their lives. The treatment of rape victims has changed to some extent but it remains a crime for which conviction is relatively low despite efforts to redefine its nature and to extend its scope into date-rape and marital rape, for example.

- In terms of the development of theory, one of the important issues is whether sex offenders are crime generalists or whether they specialise in a particular type of offence. There is evidence supporting both views but, importantly, it would appear that rapists are more likely to be crime generalists and that sexual offenders against children specialise.

- Various researchers have claimed that there are several different patterns of rape. Groth, Burgess and Holmstrom (1977) identified power-assurance rape, power-assertive rape, anger-retaliatory rape and anger-excitement rape. This typology is based on the psychological motive of the offender. Hostility, control, theft and involvement have been identified as the four major characteristic patterns in behaviour at the rape scene.

- Ideas conducive to rape are common in Western cultures. Rape myths are beliefs about women and their sexuality which place the blame on the woman rather than the rapist. However, there is no convincing balance of evidence which demonstrates that sex offenders are more extreme in their acceptance of rape myths.

- Offenders use pornography but developmental studies tend not to hold pornography responsible for creating their deviance. Furthermore, research on sexual fantasy tends to indicate that fantasy has a potentially complex relationship with offending.

- Phallometry or plethysmography is a technique for measuring the volume or circumference of a penis as an index of sexual 'arousal' in a man. There are doubts that it is sufficiently precise to identify men likely to offend and there is reason to believe that it is somewhat outmoded as alternative, simpler ways of achieving the same end are available.

Introduction

There are a number of definitions of rape. The legal definition is just one of many but is the most important in this context. Rape has various legal definitions and its precise meaning varies from jurisdiction to jurisdiction and changes over time. Although it is important to differentiate legal definitions from other definitions of rape, this is not so easily done while reading psychological and social scientific writings on rape. Feminists, in particular, tend to extend the definition far beyond its typical legal meaning to include all forms of sexual act that women may not wish (e.g. Kelly, 1988, 1989). For example, some writers may well include salacious comments to a woman about her breasts in the definition. Legal definitions refer almost exclusively to penetration by a penis. Traditionally, penetrative vaginal sex has been a crucial criterion. Increasingly, the anal penetration of either sex may be rape in some jurisdictions as can oral penetration. A conviction for rape requires that the victim has not given consent to the sexual act. In some jurisdictions, intercourse with youngsters regarded as too young to give their consent is classified as rape – *statutory rape*.

Along with domestic violence and sexual and physical abuse of children, rape was increasingly seen as a matter of social concern under the influence of feminists and others from the 1970s onwards. There are many accounts of the reasons why rape is a political issue for feminists. To take just one example, Los (1990) explained how rape laws have tended to reinforce the position of the powerful male over the less powerful female. From her Canadian perspective, although much the same may be said of other jurisdictions, Canadian law served interests of men at the expense of those of women in the following ways, among others:

- by giving the husband the unrestricted right to sexual access to his wife;

- by defining rape as heterosexual penetration and defining other forms of penetration as less serious, thus putting the risk of the wife being made pregnant by another man equivalent to the most serious offence;

- by protecting women from men who seduce them with the false promise of marriage – such as in breach of promise legislation – which essentially implies the weakness of women;

- by requiring that women report their rape immediately otherwise invalidating their case – the delay, putatively, would give them time to make up the story;

- by indicating that women's credibility in court rests on their sexual reputations whereas men's does not.

The current Canadian Assault Law of 1983 adopted a gender-neutral definition of rape. In part, this was an accommodation to a great deal of feminist lobbying. Other changes in conceptions of rape are obvious in issues such as marital rape, which previously in some jurisdictions was not a possibility or extremely difficult to prosecute, and the development of the idea of date-rape (Lees, 1995).

Frequency of rape

Not surprisingly, the frequency of rape cannot be assessed with certainty. The answer, like the answers to all such statistical questions, clearly depends on the source of information and the definition employed (Chapter 2). Sexual crimes are likely to be under-reported to the police for a variety of reasons. These include the possible (but misplaced) shame and embarrassment of the victim, fear of a particularly hostile treatment by the police or lawyers, a wish to avoid more distress, ignorance that an offence has been committed (e.g. as in the case of rape by a sexual partner) and so forth. Conviction rates and police crime reports are unsatisfactory as indicators for other reasons. For example, they partly depend on police or other officials' decisions about which crimes to prosecute and the police finding someone to prosecute. Lack of consent to sexual activity is very difficult to prove for rape on dates. Victim surveys, while possibly being the best indicators of actual frequency of rape, have their own biases since the lack of consent may be clearer to the victim than it might be, say, to police officers. Rapes in England and Wales reached only 500 cases recorded by the police per annum in 1959. By the late 1990s, the figure had reached 5,000 cases annually. Male rape began to be recorded as such in 1995 onwards. The numbers are fewer than 350 per annum – much the same as the figures for rape of females prior to the 1950s. These are *numbers* and not rates. The 2005/6 figure for recorded rapes was 13,000 offences (Home Office, 2008) and the figure for 2009/10 was 14,000 offences (Home Office, 2010).

The trends in rape in the United States are illustrated in Figure 9.1. This gives the rates of rapes per 100,000 every ten years from 1960 onwards excluding attempted rapes. These are the rates given in the Unified Crime Statistics (FBI, 2009). The rates of reported rapes to the police per 100,000 people have changed markedly over the years. In 1960 the rates were relatively low but they increased markedly in 1970 and 1980 – peaking in 1990. Since then there has been a steady decline. Of course, these are crimes reported to the police. The figures for actual rapes may be radically different. Take for example, the figures for 1999. The rate per 100,000 that year was 33. In comparison, for the same year, the US National Crime Victimisation Survey of a sample of the population, as might be expected, gave a higher figure – 90 per 100,000 of the population (Bureau of Justice, 2001d). The definition of rape given to the participants was 'forced sexual

intercourse including both psychological coercion as well as physical force. Forced sexual intercourse means penetration by the offender(s). Includes attempted rapes, male as well as female victims and both heterosexual and homosexual rape. Attempted rape includes verbal threats of rape.' Given the differences in definition, the disparity is not so great as sometimes claimed between crimes known to the police and victim survey statistics – about a third of rapes being reported to the police, it would seem. The historical trends may be different in other countries. Egg (1999) provided evidence that sex offences in Germany showed rather different trends from those of other Western countries.

The British Crime Survey is a random survey of households which attempts to assess the rates of crime, including those not reported to the police. Participants can use a Computer Assisted Self-Interviewing procedure, which is operated using a laptop computer and which may reduce interviewer influences significantly. The women in the study were asked questions that identified them as having been through some form of sexual victimisation. Other questions followed if they had. This enabled the researchers to classify whether an offence was a rape or not. The researchers defined rape as the woman being forced to have sexual intercourse (vaginal or anal penetration) though they did not require penile penetration in their definition. A sexual assault was anything identified as sexual which did not meet the requirements of rape:

- Four women in a thousand described incidents that could be classified as rape in the previous year.

- Forty-nine women in a thousand claimed to have been raped since the age of 16 years.

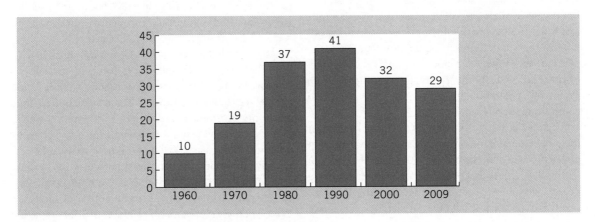

Figure 9.1 US rape rates per 100,000 population

- Nine women in a thousand claimed to have suffered some form of sexual assault victimisation in the previous year.

- Ninety-seven women in a thousand had suffered some form of sexual assault since the age of 16.

Overwhelmingly, victims of rape know the rapist: 45 per cent of rapists were the woman's current partner, 16 per cent were acquaintances, 11 per cent were ex-partners, 11 per cent were dates and 10 per cent were other intimates. In this study, only 8 per cent of rapes were committed by men not known to the victim. However, women who were raped by a stranger were more likely to report it to the police – 36 per cent of them did so whereas only 8 per cent of women raped by a date reported this to the police.

However, the woman's belief that her experience was rape was not always correct as far as the researchers could ascertain. Nevertheless, the women and the researchers agreed that the events were rape in 60 per cent of the cases.

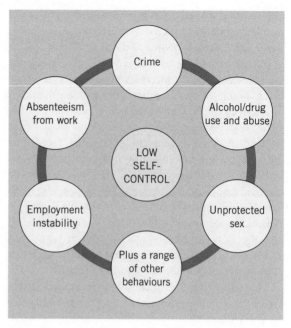

Figure 9.2 The General Theory of Crime
Source: based on Gottfredson and Hirschi, 1990

Sex offenders as specialists and generalists

There are two conceptually distinct models of sex offenders. The first is based on the general deviancy model which says that sex offenders offend sexually as part of their general tendency to engage in all sorts of deviant behaviour. The specialist model suggests that sex offenders largely specialise in sexual crimes and do not engage in other types of deviancy. Harris, Mazerolle and Knight (2009) put this slightly differently by suggesting that there is an 'implicit' assumption that those who commit sex offences are not the same as non-sexual offenders. Essentially this posits that sex offenders are exclusively/predominantly/persistently to be found committing sex offences.

The idea of the sex offender as a criminal generalist fits well with modern criminology theory especially that of Gottfredson and Hirschi's (1990) General Theory of Crime. This argues that offending is a manifestation of a broader and more pervasive antisocial character which involves not just crime but other similar behaviours (see Figure 9.2). Offenders lack self-control which means

that they engage in crime-analogous behaviours which result in other, broadly antisocial, behavioural patterns as well as crime itself. According to the General Theory of Crime, these other behaviours include absenteeism from work, alcohol and drug use and abuse, cigarettes, employment instability, irresponsible driving, marital instability, truancy, and unprotected sex (Simon, 2000). It should be added that Gottfredson and Hirschi (1990) accept that there is some crime specialisation but they believed that overwhelmingly criminals are generalists. No serious criminological analysis would deny that Gottfredson and Hirschi's General Theory of Crime is well supported by research evidence. How well it accounts for sex offending is another matter.

According to Lussier, Leclerc, Cale and Proulx (2007), sex offenders include both generalists and specialists. The case for them being generalists is quite extensive and compelling. Previous histories of non-sexual offending are common among sex offenders. Furthermore, when they reoffend following a conviction for a sex offence it is most likely that it will be for a non-sexual offence. Equally important is that the risk factors for sexual reoffending are much the same as the ones predictive of generalist patterns of a broadly antisocial lifestyle. Typical of these risk factors are any sort of prior offences, a background of involvement in violent and property crimes, an antisocial personality, and psychopathy. The specialist view of sex offenders would lead us to expect specifically sexual risk factors to be involved – such as having been charged with a sex offence, having committed sexual offences early in life, a preference for male victims and stranger/extrafamilial victims, and sexual deviance. Evidence that sex offenders can be characterised as having poor self-control can be found in Cleary's (2004) findings. Her in-depth interviews with sex offenders found that offenders were frequently injured in motor accidents, had fathered illegitimate children and were involved with alcohol and drugs.

One problem is that global categorisations such as sex offender subsume a variety of different types of offences which may mask the degree to which they are specialists. The failure to differentiate, say, rapists from child molesters in a great deal of research may mean that important differences between the two are simply not recognised. Indeed, Knight and Prentky (1990) suggest that rapists show the signs of criminal versatility of the generalist whereas child molesters tend to be crime specialists. It is of some importance that well-regarded theories of sex offending tend to treat them as sexual crime specialists and not as generalists as implied by the General Theory of Crime. For example, several theories of sex offending claim that it is the result of conditioning or, alternatively, based on social learning (e.g. Laws and Marshall, 1990). Similarly, explanations of sex offending which suggest that it is the consequence of sexually deviant experiences (Ward *et al.*, 2006) help promote the idea that sex offenders are specialists in a particular type of crime.

A recent study attempted to clarify some of the issues arising from all of this (Harris *et al.*, 2009). The study explored the extent to which:

- There is a group of generalist (versatile) sex offenders who tend to show the mix of antisocial behaviours predicted by the General Theory of Crime. For example, they are more likely to show signs of psychopathy. In addition, there is a group of specialist sex offenders who are likely to manifest characteristics associated with specialism such as emotional congruence with children, a preference for male victims and victims known to themselves, and sexual preoccupation.
- Rapists are generalist (versatile) offenders showing the characteristics of generalist criminals. Child molesters tend to be specialist offenders showing different criminal characteristics from the generalist offender.

Harris *et al.*'s (2009) study was based on a sample of 572 sex offenders convicted in Massachusetts between 1959 and 1984. Specialisation in sex crime was determined using 'the specialisation threshold'. This essentially assumes that if an offender has a majority of offences for a particular type of crime then they are a specialist in that type of crime. Charges rather than convictions were used in this study. It was found that:

- Sex offenders who were classified as generalists (versatile) tended to exhibit the characteristics identified in the General Theory of Crime. For example, school maladjustment and delinquency were much more common in the versatile offenders group and they were typically rearrested after release much more frequently.
- The victims of specialist sex offenders tend to be known to the offender.

However, the researchers subdivided sex offenders further into four groups: specialist rapists, versatile rapists, specialist child molesters and versatile child molesters. Only about 12 per cent of the rapists could be described as specialists in this sample using the criteria employed for specialism. Figure 9.3 shows this breakdown and some of the characteristics associated with each subdivision. Once again, these characteristics are associated with the General Theory of Crime for versatile offenders and indicative of specialism for the specialist subgroups of offenders:

- Versatile child molesters were more likely to abuse alcohol and other substances, to have had difficulties in their early years at school and to show behavioural problems during adolescence.
- Specialist child molesters were more likely to be sexually preoccupied, to have emotional congruence with children and to offend against male victims.

Another aspect of sex offender generalism-specialism is related to the issue of victim category crossover. Crossover is the extent to which a sex offender offends against victims in a variety of categories. For example, one offender might offend against adult women only whereas another might offend against adult women and boy children. The more crossover there is the more difficult it is to explain sexual offending in terms of different patterns of conditioning or social learning, for example. Similarly, the more crossover there is the harder it is to predict the sort of sexual reoffending that a sex offender

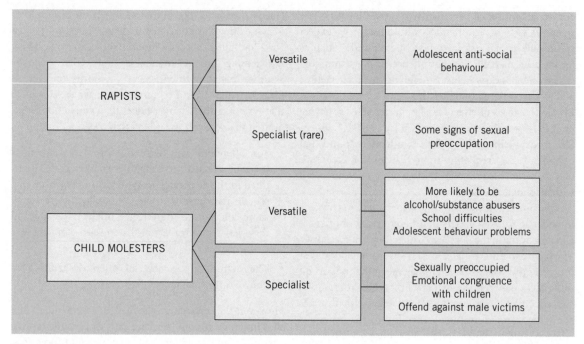

Figure 9.3 Rapists and child molesters as versatile and specialist offenders

may engage in. Of course, it is not easy to define exactly what constitutes the same type of offence and what constitutes a different type of offence. A recent study by Cann, Friendship and Gozna (2007) looked at crossover among sexual offenders in terms of their choice of victims defined by victim age, gender and relationship to the offender – intrafamilial versus extrafamilial. Their sample consisted of 1,345 adult male sex offenders. Each had offended against multiple victims and each had been sentenced to a minimum of four years for a sexual offence. The data were collected from police records at New Scotland Yard's National Identification System. These records include written offence summaries describing the offender's convictions and, usually, details of the victim. This was supplemented with data collected from the Offenders Index (OI). Twenty five per cent of the offenders showed evidence of crossover in their offending on a minimum of one dimension. Of course, this shows that the vast majority did not cross over. Some offenders crossed over on more than one dimension as is illustrated in Figure 9.4. This figure gives the percentages of all types of crossover in the entire sample. The crossover offenders were at higher risk of reoffending according to Static-99 calculations. (Static-99 is an assessment method which predicts recidivism though it is not actually in itself a measure of recidivism (see Chapter 27)).

Furthermore, cross over offenders had more convictions for any sort of offences as well as more sexual offences than non-crossover offenders. One interpretation of this is that offenders cross over from a preferred victim type

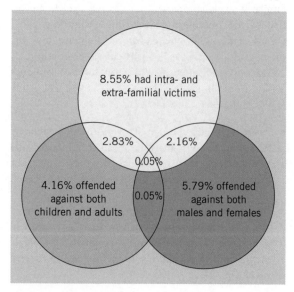

Figure 9.4 Crossover behaviours in offenders showing the percentage of crossovers of various types in the total sample of offenders

when circumstances make it difficult to find their pre-ferred victim type (Heil *et al.*, 2003).

Youthful sex offenders

We saw in Chapter 6 that it is a general trend for sex offending to begin in the early life of an offender. This sort of crime tends to follow the same sort of pattern associated with violence. Violent crime is most commonly a youthful offence that declines sharply in middle age and beyond. This suggests that rape is best conceived as a crime of violence rather than one of sexual lust. Certainly there is good reason to believe that rape is associated with anger in many offenders. Childhood abuse is also commoner in sex offenders:

- Worling (1995) carried out a study of adolescent sex offenders – one group had offended in a 'hands-on' fashion against peers and older women. The other group had offended against younger children. A range of measurements was taken including acceptance of rape myths (see pp. 157–58) and experience of physical punishment and sexual abuse. Those offending against a woman rather than a peer had experienced greater levels of physical punishment. Interestingly, sexual abuse by men tended to lead to abuse against younger children by the victims. In contrast, victims of sexual abuse by females tended to become the offenders against peers and older women.

- Haapasalo and Kankkonen (1997) studied the self-reported experiences of childhood abuse in men whose victims were women above 18 years. These were compared with violent offenders with no record of sexual offences. The two groups were matched according to a number of family problems – including matters such as being in care in childhood, having experienced parental divorce in childhood, having parents who were substance abusers and a number of other factors. Sex offenders claimed to have experienced more psychological (verbal) abuse (such as yelling, threatening, ridiculing) than the violent offenders. Furthermore, psychological rejection and isolation were commoner in sex offenders' childhoods. For example, their parents were more openly hostile and negative towards them as children, they tended to be ignored, other siblings were better favoured and they were locked up in closed environments more

frequently and isolated from other people. There were further differences:

- father threatened to hurt me;
- father belittled me;
- father did not want me near him;
- mother threatened to hurt me;
- mother belittled me;
- mother did not want me near her;
- father made me do shameful things.

- What is true of the childhoods of rapists may not be true of the childhoods of other types of sex offender such as paedophiles and child molesters. Often in research it is important to differentiate these different types. Jespersen, Lalumièrea and Seto (2009) published a meta-analysis (see Box 4.2) of publicly available research articles, theses and dissertations which examined childhood experiences of sexual abuse in offenders. The studies included in the analysis were those which compared sex offenders with other types of offender. Studies which compared sex offenders with non-offender groups were not included. The analysis compared sex offenders with offenders for other types of crime and also men who had sexually offended against an adult and those who had sexually offended against a child. The meta-analysis included physical abuse if it had been part of the original study. Sex offenders overall were much more likely to have been sexually abused but the trend for physical abuse to be commoner in sex offenders was not statistically significant. Sex offenders against adults were less likely to have been sexually abused in childhood than those who offended against children. On the other hand, those who offended sexually against adults were more likely to have been physically abused in childhood than offenders against young people.

It is easy to understand the origins of the hostility that some rapists feel. A number of researchers have commented on the role of this. For example, Hall and Hirschman (1991) suggest that there are a numbers of precursors to rape which may motivate the crime:

- sexual arousal: deviant sexual arousal;
- cognitive motivation: rape myths (see later);
- developmental problems;
- emotional factors (e.g. anger towards women).

While anger as a component of rape appears to be common, very little is known about precisely how it contributes to offending. It is generally accepted that some rapes are driven by sadistic fantasies which eventually are acted out in behaviour (e.g. MacCulloch *et al.*, 1983). Moreover, anger has been more directly associated with sex offending than this indirect route implies. For example, 94 per cent of rapists report that anger is associated with the offence, a figure that is not much lower in other types of sex offender (Pithers *et al.*, 1988).

There is a general assumption that rape is a crime committed by younger offenders and a number of surveys have demonstrated this. However, the type of rape can make a significant impact on these age trends. Muir and Macleod (2003) showed that rapes in an unspecified UK metropolitan area were generally committed by offenders under the age of 40 years, however this figure was lower for the rape of intimate partners such as spouses. In the case of rape by strangers, 61 per cent of offenders were under 30 years of age; for the rape of acquaintances, again 61 per cent were under 30 years of age; for the rape of intimates involved only 24 per cent of offenders were under 30 years of age. Furthermore, rape is an offence where the victims tend to be younger women – only 8 per cent of rapes were committed against victims of 40 years or older. Seventy-five per cent were committed against women of under 25 years of age and 30 per cent were against 14-year-olds and under. Probably a high proportion of the latter were statutory rapes. The 15- to 24-years-old age group was the most at risk but this was largely the case for stranger and acquaintance rape.

Patterns in rape

McCabe and Wauchope (2005) studied Australian rapes based on a sample of 130 police reports involving the penetration (or attempted) penetration of a woman. In this study, it was found that rapist and victim were most likely to be strangers to each other (42 per cent), which was followed by 24 per cent of rapes being perpetrated by the women's acquaintances/work colleagues and formed the second most common category. Forty-two per cent of the rapes took place at the victim's home. Just what acts take place during rapes and just how frequent are they? Surprisingly, until recently, such seemingly basic information has rarely been systematically brought together in order to obtain a picture of typical rape behaviours. Of course, these details are

valuable to offender profiles (see Chapters 14 and 15). The researchers identified different behavioural themes in these reports at the following rates:

- The *vaginal theme* which included digital penetration, foreign object insertion, hand/fist insertion and so forth (92 per cent of rapes).
- The *kissing/hugging theme* (32 per cent).
- The *oral theme* which included cunnilingus, fellatio, analingus (25 per cent).
- The *anal theme* which included foreign-object insertion and anal penetration (22 per cent).
- The *brutal-physical theme* (9 per cent) (including biting, beating, kicking, choking and strangulation).

Certain themes are more likely to co-occur in combination than others. The most common combination was the kissing/fondling with the vaginal theme which occurred together in 29 per cent of rapes followed by oral and vaginal themes which occurred together in 22 per cent of rapes.

The language used in the assaults could be largely accounted for by four themes:

- A caring, persuasion or reassurance theme – 'I won't hurt you, I just want sex' (characteristic of 24 per cent of rapists).
- A sexually abusive or explicit language theme – 'I want you on top, play with yourself' (19 per cent).
- An angry, demeaning or threatening theme – 'Keep your voice down or I will kill you' (18 per cent).
- A revenge or payback theme – 'I will kill your new boyfriend' (just 2 per cent).

Other forensic and criminal psychologists have begun to explore the different characteristics of rape. One important step in this process is attempts to identify patterns in rape offences in order to assess whether there are different types of rape. This is a form of analysis of crimes related to profiling (Chapter 15). Häkkänen, Lindlof and Santtila (2004) studied the police database for rapes by strangers in Finland. Case files included various records: witness statements, medical statements, forensic evidence, the interview with the victim and the interview with the suspect. A long list of possible characteristics of the rape was compiled and each case record coded in terms of its presence or absence. A complex statistical technique, multidimensional scaling, was used to identify what sorts of behaviours tended to be associated with each other. For example, in some of the rapes the offender had apologised to the victim. In others, the offender had bitten the victim. Do these characteristics tend to coexist or does the presence of one, an apology, tend not to be associated with biting?

Some behaviours were virtually universal in the rapes. Vaginal penetration from the front was achieved or attempted in 89 per cent of the rapes. In contrast, vaginal penetration from the rear or an attempt at this was relatively uncommon (7 per cent of rapes). The rapist revealed information, true or false, about themselves in 40 per cent of cases. In 23 per cent of rapes, the offender carried out multiple acts of violence against the victim – more than those required to simply control the victim. Among the rare characteristics were that the offender had taken a weapon to the scene of the crime (6 per cent), penetration achieved more than once (6 per cent), and the offender implied knowing the victim before the attack (5 per cent). Three separate rape patterns were identified:

- *Theft*: the offender had stolen identifiable items such as credit cards from the victim; the offender rummaged or searched through the victim's property; a condom was used; the offender stole things such as money which cannot be identified.

- *Involvement*: the offender tried to reassure the victim though this might include reassurance that he did not intend to carry out the act; the offender complimented the victim; the victim was drugged by the offender; the rapist implied that he knew the victim; the offender attempted an intrusion into the victim's home.

- *Hostility*: the offender carried out vaginal penetration from the rear; the offender bit the victim; the offender carried out a single act of violence but not to control the victim; the offender penetrated the victim's vagina digitally; the weapon had been taken from the scene of the crime.

An earlier study using British data by Canter *et al.* (2003) had generated a similar classification of rape based on the transcripts of statements made verbatim by rape victims. This provided information about a number of characteristics of rapes which could be analysed statistically for patterns in stranger rape. The terminology is much the same, though the rape characteristics used to define each pattern were not the same in every case:

- *Control*: the victim was bound or gagged, use of mask or blindfold and using a weapon were characteristic of this. About a tenth of rapes were in this category. This

pattern did not emerge in the Finnish study discussed above although the following patterns are similar in both studies though slightly differently defined.

- *Theft*: goods would be demanded from the victim, the personal property of the victim would be stolen, identifiable goods were stolen and stealing unidentifiable goods. About a twentieth of rapes were in this category.

- *Involvement*: the victim may be complimented about her appearance – for example, the offender would make sexual comments in the course of the offence, the victim is kissed, and the offender implies that he knows the victim. About a third of rapes were in this category.

- *Hostility*: the offender removed the victim's clothing in a violent manner, there was an attempt to penetrate the victim anally, the victim was threatened at some time in the offence, and demeaning or insulting the victim such as by the use of verbal insult. This amounted to about a quarter of rapes.

Some rapes showed mixed patterns.

Canter *et al.* (2003) argue from these crime activity typologies that rapists are best distinguished in terms of the sorts of interpersonal behaviours that occur as part of the rape. It is less important and profitable to study the types of sexual behaviours involved.

The nature of rapists

So, it is clearly too simplistic to regard rape as the result of an uncontrolled, intense sexual lust. There are many reasons to be dubious about this formulation. For example, there is some evidence that sexual deprivation is not an essential component of rape (Howitt, 1991a). Rape commonly involves physical violence, of course. This, in some cases, goes substantially beyond the levels required to force the victim to participate in sex. Lloyd and Walmsley (1989) found that rapes in the United Kingdom typically were accompanied by violence. Around 25 per cent contained no violence. About one in eight resulted in the victim being hospitalised owing to the level of the violence. Thus the explanation of rape must go beyond libidinous needs alone or in part.

Rape may manifest itself in a variety of forms. Hazelwood (1987), an offender profiler, suggests that the following types of rapist should be considered (following Groth *et al.*, 1977):

The power-assurance rapist:

- This describes the commonest type of rapist.
- The rape is concerned with dealing with the rapist's insecurities about his masculinity.
- As the offence may not help with the insecurities and because the insecurities are deep, there may be only a short interval before he needs to offend again.
- Force is not great and threats may be involved. Weapons are not common in this form of rape.
- Usually the rape is planned – there may be prior surveillance of the victim.
- If the victim is sufficiently passive to allow this, sexual fantasies may be expressed during the course of the rape.
- 'Trophies' such as clothing or some other article may be taken. These may be used, for example, in future masturbation.

The power-assertive rapist:

- This type of offender is sexually confident.
- Rape expresses his virility and sexuality, and power over women.
- Victims may be found in social locations such as discos, pubs or parties.
- Initially his manner may be friendly but may quickly change.
- Violence is extreme especially in the later stages. He does not appear to be the stereotypical rapist as he is socially skilled.
- Offences may be scattered and irregular in terms of frequency of occurrence.

- This pattern may be common in date-rape.

The anger-retaliatory rapist:

- The offender has extremely high levels of anger towards women such that, for example, degrading activities may be involved in the rape.
- It involves short intense attacks (blitz).
- Characteristically, there is a similarity between the victim and the woman he has a grudge against.
- Attacks may be fairly regular as a consequence of the build-up of anger.

The anger-excitement rapist:

- This is the least common type of rapist.
- The rapist gains pleasure and sexual excitement from viewing the distress of his victim.
- Thus the infliction of pain is common and violence is at such high levels that the victim may be killed. Torture is common.
- There is careful, methodological planning.
- He will bring such items as blindfolds, gags and ropes to the rape.
- Victims are usually total strangers to the offender.
- Photographs and video-recordings may be taken.
- Usually attacks are irregular, in part determined by the time at which his careful planning is complete.

Clearly then rape takes a variety of forms in terms of the motives and behaviours of the rapist. Understanding the different types of rapist may be helpful in deciphering the different crime scenes.

BOX 9.1 Forensic psychology in action

Phallometry (also known as plethysmography)

The phallometer is a device that measures the size of a penis as an indicator of sexual arousal. There are two types:

- *Volume phallometry* measures the volume of the penis. Essentially, a man's penis is put inside a glass tube. Changes in the size of his penis will cause changes in the pressure inside the tube. These changes may be measured through a meter or

recorded on a electrical, moving pen device (much like a lie-detector machine – see Chapter 18).

- *Circumference phallometry* measures the circumference of the penis with a flexible 'tube'. Changes in circumference lead to changes in the electrical signals that are fed to the recording device.

The underlying theory is obvious – the size of a man's penis is an indicator of his level of sexual arousal.

Thus, if a man is shown a pornographic video of a rape, then the potential rapists should show greater increase in penis size than so-called normal men. There are a number of practical difficulties that need consideration:

- Penises vary in size both between men and over time. One consequence of this is that the measures used tend to be expressed in relative terms: that is, rather than the change in penis volume or circumference being used, the *percentage increase* in volume or circumference would be the measure of arousal. Alternatively, the man may be encouraged to masturbate to full erection and his response to the sexual stimuli assessed as a percentage of this maximum.
- Phallometry is undertaken in circumstances that are not conducive to sexual arousal for all men. These investigations are relatively public, cold, clinical and intrusive: for example, being connected up to the apparatus by a clinician, being sat in a chair in a small room or cubicle in a corner of a hospital or clinic, and being shown pornography which might be alien to one's sexuality. These factors mean that for some men, at least, the assessment process is ineffective as little or no sexual response is produced.
- It is possible to fake responses in a number of ways. Secret masturbation may allow the offender to show apparent arousal to 'normal stimuli'. Fantasising to alternative arousing imagery and tensing muscles in the area of the anus/scrotum may allow the same control on arousal. Disinterest in certain stimuli may be faked by fantasising about non-arousing themes while the clinician is showing otherwise arousing material to the man. For example, the man may be carrying out mental arithmetic while the arousing material is being shown. Alternatively, by pressing heavily on a nail or splinter in the chair he may cause an unpleasant and distracting sensation.

Attempts may be made to detect or prevent faking. One way of doing this is to ensure that the participants are concentrating on the video material by setting them a task such as answering questions about what they have seen or, for example, to signal when a light flashes in the video.

There are a number of techniques using phallometry which assess sexual arousal to different types of 'sexual' stimulus and possibly, then, the different types of victim. For example, Abel *et al.* (1977) developed the *rape index*. This compares a man's responses to various types of erotic material including that with force and coercion. Men highest on response to the latter type of material are regarded as those with the greatest rape potential. Similarly, Avery-Clark and Laws (1984) put forward a *dangerous child molester* index which identifies the men with the greatest response to coerced sex with children.

As ever, a crucial question is that of the extent to which the different types of offender can be differentiated using phallometry: that is, if one is trying to identify paedophiles, just how many of them would be correctly identified as such and just how many of them would not be identified? Furthermore, how many normal men would be classified as paedophiles and how many would be identified as normal by the test in question? The evidence seems to be that circumference measures are fairly poor at correct identifications (Baxter, Barbaree and Marshall, 1986; Baxter *et al.*, 1984; Murphy *et al.*, 1986). Volume phallometry is better (McConaghy, 1991). Unfortunately, all that can be said currently is that if one has two groups of men, one group normals and the other group paedophiles, phallometry will help you correctly choose the group of normals and the group of paedophiles. It is rather less good at deciding for any group of men who is a paedophile and who is not.

The important question, to the clinician, is whether phallometry can identify rapists and paedophiles from the rest of the population. If high proportions of normal men are wrongly classified as paedophiles or rapists, and offenders are often misclassified as normal, then it is an ineffective test. For example, Quinsey *et al.* (1975) found that normal men showed erections to pictures of pubescent and young girls that were 70 per cent and 50 per cent of their responses to erotic pictures of adult females. In a study by

BOX 9.1 (continued)

Wormith (1986), the classification accuracy based on circumference phallometry was 64 per cent for groups of paedophiles, rapists and non-sex offenders. Only 50 per cent of paedophiles were correctly classified as such, and 42 per cent were classified as normal.

Perhaps more importantly, Hall, Shondrick and Hirschman (1993) carried out a meta-analysis (Box 4.2) of a number of published studies. These studies compared penile responses when shown sexually aggressive materials in men known to be sexually violent with appropriate control participants. These studies only used audiotaped materials, which included both consenting sexual activity and sexual violence (rape). Using tables in Howitt and Cramer (2008), the correlation (effect size) obtained over the varied studies was about 0.14. This is a rather small correlation despite showing a relationship between responses to rape stimuli and being a rapist: that is, many men would be misclassified.

Using the rape index (Abel et al., 1977), the correlation was much higher at the equivalent of 0.33. This proved to be a rather inconsistent finding since some studies obtained large relationships and others small relationships. According to Hall et al., the studies finding large effects were those comparing rapists with non-sexually violent men. Smaller differences were found for the studies in which rapists were compared with paedophiles, for example.

Other worries include the simplistic equation that links erections to sexual offending. This assumes that sexual motives underlie rape and other forms of sexual offending whereas there is considerable evidence that offenders may suffer sexual dysfunction in that they

cannot achieve penetration and that there are non-sexual motives involved in some of the crimes.

Some recommend confronting suspected sex offenders with phallometric evidence in order to elicit a confession (Travin et al., 1985). This has its own risks such as false confession. While phallometry may be effective enough for research purposes, it appears to be rather risky for clinical assessment purposes. Indeed, there is some evidence that self-reports may be at least as effective as phallometry in detecting offenders (e.g. Howitt, 1995a). Furthermore, the results appear to be better for cooperative (admitting) offenders than uncooperative (non-admitting) offenders. This again lessens their attractiveness as an objective assessment technique.

Penile plethysmography is problematic in a number of obvious ways. It involves relatively expensive instrumentation which needs time and appropriate space to administer. Furthermore, there is no universal standard way of administering the phallometry which is applied consistently from one clinical setting to another. Laws and Gress (2004), among a number of researchers, have increasingly regarded viewing time of 'erotic' imagery as an alternative to phallometry since it involves no equipment attached to a man's genitals and is equally suitable for assessing women. Viewing time measures are simply the amount of time that, say, a sex offender spends looking at particular types of erotic stimuli. It is now possible to administer viewing time procedures using computers, which can also be used to generate standard imagery without having to recourse to pictures of real people.

Rape myths

Cognitive factors conducive to rape increasingly became a focus for researchers following Burt's (1980) work on the cultural myths concerning rape. She developed the *Rape-myth Acceptance Scale* based on the observation that Western culture had essentially blamed the victims

of rape for the attacks on them. Such victim-blaming strategies have been identified as characteristic of the criminal justice system. In a male-dominated culture, ideas develop that, by essentially blaming the victim, either encourage men to rape or provide them with an excuse for their sexually aggressive acts against women. Women, it is held, deserve to be or want to be raped.

Men, according to the myths, are almost justified in raping. This is best illustrated by considering a number of items taken from the *Rape-myth Acceptance Scale*:

> If a girl engages in necking or petting and she lets things get out of hand, it is her own fault if her partner forces sex on her.
>
> If a woman gets drunk at a party and has intercourse with a man she's just met there, she should be considered 'fair game' for other males at the party who want to have sex with her too, whether she wants to or not.
>
> A woman who is stuck-up and thinks she is too good to talk to guys on the street deserves to be taught a lesson.

The final item above also illustrates the idea that rape is part of male domination/control of women. There are other measures, which reflect similar ideas such as the Mosher Scale *Sexually Callous Attitudes Towards Women* (Mosher and Anderson, 1986). This appears to measure somewhat tough, unsympathetic and heartless attitudes on the part of men towards sex with females and female sexuality:

> You don't ask girls to screw, you tell them to screw.
>
> You never know when you are going to meet a strange woman who will want to get laid.

There is evidence that this sort of measure of the cognitive aspects of rape is associated with at least expressed views about willingness to offend. The most controversial of these measures is Malamuth's *Self-reported Likelihood to Rape* measure (Malamuth and Ceniti, 1986). This is also known as the proclivity to rape. It is basically a single item measure: 'How likely do you think you would be to commit rape if you can be assured of not being caught?' This is a controversial measure because of the inherent difficulty in knowing quite what men mean if they agree with this statement. Does it mean that they are likely to rape even if they might get caught? Does it mean that they are unsure of why they do not rape so feel that they might rape in some circumstances? Or what do the answers mean? A number of researchers have shown that there is a small or modest relationship between acceptance of the rape myths and proclivity to rape. For example, Tieger (1981) found that the men who score higher on the *Likelihood to Rape* measure also tend to see rape as an enjoyable seduction for the victim and hold the victim to blame for her victimisation. Men who report regarding rape as a serious crime and who are not overtly stereotyped in their thinking about sex roles tend to score lower on the *Likelihood to Rape* measure. Some researchers stress these cognitive components and, for an extreme version of this viewpoint, Russell's (1988, 1992) model warrants attention in so far as she draws together much of the work in this area to make the case for the cognitive basis of rape.

The acid test of this cognitive model has to be whether these cognitive factors help us differentiate between rapists and non-rapists. Here the theory seems to fail. There is some evidence suggesting that such cognitive factors do not differentiate rape offenders from others. For example, Overholser and Beck (1988) found no evidence that rapists differed from non-rape offenders and non-offenders on a number of attitude scales including acceptance of rape myths as well as attitudes to sex and attitudes to the use of violence. Stermac and Quinsey (1986) found no evidence that rapists were different from other groups in terms of their attitudes to women. The finding that adolescent sexual assaulters against women did not differ from the less overtly aggressive offenders against younger children supports this. Perhaps this is no surprise given what we know about the offending and reoffending patterns of rapists. They tend to have been previously imprisoned for non-sexual offences and their reoffending is likely not to be sexual (Lloyd and Walmsley, 1989).

It is not easy to make the case that rape myths are a crucial factor in rape because of such evidence. Nevertheless, work on the cognitive aspects of sex offending, including the factors discussed in this section, is extremely common in the psychological treatment of sex offenders (see Chapter 26). There is no distinct evidence of the effectiveness of therapy on rape myths on recidivism separate from the total effects of the treatment programme. Any improvement in the social functioning that might enable an offender to establish a non-offending lifestyle is welcome irrespective of what aspect of the therapy is responsible.

Socio-cultural factors and sexual violence

Hall and Barongan (1997) argue that socio-cultural factors may be involved in rape. By this they mean that certain sorts of cultural organisation may encourage males to rape and others may reduce the risk of rape. One dimension on which cultures differ is the *individualist–collectivist* orientation. Western culture, and that of the United States especially, holds that individuals should strive to achieve the best they can for themselves. Collectivist cultures, on the other hand, value those who work for the collective good. Within a nation, of course, there may be different subcultures, especially nations built on migrant communities such as the United States. The argument is that collectivist cultures are less conducive to rape than individualist cultures. Unfortunately for Hall and Barongan, superficially their idea does not fit the available statistical evidence well. For example, despite the fact that African-American communities may be regarded as relatively more collectivist in orientation, African-American men tend to be over-represented in the rape statistics. Hall and Barongan suggest that this may be illusory – a function of socio-economic status differentials between black and white Americans. Low socio-economic status is a risk factor in committing rape and also more characteristic of black rather than white Americans.

International crime statistic comparisons are problematic since one is unsure whether like is being compared with like. For example, rape might be defined differently, women less likely to report rape, police less likely to seek prosecutions for rape and so forth. There is some evidence when American and collectivist Hong Kong Chinese college students are compared that the American men were rather more likely to report using coercion sexually such as when touching a woman's genitals against her will. Among the reasons why collectivist cultures will show lower levels of sexual violence are:

- interpersonal conflict (including violence) tends to be minimal in collectivist cultures partly because of the sharing of group goals;
- individual needs are subordinated to the well-being of the group in collectivist cultures;
- a personal sense of shame at letting down the community is a major deterrent against crime.

Similarly, socio-cultural values are intimately related to rates of rape in different parts of the United States (Baron and Straus, 1989). Their research design was statistically complex but essentially simple. They took the 50 American states and compared them in terms of rates of rape based on publicly available statistics. Of course, such statistics are gathered from official sources and are subject to a degree of error since they are dependent upon reporting by the victim, recording by the police and other factors that may lead to a degree of inaccuracy. While accepting that there is inaccuracy, Baron and Straus argue that in relative terms such indexes are satisfactory for their purposes. Some states such as Alaska and Florida tended to have high rates of rape given the size of their population and other states such as Maine and North Dakota tended to have substantially lower rates of rape compared to their population size. The crime figures were rape reports in the Uniform Crime Report statistics from the early 1980s.

The researchers also collected a number of other indexes of significant differences among the 50 states based on sociological theory. These included the following, which essentially constitute three different theories about why rape rates vary across different communities:

- *Cultural spillover*: this was measured in terms of the *Legitimate Violence Index* which involved State-approved violence such as the acceptance of corporal punishment in schools and capital punishment rates for murder.
- *Gender inequality*: this was an index of the economic, legal and political status of women compared with men. The measures included the proportion of the state's senate that was female and the average income of employed women compared with that of employed men.
- *Social disorganisation*: this was based on indicators of social instability due to weakening forces of social regulation. Factors such as geographical mobility, divorce, the proportion of lone-parent families and a lack of religious affiliation were included in these.

There was support for the *gender inequality* and *social disorganisation* explanations of rape. *Cultural spillover theory* was rejected on the basis of the data. In other words, the findings suggest that the greater gender inequality in favour of males and the greater social disorganisation then the greater the amount of rape.

BOX 9.2 Controversy

Sexual fantasy and sex offending

It is commonly accepted that sexual fantasy, especially violent sexual fantasy, has some role to play in the most serious sexual crimes including sexual murders. The work of MacCulloch *et al.* (1983) was particularly influential in this regard. Clinicians believe that there is a process by which somewhat obsessive sexual fantasies escalate in frequency and extremity. Eventually these may lead to violent and sexual criminal acts. Following this there may be satiation. This sort of escalating cycle of fantasy is described in the writings of clinicians dealing with paedophiles (e.g. Wyre, 1990, 1992). Fantasy-reduction and fantasy control is an important theme in the therapy employed with sex offenders. Some therapists employ the term *directed masturbation* in which the offender is encouraged to masturbate to sexual imagery which is appropriate (e.g. consensual sex with two adult women) in an attempt to recondition appropriate sexual preference (Cooper, 2005). It is also useful to note that research seems to have established that child molesters tend to have more fantasies about children when they are in a negative mood state (feeling depressed or miserable, for example) than at other times (Looman, 1999).

Others, dealing with non-offender populations, have taken a rather different view about the role of fantasy in sexual relationships (e.g. Cramer and Howitt, 1998). It would seem clear that in sexual relationships, there may be a big difference between the contents of fantasy and expectations about sexual relations. Sexual thoughts that lead to sexual arousal are commonplace for both men and women (Jones and Barlow, 1990). Sexual fantasy within the relationships of ordinary couples may be at variance with principles such as monogamy, tenderness and sharing. This is as true of women as it is of men. Sexual fantasy in sexual intercourse and masturbation occurs at very high rates (Knafo and Jaffe, 1984). In other words, sexual fantasy may be construed as normal and it is common to find somewhat

unacceptable themes in fantasy. For example, Kirkendall and McBride (1990) established that more than a third of men and a quarter of women fantasised of being forced into sexual relations.

A number of possible links between sexual fantasy and offending may be hypothesised (Howitt, 2000, 2004). One crucial piece of information would be to assess whether the reduction of sexual fantasy through therapeutic intervention actually reduces offending. There is little direct evidence on this. Hall, Hirschman and Oliver (1995) describe a meta-analysis of studies of the effects of sex offender treatment programmes on recidivism. There was a negative effect of behavioural therapies directed mainly towards fantasy reduction: that is, more recidivism where sexual fantasy had been reduced. Also of significance is Daleiden *et al.*'s (1998) finding that the difference between offenders and non-offenders is not in terms of having 'deviant' sexual fantasies but that offenders have fewer normal fantasies! The lack of normal fantasy is what is dangerous. Interestingly, a small study involving largely homosexual paedophiles found that those engaging in deviant fantasy were less likely to use coercion and more likely to engage in 'friendship formation' in the process of offending (Looman, 1999).

Where do fantasies come from? They seem to emerge developmentally at a quite early stage. More than 80 per cent of offenders reported having deviant sexual fantasies by the age of 15 years (Bates, 1996). Such fantasy might have its origins in childhood sexual abuse since some claim that there is a close link between early fantasy and features of their abuse (Howitt, 1995a, 1998a). Others find no such link (Waterhouse, Dobash and Carnie, 1994). Fantasy, in this formulation, is regarded as rising out of experience. If this is the case, then it becomes feasible that offenders engage in offending not because they are driven by their fantasies but in order to provide

▶

BOX 9.2 (continued)

fantasy imagery. Sex offences are quite frequently non-consummatory since penetration and orgasm do not take place (Howitt, 1995a). An offender, for example, might limit his sexual contact to touching a child through its clothes. One explanation of such behaviour may be that it is to provide the fantasy rather than to act out the fantasy.

In an attempt to see whether preventing masturbation could reduce sexual fantasy, Brown, Traverso and Fedoroff (1996) had outpatient paedophiles randomly assigned to a masturbation-allowed or masturbation-not-allowed condition. Self-report measures were used to assess the effectiveness of masturbation prevention. Only about a fifth of the paedophiles were able to abstain from masturbation for the required four-week period. There seemed to be no differences between the two groups in terms of intensity of sexual urges, urges to masturbate, urges for sex with adults and urges for sex with children. The low compliance of the offenders with the therapist's request not to masturbate should be assessed against the finding that paedophiles masturbated about four times each week. The authors regard what they see as a low sexual interest in this group as reason not to employ masturbation prohibition.

Sheldon and Howitt (2008) studied Internet child pornography offenders compared with regular contact paedophiles in terms of their use of sexual fantasy and the contents of their sexual fantasies. The most common sexual fantasies among these offenders with a sexual interest in children were the same as the typical heterosexual fantasies of men in general. So fantasies such as 'having vaginal intercourse with a willing female adult', 'giving oral sex to a willing female adult' and 'masturbating a willing female adult' were among the most common fantasies (Sheldon and Howitt, 2007, p. 195). Fantasies involving force were among the least common (e.g. 'overpowering a woman and forcing her to give me oral sex', Sheldon and Howitt, 2007, p. 197). Interestingly, the contact offenders reported fewer girl-oriented sexual fantasies than did the

Internet child pornography offenders. There was also some evidence that contact offenders had a greater tendency to use confrontational fantasies which involved things like 'exposing my genitals to an unsuspecting adult or adults' and 'making obscene phone calls' which implies that for them fantasy has to stray into the realms of experience (Sheldon and Howitt, 2007, p. 199). If anything, there seems to be a deficit in the amounts of sexual fantasy in contact offenders compared with Internet child pornography offences. This, of course, leaves open the possibility that contact offenders need to contact offend in order to stimulate their fantasy rather than offend to fulfil their fantasies.

Given that it is commonly assumed that deviant sexual fantasies are played out behaviourally by sex offenders (Williams, Cooper, Howell, Yuille and Paulhus, 2009), why does not every deviant sexual fantasy lead to deviant sexual behaviour? Sexual deviance may be defined by the criterion of an unusual source of sexual arousal. However, according to Williams *et al.*, the rates of deviant sexual fantasies are very similar for offender and non-offender samples. Given this, then just what determines whether a fantasy will be acted out in the form of a crime or not? The researchers used nine different deviant behaviours for their study including bondage, exhibitionism, fetishism involving objects, frotteurism, paedophilia, sadism, sexual assault, transvestism and voyeurism. The study involved non-offender male university students at a large Western USA university who completed a self-completion questionnaire pack anonymously. An 80 per cent return rate was obtained. The core of the research questionnaires was the Multidimensional Assessment of Sex and Aggression by Knight, Prentky and Cerce (1994). The items from this were rearranged into the nine areas of deviant sexual behaviour listed above in order to provide a measure each of them. The researchers also obtained self reports of the nine different deviant fantasies and behaviours.

Ninety five per cent of the participants reported having had at least one deviant sexual fantasy though only 74 per cent had actively engaged in one or more of these activities. The mean rate for experiencing each fantasy was 52 per cent, which was higher than the mean rate for engaging in the corresponding sexually deviant behaviour, which was much lower at 21 per cent. Despite there being a moderately high correlation between having a deviant fantasy and carrying it out this relationship was not statistically significant for paedophile fantasies. To put it another way, fantasisers were behavers in only 38 per cent of cases but behavers were fantasisers in 96 per cent of cases. Sixty-three per cent of the sample claimed to use pornography currently and the mean fantasy score was significantly greater for those who did than for those who did not. Users also reported significantly more carrying out of fantasy. The use of pornography had a partial but statistically significant mediating effect on the relationship between fantasy and fantasy-related behaviours. Pornography's influence on deviancy was mediated in part by an increase in deviant fantasy.

Are there any factors which determine whether a fantasy will be acted out in behaviour? A second study by Williams *et al.* (2009) examined the possible mediating influence of different variables including the eight personality characteristics – these were agreeableness, conscientiousness, extraversion, Machiavellianism, narcissism, openness to experience, psychopathy and stability. It emerged that the link between fantasy and deviant behaviour applied only to those individuals who reported high levels of deviant sexual fantasy. Furthermore, the association between pornography use and sexually deviant behaviours only applied to those participants who were also high on psychopathy. It has to be stressed that this research involved seemingly normal university students rather than offenders. The equivalent research has yet to be carried out on offenders. Nevertheless, it is important to know that the prevalence rates for deviant sexual fantasies in offender samples has been found to be approximately 80–90 per cent.

In a systematic review of sexual murderers which involved seven different studies and a total of 171 sexual murderers, Maniglio (2010) concluded that sexual fantasies might lead to sexual murder when the offender had early traumatic life experiences or more extreme social and/or sexual dysfunctions. There are problems for researchers since legal definitions of sexual homicide in the USA exclude many crimes which appear to have a sexual element and, in addition, sexual killing is relative rare among homicides. The research suggested that deviant sexual fantasies may lead to sexual homicide when there has been early traumatic experiences and social and/or sexual dysfunction.

More on the theory of rape

There has been one systematic attempt to compare the different theoretical explanations of rape that should be considered. Ellis (1989) identified three major theories of rape:

- feminist theory;
- social learning theory;
- evolutionary theory.

In many ways influenced by the socio-biological approach to crime (see Chapter 8), Ellis suggests that it is possible to generate testable hypotheses from each of these theories.

Feminist theory

This essentially argues that rape is built into the gender structure of society. A dense network of different ways of controlling women buttresses male power. As such, one would expect this control to be manifest in many aspects of society. It has been manifest in the law (e.g. the denial of women's property rights, considering it reasonable that a man should be allowed to beat his wife and so forth) as well as domestic relations between men and women. Basic tenets of feminist theory, according to Ellis, are the following:

- Rape should be associated with sex disparities in social status and power. (p. 20)
- Rape is primarily motivated by a desire for power and dominance rather than a desire for sex. (p. 21)

From these basic ideas of feminist theory, Ellis derives what he considers to be formal hypotheses that can be tested against empirical data concerning rape:

- Societal trends toward sexual egalitarianism should be associated with a lessening of rape victimisation. (p. 28)

The evidence does support the idea that gender equality in society is associated with fewer rapes, as we have already seen.

- Rapists should hold less egalitarian and more pro-rape attitudes toward women than non-rapists. (p. 29)

This hypothesis is not clearly supported by the studies which find that rapists are no different from other offenders in terms of their cognitions about rape and women, as we saw above.

Social learning theory

This basically suggests that rapists learn to be rapists by learning pro-rape beliefs and attitudes from their social milieu. For various reasons, rapists tend to learn the pro-rape cognitions more effectively than non-rapists do. Ellis mentions the following hypotheses based on social learning theory, among others. Notice that the hypotheses derived from social learning theory are not necessarily very different from those proposed by feminist theory:

- Rapists should hold attitudes that are more favourable towards rape, and towards violence in general, than other men. (p. 33)

We have seen that this hypothesis is not clearly supported.

- Exposure to violent pornography should increase male propensities to commit rape, and otherwise to behave violently toward women. (p. 35)

This is one of the pornography-related hypotheses listed by Ellis, who regards pornography as an almost essential learning course for rape. This is a somewhat controversial area and Ellis's views reflect just one side of the controversy (Box 10.1).

Evolutionary theory

Socio-biological theory is largely about one's adaptiveness for the transmission of one's genetic material to the next generation. Rape, according to a socio-biological perspective, should reflect this basic principle of behaviour. In other words, the hypotheses for evolutionary theory should emphasise the functionality of rape for the transmission of genetic material to the next generation. The following hypotheses are feasible:

- Tendencies to rape must be under some degree of genetic influence. (p. 43)
- Forced copulations should impregnate victims, at least enough to offset whatever risks rapists have of being punished for their offences. (p. 47)
- Rape victims should be primarily of reproductive age. (p. 50)
- Rape should be vigorously resisted by victims, especially when the offender is someone to whom the females are not sexually attracted. (p. 50)
- Rapists (especially those who assault strangers) should be less likely than other males to attract voluntary sex partners. (p. 52)

To the extent that these hypotheses are clear, there is generally some evidence to support them. Ellis's (1989) position is that basically each of the different theories has some commendable features and that a synthesis of various elements is essential to understanding rape. Unlike some recent writers, Ellis is an advocate of the view that rape is partially a sexual rather than a violent crime.

More recently, another theory about rape claiming to be based on evolutionary psychology has received a great deal of publicity especially in the United States. Thornhill and Palmer (2000) are not psychologists despite this. Their argument is that subject to conditions all men are capable of rape. Rape, they argue, has to be considered to be motivated by sex. Men who are essentially disenfranchised from society, lacking status in the sexual order, are still driven to procreate. Cognitions may play a part in that men are calculating beings capable of evaluating the benefits and costs of rape. In the theory, women are regarded as contributing to their victimisation by rapists by failing to avoid dangerous situations conducive to rape attack. The trauma that follows rape is regarded as a beneficial matter since the women would be less inclined to put themselves in any of the situations which are conducive to rape in future. Many of their ideas have placed Thornhill and Palmer at the centre of significant criticism from academics and others.

Others have recently outlined their own theoretical relationships between evolutionary concepts and crime.

A good example of this is Quinsey (2002) who relates evolutionary theory to sexual crimes as well as other types of crime. Evolutionary theory, he suggests, is environmental and selectionist in nature because the environments of our ancestors have helped select particular characteristics of individuals which are genetically transmitted over generations. Those characteristics that tend to be emphasised as a consequence of natural selection are termed *adaptations*. They are related to successful reproduction strategies since if they were not then the adaptations would die out. Quinsey gives a simple example. He suggests that a man in the 'ancestral environment' who had a genetically produced sexual proclivity for trees would have little reproductive success with females and so would not sire future offspring. So males would demonstrate features that lead to reproductive success with females which may not be the same as those that lead to reproductive success in females themselves. Males and females, in the evolutionary view, do not share reproductive interests entirely. Quinsey argues that sexual coercion illustrates this divergence between males and females. While, according to the environmental psychologists, it is in the interest of women to seek a male who provides the greatest advantage in terms of protection and care and genetic potential, sexual coercion essentially prevents women exercising choice in this respect. So one argument from the evolutionary perspective is that in circumstances where the costs of disregarding the mating preferences of females are insignificant then coercive sexual behaviour is more common. Circumstances in which this would happen include the situation of soldiers in an occupying country or when the man expresses sexually callous attitudes towards women anyway. The problem is, of course, that without the crucial evidence that links sexual coercion to genetic make-up in some way, many other explanations of sexual coercion are equally viable. For example, Quinsey points out that psychopathy and sexual deviation as measured by plethysmography together predict new sex offences. Unfortunately for this explanation, psychopaths commit many types of crime more frequently than others and not just sexually coercive crime.

Rape is a complex matter and we need to research it from a range of different perspectives. An example of alternative ways of studying the topic can be found in the work of Dale, Davies and Wei (1997). They investigated the conversations between rapists and their victims during the offence. It might be possible to analyse the discourse used at the time of the rape with the type of the rape and the psychological nature of the offender. Rape, they argue, is a constrained activity in which what the victim can say is limited by the situation as much as what the attacker may say. Information was obtained concerning over 250 offences by 55 rapists. Examples are provided by Dale *et al.* of different types of speech act that have been used by rapists. One strategy they mention is described as scripting. This 'essentially' is telling the victim just what to say and what to do:

> 'Kiss me: cuddle me: pretend I'm your boyfriend. Say something . . . Say "Hello Robert" . . . Louder.'
>
> (pp. 663–4)

Or acts of justification may be used to close the offence:

> 'You'll look back on this in a couple of weeks and think you enjoyed it.'
>
> (p. 665)

Or the victim might be told:

> 'I wouldn't have done it if you were a virgin.'
>
> (p. 665)

The co-occurrence of different discourse strategies and their relative occurrence in particular types of crime may hold valuable information for the eventual identification of offenders.

Synthesising explanations of sex offending

Certain concepts commonly reoccur in the research literature on sex offending. Lussier, Leclerc, Cale and Proulx (2007) point to three major concepts which tend to dominate in explanations of sex offending. They concentrated on empirically testing the role of the concepts of internalisation, externalisation and sexualisation using data from interviews with members of a large sample of sex offenders. According to Lussier *et al.*, each of these concepts consists of several, interrelated components:

- Externalisation is undercontrolled behaviour and involves authority conflict, recklessness, covert externalised behaviours and overt externalised behaviours.
- Internalisation is overcontrolled behaviour and is made up of social isolation, depression and anxiety/somatic complaints.

- Sexualisation is a pattern of precociously over-sexualised behaviours and can involve things like impersonal sex, sexually compulsive behaviour, and a preoccupation with sex. The view is that offenders are essentially driven to engage in deviant sexual behaviours. Lussier *et al.* use the term sexualisation to describe the lack of control offenders have over their sexual behaviour and feelings and the high strength and frequency of their sexual libido.

Examples of each of these components are given in Figure 9.5. For each of the individual concepts, the individual components are likely to co-occur. Thus depression, social withdrawal and anxiety are described as commonly occurring prior to the commission of sexual offences by offenders. Of course, not every researcher uses the same terminology in order to describe these different constructs.

The research team interviewed more than 500 convicted sex offenders in Quebec concerning their developmental history. They collected a wide variety of information but concentrated on internalisation, externalisation and sexualisation. Their analysis employed advanced statistical techniques (structural equation modelling and confirmatory factor analysis) to test various models (patterns of relationships) which might account for the

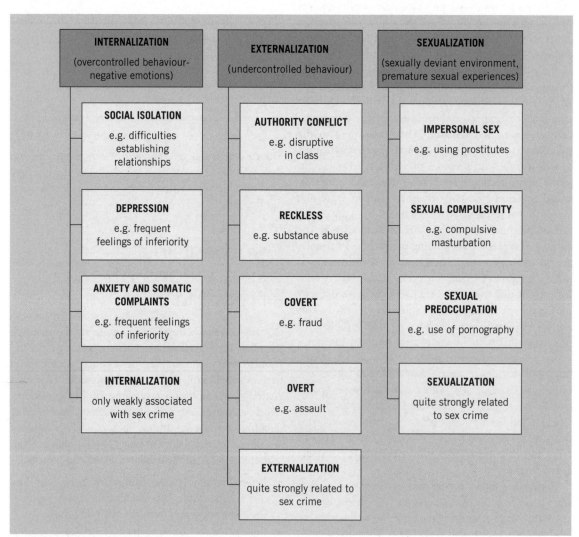

Figure 9.5 Internalisation, externalisation and sexualisation as concepts in the explanation of sex offending

data. For example, the first model they tried was based on the general deviancy model which would suggest that internalisation, externalisation and sexualisation were highly interrelated. If an offender was high on one, then he would be high on the others. This model fitted the data badly – that is, the assumptions of the General Deviancy Model found poor support from the data. The best fitting model was one in which internalisation, externalisation and sexualisation are largely independent of each other. Slight modifications had to be made to the model as it was found that impersonal sex was related to both sexualisation and externalisation (not just to sexualisation as was

originally thought) and compulsivity was related to both sexualisation and internalisation. These are empirical linkages, of course, and not conceptual ones.

You will also see in Figure 9.5 that sexualisation and externalisation were the more powerful constructs in explaining the extent of sexual offending. Internalisation was only weakly related to it. However, the construct of internalisation was important since where the victim was a child there tended to be higher internalisation. The evidence of a clear sexualisation pathway probably reinforces the importance of this in explaining why some offenders may specialise in sexual offences.

Main points

- The legal definition of rape often now includes non-consensual anal and oral penetration with a penis as well as that of a vagina. In the last two decades or so conceptions of the nature of rape have changed, especially under the influence of feminist thinking which construes rape not simply as a sexual crime but as another aspect of male control of women. Rape, defined legally, has happened to 1 in 20 women at some time in their lives although the annual rate is much lower. This is according to victim studies. Rape is a relatively under-reported crime and is much more often carried out by men whom the woman knows rather than strangers. It is a crime more commonly carried out by younger offenders and shows much the same characteristics in terms of offender characteristics as other crimes of violence.

- Anger is a component of some rapes but not all. The commonest type of rape is described as the power-assurance rape. The offender is insecure in his masculinity which he tries to assert through his use of power. As a consequence, he does not actually get the reassurance that he needs from his actions and is likely to reoffend after a short period of time. Other researchers find that other patterns can be identified in the characteristics of the rape itself without reference to psychological motives. One pattern is involvement in which the offender tries to reassure the victim throughout the act in some way or he may indicate that he knows her or try to intrude into her

home – so he may compliment her. It is commonly accepted that rape myths are conducive to rape offenders. Rape myths are exemplified by such ideas as if a woman wears sexy clothes, she is to blame if she is raped. However, there is no evidence that such ideas distinguish rapists from other men. Evolutionary explanations of rape also tend to emphasise traditional gender-stereotypical ideas and seem, in many ways, the antithesis of feminist ideas about rape.

- In the forensic setting, there are a number of issues that are especially pertinent. One is the use of phallometry/plethysmography, which is basically a technique for assessing a man's sexual responsiveness to different types of sexual imagery. It involves using a tube or cuff around the penis. Changes in the volume or circumference of the man's penis can be recorded from this apparatus and are held to be indicative of sexual arousal. In this way, a man's responsiveness to rape imagery can be assessed, for example. Sexual fantasy, although commonly accepted as a driving force in sexual offences, is poorly understood and inadequately dealt with in forensic and criminal psychology. The common view is that sexual fantasies will be acted upon and, sometimes, this will be in criminal ways in the form of sex offences. This contrasts with what we know about sexual fantasy in non-offender groups, which indicates that fantasy does not always need to be acted out in order to have erotic effects.

Further reading

Up-to-date theory and research can be found in:

Gannon, T.A. and Ward, T. (2008) 'Rape: psychopathology and theory' in D.R. Laws and W.T. O'Donohue (2008) *Sexual Deviance: Theory, Assessment, and Treatment* (2nd edn) New York: Guilford Press, pp. 336–55.

Ward, T., Polaschek, D.L.L. and Beech, A.R. (2006) *Theories of Sexual Offending* Chichester: John Wiley.

The following are classics in the field and are still worth reading:

Burt, M. (1980) 'Cultural myths and support for rape' *Journal of Personality and Social Psychology* **38**, 217–30.

Groth, A.N. with Birnbaum, H.J. (1980) *Men Who Rape: The Psychology of the Offender* New York: Plenum Press.

Visit our website at www.pearsoned.co.uk/howitt for self-test and essay questions, annotated further reading, audio interviews with researchers in the field, weblinks and more information on becoming a forensic psychologist.

Chapter 10

Sexual offenders 2: paedophiles and child molestation

Overview

- The public show considerable levels of animosity towards sex offenders against children and seem to want a mixture of punishment and therapeutic treatment for convicted offenders, although they do not want treatment centres in their own neighbourhood. Although psychologists seem less hostile towards paedophiles than some professional groups (e.g. police officers), there is a danger that forensic and criminal psychologists are affected in their professional work by this antagonism.

- The link between pornography and sex offending is a matter of some controversy. On balance, studies of actual sex crime rates and the availability of pornography reveal no causal influence of pornography on sexual offences.

- It has proven a somewhat fruitless endeavour to seek personality characteristics based on conventional measures that differentiate sexual offenders against children from other men or other offenders. It is more adequate to suggest that sex offenders against children do not stand out in the crowd. Nevertheless, paedophilia is a diagnostic category in the American Psychiatric Association's *Diagnostic and Statistical Manual*. This may make it a mental abnormality but it does not mean that paedophiles are suffering a psychotic illness. Many sex offences are committed by young people, including ones against children.

- Child molesters are often classified as fixated or regressed. Fixated paedophiles are halted in their psycho-sexual development so that they retain a sexual interest in children. Regressed offenders have matured sexually but have returned to an earlier stage of psycho-sexual development. The regressed offender is much more likely to be an intrafamilial (incestuous) offender. These categories are problematic in that it has been shown that many incestuous offenders also offend against children outside their family.

- It is difficult to assess the true rate of paedophile orientation in the general population. One study found that a quarter of men in the sample showed greater sexual response (as measured by phallometry) to erotic stimuli involving children than to those involving women. About 4 per cent claimed to have engaged in paedophile activity.

- Only a minority of paedophile acts involve penile penetration and many involve non-contact offences such as flashing and peeping. Bribery rather than other more violent forms of coercion is typical of paedophile contact with children.

- Recidivism in sex offenders against children seems to be comparatively low. Reconviction (as well as previous convictions) tends to be for non-sexual offences.

- There are a number of important theoretical models which attempt to explain sexual offences against children:

  - The *preconditions model* suggests that the paedophile needs emotional congruence with children, sexual arousal by children, blockages against social contact with other adults, and the removal of inhibitions against sex with children.

  - The *psychotherapeutic/cognitive model* is built on the idea that offenders have distorted beliefs about the sexuality of children and engage in various types of denial to minimise the psychological impact of offending on themselves.

  - The *sexualisation model* assumes that certain forms of early abusive experiences and sexual contacts with other children lead to paedophile interests and a paedophile lifestyle.

  - The *pathways model* suggests that there are several routes to paedophile offending which include intimacy and social skills deficits, sexual scripts learnt in childhood being distorted due to early sexual experiences in some individuals, and emotional dysregulation when offenders avoid guilt when offending against children or when they fail to learn the coping skills to help them deal with stress development.

- Internet paedophile offenders can commit a number of offences but ones associated with child pornography are the commonest. Few seem to have had previous convictions for contact offences against children. They are theoretically of great importance since they seem to be difficult to differentiate from other paedophiles other than by their lack of contact offences. Consequently, they appear to be desisters from acting out their sexual interest in children by contact offending, thus making the link between paedophile orientation and paedophile offending less clear-cut than is often suggested.

Introduction

Sexual offenders against children are regarded with a special hostility by the general public. This should be of particular concern to forensic and criminal psychologists for three major reasons:

- It is possible that their professional judgement will be affected by these general anti-paedophile feelings.

- That assessment of the risk of recidivism (reoffending) by paedophiles sometimes has to be made under the pressure of public opinion in particularly notorious cases.

- Treatment for sex offenders, and paedophiles in particular, may be put in jeopardy because of the public's reluctance to have treatment facilities in their communities.

From time to time, there have been public protests about the location of treatment facilities. For example, in the 1990s the UK's Gracewell Clinic's new premises were apparently subject to an arson attack. Similarly, units have been forced to close down or not allowed to start their work in other countries such as the United States. More formal evidence of the public's hostility towards paedophiles can be found in the findings of a postal survey conducted in the United Kingdom (Brown, 1999). This research investigated stereotypes about sex offenders and attitudes towards their treatment. Mostly, the public felt that the treatment of sex offenders was desirable though they nevertheless wished offenders to be punished. The basic division of opinion on the treatment of sex offenders was that:

- 51 per cent of the public felt treatment of sex offenders was a good idea;

- 35 per cent were undecided;

- 13 per cent said that sex offenders should never be given therapy.

Of those who were favourable towards the idea of treatment, a small majority (51 per cent) believed that treatment facilities should be available in both prison and the community. Nearly as many (45 per cent) thought that treatment should *only* occur as part of the term of imprisonment. Virtually no one thought that treatment should be confined to community settings. Generally, a mixture of custodial sentence together with treatment was seen as acceptable. The vast majority (88 per cent) believed that treatment without a prison sentence was unacceptable.

This may sound fine and positive, especially to those involved in treating offenders. Unfortunately, the strength of feeling in favour of remedial work with sex offenders was not so strong as that in favour of punishment-based approaches. The participants in the survey were all living in the same community and were asked their views about a treatment centre to be located there. The findings on this contrast somewhat with attitudes to treatment in the abstract:

- Only 36 per cent were in favour of a treatment centre to be located in their community.

- As many as 44 per cent said that they would not be prepared to move house into an area in which there was a treatment centre for sex offenders.

- Those who were against a treatment centre in their community expressed willingness to take action in support of their views. Twenty-six per cent would start a campaign against it and 33 per cent said that they would join an existing campaign against it; 80 per cent would sign a petition against it.

- Those in favour of a treatment centre in their community were much less willing to take action in support of their belief. Only 9 per cent of them were prepared to start a campaign in favour and just 7 per cent said that they would join a pre-existing campaign; 50 per cent said that they would sign a petition in support of the treatment centre.

There are other reasons to believe that the community is increasingly intolerant of sex offenders. La Fond (1999) suggests that, in the United States, this intolerance has resulted in extensive legislation aimed at controlling (rather than just punishing) sex offenders against children. Similar trends have been noted in the United Kingdom (Howitt, 2005). The American legislation includes sex offender registers, notification of the community about sex offenders in that community and laws encouraging chemical castration. More recently still, laws have been introduced allowing the commitment of sexual predators.

The latter, known as *sexually violent predator (SVP) laws*, can result in sex offenders being detained after their prison sentence has finished. The legal requirement is that it has to be shown that the individual both is dangerous and presents a high risk of reoffending. Furthermore, the individual in question must have either a 'personality disorder' or 'mental abnormality' which may lead to the reoffending. The process involves a trial at which the offender is legally represented. Furthermore, the offender may have an expert of his own choice to conduct an evaluation separate from that carried out for the state. Offenders who are committed to further incarceration must be given therapy and the question of their release periodically reviewed.

Similar processes can be seen in research in the USA into the registration of sex offenders. Levenson *et al.* (2007) found that nearly three-quarters of participants in their survey said that they would support sex offender registration even though there is no evidence that it reduces sexual abuse. Extending this to deal with beliefs about the registration of juvenile sex offenders in the USA, Salerno *et al.* (2010) found that family law lawyers were less supportive of registry laws for juveniles than for adult sex offenders. However, the general public (in this case represented by a sample of university students) and prosecution lawyers supported registration laws for juveniles as strongly as they did for adults. The public tend to envisage an extreme prototype of the juvenile sex offender when making their judgements. But if they envisage or are encouraged to envisage a less extreme prototype then their support for registration tends to be less extreme. These effects are mediated by the perceptions of threat posed by the juvenile sex offender (utilitarian concerns) but also by moral outrage (retributive concerns).

Not only are the attitudes of the general public important; the views of staff working in the criminal justice system have an even more direct impact on how offenders are treated in the system. Radley (2001) used the *Attitude Toward Sex Offenders Questionnaire* with samples of police officers, prison officers, and probation workers and psychologists. The sorts of items involved include (p. 6):

- sex offenders are different from most people;

- sex offenders never change;

- I think I would like a lot of sex offenders.

Although attitudes varied, it was clear that police officers were more hostile than probation workers and

BOX 10.1 Controversy

Pornography and sex offending

Ted Bundy, the notorious US serial killer, claimed to have been influenced to his violent sexual crimes by pornography. The role of pornography in creating sexual attitudes has been part of the feminist debate for two decades at least. Here, we are concerned only with the evidence that pornography might lead to sex offending. Analyses of the content of pornography indicate that at least some of it contains anti-women themes such as rape, violence and degradation. The extent differs according to the study. For example, Thompson (1994) found little to support the view that pornography was full of such imagery whereas others (Itzin, 1992) find the reverse. This is partly a matter of how a particular image is interpreted and codified.

The range of studies is wide and stretches from laboratory experiments to case studies. Here are some of the more important studies:

- *The Danish Experiment*: Kutchinsky (1970, 1973) carried out research into the social consequences of liberalising the law in Denmark in the 1960s. Pornography became increasingly available. The crime statistics over this period tended to decline. The crimes affected were those such as indecent exposure, peeping, indecent language and so forth. These are the relatively trivial crimes which might be most affected by changes of public attitude towards sex such that they are less inclined to report trivial crimes to the police. There was no such change in the reporting of rape. In later studies, Kutchinsky has claimed to find that the liberalisation of pornography laws has not brought about increases in the rates of sex crimes: things have either held more or less steady or rape rates have declined. These researches were carried out in Denmark, Germany and the United States (Kutchinsky, 1991).
- *Court's propositions*: Court (1977, 1984) put forward several hypotheses about the effects of pornography on sex crimes. For example, he has suggested that in parallel to the availability of increasingly violent pornography, the amount of violence in rapes will have increased over time. Although Court has evidence for this proposition, it should be pointed out that he is a little selective in that he does not examine every country where crime statistics are available. For example, Howitt (1998b) showed that

there is evidence that over a fairly lengthy period, rape in the United Kingdom shows trends upwards, which cannot be explained by changes in legislation (which became more controlling). Since the contents of pornography have tended to remain relatively free of violence, the steady rise in rape cannot be explained by that either (Thompson, 1994).
- *Developmental studies*: a number of researchers have studied the aetiology of interest and use of pornography in the life cycle of sex offenders. There is some evidence that masturbation comes early in the adolescent lives of sex offenders and earlier than use of pornography (Condron and Nutter, 1988; Howitt and Cumberbatch, 1990). Their deviancy seems to precede their use of pornography in general. This sequence of events suggests that pornography is not a cause of this deviancy although their interest in it may be a consequence of their deviancy.
- *Area studies*: Baron and Straus (1984, 1989) and others (Gentry, 1991; Scott and Schwalm, 1988) looked at the relationship between the amount of pornography circulating in different states of the United States and rape rates in those states. Although they found a relationship between the two, since this was strongest for the circulation of pornography aimed at women, it seems unlikely that this sort of pornography actually caused the rapes according to Baron and Straus.
- *Paedophile preferences*: in terms of paedophiles, the few available studies have concentrated on the use made of pornography by paedophiles. Marshall (1988) found, for example, that sex offenders show little preference for and arousal to pornography redolent of their offending. They tend to use a variety of pornographic stimuli. Similarly, Howitt (1995b) describes how paedophiles will use a variety of imagery in their fantasies including Walt Disney films featuring children, television advertisements for baby products and adult heterosexual pornography. This material is used to generate personal paedophile fantasy.

It would appear that, like many non-offenders, sex offenders use pornography and other imagery. It is difficult to argue that this material causes their offending. However, see Box 9.2 on sexual fantasy and sex offending.

psychologists. There was also evidence of similar differences between prison officers and probation workers/psychologists. Female staff members were more favourably disposed to sex offenders. There was also, possibly, evidence that attitudes towards sex offenders have become less hostile in recent years.

Mental illness and sexual predators

According to Howitt (1995a), there is no reason to think that paedophiles share particular personality characteristics. Apart from their offending behaviour, they are fairly typical of men in general. Paedophiles, in general, simply do not stand out in the crowd – which is part of the reason that their offending goes undetected (La Fontaine, 1990). If the US sexually violent predator laws are to be applied to an offender, the matter of the personality disorder or mental abnormality that led to the offending has to be considered. Neither of these concepts is an easy one for psychiatry or psychology. They seem more readily defined by the law. A mental abnormality legally is 'a congenital or acquired condition affecting the emotional or volitional capacity which predisposes the person to the commission of criminal sexual acts in a degree constituting such person a menace to the health and safety of others'. There is no requirement that the condition is amenable to treatment for the sexual predator laws to apply. So what is the problem for psychology and psychiatry?

No generally accepted definition or meaning for the term mental abnormality exists in psychiatry (or psychology for that matter). In the *Diagnostic and Statistical Manual of the American Psychiatric Association* (see Box 21.1) there is an entry for paedophilia. Some psychiatrists and psychologists claim that men who offend against children can be regarded as suffering from a mental abnormality on the basis of this. Without treatment, the abnormality may well lead to reoffending, they suggest. Legal concepts and psychological concepts do not always equate, as we saw in Chapter 1. Legal concepts may sometimes be extremely difficult to translate effectively into ideas acceptable to psychologists. Nevertheless, for psychologists to function effectively in court it is essential to bridge the differences between the disciplines of psychology and law. Consequently, forensic psychologists have to develop their own understanding of legal terms.

All of this may seem a reasonable approach. Nevertheless, according to La Fond (1999), there is no equivalent of paedophilia for rapists in the DSM. The idea of a personality disorder does not occur in DSM-IV – the nearest thing being antisocial personality disorder (ASPD). The difficulty is that a very substantial minority of incarcerated offenders of all sorts fit this classification – the figure might be almost as high as 50 per cent. All types of offenders may fit this classification including, but not exclusively, sex offenders. In other words, ASPD is so common that it is not really predictive of sexual reoffending. (Psychological risk assessment is discussed in Chapter 27.) In other words, although the concept of personality disorder may be 'extended' to fit dangerous sex offenders, this is at the expense of psychological rigour.

Classifications of child molesters

One of the commonest taxonomies of child molesters is the dichotomy between fixated and regressed offenders (Groth and Birnbaum, 1978):

- *Fixated offenders*: these are said to be developmentally fixated on a permanent or a temporary basis such that their sexual interest is in children rather than adults. Although they may have had sexual contact with adults, this contact is more coincidental than intentional since peer relationships are not psychologically an integral part of their sexuality.

- *Regressed offenders*: these are men who matured in their sexuality but demonstrated a return to an earlier level of psychosexual development. Their psychosexual history would show primary interest in peer age or adult individuals rather than younger ones. Interest in the latter seems to reflect almost a reversal to a more childlike sexuality.

Important differences are found between the two types especially in terms of their relationship history. This is perhaps not surprising given the above descriptions, but fixated offenders rarely are or have been married (something like one in eight have been married) whereas about three-quarters of regressed offenders have been married. Perhaps even more significantly, the fixated offenders offend most commonly against strangers or acquaintances whereas the regressed type offend commonly within the network of friends or relatives. This is the very sort of victim which feminist writers on child sexual abuse have regarded as incestuous in its broadest terms (Howitt, 1992).

While it may seem commonsensical to suggest that adult men who have sexual relationships with women have 'regressed' when they offend sexually against children, this is actually somewhat naive. Some offenders target women with children for the primary purpose of gaining access to the children. While they may engage in sex with the mother, in some cases they describe this as being accompanied by paedophile sexual fantasy (Howitt, 1995a). There are other reasons to be cautious about the taxonomy:

- Despite claims to the contrary, incestuous fathers have frequently also offended against children outside the family or raped women (Abel *et al.*, 1983). In other words, offending against children is a sexual preference, not the product of family circumstances such as stress or sexual privation. This does not mean that the groups are not to some extent different. For example, Miner and Dwyer (1997) found that incestuous offenders were more able to develop trusting interpersonal relationships than exhibitionists and child molesters.

- Incestuous offenders seem to show patterns of sexual arousal to 'erotic' depictions of children (Howitt, 1995a) despite the argument that they are 'forced' by circumstances to regress to sex with children. That is to say, explanations of family factors leading to offending against children by offenders possibly serve merely as excuses. Studer *et al.* (2002) used phallometry (see Box 9.1) in order to assess child molesters' responses to slides of different ages, sexes and body shapes. The molesters could be grouped into incestuous and non-incestuous offenders against children. It was not possible to differentiate the two groups effectively on the basis of their responses to the slides. Just over 40 per cent of each group showed their strongest erotic response to the slides that featured pubescent children. More of the incestuous offenders showed their major response to slides of adults (37 per cent) compared with 19 per cent of the non-incestuous group. More of the non-incestuous group (30 per cent) showed their primary erotic response to pre-pubescent children compared with 13 per cent of the incestuous group. So, clearly, there are some differences but equally clearly there are

sizeable numbers of incestuous offenders who show exactly the same sort of erotic attraction towards under-age persons that non-incestuous offenders do. In terms of their self-reported offending, over 40 per cent of incestuous offenders had committed sexual offences against children outside the family.

- Groth and Birnbaum (1978) argue that homosexual men are never regressed offenders. By homosexual we mean men whose adult sexual orientation is towards men. (This is in order to differentiate them from heterosexual paedophiles and homosexual paedophiles who are defined in terms of the sex of their child victim, not their sexual history with adults.) This is a remarkable claim in some ways and difficult to accept. The implication is that sexual privation and stress do not affect gay men in the same way as they do heterosexual men. This clearly needs support, if it is true, which has never been provided.

Interestingly, there are sentencing differentials between heterosexual and homosexual child molesters. Walsh (1994) studied a sample of serious sex offenders in Ohio including rape as well as sexual offenders against children. His interest was in those who offended against boys compared with those who offended against girls. The former were nearly seven times more likely to be put in prison for their offence than the latter. According to Walsh, this is only accountable in terms of homophobic attitudes and beliefs. None of his other predictor variables (e.g. previous sexual offences, victim cooperation and so forth) seemed to account for this sentencing differential.

How common is paedophilia?

There is plenty of evidence that sexual abuse of youngsters below the age of consent is common. The research surveys on child sexual abuse provide a range of different answers to the question of how common such abuse is. Depending on the definition of abuse used – e.g. self-definition by the victim or legal definition – various estimates will be obtained. Furthermore, relatively unintrusive sexual acts such as passing suggestive remarks may be very common but nevertheless experienced as abuse (Kelly, 1988, 1989) whereas penetrative sex is relatively rare in this abuse (Nash and West, 1985). Once again, studies of offenders provide alternative perspectives from studies of victims. The difficulties of under-reporting of sexual offences are particularly strong in this area. Conviction data are poor indicators of the extent of victimisation.

One theoretically important question concerns the extent to which paedophilic sexual arousal can occur in 'normal' men. Is sexual arousal to imagery of children confined to offenders? Research on this is sparse. Hall *et al.* (1995) recruited a sample of American men through a newspaper advertisement. Each man was assessed in several different ways including plethysmography (see Box 9.1) in which changes in the size of a man's penis is regarded as an indicator of sexual arousal. A number of slides of nude pre-pubescent girls, nude women and clothed pre-pubescent girls were shown in random order to each participant. Generally, there were fairly high relations between the effects of the different pictures – that is, there was a tendency for the men who were aroused by one type of stimulus to be aroused by others.

Most importantly, about a quarter of the ordinary men showed more arousal to child stimuli than to those of women. About a fifth of the total sample reported that they had 'paedophile' interests. Only about 4 per cent of the sample reported that they had actually engaged in paedophile behaviour. This is a low figure compared with the figures for physiological arousal to paedophile stimuli and interest in children sexually. Nevertheless, one should be cautious when generalising from the findings of any single study:

- It is important to note that the men who were aroused by the paedophile stimuli were also aroused by other sexual imagery. This might indicate that they were not paedophile in their sexual orientation because they found all imagery, including that of adults, arousing. The men most easily aroused by the explicit pictures of adult women often could be aroused by the paedophile stimuli too.

- The men in the study were encouraged to allow themselves to be aroused. While this is not uncommon in studies using plethysmography, it may be a limitation in that it may result in more men showing signs of sexual arousal. The researchers have no way of knowing what was actually causing the arousal – what was in the experimental stimuli or personal fantasies created by the participant in order to become aroused? (See Boxes 9.1 and 9.2.)

Despite these criticisms, this is of theoretical importance since it may mean that paedophile orientation does not necessarily have to be acted out in the form of sexual abuse – that is, it is possible to desist from sexual crime against children.

The nature of paedophile offences

The general public learn about sex offending through the media. The media, of course, have their own agenda (Los and Chamard, 1997) in which the sensational and extreme acts are presented as the image of sex offenders and what they do. Paedophiles are mainly seen as murderous child abductors. Some are. However, in the United Kingdom, for example, convictions for child abduction averaged 44 annually in the 1990s. Of these abductions, 60 per cent were motivated by sexual factors (Erikson and Friendship, 2002). Research suggests that as a group, molesters carry out a wide range of different types of activity. Some, such as frotteurism and peeping behaviour, may not be recognised by the victim as such.

Like most crime issues, the picture of paedophile offending varies according to one's source of information. The context in which data are collected is also important. Studies of victims of child sexual abuse illustrate this. In a Los Angeles study, Wyatt (1985) found non-contact incidents such as flashing, improper comments and the like formed 40 per cent of the abusive experiences. Intercourse/attempted intercourse made up about a quarter of the incidents. A study of the perpetrators of child sexual abuse coming before the court in an area of south-east London over a period of two years also reveals something of the varied nature of such offending (Craissati and McClurg, 1997). The offences with which they were charged were overwhelmingly indecent assault (68 per cent). Gross indecency (11 per cent), buggery, i.e. anal intercourse, (9 per cent) and rape (7 per cent) were much less common. Under a third (29 per cent) of the men were convicted of penetrative offences. Nearly three-quarters (71 per cent) were convicted of offences against just one child (at that hearing) and 14 per cent were involved with offences involving a total of three or more victims. Male victims tended to be abused outside the home whereas female victims were relatively more likely to be victimised by relatives at home. The methods of grooming were: 40 per cent used bribery to gain the participation of the victim, 24 per cent used verbal threats and 16 per cent used physical threats. One of the subgroups, and the one most at risk of recidivism, tended to show the following characteristic pattern:

- to have been sexually abused as a child;
- to offend against boys;
- to have more victims;
- to have victims outside their family;
- to exhibit cognitive distortions;
- to have previous convictions for sexual offences.

Whatever the overall pattern, individual offenders may have very distinctive patterns of offending. For example, Robert Black, a lorry driver who killed girls and left their bodies in locations in various parts of the United Kingdom, had a pattern of penetrating the child's vagina with his finger and then killing her (Wyre and Tate, 1995): in other words, extreme violence but less extreme sexual acts.

BOX 10.2 Controversy

Sex offenders – minor or major recidivists?

A number of initiatives have been introduced in recent years against sex offending in a number of countries. The measures include sex offender registers that require that offenders, meeting the minimum requirements for registration, report their addresses to local police. Megan's Law-type initiatives require that the locations of sex offenders be revealed to the community. These initiatives seem to presume that sex offenders are repetitive and persistent in their offending and are persistently dangerous. There are two totally opposite points of view on this matter:

- *Little reoffending*. The clearest statement of this sort of position would include West's (1987) finding that most sex offenders convicted in British courts appear only once in court.
- *Major reoffenders*. A study by Abel *et al.* (1987) is frequently quoted as support for the view that sex offenders are chronic offenders. Taking 561 sex offenders attending a private clinic for sex offenders, the total offences that these men reported was approximately 250,000. In other words, the numerical average is 446 offences per man! This gives the very clear impression that sex offending is habitual and virtually without respite. These figures disguise the actual trends. For example, if the rapists alone are considered, the mean number of rapes admitted per rapist was seven. The median number of rapes is one. The median is the number of rapes committed by the rapist who is at the top of the bottom 50 per cent

of rapes but at the bottom of the remaining 50 per cent of rapes (that is, exactly in the middle of the frequency distribution). Most rapists actually admitted to just one rape. In other words, the vast proportion of rapes are committed by a small number of rapists.

This sort of analysis is complicated by a number of factors:

- The influence of the methodology employed. For example, men attending a private clinic may be inclined to admit to more offences simply because they feel that the therapist will see them as being cooperative and *not* in a state of denial of their offending behaviour. Indeed, there may be a motive for exaggerating the number of offences since the more cooperative an offender appears, the more likely he is seen as suitable for treatment and eventual release.
- Studies using reconviction rates severely underestimate the amount of reoffending. It is known that many rapes go unreported by the victim. Thus reconvictions may only identify a small proportion of reoffenders.

Fisher and Thornton (1993) argue that neither extreme captures the truth. There are some offenders who reoffend at a high rate and others who offend on a single occasion. Thus it is impossible to predict future offending simply on the basis of 'once a sex offender always a sex offender'. It is not true to say that all sex offenders are by definition high risk and certain to reoffend if allowed to go free.

There is a question of whether sex offenders are 'trapped' in an escalating spiral of increasingly serious and frequent offences. Mair (1995) argues that some of the views about sex offenders described in the writings of professionals essentially distort the reality of such offences. She suggests that a number of the claims made about sex offenders do not adequately reflect the available research evidence. The reason why we target sex offenders is not to do with their likelihood of reoffending – that is low compared with other types of crime – but because we find their offences disgusting and we are concerned about their victims. There are some sex offenders who are extremely dangerous, but this does not reflect the typical sex offender in this context. Mair is critical about some of the 'classic' studies such as Abel *et al.* (1987) described above. This is a much-quoted study that claimed very high levels of sexual recidivism. She points out that the sample used was very unrepresentative of sex offenders:

- they were not currently being prosecuted for sexual offences;
- they were offered treatment in exchange for confessions that would not be reported to others;
- they were likely to be the most deviant and troubled sex offenders simply because they had sought help independent of arrest.

However, the broad findings of the study have been endlessly reported as factually true of all offenders.

Similarly, Laws (1994) argued that up to one-half of rapists of adult women are at risk of being sexually violent to children. What does this mean? That studies have shown that half of rapists also sexually attack children? No: it means that he is referring to phallometric studies (see Box 9.1) which showed that a minority of rapists also show sexual arousal to child images.

The Grampian sex offenders study (Mair, 1995), much like other studies (see Box 27.3), demonstrated that after a follow-up period of, for almost all, over 10 years, about a half of the men were reconvicted – but for non-sexual offences. Those convicted of a hands-on offence (i.e. a sexual offence involving

touching the victim) were *less* likely to sexually reoffend than those with hands-off offences (e.g. indecent exposure). Such reconviction trends are reflected in the most recent figures. The UK Home Office (2004) has published figures which show that 19 per cent of sex offenders are reconvicted within two years of leaving prison. However, the reconviction rate for all adult prisoners is 52 per cent in the same period. Recidivism, in this case, is recidivism for any type of offence. Some would argue that sex offences are hard to detect and largely go unreported. However, it is difficult to explain why sex offenders should be better than other types of offender at avoiding arrest for crime in general and not just sex crime.

Recidivism rates are different for different types of sex offence. Hood *et al.* (2002) investigated sex offenders in the United Kingdom who had received prison sentences of four or more years. Most (59 per cent) had been convicted for penetrative or attempted penetrative sexual intercourse. The period studied in which the men were at risk of recidivsm was up to six years following release from prison. Incestuous offenders (intrafamilial offenders) had very low reconviction rates. In fact, none of them in this study was reconvicted for a sexual offence and sent to prison. Only 2 per cent were re-imprisoned for any type of offence. Extrafamilial offenders were rather more likely to reoffend sexually – up to 26 per cent of them did so. Only 11 per cent of the incest group were reconvicted for any type of offence whereas 47 per cent of the extrafamilial offender group were. The evidence suggested that those convicted of the most serious extrafamilial offences were the most likely to reoffend.

To bring these findings up to date, it is helpful to mention a recent review of 18 UK sexual reconviction studies half of which used prison samples (Leam *et al.*, 2008). The extensive preparatory work identified all the published and unpublished studies on the topic between the years 1991 and 2005. It is important to include non-published studies as these can include data which are different from the general trend. They found that over all of the samples the reconviction rate followed up for two years was 6 per cent and at

BOX 10.2 (continued)

six years and more it was 18 per cent. There were differences which indicated that incarcerated samples were more likely to reoffend sexually than those dealt with in the community. The figures for the incarcerated offenders were that 8 per cent reoffended after two years and 20 per cent reoffended after 6 years whereas the corresponding figures for the non-incarcerated sample were 6 per cent and 16 per cent respectively.

Leam *et al.* (2008) make an important point when they argue that the risk assessment instruments used to make decisions about parole and other issues actually over-predict the likelihood of reoffending by sex offenders quite substantially. Some of these instruments do so by quite substantial factors. The use of these may have adverse consequences for the typical sex offender.

Youthful offenders

Despite the public image of sex offenders as being dirty old men, there is considerable evidence that young offenders are responsible for significant proportions of sex offences. For example, it has been estimated in the United States that up to half of child sexual abuse is carried out by persons under the age of 21 (Graves *et al.*, 1996). According to the Home Office (2003), 20 per cent of those convicted for a sexual crime are under the age of 18 years and 30–50 per cent of childhood sexual abuse is carried out by adolescents. This is important for several reasons:

- These are a substantial proportion of sexual offences, so need to be considered in any account of sex offending.

- They support the view that frequently sex offending emerges in childhood and adolescence and continues, almost career-wise, into adulthood (Howitt, 1995a).

Graves *et al.* (1996) carried out a meta-analytic review of studies of youthful sex offenders by studying empirical research studies from 1973–1993. Meta-analysis is the study of trends across different studies of similar phenomena (Howitt and Cramer, 2008) (see Box 4.2). The study concentrated on the demographic and parental characteristics of youthful offenders. The authors believed that the youthful offenders could be classified into three different, exclusive categories:

- *Paedophilic* – generally their first offence was committed between 6 and 12 years of age. They consistently molest younger children and prefer female victims.

- *Sexual assault* – these are youthful offenders whose first reported offence is between 13 and 15 years but their victims may vary substantially and include both older victims than themselves and younger victims.

- *Mixed offence* – these are youngsters who commit a variety of offences such as sexual assault, molesting younger children, exhibitionism, voyeurism, frotteurism, etc.

Overall, youthful sex offenders in general tended to have the following characteristics:

- lower socio-economic class origins;

- pathological family structures and interaction style;

- their fathers were physically neglected as a child;

- their mothers were physically abused as a child;

- substance abuse was common among the fathers.

There were considerable differences between the three different types of youngster as shown in Table 10.1. Care has to be exercised since despite the rather pathological picture painted of the families of youthful sexual offenders, these are only trends in the data. A substantial proportion of youthful sex offenders came from homes identified as healthy.

Theories of paedophilia

There have been a number of attempts to explain paedophilia. None of them is completely satisfactory in itself, although most have at least some virtues. The ones that we will consider in some detail are:

Table 10.1 The family and social characteristics of different types of youthful male sexual offenders obtained from meta-analysis

Characteristic	Paedophilic	Sexual assault	Mixed offence
Low to middle social class	✓	✓	✗
Low social class	✗	✗	✓
Lives in foster care	✓	✗	✗
Lives in lone-parent family	✗	✓	✗
Mother physically abused as child	✓	✗	✗
Mother neglected as child	✗	✗	✓
Mother abuses drugs	✗	✗	✓
Father abuses alcohol	✗	✓	✗
Father abuses drugs	✓	✗	✗
Maladaptive, dysfunctional family	✓	✗	✓
Rigid family	✗	✓	✗
Maternal neglect	✗	✗	✓
Protestant religion	✗	✗	✓

A ✓ indicates that this characteristic is especially common in that group of youthful offenders.

- the preconditions model;
- the psychotherapeutic/cognitive model;
- the sexualisation model;
- the pathways model.

The preconditions model

Araji and Finkelhor (1985) proposed the preconditions model of abusive behaviour. It is illustrated in Figure 10.1.

As can be seen, several different types of factor are listed, which are seen as partial preconditions for sexual abuse. These broad types of factor include emotional congruence, sexual arousal, blockage and disinhibition. The following points should be made:

- This model is relatively old and was developed at a time when empirical research on sex offenders was very limited in its scope.
- It is based on a number of almost common-sense assumptions, not all of which have or had been

1. **Emotional congruence with children**
Offenders lack self-esteem
Offenders are psychosocially immature
Offenders may have a need to dominate

2. **Social arousal by children**
Sexually socialised by child pornography
Hormonal abnormalities/imbalances

3. **Blockages preventing adult contact**
Lack of effective social skills
Problems in relating to adult females
Experienced repressive sexual socialisation in childhood

4. **Disinhibition of norms against adult/child sex**
Offenders may be senile
Alcohol may decrease inhibitions
Possibly in an incest-tolerant subculture

Figure 10.1 The preconditions model of molestation

supported and some have not even been adequately tested.

- It assumes that child molestation is multiply caused and does not assume that any of the preconditions are necessarily involved in any given case.

- It has the advantage of linking the theory with therapy that has tended to assume the multi-causality of abusive behaviour and, consequently, the need for complex therapeutic methods.

- Unfortunately, as was acknowledged by Arajii and Finkelhor, very few of the preconditions have been shown in empirical research to be associated with abusive behaviour.

Furthermore, it is descriptive in the sense of merely describing the characteristics of abusers rather than trying to identify the root cause of the abusive behaviour, say, in their own childhood.

The preconditions model was the first attempt at a comprehensive theory of sexual offending against children and among its achievements was its help in clarifying the goals of treating such offenders. In particular, according to Ward and Hudson (2001), the model encouraged the following: concentration on deviant sexual arousal, working with problems of intimacy, showing offenders how to effectively identify and manage situations in which they are at high risk of offending, and the incorporation of socio-cultural factors such as the possible role of pornography. However, it could be argued that the theory has merely encouraged a highly unspecific multi-faceted approach to the treatment of offenders which, consequently, has not helped develop our understanding of the process of becoming an offender.

The psychotherapeutic/ cognitive model

This model is rarely systematically described in total although elements of it are very common in the literature (e.g. Salter, 1988; Wyre, 1987, 1992). The main emphasis of this model is on the cognitive and behavioural steps involved in offending behaviour. Broadly speaking, the model suggests that there are four steps in the process:

- Cognitive distortions or distorted thinking of the sort effectively captured by the Abel Rape Index Scale (Abel *et al.*, 1977). Such distorted beliefs include

'Having sex with a child is a good way for an adult to teach a child about sex', and include other beliefs about the sexual nature of children, how their behaviour signals sexual interest and so forth.

- Grooming – these are the methods by which offenders contact children and gain their trust and confidence. Violence or threats of violence may be part of this, but probably more typical are bribes of sweets, money, trips out and the like.

- Planning through fantasy: this is the idea that the offender plans in fantasy the likely scenarios of events in, for example, finally trying to seduce the child. What will they do, say, if a child says they are going home?

- Denial is the mental process by which offenders appear to be denying the consequences of their actions and perhaps blaming someone else. For example, they would tend to agree with the following statements from the Abel scale (Abel *et al.*, 1977): 'Sex between an adult and a 13-year-old (or younger) child causes the child no emotional problems' and 'A man (or woman) is justified in having sex with his (her) children or step-children, if his wife (husband) doesn't like sex'. Denial can take a wide range of forms according to Salter (1988) and others:

  - the denial that abuse actually took place;
  - minimisation of the abuse by claiming few victims, for example;
  - denying seriousness – by admitting fondling but not anal sex, for example;
  - denying that there is anything wrong with them – they have found God so do not need therapy;
  - denial of responsibility – blaming the child for seducing the offender.

While it is fairly well established that there is cognitive distortion or distorted thinking in paedophiles and other sex offenders, this idea is often mixed together with that of paedophiles being adroitly manipulative people. They are keen to manipulate others, including psychologists and others working with them. Hence, they will try to convince the other person of whatever they think will be to their advantage. Thus it becomes a little unclear whether or not they really do think in particular ways or whether they are simply trying to manipulate their therapists, researchers and any other individuals who become involved. The writing on this is not particularly coherent in the sense that concepts are somewhat inconsistently used. Sometimes similar words are used to describe very

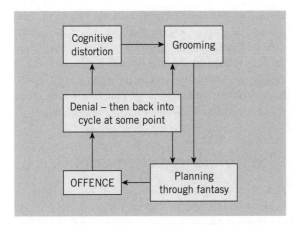

Figure 10.2 The clinical/cognitive model

different processes, so one finds the terms 'minimisation' and 'denial' used somewhat interchangeably. Figure 10.2 presents aspects of this model as a diagram.

Studies of cognitive distortions in paedophiles and other sex offenders are rather rare compared with the numerous mentions of them in the professional literature. Nevertheless, research does seem to suggest the importance of cognitive distortions. Barbaree (1998) found that substantial numbers of paedophiles and rapists denied carrying out the offences they were charged with. This Barbaree refers to as denial. Some adopted strategies that essentially minimised the offence in some way. Approximately 30–40 per cent of the offenders sought to minimise the seriousness of the offence or the extent of their culpability by strategies such as:

- blaming the victim;

- suggesting that the amount of force used was smaller than it actually was;

- holding personal factors such as stress or unemployment responsible.

Interestingly, the effects of psychological therapy on the men who initially denied the offence were quite impressive. About two-thirds changed from denying to admitting their offence. Denial of the offence was replaced by minimisation of the seriousness or their culpability for the offence. The excuses were largely about their use of force and just how sexually intrusive the sexual acts involved were. Of those in the study who initially admitted involvement in the offence but minimised other activities, the tendency was overwhelmingly for them to continue to minimise but at reduced levels. Hence, Barbaree

argues that these cognitive strategies are amenable to change through therapy and recommends that they are tackled early in therapy. At the same time, it should be noted how strongly offenders persist with minimisation despite admitting the offence itself in general terms.

Of course, there is nothing unusual about the denial of an offence since it occurs among all sorts of offenders. Any court of law will demonstrate this on a daily basis.

It has been argued that the use of denial is exceptionally common among sex offenders (e.g. Abel *et al.*, 1987). According to Nugent and Kroner (1996), clinical experience suggests that child molesters are more likely to admit to their offences than rapists, though this appears not to be supported by Barbaree's study described above. There are claims that, for example, sex offenders who admit the offence may differ from those who do not in terms of the self-justification strategies they employ. Men who are offence *deniers* tend to attribute responsibility to the victim (Scully and Marolla, 1984) whereas the *admitters* attribute the cause to their emotional problems or substance abuse, in particular. This is a further indication that the style of cognitive distortion differs although such distortion is common.

Nugent and Kroner's Canadian study concerned offenders prior to treatment. The different groups of offenders involved were rapists, intrafamilial and extrafamilial offenders. Two measures in particular are of interest. These assess the tendency of offenders to characteristically seek to present themselves in a favourable light. So the balanced *Inventory of Desirable Responding* was given as well as the defensive response style part of the *Basic Personality Inventory*. Men whose victims were under 14 years were considered molesters. They divided the offenders into four categories (although in general the type of offence affected the findings more than the style of response):

- non-admitters who claimed no illegal interaction with the victim;

- partial-admitters who admitted that they had sexual contact but believed no offence had taken place;

- partial-admitters who again admitted a sexual act such as fondling but not penetrative sexual intercourse;

- admitters who admitted the offence as on the official record.

One way of conceptualising this research is in terms of the ways in which offenders represent themselves to those in authority. The findings indicate that the child molesters were trying to manage the impression they created more actively than rapists. Interestingly, in this study, more child molesters admitted their offences than rapists (i.e. 43 per cent versus 27 per cent).

The idea that denial of the offence is a risk factor for future recidivism has a great deal of intuitive appeal among some professionals working in sex offender treatment (Howitt, 1992). By denying their offending, offenders may fail to deal with the factors which contribute to their offending. Research, however, has only shown a small relationship between denial of sexual offences and the likelihood of reoffending in the future. Nunes *et al.* (2007b) studied Canadian sex offenders (predominantly those offending against children) in an attempt to discover whether other variables might, in some way, be masking the relationship between denial and recidivism. Deniers were those who denied committing all index offences for which they had been convicted whereas admitters admitted at least one of their index offences. As part of a detailed analysis, the researchers found the offender's relationship to the victim – that is, whether the case involved an incest offender or an extrafamilial abuser – was a key factor. For incest offenders, denial correlated with increased risk of recidivism but this was not the case for extrafamilial offenders. Sexual recidivism was 17 per cent for incest offenders who denied but only 6 per cent for those who admitted their offending. The reverse pattern applied to the extrafamilial offenders. Extrafamilial deniers reoffended at a rate of 15 per cent but extra-

familial admitters recidivated at a rate of 24 per cent. Among the various explanations of this is that incest offenders need to gain the trust of their family before they can reoffend. Admitting the offence is not a way of gaining this trust and so recidivism in this group is lower. For extrafamilial offenders, regaining their family's trust is not relevant to reoffending outside of the family.

The sexualisation model

Howitt (1995a) regards paedophilic orientation as developing out of the characteristics of early sexual experiences. In particular, he suggests that experience of sexual abuse in childhood is the start of a process that ends in paedophile activity. Not all abuse is equally likely to lead to sex offending of this sort but penetrative sex, abuse by females and similar uncharacteristic abusive acts are more likely to have this effect. Furthermore, it is possible that sexual experiences in childhood with other, probably older, children may also be influential. In this approach, paedophilia is seen more as a developmental process beginning from early sexual experiences but often continuing through adolescence into adulthood. One possible consequence of this early experience is the way in which the paedophile regards sexual activity between adult and child. He will see adult–child sexual contact as normal since it is the normal thing in his experience. The following should also be considered:

Box 10.3 Key concept

Cycles of abuse

There is little doubt that the childhoods of young sex offenders often include various experiences which make them vulnerable to developing patterns of sexually harmful behaviours. Vizard, Hickey, French and McCrory (2007) studied, in depth, a substantial sample of nearly 300 children referred to a national assessment and treatment service for young people who perpetrate sexually harmful behaviours. Their sexually inappropriate or abusive behaviour began before the age of 10 years for 54 per cent of the young sex offenders. Fifty seven per cent offended against at least one victim who was five years or more younger than them. Victims were overwhelmingly known to the child offender. Most (88 per cent) had abused female victims and 57 per cent had abused male victims. Half of them had abused both male and female victims. Their childhoods were far from normal. Vizard *et al.* argue that during the development of children there is a matrix of risk factors which may contribute to the emergence of sexually abusive behaviours (see Figure 10.3). The childhoods of the children involve extremes of emotional deprivation including abuse, family instability and family dysfunction:

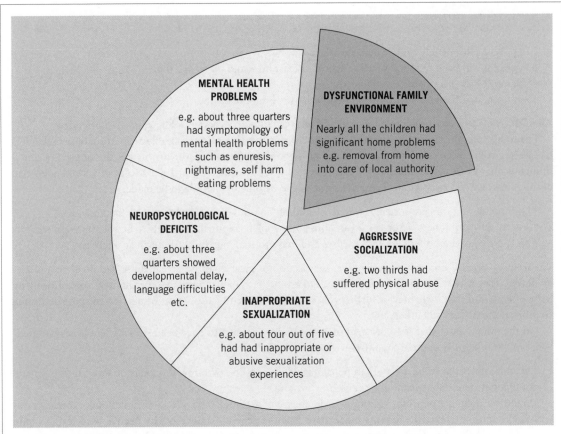

Figure 10.3 Vulnerability factors in the childhoods of young sex offenders

- 92 per cent had suffered at least one of neglect, witnessing domestic violence, or had been victims of one form of abuse from sexual physical and emotional. For three-quarters, this began under the age of six years;
- 76 per cent had been removed from home into the care of the local authority;
- 61 per cent had been sexually abused by members of their family;
- 50 per cent or more inconsistent or overly punitive parenting;
- 50 per cent approximately had been sexually abused at the age of seven years usually suffering serious abuse such as anal penetration (38 per cent);
- 44 per cent were exposed to lax sexual boundaries within the family such as access to sexually explicit materials and exposure to adult sexual behaviour;
- 35 per cent of the biological mothers had mental health problems and 29 per cent of fathers had criminal records;
- 22 per cent had been admitted into a therapeutic community or other psychiatric unit;
- 21 per cent had been abused by a female abuser;
- only 13 per cent had stayed in the same family home throughout childhood and only 5 per cent of the children were living with both of their biological parents when assessed.

This level of dysfunctionality and problems extended into the young offender's educational environment:

> ## Box 10.3 (continued)
>
> - 71 per cent exhibited disruptive behaviour in school;
> - 63 per cent had been required to move school at least once and up to five times;
> - 45 per cent had special educational needs;
> - 42 per cent had been excluded from school because of their behaviour.
>
> All of this adds to a distressing picture of the difficult childhoods experienced by young sex offenders.
>
> From this and other research, it is fairly uncontroversial to suggest that a sizeable proportion of sex offenders had been victims of sexual abuse as a child. What is controversial is the issue of whether this abuse is a causal influence on sex offenders. Imagine, for example, that there is evidence that 100 per cent of sex offenders had been sexually abused as children. These are some of the comments that might be made:
>
> - Many youngsters who are sexually abused as children do not grow up to be abusers themselves.
> - Girls are the commonest victims of sexual abuse but women are much less likely to be abusers than men are.
> - This merely provides offenders with excuses and inappropriate justification for their offending.
>
> The first two points, although correct in themselves, do not mean that the sexual abuse had no effect on later offending. They may merely imply that one needs to explore factors that insulate some children from growing up to be offenders or that there may be further characteristics of their victimisation which lead to some becoming victimisers themselves and others not.
>
> On the other hand, what if 10 per cent of sex offenders claimed to have been sexually abused as children? What might be argued in these circumstances?
>
> - This does not seem to be a very high percentage and is in line with low estimates of abuse in the general population. Hence abuse cannot be causal.
> - Offenders might be reluctant to admit their abuse or may not even see their childhood experiences as sexually abusive. Hence the data are inadequate. Men, in general, known to have been abused sexually tend not to regard their experiences as sexual abuse in a ratio of 6 to 1 (Widom and Morris, 1997).
>
> These are really the extremes. Certainly, there are a number of authorities who deny the strength of the cycles of abuse argument (Finkelhor, 1984; Hanson and Slater, 1988) for the reasons given above and others. Equally, there are a number of studies which suggest that the incidence of abuse in the childhoods of sex offenders is low. For example, Waterhouse et al. (1994) suggest that offenders are little different from non-offenders.
>
> Unfortunately, these studies are based on survey methods that tend to ask quite direct questions such as 'Were you sexually abused as a child?' This is a sensitive issue that may well elicit denial from any person abused in their childhood. It may be a matter with which they have not come to terms. Hence it is not surprising that studies that examine the question but in groups of offenders' post-treatment find that the admission rates of sexual abuse in childhood increase dramatically from 22 per cent to about 50 per cent (Worling, 1995). Howitt (1998b) provides evidence that, using a similar style of questioning, the experience of abuse was admitted by 80 per cent of young sex offenders compared with 25 per cent of non-offenders.
>
> The importance of this issue lies in the argument that sexual crime may be a re-enactment in some form of childhood experiences of being abused (Burgess et al., 1988).

- This account also partly explains the apparent relationship between the characteristic abuse experienced by the paedophile-to-be and the characteristics of his offending against children in the future. Others have noted similar tendencies in abused children. Haapasalo, Puupponen and Crittenden (1999) describe the concept of isomorphic behaviour. They point out 'Physically abused children tend to commit physically violent crimes whereas sexually abused children are prone, in adulthood, to sexual violence, including pedophilia, child molestation, and rape' (p. 98). Groth and Burgess (1978) mention that there are age and type of act similarities between offender and victim and Howitt (1995a) gives other examples. One reason for the isomorphism of sexual offending may be that it involves repetition of strategies for achieving basic feelings of safety and security. It could equally be simply a further instance of the importance of childhood experiences in determining adult behaviour.

- One potential difficulty with the explanation lies in the mixed support for cycles of sexual abuse in the literature. Box 10.3 suggests that the evidence is stronger than some researchers have indicated. Furthermore, not all acts of sexual abuse are as damaging as others.

- Another potentially crucial problem is that not all children who are abused become abusers themselves. The sexualisation model, since it assumes that the more extreme/repetitive forms of abuse have greatest effect, actually has an explanation of why some abused youngsters become abusers. Howitt (1998a), for example, points out that sexual abuse of boys by women seems to be particularly associated with later sexual offending by the victim.

There has been a growing recognition that sex offending in childhood is a matter that should not be neglected and that it is actually rather extensive in scope. Coleman (1997), for example, has mentioned the following 'explanations' of adolescent offending – that the offender is experimenting or curious, that sexual aggression is common in adolescence, or boys will be boys. She sees the denial of juvenile sex offending as a problem as part of the means by which such offending is cultivated. If it is not a problem then nothing needs to be done about it and adolescent offenders proceed to adult offending. Of course, increasingly juvenile sex offending is being recognised as a significant problem.

This sexualisation model is illustrated in Figure 10.4.

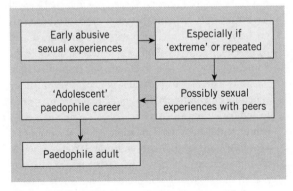

Figure 10.4 The sexualisation model

The pathways model

Ward and Siegert (2002) integrated the best features of several important multi-factorial theories of child sexual abuse into a single, comprehensive model. This they call the pathways model. The term multi-factorial means that for a particular form of behaviour, there are many determinants of that behaviour that the theoretical model needs to take into account. These determinants should be considered individually or in combination in order to understand sex offending against children. Virtually all of the theories of paedophilia discussed in this chapter accept that child sexual abuse is multi-determined in this way. They differ in important ways. Finkelhor's approach tends to imply that offenders are diverted from the path of a normal sexual interest in adults by a variety of factors which push the offender towards children or remove inhibitions against sex with children. The psychotherapeutic/cognitive model makes very similar assumptions in that it assumes that the way to stop the sexual abuse of children is to change a wide range of cognitions and behaviours which are conducive to child sexual abuse. Howitt's sexualisation model is different in a key respect. Sex offending in this model is regarded as a part of a lifestyle starting in childhood in which sexual orientation to children begins early and remains into adulthood. This does not mean that sexual abusers of children never involve themselves in sexual relationships with adults: they do. However, the model does imply that the task of the researcher is to understand the origins of the offender's sexual interest in childhood rather than regard it as a substitute for sexual activity with adults. In other words, sexual interest in children should be regarded as more akin to a sexual orientation.

Theories operate at three different levels according to Ward and Siegert. Level I is the multi-factorial level; level II is a theory which postulates a single factor though in many respects these amount to little more than a hypothesis about the relationship of a variable to the sex offending against children; and level III is the micro-level or offence process level, which is little more than descriptions of the behavioural sequence leading to offending or possibly relapsing into offending behaviour.

A distinction is made by Ward and Siegert between *distal* and *proximal* factors in relation to the offending behaviour:

- *Distal factors*: these are causal factors which lie in the predispositions of the offender. They may have a number of origins. They may be in the genetic make-up of the offender or in his childhood development and beyond. They are long-term psychological mechanisms which may lead to offending when the environmental situation encourages offending.

- *Proximal factors*: these are the factors in the environment that change the distal factors into actual offending. They, in other words, trigger the predispositions into action. Possible proximal factors could include negative mood states or stress.

Ward and Siegert (2002) propose four psychological mechanisms which may be involved in an offender's offending behaviour: (1) intimacy and social skill deficits; (2) deviant sexual scripts; (3) emotional dysregulation; and (4) cognitive distortions. These are distal factors which make the offender vulnerable to offending against children but are not the immediate trigger for offending. The four pathways constitute different aetiological factors in the sexual abuse of children though offenders will exhibit the other three with varying intensities. So there is a central pathway which may be associated with other less important pathways for a particular offender. The four pathways are then as follows:

- *Intimacy and social skill deficits*: as a consequence of abuse and/or neglect in childhood, the ways in which a child understands relationships and 'the emotional availability' (p. 331) of important others are adversely affected. They may have difficulties in emotional disclosure to others. Furthermore, other people may not be valued as people as a consequence of these adverse early experiences. The attachment style corresponding to this is best described as insecure since the offender may fail to develop the appropriate trust of others and see the social world as a dangerous place. So they lack socially and emotionally intimate contacts and avoid such contact. According to Ward and Siegert, insecure attachment can result in lasting difficulties in managing mood and problem solving.

    This sort of offender is hypothesised by Ward and Siegert to offend only at specific times such as when their normal adult sexual partner is unavailable. The child in the abuse is effectively an 'adult substitute'. The intimacy deficits are the result of insecure attachment and abuse is directly consequent on the offender failing to achieve satisfactory relationships with adults. Other pathways such as cognitive distortions will be involved. In particular, the offender may believe that he has a right to sex with whosoever he pleases.

According to Ward and Siegert, this sort of offending is likely to have its origins in adulthood. When faced with rejection or emotional loneliness, the offender diverts his attentions towards children.

- *Sexual scripts*: 'A sexual script spells out when sex is to take place, with whom, what to do, and how to interpret the cues or signals associated with different phases in a sexual encounter. These cues can be internal to the individual, interpersonal, or broadly cultural in nature' (p. 332). Sexual scripts are learnt during psychological development and represent the broad framework of understanding how complex social behaviours play out. As a consequence, the scripts in part guide social behaviour. It is argued that sexual experiences before the child is capable of cognitively and emotionally handling them lead to distortions in the script in comparison with those developed by others. The distorted script might involve inappropriate sexual partners (e.g. age discrepancy), inappropriate behaviours (deviant practices) or inappropriate contexts (e.g. sex devoid of interpersonal feelings).

    Sexual abuse in childhood may be the basis of their offending. These offenders seek emotional reassurance through sexual activity and sexual behaviour is equated with intimacy. Sexual cues are not differentiated from or confused with the cues to affection and closeness. They also fear rejection in intimate relationships. They choose children sometimes because of opportunity or because of intensified sexualised emotional needs. Sexual abuse of children is likely to emerge in adulthood in this group.

- *Emotional dysregulation*: we need to regulate our own behaviour in order to function effectively. This self-regulation allows an individual to achieve their goals. For example, we might be afraid of flying but wish to travel abroad for holidays. To achieve that goal we will have to adopt behaviours that allow us to succeed in that goal. That is, we have to control our anxieties about flying. Part of self-regulation is the regulation of emotions. Sometimes we may seek to elevate our emotional state (such as listening to particularly evocative music or watching an emotional film) but equally we may need to reduce emotions in some way. The offender may exhibit emotional dysregulation when, for example, avoiding guilt and other emotional feelings while offending against children or when they fail for whatever reason to use coping skills to deal with stress leaving them at greater risk of offending against children.

This group develops essentially normal sexual scripts. However, their emotional regulation system has substantial problems. For example, they may have difficulty in using social support effectively in times of distress or some may have difficulty in identifying particular emotional states in themselves accurately. They may have problems in dealing with anger and resort to the sexual abuse of children as part of an attempt to punish a partner who has angered them. Sexual fantasies help ameliorate negative feeling states and, consequently, increase the risk of offending. Such offenders are unlikely to attempt to develop emotional intimacy with their victim but have profound sexual arousal when they are strongly emotionally aroused.

- *Cognitive distortions*: these have already been discussed but Ward has suggested that cognitive distortions are generated by a much smaller number of schemata or implicit theories held by the offender. Ward's view is that many varied expressions of distorted thoughts which are manifested by offenders actually reflect a small number of implicit theories which the offender holds. We all have such theories or schema about the world but the offender's are maladaptive because they can lead to offending behaviour. Five important implicit theories are listed by Ward:

  – Children as sexual objects: just as the offender regards adults as sexual, children are equally regarded as able to enjoy and desire sexual relationships with adults.

  – Entitlement: offenders regard themselves as being entitled to have their sexual needs met because they are more important than other people.

  – Dangerous world: children are not seen as being the threat that other adults are and their reliability and trusting nature gives the offender comfort against the danger.

  – Uncontrollable: the offender is not in control of his actions but is driven by external factors such as those resulting in stress or the effects of drugs or alcohol.

  – Nature of harm: not all sexual activity with a child is harmful and children can benefit in a variety of ways from sexual activity with adults.

These offenders tend to be antisocial generally and demonstrate strongly criminal attitudes. These offenders are patriarchal in their attitudes towards children and believe in their own superiority. Their sexual offences against children do not reflect a sexual preference but more their general antisocial behaviour pattern.

There is a fifth group which Ward and Siegert suggest may represent the 'pure paedophile' in the sense that they have critical deficits in all four of the above pathways, not just a preponderance of just one sort of deficit. They idealise the relationship between an adult and a child in their sexual scripts.

BOX 10.4 Controversy

Cognitive distortions

Cognitive distortions are a virtually indispensable concept in most explanations of sex offending and, especially, that against children. It serves as a cornerstone of several different theories of sex offending including that of Finkelhor (see main text of this chapter). Recently, a number of researchers have begun to question its explanatory role in sex offending. For many clinicians, cognitive distortions are common in their conversations with sex offenders and can be regarded as routine in their day-to-day work. So it would be a surprise to these clinicians to know that some researchers express doubt over the centrality of cognitive distortions in the explanation of sex offending. This controversy about the value of the concept may reflect problems with the relevant research just as much as inadequacies of the concept.

Historically, there seems to have been a shift in how cognitive distortions have been construed. According to Sheldon and Howitt (2007), there are at least three distinct views of what cognitive distortions are:

▶

BOX 10.4 (continued)

- *Cognitive distortions* are beliefs held by offenders which help them overcome inhibitions about offending and serve as a defence in so far as they serve to reduce the guilt that sexual offending creates. A presumption of this view is that sexual offenders are predisposed to being sexually interested in children and that their cognitions are modified such that, for example, children and childhood sexuality are seen in ways which justify their sexual assaults on children. Such a conception of conceiving cognitive distortions reflects the original formulation put forward by Abel, Becker and Cunningham-Rathner (1984). As such, cognitive distortions can simply be regarded as a special instance of drift or neutralisation theory (Sykes and Matza, 1957). Drift/neutralisation theory argues that offenders effectively neutralise the psychological impact of their offending. Many techniques of neutralisation are similar to cognitive distortions and the denial processes which psychologists have seen as characterising sex offenders. Although the original formulation of cognitive distortions is absolutely clear, confusion has developed as to whether neutralisation through cognitive distortions comes prior to or follows after offending. However, Maruna and Copes (2005) insist that conceptually cognitive distortions can only apply post-offence and that it cannot explain the aetiology of offending.

- Cognitive distortions are *rationalisations* which emerge when offenders need to account for their crimes. Thus they are little other than justifications or excuses for unacceptable behaviour. In other words, the accounting process required in many forensic interviews yields characteristic cognitive distortions. Gannon and Polaschek (2005) describe these as 'transient post-offence justifications and excuses' (p. 184). Thus cognitive distortions do not have a significant role in offending in this conceptualisation. Instead cognitive distortions are essentially face-saving devices which come into play when the offender is held to account for their crimes by psychologists, police officers and others in the criminal justice system.

- Cognitive distortions should not be construed as altered cognitions at all but, instead, they reflect the distorted life-experiences of offenders. In this sense, cognitive distortions can be regarded as essentially narrative accounts of the sex offender's childhood experiences of sexual abuse by adults and sexual play with other children (Howitt, 1995a). In this formulation, cognitive distortions may pre-date offending but they have close links to offending behaviour. Accounts of childhood experiences are difficult to obtain from offenders and they are often and characteristically fragmentary. Nevertheless, many offenders describe their early experiences of very sexualised behaviours including histories of sexual abuse, sexual play or both. Thus cognitive distortions involving *children are sexual beings* simply reflect the sexualised childhood of the offender and the child's sexual involvement with others. Cognitive distortions, then, are consequent on particular childhood experiences which themselves are grossly different from the childhood experiences of most of us. The term cognitive distortion is, therefore, a misnomer since the cognitions reflect a child's subjective reality.

Maruna and Mann (2006) have questioned the value of the concept of cognitive distortions to sex offender research. The term cognitive distortions, they argue, lacks a singular and clear meaning. It is used as an umbrella concept for (a) a variety of attitudes which seem supportive of sex offending, (b) cognitions common during the offence sequence and (c) *post hoc* neutralisations of or excuses for offending. Cognitive behavioural treatment programmes for sex offenders focus on cognitive distortions, of course. Therapists want offenders to take responsibility for their actions and eschew rationalisations. The identification and confrontation of cognitive distortions is a major part of this. Maruna and Mann argue that the *post hoc* excuse aspect of cognitive distortions is problematic since, after all, such after-the-fact excuses for one's behaviour are regarded as part of the psychology of normal, healthy individuals. The therapeutic process should shift attention from *post hoc* excuses to concentrate, instead, on those offence-supportive attitudes and cognitive schemas which have been clearly linked empirically to offending.

Evidence abounds that in Western societies individuals formulate excuses and justification for their unacceptable actions. Furthermore, there is a wide variety of criminological research which has shown that, for offences ranging from poaching to attacks on prostitutes, offenders seek to justify their offences. Generally, these studies show that offenders tend to blame external and unstable causes as being responsible for their offending. The explanations avoid blaming the offender in terms of their personal responsibility. In other words, there is a human tendency to claim that it is not our fault when we behave badly. Bandura's (1990) theory of moral disengagement suggests that individuals avoid sanctioning themselves for their immoral behaviour through processes such as displacement of responsibility, diffusion of responsibility, distortions of the consequences of our actions, dehumanisation of the victim of our crimes, and by presenting themselves in the role of a victim.

What is strange is that what is considered as normal for most people becomes pathological when we consider prisoners and other offenders. These explanations employed by offenders have been called aligning techniques because they align the offender with the rest of society. Maruna and Mann (2006, p. 158) argue:

> Pathologizing such aligning techniques when used by criminal justice clients places them in a no-win situation: If they make excuses for what they did, they are deemed to be criminal types who engage in criminal thinking. If, however, they were to take full responsibility for their offences – claiming they committed some awful offence purely because 'they wanted to' and because that is the 'type of

person' they are – then they are, by definition, criminal types as well.

Besides conceptual problems with the concept of cognitive distortions, it has not always fared well in terms of empirical research. There has not been a consistent research finding that child molesters differ from controls in terms of their use and acceptance of cognitive distortions. There are some studies which demonstrate such differences in terms of mean scores on cognitive distortions questionnaires (e.g. Bumby, 1996). On the other hand, there are those researchers who suggest that child molesters are reluctant to overtly agree with cognitive distortions. These researchers tend to suggest the difference between sex offenders and control groups is that child molesters tend to reject the cognitive distortion less extremely than appropriate controls (e.g. Arkowitz and Vess, 2003; Marshall et al., 2003). Thus, for instance, where the non-sex offender ticks the questionnaire it is to *very strongly* disagree with the cognitive distortion whereas the sex offender is likely to just *disagree*. Among the explanations of this is the possibility that offenders fake a socially acceptable response by rejecting the distortion (Blumenthal, Gudjonsson and Burns, 1999; Horley, 2000; Kolton, Boer and Boer, 2001). Such faking 'good' is consonant with the image of sex offenders as being liars and manipulators (Wyre, 1987, 1990). Nevertheless, experimental studies with sex offenders have indicated that social desirability response sets are not responsible for the answers which sex offenders give to such questionnaires (Gannon and Polaschek, 2005). Offenders' answers are also unaffected by convincing the offender that if they lie are likely to be found out (Gannon, 2006).

An alternative possibility is that some cognitive distortions questionnaires include very extreme questions which perhaps most offenders actually disagree with. Hence low scores on such extreme cognitive distortions are to be expected if offenders are responding honestly to them.

Internet paedophile offenders

The Internet has provided the legal impetus for a range of new offences in countries throughout the world. According to Robbins and Darlington (2003), 27,000 people throughout the world go on to Internet child pornography sites each day and over 1 million images of child sexual abuse are in circulation. While child pornography involves the sexual abuse of children, Internet offences may be committed by those who have not made physical sexual contact with children themselves. So offences related to the possession of child pornography downloaded from the Internet may or may not be related to contact sexual offences against children. There are other modern offences, such as using Internet chat rooms to groom children for sex, which are not in themselves contact offences, though the intent may be to eventually meet the child for sex. Internet offences are important in that they raise the possibility that some adults may be sexually interested in children but never contact children sexually. This is theoretically important in that it suggests that there are some paedophiles who desist from sexual activity with children despite their sexual interest in children (cf. Howitt, 1995a). Understanding more about how paedophiles may desist from contact offending against children might help us to understand better how to help paedophiles cease offending despite their sexual leanings (Howitt, 2005). There is evidence that 97 per cent of UK Internet paedophiles have no previous convictions and have not previously come to the police's attention (Brookes, 2003).

Internet pornography offences have come to court in increasing numbers in recent years, mirroring the rapid growth in the spread of the Internet. In jurisdictions such as Britain and the United States, Internet pornography offenders risk lengthy prison sentences. Child pornography is a graphic representation of the sexual abuse of children and, it is argued, downloading the material contributes tangibly to the sexual abuse of children by encouraging further production of such material. However, the suggestion that Internet child pornography users will then go on to offend against children is based more on speculation than evidence. Sullivan and Beech (2003) are among the psychologists who believe that fantasising to imagery of child abuse encourages men to act out their fantasies through the direct sexual abuse of children. This, of course, does not mean that there are no contact offenders who also offend on the Internet. In this context it is worth noting Seto and Eke's (2005) study which found that although 17 per cent of child pornography offenders reoffended in some way in the following 30 months, it was just 4 per cent who were reconvicted for a contact sexual offence against a child. Sheldon and Howitt (2007) studied the explanations given for desisting from contact offending by Internet child pornography offenders. The following is a typical explanation:

> I have been in the position shall I say if I'd wanted to I could have done . . . on many, many occasions, but I always drew the line of actually touching [a child]. I got to the point where if I was looking at something that to me was my, like a drug addict, that was my fix for the day . . . my end release was looking at the pictures. I never got to the point where I would want to touch . . . looking at the images is enough, though a lot of people will disagree . . . I mean I've met people in prisons . . . who are in for the same thing and . . . their talk was never of actual sexual contact. Definitely. No. No. I would never.
>
> (Sheldon and Howitt, 2007, p. 227)

It is not easy to answer the superficially simple question of whether child pornography offenders can be regarded as paedophiles. One way of conceiving paedophiles is that they have a sexual interest in young children under the legal age of consent to sexual intercourse. Just like there are people with heterosexual interests who remain virgins all their life, there is no reason why a paedophile has to act out their sexual interest. What evidence there is suggests that many Internet pornography offenders collect substantial quantities of the material and that a good proportion of these will masturbate while at their computers to such imagery (Sheldon and Howitt, 2007). So in this sense, Internet child pornography offenders can be seen as paedophiles. However, if one insists that a paedophile is someone who commits a sexual offence directly against a child then, of course, Internet-only offenders are not paedophiles.

As yet, psychological research on Internet offenders is in its infancy. We are only just beginning to identify the ways in which contact offenders and Internet offenders differ and are similar. Sheldon and Howitt (2007) compared groups of Internet child pornography offenders and contact sex offenders against children in terms of a great many characteristics. For example, Internet child pornography offenders tend to have had a longer education than contact sex offenders. On the other hand, both types of offenders, quite contrary to the usual stereotypes, tend to be in relationships with adults at the time of their offending though there is some evidence that these relationships are fundamentally inadequate or troubled in some way. Nevertheless, Internet child pornography offenders tend to be more psychologically secure in their adult relationships than contact sex offenders against children. Both types of offender commonly experience rather adverse and neglectful childhoods. The lack of adequate relationships with their parents seems often to push the offender as a child to seek emotional warmth from other children or adults which can result in early sexual experiences or exploitation. Sheldon and Howitt (2007) indicate that sexual experiences in childhood with peers are common in both groups though abusive sexual activities were less common in Internet offenders and sexual activities with adults were more common in the contact offenders.

One promising line of research involves the cognitive distortions of these offenders – the ideas and beliefs which facilitate the offender. There is evidence that Internet offenders are cognitively similar to contact offenders in terms of the broad pattern of their cognitive distortions. For example, it has been claimed that Internet offenders who view pictures of children involved in sexual intercourse tend to interpret a child's smiles just as contact offenders do (Drake *et al.*, 2001). That is, the children's smiles are seen as indicating that children are sexual beings and are enjoying their abuse (Taylor and Quayle, 2003).

Using a conceptualisation developed by Ward (Ward, 2000; Ward and Keenan, 1999), the patterns of cognitive distortions in contact and Internet offenders have been explored by Sheldon (2004). Sheldon interviewed both Internet-only and contact offenders about many different aspects of their lives and analysed the interview transcriptions for evidence of the above, Ward's five 'implicit theories'. She found similarities throughout in terms of the use of these theories by both types of offender. For example, take the first implicit theory – children as sexual objects. One of her interviewees, who had Internet as well as contact offences, said of his victim:

> She was a bit of a tart dressed in a provocative manner the way she put herself to you verbally and physically . . . the way she walked, the clothes she wore you pick it up straight away . . . probably even blokes think she's a puller.
>
> (p. 27)

This clearly demonstrates how that offender regarded a child as a sexual being – much of the language is more commonly used to describe adult women and would not be used of a child by many people. Sheldon found evidence of similar beliefs in Internet-only offenders. For example:

> My favourite [fantasy] would be consensual sex with a child . . . the most arousing thing would be to give the child pleasure.
>
> (GA: Internet)

Notice that this ideal sex is described as consensual and that the child in the fantasy has an orgasm. If it were applied to an adult woman, such a fantasy would not be regarded as deviant in any way. Because of their similarities in the use of cognitive distortions, we should hesitate in assuming that the two groups are essentially distinct.

Main points

- Sex offenders against children, in general, are difficult to differentiate from the rest of the population in general. Various attempts have been made to categorise different types and one of the most common is that of fixated versus regressed offenders. Despite being common, there are problems with this especially when regressed offending is regarded as typical of intrafamilial offending. Some data suggest that paedophile response to erotic images of children is quite common though self-reported paedophile acts are relatively uncommon. In order to understand sex offending against children, it is important to recognise that adolescent sex offending is quite a high percentage of all sexual offending.

- An important issue is the extent to which sex offenders, and sex offenders against children, are frequent recidivists. The evidence is that sexual reoffending is relatively uncommon after conviction even several years after release (see also Chapter 25). Recidivism for other types of crime is more frequent. Similarly, the previous criminal histories of sex offenders against children are more likely to involve non-sexual crimes. Despite this, it is common to read that paedophiles have large numbers of victims. This may be so for some offenders but the majority seem to have committed a very small number of offences. It should also be noted that modern policy on sex offenders includes considerable monitoring of the lives of offenders when in the community (see also Chapter 27).

- There are a number of theories to account for sexual offending against children. The preconditions model is of historical importance for the most part and very few of its principles have been established empirically. The psycho-therapeutic/clinical model stresses cognitive aspects of the offending cycle such as fantasy and cognitive distortions. There is more support for this model and it has a degree of validity in terms of describing the abuse process, though it does not address the issue of the aetiology (development) of offending behaviour. There is reasonable evidence to suggest that offenders' early abusive and other sexual experiences are associated with sexually offending against children. However, it is clearly untrue to suggest that all sexually abused children will grow up to abuse others. Nevertheless, there are some indications that certain types of sexual abuse and repeated abuse in childhood are more conducive to the development of sexually abusive behaviour towards children. This supports the basic idea of sexualisation theory. One question is whether a single factor cause of offending is adequate. The pathways model suggests that there may be a number of different developmental routes to offending, though it accepts much of what is central to the other models of sexually abusive offending.

The treatment of sex offenders is dealt with in Chapter 26.

Further reading

The following provide very different approaches to the study of paedophiles and other sex offenders:

Seto, M.C. (2008) *Pedophilia and Sexual Offending Against Children: Theory, Assessment, and Intervention* Washington: American Psychological Association.

Sheldon, K. and Howitt, D. (2007) *Sex Offenders and the Internet* Chichester: John Wiley.

Ward, T., Polaschek, D.L.L. and Beech, A.R. (2006) *Theories of Sexual Offending* Chichester: John Wiley.

The book: D. Howitt (1995). Paedophiles and Sexual Offences against Children. Chichester: Wiley, can be found at: http://www.ipce.info/host/howitt/

Visit our website at www.pearsoned.co.uk/howitt for self-test and essay questions, annotated further reading, audio interviews with researchers in the field, weblinks and more information on becoming a forensic psychologist.

Chapter 11

Police psychology

Overview

- Within the criminal justice system, the organisation most highly regarded by the general public tends to be the police force. Since police forces are work organisations, their operation can be regarded as part of the remit of organisational psychology such that recruitment and selection of police officers, their working group dynamics, occupational stress and many other factors such as these are aspects of the psychology of policing. Other chapters pertinent to policing include Chapters 12 to 21.

- The police have a distinctive organisational culture that emphasises heterosexual, white male attitudes. It also stresses the importance of confessions obtained through interview. As a consequence, researchers have studied police interviewing techniques in some depth. Many bad practices have been identified over the years though good practice is also to be found. *Intimidation* by maximising the seriousness of the event, *robust challenges* such as accusing the interviewee of lying, and *manipulation* in which the officer suggests that the interviewee was not totally responsible for the offence or that the offence was not so serious are among the most common tactics identified in police interviews. So there is considerable doubt that police interviewing and evidence are as good as forensic training could ensure. There is a considerable body of evidence to suggest that the cognitive interview can improve the interviewing of cooperative witnesses better than other techniques such as forensic hypnosis.

- Language inconsistencies in statements taken by the police can reveal fabricated evidence.

- The *cognitive interview* consists of techniques designed to improve the quantity and quality of eyewitness evidence based on principles developed from the psychological study of memory. Some of the recommended strategies are reporting everything that they possibly can from the events that they witnessed no matter how trivial or seemingly irrelevant, trying to relive the context of the eyewitnessed events, such as their own personal feelings, and trying different methods of retrieving information from memory. The *enhanced cognitive interview* adds elements from good interview techniques in general such as establishing rapport and asking questions effectively. There is evidence from a range of studies that cognitive interviewing is effective at eliciting greater quantities of good quality information, although there is an attendant risk of more inaccurate information.

▶

- Forensic hypnosis is not held in great regard by forensic and criminal psychologists who generally prefer the cognitive interview. Although forensic hypnosis tends to increase the numbers of both accurate and inaccurate memories, this problem can be offset by limiting the number of memories elicited.

- The broad consensus, until recently, was that police officers, in general, are no better as eyewitnesses than other people. However, there is emerging evidence that where the events witnessed were stressful, the police tended to be at an advantage and produced better eyewitness testimony possibly as a result of their experience and training.

- Being witness to the consequences of offending has a stressful and traumatic effect on a proportion of the officers involved. Dealing with the aftermath of a suicide is a particularly traumatic experience. The stress of working in a bureaucratic organisation also takes a toll on officers.

- Among other issues that psychologists have raised in relation to the work of the police is the clarity of the police caution. There is evidence that police cautions are poorly understood by many of those who receive one. Furthermore, there should be concern when arrestees waive their rights in law since they may be unaware of the impact of this decision.

Introduction

Of all agencies in the criminal justice system, the police are the most highly regarded by the public (Howitt, 1998b) irrespective of objective evidence about performance (Christensen, Schmidt and Henderson, 1982). In the year 2009/10, the British Crime Survey of a general sample of the population found that 56 per cent of respondents believed that their police were doing a good or excellent job (British Crime Survey, 2011). More specifically, 50 per cent tended to agree or strongly agreed that their local police could be relied on to be there when one needed them. Furthermore, 84 per cent believed that they would be treated with respect by their local police if they contacted them. If anything, these percentages have tended to rise in recent years. In the British Crime Survey of 2000 (Mirrlees-Black, 2001), 53 per cent of the British public said that the police were doing a good or excellent job. In comparison, all of the other agencies in the criminal justice system did badly. Prisons got 31 per cent saying good or excellent, magistrates 26 per cent, the probation service 23 per cent, the Crown Prosecution Service 23 per cent, judges 21 per cent and youth courts 12 per cent. Such relative approval of the police has been found in other countries. More recently, the British Crime Survey has reported long-term trends in satisfaction with the performance of agencies in the criminal justice system including the prison service, prosecution service, prosecution service and judges. The police continue to be regarded the most favourably among the agencies (British Crime Survey, 2011). American research suggests much

the same general appreciation of the police (Graber, 1980; Skogan, 1996). On the other hand, the police tend to receive some criticism from the research findings of forensic and criminal psychologists as we shall see.

Police forces are work organisations. Thus, potentially, there is a strong role for psychology with the police as with any other organisation. In other words, police psychology could be construed as merely a subfield of organisational psychology. According to Ainsworth (2000b), psychologists working with the police fulfil much the same role as organisational psychologists in any organisation. As such, they tend to work directly with police management on matters such as assessment and selection procedures. Other types of psychologist, such as offender profilers, are not typical of psychologists working with the police. In some countries, profilers would only be brought in on an ad hoc basis as the need arises. Elsewhere, in the United States for example, profilers are found fairly commonly in regular, permanent employment with the police. Of course, it is extremely difficult to identify a distinct police psychology that does not encompass issues from other chapters in this book (e.g. lie detection – Chapters 18 and 19, effective interviewing with children – Chapter 20, false allegations – Chapter 16, false confessions – Chapter 17 and crime analysis – Chapters 14 and 15). In this chapter we will concentrate on some of the issues which are central to police work.

A distinction has to be made between psychology as used by the police and the psychology of the police. This chapter reflects both of these.

Recruitment and selection

The question of how to recruit and select effective police personnel seems deceptively easy. There is not space to review the major issues in the general recruitment and selection process as covered in organisational psychology. Nevertheless, it is possible to make a number of points specifically about police recruitment following the account given by Ainsworth (1995). It is important to note that the costs to the police of poor selection of recruits may be quite large. It is expensive to train police officers so inadequacies of selection have a direct financial cost, but there are also fewer tangible costs in terms of public relations and public appreciation that poor recruits bring to the police. Psychological tests have long been used in personnel selection. Nevertheless, the development of appropriate tests for police selection has not proven to be the easiest of tasks (Ainsworth, 1996).

- Testing could serve either or both of two functions: (a) screening out unsuitable applicants to avoid spending substantial amounts of money on intensive selection processes which may, for example, involve fairly senior police personnel, or (b) concentrating on selecting the very best applicants out of the field.

- Police work involves a multiplicity of different tasks – traffic patrolling and delivering bad news to relatives being just two examples. It is not easy to imagine a relatively simple approach to finding suitable recruits that could select the best personnel for such a variety of tasks. Conversely, it is difficult to imagine the sort of array of measures that would be needed to recruit for specific types of task.

- Detailed studies of what sorts of recruit are ideal for the police force seem not to have been carried out in all police forces. When asked, serving police officers suggest that recruits should possess 'common sense' or 'a sense of humour'. Concepts such as these are difficult to translate into known or potential psychometric tests.

The notion of a 'police personality', to the extent that it has any validity at all, is probably at least as much to do with the requirements of police work as it is to do with any pre-existing personality predispositions or any selection characteristics (Bull, 1984). Stress seems

endemic and indicators such as suicide have been claimed to show elevated levels in police officers (but see Box 11.1 for evidence of the mythical status of this claim). Another characteristic of police work is the common requirement that all officers graduate through the ranks to achieve promotion. This not only brings about problems of reorientation towards one's previous peer group but may well be the prime way in which the police occupational culture is transmitted.

Irrespective of the issue of the police personality, it seems clear that the process of becoming a police officer produces changes that even the police themselves are unaware of. Garner (2005) carried out a longitudinal study involving police trainees. They were assessed in terms of their attitudes to policing and their 'distinctive impact or effectiveness in law enforcement' during training and a year later. There was a marked shift in most aspects of their attitudes to an increasing pro-police position despite the officers in question overwhelmingly believing that they had not changed.

Police culture

Skolnick (1966) was the first to suggest that the culture of the police influences the work of the police force. It is fairly easy to recognise the different cultures typical of different organisations. Since culture is little more than the sum of the shared knowledge, behaviours and practices of members of that culture, then it should be possible to identify the particular characteristics of different organisations. The organisational culture of a hospital is obviously different from that of a school. Similarly, there are typical characteristics of the organisational cultures of police forces that are not found in the same measure or the same combination in the cultures of other organisations. While there are occupations for which relatively minimal amounts of training will prepare incumbents for the major eventualities, as we have seen, multiplicity and diversity of tasks are characteristic of police work.

Ainsworth (1995) suggests that no two days of police work are ever the same. He lists among the diverse situations with which police officers have to deal as the following: attending road traffic accidents, going in pursuit of a teenage vandal, taking drunks to the police station, attending domestic disputes, helping to police a riot and working through backlogs of paperwork. At the same time, the police officer is required to have a good working knowledge of the law and to act lawfully. Finally, the officer is expected to promote a positive image of the police force. This is a range of tasks with which, say, the average supermarket checkout assistant or psychologist does not need to cope. The training of police officers is, consequently, a compromise between what is practical to put in training and what would be ideal. While earlier generations of police officers received little training except that provided by on-the-job experience, increasingly policy is towards fairly extensive training. Ainsworth (1995) indicates that police training in the past encouraged rote learning of legislation and the powers available to police. Nowadays, it increasingly concerns how to deal with the wide variety of incidents that come under the rubric of police work.

Part of the training of new recruits is through contact or on-the-job training with more seasoned or experienced officers. At one level this can be regarded as teaching the recruits the job at a practical level. On the other hand, seasoned officers may employ practices that are less than ideal or even unacceptable to their managers. Consequently, the novice police officer may merely learn bad practice from his or her colleagues. This is particularly important when we consider the transmission of the occupational subculture or *police culture*. Police culture refers to the characteristic patterns of belief, behaviour, thinking and interaction that police officers tend to share in common. They are essentially *normative* as they are the accepted and prescribed standards of police personnel. This does not mean that they are fixed and unchanging. Although personnel may be recruited because they seem to reflect the characteristics of a 'good' police officer, they learn police culture by interacting with other police officers. The occupational culture may be in some ways at odds with what new officers have learnt at police college. There may be a painful reality shock when they try to put their college knowledge into practice. They may find that their new ways of doing things clash with what is acceptable to the transmitters of police culture – the old school of officers.

Canteen/cop culture

While police culture is a generic description of the cultural characteristics of the police, there is also evidence of the prevalence of certain sorts of attitude that characterise the general thinking of ordinary police officers. We may call this canteen or cop culture in order to differentiate it from the more general police culture. There may actually be a clash between the management subcultures and the subculture of the rank-and-file officers. Wootton and Brown (2000) summarise canteen culture as involving and valuing:

- action;
- cynicism;
- conservatism;
- mission;
- pessimism;
- pragmatism;
- solidarity;
- suspicion;
- racial prejudice.

The list might be extended further since, in addition to racism, sexism, homophobia and heterosexism are characteristic of the culture. Essentially, cop culture determines the rules abided by police officers that allow them to be seen as being effective in their work. This means that the standards of the dominant group within the police and their styles of interaction determine what is regarded as effective policing and the effective police officer. Gay and lesbian officers, for example, can then be seen as subordinate to the dominant group – their values disregarded. The nature of the canteen culture is such that homosexual officers do not 'come out'. This choice can do nothing to challenge the homophobia and, in a sense, reinforces it.

After joining the police, the processes of occupational socialisation may create a situation in which the individual's police identity is not psychologically compatible with other aspects of the individual's identity (e.g. their sexuality). In-group identification refers to the sense of a common identity shared by members of the force. This sexist, heterosexist and homophobic culture would readily identify gays and lesbians as out-groups. This may encourage hostility and discrimination by the majority group towards the out-group. Women, ethnic minorities, lesbians and gays are not readily tolerated because they are 'other' or different from the accepted norm. The problem for officers with these characteristics (e.g. they are women or homosexual) is that the dual identities of police officer and being homosexual, for example, can be extremely difficult to reconcile and handle.

Wootton and Brown (2000) studied police officers. One group consisted of officers who belonged to one minority (e.g. the officer was female). The other group had two minority positions (e.g. they were black women or they were homosexual black men). The officers were interviewed and what they had to say was coded in terms of the presence or absence of a number of themes. A grid was then created in which the different officers were listed against the different themes emerging in the interviews. This was then analysed using a complex statistical technique (multi-dimensional scalogram analysis). This essentially plots people into a chart indicating their similarity/dissimilarity across the themes. There seemed to be a cluster of heterosexual officers who shared similar experiences. Lesbians and gays were not among them. Furthermore, officers with just one minority characteristic (e.g. being black or being homosexual) tended to group together as similar in terms of their experiences. Individuals with two minority characteristics (e.g. black homosexuals) tended to be at the periphery – separate from the dominant heterosexual group and the minority group. Wootton and Brown recommend that it is members of the heterosexual core, those demonstrating the discriminatory attitudes, who should be seen as having the problem – not their victims.

One reason why the social attitudes and beliefs of police officers are important is a consequence of the considerable discretion that officers have in the way they carry out their duties. For example, there is discretion in terms, for example, of whether they make an arrest. While the police as individuals and as institutions may try hard not to let such factors influence their decisions, good intentions may not be totally effective in preventing this happening. Thus, potentially, police officers' social attitudes and beliefs relevant to a particular suspect may be influential on their decisions. Further indications about how homophobic attitudes might influence policing decisions can be found in the work of Lyons *et al.* (2005) who studied anti-gay attitudes in a sample of largely male US police officers. The officers completed an *Attitudes Towards Gay Men* subscale which includes items such as 'Male homosexuality is a perversion'. Generally speaking, homophobic attitudes tended to be typical of the officers.

In another part of the study, these police officers were given a crime scenario in which the offender's sexual orientation was described as either heterosexual or homosexual. The officers judged culpability of the offender in a scenario which incorporated a moral dilemma adapted from the work of Kohlberg on moral development. In this, a person steals from a pharmacist drugs which might help save his dying partner. The pharmacist is grossly overcharging for the drug, which the offender cannot afford to buy.

When the suspect was gay, the officers were more likely to think that he should be convicted than if the suspect was heterosexual. Those with most extreme homophobic attitudes were more likely to endorse the conviction of the offender. Most officers believed that the offender ought to be arrested (82 per cent) and the sexual orientation of the man made no difference to this. Eighty-six per cent believed that the man should be indicted (charged) but only 72 per cent thought that he should be convicted. However, this figure was only 64 per cent where the offender was described as heterosexual but 79 per cent for the homosexual offender. In the homosexual condition, there was a relationship between the level of the officer's homophobia and believing that the defendant should be convicted. This was not the case for the heterosexual condition.

There are other aspects of police culture that warrant attention. In particular, there is some evidence that the police have systematically different beliefs about the criminality of men and women. Horn and Hollin (1997) took a sample of police officers and a broadly similar comparison group who were *not* police. A lengthy questionnaire was used to extract, in particular, ideas about female and male offenders. Factor analysis, a complex statistical technique, revealed three dimensions underlying ideas about criminals:

- *Deviance* which includes beliefs such as 'Trying to rehabilitate offenders is a waste of time and money' and 'In general, offenders are just plain immoral'.

- *Normality* as reflected by agreeing with statements like 'There are some offenders I would trust with my life' and 'I would like associating with some offenders'.

- *Trust* which is measured by such matters as 'I would never want one of my children dating an offender' and 'You have to be constantly on your guard with offenders'.

There were two versions of the questionnaire – one with female offenders as the subject, the other with male offenders as the subject. Women offenders were seen as less fundamentally bad (deviant) than men who offend. This was true irrespective of the sex of the police officer. Compared with the non-police group, police officers saw offenders as fundamentally deviant or bad. The police viewed offenders as less normal than the general public (factor 2), though they tended to see offending women as more normal and like the general public than they saw male offenders. They also regarded offenders as less trustworthy than did the general public and male offenders were seen as less trustworthy than female offenders.

It should be remembered that rapid changes occur within police organisations as a consequence of the pressures on police management coming from political sources as well as legal judgments and reviews of particular policing episodes. These will differ from country to country and force to force but nevertheless they put established practices continually under review.

BOX 11.1 Controversy

False facts and forensic psychology

False facts, according to Aamodt (2008) are to be found in a number of areas of forensic and criminal psychology. By false facts we mean notions which are commonly promulgated for which there is simply no research foundation. Among these is the idea that police officers are more prone to suicide and divorce (Kappeler, Blumberg and Potter, 2000). Apparently the FBI held a conference seeking remedies for this only to find that the suicide rate among police officers may even be lower than would be expected and that much the same motives apply for suicide in police officers as in the general public. Or is this a myth too? Some beliefs – such as that the police are good at detecting deception – may have a bad influence simply because they encourage misplaced faith in the ability of the police. There is plenty of evidence concerning this in Chapter 18. According to Aamodt, perhaps the most alarming feature of these myths is that they are perpetuated despite sound evidence that they are untrue. He lists other false facts such as that crime increases during a full moon and that the typical profile of a serial killer is a white male in his twenties. These are feasible but which of us knows whether they are true or not? Aamodt argues that a number of principles might help reduce the amount of misinformation circulating. For example:

- Check the primary source for the facts – relying on secondary sources is not good
- Be sure that like is compared with like – there is no point applying what might be the case for apples to pears.

So what of the claim that police officers are more likely than people in general to get divorced? Aamodt

reports several Internet claims of this sort, e.g. 'Police officers, for example, face divorce rates averaging average between 66 and 75 per cent' (Aamodt, 2010, p. 1). What is the source of this 'fact'? No sources are given for this or numerous other examples on the Internet. McCoy and Aamodt (2010), however, used census data and found that the rates of divorce and separation for police officers are somewhat lower than the national average. Aamodt stresses primary sources because he is aware of secondary sources which are substantially inaccurate compared to the relevant primary source. For example, the Kitty Genovese murder has often been used to illustrate the principles of bystander intervention and how bystanders fail to intervene when there are several of them. The truth is that two bystanders called the police in this case despite the impression created by textbooks.

What of the claim that police officers are particularly prone to suicide? This apparently, according to Aamodt, was based on a study of insurance claims which found that the police officer suicide rate was 22 per 100,000 as opposed to 12 per 100,000 in the general population. This led to many claims including the idea that police suicide had reached epidemic proportions. The problem is that this statement simply compares apples with pears. Police officers in the USA are predominantly white males between the ages of 25 and 54 years. The suicide rate for these 'apples' in the general populations is 22 per 100,000. That is, the police suicide rate is exactly what it should be if the police are merely regarded as a random sample from the general population with those particular demographic characteristics.

Into this mix of dubious facts, Lilienfeld and Landfeld (2008) throw claims about the role of pseudoscience in relation to law enforcement. Pseudoscience has many of the superficial appearances of science but does not work by the rules of science despite this. The responsiveness of pseudoscience to negative evidence about its precepts is not the same as that which science ideally shows (no matter how reluctantly initially). Thus falsifiability does not feature as a criterion. Lilienfeld and Landfeld (2008) provide a whole list of pseudoscientific endeavours related to law enforcement such as the belief in truth serums, profiling and the polygraph. They also mention graphology – the idea that handwriting can be used to assess personality or psychopathology. There is no evidence of its validity.

Explaining police bias

Police work is an environment which is conducive to the creation of negative stereotypes of minority groups. Officers are at risk of developing negative stereotypes of groups of people with whom they interact during police work. Smith and Alpert (2007) propose that this leads to a form of unconscious racial profiling which leads to disproportionate actions against minority group members during police work. This does not mean that there are not instances of differential treatment out of what Smith and Alpert call *racial animus* or as part of an intentional strategy to deal with crime. Black (and Hispanic) people have repeatedly been shown to be over-represented in the activities of the US police. They are likely to be over-represented as the targets of police actions such as stops, searches and arrests. Why should this be the case? Smith and Alpert (2007) argue that social-psychological research concerning stereotypes can go a long way towards explaining it. The authors claim that racism is not the root of this bias but nevertheless the bias acts against black people. Instead, social conditioning and the phenomenon of the illusory correlation may lead to police officers believing that black people tend to be criminal. Because of this, at each stage black people are disproportionately involved in police activity and they are likely to receive tougher treatment and charges. Discretion is a characteristic of much police activity and it is the police's ability to employ discretion which leads to the over-representation of certain minority groups.

Unconscious racial stereotyping may be part of the explanation of these biases, according to Smith and Alpert. Attitudes, beliefs and stereotypes emerge when the police have repeated contact with people from a particular social grouping. Stereotypes are the outcome of both social and individual cognitive processes. As members of communities, police officers share with other members of the community stereotypes which appear to them as collective knowledge and beliefs about minority group members. Officers are also in regular contact with criminals and develop cognitive schema concerning black people and crime. These schema are activated to help the officer understand new situations based on familiar features of the situation. The consequence of this is that beliefs about black people as a group and crime are generalised to individuals from that group irrespective of the personal characteristics of the individual minority group member.

The illusory correlation also may be relevant. This is the idea that there appears to be a correlation between two things (e.g. race and crime) whereas in reality there is no or a smaller than believed correlation between the two. Smith and Alpert mention one study (Hamilton and Gifford, 1976) in which (1) an arbitrary majority group of 26 persons and (2) an arbitrary minority group of 13 persons was created. Each group was presented as engaging in different and unique behaviours proportionate to the size of the group such that the ratio of desirable to undesirable behaviours in the two groups was identical. In other words, the researchers created a situation in which the behaviours of the majority group and the minority group were exactly equal. Despite this, the two groups were perceived differently such that the majority group was seen as the more desirable and, also, the proportion of undesirable behaviours in the minority group was perceived as being greater than it actually was.

Of course, the consequences of such stereotyping can be serious. For example, African Americans are approximately four times more likely than white people to be killed in encounters with the police in the United States. Furthermore, simulation research suggests that decisions to shoot a person or not are more accurate for armed black men and unarmed white men (Correll *et al.*, 2002).

Confession culture

Not all people detained by the police are formally interviewed. Robertson, Pearson and Gibb (1996) found that only about 30 per cent were interviewed in London (many minor offences do not require one) and interviews are largely conducted by junior officers. Nevertheless, the interview was common for other and, particularly, serious offences. Despite the belief among psychologists that coercive interviewing by police runs the risk of false confession (Chapter 17), observers of the police suggest that the interview is regarded as a crucial stage in a criminal investigation and may encourage all sorts of tactics. The interview situation is different from a normal conversation because one person, the police officer, is the prime controller of the content, structure and direction of the exchanges. Suspects are discouraged from interrupting, initiating conversation or challenging the officer's authority at any level. In the United Kingdom, concerns about miscarriages of justice have led to legal changes. The *Police and Criminal Evidence Act* of 1984 changed the underlying ideology of interviewing to discourage practices which courts of law in the United Kingdom have found unacceptable (Sear and Williamson, 1999). This has resulted in substantial differences between the United Kingdom and the United States:

- *United Kingdom*: a number of principles underlie modern UK training in investigative interviewing. These are:
  - the function of interviewing is the search for the truth rather than justification for a prosecution;
  - the interview should be approached with an open mind;
  - the interviewing officers should behave fairly and recognise, for example, the special difficulties of the groups who may be most at risk of making false confessions – such as those with very low intelligence.
- *United States*: in contrast, in the United States very different legal decisions have meant that trickery and deception are acceptable in substantial parts of police investigative work. The training of officers involves training in these techniques as well as others. Training is frequently by outside agencies.

Part of the American approach is to present the suspect with an acceptable justification for their offending. These are appealing psychologically whether or not they have any basis in law. The self-respect of the offender is ostensibly redeemed by these 'excuses'. Examples include justifying theft by suggesting that the company is rich or that the offender was stealing to help support their family. Another example is feigning support for the offender with comments such as 'Her mother dresses her in those little tiny pants, deliberately turning you on . . .' (Sear and Williamson, 1999, p. 76). A further strategy is to minimise the crime such as suggesting that this was the first crime or that there are far worse crimes.

While it seems beyond doubt that the systems of interviewing are different, care needs to be taken not to idealise the British police in this respect. There is reason to believe that more junior officers, if not others, continue the tradition in the police of viewing confessions as very important if not central to their interviewing work. Cherryman, Bull and Vrij (2000) suggest that there are a number of substantial reasons for this, despite the growth of evidence of the risk of false confessions in interviews:

- Confessions are seen as very convincing evidence even though courts in some jurisdictions may require further corroborative evidence over and above the confession.
- Many suspects confess during an interview and so confessions may be regarded as routine and expected within the interrogation contexts. The lack of other evidence makes confession important.
- Pressures within the police organisation to meet crime clear-up targets may put a premium on any evidence including confession evidence.
- There is a curiously twisted logic that supports the use of any technique to obtain a confession: that is, if for any reason the police officer is convinced of the guilt of the suspect, then any pressure to obtain a confession is defensible.
- Confessions gained using forceful questioning were ruled inadmissible in only a third of British cases (Pearse and Gudjonsson, 1999). So, in a sense, this validates the use of forceful questioning.

In order to demonstrate the influence of confession on police officers' evaluations of interviews, officers listened to various real-life, audiotaped interviews. These varied in competence levels (as judged by researchers) and in terms of whether or not a confession was obtained. The police participants rated the interviews on a large range of factors that experts regard differentiate good from bad interviews. The following are among the characteristics of a good interview:

- all information released at the beginning of the interview;
- appropriate use of pauses or silences;
- appropriate use of pressure;
- communication skills;
- conversation management;
- development and continued rapport;
- empathy/compassion;
- information released appropriately;
- interview has structure;
- keeps interview to relevant matters;
- knowledge of the law;
- open-mindedness;
- planning and preparation;
- purpose of interview explained;
- responds to what interviewee says;
- summarises appropriately;

whereas the following are characteristics of a bad interview:

- apparent use of tactics;
- closed questions;
- closure;
- creation of apprehension;
- inappropriate interruptions;
- leading questions;
- over-talking;
- questions too complex or long;
- undue use of pressure.

The officers making the ratings tended to see the interviews as better when they resulted in a confession or admission than when no confession or admission was obtained.

According to the research of Pearse and Gudjonsson (1999), police tactics in interviews with suspects of serious crimes may be classified empirically into six main categories:

- *Appeals*: this might be appeals to tell the truth, appealing to the suspect's good character and suggesting that it is in the suspect's interest to confess.
- *Intimidation*: in this the seriousness of the event and the anxiety felt by the suspect are maximised. Long silences, attempts to manipulate the self-esteem of the suspect and the use of more than one officer to ask questions while not giving the suspect time to answer are additional features of this.
- *Manipulation*: minimising the seriousness of the offence, minimising the suspect's responsibility, suggesting themes to explain events and so forth.
- *Questioning style*: leading questions used, echoing the answer and asking more than one question in a single sentence.
- *Robust challenge*: this involves direct challenges such as suggesting the suspect is lying. This is often repeated at different stages.
- *Soft challenge*: soft, friendlier tone, challenges with questions such as the possibility that the witness is lying, and attempts to reduce shame of the acts, especially in child sexual abuse cases.

It was found that the greater use that was made of the first three tactics above (the authors call these the overbearing tactics) the greater the likelihood that the court would dismiss the evidence as inadmissible.

BOX 11.2 Forensic psychology in action

Forensic linguistics and the veracity of witness statements

There have been numerous examples of dubious convictions in recent years. Many of the most famous have been British and associated with terrorism. Obviously, dishonesty by police officers is a possibility, especially in high-profile cases in which political and organisational pressure on police officers to find the offenders is strong. Although it is not possible to quantify the dishonesty of police officers definitively

▶

BOX 11.2 (continued)

given that it may not always be easy to detect, it is clear that at least on occasion there is falsification of evidence. Just how is it possible to challenge a confession putatively taken down by a police officer? Obviously, the tape- or video-recording of the statement would reduce the possibility substantially but although this may occur in some countries, in many parts of the world it is not the practice. Even where it is the practice, disputed evidence may pre-date the use of recordings. Forensic linguistics involves a set of procedures that have been used on occasion in this sort of circumstance. An excellent example is Coulthard's (1994) analysis of the 'confession' of William Power, a member of the Birmingham Six who were accused of the IRA bombing of two public houses in Birmingham in 1974. Power claimed that his confession as produced by the police was manufactured. Coulthard examined this and related documents for evidence to confirm or reject this claim. The Birmingham Six were released in 1991 because their conviction was unsafe. We will concentrate on the confession of Derek Bentley which Coulthard also analysed. Some of the aspects of the confessions which can be analysed using forensic linguistics include the following (Coulthard, 1999).

Differences between spoken and written English

Spoken and written languages are not the same. If we take the following sentences from a confession, we can see that they may differ markedly in certain features:

I drove down to the flats and I saw him up on the roof and I shouted to him and he said that he would be down in a couple of minutes.

I wish to make a further statement explaining my complete involvement in the hijacking of the Ford Escort van from John Smith on Monday 28 May 1987 on behalf of the A.B.C. which was later used in the murder of three person (sic) in Newtown that night.

(Coulthard, 1999, p. 112)

Linguists have recognised for a number of years that written English, the language of education, varies markedly from the language of speech (Halverson, 1991; Olson, 1977). Even without this knowledge, probably most of us would correctly identify the first statement as being spoken language: (a) It has low lexical density – that is, there are a lot of words such as to, the, and, on and so forth which largely serve a grammatical function and are not altogether essential to making the sentence meaningful. If they are blanked out then the sentence remains fairly readily decipherable. (b) The clauses in the first sentence are relatively short, e.g. the first clause is 'I drove down to the flats' and the other clauses are of a similar length.

The second sentence seems to show the features of written language which, apart from lexical density and the length of the clauses, include: (a) many examples of nominalisation, i.e. turning verbs into nouns (i.e. statement, involvement, hijacking and murder) and (b) the extensive use of repeated subordinate clauses. The second sentence was part of a disputed confession – the police officer in question admitted that the statement might not be quite the order in which the suspect spoke the words.

Register

The context in which we are speaking or writing has an effect on the language that we use. We use different language in different contexts. Professions differ in terms of the way that language is used. Thus there is a risk that if a police officer attempts to fabricate a statement, elements of that officer's professional language may infiltrate the fabricated statements. Coulthard (1999) provides the famous example of the Derek Bentley case in which Bentley and the teenager Chris Craig were attempting to break into a warehouse. Bentley was arrested but his partner resisted arrest and killed a policeman. Despite being under arrest at the time of the shooting, Bentley was hung for murder whereas Craig, being young, served a prison term. The famous phrase 'Let him have it Chris' uttered by Bentley was translated by the police as 'Shoot him Chris' rather than 'Give him the gun Chris'.

Derek Bentley was virtually illiterate so his statement was taken down by a police officer. The version appearing as evidence in court was claimed to have been a mixture of what he had said and fabrication by the police. Coulthard argues that significant in the disputed statement was the frequent appearance of the word 'then' which appears 10 times in nearly 600 words. There would seem to be little odd about this except when it is revealed that the statements of other witnesses in the case contained the word 'then' once in nearly 1,000 words. On the other hand, the statements of police officers show that the word 'then' is used as frequently as once in about 80 words. In other words, the police's professional need to be precise in reporting may have spilled into the fabricated statement. Derek Bentley, posthumously, received a pardon in 1998.

Improving police work

Police psychology consists largely of attempts by psychologists to try to enhance or facilitate good police practice. Research tends to be centred on the competence of the police at their routine tasks, such as interviewing and providing testimony, and approaches to improving this competence. While many of us have obtained our knowledge of police work from the many media portrayals of police activity (Sacco and Fair, 1988), this does not necessarily reflect the reality of police work properly. Motorists may be very familiar with the role of police in road traffic matters, but what about their role in relation to crime? We have been encouraged by the media portrayals of famous fictional detectives to assume that the police operate largely through detection and theorising about the motives of offenders or unknown offenders. So it is worthwhile noting that a study by Farrington and Lambert (1997) found a more routine picture of crime detection. They explored the factors associated with arrest of suspects for different types of crime. Apprehension for burglary involved the following factors:

- Offender caught in the act by the police – 15 per cent.
- Information supplied by an informant – 13 per cent.
- Offender caught near the scene of the crime – 12 per cent.
- Articles left somewhere or disposed of by the offender – 11 per cent.
- The offender arrested when seen acting suspiciously in the crime area – 8 per cent.
- The offender arrested for another crime – 7 per cent.
- Eyewitness descriptions of the offender – 6 per cent.

For arrests for violent offences, the pattern was a little different:

- Offender detained at the scene – 16 per cent.
- Victim description of the offender – 15 per cent.
- Witness description of the offender – 13 per cent.
- Caught in the act of violence – 11 per cent.
- Vehicle description – 11 per cent.
- Number plate – 11 per cent.

In other words, Sherlock Holmes, Maigret, Miss Marple, Inspector Roderick Alleyn and Jane Tennison would have rather wasted skills in the real police force.

The cognitive interview

Much of the psychological literature on traditional police interviewing skills paints a picture of officers using less than optimum techniques to elicit information from witnesses. In contrast, the psychological research literature is replete with findings about what makes a good interview and there is plentiful advice and assistance about the best techniques to use. Often police interviews fail to meet the standards recommended in these publications. Wright and Alison (2004) analysed a number of interviews with adult witnesses in Canada. The interviews were characterised by a number of features: (a) there was frequent interruption of the witnesses by the officers, (b) more closed questions of the sort which produce short (e.g. yes/no) answers were asked than open questions designed to elicit more information, and (c) psychological techniques of the sort discussed later in this section designed to facilitate the witness's memory were not fully used. The police spoke about one-third of the time, interviewees two-thirds of the time, and lawyers scarcely spoke at all in comparison – just about a third of 1 per cent of the total time! Questions were asked at a high rate of frequency – there was on average one question posed every 16 seconds. Multiple (complex) questions were asked once in just over four minutes on average. The officers paraphrased what the witness had said once every seven minutes. In every minute of interview time, on average, 0.4 questions were asked by way of clarification, 0.3 leading questions were asked and 1.2 closed questions were asked per minute about clarification.

There was a common structure to the interviews whereby firstly the interviewing officers helped the witness to construct an account of the events and then, secondly, they used a sequence of yes/no (closed) questions to confirm that account. It appeared possible that the interviewing officers had a version of the events which they were pursuing through the interview.

From time to time, police interviewing techniques have come under major and potentially damaging public scrutiny. In Norway, a notorious child sexual abuse case led directly to new efforts to improve the police's skills in interviewing children. This is known as the Bjugn case. Seven adults were arrested for the suspected sexual abuse and rape of children in the town. The police conducted a substantial number of interviews with children and there was a judicial hearing involving 40 children. However, charges against six out of seven of the suspects were dropped, though the remaining suspect underwent a 10-week trial before being acquitted. Criticisms of the affair included the competence of the interviewers, the style of questioning adopted, and the large delay between the allegations being made until when the interviews finally took place.

Norwegian police officers' use of open and closed questions was studied during investigative interviews with children. The officers were divided into two levels based on their competence assessed through the amount of training and experience. The questions that they asked during their questioning of the children were classified as open or closed. Closed questions predominated and were 10 times more frequent than open ones. However, there was not a significant difference due to competence. Open questions became less frequent as the interview progressed, whereas the frequency of closed questions showed an inverted U distribution with most occurring at the middle of the interview.

The cognitive interview attempts to enhance recall by witnesses using techniques deriving from psychological research into memory retrieval. Recall does not just happen, it is dependent on the types of probe used to retrieve the memory. If one type of probe does not work,

then another may (Tulving, 1974). Cognitive interviewing is a practical reality, at least up to a point, since it has been adopted in police work. For example, since 1992 it has been part of the standard interview package used to train officers in England and Wales. It takes just a few hours for a police officer, for example, to obtain improvements in the information obtained from witnesses (Memon et al., 1994). The cognitive interview is not recommended for use with suspects or witnesses who are uncooperative or resistant to the interview. In this case, the recommended best practice is to use the conversation management approach (Shepherd and Milne, 1999). This involves the building of trust and confidence in the interviewer. It is known as GEMAC (greeting, explanation, mutual activity, close). Thus the initial greeting signals equality. The interviewer discusses the reason for the interview, the agenda of activities, routines employed such as the taking of notes or the recording of the events and the expectations of the interviewer, e.g. that the interviewer regards silence as positive and interruptions to these will be avoided. Mutual activities include monitoring activities such as active listening. Finally, the close of the interview can be an opportunity to summarise what has been said in order to check on the detail. Shepherd (2007) has presented in great detail a manual giving details of how to conduct an investigative interview using the conversation management approach.

The original cognitive interview adopted two basic principles (Geiselman et al., 1984):

- Recall in an environment that successfully reproduces features of the original encoding context is likely to be superior (Tulving, 1974).

- Memory is a complex thing and there is no whole representation of events stored in the brain. Instead there is a complex array of events and happenings which may not be stored in a coherent manner but will require a variety of strategies to tap in their entirety.

The cognitive interview then consists of four 'strategies' for improving the process of retrieving memory. Incorporating these simple instructions can improve eyewitness memory reports compared with standard police interview (Geiselman and Fisher, 1997). Witnesses should be encouraged to do the following:

- Report everything that they can think of about the witnessed events, even including trivial or incomplete fragments that they might feel irrelevant. Such an instruction might be 'Tell me everything you remember, no matter how big or how small a detail' (Goodman and Melinder, 2007, p. 11).

- Mentally reinstate the circumstances of the witnessing. This includes their feelings at the time (e.g. they felt scared) or external factors that they recall (e.g. the noise of the building work in the background). So it should be explained at the start of the interview that they should mentally recreate the external physical environment and their internal state including affective (emotional), physiological and cognitive states at the time of witnessing the events (Fisher, Brennan and McCauley, 2002). This instruction may be phrased, perhaps, as follows 'Think back to where you were at the time' (Goodman and Melinder, 2007, p. 11).

- Vary retrieval methods. For example, the interviewer should encourage the witness to report events in a number of different sequences and not just in chronological order. So recall could be obtained from the point that the police arrived or perhaps by recalling in reverse order. The underlying idea is based on research evidence that different components of a complex event may be recalled when different cues are present to aid retrieval from memory. Fisher *et al.* (2002) stress that these methods need care, otherwise the interviewer may be dissatisfied with the evidence presented. This might be phrased, for example, 'Now that you have told me what happened, try to remember it again but this time starting at the end and recounting it in reverse chronological order' (Goodman and Melinder, 2007, p. 11).

- Report events from alternative perspectives such as that of another witness, the offender or from another physical location. This instruction might be phrased 'What would the perpetrator have seen and heard?' (Goodman and Melinder, 2007, p. 11).

Additional considerations have been added as interest in the cognitive interview has grown. For example, witnesses should be encouraged to concentrate on their senses. Although we memorise in terms of concepts, we also memorise in terms of events' sensory features. So one simple technique for improving retrieval is to have the witness close their eyes and visualise the events.

Eventually, a number of problems became apparent that are not to do with memory directly. For example, the witness may be nervous and anxious, inarticulate and very unsure of what is expected of them in the context of the interview. For that reason, Fisher and Geiselman (1992) introduced what is known as the *enhanced cognitive interview*. This can be seen as the cognitive interview combined with techniques from communications psychology to help alleviate communication problems. For example, an interview can be ineffective because it fails to take into account the fact that people have limited mental resources to cope with the information flow. The interviewer may have a too complex task if they have to frame the questions, pay attention to the interviewee and make notes at the same time. As a consequence, they may fail to hear all of the information being provided, perhaps because they are distracted by the need to frame their next question. Similarly, if the interviewee is faced with a barrage of questions they may be so overloaded cognitively that they can only search their memory superficially (Fisher *et al.*, 2002).

The enhanced cognitive interview hands control of the interview to the witness by making it clear that they have as much time as they require to respond to questions. Instead of the police officer determining, say, when as much has been recalled as could be recalled, this among other things becomes the prerogative of the witness. Other changes included training in the following:

- The process of building rapport or easy dialogue between the officer and the witness.

- How to use appropriate body language in the interview to reduce the feeling of intimidation experienced by some witnesses being interviewed, for example.

- How to ask effective questions – that is, for example, questions asked in a way that facilitates both understanding and a clear reply.

- How to use pauses effectively – for example, allowing the witness time to think and reply rather than rushing from one question to the next.

So the main principles of the cognitive interview seem to be effectively based on detailed and well-founded research on effective memory retrieval. Nevertheless, simply knowing the basics of the cognitive interview is insufficient to effectively conduct one. Fisher *et al.* (2002) explain that the cognitive interview should be structured into five different sequential components (these are expanded on in Figure 11.1):

- *Introduction*: this is a crucial stage in that it provides the witness with an appropriate psychological and social setting for the cognitive interview to work. So it is at this stage that the interviewer must develop rapport with the interviewee, explain the need for as much information in as great a detail as possible, and

Step 1: Introduction: Building rapport with interviewee	• Make interview more interpersonal: exchange names, making sure that the witness is comfortable, confirm witness wants to remember everything • Transfer control to witness: explain that the witness is the best informed about the events, allow witness to decide where to begin their evidence, do not interrupt if possible, listen actively to the witness's evidence
Step 2: Open-ended narration: Recreation of the context of the the crime/obtaining detailed report	• Ask witness to close their eyes and imagine themself back at the scene of the crime/events • Ask the witness to recall as much detail of the crime events as possible
Step 3: Probing: Obtain open-ended narrative account of the witnessed events	• Request the interviewee to give as full as description as possible • Avoid interrupting the interviewee, though brief encouragement such as 'Can you tell me more' is acceptable • Focused retrieval are guidelines to help the witness such as (a) using open-ended questioning and (b) allowing long pauses in the narration without interrupting them • Extensive retrieval: Encourage extensive memory searching by (a) asking the witness to report the events from the perspective of different locations or (b) varying (reversing) the chronological order • Witness compatible questioning: for example, do not stick rigidly to a particular sequence of questions when the witness begins providing their answers but not in the same order
Step 4: Review evidence	• Take the witness through their evidence for checking purposes
Step 5: Closing the interview	• Outline to the interviewee what is likely to happen next • Exchange contact details • Tell the witness to get in touch say if additional details are recalled

Figure 11.1 The basic procedural steps for the revised cognitive interview according to Wells, Memon and Penrod (2007) and Fisher and Geiselman (1992)

encourage the interviewee to engage actively in the interview and freely offer information without waiting for a direct question pertinent to that information.

• *Open-ended narration*: by allowing the interviewee an opportunity to freely indicate what they remember of the witnessed events, the interviewer is provided with the basic material needed to plan what aspects should be probed using the techniques of the cognitive interview. During the course of the witness's narration, the interviewer notes what appear to be the mental images of important aspects of the events: for example, what images does the witness have of the perpetrator and significant objects such as weapons.

• *Probing*: because the interviewer has established the general features of the interviewee's recollections, the

aspects of memory which might be the best sources of information are focused on. So the interviewer 'guides' the interviewee to these aspects and provides the cognitive interview techniques which help maximise the information gathered. The interviewer might suggest that the witness closes their eyes and thinks about the best view that the witness had of the offender (Fisher *et al.*, 2002). This best view is then described in as much detail as possible. Of course, the interviewer may ask additional questions (probes) in order to get more information.

• *Review*: the interviewer takes the interviewee through the evidence that the interviewee has provided in order to find any inaccuracies in what has been recorded. Naturally, in the course of this the witness may recall more things.

- *Close*: this may include fulfilling the official requirements in respect to interview such as signing any required forms and the like. The witness may be encouraged to get back in touch with the officer when new things occur to the witness which were not recalled in the interview.

Unquestionably the cognitive interview works. Quite how it achieves its objectives and how well is not so clear. For example, there is the question of what to compare the cognitive interview with. The standard police interviewing techniques can be extremely poor and based on little or no appropriate training. So is it reasonable to compare this sort of interview with the outcomes of special training in the cognitive interview? Officers trained in the cognitive interview may be motivated by their training to interview better without the cognitive interview itself having much effect on witnesses' recall (Kohnken *et al.*, 1999). For that reason, researchers have chosen to use what is described as the structured interview as a control procedure to the cognitive interview. These interviews are similar to the cognitive interview in terms of the good and positive characteristics they possess but the mnemonic memory techniques of the cognitive interview are missing (Kohnken, Thurer and Zoberbeier, 1994). Figure 11.1 gives the basic procedural steps involved in conducting a cognitive interview.

There is some evidence that cognitive interview techniques are well received by police officers. Kebbell, Milne and Wagstaff (1998) surveyed police officers about the cognitive interview. Officers trained in the method showed evidence of using some of the techniques more often, in particular the mental reinstatement of context, changing the order of events and describing the events from another perspective. Features of cognitive interviewing such as reporting everything, establishing rapport and transferring control did not seem to differ between trained and untrained officers. In terms of the usefulness of different components of cognitive interviewing, establishing rapport was rated as the most useful. Some of the cognitive interview techniques such as changing perspective, trying different orders and transferring control were seen as much less useful even though these are key aspects of cognitive interviewing.

Memon *et al.* (1994) trained police officers in cognitive interviewing and examined their performance with witnesses to a simulated robbery. The police had some difficulties. For example, they tended to continue with the faults of conventional police interviewing such as

rapid-fire questions with little opportunity for the witness to respond and questions about specific matters. They incorporated, most commonly, the cognitive interview strategies of context reinstatement, perspective changing, reporting everything and focused retrieval. On the other hand, officers trained in structured interviewing techniques (see above) also commonly used context reinstatement and reporting everything. After cognitive interview training, context reinstatement, perspective changing and focused retrieval were used more. Overall, it would appear that despite its successes, there are problems in implementing the cognitive interview entirely.

Nevertheless, in Wright and Alison's (2004) study mentioned above, cognitive interview techniques were rarely used. For example, none of the interviews encouraged the witness to recount events from someone else's perspective and it was virtually unknown for the witness to be encouraged to mentally reconstruct the physical and emotional context of the events they had witnessed. Other cognitive interview techniques were used more frequently. One in five interviews encouraged the interviewees to report any detail or to recall events in any order. Much more common were verbal demonstrations that the interviewing officer was listening to what was being said, giving the interviewee an opportunity to contribute information which had not specifically been asked for, and questioning sequences compatible with the witness's recollections. These were found in over three out of five interviews.

These findings are broadly reflected in more recent research by Dando, Wilcock and Milne (2008). In this, over 200 young non-specialist police officers completed an anonymous self-completion questionnaire concerning the role of the cognitive interview in their day-to-day work. This is, of course, not a cross section of police officers in general. Many of the components of the cognitive interview were regarded as being effective in their interviewing work. The perceived effectiveness of some of the components of the cognitive interview is shown in Figure 11.2. It is notable, though, that the procedures of recalling in various orders and changing perspective during recall were regarded as the least effective. This pattern was reflected in the officer's frequency of use of these same techniques. Most cognitive interview elements were quite frequently used though, once again, recalling events in various orders and changing the perspective during recall were the least frequently used. They are perhaps the most psychological and least obvious aspects

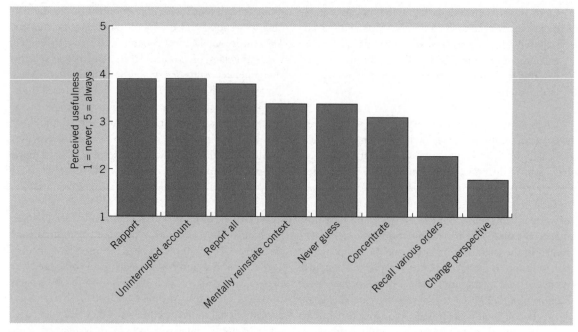

Figure 11.2 Police officers' perceptions of the effectiveness of different aspects of the cognitive interview

of the cognitive interview which perhaps do not equate with common sense as much as the others. The officers generally lacked confidence in their interviewing training and expressed a desire for more.

The evidence from studies of the impact of the cognitive interview on memory quality is broadly positive. There are numerous studies and too many to consider here individually. The technique of meta-analysis (see Box 4.2) allows trends over a range of studies to be assessed. Kohnken *et al.* (1999) put into such an analysis studies that involved recall (rather than recognition) as the measure of memory. Their main selection requirements for including a study were that a full cognitive interview strategy was employed and that the outcome was compared with some form of standard interview (non-cognitive interview). Over 40 studies were found meeting these criteria:

- The cognitive interview compared with the standard interview produced more correct details. Translated into a correlation coefficient, the type of interview correlated 0.4 with the amount of correct details recalled.

- Factors that led to poorer outcomes in the cognitive interview included the length of delay between the witnessing of the event and the interview, how little

the interviewees were involved in the events they witnessed and the research laboratory where the study took place. It was the research carried out in the laboratory of the originators of the technique that had the best effects on recall.

- There were no identifiable differences between the effectiveness of the original cognitive interview and that of the enhanced cognitive interview.

- The cognitive interview tended to increase the number of errors (incorrect recollections) made.

- The type of cognitive interview made a difference. The enhanced cognitive interview was especially error-prone. Again, the research conducted in the laboratory of the originators of the technique tended to get the highest error rates. To clarify matters a little, while increases in errors may be undesirable, an increase in the correct detail is more important as this aids detection. If one calculates the proportion of correct details remembered to the total number of details, the cognitive interview produces a 40 per cent increase in the relative numbers of correct details. It has been recommended for work with children (Milne and Bull, 1994). Milne *et al.* (1995) showed children to be resistant to leading/suggestive questioning after the cognitive interview (also Hayes and Delamothe, 1997, and Milne and Bull, 1996, for children with mild learning difficulty).

As far as can be ascertained, it would appear that the use of cognitive interviewing has not been a contentious issue in courts of law. For example, Fisher *et al.* (2002), experts in the field, indicate that they are aware of only two court cases in which the use of the cognitive interview was raised as a point of contention. One of these is American and the other British. Both occurred over 10 years ago, which is significant in itself.

Forensic hypnosis

Hypnotic suggestion as a defence against criminal charges has occurred from time to time. There is evidence that the public regard 'automatism' due to hypnosis as the basis for seeing the defendant as less responsible for the offence than a similar crime carried out under duress (Roberts and Wagstaff, 1996). Potential jurors with experience of hypnotism tend to be less believing that hypnotism had affected individuals' behaviour (Wagstaff, Green and Somers, 1997). Another aspect of hypnosis in forensic contexts is the investigation of crime. This seems to be regarded favourably by the media (McConkey, Roche and Sheehan, 1989). Many psychologists who are experts in the field are less than enthusiastic about forensic hypnosis compared with, say, the cognitive interview (e.g. Wagstaff, 1996). It also needs to be said that hypnosis has had a somewhat chequered history in courts of law. This is documented for the United States by Lynn, Neuschatz and Fite (2002). The use of forensic hypnosis only became popular in the 1960s. Even then it attracted controversy and legal ambivalence about where and when hypnosis is appropriate in testimony. The Hurd rules (or Orne rules after the famous psychologist Martin Orne) may be used as procedural guidelines and safeguards. Briefly they include, according to Lynn *et al.* (2002):

- Qualified expert: the psychiatrist/psychologist conducting the hypnotic session needs to be experienced in the use of hypnosis.

- Independence: the hypnotist should be independent of the major parties in the case (prosecution, investigation and defence) and should not be in the regular employment of any of these parties.

- Recording of information: the information received from any of the major parties should be recorded in writing (or another acceptable form).

- Pre-hypnosis gathering of facts: a full account of the events should be obtained from the witness prior to any hypnotic session. The hypnotist should not influence the description by their interview technique or add details in error to the description.

- All contact between the hypnotist and the 'witness' must be recorded.

- No other persons should be present during the hypnotic suggestion phase – including any pre-hypnotic testing and any interview after hypnosis.

Despite all of this, the American judiciary have tended to accept hypnotically obtained evidence rather than reject it.

While it would appear a reasonable question to ask 'what is hypnosis?', a clear and consensual answer is not forthcoming (Wagstaff, 1997). To suggest that it is a different or altered mental state compared with normal conscious behaviour is to ignore a lot of evidence. This would imply that people who have not been hypnotised will carry out much the same behaviours and at similar rates as those who have characteristically been seen as showing hypnotic behaviour. The latter viewpoint is the non-state view of hypnotism, which argues that it is not a distinct psychological state but basically normal psychological processes. Its proponents see hypnotic behaviours as the result of less extraordinary psychological mechanisms such as conformity, compliance and expectations. According to Wagstaff, one of the reasons why hypnosis remains a point of contention is that simply because a non-hypnotised person will do the same things as a hypnotised person (e.g. handle snakes), this does not mean that hypnosis is not a distinct state of consciousness. Any given behaviour may have a number of different determinants, of course.

Not surprisingly, there is an extensive academic research base evaluating hypnotically induced testimony. While hypnotic practitioners may have a different view, the academic consensus tends to doubt the value of hypnosis compared with other methods of improving witness recall (Kebbell and Wagstaff, 1998):

- Inaccurate recall sometimes results from hypnosis, thus decreasing the overall accuracy rate. According to Lynn *et al.* (2002), meta-analyses (Box 4.2) of a large number of studies have pointed to the conclusion that although hypnosis increases the amount of material remembered, this is at the cost of also increasing the amount of false recollections. This is much the same criticism as for the enhanced cognitive interview. The reason for this appears to be that hypnotised witnesses simply report more of both inaccurate and accurate recollections. When witnesses are required to recall a fixed number of memories, there was no difference between hypnotised and non-hypnotised individuals in terms of their accuracy.

- Confidence in hypnotised witnesses may increase without commensurate improvements in accuracy. Indeed, they may well have more confidence in what they inaccurately remember under hypnosis than the accurate information (Lynn et al., 2002). This is of particular concern in the legal context given the importance of witness confidence in persuading courts of the value of a witness's testimony. Some witnesses appear to be more suggestible to the effects of leading questions and misleading information. Nevertheless, Lynn et al. state that 'vulnerability to suggestive information' may be commoner among those who are high or medium on hypnotisability who tend to report false memories (pseudomemories) much more commonly than those low on hypnotisability. As high and medium hypnotisability is characteristic of most of the population, then Lynn et al. puts the figure of those susceptible to suggestive memory recovery techniques as high as 60 per cent. Even those low on hypnotisability sometimes report false memories.

- It should be considered that the hypnotic interview may be technically better executed than the typical police interview. So memory performance may actually be better but not because of hypnosis.

It should be stressed that most of the findings are based on generalisations from laboratory situations. Consequently, there may be some reason for caution before hypnotism is rejected entirely by forensic psychologists.

While there are advantages in using hypnotism, it has been suggested that the cognitive interview out-performs it. It is a particular concern to some that hypnotism may have a distorting effect on memory. That does not mean that it invariably does so. Wagstaff (1996) argues that without detailed knowledge of the process of hypnosis involved in a particular case and other details, it is not possible to draw firm conclusions about the degree of adverse influence of hypnosis on the witness. Others (Berry, Robinson and Bailey, 1999) suggest that hypnosis,

irrespective of its effectiveness, may have a variety of drawbacks for practitioners. These include the number of lengthy hypnotic sessions necessary and the possible need for aftercare in cases where the memories emerging in hypnosis are particularly distressing.

Although the value of hypnosis in interviewing has generally not been held to be great, as we have seen, there remains some interest in aspects of it. Hammond, Wagstaff and Cole (2006) studied two techniques which may facilitate the quality of eyewitness memory during interviews. One has its origins in the cognitive interview and the other is essentially the hypnotic method without hypnotic states being achieved. Although there is considerable evidence that other techniques may work better, it is true that hypnosis may be better than using no technique at all. Furthermore, in some studies the cognitive interview produces high levels of false recollections which may reach unacceptable levels when poorly trained interviewers are used. However, it is fairly generally accepted that the cognitive interview does not seriously increase the amount of incorrect information recalled nor does it increase susceptibility to leading questions. But there are problems with the cognitive interview especially since it leads to lengthier interviews and the amount of training officers need to become effective at using the techniques. There is evidence that officers may fail to comply with the procedures of the cognitive interview despite being trained in the method. Children seem to have difficulty with cognitive interview techniques and may be error prone as a consequence. In Hammond et al.'s study, both adults and children viewed a video of a crime which involved an armed robbery of a shop selling alcohol. They were then either put through a focused mediation procedure which derives from hypnotic interviewing techniques or the context reinstatement procedure from the cognitive interview. A control group received no memory procedure.

The context reinstatement procedure used asked participants to close their eyes and try to clear their head of other thoughts apart from the crime that the participant had witnessed. They were to picture the events as if they were happening at this very moment in front of their eyes. They were asked to replay the exents in their minds as if they were watching a film. They then had to ask themselves questions such as the location of the crime and what the environment surrounding the crime looks like. The instructions continued in this vein and encouraged them to remember as much detail as possible. The focused mediation procedure is similar to hypnotic induction but does not have the context of hypnosis, which itself might be responsible for the false alarms and mistaken confidence that hypnotic methods may create. The focused mediation group were taken through a short focused breathing mediation procedure and were asked to continue these exercises while they completed the memory questionnaire.

The sort of open-ended questions used were 'Describe the scene where the crime occurred' and 'What did the first robber look like?' whereas the closed questions were for example 'What weapon did the second armed robber use?' and 'What was on the shop counter?'. Both methods improved memory compared with the controls. This was for both open-ended and closed interview questions. Context reinstatement produced more correct responses though than the focused mediation methods and the context reinstatement group showed higher confidence levels when they gave wrong information in reply to the closed questions.

Police as eyewitnesses: how accurate are they?

Common sense suggests that the police, because of their training and experience, should be accurate witnesses. They are, after all, experienced professionals. Whether or not police officers make especially accurate witnesses is probably not the most important issue. Crucial is whether those responsible for making legal decisions believe in the superiority of police eyewitness evidence. A majority of the general public believed that officers were more accurate than people in general (Clifford, 1976). Not only that, but there is evidence that the majority of legal professionals such as judges, lawyers and police officers also believe in the superiority of police evidence. To the extent that this leads to greater acceptance of the evidence of the police, then this is a significant social fact.

Forensic and criminal psychologists have argued differently. Police officers and others were asked to identify crimes that had occurred at a street corner depicted in a video. They seemed to be no more skilful than civilians (Ainsworth, 1981). Actually, there were differences in the sense that the police officers were more suspicious that a crime was taking place when, in fact, it was not. Clifford and Richards (1977) found that police officers could give better descriptions than could civilians of a

person who stopped them to ask for directions. Briefer encounters than this produced no differences.

In Sweden, Christianson, Karlsson and Persson (1998) studied students, teachers, trainee police and police officers. These groups were shown a series of somewhat gory photographic slides of a violent incident – a man's gloved hand holding a bloody knife, a woman with slashed throat and copious bleeding, a distant shot of a woman lying bleeding. They were then shown photos of the perpetrator making his escape. The next stage was a filler stage in which participants were shown photographs of faces. The findings were somewhat different from those of earlier studies. In terms of the proportions able to recall information related to the crime slides correctly, serving police officers were clearly superior to the other groups – especially school teachers. Specifically, the police tended especially to recall more about the perpetrator. In a line-up/identity parade situation, 'hits' (correct identifications) were highest for police officers. False alarms (the wrong person selected) were little different between any of the groups. Incorrect rejects were the least for the police officers. That is to say, the police officers less often failed to identify the culprit when he was actually in the line-up. Length of service more than age or any other factor tended to be associated with better recall. While memory in general was not superior in police officers, it may be that the emotive nature of the task here worked to the advantage of police participants.

Lindholm, Christianson and Karlsson (1997) wondered whether experience in policing brings with it a knowledge of crime events which facilitates the way in which officers remember events. This would follow from early research indicating that familiarity with a particular domain of memory tends to facilitate recollection of events relevant to that domain. This is possibly because previous experience provides a structure for the organisation of memories. Swedish police recruits, police officers in service and students were shown to be similar on all measures. The memory material consisted of one or other version of a video of a robbery of a grocery store. It takes the viewpoint of an eyewitness who picks up items such as lettuce and spaghetti before arriving at the checkout. At this point, a man runs through the store, threatening the people queuing. He then robs the cashier, slashing his face with a knife. There were two versions of the robbery which differed in terms of the robber's ethnicity – in one case he had a Scandinavian blonde appearance whereas in the other he had a dark, more southern European appearance. After a short filler task, participants were asked to write down as much detail as they could remember. They were also given a multiple-choice questionnaire concerning: (a) people in the video (such as their clothing) and (b) the sequence of events in the film. A photo line-up and a line-up of the knife from the video and others were also employed. The findings were:

- Police officers were better at identifying the actual knife.
- Police officers were better at identifying relevant crime information.

One possible reason for the superior performance of the serving police officers may be that the stress of the events in the video was less for them because they were used to dealing with violent events in their work. Their lower emotional responses to the video may have provided them with more freedom to form an accurate opinion rather than rely on stereotypes. In the light of the earlier comments, it is worth noting that the police officers seemed less affected by the ethnicity of the offender than the others.

Whether or not features of the training of police officers in Scandinavia contribute to their superior performance over the public is not known. Comparative data collected in similar circumstances from police officers in other parts of the world are simply not yet available.

The police caution

The police caution is the 'warning' that a police officer is required to give when arresting a suspect for an offence. The current police caution in much of the United Kingdom is: 'You do not have to say anything, but it may harm your defence if you do not mention when questioned something which you later rely on in court. Anything you do say may be given in evidence.' In other words, it is a warning that silence after arrest may carry a message to the court. Police cautions to suspects vary from legal system to legal system. In the United States, the police caution reminds the suspect of their right to remain silent so as not to incriminate themselves. This, along with the right to a lawyer, forms the basis of informing the suspect of what are known as his or her Miranda rights. Thus British and US systems are now quite different. Previously, in the United Kingdom, citizens had the right to remain silent and exercise of this right could not be considered by the court. One

key issue, despite the variation among nations and over time, is the extent to which statements of rights are actually understood by the public.

A survey of the modern police caution in Britain (Shepherd, Mortimer and Mobaseri, 1995) found that relatively few members of the public could explain the components of the caution (Police and Criminal Evidence Act of 1984):

- 'You do not have to say anything.' This was understood by 27 per cent.
- 'But it may harm your defence if you do not mention when questioned something which you later rely on in court.' This was understood by 14 per cent.
- 'Anything you do say may be given in evidence.' This was understood by 34 per cent.

Scotland has a different tradition of caution that does not depend on quite such a precisely prescribed position, although the officer should explain it. The basic common law caution is that a suspect is not obliged to say anything but anything she or he does say will be noted and may be used in evidence. (Common law is that established by custom and the decisions of judges. It is law that is not contained as such in statutes or legislation.) Young offenders are known from previous international research to have particular difficulties with the standard cautions. In other words, suspects do not understand their basic rights. Cook and Philip (1998) studied the comprehensibility of the Scottish caution in a number of ways. One of the things they did was to ask the young offenders to decide whether phrases actually meant the same as the phrase in the caution:

- 'You are not bound to answer' was seen by 59 per cent as equivalent to 'You do not have to say anything until the police ask you questions' though its legal implications are quite different from this.
- The phrase in the caution 'Your answer may be used in evidence' was interpreted by 90 per cent as meaning the same as 'As long as you are polite to the police, whatever you say will not be used against you in court.'

The Canadian police caution includes a statement about the right to silence and one about the right to have a lawyer present. The right to silence is as follows: 'You need not say anything. You have nothing to hope from any promise or favour, and nothing to fear from any threat, whether or not you say anything. Anything you do say may be used against you as evidence.' The right to a lawyer is: 'You have the right to retain and instruct counsel without delay. You have the right to immediate access to advice from duty counsel (lawyer) free of charge. You also have the right to subsequently be represented by a lawyer free of charge if you meet the criteria set up by the Newfoundland Legal Aid Commission.' It was found in a study by Eastwood and Snook (2010) that participants in the research (and they included a very substantial minority of individuals on a programme for police recruits as well as students on a range of other degree programmes) poorly understood these two elements of the caution. Only 3 per cent fully understood the right to silence and only 7 per cent fully understood the right to a legal counsel. This is when the caution was read aloud to the participants; they were much better when the statements were in a written-form, when 48 per cent and 32 per cent understood the two elements of the caution fully. It did not matter significantly whether police recruits or the others were considered. Broken down sentence by sentence, it was clear that there were problems with the second sentences in both cases. They were poorly understood and appear to be somewhat complex but nevertheless contain important information in the context of the research. While it would seem that the caution could be presented sentence by sentence in written form in order to optimise its comprehension, this is problematic. Many of those arrested by the police may have literacy limitations so they lack the ability to deal with material in this format. In contrast, the participants in the study were well educated and well versed in reading skills. Clearly what should be done is far from obvious or straightforward.

Whether or not psychologists could develop phraseology that would improve matters in any of these jurisdictions is a moot point if the precise legal implications of the caution are to remain unchanged. Nevertheless, the bottom line is that offenders in the normal intelligence range often have difficulty understanding their legal rights.

Other studies find similar findings. For example, the UK Police and Criminal Evidence codes of practice are available at police stations. They supplement the statutory verbal and written material. Various matters are covered. These include the rules governing detention. Very few arrestees actually ask to see the code of practice. When they do, based on the observations of Joyce (1993), they read a passage or two and then discard the booklet. Readability of text can be analysed. For example, the average sentence length is a useful index. One example of this approach is the Flesch Index. This is the average sentence length adjusted by the average number of syllables in a word. Joyce took 40 passages from the code. Overwhelmingly, they fell in the fairly difficult to very difficult range. An IQ in the range above average to above 126 is needed in order to comprehend material of this level of difficulty. What is the readability of the paragraph you are reading? It is in the fairly difficult range. This means that this paragraph is easier to read than nearly all of the samples of text in Joyce's study!

In some countries such as England and Wales, there is no longer a right to remain silent with no legal consequences. In other countries such as the United States, the constitution gives suspects the right of silence with impunity. These are known as the Miranda rights in the USA. In these circumstances, the issue of understanding the police caution becomes even more salient. Kassin and Norwick (2004) report an intriguing laboratory study in which groups of 'suspects' were subjected to different styles of interviewing by a 'detective' including sympathetic and hostile styles. The 'detective' was trying to get the 'suspect' to forego their Miranda rights so that more evidence could be obtained which would be legitimate in court. The style of interview actually made no difference of note to the decision to waive one's Miranda rights. However, the researchers had included a guilty–innocent dimension into the study. Some participants 'stole' money from a nearby teaching laboratory, others did not. Actually, they had received instructions about what to do from the experimenters. Nevertheless, some were 'guilty' because they had taken the money on instruction and others were 'innocent' because they had not taken the money. When put under some pressure by the 'detective' it was found that the 'innocent' group were more likely to waive their Miranda rights than the 'guilty' group. Kassin and Norwick (2004) argue that Miranda warnings may not protect the most vulnerable from the actions of the police. False confession is not uncommon and we need to understand the process that includes waiving Miranda rights. One important case involved an 18-year-old who confessed to the murder of his mother and was imprisoned until independent evidence showed that he could not have possibly committed the crime. When asked why he did not remain silent during the interview he said: 'I hadn't done anything wrong and I felt that only a criminal really needed an attorney, and this was all going to come out in the wash' (reported in Kassin and Norwick, 2004, p. 218). Thus the innocent may be put at risk more than the guilty.

Use of lethal force

According to Blau (1994), in the United States something of the order of 100 police officers die each year at the hands of civilians. Nevertheless, the police are more likely to kill than to be killed. Nearly 300 civilians are legally killed by police officers each year. The officers were not killed by deranged individuals. The killers were not 'mad psychopaths' but, generally, criminals attempting to escape a crime scene. Blau suggests, based on this, that one of the strongest cues to danger for a police officer should be when the offender is attempting to escape arrest. It is difficult to judge danger but the following may be particularly dangerous:

- suspects who have a history of dangerousness;
- suspects who associate with people with a history of dangerousness;
- suspects who live or work in situations or settings where violent and dangerous events are likely to occur.

There is a buffer zone which when breached greatly increases the likelihood that the suspect will react violently (Blau, 1994). A dangerous stimulus moving from 4 ft (1.2 m) to closer is especially likely to produce a dangerous response in the officer. In the United States, 50 per cent of police officers are frequently required to carry guns on duty and the remaining 50 per cent of officers are permitted and encouraged to do so. Research for the 1980s discovered about 800 felonious killings of on-duty police officers:

- 40 per cent were killed while attempting to make an arrest;
- over 90 per cent were killed with firearms;
- 15 per cent were killed by their own weapons taken from them physically by their killers.

The costs of being involved in armed violence as a victim are not merely personal. In the United States, four-fifths of police officers involved in shooting incidents left their police department consequently.

Police officers who get involved in shooting incidents are not a random sample of officers. Research has shown that they tend to show certain characteristics. McElvain and Kposowa (2008) studied nearly 200 shooting incidents over a 15-year period which involved more than 300 officers in a particular Californian Sheriff's Department. The researchers obtained data concerning the shootings and the officers involved from the department. Almost all of the shooting incidents happened while the officer was on duty. The researchers selected a comparison group of officers who had not been involved in a shooting incident during that period. Among their findings were:

- College educated officers were about 40 per cent less likely to be involved in a shooting.
- Female officers were only one third as likely as male officers to be involved in a shooting.
- Lower ranking officers were more at risk of being involved than higher ranking ones.
- Older officers were substantially less likely to be involved in a shooting.
- Those officers that had previously been involved in shootings were about 50 per cent more likely to be involved in another shooting incident.

Of course, very different patterns may exist in other countries. This is especially so for countries with lower levels of violence in the community in general, or those where the police are not normally armed. Surprisingly, figures on the use of force in police work such as when making an arrest are not always available. For example, Rappert (2002) explains that such figures were unavailable for the United Kingdom. Instead, he had to rely on the data collection initiative of a particular UK police force to provide any systematic data. (The United Kingdom has no national police force.) In one area, force was used in 6 per cent of arrests. This contrasts with a figure of almost 20 per cent for arrests in the United States. In the British data, evidence was found that the arresting officers sustained injuries in about 16 per cent of these instances. In other words, in roughly 1 per cent of arrests police officers sustain an injury. Rappert puts the situation this way: 'As the police patrol the boundaries of respectability in society, the resort to the use of force is always a possibility' (p. 690). In the United Kingdom, *Armed Response Unit* personnel are likely to be called in when there is a critical incident that appears to be sufficiently dangerous. Such officers are likely to drive or be driven at high speeds to the incident. Barton, Vrij and Bull (2000a,b) argued that this sort of situation might have potential for encouraging violent responses based on the *excitation transfer theory* of aggression (Zillmann, 1979, 1982). Basically, this proposes that:

- emotional events are physiologically arousing;
- we become aware of physiological arousal from cues such as heart rate, breathing getting heavier and sweatiness;

- this internal state is generally labelled by us according to the environmental stimuli available at the time;

- failure to recognise the true cause of the emotional arousal will result in other factors being identified as the cause of the emotion.

This is relevant to the work of the Armed Response Unit since their rapid travel to the scene of the incident is physiologically arousing. If the officer attributes his or her physiological arousal to the suspect at the incident, this may well result in their acts being labelled differently.

Previous research has shown the efficiency of 'incident' simulators to research in this area. Generally, officers are very accurate in their marksmanship when they appropriately evaluate the situation as being a risk to themselves or others. When they *inappropriately* decide to shoot then their accuracy is relatively poor (Doerner and Ho, 1994). In their study, Barton *et al.* (2000a,b) had officers drive either at normal patrol speeds or at a high 'emergency' speed. Normal driving should produce less physiological arousal than high-speed driving. Based on the theory, it might be predicted that high-speed driving may produce physiological responses that may or may not be identified correctly as being the consequence of the high speed of driving. The officers were then exposed to one of two simulated incidents. In one case they would be justified to shoot under British law. In the other case shooting would not be justified:

- Shooting justified: they enter a shopping centre and see the suspect kneeling by cash machines picking up money. Following a warning of 'armed police' the suspect fires a handgun at the officer.

- The unjustified situation: the suspect pulls a small child to his body as protection, then releases the child, lifts a firearm and places it on the table and surrenders.

The findings were:

- The speed of travel affected the officers' self-rated willingness to shoot.

- Another variable known as *field dependence* (Witkin and Goodenough, 1981) (this is, essentially, the perceptual dependency of the individual on the environment around them) affected outcomes where the shooting was justified. Field-dependent officers rated themselves as more likely to shoot the suspect.

The impact of their work on the police

Practices will vary in different police organisations, but one British police force has experimented with a system of requiring members of its staff and officers to attend a 'counselling' session with an independent counsellor on a twice-yearly basis. This is recognition that stress is an important adverse factor on police performance. Karlsson and Christianson (1999) asked Swedish police officers to describe the most stressful and traumatic event that had happened to them. Commonest among the stressful/traumatic policing episodes were:

- being threatened with a weapon;

- complex investigations requiring them to deal with relatives of the victim and handle the press, and being under pressure to find the perpetrator;

- homicides and suicides;

- notifying next of kin about deaths;

- taking children into custody;

- traffic accidents, especially being the first to arrive at deaths and bad injuries.

Armed threats and traffic accidents accounted equally for a total of about half the events reported. Their memory for the events was highest for suicide but each of the other categories of events was not much different. The commonest consequences of the event were 22 per cent who felt depressed, 19 per cent who felt fear when reminded of the event and 15 per cent who mentioned feelings of guilt. Tension, sleeping problems, nightmares and overreacting were also included.

Just what is the impact of stress in police work? Police officers in Baltimore, USA were studied by Gershon, Barocas, Canton, Li and Vlahov (2009). The main components of their analysis can be seen in Figure 11.3. In this, stressful things which are perceived by the individual as stressful may have their influence modified by coping mechanisms though they may nevertheless lead to negative consequences. The main components of this model are:

- Perceived stress: The range of self-perceived stressors included the categories (a) critical incidents (e.g. violent arrests and shooting suspects), (b) workplace unfairness, (c) lack of cooperation from colleagues and (d) job dissatisfaction. The sorts of individual questions used to measure perceived stress included

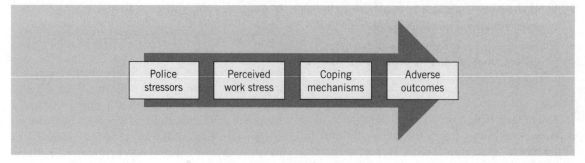

Figure 11.3 A model for the effects of police stress

'I want to withdraw from constant demands on my time and energy at work' and 'I think that I am not as effective at work as I should be.' Exposure to critical incidents had the highest rating as a stressor followed by job dissatisfaction – 93 per cent of officers in the survey reported explosure to critical incidents. The greatest emotional impact was attending police funerals (64 per cent mentioned this) and being subjected to an internal affairs investigation at work (52 per cent), and shooting someone in the line of duty (32 per cent).

- Coping strategies: Four different coping strategies were measured: (a) cognitive coping strategies such as making a plan of action and carrying it out, (b) faith-based coping strategies such as relying on religious faith to get through a difficult time, (c) avoidance coping strategies such as acting as if nothing is bothering you, and (d) negative behaviour coping strategies such as drinking, smoking and acting aggressively. Common coping strategies among the police officers were making a plan of action and following through (45 per cent), talking to family members or professionals when they felt stressed (39 per cent), and faith-based include relying on their faith in God (39 per cent) and praying (32 per cent). Less common were avoidance coping methods including acting as if nothing was bothering them when they were actually feeling stressed (27 per cent) and negative strategies such as smoking more than usual (12 per cent).

- Adverse outcomes: Measured in terms of a checklist including aggressive behaviour, anxiety, burnout, depression, interpersonal family conflict, post-traumatic stress symptoms and somatisation. Among the adverse items, the highest levels were for the post-traumatic stress symptoms, burnout, depres-

sion, somatisation and anxiety in that order. Work stress was particularly associated with feeling tired at work despite adequate sleep (84 per cent), feeling moody or irritable or impatient about small things (70 per cent), and feeling that their efficiency at work was not what it could be (63 per cent). The most commonly reported individual psychological symptoms were low energy (81 per cent), feeling blue (64 per cent), headaches and pressure in the head (58 per cent), self-blame (47 per cent), stomach pains (47 per cent), no interest in things (46 per cent) and pains or pounding in the chest (46 per cent). Post-traumatic symptoms included having intrusive/recurrent thoughts, memories or dreams about distressing work events (33 per cent) and feeling detached from people and activities that were believed to be related to the stressful events (24 per cent).

What is notable about the findings from this study is that of the five major categories of stressors the strongest relationships with stress were for common workplace issues such as the lack of fairness of the organisation and job satisfaction. That is, critical incidents and the like were less important than the general workplace environment. Of the psychological adverse outcomes depression, somatisation and PTSS symptoms were stably related to stress when demographic and similar variables were controlled. Physiological and behavioural outcomes were all associated with perceived work stress. Positive coping behaviours such as problem solving and faith were predictive of lower levels of perceived stress whereas negative and avoidant coping strategies were associated with more stress.

The finding that relatively routine workplace issues are particularly stressful led Garner (2008) into an attempt to help officers deal with such problems. Survey research had indicated to Garner that criticism from others in the workplace was difficult to deal with. Not only that, but those in a supervisory role indicated that they experienced extra stress when they had to evaluate or hand out criticism to others. To counter this Garner developed a stress-innoculation training programme for police officers which tried to help officers deal with the criticism issue among other things. It involved (a) a conceptual phase which include examining coping skills and cognitive restructuring, (b) skills acquisition including relaxation training, and (c) application and follow-through including role-playing scenarios etc. Officers following this programme reported that (a) they were better at dealing with criticism in relevant situations, (b) they felt less general job stress, and (c) they had fewer health complaints compared to a control group which did not go through the programme. Interestingly, the ratings of supervisors about interpersonal performance and conflict handling were higher for the officers who went through this programme.

Police work is built around working teams that are to a degree mutually interdependent. Consequently, it is wrong to regard police officers solely as individuals acting in isolation. Considered as part of a team, the problems of a stressed-out or underperforming colleague are actually shared by the team. The team has to cover for the inadequacies of their colleague, which will extend stress far beyond the individual officer.

Generally, the officers felt a lack of support from superiors and a lack of preparation for what they were going to experience. It was brushed aside with a joke, one should be able to deal with that sort of thing. Significantly, half mentioned fellow workers; half mentioned close family members; a quarter mentioned neighbours, friends and relatives; and about a sixth mentioned other persons at the event as those who helped with the effects of the stressful events. Doctors, psychologists and priests were mentioned by about 1 in 20. A tenth reported that nobody had helped them.

A further study compared ratings of the impact of a particular event ten months and four-and-a-half years after the event. The event was a mass shooting incident. Things remained fairly stable in terms of emotional impact – if anything getting worse or more negative with time (Karlsson and Christianson, 1999).

This brings us to the question of the impact of traumatic incidents on the officers involved. It is obvious that some of the situations faced by the police during their work are horrific. Equally, a great deal of police work involves following largely bureaucratic procedures. According to Rallings (2002), there is little direct information about the impact of the offences they come across on the police. The way in which the media tend to cover police work encourages the impression that their work is dangerous, morbid and gruesome. As a consequence, the idea is encouraged that police officers are resilient and immune to any psychological consequences that their work may have on them. Some describe this as the impervious perspective or the John Wayne syndrome. However, there is another, more realistic, view which construes police officers as hidden victims suffering from much the same adverse consequences that members of the public would suffer in similar circumstances but their problems go unrecognised. Post-traumatic stress disorder (PTSD), an extreme and debilitating response to severe trauma, is to be found within the police at a prevalence rate of about 7 per cent. (See Chapter 4 for a detailed discussion of PTSD.) This is probably a fraction of the figure that would be achieved if exposure to traumatic events invariably led to PTSD. There are far higher rates of exposure than cases in which particular events lead to PTSD, which implies that other, mediating factors may be at work. Among these factors would be good social support at home and at work.

Shooting incidents produce quite profound emotional reactions in the majority of officers. The typical reports are of crying, depression, anger, elation, nightmares, flashbacks of the incidents, bodily and emotional disturbances, loss of interest in work. Some officers had problems with adjusting back to work on the streets after a shooting incident. The sorts of incident that seem to be most associated with psychological symptoms are those in which the officer is subjected to violence, a colleague dies, children are dead, sudden deaths and mutilated bodies or decomposed ones. In this sort of study, the officers nominate the most traumatic work-related event that they have experienced. These can then be compared with the symptoms of trauma experienced by the officers.

Two recommendations made by Rallings are particularly important:

- It may be possible to focus resources on affected officers rather than all officers following a traumatic policing episode. By examining the immediate effects on physiology, emotion and mental dissociative responses then the at-risk personnel may be identified.

- Workplace characteristics have an impact on whether or not a traumatic event will lead to psychological trauma. So workplaces should be perceived by officers as supportive, morale should be good, and communications in the workplace should be improved.

There have been suggestions that vicarious traumatisation may affect an officer's ability to behave in a seemingly neutral manner when interviewing child victims. Oxburgh, Williamson and Ost (2006) researched the use of emotional language by police officers who interview both a child victim as well as the suspect during a child sexual abuse investigation. The prior expectation of the researchers was that officers who had interviewed the victim before they interviewed the offender typically would use more emotional language during their interview with the offender. It was also predicted that the amount of emotional language used would depend on the gender of the interviewer as well as the type of offence. For example, there might be differences between intra-familial offenders compared with extrafamilial offenders. Transcripts were obtained from police forces but an analysis of the numbers of negative emotional utterances such as contempt, disgust and anger indicated that those who had *not* interviewed the child before tended to use this emotional language more. Gender and type of offence made no significant difference. However, one limitation of the study was that very few officers had received specialised training to deal with child sexual abuse case. One explanation of the findings is that the experience with the child is less emotional in fact than the general view of the effects of abuse on children. Thus those who did not interview the children would have the highest levels of emotion.

Emotional labour (Hochschild, 1983) refers to the process by which all of us manage our emotions as part of our working lives. Display rules are the expectations, implicit or explicit, governing emotional display at work. In most jobs the display rules confine emotional expression to positive emotions. However, naturally, sometimes how an employee feels emotionally will not be positive at all. Thus there is a state of emotional dissonance between the two. Problems at home may lead to negative emotions but, at work, the requirement generally is for a display of positive emotions. There are many situations in which individuals may, as part of their role, need to express negative emotions. This is not normally in relation to the general public but to subordinates who may, for example, need to be reprimanded in some way. The police force seems to require more negative emotion display in daily interactions between its members than is common in other workplaces. Positive emotional expression is expected in police work with the community, for example. So it can be said that the police force demands a variety of positive and negative emotional expression which changes continually. This requires officers to know when a particular strategy is needed.

Usually two factors are held to describe the emotional labour of people whose work involves significant amounts of interpersonal contact with the public:

- Surface acting: This refers to the masking/hiding of the emotions one feels so as to meet the rules of emotional display that govern conduct in the work environment. This does nothing to reduce emotional dissonance, of course, and the outcome is that surface acting leads to emotional exhaustion according to research.

- Deep acting: This involves modifying one's emotions to meet the expectations of emotional display in that particular work environment. This requires that an effort is made to experience workplace-appropriate emotions. This might be achieved by focusing on the work situation to the exclusion of other difficulties or by reappraising the situation entirely. In effect, emotions are brought in line with what is expected in the workplace. As a consequence, deep acting protects against emotional exhaustion.

As might be expected, researchers have studied the negative psychological consequences of such emotion regulation strategies. These include burnout (i.e. the experience of chronic exhaustion and loss of interest expecially in relation to one's job). It has also been suggested that deep acting leads to a better identification with one's work. So for example, the need of a job change may be felt less soon. But more is involved than merely presenting a positive face in organisations. The research by Larissa, Grawitch and Trares (2009) involved nearly 300 officers from a US police department. The researchers distributed a survey to all employees although just over a fifth replied. An established questionnaire assessing surface and deep acting was adapted for the study. This included items such as pretending to have negative feelings that they don't really have, pretending to have positive feelings that they don't really have, and so forth. Emotional exhaustion was measured by three items asking how drained their work makes them feel, how burned out their work makes them feel, and how used up they felt at the end of the day. The researchers' analysis of the data suggested that there were three different components, not two, to the work of police officers. These are illustrated in Figure 11.4. As is commonly found, surface acting predicts emotional exhaustion. However, it was force-oriented deep acting (not service-oriented deep acting oriented towards the general public) which was associated with greater job involvement. Force-oriented deep acting involves negative emotions that have to be expressed within the police force.

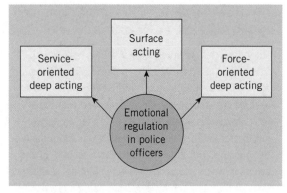

Figure 11.4 The components of emotional regulation in police officers

Why investigations go wrong

A Swedish man, Joy Rahman, was convicted for the murder of an elderly Swedish woman but the verdict was reversed by the Court of Appeal (Ask and Granhag, 2005). Rahman was identified as the prime suspect because he had bought coffee at the same time and place as two bottles of a particular brand of cigarette-lighter fuel were sold. The fuel was used in an attempt to burn the victim's body. The victim had been killed using the decorative edging from a Christmas decoration which was believed to have come from the home of a woman that Rahman had visited on the day of the murder. The appeal was granted on the basis that: (1) it had not been established that he had bought the lighter fuel or that it was the same as that found at the crime scene and (2) it had not been established that the murder weapon had been taken from the other woman's home that day or that no one else but Rahman could possibly have taken it.

This case offers some support for the idea that (1) the police when conducting an investigation are driven by theories which guide the process and evaluations of the evidence etc. and (2) the working hypotheses used by the police are not always firmly based on the facts of the case.

Causal hypotheses and theories are common in human thinking (Pennington and Hastie, 1986, 1988, 1992). Jurors, for example, tend to incorporate evidence into coherent memory structures which equate to causal explanations. The well-known processes which may affect police thinking include the following:

- Confirmation bias is a well-known and well-established phenomenon which occurs throughout human thinking. The term refers to the tendency for people to seek information which supports their existing beliefs and opinions.
- People also interpret information in a way which supports their existing beliefs and tend to avoid anything which contradicts their beliefs – things which might support alternative explanations.
- When given the opportunity to search for new information, people also tend to go for information which is more likely to confirm their beliefs and also tend to interpret new information in ways which support their existing beliefs.

Evidence supporting this can be seen in the role of confirmation bias in the interviewing of suspects (Hill, Memon and McGeorge, 2008). Scottish university

▶

BOX 11.3 (continued)

students acted as 'interviewers' whose task was to formulate questions to ask in order to assess the guilt of a suspect. One group of 'interviewers' were led to assume that there was a high likelihood that their interviewee was guilty whereas the other group were led to assume that their interviewee was more likely to be innocent. The 'interviewers' read a resumé of the events in which two people were completing intelligence tests in the same room. They were being supervised by the researcher's assistant who eventually left the room for a few minutes. The assistant had left the answer sheet for the IQ test on the desk. When the researcher's assistant returned the answer sheet had been moved. In the guilty expectation version the 'interviewers' were told that most (80 per cent) of people cheat in these circumstances (i.e. there was a high presumption of guilt) whereas in the innocent expectation version the 'interviewers' were told that most people (80 per cent) do *not* cheat (i.e. there is a low presumption of guilt). The 'interviewers' were asked individually to formulate ten questions to help them to determine whether or not cheating had occurred. A team of evaluators rated the questions on a scale from extremely presumptive of innocence to extremely presumptive of guilt. Much as the researchers expected, where there was a presumption of guilt then the questions formulated were presumptive of guilt; where there was a presumption of innocence then the questions formulated reflected this presumption.

Of course, in the context of a police investigation, the risk is that these normal, everyday cognitive processes work against the interests of the innocent suspect and affect the quality of the investigation in other ways. The concept of 'the need for cognitive closure' may also play a role since police officers can be under considerable time pressure to complete an investigation. It can be measured by statements such as 'I don't like situations that are uncertain' and 'I usually make important decisions quickly and confidently.'

In an experiment, police officers were given a vignette by Ask and Granhag (2005) about a crime in which *either* an alternative suspect was indicated as a possibility *or* a plausible motive for the murder was presented. Half of the participants were given each version. Thus, one mindset was the guilt of the potential culprit whereas the other was of the possibility of another potential culprit. This manipulation was followed by a 20-item list of things noted in the preliminary investigation of the murder. Some of these things were compatible with the one or other of the different viewpoints on the crime and others were incompatible with them. There was only mixed support for the hypotheses. Police officers' guilty ratings were in line with the hypothesis. Participants with a high need for closure tended to be less likely to notice that observations were inconsistent with the condition of the study.

Main points

- Psychologists from a wide variety of backgrounds can and have contributed to our understanding of the police and their work. It is particularly important to note that the police as organisational cultures tend to have particular attitudes and values, some of which may make the problems of a psychologist working in this context more difficult. It is commonly held that the police have a somewhat macho culture which may make helping them deal with stress or certain groups difficult.

- A major area where psychological research and theory has contributed to our understanding of the work of the police is in terms of interviewing techniques. Of particular note in this context is the enhanced cognitive interview, which is part of the training of some police officers. The enhanced cognitive interview takes concepts and techniques from laboratory studies of memory and communications psychology in an attempt to improve interviewing with eyewitnesses. The research evidence tends to point to the superiority of the enhanced cognitive interview in extracting good-quality accurate memories of the eyewitnessed events despite an increased risk of generating inaccurate memories. There is generally little support for the use of forensic hypnosis as it is felt that there are no respects in which it is superior to the enhanced cognitive interview.

- Stress affects police work in a number of ways. As in any other work organisation, aspects of the bureaucratic structure may add to felt stress levels. Stress is relevant to police work in ways that are not characteristic of other organisations. In particular, police work involves being involved in highly stressful situations such as the aftermath of crimes or suicides, for example. The requirement sometimes to use lethal force and the risk of being victims of lethal force are also characteristics of police organisations not shared by other organisations. Features of the organisation may make dealing with the stress more difficult, such as the macho-ness of police culture and attitudes towards the working team. However, the police may be better able to perform under stress than others since there is some evidence that they make better eyewitnesses of stressful events than the general public.

Further reading

The following cover important topics in relation to policing including those covered in later chapters in this book:

Gudjonsson, G.H. (2002) *The Psychology of Interrogations and Confessions: A Handbook* Chichester: John Wiley.

Kebbell, M.R. and Davies, G.M. (eds) (2006) *Practical Psychology for Forensic Investigations and Prosecutions* Chichester: John Wiley.

Kitaeff, J. (ed.) (2011) *Handbook of Police Psychology* Abingdon: Routledge Academic.

Memon, A., Vrij, A. and Bull, R. (2003) *Psychology and Law: Truthfulness, Accuracy and Credibility* (2nd edn) Chichester: John Wiley.

Shepherd, E. (2007) *Investigative Interviewing: The Conversation Management Approach* Oxford: Oxford University Press.

The Heavy Badge contains material aimed at the serving police officer's involvement in critical incidents and so forth: http://www.heavybadge.com/

Visit our website at www.pearsoned.co.uk/howitt for self-test and essay questions, annotated further reading, audio interviews with researchers in the field, weblinks and more information on becoming a forensic psychologist.

Chapter 12

Terrorism and hostage-taking incidents

Overview

- Psychologists expert in the field of terrorism suggest that the field lacks scientific rigour and has failed to provide an adequate psychological perspective on the psychology of the terrorist.

- The definition of terrorism involves the idea that force or the threat of force is being used in a political way in order to bring about social or political change. There is no universal agreement on which groups are terrorist and which are not.

- There is clear evidence that major acts of terrorist violence can have substantial psychological effects on the victims and the community from which they come. These effects can include major depression and post-traumatic stress disorder. The effects are greatest on those closest to the attack, with victims being particularly affected. There is some evidence that the police are more resistant to these psychological consequences of terrorist attack.

- While it is conventional to use terms such as 'mad' to describe those who commit extreme violence, there is no evidence that the typical terrorist is anything but a normal person. Similarly, there is no evidence that terrorists are typically psychopaths despite the apparent extreme callousness of their acts. Furthermore, suicide bombers do not conform to the usual psychological profile of the suicidal person.

- There is growing evidence to suggest that terrorists are the product of certain cognitive and social processes which are important parts of the pathway to committing acts of extreme terrorist violence. The processes of terrorist identity formation and the cognitive defences which allow them to commit atrocities are important. Cognitive distortions may be involved.

- Hostage barricade incidents are difficult situations to which psychological research has made an important contribution. However, it is not clear that the police are always well trained to accurately identify the risk factors involved in real-life incidents. Officers tend to identify the wrong features of hostage situations as indicators of risk.

- Hostage negotiation involves the psychological principles of negotiation developed in organisational psychology. Although the methods are important in that they encourage communication between the hostage takers and the police, they are by and large simple techniques which aim to defuse the situation by slowing it down.

- Hostage negotiation involves the use of 'active listening skills'. These are generally very simple techniques such as mirroring what has been said. However, research using real hostage-taking incidents suggests that active listening skills are employed in only a minority of the exchanges and then mainly using the simplest techniques.

Introduction

Terrorism's impact on governments has escalated in recent years especially following the Twin Towers attack in New York, often referred to as 9/11. But there have been other large-scale terrorist incidents, such as the Madrid commuter train and the London tube bombings. This changed security environment has escalated spending on counter-terrorism (homeland security) of from £1 billion to £2 billion between 2004 and 2009 (Mythen and Walklate, 2005) and was expected to be £3.5 billion in 2010/11 (Security Service, 2007). Before 9/11 the UK spend was only about £950,000. There has been a great deal of terrorism research over the past 30 years or so. However, in purely academic terms, much of this research lacks scientific rigour (Borum, 2004) and is often less than convincing. Empirical research is far from easy in this field for obvious reasons and many of the publications of terrorism researchers are highly conjectural and speculative. Data constitutes a challenge and many of the basic methods of psychological research cannot be employed or are meaningless in this context. Overviewing the field shows it to be dominated by a need to understand which is met rather more in terms of theory than in terms of empirical research. One leading expert put things this way:

> Research on terrorism has had a deeply troubled past. Frequently neglected and overlooked, the science of terror has been conducted in the cracks and crevices which lie between the large academic disciplines.
>
> (Silke, 2004, p. 1)

While Silke is somewhat dismissive of the psychological research in this area, suggesting that all that has been established is that terrorists are normal people, even this is actually an important achievement. To assume otherwise is dangerous and may provoke dismay and

bewilderment when other nations, for example, side with the terrorists.

Seemingly very little can differentiate the violence of the terrorist from other forms of criminal violence:

> . . . terrorism is generally understood to be the use of violence and intimidation to disrupt or coerce a government and/or an identifiable community. Terrorism has traditionally been distinguished from routine criminal violence because it is driven by a particular political and/or religious motivation.
>
> (Mythen and Walklate, 2005, p. 381)

Terrorist crimes are ones which are aimed, in some way, at changing national government or specific communities. But, of course, the boundaries between terrorist and other groups are not necessarily clear-cut and it is notable that different nations may not agree as to whether a particular grouping is terrorist or not. A terrorist from one perspective is a martyr or freedom fighter from another.

Some terrorism experts point out how the nature of terrorism changed substantially in the latter part of the twentieth century. Increasingly, religious fundamentalists (e.g. Hezbollah and al-Qaeda) began to employ the terrorism of mass destruction (Hudson, 1999). These new terrorist groups had a very different attitude from earlier ones. Previously, terrorist groups frequently showed concern not to alienate the public through the use of indiscriminate, excessive, mass violence. The IRA (Irish Republican Army), for example, usually gave specific warning of the terrorist acts that they were about to perpetrate. Another big change in recent years is the growth of suicide terrorism. The first modern example of suicide bombing occurred in 1981 and involved the car-bombing of the Israeli embassy in Beirut. Evidence of the escalation in the rates of suicide bombing can be seen in the fact that three-quarters of the suicide bombings between 1981 and

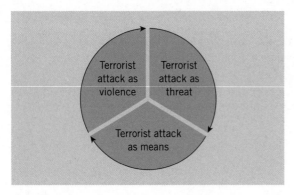

Figure 12.1 Types of terrorist attack according to Yokota *et al.* (2007)

2004 took place between the years 2000 and 2004 (Merari, 2007).

Terrorism takes numerous forms and it is difficult to discern patterns without a collecting together a substantial data set of terrorist incidents. Such databases are available including ITERATE (International Terrorism: Attributes of Terrorist Events). This together with sophisticated statistical methods (non-metric multidimensional scaling) was used by Yokota *et al.* (2007) in order to seek patterns in terrorist attacks. They coded each of this large sample of terrorist incidents along a number of dimensions. The associations between these ratings for the different incidents allowed them to identify the main clusters or groupings of terrorist types. Three strategy types emerged as can be seen in Figure 12.1. In more detail, they were:

- Terrorist attacks as threat: In this the terrorist organisation seeks to intimidate people and society. The intention is not primarily to cause casualties.

- Terrorist attacks as means: The victim is used as a way of negotiating about the goal of the terrorist group.

- Terrorist attacks as violence: In this individuals or groups of people are targeted to be injured or killed.

Terrorist organisations tended to use one of these forms of incident more than types. That is to say, one terrorist organisation would primarily use terrorist attacks as threat, another would use terrorist attacks as means, and so forth. Eighty-seven per cent of terrorist organisations had over 50 per cent of their incidents in one category. This, nevertheless, leaves some variation in strategy which Yokota *et al.* suggest may be the result of instability within the terrorist organisation. Deaths were quite common where the strategy was terrorist attack as means or terrorist attack as violence despite the fact that the motivation for terrorist attack as means was not the killing or otherwise harming of the victim. Modern policing policies in many countries now aim to resolve potential stand-offs (or barricade incidents) peacefully without harm to terrorist, hostage or police officers.

BOX 12.1 Controversy

Is fingerprint evidence unreliable?

In March 2004, terrorist bombs exploded on commuter trains in the region of Madrid, Spain. A bag of detonators was discovered, on which was found a crucial fingerprint. This was identified by the FBI's Integrated Automated Fingerprint Identification System as that of Brandon Mayfield, an American Muslim lawyer, married to an Egyptian professor's daughter. In fact, Mayfield was one of several matches identified for the crucial fingerprint and was only the fourth closest match found. Nevertheless, among the 'incriminating' facts was that he had associates who themselves were suspected of being terrorists and that once he had acted as lawyer for a known terrorist in a child custody case! Four fingerprint experts expressed complete confidence that the print from Madrid was a match for Mayfield, who was subsequently arrested – putatively because his prints were an absolute match for those on the detonator bag (Busey and Loftus, 2007).

Fortunately for Mayfield, the Spanish police had other suspects – one of whom was identified using a better fingerprint. This man was an Algerian terrorist who was believed to have al-Qaeda links. Mayfield was released and subsequently successfully sued the FBI. According to the FBI, the error was due to the poor digital image of the original fingerprint and the exceptional similarity of Mayfield's fingerprint to that on the bag of detonators. However, independent reviewers blamed the first fingerprint examiner for not completely analysing the crucial fingerprint and so failing to see the decisive differences between the two. Possibly, the judgement of the first expert influenced those of the other three. This was a public, high-profile case which pressured the fingerprint experts who probably had too much confidence in the fingerprint analysis system in use.

This is, of course, a salutary lesson for those who believe that fingerprint evidence is without problems. Recent research has looked at the influence of extraneous (psychological) factors which may affect the decisions of experts as in this case (Dror and Charlton, 2006). The researchers had the cooperation of a laboratory which employed fingerprint experts of considerable experience and capability. Consequently, they had access to fingerprints which had been involved in real criminal cases. The Tenprints system is essentially a database of 'rolled' fingerprints which can be compared with latent prints collected from the crime scene. The research design was very imaginative. The researchers had access to archival information about previous decisions made about fingerprints by the experts at this laboratory. The researchers wanted to know if the experts' previous decisions about fingerprints could be influenced by contextualising psychological and cognitive information. So the researchers might introduce biasing information such as the suspect had confessed to the crime or that the suspect was in police custody at the time of the crime. The researchers selected (for each fingerprint examiner) (a) some fingerprints that they (the fingerprint examiner) had previously judged to be individualisations (that is, the fingerprint

matched a known person's fingerprint) and (b) some fingerprints that had been judged to be exclusions (that is, the fingerprint did not match that of a known person). Independent experts confirmed that there was enough information in the fingerprints to make a definite individualisation or exclusion decision. Half of the prints were selected because they were hard to evaluate whereas the others were easy to evaluate. There was also a control sample of prints for which no contextual information was provided.

Two-thirds of the experts made inconsistent decisions compared with what they had decided previously about the same fingerprints. However, some experts (a third) were perfectly consistent with their previous decisions throughout. About 17 per cent of inconsistent decisions were made due to the biasing context.

Dror, Charlton and Peron (2006) carried out a similar study which was even more directly relevant to the Madrid bombing case. The fingerprint experts looked at what they believed to be a pair of fingerprints, one from the Madrid train terrorism case and the other being the rolled fingerprint of someone else. They were told that the prints were those which the FBI had erroneously matched with the Madrid bomber. In other words, contextual information suggested that the prints were a non-match. Only one of the fingerprint experts decided (counter to the contextual information) that the prints were a match although this expert had five years previously concluded that these prints were not a match! Of the other experts studied, three of the experts judged the 'new' pair as a non-match. Only one decided that there was insufficient information to form a judgement and only one did not change their mind at all! Dro et al. (2011) suggest that the degree of inconsistency is not consistent across experts or across fingerprints.

The consequences of terrorism

Despite ideas which abound concerning the resilience of the general population to the effects of terrorist

violence, there is considerable evidence that terrorist incidents can have quite profound effects on members of the public. DiMaggio and Galea (2006) describe the results of a meta-analysis (see Box 4.2) of the aftermaths of terrorist incidents such as 9/11 and the 2005 London tube and bus bombings. They found that the rate of

PTSD in directly affected populations was between 12 per cent and 16 per cent.

An exceptionally deadly major terrorist incident took place on 11 March 2004 with the commuter train bombings in Spain. Bombs exploded on four different early morning trains destined for Madrid's Atocha station. More than 400 people were taken to hospital and nearly 200 died from the blasts. A loosely structured Moroccan Islamic combatant group (GICM) was responsible and some of those associated with it had been trained at al-Qaeda camps. Gabriel *et al.* (2007) studied the aftermath of these terrorist attacks on three different groups of people. These were (1) those injured in the bomb blasts, (2) the residents of the local area in which many of the victims lived and in which few did not know a victim and (3) the police officers involved in the rescue operation. Members of each of these three groups were interviewed on a one-to-one basis within three months of the attacks. The researchers used standard psychiatric diagnosis instruments such as the mini international neuropsychiatric interview (which is used to assess major depression, panic disorder, social phobia, generalised anxiety disorder and agoraphobia) and the Davidson trauma scale to assess the mental health of the participants. The group of injured commuters showed the greatest evidence of current mental disorders when interviewed after the attack (58 per cent). For the local area group, 26 per cent showed signs of a current mental disorder. However, only 4 per cent of the police officer group showed mental health problems. Post-Traumatic Stress Disorder (PTSD) (see Chapter 4) was the commonest category of mental disorder manifested by the injured group (44 per cent). The equivalent figures for the local group were 12 per cent and for the police 1 per cent. One striking feature of the data was the extent of the co-morbidity (co-occurrence) of two or more mental disorders. Fifty-three per cent of the injured group showed this compared with only 22 per cent of the local group. This is, perhaps, a clearer demonstration of the impact of direct victimisation on the mental health of victims.

As one might expect, there have been numerous studies of the impact of 9/11 on mental health. One study (DiMaggio, Galea and Richardson, 2007) concentrated on mental health-related admissions to hospital emergency departments for psychological reasons before 9/11 and the changes which occurred after that date. The researchers put forward the simple hypothesis that the impact of the terrorist attacks would vary according to the distance that people lived from the terrorist incident – the closer they were the more likely they were to attend an emergency department for psychological health reasons. Four different geographical areas were selected which represented increasing distances from the target of the 9/11 incident, the World Trade Center (attacked in the 9/11 incident) in the New York and New York State areas. Also four time periods were stipulated representing periods before 9/11 and the period after 9/11. The findings were in line with other mental health studies: compared with periods prior to the terrorist attacks, after 9/11 there were 10 per cent more behavioural and mental heath diagnoses at hospital emergency departments. Furthermore, in support of the hypothesis, there was evidence that these increases were stronger in the areas closest to the 9/11 attacks.

Perhaps by way of a summary and coda to this, Jhangiani (2010) brought together and reviewed 118 research studies into the psychological consequences of the 9/11 attacks. As we have seen above, there was evidence of poorer mental health in New York and Washington DC consequent upon the attacks. However, these levels returned to pre-attack baseline levels after about six months or, it would seem from some studies, that mental health was better than before. The precise details of this varied from study to study. The effects of the terrorist attack were worse if the individual:

- had a history of mental illness
- was physically very close to the attacks
- knew someone involved in the attacks.

Outside of the target areas, research showed a much more minimal effect of the impact of the attacks on mental health. For countries outside of the USA the impact of the bombings was virtually indiscernible over the various studies. There was a positive response to the attacks, too, which included long-term increases in helping behaviours, religion, and even an increased level of life satisfaction.

Is there a terrorist personality or profile?

Just how to conceptualise people who do extreme things has long been a difficulty for psychologists. For example, are the terrorists mad who hijack aircraft, force them to another country and then hold passengers as hostages? Are suicide bombers already suicide prone? There is a temptation to label out-of-the-ordinary actions as insane since such a label seems to justify the behaviour. There is a danger of assuming that terrorists necessarily conform to particular modern terrorist episodes. For example, the media feed us with the idea that suicide bombers are religious zealots, which leads us to the assumption that religion is strongly associated with terrorist acts. However, the Tamil Tigers group of Sri Lanka is not based on religion but politics. Nevertheless this group has committed a good proportion of all suicide bombings worldwide.

Given our assumptions about the relationship between the male sex and violence, there can be surprisingly large proportions of women who become suicide bombers. There is evidence that the Kurdistan Workers Party (PKK) and the Tamil Tigers of Sri Lanka use women as frequently as men as suicide bombers (Ergil, 2001).

Psychopathology and terrorism

There is a remarkable consensus in the research literature: (a) there is no such thing as a terrorist personality and (b) that mental abnormality is simply not an important consideration when trying to understand terrorist attackers. In an early review of the mentality of terrorists, Maghan (1998) suggested that terrorists range through all character types from the self-doubting wretch to those haunted by indescribable demons. But madness, as an explanatory concept, has no role to play. Later reviewers followed suit:

- Silke (1998) summarised the findings of researchers by suggesting that terrorists are normal people but who commit acts of terrorism.

- Ruby (2002) commented that terrorists are rational, lucid people.

- Borum (2004) also reviewed the evidence about psychopathology in terrorists. He concluded that the consensus among commentators on this is that terrorism is at best poorly accounted for on the basis of psychopathology widely defined to include conditions referred to as mental disease and mental disorder. There will be terrorists with such conditions, of course, but there is no tendency for terrorists to be more likely to have these conditions.

An article in a popular psychology magazine by Perina (2002) had the subtitle 'suicide bombers have distinctive personality traits'. Despite this, Perina also points out that psychologists tend to agree that suicide bombers cannot be explained in terms of some personal psychopathology but it is also difficult to understand how other factors such as those of a religious, social or cultural nature in themselves can turn just some normal young people into suicide bombers. He reports that Ariel Merari, director for the programme for political violence at the University of Tel Aviv, studied 32 suicide bombers and found no evidence of social dysfunction or suicidal characteristics which could account for their actions. Terrorist groups such as Hamas in Palestine may take advantage of their recruits' religious fanaticism and nationalism but these fail to account for why these particular people and not others with similar characteristics become suicide bombers. Merari has made a number of observations based on his studies of terrorists (*Michigan Daily*, 2002). Like others, he argues that terrorists are just normal people who can be seen as a cross-section of their societies. There was no significant evidence of any psychopathology among them. Neither is it correct to suggest that suicide bombers can be seen in simple terms as extreme religious fanatics.

We need to consider why it is even expected that terrorists will have some sort of personality extremity or defect despite this being common in discourse about terrorists (e.g. 'these madmen', 'these fanatics'). This accords with the general tendency to associate deviant activity with madness and badness. But this is to assume that terrorism is driven by characteristics of the individual and that it needs some particular personality to commit extreme acts. However, the lesson taught by social psychology is quite different. Social psychological research has pointed to the rationality rather than irrationality of participants in extreme behaviours. The classic studies of Milgram (1974) on obedience demonstrate how ordinary citizens can obey dangerous commands that might harm others. So, the atrocities of Nazi Germany may be the consequence, in part, of normal social processes. Taylor and Quayle (1994) made the important analogy between terrorism and careers in terms of personality. One would not expect that university lecturers all had a similar personality profile or that all students shared a similar personality so why should one expect that terrorists would be any different as a group?

Psychopathy and terrorism

Many of the acts of terrorists are atrocious in nature. The humiliation of hostages and, for example, their slow decapitation which is videoed and broadcast on the Web are instances of this. This naturally has led some to ask whether psychopathy is characteristic of terrorists. After all, we know that psychopaths commit some of the most extreme murders and rapes. Borum (2004) reviewed the evidence on psychopathology and antisocial personality disorders in terrorists in the light of this general assumption that terrorists are callous, cold-blooded killers. According to Borum, however, the characteristics of psychopaths do not make them good members of any sort of organisation (although this seems to contradict the evidence that psychopaths can do extremely well in organisations, see p. 391). While dedication and selflessness may be required of terrorists, Borum argues, these are very different from the defining characteristics of psychopaths.

Suicidal characteristics and suicide terrorism

It is important to note that suicide bombing is rare in terrorism although it is responsible for a high proportion of deaths. So is it possible to regard suicide bombers as being like anyone else who commits suicide? The answer is no, according to Silke (2003). Suicide bombers do not share characteristics and motivations with the typical person who commits suicide. Suicide bombers are psychologically stable and very much ordinary personalities when judged from their own cultural context. Furthermore, suicide bombers' families regard their actions positively as being heroic, in contrast to the families of people who commit suicide for other reasons.

All of this and more is reinforced in Townsend's (2007) views on the question of whether suicide bombers are indeed suicidal. Quite evidently this is a technically difficult issue to address. Her strategy was to assess the extent of similarity and dissimilarity between:

- what we know from research on suicide in general
- known psychological characteristics obtained from research on (potential) suicide bombers.

There was little correspondence between the two. One possibility considered was that suicide terrorists are similar to 'altruistic suicides'. There is an obvious difficulty since suicide terrorists takes the lives of many others and not just themselves. Researchers have found from suicide notes and interviewing suicide attempt survivors that a variety of motivations underlie suicide. Amongst these are financial problems, mental health issues and relationship problems. Based on this, one could take the view that there is no such thing as a typical suicide but terrorism research suggests that there is no such thing as the typical suicide terrorist either.

There is plenty of evidence of a higher incidence of diagnosable mental illness in both attempted and completed suicides. Depression, not surprisingly, is particularly associated with these. In contrast, what is known about suicide terrorism strongly links it with feelings of martyrdom which are accompanied by positive feelings. These do not appear to be at all like the sense of being abandoned by everyone around and the feeling of being a burden to loved-ones and others characteristic of suicide in general. The suicide bomber regards their violent acts as being in the service of Allah. This martyrdom is known as *istishhad* (Abdel-Khalek, 2004). Suicide, itself, is not acceptable in the Islamic faith in any circumstances. Given that we know that suicide bombers (a) are religious, often to an extreme and (b) believe that their acts are supported by Islamic principles then these facts fit better with the view that so-called suicide bombers lack suicidal intent.

So is religion a factor in suicide, since it is strongly implicated in suicide bombing (though not all terrorism)? Once again there seems to be a mismatch since, according to Townsend, good modern research indicates that religion may be a protective factor against suicide. Frequency of praying and the importance of religion to the individual predict having lower levels on suicidal thoughts on average and not having attempted suicide in the past (Nonnemaker, McNeely and Blum, 2003). One clear characteristic of suicide bombers is that vengeance is frequently a motivation. For example, research suggests that terrorists have often been victims of state violence or even torture in their earlier lives. Again this does not match with the motivations of suicidal individuals in general who rarely mention revenge as a motive with the exception of some abused women. But, even these, unlike the suicide bombers, do not act violently to others prior to their suicide.

The terrorist profile

On the basis of what we have just seen it is not surprising that there tends to be little enthusiasm for the idea that terrorists can be socially or psychologically profiled. Of course, a terrorist profile is not like a criminal profile (Chapters 14 and 15) since the primary purpose of a terrorist profile would be to help identify terrorists before they have launched their attack or to disrupt terrorist activities in some other way. Once a terrorist act such as a suicide bombing has occurred there is no point in using terrorist profiling to identify possible suspects. One problem of identifying a terrorist profile is that it would constitute the focus of counter-terrorism work. Consequently, an astute terrorist organisation might choose to recruit members simply because they were very different from the target profile and so less likely to come under the attention of security forces.

But there have been attempts to describe the typical terrorist. One early study was based on information about a large number of terrorist groups and leaders from a number of countries. Their profile was of an urban-dwelling middle/upper-class, young, university educated, unmarried man (Russell and Miller, 1977). Furthermore, the typical terrorist was likely to subscribe to an extreme political ideology. Of course, such a profile is not particularly useful since its general features would apply to many young men. Furthermore, such a profile would need to be actively updated regularly since the modern pattern of terrorism seems very different from that of the 1970s.

The failure to find particular psychological characteristics to be associated with terrorism does not mean that a psychological explanation of terrorists is impossible – it may merely mean that a different sort of explanation is necessary.

The problem created for risk assessment

The question of how to rehabilitate terrorists has become a practical concern for modern governments. For example, Horgan and Braddock (2010) describe different de-radicalisation programmes employed by a variety of nations. The idea that terrorists are by-and-large psychologically normal lacking indications of mental illness leads to difficulties for any psychologist. At some stage, decisions have to be made about the release of convicted terrorists from prison. Just how should psychologists and psychiatrists go about a risk assessment of such an individual? Although risk assessment is a feature of the work of forensic psychologists (see Chapter 27) little of

what is known applies well to terrorists since it is based on psychiatric patients and prisoners. Terrorists do not represent either of these groups well. Dernevik, Beck, Grann, Hogue and McGuire (2009a) argue that, as a consequence, psychologists and psychiatrists do not have an appropriate knowledge base upon which to formulate risk assessment for terrorists. The sort of approaches taken to the prediction of violent recidivism described in Chapter 27 are simply inapplicable because the causes of terrorists violence are not the same as the causes of interpersonal violence in general. They are particularly dubious about the value of psychometric methods of risk assessment which were developed on very different groups of offenders from terrorists.

Among the problems involved in applying established risk assessment methods to terrorist prisoners are the following:

- Different groups of terrors come to terrorism through very different pathways according to Dernevika *et al.* (2009a). As we saw earlier, in the 1970s, research suggested that the typical terrorist was middle class, young, unmarried and lived in an urban location – and they were university educated (Russell and Miller, 1977). This is not the profile of the typical violent offender and is also not representative of modern terrorists.

- What about mental illness and psychopathy in modern terrorists and the possibility that terrorists are typically recidivist criminals? Dernivika *et al.* place a great deal of emphasis on the research of Sageman (2004) in addressing this. He obtained biographical data on a reasonably large sample of people who were members of the worldwide Salafijihad fundamentalist Islam network of which Al Qaeda is part. There was virtually no evidence of criminality in the histories of those who committed major terrorist incidents other than very minor petty offences. Furthermore, the outrages that they committed could not be conceived as for personal gain. Using DSM-IV criteria of mental illness (see Box 21.1), Sageman sought evidence of major mental illnesses such as psychosis or delusions as well as antisocial personality disorder among terrorists. These searches led nowhere other than to the common conclusion that terrorists do not generally have identifiable mental illnesses. Hence psychological and psychiatrists measures which predict violent recidivism discussed Chapter 27 simply do not apply to terrorists.

- The lack of significant personal criminal histories among terrorists means that criminal history cannot be used to predict recidivism. Or to be more accurate, the lack of a personal criminal history would imply that terrorists in general pose little or no risk of future violence on release.

Gudjonsson (2009) regards the views of Dernevik et al. (2009a) as somewhat negative. He suggests a number of things which potentially may be of relevance to the prediction of future risk among terrorists. For example, political changes may have removed some of the major grievances which motivated the terrorism. Alternatively, in making the risk assessment the present situation with regard to the terrorist's support network needs to be taken into account. These and similar factors may well be relevant to terrorist assessment despite the fact that they have little or nothing to do with conventional ways of assessing risk as discussed in Chapter 27. Dernevik, Beck, Grann, Hogue and McGuire (2009b) point out that both historical and psychological research indicate that some of the most appalling acts of violence during the twentieth century were committed by individuals who functioned normally in general and appeared to be mentally within the healthy range.

What makes a terrorist?

There is another consensus view in the psychology of terrorism literature (Luckabaugh et al., 1997). That is that it takes time to turn even a vulnerable individual into a terrorist. The psychological motivations of terrorist recruits tend to be the very human needs of (a) wanting to feel that one belongs and (b) the development of a satisfactory personal identification. Social alienation followed by boredom leads to dissidence or protest on a minor scale, then eventually terrorism. Although histories of childhood abuse, trauma, perceived injustice and humiliation are common in terrorists' backgrounds, Borum (2004) feels that these do not help explain terrorism (though this view is not universally shared, as we shall see). Perception of injustice combined with the need for a sense of belonging and a need for identity can frequently be seen as vulnerabilities among potential terrorists.

Merari (2007) may be referring to such general vulnerability factors when he suggests that susceptibility to indoctrination may be the key to understanding suicide bombers. Most suicide bombers that he studied were young and unattached – the very sort of person at the greatest risk of becoming involved in violent organisations of all sorts. Merari believes that suicide terrorism should be understood in terms of the consequences of the terrorist organisation systems. Terrorist groups recruit members largely through interpersonal connections and then support the recruit through to becoming a suicide bomber. Highly committed members of the terrorist group will spend hours speaking with the recruit, promoting the idea that martyrdom is the will of God and focusing on the illustrious past of Islam. The suicide bomber becomes enmeshed in a group contract which is designed to increase their allegiance to the other group members. Finally there is a 'formal contract' which constitutes a final personal commitment before the suicide bombing.

Merari (2007) makes the analogy that terrorist groups act like a suicide production line. There is empirical support for this from data on Palestinian suicide bombers. Merari refers to the stages of indoctrination, group commitment and personal commitment:

- *Indoctrination*: throughout the process leading to the suicide mission, high-authority members of the group continue to indoctrinate the potential bomber in order to maintain the motivation to engage in the terrorist act and to prevent changes of mind. For the Palestinian terrorists, the major indoctrination themes were nationalistic (such as Israel's humiliation of the Palestinian State) and religious (such as the guarantee that the suicide bomber will go to paradise).

- *Group commitment*: by mutually committing to carry out suicide attacks some of the consequences of doubts are dealt with and motivation for the suicide attacks is maximised.

- *Personal commitment*: this may take the form of a video-recording in which the terrorist describes his or her intention to engage in such a suicide mission. This is partly for the bomber's family. It is a way of getting the individual's irrevocable commitment to the suicide mission. The bomber also prepares farewell letters to friends and family at this stage for later distribution. Mirari points out that the bomber is often referred to as the 'living-martyr' at this stage.

This is sympathetic with Horgan and Taylor's (2001) view that terrorists usually do not make a conscious decision that they wish to become a terrorist. Instead they gradually become involved in a process which socialises them towards their ultimate terrorist activities. The process leading towards becoming a terrorist is not absolute since there is a high rate of turnover in membership of terrorist groups (Crenshaw, 1986). Taylor and Louis (2004) suggest that:

> young people find themselves at a time in their life when they are looking to the future with the hope of engaging in meaningful behavior that will be satisfying and get them ahead. Their objective circumstances including opportunities for advancement are virtually nonexistent; they find some direction for their religious collective identity but the desperately disadvantaged state of their community leaves them feeling marginalized and lost without a clearly defined collective identity.
>
> (p. 178)

It is easy to get into a way of thinking about terrorism which holds that terrorist acts are the consequence of group processes. However, Taylor (2010) asks whether terrorism incidents can truly be understood as group phenomena. Just what does it tell us when we say that terrorism is a group process? He makes a distinction between involvement with terrorist groups and the like and taking part in terrorist events. Group processes may be important as a backdrop to terrorism where social, political and cultural factors can be seen to play their part. But do they explain the episode of terrorist violence itself? Taylor suggests that there are two broad issues:

- Do we have an adequate definition of what terrorism is (apart from being what terrorists do)?

- Do we have a clear idea of what is meant by group processes in relation to terrorism?

To illustrate his point, he gives a number of examples of terrorist incidents in which group processes seem to be minimally or not involved. For example, Theodore John Kaczynski was the notorious Unabomber who conducted a successful terrorist campaign beginning in 1978 and lasting for about 17 years in the USA. He appears to have been a recluse living in a log cabin in Montana. During that period of time he sent 12 bombs which resulted in the deaths of three people. He had an environmentalist agenda largely of his own making. This is an extreme example, but Taylor provides others where it is difficult to understand the relevance of the idea of group processes.

Life story studies

Borum (2004) argues that the life experiences of terrorists tend to include the themes of injustice, abuse and humiliation. However, Borum suggests that these are not sufficient causes of terrorism but may help identify individuals who are susceptible to the influence of terrorist groups. In some ways this viewpoint fits in with narrative studies of terrorists in that other factors need to be brought into account to understand just what turns one potentially vulnerable young person into a terrorist while another equally vulnerable young person will fail to go down the route to terrorism.

Since 1992, suicide terrorism has been a feature of Israel's relationship with Palestine. Soibelman (2004) also subscribes to the view that terrorism should be regarded primarily as the consequence of group processes rather than individual psychological factors (such as personality). Group solidarity and shared ideologies combine to create the terrorist. Obvious ideas such as that suicide bombers are young religious fanatics are rejected by Soibelman, who believes that less extreme personality characteristics are often responsible for the creation of a suicide bomber. He bases his ideas on published research as well as his interviews with five suicide bombers who had either been arrested before they could detonate a bomb or whose bomb failed to detonate (this occurs in about 40 per cent of suicide bomb attempts) in order to understand the process by which they had become bombers. He argues that there is no single explanation of why someone becomes a bomber and that there is a mixture of circumstances that are responsible, which may be different in different cases.

Group solidarity and shared ideologies combine to create the terrorist. Mostly the interviewed suicide bombers shared at least some of the following characteristics:

- Bad direct or secondary experiences of involvements with the Israeli military forces. These included a friend being shot dead and having been beaten by them.

- Political factors were commonly mentioned as the reason for becoming a suicide bomber.

- Most had previously been involved in demonstrations or other forms of assembly.

- As the situation escalated, participants' beliefs became more extreme.

Not surprisingly, given the nature of the sample used by Soibelman, all of the suicide bombers and their families followed the secular Fatah movement. Furthermore, for this group of terrorists, there was no tendency for them to have criminal backgrounds, although a few may have had.

A much more detailed analysis of the structure of life history narrative accounts of becoming a terrorist is to be found in Sarangi and Alison's (2005) study of left-wing Maoist terrorist groups in Nepal and India. These Maoist terrorists regard the State as the instrument serving the needs of the rich and so the State needs to be violently overthrown. The use of the individual terrorist as a story teller, Sarangi and Alison suggest, may help us to understand how different life trajectories are shaped in terms of how the terrorist creates his or her own personal relevance.

The 12 terrorists studied included three women and three men who were no longer actively involved in terrorism. The terrorists' average age was about 26 years and they generally lacked a formal education. Police and court records validated the fact that they had been actively involved in violent incidents. An example of a member of the study is as follows:

> RM is 25 years old. He was involved in the assassination of a prominent political leader, explosions in two industrial units, and an attack on a police station that led to the killing of a police officer. His father died when he was a small child and so his mother brought him up. He was influenced by the personality and ideas of a prominent terrorist leader and joined the terrorist movement at the age of 15 against the wishes of his mother. His mother died in his absence. He surrendered to the police because of differences with a commander and is now in prison.
>
> (Sarangi and Alison, 2005, p. 73)

The participants were interviewed by a researcher with social scientific knowledge for whom rapport-building was a priority. This was achieved by having each terrorist talk about their childhoods together with other matters not directly involved with their terrorist activities. The researchers suggest that there are common rhetorical structures in the interviews:

- *Images of self (us)*: these include Me, parents, siblings and friends, my people, such as villagers in the community. The descriptions of the self–us are simple and naive, poor, short of food and water, exploited and cheated. These images of the self are referred to

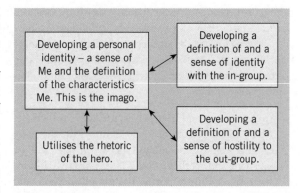

Figure 12.2 The process of terrorist identity formation

as imagoes using McAdams' (1990) concept. An imago can be seen as the personification of the self in an idealised form. The imago serves as the central character in the individual's life story. For these terrorists, the imago would be characterised as good, simple, brave, loyal and so forth. Imagoes may change according to whether it is the self in the past, present, or future which is being referred to (Figure 12.2).

- *Significant others (interpersonal figures)*: this includes the major categories of Other: (a) the descriptions of They for the Government, etc. which include characteristics such as villains, rich, powerful, exploiters, uncaring and inhuman and (b) the descriptions of They for the liked (e.g. global terrorist leaders) which would include characteristics such as heroes, saviours, brave-courageous, admired by people, knowledgeable and committed.

- *Visions of the future (the generativity script)*: the life trajectory is from the past (which included ideas such as nobody, hungry, insignificant, marginalised, suppressed, exploited and ruled by the evil They) to the present (which includes sacrificing, courageous, disciplined, fighter, cadre, and influence and significance) to the 'future' in the trajectory, which includes creator of an exploitation-free society, leaving behind a legacy, plenty of land and food, goodies of life, victory over the evil They, and powerful and respected. The terrorist accounts show a commitment to achieving an exploitation-free society in the future. They were ideologically committed to a rhetoric which justified violence of the worst sort.

Terrorist ideologies and cognitions

A common approach to explaining the development of ordinary people to terrorists is to concentrate on their ideologies and the way in which their cognitions change over as they become more involved in terrorist groups. In his important review of the psychology of terrorism, Borum (2004) includes the following as important to the understanding of terrorists:

- Terrorist ideologies are often favourable towards and justify particular behaviours.

- There is an erosion of the normal human inhibitions against killing as a result of the influence of social and environmental variables or changes in the perception of the situation.

There is reason to believe that the violent environments which are sometimes associated with the rise of terrorism may have as their consequence effects which were unintended. These unexpected consequences can be illustrated by Atran's (2003) observation based on a large study of Muslims in Gaza who were adolescent at the time of the first Palestinian Intifada which occurred between 1987 and 1993. Exposure to violence at this time was more predictive of pride and social cohesion than it was with depression or antisocial behaviour. These Gaza teens had more hope for the future than did a control sample of Bosnian Muslims. According to Borum (2004) three conditions result in an ideology being supportive of terrorism:

- the ideology must involve beliefs which both guide and justify the terrorist acts;

- rigid orthodoxies which do not allow these beliefs to be challenged or questioned in any way; and

- the terrorist acts must have clear goals which can be seen as part of a meaningful cause such as the struggle between 'good and evil'.

Part of the cognitive changes which are needed in order for normal people to engage in terrorist acts include what Bandura (1990) refers to as the techniques of moral disengagement which would allow terrorists to insulate themselves from the psychological consequences of their violent actions. These include:

- moral justifications such as the belief that the terrorist is fighting some evil;

- the displacement of responsibility to their leaders or others in the group which may allow the individual to psychologically disown their agency in terrorist acts;

- the minimisation of the suffering of victims; and

- the dehumanisation of the victims.

In a cognitive model applicable to terrorist ideologies, Beck (2002) proposed that the thinking of terrorists exhibits the sort of cognitive distortions that are often found in people who commit other sorts of acts of violence. These cognitive distortions include the tendency to over-generalise the enemy's perceived failings to encompass the entirety of the population. Perceptions of people are also dichotomised so that they are either good or they are bad with no shades of grey in between. There is a form of tunnel vision in that the terrorist focuses entirely on the destruction of their target.

Hostage barricade incidents

The phrase 'hostage barricade incident' describes the police or security forces besieging a house, business or aeroplane, for example, where people are being held against their will. A simple siege does not involve a hostage but an individual who the police are trying to get out from a particular physical location. In hostage barricade incidents, whatever intermittent communications occur are likely to be determined by the hostage takers rather than the police. Potentially, of course, the forcible release of the hostages may be extremely risky, as we have seen, so some form of assessment is necessary into the inherent risks of an immediate forceful intervention compared with the risks of continuing the barricade into the future. Just how do police officers go about assessing risk in these situations? Is there a correspondence between the risk factors identified by police officers and known risk factors obtained from real-life barricade incidents?

Research by Yokota et al. (2004) studied risk factors established from real-life hostage incidents and compared them with the beliefs that police officers have about different aspects of incidents which may make them especially risky. In two out of four of these real-life incidents firearms were present but this is a poor indicator of risk because the possession of firearms occurs very frequently in barricade situations. Hostages were most likely to be injured in domestic situations where domestic violence had led to the hostage taking or the hostage taker's purpose was to get his ex-partner to come back to him. Expressive situations such as suicides, suicide attempts or domestic situations were the most likely to lead to injuries among the hostages. The risk of injury was quite low where the perpetrator was mentally ill.

The majority (73 per cent) of the Japanese police officers studied believed that a highly excited state among the hostage takers was dangerous. In contrast, if one examines real-life hostage incidents then other factors including 'a long siege' tended to increase the risk of death. Nevertheless, the risk of death is small since fewer than 4 per cent of the real-life hostage incidents studied ended in a hostage's death. The second most common perceived risk factor was 'an incident is caused due to interpersonal problems' which was mentioned by 24 per cent of the police officers, while 16 per cent mentioned the stage at which the hostage taker was told that their demands were not to be met as being risky. About a third of the police officers mentioned offence characteristics as risk factors. Another third mentioned police activities more frequently, such as where there was no effective communication between hostage taker and the police (16 per cent). Offender characteristics such as mental illness (13 per cent), attempted suicide (11 per cent) or drug use (9 per cent) were mentioned by 27 per cent of officers.

In a second aspect of the study, the researchers presented the police officers with 22 hypothetical situations which they evaluated in terms of the level of risk inherent in each. Situations described to the officers included such things as hostages have been injured/killed, the siege duration is very long, hostage taker demands an escape route, a plane is hijacked by the hostage taker, and the hostage taker is a member of a political group such as a right-wing one. Generally the officers rated all of the situations as high risk. Where hostages had been injured/killed was the highest risk situation according to the ratings of the police officers, followed by hostage taker takes illegal drugs and hostage taker is mentally ill. Low-risk characteristics included the perpetrators making tangible demands to the police including demands for money, coverage by the media or a means of escape. Thus the officers seem to rate emotional and impulsive situations as more risky than instrumental ones.

There was only a very weak relationship between the risk assessment of situations by police officers and actual risk of deaths and injuries to hostages obtained from a sample of real-life incidents. One obvious conclusion is that the officers were unaware of the true nature of risks in these situations. This is possibly the result of inexperience but, of course, these officers may well be those responsible for at least the early stages of hostage barricade incidents.

The majority of officers managing major enquiries (80 per cent) have less than five years of policing experience. A model dealing with the experiences of senior police officers who managed significant incidents in the United Kingdom is described by Crego and Alison (2004). The lack of control the officers believed they had, together with the blame that they felt they would receive as managers, resulted in these incidents being seen as complex and difficult by them. The researchers used electronic conferencing to bring together a focus group of officers who had managed critical incidents. The method systematically explores the experiences of officers who had managed critical setting. There were several aspects to the research:

- unstructured accounts where participants considered their experiences and outlined the significant issues as they saw them;

- theme building: the officers taking part in the electronic conferencing were split into teams which were given the task of reviewing the data that had been collected in the first stage;

- plenary session where the themes developed are discussed and agreed;

- first sort: the focus group organises the items generated in the first stage into the agreed themes;

- summation in which the themes are synthesised into key statements;

- prioritisation: in which participants rate the issues according to different criteria such as, in this case, impact and ease of implementation.

Officers use two co-occurring issues as the defining features of the criticality of incidents:

- The impact of features of the situation directly on the enquiry. For example, creating a good teamwork atmosphere and keeping local and national authorities aware of what is going on.

- Whether the issue will affect how the police will be judged by others such as the community, the media or the victims. Thus the officers recognised that engaging with the community early on in the enquiry and anticipating possible leaks to the media were important. But they also appreciated that the media is a resource.

Box 12.2 Key concept

The Stockholm syndrome

The *hostage identification syndrome* (or the Stockholm syndrome) refers to the tendency in hostage-type situations for hostages to develop a psychological affinity with their captors. Negative feelings may develop against the authorities trying to rescue them. This is a two-way thing in some cases, which may work to the hostages' advantage in that their safety is improved by such positive interpersonal feelings. The Stockholm syndrome was named after the events of a robbery of the Kreditbanken in Normalmstorg, Stockholm in 1973. During the aftermath of the robbery, people at the bank and the robbers were together in a vault of the bank for the lengthy period of time of five days. Victims and robbers became somewhat close during this time and, afterwards, the hostages would defend the robbers almost as if they were the victims. De Fabrique *et al.* (2007) indicate that the characteristics of the Stockholm syndrome are as follows:

- The hostages have positive feelings about their captors.
- The hostages manifest negative feelings to the authorities including the police such as anger, fear and distrust.
- The perpetrators begin to display positive feelings about the hostages as the hostages begin to be seen on a more personal level as human beings.

So what are the conditions which lead to the development of the Stockholm syndrome? According to de Fabrique *et al.*, there are several conditions which experts generally agree are required:

- The hostage is unable to escape and it is in the hands of the hostage taker whether the hostage lives or dies. The hostage taker is in control of the hostage's basic survival needs and their life.
- The hostage is kept isolated from other people and so only has the hostage taker's perspective. The hostage taker usually discloses little or nothing about the outside world to the hostage, which further ensures the dependency of the hostage on the hostage taker.
- The hostage taker threatens the life of the hostage convincingly. The hostage then aligns themselves with the hostage taker as the safest option. The hostage realises that they simply have to accept the discomforts of being held captive and to go along with what the hostage taker wants. The alternative is to resist and risk being killed.
- The hostage taker shows the hostage kindness in some way. Without this, the Stockholm syndrome will not develop.

Given that the Stockholm syndrome may help protect the hostage, crisis negotiators encourage its formation in hostage barricade incidents.

Hostage negotiation

Hostage taking is a terrorist technique but it is also more likely to occur in domestic situations and robberies, among others. The practicalities of how to deal with such hostage situations have been addressed by psychologists, especially in hostage crisis negotiations. This is partly because of the realisation that extreme situations may have a core of normality especially so far as relations between the hostage takers and police are considered. Wilson and Smith (2000) argue that behaviour during hostage-taking situations is bound by two sets of rules: (1) rules about the 'normal' behaviour that should be followed in hostage-taking situations and (2) rules about everyday behaviour which act as a fallback if the specific rules cannot be applied. They propose the importance of the following:

- *Motivation*: although it may be a complex task to understand the motives of the hostage takers, there may be clues to motive in the actions of their behaviour in the situation. They may give information to newspapers and television about the reasons for their action. If the demand is solely for money, according to Wilson and Smith, then this suggests a personally motivated crime rather than a politically motivated one. If the hostage takers demand the release of fellow terrorists then the hijacking may be a strategic attempt to fill a gap in the organisation. On the other hand, if the demand is to release prisoners in general, then this may be a simple expression of ideological beliefs about injustice as it applies widely.

- *Planning and resources*: the amount of planning that goes into a terrorist situation may indicate various things. For example, it may indicate the determination of the terrorists to fulfil the mission. Their behaviour should be more predictable than in circumstances in which the incident occurred spontaneously. Resources and the lack of them may give other insights into the planning of the operation.

In negotiations with hostage takers, the underlying 'rules' include the following:

- Both parties should demonstrate a willingness to negotiate.
- The parties should show willingness to demonstrate 'negotiability' by, for example, being willing to extend deadlines.

The hostages are the 'currency' of exchange with which the terrorists may bargain and negotiate. The release of all hostages is a bad strategy because only things such as the aircraft remain with which to bargain. At the same time, not releasing some prisoners may also be regarded as a bad strategy. The reasons include the good publicity accruing to the terrorists if some prisoners are released, especially women, children and the sick. Wilson and Smith suggest that breaking the rules of hostage taking may lead to a direct response by the authorities. They give the example of 'bluffing' about the situation, such as the terrorists claiming to have hostages when they do not. Negotiations may break down in these circumstances.

According to Flood (2003) 82 per cent of incidents were dealt with without injury or death to the hostages or the hostage takers. This is probably in part the result of modern crisis negotiation techniques introduced by Frank Bolz and Harvey Schlossberg of the New York Police Department in the early 1970s. Schlossberg had a doctoral degree in clinical psychology (Strentz, 2006). They worked together following the Munich Olympics Massacre (where the policing tactics of a hostage incident had been disastrous) to produce soundly based guidelines for negotiators in such situations. Instead of the hard-nosed, confrontational techniques which had previously been employed, revolutionary techniques based on ideas from conflict and dispute resolution were introduced. The overriding strategy is that of buying time in order to facilitate a rational ending to the episode. The fundamental approach of crisis negotiation is to:

- negotiate with the hostage taker while at the same time containing them within their immediate environment;
- use whatever methods are available to establish the motivation of the hostage taker and the personality factors which may underlie the incident;
- proceed at a deliberately slow pace, thus stretching the timescale of the negotiations partly as a way of dealing with the stretched emotions of the hostage takers by giving them the opportunity to express their feelings. As a consequence, the hostage taker may respond in a more rational way.

The phrase 'active listening skills' describes the strategies, such as emotion labelling and mirroring, used in crisis negotiation to achieve its goals. These skills are involved in establishing social relationships between the negotiators and the hostage takers and lead to the diffusing of the situation. Noesner and Webster (1997) describe the different active listening skills used in crisis intervention negotiations, which include the following:

- *Minimal encouragements*: these are verbal demonstrations that negotiators are listening carefully to the hostage taker's words and that the hostage taker is understood. These are very ordinary, everyday responses such as 'OK' or 'I see'. These keep the conversation going and eventually may help shift control of events to the crisis negotiator.
- *Paraphrasing*: in this, the hostage taker's talk is repeated back to them by the negotiator in the negotiator's own words.
- *Emotion labelling*: the negotiator must deal with the hostage taker's emotions in relation to the hostage-taking situation. The negotiator gives a 'tentative' label to the emotions that the hostage taker is communicating. So the negotiator may say something like 'It seems that you are angry with the way the Americans have treated Muslims all over the world.' The response of the hostage taker to this emotion labelling further helps the negotiator understand his or her emotional state.

- *Mirroring*: in this the negotiator repeats just a few words of what has just been said by the hostage taker or the idea that has been expressed. For example, if the hostage taker says something like 'There's no way that I am going to be pushed around by Americans' the mirrored response might be 'You won't be pushed around by Americans.' Mirroring provides one way of avoiding confrontational exchanges between the hostage taker and the police. It may also lead to the disclosure of valuable information as well as allowing the hostage taker to vent his or her emotions.

- *Open-ended questions*: the negotiator cannot learn effectively from the hostage taker unless the hostage taker does most of the talking. So open-ended questions inviting the hostage taker to tell the negotiator more about something would be appropriate as these are known to promote lengthier replies.

- *'I' messages*: these are non-confrontational personal comments by the negotiator expressing the way he or she feels in response to the hostage taker's words or actions. Phrases suggesting that the negotiator feels frustrated at the lack of progress in the negotiations would be an example of this.

Hostage negotiation is a skill which can be taught and so is included in police training programmes. Perera *et al.* (2006) describe their evaluation study of one particular training programme in crisis negotiation. This programme involved many important topics in crisis negotiation including basic principles of effective negotiations, suicide interventions, abnormal psychology and the use of third-party intermediaries in negotiations. Apart from these psychological aspects of hostage negotiation, training in the use of equipment and technical aspects involved in the use of, for example, communication systems and command posts was included. Initial crisis negotiation training cannot be done 'on the job' for obvious reasons. So the necessary psychological skills involved in active listening are developed through role-play and enactments of risky negotiation situations. They list direct instruction, performance feedback, modelling, behavioural rehearsal and positive reinforcement as the basis of learning crisis negotiation skills.

A group of FBI special agents took part in a role-play assessment of their crisis negotiation skills prior to intensive training and afterwards in order to assess the practical consequences of the programme. The role-play test for crisis negotiation skill was based on audio-taped narrative versions of real hostage incidents. Active listening skills in general improved significantly after the training. But equally important was the fact that attempts at problem solving declined with training. It is generally regarded that making statements directed towards providing a solution to the hostage taker's problems (problem solving) is actually dangerous in crisis negotiation as it may lead to premature interventions. This is especially the case early in the negotiation before sufficient rapport between the negotiator and hostage taker has developed.

While it is clear that hostage negotiation skills can be taught, there is some evidence that active listening skills may not be commonly employed in practice. Webster (2004) obtained tapes of a number of crisis negotiations and was somewhat surprised to find that the use of active listening skills only occurred in about 13 per cent of turn-takings in the negotiations. In fact, two-thirds of these active listening skills were very basic indications of attention to what the hostage taker was saying (attending skills) or the use of minor encouragers. The sort of thing that characterises these active listening skills is the use of such expressions as 'I see', 'sure' and 'right'. The use of complex active listening skills is a rather smaller proportion of the total turns. Paraphrasing what the hostage taker has said amounted to about 12 per cent of the total, emotion labelling amounted to 8 per cent of the total, summarising what had been said so far was 7 per cent of the total, and mirroring was 6 per cent of the officer's speaking turns. If the minor encouragers are left out, the actual use of active listening skills reduces to about 6 per cent of all of the turns.

Models of hostage negotiation

One of the unexpected features of the terrorism and crisis negotiation literature is the number of models related to negotiation processes. These are predominantly theoretically rather than empirically based. Mostly psychologists tend to adopt empirically driven models rather than more hypothetical ones; however, empirical work on terrorist processes is patently very difficult or impossible. Nevertheless, crisis negotiation is a deadly serious issue which demands being better understood for the safety of all concerned. The purpose of the models is to provide a degree of conceptual clarity to otherwise intrinsically complex and confusing situations. As such, a shared framework of understanding is available to officers as well as a basis for proceeding through the negotiation.

The authors of these models almost invariably stipulate that they are to be used flexibly and that it may be appropriate to move back to an earlier stage in the negotiation process in appropriate circumstances. One such model is the FBI's Behavioural Influence Stairway Model of crisis negotiation (Vecchi *et al.*, 2005). This according to Ireland and Vecchi (2009) is the prototypical version of this sort of model. It is also a model which has influenced strategies in the United Kingdom, for example. The Behavioural Influence Stairway Model (Van Hasselt, Romano and Vecchi, 2008) is an update of the FBI's crisis negotiation process. This is illustrated in Figure 12.3. The metaphor of a stairway or steps is common in models of crisis negotiation.

The stairway starts at the bottom step where there is no relationship between the negotiator and the hostage holder/terrorist and ends at the top step where there is a good relationship between the negotiator and the hostage holder/terrorist. Progress up the steps is through the use of active listening skills over a period of time which is, of course, flexible according to circumstances. There is no reason why the negotiator should not step back down should there be difficulties advancing up the steps. There is no fixed timescale for carrying out this sort of negotiation. There is no need to have information about any mental disorders involved and it is not essential to know just what the motives of the terrorist are.

The process is about bringing the situation to a peaceful halt with no harm done to any of those involved. The staircase is a relationship-building process in which the development of a trusting, positive relationship between the terrorist and the negotiator is the underlying aim of the enterprise. The aim is not for the negotiator to understand the reasons behind the incident. Concentration on motives can divert attention onto emotionally driven aspects which can make matters worse. Neither is it about solving the terrorists problems in some way as that also is about understanding the motive of the offender and may lead to a counterproductive urgency to find a solution.

The Stairway model is intended to be dynamic since the terrorist may alternate himself between steps. Active listening is fundamental throughout and can be thought of as a way of moving from the emotional to the rational. One possibility is that the negotiator may find that the terrorist wishes to go to a bargaining stage straight away. In the process of active listening, the negotiator may appear to be making trade-offs but nothing is really given away. But doing so may help reassure the terrorist and also supply time. Terrorists in such incidents may be less concerned about themselves and their personal interests and more concerned with how they will look in the eyes of their peers. Some terrorists may be keen to die in an act of martyrdom but probably

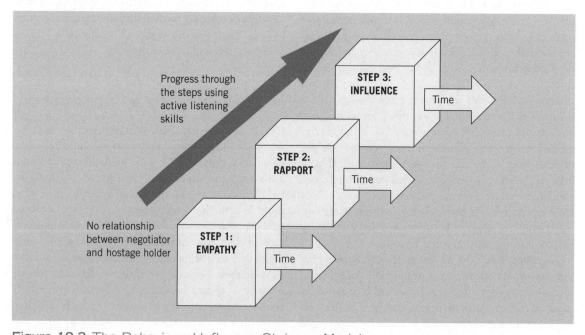

Figure 12.3 The Behavioural Influence Stairway Model

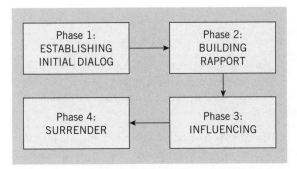

Figure 12.4 The four phases proposed by Madrigal *et al.* (2009)

many more would prefer to live to fight for their cause another day. Judgements about such matters may have a bearing on the negotiation. The flexible structure of the Behavioural Influence Stairway Model is important but nevertheless brings a sense of structure to a situation which may otherwise be chaotic to the negotiators involved.

Others have proposed not too dissimilar models. Madrigal, Bowman and McClain (2009) suggest a four-phase model of hostage negotiation which concentrates on the actions of the negotiator and indicates what style of language and talk should be used at each stag (see Figure 12.4). That is to say, the sorts of verbal statements which are utilised by the negotiator change during the negotiation process – each phase of the model is communicatively different. Generally the sequence given will be followed but this is not always the case and backtracking is a distinct possibility in this model too. The negotiator should not move too quickly through the phases since this may result in anger or some other reaction from the hostage taker. If this happens, then the situation may be corrected by backtracking to the earlier phases.

- Phase 1: Establishing Initial Dialogue: In this approach, it is assumed that the hostage taker may be reluctant to engage in negotiation and may demonstrate hostility. So the process is one of initiating dialogue through whatever means seem to be appropriate. The initial statements of the negotiator will tend to be situational or more general. The weather may be such a general topic but asking about the condition of the hostages may also be appropriate. Even sport on big match days might be a good way into the dialogue. This phase can be difficult because the hostage taker may be decidedly resistant to speaking with the negotiator.

- Phase 2: Building Rapport: Some degree of rapport has been achieved when this phase of the negotiation is instigated. The task of this phase is to create a personal relationship and trust between the hostage taker and the negotiator. In this way a free exchange of personal information becomes possible. If Phase 1 requirements have not been achieved then problems may occur in Phase 2 and the hostage taker's response may become very negative. If this is the case, backtracking to Phase 1 may be necessary. This phase will involve many of the active listening techniques which have already been discussed. Mirroring, paraphrasing, minimal encouragers are all part of this. If Phase 2 is executed successfully then it will result in personal information including emotional information being revealed by the hostage taker who holds the negotiator in some sort of positive regard if not friendship. These may appear to be reciprocated by the negotiator. This signals the possibility of moving on to the third phase.

- Phase 3: Influencing: Building on the achievements of the previous phase, the negotiators' task is to persuade the hostage holder to free the hostages and bring the stand-off to a peaceful end. The risk is that the hostage taker will perceive the negotiator as engaging in trickery. This stage involves little active listening since the necessary personal relationship will have been developed. The negotiator may make suggestions and promises, and reframe the situation to present a positive outcome from surrender. The primary task of this stage is to reassure the hostage taker of their safety should they decide to end the stand-off by surrendering. It is not really about bargaining or providing solutions to problems though sometimes these may be part of this phase.

- Phase 4: Surrender: In this phase the hostage taker will have decided to surrender. The task of the negotiator is to give the hostage taker the important instructions about how to do this in a way in which they will stay safe and also ensure that the hostage taker fully understands what is required. This is a relatively pragmatic stage since the major negotiation skills will have been used in order to get to this final phase. But this is regarded as a very risky phase for both the hostage taker and the police officers involved so everything needs to be done with great care.

Models like this are not built on vast bodies of research work but they are extremely useful in helping to clarify and conceptualise the negotiation process such that those involved can structure their experiences around a meaningful framework.

Main points

- It is a moot point whether psychological terrorism research has lacked achievements. The problem with research on terrorists is that it has tended to adopt a traditional personality/mental disorder model to explain why individuals become terrorists. Increasingly it is becoming clear that terrorists are normal people who commit extreme violence. Recent work into the cognitive processes of terrorists, their identity development, and the influence of group socialisation practices may form the basis of future research in this field.

- Adopting psychological principles from organisational psychology and the psychology of negotiations has provided police with skills to deal with a range of situations, not all terrorism-based, where hostages are being held. Although these methods are essentially simple ways of maximising talk between the authorities and the terrorists, it is notable that very few hostage-taking situations end in the death of or injury to the captives.

- The Stockholm syndrome describes the situation in which hostages begin to have a positive perception of their captors and are prepared to side with them against the police and other authorities. The Stockholm syndrome is a product of situations in which the hostage takers have complete power over the hostages but show a degree of kindness. Hostage negotiators are said to encourage the formation of the Stockholm syndrome because it is a two-way process between the hostages and the hostage takers which can serve to protect the hostages.

Further reading

Broad issues related to psychology and terrorism are to be found in the following:

Bongar, B., Brown, L.M., Beutler, L.E., Breckenridge, J.N. and Zimbardo, P.G. (eds) (2007) *Psychology of Terrorism* Oxford: Oxford University Press.

Silke, A. (ed.) (2010) *The Psychology of Counter-Terrorism* Abingdon, Oxon: Routledge.

The following have extensive reviews of the literature on the psychology of terrorism:

Borum, R. (2004) *Psychology of Terrorism* Tampa: University of South Florida: http://www.ncjrs.gov/pdffiles1/nij/grants/208552.PDF

Hudson, R.A. (1999) *The Sociology and Psychology of Terrorism: Who becomes a Terrorist and Why?* Library of Congress. http://www.loc.gov/rr/frd/pdf-files/Soc_Psych_of_Terrorism.pdf

Visit our website at www.pearsoned.co.uk/howitt for self-test and essay questions, annotated further reading, audio interviews with researchers in the field, weblinks and more information on becoming a forensic psychologist.

Chapter 13

Eyewitness testimony

Overview

- DNA evidence has proven beyond doubt the innocence of some people wrongfully convicted of a crime. Two-thirds of these wrongful convictions in the most recent US study involved incorrect eyewitness evidence. Despite this, surveys of police officers show that they value eyewitness evidence and believed that eyewitnesses are usually correct. It should be remembered that in some jurisdictions convictions based solely on eyewitness evidence are not acceptable.

- Eyewitness evidence can be accurate or inaccurate. There is evidence that for certain features such as gender and eye shape there are high levels of accuracy whereas for beards and moustaches accuracy is low. It is possible that offenders change some of their characteristics as disguise.

- There is a considerable literature on the characteristics of eyewitness memory. Of importance is the evidence that events following the incident (e.g. interviews) may affect what is remembered as well as the type of questioning. This is of importance, for example, when examining issues such as allegations of sexual abuse that occurred many years before.

- The confidence of eyewitnesses in their testimony and their accuracy are quite distinct things. At best, there is a weak relationship between the two. One implication is that witnesses who seem less than confident would probably provide as accurate identifications as any other witness. Certainly, one should be careful about legal suggestions that confidence is a sign of a good witness.

- The line-up or identity parade needs to be planned and executed following a number of rules to minimise errors. It has been suggested that some of the care that goes into designing laboratory experiments in psychology could benefit line-ups. For example, the person conducting the line-up should be unaware of the identity of the suspect in order to avoid the risk of biasing the situation. Experimental studies tend to suggest that eyewitnesses who make their decisions quickly tend to be the most accurate.

- Relative judgement theory suggests that an eyewitness tends to choose someone similar to the culprit if the culprit is not in the identification parade. Eyewitnesses, therefore, do not apply absolute criteria for matching their memories with the members of the line-up. The use of procedures which indicate that the culprit may not be present in the line-up may reduce the relative judgement effect.

- Some police tools such as CCTV and the use of facial composites have been under critical scrutiny. CCTV footage does not readily lead to the identification of individuals unknown to the person viewing the tape. Facial composites are not particularly recognisable even for well-known individuals.

- Despite a great deal of empirical research, it is not possible to evaluate with any precision a particular witness's evidence. Even well-researched topics, such as the effects of length of exposure to the offender, on the accuracy of eyewitness evidence are difficult to translate from the psychological laboratory to real life.

Introduction

Few would doubt that human memory is fallible. An intriguing demonstration of this was a study of memory concerning the crash of an El Al Boeing 747 jet onto a residential area of Amsterdam (Crombag, Wagenaar and Van Kopen, 1996). The crash had only been verbally reported on news bulletins as no film or video of the plane crash exists. Apart from eyewitnesses, no one could have seen the events. Nevertheless, participants in the research were misled into thinking that they may have seen such images on television by asking them about their recollections of the news coverage. Substantial numbers of participants in the study readily provided visual details of the crash as if they had seen it on film. One can only presume that they gleaned this information from film of crashes that had been broadcast. The key finding of the research is the failure of participants to recognise the falsity of their claims. That is to say, they did not realise that they were manufacturing memories. More recently, Ost *et al.* (2008) asked samples of British and Swedish people about the events in Tavistock Square, London, when on the 7 July 2005 a number 30 bus was blown up by a terrorist at roughly the same time as tube trains were bombed. Within three months of the events, the researchers asked whether the participants remembered seeing the video of the bus being blown up. Again no such video exists but some participants claimed to have seen it. For the combined samples, 28 per cent claimed to have seen the material which did not exist though this was more common in the British sample than the Swedish sample. When adjustments were made for the percentages of the two samples who had seen any coverage of the events (the Swedes were less likely to

have seen such material), the trends remained much the same.

The implications of these studies for forensic and criminal psychology are obvious. Imagine the following circumstances. Police officers show a photograph to a woman who had witnessed a crime. They ask her whether the man in the photograph is the offender. She decides that it is the man who committed the crime. Just what degree of confidence should one have in a conviction based solely on this identification? There are many reasons why the witness identified the photograph as being that of the offender. She might feel that:

- the police must have strong reasons to suspect this particular man;

- the man in the photograph may have a passing resemblance to the offender;

- she has seen the man in the photograph somewhere before;

- she would appear foolish if she says that she cannot remember whether or not this is the man.

Clearly this is a very unsatisfactory procedure for identifying the offender. Nevertheless, this was common practice until the Supreme Court of the United States recognised the risk of a miscarriage of justice brought about by such procedures (*Simmons v. United States, 1968*). Any procedure used to obtain identification evidence needs to be much less risky than this.

Nevertheless, there is evidence that police officers have great faith in eyewitness evidence. A survey of British police officers found that, generally speaking, they valued witness evidence positively. The majority believed that witnesses are usually correct and three-quarters thought that they were never or rarely incorrect. On the other hand, about half felt that witnesses did not remember as much as the officer wanted (Kebbell and Milne, 1998). In other words, witness evidence may have an important role in police investigations irrespective of its validity.

Of course, risky identification evidence is an issue in only a minority of crimes. Criminal statistics, as we have seen, show quite clearly that many victims already know their victimisers socially. Thus the risk of innocent misidentification in these circumstances is minimal. In other words, identification evidence is unproblematic in the vast majority of these cases. It is in circumstances in which the witness and the offender are strangers that difficulties arise.

BOX 13.1 Forensic psychology in action

CCTV video evidence

There has been a vast increase in the use of closed-circuit television (CCTV) video cameras in public areas such as town and city centres. One of their prime purposes is to act as deterrents to crime. They can also be considered as evidence collection systems. We are all familiar with footage of crimes observed in this way. Figure 13.1 presents a model of the influence of CCTV cameras based on Williams (2007) which features aspects of policing an area but also the influence of such cameras on the general public. Cameras do not provide irrefutable evidence of a crime and offenders in practice. This is partly the consequence of the very poor images produced due, for example, to the amount of enlargement of the image required. Image

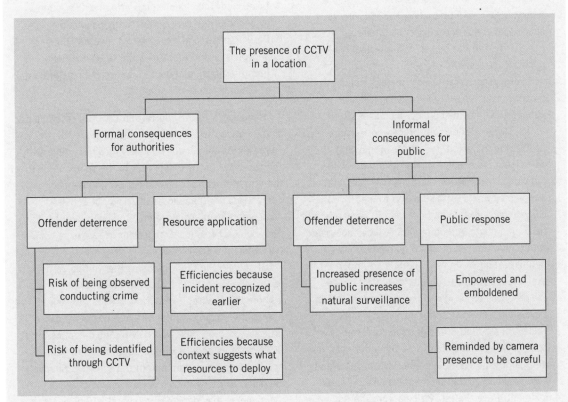

Figure 13.1 A model of the effects of CCTV loosely based on Williams (2007)

BOX 13.1 (continued)

enhancement techniques are available but they do this at the expense of movement in the image. The current psychological research suggests that the problems are substantial with current technology:

- There is evidence that CCTV systems do reduce crime in the *short term* in locations where they are installed although there is a return to previous levels in the longer term (Brown, 1995). The growing awareness that the system is not altogether effective in ensuring arrest leaves some people willing to take the risk. There are rather mixed findings from research on CCTV as a crime deterrence and reduction method. Welsh and Farrington (2002) found that the majority of studies did not demonstrate that the cameras led to a decrease in crime. Actually, three studies out of 13 showed an increase in crime rates following CCTV's introduction and four others showed no effect one way or the other.
- Familiarity with the person in a low-quality video makes it far easier to recognise them compared with strangers. Nevertheless, there is not a proportionate increase in the recognition of strangers as the video quality increases (Burton *et al.*, 1999). Henderson, Bruce and Burton (2000a) investigated the effects of allowing participants to become modestly familiar with individuals by showing them a short video clip of a face they would later be asked to identify. The consequence was no improvement in recognition of faces in a photo line-up of similar faces compared with circumstances in which no opportunity for familiarisation was given. There is an important exception to the general rule that CCTV images are problematic for identification (Davies, 2003). Davies cites the court case involving a soldier who was assaulted in a nightclub surveyed by a poor-quality CCTV system. The video did not show the features of the assailants clearly. The assault had been carried out by members of a different regiment. Nevertheless, officers from the regiment in question were able to identify the culprits independently of each other. They all agreed

on the assailants! If familiarity with the person in the video is associated with very accurate identification then the question is what degree of familiarity is required before acceptable accuracy in identification is achieved.
- With strangers, it is very difficult with even high-quality videos to determine whether two different images are of the same person (Kemp, Towell and Pike, 1997). For example, Davies and Thasen (2000) found that only 65 per cent of viewers of a CCTV video of a woman in an 'incident' in a car park in which she was seen in close-up actually picked out another 'innocent' person from a line-up. Only 29 per cent correctly identified the woman, the remainder made no choice.
- When they compared various measures of the recognition of CCTV-simulated video and stills taken from the video, Kemp *et al.* (2000) found evidence of the superiority of the video clip. Participants made more correct identifications and were less likely to make false recognitions from the (moving) video. This involved recognition of familiar faces, *not* strangers.

Henderson, Bruce and Burton (2000b) recommend that great caution is needed in assessing evidence from CCTV from people who are not very familiar with the person(s) in the video. Part of the solution lies in the improvement of CCTV images which are poor in comparison with broadcast television or domestic camcorders, with which many of us are more familiar. They see CCTV as more important in assessing what happened at a crime scene.

Of course, the CCTV cameras themselves do not identify which activities are worth monitoring and possible subsequent action. This is the task of human monitors using them. There has only been a little research on this. Just how do the operators of CCTV systems decide what is potentially criminal? The information available from the screen is relatively degraded by many things. A person who is aware of the cameras may decide to modify their behaviour according to whether or not they have any criminal intent. Playful behaviours within the context of a light-hearted conversation may appear to be aggressive or potentially violent on screen. The lack of sound to further inform the human monitors can make interpretation difficult. There is evidence from Lassiter, Geers, Munhall, Handley and Beers (2001) that persons depicted in relative close-up with the wider situation excluded tend to be perceived as problematic. The persons selected for closer observation are those who fit a criminal stereotype – such as younger males or younger black men (Norris and Armstrong, 1997). Williams (2007) studied such decision making in a control room and made comparisons with demographic and similar information collected directly from the locations where the cameras were in use. Much as in other studies, it became obvious that it was young men of a scruffy appearance who were disproportionately selected by the operators. The operators' justifications for selecting them as targets tended to be that they were loitering. Males were selected and followed by the cameras for rather longer, on average, than females.

Grant and Williams (2011) investigated the extent to which the visual cues in CCTV images could accurately be used to predict whether a criminal act was taking place. They used a group of CCTV operators and a group of novices who were shown some video scenes leading to antisocial acts and others not leading to antisocial acts. As far as was possible, the scenes were matched on things such as location and the number of people to be seen. That is, scenes leading to crime were broadly similar to those which did not. The videos were obtained from YouTube. The research utilised actual control rooms. An eye-gaze direction tracker was used to understand what visual cues were attended to by the observers. That is, measures were taken of the point of gaze during viewing the video. The observer's task was to predict which scenes led to criminal behaviour. A specially constructed measure of Criminal Intent Prediction was used. The participants reported suspicious aspects of the scenes that they observed. Good predictions about criminal actions to follow were associated with visual concentration on the face or head of a lone individual and the bodies of individuals interacting socially. Not unexpectedly, an awareness of the more general social context of the scene led to better predictions of criminal behaviour. Experienced and inexperienced operators were similar in terms of their accuracy of predicting which incidents would lead to crime.

Eyewitness testimony as a central issue in forensic and criminal psychology

As we saw in Chapter 1, as long ago as 1896 the German psychologist Albert Von Schrenk-Nortzing testified at the Munich trial of a triple murder. Basing his argument on the then emerging academic research into the nature of suggestibility and memory, Von Schrenk-Nortzing unsuccessfully argued that witnesses confuse real-life events with events they read about in the press. He used the phrase 'retroactive memory falsification'. Just a few years later, Munsterberg, who may be seen as the founder of the field of applied psychology, returned to this field. He argued that there was probably no relationship between the accuracy of an eyewitness and the eyewitness's confidence in the accuracy of his or her testimony. This conclusion still, more or less, accurately reflects available research findings.

The topic remains important in terms of justice. This is graphically illustrated by work on wrongful convictions (Wells et al., 1998, which extended an earlier review by Connors et al., 1996). This is an account of the false convictions established in American courts on the basis of genetic fingerprint (DNA) testing. Forty trials that led to wrongful conviction were available for review. In each of these the testing of genetic material with new techniques established the unjust conviction beyond any doubt. These were serious miscarriages of justice. All of the men who were convicted served prison sentences. Five of them spent time on death row awaiting execution. The testimony of at least one eyewitness was in 90 per cent of these proven miscarriages of justice. In one instance, as many as five eyewitnesses were involved. The case of Ronald Cotton is typical. Cotton spent 10 years in prison for a rape actually committed by another man, Bobby Poole. There was remarkably little evidence against Ronald Cotton. One victim had identified him from a photographic line-up (a selection of photographs possibly including the offender). In a line-up/identity parade, just one witness identified him as the rapist. Eventually, the DNA evidence from semen left by the actual rapist resulted in Cotton's release. Remarkably, the real rapist, Bobby Poole, had already confessed to the crimes and this confession had been rejected by a court as reason to release Cotton. More recently (Weber, Brewer and Wells, 2004), the Innocence Project found that two-thirds of 138 cases of DNA-exonerated convicted offenders involved wrongful eyewitness identifications. The Innocence Project deals with cases in which a conviction might be challenged on the basis of DNA evidence. Partly this study involved some of the same cases that were included in the earlier DNA study.

DNA evidence is minimally relevant to a great many crimes. So naturally, for crime in general, it would seem impossible to know the extent to which eyewitnesses make errors which incriminate innocent people in a line-up/identification parade. Nevertheless, Wells, Memon and Penrod (2007) suggested a novel way of obtaining minimum estimates of this. Their approach is based on the frequency with which a filler (stooge) is picked out erroneously as the target from line-ups/identity parades. They refer to a number of studies of real police line-ups in which the rates of identifying a filler as the suspect incorrectly ranged from about 20 per cent to about 24 per cent (i.e. in about 20 per cent of line-ups a filler is erroneously selected). In these studies, a filler was picked out in about a third of the line-ups in which someone was selected by the eyewitness (some line-ups would result in no one being identified). These filler identification rates provide a conservative estimate of the likelihood of an innocent party being picked out. This is on the assumption that the innocent party was at the same level of risk of being selected as any of the filler persons. So if the line-up consisted of six people (the suspect plus five filler people) then the five fillers would have a 20 per cent chance of being picked out *in total*. Since there are five fillers in this example then, overall, a particular filler has a one fifth of 20 per cent chance of being picked out – that is a 4 per cent chance of being identified as the criminal erroneously. The quite reasonable assumption is that the innocent person has the same risk of being picked out.

BOX 13.2 Forensic psychology in action

Facial composites and identification

One investigative technique familiar to the general public is the police's use of facial composites. That is, images of the 'suspect' based on the reports of victims and other witnesses. These have changed with changes in technology. Originally, an artist would sketch a picture of the face based on the information supplied by the witness, then in the 1970s Identikit (based on 'sketched' material) and Photofit (based on photographs) approaches were used. These used 'kits' of facial features from which, say, a nose with the appropriate shape was selected from a range of noses in the kit. The different elements of the face were then built into the total image. More recently still, technological advances have enabled the use of computer techniques to produce the images. These allow the size, for example, of the feature to be adjusted quickly so increasing the flexibility of the approach. Such computerised facial composite approaches include E-FIT and PRO-fit which are used by some police forces. Research into earlier methods of creating facial composites before computerisation generally found that the quality of the composites was not good. So are the newer methods more satisfactory?

Frowd *et al.* (2004) had the 'witness' work with a facial composite operator to produce an image of a target person (popular personalities but ones identified as not being known to the 'witness'). The image of the target was shown for about one minute and there was a delay of three to four hours before the next stage of the research. The operator did not know the identity of the 'target' and worked solely on the basis of the descriptions given by the 'witness' and the normal interactions between the witness and the operator. These facial composites could then be shown to people who were asked to identify who the celebrity was. Accuracy was not outstanding. E-FIT and PRO-fit produced 20 per cent of recognition from the composite, artist's sketches resulted in 10 per cent recognition, and Photofit yielded 5 per cent recognition. The results were essentially replicated when participants were asked to match the facial composite to an array of photographs including that of the target. In other words, the composites were not very good matches to the original photographs. One other feature of the design should be mentioned – the 'witnesses' underwent a cognitive interview before engaging in the facial composite construction task. Of course, a delay of three or four hours between exposure to the target and reconstruction was relatively short compared to most forensic situations.

A study by Frowd et al. (2005) followed many of the above procedures but extended the delay between exposure and facial reconstruction. The witnesses were showed pictures of celebrities (in this case, actors and pop music performers) until they came across one which the witness did not recognise. They looked at this for one minute. Two days later the facial composite recognition task was carried out. This again involved a cognitive interview (see Chapter 11) and witnesses were asked to think of the time that the target photo was seen and the context of this. This is the reinstatement of context procedure from the cognitive interview. Then, once a clear picture had been formed, the witness described the face, taking as much time as they needed. This was then followed by cued recall where the descriptions of each feature were read to the witness who then added anything further that came to mind. The precise procedures used for creating the 'likeness' varied but were similar to the standard practice employed with each particular method.

A separate group took part in the 'identification' process based on the composites. Overall, only a small percentage of composites were correctly named (2.8 per cent). This is partly a function of the composite method employed. Actual sketches were the most frequently recognised. Of course, this could be a consequence of the target individual not being recognisable from the original photograph. However, this group of participants were asked a number of questions about the person in the photograph. The recognition figures for the composites were adjusted on the basis of the answers to these questions to allow for these differences in recognisability of the

personalities. This resulted in a modest increase in naming to 3.3 per cent over all the composites. Once again, sketches were the best named (8.1 per cent) with E-FIT and PRO-fit only being recognised by less than 2 per cent.

Just why do facial composite methods produce such inadequate composites? The temptation is to regard the problem as being the consequence of weaknesses in the methods and the inadequacy of memory for faces. There is another possible explanation which suggests that the problem may partly lie in the communications between the witness and the facial-composite operator. Brace et al. (2006) also used recognisable famous faces which had been created by a computerised facial composite system (E-FIT). The facial composites were either produced by the E-FIT operator following the verbal instructions of the 'witness' (describer) or by the E-FIT operator working alone without a 'witness'. In some conditions the facial construction was done from memory and in others a photograph of the famous person was used. Thus the composite was produced by (1) the E-FIT operator working alone from memory, (2) the E-FIT operator working alone using a photograph, (3) the E-FIT operator following the instructions of a 'witness' who worked from memory, and (4) the E-FIT operator following the instructions of a 'witness' who could see a photograph when the operator could not.

This was followed by an evaluation phase in which the E-FIT composites were shown to a large group of evaluators who made judgements about the quality of the composites in one study or had to name the famous person from the composite in another study. The general pattern of results was the similar for both studies. Where the operator worked alone, the composites were more accurate and it made no difference whether they worked from memory or photographs. On the other hand, where the operator followed the verbal description of the 'witness' the facial composite was more accurate when the 'witness' was working from a photograph than from memory. The implication of these findings is that part of the difficulty in constructing good facial composites lies in the communication between the operator and witness; it is not simply problems to do with the witness's memory or the facial composite system in use.

The accuracy of witness evidence

Eyewitnesses, of course, can be very accurate in their descriptions despite failing to identify offenders precisely. Very little research is available that compares the characteristics of offenders with those descriptions given to the police. What evidence there is suggests that witnesses can be accurate in terms of describing individual characteristics but not always so. One of the best studies in this field was carried out in the Netherlands (Van Koppen and Lochun, 1997). Data were obtained from official court records in store at the offices of prosecutors. The researchers targeted offences involving robberies of commercial buildings and dwellings. Street robberies (muggings) were not included. In the Netherlands, witnesses are rarely questioned in court. Instead, the prosecution depends on statements obtained by the police from witnesses. In the cases studied, there was very little delay between the offence and the collection of witness statements:

- 80 per cent had been collected within two days – about two-thirds in one day;
- over 400 different robberies were studied;
- 1,300 witnesses were involved;
- 2,300 offender descriptions were obtained;
- only 1,650 descriptions could be used since not all could be verified against the robber's true appearance;
- mostly the witness had seen the robbery (over four-fifths);
- the remaining witnesses had seen the escape or preparations being made for the robbery.

Other information was available from various sources on the characteristics of the witness and the circumstances of their evidence:

- witness characteristics such as their sex and age;
- the amount of delay before they gave their statements;
- the quality of the lighting conditions at the robbery;
- whether the witness's view was obstructed;
- the estimated distance between the witness and the robbery.

The actual offender characteristics were assessed using the police's own descriptions of the arrestee, which were available from official forms designed for that purpose. The correspondence between the witness description and the police description of the suspect varied according to the physical feature under consideration. The greatest correspondence was found for:

- sex (100 per cent agreement);
- eye shape (100 per cent);
- hair colour (73 per cent);
- face shape (69 per cent);
- race (60 per cent);
- height (52 per cent);
- ears protruding (50 per cent).

While the correspondence for some of the above is generally impressive, some features were rarely mentioned in the witness descriptions. Sex and height were the most commonly mentioned features. Overall, the witness descriptions were relatively sparse. So, out of the maximum of 43 different characteristics that could be mentioned, on average each witness mentioned only eight features.

Of course, offenders have an interest in altering their physical appearance either specifically for the offence or after the offence. So it is of some interest to note that the characteristics that are the most easily altered tend to be those with the lowest agreement:

- beards (1 per cent);
- moustaches (3 per cent);
- accents and dialects (32 per cent).

Some variables predicted the accuracy of the eyewitness description. For example, the longer the statement, the greater the eyewitness accuracy. Given the large sample size involved, the relationships between predictors and accuracy were not strong despite being statistically significant. Generally speaking, the relationships were much as would be expected. Factors such as the distance between the offender and the witness, the duration of the crime, the physical position of the witness in relation to the offender and the feelings of threat experienced by the witness all had predictable relationships with witness accuracy. Counter-intuitively, the longer the delay between the crime and the statement by the witness, the better was the accuracy of the witness's description.

The overall impression, nevertheless, is of rather vague descriptions that are dominated by very general characteristics such as the offender's sex, race, height and age.

The witnesses are accurate in their description of these characteristics. However, these are the very characteristics that are poor at distinguishing offenders from others who are suspects. For example, knowing that the offender is male is not very much use in identifying the particular person in question.

This is about accuracy in describing characteristics of offenders; who gets picked out in line-ups is a different issue.

Later intrusions into eyewitness memory

The early studies of human memory in the first part of the twentieth century largely consisted of the memorising of nonsense syllables following the work of Ebbinghaus (1913): hardly a situation conducive to the study of eyewitness testimony. Things gradually changed from the late 1960s onwards in ways that encouraged psychologists to investigate eyewitness psychology. Increasingly, the importance of studying real-life memory was recognised, e.g. Neisser (1982) and Neisser and Winograd (1988) published seminal work on human memory in real-life contexts. Consequently, from the 1970s onwards, academic memory researchers carried out numerous studies of eyewitness memory. Nevertheless, coming, as they did, largely from the laboratory tradition of psychology, their emphasis was on theoretical rather than practical matters.

Some of the most important theory in this area emerged from the work of Elizabeth Loftus. Her interests eventually extended into practical matters such as recovered memories (see Chapter 16). Perhaps the most famous of her studies were demonstrations that subsequent events influenced testimony about incidents. Witnesses to a robbery or accident may be exposed later to new information – perhaps during a police interview, for example. In some circumstances, that new information can influence recollections of the incident. Furthermore, information in one modality may affect memory for events held in a different modality. Thus verbal information may affect visual recall. The most familiar study is that of Loftus and Palmer (1974). Participants witnessed film of a car accident and were later asked a series of questions in which key information was embedded. There were alternative versions of the key question:

- 'About how fast were the cars going when they *hit* each other?'
- 'About how fast were the cars going when they *smashed* into each other?'

Other variants on this theme had the cars colliding, contacting each other, bumping and so forth. Estimates of speed were affected by the word used in the questioning. The estimates were of speeds about a third faster when the word smashed was used than when the word contacted was used. It might be objected – and it was – that, in itself, this does not mean that what was stored in the brain changed. Subtly leading questions may have simply encouraged faster estimates without affecting the 'memory trace'. It is not possible to get into the mind of the witness to measure the speed the cars are travelling in the brain trace. Perhaps this is a theoretical issue rather than being of practical importance. Nevertheless, researchers, including Loftus herself, pursued this issue with some vigour.

In this series of studies, a visual recognition procedure replaced the problematic verbal statement (Loftus, Miller and Burns, 1978). Participants in the research were shown a series of colour slides of the stages of a car–pedestrian accident. The car in question was a red Datsun that was seen driving towards a road intersection where there was either a stop sign or a yield sign (give way sign), depending on the experimental condition. Later a series of questions was asked in which was embedded one of two variants of the key question:

- Did another car pass the red Datsun while it was stopped at the stop sign?
- Did another car pass the red Datsun while it was stopped at the yield sign?

After a short diversionary activity, a yes/no recognition test was administered immediately or a week later. The crucial recognition slides were the stop and the yield slides. Essentially, then, the experimental design was as follows:

- Some participants saw a stop sign and were asked about a stop sign.
- Some participants saw a stop sign but were asked about a yield sign.
- Some participants saw a yield sign and were asked about a yield sign.
- Some participants saw a yield sign but were asked about a stop sign.

In other words, some participants were asked questions *consistent* with what they had seen and others were asked questions *inconsistent* with what they had seen. Some of the findings were:

- Questioning consistent with the contents of the original experience enhanced correct visual identification for the crucial slide immediately after exposure.

- Questioning inconsistent with the original experience depressed correct identification initially.

- Generally speaking, these effects tended to reduce after a week such that the initial differences disappeared.

Given the great numbers of laboratory studies of eyewitness testimony, it is not possible to review all of the findings. We can, nevertheless, turn to some major forensic issues that illustrate the implications of research findings for court decisions.

Eyewitness evidence in court

Witness confidence

The issue of eyewitness confidence markedly divides the legal and the psychological views. In the United States, the Supreme Court decided in 1972 that witness confidence was an indicator of witness accuracy. Thus witness confidence can be regarded as 'markers' (Weber, Brewer, Wells *et al.*, 2004) or assessment variables (Sporer, 1993) which might help when assessing the value of any witness's testimony. Equally, confidence should also be taken into account when assessing the risk of misidentification. Furthermore, it is known from other research that lawyers in general accept the validity of this link and jurors tend to subscribe to this view too. In contrast, research has demonstrated that confidence is a rather poor predictor of accuracy. Cutler and Penrod (1989) studied a wide range of investigations of confidence expressed prior to identity parades/line-ups and correct identification of the offender. The overall correlation between confidence and accuracy is 0.20 or less for these studies. While this is evidence of a relationship, it is nevertheless a rather weak relationship, statistically speaking. Consequently, Cutler and Penrod felt it important to stress that the poor relationship is a good reason not to ignore the evidence of witnesses who

express a lack of confidence. Confident witnesses are not much better, in general, than non-confident ones in their identifications.

An observant reader will spot various values of the size of the confidence–accuracy relationship. Superficially this seems a little confusing but the problem boils down to whether we are comparing like with like or apples with pears – that is, the figures vary according to precisely what is being studies. For example, the correlation between confidence and accuracy may be different if all witnesses are included whether or not an identification is made compared to when only witnesses who make an identication are included. So you will find different estimates in this chapter. If the calculation is confined to witnesses who actually made a choice (but not those who do not make a choice) then the correlation between confidence and accuracy could be as much as 0.4 according to studies. This is quite a respectable value given what typically happens in psychological research though, of course, it could be regarded as the best case scenario. Of course, including non-identifying witnesses would lead to a much lower correlation.

Just what does this correlation of 0.4 mean? In order to make things more intuitively meaningful, Wells and Quinlivan (2009) compare the witness confidence–accuracy correlation with another, more familiar, relationship. Predicting someone's eyewitnessing accuracy from their confidence is about the same as predicting their gender from their height! So if you imagine predicting someone's gender from their height then this provides an indication of just what that 0.4 forensic figure means. Nevertheless, this does not mean that a correlation of 0.4 between accuracy and confidence is useless. Wells *et al.* point out that in a sample of 100 eyewitnesses, half of whom had accurately made an identification and the other half inaccurately, approximately 70 per cent of the witnesses who were above average on confidence would be accurate in their selection and only 30 per cent who were below average on confidence would make an correct identification.

As might be expected, witnesses after the line-up (identity parade) demonstrate a slightly better association between confidence as measured after the line-up and accuracy. Nevertheless, this remains a small correlation (Bothwell, Deffenbacher and Brigham, 1987). In eyewitness testimony, the size of the confidence–accuracy relationship may be affected by a range of factors. In line-ups or identification parades there is a slightly bigger relationship between confidence and accuracy in the target present line-up than in the target absent line-up. A comparison of target present and target absent line-ups reveals differences but this is starting from a low base and does not get very strong. According to Krug's review (2007), the correlation between confidence and accuracy is only about 0.3. Of course, in reality, target present and target absent line-ups are a research notion and not a practical one since the police simply do not know which applies to line-ups in their day-to-day work as opposed to the psychology laboratory. The relationship between confidence and accuracy tends to be lower for recognition memory tasks – the line-up is of course a recognition memory task for the witness. The relationship is higher for recall tasks, which is the sort of activity a witness does when he or she describes the offender to a police officer.

Kebbell, Wagstaff and Covey (1996) were among those to question such a counter-intuitive finding as the suggestion that there is only a poor correlation between confidence and accuracy. They pointed out that researchers have avoided memory tasks that are either very easy or very hard. So, for example, witnesses may be asked the culprit's sex or their eye colour. Sex is a relatively easy thing to identify but in the circumstances of the witnessed events, the witness may have no opportunity to register the offender's eye colour. The optimality encoding hypothesis (Deffenbacher, 1980) suggested that the confidence–accuracy relationship will be at its highest level in circumstances where encoding, storage and retrieval conditions are optimal. Eyewitnesses may well be less confident in circumstances which are suboptimal for any of these aspects. The witness to a crime which took place in the night in the dark might understandably be reluctant to claim great confidence in their ability to pick out the offender. In Kebbell et al.'s (1996) study, student eyewitnesses watched a short video showing the implied murder of a man by a woman. Following a filler or distracting task, they were asked to complete a 33-item questionnaire about the film. The questions were open-ended and varied in terms of difficulty. Confidence was fairly closely related to item difficulty – that is, easy questions produced a high correlation between accuracy and confidence. Difficult questions produced a low correlation between accuracy and confidence. Interestingly, virtually every time that a participant rated themselves as being absolutely certain about the accuracy of their answer to a question they were correct – that is, their accuracy was 97 per cent in these circumstances.

Memory confidence is an instance of the general phenomenon of meta-memory which refers to the way in which we monitor, predict and control our own memory. There are many instances of this, such as our assessment of how much we have learnt, the feeling that we know something well, or even that our memory for names has declined as we have got older. It is difficult to be precise about the relationship between how good our memories are and our meta-perspective on our memories (Krug, 2007). In some areas of memory, there is quite a strong relationship between our confidence in our memory and the accuracy of our memory. So, for example, confidence and ability are fairly well related in the domain of general knowledge. On the other hand, school students when assessing their own knowledge show a poor relationship between confidence and their true level of knowledge.

Some researchers have suggested that eyewitness confidence–accuracy correlations are not the ideal way of indicating exactly what the relationship is. Calibration is recommended as an alternative. Essentially, calibration is about how well the eyewitnesses' assessment of the likely accuracy of their recollections corresponds with the probability that the answer given is correct. So a perfectly calibrated relationship between confidence and accuracy would be one where the individual's confidence rating is the same as their actual accuracy. So if an individual says that they are 80 per cent confident that they are correct then they are correct 80 per cent of the time. Similarly, if someone says that they are 60 per cent confident that their answer is correct then their answer should be correct 60 per cent of the time. Perfect calibration occurs then when there is a perfect relationship between the objective and subjective probabilities concerning the correctness of an answer (see Figure 13.2). Metacognition – our cognitions about our cognitive processes – come into play in this (Nelson, Gerler and Narens, 1984). For example, we may feel that a lower confidence estimate is appropriate where the questions are about a topic we know little about, or we may not feel confident because what we saw was over so quickly, or we may feel very confident because it was a bright summer day and everything was very clear. Luna and Martin-Luengo (2010) carried out a number of studies into recognition and recall of a criminal event. For example, in one study they asked 'witnesses' direct questions concerning events which happened in a video of a bank robbery. A typical question would be what the robber had in his hand while he was in the car. Participants had

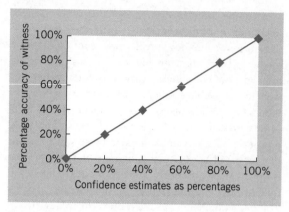

Figure 13.2 The perfect calibration between confidence and accuracy

to rate their confidence on a percentage scale with 0 per cent being the rating for a guess. Overall the findings suggested a good calibration between confidence and accuracy at the higher and lower levels – though it was not so good at the middle levels of accuracy. Witnesses appear to be over-confident in general. Calibration has one important advantage over correlation – if calibration is good then one can say things such as if the witness is 60 per cent confident then it is 60 per cent likely that the witness is correct. On the other hand, if we know that the correlation between confidence and accuracy is 0.2 then that does not directly communicate just how likely to be accurate a very confident person is, for example.

The 10–12 second rule

Another possible 'marker' or criterion for distinguishing between the good eyewitness testimony and the poor eyewitness testimony lies in the '10–12 second rule' (Dunning and Perretta, 2002). This is an idea derived from a great deal of evidence from experimental research on eyewitness psychology which has tended to find that eyewitnesses who identify someone from a line-up quickly tend to be more accurate than an eyewitness who takes rather more time. In other words, there is a negative relationship between response latency and identification accuracy. One possible explanation of this is that the eyewitness who correctly identifies the offender needs to match the characteristics of each member of the line-up against the characteristics of the offender held in memory. This takes time but is relatively speedy because the major characteristics can be identified quickly – where the offender is not in the line-up the process takes longer since each line-up member has to be checked against the remembered characteristics. Similarly, if the memory of the characteristics of the offender is weak, then it takes a longer time to check these weak memories against the actual characteristics of people in the line-up. However, eyewitnesses who correctly fail to find a target in an identification parade (line-up) do not do this quicker than those who incorrectly decide that their target is not in the line-up. This makes sense in terms of the matching process just described since in both cases all of the checking process has to be gone through.

BOX 13.3 Controversy

Critiques of expert evidence in court

Ebbesen and Konecni (1997, also Konecni, Ebbesen and Nehrer, 2000) wrote a fierce critique of eyewitness testimony research. Apart from its implications for forensic psychology, this critique contains food for thought for any psychologist working in any applied field of psychology. The critique makes the serious charge that psychologists acting as expert witnesses have systematically misled courts of law about the validity, consistency and generalisability of research findings on eyewitness testimony. This is primarily the result of researchers' over-confidence in their expertise. They argue that there is no generally accepted theory of eyewitness testimony. This is despite a number of sophisticated models of memory available to psychologists. So it is not valid for predictions to be made about the accuracy of eyewitnesses in particular cases in which eyewitness evidence may be vital.

Part of the difficulty is the vast difference between the circumstances of real eyewitness testimony and those of research studies – especially the psychology laboratory and other factors that limit their usefulness in court according to Ebbesen and Konecni (1997):

- Studies of eyewitness testimony show many inconsistencies in their outcomes.
- The vast majority of eyewitness testimony research involves the use of only college students (Yuille and Cutshall, 1986).
- The lengths of exposure to the criminal events vary substantially between real life and research. The median duration in real life lies somewhere between 5 and 10 minutes. Remarkably, in research studies the typical length of exposure to the criminal is 6 seconds, give or take a little. In other words, research studies involve exposure times of a fiftieth to a hundredth of exposure in real crimes (Moore, Ebbesen and Konecni, 1994).
- Researchers are not in a position to translate such key variables as length of exposure to the crime into the likelihood that the witness is wrong. Although it is correct to suggest in broad terms that greater exposure leads to greater accuracy, the precise risks of error cannot be calculated. So it is not possible to say that after two minutes of exposure the rates of being correct are 60 per cent or any other figure.
- Research generally shows that increasing exposure time is associated with increased accuracy in offender identification (Shapiro and Penrod, 1986). A precise mathematical function describing the relationship between these two factors is not known. Even if it were, things are not simple. Increasing exposure time for the witness to the crime is also associated with an increased risk of identifying the wrong person as the criminal (Ebbesen and Konecni, 1997).
- An analysis of transcripts of trials involving expert testimony on eyewitness accuracy shows overwhelmingly that these problems in interpreting the implications of longer exposure to the crime are not mentioned.

Ebbesen and Konecni (1997) argue:

Because the evidence is either inconsistent or insufficient in almost every area in which eyewitness experts testify and because there is no research that provides the experts, much less the jurors, with rules to use when translating the evidence to particular decisions in particular cases, we believe that eyewitness expert testimony is more prejudicial than probative and should not be allowed in courts. (p. 24)

Faigman (2008) argues that:

The task of applying general research findings to specific cases is, to be sure, a monumental intellectual challenge. Hard tasks are easy to ignore, but ignoring them does not make them go away. In a sense, then, this comment is a cry for attention, imploring psychological scientists to begin considering more carefully the inferential leap they make when they bring population level research to individual-based trial processes. (p. 313)

Of course, this is a problem which applies to most if not all psychological research findings. Trends are found in conglomerates of data and what may be true, in general, may not apply to specific instances. So although many psychologists may have the skill to comment effectively on the general case, where do their skills to comment on individual cases come from? Are psychologists taught this skill? So the issue is in two parts: (1) general application – does the scientific evidence support a particular perspective on an issue? and (2) specific application – does the psychological scientist have any basis for taking an established general finding and applying it in a particular case? Passive smoking is a useful analogy here – while the evidence may be that passive smoking increases the risk of lung cancer, the question remains whether it was passive smoking or some other factor which caused the lung cancer in a particular individual. So, in court, can a psychologist legitimately say that a woman's post-traumatic stress disorder was the result of a violent sexual assault or is it merely possible to say that her post-traumatic stress disorder was simply the consequence of some other severe stressor that has occurred in the woman's life? Faigman proposes two ways in which the psychologist may operate:

▶

BOX 13.3 (continued)

- *The limits model*: in this approach it is inappropriate for the researcher to testify on matters about which there is no empirical support. Furthermore, where there is support for a particular proposition, the researcher would need to provide evidence that in a particular case it is appropriate to generalise to a particular individual case.
- *The no-limits model*: this approach would allow the researcher to comment on the individual case even where there is a lack of data to establish that opinions about individual cases can be validly made.

The question is who should apply the general research findings to the specific case? Of course, in a court of law a psychologist may make an assessment based, say, on the research on eyewitness testimony that a particular eyewitness may not be reliable but the alternative is to leave this to the judge and jury – the triers of fact.

This is clearly an issue that all psychologists working as expert witnesses in courts of law should address. But according to Yuille, Ternes, and Cooper (2010) psychologists still fail to distinguish between laboratory witnesses and crime witnesses and ignore the problems of generalising from research on the former to research on the latter. They acknowledge the feeling among some psychologists that certain laboratory-based findings are robust enough to use in court but point out some very relevant areas of memory research where the opposite appears to be true. The Weapon Focus Effect has generally shown that laboratory witnesses are affected adversely by the presence of a weapon. They report fewer details of the events and are less able to identify the culprit (e.g., Davies, Smith and Blincoe, 2008; Pickel,

Narter, Jameson and Lenhardt, 2008). In comparison, the presence of weapons seems to have very different effects on witnesses to real crime (e.g., Behrman and Davey, 2001; Wagstaff *et al.*, 2003). Sometimes the detrimental effects found in laboratory studies are not found – sometimes more detail is recalled where weapons are present. The presence of a weapon risks distressing or traumatising real-life crime eyewitnesses whereas it is unlikely to do so in laboratory conditions. Consequently it may not be surprising that the effects of weapons found in laboratory studies are not the same as those found in real crime incidents. Also, in the typical laboratory experiment the presence of the weapon is actually drawn to the attention of laboratory witnesses – which may be the reason why they notice other things less. Yet, according to Yuille *et al.*, the findings obtained in laboratory studies have been discussed in court without reference to these problems.

Generally speaking, research shows that stress in laboratory memory experiments worsens the accuracy of witnesses in the laboratory (e.g., Bornstein, Liebel and Scarberry, 1998; Payne *et al.*, 2006). By way of contrast, crime witnesses demonstrate very mixed findings in terms of memory improvements and detriments (Yuille and Daylen, 1998). Nevertheless, despite the disparity, one expert witness said in court:

> it's my opinion, and I think it's shared by most, that when we are looking at the very high levels of stress, fear and arousal, witnesses are scared to death, in fear of their lives, that eyewitness memory for faces, facial identification accuracy is decreased.
>
> (*People v. Bacenet*, 2002 cited in
> Yuille *et al.*, 2010, p. 244)

Weber, Brewer and Wells (2004) studied the applicability of the 10–12 second rule using a number of data sets involving adults and children. A major finding is that the optimum delay differentiating accurate from inaccurate identifications was not constant and varied somewhat from the 10 seconds according to the age groups involved, for example. At best, they found a figure of 80 per cent accuracy using the optimally differentiating

time for any of their studies. They say that this makes the rule problematic for application in forensic settings. Indeed, they specifically suggest that the 10–12 second rule is an inadequate indicator of the accuracy of identification evidence (Weber, Brewer and Wells, 2004). Nevertheless, the evidence did support the idea that decision speed was a good indicator of witness accuracy. The problem is that quite what decision speed is indicative of is, as yet, not clearly identified with any particular aspects of research design. However, when a witness's confidence as well as their speed are both used in the assessment of accuracy, it became clear that accuracy of identification neared 90 per cent for the confident witness who answered within the optimum time limit for accuracy.

Improving the validity of the line-up

Practices concerning line-ups or identification parades vary from country to country. The United Kingdom is particularly advanced in its thinking on identification evidence largely because of a record of wrongful convictions on the basis of identification evidence. In the 1970s, critical reviews of identification evidence were published, including the influential *Devlin Report*. Other countries do not have quite the same procedural protection for suspects as the United Kingdom. Penrod (2003) argued on the basis of data from US line-ups that even in cases where the guilty party is identified by the witness, perhaps as many of 20 per cent of these are lucky guesses and not actual identifications as such. Furthermore, he estimates that as many as 50 per cent of witnesses who made a choice were guessing.

There are a number of problems with line-ups, some of which are more intractable than others (Busey and Loftus, 2007). These include the following:

- *Inadequately matched fillers*: in this, the foils or fillers do not match the descriptions of the offender provided by eyewitnesses. Busey and Loftus suggest that having poorly matching fillers effectively reduces the functional size of the line-up. That is, one should subtract the number of foils who do not match satisfactorily with the witnesses' descriptions from the total of foils to yield the number of effective foils.

- *Physical or bias (oddball)*: the suspect's picture in a photo line-up may be noticeably physically different from the others (e.g. it may be larger or the background may be different). The witness infers that the odd picture must be the suspect. It has been suggested that facial expression may have a similar sort of influence.

- *No double blind procedure*: this is the idea that the officer conducting the identity parade should not know which member is the suspect. Busey and Loftus describe a situation which one of them was present

at a two-witness line-up in which the first witness was concentrating on one of the filler photographs in a photo line-up. The officer was aware of whom the suspect was and asked the witness if there was anyone else in the line-up that it could be. That is, the officer essentially indicated that the witness had chosen the wrong person. The second witness was concentrating on the actual suspect whereupon the officer told that witness to sign across this photo (which is the way of indicating that this is the person that has been identified).

- *Unconscious transference*: this occurs when the witness has seen the suspect before but not at the crime scene, though the witness does not realise this. For example, they might both live in the same neighbourhood. Thus the witness has seen the person before but *not* at the crime scene.

Consequently, it is important to note that there have been attempts to lay down working procedures that would help reduce the problems associated with identification evidence. Wells *et al.* (1998) proposed four general principles given below, to protect the suspect. They are intended to guide the procedures used in line-ups/identification parades as well as photospreads. All of these seek to identify the offender. An analogy is drawn between a good line-up and a good psychological experiment:

- A properly designed experiment should be a fair test of the research hypothesis.

- A good experiment should be, as far as possible, free from biases.

Wells *et al.* suggest that two broad issues need to be taken into account:

- Structural properties, e.g. the appearance of the line-up in terms of how similar to and different from each other its members are.

- Procedural properties, e.g. the instructions given to the witnesses, the numbers in the line-up and so forth.

Consider some of the ideal characteristics of a study of human memory. The participants in the research listen to a list of words. They are then shown a sequence of words that may or may not have been in the original list. If the researcher testing their memory knows which words are in the original list then he or she may subtly and non-consciously give clues as to what these words were. For example, the researcher might pause fractionally longer over the critical words. There are indications that researchers are able inadvertently to bias an experimental outcome such that it favours the favoured hypothesis (Jung, 1971; Rosenthal, 1966). One way of reducing this influence is to keep the actual researcher in the dark about the hypothesis or leave them blind as to other aspects of the procedure (such as the list of words to be remembered). The rule for line-ups and photospreads is:

> Rule 1: The person who conducts the line-up or photospread should not be aware of which member of the line-up or photospread is the suspect.
>
> (p. 17)

Even where the experimenter does not have knowledge about the list of words to be remembered, the participants may think that they do. Thus participants might inadvertently and wrongly read into the experimenter's behaviour what they believe to be cues about the correct words. For example, the experimenter might find certain words amusing and respond differently to these. Explaining to participants that the experimenter is unaware of what words are correct may reduce the effect.

> Rule 2: The eyewitness should be told explicitly that the person administering the line-up does not know which person is the suspect in the case.
>
> (p. 19)

The participant in the memory research might be inclined to pick out certain words simply because they are more interesting, more dramatic or in some way different. They may be inclined to pick these words as the correct ones as a consequence:

> Rule 3: The suspect should not stand out in the line-up or photospread as being different from the distracters based on the eyewitness's previous description of the culprit or based on other factors that would draw extra attention to the suspect.
>
> (p. 19)

In the light of what we know about eyewitness confidence (see above), the recommendations also include the following:

> Rule 4: A clear statement should be taken from the eyewitness at the time of the identification and prior to any feedback as to his or her confidence that the identified person is the actual culprit.
>
> (p. 23)

Kassin (1998) feels that there is an omission from these recommendations. He recommends that the identification parade/line-up and witness identification should be videotaped. This is because records of the line-up are often not carefully kept such that the police and eyewitnesses differ markedly in terms of their recollections of events at the line-up. He points out that police procedures in relation to evidence of various sorts have been subject to a variety of criticisms. For example, in the United Kingdom, the Police and Criminal Evidence Act of 1984 requires that all custodial interviews with crime suspects are taped. This, of course, is primarily to protect individuals against police malpractice.

Relative judgement theory answers the question of how eyewitnesses choose the culprit from a line-up/identity parade. In the absence of the culprit, the theory suggests that the line-up members most similar to the culprit will be picked out. In other words, the eyewitness acts as if the culprit is present and forms a judgement on the best of what they recall of the culprit. No mechanism exists for deciding that the offender is not in the line-up (Wells, 1984). If participants were responding using absolute judgements, then each line-up member would be compared with the memory of the culprit. Then unless the line-up member meets the criteria they will be rejected. Evidence demonstrating the validity of relative judgement theory comes from studies such as that of Wells (1993). In this, some witnesses were shown the line-up including the culprit and others were shown exactly the same line-up with the culprit absent. Despite being told that the culprit may not be present, 54 per cent of those who identified the culprit when the culprit was present would have identified someone else in the culprit's absence! When the offender was present, 21 per cent failed to make a choice but this increased to only 32 per cent when the culprit was actually absent. In other words, mostly when the offender is absent other, innocent, line-up members are chosen.

Obviously a major factor in this is that explicit warnings that the culprit may not necessarily be present substantially reduce wrongful identifications (Malpass and Devine, 1981). They do not affect rightful identifications when the culprit is present.

A number of studies have shown some of the factors that affect relative judgements in real cases. For example, Doob and Kirkenbaum (1973) reported on a Canadian robbery at a department store. The accused was said to be one of two men who had committed the crime. The cashier who witnessed the events recalled that the offenders were neatly dressed, good looking and could be brothers. Despite this somewhat sketchy recollection, she picked out the accused from a line-up. One of Doob and Kirkenbaum's studies had 20 women pick 'a rather good looking man' out of 12 parade participants from the original line-up. The women chose the accused extremely frequently despite not having witnessed the crime. This would appear to be evidence of the unfairness of the system employed.

Similarly, in Poland, Wojcikiewicz et al. (2000) were involved in a pertinent court case. The suspect was actually a man of 29 years of age. They were asked by the defence to assess how likely it was that a particular man, from the viewpoint of a 12-year-old rape victim, could be described as being a 40–50-year-old man with a rat-like face. Adult participants in the research did see him as the 29-year-old that he was. About a fifth of the children saw the accused as being in the 40–45-year-old age group. Adults described him as having a rat-like face although children did not have a significant tendency to do so. In view of this evidence, it remained possible that the accused was indeed the perpetrator. Nevertheless, the research evidence is indicative of a possible problem and was used in court by the defence.

One way of assessing the likelihood that a person will be susceptible to relative similarity effects when choosing is their performance in the *dual line-up*. This involves an initial (or blank) line-up containing only people known to be innocent followed by a second line-up containing the suspect. Wells (1984) showed that:

- if a witness resists choosing from the blank line-up, it is more likely that they choose accurately in a proper line-up later;
- witnesses who did not go through the blank line-up first were more likely to make mistakes in the second line-up.

Sequential procedures (though this is a somewhat controversial matter) are claimed to work better than conventional line-ups. In these, the group of people selected to be in the line-up is shown in sequential fashion – one individual at a time. This makes it much more difficult simply to use a process of elimination in choosing the guilty party (it cannot be a, b or d so it must be c). It is less likely that relative similarity will operate in the sequential line-up (Dunning and Stern, 1994). Another identification method, very common in parts of the United States, is the show-up. This is a single individual who the eyewitness has to identify as the culprit or not. In one sense,

this should be more effective than a line-up since relative judgement cannot apply when there is just person to decide about. On the other hand, the fact that the police have picked out this individual for the show-up may be strongly suggestive that he or she is the prime suspect.

Steblay et al. (2003) carried out a meta-analysis (Box 4.2) of studies which compared the single-person line-up (the show-up) with six-person line-ups (these included both sequential and simultaneous versions). Furthermore, both single-person show-ups and six-person line-ups included conditions in which the target suspect was present in the majority of the studies. Interestingly, the line-up was much more likely to result in a choice by the eyewitness than the show-up. If the target were present, on average 71 per cent out of 10 line-ups resulted in a choice whereas the figure was only 46 per cent for the show-up. Where the target was absent, 43 per cent of line-ups resulted in a choice as opposed to 15 per cent of show-ups. Correct identification where the target was actually present did not differ between line-ups and show-ups. Around 46 per cent correctly identified the suspect when the suspect was present in either type of identification procedure. Furthermore, when the target is absent, the false identification rate is approximately the same at about 16 per cent for both show-ups and line-ups. What is happening when the eyewitness makes a wrong identification in a target absent line-up? Simply the errors are spread across all of the foils. This results in a situation in which if one classified all of these latter errors into a non-identification category with other non-identification outcomes, then line-ups show no difference from show-ups in terms of outcomes. It is important to note that those studies in which the foil is more similar to the target resulted in a worse performance in show-ups than in line-ups. False identification of an innocent foil is more common in show-ups than in line-ups.

The procedures actually employed by police officers when they plan identification line-ups have been investigated by Wogalter, Malpass and McQuiston (2004). Over 200 police jurisdictions in the United States were surveyed about their practices. There were examples of good and bad practice as verified by laboratory studies. Some of the common good practices included:

- Officers tended to choose line-up foils on the basis of upper facial features such as race/ethnic group, facial hair characteristics, colour of hair and overall shape of face. Whatever the reason why the officers chose to do this, it is important to note that there is a substantial amount of research evidence which suggests that people recall such upper facial features more readily than lower facial features (e.g. shape of the chin).

- Substantial numbers of officers report that they gave witnesses the option of not choosing anyone from the identification line-up which is known to reduce errors as we saw above. Very few warned eyewitnesses that facial features may change or that photographs may be of poor or insufficient quality. These factors may affect eyewitness accuracy according to research.

Examples of bad practice included the following:

- Most respondents (83 per cent) claimed to base their choice of foils in the line-up on their similarity to the suspect. In contrast, only a small number (9 per cent) based their choices of foil on the verbal descriptions provided by eyewitnesses. Research evidence has suggested that there may be problems with the use of similarity to the suspect as a criterion for choosing foils. This may seem to be a strange assertion given that it would seem common sense to use identification line-ups of similar-looking people. The problem is not in the theory but the practice. What actually happens is that the foils are chosen because of their similarity to the suspect rather than to each other. As a consequence, the suspect stands out because they have characteristics in common with many of the foils but the foils do not look too much like each other. In other words, there is a powerful clue in the situation which encourages the selection of the suspect.

- Generally, assessments about the fairness of the procedures being used by an officer are made by that officer (94 per cent). They also might ask the advice of another officer (77 per cent) or a prosecution lawyer (51 per cent). These are not completely independent judgements as they are all on the side of prosecuting the suspect. Asking the advice of the defence lawyer was fairly uncommon (only 15 per cent) although this sort of advice might be regarded as a much more acid test of fairness.

- The use of video line-ups that do not require the direct recruitment of foils was relatively uncommon. But this is the sort of line-up that enables things like the editing out of any biasing behaviours on the part of members of the line-up.

One view of the field based on the research literature is to be found in Brewer and Palmer's (2010) guidelines for line-ups/identity parades. This is summarised in Figure 13.3. They do not offer their guidelines as a cure-all for the mistakes that witnesses make when providing identification evidence. Nothing can entirely prevent such errors. Nevertheless, it is possible to do something about arrangements which are more likely to lead to errors and the way in which courts respond to eyewitnesses claims about the accuracy of their evidence.

Increasingly video-based systems are being used by police forces. Setting up a line-up or identity parade is a time-consuming matter. Pike, Brace and Kynan (2002) carried out a major survey of identification parades in the United Kingdom using several different police forces. They found that the typical delay (median) between a parade being requested and its being run was about 10 weeks. Over half of the parades were cancelled before they had even begun. There are many reasons for this. The commonest reason was the absence or late arrival of the suspect (51 per cent) followed by the witness not showing up or refusing to take part (21 per cent) and the problems associated with getting suitable foils or sufficient numbers for the parade (7 per cent). Video-based alternatives such as the VIPER system used increasingly in the United Kingdom have enormous advantages, especially the fact that they are 10 times *less* likely to be cancelled than a normal (live) line-up. In the VIPER system, a short video film of the suspect is shot. The VIPER database contains many thousands of video clips of volunteers which can be used to find suitable foils or fillers (non-suspect members of the line-up) which are similar to the suspect in important respects. What happens is that the video clip of the suspect plus about 10 clips selected from the database are sent by computer to a national centre which edits the clips into an electronic identity parade and returns the images to the police officers who can then run the identity parade with the witness. This is a very speedy process. Furthermore, the costs are a fifth or less of the regular live line-up.

A further advantage of the VIPER system is that it may result in less stress for participants compared with the traditional line-up/identification parade. Brace, Pike, Kemp and Turner (2009) carried out a study using student participants in which a live incident was staged involving two men fighting over a bag. There was some degree of pushing and shouting involved but no further violence. The identification stage was a month later. A regular line-up/identification parade was completed and then a video identification parade based on the VIPER system. In half of each of the two identification procedures the target suspect was included and in the other half the target suspect was

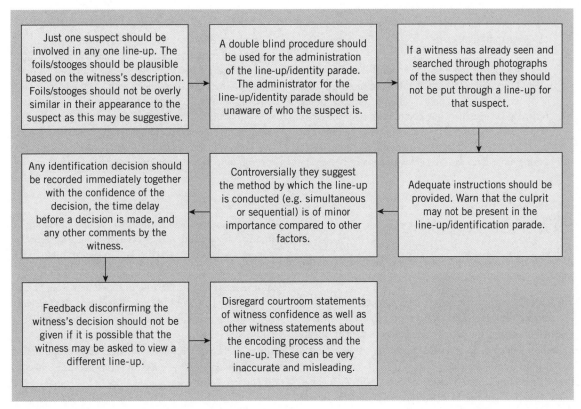

Figure 13.3 How to plan a satisfactory line-up according to the suggestions of Brewer and Palmer (2010)

not included. Police officers of inspector rank conducted all of the identification procedures using standard police procedures. The VIPER-style procedures involve more of the witnesses' time than the line-up/identification parade which only involves a witness walking up and down the line. The findings were that the participants believed that the line-up/identification parade was rather more stressful a procedure than the VIPER video method.

Main points

- Eyewitness testimony is a proven source of wrongful convictions in jurisdictions in which conviction is possible on the basis of such eyewitness evidence alone. Police officers place a great deal of reliance on it. It should not be assumed that eyewitness evidence is without worth. Research has shown that for some types of physical features, eyewitness descriptions can be quite accurate. However, little credence has until recently been placed on the idea that confident eyewitnesses are also accurate eyewitnesses.

- Memory can be influenced by a range of factors and there is evidence to show that memory can be affected by later events and questioning style. Much of the pertinent research tends to come from laboratory studies, which can be problematic to apply to real-life situations with precision. For example, it is difficult to generalise the effects of time of exposure to the witnessed event from the laboratory to real-life settings for very mundane reasons such as that exposure times in laboratory studies are a

▶

fraction of the time that a real-life eyewitness observes the offender for.

- The planning of the line-up or identification parade should proceed with care as there are many pitfalls. There is evidence that police line-ups may sometimes reflect good practice but sometimes bad practices prevail – for example, it is much more common to choose the foils (stooges) in a line-up on the basis of their similarity to the suspect whereas good practice holds that they should be like the eyewitness's description of the offender. In line-ups, eyewitnesses tend to identify someone who is like their memory of the offender even when the offender is not present in the line-up. This is in accordance with the theory of relative judgement. Factors that may improve eyewitness performance in line-ups include informing the eyewitness that the person administering the line-up does not know who the suspect is and making sure that that person indeed does not know who the suspect is.

Further reading

Although there are many books on this topic from earlier times, the following are worthwhile recent sources:

The following publication by the British Psychological Society is a quick to read, thorough and comprehensive account of research on memory especially in relation to the law. It can be recommended as an accessible summary of the relevant conclusions from research:

British Psychological Society Research Board (2010) 'Guidelines on Memory and the Law: Recommendations from the Scientific Study of Human Memory' *British Psychological Society*. http://www.bps.org.uk/document-download-area/document-download$.cfm?file_uuid=FE115F56-F2E3-4B36-C9A3-D577D9000015&ext=pdf

Castelli, P., Goodman, G.S., Edeltein, R.S., Mitchell, E.B., Alonso, P.M.P., Lyons, K.E. and Newton, J.S. (2006) 'Evaluating eyewitness testimony in adults and children' in I.B. Weiner and A.K. Hess (eds) *The Handbook of Forensic Psychology* (3rd edn) Hoboken, NJ: John Wiley, pp. 243–304.

Heaton-Armstrong, A., Shepherd, E., Gudjonsson, G. and Wolchover, D. (2006) *Witness Testimony: Psychological, Investigative and Evidential Perspectives* Oxford: Oxford University Press.

Yarmey, A.D. (2003) 'Eyewitnesses' in D. Carson and R. Bull (eds) *Handbook of Psychology in Legal Contexts* (2nd edn) Chichester: John Wiley, pp. 533–58.

Elizabeth Loftus, Gary Wells, and the Eyewitness Identification Research Laboratory separately, have websites with some downloadable materials: http://faculty.washington.edu/eloftus/, http://www.psychology.iastate.edu/faculty/gwells/homepage.htm, http://eyewitness.utep.edu/

Visit our website at www.pearsoned.co.uk/howitt for self-test and essay questions, annotated further reading, audio interviews with researchers in the field, weblinks and more information on becoming a forensic psychologist.

Profile analysis 1: FBI-style offender profiling

Chapter 14

Overview

- There are two main styles of offender profiling – FBI-style profiling which is described in this chapter and the more actuarial or statistical style associated with the British psychologist David Canter which is described in Chapter 15.

- Offender profiling dates back to the nineteenth-century case of Jack the Ripper although its modern origins are in the work of the Behavioral Science Unit of the FBI located in Virginia in the 1970s. This form of profiling is based on clinical intuition whereas more recent approaches have been more research-based and statistical in nature.

- Offending profiling of all sorts is based on the work of the police in gathering information especially from the scene of the crime. Most homicides are seen by police officers as 'self-solvers' in that the witness evidence points to the culprit or the culprit reports their crime to the police, for example. Obviously, offender profiling would only help where the police have problems identifying suspects and organising the information collected.

- FBI-style offender profiling is based on information recorded by the police. This is used to classify the crime scene into organised (where there is evidence that the crime has been carefully planned) or disorganised (where the crime scene looks chaotic and there is little sign of preparation for the crime). It is held that organised and disorganised crime scenes indicate some broad characteristics of the offender. An organised crime scene suggests, for example, a sexually competent, charming person who lives with a partner. The disorganised crime scene is indicative of an offender with low intelligence, unskilled occupation and who lives alone.

Introduction

Offender profiling uses information gleaned from the crime scene in order to identify the characteristics of the offender. Sometimes it is referred to as criminal investigative analysis. Controversy surrounds offender profiling for several reasons:

- Its nature – is it and should it be an art or science?
- The paucity of evidence that profiling is effective.
- The role of profiling in police work.
- Its high profile in the public imagination through media attention.

Box 14.1 Key concept

Defining terms

Profile analysis: 'Behaviour is exhibited at a crime, or a series of similar crimes, and studying this behaviour allows inferences to be made about the likely offender' (Jackson and Bekerian, 1997, p. 2). Jackson and Bekerian suggest that profile analysis includes offender profiling, psychological profiling, criminal profiling and criminal personality profiling.

According to Homant and Kennedy (1998), the following three types of profiling should be carefully distinguished among others:

- *Crime scene profiling*: uses information from the scene of the crime (physical and other evidence) to generate a full picture of the unknown offender.
- *Offender profiling*: the collection of empirical data in order to collate a picture of the characteristics of those involved in a certain type of crime.
- *Psychological profiling*: the use of standard personality tests together with interviewing in order to assess the extent to which the individual fits the known personality template of a certain type of offender such as child sex abusers.

Terminology is not always rigorously applied in this field and other terms are used to refer to much the same type. For example:

- Specific profile analysis: '. . . constructing a hypothetical picture of a perpetrator of a crime on the basis of data from the scene of the crime, witness statements and other available information' (Davies, 1997, p. 191).

In profiling work there is a marked disparity of opinion between two extremes. One extreme holds profiling is akin to clinical judgement – informed by research but inevitably a subjective matter dependent on the insight and skill of the profiler. The other extreme regards that profiling must be led by research and aspire to objectivity. The former best reflects the FBI approach which is featured in this chapter and the latter is David Canter's approach which is dealt with in Chapter 15.

Crime fiction is littered with numerous insightful, subjective profilers who make amazing interpretations of evidence. Remarkable deductions lead inexorably to the culprit. Fictional detectives have incredible insight into the psychological motives behind crime. It might be mentioned that the great fictional detective Sherlock

Holmes was inclined to make statements redolent of the ideas of offender profiles. A good example is that a criminal returns to the scene of the crime – which is echoed in the writings of modern profilers (Canter, 2004). Modern movies and television are replete with psychological detectives adroit in the psychology of the criminal mind. Much of this media coverage has produced somewhat hostile responses from psychologists concerned about what they see to be extremely weak psychology (e.g. Williams, 1994).

According to Canter (2004), offender profiling probably has its origins in 1888 when the medical doctor Dr Thomas Bond provided what might be regarded as a profile of Jack the Ripper. Bond was of the opinion that:

[t]he murderer must have been a man of physical strength and great coolness and daring. There is no evidence he had an accomplice. He must in my opinion be a man subject to periodic attacks of homicidal and erotic mania . . . The murderer in external appearance is quite likely to be a quiet inoffensively looking man probably middle-aged and neatly and respectably dressed. Assuming the murderer be such a person as I have just described, he would be solitary and eccentric in his habits, also he is likely to be a man without regular occupation, but with some small income or pension.

(cited in Canter, 2004, p. 2)

Canter suggests that the profile of The Ripper provided by Dr Bond is remarkably similar to profiles of sexual murderers in recent times.

The modern origins of offender profiling in psychology are usually traced back to 1956 and the work of the psychiatrist James A. Brussel on the New York Bomber crimes of that time. Brussel, basing his theorising on psychoanalysis, studied the crime scene. Based on his assessment of this, Brussel gave a description of the bomber containing the following features:

- heavy;
- middle-aged;
- male;
- single;
- living with a sibling.

This is held by some to be a convincingly accurate picture of George Metesky who was eventually convicted of the crime. He was actually living with two siblings but this is held to be of little consequence. Brussel, at first sight, had demonstrated the power of psychological approaches to detective work. Accounts vary but the general consensus is that Brussel's profile was not responsible for Metesky's arrest. Nevertheless, the case demonstrates another feature of offender profiling – the seemingly mysterious nature of the profile. Just how can this information be gleaned simply on the basis of the characteristics of the crime scene?

The more direct origins of offender profiling lie in seminal work at the US Federal Bureau of Investigation's Training and Development Division at Quantico, Virginia. This housed, in a nuclear bunker, the Behavioral Science Unit that, to this day, provides research, consultation and training in the application of psychology and the other social sciences to crime and detective work. During the 1970s, the unit began to research the personality, behaviours, crimes and motivations of serial killers showing sexual aspects in their crimes. This formed much of the research base for their method of profiling (Douglas *et al.*, 1992). The term 'serial killer' is held to be an innovation of members of the Unit. It should be stressed that there may well be serial killers who do not show sexual elements in their crimes. For example, a bank robber may kill on several different raids yet it would be difficult to identify this as being in any way sexually motivated. The FBI investigators defined serial homicide as 'three or more separate events in three or more separate locations with an emotional cooling off period in between homicides' (Douglas *et al.*, 1992, p. 21). Ferguson *et al.* (2003) argue that there is a lack of an agreed definition of serial murder that makes progress in the field difficult. He rejects the idea put forward by Douglas *et al.* (1992) that serial killers seek to express their need for power since it could be argued that every crime is an expression of power. Instead, Ferguson *et al.* (2003, p. 4) suggest the following three elements are crucial to the definition of serial (sexual) murder:

- Three or more victims killed during multiple and discrete events.
- Causing death to the victim, at the time of the killing, was considered to be pleasurable, stress relieving or otherwise consistent with the perpetrator's internal set of values. The attacks themselves did not fulfil only functional purposes.
- The murders did not occur under the direction or blessing of any political or criminal organisation.

Notice that this definition does not necessarily define the crime as sexual. However, it is questionable whether it achieves a great deal other than excluding the serial killings that occur for reasons of gain, for example.

In strict social-scientific terms, the methodology employed by the FBI team while developing ideas about serial killing was not the most rigorous. Indeed, one of the most remarkable things is the extent to which so much developed out of a study of just 36 offenders. However, the methodology not only involved the collation of research findings but also drew on the Unit's collective experience in developing offender profiling.

This form of profiling is still practised today – crime scene profiling. Several popular accounts of the work of ex-FBI profilers have been published (e.g. Douglas and Olshaker, 1995, 1997; Ressler and Shachtman, 1997). The

FBI style of profiling is presented more as a 'special art' (Canter, 2004) rather than a scientific endeavour. FBI profiling's main features are as follows:

- A willingness to encompass experience and intuition as a component of profiling.

- A relatively weak empirical database which is small in comparison to the extent to which the method is used.

- A concentration on the more serious, bizarre and extreme crimes such as serial sexual murder.

- It tends to involve an extensive contact with the investigating team of police officers at all levels of the investigation rather than simply providing a profile. For example, the profiler may make recommendations on how to respond to letters and similar communications from what appears to be the offender.

Figure 14.1 is a schematic diagram of some of the similarities and differences between FBI-style clinical profiling and statistical profiling. Some profilers would dispute certain points. What sorts of crime should be profiled? This may be decided on a number of bases:

- There is little point in profiling trivial crimes since by their nature they are unlikely to be actively investigated. Similarly, there is little point in profiling a crime that shows few distinguishing characteristics at the crime scene.

- Are the investigating officers unaware of a likely offender? Frequently, offenders are friends or family members of the victim. Thus there is an obvious pool of possible suspects without even considering strangers.

- Profile analysis is especially appropriate if the crime scene indicates pathological psychological features. For instance, objects may be found inserted in the victim's genitals or even body parts taken as 'trophies'.

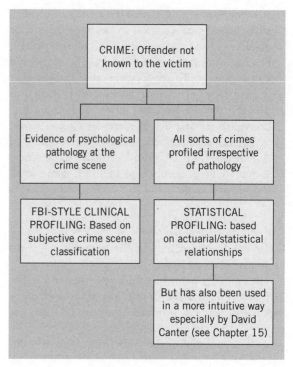

Figure 14.1 Features of FBI-style clinical profiling and statistical profiling

Nevertheless, some psychologists consider that crimes lacking such bizarre features may also be suitable for profiling. Increasingly, profiling is carried out for crimes that traditionally would not be regarded as particularly suitable for profiling (e.g. fraud).

As will be seen in Chapter 15, profiling has been extended to a much wider variety of types of crime than the FBI profilers ever considered. Nevertheless, in terms of the practical application of profiling to policing work, the above provisos would seem to apply.

Box 14.2 Key concept

Crime signature and *modus operandi*

Two concepts which have a bearing on offender profiling need to be distinguished: (a) modus operandi (MO) and (b) crime signature:

- *Modus operandi* simply refers to the particular way by which a person performs a particular task although it is commonly specifically applied to the way in which an offender commits a particular crime. According to Keppel *et al.* (2005, p. 14) a *modus operandi* refers to 'the offender's actions during the commission of a crime that are necessary to complete the crime'. (The plural of *modus operandi* is *modi operandi*.) *Modi operandi* are not necessarily fixed and offenders may well change their *modus operandi* in the light of their experiences while committing a crime or on the basis of what they learnt from previous crimes.

- A criminal *signature*, in offender profiling, actually uses an archaic meaning of the term signature which is 'a distinctive action, characteristic, etc.' (*The Concise English Dictionary*, 1990, Clarendon Press, Oxford p. 1129). A crime's signature characteristics reflect things which happen during the commission of a crime but which are more or less idiosyncratic to or characteristic of the offender. The criminal signature is believed to reflect aspects of a particular offender's nature. Unlike the *modus operandi*, a criminal signature is believed to be a relatively fixed and unchanging thing at its core. However, it may evolve in certain respects during a sequence of crimes.

Of course, this distinction is not absolute in practice but it is helpful in the sense that signature characteristics are more likely to be associated with a particular offender than is their *modus operandi*. According to Keppel *et al.* (p. 14), signature analysis is widely used in the United States and it is also the only crime scene assessment technique that courts in the United States accept as part of testimony and may be used in appeals.

It is helpful to consider the 11 Jack the Ripper killings which occurred in Whitechapel, London, between 1888 and 1891, since they illustrate the difference between the concepts of *modus operandi* and crime signatures. There has been controversy as to just how many killers were involved in the Jack the Ripper murders. Nevertheless, there is some consensus that five of the murders were committed by the same killer. However, Keppel *et al.* suggest that six crimes were committed by the same offender on the basis of their signature analysis of various Scotland Yard case files.

The earliest of the cases attributed to this killer is that of Martha Tabram. She was found face-up with clothing disarranged in a way which exposed the lower part of her body and genitals as the killer left her with her legs wide open. The evidence clearly established that she had been killed at a spot on a landing at the Working Lads' Institute in Whitechapel. There was no indication at all that the body had been dragged from one location to another. Her body was found at around 4.45 a.m. – probably three hours after the time of death. Martha was a heavy-drinking, known prostitute of about 36 years of age. She had about 39 stab wounds especially to the left-hand side of her body. There were 17 stabs to her breasts and 13 in her lower body. There were wounds to her neck, liver, spleen and stomach as well as her genitals. All of the wounds were inflicted before she died from a stab to her heart.

The last of the series of murders believed to have been committed by the one killer was that of Mary Jane Kelly. She was found in a room of a house in Spitalfields, London. Again she was a known prostitute and heavy consumer of alcohol. Her body was found on its back on a bed. There were considerable levels of mutilation: her nose and ears were severed and the flesh had been removed from the body to leave it in a skeletal state. Her heart and other organs were missing, though some body parts had been left on a table nearby. She had been disembowelled and her viscera placed around the body. Her uterus and one breast were placed under her head. Her neck was severed down to the bone and her right thigh was revealed down to the bone. Mary Jane's vulva and right buttock had been removed. It was concluded that some of the mutilation had occurred after the death of the victim.

Of course, to appreciate the murder series in full, each should be carefully considered in its entirety. The *modi operandi* of the six murders in question, while not identical, were highly similar in certain ways. Each victim was a poor woman prostitute almost invariably in the 24–45 year range. Once they lifted their clothing to have sex with the killer they were strangled and lowered to the ground. Usually their heads were facing to the left of the killer. The attacks took place during the night after midnight and before 6 a.m. The geographical locations of the murders were within a one square mile (2.6 km^2) area and it was no more than a mile (1.6 km) from each successive murder to the next. The victims were found where they were killed, which was by a sharp, long-bladed knife after they had been strangled near to death. The first victim (Martha Tabram) was stabbed from the front, which meant that the killer was covered in a great deal of blood, putting him at risk of detection.

▶

Box 14.2 (continued)

Consequently, his *modus operandi* changed to attacking his victims from behind, which meant that less blood was transferred to his body.

Interestingly, there was a change in the location of the killings. The early killings took place outdoors and the killer had been interrupted by the arrival of others at the location. The later killing of Mary Jane Kelly took place indoors as she lay on a bed. This change in the *modus operandi* meant that the killer was less likely to be disturbed but it also enabled him to extend the process of mutilation, as revealed by the extensive cutting up of her body.

According to Keppel *et al.*, the signature for the six linked Jack the Ripper killings includes the following:

- *Picquerism*: this describes the sexual pleasure that some obtain from cutting or stabbing others or observing such acts. It should be stressed that there was no evidence at all of physical sexual activity on the part of the killer in any of these crimes.
- *The killer needed submission of the victim*: all of the victims suffered multiple stab wounds, slashing of the throat, etc. which would incapacitate and subdue them.
- *Overkill to have complete domination of the victim*: the violent acts of this particular Ripper were far in excess of what was needed to kill or subdue the victim.
- *Degradation of the victim*: this was exemplified by the killer's leaving of the bodies in very public places which might suggest that he felt invincible and beyond the authority of the police.
- *Posing of victims' bodies*: except in circumstances in which he was disturbed in the course of his crime, the killer posed the bodies of his victims in a characteristic and sexually revealing manner.
- *Escalation of violence*: the violence became more extreme as the series of killings progressed.
- *Planning*: the killer left no evidence at the crime scene other than the remains of the victim and took his weapon to the crime and carefully removed it.

Finally, a signature is helpful only if it reveals very idiosyncratic behaviours. Keppel *et al.* compared this signature with a database of homicides. It is important to note that, for example, only 0.03 per cent of the murders on this database involved mutilated prostitutes, and there were no cases of prostitutes who had been mutilated and their bodies left in unusual poses. In other words, the Ripper signature for these cases is very unusual.

The process of police investigation

Profiling is seen as an adjunct to the police investigation process. Innes (2002) carried out a qualitative study of how the police in an English police force investigated homicides. The national clear-up rate for homicide is very high with approximately 90 per cent of cases being 'solved'. This is less than surprising since most homicides are committed by associates of the victim. Nevertheless, there may be problems in solving some crimes that often lie in the complex set of events involving a number of people which culminates in the murder. This can make it difficult to know precisely who did what and the reasons for this. The police make an informal distinction between cases which are 'self-solvers' and those that might be termed 'whodunnits'. Different processes of investigation would be involved in the case of the self-solvers from that of the 'whodunnit'. Something like 70 per cent of cases of homicide could be classified as self-solvers. A suspect emerges very early because there are witnesses, or the offender goes to the police, or the physical forensic evidence points to a particular individual. However, these are not always easy cases – they can be highly emotive – and deconstructing the events to provide a 'coherent, explanatory account' (p. 672) taxing. Often self-solving cases are investigated using a three-stage approach:

- The collection and analysis of information from the crime scene.
- Pursuing lines of enquiry relevant to the suspect, such as a formal interview with the suspect, tracing and interviewing witnesses who may have seen the suspect

with the victim earlier, inquiries from neighbours, and inquiries into the family background.

- Case construction: selecting and organising the material into an account of the events which is appropriate to the needs of the legal system and presented in appropriate legal language. For example, it can be important to carefully define the events as murder or manslaughter in the UK.

The 'whodunnit' investigation is somewhat more complex and involves five stages:

- *The initial response*: the primary task is to deal with the evidence available at the crime scene. Witnesses are interviewed and the area of the crime scene subjected to a systematic search for forensic evidence.
- *Information burst*: the police quickly generate substantial amounts of information. There may be a variety of sources, including interviews with the immediate relatives of the victim and ex-partners, business associates and local house-to-house inquiries. Other sources include criminal intelligence resources to identify the victim's criminal connections. A number of suspects might be arrested and released without charge on the basis of having committed similar crimes in the past.
- *Suspect development*: the police proceed to elicit more detail about possible suspects. Some suspects may be dropped at this stage and others may come under suspicion as the evidence becomes clearer. A prime suspect is being sought even on the basis of hunches.
- *Suspect targeting*: once other suspects have been eliminated or a prime suspect has been identified, the

police will change their approach and start targeting this particular individual in terms of their information gathering.

- *Case construction*: this is the stage at which the police attempt to formulate an account of the events of the homicide in a way that is in keeping with legal considerations.

The FBI profiling process

There are several stages in a Federal Bureau of Investigation profile.

Stage 1: Data assimilation stage

The earliest stage of FBI profiling involves the collection of a variety of information as seen in Figure 14.2. A crime usually has a variety of associated documentary materials: for example, the pathologist's report about the medical circumstances that led to death, photographs taken at the crime scene, witness statements and police reports and so forth. This information may not appear at first sight to be of any value at all. Nevertheless, there is always the potential for unpromising materials to be crucial in terms of the ultimate profile. The time of death, for example, may have an important implication for the psychology of the offender. Basically, the process is one of seeking to identify the psychological signature

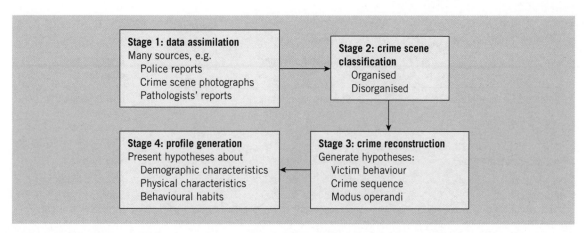

Figure 14.2 Major stages of FBI crime scene profiling

of the offender. This psychological signature is different from the *modus operandi* (see Box 14.2) – the latter broadly refers to the style of committing the crime. It is the characteristic way in which that particular criminal works. The psychological signature concerns what can be gleaned from the crime scene about the personality of the offender. This is most likely to include the fantasies of the offender.

Stage 2: Crime scene classification

Remember that serial sexual murders are the most important crimes profiled by the FBI psychologists. Profilers developed a dichotomy to describe two characteristic crime scenes – the *organised* and the *disorganised* crime scenes.

- Organised = evidence of planning.
- Disorganised = chaotic.

The organised/disorganised crime scene classification was based on offenders' reports of their crimes in the early study by profilers (Douglas *et al.*, 1992). Early research indicated that crime scenes could be reliably classified by profilers (Ressler and Burgess, 1985). There was, on average, nearly 75 per cent agreement between different profilers on whether a crime scene was organised or disorganised. However, there was considerable variation among profilers and some profilers made a very different assessment of the sort of crime scene involved than others did.

The two types of crime scene reveal different aspects of the psychology of the offender. According to Geberth (1996), the organised offender is characterised by features such as following the news media, has a decent car, alcohol is associated with the crime, his father had a stable pattern of employment, experienced inconsistent childhood discipline, and that the offender controlled their mood during the crime. The disorganised offender demonstrates virtually the reverse pattern: little or no interest in the news media, lives or works close to the crime scene thus a vehicle is not needed, alcohol was uninvolved in the crime, the offender's father had an unstable employment pattern, their childhood discipline was harsh, and exhibits anxiety when committing the crime. Further, perhaps more important, differentiating characteristics of organised and disorganised offenders are to be found in Table 14.1. This is based on the work of Holmes and Holmes (1996) which, as can be seen, extends into matters such as which interview techniques are appropriate to which type of offender. Gierowski, Jaskiewicz-Obydzinska and Slawik (1998, 2000) studied 120 murderers classified by their crime scenes as planned or not planned which appears to be very similar to the FBI profilers' organised versus disorganised dichotomy. The factors associated with a planned crime include the choice of weapon and the manner in which death was inflicted, the location and time at which the crime occurred, and other aspects intended to hide the identity of the culprit. Disordered socialisation factors (e.g. inconsistent upbringing methods and running away from home) were associated with the organised crime scene. Organised crime scene offenders had frequent changes of sexual partners, were low on alcoholism and showed evidence of psychopathy.

Table 14.1 The relationship between crime scene type and aspects of investigation

	Organised offender	Disorganised offender
Personal characteristics	Sexually competent Lives with partner Has charm	Low intelligence Unskilled Lives alone Poor personal hygiene
Post-offence behaviour	May move body Police 'groupie'/follower	May turn religious May change job
Recommended interview technique	Use direct strategy Be accurate about details	Show empathy Interview at night

Source: Holmes and Holmes (1996)

They also tended to have higher regard for their personal appearance.

Stage 3: Crime scene reconstruction

The crime scene is not a simple fixed event. Instead, it is the result of a complex set of circumstances. Consequently, there are aspects of the crime scene that cannot be understood unless attempts are made to understand the events as a dynamic process involving a minimum of two people – offender and victim. There may be witnesses, actual or potential, to consider. The information collected in *Stage 1* is essential to the reconstruction. Inference and deduction are involved. Reconstruction does not have to involve playing out the events as in a television reconstruction. The purpose of the reconstruction may be to clarify the offender's *modus operandi*. K~~~~~~ this may help tie the crime to other crimes.

are
red.
the
then
out

rawn
ycho-
emo-
nent/
ing in
iixing
s (e.g.

if pos-
police
ng by
iarrow
ofiling
is to help answer questions ~~~~~~~~ eries of crimes and the possible number of different offenders involved. Linking crimes to offenders in this way means that information and resources can be pooled by different police teams investigating seemingly unconnected crimes.

An example of FBI profiling

Characteristically, it is quite difficult to explain exactly how a profile emerges out of the different inputs available. FBI profilers have rarely, if ever, made totally clear the inferential processes involved and there is plainly a degree of subjectivity inherent in the method. Some insight into profiling can be obtained by comparing the inputs with the actual profile. The following case is reported in detail in Ressler, Burgess and Douglas (1988):

- A nude female body was found at 3 p.m. on the roof of the apartment block where she lived.
- She had left home for work at 6.30 in the morning.
- She was 26 years of age, 90 pounds in weight, her spine was deformed and she was not dating men.
- Both of her nipples had been removed and placed upon her body.
- Her face was severely beaten.
- She had been throttled with the strap of her bag.
- A blunt instrument had caused many face fractures.
- Virtually all items used came from the victim's bag.
- The phrase 'You can't stop me' was written in ink on her inner thigh and 'Fuck you' on her torso.
- The pendant that she usually wore was missing.
- The victim's underwear had been taken down and pulled over her face.
- Her stockings were tied around her ankles and wrists but very loosely.
- A pen and an umbrella were inserted into her vagina.
- A comb was stuck in her pubic hair.
- There was no semen in the victim's vagina. The offender had ejaculated over her body from a standing position.
- There were bite marks on her thighs and various bruises/lacerations all over.
- Faeces from the murderer were very close by. They were covered with the victim's clothes.
- There was no evidence of similar crimes being carried out in the area.

This is obviously an incomplete account of the information available. Nevertheless, there is enough, perhaps, to form an impression of the murderer.

The psychological profile developed included the following major features:

- A white man.
- Aged between 25 and 35 years – similar in age to the victim.
- Alcohol and drugs were not material factors in the crime.
- Any dates would be younger so that they could be more easily controlled and dominated.
- Average intelligence but dropped out of education.
- Difficulties in personal relationships with women.
- Disorganised offender – confused and perhaps mental difficulties in the past.
- He would fit into the context well – might reside in apartment or could be employed there.
- Never married.
- No military background.
- Possibly unemployed.
- Sexual fantasies have been harboured by the offender for a long time and he possibly uses and collects sadistic pornography.
- Sexually inexperienced and inadequate.
- Unskilled or skilled occupation.

So what is it about the information we saw earlier about the crime scene and the associated information that leads to the profile above? The answer is that at least some of the profile can be understood in the light of the following considerations:

- Killers tend to be similar in terms of age and race to their victim.
- Fantasy tends to be embedded at the core of such extreme cases. The crime may be the result of the offender using the fantasy as a plan or blueprint for offending. Extreme cases such as this are substantially founded on fantasy, which serves as a guide for the crime. Thus the contents of the fantasy may be seen in the characteristics of the offence. Hence the sadistic nature of this crime is indicative of the contents of the offender's sadistic fantasy. Keeping a pendant as a 'trophy' indicates that the offender has a need to fantasise in the future.
- There is little evidence that this crime was prepared for – except in fantasy. The crime scene was disorganised. The offender used whatever was to hand in the course of the crime: things were taken from the victim's bag.
- Although the crime was clearly sexual in nature, the offender used substitutes for sexual penetration. This suggests that he had sexual inadequacies. Consequently, the likelihood is that he lacked sexual experience and had never married.
- The offence has elements of control and domination, thus explaining his choice of victim.
- That the offender defecated near the crime scene indicates that the offence took place over a lengthy time period. Remember, though, that the murderer was in an exposed location and there was a great risk that he might be seen. One explanation linking these features together is that the killer is very familiar with that locality. Perhaps he is an employee or resident in that area.

Once this profile was available to the police, they studied their investigation records. They found a prime suspect – a man whose father lived in the apartments. Although they had been led to believe that the man was in mental hospital, it was discovered that security there was not perfect. He was convicted on the evidence of the bite marks on the body which matched his dental pattern.

Studies that have investigated the nature of profiles reveal a number of problems. In a nutshell, the profiles lack justification for the claims and assertions made about the offender based on the profiler's analysis. In the United Kingdom, the Association of Chief Police Officers has required that the profiler must explain the thinking behind their claims in the profile. Alison, Smith and Morgan (2003) and Alison, Smith, Eastman and Rainbow (2003) obtained a selection of real offender profiles largely from the United Kingdom and the United States. Using a systematic coding scheme, they analysed the 3,090 statements found in these profiles. The vast majority of the statements were merely reiterations of facts that were already known to the police, statements about the profiler's professional competence, or statements about the limitations of the use of the profile. This left only 28 per cent which were profiles of the offender. Mostly these were unsubstantiated claims (82 per cent of the 28 per cent). About 16 per cent provided some justification for the statement being made. A further 1 per cent were simply illogical.

BOX 14.3 Controversy

Is criminal profiling just common sense?

Just what is the status of criminal profiling as presented in the professional literature? Snook *et al.* (2007) systematically reviewed publications discussing criminal profiling literature by employing what they refer to as a narrative review. The concept of narrative review is based on the work of Gendreau *et al.* (2002) who classified publications into whether the author used common-sense or empirically based arguments to make their case or evaluate an idea. Common-sense sources of knowledge are those which essentially regard criminal profiling as a skill or art based on experience or intuition. This would be exemplified by references to authorities, testimonials, intuition and anecdotal information to make the case for criminal profiling. Such common-sense rationales are very different from an empirical rationale in which the following, for example, might be used: (1) empirical research drawn from scientific writings, (2) data based on surveys, (3) experiments or similar scientific methods and (4) the issue of causality is regarded as problematic. Another aspect of this more scientific perspective is that theory needs to be revised in the light of new empirical findings. Snook *et al.* (2007) searched the electronic databases *PsycINFO* and *Criminal Justice Abstracts* using the keywords criminal, psychological and offender profiling. A wide range of different sorts of publications were included, namely peer-reviewed journal articles, book chapters (including those from a previous edition of this book), research reports, published conference papers and magazine articles.

Coders independently coded the materials using the following broad categories:

- Knowledge source (e.g. quantitative versus qualitative).
- Analytic processes (e.g. experimental or biased towards hindsight).
- Evidence integration (e.g. idiographic versus nomothetic focus).

In addition, *post hoc ergo propter hoc* (often shortened to post hoc) reasoning (i.e. reasoning after the event – the phrase literally means 'after this, because of this') was added into the codings. The coders were generally good at coding material into the same categories since overall inter-coder agreement was 76 per cent though there was more disagreement on some of the codings than others.

In many ways, the findings were remarkable. Out of a total of 130 articles on criminal profiling, the *sources of knowledge used* tended to be greater for common-sense types of arguments than the use of scientific evidence. For example, 42 per cent of the articles used scientific evidence but anecdotal arguments (60 per cent), testimonials (45 per cent) and authority (42 per cent) were all at least as common or more common. Common sense rather than science was also dominant in the analytic processes used. Hindsight biases, illusory correlates, availability heuristic, *post hoc ergo propter hoc* and self-serving biases were all more common than the scientific processes of surveys, correlational methods, case histories, quasi-experimental procedures and experiments. It was only for the category of integration of evidence that scientific categories were found to be generally more common than for common-sense ones. So the commonest categories in this broad category were 'recognition that causality is complex' and 'the expectation that theory will be revised'. A simple summary of all of this is that over all of the articles, common-sense arguments were used in preference to empirical evidence on 58 per cent of occasions.

Snook *et al.* found, not surprisingly perhaps, that the use of common-sense arguments was associated with publications which were generally more favourable to criminal profiling. Interestingly, articles from the United States were substantially more common sense-based than, for example, those from the United Kingdom. This may reflect the more objective forms of criminal profiling that are used by British profilers. Snook, Cullen, Bennell, Taylor and Gendreau (2008) describe FBI-style offender profiling as 'smoke and mirrors' with nothing behind them. They suggest that people are led to believe that profiling is effective because of dramatic anecdotes describing its success, the idea that there are profiling experts and the concentration on a few correct predictions when there may be many more incorrect predictions to counterbalance these.

Does profiling work?

There is a substantial body of research into profiling as a means of exploring, especially, the relationship between crime scene characteristics and offender characteristics. Long term, such research might contribute to more effective profiling; short term the problem is that the issue of the effectiveness of profiling in terms of policing has been much neglected. Equally noteworthy is the neglect of empirical evaluations of FBI-style profiling's theoretical adequacy which is criticised by some psychologists for a lack of scientific rigour. The glaringly minimal research base in support of FBI profiling is not rectified simply by repeatedly reiterating this criticism. Research is needed to extend the research base of FBI profiling appropriately. Of course, it could be argued that any research on profiling extends the database. However, by focusing on FBI profiling concepts, researchers would more rapidly make progress in understanding just what there is of value in that approach. Unfortunately, little work has been done in this spirit.

One notable exception is Canter and Wentink's (2004) attempt to test Holmes and Holmes' serial murder classification scheme (Holmes and Holmes, 1998). Five types of serial murder were proposed based on case material from serial killings. These are visionary, mission, lust, thrill, power/control. Canter and Wentink used archival data of public domain accounts of serial killings. All of the cases were from the United States. In order to give Holmes and Holmes' typology the maximum possible chance of success, the researchers coded each of the serial cases in terms of the presence or absence of characteristics relevant to the typology. There were 37 such characteristics. The researchers then identified which of these variables are pertinent to each serial killing type. The following is indicative of the type and the sorts of variables that Canter and Wentink identified as being especially relevant to each category:

- *Visionary killers*: this type of killer is largely acting on voices or visions from God, angels, devils and the like which tell him that he should kill a particular person or type of person (e.g. prostitutes). Thus, for example, the visionary killer is claimed by Holmes and Holmes to leave behind a chaotic crime scene – the typical disorganised pattern. Variables such as scattering of belongings, clothing spread around, weapon left in victim, ransacking and bludgeoning should help identify this type.

- *Mission killers*: this type of killer has decided that a certain group or type of person is unacceptable or valueless and that the world should be free of them. The crime scene characteristics that should identify this type in Canter and Wentink's data include murder weapon missing, firearm use, bludgeoning, throat cutting.

- *Lust killers*: this type is a subcategory of hedonistic killers. Lust killers kill as part of the process of fulfilling their sexual lusts. Sex is the point of the process. As a consequence, typical crime scene characteristics would include multiple sexual acts, penetration with object, vaginal rape, abdominal mutilation, torture and violence to genitals.

- *Thrill killers*: this is another subcategory of hedonistic killers. The thrill killer basically enjoys the process of killing in the sense that they get pleasure and excitement from killing. The death may deliberately be extended to take a long time and may involve torture. Characteristics of thrill killing can be similar to those of lust killing (e.g. torture, vaginal rape and penetration with objects) but others are different (e.g. bite marks, manual or ligature strangulation, body covered after death and concealed perhaps in an isolated spot, and burns on body of victim).

- *Power/control killers*: the gratification in the killing is that the killer has control over the victim. Dominance over another person is the motive. Enjoyment of the killing is maximised by extending the process over time as a consequence. Typical crime scene characteristics include the use of restraints, torture and gagging, body parts missing, evidence tampered with, decapitation. Some of the characteristics it shares with thrill killing such as vaginal rape, ligature strangulation and the body concealed.

Canter and Wentink (2004) claim that their data offered some rather limited support for the typology. Nevertheless, simple, direct support for the typology categories did not emerge. The following summarises some of the more important findings:

- Power/control killing characteristics were actually very typical of the entire sample of cases and did not form a distinct group. Such acts as bludgeoning, attacks on the face, strangulation and violence to the genitals, then, are a feature of the other types of serial killing.

- There did appear to be a group of thrill killing variables which tend to go together though these seem to be best considered largely in terms of the restraint pattern that the killer used. For example, gagging, ligature use and covering the dead body seem to form a cluster. However, other characteristics which seem to imply an inferred thrill according to Canter and Wentink were not so clearly identified with this particular pattern. So details such as the weapon being missing and the victim being alive during the sexual attack were likely to be part of other patterns.

- There did appear to be some support for the idea of visionary killers. Characteristics such as bludgeon-ing the victim to death and leaving a trail of clothing around tended to co-occur frequently in crime scenes. On the other hand, some of the key characteristics of visionary killers according to Holmes and Holmes were not particularly close to this core of variables – e.g. leaving the weapon in the victim. The researchers add that facial disfigurement, which is characteristic of lust killing according to Holmes and Holmes, seems to be more associated with the core of visionary killer variables.

This is, of course, progress in academic terms. That it may make Holmes and Holmes' ideas more difficult to use by profilers is not the point. Canter and Wentink's findings indicate that the simple typology lacks sufficient clarity and empirical justification to be used without further modification.

Nevertheless, perhaps the most important aspect of profiling at least in the minds of the general public, is its contribution to the work of the police. There are a number of points to be made about the seemingly straightforward issue of the adequacy of profiling for police work: it is a deceptively simple question to ask whether profiling is effective. Try to imagine a research study to definitively answer the question of whether pro-filing is worthwhile. How would such a study be done? What crimes would be studied? Would a profiler be randomly assigned to some cases and not others? What is the criterion of success – arrests, reduction in time to arrests, the satisfaction of the senior investigating officers with the profiler, or what?

- Purely in terms of psychological research methods, the issue might be thought of as a simple technical exercise in evaluation research. As soon as we plan this research in detail, the practical and conceptual diffi-culties grow. A researcher might select, say, crimes and assign a profiler at random to half the crimes and no profiler to the other half. The outcome of this might be evaluated in terms of the proportion of crimes that

were solved with and without a profiler. Even if the profiler condition seemed more successful, this in itself would not be definitive evidence that profiling itself worked. Profilers are usually very familiar with police methods and their apparent success might be the result of their good advice on how to conduct and prioritise the investigative operation. The profile itself may well be poor. Profiling has traditionally been applied to extreme crimes. Serial rapes and serial sexual murders may result in pressure on the police for an arrest. At the same time, the investigating police officers may have little experience of such rare crimes. Expert profilers may simply bring wider experience of such crimes. Their profiling skills, as such, may not be very helpful.

- The involvement of a profiler may be diverting resources away from other lines of enquiry. If other options are ignored simply because of the profile then this might reduce the success.

- Claims about the importance of profiling in a par-ticular high-profile crime may appear impressive because an arrest is achieved. What does this tell us about crimes in which profiling was used but no arrest achieved or about the improvement in the chances of arrest due to profiling? It is a bit like a heart surgeon parading their living patients as evidence of the success of their techniques while ignoring those who ended in the graveyard.

- It is generally believed that only certain crimes are suitable for profiling or potentially helped by profiling. People with certain characteristics, for example, may commit car break-ins, but it is unlikely that resources will be found to mount an investigation of the vast majority of these crimes. So profiling could not make a contribution.

- Is detection of a particular crime the main objective of profiling? There are circumstances in which the role of the profiler is rather different: for example, when trying to assess whether crimes are linked to a particular offender or whether they are the work of several different offenders. Sometimes in high-profile cases there is the need to assess the likely validity of letters of confession which may be hoaxes. The hoax potentially could waste much police time. Just what strategy should the interviewing officers take when interviewing suspects? All of these seem worthwhile profiling endeavours but may impinge little on the question of whether the offender is arrested.

- The information provided by profiling research may be operationally useful in general without it having a discernible impact on individual cases. Potentially, ideas of what sorts of rapist are associated with particular crime scenes may generally inform police work without the direct input of a profiler, for example.

- Profiling can inform the sorts of data collected at the crime scene and lead to improvements in the collection and recording of information. There is potentially a symbiotic relationship between profiling and crime scene information collection. The better the crime scene information, the better profiling research can be, and the better profiling research becomes, the more we will know about what crime scene information is useful.

- There have been studies of user satisfaction with profiling. By user satisfaction we mean in this case the senior officers managing a particular crime. It is notable in these that relatively few offenders are arrested as a result of the profile. Gudjonsson and Copson (1997) found that 3 per cent of detections were attributed to the profiler's work. Do not forget that these figures are based on what the senior officers say and it may be that they are not keen to give credit to the profiler. It is interesting to note, nevertheless, that most senior officers express positive attitudes to profilers for other reasons.

- Of course, a profile may be good but the offender arrested without its help. In these circumstances, comparing the fit of the profile to that offender might better assess the validity of the profile. The difficulty is the lack of a clear standard for doing this. For example, is a count or tally of the similarities between the profile and the offender sufficiently sound for evaluating profiling? For example, if the profile of a killer was young, male, of average education, lived near the crime scene and has at least one previous arrest, most of us would not be impressed with the profile even if all of the listed characteristics proved to be true. On the other hand, if the killer was predicted to be a hotel worker, supporting his arthritic mother, living within two minutes of a railway station, with a history of exhibitionism and transvestism and it all turned out to be correct, we would be more impressed.

- Despite allegations of its less than scientific status, FBI crime scene profiling has been subject to more validity assessment than the statistical or actuarial approach discussed in the next chapter. By validity assessment we mean its validity in relation to police work rather than its psychological methodological validity. Few, if any, studies have been conducted on the operational value of statistical profiling.

One of the perplexing findings on offender profiling is the claims made by the police that the profiles were useful but did not lead to the arrest. Alison, Smith and Morgan (2003) carried out a study in which they took a genuine FBI profile and asked police officers to evaluate the accuracy of the profile against the known facts about the criminal finally convicted. In this particular case, the offender was 19 years of age, a stranger to the victim, was unemployed in his work as an actor, had attempted suicide and suffered depression, had no previous convictions, had no relationships in his life, had no sibling, denied the offence and had not suffered abuse within the family. Among the statements that the profile contained were the following:

- The offender will be a white male between 25 and 35, or the same general age as the victim and of average appearance.

- He will be of average intelligence and will be a secondary school (high school) or university (college) dropout.

- He will not have a military history and may be unemployed.

- He will have a pornography collection.

- The subject will have sadistic tendencies.

- The sexual acts show controlled aggression, but rage or hatred of women was obviously present.

- He did not want the woman screaming for help.

- He probably will be a very confused person, possibly with previous mental problems.

The police officers overwhelmingly claimed that the profile was useful for crime investigation. Another group of forensic professionals tended to be less enthusiastic.

However, the study went further than this and for another similar group of officers the procedure was varied and a fabricated picture of the offender was provided. For example, in this condition he was 37, he knew the victim, he worked for the water board but had just been made redundant, he was an alcoholic, had several previous convictions for assault and burglary, had lived with a girlfriend and had had several relationships with women but each one was violent, he has two sisters, admitted the offence, and suffered an abusive family background. Despite the fact that the two descriptions of the offender were virtual opposites, the officers were just as likely to see the profile as being as useful for the bogus description as the real description. In other words, accuracy had no impact on how useful the officers regarded the profile!

Not surprisingly, FBI-style profiling is treated with a degree of scepticism by psychologists and others. For example, Torres, Boccaccini and Miller (2006) describe the findings of an Internet-based survey of American forensic psychologists and psychiatrists. These professionals were likely to believe that profiling was a useful tool in law enforcement. Ninety-five per cent of the psychiatrists and 85 per cent of the psychologists believed this. Nevertheless, there were doubts about its scientific basis. Over 97 per cent of the psychologists and psychiatrists thought that profiling needed empirical research to support it. It was only a minority who thought that profiling was a scientifically valid method for linking a defendant to a crime and even fewer believed that profiling was scientifically reliable. Interestingly, the group of forensic psychologists and psychiatrists generally did not feel themselves to be knowledgeable about profiling and only about a quarter claimed to be knowledgeable. Similarly, only about one in eight of these forensic practitioners had testified in court concerning profiling or had been asked for their opinion about profiling in court.

Scepticism about profiling sometimes manifests itself in somewhat hostile exchanges between its proponents and opponents. For example, there is some evidence that profilers, psychologists and the police produce more informative and detailed reports containing more predictions than non-experts such as comparison groups of students (Kocsis, 2003; Kocsis, Middledorp and Try, 2005). In a similar vein, Pinizzotto and Finkel (1990) found that profilers and other expert groups produced profiles which were better than chance in terms of their accuracy of their contents compared with the known facts. Profilers were the best with 67 per cent accuracy to no more than 57 per cent for the other expert groups. The research design is essentially quite simple. Groups of experts in profiling and non-expert comparison groups read the details of a criminal case. The usual research design compares expert profilers with non-profilers such as students and others. Then the participants rate the characteristics that they think the offender is likely to have using a standard form. The offenders' known characteristics are then compared with these predictions. Basically, then, the research tests the hypothesis that the expert profiler is more accurate in their assessments than the non-expert. Generally speaking, these studies suggest that expert profilers are better profilers than non-profilers. This hardly sounds controversial. Nevertheless, there are some limitations to the method employed and, consequently, the findings are only partially convincing. For one thing, the situation in which the profiles are generated is somewhat artificial with the participants completing a checklist rather than generating their profiles themselves.

Figure 14.3 summarises available data on the accuracy of criminal profiling using this sort of methodology

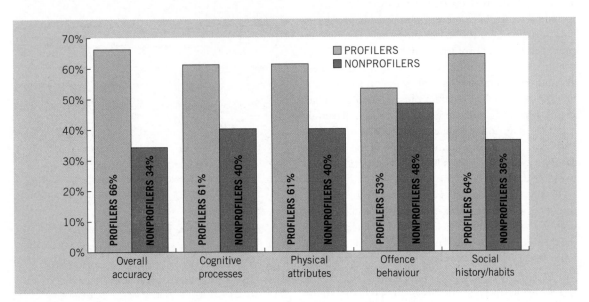

Figure 14.3 Comparing profilers with others in terms of accuracy

according to Kocsis, Middledorp and Karpin (2008). It is a composite of several different studies. It would seem to show that profilers, overall, are substantially more accurate in the profiles that they generate. The superiority of experts, nevertheless, is nevertheless, not consistent across all aspects of profiling. For example, there is very little difference between the expert and non-expert profilers in terms of the quality of their predictions about offence behaviour. It has to be said that Kocsis, Middledorp and Karpin make relatively modest claims about the trends shown in the data. However, offender profiling is not the most neutral of topics for researchers to study. Perhaps, then, it is not surprising that others chose to dispute Kocis, Middledorp and Karpin's conclusions. In particular, Snook, Eastwood, Gendreau and Bennell (2010) evaluate the data differently and argue that the profiling groups 'did not decisively outperform' the comparison groups. This disagreement is difficult to explain briefly and it is even more perplexing because Kocsis (2003) and Snook *et al.* (2010) largely use data from the same set of studies in their analyses but reach radically different conclusions. Partly the issue is of just what is strong evidence in favour of offender profiling. But there are other difficulties. For example, just who is an expert profiler and who is not (Kocsis, 2010)? If we exclusively define an expert profiler to include those who have clear training and expertise in the FBI style of profiling then the evidence that profiling experts are better than non-profilers at producing accurate profiles is stronger. On the other hand, if we include serving police officers who provide profiles to courts in the USA but who lack the formal training then the expert group of profilers is little different from non-profilers in their profiling ability. Just which of these alternatives is correct? Well neither is correct since the issue of definition is a complex one and involves judgements which are not consensual. One cannot simply claim the superiority of one approach over the other. Factors such as these account for some of the disagreements between researchers looking at essentially much the same data.

Finally, any evaluation of any form of profiling needs to assess the theoretical underpinnings of profile generation. We will return to this in the next chapter. Among the theoretical assumptions of FBI-style profiling are the following:

- the characteristics of the offender are reflected in the characteristics of the crime scene

- crime scenes can be effectively categorised
- an offender's crimes tend to show characteristic patterns.

One approach to evaluating is to examine what has increasingly been termed the homology hypothesis (see Figure 14.4). Quite simply, this asserts that crime scene characteristics and offender characteristics converge. Snook *et al.* (2008) argue that typologies commonly used in offender profiling actual have no substance in terms of the relevant empirical literature. So they point to the example that the organised/disorganised crime scene typology has not been empirically validated by the little research that has so far been carried out into it. Snook *et al.* suggest that it is intrinsically a problem that FBI-style profiling is built on trait approaches to personality. Modern conceptualisations in psychology recognise that situational characteristics are probably more important determinants of a person's behaviour than whether they do or do not possess a particular personality trait. For the homology hypothesis to work, the offender should show consistency in terms of their style of offending over the course of a number of offences. This often is not the case because, for example, the offender learns by experience what does and does not work. This may lead to the abandonment of ineffective strategies while effective ones are repeated subsequently.

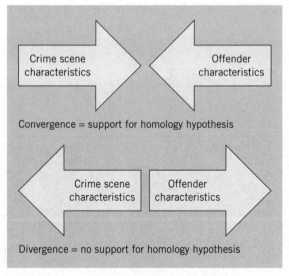

Figure 14.4 The homology hypothesis that there is a convergence between characteristics of the crime scene and the characteristics of the offender

Main points

- Offender profiling seeks to use information from the scene of a crime to assess characteristics of the sort of offender likely to have committed the crime. It ranges from somewhat intuitional approaches to those based on the careful analysis of aggregate statistical data. The latter is becoming increasingly characteristic of research in the field as is discussed in Chapter 15. All forms of profiling assume that there is some sort of homologous relationship between the crime scene and the offender in question. It is unclear whether the simple distinction between organised and disorganised crime scenes stands up to empirical scrutiny despite its impact on the work of FBI profilers.

- There is considerable evidence that the police regard offender profiling favourably. There is evidence that police officers find profiles equally useful even when they are given virtually opposite profiles for the same crime! There is evidence that FBI profiling is less accurate than statistical profiling in circumstances in which it is possible to assess the validity of elements of the profile. Research indicates that some profiles may contain a very high proportion of information which is little more than the facts already collected by the police themselves. Only a small proportion of statements in profiles include some justification for what was being claimed. There are clear signs that offender profiling is regarded as useful though it is just one of many sources of support that supervising officers find very useful without it necessarily leading to an arrest.

- Profiling has had a high public profile in recent years thanks to the various media depictions of profilers. Furthermore, profiling is intimately associated with the concept of serial killing. Given this, one would expect that public interest in the topic will continue to be disproportionate to the tangible achievements of profilers. One of the achievements of profiling is that it has moved research into serious crime away from the search for psychological abnormalities to the manifestation of individual characteristics in the behaviours of criminals when committing crimes.

Further reading

Accounts by FBI-style profilers of their own work are to be found in the following:

Britton, P. (1997) *The Jigsaw Man: The Remarkable Career of Britain's Foremost Criminal Psychologist* London: Bantam Press.

Douglas, J.E. and Olshaker, M. (1995) *Mind Hunter: Inside the FBI's Elite Serial Crime Unit* New York: Pocket Books.

Douglas, J.E. and Olshaker, M. (1997) *Journey into Darkness* New York: Pocket Star.

Ressler, R.K. and Shachtman, T. (1997) *I Have Lived in the Monster* New York: St Martin's Press.

And for a more systematic introduction to their thinking try:

Douglas, J., Burgess, A.W., Burgess, A.G. and Ressler, R.K. (2006) *Crime Classification Manual: A Standard System for Investigating and Classifying Violent Crimes* (2nd edn) Chichester: John Wiley.

Or for the work of other profilers:

Holmes, R.M. and Holmes, S.T. (2002). *Profiling Violent Crimes: An Investigative Tool* (3rd edn) London: Sage Publications.

Visit our website at www.pearsoned.co.uk/howitt for self-test and essay questions, annotated further reading, audio interviews with researchers in the field, weblinks and more information on becoming a forensic psychologist.

Chapter 15

Profile analysis 2: investigative psychology and statistical profiling

Overview

- The actuarial or statistical approach to offender profiling is most closely associated with the work of David Canter. His approach is set within the broader framework of investigative psychology. Increasingly, offender profiling has been applied to a wide variety of crimes beyond the initial FBI focus (serial sexual homicides and rape) such as arson and property crimes. A slightly broader term to describe the activities of psychologists working with the police is, in the UK especially, behavioural investigative advice (BSI). Nevertheless, the statistical approach to offender profiling is built on the assumption that patterns in crime scenes may be linked to characteristics of the offender. However, the patterns in the crime scenes are sought using empirical evidence of what crime scene characteristics tend to co-occur.

- The basic characteristics of Canter's approach emerged in his earliest work on offender profiling. These can be seen as statistically based attempts to identify patterns in different crime characteristics and the consideration of geographical factors in the commission of crimes.

- Statistical profiling uses statistical techniques such as smallest space analysis in order to plot the relationships between crime scene characteristics on a diagram or plot. The crime scene characteristics that tend to co-occur most frequently are physically close on the plot. Characteristics that are common in crime scenes are at the centre of the plot, those that are relatively uncommon in crime scenes are at the periphery of the plot. The researcher then identifies the major segments of the plot and identifies their linking characteristics.

- Generally, there has been little success using standard psychological measures of personality when assessing the relationship between the crime scene and offender characteristics. This is a different issue from whether or not there is a criminal personality which is different from normal personality.

- Currently, considerable research attention is devoted to the statistical profiling of crime. There seems to be less interest in evaluating profiling in the context of actual police work. The evidence of the effectiveness of profiling is varied. It would seem that the police like and value it although it seldom is the basis for an arrest. What seems to be important is what the profiler contributes to dealing with the mass of information available to the police and in providing the police with advice that facilitates other aspects of the policing process.

Introduction

Before his work on investigative psychology, the social psychologist David Canter made important contributions to developing the research field known as environmental psychology. This seeks to understand the interaction between people and the environments within which they live. Some of the basic principles of environmental psychology were incorporated into a distinct approach to offender profiling which Canter developed. In the 1980s, he had begun to meet with senior police managers about using psychology as an aid to police work (Canter, 1994). According to Canter, shortly after, he became intrigued by a number of unsolved rapes in the London area which were the focus of newspaper articles. In 1986, Canter began to assist the police in the investigation of these crimes – that is, the series of rapes which eventually were known to have been committed by John Duffy either alone or with David Mulcahy. The media labelled these rapes as the railway rapes and, later, the railway murders. During the course of this investigation, Canter created the first offender profile created in the United Kingdom.

Characteristically, Canter incorporated quantitative data into his analysis and had drawn up simple information such as (a) maps showing the locations where the crimes had taken place and (b) chronologies of when the offences occurred. Initially, Canter was faced with a list of rapes which may or may not have been committed by the same person(s). So in order to assess which rapes had been committed by the same person(s), he examined how similar each of the rapes was to the others in terms of their manifest characteristics. The essential features of each crime (such as precisely what sort of things took place during the sexual activity) were coded and then the data collated. Using computers, it was then possible to generate an index of how similar the different crimes were to each other in terms of the characteristics that they manifested. Some crimes were very similar (i.e. contained many of the same elements) and so they were likely to have been committed by the same person. Features of the highly similar rapes, for example, were acts like tying the victim's thumbs together behind her back and asking her questions about herself and her home's location. In this way, Canter had isolated a group of rapes from the series which appeared to be very similar and likely to have been carried out by the same offender(s). These rapes became the focus of his attention and, eventually, resulted in his first, tentative offender profile.

The profile Canter sketched out for the police included 17 different elements, most of which are now known to be accurate. The profile included:

> Has lived in the area circumscribed by the first 3 cases since 1983.
> Possibly arrested some time after 24 October 1983.
> Probably semi-skilled or skilled job, involving weekend work or casual labour from about June 1984 onwards.
>
> (Canter, 1994, p. 39)

How did Canter reach such highly specific conclusions as these? By gradually superimposing maps of successive years of offences in this series on top of each other, it could be seen that there was no offending at certain times. Hence, because of the length of the gap in offending, the possibility that the offender had been arrested fitted the data. Furthermore, the geographical locations of the crimes in relation to their chronology did not seem to indicate that the offender was moving from area to area committing several crimes before moving on to another area. Instead it looked like the offender was increasingly willing to travel further in whatever direction from his home to commit the offences. Therefore Canter believed that the location of the first three offences mentioned in the profile essentially determined where the offender lived. Duffy, although he had been a bottom-of-the-list suspect for quite a while, was arrested shortly after the profile was discussed with the police. His co-offender was not found until many years later when Duffy finally revealed his identity.

Some of the characteristics of Canter's approach to offender profiling can be seen as originating in this early investigation. In particular, his emphasis on the empirical search for patterns which are associated with different types of offenders and the consideration of geographical factors are strong features of his work. See Box 15.1 for a discussion of geographic profiling which extends Canter's use of geographical data in the railway rapes case. Recently, some have preferred to replace the term offender profiling with that of Behavioural Investigative Advice (BIA). This refers to the evidence-based methods that psychologists, especially in the United Kingdom, provide to the police to help with particular investigations (Alison, Goodwill, Almond *et al.*, 2010).

Box 15.1 Key concept

Geographical profiling

Criminologists have long recognised the importance of environmental factors in crime. It is known that crime is not spread out evenly throughout cities but it tends to be concentrated in crime hot-spots which attract much police attention relative to the size of the area (Sherman *et al.*, 1989). The Chicago School of Sociology (Shaw and McKay, 1942) established that offenders tend to be concentrated in particular zones of a city. Another example, Routine Activity Theory (see also Chapter 7), stresses the relationship between a criminal's general, daily activities and the crimes which are committed. In other words, crime is often the result of everyday opportunities combined with three key factors occurring together: (1) there being a suitable target for the crime, (2) the risks of being seen are minimal since, for example, a property has no neighbours who can act as guardians of the property perhaps because it is secluded, and (3) there is a potential offender available. Routine Activity Theory originated in the work of Lawrence Cohen and Marcus Felson. Their main interest was in the theory of crime prevention and not crime investigation. However, geographical profiling, which aims to suggest the likely base (home usually but could be the place of work or some other frequently used place) of the offender seems to have somewhat different origins.

The earliest use of geographical profiling is a matter of debate. It has been suggested that it first occurred in the infamous UK Yorkshire Ripper case in 1980 when an investigator examined the locations of the Ripper's attacks and calculated a sort of central point in this distribution which turned out to be the city of Bradford where the Ripper actually lived. Others attribute its invention to the work of Detective Kim Rossmo of the Vancouver Police Department in Canada. He uses a computerised algorithm technique called RIGEL to analyse the spatial locations of serial crimes. Rossmo (2000) summarised the early findings of geographical profiling as including: (a) criminals tend to offend close to their homes, (b) there is a decline in the number of offences the further away one gets from the offender's home and (c) the precise patterns vary with the crime type in question. Of course, sometimes a close-by target is less desirable than, say, an affluent city centre (see Figure 15.1).

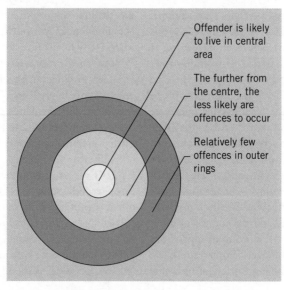

Offender is likely to live in central area

The further from the centre, the less likely are offences to occur

Relatively few offences in outer rings

Figure 15.1 The basics of geographical offender profiling

Of course, a psychological approach to geographical profiling would seek to examine the association between crime geography and more psychological factors. For example, Snook *et al.* (2005) studied the way in which a group of 53 German serial killers' location decision making was mediated by their social, economic and cognitive characteristics. On average each killer had killed 4.6 times. In 63 per cent of murders the killer lived within 10 kilometres (6 miles) of the place where the body was found. Younger killers tended not to travel so far from their home base and killers with a higher IQ travelled further. Not surprisingly, those with their own transport travelled further than those with access to public transport only. There is reason to question whether the initial killing is the best indicator of where the killer lives since fewer than one in five of initial killings were the closest of the series of killings to the killer's home. Of course, it is important to realise that averages (means) can be a little misleading. The mean distance between the killers' homes and the body sites was 30 kilometres (19 miles) whereas the median distance was only 8 kilometres (5 miles). This suggests that some killers murdered a long way from home although very few homicides were in excess of 100 kilometres (62 miles) away.

One approach has attempted to link crimes together in order to assess the extent to which crimes by the same offender can be identified using spatial characteristics of crimes. Bennell and Canter (2002) found that there is a degree of stability in an offender's choice of crime site locations, which may be useful in helping identify linkages between crimes. In particular, linked burglaries tend to occur closer together. Of course, depending on what cut-off point is selected, more or less serial crimes would be identified as linked by inter-crime distances. So if the criterion was 0.7 kilometres then 52 per cent of linked and 93 per cent of unlinked burglaries would be correctly identified. However, using a less stringent threshold of 2.5 kilometres then 62 per cent of linked burglaries but only 68 per cent of the unlinked would be correctly identified as such. In other words, great care needs to be exercised in the setting of the decision point which differentiates the likely linked crimes from the likely unlinked crimes. Bennell and Jones (2005) followed up this by studying commercial and residential serial burglaries using different elements from the *modus operandi* exhibited. They claim that the distances between crime sites were a better way of assessing whether crimes were linked than more traditional crime scene behaviours. They used a variety of types of crime characteristics such as the way in which the property was entered, characteristics of the target location of the burglary, and the type of item stolen. In addition, the distance between the crime sites in kilometres was used. By using data from crimes where the offender was known, it was possible to distinguish between isolated crimes and those in which there was a serial offender. The factor which best distinguished isolated from serial burglaries was shortness of distances between the crimes. Linked burglaries tended to have the smallest inter-crime distances.

The way of optimising the decision criterion is to use a Receiver Operating Characteristic or ROC curve. This is used for binary decisions such as whether a crime is a linked or unlinked one. Basically it is a graph of the true positive rates against the false positive rates for the different values of the decision criterion. The ideal decision rule is the one which maximises the true positive rate and minimises the false negative rate. The true positive rate is the number of linked offences detected whereas the false negative rate is the number of linked crimes wrongly identified as being unlinked crimes. Of course, these are assessed against crimes which are already known to be linked and those known not to be linked.

What about other questions which may be important to crime investigators? For example, can geography be used to help differentiate between crimes committed by a single offender and those committed by multiple offenders? Bernasco (2006) looked at whether co-offending burglars were different in terms of their choice of target areas for crimes. The study was carried out on data from The Hague. The assumptions underlying the research were that areas are more likely to be targeted if they are affluent, the properties are physically accessible, where social disorganisation is rife (which tends to reduce the number of guardians to watch over neighbouring properties), the proximity of the neighbourhood to the city centre and the proximity of the neighbourhood to the offender's home. Of course, some of these factors may be particularly salient to burglar groups rather than solo burglars. For example, a group of burglars is more visible than a single burglar so it

▶

Box 15.1 (continued)

could be that burglar groups are more likely to offend in areas of social disorganisation where neighbours are less likely to watch over each other's properties. The findings were clear-cut. No matter how the distance from the burglars' homes to where the offence was committed was calculated (i.e. which member of the group of burglars was chosen), these distances failed to differentiate the solo from the group burglar. Burglars, however, tended to recruit their burglar partners from their own neighbourhood.

One rather unexpected use of geographical profiling has been that of obscene telephone calls made to children in southern Sweden. Dragnet, a geographical profiling program, was to estimate the most likely area that the obscene telephone caller lived. Remarkably, given that the telephone calls potentially could have been made to any part of Sweden, the program identified very precisely the area in which the offender lived (Ebberline, 2008).

Statistical profiling

Importantly, Canter recognised how little was known about the behaviours of criminals in their real-life environments. This contrasted with the great deal of information that was available about offenders after they had been arrested and processed through the criminal justice system. As we have seen, empirical, statistically based methods in conjunction with careful attention to theory had served Canter well in relation to the railway rapes. Subsequently he turned his attention to systematically studying the behavioural characteristics of offences. The statistical model of offender profiling is illustrated in Figure 15.2, which is based on data collected by House (1997). As with FBI profiling, the assumption is that features of the crime scene contain evidence of salient behaviours carried out by the offender while carrying out the crime. These then may help reveal the distinguishing features or characteristics of the offender. The essential difference between statistical profiling and FBI profiling is that the former concentrates on establishing the relationships empirically using statistical techniques which identify patterns in large data sets. FBI-style profiling lacks this empirical core. Thus, statistical profiling is based on its own distinct ethos despite the overlaps between it and the FBI profiling approach. It is much more empirical and is nowhere near so reliant on intuition and clinical

insight. Indeed, the application of research directly in the police setting would not seem to be a primary objective of much research on statistical profiling and it is increasingly geared to addressing theoretical issues.

There are a number of issues that manifest themselves much more clearly in statistical profiling than the FBI approach:

- How best can the crime scene be classified? This really refers to two distinct things: (a) the information that is collected about the crime scene and (b) whether there are features of certain crime scenes which warrant them being classified as being of a particular type, grouping or cluster.

- Do these types, groupings or clusters of crime scenes reveal psychological and other features of the offender?

- What degree of stability is there in the crime scenes of individual offenders? Will an offender leave similar patterns behind at a crime scene? To what extent do patterns remain stable and consistent over time?

There is no full and definitive answer to these questions.

In Canter's statistical approach, the classification of crime scenes is empirically based, using specialised statistical methods such as smallest space analysis. This is a method of identifying just how likely features of crime scenes are to exist and coexist with another feature at a particular crime scene. Take the following features of rapes:

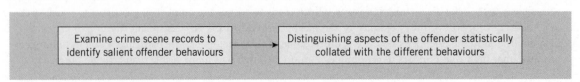

Figure 15.2 The statistical approach to profiling

- apologises
- binding limbs
- clothing removed
- disguise
- element of surprise
- fellatio of the offender
- gratuitous violence
- humiliation
- inquisitive
- kisses
- multiple violence
- offender confident
- reassures victim
- sex language – victim
- sodomy
- takes time
- theft of money
- theft of personal belongings
- torture

- use of blindfold
- vaginal penetration
- verbal aggression.

Some of these features are very common in rape (e.g. vaginal penetration is practically universal in rapes of women) whereas others are quite rare (e.g. cunnilingus). Some of the behaviours frequently occur together if they occur in a rape; other behaviours are rarely found together. House (1997) analysed the co-occurrence and frequency of these behaviours in rapes. The statistical analysis produced a pattern shown stylistically in Figure 15.3. This gives a visual representation of a smallest space analysis of data on the above and other characteristics of rape crime scenes. Vaginal penetration, the element of surprise and clothing removed are central in the diagram – this indicates that they are very common features of rape. As such they are not very useful for differentiating different types of rape crime scene:

- Characteristics at the extremities of the diagram (such as the rapist apologises) are relatively rare in rapes.

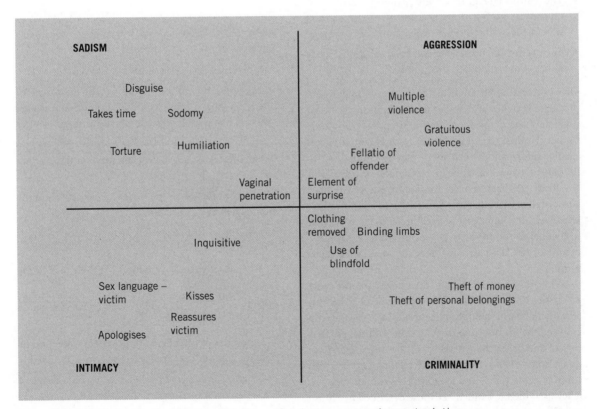

Figure 15.3 Schematic representation of crime scene characteristics

- Characteristics that are close together occur together relatively often, such as theft of the victim's money and theft of the victim's personal property. Theft of the victim's money and sodomy rarely occur together. This is shown by the distance between them in Figure 15.3.

Also notice that labels have been given to the characteristics in the four different quarters of the diagram – sadism, aggression, intimacy and criminality – which seem to reflect the major integrative themes underlying the pattern of associations among characteristics. This is as if there are several major themes in rape – a variety of scripts for carrying out rape.

One practical implication of House's work is his finding that the type of rape is associated with the offender's past criminal history:

- The sadistic group were less likely to have an arrest and conviction history; the criminality group were the most likely to have been imprisoned (they are committing other types of crime alongside the rape, after all, as can be seen from Figure 15.3).
- The sadism and intimacy groups tended to be low on convictions for property crime; the sadistic group were the least likely to have convictions for violence.
- The sadism and intimacy groups were the most likely to have convictions for deception.

One potential application of this is that it might help prioritise searches of offender databases in the hunt for possible suspects for a rape attack. If rapists commonly have a criminal record and these records contain good quality information, then there may be something to be gained from searching the criminal records. This would merely help manage routine investigative police work of interviewing, record keeping and so forth more effectively. It could never in itself prove that a particular individual is the rapist – unless, of course, there is a record of his DNA that matches the new crime scene sample.

While this is interesting and does point to some characteristics of the offender, it is desirable to extend this sort of analysis to include indications of the relationship between the major crime scene 'scripts' and the psychological and other characteristics of the offender. Salfati and Canter (1998) examined the relationship between murder crime scenes and the murderer's characteristics. They used methods much like those described by House (1997). A major hypothesis was that the murderers would show similar modes of interaction during the homicide as in much of the rest of their lives.

A sample of 82 British homicides in which a single offender attacked a stranger was studied. These were murders in which the police did not know the assailant at the time of the discovery of the crime. Although these are described as stranger murders, this is something of a misnomer. Seventy-four per cent of the offenders knew the victim at least slightly. Information about the crimes was drawn from police records. Some 48 variables were extracted from these records. Broadly speaking, they fell into the following categories:

- Characteristics of the victim.
- Information which reflected characteristics of the offender.
- Things or actions done by the offender to the victim.
- Traces of behaviours left at the crime scene.

There were a number of informative features of the crimes:

- 12 per cent of offenders had served in the armed forces.
- A further 23 per cent had previously been married.
- About half of offenders were married or cohabiting (48 per cent).
- Few involved sexual elements (12 per cent).
- Imprisonment was common in the histories of offenders (40 per cent) with the commonest previous offences being theft (22 per cent), burglary (18 per cent) and violence against people (15 per cent).
- Mostly the homicides had taken place in the evening (66 per cent).
- Mostly the offenders were male (72 per cent) and the victims female (55 per cent).
- Mostly the victims were left at their place of death (76 per cent).
- Nearly half of victims were found in their own home (44 per cent).
- Offenders were much younger with an average age of 27 years and a range of 15 to 49 years.
- The majority of offenders (79 per cent) were local or familiar with the area in which the crime occurred.
- The victims averaged 45 years of age with a range of 1 to 70 years.
- Unemployment was common in offenders (41 per cent).

Box 15.2 Key concept

Facet theory and smallest space analysis

Shye and Elizur (1994) and Borg and Shye (1995) provide excellent and detailed summaries of facet theory and Canter (1983) describes its role in psychology. Canter explains how the use of facet theory requires the researcher to abandon many of the ideas which are held dear by psychologists. In particular, it involves the exploration of the area being researched thoroughly rather than quickly and developing a simple hypothesis which can be tested using simple tests of statistical significance. Those who can act on the findings of research (policy makers of all sorts) are usually only concerned about things under their control. Isolating factors in a situation (variables) one from another may be part of psychologists' training, but policy makers may be much more concerned with the total situation. Furthermore, Canter believes that facet theory allows the researcher to explore the definition of concepts at a theoretical level so eschewing the tendency of researchers to define concepts operationally by reference to the measurement procedure and other similar measures of similar concepts. He stresses that facet theory is a broad method for research – it should not be regarded as a narrow measurement technique or way of analysing data.

Consequently, there are a number of ideas that need to be understood a little before one can begin to appreciate the role of facet theory in crime scene analysis which tries to assess the psychological characteristics of the offender from characteristics of the crime scene. Facet theory can be used to relate crime scenes with offender characteristics:

- What is a facet? In facet theory, any domain of interest is a complex system. Research can only partially sample this system. Variables are seen as continuous throughout the system in facet theory. Each variable has other variables that differ only slightly from that variable and other variables. This is just like the faces or facets of a diamond, which are just one view of that thing that is the diamond. The same diamond can be cut in many ways and each facet is merely one of many minutely different ones that might have been cut.
- In crime scene analysis, the presence of multiple stabbing of the victim, for example, in itself fails to capture the fullness of the crime scene. Bloodiness, depth of penetration, the multiplicity of weapons used and other variables would be needed to capture crime scene ferocity more completely.
- Shye and Elizur (1994) describe a facet as 'A set playing the role of a component set of a Cartesian set' (p. 179). Cartesian means that facets can be represented in terms of a physical space. Usually, it implies the use of axes at right angles to each other. Put this way, a scattergram or scattergraph would represent the position of individuals in a two-dimensional physical space defined by the horizontal and vertical axes. In terms of crime scene analysis, the two axes might be:
  - Amount of effort by offender to hide own identity (rated on a scale from very high to high to fairly high to fairly low to low to very low).
  - Amount of effort by offender to hide the identity of victim (rated on a scale from very high to high to fairly high to fairly low to low to very low).

Crime scenes could be rated on these facets and each crime scene represented on a scattergram by a single point. This would roughly correspond to the Cartesian approach. The analogy is with a map and facet theorists speak of mapping.

The matrix overleaf (Table 15.1) takes a simple case of three murders A, B and C and four different characteristics of the crimes such as whether they took place at night.

It is obvious that there are patterns in this matrix – Murders A and B are similar in terms of the presence of three of the four characteristics, whereas Murder C is rather different. One step onwards is to produce a matrix of the correspondence of the four facets across the three murders in order to see what sorts of thing tend to

▶

Box 15.2 (continued)

Table 15.1 Crime scene characteristics at three different murders

	Murder A	Murder B	Murder C
Multiple weapons	1	1	2
Sexual humiliation	1	1	2
Night-time	2	1	2
Victim left naked	1	1	2

1=yes, 2=no

Table 15.2 A simple matrix of the co-occurrence of crime scene characteristics

	Multiple weapons	Sexual humiliation	Night-time	Victim left naked
Multiple weapons				
Sexual humiliation	3			
Night-time	2	2		
Victim left naked	3	3	2	

occur together. So, if we consider Multiple weapons and Sexual humiliation, the three different murders show complete agreement as to whether these things co-occurred or not. There is a match for these variables on the three murders so there is a score of 3 entered into Table 15.2.

Night-time and Multiple weapons match twice over the three murders so 2 is entered as the amount of match or similarity between Night-time and Multiple weapons in the table.

Each of these numerical values (similarity scores if you like) can be represented in space. The Cartesian basis of the approach comes into play here. It is not quite like drawing a scattergram since we do not know where the axes should be. Nevertheless, the information in the above table can be represented in physical space. All that we know is how close or distant the points representing the table would be. Three of the four facets (Multiple weapons, Sexual humiliation and Victim left naked) are at the identical point in space. The remaining facet (Night-time) is 1 away from a complete match with the other three facets (according to the data in the table). We can arbitrarily place any of the facets and plot all of the other facets in relation to it. This plotting would look something like this:

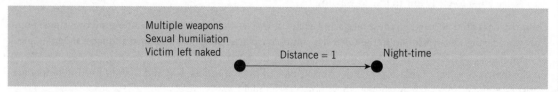

In this simple example, Multiple weapons, Sexual humiliation and Victim left naked all lie at the same point in space – there is no difference between them and they match perfectly. Only Night-time fails to match completely with the other three. The maximum match for this and the other three variables is 2 so it is different by just 1.

It may take several dimensions in order to reproduce the case. Take for purposes of illustration this little puzzle: Greater Aston, Middle Aston and Little Aston are three different villages. Each of them is four miles by foot as the crow flies from each other. You can probably work out that the three villages would look like they were at the points of an equilateral triangle on a map. The sides of the triangle are four miles long each. There is another village – Great Spires – that is three miles exactly from each of the other three villages. How can that be? Well the answer has to be that either Great Spires is on the top of a hill in the middle of the other three villages, or that it is in a valley with the other three on the ridge above. In other words, the first three villages can be represented by a two-dimensional map (a triangle is two-dimensional) but the four villages require an extra dimension to represent their relative distances from each other.

Statistical techniques, in an analogous way, can plot a multitude of distances or differences into Cartesian space. We need not know precisely how it is done and it is best left to computer programs. There are numerous techniques available. They are all built on indexes of similarity or closeness or correlation between the variables. In the case of crime scene analysis, they are based on whether Variable A and Variable B tend to occur *together* at different crime scenes. This is then extended to include the relationships between *all* possible pairs of crime scene variables. This can be expressed as a matrix of similarity or a matrix of correlation. Smallest space analysis (often just referred to as SSA in research publications) is one of the statistical techniques available that will represent matrices of similarity or correlation matrices in multidimensional space. As mentioned earlier, this process is known as mapping. One important question is that of how many dimensions? 1, 2, 3, more? (Yes, it is possible to have more.) The computer programs doing smallest space analysis will produce the best outcome they can for the number of dimensions specified by the researcher. If the researcher wants a two-dimensional plot then that is what they should request from the computer. The computer gives something called the coefficient of alienation. This is simply an index of how well, say, the two-dimensional plot fits the data. If the coefficient is zero then this means that the data fit the two-dimensional plot perfectly. The poorer the fit, the greater the need for more dimensions. There is something of a trade-off between the adequacy of the plot and how useful it is for most analysts.

What emerges is a two-dimensional map. On this map are placed the attributes of a crime scene. The closer two attributes are to each other, the more likely they are to coexist at the crime scene. Attributes that are common to crime scenes tend to be at the centre of the map. The more central, the more crime scenes they are found at. The figure illustrates this using a few facets of a crime scene.

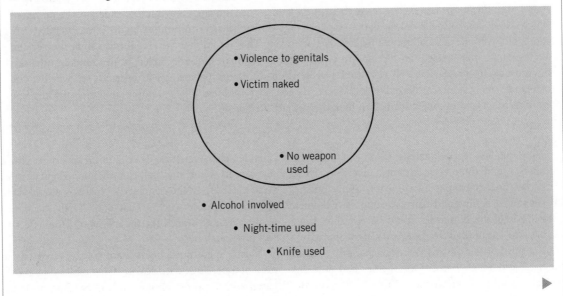

Box 15.2 (continued)

This (imaginary) plot tells us the following:

- Where a knife is used it is likely to be night-time and that alcohol is involved since these three things tend to be close together on the plot.
- That typically no weapons are used in the murders (since No weapon used is close to the centre of the plot).
- Where the victim is naked and there are signs of violence to the genitals, then it is unlikely to find a knife used.

The researcher is also likely to segregate or partition the plot into sectors, largely subjectively, in order to identify the broad types of crime scene. This is somewhat difficult with the simple example above but one obvious sector consists of the murder crime scenes with a sexual component. That is, lines would be drawn (usually from the centre) to enclose the aspects of crime scenes that are sexual in nature (i.e. a naked victim, violence to the genitals). Examination of real analyses will demonstrate the value of this better.

Profile analysis is dependent on the measures of similarity used. The simple total of matches between two crime scenes is not the only possibility. Woodhams, Grant and Price (2007) consider two methods:

- Jaccard coefficient: this method is quite well established. The Jaccard coefficient is simply the number of crime scene characteristics shared by two crime scenes divided by the total number of different crime scene characteristics present in at least one of the two crime scenes. In this way, crime scene characteristics which are present at neither crime scene are not used in the calculation of crime scene similarity.
- Taxonomic similarity: in this procedure, the similarity calculation is calculated in a way which considers that certain behaviours are similar despite the fact that they are nominally different. So, for example, a crime scene behaviour such as 'bites victim's breasts' can be seen as very similar to 'bites victim's buttocks' even though they are not exactly the same. Both, for example, can be seen as very different from say 'cuts off some hair from the victim'. Taxonomic similarity thus takes into account the fact that some crime scene characteristics can be seen to belong to much the same category.

The researchers used offence information which was on file with a Social Services Department in the United Kingdom. Seven young offenders under the age of 16 years were studied. A list of 55 offence behaviours were coded from this information. The researchers knew from police information which offenders had committed which crimes. So they explored the data to find out how similar offences committed by the same offender were compared with offences committed by different offenders. They found that the taxonomic similarity measure worked somewhat better than the Jaccard coefficients at distinguishing the linked from unlinked offences. Interestingly, the researchers also omitted a proportion of offence behaviours in order to see whether the indexes of similarity were affected by incomplete data. They found that the taxonomic similarity measure was more resistant to dropping information than the Jaccard coefficient.

Using smallest space analysis (Box 15.2), the researchers found three major groups of crime. These were classified as having instrumental opportunistic, instrumental cognitive and expressive impulsive themes. Two-thirds of the homicides could be classified fairly readily into one of the three categories. Very approximately, a third of the classifiable crimes fell into each of the three groupings. Each of the themes had different typical offender characteristics. Table 15.3 gives the major crime scene characteristics and the associated offender characteristics. This is impressive but with a few caveats – just how well can offender characteristics be predicted from the crime scene? Just how useful is the analysis in police work? What does it tell the police about where to search for the offender? How effective will this search be?

Mostly these questions cannot be answered at the present time. Most statistical profiling remains research-based with no direct input into the conduct of police investigations. So, in that s ense, it is not known whether

Table 15.3 The relationship between crime scene theme and offender characteristics

Crime theme	Crime scene characteristics	Corresponding offender characteristics
Instrumental opportunistic	Face hidden Female victims Manual attack Multiple wounds in one area Neck attacked Old victims Partially undressed Premises of the victim Sexual	Previous theft offences Familiar with the area of the crime Having previously come to police notice Knew victim Unemployed Knew victim Previous vehicle theft offences Knew victim Previous burglary offences
Instrumental cognitive	Body transported Body hidden Body carefully placed Blunt instrument Face up	Served in the armed services Served a prison sentence
Expressive impulsive	Limbs attacked Multiple wounds all over body Single wound Slash/cut Torso attacked Weapon taken to scene and also removed	Previous traffic offences Married at the time of the offence Previous marriage Female offender Previous offences for public disorder Previous violent offences Previous drugs offences Previous marriage Previous offences for damage to property Previous sexual offences

such profiling could enhance police work. The potential is there but the success of the application of the methods may be a matter for future collaborations between researchers and the police. Importantly, Canter's statistical profiling recognises better than FBI profiling that relationships established between crime-scene and offender characteristics are only probabilities and not certainties. Thus an instrumental cognitive crime scene merely indicates that the offender has an enhanced probability of having served in the armed forces.

BOX 15.3 Forensic psychology in action

Profiling past crimes

Davies (1997) studied a sample of rapists from the British National Crime Identification Bureau records. Their average age was 27 years, and three-quarters were under 33 years of age although they ranged from 14 to 59 years. Most significantly, 84 per cent of them had criminal records. Bear in mind, though, that sexual offences were the *least* common previous offences. Burglary and violence offences were the most common previous offences. Perhaps the fact that the vast majority of rapists had previous convictions is the crucial thing. It means that there should be police records existing on the offender in most cases.

BOX 15.3 (continued)

Davies concentrated on available information from the rape scenes that she describes as non-sexual aspects of rape. These are types of behaviour relatively easily identified, especially with the help of the victim. The important thing is that these different types of behaviour have different associations with past criminal behaviours on record. In other words, the type of behaviour at the crime scene can suggest what sort of past offences to search for. This is illustrated in the table below.

Relationship between crime scene behaviours and criminal record

Type of behaviour	Previous record
Fingerprint precautions: 15 per cent of offenders had worn gloves, or wiped off fingerprints, or some similar activity	4 times more likely to have burglary convictions if used, 3 times more likely to be one-off rapist if *not* used
Semen destruction: 5 per cent of offenders had made efforts to make sure that no useful forensic evidence was left by their semen	4 times more likely to have a conviction record
Reference to the police: 13 per cent made some comment about the police	4 times more likely to have been in custody, 5.5 times more likely to a have a conviction, 2.5 times more likely to have a conviction for violence
Theft from victim: 20 per cent stole money or property from the victim	4 times more likely to have prior convictions for property crime
Forced entry: 25 per cent of the rapes were accompanied by a forced entry to the property where the rape took place	5 times more likely to have burglary convictions
Extreme violence – striking the victim twice or more – was used in 20 per cent of cases	3 times more likely to have prior convictions for violent offences

Davies went on to show through logistic regression analysis that combining features of the crime scene could make good predictions:

- A previous record for burglary could be predicted with almost complete certainty on the basis of fingerprint precautions being taken, theft from the victim, a forced entry to the premises and the presence of alcohol at the scene or immediately before the crime.
- Previous convictions for violent offences are predicted by the use of extreme violence, comments about the police and deliberately lying to mislead about the offender's identity.
- A lack of previous convictions for sexual offences is predicted by a lack of fingerprint precautions, a lack of precautions about departure from the crime scene to ensure that they are not arrested, the presence of alcohol at the scene or immediately prior, and either a forced entry

or a confidence (trickster type) approach, although both of these cannot be possible at the same time.

Some caution is needed over what would otherwise seem to be a valuable approach to profiling. In particular, the idea that only one in seven rapists has no previous criminal record needs care. There may well be an interaction between an offender having a previous criminal record and the willingness of the police to prosecute. Only small proportions of rapes and rape allegations ever reach court and end in conviction. The criminality of rapists may be an artefact of police practices rather than a feature of all rapes. In this connection, date-rape might be mentioned since it has only recently been generally recognised as a major aspect of rape and a matter for police prosecution. On the other hand, victims know date-rapists so their identification is easy.

The homology issue and basic theory

The concept of homology in relation to offender profiling was introduced in Chapter 14. The basic theoretical assumption in offender profiling is that there is a relationship between crime scene characteristics and the characteristics of the offender. We have seen evidence for such a relationship already in this chapter but conceptually there are a number of matters that relate to this. The evidence as it stands currently in the literature tends to be rather mixed but, generally, can be said not to strongly support the homology hypothesis. So, to be clear, the basic assumption that the characteristics of the offence (crime scene) are predictive of the characteristics of the offender is known as the homology hypothesis. This assumption can manifest itself in various forms (see Figure 15.4):

- Crime linkage: The first type of assumption is the crime matching approach which is built on the assumption that there is a consistency in the characteristics of the offences of a particular offender. This is sometimes referred to as the consistency hypothesis (Canter, 1994) which refers to the expectation that the manner of carrying out a crime on one occasion will be reflected in the characteristics of the manner of offending on a later occasion. It is primarily used to assess the likelihood that a particular offender was responsible for a series of crimes or whether different offenders were involved in the different offences.

- Matching: The second type of assumption is that there is a simple matching between a characteristic of the offence and the characteristic of an offender. This type of research is illustrated by the suggestion that there

is a relationship (negative) between the age of the victim of a sex attack and the age of the offender. Of course, the potential for such research is big as there are so many different measurable aspects of crime scenes and a multitude of characteristics than may be ascribed to the offender.

- Homology: The third type of assumption seeks more than relationships between aspects of the crime scene, looking for relationships between particular patterns of crime scene characteristics and particular characteristic patterns (usually traits) in the offender.

No simple summary can describe the findings into the various studies of these various approaches. Although, as we saw at the end of Chapter 14, Snook *et al.* (2008) argued strongly that the evidence for these relationships is very weak – so weak that they suggest that the fundamental theory underlying traditional FBI offender profiling is invalid – but this does not adequately reflect the range of findings and expert opinion on this matter. Probably the better conclusion is that the situation overall is of some tentative support for the idea that crime scene characteristics reflect offender characteristics to some extent but sometimes at only modest levels. However, better methods and data may well improve our understanding.

There are a number of reasons why the crime scenes of an offender may change over a period of time:

- Criminals change and develop new tactics and become more effective with time – their confidence in their ability to commit the crime increases

- The offenders' goals may change over time – maybe their sexual fantasies have changed

- The victim's resistance may change what the offender needs to do in order to complete the crime for a particular crime.

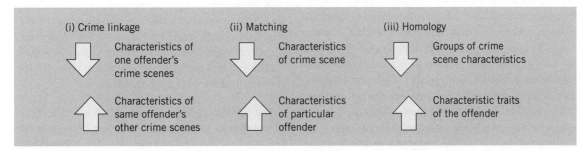

Figure 15.4 Some of the different types of consistency between the crime scene characteristics and the offender

The research in this area tends to be rather technical and it is easy to overlook the successes of profiling. So it is worthwhile starting with what appears to be a successful demonstration of the effective use of profiling. The basic idea is to calculate the mathematical similarities between one crime scene and other, possibly related, crime scenes. Thus Yokota *et al.* (2007) created a profiling system based on a general crime data base. Ninety-six variables concerning different aspects of the crime were recorded including things such as the type of victim, the place of victimisation, the time of victimization, interaction with the victim and the sexual behaviours. Each variable with the exception of age was dichotomously coded into one of two categories for each crime. Age was coded in approximately ten-year bands. The information stored on the computer was the records of individual offender's crimes. The data base contained about 1,250 incidents of rape and forced indecency from 868 offenders. Most of the offenders (78 per cent) had just one record. The computer program allowed the researchers to compare a new crime scene with all of the other crime scenes in the data base. It picked out those old offences which were most like the new offence. Since this particular database involved old offences where the offender was known then this essentially generated a list of likely suspects. Actually, the method was slightly more sophisticated than all of this implies. Because this was a research trial, the 'new' offences were really the most recent offence in the series of offences where the offender had committed three or more crimes. Thus, the offender for the 'new' offences was actually known to the researchers. The 'new' offences were not included in the database for the trial. The computer calculated similarity scores between the old offences (those in the database) and the new offences (the most recent offences of 81 offenders).

The system showed a lot of promise in terms of identifying 'potential offenders'. For 81 'new' offences, the system picked out the actual offender from the other records on 30 per cent of occasions and the actual offender was picked out as in the top four likely suspects for half of the 'new' crimes. The hit rate for the actual offender being the number one suspect increased to 56 per cent when the area of Japan involved was added into the calculations. The researchers could also use the most likely offenders to generate a profile of the sort of offender who was most likely to be involved. Interestingly, this approach allows for the inclusion of low-frequency behaviours which are dealt with by the similarity calculation (algorithm).

Most studies tend to dispense with very infrequently and very frequently occurring behaviours.

Sorochinski and Salfati (2010) provide an analysis of what they term the 'consistency of inconsistency' in serial homicide. They point out that some research has painted a rather muted picture of the consistency between crime-site behaviours in serial homicide offenders – the very sort of offenders for which offender profiling was developed. Earlier research by Bateman and Salfati (2007) found just four crime scene behaviours which showed consistently over all of the offences (bringing equipment to the crime scene to help them commit the crime, destroying evidence, oral sex by the victim and using a ligature). This is only very modest evidence of crime scene consistency. Sorochinski and Salfati essentially replicated this research but using groupings of different types of crime scene behaviours rather than individual crime scene behaviours. Three groups of behaviours were used. Each of these was broken down into two different themes. These were:

- Group 1: Planning: A strategy to complete the crime and avoid arrest (e.g body transported, evidence of forced entry, forensic evidence removed, and weapon brought to scene). It was found that this group could be fairly effectively differentiated into pre- and post-planning themes.

- Group 2: Wounding: The strategy for killing the victim (e.g. biting, blunt instrument, injury to face, injury to neck – stabbing, and ligature strangulation). It was found that this could be differentiated into (a) process-oriented and (b) goal-oriented themes which strongly separated wounding behaviours into one of the two dominant themes.

- Group 3: Offender–victim interaction behaviours (e.g. body posed, face covered after death, masturbation at the scene, necrophilia, and prostitute victim). It was found that this group could be differentiated into the themes of (a) the victim as object were basically acts which treated the dead victim as an object such as necrophilia and (b) the victim as vehicle included various types of sexual acts with the live victim and the victim being a prostitute.

The different crime scenes were coded using these three different groups and themes for 19 serial homicide cases with solo killers in the USA (Sorochinski and Salfati, 2010). On average, each offender had killed more than five people. However, for the purposes of

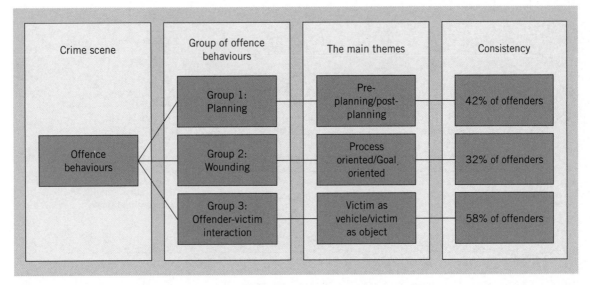

Figure 15.5 Consistency of crime scene themes over serial killings

the analysis, only the first three killings were studied. The question is just how consistent the offenders were in terms of their behaviours over these three groups. As shown in Figure 15.5, the consistency of the offender's placement in each of these groups and their themes was most evident for the victim–offender interaction behaviours group. It was found that there was 58 per cent consistency for crime scene categorisation for this group into the different themes. Consistency for planning was 42 per cent and for wounding 32 per cent. However, consistency was not a characteristic across all three crime behaviour groupings. That is to say, for example, if an offender was consistent in terms of victim–offender interaction they were unlikely to be consistent for planning and wounding as well.

Of course, the classification of crime scene behaviours into groupings and themes has consequences. Most importantly, it inevitably loses some of the specific detail which, in some circumstances, might show consistency. Grouping variables together is only clearly advantageous if the research outcomes are more informative as a consequence. One study suggests that grouping crime scene behaviours may be a problem (Goodwill, Alison and Beech, 2009). They used data from a sample of stranger rapists acting alone in order to evaluate the extent to which three different profiling models predicted previous rape offences from crime scene information. The three models were:

- Hazelwood's (1987) Power and Anger model. The basis of these ideas is discussed in Chapter 9.
- Behavioural Thematic Evaluation (Canter, Bennell, Alison and Reddy, 2003). This suggested that there are four styles of rapist plus a mixed group.
- The Massachusetts Treatment Centre's Rape classification scheme which involves five types of rapist.

Details of the different subcategories in each of these models may be found in Figure 15.6.

Each of these three models are commonly used when profilers give advice about sex offences (Goodwill, Alison and Beech, 2009). The researchers used the coding schemes developed by the original authors of the three models. In order to ensure high-quality coding, the coders underwent a period of training involving practising and obtaining feedback on how they coded the data for each of these three models. Then the coding stage proper began. Information about the rapists' previous convictions was obtained from the UK Police National Computer. The researchers were looking for previous convictions for the same type of offence – that is sexual, violent, drug and/or weapon, property, or other offences.

Hazelwood's Power and Anger model and the Massachusetts Treatment Centre's Rape classification scheme were just about equally as effective at predicting whether or not the offender had previous offences though

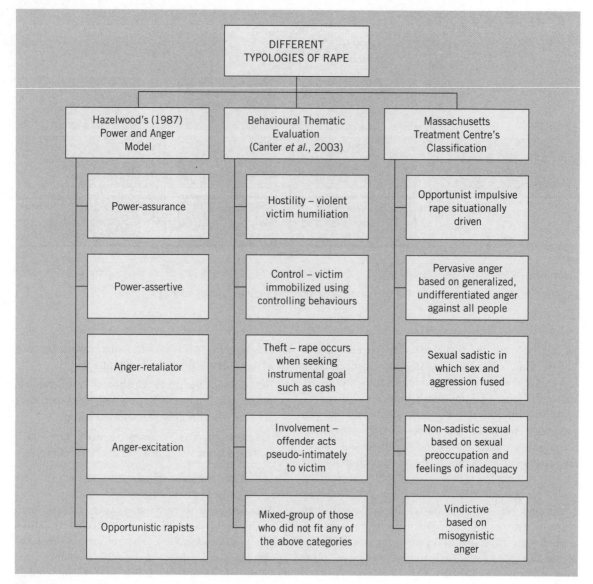

Figure 15.6 The different typologies of rape evaluated in Goodwill *et al.*'s (2009) study

this was fairly modest. Canter's Behavioural Thematic Model was decidedly less effective. This is fairly typical of the findings in this broad area of research. But Goodwill *et al.* (2010) decided to analyse the data but without organising it in terms of the requirements of the three models. By using the raw data to make predictions (as opposed to using the raw data to code into theoretical models) far better accuracy of the predictions could be achieved. Thus the categorisation process in this case may be responsible for the relatively poor fit between the crime scene data and previous offences.

Profiling and personality

Anyone examining the research on profiling will find relatively little which relates criminal activity to conventional personality theory. There is, of course, some research which tries to make the link between criminality and personality such as Eysenck's biosocial theory (see Chapter 5). The profiling literature does make reference to personality characteristics but these are rarely based on theoretically advanced understanding of human personality. According to Youngs (2004), little research is available into the relationship between *styles of offending* and personality as opposed, for example, to studies of the personality of, say, violent offenders. Perhaps not surprisingly, most of the measures of personality used in these studies are ones created for clinical purposes. Their value, then, is limited to the extent to which clinical (abnormal) factors are responsible for criminal style. The alternative is to use non-clinical measures of personality. The upshot of these studies is less than clear. Some studies claim a relationship whereas others suggest that there is no relationship. Quoting Youngs (2004), 'it remains unclear, then, whether personality is differentially related to offending style and, if so, which aspects of personality will relate to which aspects of offending style' (p. 101). Youngs argues that the circumstances in which there will be a differentiating relationship between personality and style of offending are as follows:

- Conceptions of personality employed must be appropriate to criminal behaviour.

- Empirical research must be informed by an understanding of the way that behaviour is shaped by personality.

- Offending styles must be empirically defensible and defined.

In other words, the researcher needs a sophisticated understanding of both personality and criminal behaviour.

Modern ideas about personality have been introduced into profiling by a number of researchers. In an expert review of the evidence on crime linkage involving psychological methods, Woodhams, Hollin and Bull (2007) carefully evaluated the evidence and concluded that the assumption of some consistency in an offender's behaviours across crimes is supported. Not only this, they suggest that the variation between different offenders in their crime patterns is sufficiently great that the offences of a particular offender can be differentiated from the other offenders' crimes with a degree of confidence. Nevertheless, consistency in the successive crimes of criminals is not always the rule. That is, there is both usable consistency but problematic inconsistency. Researchers need to develop understanding of the latter. Woodhams *et al.* argue that profilers have tended to adopt an outmoded conception of personality which was abandoned by personality researchers several decades ago. They argue that if forensic researchers adopted a more modern approach to personality, then a better fit

could be achieved between personality and the different crime scenes of the same offender. There are two fundamental aspects to all of this:

- Consistency across an offender's successive crime may not be the same irrespective of the behaviour in question.

- Situation-dependent behaviours show less consistency than the behaviours initiated by the offender.

Woodhams *et al.* argue that that research trying to link different crimes has ignored the 'if' in the 'if-then' relationship (Mischel, 1999). What this means is that people respond in distinctive but stable ways to situations but that this response is dependent on the type of situation under consideration. A person may be open and communicative when interacting with their friends but quiet and unresponsive when in a meeting with their boss at work. The situations are the 'if' and the stable behaviour patterns are the 'thens'. Crudely, this can be expressed as in Figure 15.7. Essentially, the argument is that by taking into account the general situation of crimes then one can make better assessments of whether the same offender carried them all out. Generally, the situation is that psychologically defined by the offender rather than some more objective situation. Consequently, the situation that the offender is responding to is not totally reflected in the crime scene. Even where the offender chooses a crime scene to be similar to the others, events may happen to cause changes. For example, a victim may resist the attack, a passerby disturbs the offender, and so forth.

Goodwill and Alison (2007) make a similar argument about the incorporation of the situation into profiling. They stress that profiling is only possible if (a) offenders

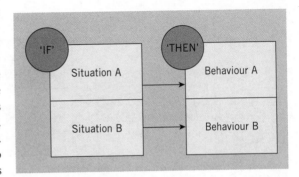

Figure 15.7 Behaviour involves personality characteristics plus situational characteristics

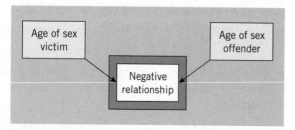

Figure 15.8 Illustrating the negative relationship between victim and sex offender age

are consistent in the manner in which they commit their crimes and (b) they are differentiable from other offenders in their offending behaviours. Some things are so unique to a particular offender that they can do nothing to help when comparisons are being made between a number of offenders. Nevertheless, a feature which is exclusive to an individual is a 'signature' of that individual and so reliably indicates that this particular individual was responsible for the series of crimes. Goodwill and Alison explored the simple idea of an inverse relationship (negative correlation) between the age of the offender and the age of the victim in sex offending (Figure 15.8). Thus if the victim of a sexual attack is young then the offender is more likely to be older and vice versa.

Other relevant features of a crime which can be assessed from the crime scene are:

- Planning: Has the crime been planned and organised in advance? Planning may be assessed by such factors

as whether the offender brings to the scene equipment to help carry out the rape such as handcuffs to control the victim, a gag for the victim, or a disguise or blindfold for himself. Research has shown that such planning enables the offender to target a victim of choice rather than someone at random. In these circumstances, the relationship between the age of the offender and victim may be apparent. Where the crime is unplanned, then the expected relationship between offender and victim age may not be apparent.

- Gratuitous violence: The level of aggression/violence involved in the sexual crime is predictive of the age of the offender. Younger sex offenders tend to be more violent than older ones against (Grubin and Kennedy, 1991), for example. Gebhard *et al.* (1965) found that violent sexual aggressors were typically younger than non-violent sexual offenders. The fact that these findings tend not to be consistent across different studies suggested to Goodwill and Alison (2007) that the level of aggression/violence may be a moderating factor in the relationship between offender age and victim age.

Goodwill and Alison investigated data from 85 stranger rapes in order to examine the question of whether the situational factors strengthen the relationship between victim age and offender age. The researchers' expectations and the findings of the research were as shown in Figure 15.9. Their analysis showed that there was the expected, modest negative relationship between victim and offender age. If one simply takes either the gratuitously violent group or the planning group then the

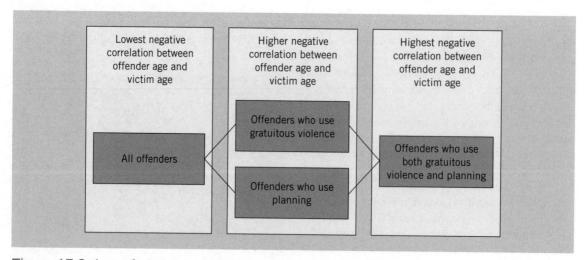

Figure 15.9 Age of victim and offender relationships taking into account the moderating effects of planning and gratuitous violence

relationship gets stronger. This indicates that gratuitous violence and planning separately have a moderating effect. However, the relationship between age of offender and age of victim is strongest when the moderating effects of gratuitous violence and planning are considered. Where there is evidence of both planning and gratuitous violence then it is possible to predict the offender's age from that of the victim to within less than three years.

It can be argued that criminal behaviour is an interpersonal activity. The extent to which crimes differ in this regard is enormous and in some cases, the relationship is extremely remote. For crimes such as rape and murder there has to be some sort of direct relationship whereas for other crimes, such as burglary, the relationship is not direct but 'implicit'. So, for example, a burglar is affected by the behaviour of a victim even if this is merely in terms of when the victim is away from home. This is a very indirect level of interpersonal activity. It might be noted also that many of the concepts used to explain the characteristics of offenders really describe interpersonal relationships – controlling, dominant and hostile are examples.

Youngs (2004) suggested that, potentially, Fundamental Interpersonal Relations Orientation (FIRO) theory could be a means of assessing interpersonal interaction characteristics which might have a bearing on criminal style (Shutz, 1994). A person's interpersonal style will be reflected in the characteristic behaviours they receive from others. The theory's core personality characteristics of control, inclusion and openness may be defined as follows:

- *Control*: this consists of two components that are not strongly related to each other. Expressed control is essentially the exertion of control over others whereas received control is the individual's willingness to submit to the control attempts of others. Someone who attempts to control others may be willing to be controlled or resistant to control.

- *Inclusion*: expressed inclusion is basically the manifestation of the desire to receive attention, interact and to belong to others. High received inclusion refers to those persons who tend to receive the attentions of others.

- *Openness*: expressed openness refers to those who relate to others with affection and closeness. So they are not private and withdrawn in their relationships. Received openness refers to those who tend to receive the affection and closeness of others.

The offending behaviours of young men in the age range of 14–28 years (the median age was 19 years) were studied using a lengthy questionnaire. This included behaviours such as cheating at school in tests, being drunk regularly under the age of 16, trying to pass a cheque by signing someone else's name. A statistical analysis found two major modes or styles of offending behaviour. Expressive behaviours included breaking into empty buildings to cause damage, arson and sex in public. They are expressive since these acts are the aim of the behaviours. Instrumental behaviours included forging a cheque, shoplifting and burglary. Another dimension of the offence concerned the seriousness of the behaviours.

Among the findings was that the expressed control group tended to target their offending against others – commonly through the use of violence. Offences involving the use of a weapon and the carrying and use of a gun were especially common in this group. In terms of the received control dimension, higher scorers tended to be more involved in property offences with the highest levels being for vandalism. These, taken with other findings, are suggestive support of Youngs' assertions about the circumstances in which offence style might relate to personality.

Main points

- Canter's approach to offender profiling, although originating in an interest in solving the railway murders, is probably best regarded in terms of its characteristic empirical basis involving the collation and analysis of substantial systematic data sets describing numerous crime scenes and of descriptions of crime scenes and characteristics of known offenders. As such, it can be seen as systematically testing some of the basic assumptions of FBI-style profiling rather than being aimed at directly supporting specific criminal investigations.

▶

- Statistical profiling has abandoned many of the shibboleths of FBI-style profiling. This can be seen most easily in the much wider range of types of crimes which it covers compared to FBI-profiling's emphasis on serial violent sexual crimes containing 'bizarre' elements. So statistical profiling is increasingly likely to look at crimes such as arson and fraud which are very different from the focus of the original FBI profilers.

- It would be wrong to describe Canter's approach to offender profiling as a purely empirical endeavour as researchers adopting his methods have emphasised new and different theoretical perspectives in their writings as we have seen, for example, in the work of Youngs (2004) described above. Nevertheless, many of the writings in this field are dominated by statistical approaches to pattern finding which are characteristically a little inaccessible. Consequently, it is important to understand how these methods are used following explanations such as those in this chapter and not to be overwhelmed by the detail of the analysis. There is a great deal of work to be done if the statistical approach is to inform police investigations in ways as influential as those of the FBI profilers.

Further reading

The following contain practical accounts of offender profiling linked to David Canter's approach:

Alison, L. (2005) *The Forensic Psychologist's Casebook: Psychological Profiling and Criminal Investigation* Cullompton: Willan Publishing.

Canter, D. (1995) *Criminal Shadows: Inside the Mind of the Serial Killer* London: HarperCollins.

Canter, D. (2007) *Mapping Murder: Walking in Killers' Footsteps* Virgin Books.

Canter, D. and Youngs, D. (2009) *Investigative Psychology: From Offender Profiling to the Analysis of Criminal Action* Chichester: John Wiley and Sons.

Researchers in the field have a number of downloadable publications at the following link: http://www.liv.ac.uk/psychology/ccir/op.html

Visit our website at www.pearsoned.co.uk/howitt for self-test and essay questions, annotated further reading, audio interviews with researchers in the field, weblinks and more information on becoming a forensic psychologist.

Chapter 16

False allegations

Overview

- Miscarriage of justice is a legal rather than psychological concept and may involve procedural rather than factual matters. Psychologists have tended to focus on more limited issues such as false allegations and false confessions (see Chapters 16 and 17). False allegations may be made for a number of reasons – they are not simply motivated by malice in every case.

- Bad interviewing practices can lead to false information. There is clear evidence that at least in some circumstances, persistent leading questioning can result in individuals being falsely implicated in crime. Some children, especially, seem vulnerable to the implantation of false memories of events that are resistant to challenge in some cases.

- The recovered memory/false memory debate reflects opposite ways of understanding some allegations of sexual abuse dating back to childhood experiences. Recovered memory implies that the abuse happened and was lost to memory for a while whereas false memory implies that the memories are of events which did not take place. The debate centres around radically different perspectives on memory. A rather sceptical view on recovered memory comes from those experimental psychologists who have been inclined to use laboratory-style experimentation in developing theories of memory. The more accepting approach comes from those who regard memory as being affected by repression, especially following trauma. Some individuals retract claims of having had memories of childhood recovered in adult life.

- There are a number of graphic experimental demonstrations that children can be encouraged to make false claims about happenings which might be interpreted as sexually abusive. The *Mr Science* studies involved a classroom visit and later stories told to the children by their parents about that visit which contained inaccurate information. Some children claimed to remember events that happened in real life which were only to be found in the stories. 'Experts' in interviewing were not able to distinguish between the children's accounts of the real and fictional events.

- Professionals may make false allegations because they fail to understand the limited value of certain signs in diagnosing child sexual abuse, for example. The risk of false positives and false negatives should be part of any such assessment. However, there is a secondary problem in that when it becomes commonly believed that children are suggestible and easily influenced by interviewers, confusion may be caused by professionals about the adequacy of their interviewing technique.

Introduction

Miscarriages of justice are identified when an appeal court overturns a conviction (Naughton, 2005). Consequently, the processes and procedures of the court of appeal determine what becomes classified as a miscarriage of justice. The concept of miscarriage of justice has tended to be used for those cases that failed on the first occasion they went to an appeal court but were overthrown at a later appeal hearing. Such cases tend to be high-profile and receive considerable media publicity. Nevertheless, these are extremely infrequent since they amount to less than 0.001 per cent of the annual number of criminal convictions in the United Kingdom. Unfortunately, this disguises the fact that courts of appeal regularly quash many thousands of convictions each year. Furthermore, in law, overturning a decision does not mean that the appeal court has decided that the convicted person is, in fact, innocent. The requirement for a conviction (in England and Wales) is that the legal standard of proof has been met – that there is sufficient evidence that establishes beyond reasonable doubt the guilt or otherwise of the accused. So miscarriages of justice do not exclusively concern wrongful convictions of individuals who did not commit a crime but are also about the procedures that led to a conviction (and sometimes acquittal). Many aspects of miscarriage of justice have been ignored in forensic and criminal psychology. So most of the research in forensic and criminal psychology pertinent to miscarriages of justice has concentrated on false accusations and false confessions. The latter are dealt with in Chapter 17. Neither of these, necessarily, leads to a miscarriage of justice. For example, the accusation may not be believed or the confession may be retracted and this retraction accepted in court or by the police.

The true rate of false allegations is somewhat difficult to estimate for the reason that one's definition of false allegations partly determines that estimate. For example, it would be highly problematic to define false allegations in terms of the proportion of trials that end in not guilty verdicts. A not guilty verdict may or may not mean innocence and there is an obvious distinction to be made between false allegations and false convictions. There is a big conceptual difference between false allegations and unfounded claims since the latter may, for example, refer to sexual harassment which actually happened but the evidence to support the claim is not sufficient. Furthermore, recanted claims do not necessarily mean

that the offence did not take place since there are numerous reasons for recanting – such as a reconciliation between partners. Probably researchers have studied false allegations in relation to child sexual abuse more than in any other topic. The main areas of concern have been as follows:

- *False allegations of child physical and sexual abuse* made by professionals against parents. Perhaps the most noteworthy of these are the events in Cleveland, England, in the late 1980s (Bell, 1988; Howitt, 1992) when doctors and social workers made charges of child sexual abuse – largely sodomy – against a number of families in northern England. These allegations appear to be based on a faulty medical test of sexual abuse. The test, supposed to measure anal penetration, was eventually found to lead to a high proportion of misdiagnoses. This led to a public inquiry, as did a number of subsequent cases such as those involving satanic abuse.

- *Allegations of sexual abuse made against the conflicting parent in divorce cases* – especially cases in which the custody of children is in dispute.

- *The so-called false-memory syndrome* in which adults undergoing therapy come to 'recall' sexually abusive experiences in their childhood (see Box 16.1).

Of course, these are not the only circumstances in which false allegations may be made. They just happen to be the circumstances that have attracted the interest of researchers. Poole and Lindsay (1998) suggest that false allegation rates might vary from 5–8 per cent for child sexual abuse – if we take into account only *intentional* false allegations. Such malicious motives exclude a great number where the police and social workers among others raise suspicions of abuse against families. When false suspicions of this sort are included, the false allegation rate increases markedly to between 23–35 per cent according to the study in question (Howitt, 1992). Underlying these figures may be a reality of trauma, stress and distress for the child and its family. Risks include children being removed from their homes, fathers being forced to live away from home and imprisonment. Even if they do not lead to criminal convictions, well-intentioned false allegations may still take their toll on family life (Howitt, 1992). So, in this way, they cannot be regarded as trivial.

The reasons why false allegations seem to be common in allegations of sexual abuse include the following:

- In many cases, no physical evidence of sexual abuse can be detected. While penetrative sexual intercourse might damage the sexual organs of a physically immature child or its anus, sexual abuse takes many other and less invasive forms. Almost certainly, oral sex will leave no physical signs.

- What evidence there is often comes from an interview with relatively young children.

- Professionals and the public in general are sensitive about the dangers of abuse and feel it is important to protect children wherever possible.

In some circumstances, children may make false allegations of sexual abuse according to Lipiana, Mills and Brantman (2004). These include the following:

1. During the course of divorce proceedings, one parent influences an impressionable child in some way to make false claims related to abuse.

2. In dysfunctional families, an adolescent makes allegations of sexual abuse for secondary gain. For example, as a way of getting back or deflecting family outrage in family conflicts about a teenage pregnancy or unacceptable boyfriends/girlfriends.

3. A child has learned from past abuse about the power that the disclosure of abuse brings. So years later that make an allegation of abuse as a bombshell to try to stop something from happening that they don't want to happen.

4. The child in a dysfunctional but non-abusive family makes allegations of sexual abuse as a sort of cry for help.

5. There can be contagion effects when other youngsters have come forward claiming abuse.

There is a great deal more to be found in Chapter 20 on the problems of interviewing children and getting the best quality testimony from them.

It is important to bear in mind the problems facing investigators in difficult cases such as the sexual abuse of young children. Not only is independent evidence of sexual abuse often difficult to find but, also, the offender is unlikely to confess. Lippert, Cross, Jones and Walsh (2010) are among the researchers who have studied the confession rates in those suspected of sexual abuse. Included among the cases studied were 38 per cent involving allegations of vaginal or anal intercourse. The children averaged 9 years of age at the time of their abuse and 88 per cent were girls. Only 30 per cent of the participants confessed during the stages of the criminal justice process either to the allegations in full or partially. This sort of figure is typical of the findings of similar studies too except where polygraph testing is used in the community when higher confession rates are found. A number of factors seem to encourage confession: (a) the suspect is young, (b) there is a greater amount of evidence, (c) the victim is older, (d) if it is a case of abuse outside of the family, (e) the more severe the abuse, (f) the child discloses the abuse fully, (g) if another child alleges abuse by the same person, and (h) where there is collaborating evidence. Quite clearly, then, in many cases the investigators can expect denial from the suspect and the optimum circumstances for a confession simply are not present.

Pathways to false allegations

There are any number of potential reasons why individuals are falsely accused of crimes which they did not commit or simply did not happen irrespective of the perpetrator. Psychological research has yet to embrace the full range of motivations and processes involved. A useful perspective on the complexity of false allegations is O'Donohue and Bowers' (2006) theoretical analysis in relation to sexual harassment allegations. O'Donohue and Bowers include in their list of pathways to false allegations a wide variety of factors including lying, psychosis, substance abuse, dementia, false memories, false interpretations, biased interviews and mistakes in the investigation. But most of these pathways are themselves very complex. So, for example, what are the reasons why people knowingly lie by making false allegations of sexual harassment? They include the possibility of financial gain, that some people enjoy the status of being a victim, simply to hurt an individual or organisation, and to serve as an excuse for poor work performance.

Of course, these pathways are speculative and we simply do not know how generally they apply either in terms of their extent or the crimes that they are relevant to.

Child sexual abuse

It is hard for the inexperienced to believe how, in some cases, bad interviewing technique can create false evidence.

The psychiatrist Bernet (1997) described a case in which an allegation was made against a parent through repeated suggestive questions (i.e. leading questions). A babysitter developed suspicions about the family for whom she worked. She, as a precaution, taped an interview she conducted with their child, known as Betsy, then five years of age. As a consequence, the parents were reported to child protection services and Betsy was removed from the family home for nearly two years. Generally speaking, repeated sessions of suggestive interviewing are not necessary to produce such effects. Notice how in the following extract the child very quickly begins saying untrue things. The babysitter had formed the opinion (or developed a theory) that Betsy was afraid of sweeping brushes or brooms because her parents played a game they called 'sweep the bootie' with her. There were several hundreds of questions on the tape. The following is representative of some of the things that can be heard on the tape:

Joyce [the babysitter]: Okay. So Daddy plays sweeping the bootie with his hand. How does he use his hand? What does he do with his hand?

Betsy: Touches.

Joyce: He touches you. Did he touch your pee-pee where you go number one or did he touch where you go number two?

Betsy: Number two.

Joyce: Okay. You're saying he touched you where you go do-do at or where you go pee-pee at?

Betsy: Do-do.

(Bernet, 1997, p. 968)

Notice the way the babysitter gives forced-choice alternatives that gradually shape in the mind of the child the idea that the parents had molested the child's genitals and anus. The net effect of all of the questioning is that the parents appear to be being accused by the child of molesting her genitals and anus with a sweeping brush.

BOX 16.1 Controversy

The recovered memory/false memory debate

One of the most perplexing but familiar issues in forensic and criminal psychology is that of recovered memories/false memory. Legally this is a complex issue in some jurisdictions because conventional time limitations on prosecutions have to be set aside in order to try the accused. A very significant factor in the origins of the debate was the allegations made by an American professor of psychology, Jennifer Freyd (1996), against her parents, John and Pamela Freyd, concerning sexual abuse (Calof, 1993). These claims led to the False Memory Syndrome Foundation being set up. In adulthood, she had undergone therapy and her recollections of the events emerged following this. The basic issue is whether such memories are simply the product of suggestions made during psychotherapy (false memories) or reflect the uncovering of true childhood memories of repressed, stressful events (recovered memories). The language used to describe the 'phenomenon' is potentially value-ridden and evaluative. The so-called false memory syndrome is a severe psychopathology involving

pseudomemories relating to beliefs about early sexual abuse. It is identified in terms of a belief in their memories concerning their abuse, the patterns in their current interpersonal relationships, symptoms of trauma in their life history and characteristics of their therapeutic experience (Hovdestad and Kristiansen, 1996a). Only a small proportion (less than about one in eight) of women with claims of recovered memories actually meet the diagnostic criteria.

Central to the debate is the idea that therapy instils the belief in some clients that the repression of sexual abuse is common and is the cause of the client's problems. In a sense, the issue is one of diagnosticity of signs, since some therapists believe that a wide range of emotional and psychological problems result from untreated child sexual abuse. One client has expressed this in the following terms:

He [therapist] kept pressuring me by telling me that if I wanted to recover from my depression at that point and become a better mother, then I better look at these memories and do some work with them. He also thought if I left my children with their grandparents, they might be in danger. He kept insisting that I had all of the symptoms and I might as well admit it. He acted like he could see right through me and that he knew my story better than I did.

(Ost, Costall and Bull, 2002, p. 4)

The recovered memory issue became important in legal settings. The fairly acrimonious debate within psychology has been rehearsed in front of judges in many courtrooms. MacMartin and Yarmey (1998) regard the debate as being a dispute over who possesses the expertise on the matter. The battle involved confrontations between academic psychology (experimentalists for the most part) and clinician/ practitioners (including clinical psychologists and psychiatrists):

- Support for the idea that recovered memories are reliable evidence of childhood sexual abuse comes largely from practitioners – the people who counsel the victims of abuse. They believe that through repression and dissociation, early memories of real events become unavailable to memory. The writings and evidence of this category of expert suggest that repression and dissociation help the traumatised victim of sexual abuse defend themselves psychologically against the resulting psychological pain. Broadly speaking, repression is regarded as the burial of memories of abuse deep in the mind whereas dissociation is a sort of laying to one side, or setting aside from memories normally available within our conscious experience. There are a variety of positions within the clinical perspective. The primary evidence for this idea is, of course, the case studies of recovered memories. There is also a long tradition in clinical theorising (starting with Freud and Janet) which adopts such a perspective. In addition, there are some examples from the research tradition of experimental laboratory studies that can be or have been used in support of this. While these do not directly study trauma for obvious reasons,

these include studies in which forgetting is directed under hypnosis and could be seen as evidence of similar processes. Sheehan (1997) suggests that the cases in which a woman has forgotten her abuse but the offender validates that she was abused are persuasive evidence of repression.

- Academic psychologists are more likely to be dismissive of the value of recovered memories as evidence of childhood abuse. Some of them, according to MacMartin and Yarmey (1998), claim that clinicians work with what could be described as 'robust repression'. They are suggesting that repression in the clinical formulation screens off what is an accurate memory trace of the traumatic events of the sexual abuse. The difficulty with the notion of robust repression is that it relates poorly to the beliefs of experimentalists researching memory. Experimentalists tend to view memory as a reconstruction that blends fact and fiction. Experimentalists may be rather more accepting of the notion of dissociation. Doubters of the veracity of recovered memories sometimes point out that a person in a dissociative state is usually aware that there is something missing from their memory. This does not seem to apply to the cases of recovered memories. These sceptics generally believe that there is no definitive evidence favouring repression and dissociation as applied to multiple repeated experiences of sexual abuse. One of the fiercest critics of the idea of recovered memories is Elizabeth Loftus (Loftus, Garry and Hayne, 2008) who views the evidence of the process of repression as central to the debate. She argues that 'there is no empirical evidence for repression and that claims of repression (in cases where the event really happened) are merely instances of plain old everyday forgetting' (p. 178). Nevertheless she points out that the majority of people in forensic settings such as judges (50 per cent), jurors (73 per cent) and police officers (65 per cent) believed that the phenomenon of repression exists (Benton et al., 2006) whereas only 22 per cent of psychologists of a scientific orientation did.

▶

BOX 16.1 (continued)

While not feeling able to prefer one side of the debate over the other, Memon and Young (1997) stress the importance of exploring the possible mechanisms of recovered memories. Their conclusions echo those of others:

- They describe the 'grand' idea of repression to be of dubious validity if by repression we mean something other than the gradual forgetting of events.
- Repression in the sense of cognitive/emotional processes which essentially 'keep the lid' on events and memories that we would otherwise remember lacks laboratory evidence convincingly mimicking the process.
- There is evidence in favour of the ideas that memories may be suppressed, the dissociation of memories (as in multiple personality disorder) and inhibition.

It can be added that although repression is regarded as a consequence of the emotion surrounding the acts of abuse, there are a number of studies which indicate that highly emotional events can be remembered with high levels of accuracy as in flashbulb memory (Brown and Kulik, 1977).

Of course, the task of sceptics includes explaining the processes involved in false memories. These include the mechanism by which these 'memories' are recovered. This may be through a retrieval process of the sort that has frequently been described in the research literature. An especially graphic example of this is a study by Loftus and Pickrell (1995). Their study involved stories apparently recalled by older relatives about the early childhood of each participant. Three of the stories were in fact true recollections by the relatives but the fourth one was untrue. The participants remembered 68 per cent of the true stories. Many fewer claimed to remember the fictitious events but, nevertheless, a quarter of them indicated that they at least partially remembered the fictitious events. Figure 16.1 provides a summary of some of the possible mechanisms of repressed memory.

One difficulty with the debate on the false/recovered memory debate is that memory as studied by most experimentalists is factual, conscious and reflective. This is termed explicit memory. Hovdestad

and Kristiansen (1996b) argue that there is another form of memory – implicit memory – that is different in many respects. For example, it involves conditioned emotional responses, it is unconscious, it is not reflective, it appears from birth rather than infancy and it appears to be associated with the more primitive brain structures. This suggests that the traumatic experience of child sexual abuse may be processed totally differently from the way that experimentalists suggest.

Kassin (1997a) suggests that there is a strong resemblance between false memories of victimisation and some false confessions of offending where memories are confabulated and turned against oneself.

Not only are claims of recovered memories made, they are also sometimes retracted. De Riviera (1997) suggested that retraction of claims of abuse may be the result of a set of circumstances in the creation of these memories:

- an authority figure used techniques of emotional, information, behavioural and thought control to control their thoughts;
- the client creates a narrative that helps put their lives into a meaningful systematic structure aided by a few suggestions from the therapist.

Ost *et al.* (2002) also studied retractors. Almost by definition, their evidence might be suspect given their lack of consistency (the change from not remembering the events, then recovering memories of the events and finally denying their recovered memories). Only a few retractors had any indication of memory of abuse before they recovered memories of abuse. Mostly the recovered memories were their first memories of abuse. The overwhelming majority claimed that there had been *no* pressure on them to retract the false memories. This contrasts with their claim that they were under pressure when they recovered their memories of abuse. Generally, they were not confident in the veracity of their recovered memories even at the time of making their allegations. Virtually all were firmly confident in their retraction of the recovered memories. The more pressure they had felt to remember abuse, the more likely they were to be confident in their retraction of

Model 1 CLASSICAL REPRESSION	Model 2 EMOTIONALLY CHARGED MEMORY PROCESSES	Model 3 RETRIEVAL PROCESSES FROM MEMORY
Origin: Later writings of Sigmund Freud regarded repression as an unconscious response to distressing memories	Origin: Studies of the accuracy of eyewitness testimony about stressful situations. Emotion adversely affects memory of abuse.	Origin: Encoding specificity theory concentrates on the role of memory retrieval cues.
Experimental support: Many studies have failed to show unconscious repression.	Experimental support: Eyewitness studies support the opposite view – emotionally charged events are better remembered. However, even when clear they are subject to distortions of memory.	Experimental support: A multiplicity of studies show that memory is a reconstruction rather than a pure trace of an event.
Clinical support: Repression is a central concept in psychoanalysis and clinical psychology.	Clinical support: This is not really a clinical issue distinct from the concept of repression.	Many psychoanalytic approaches are intended to uncover repressed memories. Psychotherapy is held to cause false memories by some.
Status of recovered memories: Reflect true events hidden by the memory.	Status of recovered memories: May reflect true events or distortions.	Status of recovered memories: Provide evidence of the creation of entirely spurious memories though as yet no easy way of distinguishing fabricated from true memories.
Other comments: Evidence seems to suggest that some individuals consciously suppress memories more than that unconscious factors are at play.	Other comments: Source monitoring theory suggests that emotion reduces concentration on peripheral informations, such as the source of the memory that makes recollection difficult.	Other comments: Establishes the plausibility but not the actuality of claims that memories are false memories.

Figure 16.1 Possible mechanisms of repressed memories

BOX 16.1 (continued)

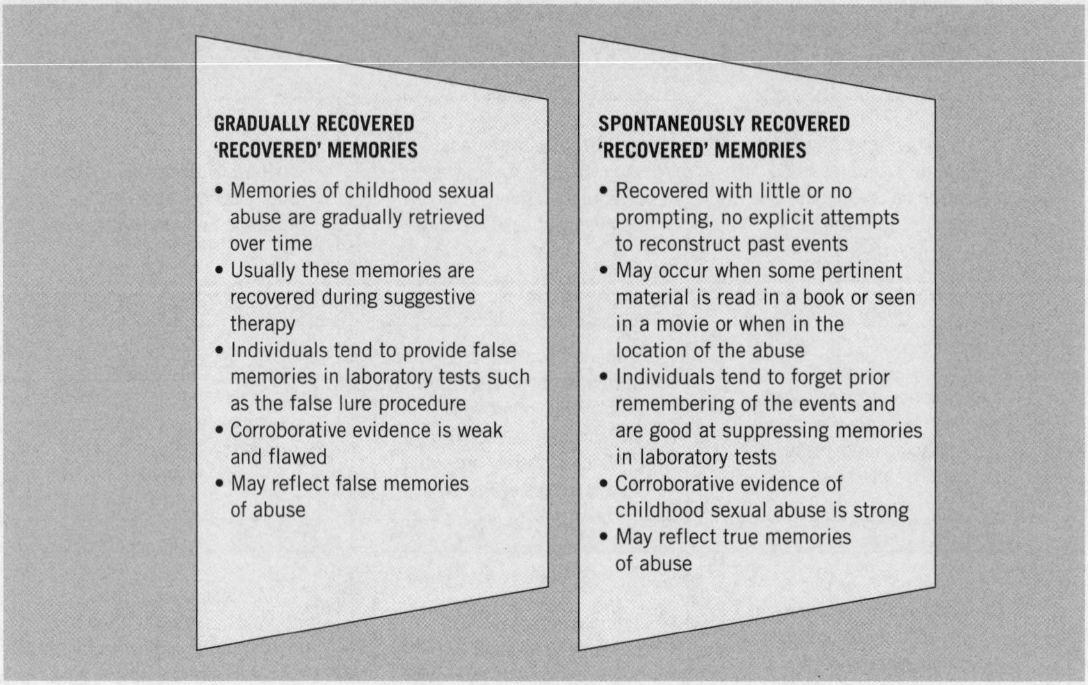

GRADUALLY RECOVERED 'RECOVERED' MEMORIES

- Memories of childhood sexual abuse are gradually retrieved over time
- Usually these memories are recovered during suggestive therapy
- Individuals tend to provide false memories in laboratory tests such as the false lure procedure
- Corroborative evidence is weak and flawed
- May reflect false memories of abuse

SPONTANEOUSLY RECOVERED 'RECOVERED' MEMORIES

- Recovered with little or no prompting, no explicit attempts to reconstruct past events
- May occur when some pertinent material is read in a book or seen in a movie or when in the location of the abuse
- Individuals tend to forget prior remembering of the events and are good at suppressing memories in laboratory tests
- Corroborative evidence of childhood sexual abuse is strong
- May reflect true memories of abuse

Figure 16.2 Two types of recovered memory claims (Geraerts *et al.*)

those memories. See Figure 16.2 for an outline of the possible mechanisms of repressed memories.

One fascinating piece of evidence puts the recovered memory/false memory debate into perspective. Quite clearly it is an issue that has attracted the interest of the public and is not confined solely to an crimonious debate between squabbling professions. It is also a socio-political issue. Kristiansen (1996) has shown that for two different Canadian samples, participants who believed in the false memory syndrome (i.e. the invalidity of some abuse allegations) tended to have more anti-women ideas such as 'women who stay in abusive relationships obviously like to be beaten' or 'many women are unsuitable for top management positions because, for a few days each month, they simply can't function at their best' (p. 26). Similarly, Griffith, Libkuman and Poole (1998) found that women jurors were less likely to believe the defendant than male jurors in a simulated repressed memory trial.

One useful account of the US legal experience of 'recovered memories' especially in relation to the statute of limitations (i.e. time elapsed before reporting crime) is Taub (1996). There is good reason to accept Kristiansen, Felton and Hovdestad's (1996) caution that beliefs about recovered/false memories are '[more] closely tied to autocratic misogynism and self-interest than they are to social values or science' (p. 56). It is an area where 'facts' can be readily supplied for any position that one wishes to defend.

Geraerts, Raymaekers and Merckelbach (2008) recount the story of famous clarinettist Binjamin Wilomirski who published his autobiographical memoir in 1996. In this he describes his childhood in a German concentration camp. He became something of a hero among Holocaust survivors. During his adult life he did not recall these events until he went through something called dream interpretation therapy. However, a journalist discovered that Binjamin had spent his childhood in the home of his foster parents who lived in Switzerland. Some began to regard Wilomirski as a fabricator but he, himself, remained convinced of the truth of his childhood ordeal. Research laboratories have begun to examine the question of the people who report 'recovered' memories might also be those who are prone to the induction of false memories by researchers. There is a cognitive test known as the Deese-Roediger-McDermott (DRM) paradigm (Deese, 1959) in which participants look at a list of words which are strongly associated with another word not included on the list. This word is the *critical lure* and reflects the essential features of the whole list. Geraerts *et al.* (2008) give the example of the list awake, bed, rest, tired etc. and its critical lure word 'sleep'. Tested later, some people claim to have seen the critical lure word 'sleep' among the words presented on the list.

Geraerts *et al.* found that people who had experienced recovering child sexual abuse memories tended to erroneously recall the critical lure as being on the list compared with a control group of people with no history of abuse or those who had been abused but had never forgotten these events (also Clancy, Schacter, McNally and Pitman, 2000). Of course, such a research procedure may be criticised for its artificiality compared to the recovered memory phenomenon – a problem which Geraerts *et al.* partially address by using more emotional, sexually charged lures such as assault, rape and violence. Much the same findings emerged for people claiming recovered memories of sexual abuse to believe that they remembered the (emotional) lure as being on the list.

Case examples suggest that some people who claim to have recovered memories of childhood sexual abuse had actually talked to others previously about this abuse. Although the other people clearly remember these discussions, the person themselves claim to have no recollection of these discussions and so believe that they had no recollection of the abuse since childhood until the memory was eventually recovered – apparently spontaneously.

According to Geraerts *et al.* (2008), interviews with those who had recovered memories suggested that there are two types of recovered memory as illustrated in Figure 16.2:

- One type of recovered memory experience is fairly slow and is usually associated with involvement in suggestive therapies including hypnosis. This is the gradual type of recovered memory.
- The second type of recovered memory is much quicker and almost takes the individual by surprise. This is the spontaneous type of recovered memory.

The two types may begin to explain why some adult recoveries of memories of childhood abuse seem to be accurate whereas others seem to be false. In order to examine this further, the following four groups of participants were used:

- A control group who had never claimed as an adult or child memories of child sexual abuse.
- A spontaneous recovery group who reported forgetting memories of their sexual abuse as a child with no prompting from others.
- A group who recovered memories of child sexual abuse during therapy perhaps encouraged by suggestive therapeutic techniques – that is, sexual abuse memories were actively reconstructed.
- A continuous memory group who had never forgotten their childhood experiences of sexual abuse.

It was expected that the group recovering memories of child sexual abuse during suggestive therapy would be particularly prone to showing source monitoring deficiencies as assessed by the DRM or false lure test and that the spontaneous memory recovery group would be show a tendency to underestimate their prior remembering of events as assessed by the false lure test. The spontaneous recovery group was expected to be more capable of suppressing memories when asked to do so under laboratory conditions. Both of these expectations proved to be true. Of course the implication is that the memories recovered under suggestive therapy are mistaken and fabricated whereas the spontaneously recovered memories are not really recovered memories at all but memories that have been accessed before but forgotten about (see Figure 16.2).

▶

BOX 16.1 (continued)

The minefield that can be research into recovered memories is epitomised by the experiences of Elizabeth Loftus (Geis and Loftus, 2009). Briefly, Loftus is somewhat sceptical of the idea that there are of repressed memories of sexual abuse which can be recovered or retrieved during therapy. She was interested by a published article by a psychiatrist concerning the pseudonymous 'Jane Doe' who was first interviewed at five years of age and again at the age of 17 years. Jane Doe had putatively recovered memories of sexual abuse by her mother. Loftus and Guyer (2002) reviewed this article and critically evaluated the evidence that it contained. A psychiatrist involved in this case had claimed that Jane Doe's experiences represented an example of recovered memories (Corwin and Olafson, 1997). One oddity was that the Jane Doe was known to the mental health authorities from when she was a young child and had told them of the abuse by her mother – and of abuse by her father which she eventually retracted. There was documentary evidence that the allegations were repeated. However, the psychiatrist claimed that Jane Doe had suffered traumatic amnesia and the abuse was eventually revealed during interviews with him. Loftus and Guyer decided to track down Jane Doe which they did from clues to her identity in video of the interviews and so forth. On the basis of their investigations, Loftus and Guyer (2002) not only doubted the evidence of recoovered memories but also whether the alleged abuse had ever happened.

Jane Doe sued Loftus and Guyer and others for alleged harms that had been done to her in terms of emotional distress, defamation and invasion of privacy among other things. The basis of the claim of defamation was that Loftus had supposedly publicly questioned Jane Doe's mental health and fitness. The point of describing all of this is not only that it led to lengthy proceedings against Loftus and others in the courts but it also led to obstacles being placed before Loftus and Guyer's academic research by their then respective academic institutions. This was a tricky, thorny road indeed for academic researchers.

False claims of abuse and young children

It seems relatively easy to demonstrate how false claims of abuse can be obtained from pre-school children (e.g. Bruck *et al.*, 1995; Ceci *et al.*, 1994). Essentially, researchers interview children about events that had happened to the child and also what were actually fictions (according to the child's parents). The studies involve, for example, a fictitious episode in which the child was supposed to have caught his or her finger in a mousetrap. As a consequence, a hospital visit was necessary to deal with the injury. For all (or the vast majority) of children in the studies these events had not happened.

How resistant are pre-school children to the pressure of the interview? During the course of an interview, children were read a list of things that might have happened to them. They were required to think hard about each of them and to try to remember if the event really happened. About a third of children accepted fictitious events as real. This percentage remained much the same when they were interviewed on several occasions. There was some inconsistency since a number of the children switched one way or the other at each stage, balancing the changes in each direction. If the children were told by the interviewer that the fictitious events really did happen to the child, there were increases in the percentage of the children accepting the fictitious experiences as real (Ceci *et al.*, 1994). The extent of 'false memory induction' depended somewhat on the age of the child. Children who accepted the fictitious event as real would sometimes provide additional detail about the events. The event would be elaborated and they would describe the emotional feelings associated with it.

Of course, such evidence as this is only suggestive of the extent to which, in interview conditions, young children confuse fiction with fact. Limitations include the following:

- This age group is not representative of those involved in sexual abuse allegations and false memory induction may not apply to these older children.

- The questioning by the interviewers in these studies went way beyond what would be expected in a police interview or social work interview of a child involved in possible sexual abuse.

That is to say, the findings of the studies might not generalise to real-life situations. In order to disregard the suggestion in the question, the child must be able to do the following, according to Poole and Lindsay (1998):

- Understand that the interviewer actually wants them to report only their individual, personal experiences.

- Know what the sources of their knowledge actually are (i.e. they require source monitoring ability).

An important experiment in this context is Poole and Lindsay's *Mr Science* study. In essence, this can be summarised as follows:

- At school, a group of 3- and 4-year-olds experienced vivid science lessons given by Mr Science.

- Closely afterwards, they were interviewed and requested to tell the interviewer everything about the science lesson. Their reports were extremely accurate and very few of them made false claims.

- Three months later, the parents of the children were sent a storybook to read to their child. It contained descriptions of the Mr Science lessons that had actually happened, but also descriptions of lessons that had not happened. The fictitious material, for example, describes how the child was touched by Mr Science who then put a 'yucky' object in their mouth. The stories were told to the child three times.

- This was followed by another interview session in which open-ended and then leading questions were put to the child about whether or not the events were real or just from one of the stories.

The major findings from the study were as follows:

- Two out of every five children mentioned as if real events that originated only in the stories.

- Leading questions increased the rates of false reporting. Over half of all children answered yes to a question about whether Mr Science had put something 'yucky' into their mouths. When requested by the interviewer, the majority of these children went on to describe details of the fictional event.

- The interview also included quite severe challenges to the children about the truth of what they said. Nevertheless, the majority of the children when challenged

in this way continued to maintain that Mr Science had truly put a yucky thing into their mouth.

- Increasing the age range from 3 to 8 years of age did not result in a decline in false reports. These remained stable in free recall conditions.

- Challenges about the truth of their claims meant declines in false claims for the older children but not the younger ones.

- There was a fairly high degree of stability in the false claims. Follow-up of those who had made false claims a month later revealed that two-thirds were still making the same false claims.

There is another important study which reinforces the view that even young children are somewhat resistant to suggestive or leading questioning. It also shows that as children get older then even the simplest of challenges to their false claims rapidly produces recantation. Leichtman and Ceci (1995) had children aged 3–6 years watch as a stranger named Sam Stone visited their pre-school, walked about and left. They were interviewed four times about Sam Stone's visit. There was no leading or suggestive questioning up to this point. Then the children were asked about two fictitious events: did Sam Stone do anything to a book or a teddy bear? A high level of accuracy was produced. Only 10 per cent said that he did do something and this figure reduced to 5 per cent when they were asked if they actually saw him do it. When they were gently challenged about their false claims – you didn't really see him do anything to the book/teddy bear, did you? – this figure declined further to 2.5 per cent. For the older children, this sort of challenge was especially effective.

Another group of pre-schoolers was exposed to repeated conversations about Sam's clumsiness and proneness to breaking things. They were subsequently interviewed with suggestive questions such as 'Remember the time Sam Stone visited our classroom and spilled chocolate on that white teddy bear? Did he do it on purpose or was it an accident?' In the final interview:

- 72 per cent of the youngest pre-schoolers reported that Sam did something to the book or teddy;

- 44 per cent said they actually saw him do these things;

- 21 per cent maintained their false stories when gently challenged;

- 5–6-year-olds were less malleable since only 11 per cent said they actually saw the misdeeds and less than 10 per cent maintained the story when challenged.

Forensically, the issue is more complex than this. Children in sexual abuse cases are in the hands of professionals such as the police, social workers, psychologists and psychiatrists, all of whom must form judgements and make decisions. So one question must concern us: just how good are professionals at detecting false information? Poole and Lindsay (1998) argue that the ability of professionals is relatively poor. For instance:

- When clinical and research psychologists specialising in interviewing children were shown videos of children in the mousetrap experiments described above, they were unable to differentiate between fictional and real experiences at better than the chance level (Ceci *et al.*, 1994).

- Horner, Guuyer and Kalter (1993) showed workers in the mental health field a two-hour case study containing interviews with the parents, interviews with the child and child–parent interaction, and they could request additional information. In addition, groups of the workers discussed the case together for over an hour. The researchers found no relationship between whether or not the health worker believed that child abuse had taken place and recommendations about future contact of the child with its father – they all recommended that the child–father contact should be supervised irrespective of their judgements about abuse!

Bruck and Ceci (1997) construe the above research and others as evidence of the creation of suggestive interviews based on interviewer bias. Such biases are seen as involving a failure to challenge what children say when it supports the interviewer's preconceptions, and events inconsistent with the interviewer's preconceptions are not touched upon.

The concept of suggestibility has a long history in psychology but, perhaps more importantly, it is a notion familiar to professionals working in the criminal justice system and child protection. Over 100 years ago, William Stern (1904) regarded the predisposition to succumb to suggestion as suggestibility. Nevertheless, it was important to differentiate two different types of suggestion:

- Active suggestion: the activity of suggesting something to another person.

- Passive suggestion: the state of a person who is currently under the influence of suggestion.

These can be totally unrelated processes since (1) a suggestion may be made but it is *not* responded to but (2) a suggestion which has *not* been made may be responded to. In other words, one cannot simply find suggestion's influence in circumstances in which a suggestion has been made. According to Ceci and Bruck (1993), suggestibility refers to the extent to which all aspects of a child's memory for events are influenced by a variety of social and psychological factors. Suggestibility may influence the ways in which events are encoded into memory, the processes of retrieving the memory, and just what is reported to others in interviews and elsewhere. Thus it is a mistake to assume that suggestibility is exclusively the consequence of a particular interview or interview style.

Motzkau (2004) argues that 'suggestibility is itself suggestive' (p. 7), meaning that the widespread knowledge of the concept of suggestibility itself has an effect within the criminal justice system over and above what could be warranted by our current research-based knowledge. Some psychological concepts spread into common knowledge among other professions and the general public. The public finds out about psychological ideas in part through the media. Of course, the concept as understood by the public may be quite a simplistic one and involve rather overstated accounts of the findings of research (Motzkau, 2004). So, for example, the general public may be led to believe that children are extremely suggestible and easily influenced by parents and misguided professionals into making allegations that are simply untrue. The danger in this is that because of high-profile cases in which children have made unfounded allegations of abuse, others will be reluctant to report the abuse simply because it is felt that no one will believe their story. As a consequence, there will be a decline in the number of reported child abuse cases. In Germany, argues Motzkau, people became concerned that the criminal justice system could be undergoing an 'epidemic' of false allegations of child sexual abuse especially in relation to child custody disputes since there had been a great deal of scientific, media and public interest in the issue of suggestibility. Objectively, this was totally unfounded as there were virtually no cases in which false allegations of sexual abuse were an issue. The issue focused on the disputed child custody cases in which allegations of abuse could result in unfair child custody decisions.

The important practical consequence of this can be illustrated by one of Motzkau's interviews with a police officer. The police had been called in by staff at a care home. A 12-year-old girl with learning disability had apparently reported to one member of staff another staff member for behaving inappropriately sexually towards her. The alleged perpetrator denied this. The police officer was concerned about his role as an interviewer, fearing that he might not have interviewed the girl correctly since she disclosed nothing about her apparent abuse. The officer was also apprehensive about interviewing the girl again since this repeated interviewing might devalue the evidence in the eyes of others. It finally emerged in a chance comment from a different child that the alleged perpetrator had actually accidentally hurt the putative victim of abuse with a food trolley. With this information, it was possible to clarify with the 'victim' that this was the incident that had resulted in the allegation. Furthermore, the staff member who had reported the matter to the police initially had decided not to discuss the matter with the girl because she feared the suspicion that she had suggested the allegation to the girl in some way!

BOX 16.2 Forensic psychology in action

Testing for suggestibility

While it is extremely important to understand just how questioning styles, age and other factors influence responsiveness to suggestibility, there is another fundamental issue – do certain individuals tend to be more suggestible than other people in more situations? That is, is it reasonable to regard suggestibility as a characteristic of the individual rather than the situation? Gudjonsson (2003) explored this route using the Gudjonsson Suggestibility Scale (Gudjonsson, 1984), which attempts to establish the general suggestibility level of an individual. Quite clearly, if suggestibility is a characteristic of individuals then a test that measures it would have potential in the context of the work of forensic psychologists. The Gudjonsson Suggestibility Scale is more than a questionnaire – it is a procedure in which the practitioner gives the individual material to learn and then examines the way in which that individual responds to leading questions and other pressures. The point is, however, that the procedures are reasonably standardised. The steps in the process are as follows:

- Material presentation: a tape-recording of a short piece of narrative is played to the person being assessed.
- Immediate recall: the person being assessed is requested to remember as much of the narrative as possible in as much detail as possible.
- First asking of list of leading questions: the assessor asks a standard list of 20 questions about the narrative. Fifteen of these questions are actually leading questions that imply an answer which is actually inaccurate. A score is computed known as 'Yield 1' which is simply the number of the leading (inaccurate) questions that the person being assessed agrees with.
- Negative feedback: once the questions have all been answered, then the assessor says things like 'You have made a number of errors. It is therefore necessary to go through the questions once more, and this time try to be more accurate.' This is an attempt to influence the individual being assessed further.
- Second asking of list of leading questions: the assessor reads out the same list of leading questions again. After this stage, two additional different scores are calculated: 'Shift' is simply the number of questions that the person being assessed actually gives a different answer to from the first time. It does not matter if the question is a leading question or one of the five other questions. 'Yield 2' is the number of leading questions which the person being assessed agrees with after the negative feedback. It indicates the direction of any change from the first leading question stage to the second.
- There is another measure – total suggestibility – which is simply the sum of 'Yield 1 + Shift'.

Research suggests that 'Yield 1' and 'Shift' are two quite distinct aspects of suggestibility. They are

▶

BOX 16.2 (continued)

independent dimensions. Of course, this is a quite complex assessment and it is perhaps not surprising to find that procedural differences may have some but not necessarily a crucial influence on the outcome. For example, the negative feedback can be expressed in a more or a less hostile fashion (Boon and Baxter, 2004). It is also valuable to know that it is difficult to fake suggestibility on Gudjonsson's test (Baxter and Bain, 2002) since of course it would be in some offenders' interests to be able to appear suggestible when they are not. Some participants in a study were requested to pretend to act like a suggestible person on the test. The researchers found that it was possible to fake suggestibility well on the 'Yield 1' measure but, having done this, then their 'Shift' scores did not correspond to the pattern of a suggestible person. So, quite clearly, the participants knew some of the things that they needed to do in order to appear suggestible but they could not anticipate all of

what was needed to put on an entirely convincing display.

Does the scale work with children? Scullin, Kanaya and Ceci (2002) studied an adaptation of the Gudjonsson measure which is known as the Visual Suggestibility Scale for Children. This is very similar except that the material is presented visually as well as aurally and a number of other modifications were made to ensure that the measure was suitable for this younger age range. What they did was to set up an independent field study in which the children were repeatedly interviewed about an event that occurred at school and things that did not actually happen. The question was, then, whether being influenced in these interviews actually was predictable on the basis of scores on the Visual Suggestibility Scale for Children. The 'Yield' and 'Shift' measures both independently predicted aspects of suggestibility in the field interviews.

Great care needs to be exercised over the question of the level of young children's suggestibility. As we saw above, there is evidence that they can be influenced to make accusations that emerge to be simply not true. However, just because they may be influenced, say, by leading questioning does not mean that they are always influenced or that they are more susceptible to suggestion than older children or even adults. Similarly, just because young children may be susceptible to influence on some matters does not mean that they are equally susceptible on all matters. A good example of this is Eisen *et al.*'s (1998) research. They studied a group of children who had been hospitalised for several days for assessment of abuse. This involved a medical examination which included an analysis of their genitals and anus as well as an interview concerning their possible abuse or neglect. Before they left hospital, they were subjected to an interview which included misleading questions about the genital and anal examination and about other much more mundane matters. There were clearly signs that younger children were more susceptible to suggestion than older children. When asked suggestive questions about mundane matters, pre-school children were led to give untruthful responses nearly one-third

of the time whereas the figures for older children were half this and for teenagers a fifth of this. But when faced with leading questions on the topic of abuse such as 'The doctor did not have any clothes on, did he/she?' then pre-school children succumbed one-fifth of the time, older children rarely and teenagers never. That is to say, that the youngsters were not so suggestible about the crucial issue of abuse.

There is little consistency across studies in terms of the percentages of children who succumb to suggestive questions. Poole and Lindsay (2002) describe the proportions across different studies which are affected by suggestive questioning as showing 'vast variability' (p. 369). Consequently, it is difficult and perhaps impossible to assess the likelihood that suggestion plays a role in real-life cases involving children. One remarkable suggestion they make is that there is a case for the use of leading questions in some circumstances. They urge professionals such as social workers not to use leading questions when working in areas where the baseline rates of abuse are low. Children disclose about abuse without interviewers using leading questions, which risk increasing the risk of false claims by the child. On the other hand, professionals working in areas where sexual abuse is common may be justified in using leading questioning as their 'hit' rate is likely to be high. They can reduce the risk of false information by the use of instructions or procedures which clarify to the child what is expected. For example, they can be told that they can give answers such as 'I don't understand' or 'I don't know.'

The problem with this is that it is difficult to make a judgement about just what proportion of false allegations are tolerable. If one seeks to minimise the number of false allegations then what Poole and Lindsay have to say is unacceptable. On the other hand, if the objective is to maximise the number of correct identifications of child sexual abuse then what they have to say is appropriate. These are not matters for psychology but are issues such as fairness, justice and ethics.

The diagnosticity of signs of abuse

Forensic and criminal psychologists and other clinicians usually spend their time forming judgements about a limited range of individuals. For example, they may work almost exclusively with sexually abused individuals. It is not surprising, therefore, to find that their expertise is largely limited to this group. They may take character-istics of such clients as indicators that there is a problem in people in general. For example, many of their sexually abused clients may report bed-wetting or enuresis in childhood and assume that this indicates a relationship between sexual abuse and bed-wetting. In other words, the psychologist may come to believe that bed-wetting is symptomatic of child sexual abuse. The trouble is that this is an illusory correlation since no comparisons are being made with non-abused children. If the psycho-logist dealt with non-abused individuals then he or she might well find that bed-wetting is just as common in this group. Hence bed-wetting has no power to differentiate between the abused and the non-abused.

So clinical experience may result in practitioners hav-ing false beliefs that certain indicators are signs of abuse. Denials by a child that they have been abused do not always seem to carry the evidentiary weight that might have been expected had the denial been made, say, by an adult. It is widely assumed that children are reluctant to disclose abuse for many reasons. A study, in Texas, took children in the age range of pre-school to 18 years on the files of the local child protection service (Bradley and

Wood, 1996). Nearly three-quarters of them had already disclosed to someone that they had been abused. Only later did most of them come to the attention of the police or the child protection service. Denial of abuse by the children was rare at 6 per cent of the cases. The recanta-tion by the child of their claim to have been abused was also rather rare at 4 per cent of the cases. One simple lesson to be drawn from these statistics is that children who deny abuse are probably not hiding the fact that they have been abused. It is more likely that abuse simply did not happen.

Berliner and Conte (1993) argue for caution when implementing the conclusions of studies that find a greater prevalence, say, of behavioural disorders in clinical samples of sexually abused individuals than in community controls. Most behavioural correlates of abuse are non-specific to abused children. That is to say, there are few, if any, factors that manifest themselves only in the behaviours of sexually abused children. Furthermore, the behavioural differences between abused and non-abused children are rather stronger when the behaviour is assessed through parents' ratings than when they are assessed through the children's ratings. It is possible, then, that the parents are aware of the possibility of abuse and consequently their ratings are affected by that knowledge. In this context, some of the indicators that have been claimed to be characteristic of sexually abused children do *not* emerge in the self-reports of those children. These are depression, anxiety and low self-esteem.

A key concept in understanding false allegations is that of diagnosticity. Broadly speaking, this is the extent to which certain features of a child's behaviour indicate that he or she has been sexually or physically abused (but see below). Howitt (1992) listed some of the many factors that have been suggested as indicating abuse. Textbooks for teachers about abuse, for example, sometimes sug-gest that regularly being late for school is a sign of abuse. Medics in Cleveland, location of the first major sexual abuse scandal (Butler-Sloss, 1988), similarly accepted that the response of a child's anus to being touched by a doctor was a sign that that child had actually been abused (Hanks, Hobbs and Wynne, 1988). These are examples of the indicators approach to the identification of sexual abuse.

Their use may be flawed in practice, but it is encouraged by research findings. For example, Slusser (1995) review-ing six studies concluded that overt sexual behaviour that is inappropriate for a child of that age is an indicator of sexual abuse. Nevertheless, any practitioner working with children should be aware that the baseline rates of childhood sexual activities are sometimes high. Gordon, Schroeder and Abrams (1990a,b) obtained parental reports on 2- to 7-year-olds:

- 29 per cent of the families claimed that their child had been exposed to sexually explicit materials;

- half of the children were known to have masturbated;

- 30 per cent of the children had been involved in exploratory sex-play.

The value of any indicator of sexual abuse is dependent on the following factors:

- The frequency of this possible indicator of sexual abuse in the group in question.

- The frequency of the indicator in similar but non-abused children.

It is particularly important for an indicator to be common among abused children but rare or non-existent among non-abused children. Very often, the relative frequency of the indicator in the population is unknown. Diagnosticity of a sign of sexual abuse depends on how common the sign is in abused children compared with its frequency in non-abused children. If the sign is equally common in both groups of children then it is useless in the diagnosis of sexual abuse. Munchausen's syndrome by proxy is a condition in which the offender fabricates symptoms and may deliberately injure a child in order to obtain repeated medical attention (Plassman, 1994). Some of the suggested indicators of the syndrome are actually diametric opposites (Howitt, 1992). So, for example, it has variously been suggested that evidence of the syndrome is demonstrated by confession to the crime but also by denial of the crime, or by over-concern about the child's health on the part of the parent as well as unconcern about the child's health!

A study of paediatric psychologists (Finlayson and Koocher, 1991) suggests that their interpretation of the extent to which an indicator may be indicative of abuse varies enormously. The psychologists were, for example, given a short description of a child whose school performance declined fast, who wet its bed, who was saying things about a bad man and who became anxious at the prospect of separation from its parents. On the basis of this evidence, 9 per cent believed that the likelihood of abuse was above 75 per cent certain, and 35 per cent suggested that the probability of abuse was less than 25 per cent certain. According to Slusser (1995), certain indicators such as bed-wetting may be the result of a multiplicity of different aetiologies. Consequently, especially because they are common among children (i.e. high base rate of occurrence), these indicators are of little diagnostic value at all. Why is this?

The diagnosticity issue is illustrated in Table 16.1. This shows the possible outcomes of using an indicator to predict whether abuse has occurred. For an indicator to be useful, true positives and true negatives should be maximised but false positives and false negatives should be kept to the minimum. Otherwise the guilty will escape detection and the innocent will be falsely accused.

The lack of knowledge of how common an indicator is in the non-abused population affects the confidence that one can have in its diagnosticity. So, for example, it is fairly widely held that precocious sexual behaviour is an indicator of sexual abuse. Just how common is it in the non-abused population of children? Research is the only sure way to answer the question. Friedrich *et al.* (1992) have carried out extensive investigations into parents' reports of sexual behaviours in abused and non-abused children. Certain sorts of behaviour seem to occur at similar rates in groups of abused and non-abused children. So, for example, touching the breasts of a woman is equally common in both sexually abused girls and non-abused girls. Thus any psychologist who took such touching as an indicator of sexual abuse would be profoundly wrong. There are dangers in inadvertently choosing a variable as an indicator of abuse which, actually, does not discriminate between abused and non-abused children.

Even if we take an indicator such as masturbation that does differentiate between the two, there remain dangers,

Table 16.1 The outcomes of using an indicator (or sign) to predict abuse

	Child abused in reality	Child not abused in reality
Indicator of abuse present	True positive	False positive
Indicator of abuse absent	False negative	True negative

despite the fact that this is commoner in abused children. Data collected by Friedrich (undated) demonstrated that in the 2–5 years of age female group, 28 per cent of the sexually abused children masturbated whereas 16 per cent of non-abused children did. In conventional psychological research terms this suggests that there is clearly an association between masturbation and sexual abuse. In terms of diagnosticity of indicators, things are not this simple. Take, for example, a class of 30 children. It is difficult to state precisely just how many of this class will have been sexually abused on average. Given the age group and the results of a variety of surveys, it is not unreasonable to suppose that 10 per cent of the class will have been abused whereas the remaining 90 per cent will not have been abused. Taking Friedrich's figures on rates of masturbation, we would expect the following outcome:

- *True positives* – one child correctly identified by the indicator as sexually abused.
- *False negatives* – two children who were abused are not correctly identified as such by the indicator (because they do not masturbate).
- *False positives* – four children wrongly identified as abused (because they are in the non-abused sample but masturbate).
- *True negatives* – 23 children correctly identified as not being abused.

Thus using this test, only a third of abused children are identified as being abused. For every abused child the test picks out, a further four are identified incorrectly as being abused. This is an unimpressive outcome, especially given the distress that follows from false accusations.

Thus the requirements of the indicator approach are much more demanding than would appear initially (Wood, 1996). It has been suggested that an indicator that is three times commoner among abused children than non-abused children nevertheless is only very weak evidence of abuse. An indicator that is 14 times more common in abused than non-abused children might be described as a moderate to strong indicator. It is far from being perfect proof (Poole and Lindsay, 1998). The interpretation of ratios such as this may be difficult for practitioners and other professionals to appreciate and apply. It may be helpful to point out that Friedrich *et al.* (1992) found that imitation of intercourse occurred in precisely this ratio. Imitation occurred in 14 per cent

of abused children but only 1 per cent of non-abused children. Another reason for caution about such indicators is that sexual interest in sexually abused children may be heightened by the child sexual abuse investigation itself: that is, that part of the apparent effect of child sexual abuse is actually a consequence of the interest in sexual matters among the professionals and parents involved.

Of course, it might seem sensible to seek two indicators rather than a single indicator of abuse. But the consideration of two indicators may not be much of an advance given the weak predictive strength of most predictors of abuse. Furthermore, the indicators may almost always occur together, which would do very little to improve the diagnosticity of the indicators.

Assessing the accuracy of young children's reports

Berliner and Conte (1993) suggested that there are two main strategies for improving professional judgement in child abuse cases:

- *Indicators approach*: this involves the search for evidence that distinguishes the true from the false report. As we have seen, one difficulty with this is the weakness of some of the indicators in use by practitioners.
- *Standards approach*: this specifies rules of conduct for those who carry out assessments. It seeks to minimise contamination of the child's reports through the use of best-practice procedures when dealing with children.

In what ways are genuine allegations different?

Obviously, if there were simple ways of differentiating a true allegation from a false allegation then false allegations would be easily dealt with. But, of course, there is no way of doing this with complete certainty in every case. Chapter 18, which deals with the assessment of truth, is clearly pertinent here and, for example, it discusses how statement validity analysis has been used to differentiate rape allegations which the police believe to be genuine from those which appear to be false. In a similar way, Marshall and Alison have used what they term structural behavioural analysis to differentiate the characteristics of genuine rape allegations from simulated ones. Marshall and Alison (2006) obtained actual rape allegation statements held by the police and compared them with the manufactured accounts of women instructed to imagine that they were trying to convince the police that they had been raped. None of this group had been the victim of any form of attack in their lives. The analytic task was straightforward – what characteristics differentiate the genuine rape allegations from the manufactured ones? The researchers examined each of the accounts, real or fabricated, for the presence of 37 different characteristics. These characteristics included things like the offender made sexual comments, kissing was involved, fellatio occurred, cunnilingus occurred, the victim was bound, something personal was stolen from the victim, the offender was apologetic, and there was anal penetration. There were points of difference between the two. For example, there were more different behaviours reported in the real accounts, pseudo-intimate features (such as

the offender giving the victim compliments and telling the victim details about himself) occurred more frequently in the genuine accounts, and there was a tendency for genuine accounts to describe more behaviourally coherent accounts than fictitious ones.

Fictitious accounts tended to involve sexual acts which were 'normal' such as vaginal intercourse whereas other acts such as anal intercourse, fellatio and cunnilingus were relatively uncommon in fictitious accounts. Fictitious accounts were also more likely to include violent acts such as the victim's clothes being torn, the woman subjected to insulting or demeaning language, and more different acts of violence. There were indications from the analysis that the methods employed were much better at identifying truthful allegations than they were at identifying fictitious allegations.

In this chapter we have largely examined the bad practice aspects of these approaches. Forensic and criminal psychology has made a more positive contribution. Chapter 20 discusses methods of assessing the value of a child's evidence and provides more information about how interviews can be better constructed to prevent the influence of suggestive and leading questions.

Main points

- The problem of false allegations is only one component of miscarriages of justice. It has proven particularly problematic in relation to allegations of child sexual abuse given the young age of many victims and the difficulty in interviewing them adequately. There is considerable evidence that some false memories for events may be created in children. Persistent leading questions can have an effect. One can overstate the fallibility of children's memories since there is plenty of evidence that they can be very accurate at recalling events. Nevertheless, some children in some circumstances will be affected by suggestion and make incorrect reports. However, a proportion of these will be retracted by the child when the interviewer questions their answer.

- There are a number of mechanisms that lead to repressed memories according to the theoretical approach in question. Freudian/classical repression refers to an unconscious process by which the person

is protected from distressing memories. An alternative are those studies that investigate the accuracy of eyewitness memory for emotionally charged events although the evidence seems to suggest that these tend to be well remembered. The repressed memory/false memory debate in psychology has attracted a great deal of public attention. Fundamentally, it sets different theories of memory in opposition to each other. It seems likely some recovered memories are indeed false memories because they are retracted.

- The issue of the diagnosticity of signs ought to be understood better by professional groups working with children. There are frequent claims in the professional literature of various professional groups that certain things are predictive of, say, sexual abuse. These include, for example, precocious sexual behaviour. Thus, say, a teacher who sees such behaviour exhibited by one of their students should be alerted to the risk that the child is being sexually abused. While it may be true that sexually abused children do demonstrate this more often, precocious sexual behaviour may not be a good indicator that a child has been sexually abused. The balance between the correctly identified abused and non-abused is important. A seemingly good indicator may result in many more false positive identifications of abuse than correct ones. The number of errors depends on the base rates of sexual abuse in the population and the frequency with which a sign occurs in the population in question.

Further reading

For a short but up-to-date review of the false-recovered memory debate try:

Loftus, E., Garry, M. and Hayne, H. (2008) 'Repressed and recovered memories' in E. Borgida and S.T. Fiske (eds) *Beyond Common Sense: Psychological Science in the Courtroom* Oxford: Blackwell, pp. 177–94.

For an in-depth discussion of false allegations:

Howitt, D. (1992) *Child Abuse Errors: When Good Intentions Go Wrong* Hemel Hempstead: Harvester Wheatsheaf.

Details of many UK miscarriages of justice can be found on the following site together with other materials: Innocent: Fighting Miscarriages of Justice Since 1993: http://www.innocent.org.uk/index.html

Visit our website at www.pearsoned.co.uk/howitt for self-test and essay questions, annotated further reading, audio interviews with researchers in the field, weblinks and more information on becoming a forensic psychologist.

Chapter 17

False confessions

Overview

- There is plenty of advice available to police officers about how best to elicit a confession. The environment for the interview should isolate the suspect and leave the officer in total command. The suspect may be intimidated by overstating the crime's seriousness or the strength of the evidence against them or by making claims which are simply not true. Alternatively, a more sympathetic approach can be used in which excuses for the crime are provided.

- It is argued that the decision to confess is a rational process and false confessions follow similar rational processes. However, there are a number of different processes leading to false confession. Stress-compliant false confession is where the suspect confesses falsely merely to escape the stress of the police interview. Coerced-compliant false confessions may be induced by threats or offers of leniency subject to a confession being made. Persuaded false confession involves the suspect becoming persuaded that they may have committed the crime perhaps because they were drunk at the time and cannot remember it.

- False confession seems to be commoner among those with previous convictions in real life. Nevertheless, laboratory studies have shown how remarkably easy it is to induce someone to confess falsely and sometimes the confessor comes to believe their confession.

- There are very serious consequences that follow from confessions and this is true for false confessions. The evidence in the United States shows that as many as half of the confessions which eventually were established to be false nevertheless led to criminal convictions. Furthermore, there is evidence that a jury, knowing that certain confession evidence has been obtained by illegal means, nevertheless may be affected by that evidence even when warned by a judge of the inadmissibility of such evidence.

Introduction

It is claimed that false confessions are much the same as any other confession. Confession is the main aim of police interviews with a suspect and serves both as evidence and to speed a case through the criminal justice system. Gudjonsson (2003) suggests that between 40 and 76 per cent of police interrogations end in a confession. While the factors which lead to confession and false confession may be very similar, the fall out from a false confession has the greatest number of ramifications for the legal system. Kassin (2008) presents a detailed argument about false confessions in relation to the criminal justice system. This is summarised in Figure 17.1. Kassin's argument is that a confession, true or false, has a powerful effect on the criminal justice process. There are many factors in confessions but police interrogation techniques are important ones. The inability of the police to effectively and accurately distinguish the truth from a lie means that innocent people may be at risk of being subjected to interrogation techniques designed on the assumption of guilt. A false confession may be made for many reasons but once made it is often difficult to reverse. It has consequences in the courtroom and the jury room. The long-term consequences of a confession made for short-term reasons may be immense.

Police interrogation methods

Confession evidence is significant evidence and, in some cases, constitutes the most important evidence available to the police. In the American system, in particular, once the police have collected evidence leading to a particular suspect, a process of interrogation takes place with the major objective of obtaining a confession. As a consequence, American police investigation manuals (Inbau, Reid and Buckley, 1986; Inbau, Reid, Buckley and Jayne, 2004) contain a great deal of advice on how to encourage a suspect to confess. This approach is known as the Reid model. In the Reid model, a two-phase approach is taken. The first phase is an information gathering exercise during which the interviewer gathers information relevant to the investigation and behavioural information based on a behavioural analysis interview. Information gathered in this way is then used to assess the guilt of the suspect and whether an interrogation is necessary. If the suspect is believed to be guilty, then the second phase – the nine-step interrogation – begins. The interrogator avoids using legal terms to refer to the crime according to one recommendation but there are many others. King and Snook (2009) describe the characteristics of Reid-style interrogations carried out by the

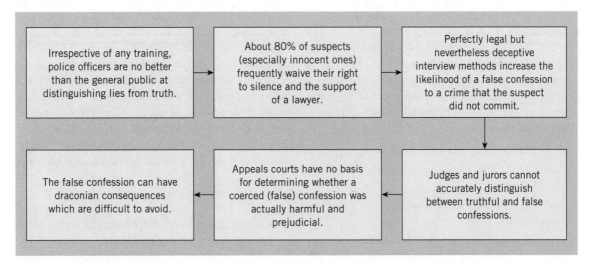

Figure 17.1 Kassin's argument concerning the power of confession evidence

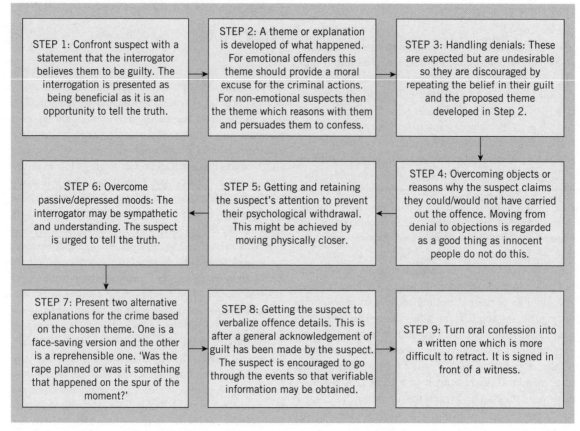

Figure 17.2 The Reid steps during the interrogation process

Canadian police. The procedure is not rigidly adhered to but most of the elements of the Reid system seem to be utilised. The Reid Interrogation approach is not universal but some of its consequences are well researched especially in relation to false confession.

Inbau *et al.*'s advice based on the Reid Interrogation approach includes suggestions about the arrangement and style of the room in which the interview is conducted. Recommendations include:

- It should take place in a small, bare room.
- Controls for things such as lighting should be inaccessible to the suspect.
- Invasion of the suspect's physical space by the officer is desirable.
- If possible, the room should be fitted with a one-way mirror so that another officer can secretly view the suspect for signs that he or she may be becoming distressed or tired. These times are when the suspect may be especially vulnerable to pressure to make a confession.

Generally speaking, such an environment will make the suspect feel socially isolated, and experience sensory deprivation. They will feel not in control of the situation. Figure 17.2 gives a résumé of the nine steps in obtaining a confession as put forward in the police manual. Advice is also given on how to differentiate guilty and innocent suspects. The manual suggests that there are verbal and non-verbal cues to lying. Innocent people give concise answers, sit upright but show little rigidity of posture and they make direct eye-to-eye contact (see Chapter 18 for a discussion of the characteristics of lying).

Two processes are involved in the interview:

- *Maximisation*: this consists of 'scare' tactics employed with the intention of intimidating the suspect. The officers overstate how serious the crime was and also the charges involved. Sometimes false or exaggerated claims are put forward about the evidence or its nature.

- *Minimisation*: this consists of the soft-sell techniques designed to encourage a sense of security. The techniques include offering sympathy, tolerance, giving face-saving excuses and moral justification by, for example, blaming the victim for the crime. The seriousness and extent of the charges may also be minimised.

Kassin and McNall (1991) found evidence that these strategies were effective in communicating high and low sentence expectations respectively, as might be expected. While these practitioner-oriented guidelines are of interest, there is more systematic information available about the process of confession. Ofshe and Leo (1997) regard false confessions as being the result of much the same type of factors that result in any other type of confession. Confession is largely the result of a *rational decision-making process* in which people optimise any situation for themselves in the context of the possible alternatives. Just as the police manual suggests, the police obtain confessions by leading the suspect to believe that the evidence against them is insurmountable. For example, it is certain that they will be convicted irrespective of any additional confessional evidence. By confessing, the suspect may gain some advantage such as a sentence reduction or a lesser charge. Following the confession, it remains possible that the suspect may be found to be innocent. For example, their confession may contain inaccurate information – they may describe using a weapon different from the one the police believe it to be. Leo (1996) likens the process to a confidence game in which the suspect exchanges trust and confidence in the police for the confession or other evidence. Only in this way, he argues, does the irrationality of not remaining silent (the suspect's right under the US Miranda rules that govern police interviews) become understandable.

There are a number of different deception ploys used by American police according to Woody and Forrest (2009):

- False evidence ploys such as where the police tell a suspect that they have a DNA match and that they never fail in court when they have.

- Demeanour ploys occur when the police fabricate evidence gleaned from the suspect's behaviour, such as when they suggest that the suspect's posture etc. indicates guilt.

- Testimonial ploys are where, for example, the person is told that others have identified them as being present at the scene of the crime, and

- Scientific ploys where it is claimed that fingerprints have been found at the crime scene. While these are legal, they do have a bearing on the value of any confessions which they encourage.

Another more elaborate example of police techniques of this sort is the 'Mr Big' technique that has been used in Canada and is also apparently used in the USA (Kassin, Drizin, Grisso, Gudjonsson, Leo and Redlich (2010). It involves setting a complex and elaborate trap which may unfold over weeks or months. The aim is to obtain a confession from the suspect away from the custodial setting. It requires massive deceptive input from the police together with the necessary social and financial support. There are (possibly) implied threats involving harm to the suspect or some form of punishment. Like other confession-inducing techniques, it is likely to be effective when used against a crime perpetrator but it has clear risks in relation to innocent suspects. The dangers are well illustrated by the case of Kyle Unger, a Canadian, who confessed and was convicted along with another man in 1992 for sexual assault and murder but was eventually exonerated on the basis of DNA evidence. He was convicted of beating and sexually assaulting a 16-year-old girl, Brigitte Grenier, at a rock music concert. He was young and naive and financially in poor circumstances. Two undercover Canadian police officers posed as tourists who gave him copious amounts of money for doing odd jobs. They also went drinking with him and provided him with luxurious accommodation. Eventually they offered that he could join their criminal organisation. He falsely confessed to Brigitte's murder to impress a fictitious gang leader who was looking for someone with the capacity for violence. The confession contained numerous factual errors but Kyle Unger was nevertheless convicted. Other evidence was jailhouse evidence of a confession told to another prisoner and a wrongful claim by a forensic expert that one of Unger's hairs was found on the victim's body.

Various types of false confessions have been identified by Ofshe and Leo (1997) based on the activities of the police who obtain the confession:

- *Stress-compliant false confession*: being accused of a crime is a stressful situation that may be compounded by insistent and seemingly endless questioning by the police. The suspect may have no answer to what they say. In an attempt to escape such a punishing situation, the suspect may confess.

- *Coerced-compliant false confessions*: threats of harm or promises of leniency may coerce the suspect into confession. For example, the detectives may appear to agree that the offence is an accident rather than a crime. Nevertheless, they insist on a confession in order to confirm this.

- *Persuaded false confession*: the suspect becomes convinced that the chances are that they actually committed the crime although they have no recollection of doing so. For example, the suspect may be persuaded that drugs or alcohol have induced a blackout, thus explaining the lack of memory of the event.

One false confessor describes his interaction with the interviewing police officer as follows. It clearly shows some of these techniques in action:

> He goes, 'If you'd just say it was an accident,' he said 'you all were having rough sex,' you know, 'and just got carried away and you accidentally killed her, they won't charge you with first degree. They will charge you with second-degree murder and then,' you know, 'your future looks so much brighter,' you know, he goes, 'because you're a clean-cut, respectable man from what I see. Your bosses think highly of you, and so do all the people I've talked to.' He goes, 'Now why would you throw your life away for some drunken coke whore who is nothing but a piece of white trash,' you know. And he goes, 'Well, if you say it was an accident I think I can possibly talk these guys into letting you go home.'
>
> (Ofshe and Leo, 1997, pp. 1103–4)

Many reasons are given by people for falsely confessing. Gudjonsson and Sugurdsson (1999) analysed data from the Revised Gudjonsson Confession Questionnaire which offers a wide variety of possibilities which respondents indicated applied to them or not. The researchers found that these clustered around the themes of external pressure, internal pressure and perceptions about the proof surrounding the case. Figure 17.3 gives examples of each these.

Another, but rather different, approach to understanding why people falsely confess involves the analysis of conversation between an interrogator and a suspect (as an interview may be regarded). It is based on the classic linguistic theory of speech acts – that is, the way that language does things. Shuy (1998) argues that:

- confessions are constructed through dialogue;
- the suspect and the interrogator each contribute to the dialogue;
- the dialogue will contain uncertainties and lead to questions about what was actually confessed and what is admitted, i.e. things may be admitted ('I did have sex with the woman') but these may not be seen as a confession to the crime ('She readily agreed to having sex').

The interrogator may make rather different inferences about what is admitted. This interpretation forms the central thrust of subsequent legal action.

Shuy (1998) provides an analysis of a number of transcripts of police interrogations. The transcripts of the interrogation were analysed linguistically by Shuy for

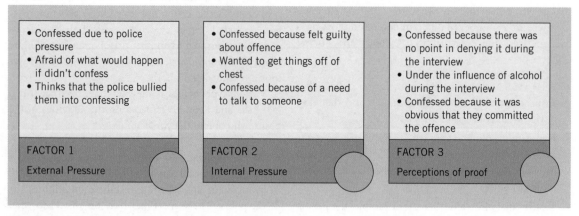

Figure 17.3 The major types of reasons given for confessing based on Gudjonsson and Sigurdsson's (1999) analysis

inconsistency. In the example to follow, he points out that the police may have misunderstood the language of the suspect. The verb 'to know' has a series of dictionary meanings but, in addition, it has a number of non-dictionary meanings. The verb may be used in the following contexts to mean rather different things such as in the sentences 'I know that Jones is going to win the election' and 'I know it's going to rain tomorrow when we have our picnic.' A strict dictionary definition of these words actually makes these sentences unintelligible.

In the case in question, Jerue is one of the suspects for a crime. The investigator asks him a question that uses this verb 'to know'. Jerue's reply is:

No
Yea, but I didn't know he was gonna shoot him though
We didn't plan to kill him when we were goin' over there.

This can be interpreted as a statement by Jerue that there was no intent to murder. That is the implication of saying that he did not know that the other man was going to shoot the victim.

This theme of intent occurs at other stages in the dialogue. The police, in their attempts to obtain an admission of the intent to kill the man, employed other words. Read through the following exchanges – it may be useful to read the passage first of all as the police seeking an admission of intent would and then in terms of the perspective of the accused who was essentially trying to deny intent:

You guys intended to go over there and rob him and kill him, didn't you?
No, we didn't plan to kill him at all.
But it was an understanding and a plan between the two of you for him to do it, right?
Yeah.

You both planned to do it – before – up to two hours before you and Lavon actually shot him, you both planned on shootin' him, right?
Right.
OK, that's what we thought, and you just had to kill him to rip his stuff off.
No, we were just gonna hold him at gunpoint, that's what I thought.
But about two hours before he actually shot him is when he changed your mind and decided to shoot him, right?
Right.
Then, if I understand you right, you guys changed your mind from robbin' him to shootin' him about two hours before he actually shot him, right?
Yeah, about that, yah.
That's when both of you changed your mind, you both agreed on it at that point, right?
Right.

(Shuy, 1998, pp. 35–6)

Early on, the suspect seems to be admitting intent but the interpretation depends on how the word 'it' is to be understood in the officer's second question. Does 'it' refer to killing the man or to going to his house with the intent to steal? Similarly, how is one to understand the penultimate sentence just before the suspect's comment 'Right'? It might appear to indicate that the suspect had finally capitulated and admitted the intent to kill. This may be an erroneous interpretation. Notice the structure of the final questions from the police officer. They are somewhat complex and it is not definite exactly what the suspect is agreeing to. It could be planning to kill but it may be that he was a little confused by the structure of the question and thought he was agreeing that the decision to rob was made two hours before.

The suspect was convicted of aiding a planned homicide.

BOX 17.1 Forensic psychology in action

Who confesses falsely?

False confessions are the result of the interaction between the police and the suspect: that is, they are a consequence of the situation. A good example involves the factors which lead investigators to suspect individuals of a crime. Obviously, the available evidence at the time is a factor but some evidence is suspect in itself. For example, Heath (2009) points out that there is a considerable amount

▶

BOX 17.1 (continued)

of evidence that the emotionality of suspects and accused is often regarded as appropriate and indicative of their innocence or truthfulness. Lacking appropriate emotionality may be regarded as a sign of guilt. Heath reports the case of the American Marty Tankleff who was just 17 when he reported to the police that his mother and father had been attacked. This was a homicide case as both were to die from their wounds. The officer leading the investigation grew suspicious because of the remarkable calmness of Marty and his lack of emotion. This suspicion was not altered by comments from relatives that Marty's demeanour was always like this. The officer then used the tactic of (falsely) claiming that Marty's father had come out of the coma and claimed that Marty had attacked him. The only way Marty could understand this was to assume that he had blacked out or something since he remembered nothing of the (false) attack. Following this, Marty made a confession (but never signed it) and recanted it soon afterwards. He was sentenced to 50 years in prison and only was released after 17 years.

What sort of person is most likely to falsely confess? The Birmingham Six were the group of men convicted of the Irish Republican Army's bombing of a Birmingham pub, killing several people. Flawed forensic evidence suggested that they had been involved with explosives. There was a serious degree of ill treatment of the men by the police. Four of the six had made confessions. Eventually, they were acquitted of the crime after many years in prison. Gudjonsson (1992) had collected psychological data from the men in 1987. His data on compliance and suggestibility indicated that the two men who were the most resistant to the pressure of the police to confess were the two men who scored lowest on these measures.

Another study examined 56 prison inmates in Iceland who had claimed to have made a false confession and compared them with over 400 other prisoners (Sigurdsson and Gudjonsson, 1997). The researchers suggest that there are two types of explanation of false confession:

- Inexperience of police methods and procedures makes some suspects especially susceptible to police manipulation and attempts at coercion. It is known from previous research that those who score highly on interrogative suggestibility as measured by Gudjonsson's Susceptibility Scale had fewer previous convictions.
- False confession is part of the criminal lifestyle of some offenders. It is known from previous research that false confessors tended to be illicit drug users and to have a history of drug dependency.

The findings of the research included the following:

- The false confession concerned only their current sentence in 5 per cent of cases.
- False confessors had previously served prison sentences more often than the control group (65 per cent versus 38 per cent).
- False confessors were younger than people who did not falsely confess when first convicted.
- False confessors were younger when they first went to prison.
- False confessors had more previous prison sentences.
- False confessors had spent more time in prison prior to their current offence.
- Nearly all had a criminal record before the false confession (88 per cent).
- The commonest offence associated with false confession was property crime (59 per cent). The second category was serious traffic violations. Violent offences amounted to 7 per cent.

Pearse *et al.* (1998) carried out forensic clinical interviews with suspects at a police station in order to assess their psychological vulnerability. Measures included anxiety, intelligence and reading as well as suggestibility. There was no evidence to indicate that such clinical assessments of vulnerability related to confession. Indeed, the best predictor of confession was whether the suspect had taken illegal drugs in the previous 24 hours. The reasons for this are not yet clear – it could be merely that they confessed so as to get out of the police station into an environment where they could obtain drugs. They tended to confess less if a solicitor was present.

Of course, it is not possible for researchers to validate claims of false confession among those subject to police interrogations. But such claims are useful data nonetheless when no better data exists. Gudjonsson, Sigurdsson, Asgeirsdottir and Sigfusdottir (2007) obtained questionnaire data from nearly 1900 Icelandic students aged between 15 and 24 years. These were youngsters who had reported having undergone police interrogation. Seven per cent said that they had made a false confession to police officers. The major predictive factors for false confessions were multiple experiences of victimisation (e.g. bullying, death of a significant other) and substance abuse (i.e. having had substance abuse therapy or used LSD). In other words, having experienced a lot of unpleasant or traumatic experiences was conducive to falsely confessing. Figure 17.4 gives more details about this.

Some factors such as alcohol use, cannabis use, parental separation/divorce, and having serious arguments with their parents did not differentiate false confessors from others, however. A similar study by Gudjonsson, Sigurdsson and Sigfusdottir (2009) involved a smaller age range – just Icelandic 15–16 year olds. Eleven per cent had been questioned at a police station as a suspect – this was commoner for boys than girls. Mostly they had been questioned just once. However, some 7 per cent of those who falsely confessed had been questioned six or more times. In this study too, life adversity variables seemed to discriminate between the false confessors and the rest quite effectively. The most discriminating aversive factors were sexual abuse within the family, death of a parent or sibling, sexual abuse outside of family, and witnessing serious violence between adults at home.

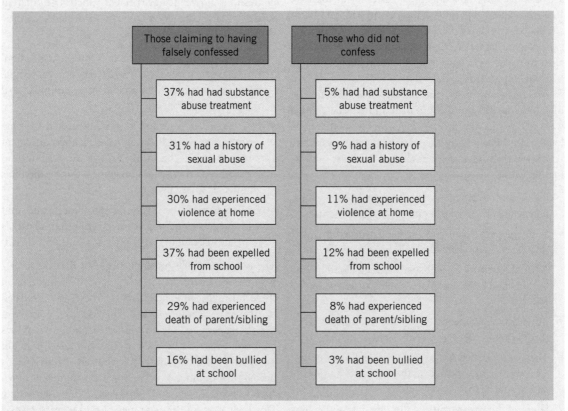

Figure 17.4 Some of the differences between false confessors and other youngsters according to Gudjonsson *et al.* (2007)

Types of false confession

Kassin and Kiechel (1996) classify three different types of false confession:

- *Voluntary false confession*, which is personally motivated and which occurs in the absence of external pressure from others.
- *Coerced-compliant false confession* in which the suspect confesses in order to escape an aversive interrogation, secure a promised benefit or avoid a threatened harm.
- *Coerced-internalised false confession* in which the suspect comes to believe in their own guilt of committing the crime.

It is difficult to believe that individuals come to believe in their own guilt over something that they have not done. Perhaps it is more understandable that people may confess when they find themselves in a no-win situation and are offered a way of making things easier for themselves. In an intriguing experiment, Kassin and Kiechel (1996) simulated aspects of false confession in a laboratory experiment. Remarkably, participants could be encouraged to make up details of an offence that they simply had not committed.

American university students were assigned to one of four different groups by Kassin and Kiechel. These were defined by the independent variable high versus low vulnerability and by a second independent variable, which was the presence versus absence of a false incriminating witness:

- Participants worked on an individual basis with a female 'plant' or confederate of the experimenter.
- Both the participant and the plant worked together on a reaction time study.
- A list of letters of the alphabet was read aloud by one of them and typed on the computer keyboard by the other.
- Initially, the confederate did the typing but after three minutes the roles were reversed.
- They were warned not to press the ALT key because a software fault would crash the computer and so the data would be lost.
- Some of the participants had to type fast and others could type slowly because of the speed of reading out the letters. This is known as the vulnerability

manipulation – the speedier one works then the less opportunity one has to self-monitor what one is doing.

- Typing errors were greatest for the high rate, confirming the validity of the procedure in this regard.
- After 60 seconds the computer crashed as had been planned by the experimenter.
- The experimenter accused the participant of pressing the forbidden key – all denied this.
- At this stage, false incriminating evidence was introduced for some participants. The confederate admitted that she had seen the participant hit the ALT key on the computer. In the control condition, the no witness condition, the same confederate said that she had not seen what had occurred.

So, the experimental situation had resulted in the participant being accused of doing something that they had not. In some cases, there was also a witness claiming to have seen the participant doing that thing. These are much the same circumstances as those in which false confessions in real life have been obtained. The different aspects of false confession could be identified according to the participant's behaviours:

- *Compliance*: the experimenter wrote a 'confession' for the participant ('I hit the ALT key and caused the program to crash') which counted as compliance if the participant then agreed to it.
- *Internalisation*: a second confederate asked the participant later what had happened. If the participant said they had hit the wrong key without qualification (i.e. without saying something like 'I think') then this counted as internalisation.
- *Confabulation*: the experimenter reappeared and asked whether the subject could recall specific details to fit the allegation.

The outcome of the research suggested that the fast or pressurised version of the study tended to increase all three forms of influence. Each of these was increased by the presence of the witness who claimed she had seen the participant hit the wrong key. Confabulation was common where there was a witness and a fast pace but not otherwise. These findings have been effectively replicated on a number of occasions. For example, Candel, Merckelbach, Loyen and Reyskens (2005) used young Dutch children in the age range of 6 to 9 years. Over a third of the children falsely confessed when they were questioned and there was evidence that the vast majority of these internalised their confession. Interestingly, a measure of suggestibility used by the researchers did not predict false confession in this study.

One criticism of this research is that falsely confessing to something one had not done had no adverse consequences. Falsely confessing in a police interview may lead to punishment in the form, say, of a prison sentence. Horselenberg, Merckelbach and Josephs (2003) essentially replicated the Kassin and Kiechel (1996) study but added a punishment in that the false confessions led to a financial loss by the confessor. That is, they lost part of their fee for participating in the study by accepting that they caused the computer to crash. Despite this, the findings of the new study were much the same as those of Kassin and Keichel's. That is to say, the majority of participants falsely confessed. However, despite the evidence that there are personality factors that might lead to false confession (see Box 17.1 for details), falsely confessing in this study was not associated with Gudjonsson's Compliance Scale and a measure of compliance tendencies. In circumstances in which over 80 per cent of people will falsely confess, would one expect that personality traits would be a factor? The situation is enough to create the confession so this will be little affected by some people being more prone to confess falsely than others.

There are a number of fairly self-evident limitations apparent in the Kassin and Kiechel study (Russano et al., 2005):

- The participants may be uncertain or confused about whether they did press the 'ALT' key accidentally since it is very plausible that they did in these circumstances. This is rather different from what happens in real cases where the accused would be accused of deliberately committing a crime.

- All of the participants in the study were actually innocent of the misdemeanour they are accused of so it is not possible to compare true confessions with false confessions.

Recently, attempts have been made to address these issues. Horselenberg et al. (2006) replicated the essence of the Kassin and Kiechel study but cleverly designed procedures which meant that the participant actually may have done something wrong. Participants had the opportunity to cheat by taking a look at an exam paper which had been left accessible to them. The researchers found that it was possible to get participants to confess to cheating (i.e. looking at the examination paper) even

though they had not actually looked. Only a small number confessed falsely but, even so, this limited evidence effectively neutralises this criticism of the Kassin and Kiechel study. In perhaps a more effective approach, Russano et al. (2005) also attempted to address the issue of the lack of culpability in the Kassin and Kiechel study. In this method, guilty and innocent participants were accused of cheating since they broke one of the rules of the experiment in which they were participating. In the study, participants were paired with a confederate and they were required to solve a number of logical problems. Some were asked to solve the problems on their own whereas some were required to solve the problems together in a 'team'. The manipulation of guilt was achieved by having the confederate of the experimenters ask the real participant for help. Some participants gave the confederate the answer and could justifiably be accused of cheating. In the innocent condition, the confederate did not ask for help. It could be argued that this cheating is a serious infringement knowingly committed by the participant. That is, a very different situation from accidentally pressing the 'ALT' key on a computer keyboard.

In one of Russano et al.'s studies, the researchers investigated the influence of the police interrogation tactics of (a) maximisation versus minimisation and (b) offering a lenient deal in return for a confession. Maximisation techniques are intimidating since the suspect is accused of guilt, the police officers will not accept denials of guilt of the crime, and the seriousness of the situation is inflated by the police officers. In contrast, minimisation is essentially the reverse of this so the officers present the crime as being relatively trivial. When dealt with by the minimisation and lenient-deal tactics, guilty individuals were three-and-a-half times more likely to confess than innocent individuals. Nevertheless, a significant main effect on confession was produced by guilt versus innocence – guilty persons were 3.5 times more likely to confess (72 per cent confessed). Compared with the condition in which there was no tactic used, offering a deal, minimisation tactics and deal plus minimisation tactics all resulted in more confessions. True confessions were nearly doubled from 46–87 per cent with the use of a deal and minimisation. The risk of a false confession increased from 6 per cent with no tactic to 43 per cent with minimisation and a deal! In other words, confession evidence is seriously degraded by the use of this sort of interrogation tactics since they disproportionately raise the likelihood of a false confession. On the basis of this research, Russano et al. argue that police officers should not be involved with any suggestion of leniency as this tends to reduce the diagnostic value of any confession resulting.

Consequences of a false confession

Confession is common. It has been estimated that in the United Kingdom something like 60 per cent of all police detainees confess (Pearse *et al.*, 1998). Just how many of these are likely to be false confessions is anyone's guess. Not all false confessors are victims of police interviewing methods. Some false confessions are nuisances and in no way solicited by the police. There is such a phenomenon as voluntary false confession. For example, 200 people confessed to the kidnap of the US aviator Charles Lindbergh's baby in the 1920s. The Innocence Project in the United States has identified wrongful convictions using DNA evidence. In about 20 per cent of these proven wrongful conviction cases there was a false confession (Russano *et al.*, 2005). Berger (2008) argues that false confessions are likely to come to the attention of authorities when (1) the inconsistency of the confession causes charges to be dropped, (2) the false confessor tries to recant or retract the confession, (3) a claim of false confession is made in proceedings occurring after the conviction or (4) when the real perpetrator is found, though this is exceptional.

At one extreme is the anonymous false confession which, if followed up by the police, may take up a lot of time. The classic example of this in Britain was the Yorkshire Ripper case of the 1970s. The police investigating this case were hampered severely by a number of highly publicised tape-recordings purporting to be from the Yorkshire Ripper himself. He appeared to be taunting the officers. Senior officers mistakenly regarded them as genuine. This diverted police resources along a false trail. It, possibly, may have delayed arrest and allowed further murders. McCann (1998) mentions another example of false confession that is not the result of police pressure. Young members of gangs may be pushed into confessing by other members of the same gang in the belief that the court will deal leniently with young people.

Leo and Ofshe (1998) studied some of the numerous documented cases of police-induced false confession. They systematically searched media, case files and secondary sources for examples of false confession. All cases selected for inclusion in the study satisfied the following criteria:

- no physical or other credible evidence indicated the suspect's guilt;
- the state's case consisted of little other than the suspect's confession;
- the suspect's factual innocence was supported by evidence.

In this way, they found 34 proven cases of false confession: for example, the murder victim turned up alive after the trial, or the true offender was eventually found guilty, or scientific evidence proved the innocence of the false confessor. In addition, there were another 18 cases that seemed highly likely to be false confessions. Eight cases were classified as probably false confessions – since the majority of the evidence indicated the innocence of the accused.

Whatever the reason for false confession, the consequences of doing so in the United States are often great as these US data show:

- 8 per cent were fortunate and suffered only arrest and detention by the police;
- 43 per cent were prosecuted but the case was eventually dismissed;
- 48 per cent of the cases ended up with a criminal conviction.

This final figure included:

- 17 per cent who were sentenced to more than 10 years;
- 5 per cent who were given death sentences;
- 2 per cent who were actually executed.

Nearly three-quarters of all of the false confessors were found guilty if they went to trial. Considering the certain false confessors alone showed that 55 per cent were released prior to going to trial. Of this group who were eventually established as not guilty by further evidence, 3 per cent were acquitted by the court, 29 per cent were convicted despite their not guilty plea, and 15 per cent pleaded guilty in court despite their eventual proven innocence.

The consequences of wrongful convictions for crime can be serious in other respects. Grounds (2004) gives evidence from a British sample exonerated after they had wrongfully been convicted for a crime. Among the serious symptoms found which appeared after incarceration were lasting anger, panic disorder, permanent personality change, substance abuse, and post-traumatic stress disorder. Two-thirds showed the symptomology of PTSD. Others argue that the consequences of miscarriages of justice can spread beyond the individuals immediately affected. The high-profile nature of some wrongful allegations and miscarriages of justice can affect the public's beliefs about the nature of crime and facts about crime and its perpetrators (Cole, 2009). He gives the example of the false cases of organised sexual abuse of children which led to numerous reports and prosecutions in the 1980s and after. These included claims of human sacrifice and cannibalism as well as satanic ritual abuse. In terms of US cases alone, there were ten or more mass prosecutions for organised sexual abuse and a minimum of 72 people were found guilty. Most of these were released though mostly without exoneration. The public's belief in organised ritual abuse waned as a consequence of this as well as confidence in the child protection system.

Can confession evidence be disregarded?

On the face of things, it is hard to understand why people confess to horrific crimes which they simply did not commit. Nearly two thirds (64 per cent) of members of the public agreed or strongly agreed that a confession

is a powerful indicator of guilt (Henkel, Coffman and Dailey, 2008). Just about half (51 per cent) believed that if a person confesses to a crime then they are probably guilty. People in general agreed with the statement 'Criminal suspects sometimes confess to crimes they did not commit' and only 14 per cent disagreed to some extent. Perhaps more troubling is that even more people strongly agreed that 'Once someone has confessed to a crime, there is no need to continue searching for other evidence, such as fingerprints.' The public tended to believe that they would be unlikely to confess to a crime they had not committed and believed that they would only do so under torture.

Just what do the public understand about the factors which lead to false confessions? Their knowledge is vital when they come to serve on juries where this might be an issue. Leo and Liu (2009) surveyed a sample of 264 jury-eligible students about the likelihood that a range of interrogation tactics would lead to a false confession (Leo and Liu, 2009). Some details about the factors they thought might induce false confession can be found in Figure 17.5. Quite clearly potential jurors believed that torture and the like were likely to encourage people to confess falsely. However they were far less likely to believe that psychological tactics such as repeatedly interrupting any denials that the suspect tries to make would work. Leo and Liu argue that these findings demonstrate the failure of the public to fully understand the power of coercive interrogation to encourage false confessions.

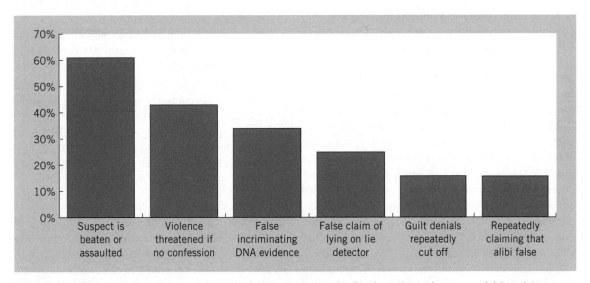

Figure 17.5 Interrogation tactics and the percent believing that they would lead to false confessions

There is evidence from experimental studies that confession evidence is especially potent. Studies by Kassin and Neumann (1997) found it to produce higher conviction rates than character testimony and eyewitness identification. Confession evidence is subject to rules. In the United States, confession evidence is not normally admissible in court if it was elicited by any of the following (Kassin, 1997b; Kassin and Sukel, 1997):

- brute force
- deprivation of food or sleep
- prolonged isolation
- promises of immunity or leniency
- threats of harm or punishment
- without notifying the suspect of his/her constitutional rights except in exceptional circumstances.

Of course, this confession evidence may be given in court before its admissibility is challenged. This begs the question of whether in these circumstances the jury members can completely disregard the confession evidence as is required in accordance with legal principles. The alternative, of course, is that the confession evidence, despite its inadmissibility, sways the jury.

Kassin and Sukel (1997) set out to test, experimentally, this hypothesis. In one study, introductory psychology students in the United States were randomly assigned to one of four confession groups. The groups were those produced by the following variables:

- high-pressure versus low-pressure interrogation
- admissible versus inadmissible confessions as ruled upon by the judge during the 'trial'.

Each 'mock' juror studied a trial transcript that took 20–25 minutes to read. They then completed questionnaires without jury deliberations.

The transcript was of the trial of a man charged with murdering his estranged wife and a male neighbour. The district attorney charged that the man, Wilson, killed the pair after coming across them together. The defendant, on the other hand, claimed that he merely found the bodies when he went back to his former abode to collect financial papers. With the exception of the confession, the evidence against Wilson was entirely circumstantial (the killer was 6 feet tall and left-handed), incomplete (there was no murder weapon) and ambiguous (before calling the police he fled the scene and phoned his attorney). The transcripts consisted of opening statements, closing arguments, the examinations of five witnesses and a brief judge's instruction on the charge of first-degree murder and the requirements of proof: presumption of innocence, burden of proof and reasonable doubt.

Other participants rated interrogation situations based on Inbau et al.'s (1986) manual for police officers:

- The high-pressure condition: 'They drove me back to the police station, where Officer Heffling handcuffed me, took out his gun and started asking me questions about the murders. My arm really hurt from the handcuffs, but he wouldn't remove them . . . I told him that my right arm had just come out of a cast and was very sore.' When asked 'were they trying to pressure you to confess?', the defendant replied that 'yes he was angry and yelling'. The police officer also testified but rejected the suggestion that Wilson was under so much stress that he would confess to a crime he did not commit.

- In the low-pressure condition, the defendant was said to have confessed immediately upon questioning. He was not handcuffed, verbally abused or threatened with a weapon.

- In the no-confession control group, the defendant and police officer both testified that Wilson denied murdering his wife and neighbour during his interrogation.

The remaining condition to be manipulated was the admissibility or not of the confession:

- Admissible condition: the defence lawyer raised an objection to the police officer's mentioning the confession material. The judge overruled the objection. The prosecuting lawyer mentioned the confession in the closing argument.

- Inadmissible condition: the judge supported the defence's objection to the police evidence about the confession. The confession was deemed inadmissible and struck off the transcript of the trial though, of course, the jury was aware of it. The jury was then instructed by the judge to disregard the police officer's remarks about the confession.

The evidence showed that the inadmissible evidence affected the mock jurors' perceptions of the guilt of the accused. They gave more guilty verdicts when they knew of this evidence. This was the case even in circumstances where they believed that the confession was a coerced one and they knew that information about that confession was inadmissible in court. A second study that contained more evidence in support of the prosecution produced similar findings. The US Supreme Court's view is to describe the admission of coerced confession as a harmless error. Kassin's findings are clearly at variance with this.

Jurors seem to discount confessions where the false evidence ploy was used. However, the extent to which this ploy is totally counterproductive in the juryroom is not clear. Woody and Forrest (2009) gave mock jurors transcripts of an interrogation to read. The transcript either did or did not include a false evidence ploy and either did or did not involve an expert witness commenting on the false evidence strategy. Although the evidence and the confession were were the same in all conditions, the presence of false evidence ploys resulted in a lowering of the likelihood of conviction and shorter prison sentences. The transcripts with ploys were rated as being more coercive and deceptive. The presence of an expert witness commenting about ploys cut down the convictions and increased perceptions that the interrogation involved deception and coercion.

What should be done?

Kassin and other experts on police drew up a list of recommendations which, if implemented, would help ensure that the problem of false confession is reduced. This was published by the AP-LS (American Psychology and Law Society) and is generally referred to as a white paper (Thompson, 2010). The main recommendations (reforms) are as follows (Kassin, Drizin, Grisson, Gudjonsson, Leo and Redlich, 2010) though it cannot be stressed too much that they are specifically aimed at the American context and may already be employed elsewhere:

- Electronic Recording of all Interrogations and interviews: The requirement is for every custodial interview/interrogation to be videotaped entirely using a camera position which places equal focus on the suspect and the interrogator.

- Limit custody and interrogation time: There should be movement towards restricting the maximum length of interrogations such that it can only be exceeded with the permission of an authority (e.g. a senior police officer). This is already a requirement in the United Kingdom.

- Presentation of False Evidence: The white paper encourages the criminal justice system to be more

sensitive to the effects that false evidence in the context of interrogations can have. For whatever reason, perhaps political, the white paper falls short of recommending a complete ban on the use of false evidence in interrogation. It suggests that vulnerable groups such as young people and those with intellectual restrictions perhaps should not be subjected to the presentation of false evidence.

- Protection of vulnerable suspects: A trained professional advocate (ideally a lawyer) should sit in on interrogations involving juveniles. Similar, those who conduct interviews with vulnerable group members should be required to have specific training with the objective of maximising their sensitivity and skills when dealing with the problems that vulnerable suspect brings.

- Reform of Interrogation Practices: In many countries, there should be a move from the Reid model of interviewing (as found in the police training manual) and its assumption of guilt to an investigatory style of interviewing (more characteristic of the United Kingdom's approach).

These seem wise suggestions. Nevertheless, there are problems with them especially in terms of the recommendation about electronically recording interviews and interrogations and, especially, the suggestion of a side-by-side picture of the suspect and interrogator despite. Why is this recommendation necessary? There is a growing use of video in some states of the USA (Snyder, Lassiter, Lindberg and Pinegar, 2009). It is felt that videoing (a) encourages the police not to employ the most extreme coercive methods of getting a confession and (b) the video may be evaluated later by the judge and jury. Besides these advantages, there can be a number of problems with video. If only part of the interrogation is recorded then the result may be misleading since it omits important information about what happened earlier in the interview. Furthermore, the use of 'recap' videos is problematic – these are essentially videos in which the suspect is asked to repeat their confession for the camera. As such, they may lack the important evidence about the emotionality accompanying the original confession. Entire interview recording, then, is important.

In addition to all of this is the camera position chosen. Frequently the video shows the suspect clearly but also part of the interrogator's body as the camera points from behind them. Researchers have identified a difficulty with this known as the *camera perspective bias*. Videoing from behind the interrogator puts the emphasis on the suspect and this leads to the camera perspective bias. It was first identified by Lassiter (2002) and repeatedly demonstrated by researchers since. The conspicuousness of the suspect compared to the interrogator is perceived by people viewing the video in terms of the suspect having a causal role in what happens during the video. If this was reversed and the interviewer dominated the video then the interviewer would be perceived as having the causal role in determining what happens. This is all down to the higher salience to the action attributed to the most conspicuous person. This is known as illusory causation and goes by to the work of Taylor and Fiske (1975, 1978). Most of the evidence for the camera perspective bias is based on simulated confessions but recently Lassiter, Ware, Ratcliff and Irvin (2009) have demonstrated it using real confession interviews.

So the solution would appear to be to have both the suspect and the interrogator portrayed with equal conspicuousness by using two cameras simultaneously and a split screen format for the video. Snyder, Lassiter, Lindberg and Pinegar (2009) carried out such a study and found that the dual camera yielded largely unbiased judgements of both the guilt of the suspect and the voluntariness of their confession. However, things are not quite straightforward since the researchers obtained actual videos of true and false confessions. The participants then watched these confessions and had to say whether or not each one was true. There were a variety of video formats. It transpired that the dual presentation was poor at obtaining accurate decisions about the truth or falsehood of the confession. This would seem to be because the participants concentrate on facial cues and ignore other information which might be more pertinent in making the decision. In other words, the white paper may require revision in this respect.

Main points

- False confessions may be motivated by a range of factors. Particularly serious are those that are the consequence of police interrogation methods which are designed to encourage confession by the guilty but may encourage confession by the innocent. Although in some cases false confessions may be made simply to obtain relief from the interview situation with the police, sometimes the decision to confess falsely is the result of a rational decision faced with apparently strong evidence.

- There are some remarkable demonstrations of false confessions based on laboratory experiments. These are important since they suggest that virtually anyone, given appropriate circumstances, can be put into a situation where they confess to doing something that they have not done. What is more remarkable is that some false confessors do not simply acquiesce under certain circumstances but that they seem to believe that they did what they confess to.

- The consequence of falsely confessing may be as serious as those for a true confession. People who are eventually proven to have falsely confessed stand a high risk of retractions not being accepted and a high risk of being convicted by a court of the crime they did not commit. Perhaps even more disturbing is the evidence that juries can be influenced by inadmissible confession evidence that a judge has warned them to disregard.

Further reading

Berger, M.A. (2008) *Eyewitness Testimony and False Confession. Beyond Common Sense: Psychological Science in the Courtroom* Oxford: Blackwell, 315–26.

Gudjonsson, G.H. (2003) *The Psychology of Interrogations and Confessions: A Handbook* Chichester: John Wiley.

Herbert, I. The Psychology and Power of False Confessions. http://www.psychologicalscience.org/observer/getArticle.cfm?id=2590

Inbau, F.E., Reid, J.E., Buckley, J.P. and Jayne, B.C. (2004) *Criminal Interrogation and Confessions* (4th edn) Boston: Jones and Bartlett.

Kassin, S.M. and Gudjonnson, G.H. (2004) 'The psychology of confessions: a review of the literature and issues' *Psychological Science in the Public Interest* 5(2), 33–67.

King, L. and Snook, B. (2009) 'Peering Inside a Canadian Interrogation Room: an examination of the Reid Model of Interrogation, Influence Tactics, and Coercive Strategies' *Criminal Justice and Behavior* 36, 674–94.

The Innocence Project has examples of DNA exonerated miscarriages of justice including those involving false confession (see, for example, the case of Eddie Joe Lloyd): http://www.innocenceproject.org/know/Browse-Profiles.php

Visit our website at www.pearsoned.co.uk/howitt for self-test and essay questions, annotated further reading, audio interviews with researchers in the field, weblinks and more information on becoming a forensic psychologist.

Chapter 18

Lies, lie detecting and credibility 1: the psychology of lie detection

Overview

- The assessment of the accuracy of testimony is a complex process. No serious researcher nowadays would suggest that there are simple, infallible indicators of untruthful testimony such as characteristic body language. Lying might be defined as the intention to deceive without making the other person aware of this intent.

- Most forms of lie detection do not detect lies at all but the emotion that may go alongside lying and the fear of its detection.

- Good indicators of false emotion are asymmetrical facial expressions and the overly quick facial expression of emotion.

- It used to be claimed by researchers that most professional groups – police officers and psychologists, for example – are little better than chance at detecting lies without specialised training. This point of view is currently being re-evaluated and careful analyses are beginning to suggest that given the right sort of circumstances the police, in particular, can do rather better than students, in particular, and the general public.

- Experience may lead to confidence in one's abilities to detect lies irrespective of actual ability. The sheer complexity of interview situations may make it difficult for the interviewer to concentrate on key aspects indicative of lying or truth telling. There are problems in detecting lying due to our mistaken ideas about cues to deception – this is an issue in relation to police work too. For example, police officers may believe that making a lot of body movements is a good indicator of lying but liars actually make fewer body movements. The lack of accurate feedback about whether they have successfully identified a liar or not is one reason why professionals cannot improve their lie-detection ability.

Introduction

Not all of the problems of the criminal justice system would be solved if psychologists could identify liars accurately. But some of them would, of course. An efficient, infallible detector of lies would, of course, free the criminal justice system enormously from much of its work. Judges and jurors, for example, routinely have to make informal assessments of who is telling the truth and who is lying without their ability to do so being questioned. Of course, this is partly done on the basis of the detail of the evidence presented but, as discussed in Chapters 23 and 24, this is not always the case. There is no perfect way of distinguishing the liar from the truth teller. Nevertheless, psychological research has provided at least some insights about how to improve (but probably never perfect) the ability of trained people to differentiate liars from truth tellers. Many of the established ideas about lies and lie detecting are currently in a state of flux and what appeared to be facts just a few years ago now are disputed and challenged. Inevitably, this chapter needs to reflect the changing nature of the field while respecting the contribution of earlier research. A good example of this is the long-held conclusion that professionals such as police officers and others were no better than the general public at detecting lies. While it is true that people in general do little better than chance at detecting lies, nevertheless, some police officers in some circumstances seem to be able to do rather better than this.

The psychology of lying

According to Ekman (1992, 1996) a lie has to include two components:

- the intention to mislead the victim of the lie;
- the victim is not informed about this intention.

It follows from this that not all forms of deception are lies – magicians, for example, are open about their intention to deceive. Keeping secrets is not a lie if the secret is known to be a secret – such as consistently refusing to reveal one's age. Giving false information with no intention to deceive is not lying. Not revealing information may be a lie if the intention was to deceive.

However, such a definition seeks to differentiate liars from truth tellers. It disregards the accuracy of statements made if there was no intention to deceive. That means that false memories of child abuse would not be considered a lie despite their extreme consequences for the accused. The accused is probably more concerned about the accuracy of the claims made against him or her in general than the motivation for the false allegation.

Assessing truthfulness is central to much professional work in psychology as well as forensic work more specifically. Nevertheless, few psychologists are formally trained in any of the methods of detecting lies. There is good reason to be suspicious of rigid systems of lie detection. None of the techniques discussed *favourably* in this chapter are based on the detection of lies from signs or signals as such: that is, body language, language and physiological signs are often poor and misleading indicators of lying. Successful detection of lies requires the examination of the total context and a broad variety of evidence.

Ekman's theory of lie detection

While some individuals are better than others at lie detecting (Ekman, O'Sullivan and Frank, 1999), there is no simple way of detecting lies with a single indicator – such as body posture – which will work with all people. Problems in detecting lies include the following (Ekman, 1992):

- The sheer complexity of the task of monitoring all aspects of what the possible liar is doing – their talk, their facial expressions, their voice expression, their hand movements, their posture, their gestures and so forth. It is simply impossible to focus on all of these at the same time. Sometimes, as a consequence, we may concentrate on the verbal and facial aspects of their behaviour. Unfortunately, these aspects of lying are the ones that the liar him- or herself is most able to monitor and change. Thus they are concerned to disguise their lying through these modalities.

- There are considerable individual differences in all of these bodily processes. For example, there is some evidence that an increase in manipulators (touching, stroking and otherwise manipulating one's own body) is a cue to deceit. That is because negative emotions increase. There are many individuals who normally use few manipulators so they are judged honest when they are in fact lying. So it is important to have some knowledge of the individual's baseline behaviours when assessing for lying.

- Unless the truth is known, the detection of a lie takes convoluted pathways. The majority of clues to deceit are actually signs of strong emotion. The deceitful person may fear being caught telling a lie. As a result, they may show physiological signs of emotion at the point of telling a lie. The difficulty for the observer is that these same emotions may be raised because of factors other than lying. For example, many of us will become angry if we are accused of lying. Consequently, on their own, emotions can be misleading guides to deceit. A great deal of other information is required.

- The context of the lie may vary enormously. So, for example, it is easier to tell a lie if one can anticipate when it will be necessary to tell a lie. If one has to lie unexpectedly, then there is little time to formulate a convincing lie.

- The spillage of inappropriate emotion given the context and contents of the lie is the real clue to deceit. Emotion, itself, is an unreliable indicator.

Nevertheless, despite all of these difficulties, individuals may be trained to be better at detecting lies. This is because, according to Ekman (1992), the emotions which lying arouses manifest themselves in *leakages* – that is, in the form of observable characteristics. These are the clues to emotion that may (but not invariably) reveal that someone is lying. Included among the clues that should be examined are:

- Frequent swallowing, faster/shallower breathing, sweating, increased blinking, pupil dilation – all of these are signs of emotion although it is not possible to say which sort of emotion.

- Louder speech – most likely anger.

- Pauses and speech errors – these suggest a lack of preparation of the 'story' or strong negative emotions, especially fear.

- Raised pitch of voice – associated with anger and/or fear.

- Whitening of the face – anger or fear.

Furthermore, there are clues that the facial expression of emotion is *not* real. These offer additional clues to deceit:

- Asymmetrical facial expressions are indicators of falsehood: that is, if both sides of the face do not reveal the same emotion.

- The onset of the emotion should not be too abrupt as this is a sign of falseness.

- The emotional expression should be at an appropriate place in the verbal account.

- *Negative* emotions that do not involve sweating, breathing change or increases in the use of manipulators are more likely to be false.

- Happiness should involve eye muscles, otherwise it is false.

- Fear and sadness involve a characteristic forehead expression especially involving the eyebrows. If this is missing then the emotion is false.

All of this can be fairly difficult to apply in practice as recent research shows. For example, there is fairly consistent evidence that liars tend to express more negative emotion than do truth tellers. But among the emotions, anger is very difficult to fake according to Ekman's (1985) theory. The muscles involved in expressing anger are very hard to control. It seemed to Ekman that genuinely expressed anger is likely to be indicative of the innocence of an accused person since the innocent accused person may find their anger difficult to control and the guilty accused person will find it difficult to feign anger realistically. Of course, anger should be more common in high-stake situations than for trivial matters. In the first part of their study of this, Hatz and Bourgeois (2010) used both real transgressions and mock transgression scenarios in order to induce lying (and truth telling). In the real transgressions scenario, college students were asked to cheat or otherwise. The task involved working independently and then collectively with another 'student' on a series of mathematical problems. The other student was a confederate of the researchers and asked the other for help – which was against the rules. Because the cheating pairs submitted identical answers they were accused of cheating by the researcher. The cheating was 'reported to a professor' who said that it could be considered as a case of academic dishonesty and could involve the academic disciplinary committee. Although cheating was a matter of choice in the study, all of the participants did cheat given the opportunity and all of them chose to lie about cheating. The design also included a mock transgression situation in which participants largely went through the same procedures as before but instead they were told that the confederate was the researcher's assistant – and the researcher's assistant told some of them that they should cheat. The participants in all conditions were secretly videotaped as they replied to a number of questions such as 'Did you two cheat on these problems?'

The videos were shown to a panel of judges in order to have the behaviours of the participants assessed. The findings were clear. First of all, the judges perceived the truth tellers in the real transgression situation as being significantly more angry than the liars. For the mock transgression groups there was no difference between liars and truth tellers in this respect. The researchers also examined the numbers of anger-related words used by participants. In the mock transgression situation, the mean number of angry words used by truth tellers was much the same as the mean number of angry words used by the liars. On the other hand, in the real transgression situation, the truth tellers used more angry words than the liars. Actually, the liars basically used far fewer angry words than the truth tellers for the real transgression and the truth tellers and liars for the mock transgression.

To help effective thinking about possible deceit, Ekman developed a 38-item lying checklist (Ekman, 1992, pp. 335–40) which considers many questions about 'the lie' and the ease with which it can be detected. If the following questions and others are answered with a yes, then this indicates that there is an increased difficulty in detecting the lie:

- Does the lie involve concealment only, without any need to falsify?
- Is the situation one in which the target is likely to trust the liar, not suspecting that he or she may be misled?
- Is the lie authorised? Lies that are socially permitted are harder to detect because there is less guilt involved in telling such lies.
- Does the liar have a good memory?

It should be evident from this that the detection of lying is not easy but not impossible. Perhaps the most important lesson is the multi-faceted approach to lie detecting. The idea that there is a single indicator of a liar is patently absurd from this perspective.

BOX 18.1 Forensic psychology in action

Are people good at telling lies to the police?

One of the common activities of the police is that of taking the names and addresses of people. This maybe because they have been a witness to a crime or maybe they have been a stopped on suspicion. Much of the time most of us would have no reason to lie about our home addresses but this is not always the case. A person acting suspiciously may provide a false address in the hope that this will help them avoid further police action. A perfectly innocent young person might choose to give a false address simply because they do not want their parents to know where they were at a particular time.

Just what is the psychology of making up a false address? It sounds like an easy thing to do but there are problems. Roach (2010) researched the fabrication of addresses in situations like this. The act of giving a false address, suggests Roach, is likely to be spontaneous rather than planned as one cannot predict being asked for one's address by a police officer. Research on human memory suggests that it is cognitively quite difficult to fabricate an entirely false address – remember that while fabricating the address the individual needs to avoid arousing any suspicions. When they choose to give a false address, people are likely to resort to using something relatively familiar since they employ established schemas in their thinking. Another way of putting this is that there is likely to be more than just a mere element of truth in this sort of lie. So just how is the false address fabricated? To understand this further, Roach (2010) adopted a simple strategy – he asked members of a substantial sample of university students in the North of England to respond to a scenario in which they had been stopped by a police officer and asked for their personal details. They do not wish to give their correct address. They are to generate a false address very quickly within a space of ten seconds. The address was required to include the number of the house, the name of the street or road, the town, and country plus the postcode (zip code).

It was often very clear that elements of the address actually gave clues about their real addresses. In other words, many of the false addresses were only partially fabricated. Participants also indicated the nature of their thought processes which led to the false address. Eight per cent said that they gave an old address of

▶

BOX 18.1 (continued)

theirs, 21 per cent gave the address of someone they knew, 16 per cent used an address made up of real and fabricated elements such as giving their own address but with a different house number, 20 per cent claimed that the address was created randomly although this is doubtful in some cases as they contained recognisable elements, and 36 per cent gave complex explanations sometimes of a rather fanciful nature. Quite a high proportion, then, of putatively false addresses contained information which might be useful in tracking down the person in question. Of particular interest were the data on postcodes (zip codes). These in general locate a house within quite a small geographical boundary. Roach found that the majority of the postcodes given were real in terms of the first two letters of the code at a minimum (see Figure 18.1) and a small number gave exactly their own postcode. In other words, the postcode given was a good predictor of the town in which the individual lives but sometimes located the individual even more precisely than that. See Figure 18.1.

Another analysis checked whether or not the postcodes given were real ones despite being part of a false address. The 'false' postcodes were checked against an available list of postcodes. It was found that where the participant had given a postcode based on reality, they overwhelmingly checked out against the list of postcodes. However, where the participant had given a totally fictitious postcode then this only existed in about a third of cases. See Figure 18.2.

These findings do not simply fit with established theory about memory but they are practically of some significance. First of all they imply that an individual may be found because the false address reflects aspects of their current address or it is an address of someone known to the individual or it is a previous address. Secondly it might be expected that if someone lies by giving a non-existent postcode then they may be more generally untrustworthy. This is a matter for further research, however.

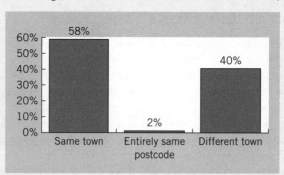

Figure 18.1 Showing the tendency to invent a 'false' postcode but which reveals the place lived in

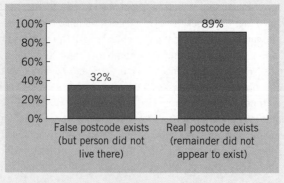

Figure 18.2 Illustrating how false postcodes do not correspond to real ones

Are professional lie detectors really no better?

It is hardly surprising that lies are hard to detect – their function is to mislead. There is a general consensus that the detection of lies is a skill that can be taught but is nevertheless a rare talent. The traditional view based on research has been that that the police, psychologists, lawyers and the medical profession can detect lies only marginally better than the chance level (Ekman, 1992, 1996). Indeed, contact with liars seems to have little impact on improving the ability to differentiate them from truth tellers. The standard research methods in this area have more recently been criticised for failing to reflect the sorts of situations in which police officers make their serious assessments of lying. At this stage it is worth mentioning Garrido and Masip's (1999) review of police lie detection skills based on studies from many parts of the world. In this review, they concluded as follows:

- Confidence about their lie-detecting ability was unrelated to actual ability to detect lies.

- Experienced officers are over-confident about their lie-detecting ability.

- Experienced police officers and newly recruited ones do not differ in their lie- and truth-detecting ability.

- Police officers are no better than the general public at detecting lies.

- Police officers use worthless indicators that a person is lying (e.g. social anxiety and assertiveness).

- Usually police officers are no better than chance at identifying truth telling and lying.

As a yardstick, this is a damning summary of the ability of police to distinguish between honesty and deceit. Increasingly research is indicating that the pessimistic conclusions from such early research may have to be modified.

There is a degree of variability in the research findings concerning the accuracy of police professionals' lie detection ability. Some studies have suggested that the police are reasonably accurate lie detectors while others suggest that their ability differs little from chance just as Garrido and Misip had concluded. Sullivan, Hurley and Tiwana (2009) argue that some conditions are sub-optimal in terms of lie detection accuracy and others are

nearer optimal. There are a number of issues – not least that in some studies the police are required to make judgements about lying in contexts very dissimilar to those of the typical police interview. Sullivan *et al.* also point out that meta-analyses (see Box 4.2) have tended to involve studies using students as participants. Young people are poorer at lie detection than older people. Meta-analyses (e.g. Aamodt and Custer, 2006) may be 'swamped', Sullivan *et al.* suggest, by data from students such that overall they misleadingly indicate that all people are poor lie detectors. The studies also often involve relatively low-stake outcomes if the lie is detected – that is, in the studies the unsuccessful liar often does not get punished. There are some studies in which the consequences of lying are much more serious such as where major crimes are involved. Sullivan *et al.* suggest that these variations in the characteristics of studies may be responsible for the rather confusing array of research findings.

One of the problems is that researchers tend to write as if a simple signal detection theory applies to the detection of lies. Signal detection theory literally developed out of situations in which a radar operative had to decide whether a signal had been detected in circumstances where there may or may not have been a signal. So the basic task of lie detection is conceived as shown in Figure 18.3 from the signal detection perspective. Sullivan *et al.* (2009) argue that the lie detection situation needs a more complex model than that implies. Since there are no universal indicators of lying, a model of

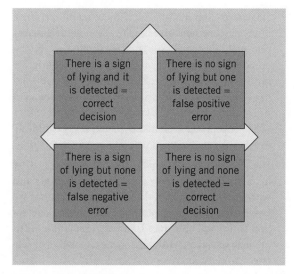

Figure 18.3 Signal detection theory applied to lie detection

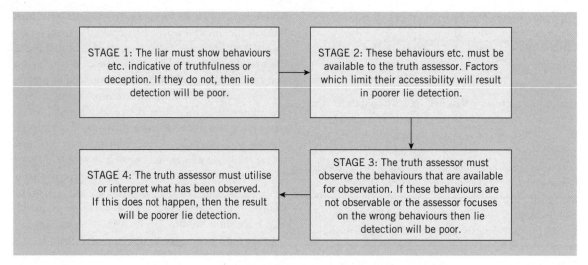

Figure 18.4 The lie detection process according to the RAM model

the lie detection situation has to be more complex than the signal detection model implies. They adopted Funder's (1999) Realistic Accuracy Model (RAM) which was originally developed in order to study the accuracy of people's assessments of another person. One advantage of the RAM model is that it does not assume that there is a signal (indicating a lie) which has to be detected in order to decide whether or not the person has lied. The features of Funder's RAM model applied to lie detection are illustrated in Figure 18.4. Each of the four stages illustrated can potentially improve or worsen the truth assessor's accuracy:

- Stage 1 requires that the liar should manifest a range of behaviours indicative of lying, otherwise lie detection will be poor. Research suggests that where the outcome or stake is trivial the cues to deception are much less likely to manifest themselves. That is, the liar has to be motivated to deceive before deception cues will manifest themselves. Furthermore, any procedure which encourages their manifestation (e.g. cognitively overloading the suspect) will improve lie detection.

- Stage 2: The signs which are indicative of lying involve potentially many parts of the liar's body and what they have to say. If the truth assessor cannot see or hear these things, for example, then their lie detection ability will be reduced. So fuzzy, inaudible video or video solely concentrating on the face will adversely affect lie detection.

- Stage 3 is more about the activity of the truth assessor when observing the suspect. The truth assessor may

simply fail to concentrate properly or they may concentrate on the suspect's face when the cues to deception are in what the suspect does with their hands.

- Stage 4 is about what the truth assessor does with what is observed in the previous stages. If the truth assessor does not know what behaviours are truly indicative of lying and so uses invalid signs then, of course, the detection of lies will be poor.

It is fairly easy to see from the theory how problems at any of these stages can hamper the detection of lies. Furthermore, the theory also gives strong hints about how the particular methodological features of a research study may mask the true level of lie detecting ability among professions such as police officers.

Laboratory induced lies, because of their lack of serious implications for the liar, quite clearly are problematic. It is probably inevitable that research relies on a fairly narrow range of procedures when a research field is new. Nevertheless, studies using significant lies with significant risks and police officers as lie detectors are much needed though at a premium. Vrij and Mann (2001) used videos of press conferences in which a relative of a missing or murdered person appealed for help in finding the missing person or their killers. These televised appeals in some cases are highly deceptive since the relative involved was actually the killer. These obviously involved high stake lies of the sort that might heighten the number of cues to deception available. So are such high-stake lies more readily detectable? Dutch police officers were shown videos of a number of such press conferences as well as similar ones that did not involve such lies as 'fillers'. The murders were all British ones, hence the decision to carry out the research with Dutch police officers who were much less likely to have prior knowledge of the events. These officers identified the liars at exactly chance level – 50 per cent accuracy. As with other studies, accuracy was unrelated to (a) the amount of time served as a police officer and (b) the amount of experience interviewing suspects. Confidence in these decisions was also unrelated to accuracy; although officers with more interviewing experience were more confident about their judgements. A variety of reasons were offered by the officers to explain their decisions about lying and truth telling. For example, they frequently mentioned fake emotions, real emotions and gaze aversion. Nevertheless, there was no correlation between these reasons and accuracy with one exception. That is, those who mentioned real emotions were actually less accurate in detecting lies than those who did not! The tempting conclusion from this study is to suggest that perhaps the original laboratory experiments had come up with the right answers about police accuracy after all.

In a way, all of this is curious since it is well known now that there are quite simple principles involved in detecting lies to be found in forensic psychology research reports. From the point of view of forensic and criminal psychology, the fact that many 'experts' in the criminal justice system remain convinced of their ability to detect lies means that the research has not reached one of its appropriate targets. Stromwall and Granhag (2003) studied three separate groups of legal professionals in Sweden – judges, prosecutors and police officers. The researchers compared what the professionals believed with what had been found by researchers. For example, Stromwall and Granhag mention such cues as higher pitched voices when lying and fewer body movements of the leg, foot, hand and arm. To what extent are the beliefs of professionals working in the criminal justice system accurate or misleading? The evidence from a survey of these professional groups demonstrates major discrepancies between what research evidence suggests overall and the beliefs of the professionals:

- *Body movements*: police officers tended to believe that liars made more body movements whereas the prosecutors and judges believed that body movement could not be used as a sign of lying. The research evidence suggests that liars may actually make fewer body movements than truth tellers.

- *It is easier to detect a liar in face-to-face situations*: the professionals tended to believe that interrogators interacting with witnesses in face-to-face situations would be better at identifying lying. Observers would be worse at detecting lying. This view held by professional groups in the criminal justice system reverses what research evidence suggests. That is, objectively, observers are better at detecting liars than interrogators.

- *Lack of detail*: all three groups of professionals tended to believe that untruthful statements contain little detail. This is supported by the mass of relevant studies into the relationship between truthfulness and the amount of detail.

- *Liars avoid eye contact (are more gaze aversive)*: most police officers subscribed to this belief. However, the prosecutors and judges tended to believe that there was no difference between liars and truth tellers in gaze aversion more often than any of the alternatives. The research evidence is that there is no relationship between lying and gaze aversion – some studies even suggest that liars make more eye contact.

- *Pitch of voice*: this was not generally seen as an indicator of lying in any of the groups of professionals. The most common belief was that pitch of voice made no difference to whether or not a person was lying. The research evidence does, however, suggest that there is a relationship.

- *Untruthful statements are less consistent over time*: all professional groups tended to believe this. There is some research evidence to suggest that this idea is correct.

It is not surprising then that incorrect decisions are being made about deceit if those decisions are based on worthless indicators of lying.

One of the problems with any form of professional decision making lies in the adequacy of the feedback that follows the decision. In the case of assessment of deceit and truth-telling, the problem is that there is no accurate feedback as to whether the decision was correct. This lack of feedback means that they cannot improve and, worse still, may come to believe that their strategy for detecting lies is a good one. Granhag *et al.* (2004) carried out a study in Sweden which was founded on this idea that adequate feedback is required in order that skills at detecting deception may be improved. They reasoned that among the groups of people who actually get feedback about the best cues to deceptions would be criminals who gain from telling lies successfully but are punished if, for example, the police do not believe them. So the researchers compared three groups – prisoners, prison personnel and students – in terms of their replies to a questionnaire concerning beliefs about the characteristics of lying. The questionnaire included a number of questions that had several responses from which to choose. For example:

> Liars include fewer details than truth tellers.
> Liars include more details than truth tellers.
> There is no difference in the amount of details given by liars.
> Don't know.

(p. 108)

The answers to the various questions could be assessed against the findings of research. So, for the above question, the correct answer according to research was the first option – liars include fewer details than truth tellers. Other research-based correct answers would include that liars move less than truth tellers and that planning of deceptive things to say increases the impression of honesty. The findings of the study tended to indicate that the prisoners did have different beliefs about the cues to deception from prison staff and students. They tended to have fewer stereotypes about cues to deception than the other two groups. Relatively, prisoners had the greatest insight into deception psychology – evidence in favour of the feedback hypothesis. Suspects who cannot lie effectively will quickly get feedback on their lack of skills by being charged with the offence. Those who lie effectively will have positive feedback of this as they walk out of the police station without being charged.

If there are some criminals who are more expert in detecting lies, then are there some police and related personnel who might be particularly good at this too? There is a tradition in the research literature which accepts that there are expert lie detectors despite the general lack of lie detection ability among people. The idea of lie detection wizards has little to do with the general view that police officers are just about as poor as the average student at detecting lies. Ekman's research (O'Sullivan and Ekman, 2004) which is held to demonstrate such lie detection skills contained very obvious weaknesses since it involved self-scoring by participants and a show of hands to indicate how accurate they were! Methodological objections to this procedure are obvious and need no explication here. Ideally, to search for lie-detection wizards involves assessment over a number of occasions. Those who are very good lie detectors in each

of the sessions can be designated as being experts. Of course, given a big enough sample, there is a probability that some people will consistently do well simply on the basis of chance – that is guessing.

Bond (2008) set about addressing the question of whether there are deception detection experts using more demanding methods and criteria. Four lie detection tests were given over two occasions. Participants who showed 80 per cent or better accuracy over each of the two assessments at the first session were invited back for more tests the next day. They were classified as deception detection experts if they did better than this criterion again. These experts were further studied in order to try to understand just why they were so good, using eye gaze tracking of them viewing suspects giving evidence and think aloud data where they attempted to say what they were doing in their observations of the suspects. The liars and truth tellers were former prison inmates with histories of serious offending. They were required to lie and truth tell in four different contexts: (a) a mock crime interrogation, (b) their work history during a job interview, (c) talking about people who had had a positive or negative impact on their lives, and (d) when describing videos they had watched. An elaborate counter-balanced procedure was used to obtain video of the each of the offenders lying and truth telling. These offenders were videoed during the lying and truth telling episodes showing their body in full except where occasionally their feet went out of shot.

Potential lie detection wizards were recruited from various locations where police officers and other front-line personnel from the criminal justice system were to be found. A total of 112 participants were involved. A similar number of American university students were also recruited to go through the testing procedures. At their first testing session, the participants were shown 14 video excerpts which they had to assess for truthfulness or lying. There were equal numbers of truthful and deceitful video clips. Accuracy scores (based on accurately detecting lies and deceit) were calculated for the participants. The range was from 34–63 per cent correct for students and from 31–94 per cent correct for the police officers. There was a tendency for the police officers to suggest that the 'suspect' was lying which, if they said lying all of the time, would ensure perfect accuracy for the detection of lies – but perfect inaccuracy for the detection of truth. However, this sort of bias is more or less controlled for by using figures for overall accuracy and not just lie detection accuracy.

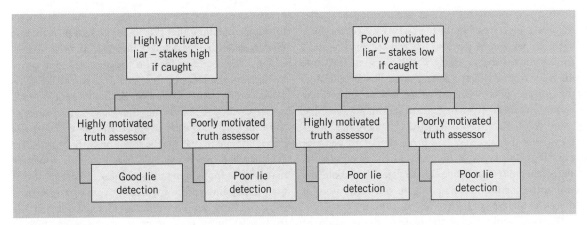

Figure 18.5 Possible circumstances where lie detection would be good

After the first session (i.e. two lie detection trials) it was found that 10 per cent of the police officers achieved more than 80 per cent accuracy on both occasions. These were invited to take part in the second day of assessment. For the students, basically a random sample of the better performing individuals were invited back for their second day. None of the students actually reached anywhere near the 80 per cent accuracy of the best of the police officers. In the second session, the participants' accuracy was again assessed and some police officers who continued to perform very well were invited to take part in an eye tracking study and other investigatory procedures on yet another occasion. Two corrections officers, both female, performed at better than 80 per cent accuracy on all of the testing sessions. The chances of this occurring on the basis of random guessing are incredibly small and so it is unlikely that chance is the explanation of their skill. The research found that the lie detection wizards were very quick to come to a decision about truth or lie. They also showed distinctly expert strategies in terms of their eye gaze pattern on the 'suspect'. That is to say, they focused rapidly on non-verbal cues which they had found helpful in lie detection in their careers which led to them not only making fast decisions but also extremely accurate ones.

These findings are a little more promising in terms of the accuracy of police officers and related professionals when assessing for deceit or truthfulness than the traditional view. But it remains something of a difficulty that some reviews of the evidence seem to suggest that inaccuracy typifies truth assessors. O'Sullivan, Frank, Hurley and Tiwana (2009) also argue that the stake of the liar in the outcome is an influential factor in the detection of deceit. Of course, most police interviews involve higher stake outcomes than the average laboratory experiment in this area. Where the stake was high because the lie was personally very involving or it would lead to substantial rewards or punishments, they argue that police lie detection ability would be high compared to circumstances in which the stake was low. The broad scheme of this is given in Figure 18.5. Furthermore, it is likely that the high stake situation should be one which is also be relevant to the occupation of the truth assessor. From a total of eight different countries, 23 research studies were located which involved the police as participants.

Some of the characteristic high-stake scenarios would be:

- Having to lie about something important personally to themselves.

- Having to lie when they are in an intense emotional state.

- Lies told by real suspects under police interrogation are high stake whereas the ex-prisoner who is encouraged to lie under laboratory conditions will be telling low-stake lies.

- Where there is a (personally) big reward for a successful lie as opposed to a minor reward (such as a cinema ticket).

The scenarios used in the studies identified for inclusion in the new analysis were rewritten in a more standard form and assessed by a panel of raters in terms of how distressed or afraid or upset or feeling guilty the person telling the lie would be. This resulted in a group of studies involving high stakes and a group of studies involving low stakes. For the high stakes studies the average accuracy was 64 per cent whereas for the low stake studies the average accuracy was 55 per cent (i.e. little different from chance). Quite clearly, this is indicative that some police when assessing lies in appropriate conditions are far from being the random guessers that some researchers have suggested. Furthermore, there is evidence that some types of professionals are better at assessing some types of lies than others. For example, expert therapists are better able to detect lies about the emotions a person is feeling but the police are poor at detecting this type of lie (O'Sullivan, 2008).

It is doubtful whether the issue of the accuracy of police lie detection is yet settled, but the balance of probabilities seems to be beginning to change.

Improving lie detection hit rates

More researchers have begun to address the question of how a professional lie detector could improve their 'hit' rate above what often seems to be derisory levels in research studies. By and large these newer developments have involved improving or otherwise changing the interview situation in which lie detection is to take

place. For example, the interviewee could be asked to go through something that they had just said or elaborate on it in much greater detail (Vrij, 2004). In other words, increase the cognitive load on the interviewee in order to increase the chances that they will reveal the signs of deception (see Figure 18.6). Basically cognitive load is increased by demands that the suspect multi-tasks in some way. The cognitive overload ensures that suspects find it difficult to manage the situation without revealing evidence that they are lying. There is reason to believe that lying is more demanding on our mental resources than telling the truth – the liar has to do more mental work and carry out more different kinds of task than the truth-teller in most circumstances. This multi-tasking simply gets too much. This increase in cognitive load is the result of a number of factors including:

- it is cognitively more demanding to invent the lie than to merely report the truth
- truth-tellers will assume that the other person sees what they say as truthful whereas the liar may feel it necessary to put more effort into appearing credible
- the liar may need to monitor the other person more actively and carefully for indications that the liar is being believed or not
- the truth has to be suppressed by the liar which itself may be cognitively demanding. This does not mean that all lies are cognitively more demanding than the

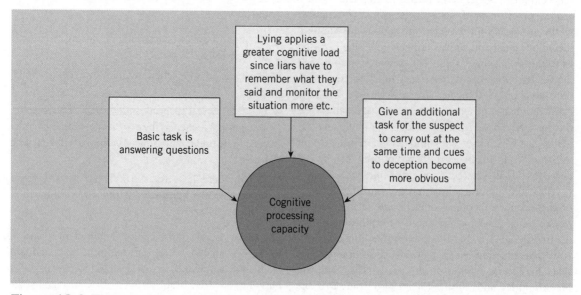

Figure 18.6 The cognitive load approach to making lie detection easier

truth, but they will be in certain circumstances. For example, lying may not be more demanding where the liar has no strong motivation to be believed. On the other hand, the liar needs to be able to access the truth from their memories quickly and easily otherwise it will be more difficult for them to suppress the truth. There are some circumstances in which the cognitive load on the truth-teller will be bigger than that on the liar. For example, if the truth-teller is trying to recall largely forgotten events then their cognitive load may be higher than that for the liar simply making up events.

Generally, however, all of this implies that any procedure which increases cognitive load will result in the liar revealing more cues that they are lying all other things being equal. To demonstrate this Vrij, Mann, Fisher, Leal, Milne and Bull (2008) set up a situation in which the participant was playing a game with another person during which a wallet belonging to a third person was recovered but the owner claimed that £10 was missing. The participants in this scenario were the truth-tellers. Other participants were simply asked to take the money physically out of the wallet and to lie and deny that they had done so. The truthful and lying participants were also provided with a scenario of the events which the truthful participants had participated in. So the truth-tellers actually participated in all of the events whereas the liars did not do so although they knew about the events. Both truth-tellers and liars were interviewed using a standard protocol. They were promised a cash reward if they convinced the interviewer that they were telling the truth but an additional chore if they did not do so. The instructions were slightly different for some participants in order to increase their cognitive load. They were required to recall the events in reverse order of their actual occurrence.

The interviews were videotaped and transcribed. The videos were coded for visual cues to lying (e.g. 'He went to the whiteboard') and the transcriptions were coded for verbal cues to lying ('She said to sit down'). The coding was done by persons unaware of the nature of the hypotheses underlying the study. Other features were also coded such as the time delay between the question being asked and the start of their account of the events, the number of errors of speech, the number of pauses, the use of illustrators, hand and finger movements, and the number of seconds of gaze aversion. The analysis of these data showed very clearly that many

more cues to deceit were to be found in the interviews of the liars than the truth-tellers.

Using these same videos, the researchers also had a group of British police officers make judgements about the person in the video relevant to an assessment of their truthfulness. The reverse order – the high cognitive load – interviews proved easier for the officers to detect truth or lies in than the forward order interviews.

Vrij, Mann and Fisher (2006) provide further evidence that the style of interviewing that the police adopt may have a bearing on the extent to which cues to deceit are present in the interview and, consequently, the likelihood that the interview will reveal cues to deceit. Three different interview styles were used – (a) information-gathering, (b) accusatory and (c) behaviour analysis:

- The information-gathering style of interview involves the police officer requesting a detailed statement about the suspect's activities such as what they did on the day that the crime was committed. This is an open-ended form of questioning in order to elicit as much information as possible and generally it is reasonably successful in this regard.

- In the accusatory style of interview, the police officer is much more confrontational ('What are you trying to hide from me?'). Perhaps not surprisingly, accusatory interviewing styles tend to produce cryptic denials of such accusations ('Nothing!'). Of course, the more that the suspect says, the greater the possibility that the cues to deception will be revealed.

- The third type of interview studied was Behaviour Analysis Interview as proposed by Inbau et al. (2001). This form of interview begins with exploratory open-ended questions much like the information-gathering interview but then introduces a standard, predetermined list of 15 questions. The theory underlying the Behaviour Analysis Interview includes the idea that those suspects who are innocent expect to be eventually seen as innocent and as a consequence they are more likely to try to be helpful to the police. So, for example, the suspect is asked to answer questions about who would seem to be the person who had the opportunity of committing the crime – truth-tellers are more likely to suggest names. However, there is some doubt whether this assumption is adequate (Vrij et al., 2007).

As might be expected, the different types of interview differed in terms of (a) the amounts of cues to deception that were available to the interviewers and (b) the extent to which false interpretations of guilt were made on the basis of these cues. The accusatory interview fared the least well in this regard although the rates of positive detections of lying did not differ significantly between the three types of interview.

There seems to be emerging a much more optimistic view about the possibility of improving interviewers' ability to detect deception (Granhag, Strömwal and Hartwig, 2007). The essence of their approach depends on the findings of various research studies which suggest that innocent suspects may volunteer information which might incriminate themselves, whereas guilty suspects employ strategies of trying to avoid confrontation with incriminating information or otherwise try to escape the situation. Granhag *et al.* report that guilty suspects are more likely to have a strategy to deal with an interrogative interview than innocent suspects. Innocent people tend to believe that the truth will prevail ultimately. As a consequence, innocent suspects, if they have any strategy in the interview at all, are likely to simply 'tell it like it is' on the assumption that the truth will shine through. The guilty suspect, though, needs a strategy by which they can avoid referring to incriminating information if at all possible. However, if the guilty suspect is 'cornered' in the interview they deny that they are in possession of the incriminating evidence.

The SUE (Strategic Use of Evidence) technique is based on these ideas. The technique basically involves the interviewer planning the interview very carefully in the light of any information that is available which potentially might incriminate the suspect (who, for much of the interview, remains unaware of the fact that the interviewer has this information). So, for example, a fingerprint belonging to a suspect might be found on a bag in a room from which something was stolen. If the suspect does not mention visiting the room or seeing a bag when asked about their activities on the day of the crime, this suggests that they are avoiding revealing potentially incriminating evidence. There may be innocent reasons why the fingerprint is on the bag but the innocent suspect is more likely to reveal this potentially incriminating evidence. The interviewer needs to carefully check with the suspect any statements that the suspect may make relevant to the potentially incriminating evidence. Towards the end of the interview the interviewer may ask the suspect to account for discrepancies in his or her evidence and the potentially incriminating evidence. This technique when used with

a guilty suspect is likely to produce elements of the statement which is at variance with the known incriminating evidence. When used with an innocent suspect the technique produces statements which are consistent with the known incriminating evidence.

Hartwig *et al.* (2006) used two groups of Swedish police, one of which received training in the SUE method and the other did not. The suspects were either guilty or innocent of stealing a wallet from a campus bookstall though both the guilty and innocent suspects had been to the bookstall. The officers participating in the study had a file containing such incriminating evidence as the suspects' fingerprints were found on the briefcase. So an officer using the SUE technique would perhaps encourage the suspect to talk about what they had done that day to see if any mention of the bookstall was made or, say, if they had seen a briefcase. The outcome of the study was that the accuracy of the trained officers in detecting the guilty and innocent was 85 per cent compared with only 56 per cent for the untrained officers. The latter figure is little different from chance but trained officers were doing extremely well once undermining the arguments of poor lie detecting accuracy among police officers.

Probably the most important focus for researchers into the assessment of lying and truth telling must be on high stake lies researched in natural conditions. As we have seen, this sort of research simply was not available in adequate quantities until now. Porter and ten Brinke (2010) have reviewed progress to date and present a cautious optimistic view of the future. They argue that it is important that practitioners are realistic about what is possible and understand the likely limitations of current lie detection knowledge. There is unlikely to be a Pinochio's-nose indicator of lying but that does not mean that important progress has not or cannot be made. Porter and ten Brinke (2010), in their review of the field, suggest that changes from baseline measurements for facial expression/information, verbal behaviour and non-verbal behaviour/body language can be useful indicators of lying. Among the specific indicators which may help guide the lie detector are:

- Facial cues especially involving the top or bottom of the face

- Increased delays before answering a question

- Increased or decreased use of illustrators (hand gestures which emphasise or illustrate the point being made)

- Involuntary, fleeting emotional expressions of the face
- Little contextual embedding and reproduced conversation where the incident involves more than one person
- More frequent and longer pauses in speech
- Reductions in the rate of blinking
- Repetition of details
- Slowing down of the rate of speech
- Vagueness of descriptions given

- Verbal slips such as tense changes (they give the example of speaking of the missing person in the past tense).

Some of these are better supported than others by research but they do serve to focus attention in potentially profitable directions. There have been developments, they point out, in terms of brain scanning approaches but, whatever the promise of these, they are far from properly validated and far from being practicable as yet for day-to-day police work.

Main points

- There is no simple way of detecting a liar. There is considerable evidence to suggest that for the most part, such groups as the police and psychologists do little better than chance when assessing the truthfulness of those they interview. Nevertheless, given appropriate circumstances, it is possible to improve on this. Most methods of detecting lies rely on detecting the emotions that may go along with lying. By concentrating on this, rather than relying on unproven ideas of the signs of lying, a better hit-rate may be achieved. There is reason to think that observers at an interview do better than the interviewer at detecting lies – presumably because they are faced with a simpler task and can concentrate more on the hard-to-detect indicators of lying.

- Increasingly researchers have focused on procedures which increase the cognitive load on the suspect during interviews. This increase in cognitive load has an important effect of making some of the cues to deception more apparent and, thus, improves the hit rate of anyone who focuses on valid cues to deception.

- Research involving high-stakes situations resembles the typical situation in a police interview and should increasingly be the focus of researchers' efforts. Changes such as these to the way in which research is done are partly responsible for some of the radical revisions in dominant views about the ability of professionals to detect lies.

Further reading

An in-depth account can be found in:
Vrij, A. (2008) *Detecting Lies and Deceit: Pitfalls and Opportunities* (2nd edn) Chichester: John Wiley.

Visit our website at www.pearsoned.co.uk/howitt for self-test and essay questions, annotated further reading, audio interviews with researchers in the field, weblinks and more information on becoming a forensic psychologist.

Chapter 19

Lies, lie detecting and credibility 2: the polygraph test and statement validity analysis

Overview

- This chapter is about two techniques which raise controversy to high levels – the lie detector or polygraph test and *statement validity analysis*, a less well-known technique to the general public.

- The polygraph test is a controversial technique depending on the physiological response to the fear of being caught lying. While it has some success, it also risks relatively high rates of wrongful accusations against innocent individuals. The threat of the polygraph or its findings can be effective in inducing a confession. Although the use of the polygraph may be unacceptable in court in a number of jurisdictions, there is a trend to using it as part of the supervision of sex offenders.

- The polygraph is more than simply a physiological instrument since the administration of polygraphy is more complex than that implies. In particular, it should be noted that the polygraph examiner knows a great deal about the case generally and is not unaware of the strength of the other evidence against the suspect.

- The validity of the normal police polygraph test is good for the guilty but rather poorer for the innocent.

- European psychologists have developed statement validity analysis as a way of assessing the competence of witnesses in giving evidence. This is a complex set of procedures that yield probabilistic statements about the evidential competence of the witness. It consists of criterion-based content analysis and the lesser-used validity checklist.

- Criterion-based content analysis is based on the working assumption that the way we present memories of real events is different from that for fictitious events. There are approximately 19 different criteria which may be used. For example, accounts of true events tend to contain indications that the person accepts that aspects of their account may be flawed. Generally, the evidence seems consistently to point to the value of statement validity analysis in the assessment of the value of some forensic evidence. There is evidence from both laboratory experiments and forensic settings that the methods are of value.

Introduction

This chapter turns attention on two techniques for evaluating evidence which differ in terms of the value as assessed by psychologists:

- The polygraph test, which can be used to assess the physiological arousal patterns manifested by a person anxious about the risk of identification as a liar. In recent years this has been applied in new contexts within the criminal justice system.
- Statement validity analysis, which takes a broad view of the differences between memories for real events and lies. This approach attracted enormous attention from researchers and practitioners in the 1990s and before. The debate surrounding its use has waned somewhat in recent years.

The polygraph test is well known to most people but the evidence of its worth is rather scarce and generally it is held to be an insufficiently valid technique by most psychologists for many practical purposes. Despite this, it is used in some jurisdictions such as much of the USA as a central part of the criminal investigation process. We will learn why many psychologists are concerned about its use and of its current revival in the management of convicted sex offenders.

Statement validity analysis is far less widely known outside of the field of forensic psychology. It consists of methods designed primarily to assess the credibility of the evidence of children. The intellectual roots of statement validity analysis are very different from those of most of the tests and measures with which psychologists are familiar. It is of continental European origins and is a more holistic procedure than psychologists' usual concerns about reliability and validity and item analyses are relevant to. Nevertheless, this has not stopped some researchers from putting statement validity analysis under the same scrutiny that psychometrically inclined researchers would apply to their measures.

The polygraph process

It is frequently suggested that the polygraph or lie detector works because of the fear of offenders of being found to be lying. The Federal Bureau of Investigation in the United States maintained a website where it claimed that the polygraph or lie detector has a variety of uses (now unavailable):

- It can identify guilty people.
- It can eliminate suspects.
- It can establish the truth of statements made by witnesses or informants.
- It can save money by shortening investigations.
- It can increase conviction rates by encouraging confession by those who have lied prior to the polygraph examination.

This would seem to be a remarkable achievement for a device that does little more than measure some autonomic responses of a person's body when answering questions. The polygraph is a surprisingly elderly piece of equipment. Its foundations were in attempts around 1914 to assess lying using the pneumograph – a device that measured breathing patterns. The work of Larson (1922) and Keeler (1934) resulted in the polygraph machine, which is more or less the same as is used today. Sensors are attached to various parts of the body to detect various responses:

- Blood pressure variations reflecting cardiovascular (heart and veins) changes. These are measured using a version of the blood pressure cuff, which is placed around the arm when a nurse or doctor measures our blood pressure.
- Respiration rates and amplitude are measured by changes in pressure on inflated tubes placed strategically around the individual's torso.
- Sweating in the palms of the hand. This is part of the galvanic skin response.

The word polygraph merely means many drawings – several 'pens' draw lines on a moving paper chart in the technique. These pens move under electrical control determined by a variety of physiological responses of the body. Physiological changes produce wave patterns that may become more frequent (e.g. the suspect breathes more rapidly) or increase in amplitude (e.g. the suspect breathes more deeply). Nowadays the apparatus is small enough to be stored in an attaché case. Furthermore, advancing technology has meant that computers may be connected to the polygraph. In this way, complex waves may be broken down into their component parts for easier interpretation. Increases in the physiological responses to a question, as measured by the polygraph, are held to be indicators of lie telling.

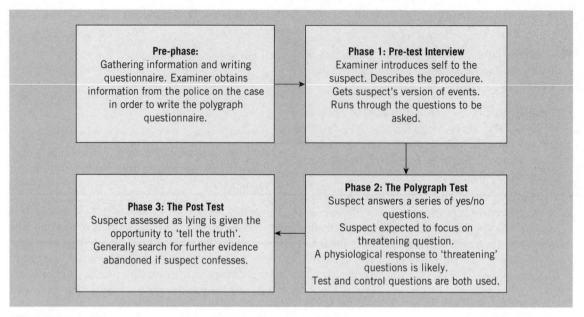

Pre-phase:
Gathering information and writing questionnaire. Examiner obtains information from the police on the case in order to write the polygraph questionnaire.

Phase 1: Pre-test Interview
Examiner introduces self to the suspect. Describes the procedure. Gets suspect's version of events. Runs through the questions to be asked.

Phase 3: The Post Test
Suspect assessed as lying is given the opportunity to 'tell the truth'. Generally search for further evidence abandoned if suspect confesses.

Phase 2: The Polygraph Test
Suspect answers a series of yes/no questions.
Suspect expected to focus on threatening question.
A physiological response to 'threatening' questions is likely.
Test and control questions are both used.

Figure 19.1 The phases of the FBI polygraph process

Figure 19.1 gives the phases in the FBI interview using the polygraph. Note the following points:

- The test itself, Phase 2, is just one component of the procedure using the polygraph or lie detector test.

- The examiner develops the list of questions to be used in a particular application in a pre-phase, partly in collaboration with the investigating officers.

- The process involves rapport building with the suspect that is different from the element of surprise we might expect from movies and video. In particular, the questions to be asked are not entirely unknown to the suspect before the polygraph test. It is the threatening nature of certain questions that is mainly the focus since these are the ones that make the suspect fear that they will be caught lying by the machine.

- Most importantly of all, the polygraph examiner does not merely make an assessment of the truth telling of the suspect: the examiner (or the police officers involved) may confront the suspect with evidence that they were lying on the test. At this stage they are encouraged to tell the truth in various ways.

- Suspects who are deemed to be innocent by the test are unlikely to receive any further questioning.

Thus rather than speaking of 'the polygraph test' it is more appropriate to describe it as 'the polygraph process'.

Not only does this give a better idea of the context but also it relates to the major criticisms of the technique. Few would argue that the polygraph is anything but controversial. In parts of the world polygraph evidence is not acceptable in court; elsewhere it is. The polygraph is a notable feature of the legal system in the United States despite there having been legislation which restricts of use of polygraph testing in terms of the selection of employees. So, although many thousands of polygraph tests are still given each year, in the United States the *Employee Polygraph Protection Act of 1988* essentially reduced pre-employment polygraphs to a trickle of 15 per cent of their use prior to the Act. There are at least 70 countries in the world where the polygraph test is used extensively (Grubin and Madsen, 2005).

Nevertheless, before concluding that the polygraph is a good thing, a number of issues concerning its use should be considered. One of the problems of risk assessment (see Chapter 27) is that some of the information used comes from what the offender tells the psychologist or other practitioner; for example, it is well established that the extent of previous offending is a predictor of future offending. The question is just where the information about previous offences should come from. Obviously the information on file for a particular offender might be a good starting point. This information would be obtained from previous disclosures at interview and conviction records, among other sources. For any number of reasons, this information might be partially incomplete. Research studies have demonstrated that polygraphy can be used to increase the amount of information available – for example, it can lead to a several-fold increase in the number of known offences on record. There is evidence that polygraphy can increase the number of crossover reportings (crossovers refer to the variety of sexes, ages and relationships involved in a perpetrator's offending). Crucially, it is known that offences against a wide variety of victims increase the risk level posed by the offender. Unfortunately, much of this research is confounded by the fact that the typical research design takes place in relation to treatment and offenders are given immunity from prosecution for new offences that they reveal. This raises the possibility that factors other than the polygraph itself are actually responsible for the offender disclosing additional offending. In many ways, what is known so far is encouraging as it seems to suggest that offenders will disclose further offences under the influence of the polygraph. The problem is that it is not known (a) whether those disclosures are factually correct and (b) whether this increase in disclosures actually leads to more accurate predictions of risk.

Problems with the polygraph

There is little doubt that those who use the polygraph are convinced of its value. There is quite clearly a value in the technique even though it might be incapable of distinguishing between lies and the truth. People, in general, believe that it can detect lies and, more to the point, so do some offenders. Consequently, to tell a suspect that

he or she has failed the lie detector test may induce confession in the guilty and false confession in the innocent. Ianoco (2008) put it this way:

> a polygraph test could have no better than chance accuracy and still have utility. If one used a 'lie detector' that was no more accurate than a coin toss to adjudicate guilt, half of all guilty individuals would be accurately identified as liars. Confronted with the results of this lie detector by a skilled interrogator, guilty individuals would on occasion confess, demonstrating the utility of the lie detector. In the absence of knowledge that this device worked by chance, those using this technique could naturally be expected to come to believe in its validity.
>
> (p. 231)

Because failing the polygraph test may induce such confessions, the examiners who use the polygraph may regard this as clear evidence of its validity – they decide that someone is showing signs of lying and that person subsequently confesses. In this sense, it is not surprising that police officers used to polygraphy see value in its use. Nevertheless, this may be merely an example of confirmation bias – the disproportionate emphasis we put on evidence that supports our point of view and the relative underplaying of evidence that contradicts our view. Probably more important, and systematically excluded from the FBI-style process, are the individuals who are 'cleared' by the polygraph process. Does this group consist solely of the innocent? If not, just what proportion of this group is in fact telling lies? What is known as the 'ground truth' (objective reality) cannot ever be known, of course. Without examining the evidence of the shortcomings of polygraph evidence, we may confuse ground truth with what the operator decides is the truth.

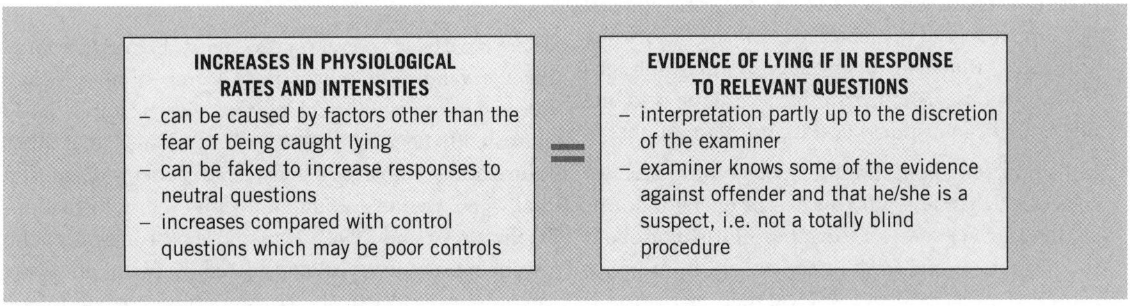

INCREASES IN PHYSIOLOGICAL RATES AND INTENSITIES		EVIDENCE OF LYING IF IN RESPONSE TO RELEVANT QUESTIONS
– can be caused by factors other than the fear of being caught lying – can be faked to increase responses to neutral questions – increases compared with control questions which may be poor controls	**=**	– interpretation partly up to the discretion of the examiner – examiner knows some of the evidence against offender and that he/she is a suspect, i.e. not a totally blind procedure

Figure 19.2 The basic polygraph equation

The basic polygraph equation is given in Figure 19.2 together with some of the issues raised by the equation. The most serious of the problems are (partly based on Iacono and Lykken, 1997; Iacono and Patrick, 1997) as follows:

- In the normal polygraph process, the adequacy of the control questions is vital and it may be difficult to get them right. So, for example, the question 'Have you ever thought of taking revenge against someone who has done you a wrong?' is intended to encourage a lie in everyone, including the innocent. Most of us have done this although we do not care to admit it. On the other hand, some may answer 'no' to this question – not because they are wilfully lying but because they had forgotten the occasions when they had.

- To be accused during the course of polygraphy of, say, murdering one's wife may be emotive for both the guilty and innocent. In these circumstances, there is reason to believe that the polygraph may fail to differentiate between lying and 'honest denial' (Iacono and Patrick, 1997).

- The control questions may disturb the guilty more than the innocent. For example, if asked in the context of a homicide, 'Have you ever stolen anything?' the guilty might remember a series of armed robberies they had committed. Thus they show the same emotional signs to the control question as they do to the relevant question since, for them, the control question is also a relevant question.

- Faking and countermeasures are possible in response to a polygraph test. Indeed, some experts advertise such claims as that they can teach their clients to deceive the lie detector in half an hour on the Internet. The essential theory of this is simple: manifest the same physiological response to the control questions as the relevant questions. Thus practical advice might be to press down hard with one's toes to the control questions or to engage in a complex task such as mental arithmetic, which might produce a similar physiological response. Another simple technique is to bite one's tongue in response to the control questions.

- In its practical application, the polygraph test is not subjected to 'fair test' procedures. The operator normally does not operate 'blind' to other information about the suspect coming from interview and from police sources. Furthermore, it is known that the suspect is a suspect so it is likely that there is other evidence against him/her. In normal practice, the polygraph is not tested against groups of known innocent people.

- Even the basic theory of the polygraph may be challenged since it has not been established that the only way that the body responds to fear of detection in lying is increases in the physiological measures assessed by the polygraph.

In the defence of polygraphy, the following points are worth considering:

- The polygraph questionnaire normally consists of several sets of questions. Inadequacies in any question may be compensated for by the other questions.

- There is a distinction to be drawn between the practical utility of the polygraph and its scientific adequacy. If polygraphy encouraged more guilty individuals to tell the truth then this could be seen as an advantage. But this has nothing to do with the validity of the polygraph to detect the fear its advocates claim is the basis of its success. Actually, to play the devil's advocate, it could be argued that it would be more useful if all suspects were adjudged liars by the polygraph. Then all suspects could be confronted with the evidence of their guilt and encouraged to confess. Provided that one is prepared to accept the consequences in terms of increased numbers of false confessions – and it is anyone's guess how many this would be – then one would maximise police success.

- The criticisms of present practice do not mean that the concept of polygraphy is worthless – there are other approaches to polygraphy such as the *guilty knowledge test* that have yet to be generally adopted.

Studies of the validity of polygraphy

There have been several surveys of psychologists regarding the validity of polygraphy. Members of a society devoted to psychological physiological research fairly consistently rejected its sole use in the absence of other information, but it was considered a useful diagnostic tool when used in conjunction with other information. In the 1980s and 1990s as many as 60 per cent of the psychologists surveyed considered it useful in those circumstances. Virtually no one considered it totally worthless (Iacono and Lykken, 1997). A more recent survey specifically mentioned the different types of polygraph test. The common *control question technique* (relevant versus control questions) was seen by only about a third of two separate groups of psychologists to be based on sound psychological principles. Only about a quarter were in favour of the use of the polygraph in courts of law. On average, the psychologists thought that the control question technique was 63 per cent accurate with innocent suspects and 60 per cent accurate with guilty suspects. These figures would indicate a high proportion of errors.

There are a number of laboratory studies that have investigated the validity of the polygraph when the control question technique is employed. Essentially, the procedure is to inculpate some participants in the research, for example in a 'mock crime', and not others, the control group. The polygraph examination is then used to assess which group each participant was in. This seems a reasonable procedure although there are a number of problems:

- In real life, failing the polygraph test may have very serious consequences. Failing the laboratory set-up's polygraph test simply does not carry the same implications about punishment. There is no obvious strong motivation to pass the test. Indeed, the motivation may be to fail the test if you are in the guilty group as it is fairly obvious that the researchers are interested in the validity of the test.

- Because there is no cost of failing the test, it is possible that the control questions are relatively more intrusive and anxiety provoking. For example, as the experiment is possibly seen as play-acting, the participant may be more concerned about questions that bring into question their integrity and morality. So a question such as 'Have you ever told a lie?' might produce a more physiological response than 'Did you take part in the (mock) crime?'

- Iacono and Patrick (1997) are critical of the so-called friendly polygraph test organised by the defence. Failure on the test would not be publicised whereas passing the test would be lauded as evidence of innocence. Furthermore, in the friendly test the examinee has nothing to fear from detection. Remember that it is the fear of detection that is crucial to the success of the polygraph.

One obvious major advantage of the laboratory experiment is that the 'ground truth' (whether the suspect was actually involved in the crime) is easily established – indeed it is imposed by the researchers. Field studies of real-life polygraph examinations have severe problems in establishing ground truth. The normal criterion of confession is hardly adequate for reasons already mentioned. Primarily, the confession is a response to the outcome of the polygraph test so it could hardly fail to support the validity of the polygraph test. The failure to examine the 'cleared' suspects any further is a less obvious problem but nevertheless crucial. If we look at Figure 19.3, only the true positives and the false positives are encouraged to confess. The false negatives and true negatives are essentially ignored. All of this contributes to a spurious enhancement of the apparent validity of the polygraph.

It would obviously be very useful to examine the guilt and innocence of those excluded by the polygraph

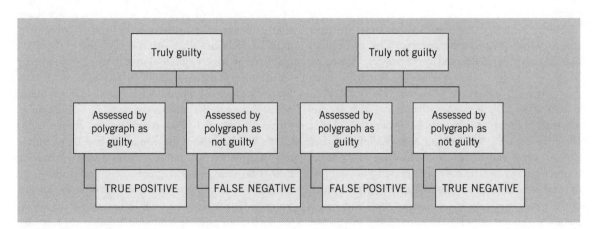

Figure 19.3 Possible outcomes of the polygraph test

test – those whom we have classified as true negatives and false negatives. Ideally, then, field studies of the validity of polygraphy should do the following:

- Explore the group of individuals who passed the test as innocent for later evidence of guilt or innocence, e.g. later confession to the crime.
- Independently re-score the polygraph charts blind to the original examiner's conclusions and other information that might have influenced the examiner to decide that the suspect was guilty.

Few studies have met these requirements. Patrick and Iacono's (1991) study involved finding all of the cases from a large Canadian metropolitan area which had involved polygraph testing over a five year time period. Ignoring the outcomes of these polygraph tests, the researchers scoured police records in order to find evidence that someone had later confessed to the crimes and also cases where it was later found that a crime actually had not actually occurred (e.g. putative stolen property had actually been misplaced). In this way, the results of the polygraph test were not confounded with the confession, for example. They found that the blind polygraph reassessment correctly classified individuals as innocent in only 57 per cent of cases, which is scarcely different from the chance level of 50 per cent. The researchers also identified instances where the suspect failed the initial polygraph test and then confessed. In these circumstances there was a 98 per cent success rate for identifying the 'guilty' individuals. This may be because the criterion of guilt and the initial polygraph findings are confounded since those who were found guilty by the polygraph would have had good reason for confessing. In other words, the innocent are very poorly identified as such by the polygraph test.

These findings are similar in some ways to earlier studies where ground truth was based on confessions that may have been influenced by the polygraph outcome. These, of course, do not involve the search for later, non-polygraph influenced confessions. The best of these studies showed 76 per cent (Kleinmuntz and Szucko, 1984) and 77 per cent (Horvath, 1977) of the guilty were correctly classified, while 63 per cent (Kleinmuntz and Szucko, 1984) and 51 per cent (Horvath, 1977) of the innocent were correctly classified. These trends are true of studies involving the control question test which is the typical situation in forensic settings. But this is not the only form of polygraphy. Table 19.1 gives some information on the different types of polygraph test

which are based on different questioning techniques. A British Psychological Society report (British Psychological Society Working Party, 2004) gives a detailed comparison of these techniques together with the directed lie test (Raskin and Honts, 2002) in which the suspect liar is told to answer no to questions which everyone should say yes to. There are other questions that are more pertinent to the 'crime' in question. The idea is that innocent people should be more concerned about the first sort of question than those questions about the 'crime'. Unfortunately, as the control question technique is almost exclusively the one used in forensic settings, the research on the other techniques is of lesser forensic interest. Fiedler, Schmid and Stahl (2002) provide an evaluation of the scientific validity of the polygraph employing the Control Question Technique. Their review led the German Supreme Court to stop using the technique in relation to penal matters.

In contrast, research into the accuracy of the guilty knowledge test tends to demonstrate exactly the reverse trend. Elaad (1990) and Elaad, Ginton and Jungman (1992) found that the guilty knowledge test was extremely accurate in identifying the innocent – over 90 per cent were correctly classified. The guilty, on the other hand, were correctly identified in only 42 per cent of cases in the first study and in 76 per cent of cases in the second.

Polygraphy and the post-conviction sex offender

Even in countries where the polygraph test cannot be used as evidence of guilt in courts of law, it may have alternative uses. A few years ago, the British Government initiated trials into the post-conviction use of the polygraph in the supervision and management of convicted sex offenders in the community. In the UK the scope of its use is much more limited than, say, in the United States where it is used in a majority of states as a condition of probation and parole. Post-conviction sex offender polygraphy is largely about the management of sex offenders following conviction rather than finding evidence for further prosecutions. Polygraphy used in this way is far from new since it dates back to the 1970s in the United States (Grubin and Madsen, 2005). Its uses include assessing the truthfulness of what paedophiles say to probation workers about their day-to-day activities. So denials

Table 19.1 The different types of polygraph test question

	Guilty knowledge test	Relevant/irrelevant question technique	Directed lie test	Control question technique
Type of questions used	'If you killed your wife, then you will know the sort of weapon. Was it a craft knife . . . a kitchen knife . . . a chisel . . . a Bowie knife . . . a hatchet?'	**Irrelevant question:** 'Is today Friday?' **Relevant question:** 'Did you kill your wife?'	**Control questions** such as 'Before age 27, did you ever break even one rule or regulation?' Instructed to answer 'No'. **Other questions** relevant to crime.	**Control question** (emotive question for most people): 'Have you ever plotted revenge on an enemy?' Relevant question: 'Did you kill your wife?'
Evidence of its validity		None		
Basis of interpretation	Does not detect lying as much as being aware of information which is only available to the offender and the police normally.	Truth is indicated by similar physiological response to relevant and irrelevant questions. The examiner questions the suspect in order to ascertain whether the suspect has an appropriate demeanour and explanation.	Innocent persons will be more concerned about lying in response to the control questions than to questions relevant to the crime.	Guilty will show more response to the relevant question, innocent will show more response to the control question.
Limitations	Needs careful knowledge of the crime scene to write questions. Not all crimes are amenable to the construction of guilty knowledge questions.	Confounds lying and emotive questions – many people would feel troubled by being asked if they had murdered their wife.		
Popularity	Rare.			Common in forensic applications.

by paedophiles that they are targeting playgrounds in public parks may be evaluated against their responses on the polygraph. It is claimed that the polygraph used in this sort of way has prevented the sexual abuse of a number of children and led to the reimprisonment of some offenders (BBC News, 2005). However, the validity of the polygraph in this context is largely unresearched compared to the extensive research base in criminal investigations. One of the problems in dealing with sex offenders is their denial and avoidance of confronting their offending behaviour (see Chapter 10). Proponents of the use of post-conviction sex offender polygraphy argue that (a) it can be used to ensure more reliable information from offenders about their

activities and (b) it can motivate offenders to avoid high-risk situations that might lead to reoffending against children (or other targets). For example, if an offender carries on masturbating to sexual fantasies about children, the belief is that he is much more likely to carry out that fantasy in real life. Without polygraphy, it is harder to assess behaviours like this though, of course, not impossible in a conversation between the offender and their probation worker. Similarly, it is hard to know whether an offender gravitates towards children's play areas which may increase his risk of reffending just by asking. Thus there are alternatives to the polygraph though they may not be so effective given what we know about denial and avoidance in sex offenders.

There are four types of use of the post-conviction sex offender polygraph test according to Grubin (2008):

- To help obtain a more complete disclosure of the sex offender's history. The offender will be questioned under polygraphy about aspects of his sex offending history. Having more information inevitably enables better assessments of the offender's risk and also contributes to setting relevant and appropriate treatment targets.

- To help with the maintenance of the offender during treatment and supervision. Maintenance will involve a number of requirements set between the offender and his supervising probation worker or therapist. Regular polygraph testing can help check that these requirements are being abided to. Grubin (2008) suggests that maintenance polygraph testing is to prevent reoffending rather than detect that it has happened.

- To help overcome denial. This involves testing to obtain a more complete account of the index offence for which he has been convicted. The aim is to obtain a more complete account of the nature of that offence. This sort of polygraph testing may help overcome behaviours such as the offender's denial or minimisation of his offending. Again the outcome of the polygraph testing may be useful during treatment and management of the sex offender.

- Specific issue testing or monitoring examinations concentrate on a particular matter of concern in relation to a particular offender. One example, mentioned by Grubin, would be the issue of whether the offender might have contacted his victim while under supervision.

Some sex-offender participants in a study (Grubin et al., 2004; Madsen, Parsons and Grubin, 2004) were told that they would retake a polygraph test after three months whereas the other offenders were not told this. At the polygraph reassessment they were asked questions like 'Have you done anything over the last three months that would concern your probation officer?' Out of the men who took the second polygraph test, the vast majority (97 per cent) admitted engaging in this sort of high risk of reoffending behaviour. This means that only one man did not admit any high-risk behaviours – and he failed the test anyway. One way of looking at all of this is that where the offender wishes to reduce their risk of reoffending, the polygraph can be helpful in helping them maintain a reduced-risk-of-reoffending lifestyle. There was evidence of a great deal of resistance to taking part

in the polygraph testing on the part of some offenders and significant numbers of failures to turn up for the second polygraph test. The researchers suggest that these concern individuals with little or no motivation to change their offending behaviour. In contrast, those motivated to change seem to have found it helpful in avoiding risky situations and reoffending.

Despite its long-established use in the United States, post-conviction polygraphy for sex offenders remains somewhat controversial elsewhere. A good example is Ben-Shakhar's (2008) critique. His argument is largely redolent of the criticisms of the use of the controlled question polygraphy technique in police investigations. He is particularly concerned with false positive and false negative outcomes. The post-conviction sex offender who beats the lie detector and appears to be behaving appropriately, he argues, may be an increased risk to children and women because his denials have been reinforced. Grubin (2008), in defence of post-conviction polygraphy, first of all points to the major uses of polygraphy in criminal investigation settings as well as security vetting and, even, in pre-employment vetting. The question in these settings is whether the individual passes or fails the lie detector test. The consequences of failure can be significant just as the rewards for passing can also be considerable. In these circumstances, issues such as the error rate (false positives and false negatives) become important. Post Conviction Sex Offender Testing, however, is rather different and does not depend of passing or failing for its effectiveness. Instead it may be evaluated in terms of the extent to which the offender is encouraged to disclose information which otherwise may not be available. This information may be helpful in the supervision and management of the sex offender as well as his treatment. Grubin compares sex offender polygraphy with an investigative interrogation which is essentially confrontational in nature. Grubin suggests that the post-conviction sex offender polygraph test is rather less extreme in its style and consequences. He argues that disclosures made during testing are therapeutically helpful and that they result in rewards for the offender rather than punishment. The sex offender who is open and discloses can be seen to be making progress in treatment and given positive feedback. Apparently, indications of lying on the polygraph test are not acted upon – it is the additional information that is provided that is important, claims Grubin. For this reason, if the polygraph is 80 per cent effective in encouraging disclosure then this is good enough to inform the treatment and management of the sex offender.

The accuracy of these sorts of polygraph testing results is not an entirely meaningful concept to apply. How does one validate statements about whether or not the offender has masturbated to deviant fantasy, for example? Grubin suggests that quite high error rates are not really critical in this context whereas they would be in the crime investigation context. The polygraph test is merely part of a range of information available to those involved in the treatment and management of the sex offender. As such, Grubin regards the outcome of the polygraph test as largely benign though it is impossible to know whether all post-offence sex offender polygraph tests are evaluated in such a balanced context. Falsely confessing to offending or behaviours merely to please their probation supervisor or therapist is a risk but Grubin indicates that only about 10 per cent of offenders admit in any anonymous survey to doing this (Grubin and Madsen, 2006). Grubin adopts a generally pragmatic approach to sex offender polygraph testing. So on the issue of whether a sex offender can fool the polygraph test, he writes that this is a possibility but indicates that they may fool their therapists and supervisors equally well or better.

Another use of the polygraph is in attempting to improve risk prediction for sexual offenders. Gannon, Beech and Ward (2008) review this research literature thoroughly.

Statement validity analysis: criterion-based content analysis and the validity checklist

Since lying is a verbal process then the use of physiological techniques would appear to be indirect compared with examining language itself for lies. The difficulty, though, should be obvious by now – most of us are fairly bad at recognising lies. In continental Europe, research interest has focused on a group of techniques known as *statement validity analysis*. This derives largely from the pioneering work of German psychologists, especially Undeutsch (1992), as well as Swedish psychologists. Statement validity analysis is accepted in a number of European legal systems, including the Netherlands in addition to Germany and Sweden, and also in some American states (Vrij, 2005). Researchers speak of the Undeutsch hypothesis as being fundamental to the method. The hypothesis essentially states that witnesses' descriptions of experienced and fictitious events are different in a number of ways. Truthful narratives are not the same in form and structure as untruthful ones. These differences are potential indicators differentiating truthful accounts from falsehoods.

Statement validity analysis is important in sexual abuse assessment because rarely can sexual abuse be determined on the basis of physical evidence. Despite popular beliefs about the nature of sexual abuse of children, much of it leaves few or no physical signs. Thus touching and stroking, for example, leave no independent evidence such as semen for DNA testing or injury to the anus or genitals. In the absence of physical evidence, it is necessary to depend on the victim's testimony. This may be contaminated in a number of ways. Adults may suggest events that never occurred to the child or sometimes there may be a deliberate lie by the child who is, say, angry with an adult for some reason. These matters were discussed in Chapter 17 in more detail.

Statement validity analysis consists of the two major components shown in Figure 19.4:

- *Criterion-based content analysis* involves an analysis of the content of a statement about the crime to see which of about 19 different criteria of 'truthfulness' are present.

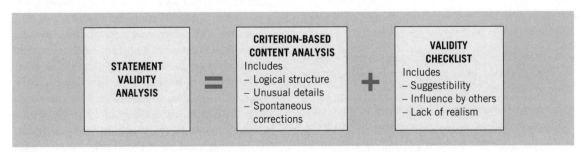

Figure 19.4 The components of a statement validity analysis

- The *validity checklist* is much more of an in-depth psychological assessment of the possible victim for motivations for giving a false statement. It may incorporate wider knowledge from other sources about the crime.

Of the two major components of statement validity analysis, research has concentrated on criterion-based content analysis with the validity checklist largely ignored.

Statement validity analysis should not be evaluated in terms of traditional North American assessment techniques. It does not provide a numerical score that can be judged against normative data of statement validity. Thus it is not possible to say that if a witness statement has 14 of the characteristics of a truly experienced account then they are telling the truth. It is impossible to use the method to differentiate truth from fiction in a simplistic way. Instead, the psychologist must gather information about the child's general competence in narrating memories of events to compare with the specific statement that is forensically of interest (Greuel, Brietzke and Stadle, 1999). There are several stages in statement validity analysis which help assess whether a witness is probably credible. To concentrate on individual components of statement validity analysis such as criterion-based content analysis is to misunderstand the method's intent and fundamental strategy. A child can be judged a competent witness only by reference to a number of features. The concept of credibility refers to a cluster of three essential components: (1) the individual's competence to testify in court; (2) the quality of the witness's statement; and (3) the reliability of the statement. The process of assessing credibility is illustrated by the flowchart in Figure 19.5.

What differentiates credible from fictitious testimony? These differentiating characteristics are usually classified into general characteristics, specific contents, peculiarities of content, motivation-related content and offence-specific elements (e.g. Bekerian and Dennett, 1992). The major features of narratives based on experience are presented diagrammatically in Figure 19.6. Generally speaking, truthful accounts are ones that:

- contain evidence that the witness regards their account as possibly flawed because of poor/incomplete memory for events;
- contain a greater amount of detail of context, conversations and interactions relevant to the narrative;
- contain a greater amount of irrelevant detail in describing the events that occurred;

- describe logically feasible events in a somewhat unstructured or disorganised fashion.

Criterion-based content analysis uses these features, in conjunction with other evidence, in order to assess the likelihood that the witness's account is credible as an account of experienced events. Most of these criteria seem to be reasonably valid since many of them are based on empirical evidence from cognitive psychology. Psychologists using the method tend not to write of lies and truth but to refer to credibility instead. A child influenced by an adult into making allegations of abuse is not lying by the criterion of a deliberate intention to deceive. On the other hand, that child is not giving an accurate account of events that they experienced.

Comparison with *other* people is not a feature of statement validity analysis as it would be in a typical psychological test. In statement validity analysis comparisons are made but they are with other data collected about the child in question. There are numerous reasons why it is necessary to compare individuals with themselves rather than others. For example, some credible witnesses will be extremely good at telling narratives about their experiences whereas other credible witnesses will be less good at telling narratives about their experiences. Some witnesses will have a good memory for detail, for example, whereas others will have a poor memory for detail. As you can see in Figure 19.6, some of the criteria of credible statements are partly dependent on good memory. Thus you would expect a credible witness statement about a crime coming from an individual with a good memory to have high memory content whereas a credible witness statement about a crime from a witness with a relatively poor memory will start at a lower baseline. The three major stages in a statement validity analysis are as follows:

- *Stage 1: witness competence to testify*. Returning to Figure 19.5, you will see that the initial stage of statement validity analysis is to assess the competence of a witness to testify. There is little point proceeding any further with a non-competent witness. There are a number of reasons for non-competence. A witness who shows poor ability at giving narrative accounts of recent events in their lives may have a brain disease, for example, which makes their statements suspect. Another witness may give the impression of being unable to tell the truth about anything. On the other hand, yet other witnesses may give the impression of being unable to give a false account

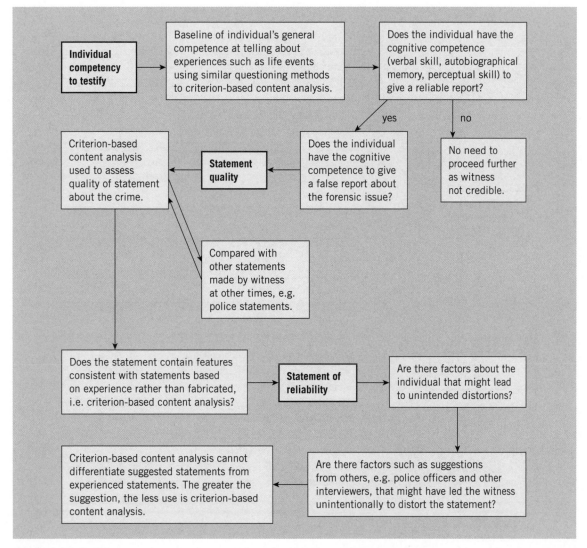

Figure 19.5 The structure of a statement validity analysis

about anything. In addition to this sort of assessment, this initial stage provides the opportunity to obtain baseline indications of the ability of the witness to give good narrative accounts of their experiences as well as gathering an impression of the characteristics of their narratives.

- *Stage 2: statement quality.* This involves the assessment of statement quality. This is essentially criterion-based content analysis. This is done in two ways: (1) internally to the statement collected from the witness (known as the immanent view) or (2) comparatively between that statement and ones obtained in other

circumstances such as in court or during the police interview. This means, first, that it is possible to assess the extent to which the statement contains criteria indicative of experience-based statements relative to one's expectations of the individual in question. Secondly, it is also possible to assess whether these criteria are stable in all accounts of the events provided by the witness.

- *Stage 3: statement reliability.* Witnesses may unintentionally provide testimony that departs materially from the credible. This may be the result of the witnesses' personal characteristics. Distinctive styles

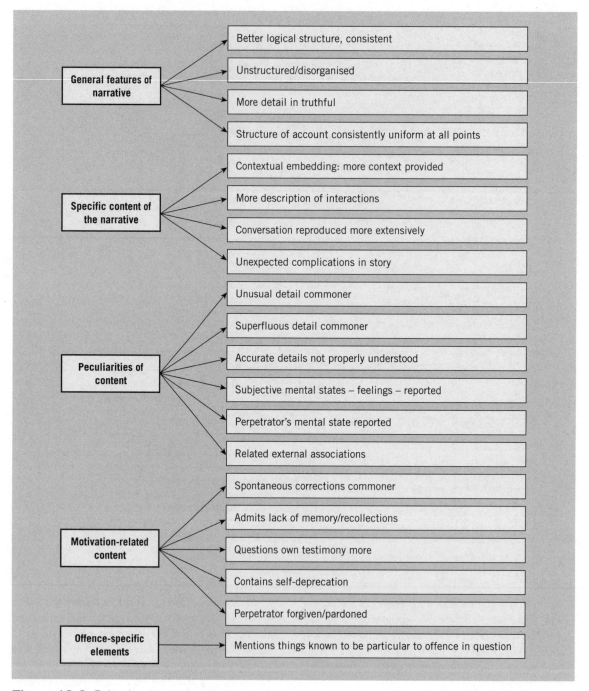

Figure 19.6 Criterion-based content analysis: some aspects of truthful narratives

of attribution, perceptual styles or motivations may be involved. Childhood victims of sexual abuse, for example, sometimes have distorted perceptions of who was responsible for initiating the abuse and blame themselves rather than the adult who perpetrated the crime. Other victims may consistently embellish or dramatise the truth. The major part of assessing statement reliability involves the issue of suggestibility.

This might be the tendency of the witness to be influenced by distortions due to leading or suggestive questioning by other people such as police officers, social workers or others. However, more important is whether or not the previous interviews and interrogations involved suggestion. So, for example, is there evidence of a suggestive interviewing style in the transcripts of previous interviews? Does the narrative provided by the witness change markedly following an earlier interview? The answers to these questions have an important bearing on how the criterion-based content analysis from the previous stage is to be interpreted. There may be no evidence at all of suggestion being involved in the statement. For example, there may have been no previous interrogations and so no opportunity for suggestion to have an influence. In these circumstances, criterion-based content analysis can be directly interpreted according to what criteria it contains together with the psychologically based expectations of that individual developed in Stage 1 – competence assessment. If there is evidence of suggestion then caution is necessary. Criterion-based content analysis cannot distinguish suggestion-based narratives from experientially based ones. The greater the suggestion, the less can be said on the basis of the content analysis.

The forensic use of statement validity analysis has largely been confined to certain parts of Continental Europe and Germany in particular, although research on it has been much more international.

However, there has been an intriguing analysis of eyewitness evidence surrounding the claims that a UFO (unidentified flying object) crashed near Roswell, New Mexico, USA (Houran and Porter, 2005). An investigation by the military claimed that the fragments found were those of a weather balloon, not a flying saucer. Jim Ragsdale provided a deathbed 'eyewitness' account of the crash and the contents of this flying saucer. He was with a woman who was later killed in a car crash. Ragsdale provided two accounts – one of 600 words and the other an affidavit of 1,000 words – which he published in 1996. The delay between 'witnessing' the events and his description was 48 years. This is the sort of material that might be assessed using statement validity analysis for its veracity as a product of human memory. Part of Ragsdale's testimony was as follows:

Since it was the Fourth of July weekend, I had several days off work. I was working driving a truck, transporting heavy equipment for a gas line. My girlfriend was from Las Cruces, and I lived in Carlsbad. We decided to go to the perfect place near Boy Scout Mountain in a campsite where we could have some solitude. We went up Pine Lodge Road and turned onto a gravel road heading toward the campsite. We went where there is a picnic ground and we had access to water. I parked my pickup behind a clump of trees, got the quilts out and put them in the back of my pickup, and we started drinking and making-out. We were lying in the back of my pickup truck, buck naked, drinking beer, and having a good ole time when about 11:30 the night of July 4, 1947, all hell broke loose. From the northwest, there was a big flash, an intense, bright explosion, and then, shortly thereafter, with a noise like thunder, this thing came plowing through the trees, sheering off the tops, and then stopped between two huge rocks. It was propped up against one rock. It was about twenty feet around. As it was approaching, huge streams like fire were coming out from behind. After the impact, silence. There was a hole in one side about four feet wide and two feet high. There was junk scattered around the disc, and we picked some of it up. I looked inside the hole, and inside, there was a chair that looked like a throne. It looked like it was made of rubies and diamonds. There were other little chairs – four or five and a lot of instruments on a panel. There were also the little people, four of them. They looked like midgets, about four feet long. Their skin, if it was skin, was sort of gray and when I touched one of them, it felt like a wet snake.

(pp. 68–9)

Houran and Porter (2005) suggest that the following were missing among other features of truthful accounts, though the accounts were, for example, coherent and also showed a degree of contextual embedding such as the detail of the couple's activities in the back of the truck:

- Description of interaction: although the events prior to the *explosion* do contain detail of the interaction between the couple, the description following these events contains nothing of contact or interaction that the couple may have had.

- Reproduction of conversation: no conversation between the couple is described in Ragsdale's account.

- Spontaneous corrections: Ragsdale corrected his memories on *no occasion* during the two reports.

- Admitting lack of memory: Ragsdale did not question his ability to recall the events in any way during his account.

Other criteria of truthful accounts were also missing as can be seen. Thus the analyst concluded that the accounts were not characteristic of memories of real events since very few indicators of truthful accounts according to statement validity analysis were present.

The validity of statement validity analysis

Forensic validity

The origins of statement validity analysis were in practical forensic applications of psychological research, especially in child sexual abuse cases. As such, the forensic rather than the laboratory validity of the approach is important. Udo Undeutsch made great claims about the effectiveness of the methods as he employed them within the German court system. For example, he suggested that of the cases assessed by him in order to provide evidence of the guilt of the suspect, no instances have emerged to indicate that statement validity analysis was wrong. Acquittals on appeal after new evidence has emerged of the innocence of the accused would indicate that statement validity analysis was leading to false convictions. But there was no evidence of acquittals on appeal. As Undeutsch was involved in thousands of cases, this appears to be strong evidence of the validity of the method. However, Undeutsch's, and similar, assertions have not been extensively or adequately documented (Bekerian and Dennett, 1992). Basically, the claim is that statement validity analysis is effective and leads to no false convictions but there are a number of considerations that reduce the impact of the claim:

- The *evidence* is that false allegations of child abuse possibly amount to no more than about 10 per cent of allegations (Howitt, 1992). Thus an allegation is a good sign of guilt and reversals of a conviction are only likely in this small percentage of cases.

- It is unclear what aspects of statement validity analysis led Undeutsch to his conclusions. Statement validity analysis can draw evidence from a wide variety of sources, as we have seen. Could it be that Undeutsch was more influenced by other forensic evidence than, say, criterion-based content analysis?

- It is not known what numbers of false negatives the *method* produces. If Undeutsch decided that the allegation was not very credible, this might result in a decision not to prosecute despite there being other evidence of guilt – leaving a guilty individual unpunished. The potentially more risky prosecutions are thereby excluded from trial, which obviously minimises the potential for appeals.

- It could be that the decision to obtain a statement validity analysis from Undeutsch was only made if the evidence was strong enough to make a conviction likely, Undeutsch's support being requested merely to strengthen an already strong case. In these circumstances, later reversals of the conviction would be unlikely.

These are conjectures that merely serve to reinforce the view that statement validity analysis needs more evaluation in its practical application. For example, Lamers-Winkelman and Buffing (1996) provide evidence from the Netherlands that certain of the components of statement validity analysis show age trends so that if the child's age is not taken into account, the validity of the method is reduced.

Laboratory validity

The ideal study of the validity of statement validity analysis is impossible. It would probably involve psychologists, well experienced in the method, making judgements of the credibility of witnesses to apparently the same event – one witness telling the truth, the other lying. Using statement validity analysis, the psychologists would decide which was the credible witness. Of course, this sort of situation does not normally occur. Furthermore, unless the 'witnesses' were randomly allocated to truth-telling or lie-telling conditions even this would not be fully capable of providing evidence of the value of statement validity analysis. Perhaps naturally honest people would choose to tell the truth and dishonest people would choose to lie. In these circumstances, it may be that the psychologists pick the truthful account from the angelic faces of the honest people and the fictitious account from the scowling demeanour of the naturally dishonest person. Clearly, certain issues can be resolved only by using random allocation in controlled experiments. Unfortunately, this does not work very well in other respects. One of the major difficulties is that laboratory experiments cannot involve the serious crimes perpetrated against the witnesses in non-laboratory settings. Another difficulty is the desire of the researchers to simplify the procedures as much as possible by concentrating on the criterion-based content analysis and ignoring the validity checklist. As we have seen, this is to do an injustice to the assumptions of statement validity analysis. Consequently, the laboratory studies can often be criticised as failing to employ the full potential of statement validity analysis. In other words, we should not be surprised that statement validity analysis appears only moderately effective if we rely on research that does fundamental disservice to the approach. Others have noted that the quality of forensic interviews with children may be so poor as to mask the worth of the method to a degree (Lamb *et al.*, 1997).

Nevertheless, it is unlikely that the North American tradition of psychological testing will readily yield to the requirements of this European approach. For example, Lamb *et al.* (1997) argue that trained assessors using criterion-based content analysis fail to show satisfactory levels of inter-rater reliability on many of the dimensions of the technique (see Figure 19.5). Some should be dropped as of no value and others need to be more carefully defined. Criterion-based content analysis dimensions that were not useful in differentiating truthful from false accounts included logical structure, complications, superfluous details, misunderstood details, external references, subjective feelings, perpetrator feelings and spontaneous corrections.

However, the following criterion-based content analysis dimensions were helpful in differentiating between allegations believed to be true according to independent judgements and the false allegations:

- unstructured production;
- quantity of details;
- contextual embedding;
- interactions;
- conversations;
- unusual details.

All of these were more common in the plausible accounts.

In this context, some American research findings may be even more positive than it at first appears. Porter and Yuille (1996) studied a range of verbal indicators of deception in interrogations. The verbal indicators were partly taken from criterion-based content analysis or one of three other approaches to differentiating truth from lies (such as reality monitoring, and a training programme in detecting lying). The participants in the research were required to give accounts of events that were either truthful or deceptive. Of a substantial list of verbal indicators of lying, only those of quantity of details, coherence (that is, what others call logical structure) and admission of lack of memory were effective. These are all from criterion-based content analysis. The other three methods failed to distinguish truthful from false accounts.

Evidence of the validity of the validity checklist is much less common, perhaps rare. Lamers-Winkelman (1997) is one of the very few researchers to have studied this aspect of statement validity analysis. His Dutch team studied over 100 possible sexual abuse victims in the 2- to 12-year-old-age range. While we might assume that the vast majority of these allegations are truthful, a small percentage are likely to be false allegations, the researcher suggests. Because the normal medical practice in the Netherlands is not to physically examine child victims of sexual abuse, no independent evidence of abuse exists. Of course, physical signs of abuse are not common. By the usual criteria of psychological assessment, there was good agreement between different raters both in terms of criterion-based content analysis and the validity checklist. Both of these had inter-rater reliabilities of over 0.8, indicating good consistency between raters. It should be stressed that the interviewers were trained by the leading experts in the method (Udo Undeutsch and Max Steller). We might expect that this led to greater reliability. A number of validity checklist items were explored in these interviews:

- *Age appropriateness of language in general*: a child who uses language more advanced than his or her chronological age may be reporting under the influence of older people. Generally speaking, in this sample there was no evidence of age-inappropriate language.

- *Age appropriateness of sexual knowledge*: sexual knowledge too advanced for the child's chronological age and level of development might be an indication that sexual abuse had taken place. Age inappropriateness was common among all of the age range. Thus, the minimum at any age level was 50 per cent but with younger children the figures went much higher: for example, 95 per cent of the 4- to 5-year-olds had knowledge too advanced for their age and level of development. These high figures might be expected in a group of sexually abused children; it is difficult to judge without the benefit of interviews with a group of non-abused children. There was a further problem. The interviewers found it difficult to decide what was sexually appropriate knowledge for the older age groups. Boys in the 9- to 11-year-old age group are mentioned as a particularly difficult group. Be cautious about these figures. Remember that in Chapter 16, it is pointed out that some sexual behaviours such as public masturbation do not differentiate sexually abused children from other children very effectively.

- *Resistance to suggestive questioning*: as part of the validity analysis, the children are examined to see whether they are susceptible to the interviewer's 'planting' ideas in their mind. A child who is susceptible to leading or suggestive questioning may be a child who has previously been led by another adult to make the allegations of abuse falsely. From quite an early age – 4 years – the children demonstrated high levels of resistance to suggestive questions. Younger children than these were more influenced by such questions: 29 per cent of children under 4 years failed to resist suggestive questions.

- *Appropriateness of affect*: the emotional signs accompanying descriptions of abuse should be appropriate to the abuse and general signs of emotionality may be present. In the study, about half of the children supported their descriptions of abusive events with gestures signalling emotion.

The performance of children when assessed using criterion-based content analysis varies according to the age of the child. The characteristics of the testimony of 2-year-olds and 14-year-olds are different. Criterion-based content analysis has no specific way of dealing with age trends of this sort. Buck *et al.* (2002) obtained transcripts of real-life child sexual abuse interviews and had them rated using criterion-based content analysis. The reliability between different raters was modest. Use of most of the criteria of criterion-based content analysis correlated with age. So older children, for example, demonstrated greater logical structure, quantity of details and contextual embedding. Only criteria such as the amount of unusual detail, references to the offender's mental state, doubting own testimony, self-deprecation and pardoning perpetrator showed no overall correlation with age. So, in general, indicators of truthfulness were commoner in the older age groups. Some of the criteria of truthfulness simply did not appear for some ages of children. For example, comments doubting their own testimony did not appear until the 12- to 14-years-of-

age group and pardoning perpetrator only appeared in 9- to 11-year-olds. This, of course, raises the question of precisely how to deal with age when assessing children's accounts. The temptation might be to assume that older children are simply more honest in their reports but there is no evidence on this one way or the other. They may simply have a different style of reporting events which corres-ponds better with the criteria of truthfulness. (This is a complex issue – see Chapters 16 and 20 for more on children's age and testimony.) One should also be aware that the interviews subjected to analysis in this study were not the sort that criterion-based content analysis usually employs – they were standard child sexual abuse interviews instead. Thus the comments actually only apply to standard child sexual abuse interviews.

Finally, it should be mentioned that some researchers have used statement validity analysis and criterion-based content analysis in attempts to detect deception in adults. One particularly important study made use of London police interviews with rape victims. Some of these interviews contained demonstrably false claims since, for example, the 'victim' freely acknowledged that their allegations were false, there was evidence of the falsity of the claims from eyewitnesses or medical evidence and so forth. The interviews were studied using relatively structured scoring sheets. Correct identifications of true rape victim statements were high based on criterion-based content analysis (88 per cent correct) and the validity checklist (100 per cent correct). The figures for interviews correctly identifying false statements as being false were 92 per cent for criterion-based content analysis and 58 per cent for the validity checklist. Combining criterion-based content analysis with the validity checklist led to a 100 per cent correct identification for true statements and a 92 per cent correct identification for false statements. False statements tended to be much more organised in style whereas true statements tended to present a mixed range of emotions and unstructured delivery of the account. There is a lack of confusion in a false account. The validity criteria that differentiated the two types of interview included 'inconsistencies within physical evidence', incongruous affect during interview and 'inconsistent statements'. The researchers also had experienced detectives evaluate the interviews. They concluded that the police officers demonstrated 'little consistency' (p. 249) in their decisions about the truth or otherwise of the statements. Statement validity analysis did better at identifying false statements than any of the individual officers or the group of officers as a whole.

BOX 19.1 Controversy

Statement validity analysis in forensic settings

Statement validity analysis was used by European forensic psychologists long before its validity in research terms was assessed. In an important and thought-provoking review, Vrij (2005) asks some very searching and demanding questions about the method. He reviewed 37 studies into the 'accuracy' of statement validity analysis. The 'ground truth' of whether a child's evidence is truthful or not really needs to be known before the validity of statement validity analysis can be assessed but obviously obtaining information about this is far from easy. Evidence of the 'ground truth' of witness statements has included (a) the confession of the accused person, (b) that the accused was convicted by the court and (c) whether a polygraph examination confirms the guilt of the accused. Unfortunately, none of these is independent of the information which statement validity analysis also depends upon. For example, if the child's evidence appears to be very strong or if the statement validity analysis expert feels that the child's evidence is true then the accused may feel under pressure to confess simply in order to obtain a possible reduction in sentence.

Vrij identifies much subtler problems. For instance, how do we classify the situation in which a child's evidence is overwhelmingly accurate but the wrong person is identified as the perpetrator by the child? It is a false accusation but only in terms of the offender's identity since the rest of the detail may be very accurate. Laboratory experiments into the efficacy of statement validity analysis, of course, do not have problems in establishing the ground truth simply because the researchers have manipulated the situation so that who is telling the truth and who is lying is built into the research design. Unfortunately, the artificial nature of such laboratory experiments is also built into the experiment's design. Despite there being many inherent problems in the way in

which the accuracy of child witness statements is assessed, research evidence is fairly consistent in showing that the criteria used in statement validity analysis generally tends to effectively differentiate truth from fiction.

So how powerful is statement validity analysis and, in particular, criterion-based content analysis, at identifying truth tellers and liars? The evidence is that criterion-based content analysis employed by trained persons is better at identifying truth telling than such assessment made by untrained individuals. But the problem is that often the training given to people in the use of criterion-based content analysis in many of the studies appears to be fairly minimal compared with the complexity of the task. The lowest period of training given in any of the studies surveyed was 45 minutes! Remarkably, most field studies of statement validity analysis fail to provide useful information of the accuracy of the procedure. Consequently, Vrij had to turn to the findings of laboratory studies where the ground truth of guilt versus innocence is known. Virtually all laboratory studies gave overall accuracy rates between 65 per cent and 90 per cent for criterion-based content analysis. In finer detail, the accuracy rate for detecting lies was between 60 per cent and 90 per cent, according to Vrij (2005), and that for detecting truth was between 53 per cent and 89 per cent, though the average accuracy was hardly different at 73 per cent accuracy for truth and 72 per cent accuracy for lies.

Finally, Vrij raises the question of the legal implications of the research findings that he reviewed in relation to the American Daubert criteria (Box 1.1) concerning guidelines for the permissibility of expert scientific evidence in court. One of the Daubert criteria is whether there is a known error rate for the assessment methods used. Vrij doubts whether this criterion is met by statement validity

▶

BOX 19.1 (continued)

analysis research as there is no satisfactory research in field settings which would supply forensically valid error rates. But if we use the findings of laboratory studies we get an error rate of 30 per cent or so. This may be accurate or not as an estimate of the error rate in forensic settings. Assuming that it is, then this implies a big risk of the expert getting it wrong. Statement validity analysis assessment simply fails to meet reasonable criteria of being error free. Another Daubert criterion is that scientists accept the theory underlying the technique. Statement validity analysis theory has been seriously questioned by some researchers so this form of analysis may not meet this second Daubert criterion. Vrij suggests that although the method may not be adequate for use in courts, it may still be useful to the police in their work.

Of course, this perspective itself is not without its limitations.

- The error rate of statement validity analysis may not be the same as the risk that the expert's conclusions will be accepted by a court of law. The court may use other information over and above that supplied by the statement validity analyst which reduces the impact of the big error rate.
- Other legal jurisdictions outside the United States may not accept the Daubert criteria. So different criteria must apply to these countries.
- Vrij's argument might be seen by some as more of a condemnation of the use of laboratory studies for forensic research than a decisive verdict on statement validity analysis. This is merely to question the value of laboratory studies in this field.

Main points

- The polygraph test may become a more common feature in jurisdictions that do not allow it in court. There is increasing interest in its use in the monitoring of sex and other offenders while out in the community. There are several different ways of asking questions in the polygraph examination and they do not necessarily generate the same outcomes. Not all of the methods are used in practice by professional polygraph operators. The polygraph is more than a piece of physiological apparatus and is better seen as a process in practice. The operator usually has rather more information about the case and the suspect than a totally 'blind' procedure would require. The polygraph can be effective at generating a confession irrespective of the validity of the technique. The major problem with the polygraph is its error rate, which in polygraph assessment tends to produce more false positives in that a proportion of innocent individuals are judged guilty by the polygraph operator.

- Statement validity analysis is a set of techniques which attempt to establish the credibility of witness evidence and is especially pertinent to the evidence of children in sexual abuse cases. It consists of a mixture of various matters to consider in relation to the testimony. Central to the approach is the idea that memory for events that were truly experienced is different from that for imaginary events. In addition to features of the situation such as the child's apparent resistance to suggestive questioning, the appropriateness of the language used to the child's age group may indicate adult influences on the child. There is evidence of the effectiveness of the approach and there are examples of its use with adult victims of rape in which statement validity analysis seemed able to distinguish 'known' false witness statements from true ones.

Further reading

A report on the status of polygraphy produced by the British Psychological Society can be found at: http://www.bps.org. uk/sites/default/files/documents/polygraphic_deception_ detection_a_review_of_the_current_scientific_status_ and_fields_of_application.pdf

Visit our website at www.pearsoned.co.uk/howitt for self-test and essay questions, annotated further reading, audio interviews with researchers in the field, weblinks and more information on becoming a forensic psychologist.

Chapter 20

Children as witnesses

Overview

- Social and legal perceptions of children as witnesses have changed markedly in the past century or so. They were once regarded as dangerously unreliable witnesses whereas the modern view is that, given appropriate interviewing and support, they can supply good quality evidence. Countries differ markedly in their presumptions of the competence of children as witnesses.

- Bad professional practices in interviews with abused children can create problems in terms of the value of the evidence produced. It is the case that children present characteristic problems as witnesses but it is equally true to suggest that the interviewer may also create problems by not using an appropriate questioning style.

- Anatomically correct dolls can have a place in forensic interviews with children for a number of reasons to do with the enhancement of communications. They allow discussion of topics. Sexual play with such dolls is not a risk indicator of child sexual abuse and it is not appropriate to use the dolls to make such assessments.

- It is possible to suggest improvements to all aspects of professional work with children that improve the quality of the information provided. Generally speaking, open-ended questioning tends to produce the best quality information for child witnesses. However, the extent to which a question is leading is only partially determined by the structure of the question. Some would argue that leading questions have a role to play.

- There is evidence that lawyers in the courtroom do not modify their questioning appropriately for the age of the child witness. Typical problems include overly complex language, the use of legal terms that the child may not know or fully understand, and dwelling on concepts of time and distance which are not fully developed in early childhood.

- Further material pertinent to this chapter may be found in Chapter 19 (statement validity analysis) and Chapter 16 (false allegations).

Introduction

The past century has involved major changes in the way that childhood is conceived and understood. Alongside these changes, the past century has seen remarkable changes in the way that children's evidence has been viewed. In the nineteenth century children were seen as dangerous witnesses who could not be relied on, or worse (Baartman, 1992; Myers *et al.*, 1999). This view has changed so substantially that towards the end of the twentieth century it became the fashionable professional view to claim that children never lie (Silas, 1985; Driver, 1989). Children were increasingly regarded as young people with rights during the last century (e.g. Kitzinger, 1988). In this context, it should not be forgotten that, in some jurisdictions, quite young children are tried for criminal acts, not infrequently in adult courts. Consequently, there may be issues, in some cases, concerning the competence of a young person to stand trial (see Chapter 22). Arguments concerning aspects of this, such as whether juvenile competence is different from adult competence, are discussed in Heilbrun, Hawk and Tate (1996).

Courtrooms have traditionally been very adult environments. Generally speaking, in the past they lacked any recognition of the needs of children in that environment. Perhaps this is hardly surprising given the suspicion with which the evidence of children was regarded historically. In some states of America, for example, jurors would be instructed by the judge to consider the evidence of children especially carefully. Public disquiet about child abuse and child sexual abuse in the 1970s and 1980s respectively inevitably meant that the needs of child witnesses in the courtroom became a prime focus for research and reform of the system. Without the evidence of children, a lot of sexual abuse of children could not be prosecuted. Much the same process applied to the treatment of victims of rape in the criminal justice system. Numerous changes have been made in recent years as far as the evidence of children is concerned in a lot of countries. Myers (1996) reviewed many of these changes.

Myers argues that a distinction has to be made between legal systems based on common law (United States, United Kingdom, Australia, Canada, New Zealand, South Africa, Republic of Ireland) and those based on civil law (Germany and France). The common law systems have adversarial court systems in which the prosecution is pitted against the defence in front of judge and jury. The civil law system gives courts an inquisitorial role and the responsibility of uncovering what has happened. This is quite different from the role of a court being to decide which is the more convincing of two opposing arguments. In the inquisitorial system the judge would normally be the leading figure in questioning the witnesses, rather than the lawyers. Adversarial systems have more difficulty in coping with the needs of the child witness. For example, examination and cross-examination by lawyers is not constructed to be much other than a battle. In the United States, for one example, the right to have witnesses cross-examined is incorporated into the constitution.

Children may not have the ability to cope with what may be fairly oppressive cross-examination. Special arrangements may have to be applied to child witnesses. One or both of the following are to be found in some jurisdictions:

- *Preparation for court*: youngsters can be given professional help to understand court procedures, to deal with stress and anxiety about court as well as their abuse, and to testify competently in court. They may also be provided with an official advocate who works on their behalf with agencies. Sattar and Bull (1996) surveyed professionals working with children in a legal context in the United Kingdom. These professionals were well aware of the problems for child witnesses including the children's fears and anxieties. The provision of support for children in this context included special child witness preparation provided by agencies. Facilities for the support of children after the hearing were not so good.

- *Children's hearsay statements*: usually hearsay (essentially second-hand evidence) is disallowed in adversarial systems except in exceptional circumstances. Some states of the United States, England and Wales and Scotland now allow hearsay in proceedings for the protection of children.

Competence to testify and give the oath is a key issue with child witnesses. A child witness is required to meet standards of cognitive and moral ability if they are to testify. Three different arrangements seem to apply:

- Some jurisdictions impose a presumptive incompetent criterion. This means that under a certain age (say 10 years but it does depend on location), the child has to be examined on competence to testify. If they meet these criteria, they can give evidence.

- In other jurisdictions, everyone is accepted as competent irrespective of their age. Should an individual's competence become an issue, then it can be evaluated.

- Still other jurisdictions judge all victims of abuse as competent although they may not be assumed competent in other circumstances. In some jurisdictions (e.g. Canada, United Kingdom, France and Germany), the child does not have to be sworn in before they can provide evidence.

Other changes involve methods of altering the court physically and in other ways to be rid of the intimidating, over-powerful aura of traditional courtrooms. For example, expecting lawyers to remain seated when examining child witnesses may make a less daunting arrangement. The court may allow the use of leading questions with young children. The court may sit in a simpler, more comfortable and relaxed environment for the child. Other changes may include the following:

- Closing the court to the public/press.

- Video testimony: interviews with the police or social workers as part of the investigation process may be shown through video. In England and Wales, interviews with police or social workers may be used as a substitute for the child's in-court evidence. This has been adopted by, for example, some American states; video may be used to present either live or pre-recorded testimony from the child. Many countries allow closed-circuit television to help the giving of evidence by children. This was first developed in the United States in 1983 but Britain, New Zealand and Australia, among others, followed suit. Not only is there evidence that children are happier using the video links, but the quality of their evidence seems better (Davies and Noon, 1993).

What is difficult about forensic interviews with children?

This chapter is about the voice of children in courts of law, so it is appropriate to examine the problem from the point of view of the child who has been abused but then has to face the criminal justice system. Westcott (1995) studied a small group of children and young

people, each of whom had experienced sexual abuse investigation interviews. For the most part, these children had disclosed their abuse. The comments made by the children give some indications of what would be good practice in such interviews – a different but equally valid approach from what researchers and practitioners have suggested:

- *Language and questioning styles*: complex words and sentences were mentioned as well as the interviewer talking extensively and interrupting the child.

- *Cognitive issues*: sometimes the children and young people had problems with the amount of detail they were being asked about their abuse. This may well have involved their recalling events that had happened a few years before. One of the sample mentioned being asked about the frequencies and dates of their abuse!

- *Personal issues*: discussing the detail of what happened in the abuse may be embarrassing to some children and young people. They were also scared of giving information for fear that their abuser would take revenge on them for disclosing the abuse.

- *Motivational issues*: who was present at the interview could influence the victim's willingness to talk. For example, not all children wanted their parents present. Neglect of the child's feelings by the interviewer who might appear to be mainly interested in the punishment of the abuser was perceived by some of the children.

- *Social characteristics*: some interviewers were disliked for reasons such as: made it feel unimportant, disbelieving, bored, treated me younger than I am.

From the researcher's and practitioner's point of view some of these comments may be a little uncomfortable. They appear to put the onus on them for some of the problems interviewing child witnesses. To deal with many of the points made by the children, an interviewer would need to be sensitive to the needs of children and accepting of their personal responsibility for the inadequacies of their interviews. So with this in mind, we can turn to some of the research-based ideas about the nature of children's testimonies. Lamb, Sternberg and Orbach (1999) suggest that the following factors may have an influence on the quality of children's evidence:

- *Fantasy*: some believe that children are especially prone to fantasise events and report them as fact. The research evidence, though, is that certainly by the age of 6 years, children are probably little different from adults in terms of their ability to differentiate reality from fantasy (Woolley, 1997). If an interviewer asks a child to imagine or pretend, the child will respond appropriately by being imaginative and pretending. Similarly, the presence of dolls and toys encourages fantasy behaviour, it is argued (see Box 20.1). Forensic interviews should be planned to exclude these possibilities. However, Lamb *et al.* (1999) indicate that the children who have a tendency to fantasise are no more likely to make false reports or fabrications when giving evidence.

- *Language*: children's accounts of events tend to be short and lacking in much detail. Their speech can be difficult to follow because of their inconsistencies in enunciation and sometimes they use words which they do not understand the use of properly. These can be quite simple words such as 'yesterday' or 'before', which are readily understood by adults.

- *Interviewers*: it is too easy for adults to pose questions in ways that are difficult for even adolescents to understand. The consequences are obvious. Children do not always correct an adult who has failed to understand what the child is saying. So, with support from the research literature, it can be recommended that children should not be expected to:

  - have a complete mastery of adult vocabulary; or confirm complex summaries of the information that the child has provided;

  - reverse negative statements by adults (Is it not true that you stole the apples?);
  - understand passive wording (Was the apple taken by her?) as opposed to active wording (Did she take the apple?).

There is evidence that about one-third of questions asked by lawyers in court were not understood by 6- to 15-year-old children (e.g. Brennan and Brennan, 1988).

- *Memory*: the brevity of young children's accounts does not mean that their memories are bad. In fact, their memory is quite good. There is a distinction to be made between memory performance and memory capacity. Thus a young child may appear not to have a good memory capacity simply because they provide only a brief account of events. This may really be an issue of memory performance – they have poorer vocabularies, they lack motivation to provide the account, and they are less capable of using analogy to elaborate their descriptions.

- *Suggestibility*: in some settings even 3- and 4-year-olds are very resistant to leading questions that were irrelevant to the actual events. Questions such as 'Did he kiss you?' and 'Did he keep his clothes on?' failed to lead the children.

- *Interviewer characteristics*: the characteristics of the interviewer such as their friendliness or accusativeness do not appear consistently over studies to influence the suggestibility of the children they interview.

BOX 20.1 Controversy

Anatomical dolls and the diagnosis of abuse

It is an obvious idea to use toys as an aid when interviewing children. Anatomical dolls have been used extensively in child sexual abuse assessment. Quite simply, they are dolls with 'extra' anatomical details – genitals, anuses, mouths. According to the *American Professional Society on the Abuse of Children* Practice Guidelines (APSAC, 1996), research shows that the use of such dolls does not increase sexualised behaviour in non-abused children and their use does not seem to encourage suggestibility and

error in recall. The doll is almost invariably clothed apart from exceptional circumstances in which the child has previously said that sexual abuse had taken place with naked individuals.

Anatomical dolls should only be used by skilled interviewers. 'Sexual' play with dolls such as inserting another doll's penis into a doll's mouth, anus or vagina is *not* diagnostic of sexual abuse. While such behaviour may be more common among sexually abused children, the risk of misdiagnosis is too

▶

BOX 20.1 (continued)

great to interpret it as such (see Chapter 16 on diagnosticity of signs). Four-year-old boys from low social class families are the group most likely to display such behaviour. Exploration of a doll's genitals or anus with the finger is not infrequent among young children. However, the interviewer should be sensitive to other possible indications of abuse. In short, it would be a mistake to attempt to diagnose sexual abuse on the basis of play with anatomical dolls in the absence of other supportive evidence.

The use of the dolls should not be presented as pretend or play. Instead, the interviewer should encourage the child to talk about 'things that really happened'. Putting pairs of dolls in sexual positions and asking whether this had ever happened to the child is tantamount to a leading question and should not be done. On the other hand, anatomical dolls help communication and promote better recall of events though drawings or ordinary non-anatomical dolls may be equally effective:

- The dolls can be used as an *icebreaker*, allowing the child to talk about sexual issues that might be taboo to the child normally.
- The dolls can be used as an *anatomical model* to find out the names used by the child for the different parts of the body and what they know about their functions.
- The interviewer might also use the dolls to make clear just what it is the child has said about the acts of abuse (i.e. as a *demonstration aid*).
- The doll may also be used in a non-threatening setting to gain insight into the child's sexual interest and knowledge (i.e. as a *screening tool*). After a period of free play, the interviewer may add questions to elaborate on what had been observed. The guidelines suggest that spontaneous 'suspicious' comments by the child should be followed up. For example, 'Daddy's pee-pee gets big sometimes'.

According to Everson and Boat (2002), anatomical dolls may also be used as a *memory stimulus*. Seeing the doll's sexual characteristics (genitals and breasts) may help the child remember sexual episodes in

which they were involved – for example, as victims of sexual abuse.

The Guidelines suggest that other matters of good practice when using anatomical dolls need to be considered, including the following:

- The interviewer should recognise that children of less than 4 years may be unable to re-enact scenes well.
- Interviewers using anatomical dolls should be trained in their use and regularly updated on new research findings relevant to the use of the dolls.
- Videotaping interviews using anatomical dolls is a wise precaution as it is with other aspects of forensic investigation.

There is a substantial body of research on the usefulness of anatomical dolls and similar props (such as drawings) in sexual abuse interviews with young children. Everson and Boat (2002) address two critical issues concerning anatomical dolls which have arisen in research: (a) anatomical dolls are so suggestive that sexual fantasy and sexual play will be encouraged by the dolls in a way that some interviewers will interpret as sexual abuse in children who have not been abused and (b) evidence that the use of the dolls facilitates disclosure of abuse is required:

- *Suggestibility of dolls for non-abused children*: Everson and Boat (2002) mention 11 studies concerning the behaviour of non-sexually-abused children (2- to 8-year-olds) when playing with anatomical dolls. Some interest in the doll's genitals was fairly common, explicit play involving sexual intercourse with the doll or oral sex was fairly rare. Only 4 per cent of children in all of the studies combined demonstrated such heavily sexualised behaviours. Furthermore, there may be other sources of sexual knowledge even where the child displayed sexualised behaviours of this sort. These sources would include pornography or observing sexual activity at home, for example. This could account for the majority of instances of such sexual knowledge in non-sexually-abused children.

- *Efficacy of the use of anatomical dolls*: the better research relevant to this tends to use real medical examinations/procedures which would necessitate the medic to touch the child's genitals or anus, for example. In other words, a situation which is realistic and pertinent in that it involves what in other circumstances would constitute sexually abusive acts. Children can be interviewed some time after the medical procedure in order to see whether they reveal the genital or anal touching. Whether interviews using anatomical dolls are more successful at identifying the touching can be assessed. Steward and Steward (1996) carried

out a study along these lines. About a quarter of the children revealed the touching without the anatomical dolls. This figure more than doubled to three-fifths of children in interviews using anatomical dolls. It increased to nearly three-quarters when the children were interviewed with the anatomical dolls and the interviewer asked direct and suggestive questions. False reports were not very common. No false reports were made in the simple verbal interview. This increased to 3 per cent in the anatomical doll interview and 5 per cent where the anatomical doll interview included the direct and suggestive questions.

Improving forensic interviews with children

According to researchers, open-ended questions produce the most accurate answers from children. This is partly because open-ended questions encourage children to give as much detail as they can in their replies. They act as recall probes. In contrast, focused or closed questions, directive questions or leading questions involve the child in a recognition task that can be answered completely with merely a yes or no. That is, leading and similar questions act as recognition probes about the things on which the interviewer wishes to focus. As such, they may pressure the child into a response even though the child does not know what that response should be. Figure 20.1 illustrates the differences between the two different forms of questioning.

Most lawyers and psychologists are familiar with the concept of leading questions. These are questions that encourage a particular reply. Myers, Saywitz and Goodman (1996) argue that there is a continuum of suggestiveness in questioning:

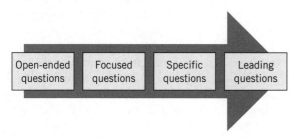

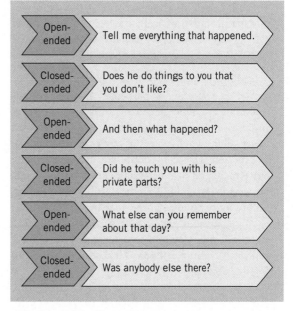

Figure 20.1 Open-ended versus focused/closed questions as they might appear in a child sexual abuse interview

Source: Based on Lamb, M.E., Sternberg, K.J. and Orbach, Y. (1999) 'Forensic interviews of children' in A. Memon and R. Bull (eds) *Handbook of the Psychology of Interviewing*. © 1999 John Wiley & Sons, Ltd

This is very important since there is a tendency to concentrate on the two questions – open-ended and leading. This, to a degree, misrepresents the situation in interviews. By considering more types of question then we begin to appreciate how structuring can take a number of different forms. The underlying order is from the least to most suggestive questioning style:

- An open-ended question is a fairly general question which is little other than a request for the interviewee to speak as in 'Did anything happen?' or 'Tell me about that'.

- A focused question brings a child's attention to a particular issue such as a location or a person. So a question such as 'Shall we talk about school?' brings a child around to the topic of school without suggesting anything about the sorts of information that the interviewer wants. Questions such as 'where' or 'who' and 'when' are other examples.

There is no rigid dividing line between focused and the next level of specific questioning.

- Specific questioning may be similar though generally specific questions call for a greater level of detail. Questions in this category include 'What is her name?' or 'What colour dress did she have on?'

- A leading question is one that implies that the interviewer is expecting a particular answer. Leading questions are often statements of fact to which the interviewee is expected to agree. So 'You felt very angry, didn't you?' makes it very clear what answer is expected. This is a continuum of suggestiveness since each level has increasing likelihood to suggest answers to the child. Even the open-ended question, according to circumstances, may be suggestive. For example, a parent who asks a child what happened in school yesterday might be suggesting the sort of reply if, for example, the child had been caught cheating in an exam.

It is overly simplistic, some argue, to regard open questions as good and closed questions as bad. Professionals who carry out sexual abuse interviews are presented with a serious dilemma: that is, using only open-ended questions may well fail to obtain the necessary information from a child who has been abused (Myers *et al.*, 1996). Unfortunately, there may be a trade-off between the poorer disclosure coming from open-ended questioning and the contamination of evidence emerging out of leading questions. The issue, then, is somewhat intangible. Is it better to have some false allegations in order to maximise the detection of actual abuse, or is it better to

have no false allegations but fail to maximise the detection of abuse? The answer depends, in part, on one's perspective. Is it more important to have abuse disclosed or is it more important to be able to prosecute abusers successfully in court? This dilemma cannot be addressed by research evidence on different questioning styles. It is a moral, ethical and political issue.

Of course, there is always a great need for research into the way practitioners work. The following study generally supports the conclusion that open-ended questioning tends to produce superior evidence from children. However, more importantly, it reveals some of the problems in encouraging practitioners to use this form of questioning. The research took place in Israel and the United States and involved coding recordings of real-life interviews with children (Sternberg *et al.*, 1997). The interviewers' utterances were classified into a number of categories:

- Invitations to open-ended responses.

- Facilitators such as okay, feedback of the child's previous statement, and general encouraging comments.

- Directive utterances – directing the child towards certain aspects of the events already mentioned by the child.

- Leading utterances – directing the child towards things *not* already mentioned by the child.

- Suggestive utterances which could indicate strongly to the child what reply is expected by the interviewer or include references to details that have not previously been mentioned by the child.

The children's answers were coded in terms of the number of new details supplied by the child. These details would include such matters as identifying and describing individuals, objects, events and actions relevant to the incident under investigation. Irrespective of the age of the child being interviewed, the findings showed that open-ended questions encouraged the child to give longer replies (that is, up to four times longer), containing about three times the amount of new detail.

Despite the superiority of open-ended styles of questioning in this regard, experienced interviewers generally used the least productive, closed interview techniques. The majority (over four-fifths) of the interviewers' dialogue consisted of focused or closed prompts. Only 6 per cent were invitational (open) questions and statements. The researchers attempted to improve interviewing technique during intensive interviewing workshops over the period of a week. In these workshops children's memory capacity was explained, what factors might encourage suggestibility were discussed and advantages of open-ended questioning explained. Unfortunately, this made little or no difference as the interviewers carried on using their focused questioning style!

In an attempt to find a solution to what was seemingly an intangible problem, Sternberg *et al.* (1997) provided introductory scripts to the interviewers. Some of the scripts were open-ended whereas the others were closed-ended. This led, irrespective of the questioning style adopted by the interviewer later in the interview, to lengthier narratives from the children in the open-ended condition. In other words, once the children had begun to respond to questions in detail, they then continued to do so irrespective of the nature of the later questioning. When the introductory script was used, the children on average provided 91 details compared with the five or six details obtained when the script was not used.

Questioning styles are not the only way in which interviewers can adversely affect the information obtained. Poole and Lindsay (2002) explain that sometimes an interviewer can produce ambiguity in ways that are very different from leading the child. Young children drift readily off topic and fail to appreciate what is actually being discussed so they can be difficult to interview. Poole and Lindsay (p. 358) highlight the following excerpt of transcript of an interview with a child originally reported by Warren *et al.* (2002):

Interviewer: Is it good or bad to tell a lie?
Child: G.A. touched me.
Interviewer: Jesus loves me? Is that what you said?
Child: Yeah.

This is clearly a situation in which the difficulty of interviewing the child led the interviewer to offer the child an interpretation which amounted to a suggestion. However, there was no intent to produce that outcome. In this case, what appears to be a claim of abuse was essentially turned into something very different.

The trade-off of accuracy against completeness

There is an obvious but extremely important distinction to be made between:

- the amount of accurate information collected in an interview;
- the amount of inaccurate information collected in an interview.

Unfortunately, in real life, it is often more or less impossible to know what is accurate information and what is inaccurate information. Nevertheless, the distinction means that there is an important choice between the risk of incorrect information and the risk of incomplete information. There seems to be little doubt that general, non-directive questions encourage children to give testimony that is accurate and low on inaccuracy. Unfortunately, this is at the expense of answers that are complete. The question is which is to be accepted – inaccuracy or incompleteness? Both reflect adversely on the quality of the evidence of child witnesses. Hutcheson *et al.* (1995) accept that there is such a dilemma when questioning young children. They found that the age of the child makes a considerable difference to the effect of questioning. The researchers found that interviewers who tended to ask a high proportion of focused or specific questions obtained success according to the age of the child:

- Focused and specific questions addressed to 5- and 6-year-olds produced more inaccurate answers. There was no benefit of increasing the completeness of the answers.
- Interviewers who asked 8- and 9-year-olds a high proportion of focused questions obtained more complete answers. In this case accuracy was not affected.

It should be noted that not all researchers see a simple contrast between open and closed questions, one being good and the other being not so good. We will discuss some recent examples of research which produces a more complex answer in the next section on errors of omission and commission.

BOX 20.2 Controversy

Communicative competence in the courtroom and those working with children

Adult language can be complex especially when sophisticated users of language such as lawyers and forensic psychologists are involved. There is good reason to believe that the language of the courtroom is inappropriate for many children. Some of the following issues have been raised in connection with other forms of interviewing, but they bear repetition because they are drawn from courtroom experience:

- *Linguistic complexity*: the following question in a court transcript: 'On the evening of January third, you did, didn't you, visit your grandmother's sister's house and didn't you see the defendant leave the house at 7:30, after which you stayed the night?' (Myers *et al.*, 1996). The child expected to answer this was 4 years of age!
- *Children may not understand legal terms*: Myers *et al.* (1996) point out that quite young children of 5 or 6 years do understand some terms, so they know words such as lie, police and promise. This does not mean that they have full understanding of the terms. So a child may have an idea of what the police do but will certainly not know the full ramifications of the job. Other words are beyond the understanding of even teenagers in the forensic setting. There is a potential for misunderstanding legal terms such as court (which is a place where tennis is played), charges (which are to do with money), hearing (which is listening), party (which is a social gathering) and swear (which is to say a rude word).
- *Time, date and distance*: these are concepts built up gradually in the school years. It is pointless, for example, to ask a 7-year-old child the time that something happened because they do not have sufficient knowledge of the concept.
- *Comprehension*: monitoring is being able to assess how well we understand things that are said to us. Children are not particularly good at this and they may believe that they understand questions

which, in fact, they do not. Furthermore, children rarely ask for clarification about the meaning of a question.

Lawyers' use of language in their dealings with victims in child abuse cases may be seen as oppressive and abusive from some perspectives. Brennan (1994) lists 13 different verbal tactics that are difficult or impossible for young witnesses to deal with effectively because they stretch their linguistic competence. For example, the following is an example of a multi-faceted question: 'And did your mother ever say to you that if somebody asks you the questions I am asking you, you should say that we didn't say what was going to be said?' (p. 213). It should be stressed that this is a question addressed in court to a 10-year-old. A good illustration of the problem is reported in Carter, Bottom and Levine (1996). Children were asked two versions of a question. One version was in legalese: 'To the best of your knowledge, X, in fact, kissed you, didn't she?' and the other version was simpler: 'X kissed you didn't she?' The version in legalese was much more likely to produce inaccurate replies in 5- to 7-year-olds than the simpler wording. Actually, even this version of questioning introduces a feature that may be problematic – the tag – as in a question like 'Amy touched your bottom, didn't she?' as opposed to the direct version which is 'Did Amy touch your bottom?' With questions such as these, the child's answer is vital in that a case of abuse could rest on it. Krackow and Lynn (2003) investigated this very tag question and others in a sample of 48- to 70-month-old children. They set up a situation (actually an innocuous game) that included either innocuous bodily touch or no such touch. All that happened actually was that half of the children were touched on their hands, arms, calves or feet by an assistant whereas the others were not touched at all. A week later the children were interviewed about the events using tag and direct questioning techniques. 'Did Amy touch your bottom?' produced fewer erroneous yes answers than the corresponding tag-question version 'Amy touched your bottom, didn't she?' It did not matter whether there had been any touch at all during the play session with Amy. In fact, the children who answered the direct question were almost always accurate in their answer, those answering the tag question seemed responding almost at random since nearly 50 per cent falsely agreed that their bottom had been touched when none of the children's bottoms had actually been touched.

While it may be easy to understand why some lawyers may not be good at communicating effectively with children, there is considerable evidence that those whose professional lives involves working with children may not be very much better. Korkman *et al.* (2008) studied the investigative interviews which Finnish mental health professionals conducted with children concerning suspected child sexual abuse. These children were in the age range of 3–8 years and the question was whether these key mental health professionals were using age-appropriate language with the children. One would expect that they would make fewer demands on the language ability of young children than the older ones. The researchers obtained interviews from child sexual abuse investigations. Nearly all of them had been video-recorded. Generally the researchers found that the interviewers failed to use age-appropriate language. For example, children of this age group have generally poor concepts of time. The researchers noted that when dealing with

the issue of time, the interviewers had a tendency to give the child a string of unproductive options as in the following interview involving a 5-year-old:

Interview: Do you remember when this happened?
Child: [no response]
I: Do you? Was it in the summer or in the winter?
C: [no response]
I: Was it long ago or a short time ago?
C: [no response]

(p. 53)

Overall the researchers found that about a fifth of the utterances of the interviewers included some form of unsuitable language structure: for example, sentences using complicated, multiple and long questions or unclear material about people or places. The interviews tended to be somewhat unstructured with a lack of consistent focus on topic. There are a number of possible explanations for this. Sexual matters are sensitive and the interviewers might not feel confident in talking about them irrespective of the age of the interviewee. Furthermore, this is an emotive area and the emotional reactions raised in the interviewer may detrimentally affect their cognitive processes. As a consequence they may fail to apply the knowledge they have about interviewing children appropriately. Whatever the reason, this is an area where there is still a substantial amount of work to be done to ensure good quality interviews with children.

Errors of omission and commission

There is a basic difference between two major types of error in recall – errors of omission versus errors of commission. Much of the work on children's evidence has concentrated on errors of commission where the child recalls things or events which did not actually happen. In contrast, errors of omission are when the child fails to recall something which did happen. Otgaar. Camdel, Smeets and Merckelbach (2009) argue that errors of omission are especially relevant to some child sex abuse

cases. In particular they mention those cases where the child is told by their abuser or even their parents that the abuse did not happen. The researchers used an intriguing methodology to encourage errors of omission and commission. Basically their research involved children in two age groups – one group was around 4 years of age and the other group was around 9 years of age. They were introduced to an 80-cm doll named Lucy dressed in a variety of pink items of clothing such as a hat, jacket, pants, shoes and skirt. The children's task was to take off *three* of the items of Lucy's clothing. Immediately afterwards, the children's recollection of what items they had removed was virtually perfect – 95 per cent of children

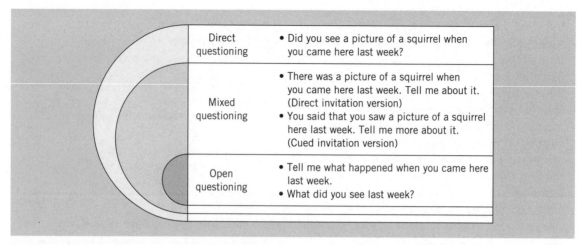

Direct questioning	• Did you see a picture of a squirrel when you came here last week?
Mixed questioning	• There was a picture of a squirrel when you came here last week. Tell me about it. (Direct invitation version) • You said that you saw a picture of a squirrel here last week. Tell me more about it. (Cued invitation version)
Open questioning	• Tell me what happened when you came here last week. • What did you see last week?

Figure 20.2 Types of question

correctly recalled the three removed items accurately. In half of the cases the children were next led to believe that they had taken off just two pieces of clothing and the other children were led to believe that they had removed four items. That is, in a separate room they were asked about the items of clothing removed. In the omission condition they were told that it was impossible that they had removed that many pieces of clothing. Furthermore, they were taken to the other room where they were shown the doll, Lucy, but one of the items of clothing that had previously been removed by the child had been replaced by the researchers. In the other condition – the commission condition – the children were told that they had forgotten one item of Lucy's clothing and taken to see the puppet to 'prove' it. That is to say, the researchers had removed an item of clothing in addition to the three that the child had.

Then the children were interviewed by a female interviewer on a total of three occasions at one week intervals. This, of course, emulated the repeated questioning that a child victim would experience in real cases. The children were asked to name the items of clothing that they had to take off. Both errors of omission and commission decreased over time – though the authors say that errors of commission tended to be persistent. Forty five per cent of children in the omission suggestion condition failed to report taking off items of clothing which in fact they had removed. This tendency became less strong over time. Age made no difference in the likelihood of making omission errors but commission errors were substantially more typical of younger children. Errors of commission

were also more likely to occur as a result of the experimental manipulation. This study therefore demonstrates the creation of errors of omission and commission in children using misinformation techniques.

In another study of both errors of omission and commission, Horowitz (2009) looked at three styles of questioning – direct (closed) questions, open-ended questions and mixed questions including cued invitations. The meaning of each of these is illustrated in Figure 20.2. The mixed-question format has not been mentioned so far in this chapter and so it warrants explication. A mixed question consists of both a direct question and an opportunity to say more or explain just how things happened. So a mixed question might be 'Did you see the policeman's hat blow off? Tell me more about what happened.' One particular type of mixed question is termed a cued invitation. In this the child is reminded of something that they had said earlier and then invited to say more. An example might be 'You told me earlier that you laughed when the policeman's hat blew away. What happened?' There is an alternative version of the mixed question in which the first direct part of the question is based on something that the child has already mentioned which the researcher reminds them of before asking them to say more about it.

Are the different forms of questioning in Figure 20.2 equally good at eliciting accurate information? In order to answer this question, Horowitz (2009) obtained samples of children in the 6-year-old (approximately) and the 11-year-old (approximately) categories. The basic design was as follows:

- In the first week of the study, the children were shown a series of pictures of animals engaged in various activities. Collectively these pictures told a story.
- One week later, the child was sat down with an interviewer. The interviewer first of all built up rapport and generally got the child used to the interview setting. An interview then began which used the three different styles of questioning (direct, mixed and open) in a counterbalanced design.
  - The direct questions were like 'Were you shown a picture of a Kangaroo?'
  - The mixed questions were like 'Was there (or "You mentioned") a picture of a Kangaroo? Tell me more about that.'
  - The open questions were like 'Tell me about the pictures you saw.'

The interviews were videoed and later transcribed. Where there was an incorrect answer it was classified as being either an error of omission or commission. In order to do this, the researcher created an arbitrary list of items of information some of which were part of the direct questioning and the rest were not part of the direct questioning though they had happened in the first week. This strategy made the researcher's task manageable.

As had been found in many studies before, direct questions resulted in shorter answers and open questions resulted in longer answers in terms of the number of words. Mixed questioning produced answers of an in-between length. The children in the older age group tended to say more when giving their answers though this was only statistically significant when open-ended questions are considered. The following were among the main findings:

- Remember that some of the events had been mentioned when the children were prompted using direct questioning. In these circumstances, if the direct questioning came before the open-ended questioning then there was an increased number of errors of commissioning in the open-ended answers. Cued invitations which used the replies to the direct questions as part of the mixed questions led to fewer errors of omission but did not increase the number of errors of commission.
- For the details which were *not* prompted by the direct questions, the direct questioning produced more errors of omission followed by the mixed questions followed by the open-ended questions. Younger children tended

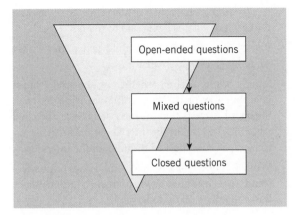

Figure 20.3 The inverted pyramid of questioning

to make more errors of omission except for the direct questions. Direct and mixed questions generated more errors of commission than open questions.

Considering these and other findings, Horowitz (2009) argued for what he describes as an inverted pyramid approach to questioning. This is illustrated in Figure 20.3. The interviewer should begin with open-ended questions but if the outcome from this is unsatisfactory then mixed questions may be used, followed by direct questions if the required information is still not obtained.

How to interview child witnesses

There are problems in interviewing child witnesses which are greater the younger the child involved. However, this does not mean that children under the age of 5 years cannot be interviewed, for example, it merely means that the skills of the interviewer and the assumptions made about the language ability of the child have to be borne in mind. Shepherd (2007) gives a great deal of advice on this. For example, among the information that might surprise some adults are the following (p. 272):

- Children know that adults want children to reply since they understand that when a powerful adult stops speaking then it is the child's turn to speak.
- It is only older children, in general, who will tell the adult in some way that they don't understand what is being said to them.

- It is the responsibility of the interviewer that the child understands what is being said to them.

- Rather than say nothing a child will prefer to say something, no matter what it is.

- Simply asking a child whether he/she understands is a poor way of checking comprehension. Instead, Shepherd suggests that the interviewer asks the child what the child thinks the interviewer means. This has to be repeatedly checked throughout the interview.

- While it is often the case that a child does not understand what an adult is saying to them, children do not know that they don't understand.

Saywitz (1994) also had a number of practical guidelines for interviewing very young children under the age of 7 years although there are lessons for interviewing older children contained within them.

- Avoid complex grammatical constructions such as double negatives (e.g. 'You're not saying you didn't steal the apple, are you?').

- Avoid questions requiring counting ability if the child is too young to be able to count. Similarly, time, linear measurements and similar concepts may be beyond the child's cognitive ability.

- Avoid using personal pronouns (him, her, they, she) in favour of proper names such as Darren or Sue. Personal pronouns can cause confusion about what they actually indicate during speech.

- Children may appear to be uncooperative and uninformative because of their emotional and psychiatric states. Social withdrawal, as a consequence of abuse, should not be confused with uncooperativeness, for example.

- Concrete terms are better than abstract ones (e.g. 'gun' is better than 'weapon').

- Jargon words should not be used (e.g. legalese such as 'sentence' and 'charge' which also have more obvious meanings).

- Make it absolutely clear to what you are referring (e.g. 'When did your mother go to work?' is better than 'When did that happen?').

- The passive voice should be avoided (e.g. the active voice 'Did Adam steal the money?' is clearer than the passive voice 'Was the money stolen by Adam?').

- Use short sentences. Break down compound or overloaded questions into several simple questions.

- Use short words rather than longer ones (e.g. 'mend' rather than 'repair').

- Use simple verb constructions. Avoid complex verb structures (e.g. 'Do you think it possibly could have been?').

- With younger children, concrete, imaginable and observable things are better than abstract things.

While good advice is readily available, what is the evidence that it is followed? Warren *et al.* (1996) investigated the adherence of interviewers to such good practice guidelines. They obtained transcripts of child protection workers' videotaped interviews with children. Typically, the interviews were conducted by a single interviewer but in some cases more than one additional person was present. The following are some of the more important findings:

- Establishing rapport in order to relax the child and make them feel comfortable: most (71 per cent) of the interviews studied included an attempt to establish rapport. However, rather than encouraging the child to talk, the interviewer would do something like three times the amount of talking during the rapport stage. Equally important is the fact that in nearly one-third of interviews no attempt was made at all to build rapport with the child.

- Establishing interview ground rules: only a minority of the interviewers (29 per cent) made any reference to the sort of ground rules that establish in the mind of the child just what is expected by the interviewer. Children erroneously assume that they have to give an answer to every question, that there is a right and wrong answer to every question, that the interviewer knows exactly what happened and so the child defers to the 'superior' knowledge of the interviewer where the interviewer seems to differ from the child, and that it is inappropriate to ask for clarification or say that they do not know in response to a question. In various ways, the interviewer can indicate that such assumptions may be wrong. But they rarely did. In only 29 per cent of the interviews were the children told to tell the truth, in 14 per cent of interviews was it explained to the child that it was appropriate to say 'Don't know' in answer to a question, and in only 7 per cent of cases was the child told to tell the interviewer that they didn't understand a question. Other ground rules were never or rarely mentioned.

Quite simply, the relatively clear messages from research may be ignored in practice.

Care needs to be taken not to assume that simply because the child is given instructions not to lie, for example, that this will be completely effective. Huffman, Warren and Larson (2001) carried out research into the effectiveness of such warnings with young children. They point out that this is far from easy with the youngest children. They report the following exchange between an interviewer (I) and a child (C):

I: Now, B., do you know the difference between the truth and a lie?

C: [Nods]

I: If I told you that – that you were standing on your head right now, what would I be telling you?

C: Old McDonald said that at the police station.

I: Uh-huh. At the police station?

C: You've got to take his shirt off. [Referring to small boy doll]

(p. 10)

Problems similar to these can even emerge when trying to establish interview ground rules with older children.

The researchers obtained a substantial sample of transcripts of interviews with children, largely of pre-school age. A small majority (56 per cent) of these interviews actually contained a discussion between the interviewer and child about the difference between the truth and a lie. Not only this, but this analysis provided information about the standard procedures used by interviewers in this context. Consequently, a further study actually investigated the effectiveness of the discussion about lies on the quality of the information supplied by the child. Two procedures were employed:

- *The standard protocol*: this was based mainly on the transcripts which contained a discussion with the child about truth and lies. So one question was included which asked the child if they understood what is different between lies and truths. Then they would have to answer a real example such as 'If I said that you were a boy, would that be a truth or a lie?' Finally, the interviewer would ask the child only to give truthful answers.

- *The elaborated protocol*: this was much more open-ended in terms of questioning and focused on the concept of a lie by the use of examples of lies and definitions of lies. The researchers believe that the concept of truth is too abstract to communicate. The children were given three different scenarios involving possible lies and they had to judge them. The following is an example:

> One day Jane/Jim and his/her mother were at home and the phone rang. Jim/Jane's mother did not want to talk on the phone and asked Jim/Jane to answer the phone but say she was not at home. When Jim/Jane answered the phone and the person asked for Jim/Jane's mother, Jim/Jane said, 'My mother is not at home.' Did Jim/Jane tell the truth, a lie, or something else? Why is that a _____? Was it okay for Jim/Jane to say his/her mother was not at home? Why/Why not?

It was found that the value of the children's evidence was enhanced by the elaborated protocol. There was little difference between using the standard approach and not having any discussion of the difference between truth and lies.

BOX 20.3 Forensic psychology in action

More evidence of the competence of children as witnesses

There is a great danger in overlooking the abilities of children. While one might expect that younger children may not be as good as adults at all tasks relevant to forensic work, this does not mean that their contribution is not of some value. What about facial composites? We know that facial composites produced by adult witnesses are less than perfect (see Chapter 13) yet may be helpful in police investigations. So a degree of imperfection does not necessarily preclude the child as an eyewitness. Paine *et al.* (2008) investigated whether children under the age of 10 years could produce worthwhile facial composites using modern computer-based facial composite creation techniques (E-FIT).

▶

Previous research had shown that children could perform reasonably well when older methods of facial composite construction were used. Paine *et al.* recognised that children's composite building might be affected by vocabulary limitations. So they developed a technique for using visual prompts to help the communication between the child and the composite-maker. So, for example, take the matter of the distance between the eyes of the facial composite target. Verbal prompts might ask how wide the eyes were apart, which then means that the child has to be able to respond appropriately verbally. In the visual prompts condition the children were presented with stylised pictures of faces with the eyes different distances apart. Their task in these circumstances was simply to pick the picture which best represented the face that they were reconstructing. Although the evidence suggested that indeed younger children's composites were not so good as those of older children and adults, they were nevertheless able to help create a facial composite of an unfamiliar face. Indeed, in some cases, children produced facial composites which were better than those of some adults. The authors indicate that although the police use 10 years and below as the cut-off point below which facial composites are not attempted, there is reason to think that this is unduly cautious.

Long-term influences of questioning

It is clearly important to understand the long-term influence on questioning on children's memory for events. A study by London, Bruck and Melnyk (2009) investigated the effects of post-event information given by interviewers on young children's memory for events. Their research design is a little complicated so it is summarised in Figure 20.4. The most important aspect of this study is that it investigated the children over a period of about 15 months. Children of 4–6 years living in Montreal watched a standardised magic show containing a number of target events which they would be questioned about in the successive stages of the study. These target events included such things as the magician tripping over her shoelaces, falling over and then requesting assistance from the child. Sometime later (see Figure 20.4), the children were subjected to two sessions of suggestive interviewing. This was done by using true and false reminders of what happened at the magic show in the questions. So the child might be asked about the boots they wore at the show using correct or incorrect detail. This incorrect detail was the post-event information. Subsequently the children underwent memory tests for the events on two occasions. Among the findings were the following:

- In free-recall where the children basically recounted the magic show events, the post-event information initially clearly had influenced what was recalled though this declined markedly at the 15-month follow-up session.

- For correct spontaneous utterances during free-recall, there a decline in the information related to the correct reminders over the two memory testing sessions 15 months apart. They dropped from 29–4 per cent of the correct utterances. This was entirely responsible for the decline in correct utterances by the child over the 15-month period.

- For incorrect spontaneous utterances during free-recall, there was no significant decline over the 15-month period. However, incorrect spontaneous utterances were initially 75 per cent based on the misleading questioning at the first memory testing stage but then declined to absolutely none of the incorrect recollections 15 months later! That is to say, the children made incorrect statements when tested more than a year later which were generated by other memory phenomena and not the influence of misinformation provided in the two interview stages.

- For correct reminder items assessed using yes/no questions, there was a decrease in correct answers over the 15-month period. However, there was no decline in the accuracy for correct items which had not been subject to the correct reminders at the interview stages.

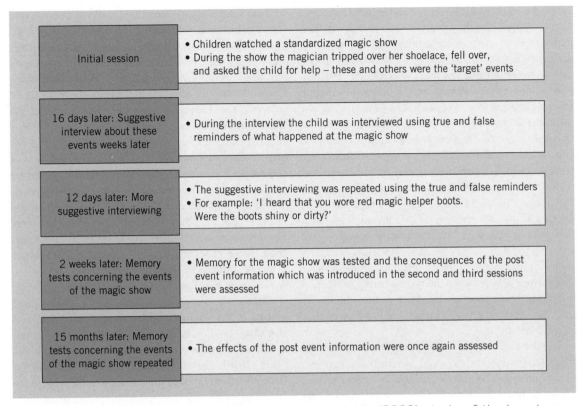

Figure 20.4 The design of London, Bruck and Melnyk's (2009) study of the long-term effects of suggestive interviewing

- For false reminder (misinformation) items assessed using yes/no questions, there was evidence that the misinformation affected the accuracy of recall at both memory assessment stages although there was evidence that the effect of the interviewer's misinformation was less at 15 months than earlier.

Thus it is fairly clear that misinformation effects in interviews following events tend to decline with a longer interval between the interview and the recollection stage. Nevertheless, the data is fairly complex. London, Bruck and Melnyk (2009) argue that, forensically, it is better to rely on spontaneous recollection of events by children. Questioning based on yes/no answers to questions (closed questioning), they suggest, is better reserved for situations where additional information is needed. All of the time, however, the interviewer needs to be aware of the possibility that previous interviews had been suggestive. Of course, this is an issue where we need to await further research findings.

Interviewer features

It is too easy to assume that the only difficulties in interviewing children are to do with the characteristics of children and the way in which questions are posed. Researchers are beginning to question whether cognitive factors such as these, alone, provide us with a full account of the difficulties associated with interviewing children. In other words, the cognitive approach is a too focused view of the interview situation and it is suggested that social and individual factors have a bearing on the quality of the evidence that the child provides. For example, Almerigogna et al. (2008b) found that children in the 8–10-year-old range perceived interviewers more positively when they were smiling and more negatively when they fidgeted. Building on this finding, the researchers had children of this age engage in an educational activity concerning vocal cords. The children were interviewed a week later but the interviewer either adopted a supportive (they smiled and avoided fidgeting) or non-supportive (they fidgeted such as tapping their hands and feet and avoided smiling) style of behaviour during the interview. The supportive interviewer yielded better-quality information from the children. The supportive interviewer obtained more accurate information from the children who were also less likely to give the false information that they had been touched in the educational activity ('Where on your body did the lady touch you to feel the vibrations'). None of the children had been touched. Children interviewed by the supportive interviewer also gave proportionately nearly four times the number of 'don't know' answers to questions. In another study, Almerigogna et al. (2008a) found that the children who were characteristically anxious (trait anxiety) and those who showed higher levels of anxiety following the interview (state anxiety) tended to give more wrong answers when interviewed using misleading questions. It is important to note that non-supportive interviewers could produce higher levels of state anxiety in children.

Children are interviewed for particular purposes and the interviewer often will need to report the contents of the interview to others – perhaps in a court of law. Evidence based on what the child says in interview when discussed in court is 'hearsay' since it is passed on by a third party and not the child's direct evidence. So a crucial question is that of how accurate are professionals carrying out interviews with children? Warren and Woodhall (1999) studied this question by asking a group of mainly child protection workers with between 4 and 21 years of experience to conduct interviews with 3- to 5-year-olds. The children were to be questioned about a magic show (which involved a disappearing book and lights pulled out of the magician's ears among other things) and a silly doctor session in which the child played with Dr Tracy who took their blood pressure, checked their ears, tested their knee jerk response, and measured the child's muscles among other things. The interviews took place a month after these experiences. The interview started with a cue question such as 'Tell me about the time you went with Tracy to play silly doctor' (p. 360). The task for the interviewer was to find out as much as possible about the events that the child had experienced. The interviews were recorded. The interviewers were asked to give a written account from their memory of the interview, its contents and sequence as accurately as they could. They were to use as accurate wording as possible.

Each interview was transcribed and broken down into 'units' which was the number of aspects of the events that the child recounted in the interview. So, for example, mentioning the lights being pulled out of the magician's ear would be one unit. Each unit was broken down into more specific subunits and involved greater detail of things that happened when the magician pulled the lights out of their ears. The interviewer's recollections of what had been said were good. They recalled 83 per cent of the major units of the events and 65 per cent of the detail. They also recalled 60 per cent of the errors made by children when they recalled the events such as claims that the magician had a magic wand which he did not have. So, according to Warren and Woodhall, there is some degradation of the child's testimony such that some of the important detail is omitted in the 'hearsay' evidence supplied by the interviewer.

Research has demonstrated quite frequently that children make more false identifications – guess more – than adults do faced with the same circumstances (see Chapter 13). The question of just why they do this is addressed in the research of Lowenstein, Blank and Sauer (2010). They investigated and found that in the United Kingdom, police officers sometimes dress formally in uniform and sometimes they dress using more informal, civilian clothing. Does wearing of a uniform act as a sort of cue concerning authority which adversely affects the quality of children's eyewitness evidence? The problem is that children tend to assume that they must provide an answer or make an identification. The consequence is that they make risky, error-prone decisions because of their assumption that adults are requiring them to make an identification. To explore this further, Lowenstein et al. staged a theft in front of 9–10-year-old participants in which a computer monitor was stolen before their very eyes. However, none of the children mentioned to the researcher that this had happened at the time. About one week later they were asked to identify the culprit from an array of black and white photographs – i.e. a simultaneous line-up/identification parade (see Chapter 13). Some of the line-ups included the offender's photo and others did not. The children were asked to say which was the offender if he was present but otherwise to say that he was not present. In some cases the parade was conducted by a uniformed 'police officer', in other cases by the same individual but more casually dressed. More choices were made in the presence of the uniform. Most importantly, children made more errors for the target-absent parades than the target-present parades. Children seem to be uncertain in the target-absent situation but do not express this uncertainty in the presence of the authority of a uniform. In the target-absent condition the children took much longer to reach a decision and they were less confident in the decision they made than in the target-present condition. Where there was no uniform there was a relationship between the identification time, confidence and accuracy but this was not the case where the officer was in a uniform. Less time is needed in a target-present line-up because the search can end as soon as the offender is recognised. The children's task seems to have been become more complex with the uniform present and they seemed to be wanting to find a culprit irrespective of what their memories told them. Clearly there is a case for not using uniformed officers in line-ups/identity parades

involving child witnesses and possibly the same applies to child interviews in general.

It is worthwhile mentioning the suggestive evidence from a 'laboratory' study which compared how mock student jurors evaluated evidence presented as if it were that of a child with the same evidence but presented as hearsay evidence from an expert interviewer of children (Warren *et al.*, 2002). Although the evidence was not perfectly consistent, there were some indications that the jurors tended to regard the evidence of the interviewer as more believable – but largely in a condition where they only presented the gist of the child's evidence rather than the detail. In other words, interviewer testimony may be effective, so care must be needed over the degradation of that testimony compared with that of the child's original interview.

Main points

- In order for child victims to gain justice under the law it is necessary for them to provide evidence that is credible in a specific case. There are a number of procedures that have been adopted which may reduce some of the stress of appearing in court – a very adult environment normally. In some jurisdictions, video links of either the children giving testimony live or pre-recorded links may reduce the stress, as does making the court less formal by allowing lawyers to be seated when they ask the child questions.

- Experienced interviewers of children may employ closed questions a lot despite the research evidence which suggests that this tends to generate a much smaller amount of material from the children involved. It may be advantageous to use scripted introductions to interviews, which use open-ended questioning, as once children are freely answering they tend to carry

on in the same way no matter the type of questioning style used. It should not be forgotten that children at different stages of childhood may have very different communication skills. Some types of question – tag questions for example – may cause inaccurate testimony.

- Many of the problems in interviewing children are not ones of the child's competence and accuracy but matters to do with the interviewer. For example, there is evidence that lawyers in court have difficulty in consistently phrasing questions in a manner appropriate to the child's developmental stage. Furthermore, when interviewers were asked to recall the detail of interviews with children they are less than perfectly accurate despite the importance of being able to do so. The way in which the interviewer raises issues of truth and lying can have an influence on the accuracy of the child's testimony.

Further reading

The following cover the field of interviewing especially child witnesses thoroughly taken collectively:

Bull, R., Valentine, T. and Williamson, T. (eds) (2009) *Handbook of Psychology of Investigative Interviewing: Current Developments and Future Directions* Chichester: Wiley-Blackwell.

Lamb, M.E., Hershkowitz, I., Orbach, Y. and Esplin, P.W. (2008) *Tell Me What Happened: Structured Investigative Interview of Child Victims and Witnesses* Chichester: John Wiley.

Milne, R. and Bull, R. (1999) *Investigative Interviewing: Psychology and Practice* Chichester: John Wiley.

Smith, K. and Tilney, S. (2007) *Vulnerable Adult and Child Witnesses* Oxford: Blackstone.

Westcott, H.L., Davies, G.M. and Bull, R. (eds) (2002) *Children's Testimony: A Handbook of Psychological Research and Forensic Practice* Chichester: John Wiley.

The UK Home Office has published guidance for interviewing vulnerable witnesses including children produced, in part, by psychologists: Guidance for Vulnerable or Intimidated Witnesses, including Children: http://www.cps.gov.uk/publications/docs/achieving_best_evidence_final.pdf

See also: Guidance on Interviewing Child Witnesses in Scotland – Supporting Child Witnesses Guidance Pack: http://www.scotland.gov.uk/Publications/2003/09/18265/27045

Visit our website at www.pearsoned.co.uk/howitt for self-test and essay questions, annotated further reading, audio interviews with researchers in the field, weblinks and more information on becoming a forensic psychologist.

Chapter 21

Mental disorders and crime

Overview

- In popular culture, the link between mental illness and crime has consistently been made. This is true of fictional and news media. The media, through selectivity, exaggerate the violence and extreme nature of crimes perpetrated by the mentally ill. Individual dramatic news events increase public antagonism towards the mentally ill. However, the evidence of major mental illness in a substantial minority of killers is quite strong.

- The relationship between mental illness and crime is complex and there are a number of confounding factors which can cloud the evidence: (1) the mentally ill tend to drop in socio-economic status, which means that they may live in more violent communities; (2) psychiatric categories of mental illness tend to involve violence in their definition, consequently, the mentally ill are violent because they are required to be if they are so categorised; and (3) the public may be more alarmed by a given level of violent behaviour if that person shows signs of mental illness. As a consequence, the violence of the mentally ill may more readily be reported to the police.

- Surveys involving general population samples and objective measures of psychiatric illness are the ideal to avoid the biasing effects of using clinical/hospital/prison samples. Mental illness does increase the risk of violent crime in these studies but other factors such as substance abuse have much greater influence.

- Late starters in criminal behaviour tend to be identified in the criminal justice system as mentally ill. It should not be overlooked that the mentally ill people are themselves more likely to be victims of violence. Nevertheless, reoffending by those with a criminal history which led them to be confined in high-security special hospitals is quite frequent after release from the hospital. A quarter of those discharged are reconvicted for serious (largely violent) offences.

- Other pertinent material may also be found in Chapter 22 on mental problems in court and Chapter 27 on risk and dangerousness.

Introduction

The professions of law and psychology share little in terms of how they conceptualise their subject matter – people. The causes and motivations of behaviour are central to both; nevertheless the two professions are essentially split by the way they construe human nature. This sometimes causes great confusion. Even a concept such as 'mental illness' means different things in the law and in psychology. Thus a definition of mental illness, for example, from clinical psychology or psychiatric textbooks tells one little about the legal meaning of the term. Under English law, for example, mental illness is not a technical phrase. It means what it means in ordinary language to ordinary people. It is for the jury or court to decide whether the term applies to a particular defendant (Pilgrim, 2000).

Belief in an association between mental illness and violent crime has a long history (Howitt, 1998b). As long ago as 1857, a Dr John Gray suggested that serious mental illness is associated with attempted or actual homicide. This theme became common in the mass media. As early as 1909 *The Maniac Cook* movie had the mentally ill as homicidal maniacs. Modern cinema continues exactly the same themes in *Psycho* (1960), *Silence of the Lambs* (1991), *Black Swan* (2010), *Shutter Island* (2010) and many others. Dangerousness and unpredictability have been shown to be the dominant characteristics of the mentally ill in the media (Day and Page, 1986; Wahl and Roth, 1982). Furthermore, public opinion surveys indicate that mentally ill people (especially those with schizophrenia) are perceived as violent and dangerous. In other words, the idea that the mentally ill are dangerous is well supported in Western cultures.

Not surprisingly then, research indicates that the media may shape the public's beliefs about the dangerousness of the mentally ill. A German study concentrated on the way in which daily newspapers portray the mentally ill (Angermeyer and Schulze, 2001). A German tabloid newspaper (*Bild-Zeitung*) with daily sales of 11 million copies was analysed in terms of its coverage of mental illness in relation to crime. The largest proportions of stories about the mentally ill concerned murder, multiple murder, physical injury/grievous bodily harm, attempted murder, rape/sexual abuse, multiple infanticide and infanticide. This amounted to a total of 68 per cent of all of the reported crimes being in this category, which is essentially the more extreme forms of violence. Indeed, 49 per cent involved some form of homicide. The researchers also showed that individual news events in which public figures were violently attacked by mentally ill people seemed to affect the public's attitudes to mentally ill people in general. The public's attitudes to the mentally ill became more negative after highly publicised violent incidents involving the mentally ill such as the knife attack on court against the tennis star Monica Seles in 1993.

The criminal justice system (the police, courts, prison, probation services) is only one aspect of a complex structure dealing with mental illness. Medical services such as hospitals clearly have a part to play, as do voluntary services, say, dealing with mental health issues or homelessness. Furthermore, we should not forget that the community and family also have a central role and that some individuals with mental disturbances never seek or receive psychiatric or psychological help. The relationship between different parts of the system is dynamic and changing and there is an interplay between the medical system and the criminal justice system: that is, problematic individuals will be diverted into one or other system according to what capacity there is in the medical system. It has been shown, for example, that British mental hospital admissions correlate negatively with rates of prison imprisonment (Weller and Weller, 1988). The prisons were apparently receiving cases who previously would have entered psychiatric institutions. In this context, one should note the findings of Robertson *et al.* (1996) concerning people detained at London police stations. About 1 per cent of detainees were acutely ill. They tended to get diverted to other services and not to go through the criminal justice system. Violence, at the time of arrest, tended to lead to processing through the criminal justice system.

To get matters into proportion, it is useful to quote a few statistical findings. Based on data from 500 homicide cases in England and Wales in 1996–7 for whom psychiatric reports could be obtained, the levels of mental disorder were (Shaw *et al.*, 1999):

- 44 per cent had a record of mental disorder at some time in their life;
- 14 per cent had symptoms of mental illness at the time of the offence;
- 8 per cent had had contact with mental health services in the year before the offence.

Only in a small proportion of homicides did the offender show signs of mental illness at the time of the offence.

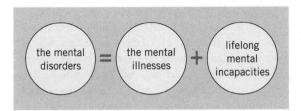

Figure 21.1 How the concept of mental disorder includes mental illness and mental incapacities

According to Hodgins and Cote (1993), studies using 'unbiased' samples of killers find rates of major mental illness among them from about a fifth to over a half. One should bear in mind that mental disorder is very common in the general population when assessing these trends. Relatively frequent problems include depression.

In passing, it should be noted that the terms mental illness and mental disorder are not synonymous. Mental disorder incorporates the mental illnesses which are regarded as treatable and changing but includes, in addition, long-term and unchangeable conditions such as learning disorder. Figure 21.1 illustrates this. So one might say that mental illness involves an interruption of mental functioning. This has the implication that the individual had functioned normally at some stage and may function normally in the future. Mental disorder is a general term for various problems in mental functioning including lifelong problems like learning difficulties as well as familiar mental illnesses such is cyclical disorder and depression. Much of the research and theory described in this chapter is specifically about mental illness.

The question 'What is the relationship between mental illness and crime?' is relatively simple to answer compared with the methodological and conceptual difficulties inherent in the question 'Does mental illness cause violent crime?' (Arboleda-Florez, Holley and Crisanti, 1996). There are a number of other difficulties that need to be resolved.

Controlling for confounding factors

No matter what the statistical association between mental illness and violent crime (positive, negative or none), there remains the possibility that the apparent relationship is an artefact of the influence of third variables or confounding factors. So, to give a somewhat unlikely example, it is possible that the mentally ill appear to be more violent because they respond to taunts about their behaviour. Without these taunts, there might be no violent response. There are other possibilities:

- Some variables cannot be considered to be alternative causal variables. Mental illness cannot cause a person's age or sex, for example. This is not to say that mental illness does not correlate with age or sex. Schizophrenia was originally called *dementia praecox* because it was seen as an illness of young people. It is a common observation that, for whatever reason, women appear more frequently than men among the statistics on rates of mental illness. Such variables as gender can be appropriately partialled-out or controlled using common statistical techniques.

- Other factors that initially appear to be appropriately dealt with by statistical methods may actually be somewhat problematic. What is considered to be a confounding factor is a complex matter. Social class is a case in point. It is known that there is downward social drift among the seriously mentally ill (Monahan, 1993). A company director who becomes mentally ill may be launched into a downward spiral because of being unable to keep a job, say, because they can no longer cope with the stresses of a managerial career. Their consequent income drop may cause them to lose their homes and any work they obtain will be poorly paid. Once their socio-economic status has dropped markedly, they may find themselves in contact with violent subcultures (e.g. from living on the streets if they become homeless). The net effect of the downward spiral is that the mentally ill will tend to be disproportionately of lower socio-economic status. In this sense, mental illness can cause their social class. Removing socio-economic status from the association between mental illness and violent crime statistically would distort the findings in this case.

- Things can be even more complicated than this implies since such downward drift does not always happen and may be caused by factors other than mental illness anyway. For example, what if mental illness is sometimes the consequence of stress caused by bad housing or financial difficulties? In these circumstances, there is potentially a need to control for socio-economic status since it is part of the chain of factors causing mental illness.

- Neither of the preceding points of view is wrong. Nevertheless, they lead to very different approaches to statistical control in the data. Of course, if both approaches lead to the same broad conclusion, then interpretation is easy.

Confounding by overlapping definitions

Mental illnesses are largely defined in terms of a number of diagnostic categories. Imagine that among those diagnostic features is violence itself. One possible consequence is that there will be an association between mental illness and violent crime. People who are violent then have a greater chance of also being defined as mentally ill since they show one of the symptoms of mental illness – violence. For many of the psychiatric disorders described and defined in the *Diagnostic and Statistical Manual of the American Psychiatric Association*, the 'bible' of psychiatric classification, violence is listed as a key diagnostic feature. Illnesses such as *antisocial personality disorder* and *borderline personality disorder* are partly defined in terms of violence. For other disorders, such as schizophrenia, violence is mentioned as an associated feature although not a diagnostic characteristic (see Box 21.1 and Chapter 22):

- A study of DSM-I (published 1952) showed that only 2 per cent of the listed disorders characteristically involved violence. In DSM-II (published 1968), this percentage increased slightly to just 13 per cent of disorders. Things changed markedly with the issue of DSM-III in 1980. This time, 47 per cent of the psychiatric categories listed violence as a characteristic (Harry, 1985).

- These changes in definition coincided with changes in research findings. Prior to this time, research studies tended to show *no* relationship between mental illness and violent crime. After that time a relationship was more often shown (Link, Andrews and Cullen, 1992).

The confounding effects of medication

Psychiatric drugs are often prescribed to the mentally ill to control the symptoms of their illness. These drugs may have side effects leading to violent behaviour. For example, it is known that certain tranquillising drugs with neuroleptic effects can make users more aggressive. In other words, the drugs that the mentally ill take to alleviate undesirable symptoms are the actual cause of their aggressiveness, not the mental illness as such. Thus aggression in this case is not a direct effect of mental illness.

The clinical sample problem

Imagine that there is no relationship between mental illness and violence. It would still be possible to produce an association by selecting one's sample of mentally ill people in such a way that the mentally ill who are also violent have a better chance of being sampled. One way in which this might happen is to draw one's samples from mental hospitals. These people may be in hospital because they drew attention to themselves in the community – perhaps they were violent and so were arrested. In reality, violence may be no more common in the mentally ill than the general population. Any selection method that favours the violent mentally ill may be responsible for a spurious association.

Misclassification of the mentally ill and violent

The use of hospital and crime records to classify people as mentally ill and violent may depend on a flawed classification system. For example, the general public may be more likely to report violence or threats of violence by people who show signs of mental illness. This is because their psychiatric symptoms make their violence more disturbing. As a consequence, the relationship between mental illness and violent crime would strengthen.

Effects of general social trends

It is possible that the apparent relationship between mental illness and violent crime will vary with major changes in social policy. Since the early 1980s there has been a policy of retaining fewer of the mentally ill in mental institutions in favour of supporting them within the community (Bachrach, 1984, 1989; Shadish, 1984). This is known as deinstitutionalisation. This, in itself, places the public at greater risk. Intriguingly, opinions have changed about violence carried out by the mentally ill. Prior to the 1980s, researchers tended to conclude that the mentally ill were, if anything, less violent than people were in general. This could have been an artefact of the likelihood that the violent mentally ill were kept institutionalised and not allowed to return to the community. Since then, the view has been that mental illness has a slight tendency to be associated with violence.

BOX 21.1 Controversy

Psychiatric diagnosis

Forensic and criminal psychologists associate professionally with a variety of other professions – the law, social work, policing, prison administrators, prison officers and psychiatrists. This means, inevitably, that forensic and criminal psychologists should be able to communicate effectively across professional boundaries. This poses special problems in relation to psychiatry. Psychiatry overlaps with psychology in seeking to understand and explain human behaviour including criminal activity while at the same time the two disciplines are very different in their practical and theoretical base. One particularly problematic area is that of psychiatric diagnosis in which individuals are classified as manifesting the characteristics of particular mental illnesses, for example, or not. This is much the same as diagnosing physical diseases such as typhoid, carcinoma and the like.

Psychiatrists have mainly worked with diagnostic schemes based on the work of Emil Kraepelin in nineteenth-century Germany. For Kraepelin, each psychiatric disorder should demonstrate a cluster of symptoms that tend to occur together invariably. The prognoses of people classified as having the same 'mental disease' should be similar since the same pathological root is shared by all of them. Kraepelin believed that there were three major types of psychosis:

- dementia praecox or schizophrenia – hallucinations and delusions;
- manic depression – extremes of mood including depression and mania;

- paranoia – delusions of a persecutory or grandiose nature.

Given the origins and rationale of this psychiatric classification, it is hardly surprising that many psychologists regard it as the epitome of the medical model of *mental illness*. According to Eastman (2000), any conception of mental illness in terms of diseases such as lesions or disturbances of the function of a part of personality are indicative of the underlying acceptance of the medical approach. His term for this is the psychiatric phenomenological approach. Control of symptoms is an important part of the 'treatment' of such conditions and one may seek a 'cure'. In contrast, what he terms the psycho-understanding approach sees psychological content as valid and enlightening (rather than the outcome of a fault in the system as it is in the medical model).

Currently, there are two standard diagnostic systems. The most famous is the *Diagnostic and Statistical Manual of the American Psychiatric Association* (DSM-I to DSM-IV have been published to date) and the *International Classification of Diseases* (World Health Organization, 2011).

DSM-IV uses a system of classification involving five broad aspects of psychiatric diagnoses which are labelled from Axis I to Axis V. These are shown in Figure 21.2. The various categories of mental illness are defined by various characteristics. So, for example, *schizophrenia* would be defined by the demonstration of the following things:

▶

BOX 21.1 (continued)

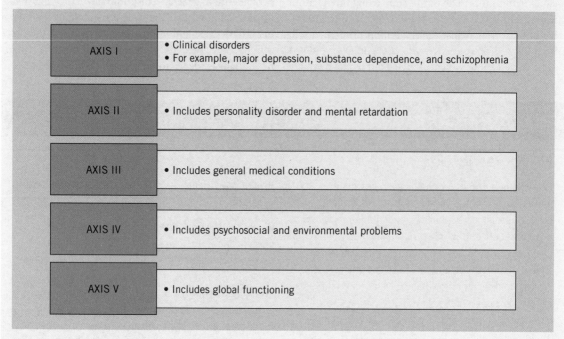

AXIS I	• Clinical disorders • For example, major depression, substance dependence, and schizophrenia
AXIS II	• Includes personality disorder and mental retardation
AXIS III	• Includes general medical conditions
AXIS IV	• Includes psychosocial and environmental problems
AXIS V	• Includes global functioning

Figure 21.2 The five axes of the Diagnostic and Statistical Manual

- Two or more symptoms from the following shown over a month:
  - delusions;
  - disorganised speech;
  - grossly disorganised or catatonic behaviour;
  - hallucinations;
  - negative symptoms such as flattened emotions.
- Social and/or occupational dysfunctions.

The World Health Organization's (2011) system is briefly summarized in Figure 21.3. The system contains a greater description of the characteristics of each of the subcategories of each of the diagnostic categories. The system contains a wide range of medical conditions although Figure 21.3 concentrates on those related to mental illness etc.

The problems for a psychologist using these diagnostic manuals include the following (Pilgrim, 2000):

- Diagnostic categories are created by psychiatrists and others. Consequently, they may change, get abandoned, subdivided and so forth based largely on expert opinion rather than scientific utility.

- Unlike many diagnoses of physical illness, even for major psychiatric classifications of illness such as schizophrenia, the utilitarian value of the diagnosis is unclear. For example, the bodily causes of schizophrenia have not been clearly identified despite years of research. This is quite different from the situation with physical illnesses such as typhoid and carcinoma for which the physical mechanisms are known.

- There are major difficulties when the user tries to differentiate one diagnostic category from another. Different diagnosticians may put the same patient in very different categories. Similarly, simply diagnosing people as normal or abnormal is far from an objective process with different clinicians reaching different conclusions.

- Some would argue that these diagnostic systems have nothing extra to offer than does ordinary language. So to suggest people are mad, bad, sad or afraid may be to effectively offer the equivalent of diagnoses such as schizophrenia, antisocial personality disorder, depression or phobia.

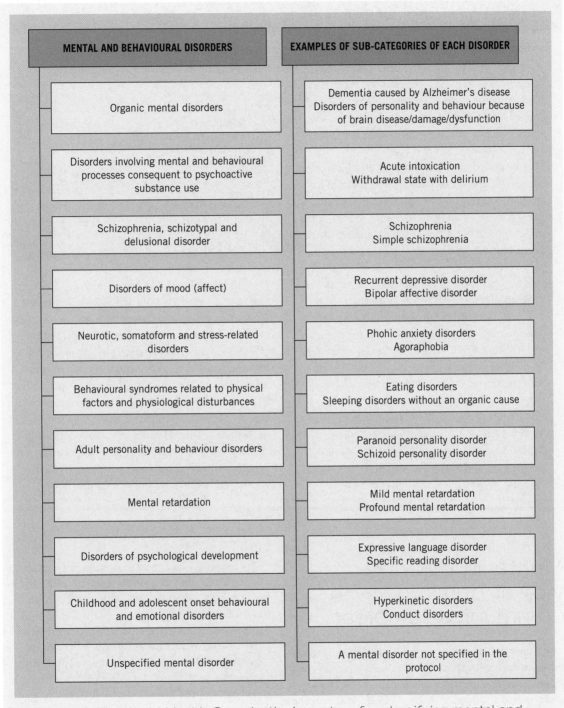

Figure 21.3 The World Health Organization's system for classifying mental and related disorders

BOX 21.1 (continued)

Pilgrim (2000) suggests that the psychiatric diagnoses tend to stigmatise people more than ordinary language does. The descriptions of ordinary language tend to be associated with relatively subtle explanations of why a person is a particular way and often a variety of notions about what can be done to help the person with the problem.

- The diagnoses may merely present technical terms that fulfil no other function than to enhance the technical reputation of diagnosticians. The ordinary person in the street understands the violent, often repetitive and antisocial nature of rape, so what extra is gained by diagnosing such a person as a psychopath?

- There is circularity in the definition of mental illness. A person is classified as mentally ill on the basis of their behaviour, then this diagnosis is used to explain their behaviour. This circularity is illustrated below. Notice that things are different in medical diagnosis since although the disease is often defined by its symptoms, frequently there is an independent test to determine the correctness of the diagnosis. Interestingly, Pickel (1998) found evidence that simulated jurors tended to make judgements about the insanity of defendants accused of homicide if there were unusual features about how the crime was

committed, e.g. that the body was covered with strange designs done with yellow mustard.

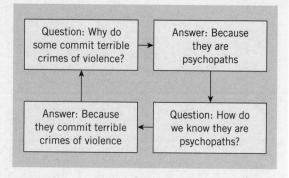

To these we should add a very important point of great relevance to forensic practitioners. That is, the way in which people with mental disorders are conceived psychologically and psychiatrically is simply not the same as the legal categories used in relation to the same people. That is, legal definitions are not simply the application of psychological concepts or psychiatric classifications. In other words, there is no common language between psychiatry or psychology and the law on these matters. The law is made by legislators and can reflect profound ideological changes in the way in which mental disorders are understood (Forrester, Ozdural, Muthukumaraswamy and Carroll, 2008).

Mental illness and violent crime in community samples

Two important studies have been carried out involving substantial samples from the community (as opposed to, say, prisons or mental hospitals). This design removes some potential artefacts (McNeil, 1997) and may be regarded as the ideal type of study to answer the question of whether mental illness is linked to crime:

- Link *et al.* (1992) studied representative samples of 500 never-treated community residents in New York

City together with a mental patient sample. As might be expected, mental patients had the highest levels of a variety of official and self-report measures of violent and illegal behaviour. Statistical control for socio-demographic and community context variables still left the mental patient group more violent and more criminal. The researchers employed the *Psychiatric Epidemiology Research Interview* with both samples. This assesses the extent of mental illness symptoms independently of the mental health system. There was a relationship between having psychotic symptoms and violence. Despite this, the presence of psychotic symptoms was a weaker predictor of violence than other variables such as age, education level and gender.

- Swanson *et al.*'s (1990) study was similar in that psychiatric symptoms were assessed using the *Diagnostic Interview Schedule*. They obtained a sample from the communities of Baltimore, Raleigh-Durham and Los Angeles in the United States. Socio-demographic variables including age and sex were statistically controlled. Following this, it was clear that schizophrenia and major affective disorders were associated with an approximately fourfold increase in the likelihood of violence in the year following assessment. These findings need to be set against the 14-fold increase in the likelihood of violence associated with substance abuse. The presence of mental disorder and substance abuse together increased the likelihood of violence to 17-fold. Mental disorders differ in their relationship with violence. Psychotic illness (i.e. schizophrenia and similar) resulted in higher levels of violence than affective or anxiety disorders. Nevertheless, serious mental illness is rare compared with, for example, substance abuse. Consequently, the relative risk is far greater from substance abusers than the mentally ill.

Clinical aspects of violence

There are other factors in mental illness that affect the likelihood of violence (McNeil, 1997). Mental illnesses, as we have seen, are not all associated with violence and in the same way. Furthermore, mental illness is not an invariant feature of a person's life. It changes in intensity and form over time. Consequently, studies of patients in the acute phase of a mental illness may find higher levels of violence. Studies of patients in remission (the non-acute phase) may find lower levels of violence. In particular, people with schizophrenia in stages of frequent and intense symptoms (i.e. during acute exacerbation) are more violent than groups of patients with a different psychiatric classification. In the case of mania (manic depression/bipolar disorder), the manic phase may show the highest levels of violence.

Mental disorders can be the consequence of traumatic injuries or physical disease. Head injuries tend to elevate the risk of violence – in particular, damage to the temporal or frontal lobes may encourage aggressive behaviours.

Other factors need to be taken into account. *Command hallucinations* (the hearing of voices instructing the patient to commit violence or other harm against a third party)

seem to heighten the risk of violence. The famous case of the Yorkshire Ripper who, in the 1970s, murdered at least 13 women, generally prostitutes, featured such hallucinations. It was claimed at Peter Sutcliffe's trial that he was instructed by the voice of God to carry out the murders. This may have been a failed attempt to be pronounced mentally ill by the court (Ainsworth, 2000a). However, a study of schizophrenic men detained under the UK Mental Health Act of 1983 for serious sexual offences against women considered by the courts to be a special risk to the public, found a poor relationship between their delusions and their sexual offending. Ninety-four per cent had some sort of delusions and hallucinations at the time of the offence but did the contents of these have any relationship to the offence? For 51 per cent of these offenders the delusions were just coincidental and had no bearing on the attack. Another 25 per cent had delusions that were of a sexual or persecutory nature but which did not reflect the characteristics of the sexual assault. Eighteen per cent had delusions that appeared to be directly related to the sexual attack (Smith and Taylor, 1999). O'Kane and Bentall (2000) concentrate on severe psychotic disorders, which they see as characteristically involving hallucinations, delusions and apparent loss of contact with reality. They discuss the symptom approach to violence in the mentally ill in which the search is for the symptoms associated with violence (as opposed to the diagnosis approach, which concentrates on the psychiatric diagnoses associated with violence). The sorts of symptoms they implicate in violence are already partly familiar:

- Delusions and passivity delusions with paranormal influences.
- Psychotic individuals with organised delusions are especially likely to commit either lethal or near-lethal acts.
- Paranoid symptoms are associated with violent behaviour.
- Command hallucinations often involve aggression and self-punishment. They have also been implicated in sexual offences.

Among the most interesting of these symptoms are command hallucinations. In general, auditory hallucinations of various sorts are a main symptom of psychotic disorders in general. Command hallucination is merely one particular type of auditory hallucination and involves a voice commanding the person to do a particular thing.

Other voice hallucinations may involve the comments of the 'voice' but what is said lacks directions. Research suggests that the prevalence of command hallucinations depends on the particular type of sample being studied. The figure is in excess of 50 per cent for those who experience auditory hallucinations of any sort (e.g. Mackinnon *et al.*, 2004). However, perhaps surprisingly, the rates of command hallucinations are no different in forensic and non-forensic populations. Command hallucinations can be categorised as belonging to three different types:

- benign commands involving no harm to oneself or others
- other-harm commands instructing the hearer to do something harmful to another person
- self-harm commands instructing the hearer to do something damaging to oneself.

But just what leads to a command being carried out? There is some evidence to suggest that this is partly dependent on the individual's beliefs about the voice that they hear and not the particular content of the instruction. The voice may be perceived as powerful compared to the vulnerable self. Such circumstances have been found to relate to compliance to the instruction of the command hallucination and particularly so where the instruction is for inflicting harm on others (Fox *et al.*, 2004). Those who obey other-harm commands tend to perceive the voice as all-powerful and controlling. One possibility is that if the hearer regards themself as being of low social power then they will be more inclined to implement self-harm commands than other-harm commands. The hearer who regards themself as being higher in social power is more likely to obey other-harm commands.

Reynolds and Scragg (2010) researched two groups of men who heard command hallucinations. One group was compliers to the commands and the other group resisted commands. All the men were recruited from a variety of types of forensic location. The researchers were interested in three aspects:

- the hearer's perceptions of the perceived power of the voice
- the hearer's perceptions of the social rank of the voice compared to their own
- the hearer's perceptions of their own social rank compared with that of others.

The focus of the research was solely on the other-harm command. The men were interviewed and a number of psychiatric tests administered. These included the Voice Power Differential Scale which includes the aspects of ability to inflict harm, confidence, knowledge, respect, strength, and superiority and the Social Comparison Scale which assesses the individuals' perceived social rank relative to others. It was found that compliance with voices did not depend on the severity of an individual's psychiatric symptoms or psychopathy. However, compliers with the voices saw the voice as more powerful than did resisters and compliers saw the voice as being of a higher social rank compared with themselves. These findings were as the researchers predicted. Nevertheless, the expectation that the individuals who complied with the command of the voices would perceive themselves as of higher social rank compared with other people was not supported.

McNeil (1997) believes that the following should be considered when trying to understand the violence of individuals with psychiatric difficulties:

- A previous history of violence is the best single predictor of future violence in both clinical and non-clinical populations.
- Among the mentally ill, homelessness is associated with violent behaviour.
- Being victimised by child abuse or observing adults being violent to each other at home increases the risk of acting violently.
- Care-givers and nurses are at the greatest risk of violence from the mentally ill.
- Gender is a poor predictor of violence. Violence by male psychiatric patients may be perceived as more fear-provoking because they are more likely to threaten and damage property. Nevertheless, women psychiatric patients would appear to commit more assaults. Studies of people *living in the community* who attend psychiatric emergency facilities generally suggest that the genders are comparable in violence levels.
- Poor social networks are associated with violence.
- Race, ethnicity and culture are inconsistent and so worthless predictors of violence in the mentally ill. This is the case after social class and similar variables have been taken into account.
- Some environments are actually threatening, which may encourage violence.
- The availability of weapons increases risk.

While some forms of mental illness carry an increased risk of violence to others, caution is needed about the issue.

The rates of serious mental illness are small compared with people manifesting other risk factors for violence (e.g. substance abuse, youth). In other words, the likelihood of an individual being assaulted by someone with a serious mental illness is less than that of being assaulted by someone with a different risk factor.

So what are the characteristics of the offending associated with different types of mental illness? One area of particular interest is homicide. In Finland, Häkkänen and Laajasalo (2006) obtained samples of forensic psychiatric statements for four different DSM-III-R diagnostic groups – schizophrenics, abusers of alcohol or drugs, offenders with personality disorder, and offenders with no diagnosis or a relatively minor disorder. There were some characteristics particularly associated with these different groups:

- *Alcoholics*: they were all drunk when committing the homicide; they were the group most likely to use a weapon present at the crime scene; they were most likely to kill following an argument; they were the most likely to give themselves up; they were very unlikely to use a handgun.

- *Drug addicts*: these stole more frequently from their victims and they killed in the context of another crime more frequently; surprisingly, they showed some of the pattern as schizophrenics since their choice of weapons was very similar and the killings of both of these groups seem not to be the consequence of external events such as quarrels.

- *Personality disorder*: guns and blunt and sharp weapons were associated with this group as was kicking and hitting; there were few other characteristics that may reflect the tenuous nature of this classification.

- *Schizophrenics*: sharp and blunt weapons are used more often than guns perhaps because their crimes are more impulsive; they injured their victim's face more frequently than the other groups of mentally ill offenders possibly because the face is symbolically the essence of a person or because they find facial expressions threatening; their attacks were less likely to follow arguments; mostly they suffered from hallucinations/delusions at the time of the attack; their victims were frequently relatives.

BOX 21.2 Controversy

Does research on violence and psychosis need a change of direction?

Do we know enough about the mechanisms which link psychosis to violence? Taylor (2005) argues that research showing that the risk of violence in society attributable to people with schizophrenia is very low at 4 per cent of violent incidents does not help us clinically when it comes to the risk presented by a particular individual with schizophrenia. She suggests that we need to look at the symptoms which increase the risk of physical violence. However, studies of such symptoms are beset with the sort of methodological difficulties which characterise studies of the relationship between psychosis and violence in general. Taylor's view is that there is too much emphasis on the statistical correlation between violence and psychosis which may reflect that researchers have been concentrating on the wrong question. Evidence suggests that violence is generally an interplay between the individual and the social context. For example, we need to understand what sort of person becomes the target of the violence of psychotic persons.

What is it about some individuals with psychosis which makes it more likely that they will exhibit violence whereas others do not act violently? Taylor makes three main points about this:

- Persecutory delusions and passivity delusions are known to be associated with violence, but we need to know whether there are different factors which result in these different delusions resulting in violence.
- Some offenders reoffend many times violently whereas others reoffend just once but extremely seriously – so are these very different patterns of violence to be understood in very different ways?
- Very little is known chronologically about the changes in factors such as family environment and peer relationships which may lead to later violence.

In other words, there is a great deal yet to be learnt about why a small proportion of people with psychosis actually act violently.

Who among the mentally ill is violent?

The origins of criminals with major mental disorders (schizophrenia, major depression, bipolar disorder, other non-toxic psychoses) are not uniform. There are two clearly definable groups (Hodgins, 1997; Hodgins, Cote and Toupin, 1998):

- *Early starters* have a stable history of antisocial behaviour from childhood and throughout their lives. Interestingly, within the criminal justice system, they are not usually identified as mentally disordered. When they are in the acute stages of mental illness, they show no pattern of antisocial behaviour so they are not seen by the psychiatric services as criminal or antisocial.

- *Late starters* do not have the early history of criminal and antisocial behaviour. Such behaviours emerge only at about the same time as symptoms of the mental disorder appear. The late starters are more likely to be positively helped by treatment of the mental disorder.

Laajasalo and Häkkänen (2004) studied the schizophrenics in their sample by subdividing them into those whose criminal convictions started by the age of 18 years (early starters) and those whose criminal convictions began after that age (late starters). Early start offenders, compared with the late start offenders, were more likely to have killed following an argument, were less likely to kill an acquaintance, and were more likely to kill their victims by strangulation using some object. Overall, however, despite these differences, the use of crime scene characteristics was only modestly successful in predicting the age of onset of their criminal career.

It is possible that at least some of the violence of the mentally ill has not been included in the analysis of the relationship between violence and mental illness. If we concentrate our attention on the sort of violence that is measured by criminal convictions and recidivism, we probably underestimate the violence of the mentally ill. The violence of the mentally ill when inpatients in clinics and hospitals is unlikely to lead to prosecution and conviction. It probably leads to prosecution only when it is very extreme. Inpatient violence ranges from 3 per cent for hospitalised patients to 45 per cent for outpatients to 62 per cent for committed individuals (Dernevik, Johansson and Grann, 2000). Obviously, this

is a clearer issue in relationship to violence in an institution or prison than out in the community. For instance, Dernevik et al. (2000) found some evidence of the effectiveness of risk management on violent incidents. High-risk management was the amount of time spent on a high-security ward with no community access. Medium-risk management was an amount of time spent living in the hospital but with some access to occupational and recreational activities in the community. Low-risk management was time spent in a less secure living arrangement and having access to the community while still being regularly monitored. While a standard risk assessment measure predicted violence in the final two risk situations well, it was a poor predictor within the high-security arrangement.

Mental illness and crime in general

While the threat of violence by the mentally ill has been a major aspect of this area of study, there is a more general question of the general criminality of those suffering from a major mental illness. According to Hodgins (1997), three different types of evidence support the association between major mental illness and criminality:

- Major long-term studies of people born in a particular time period which show that those who develop a major mental illness also tend to have higher levels of criminality.

- Studies that compare the criminality of those suffering a major mental disorder on release into the community with members of that same community with no mental disorder.

- Studies showing the higher levels of mental illness in convicted offenders.

A good example of the relevant research is a study of the 15,000 people born in Stockholm during 1953 (Hodgins, 1992). This was an unselected sample except in so far as people no longer living in Stockholm 10 years later were excluded. The figures varied somewhat by sex, but there was an association between the development of a major mental disorder and having committed a criminal offence by the age of 30. For men, 32 per cent with no mental disorder (or mental retardation) became criminal but 50 per cent of those with a major mental disorder were criminal. For women, 6 per cent of the non-mentally-ill compared with 19 per cent of the mentally ill became criminal. The risks were somewhat greater for violent than non-violent crime. This and other research (Hodgins *et al.*, 1996) suggests that many of the mentally ill commit their initial crime at the age of 30 plus. About a third of the mentally ill men and two-thirds of the mentally ill women demonstrated this pattern.

Why should there be greater criminality among the mentally ill?

The question of why criminality should be commoner among those with a major mental disorder needs to be addressed. There are a number of explanations (Hodgins, 1997):

- The police easily detect mentally ill offenders because they tend to offend in public, do not flee the crime scene too readily and are more likely to confess their crimes. Research evidence on this is equivocal.

- The co-morbidity of major mental disorders with alcoholism and drug abuse. In other words, alcoholism and drug abuse can lead to criminality. These conditions seem to exist in high proportions among offenders with a major mental disorder.

- Treatment delivery is more problematic with deinstitutionalisation. This may be made worse by the greater rights of patients to refuse treatment.

Violent victimisation of the mentally ill

One intriguing possible explanation of the link between mental illness and violent crime emerges out of the observation that the mentally ill are actually more likely to be victims of crime than members of the general public. Hiday *et al.* (2001) interviewed severely mentally ill patients (e.g. schizophrenic or another psychotic disorder) who had been involuntarily admitted to a psychiatric unit. Some of them had substance abuse histories. In the four months prior to the interview, over a quarter (27 per cent) had been the victim of any sort of crime, 8 per cent had been a victim of a violent

crime and 22 per cent had been a victim of a non-violent crime. However, half of the sample was known to have acted violently in the same time period. Thus it cannot be said that these violent acts were simply fights involving a mentally ill person rather than attacks on a mentally ill person, for example. Compared with the general population, the rates of non-violent victimisation of the mentally ill were average in this study though this is not the usual finding of research (see below). On the other hand, the mentally ill were rather more likely to be victims of violent crime than a member of the general population. This was still the case when demographic variables were controlled in the analysis. Consequently, it seems unlikely that the relationship between mental illness and being a victim of violent crime is a spurious one. However, since this was a cross-sectional study, one should be cautious about inferring exactly what the causal relationship is. Nevertheless, the findings of this study are consistent with the view that a mentally ill person may be violent because of their earlier violent victimisation.

Maniglio (2009) searched major research data bases and found nine studies published between 1966 and 2007 concerning the prevalence of crime victimisation among the severely mentally ill. His search keywords included depression, mental illness, psychiatric/mental disorders, psychosis, and schizophrenia. The retrieved studies involved research on 5,000 patients. The mentally ill faced a high risk of victimisation by others. Prevalence rates for violent criminal victimisation based on self-reports were found to be between 4–35 per cent according to the study and non-violent victimisation ranged from 8–28 per cent unlike the findings of Hiday *et al.* above. It is not easy to find explanations of the considerable variation in prevalence estimates from study to study. Possibilities include the at-risk period of time which was used for victimisation and whether an urban or rural location was involved. Remarkably, criminal victimisation was between 2 and 140 times higher than figures for the general population. There was evidence that a number of factors such as alcohol and or illicit drug use, homelessness, more extreme symptoms and involvement in a criminal lifestyle were associated with increased levels of victimisation.

Just why should the mentally ill be prone to suffer from violent victimisation? One possibility is that an intervening factor in the relationship is stress. So the suggestion is that the mentally ill tend to be more susceptible to victimisation at times when they are under stress. For example, at times of stress the mentally ill may lack the resources to deal effectively with interpersonal relationships. In other words, they may fly off of the handle more easily at times of stress, for example, which leads to interpersonal conflict and friction. Teasdale (2009) tested this possibility in the USA but found no evidence to support the idea that violent victimisation increased at times of stress in a simple, direct fashion among the mentally ill. However, some other possible mechanism linking mental illness and victimisation were investigated:

- Stress and gender interact in ways which leads to different patterns of response to stress in men and women. Men tend to adopt flight or fight strategies during stress but women, in contrast, use coping strategies involving tending and befriending. Thus stress should increase male victimisation but decrease female victimisation.

- Violent victimisation of the mentally ill increases when things happen or they do things which decrease the guardianship (the watchful eye) that others have over them. So mentally ill people are better protected from violent victimisation if they are married or working. This is because their partner and their supervisor, for example, provide a certain amount of guardianship.

- Increased levels of symptoms may indicate to others the vulnerability of the mentally ill person which makes them more exposed to victimisation. Furthermore, they may not be able to look after themselves effectively. Another alternative is that their symptoms may involve making them more socially conflictful or a failure to engage in normal social protocols.

The research was based on data from the MacArthur Violence Risk Assessment Study which was a longitudinal study of people released from psychiatric hospitals. The researchers found support for all three of the mechanisms listed above.

Although these research studies and conceptualisations of the processes involved constitute progress, a great deal more work will be needed before this area of victim research is well understood.

The special issue of psychopaths and crime

There is no doubt that some psychopaths engage in criminal behaviour. There is also no doubt that there are many psychopaths in prison. However, this leads to the important issue of just what it is about psychopathy which leads to crime? Is criminal behaviour a symptom of psychopathy or is criminal behaviour a consequence of the abnormal personality characteristics which define psychopathy? One can see, for example, that since psychopaths are impulsive and irresponsible this may lead to them getting in trouble with the law. The concepts of the psychopath and psychopathy have been among the most researched topics in recent years in forensic and criminal psychology. They have developed over a long period of time starting from the beginning of the nineteenth century (Forrester, Ozdural, Muthukumaraswamy and Carroll, 2008). Pinel (1809) formulated a condition which he termed *manie sans délire*. This was primarily a disorder of the emotions rather than thinking and, as such, was an important breakthrough in the way psychiactric disorders were conceived since it extended conceptions from mental conditions to emotional conditions. Various monomanias were proposed by Esquirol (1838) – one of which included *lesions of the will* which allowed the individual to carry out bad acts which were based neither on reason nor emotion. These developments gradually led to the concept of the psychopath. Partridge (1930) was responsible for developing the closely related concept of sociopathy which had all sorts of social maladjustment as a defining essential feature. Most important of all, Cleckley in *The Mask of Sanity* (1941) provided clear criteria for the diagnosis of psychopathy. This, however, describes psychopathy in terms of deceitfulness, egocentricity, failure to follow a life plan, grandiose interpersonal style, inability to experience anxiety, inability to love, manipulativeness, shallowness and superficial charm. Criminality was not particularly germane to Cleckley's defining features of the psychopathy.

It was Cleckley's conceptualisation which Robert Hare turned to when developing his highly influencial Psychopathy Checklist (PCL) and the Psychopathy Checklist Revised (PCL-R) (see Chapter 27). It is fair to suggest that these measures have dominated in research into psychopathy and the checklists have been referred to as the gold standard for assessing psychopathy. There is good evidence of its power as a predictor of violent recidivism (see Chapter 27). Despite acknowledging Cleckley's influence on his work, Hare elevates criminality to a more central position in the conceptualisation of psychopathy than Cleckley had. For example, Hare's PCL and PCL-R questionnaires include items referring to aspects of anti-social and criminal behaviour.

This has led to a debate among researchers which is of considerable importance. Skeem and Cooke (2010) argue that the massive amounts of research generated by the PCL and PCL-R have largely concentrated on its predictive power in relation to criminal recidivism. They believe that Hare's concentration on criminality in relation to psychopathy has been the basis of substantial conceptual confusions. In particular, they say, there is a risk of equating the theoretical construct of psychopathy with the means of measuring that construct (usually the PCL-R). For them, the question is whether criminal behaviour is at the core of psychopathy or what they refer to as merely a 'downstream correlate' of psychopathy. This is ultimately not a matter that can be resolved by statistical analyses of the PCL-R since these can only inform us about the nature of the PCL-R – the more fundamental question of what psychopathy is cannot be dealt with in this way. The construct of the psychopath was to be found in the clinical and research literature long before the PCL was created. In the early writings on psychopathy, it was not discussed in tandem with criminality. Instead the focus was on trying to understand the interpersonal and affective characteristics of the psychopath – what might be termed the psychopath's emotional detachment. Provocatively, Skeem and Cooke argue that a person with all of the characteristics of psychopathy as defined, say, by Cleckley is nevertheless unlikely to be diagnosed as a psychopath. In addition, they need a history of violent and criminal behaviour.

Despite this fundamental argument, Cooke and others have debated the use of the PCL-R with Hare. Essentially Cooke argues that items related to criminality should not be part of the measurement of psychopathy. Leaving these out means that the PCL-R corresponds more closely to Cleckley's conceptualisation of psychopathy. Cooke and others (e.g. Cooke and Michie, 2001) simply deleted items to do with criminality from the PCL-R. They found that this revision led to there being three different components or factors underlying the measure. These correspond to the first three factors of the model shown in Figure 21.4. Hare (2003) then more or less reinstated the criminality items which resulted in all of the four factors shown in Figure 21.4. The difference is that Cook's three-factor model concentrates on psychopathy in terms of personality pathology and personal dispositions whereas Hare's four-factor model involves social behaviours (including criminality) as well. Of course, this highlights the issue of what the concept of psychopathy is and what its relation to crime is. Take a look at Factor 4 in Figure 21.4 and you will see that it is measured, in part, using items about delinquency and offence versatility. So it is not surprising that psychopathy as measured by the PCL-R predicts criminality – the relationship is a tautology in this sense.

Perhaps a little futilely given Skeem and Cooke's insistence that the conceptualisation of psychopathy is a theoretical issue rather than an empirical one, Roberts and Coid (2007) chose to address some of the issues

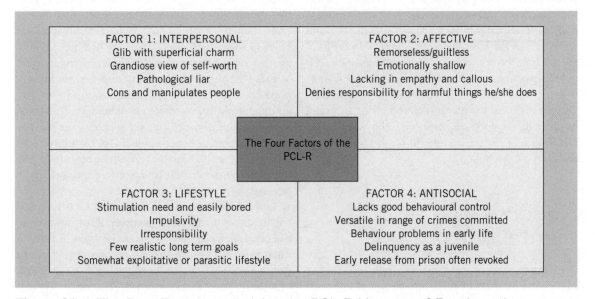

Figure 21.4 The Four Factors underlying the PCL-R Measure of Psychopathy

empirically. Their study was based on a major national sample of prisoners in England and Wales. The final sample included almost 500 male and female prisoners. They were interviewed extensively and assessed for psychopathy using Hare's PCL-R. The relationships between the overall PCL-R score, scores on Hare's four factors of psychopathy and criminal offences were explored using multiple regression. Briefly, the researchers looked at the relationships between the total score on the PCL-R and lifetime offending and controlled for the influence of Factors 1 to 3 as well as the additional variables of age, ethnicity, alcohol problems and drug problems on the relationship. So is there any relationship between the PCL-R fourth factor when the influence of the other three (undisputed) PCL-R factors is removed? The researchers found that even after all of these controls had been applied, total scores on the PCL-R were correlated with many offending categories such as robbery/blackmail, burglary and theft, violence and so forth with the exceptions of murder and manslaughter, sex offences and drug offences. A further analysis adding in the disputed Factor 4 as a further control variable resulted in virtually all of the associations between PCL-R total score and the various criminal behaviours becoming insignificant. This, to the authors, is indicative of the need for Factor 4 in the conceptualisation of psychopathy but, equally, it could be argued that the key defining features of psychopathy (the first three factors which Hare and Cook both agree upon) have no particular relevance to criminality. However, there is a problem. That is, Factor 3 (which Cooke accepts as a measure of psychopathy purely defined) is highly correlated with Factor 4 (which Cooke does not see as part of the basic conceptualisation). In terms of the research, the two were very difficult to separate. This is, perhaps, stronger evidence that criminality (Factor 4) is a necessary part of the construct of psychopathy. Of course, this is a matter of the underlying theory of psychopathy; it does not undermine the value of the PCL-R as a predictive measure in the field of forensic and criminal psychology.

Reconviction and mental illness

Of particular public concern are those groups of offenders who commit serious offences but are found to have a major mental disorder. There have been a number of high-profile cases in which it would appear that offenders seek to use provisions for dealing with offenders with such problems to avoid prison. In England, many such offenders would be detained in high-security special hospitals such as Broadmoor and Rampton. Among the criteria for such admissions would be that the offender has one of the major psychiatric classifications according to DSM-IV (see Box 21.1) and is an immediate danger to the public. The majority in such hospitals have a psychotic illness, a smaller proportion have personality disorders (e.g. borderline personality disorder, antisocial personality disorder, schizoid and paranoid), and a very small proportion have general learning disability. Jamieson and Taylor (2004) studied a complete cohort of patients discharged from special hospitals in a single year (1984). A 12-year follow-up period was possible and the releases were after the implementation of important legislation in the Mental Health Act of 1983. Some would have been discharged to another type of hospital, some would be returned to a prison following hospitalisation in the special hospital because of a major crisis in their behaviour in prison or returned to court for sentencing, and others would be discharged into the community.

Reconviction data were obtained from a variety of sources including the offenders' index and the police national computer. A quarter of patients were reconvicted of a serious offence (e.g. homicide, violence and sexual, though the commonest by far were grievous bodily harm/actual bodily harm, robbery and assault) after discharge from the special hospital. Overwhelmingly, they were in the community at the time of the reconviction (86 per cent) though, of course, others were reconvicted for offences which took place when they had moved on to another type of institution. Predictors of reconviction included having a psychopathic disorder, number of previous court appearances, younger age on discharge and amount of time spent in the community. Those with a psychopathic disorder were seven times more likely to commit a serious offence on discharge than those with a mental illness. Those with mental impairment and those with a psychopathic disorder were equally likely to be reconvicted.

In the United States, Gagliardi et al. (2004) studied recidivism in a sample of mentally ill offenders who had been released from Washington prisons in 1996–7. These prisoners were defined as mentally ill on the basis of having at least two of the following: (1) a diagnosis of a major mental illness recorded; (2) a prescription for indicative psychotropic medications; and (3) spent over

30 days on a residential mental health treatment programme while in prison. Quite clearly, this is a different sort of mentally ill sample from the one used in the special hospitals study just described. Presumably the members of the US sample were regarded as less dangerous. Also, the follow-up period in the US study was only 27–55 months. Nevertheless, after release the mentally ill offenders demonstrated high levels of arrest or charge for crime. Over three-quarters (77 per cent) came to the attention of the police in this way. Forty-one per cent of the entire sample were found guilty of a new crime, which is much the same as the 38 per cent of a similar sample of offenders who were not mentally ill. The figures for violent crimes are particularly relevant – 10 per cent of the mentally ill committed a violent felony offence, exactly the same percentage of the comparison sample of non-mentally ill offenders. Felonies are grave – that is, serious – offences.

Main points

- There seems to be little doubt that some forms of mental illness and certain patterns of symptoms elevate the likelihood of violent crime and crime in general. A major difficulty is in identifying exactly what the pattern of risk is and who among the mentally ill is the most likely to be violent and criminal. It is also difficult to form a clear impression of the risk posed by the mentally ill. Other factors such as drug or alcohol abuse seem to have much greater effects relative to mental illness simply because there are proportionately fewer mentally ill people compared with those who drink excessively. So, the relationship between mental illness and crime is relatively small and, in general, the public is at greater risk from, for example, young men and substance abusers than from schizophrenics. The latter are relatively rare in the population.

- Exactly why mental illness is associated with violence is equally difficult to explain. It is a little too simplistic to suggest that mental illness is a cause of violence. There are many reasons for this. For example, some of the drugs used to treat mental illness are known to cause aggression. Furthermore, the extent of the relationship between mental illness and violence can change with changes in social policy dealing with the mentally ill. With the use of care in the community, the risk to the public may increase.

- The risk factors that predict the likelihood that a mentally ill person will commit a violent offence are increasingly understood. Factors which affect the pattern, apart from type of diagnosis, include whether antisocial behaviour began in childhood or much later and hallucinations and delusions. The mentally ill may have an elevated risk of being victims of violence though whether this is the consequence of their aggressive behaviour is not known.

Further reading

This is covered in general in:

McMurran, M., Khalifa, N. and Gibbon, S. (2009) *Forensic Mental Health* Cullompton: Willan.

Shea, P. (1996) *Psychiatry in Court: Psychiatric Reports and Psychiatric Evidence in Court Proceedings* Cullompton: Federation Press.

And a good account of the problems of researching mental illness and crime is at the following website:

Arboleda-Florez, J., Holley, H.L. and Crisanti, A. (1996) *Mental Health and Violence: Proof or Stereotype?* http://www.phac-aspc.gc.ca/mh-sm/pubs/mental_illness/index-eng.php

Visit our website at www.pearsoned.co.uk/howitt for self-test and essay questions, annotated further reading, audio interviews with researchers in the field, weblinks and more information on becoming a forensic psychologist.

Chapter 22

Mental, personality and intellectual problems in court

Overview

- Courts make decisions partly on the basis of certain legal requirements related to certain psychiatric and intellectual states. The nature of the issues varies according to the matter in question. Competency to stand trial refers to mental state at the time of trial whereas, for example, the psychological state of the defendant at the time of the crime may be mitigating circumstances relevant to sentencing (e.g. diminished responsibility/capacity and insanity pleas).

- Defendants have to be competent at the time of their trial. The definition of this depends on the legal jurisdiction in question and the differences are often quite subtle. Typically, a fundamental requirement is that defendants should be able to partake in their defence (with the aid of a lawyer) and understand the court procedure. There is evidence that substantial minorities of juvenile offenders seem to fail the competency requirement when assessed by a standardised test of competency.

- The most familiar competence assessment test is the MacArthur Competence Assessment Tool for Criminal Adjudication which deals with the American standard of competence. Nevertheless, it is more likely that competence will be assessed by judgements of clinicians such as psychiatrists and psychologists. There is evidence that a psychotic illness diagnosis, non-psychotic diagnosis and being unemployed are predictive of an incompetence assessment by the clinician. Other research suggests that, generally, psychiatrists are unaffected by legally irrelevant factors when coming to their decisions. For example, having had a spell of time in a psychiatric hospital is not relevant to current competency to stand trial but sometimes can affect decisions.

- Individuals with learning disability are often vulnerable and may be subject to various forms of sexual abuse, for example. As such, their testimony may be essential for justice to be done. There is evidence that they can supply good quality evidence and can make legally competent witnesses. However, the style of questioning adopted should be open ended as closed or leading questioning can lead to poor-quality evidence. In court, too, little appropriate questioning seems to be employed and judges seem reluctant to intervene to support these witnesses when they are giving testimony.

- Psychopaths do not always manifest the criminality which is frequently used to characterise them. As such, since the condition may be adaptive, it is difficult to equate it with the idea of a dysfunctional mental disease. The McNaughten rule suggests that a person is not criminally responsible if at the time of the crime they did not know the nature and quality of the act they did. Despite this, some experts believe that psychopathy should be regarded as a reason for more punishment not less. Others argue that psychopaths do not pass through crucial stages of moral development which leads them to be incapable of knowing right from wrong; thus punishment is inappropriate since they cannot learn from it. This does not mean that they should go free but should be treated appropriately to their condition.

Introduction

There are a number of circumstances in which a defendant's psychological state may be taken into account in court. These do not necessarily apply at the same stages of a trial. For example, competence to stand trial needs to be considered prior to the start of the trial as this decision determines what happens next. The reasons for judging a person incompetent to stand trial may be to do with poor cognitive functioning or mental illness. Competence to stand trial has nothing to do with the reason why an individual committed a criminal act, it refers solely to a person's situation at the time of their trial. If someone is judged incompetent to stand trial, it does not mean that they will go free but merely that they will be processed differently – for example, they might be sent to a psychiatric facility.

Sentencing decisions may be influenced by psychological factors which were present at the time of the offence. That is, there are some psychological factors which might work in mitigation of the sentence. Of course, simply because an individual has a psychological condition is not necessarily a reason not to punish or punish more leniently. Courts of law are not psychologists' consulting rooms; arguments appropriate in court are not necessarily ones that would be appropriate in a psychology lecture. Consequently, there are controversies, as we shall see, about the standing of diagnoses such as psychopathy as a mitigating factor. Indeed, some argue that psychopathy is an aggravating factor and may warrant greater punishment.

There are actually rather more points in the criminal justice system where the individual's mental state may be considered (Gunn and Buchanan, 2006):

- during the police investigation
- when making the plea of guilt or otherwise

- during the trial
- when deciding the sentence.

Figure 22.1 summarises Gunn and Buchanan's argument about differences between the United Kingdom and the USA.

Competence/capacity to stand trial

Many different criminal justice systems require that defendants should be able to contribute effectively to their own defence (Hollin and Swaffer, 1995). Competency requirements to assist in one's own defence during legal proceedings date back to the fourteenth century and possibly earlier. Historically, common law courts refused to try those who were incompetent because of mental illness or mental defects (Otto, 2006). Ultimately it is the accused and not lawyers who makes the decisions relevant to the trial. The requirement of competence is necessary in adversarial systems of justice. In these, winning in court is the key objective of the court appearance. As such, the opposing sides of prosecution and defence line up against each other, much as in a battle. Should the defendant be a hapless individual incapable of understanding and coping with this affray, then is it possible for him or her to have a fair trial? It is clearly important for the public credibility of the legal system that their trials are fair, that the legal process is dignified and demonstrates integrity, and that the defendant understands the reason why they are being punished (Zapf and Roesch, 2001). A 'reasonable and legitimate' justice process would be severely compromised without the requirement of competence to stand trial. In contrast, the inquisitorial

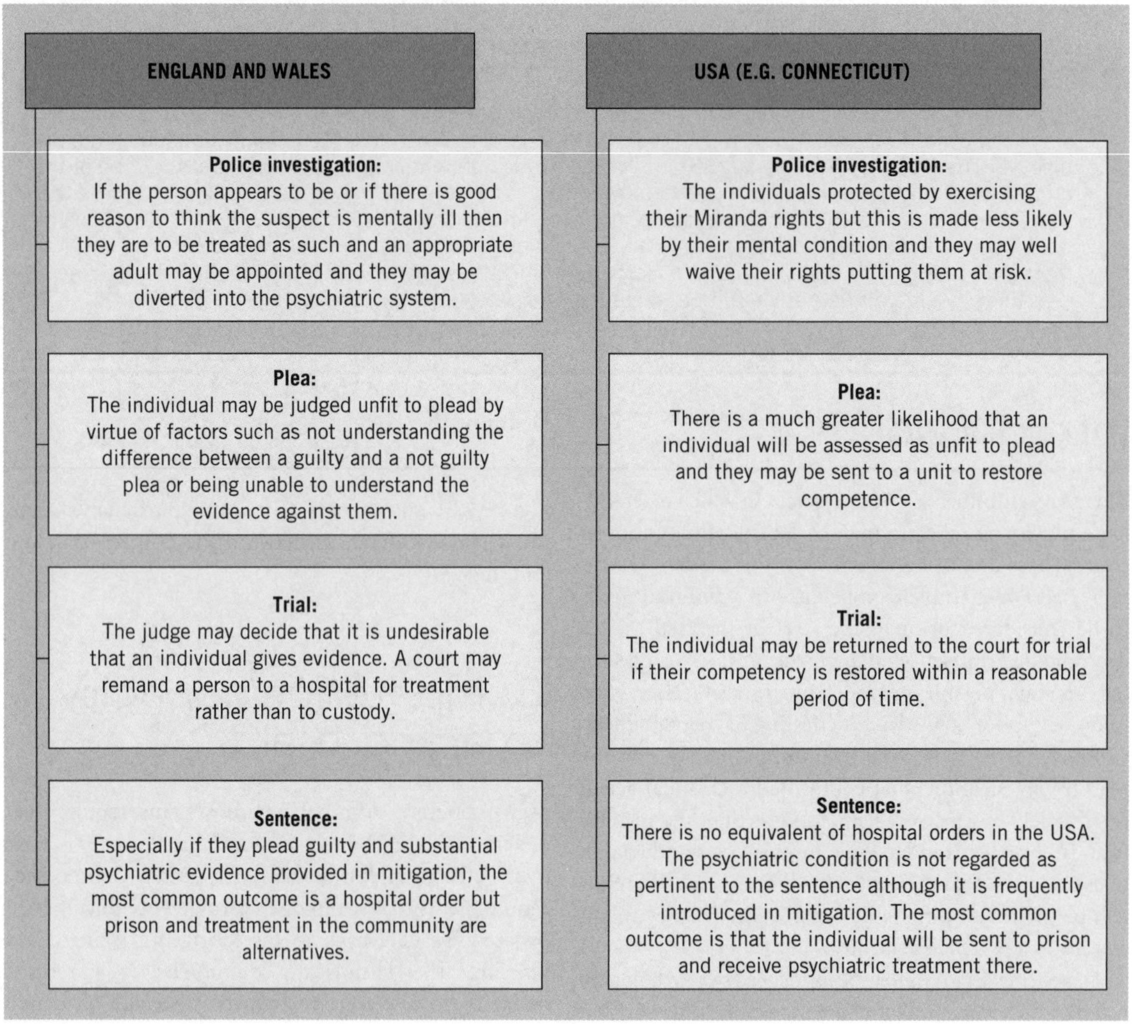

ENGLAND AND WALES	USA (E.G. CONNECTICUT)
Police investigation: If the person appears to be or if there is good reason to think the suspect is mentally ill then they are to be treated as such and an appropriate adult may be appointed and they may be diverted into the psychiatric system.	**Police investigation:** The individuals protected by exercising their Miranda rights but this is made less likely by their mental condition and they may well waive their rights putting them at risk.
Plea: The individual may be judged unfit to plead by virtue of factors such as not understanding the difference between a guilty and a not guilty plea or being unable to understand the evidence against them.	**Plea:** There is a much greater likelihood that an individual will be assessed as unfit to plead and they may be sent to a unit to restore competence.
Trial: The judge may decide that it is undesirable that an individual gives evidence. A court may remand a person to a hospital for treatment rather than to custody.	**Trial:** The individual may be returned to the court for trial if their competency is restored within a reasonable period of time.
Sentence: Especially if they plead guilty and substantial psychiatric evidence provided in mitigation, the most common outcome is a hospital order but prison and treatment in the community are alternatives.	**Sentence:** There is no equivalent of hospital orders in the USA. The psychiatric condition is not regarded as pertinent to the sentence although it is frequently introduced in mitigation. The most common outcome is that the individual will be sent to prison and receive psychiatric treatment there.

Figure 22.1 Possible relevance of mental health considerations at the various stages of the criminal justice system

systems employed in many parts of Continental Europe and elsewhere involve much more of a guided search for the 'truth' by the inquiring judge. So, in the inquisitorial court system, the issue of fitness is not so important as it is in the adversarial system. It is noteworthy, then, that the inquisitorial legal systems of Austria and Denmark, for example, have no fitness-to-stand-trial criteria. As might be expected, psychiatric reports may be called for if there appear to be any problems with the mental state of the accused that may help inform the judgment of the court.

The issue of competence is more frequently raised in some jurisdictions than in others. Competence is a commoner issue in the United States than in the United Kingdom, for example (Hollin and Swaffer, 1995). In England and Wales, the annual numbers of defendants judged unfit to stand trial is very small – around 20 cases per year. This is not because there are few offenders with poor capacities, but because many would be taken out of the justice system at an earlier stage under mental health legislation. In other countries, such as the United States, the competence to stand trial decision is much more common. For example, Bonnie and Grisso (2000) estimate that there are about 60,000 competency evaluations in the United States annually. Sometimes competence to stand trial is referred to as the capacity to stand trial.

The following case from the United States demonstrates graphically some of the problems associated with the issue of competence:

> Andy was just 11 when he started hanging around with the teenage gang members in his neighborhood. They used him as a lookout when they sold drugs . . . until one drug deal turned violent and two people were shot. That's how Andy ended up facing a charge of murder. The prosecutor offered a deal: Andy could admit he was there, testify against the others, and face a few years in juvenile detention. Otherwise he would be transferred to adult court and, if found guilty, spend a much longer time in detention and prison. Andy had just a few minutes to make a decision that would determine the rest of his life. He chose to take the risk: he would go to trial.
>
> (Steinberg, 2003)

The psychologist who assessed Andy's competence to stand trial asked him whether he understood what would happen if he was found guilty of the crime. 'I'll go to prison for a long, long time,' was his reply. He was assessed a few weeks later by another person and asked the identical question. Andy gave much the same reply but he was then asked to explain what he had said. His reply was that 'It's like when you do something bad and your mother sends you to your room for the whole weekend.' Andy seems not to understand the nature of the process of which he was part, since his conception of imprisonment is inadequate. This is not an exceptional circumstance. Steinberg (2003) reports the findings of a study of the competence of young Americans to stand trial using a standardised competence assessment procedure. Thirty per cent of 11- to 13-year-olds were not competent to stand trial, as were 19 per cent of 14- and 15-year-olds and 12 per cent of later adolescents and young adults. This is of major importance in a country such as the United States where increasingly young people have been tried in adult rather than juvenile courts.

There is a concept in English law that dates back to the fourteenth century and is also found in Australian law, for example. *Doli incapax* refers to the assumption that children below a certain age are incapable of being evil, which may be equated with an incapability of committing a crime because they do not know the difference between right and wrong. *Doli incapax* is a presumption and it does not mean that children cannot be tried for crimes but it has to be established that they did know what they were doing when they committed the offence. Without using the *doli incapax* phrase, other countries may have ages below which children may not be tried in an adult court. This varies substantially from legislature to legislature.

The United Kingdom

The court, prior to the commencement of the trial proper, assesses competence. The criteria vary according to jurisdiction. The criteria in the United Kingdom determining whether a defendant is fit to stand trial include the abilities to:

- comprehend the details of the evidence;
- follow court proceedings;
- instruct lawyers effectively;
- understand that jurors may be challenged (objected to);
- understand the meaning and implications of the charges (Grubin, 1996a).

A number of matters are important (Grubin, 1996a):

- Competence is judged by the jury in the United Kingdom (elsewhere it may be an issue for the judge solely).
- The consequences of being found unfit to stand trial are drastic. In the United Kingdom, the defendant may be compulsorily detained in some sort of hospital for indeterminate periods of time. Given this serious outcome, the issue of fitness to stand trial or competence is far more frequent for trials of extremely serious offences. In the United Kingdom, modern legislation requires the following. After the decision that the defendant is not competent to stand trial, a hearing is held to determine whether it is likely that the defendant committed the offence. If unlikely or disproved, then the accused will be discharged. This ensures that the judgement of incompetence for the innocent is not followed by extremely serious consequences.
- Poor mental functioning is not the main reason for classifying an offender as unfit to stand trial. British evidence (Grubin, 1996b) indicates that the majority are classified as having schizophrenia.

The United States and Canada

Recent court rulings in Canada and the United States have established that decisions to waive counsel, decisions to confess and decisions to plead guilty all require a certain and invariant level of competency, which is unaffected by particular circumstances (Coles, 2004). In some parts of the United States, expert witnesses can only advise the court about an individual's abilities relevant to their competency – not on the matter of their competency to stand trial directly. In the United States, competence to stand trial, according to the US Supreme Court, is whether (the defendant) has 'sufficient present ability to consult with his lawyer with a reasonable degree of rational understanding' – and whether he has a 'rational as well as factual understanding of the proceedings' against him. This standard was established in the Supreme Court ruling of *Dusky v. United States (1960)* (Heilbrun *et al.*, 1996). In practical terms, competence to stand trial requires that the accused can comprehend the charges against them and understand what the judge, jury and lawyers do. Variants of this definition of competence are used by most states though in these no mental conditions are defined as limiting this capacity. The courts may take the advice of professionals in the field but ultimately it is a decision of the courts and not experts. Furthermore, a defendant may be competent to be tried on one charge but incompetent to be tried on another. For example, drunken driving might need a lower competence level than a complex case of fraud (Otto, 2006). However, in Canada, there is a different competency that does not include the criterion of rationality. Zapf and Roesch (2001) suggest that the Canadian standard only requires the defendant to be able to communicate with and understand their lawyer.

Assessing competence is a specialist skill and there is a risk that different practitioners would not agree on an individual's competence to stand trial. There are, of course, guidelines to help establish common standards in the United States (e.g. Baker, Lichtenberg and Moye, 1998). However, one important development in the United States is the *MacArthur Competence Assessment Tool for Criminal Adjudication*. This is a standardised instrument to assess fitness to participate in legal proceedings within the US legal system (Otto *et al.*, 1998). There are other MacArthur competence measures (e.g. for competence to agree to medical treatment). The MacArthur charity funded the *MacArthur Research Network on Mental Health and the Law* which developed this competence measure. The assessor using the competence assessment tool presents a short description of a crime and consequent events. The administrator then asks a series of questions concerning court procedures, the roles of

various people (e.g. the jury), and the reasoning processes underlying the decisions made in court.

Strictly speaking, the *MacArthur Competence Assessment Tool for Criminal Adjudication* is applicable only to the United States. It may assess people incompetent to stand trial who would be competent in other jurisdictions. Zapf and Roesch (2001) compared the *Fitness Interview Test (FIT)* with the *MacArthur Competence Assessment Tool*. The FIT test measures competence in terms of Canadian legal definitions whereas the MacArthur tool measures competence in American terms. Both measures were given to a sample of males remanded in a forensic psychiatry institute. Although the two measures correlated moderately well, it was clear that the MacArthur measure was more likely to classify individuals as unfit to plead than the measure based on the Canadian standard of competence. This confirms that the American criteria for competence are stricter than the Canadian. This is a reminder, if a further one is needed, that forensic and criminal psychologists must be aware of the legal codes and practices of the jurisdiction in which they operate.

Since there is clearly a degree of discretion in any clinical assessments and in assessments of competency to stand trial in particular, is the process of decision making a biased one? It is important to note that clinical assessments of competence to stand trial and court decisions concerning competency concur highly. Of course, such a high degree of overlap may simply reflect that clinicians and courts share the same biases. Cooper and Zapf (2003) looked at the question of how competency decisions are made by clinicians by using a variety of demographic, clinical and criminological measures extracted from files on over 400 individuals assessed for competency. Only about a fifth of those assessed had been previously classified as unfit to stand trial. Those with a psychotic disorder (e.g. schizophrenia) or with a major non-psychotic disorder were much more likely to be classified as unfit to stand trial. However, those who had an alcohol or a drug-related disorder were less likely to be deemed 'unfit to stand trial'. Four variables were strong predictors of the classification as incompetent when the researchers tried to develop a statistical model of the decisions. These were psychotic diagnosis, non-psychotic major diagnosis and non-psychotic minor illness diagnosis – all clinical dimensions – together with unemployment. Based on this model, it was possible to predict the actual classification of 89 per cent of the competent cases and 47 per cent of the incompetent cases. Thus prediction was substantially superior for the competent cases. The authors argue that because the clinical variables are so important in the decision-making model, there is no evidence of bias in the judgements. This, however, assumes that there are no biases in these clinical assessments in the first place. Furthermore, there are a lot of instances where these seemingly rational judgements fail to apply – for example, 53 per cent of the incompetent cases could not be predicted on the basis of the clinical variables plus unemployment.

Some research provides a more reserved interpretation. Plotnick, Porter and Bagby (1998) used an experimental design. Psychiatrists rated a number of vignettes relevant to fitness evaluations. In some conditions, the vignettes actually contained legally irrelevant information which should not be considered as part of the evaluation of fitness to plead. These potentially biasing but legally irrelevant variables were a previous psychiatric hospitalisation (or not), the nature of the current crime (violent versus petty larceny) and prior legal involvement (six prior arrests versus no prior arrests). In addition, there were several conditions that were legally pertinent to fitness evaluations. For example, the unfit condition involved the defendant having psychotic symptoms in abundance and being incapable of communicating with their lawyer. The research findings suggested that overwhelmingly the fit and unfit categories were correctly used. Over 70 per cent of both the fit and unfit vignettes were correctly classified. Nevertheless, for the legally fit vignettes, sometimes legally irrelevant factors affected the psychiatrists' judgements. The psychiatrists tended to misclassify legally fit individuals if they had been charged with a violent crime and had a lot of previous psychiatric admissions to hospital but no previous arrests. In other words, classification as fit or unfit to plead could be affected by legally irrelevant information but, nevertheless, the psychiatrists tended to make correct classifications in general.

For anyone wishing to understand the similarities and differences between the British and USA systems, Gunn and Buchanan (2006) describe how a fictitious case would be treated in the two countries.

BOX 22.1 Forensic psychology in action

Mental illness in court

Mental illness is common among non-convicted and convicted prisoners. Indeed, there may be more persons with serious mental illnesses in prisons than in mental hospitals (Blaauw, Roesch and Kerkhof, 2000). Furthermore, current prevalence rates for any psychiatric disorder for those in European prison systems have been estimated as anywhere between 37 per cent and 89 per cent according to the study in question. Not surprisingly, then, mental states may be significant in relation to certain trials. Issues related to mental illness and limited cognitive functioning may influence the course of a trial. This can be both in terms of the requirements of proof and mitigation of punishment. Two Latin phrases cover the requirements of proof in a criminal trial: (1) *actus reus* and (2) *mens rea* under British law. These are not universal to all legal systems, of course, but they are important concepts in their own right:

- *Actus reus*: this is the requirement in some jurisdictions that the prosecution needs to show that a crime has indeed been committed and, further, that the accused was the person who committed that crime. This may be a matter for psychologists since forensic practitioners may be asked, for example, to evaluate the confession evidence that implicated the accused. The self-confession may have been obtained unfairly or from a person incapable of understanding the police caution, for example.

- *Mens rea*: this is the legal requirement in some jurisdictions that the accused actually understood that what they did was wrong or that they had behaved recklessly. Intentionality or recklessness is the important factor. Actually, this requirement does not apply to all crimes. Some offences are *strict liability* to which matters of recklessness or intentionality are inapplicable. Road traffic

BOX 22.1 (continued)

offences are often strict liability offences (see Ward, 1997). Lack of criminal intent can be used in strict liability cases, but only in mitigation.

Diminished responsibility (diminished capacity in the United States) is an excuse offered by the defence that although the defendant broke the law they are not criminally liable since their mental functioning was impaired in some way. An obvious situation in which diminished responsibility might apply is where the defendant is intellectually very challenged. There are other defences such as insanity that may be very similar. However, the choice between diminished responsibility and insanity defences may depend on the jurisdiction in question. Beck (1995) points out that in the United Kingdom, the defence of *insanity* had hardly been used. This was because disposal after a decision of not guilty by reason of insanity meant indefinite diversion into a mental hospital until the new legislation in 1991. Legislation has changed things to allow commitment to a mental hospital for a limited time or, even, release back to the community given certain provisions. *Diminished responsibility* is used as a defence only in murder trials since, if accepted, murder becomes the less serious crime of manslaughter. The only sentence for murder is a mandatory life sentence. There are a variety of options for manslaughter – probation, prison or hospital. In the United States, the use of the insanity defence is also rare and where used is rarely successful. So less than 1 per cent of felony charges would meet with an insanity defence and acquittals on the grounds of insanity occurred in about 1 in 400 felony cases (Lymburner and Roesch, 1999).

Defences of insanity and diminished responsibility/ capacity (among others) may be supported by psychiatric or psychological evidence of mental disorder in the accused. This is true also of the crime of infanticide, which is a lesser form of homicide. The distinction between insanity and diminished responsibility, according to a survey of psychiatrists (Mitchell, 1997), is not something that causes difficulties for the majority of practitioners. It is also worthwhile noting

that there is some question as to whether psychiatric assessment that an individual demonstrated diminished responsibility actually is acted on by courts when sentencing. Ribeaud and Manzoni (2004) suggest that taking into account the legal seriousness of the crime, psychiatric assessment of diminished responsibility slightly *increases* the likely sentence in the Swiss cases they studied. This is clearly an issue about which more research is needed.

In Britain (as in other countries such as the United States), an offender may be placed on probation subject to the condition that they undergo psychiatric treatment. Treatment is voluntary and those who refuse it will be disposed of otherwise by the criminal justice system. In different countries, different standards apply about the involuntary treatment of the mentally ill. The British allow the mentally ill (and mental illness is not defined by law or regulation) to be identified solely by psychiatric opinion. Forced medication for up to three months is also allowed. This is different from the United States where substantial legislation surrounds any attempt by the authorities to deny citizens their liberty (Beck, 1995).

In the United Kingdom, recent legal provisions limit the 'right to silence' which means that a jury may interpret the silence of a witness in whatever way it wishes (Criminal Justice and Public Order Act, 1994). If it appears that the mental or physical condition of the accused means that if they do not give evidence, then the court may not make such an inference (Grubin, 1996a). This is clearly an area in which forensic experts may be expected to provide evidence on the mental condition of the accused.

Temporary psychiatric states are particularly problematic in court. For example, dissociation is the term for the experience in which the individual ceases to be fully aware of their self, time or the external environment. Dissociation may be a fairly normal everyday experience such as when the indvidual becomes lost in a television programme so that the sense of the passage of time is lost and with it a sense of the surroundings. Dissociation may be a feature of post-traumatic stress disorder, for example (see Chapter 4). Bert Stone murdered his wife in Canada in 1993. Part of his account of the murder is as follows:

> I sat there with my head down while she's still yelling at me that I'm nothing but a piece of shit and that when she had talked to the police, that she had told them lies, that I was abusing her, and that they were getting all the paperwork ready to have me arrested, and that all she had to do was phone them, and once they had me arrested, that she was going to get a court order so that I wouldn't be allowed back onto our property and that I would have to go and live with my mother and run my business from there, that she was going to quit working and she was just going to stay in the house with her children and that I would have to pay her alimony and child support . . . Well, she just continued on and she just said that she couldn't stand to listen to me whistle, that every time I touched her, she felt sick, that I was a lousy fuck and that I had a little penis and that she's never going to fuck me again, and I'm just sitting there with my head down; and by this time, she's kneeling on the seat and she's yelling this in my face.
>
> (McSherry, 2004, p. 447)

His wife was killed by 47 stab wounds to her body. Stone was unaware of the moments during which he stabbed his wife repeatedly. Bert Stone describes how his wife's voice faded away and a 'whooshing' sensation enveloped him. The defence argued that under extreme provocation, Stone demonstrated a degree of loss of self-control 'and the dissociation which resulted in automatism was the result of extreme levels of external stress'. The jury decided that Stone was provoked, which led to a partial loss of self-control though they did not accept that he was experiencing dissociation, which would have made his actions involuntary.

Psychopaths and mental illness

Criminal jurisdictions commonly employ rules in order to protect some offenders suffering from insanity. The M'Naghten or McNaughten case of 1843 led to a rule to protect such individuals in the United Kingdom. The McNaughten rule indicates that a person is not criminally responsible if:

> at the time of the committing of the act, the party accused was labouring under such a defect of reason from disease of the mind, as not to know the nature and quality of the act he was doing; or if he did know it, he did not know he was doing what was wrong.

This is a difficult rule for psychologists because it promulgates a nineteenth-century view of mental illness as a disease and a defect. Not all, perhaps not many, psychologists subscribe to this medical view of mental illness. The American Law Institute proposed a different rule to accommodate the mentally ill offender in the 1960s:

> a person is not responsible for criminal conduct if at the time of such conduct as a result of mental disease or defect he lacks substantial capacity to appreciate the criminality of his conduct or to conform his conduct to the requirements of law.

This 'rule' also causes problems since it promotes the idea that the bad can be excused as mad. To offset this, the American Psychiatric Association offered the Bonnie rule in 1983 which identifies a person as mentally ill if:

> as a result of mental disease or defect he was unable to appreciate the wrongfulness of his conduct at the time of the offence.

This seems to hark back to the original McNaughten rule.

The question of 'mad or bad?' is particularly difficult in relation to the concept of psychopathy. Just what is a psychopath? The answer to this question has changed constantly over the years. Hodgins (1997) suggests that there are a number of reliable research findings concerning psychopaths. In particular, there is physiological evidence to suggest that when threatened with a noxious/unpleasant stimulus, the psychopath shows few or no physiological signs. Thus the indicators of emotional arousal (e.g. skin conductivity or heart rate) hardly or do not change. Psychopaths generally fail to anticipate emotional noxious events. So they might learn to avoid touching a hot stove through experience of touching one; they do not learn to avoid criminal activity through anticipating the aversive consequences of being arrested and imprisoned.

One important debate concerns the following:

- Is psychopathy a dimension of personality along which people can be placed in terms of degrees of psychopathy?
- Is psychopathology a discrete unit or class when applied to a person? (The term 'taxon' is proposed for such a discrete class.)

Some have proposed that psychopathy is not a mental disorder but a cheating lifestyle that has evolved over history (Rice, 1997). The characteristics of psychopaths suggest that they should make excellent cheats – things such as glibness and charm, pathological lying and so forth. The idea is that psychopathy is adaptive and facilitative in many environments. So some highly successful business people are psychopaths and not involved in the violence of the typical psychopath. Perhaps a violent and hostile upbringing leads some psychopaths down the violent route.

It has been argued by Hare (1998) that psychopathy is the most important clinical psychological concept relevant to the criminal justice system. He also claims to be able to assess it with a high degree of certainty. Hence the ironic quote from one prisoner talking to Hare: 'So what if 80% of criminals with a high score on your psycho test, or whatever the hell it's called, get nabbed for a violent crime when they get out. What about the other 20% who don't screw up? You're flushing *our* lives down the drain' (p. 101). Hare's conception of the term psychopath is relatively exact and so his measure cannot be used to assess psychopathy in terms of anyone else's conception of what psychopathy is (Hare, 1998). This is very important in connection with any forensic use of the scale. For example, in one case, a forensic psychiatrist claimed a very high score on Hare's Psychopathy Checklist Revised (PCL-R score) for an offender using his own personal understanding of the term. A proper examination by trained personnel found the man to have a very much lower score. The judge directed the dismissal of the psychiatrist's evidence in this case. According to Hare (1998):

- Psychopaths readily engage in predatory, dispassionate and instrumental violence (p. 104).
- The violence of psychopaths is remorseless, frequently motivated by vengeance, greed, anger, money and retribution.
- Psychopaths tend to attack strangers.
- Psychopaths are responsible for half of the deaths of police personnel who die on duty.
- Probably 1 per cent of the general population is a psychopath.
- Psychopaths are much commoner than this in prison populations.

Antisocial personality disorder and psychopathy are sometimes confused even in professional writings. According to Fine and Kennett (2004), antisocial personality disorder is very common in prison populations at somewhere between 50–80 per cent of prisoners. In contrast, psychopathy is present in 30 per cent of the forensic population. The antisocial lifestyle is only part of the diagnosis of psychopathy but it is the defining feature of antisocial personality disorder. Furthermore, neither is Hare's concept of psychopathy the same as *antisocial personality disorder* as discussed in the *Diagnostic and Statistical Manuals* of the American Psychiatric Association (1987, 2000). Hare's ideas about the nature of psychopathy are discussed more extensively in Chapter 27. A few people classified as manifesting antisocial personality disorder can also be classified as psychopaths. The vast majority of the research on psychopaths has been carried out on offender populations (as opposed to clinical populations, for example) so it is not surprising to find that the concept of psychopath is regarded as associated with antisocial behaviours. The *Diagnostic and Statistical Manual of the American Psychiatric Association IV* (DSM-IV) published in 1987 deals with antisocial behaviours in terms of the diagnostic category antisocial personality disorder.

Blackburn (1995a) suggests that the question of whether psychopaths are bad or mad is nonsensical. Psychopaths can be both mad and bad, or just mad or just bad. Mad and bad are not opposites, they are different. Reduced to its elements, the real question for the forensic psychologist is whether the presence of a personality disorder should affect the eventual disposal of the offender. The essential problem, for forensic and criminal psychology, is that the concept of psychopath brings together a personality concept with deviant and criminal activities. This fails to differentiate between the following two distinct things:

- the medical/psychiatric state of psychopathy;
- the behaviour which amounts to its symptoms.

Despite the concept of *antisocial personality disorder* being listed in the DSM-IV, is it only possible to recognise the disorder by the antisocial and criminal behaviours that its victims possess? If so, then how can one differentiate between the different causes of those behaviours: ASPD, unemployment, poor parenting and so forth?

According to Blackburn (1995a), the English Mental Health Act category of psychopathic disorder is similar. The only way in which psychopathic disorder can be defined is using the symptoms of serious antisocial conduct that are also the consequence of having psychopathic disorder. Blackburn, in his research, noted that legally defined psychopaths are a varied (heterogeneous) selection of individuals. This observation strengthens the view that the antisocial behaviour of legally defined psychopaths is not dependent on any single psychological state. Furthermore, there appears to be a great difference between:

- legally defined psychopaths confined to special hospitals;
- psychopaths defined psychologically by the Hare Psychopathy Checklist.

The latter includes characteristics such as superficial charm, unreliability, lack of remorse and egocentricity. Blackburn suggests that no more than a quarter of the psychopaths studied by him would be also defined as psychopaths using Hare's Psychopathy Checklist.

For Blackburn, the ultimate question appears to be whether or not a disorder of personality, such as psychopathy, as is apparent in terms of modern psychological research, can also be regarded as a mental disorder. The *Diagnostic and Statistical Manual of the American Psychiatric Association* (DSM III-R) defines a mental disorder as a syndrome: 'that is associated with present distress or disability or with significantly increased risk of suffering death, pain, disability, or an important loss of freedom.' Thus many have taken the view that psychopathy should not be a mitigating factor in court but, instead, should be treated as an aggravating factor perhaps deserving of greater levels of punishment. This is a view expressed by Robert Hare, the leading researcher

in the field of psychopathy, too, given that psychopaths show callousness, indifference to the rights of others and lack remorse for what they do. In this way, the diagnosis seems to lack any mitigating aspects (Fine and Kennett, 2004). However, Fine and Kennett take the view that there is considerable evidence that psychopaths do not pass through crucial stages in normal moral development and perhaps can be considered as not criminally responsible in the sense that they have not got a proper understanding that what they do is wrong or immoral. This does not mean that they go free, it merely means that to punish them is wrong as they cannot respond to punishment. Nevertheless, detaining psychopaths proven to have committed serious crimes serves as self-defence for society.

The concepts of psychopathic personality and personality disorder have been dominant aspects to consider when trying to decide who are dangerous offenders. However, use of the terms has been inconsistent and Blackburn (2007) describes the situation as 'confusing'. Sometimes the two concepts appear to be interchangeable but the development of Axis II classification in the APA diagnostic manual has resulted in a clearer separation. As stated in Box 21.1, in DSM-IV the psychiatric diagnoses are sorted into five different levels known as axes. Axis I refers to clinical disorders and includes mental disorders, such as depression, schizophrenia, bipolar disorder and anxiety disorders. Axis II refers to pervasive or personality conditions such as borderline personality disorder, antisocial personality disorder and mild mental retardation. Personality disorder is more relevant to the mental health system whereas psychopathy is more relevant to the criminal literature.

Although psychopathy literally means psychologically damaged, its usage refers to someone who is antisocial or socially damaging (Blackburn, 2007). DSM-IV criteria for antisocial personality disorder are lists of 'socially undesirable activities' rather than personality characteristics of the sort that the PCL-R deals with. Psychopathy, as such, is not a category in the *Diagnostic and Statistical Manual.*

Some have said that antisocial personality disorder and psychopathy are just different ways of describing the same thing. In contrast, Blackburn suggests 'Defining a disorder of personality in terms of social deviance confounds the dependent with the independent variable and precludes any understanding of the relationship' (p. 10).

BOX 22.2 Forensic psychology in action

Victims and learning disability

The level of intellectual functioning of those with learning disability can be extremely low. Three-quarters of learning disability individuals in Texas replied 'yes' when they were asked 'Does it snow here in summer?' Despite the fact that none of them was Chinese, 44 per cent said that they were Chinese when asked 'Are you Chinese?' (Siegelman *et al.*, 1981).

Individuals who suffer mental or intellectual disabilities (the term mental retardation is generally considered unacceptable nowadays) amount to 1 per cent of Western populations. Competence to stand trial may be separated conceptually from competence in terms of giving evidence. Some countries allow evidence from people with limited intellectual ability without requiring them to swear an oath (Kebbell and Hatton, 1999). Nevertheless, the full picture suggests that there is a serious risk that people with limited intellectual powers will be served extremely poorly by the criminal justice system. See Figure 22.2 for more information about

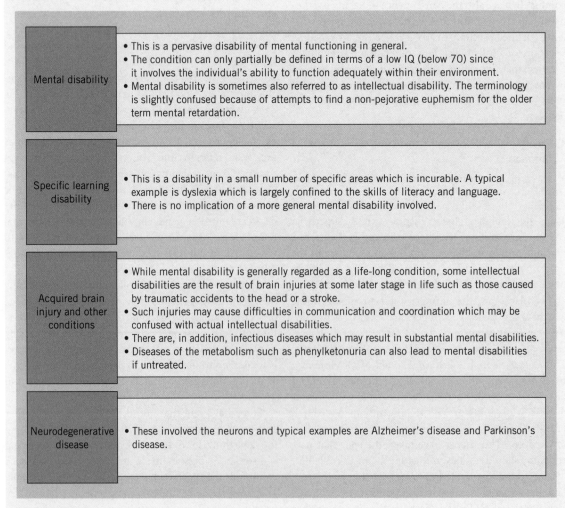

Mental disability	• This is a pervasive disability of mental functioning in general. • The condition can only partially be defined in terms of a low IQ (below 70) since it involves the individual's ability to function adequately within their environment. • Mental disability is sometimes also referred to as intellectual disability. The terminology is slightly confused because of attempts to find a non-pejorative euphemism for the older term mental retardation.
Specific learning disability	• This is a disability in a small number of specific areas which is incurable. A typical example is dyslexia which is largely confined to the skills of literacy and language. • There is no implication of a more general mental disability involved.
Acquired brain injury and other conditions	• While mental disability is generally regarded as a life-long condition, some intellectual disabilities are the result of brain injuries at some later stage in life such as those caused by traumatic accidents to the head or a stroke. • Such injuries may cause difficulties in communication and coordination which may be confused with actual intellectual disabilities. • There are, in addition, infectious diseases which may result in substantial mental disabilities. • Diseases of the metabolism such as phenylketonuria can also lead to mental disabilities if untreated.
Neurodegenerative disease	• These involved the neurons and typical examples are Alzheimer's disease and Parkinson's disease.

Figure 22.2 Varieties of intellectual disability

different types of mental disability. According to Willner (2011), people with intellectual disabilities experience in the criminal justice system organisations among the least adapted to their needs. They are less integrated into courts of law and so forth than any other part of their lies. In particular, they are victimised by crime in ways more extreme than other people:

- People with intellectual disabilities are a high-risk group and are more likely to become victims by a factor of two and possibly as much as ten times. In particular, they have a greater risk of suffering personal crimes such as assault and robbery. They often have little property which may account for them having a much smaller greater relative risk of suffering property crimes.
- The crime which people with intellectual disabilities suffer is rather less likely to be reported to the police than that against people in general. The likelihood of reporting is lower for those with greater intellectual disabilities. The figures for non-reporting of sexual assaults may be as high as 97 per cent.
- They are also systematically excluded from the criminal justice system even when crimes against them have been reported. The probable reason for this is that they are assumed to lack competency to act as reliable witnesses.

Things have improved in general, though. For example, in the United Kingdom vulnerable adults can give evidence using closed-circuit video systems and clear guidelines for the investigation of allegations of abuse against them. Nevertheless, substantial disadvantages persist (Willner, 2011).

There are other reasons why people with an intellectual disability may witness more crime than people in general. The practice of deinstitutionalisation, which ensures that many of them live in poor neighbourhoods, puts them at increased risk of being victimised by others in the community. Sexual assaults on people with a mental impairment can often only be prosecuted if they can provide evidence in court or in interview (Kebbell and Hatton, 1999). The quality of witness evidence from people with mental impairment varies but nevertheless may be valuable. Gudjonsson, Murphy and Clare (2000) assessed approximately

50 men and women residents at two private residential homes. These were clients incapable of surviving independently. There were allegations of ill treatment by members of the staff. These allegations were eventually proven in court. As part of the assessment the following were administered:

- the Wechsler Adult Intelligence Scale;
- the Gudjonsson Suggestibility Scale, which measures memory, suggestibility and confabulation;
- a measure of acquiescence specially developed for the purpose.

Pairs of incompatible statements were given and the resident replied whether each was true or false. For example:

- I am happy most of the time.
- I am sad most of the time.

A yes to both statements was scored as acquiescence. Acquiescence is the tendency to agree irrespective of the content of the statement.

Under British case law, a witness is classed as competent if the judge is satisfied on two main issues for which the advice of psychologists and psychiatrists may be sought. They are:

- Does the witness understand the oath and its implied sanction, i.e. I swear by Almighty God, that the evidence I shall give will be the truth, the whole truth, and nothing but the truth?
- Is the witness capable of giving an accurate account of what they have seen?

The potential witnesses among the residents were assessed. The highest IQ for 'mental retardation' is 70. Many of the residents assessed could not complete the IQ test because they lacked the verbal ability to do so. More than a third of them were right at the bottom of the IQ scale since they did not achieve any score on the items or subtests of the intelligence scale. Similarly, they generally showed poor ability to recall either immediately or on a delayed basis a story read to them by the assessing psychologists. For example, over a quarter were unable to remember any of the story in an immediate recall test. Delay before being asked to recall the story

▶

BOX 22.2 (continued)

resulted in nearly half of the residents being unable to remember anything from the story.

The residents were asked to say what the standard oath, as given above, meant. Some were capable of doing this and said things like:

> You swear on the Bible to tell the truth. You must tell the truth. The whole truth means you give a complete picture of what happened.
>
> A lie is when you are not telling the truth.

About a fifth could explain the oath to the satisfaction of the psychologists' standards. Almost without exception these had an IQ score of 60 or over. Of course, some of the clients had difficulty answering the question, so they were presented with alternative questions:

- If I said your name was (the client's actual name given) would that be true or a lie?
- If I said your name was Fred (or the female equivalent) Bloggs would that be true or a lie?

A resident who could answer these questions was considered to have some understanding of the concepts of lies and truth. This may be considered as part of understanding the oath entirely. Another fifth of the residents could answer at this level. Almost without exception, those who could explain a lie in this concrete situation had an IQ of 50 or more.

According to Kebbell and Hatton (1999), the style of questioning used with people with mental limitations may have an influence on the quality of the testimony elicited. The most accurate answers by witnesses with mental retardation are open-ended free recall ones: for example, 'What can you tell me about what you saw?' Accuracy may be regarded as the ratio of correct to incorrect information. As the question becomes increasingly specific, the answers become less accurate. So, for example, the question 'What was he wearing?' would produce better results than 'What colour jacket was he wearing?' Similar trends are found in the general population but the trends are a little more extreme for people with mental retardation. Another characteristic of people with

mental impairment is their tendency to respond more to leading questions. This is only a minor trend since many people with limited intelligence can be accurate even with such leading questions. The reason for their greater suggestibility might lie in their poorer memory capacity. These individuals may only be suggestible on matters about which they are unsure. They also have less intellectual resources to cope with unfamiliar and stressful tasks such as those involved in providing eyewitness testimony.

People who are classified as 'mentally retarded' are often able to provide accurate enough testimony (Kebbell and Hatton, 1999). Lawyers' tactics as employed in examination and cross-examination interfere with the quality of the information obtained. The use of complex questions, such as those involving double negatives, is especially problematic. People in general tend to reply 'don't know' to such questions but will reply accurately to similar but simply expressed questions. The language used by the criminal justice system is complex for even intellectually able people:

- An IQ of 111 is needed to understand the rights notice used to inform detained suspects of their legal rights (such as the Miranda in the United States).
- People with mental disability understood only about a tenth of the sentences in some of the rights notices.
- The closed questions used in cross-examination are a strain for verbally fluent, well-educated and trained expert witnesses to deal with effectively.

Milne, Clare and Bull (1999) describe research which suggests that the cognitive interview (see Chapter 11) may be helpful in obtaining information in adults with mild learning disabilities.

This is an area in which great care is needed – the risk is always that witnesses with a mental disability are regarded as potentially unreliable. With this in mind, it is worthwhile to consider a case study reported by Willner (2011). This describes 'Joan' who was a 38-year-old victim of a theft against her by a person she knew. A clinical psychology unit assessed her in terms of a capacity to testify should it be necessary. This involved the use of a number of psychometric tests together with formal clinical interviews. Her intellectual ability was assessed to be in the lower range of 'mild learning disability'. This means that she was likely to be able to take the oath. She understood the concept of truth and the requirement to tell the truth in court, and the solemnity of the proceedings of a court of law. She also understood that there was a possibility that the accused might be acquitted in a court of law and she demonstrated that she would be able to cope with this. These are the positive signs. However, there were doubts about her ability to withstand the cross examination of a lawyer for the defence so special arrangements would be needed for her evidence. She also performed badly on the Gudjonnson Suggestibility Scale (see Box 16.2) which involves a practical test of being influenced by leading questions and other pressures. That is, like many others with an intellectual disability she was very suggestible. This might have been sufficient for authorities to decide that she would not make a reliable witness. In this test, a story is read which basically has to be memorised and then the suggestive pressures are applied to this. So memory is involved. The clinical psychologists, however, tried another approach. Joan had provided a lot of information about her own life during the course of the interviews. The psychologists applied similar suggestive pressures to this information. It was found that Joan was very resistant to suggestion when important facts in her life were involved. On the basis of this, it was recommended that the trial go ahead. The thief pleaded guilty in court in this case.

Of course, false confession under, say, police pressure, is a risk with such a vulnerable group. The law will vary under different jurisdictions: in the United Kingdom, three criteria were set out to help deal with this situation. In the case of confessions, the judge should consider the following:

- Does the prosecution case solely depend upon the confession?
- Does the defendant exhibit a significant degree of mental handicap?

- Is the confession unconvincing? Would a properly directed jury be unable to convict because of these inadequacies?

In these circumstances, the judge's responsibility is to withdraw the case from trial by the jury (Torpy, 1994).

This brings us to the question of how people with learning deficiencies are dealt with as witnesses in court. Are their needs accommodated by judges and lawyers? As we have seen, in appropriate circumstances, people with intellectual deficiencies give accurate information though this is highly dependent on the way in which they are interviewed or questioned. The accuracy of their testimony was best when they were asked open-ended 'free recall' questions such as 'What happened?' Questions that are very specific ('tell me about the shirt the man was wearing') produce poorer quality information. They may produce more details with the latter form of question but the information is more likely to be inaccurate. Kebbell, Hatton and Johnson (2004) located transcripts of British trials, half of which contained evidence provided by a person with intellectual disability. These witnesses were matched as closely as possible with witnesses who were not intellectually impaired in terms of type of crime and the court. A high proportion were trials for rape and sexual assault but some were for assault. The researchers coded the types of questions asked of the witnesses including open questions ('What was Mr Jones wearing?'), closed questions ('And what was he wearing on top?'), yes/no questions ('And your keyworker does the shopping for you?'), either/or questions ('And when you lived at St Anne's, did you have your own bedroom or did you share a bedroom?'), leading questions ('I suggest that on this occasion Kate did not come into the flat at all, that you left before Kate had come home?'), negative questions ('Did you not think it might be important to tell somebody?'), double-negatives ('Now, did you say that you did not say that it was something that you did not like?'), multiple questions (two plus questions without allowing a chance for the reply to be given before the next question is asked) and repeated questions (when the same question is asked more

▶

413

BOX 22.2 (continued)

than once). There was virtually nothing to differentiate the questions asked of witnesses with intellectual limitations and those asked of members of the general population. In other words, lawyers were making no adjustments in their questioning style in order to meet the special needs of those with low intellectual abilities. However, fewer leading questions were asked of people with intellectual limitations but they tended to have questions repeated more often. The most disturbing feature of Kebbell et al.'s findings was that those with intellectual limitations were the most likely to agree with the implied direction of the leading in response to leading questions and were less likely to provide additional information.

In a further analysis of the same data, O'Kelly et al. (2003) studied the judge's interventions in the court hearings by coding the transcripts of the hearings into three broad categories – interactions with witnesses, interactions with lawyers and interactions with the jury. The most frequent interventions with those with learning disabilities were clarifying issues with witnesses, calling breaks and asking additional questions about issues not raised by the lawyers. Overall, there were actually fewer such interventions with witnesses with learning disabilities, though this was not statistically significant. The same is true of interventions directed towards the lawyers, though, once again, this was not statistically significant. Probably most important among the findings was that the judge did not intervene more with people with learning difficulties to simplify the questions or to stop oppressive questioning.

Main points

- Legal concepts such as competency/capacity to stand trial and diminished responsibility are not simple to equate with psychological variables and are not exactly the same in different jurisdictions. In practice, such concepts will largely be assessed on the basis of clinical judgement although, gradually, more objective psychological measures are becoming available though clinical judgement is probably the main method. A person may be incompetent to stand trial for reasons of low intellectual functioning or as a consequence of suffering certain psychiatric conditions both of which make it difficult to be a party to one's own defence and to understand the procedures of the court. Only factors relevant to the individual's psychological state at the time of trial should be part of the assessment of competency.

- The extent to which practitioners who assess competence are objective in their judgement is clearly an important question. Doubts have been cast on the validity of clinical assessment in other contexts. The evidence that practitioners use psychiatric variables in making their assessment rather than other information such as criminal background is indicative of the objectivity of these assessments. There are many decisions that are poorly predicted by these psychiatric variables so we do not know the basis of the decision. There is evidence that practitioners can be influenced by inappropriate factors from experimental studies but generally factors irrelevant to the assessment of competence are ignored.

- Psychological and intellectual problems can affect the likelihood of obtaining justice. Victims of crime who have limited intellectual resources may be victimised (e.g. sexually abused) in order to make a prosecution possible. As with many issues in forensic and criminal psychology, it is not possible to state absolutely that such individuals do or do not provide good evidence. If interviewed appropriately, especially using open-ended questioning, the quality of the evidence provided may be perfectly satisfactory. Nevertheless, there is emerging evidence that judges and lawyers in court do not always behave appropriately towards people with intellectual limitations. The questioning style of lawyers tends to be too complex and lacks adaptation to the needs of the witness, and judges tend not to intervene in these cases in support of the witness's needs.

Further reading

For extended material on key concepts in this chapter see:

Lindsay, W.R., Taylor, J.L. and Sturmey, P. (eds) (2004) *Offenders with Developmental Disabilities* Chichester: Wiley.

McMurran, M., Khalifa, N. and Gibbon, S. (2009) *Forensic Mental Health* Cullompton: Willan Publishing.

Rogers, T.P., Blackwood, N.J., Farnham, F., Pickup, G.J. and Watts, M.J. (2008) 'Fitness to plead and competence to stand trial: a systematic review of the constructs and their application' *Journal of Forensic Psychiatry and Psychology* **19** (4), 576–96.

Also see: Crown Prosecution Service: Mentally Disordered Offenders in Court: http://www.cps.gov.uk/legal/

Visit our website at www.pearsoned.co.uk/howitt for self-test and essay questions, annotated further reading, audio interviews with researchers in the field, weblinks and more information on becoming a forensic psychologist.

Chapter 23

Judges and lawyers

Overview

- The public are reasonably satisfied with the criminal justice system. Yet a considerable minority believe that not all accused persons are treated fairly and have their rights respected by courts of law. Victims are seen as being poorly served by the system (Chapter 4) and a majority feel that the system does not bring criminals to justice. Substantial numbers of the public have attended court in some capacity – one in ten of the British public has been accused of committing a crime.

- The roles of judges and lawyers in the Anglo-American adversarial system are different from those of the inquisitorial systems where the prosecution and defence are not in battle. Nevertheless, even within the adversarial system, the styles of trial can be very different. For example, in the United Kingdom, lawyers' objections are not dealt with in the presence of the jury whereas in the United States they can be. The differences lead to differences in the relative strengths of the two systems and outcomes do not seem to be materially affected overall. Nevertheless, there is evidence that the mechanisms of persuasion may be different in the two contexts.

- There is evidence that outcomes of trials are only modestly predictable from a range of relevant variables. However, most of us will consult a lawyer in the hope that he or she will be able to accurately assess the outcome of a particular legal situation we face. Lawyers' assessments of likely outcomes follow the principles of the psychology of decision making under conditions of uncertainty. There is evidence that the way the issue is framed in terms of the numbers of factors to consider, for example, affects the probabilities of different outcomes as assessed by the lawyer.

- Considerable attention has been given to how evidence can be more effectively presented in court. There is advice that is based on general psychological developments in understanding effective communications, although their adequacy in the legal context needs to be assessed more thoroughly. For example, the use of powerful speech styles in which directness, assertiveness and rationality are characteristic tend to be perceived as delivering the more credible message.

- Many researchers have pointed to the importance of studying the effectiveness of narrative when trying to understand legal arguments. The effectiveness of evidence depends on the narrative context in which it is placed rather than its 'factual value' in order to achieve its impact. The better the narrative is based in common-sense notions, the more positive the outcome. However, effective structures for the presentation of evidence can involve concentrating in part on the legal context in which the jury has to reach a decision.

- Legal judgments may be seen as ideological in nature. They often appear to reinforce dominant social ideologies. This is especially easily demonstrated by reference to the work of feminist analyses of courtroom interactions.

- Various models have been proposed to account for judges' decision making. To a degree these utilise extra-legal considerations just as was the case for jury decision making.

Introduction

According to the British Crime Survey (Home Office, 2001), a third of British adults had been to court as a witness, spectator or juror at some time. Ten per cent of the population had been to court accused of a crime. About two-thirds of British people believe that the criminal justice system respects the rights of and treats fairly people accused of committing a crime. The figure is slightly lower for those who have been in trouble with the law but, nevertheless, even they remained as a group very satisfied with the criminal justice system. However, only about 40 per cent of the population believed that the criminal justice system brings people who commit crime to justice. There is an obvious need to understand better what happens in courts of law. However, one must be realistic about the direct impact of courts on much crime. In the majority of cases, questions of guilt have been already settled by the admission of the accused. Williams (1995) pointed out that in some jurisdictions something like 90 per cent of cases are settled by a plea of guilty. Of course, in the United States, this may involve plea bargaining – that is, prosecution and defence agreeing a guilty plea to a less serious charge than the prosecution originally intended (Colvin, 1993). This encourages more guilty pleas.

Types of trial

The Anglo-American adversarial system was described by Dabbs, Alford and Fielden (1998) as 'lawyers arguing, judges refereeing, and juries deciding the outcome.

Litigation is a form of combat, and good lawyers excel at combat' (p. 84). Trial lawyers have many similarities with the blue-collar worker of industry and commerce. They work in a place where concrete demands are made on their services rather than with abstract concepts involved in, for example, giving advice that does not demand delivery of results. They have to achieve and this requires knowledge and skills that are not taught in law school. Based on this analogy with the blue-collar worker, Dabbs *et al.* anticipated that trial lawyers will show characteristics that are similar to those that have been found in other studies. One possibility is that they will show higher levels of the hormone testosterone. This has been linked to heightened interpersonal dominance as well as sexual activity. Trial lawyers of both sexes were studied by Dabbs *et al.* (1998) as well as other lawyers who had not been trial lawyers for a period of at least five years. Saliva samples were analysed for testosterone and it was found that in all the cases studied, irrespective of gender, the trial lawyers had higher testosterone levels than non-trial lawyers. In another study, they compared trial lawyers and appeal court lawyers with similar outcomes.

The institution of the jury has a history that goes back to Socrates but, more importantly, the Norman (French) law of trial by jury (Arce *et al.*, 1996). The jury is associated with British and US developments and other countries whose legal systems derive from these roots. History took rather different routes in Continental Europe. There, legal experts working with lay people decided on matters such as guilt. (The mixed jury is different since in this, lay people working as a group reach the verdict but the judge(s) also contributes in terms of deciding sentence.) The *escabino* jury refers to systems in which qualified legal experts and lay people jointly make decisions. The *escabinato* system first developed in Germany. However, today, in Germany, the system deals mainly with rather minor offences. In France and Italy the development of *escabinatos* was associated with Fascism in the first half of the twentieth century.

Naturally, one of the questions is whether the legal professional has undue power over the other members in such a 'jury'. Arce *et al.* carried out research into the escabinato system using a real rape case that was video recorded and edited down to 75 minutes of tape. The escabinato juries were composed of five lay persons together with a judge. The results showed that the judge's initial verdict was usually very persuasive for the lay persons. No lay member changed to be against the judge. Given the two-thirds majority rule for the verdict applied in this study, the groups overall tended to adopt the judge's stance.

It is believed that the adversarial system of England was a response to the historical shortcomings of the European inquisitorial system. Torture was used sometimes in some secular judicial proceedings using the inquisitorial model (McEwan, 1995). The contrast between the Continental European inquisitorial legal system and those

based on the British adversarial system is marked. The latter is common to other parts of the world including the United States and judicial systems emerging out of British colonialism. The adversarial system can be seen to have the following characteristics:

- The judge's role is minimised as far as deciding the question of guilt is involved.
- The lawyers or advocates are partisan and act for opposed parties.
- The jury is commonly employed although it is not strictly a requirement of the adversarial system.
- Evidence is presented orally rather than as written evidence or submissions.

Nevertheless, the two systems are not quite so distinct as they might appear. Sometimes the two systems are employed within the same jurisdiction. For example, proceedings concerning the care of children are often closer to the inquisitorial model than the adversarial model. Coroner's courts, which deal with matters of the causes of death (and treasure trove) in England, employ something closer to the inquisitorial approach.

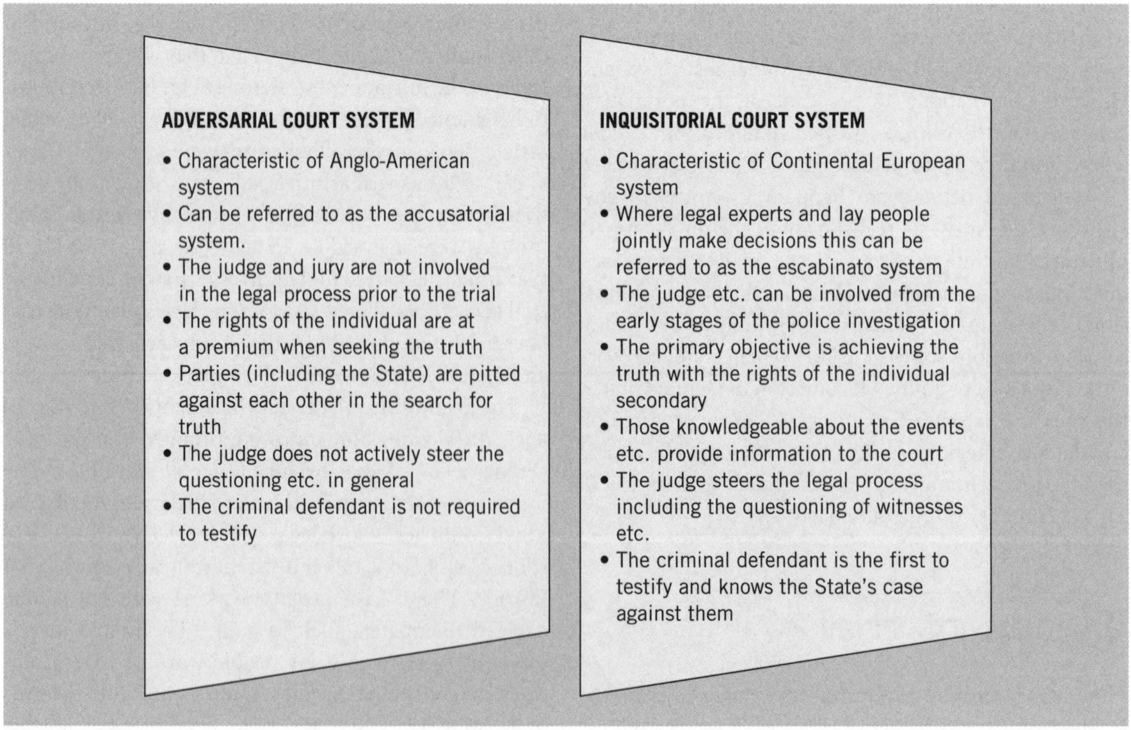

ADVERSARIAL COURT SYSTEM

- Characteristic of Anglo-American system
- Can be referred to as the accusatorial system.
- The judge and jury are not involved in the legal process prior to the trial
- The rights of the individual are at a premium when seeking the truth
- Parties (including the State) are pitted against each other in the search for truth
- The judge does not actively steer the questioning etc. in general
- The criminal defendant is not required to testify

INQUISITORIAL COURT SYSTEM

- Characteristic of Continental European system
- Where legal experts and lay people jointly make decisions this can be referred to as the escabinato system
- The judge etc. can be involved from the early stages of the police investigation
- The primary objective is achieving the truth with the rights of the individual secondary
- Those knowledgeable about the events etc. provide information to the court
- The judge steers the legal process including the questioning of witnesses etc.
- The criminal defendant is the first to testify and knows the State's case against them

Figure 23.1 Adversarial versus inquisitorial trial systems

Similarly, in France and other countries there is no pure inquisitorial system since a large proportion of cases do not go through the examination by the investigating magistrate. In the inquisitorial system, the police may be called on to investigate matters pertinent to the defence and not just the prosecution.

There are two broad types of jury:

- The lay person jury consisting only of lay persons. This often has 12 people but the number can vary and we will see in Chapter 24 that some jurisdictions use juries as small as six persons. It is 15 in Scotland.

- The escabinato jury which has a mixture of lay persons and legal experts. For example, there may be one legal expert and two lay persons. This is the system used in Germany (Arce, 1998).

Chapter 24 is devoted to the Anglo-American type of jury.

British and American trial procedures are different despite both being based on the broad adversarial strategy (Collett and Kovera, 2003). There are many differences between the two. For example, in the British system, the lawyers are confined and are not free to roam around the courtroom while presenting their case; the opening statement from the defence is given after the other side has presented its case and not right at the beginning of the trial; objections from lawyers are not dealt with in the presence of the jury; British judges are more active in the general flow of evidence during the trial than American judges who may be described as being more reserved. All of this led Collett and Kovera to the view that these differences in the demeanour of both judges and lawyers in the two systems may have consequences for how the proceedings affect the jury.

One possibility is that the process of persuasion in the two systems is different. Modern theories of persuasion suggest that there are two methods by which information is processed (Petty and Cacioppo, 1981). One is the central route in which people actively process all the information that is pertinent to their situation. Since this is a relatively cerebral and rational process, the quality of the arguments determines the level of persuasion. The peripheral route involves considerably less effort since it involves relatively simple decision-making rules or procedures when coming to a decision. For example, in the peripheral route to persuasion, aspects such as the status of the person making the argument affects acceptance of that argument. Distractive US courtroom environments would encourage the peripheral route to be more

influential, say on the jury, than the more orderly British system which would favour the more central route to persuasion. On the other hand, the greater level of involvement of the British judges may mean that jurors are more influenced by their non-verbal cues concerning the case than would be a jury with an American judge.

In an experiment testing this possibility, Collett and Kovera (2003) set up mock trials, some of which followed the British ways outlined above while others followed the American way. All other things were standard to all of the trials. The amount of non-verbal behaviour expressed by the judge was varied as well as the strength of the evidence in the trials. Those who were subject to the British-style trials could remember the evidence presented in the trial better than those who experienced the American-style trial. However, there was no evidence that the British-style trial allowed the jurors to be more influenced by the stronger evidence than did the American-style trial. The non-verbal cues given by the judge were clearly drawn attention to by the British-style procedures since participants rated the judge's non-verbal cues as more salient. There was also evidence that the British-style trial resulted in the jury being more confident in their verdicts. However, the study failed to demonstrate that the two systems differentially affected the trial outcomes. The study does not show the superiority of one system over the other. The strengths of the British system in terms of allowing the jury to focus unfettered on the evidence are offset by the apparently greater risk that non-verbal signals from the judge will affect the jury.

Are trial outcomes predictable?

If the court process is capable of being studied and analysed effectively, one would assume that the outcomes of trials are predictable. Fitzmaurice, Rogers and Stanley (1996) studied how accurately sentencing could be predicted for a sample of 4,000 cases in England. The possible sentences included discharge, fine, probation order, community service order, fully suspended sentence, partially suspended sentence and custody. Over 30 variables were assessed for each case. Different combinations of predictor variables predicted different types of sentence most effectively. In general, the predictions were not particularly good. Thus the percentage of correctly predicted sentences (i.e. the sentence matched that predicted by the measures) could be as low as 20 per cent and no higher than 60 per cent. The correlation between the prediction and the actual sentence similarly could be lower than 0.2 and no higher than 0.5.

However, despite these relatively modest sentencing predictions, one of the most important functions that lawyers have in relation to courts of law is making predictions about the most likely outcome of taking a case to court or appealing a court decision. Clients go to lawyers partly for advice on what the law is, but also for an assessment of the consequences of legal processes. So, a client who wishes to sue another person for damages needs to know from their lawyer some sort of forecast of the likelihood of success. The advice offered by lawyers may be extremely influential on whether a case goes to court. So lawyers' advice needs to be understood. As yet, not a great deal is known about this. There is a small number of exceptions to this: Fox and Rirke (2002) argued that the task facing a lawyer when making predictions about the outcome of a trial is analogous to any other decision-making process under conditions of uncertainty. Supporting theory is built on the research into such judgements. The theory assumes that probabilities are attached to descriptions of events (or hypotheses) rather than the events as such. Since descriptions of what constitutes a set of events are different from each other, the probabilities assigned to what is otherwise the same event will also differ.

Imagine the client wants to know whether seeking damages would be successful in court. The lawyer has to judge the probability of outcome A (damages awarded) versus the probability of outcome B (no damages awarded). The theory assumes that the lawyer's estimate of the probability of outcome A plus the probability of outcome B should equal 1, just as it would in statistical probability theory where the probability of a head or a tail when tossing a coin sums to 1. That is simple. However, the theory suggests that where the possible outcomes are more finely subdivided, the principle of sub-additivity should apply. For example, imagine the lawyer decides that the probability of winning the damages cases is 0.6 (that is, that the client would win in 6 out of every 10 cases like this). What would happen if the probability of winning damages were calculated for two subdivisions of damages, for example, where the damages are more than €10,000 and where the damages are less than €10,000? What happens is that the sum of the two probabilities actually sum to more than the 0.6 that they should in theory. The lawyer might assess the probability of getting over €10,000 at 0.4 and the probability of getting under €10,000 at 0.5.

Adding these together, this amounts to a probability of 0.9, which is bigger than the rational outcome of 0.6. The more subdivisions of a category, the more the sum of the probabilities of the individual categories would be. There is a further idea – that of implicit sub-additivity. This basically says that the more subdivisions of a category that are listed, the greater the probability that will be assigned. So, for example, if asked the probability that a case will end in a guilty verdict and the defendant put on probation, fined or sent to prison then the probability given will be greater than for when a laywer is asked simply what the probability is of the case ending in a guilty verdict.

In one study, a group of lawyers were asked to give an estimate of the probability of one or other of a variety of trial outcomes. So one set of lawyers were asked to make some judgements about the outcome of an antitrust case involving Microsoft in the United States. Some estimated the probability that the case would go directly to the Supreme Court. The average probability assigned to this was 0.33. However, when the other group were asked to assess the probability that the case would go directly to the high court and be affirmed, reversed or modified then the probability was judged to be 0.40. This difference supports the principle of implicit sub-additivity. Of course, there is a great deal more that needs to be known but even this one study points in the direction of improving decision making in relevant legal situations by compensating for the biases in lawyers' judgements.

Another study into the predictability of sentencing was that of Cauffman, Piquero, Kimonis, Steinberg, Chassin and Fagan (2007). This investigated factors predicting the disposal of serious juvenile offenders by juvenile courts. There are two main models which might account for this: (a) The protection of the public from further criminal activity by the offender and (b) attention to the criminogenic needs of the individual youngster. Are demographic, psychological, contextual and legal factors equally involved in decisions to award a custodial sentence rather than probation? The researchers obtained a large US sample of over 1,300 juvenile offenders in the age range 14–18 years. Both genders were included and they had committed serious offences (felony offences against persons and property, or a misdemeanor offence involving weapons, or sexual assault). The following were amongst the data collected by the researchers:

- Sentence received (disposition) – either probation or confinement (i.e. prison/secure unit)

- Demographic characteristics such as age, gender, parents' education level and race
- Legal considerations: current and past involvement with the criminal justice system including whether most serious crime was violence, the number of court referrals they had ever had, and whether previous disposition was probation or not
- Individual factors – psychosocial maturity and mental health problems as well as gang involvement; psycho-social maturity (self-reliance, identity, and work orientation) and IQ; resistance to peer pressure; perspective taking; control over one's impulses; environmental matters to do with school and family.

The participants were interviewed about 37 days after the sentencing on average. Those taking part were mainly from the lower socio-economic status groups. The findings indicated that legal factors were the most important in determining whether a prison sentence or probation was awarded. The more previous court referrals the offender had the more likely they were to be confined in a prison. Gender was a factor in disposal since males were more likely to receive a prison sentence though there was no evidence that race was related to the disposal method used. However, previous experience of probation increased the likelihood of a probation disposition. Individual factors such as developmental maturity were poor predictors of disposal.

It might be useful here to point out that there is a variety of evidence about the impact of particular lawyers on trials. Williams (1995) reviewed the evidence on this matter and found that the lawyer did not matter much or at all in the majority of studies. His own research was on appeal level courts. Whether the lawyer was privately employed or a counsel supplied by the public defender made no difference overall. Private attorneys, then, were not more likely to win the appeal. One of the reasons for this may be that many criminal appeals (these were in Florida) are seen as hopeless, frivolous or routine, i.e. unlikely to be affected even by the most brilliant of courtroom performers.

The presentation of evidence in court

It is not possible to present just any evidence in court. Structural constraints are defined which essentially prescribe how, what, where and when evidence may be provided. The precise nature of these constraints varies according to jurisdiction, who and what is being tried. There are usually constraints on the *order* in which evidence may be presented in court (Bartlett and Memon, 1995). For example, the accepted structure may involve one-way questioning by lawyers and judges exclusively. The answer may also have an accepted form. Replies such as 'I would say so, wouldn't you?' violate such principles. There are other requirements:

- In adversarial systems, restrictions on the use of information about previous offences are common. Such evidence may be admissible only in circumstances where there are common features between the present charge and the past offences. Even in these circumstances there are constraints. The prejudicial effect of the information should not exceed the benefits of its provision.
- Furthermore, again commonly in adversarial systems, the accused may only be cross-examined about their past convictions if the character of prosecution witnesses is contested or if the defence concerns evidence of the good character of the defendant (McEwan, 1995).

The procedure is for the prosecution to give its case first which is then followed by the defence evidence. Many psychologists will be reminded of the research on the effectiveness of different orders of presenting opposing persuasive communications. It has been demonstrated that arguments presented first differ in their persuasive impact from arguments presented second. This is known as the primacy-recency effect. The findings of different studies reveal a complex picture and it is difficult to say that the first argument has greatest impact. Similarly, with court evidence, the research does not result in a simple formula such as the case presented first always has the advantage. The longer the trial, the greater the advantage to the more recent case; the shorter the trial, the greater the advantage of the case presented first (Lind and Ke, 1985).

Bartlett and Memon (1995) suggest a number of strategies that may help a lawyer to persuade jurors and judges of the strength of their case. The first few can be regarded as means of increasing persuasiveness in the argument:

- *Vivid language* enhances the impact of important testimony. Thus they regard 'He came towards me' as bland whereas 'He lunged at me with flashing eyes and a contorted grimace . . .' (p. 546) might have more effect on the listener.

- *Repetition* of particularly important pieces of information may be an effective strategy.

- *Loaded questions* such as 'Did you see the broken window?' (p. 546) contain an implication that the unwary might accept – that indeed the window was broken. The question 'Did you see the window in question?' contains no such implication.

- *Subtle shifts in wording* may profoundly influence what meaning is chosen for a sequence of events. For example, the phrases 'to sit with you' and 'to sit near you' can have rather different meanings. Nevertheless, despite this, an unwary witness might accept either.

The following strategies concern the manipulation of the credibility of the witness:

- *Powerful speech* styles are characterised by directness, assertiveness and rationality. In contrast, powerless speech contains a high density of 'intensifiers' such as 'so', 'well' and 'surely' together with many words dealing with hesitations such as 'you know' and 'well'. It is also characterised by polite words such as 'please' and 'thank you very much'. According to Bartlett and Memon (1995), the powerful typifies male speech and the powerless typifies female speech. Generally speaking, males using powerful speech were regarded as more credible and much the same was true for female speakers.

- *Making witnesses appear incompetent* by providing, say, expert testimony that casts serious doubt on whether they could possibly have seen what they claim to have seen. For example, it might be impossible to see a face at a given distance in the dim lighting at the time.

The major advances in understanding powerful legal arguments have come from trying to understand the narratives that underlie lawyers' cases. Decision making in a legal context is an example of a top-down process (Van Koppen, 1995). One can consider the hypothesis presented in court (the allegation of a crime) as preceding the fact-finding to support or reject that hypothesis. There is not a body of facts that is sifted through and then the most likely person to accuse selected on the basis of the facts. Quite the reverse: someone is thought to be responsible for a crime and then the facts sought that explain the accused's responsibility for the crime. The evidence verifies the charge rather than the charge verifying the evidence. The evidence, as such, though is not the key. The important thing is the story that links the evidence together. Take the following instance from legal writing that begins with the observation that in car accidents the facts are interpretable in more than one way:

> The fact that the driver did not see the pedestrian is at once an explanation of the collision in terms of accident rather than recklessness, and also a suggestion that he was not keeping a proper lookout.
>
> (Abrahams, 1954, p. 28)

Research evidence has demonstrated that the quality of the narrative is vital in making judgements. In a classic study, Bennett and Feldman (1981) adopted a very simple methodology. They simply asked students to tell a story to other students – half of them had to tell a true story and the other half were told to invent a story. As might be expected from what we know about lie detection (Chapter 18), listeners could not differentiate between the true story and the invented story at better than the chance level. But, of course, they believed some stories but not others. So here was an opportunity to study the features of stories that made them appear truthful. Stories that were believed contained what might be termed 'a readily identifiable central action'. This provides an easily believed context for the actions of the participants. Pennington and Hastie (1981, 1986) found that the following were crucial to a good narrative:

- goals of the participants.
- physical conditions;
- psychological conditions.

Bennett and Feldman (1981) give the example of a story that was seen as made up by persons listening to it. It was a story about a birthday party:

> Ummm – last night I was invited to a birthday party for a friend her name's Peggy Sweeney it was her twenty-fourth birthday. At the party we had this just super spaghetti dinner – you know – just great big hunks of meat and mushrooms and what not – a nice salad. And then for dessert we had a um cherry and blueberry um cheesecake. It was really good.
>
> (p. 75)

The researchers argued that this story can be broken down into a number of structural elements: the connections between them being ambiguous. The two elements – I was invited to a birthday party and last night – are joined together as a meaningful connection. Others are not:

I was invited to a birthday party – At the party we had this just super spaghetti dinner

The significance of the phrase *At the party we had this just super spaghetti dinner* does not lie in the context of the birthday party. The spaghetti dinner is ambiguous in terms of its relevance to the birthday party story. Similarly, what is the relevance of the phrase 'her name's Peggy Sweeney' to the spaghetti meal? Why mention it? Unless the hearer knows who Peggy Sweeney is, her mention just complicates the picture. If the hearer thought that Peggy Sweeney was an expert in fine food then the ambiguity might be resolved.

> It is not clear what facts, logic, norms, or the like, would yield a clear inference about the relationship between these story elements.
>
> (Bennett and Feldman, 1981, p. 78)

Story ambiguities can be of three distinct types:

- If an obvious interpretative rule (fact, language category, norm, etc.) is not available to provide a meaningful link between two elements of the story.

- The listener can see many possible links between the two elements but the rest of the story fails to provide the information to support any of these plausible links.

- When the listener can make sensible, that is unambiguous, connection between the story elements but then realises that it is inconsistent with the most obvious connections among the other elements of the story.

Bennett and Feldman suggest that the number of ambiguous linkages of this sort (what they term 'structural ambiguities') partly determines and undermines the credibility or perceived truthfulness of the story. Indeed, they studied a number of predictors of story credibility. Of these, only structural ambiguity showed a substantial relationship with the credibility of the story. The length of the story, the number of actions performed in the story, the number of pauses in the story, and the length of the pauses each had no bearing on story credibility. The structural properties of the story far outweigh factors such as witness credibility, lawyer histrionics and so forth in perceptions of its truthfulness, claim Bennett and Feldman.

The birthday party story, by the way, was true despite being perceived otherwise. Bennett and Feldman's argument then suggests that the following areas are employed by lawyers in the courtroom when constructing plausible accounts of reality:

- *Definitional tactics*: the language used by witnesses (elicited by lawyers) to define pieces of evidence. Bennett and Feldman give the example of a drunk driving case in which the prosecution lawyer tried to establish the number of beers the defendant had had prior to the offence. The defence tactic was to stress the extended period of time in which drinking had taken place:

Prosecution: How much did you have to drink that evening prior to being stopped by these police officers?
(Objection by the defense)
Prosecution: Answer the question, Mr. H_____
Defendant: Well, now, I was working (at) my locker the whole day on Fisherman's Wharf. I have a locker there.
Prosecution: How much did you have to drink?
Defense: May he be permitted to answer the question, be responsive. Your Honor? He started to . . .
The Court: Go ahead. Let him explain.
Defendant: Well, it will have to all come into this now, what I am going to say.
Prosecution: Fine.
Defendant: I left Fisherman's Wharf . . .
(Bennett and Feldman, 1981, p. 119)

Notice how the defence lawyer shaped the defendant's testimony despite not actually asking the questions. Furthermore, the definition of the drinking behaviour was extended to provide a different picture from the negative impression that would have been created by a simple tally of the number of beers drunk.

- *Establishing and disrupting connections in stories*: inferential tactics. The structural location of a piece of evidence is made in relation to the remaining elements of the story. Bennett and Feldman give the example of the woman prosecuted for robbery. One of the salient facts was that the defendant gave her shoulder bag to a friend before committing the robbery so that she would be able to make a better robbery without this encumbrance. Under questioning, she explains that the bag kept slipping because of the leather coat she was wearing, the implication being that this was the reason for handing the bag over:

Q: You could ball the strap in your hand like a leash, couldn't you?
A: Yes.

Q: Isn't it true, Miss V_____, the reason you gave the purse to D_____ was because you wouldn't be burdened down with it when you ran?

(Bennett and Feldman, 1981, p. 126)

In other words, the lawyer made explicit the connection between handing over the bag and the crime.

- *Establishing the credibility of evidence*: validational tactics. Can (a) and (b) be validated by other information and explanations, or can they be invalidated by showing plausible alternative definitions and connections between the elements of the story? An example of this is the use of objections. These serve three purposes: one is to stop prejudicial evidence being presented, a second is to build up a catalogue of errors on which to base an appeal, and the third is really to address the jury:

Prosecution: Isn't it true that in February of 1964 you were convicted of manslaughter and sentenced to twenty years in the state penitentiary?
Defendant: Well, yeah.
Defense: We object to that for the record.
The Court: Overruled.

(Bennett and Feldman, 1981, p. 133)

The prosecution lawyer was acting properly in terms of the location of the court studied. By objecting 'for the record' the impression is deliberately created that such questioning is on the margins of acceptability and that, as such, it should not be given too much weight for fear of inadvertently prejudicing the case.

Anchored narratives are also based on narrative theory that emerges out of cognitive psychology. This argues that evidence is meaningless without being placed into a narrative context. The story is decided upon, not the evidence. The story may have gaps but these are filled automatically by the listener. Wagenaar, van Koppen and Crombag (1993) point to some of the gap-filling in the following:

Margie was holding tightly to the string of her beautiful new balloon. Suddenly, a gust of wind caught it. The wind carried it into a tree. The balloon hit a branch and burst. Margie cried and cried.

(p. 33)

Now this you probably took to be the equivalent of the following:

Margie, *a little girl*, was holding tightly to the string of her beautiful new balloon. *The wind was so strong that* suddenly a gust of wind caught it. The wind carried it into a tree. The balloon hit a branch and burst *on a sharp twig*. *The loss of her balloon made* Margie cry and cry.

But, equally, the story that fits the facts could have been:

Margie, *a young mother*, was holding tightly to the string of her beautiful new balloon. *Forgetfully, she let go of the balloon.* Suddenly a gust of wind caught it. The wind carried it into a tree. The balloon hit a branch and burst *when a boy managed to hit it with a stone from a catapult.* Margie cried and cried *when the boy turned the catapult on her.*

The story context determines the meaning of the central factors of the story. As a consequence, it is possible to find two radically different stories in which to set the facts to different effects. This is, after all, what prosecution and defence lawyers do to try to achieve opposite ends.

Wagenaar *et al.* (1993), working within the context of earlier 'good story' theories of evidence, suggest that good stories are 'anchored' into a system of general rules which are most of the time valid. This knowledge of the world helps determine the truth-value of the evidence to the listener. Evidence, in itself, does not have this truth-value in the absence of these rules. For example, suppose that the evidence from DNA testing says that X's semen was found in the victim's vagina. This does not prove, in itself, that X murdered the woman. It does not even prove that the pair had intercourse, forcibly or not. The victim might have been a lesbian wanting a child who obtained the sperm from her friend X. She might have inserted the semen using a spatula as she could not bring herself to have sex with a man.

Among the common-sense or legal rules that firmly anchor some stories as true are the following:

- Drug addicts are thieves.
- If a witness has a good sighting of the perpetrator then they will accurately identify the offender.
- Once a thief always a thief.
- Police officers are the best witnesses.
- Prosecutors usually do not take innocent individuals to trial.
- The associates of criminals are criminals themselves.
- Witnesses rarely lie under oath in court.

These rules need not have any factual basis at all in order to be effective.

There is another way of construing lawyers' activities. From a social-psychological perspective they could be regarded as attempting to manipulate guilt attribution. So the job of the lawyer for the defence is to present his or her client's behaviour in a way that minimises guilt attribution. Schmid and Fiedler (1998) suggest that the social-psychological notion of the peripheral route to persuasion (as opposed to the central route) is appropriate to lawyers' arguments. The central route presents the substantial arguments that are listened to and evaluated. The hearer would normally be critical in their evaluation of these arguments. In the case of the peripheral route, influence is achieved far less directly in a way that does not arouse this critical evaluation. Subtle cues of an evaluative nature, which suggest the response hoped for by the lawyer, become the basis for persuasion. Schmid and Fiedler argue that most listeners in court will be skilled language users who recognise the sorts of strategy for peripheral persuasion employed by the lawyers. If too positive, the risk is that the hearers will simply discount the argument the lawyer is making. The researchers videotaped the closing speeches of lawyers in training. Listeners (jurors, had this been real life) responded to the arguments in terms of a composite of blame attributed to the defendant, the competence of the lawyers, the fairness of the lawyer and so forth. Severity of punishment for the offences was, predictably, dependent on how serious was the crime involved. But there was evidence that subtle language strategies also played a role:

- *Intentionality of negative behaviour*: this is defined in terms of the internal attribution of the negative behaviour to the offender. The focus of the cause of the offence is on the offender rather than the victim. This corresponds to different language characteristics. For example, more punishment was suggested when the lawyer used more negative interpretative action verbs (such as hurt as opposed to help) to the offender and less to the victim.
- *Dispositionality of negative behaviour*: language characteristics that brought about higher punishment recommendations included descriptive action verbs (such as push and shout).

Do not assume that good narrative accounts of the evidence which favour one side are the only requirements of a good legal case. Spiecker and Worthington (2003) studied the influence of what they call the lawyers' organisational strategies on decisions made in simulated civil courts in the United States. The organisational strategies are the ways in which the lawyer chooses to organise the evidence. Two broad structures were identified – the narrative structure and the legal-expository structure. The narrative organisational structure emphasises such matters as describing the setting of events, describing the series of events in a meaningful and interrelated way, describing the important people in the narrative and organising the narrative in a meaningful temporal fashion. The legal-expository structure emphasises the legal requirements of the decision to be taken. These legal elements may include a description of the relevant law to the case, the nature of the burden of proof required for such cases, and the identification of the legal elements needed in order to establish the case. Both sides may take different views as to whether or not the case in question meets the requirements of proof. Of course, lawyers have more than one opportunity to make their argument. For example, they make opening statements and closing statements. So it is possible to mix the organisational strategies within a case – the opening statement could be narrative and the closing statement legal-expository. In the study in question, various possible combinations of strategies by both sides of the case were studied in terms of their effects on the jury. Broadly, it was found that both sides benefit from having the closing statement centred around a legal-expository format. That is, the lawyer should identify the legal aspects that should govern the case and offer an interpretation as to how well the evidence in a particular case meets these requirements. In terms of the overall strategy, this study showed that using a narrative opening and a legal-expository closing was more effective for the plaintiff's side than using the narrative approach for both. In contrast, the defence fared better with mixed strategy or a legal-expository approach throughout. In other words, the situation is not simply one of the narrative approach being best, it is one in which ignoring other strategies can lead to poor outcomes – strictly narrative approaches were not in the interest of the defence in this case.

Other lawyer tactics

Although it would be incorrect to suggest that there has developed a truly systematic research literature of the tactics of lawyers in court, there are signs of an increasing interest in the psychological processes underlying courtroom battles. The role of the expert witness in the adversarial system requires countermeasures from lawyers of the opposite side. This could be simply using an expert with views contrary to those of the opposition. However, in some locations at least, a more direct attack can be tried. Expert witnesses can be targets of various forms of discrediting strategy from the other side's lawyers. For example, should the expert witness be a psychologist then their training and educational background might be criticised, their evidence discredited by questioning psychology's scientific status, and more finely tuned matters such as the controversies associated with the diagnosis of mental illness emphasised. Larson and Brodsky (2010) point out that some of the strategies used in the USA involve more personal attacks on expert witnesses. These personal attacks highlight the expert witness's shortcoming. Quite scurrilously the expert might be asked about their personal substance abuse problems or the circumstances of their divorce. Apparently this style of questioning tends to be reserved more for females acting as expert witnesses. Larson and Brodsky (2010) evaluated the effectiveness of such attacks. In their study, US university students were shown a videoed summary of a murder trial including part of the cross-examination stage. It concerned a multiple murder in which a father was tried for killing his son, niece, and wife and attempting to kill his daughter. A psychologist acted as an expert witness assessing the father's state of mind at the time of the killings. The gender of the psychologist was varied across the different conditions of the research design as was the presence or absence of intrusive personal questioning. Examples of this sort of question included 'To your knowledge, Dr. Jeffries, has your own husband/wife cheated on you, or have you ever cheated on your own husband/wife?' and 'Isn't it true that you psychologists often have sexual feelings toward your clients?' In the transcripts presented to participants of the research, Dr Jeffries essentially rebuts the questioner. The mock jurors tended to rate the female expert witness as less trustworthy, reliable, believable and credible than male ones. However, the gender intrusive questioning was counterproductive to the lawyer's apparent intent. Experts subjected to this sort of questioning were seen as being more credible, trustworthy and believable than those who were treated more fairly. Apparently the jurors developed a negative impression of the prosecuting lawyer when his case included these personal attacks.

Another tactic used by lawyers in the USA is to use abstract language when examining child witnesses (see Chapter 20). Generally previous research has shown that the abstract nature of some lawyer language affects the accuracy of the testimony provided by a child. Typically defence lawyers ask more complex questions than prosecution lawyers. Such a strategy potentially may lead to less favourable juror perceptions of the accuracy of the child witness. But none of this research has focused on whether the complexity of the questions predicted the outcome of the trial. Evans, Lee and Lyon (2009) addressed the issue of whether the outcome of a trial is predictable from the complexity of the questions asked using a novel, innovative method involving a computer program which automatically carries out a linguistic analysis of text. The researchers studied the transcripts of 46 Californian child sexual abuse trials. Half of the trials ended in conviction and half ended in acquittal. The average ages of the child witnesses were also equalised across conditions.

The Connexor Functional Dependancy Grammar (FDG) program was used to obtain measures of the complexity and wordiness measures for both the prosecution and defence lawyers in each of the trials. This software provided an in-depth analysis of the syntactical relationships between words in the transcripts. Each question is broken down into noun and verb phrases using a visual tree diagram output and then each of these phrases is broken down into tokens (i.e. words). Every time a sentence is broken down a new layer of the tree diagram is produced. This number of layers was used as the measure of question complexity. The relatively simple sentence 'Do you recall testifying in April and saying that your mother cleaned up after you threw up?' has 4 layers. In contrast, a similar but more complex sentence 'Do you recall telling us that your mother had cleaned up after you throwing up back in April when you testified?' has six layers.

The trial verdict could be predicted accurately in 83 per cent of cases from the complexity of the defence lawyers' questioning. However, contrary to expectations, complex questions characterised convictions and not acquittals. The defence lawyer's complex questions were related to the verdict depending on the response that the child makes. If a complex question leads to an answer such as 'I don't know' or no expansion in the response, a conviction was more likely to occur. Simply responding yes or no to complex questions did not relate to conviction. Replying with no and expanding the response was related to a conviction. Possibly the 'I don't know' answer is seen as an indicator of the child's competency by the jury since they have coped with a complex question with an appropriate response as they have not let the question confuse them.

Another strategy involved in lawyers' work is the advice that they give to their clients about whether or not to agree to a plea bargain whereby the lawyer's client agrees to plead guilty usually to a lesser charge in return for a lesser punishment. This is a common practice in the USA. Of course, most crimes end with a guilty plea though the extent to which this is encouraged by plea bargaining agreements is not known. Similar decisions would be necessary in countries where there is an automatic reduction in the punishment tariff if the accused admits guilt at the start of a trial. One implication of this is that jury trials are actually relatively uncommon ways in which to deal with a case. The 'in the shadow of the trial' model of plea bargaining (Mnookin and Kornhausr, 1979) assumes that plea bargaining decisions are based on the strength of evidence in the case and the expected sentence for the crime. This model has come to dominate the literature though there is good reason to think that it lacks something in sophistication and completeness. Bibas (2004) identified a whole range of influences on plea bargaining over and above evidence strength and expected sentence including:

- Lawyers on a flat fee may prefer a plea bargain because it means that they can get the job done without spending more time in court.

- Sentencing guidelines strongly push towards plea bargaining in cases like this.

- The defence may be keen to use plea bargaining as a way of encouraging good relations with the judge and the prosecuting lawyers.

- The judge may be keen as a workload-reducing procedure.

- The prosecution may strongly push for a plea bargain because it can reduce time pressures and the like.

Kramer, Wolbranksy and Heilbrun (2007) studied lawyers' decision making when advising a client about plea bargaining. The research extended the situation by having the defence lawyer's client already having expressed a preference concerning plea bargaining. The participants were US attorneys including private criminal defence lawyers and lawyers working for the public defender's office. They were presented with one of eight versions of the experimental conditions created by the variables (a) high or low likelihood of conviction (i.e. strong or weak evidence), (b) the preference of the client for possible plea bargaining or not, and (c) high sentence versus low sentence. The sentences were 10 years or 3 years if convicted which reduced to 5 years or 18 months with plea bargaining respectively. Attorneys rated the likelihood of recommending a plea on a five-point scale from very likely to very unlikely. Where the evidence was strong, where the likely sentence was long and where the defendant had a preference to go to trial then the lawyers were most likely to recommend plea bargaining. Not surprisingly, when the evidence was weak but the likely sentence, if convicted, long and the defendant had a preference to go to trial then there was a low likelihood of the lawyer recommending a plea bargain deal.

There have been high-profile cases in which the defendant did not appear in the witness box to give evidence in their own defence. The decision by a lawyer not to expose their client to questioning in court is another way in which a lawyer can try to influence the outcome of a trial. Defendants are not required to give evidence in many jurisdictions including the USA, UK and elsewhere. There is clearly potential for the jury to be suspicious of the reasons why the defendant does not take the witness stand despite it being a right not to do so. At the same time, if the defendant chooses to go into the witness stand to give evidence, then the court may admit into evidence their criminal record (if it is pertinent to the evidence). So there is a risk either way of making things worse for the defendant. It has been commonly and consistently found in research studies that a defendant with a criminal record is perceived more negatively – as lacking somewhat in trustworthiness and credibility. Where any previous offences revealed in court are similar to the current charge then the effects are even stronger. The purpose of introducing the criminal history is to discredit their evidence but the jury takes things beyond this and makes more general assumptions concerning the character of the defendant. That is, they assume that because a defendant has previously committed a crime then they are likely to have committed the current one also. Thus they attribute the crime to dispositional factors not situational ones. A whole series of studies by Shaffer (Shaffer, 1985; Shaffer and Case, 1982; Shaffer and Sadowski, 1979) showed that defendants who do not take the stand are more likely to be judged negatively. However, simply taking the stand to claim one's innocence is equally risky (Shaffer and Sadowski, 1979). The

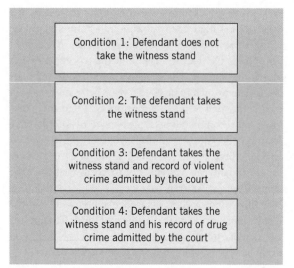

Figure 23.2 The Four Conditions of Jones and Harrison's (2009) study

jury members may feel that this is merely self-serving rhetoric which is readily discounted.

Jones and Harrison (2009) designed a study to examine the consequences of a defence lawyer's decision to take the witness stand. There were a total of four different conditions in their study (see Figure 23.2) since not all possibilities are legally possible or meaningful (e.g. not going on the witness stand but, nevertheless, a criminal record being revealed). The study involved US students serving as a mock jury in a fictitious case. Two men had got involved in a fight in a bar and one was charged with assault and battery against the other. A short transcript of the court hearing was provided. The evidence was ambiguous about which of the two men started the fight. The four conditions of the study were:

- the accused did not take the stand
- the defendant took the stand and said that the victim had started the fight and that he, personally, had acted in self-defence
- the defendant takes the witness stand and the evidence that he had a previous record for similar crimes was introduced
- the defendant takes the witness stand and his previous record for a drugs-related crime was introduced

There was evidence that jurors who thought the defendant was guilty could be influenced by their failure to take the witness stand. They were also more likely to see the offender as guilty if they perceived him as aggressive, less

trustworthy and less credible as a witness. These findings were not dependent on the research manipulations in any way. The jurors were suspicious of the defendants irrespective of them having a criminal record or taking the witness stand. In other words, the study gave no general indication either way of whether it is best to go on the witness stand or to remain silent as a defendant. However, the trial transcripts did not, in this study, include any instructions from the judge to the jurors about disregarding any implications they might draw from the failure to take the witness stand. This may have affected the outcome somewhat since it is known from past research that such warnings, perversely, merely make jurors more suspicious about the defendant who does not testify (Diamond et al., 1989; Wissler and Saks, 1985).

Judgments

From the perspective of forensic and criminal psychology, the judges and courts are largely of interest in terms of consequences for the individuals who pass before them. This is a somewhat limited perspective. Feminist writers, on the other hand, note that the higher courts, especially, have great power to define the parameters of a range of important topics. For example, Williams (1991)describes the role of the US Supreme Court in relation to gender equality. She suggests that legal cases are a 'focal point' where the issue and meaning of equality may be argued.

Courts of law work through the rather formal language of legal experts including judges and lawyers. Inevitably, then, a primary focus of research into that work must concentrate on their language use. Considerable efforts have been made to understand the narrative structure of evidence, as we have seen. Other aspects of language in court have received attention from socio-linguists, discourse analysts and feminist writers. Harris (1994) argues that the language of the law is basically and effectively highly ideological. So she regards concepts such as equality before the law and impartiality of judgment as the meat of ideological conflicts in courtroom exchanges. She suggests that the magistrates in the courts she studied use propositions that are inevitably ideological in that they are not verifiable for their truth. They reinforce power and domination relationships, and are effectively presented as common sense. However, this is expressed in complex ways. Clear examples of similar processes have been found in other legal texts as we will see.

If judges do ideological work then just how is this achieved? The lack of a repertoire of discourse appropriate to certain crimes may result in them being interpreted through other inappropriate frameworks (Coates, Bavelas and Gibson, 1994). These authors mention a Canadian trial judgment concerning a man who went into a room and put his penis in the mouth of a sleeping woman. How one describes these events may vary according to perspective, but the trial judge described this as 'the act of offering his penis' (p. 189). Now this is a rather strange use of the verb 'to offer'. Had the woman been sexually attacked in the street it is inconceivable that a judge would use a phrase such as 'the accused offered the victim his penis' if he had put his

penis in her mouth or told her to fellate him. That is, in terms of our usual discourse about stranger rape, the phrase 'to offer' has no meaning. It implies choice on the part of the woman. The language might be more appropriate if the events are interpreted using the discourse repertoire of erotic/affectionate relationships. In the context of a long-standing relationship, it is just about possible to understand the use of the verb 'to offer'. That is, it was a direct and forthright sexual invitation in a relationship in which the partners had previously established a mutually acceptable robust approach to sex and the man was 'offering' sexual intercourse. The authors surveyed a number of relevant judgments and suggested five 'anomalous' themes in similar trials:

Box 23.1 Key concept

The hypothesis testing model

According to Van Koppen (1995), it is inappropriate to regard judicial decision making as being based on a hypothesis-testing model. Nevertheless, such a model has been put forward a number of times. The hypothesis-testing process (that X committed the crime they are accused of) is evaluated firstly in terms of the prior odds that the hypothesis is true in advance of consideration of the evidence. The hypothesis is essentially the charge or indictment.

The prior odds

$$\text{Prior odds that charge is true} = \frac{\text{probability that charge is true}}{\text{probability that charge is false}}$$

Thus the prior odds have a theoretical numerical value. One difficulty is deciding what these probabilities are in any given set of circumstances. A total presumption of innocence until proven guilty would have values of 0 and 1 for the respective probabilities. In these circumstances, the prior odds are 0/1 or zero. An experienced judge may set the probabilities otherwise – that the probability of the charge being true = 0.9 and the probability that the charge is false = 0.1. Thus the prior odds that the charge is true are 0.9/0.1 = 9. The assessment of such prior odds is difficult and, given that most people probably do not express themselves well in terms of probabilities, it may be a fruitless task. The statistical procedures are based on Bayesian statistics.

Revised odds – posterior odds

The next stage is the introduction of evidence. Let us assume that it is a fact that the accused was picked out in a line-up/identification parade by a witness. This information will have a diagnostic value that indicates the probability that a person picked out at an identification parade is in fact accurately identified rather than wrongfully identified. Perhaps the judge has had a lot of experience of poor procedures for conducting the line-up being used and regards their accuracy as being relatively low. The judge believes that 7 in 10 identification parades accurately identify the individual in question. Thus the accuracy expressed as odds will be 7/3 (i.e.

Box 23.1 (continued)

7 correct identifications for each 3 incorrect ones), which equals 2.33. Thus it is 2.33 times more likely that the accused is the offender than without this evidence. This will increase the odds that the accused is guilty as charged.

$$\text{Posterior odds} = \text{prior odds} \times \text{certainty of the evidence} = 9 \times 2.33 = 21.0$$

The posterior odds are merely the odds after evidence has been introduced. Thus our prior odds (of 9) need to be multiplied by 2.33. Since this equals 21.0 then the probability that the accused is guilty increases.

Further evidence may be introduced, thus adjusting the odds. This is achieved merely by multiplying the existing odds at that stage (that is, the new prior odds which are, of course, the posterior odds calculated above) by the certainty of the further evidence. The new evidence may be the defence witness's claims to have seen the accused in a bar at the time of the offence. This should reduce confidence in the guilt of the accused. So the odds based on this information alone would suggest that the probability that the witness is mistaken should be relatively low. Turned into the ratio of the probability of being right over the probability of being wrong, the odds of the accused being guilty might be 0.5. We simply multiply the odds prior to the introduction of new evidence (i.e. 21.0) by the odds ratio for the new information. This gives us a new posterior odds value of 10.5: that is, it is substantially less likely that the accused is guilty.

The decision

In such a model, the decision is assumed to be guilty – that is, the hypothesis of guilt supported – if the posterior odds exceed a critical value. Below that value the decision will be not guilty.

Critique of the model

- The model seems not to resonate with our experiences of decision making – most of us are not skilled at expressing ideas in terms of statistical probabilities.
- As a purely statistical model (rather than a psychological model) it would have value only if it were possible to stipulate the odds ratios of various types of evidence sufficiently precisely for the model to be predictive of actual court outcomes.
- The probability of guilt assessed before the submission of evidence is conceptually difficult to define. A literal presumption of innocence until proven guilty would set the prior odds ratio at zero (0.0/1.0) since there is no chance of being guilty and a certainty (i.e. 1.0) of being innocent. The consequence of this is that no matter what the new evidence, no matter how indicative of guilt it is, the posterior odds will have to be zero. This is obviously ludicrous. It is more likely that we assume that there is a likelihood that the accused is guilty. Reading newspapers would suggest that a high percentage of prosecutions result in convictions. Should this be the figure we use? There seems to be no way of answering the question satisfactorily.
- The value of a piece of evidence is not normally easily translated into an odds ratio that can be taken as indicative of guilt. So what would we make of the testimony that the accused had been seen elsewhere at the time of the offence if the witness were the man's wife?
- The question of the odds that are high enough to convict demands a complex answer that cannot be provided by the model. Does it vary with offence type? What other factors might it vary with?

In short, the mathematical underpinnings of the model do not overcome its psychological inadequacy.

- *Appropriate resistance*: this is the idea that victims have certain obligations to prevent or resist the attack on them. Physical struggling is part of the appropriate actions of a victim, it would appear from the judges' comments. In one of the judgments, the victim is described as eventually acquiescing to her own rape once she ceased struggling: 'She testified that after the first bout of intercourse she stopped struggling and that she acquiesced in the second bout, although the intercourse was still without her consent' (p. 195). Ehrlich (1999), dealing with a university disciplinary hearing, describes related linguistic effects. One woman was questioned in the following way: 'You never make an attempt to put him on the floor or when he leaves the room, to close the door behind him or you know you have several occasions to lock the door. You only have to cross the room. Or move him to the floor, but these things are offensive to you?' (p. 244). Ehrlich suggests that this actually contains forceful illocutory assertions rather than questions. In other words, 'You should have put him on the floor; you should have closed the door; you should have locked the door' (p. 244).

- *Avoidance of agency for assault*: the actions involved in the sexual violence were frequently ascribed to the events themselves rather than to the offender, in phrases such as 'the struggle got into the bedroom' and 'there was advantage taken of a situation which presented itself' (p. 196). The acts seem to be doing themselves rather than being done by the offender.

- *Erotic/affectionate characterisation*: judges who described sexual crimes in terms of a man carrying out an offence against women or children as for the man's sexual gratification. This is to minimise or deny that the crime is an assault and also to suggest that it is sexual in nature rather than violent. Similarly, the language used to describe the attacks carries very different implications from what had actually happened. For example, forced oral contact was described as 'attempted unsuccessfully to kiss'. Forced oral/genital contacts were described as 'acts of oral sex'. Forced vaginal penetration was described as a 'bout of intercourse' (p. 192).

- *Offender's character*: the judges often described the man's character in very positive terms. For example, a man who raped a woman on two occasions was described as being of 'impeccable character' (p. 196).

- *Sexual assault distinct from violence*: especially from a feminist viewpoint, to describe a sexual assault as non-violent is to undermine the notion that sexual assault is a violent act: for example, 'there was no violence and no physical force' (p. 194).

In a similar vein, Cederborg (1999) shows how in the context of child abuse trials, Swedish judges construct children's credibility as witnesses. Overwhelmingly, the judgments encouraged the view that the children were credible. Such children, according to Cederborg, were perceived as credible because they fitted the judge's common-sense theory of what behaviour is normal. For example, 'Nancy told her story calmly and clearly and with no contradictory details. Her stories at the main hearing agreed well with her previous statements' (p. 151). The material in the judgment relevant to Nancy's character included 'It must be regarded as out of the question that at the age of 11 Nancy would have been sexually interested in him and should have even suggested that they have intercourse' (p. 151). Nancy's case was one of the majority in which the accused was convicted. In cases in which there was not a conviction, the judgment almost always lacked any assessment of the character of the child. An instance of the sorts of terminology and style used by the judges in these cases is the following: '. . . despite the efforts of the interrogating officer, this questioning does not give any clear impression that Hilda F actually experienced the events about which she answered questions' (p. 153). The judge's assessment of the child cannot be validated by any existing test so the interpretation becomes a subjective reality.

Decision making in court

Legal decision making is governed by a variety of formal aspects such as the use of case law, precedents, guidelines and so forth. So any discussion of the psychology of legal decision making needs to be considered in this wider context. In other words, the work of judges in courts of law is highly structured which may limit the potential influence of psychological factors. Even so, the psychological research literature concerning how judges reach decisions is not extensive. Of course, judges are a hard-to-reach research population and the opportunities to study them directly are limited for obvious reasons. Consequently, sometimes the research literature concerning legal decision making by judges elides into that on how jurors make decisions in courts of law. It is far from clear that there are distinct psychological approaches to juror and judge decision making. Often similar theoretical ideas could apply equally to the two. Nevertheless, there are occasions when researchers obtain access to judges as participants in their research. Such examples are particularly to be welcomed though their scarcity value is much greater than their value as a body of knowledge.

One example of this rare sort of research concerned the influence of the label 'psychopathy' on the judgments of young offenders (Jones and Cauffman, 2008). The concept of psychopath refers to a glib, charming, callous, self-centred, irresponsible and amoral cluster of personality characteristics. This is discussed elsewhere in Chapters 21 and 27. As a concept applied to young offenders it is controversial and debated with an unusual degree of passion on each side. One of the issues is that the term psychopath serves as a label which may steer the way that the individual is treated by the criminal justice system into their adult lives. The study by Jones and Cauffman showed that the label of psychopathy changed perceptions of amenability to treatment and dangerousness together with recommendations for placement made by US judges. The study involved 100 well-experienced judges working in juvenile and adult courts in South Eastern USA. Judges from adult courts would be involved in judgments where a young person has been sent to adult court for trial by a juvenile court. Various scenario cases were distributed at random the judges who read them and then responded to a series of questions. The basic scenario was one involving an aggravated assault between two 15-year-old male youngsters involving a mutual assault of one on the other. Aggravated assault allows for considerable legal discretion in terms of disposal (sentencing etc.) in the USA. This discretion makes aggravated assault ideal to show extra-legal factors in the decision making of judges. The manipulation of psychopathy appeared in information concerning a mental health expert's testimony. Of the four scenarios, one contained no mental health information, the second indicated that the defendant was a psychopath, the third was attributed the characteristic of psychopathy (such as manipulativeness, pathological lying, lack of emotion or remorse, refusal to accept responsibility for their own actions, difficulties in controlling anger, etc.), and the fourth condition included both the attribution of these traits

together with the label of psychopath. The judges rated the youngster on four characteristics – culpability, restrictiveness, amenability and dangerousness. Young people labelled as psychopaths and those who had psychopathic traits applied to them were seen as less amenable to treatment and were recommended for a disposal which involved restrictive placements. However, judgements about their culpability were NOT influenced by such ratings. When perceptions of dangerousness were controlled, this relationship was no longer significant. This suggests that psychopathy is equated with dangerousness in the minds of the judges.

Ideally one would like and expect professionals within the criminal justice system to be open to the possibility that where there is a suspect that that suspect is innocent. But we know from well-established psychological research findings that there is a tendency or bias towards confirming our beliefs rather than disconfirming them. This is known as the confirmation bias and was first demonstrated in a classic, early study by Wason (1968) which had nothing at all to do with crime. Participants in the study were given a set of four cards and asked to decide whether the set fitted a rule supplied by the researcher. They were told that each of the four cards had a letter on one face and a number on the other, hidden, surface. The rule for their consideration was that if one side showed a vowel then the other side had to show an even number. Imagine that the participant is shown four cards with the following on the visible surface – E, B, 2 and 5 (see Figure 23.3). The task for the participant is to turn over as few cards as possible to determine whether the vowel–even number rule is true. The most effective strategy would be to turn over just two of the four cards – the one showing the vowel (E) and the one showing the odd number (5). The other two cards logically have nothing to do with testing the rule. The findings indicated that most people basically make choices which confirm the rule. So they tend to turn over cards which at best can only confirm the rule

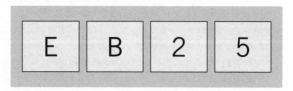

Figure 23.3 What cards need to be turned over to test the rule that if there was a vowel on one side there is an even number on the other?

– they ignore the important cards which could disconfirm the rule. Thus they do not usually turn over the card with the odd number (5) despite the fact that if there is a vowel on the hidden side then the rule is disproven.

Evidence over the years has supported the idea of confirmation bias in people's thinking. That is, they do not seek the evidence to disconfirm what they think but they have a preference for the evidence which supports what they think. Hence the importance of the confirmation bias in the criminal justice system. The research by Ask and Granhag (2005) using police officers which found that they were not affected by the knowledge of a alternative suspect when judging the incriminating power of the rest of the evidence available to them was discussed in Chapter 11. Rassin (2010) carried out two studies, the first of which replicated Ask and Granhag's study with a sample which included judges and district attorneys as well as police officers as in the original study. Participants were given one of alternative vignettes describing a crime. The first was called the motive version and was as follows:

'A woman is found dead in an apartment. A second woman, Eva, is encountered in the apartment, and is hence a suspect in the case. The victim is a psychiatrist who was acquainted with Eva and who had her office in the apartment. Eva's partner was a client of the victim, and hence (the partner and the victim) had regular contact. According to the victim's assistant, Eva had expressed suspicion about a sexual relationship between the victim and Eva's partner and was deeply jealous. The following observations have been made thus far in the investigation. . . .'

(pp. 155–6)

The 'alternative suspect' version read:

'A woman is found dead in an apartment. A second woman, Eva, is encountered in the apartment, and is hence a suspect in the case. The victim is a psychiatrist who was acquainted with Eva and who had her office in the apartment. The victim had recently received several phone calls from an anonymous man who each time threatened to kill her with a knife. These phone calls are known to the police from before. The victim had told the police that she thought the man must be a patient or a former patient. The following observations have been made thus far in the investigation . . .'

The vignettes then went on to list some facts about the crime such as:

- it happened at lunchtime,
- when she returned back to work after lunch, the victim's assistant found the apartment door was locked from the inside
- worried, the assistant phoned for police assistance
- the police banged on the door which was eventually opened by the suspect, etc.

Twenty items of information like the above were rated separately on a scale from exonerating to incriminating by participants. They then rated the guilt of the victim and whether they would convict the suspect. All of the professional groups studied gave much the same evaluations of the incriminating power of the known evidence. Most importantly, judgements about the incriminating power of the evidence were not affected by the suggestion that there was another suspect. That is to say, this is evidence of the confirmation bias in operation. Quite clearly, confirmation bias has to be regarded as worthy of inclusion in explanations of judicial decision making.

Legal systems are different in different part of the world. Understanding of how these different systems work contributes to the broad process of understanding judicial decision making. In Norway, there are three possible legal outcomes to a criminal court case – (a) conviction, (b) acquittal by the court, and (c) insufficient evidence to proceed. According to Myklebust and Bjørklund (2009), investigative interviews of children in child abuse allegation cases are videoing in their entirety to be shown in court instead of the child being present in court. This is standard practice in Nordic countries. Myklebust and Bjørklund's study involved 100 such interviews carried out by different police interviewers. The interviewees were schoolchildren between 6 and 16 years of age and all showed normal linguistic development. The interviews were transcribed using standard proscribed procedures and then coded by the researchers. It was found that interviews with older girls always produced convictions. The big difference was that where the trial ended with a conviction the average length of what the child said in their interviews was about twice as many words as for the acquittal and insufficient evidence outcomes. The apparent competency of the child may be the reason for this according to the authors.

As mentioned earlier, the opportunities of researchers to study actual judges are somewhat limited. So any evidence, no matter how preliminary, warrants consideration. De Keijser and van Koppen (2007) proposed two possible psychological mechanisms which may affect

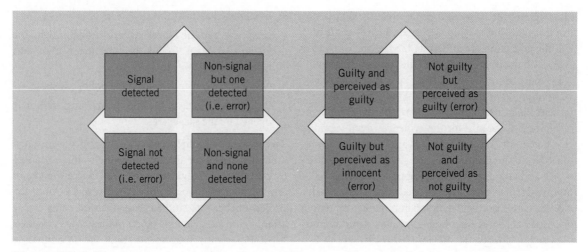

Figure 23.4 The basic signal detection problem applied to judicial judgments

the decisions judges make about guilt or innocence and the appropriate punishment for a particular crime.

- The conviction paradox: according to de Keijser and van Koppen, the conviction paradox suggests that for very serious cases, judges adopt a lower standard of proof than they ordinarily would for less serious offences. De Keijser and van Koppen relate this suggestion to signal detection theory (see Figure 23.4). Signal detection assumes that there are two kinds of stimuli – the signal and the non-signal. The decision maker has to decide between each of these two. However, the problem is that there is a background of noise and that most signals are continuous and not discrete so signal detection is prone to errors. Two types of error are possible – a false positive where a non-signal is detected as being a signal and a false negative where a signal is detected as being a non-signal. In judicial decision making there is a choice between guilty and not guilty. The characteristics of the guilty and the not-guilty overlap quite considerably. This requires decision criteria of guilt to be established. There is a trade-off between the risks inherent in a false not guity decision and a false guilty decision. Legal rhetoric has it that is is 'better to acquit ten guilty persons than to convict a single innocent'. There is evidence from research that jurors tend to go for a guilty decision where the charge is more serious, all other things being equal. Although one would tend to think that judges are more stringent in serious cases where the punishments can be expected to be large, the risks of letting a terrorist go free are much greater than letting a shoplifter go free. So criteria become less stringent not more stringent where the crime is serious and the risks of acquittal for the public greater.

- Compensatory punishment mechanism: this suggests that where the evidence is relatively weak, judges who decide on a guilty verdict will tend to compensate for their initial doubts by giving lesser punishments. The authors indicate that psychological research has demonstrated the influence of anticipated regret for the possible outcomes. Generally speaking, the judge goes for the safe option in their decision making. This means that the judge when choosing a punishment will opt for a more lenient sentence in the case of a serious crime. There is evidence of this from studies of negligence cases but none for criminal cases.

De Keijser and van Koppen's study involved Dutch judges and justices serving in criminal courts. They were supplied with fictitious but very realistic dossiers on criminal cases. The crimes involved were aggravated assault, simple assault and burglary. The strength of the evidence was manipulated with some versions involving strong evidence and others minimal evidence but legally sufficient to allow a conviction. Where the evidence was strong a guilty decision was given no matter whether it was a serious case or not. There were no differences in the pattern of decisions made for the cases were the evidence was weak whether or not the offence was serious. There was no support for either of the proposed mechanisms in de Keijser and van Koppen's research. This may be disappointing theoretically but the fact that the data were from real judges compensates for this somewhat.

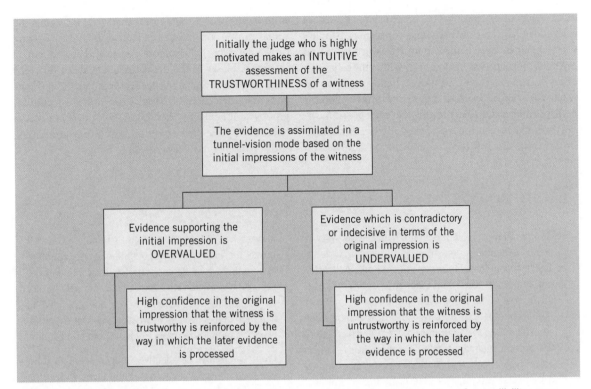

Figure 23.5 The Dangerous Decisions Theory of how assessments of credibility are used in the courtroom

Judges (and jurors too) need to evaluate accurately all kinds of witnesses including defendants. There are, however, doubts as to their ability to do that. Why should it be so difficult? According to Porter and ten Brinke (2009) part of the explanation may be found in Dangerous Decision Theory (DDT) which may help us understand just how injustices occur in the courtroom (see Figure 23.5). The starting point of the problem lies in the initial interpretation of information gleaned from the face of the defendant or their expressions of emotion. For many reasons judgements made in this way are risky since, for example, there are no perfect indicators of honesty and many misleading indicators (as discussed in Chapter 18). Research has shown that judges, when sentencing, are influenced by ways of thinking based on their previous experiences in court. Judges are highly influenced by initial impressions. Motivation will lead to close scrutiny of evidence but initial impressions colour the entire decision-making process.

Witness demeanour and the 'face of deceit' may well be involved. This means that if judges concentrate on aspects of the face and demeanour which are incorrectly understood as indicating lying then errors may dominate in their decision making. So such impressions are risky but they nevertheless initiate a whole sequence of dangerous decisions about credibility. Although these initial judgements are highly influential, they are perceived as being intuitive and not, for example, based on prejudices or biases. An informal survey of judges in Canada about the characteristics indicative of deception found virtually a complete lack of consensus about what such indicators are, though things like body movements, fidgeting and eye contact were mentioned (Porter, Woodworth and Birt, 2000). Nevertheless the judges expressed a high level of confidence in their own ability to detect deception. Judges commonly self-report using strategies which seek the ring of truth in the testimony. This is relying on intuition or gut instinct, according to the authors of the paper. Porter *et al.* found that self-reported reliance on intuition was inversely correlated with their accuracy at identifying deception! The initial judgement – whatever it is and however accurate it is – tends to persist and influence the interpretation and assimilation of subsequent evidence about the defendant. These later interpretations of the evidence are irrational but appear rational because each judge has their own schemas concerning people's trustworthiness or schemas about trustworthiness and methods (or heuristics) for deciding whether the behaviour of a witness is deceptive. The judge is highly motivated to reach a decision or conclusion. A sort of tunnel vision (or perhaps confirmation bias) ensures that evidence supporting the initial perception is preferred and so takes a hold. In contrast, disconfirming or ambiguous information is underplayed. The outcome is that, right or wrong, the initial impression influences later evaluations. Relying on stereotypical beliefs about deceptive behaviour may introduce biases in the decisions made about different cultural groups. Social science research (Vrij, 2000) suggests that detection of lying across different cultural groups is difficult. For example, Aboriginals in Canada tend to suppress their emotions which may undermine their credibility in the eyes of some judges.

Main points

- Courts of law provide procedurally based settings in which evidence is presented and judgments made. The procedures in different jurisdictions will differ markedly but the two broad approaches are the adversarial system employed in the Anglo-American approach in which opposing sides do battle against each other, and the inquisitorial system which is largely led by the judge/magistrate who may be involved at an early stage of police work. Nevertheless, even within a particular system, there are many procedural and other variations. All of this makes it very difficult to study the processes involved in courts of law.

- Despite there being a great deal known about persuasive communications from the psychology of communications and attitude change, for example, the modern emphasis when applying psychology to effective presentations of evidence has tended to emphasise the importance of narrative structures rather than, for example, peripheral factors such as the authority of the lawyers involved. A good narrative structure is one that unites the individual components of evidence into a coherent story which supports one's own side in the case. Anchored narrative theory goes one step further by suggesting that notions which are grounded in common-sense notions of what is true, for example, will tend to make for more effective communications.

- From a feminist perspective, judges seem to do a great deal of ideological work when faced with cases involving women victims. So commentaries made about particular events tend to present the evidence in terms favourable to the man's point of view. So, a man who had a history of raping women might be described as having an impeccable character. These tendencies can be contrasted with the idea that decision making in court follows a hypothesis-testing model in which probabilities are calculated mentally about each stage of the evidence. There is no reason to believe that such a model applies in court.

Further reading

Posey, A.J. and Wrightsman, L.S. (2005) *Trial Consulting* Oxford: Oxford University Press.

Waites, R.C. (2003) *Courtroom Psychology and Trial Advocacy* New York: ALM Press.

Wiener, R.L. and Bornstein, B.H. (2011) *Handbook of Trial Consulting* New York: Springer.

Also all of the chapters in Section Three of the following:
Carson, D. and Bull, R. (2003) *Handbook of Psychology in Legal Contexts* (2nd edn) Chichester: John Wiley.

The following site by Steven Penrod has many of his articles on courtroom and eyewitness psychology. The site tells you how to e-mail for the 'key' so that you can access the materials: http://web.jjay.cuny.edu/~spenrod/papers/

Visit our website at www.pearsoned.co.uk/howitt for self-test and essay questions, annotated further reading, audio interviews with researchers in the field, weblinks and more information on becoming a forensic psychologist.

Juries and decision making

Overview

- Only a small percentage of criminal cases are heard before a jury. The jury system has been subject to criticisms in some notorious cases. Trials with juries reduce the importance of the judge on decisions of guilt or innocence. Evidence is presented orally in jury trials so there is less reliance on written documentation than in inquisitorial systems.

- In the US legal system there is some scope for lawyers to influence the make-up of the jury by peremptory challenges of some jurors. There has been some research on improving the effectiveness of these challenges by using social-scientific surveys to assess what sorts of juror are sympathetic to, say, the defence. This is known as scientific decision making. The evidence on this is not compelling though such services are often offered.

- Some problems for jurors can be alleviated by simple changes such as permitting note-taking by jurors and allowing them to ask questions in court.

- Jury decision making is governed by rules which can affect the permissible size of the jury as well as the size of the majority on which a guilty verdict can be reached. The larger the jury, the longer the decision time. Where a majority decision as to guilt is required, the jury makes more effort to try to reach a verdict.

- Pre-trial publicity can influence potential jurors. However, in law, prejudice is not conceived in the same way as it would be in a psychological study. For example, in the United States this influence would need to be accompanied by a resistance to change of mind in the light of new information. Mass media are so pervasive that for some trials it is unlikely that a location for the trial could be found where media publicity has not had an effect. Researchers may help to find a relatively unaffected venue for the trial.

Introduction

Trial by jury became part of English law in twelfth century as an alternative to trial by ordeals such as walking on hot coals. In England and Wales about 95 per cent of criminal cases are tried in a magistrates' court before three lay magistrates supported by expert legal advice. Only about 5 per cent are tried in a higher court with the possibility of a trial by jury (Crown Prosecution Service, 2011). Thus the role of the jury trial can be overstated although the figures may be higher in other jurisdictions. Everyone is familiar with well-publicised instances of juries acquitting a defendant whom seems to be guilty beyond any question of doubt: one famous instance of this is the case of Rodney King, a black American, who was seen around the world on videotaped being beaten up by white police officers in 1991 (this may be viewed on YouTube: http://uk.truveo.com/search?query=rODNEy%20king %20youtube#rODNEy%20king%20youtube). They were acquitted. Inevitably, such cases lead to questioning of the jury system. Nevertheless, we can all appreciate the complex task of jurors and the pressure that they can sometimes be under. This is especially so in complex trials with weeks if not months of evidence. Is there anything that can be done to aid jurors in these circumstances? Very simple procedural changes, such as allowing jurors to take notes or perhaps to ask questions, might be advantageous.

Like many other forensic issues, there is considerable doubt about the worth of laboratory experiments for addressing research questions such as these. It matters little if psychologists are happy with such procedures if those responsible for policy will not accept the findings of their research. The procedures are easily defined as artificial since real juries are not involved. Field studies, because they usually lack random allocation to experimental and control conditions, are similarly beset with problems in terms of interpretation. In this chapter we will spread widely into the limited research into the jury and, especially, how the jury seems to reach decisions. Wherever possible, we will concentrate of research that involves real juries but this is fairly rare. There is a great deal more work involving mock jurors of various sorts. There is no single type of mock jury and the term can refer to individuals making judgments in isolation in a psychological laboratory as much as to a fairly realistic representation of a typical jury in a particular deliberating in a research setting which is very close to the situation in a real court of law. Anything which is not a real jury in a real court with real evidence making decisions which affect the future of individuals is a mock jury. For that reason, when reading about mock juries one has to carefully evaluate how convincing a particular mock jury is.

In addition to discussing how juries make decisions, we will also consider what can be done to enhance the likelihood that the evidence of one side of the case will prevail.

Scientific jury selection

In the legal world there is a plethora of advice to lawyers written by prominent lawyers about juries and jurors (Fulero and Penrod, 1990). This advice alludes to many 'theories' about what sorts of people make 'good' jurors for the prosecution or defence. Take, for example, the following advice taken by Fulero and Penrod from a number of texts about female jurors:

- Avoid women as they are unpredictable and influenced by their husbands
- Old women wearing too much make-up are unstable and bad for state prosecutors
- Women are not good for the defence of attractive females
- Women are sympathetic and extraordinarily conscientious jurors
- Women's libbers may be antagonistic to male defendants.

It should be taken for granted that none of this advice is based on empirical research. They may or may not, however, be believed by lawyers.

Advice and help about jurors and other aspects of trials is available through various commercial companies. It is worthwhile exploring the Internet for information about the sorts of services that are offered. The following are just a few:

- *Community attitude surveys* – which are used to develop jury profiles and accurately assess the quality of the lawyer's case.
- *Focus groups* – which are recommended in order to identify themes for test cases.
- *Jury selection* – a senior consultant will assist the lawyer when selecting a jury.

- *Mock trials* – which are described as formal exercises that reliably find the likely outcome for a particular case.

- *Prospective juror questionnaires* – which will give the lawyer a strategic advantage when selecting a jury.

The voir dire is the stage at the beginning of a trial at which judges (and lawyers according to the jurisdiction) seek to identify biases or prejudices among potential jurors. The phrase 'voir dire' is French and means to speak the truth. There is no common systematic way of assessing bias so different questions may be asked of each potential juror on the venire (the list from which the jury is selected). Lawyers are more concerned about prejudice that might adversely affect their side rather than a just outcome, no matter what that is. Scientific jury selection is built on the voir dire and the wish to gain advantage for a particular side. In areas of the US system, the lawyer makes a challenge for cause when it is felt that there is overt prejudice on the part of the potential juror or for some other reason. Nevertheless, it is for the judge to decide whether the challenge is accepted and the judge may choose to ask the potential juror if they can put their prejudice aside. Peremptory challenges require no stated reason and lead to the dismissal of the potential juror (Kovera, Dickinson and Cutler, 2002). Scientific jury selection uses research evidence on the sorts of juror who are likely to favour a particular side. Figure 24.1 illustrates the steps.

The voir dire is often described as a 'trial within a trial'. It is the stage at which judges and lawyers sort out legal matters between themselves, including who should be excluded from the jury.

The first major account of scientific jury selection comes from the group of social scientists, in the United States, who helped the defence of the Harrisburg Seven for conspiracy. The accused included priests and ex-priests, nuns and ex-nuns! The trial took place in 1972 against the backdrop of America's war in Vietnam. Philip Berrigan and others were accused of various plots against the State – for example, they were accused of planning to bomb heating tunnels in Washington and to kidnap Henry Kissinger, Assistant to the President for National Security Affairs. The problem for the defence was that the trial was taking place in an area that was fundamentally conservative (and generally pro the war) but the defendants were anti-war activists.

The researchers became actively involved in the case because they were unhappy that informers and *agents provocateurs* were being used against the accused. They believed that the location of the trial in Harrisburg, Pennsylvania, was favourable to the prosecution. A survey was carried out around Harrisburg using a sample matched to be similar to the panel from which the jury was to be selected (Schulman *et al.*, 1973). So factors such as age, occupation, education and race were taken into

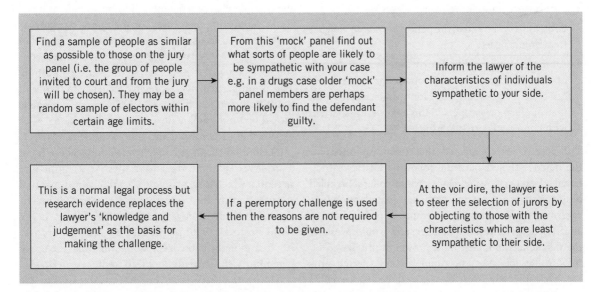

Figure 24.1 Scientific jury selection. The voir dire is often described as a 'trial within a trial'. It is the stage at which judges and lawyers sort out legal matters between themselves, including who should be excluded from the jury

account. Over 1,200 individuals were obtained by random sampling from similar voters on the voting list.

The questionnaire was detailed and covered a range of issues – including the matter of the influence of the media. The participants' choice of media to use, their knowledge of the defendants, and their knowledge of their case were measured and the following covered:

- the acceptability of certain anti-war activities and other political indicators;
- the ages and activities of their children;
- the organisations to which they belonged and so forth;
- their degree of trust in government;
- their religious attitude and commitment;
- their spare-time activities;
- who they saw as the greatest Americans during the past 10 to 15 years so that their social values might be assessed.

Religious attitudes had a bearing on trial-relevant predispositions. Religions bad for the defendants were Episcopalians, Presbyterians, Methodists and fundamentalists; religions better for the defence included Catholics. Other trends included the following:

- Overwhelmingly, the public in Harrisburg agreed with the statement that the right to private property is sacred.
- Nearly two-thirds thought that a citizen should support his/her country even when it was wrong.
- Four-fifths believed that the police should use violence to maintain order.
- Although sex and political party were weak predictors of attitudes, Democrats and women were more liberal on certain questions. Education and contact with metropolitan newspapers in this area were associated with conservatism/republicanism.

The researchers considered that the ideal juror for the defence should have the following characteristics: female, Democrat, no religion, a white-collar job/skilled blue-collar job, sympathy with the defendants' views regarding the Vietnam war, tolerance of peaceful resistance to the government's policies, and would presume the defendants innocent until proven guilty. Based on this profile, the researchers and lawyers selected prospective jurors who were closest to these requirements although the choices were also partly informed by the responses made by potential jurors in court. Of the final jury of 12, seven could be rated as good prospects from the point of view of the defence. A typical example of these good jurors was:

> Pauline Protzline, a housewife in her late 40s or early 50s, whose son-in-law had been killed in Vietnam. Concerning the war, she had said: 'I wasn't too much at first, but the last few years I've been against it.' We considered this statement to be a good sign. She listed no church affiliation.
>
> (Schulman *et al.*, 1973, p. 25)

The researchers re-interviewed a sample of the original survey chosen as being a match to the real 12-person jury. Of the three-quarters who were prepared to give further opinions, the following were found:

- Just over half presumed the defendants to be guilty. The others were classified as having only low to moderate presumptions of the guilt of the defendants.
- Age and political preference made little difference to presumptions of guilt.
- Only 37 per cent of women thought the defendants guilty on all or most counts. For men, the figure was 57 per cent.
- Of the respondents with high-school education and the preferred religious stance favouring the defence, only about a fifth had a strong presumption of guilt.

At the trial, the defence chose to offer no defence and the defendants, consequently, did not provide any evidence supporting their case. For the minor charges, the jury found the accused guilty of smuggling letters out of a federal prison. They could not agree a verdict on the conspiracy charge. Of the jury, ten were against conviction. This is not particularly impressive evidence in favour of scientific jury selection. Nevertheless, the surveys certainly picked up on the ambiguity of the jury's position.

Whether or not this is the best way in which lawyers can help their clients is also in some doubt. There is not a lot of research into the effectiveness of scientific jury selection, which is surprising since it is claimed that trial consultation in the United States has over 700 practitioners and has a turnover of $400 million (Strier, 1999). Lloyd-Bostock (1996) points out that research on over 2,000 cases in the United Kingdom found that the use of peremptory challenge did not lead to more acquittals.

Horowitz (1980) is an important exception to the general lack of convincing evidence in this field. The important details of Horowitz's study are given in Figure 24.2.

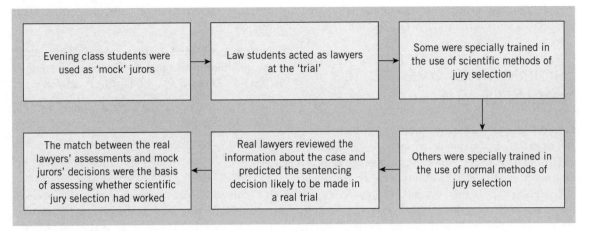

Figure 24.2 The key features of Horowitz's design to investigate scientific jury selection

In terms of the two different methods of jury selection, the following were found:

- Scientific jury selection methods were most accurate (i.e. agreed with the real lawyers' view) for drug and courts martial crimes.
- These were the cases studied for which the survey produced the most accurate results.
- Conventional methods of jury selection were the most accurate for murder.
- The survey was of low accuracy for the murder case.

Generalising from just this one study would be risky. Other research suggests that experts are often poor at identifying biased potential jurors. One study had groups of potential jurors who had been challenged in court as biased for a trial and compared their verdicts with those of the actual jurors who had not been challenged (Zeisel and Diamond, 1978). Essentially, there was no difference between the verdicts of the 'actual' and the 'biased' juries thus indicating that scientific jury selection was ineffective in these examples. This may not be surprising given that lawyers use little more than stereotypes in making their challenges.

As ever, due regard should be exercised for the fact that jurisdictions differ in terms of procedures used. The peremptory challenge in which no reason is given for wishing to reject a potential juror is a feature of the US legal system. Peremptory challenges are not possible in some other jurisdictions. In England and Wales, the right to make peremptory challenges was abolished in 1988 (Lloyd-Bostock, 1996). This means that the US style of

scientific jury selection is not possible for the defence in the UK. Commenting on the American situation, Van Wallendael and Cutler (2004) express some reservations about the general efficacy of scientific jury selection methods in the United States. One issue they mention is that very little is known about the activities of lawyers in voir dire situations. For example, it is not known whether lawyers actually effectively assess trial-relevant attitudes during the voir dire process. Furthermore, there are many situations in which the lawyer has little influence on the process of jury selection: courts in some states do not allow lawyers to assess the attitudes of members of the venire panel (the pool of potential jurors).

A number of ethical issues have been raised about the use of scientific jury selection by Saks (1987):

- The researchers need to explain to respondents just what purposes the survey is to be used for. It is not appropriate to say that the information was for research purposes when, in fact, the intention is to use it to help the defence.
- A further ethical issue concerns the fact that most defendants could not afford to employ researchers (the interviewers in the Harrisburg study, for example, were volunteers). Consequently, in the long run, the prosecution is normally much more likely to benefit from this sort of research. They are the side most capable of funding the research.

Furthermore, Lecci, Snowden and Morris (2004) argue that trial consultants are largely an unregulated group of practitioners who have not been required to establish the validity of their procedures. They should be required to employ standardised measures to assess juror bias.

Simple improvements to aid jurors

Research into jury decision processes has been based almost exclusively on simulations of trial (mock trials). These simulations are unrealistic to varying degrees. Perhaps the most realistic mock jury is the use of shadow juries. Shadow juries sit in on the court proceedings at the request of the researcher, so they hear exactly the same evidence delivered in the same manner as the real jury, and then retire to reach a verdict. Nevertheless, there is evidence of considerable inconsistency between the real jury verdict and that of shadow juries. The difference is that they can be studied by researchers whereas normally researchers do not have access to real juries. Once in a while the courts in the United States have allowed research into the effects of various sorts of change to the system – for example, permitting jurors to take notes, which has not been permitted in the US system since the times of high illiteracy. With the complexity of modern legal evidence, one can imagine that note-taking is a tempting option. Penrod and Heuer (1997) review the evidence coming from field experiments involving a fairly large number of different judges, trials, lawyers and jurors. In one national study, judges gave the jurors permission to take notes as soon as was practicable in the trial. The majority of jurors took up the option although as many as a third chose not to in some instances. On average, taking into account the civil and criminal trials, just over half a page of notes were taken each hour of the trial. While studies do not show a spectacular effect of note-taking, some of Penrod and Heuer's conclusions are of particular interest:

- Note-takers do not concentrate more on the evidence in their notes than on the other evidence available.

- Note-taking does not interfere with a juror's ability to keep up with the proceedings.

- Note-taking jurors are not more satisfied with the trial, the judge or the verdict than those who do not take notes.

- Note-taking seems to be neutral in regard to the prosecution and defence cases in terms of its effects.

- The notes are at best a small assistance to remembering aspects of the evidence.

- The notes taken tend to be accurate records as far as they go.

Similarly, research into the effectiveness of allowing jurors to ask questions using much the same sort of methods led Penrod and Heuer to the following conclusions:

- Jurors do understand the facts and issues better if they ask questions.

- Allowing questions seems to make no difference to the jurors', judge's and lawyers' satisfaction with the trial and verdict.

- If a juror asks an inappropriate question, lawyers will object and the jury does not draw inappropriate conclusions from this. However, generally speaking, the jurors ask perfectly appropriate questions.

In other words, research of this sort tends to demonstrate little or no negative consequences of the potential innovations of note-taking and juror questions, and modest, at best, improvements. Of course, the more research of this sort the better will be our understanding of the difficulties facing jurors.

The effect of jury size and decision rules

Jury decision rules are the formal constraints applied to jury decision making including the size of the majority required to reach a verdict and the size of the jury itself. Interest in the influence of jury size on the verdict was partly the result of *Williams v. Florida* (1970). In this case, the US Supreme Court decided that 6-person juries were as good as 12-person juries. Factors considered included the quality of deliberation, the reliability of the jury's fact finding, the verdict ratio, the ability of dissenters to resist majority pressure and the capacity of the jury to involve a fair cross-section of the community.

A jury may vary in terms of its size but also in terms of the proportion of the jurors who must agree in order to decide on the guilt of the accused. These rules may vary according to the jurisdiction involved but may also vary within a jurisdiction (Arce *et al.*, 1998):

- In the United Kingdom there is sometimes a combined decision rule. Unanimity may be required at first followed by a 10 out of 12 majority after a period of deliberation.

- In Spain, a qualified majority decision rule has been used. A not guilty verdict requires a simple majority of 5 out of 9 but a guilty verdict needs 7 out of 9.

Other jurisdictions employ different rules. An important question is whether factors such as the size of the jury and the decision rule in force make a substantial difference to deliberations and outcomes.

Zeisel (1971) suggested the greater the size of the jury, the greater the risk of a hung jury. A hung jury is one in which a verdict is not possible. There is some evidence that a requirement of unanimity in the decision increases the likelihood that the jury will be hung. Similarly, it is possible that complex cases are more likely to result in failure to reach a decision. In research to test these ideas (Arce *et al.*, 1998), participants eligible for Spanish jury service were selected at random from the electoral register. Gender was equalised in the juries. Participants viewed the re-enactment of a real-life rape trial including the testimony of eyewitness and forensic experts, opening and closing defence and prosecution arguments, and the judge's definition of the legal terms involved and the decision rule. The participants were randomly assigned to one of a number of juries that were then studied through the use of questionnaires. Among the findings were the following:

- Hung juries deliberated longer.
- Hung juries report perceptions of intransigence, lack of dialogue and irrelevant deliberations.
- Hung juries tended to manifest more simultaneous interruptions.
- Hung juries tended to use less of the trial evidence.
- Hung jury members employed more assertions in their communications with each other.

One way of summarising the wide range of findings into the effects of jury size on verdicts and other matters is a meta-analysis (see Box 4.2) by Saks and Marti (1997) which brought together findings of 17 studies. The following trends were found over the various research studies:

- Deliberation time is longer for larger juries.
- For civil cases, smaller juries tend to award more to the injured party.
- Guilty verdicts are not more common in large juries.
- Hung verdicts are commoner for larger juries. This is a finding that is really only true for studies that used a mock jury. In studies involving real juries, hung verdicts were rare – they occurred in only about 1 per cent of instances.

These findings emerged for studies that have a unanimous decision rule (that is, all of the jurors must agree for a guilty verdict). There is evidence to suggest that such juries tend to be evidence driven. For example, they make more references to the evidence, establish more connections between the evidence and legal issues, examine the evidence in detail, and their deliberations are more exhaustive and detailed. Juries operating with a majority decision rule are more driven to reach a verdict. So majority verdict juries are more likely to begin their deliberations with a vote. For example, Arce *et al.* (1998) compared 6- and 12-person juries that used unanimous decision criteria. The smaller juries made rather fewer references to the evidence and seemed to make fewer pro-defendant arguments.

A related aspect of jury rules is the range of different verdicts available. Generally researchers have concentrated on guilty versus not guilty choices but there are others such as the *not proven* verdict. A study by Smithson, Deady and Cracik (2007) investigated the impact of having this *not proven* alternative which is probably most familiar from the legal system in Scotland. One possibility is that the not proven category might be used as an alternative to the guilty verdict where it is available. The researchers employed a counterbalanced design with different ranges of alternative verdict options for the different conditions. Participants were students and public servants eligible for jury service at two Australian universities. The research findings suggested that, contrary to expectations, the not proven choice replaced some not guilty decisions. It did not replace the guilty decision. That it is to say, there were just as many guilty decisions when there were the additional *not proven* alternative as when there was just guilty and not guilty choices. There were also indications from the study that jurors found the *not proven* verdict somewhat more difficult to choose than any of the other verdicts.

How juries make decisions

Relatively little is known about the psychological processes that happen in real juries as opposed to the mock juries of the psychological experiment (McCabe and Purves, 1974). There are a few rare instances in which courts have allowed access to recordings of jury deliberations but these are very much exceptions. For the most

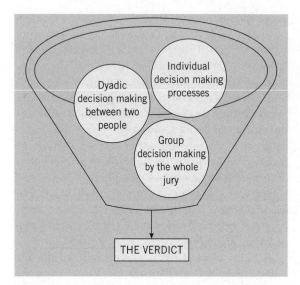

Figure 24.3 Different levels of jury deliberation in psychological research

part, researchers have had to find approximations to real juries. Figure 24.3 illustrates some of the main alternatives. All of these suffer from a degree of artificiality – the extent of which depends on the study in question. Sometimes the mock jury will merely consist of indi-

viduals making individual decisions in isolation – sometimes a group of interacting persons will be used. No matter what, the mock jury is always a pale reflection of real juries. For example, often the mock juror will merely read a scenario of a crime and trial rather than experience the full spectacle of a court of law in session.

Myers (1979) chose a somewhat circuitous approach to investigating the features of trials that increase the likelihood of a guilty verdict. She did not have access to the jury room and so obtained her data in other ways. Her research involved the cases of about a thousand defendants on felony charges in Indiana. Two-thirds of the cases involved trials by jury. Myers obtained qualitative data from a variety of sources:

- file folders of the assistant prosecutor;
- police arrest records;
- telephone interviews to obtain any necessary supplementary data.

She was on the prosecutor's staff at the time so was also able to conduct informal discussions with prosecutors and court personnel. It emerged that the following factors influenced the jury's decision of guilt:

- a weapon was recovered;
- a large number of witnesses were specified;

BOX 24.1 Forensic psychology in action

Pre-trial publicity

O.J. Simpson was tried for the murder of his wife and a male companion. Shortly after the murders, the sportsman/actor was seen on national television apparently speeding along American freeways trying to avoid arrest. Thus the issue was of the effects of pre-trial prejudicial events communicated through the media on the outcome of a trial. Does pre-trial publicity prejudice the result of a trial?

- Different countries/jurisdictions have different practices about media coverage of crime. In the United States, the constitutional guarantee of freedom of speech effectively reduces controls over media coverage as also does courtroom television.

In other countries, restrictions are in place. So, for example, in the United Kingdom, media coverage is limited once a suspect has been charged. Offending media may be charged with contempt of court and the criminal trial of the suspect abandoned. Civil trials are not subject to pre-trial publicity restrictions.

- Factors limiting the influence of pre-trial publicity include the facts that: (a) most suspects plead guilty at trial anyway and these cases cannot be influenced by prejudicial publicity and (b) very few trials receive any coverage in the national press. In the United States, the figure may be as low as 1 per cent (Simon and Eimermann, 1971). There is five times the likelihood that the trial will be covered by the local press. A trial tried by jury has at least twice the baseline probability of being reported.

- Prejudice, in legal terms, should not be seen in social-scientific terms which would suggest that prejudice leads to biasing the outcome of the trial (Howitt, 1998b). In the United States, the Supreme Court has ruled that prejudice involves both (1) a preconceived notion of the defendant's guilt and (2) this opinion being fixed and resistant to change (Moran and Cutler, 1991). In other words, what is prejudicial to a psychologist may not be prejudice in the eyes of a US judge.

Research into the effects of media on verdicts goes back to the origins of forensic psychology in nineteenth-century Germany. More intensive research began in the 1960s. Some of the research is problematic as it was based on 'mock' juries assembled solely for research purposes. Obviously this has the inevitable ecological validity problem – just how representative are the verdicts of mock juries of the verdicts of real juries? Some research involved exposing the participants to a fictitious news story and then obtaining their views about the guilt of the accused and so forth without even allowing jury discussion.

Studebaker and Penrod (1997) point out how complex the modern media environment is and how voracious the demand for news. This means that often there is nowhere the trial could be held where the jurors are unaware of the publicity given to the crime. However, some venues may be less prejudiced than others. One suggestion is that researchers could help by investigating factors in pre-trial publicity that may lead to prejudice in laboratory studies and then seeking evidence that this sort of publicity is especially common in the area where the case would normally be tried (Studebaker et al., 2000). They undertook research relevant to a hearing for a change of venue for the trial of those accused of the Oklahoma City bombing (Timothy McVeigh and Terry Nichols). Newspapers in the Oklahoma City area were analysed as were those for a number of possible alternative locations for the trial. The researchers coded the contents of these newspapers along a number of dimensions known to be relevant to pre-trial publicity

effects from experiments. These aspects were: (1) measures of the general amount of publicity given to the crime; (2) negative characterisations of the defendants; (3) information about the emotional suffering of those involved as victims of the crime; (4) information about putative confessions; (5) suggestions about the defendants' motives for the crime; and (6) information about eyewitness identifications.

Compared with *The Denver Post*, newspapers in the Oklahoma City area had more negative pre-trial publicity about the defendants and the suffering of the victims.

The researchers then compared their content analysis findings with those of surveys of the general public carried out at the time. There were parallels between the content analysis and the findings of the survey. For example, respondents in Oklahoma were much more likely to believe in the guilt of one of the defendants, McVeigh. Respondents in Denver, away from the possible venues for the hearing in Oklahoma, were relatively unlikely to claim that they were absolutely confident of McVeigh's guilt – less than 20 per cent did so. In contrast, about 50 per cent of the Oklahoma respondents were absolutely confident of his guilt. They were also more likely to follow the news of the crime and trial carefully and they knew a great deal more about the events. The findings are indicative of the value of the content analysis approach to venue selection according to Studebaker et al. (2000).

However, researchers do not always have an easy time in court when they argue that, based on their data, the venue of the trial should or should not change. Posey and Dahl (2002) describe some of the problems, including the likelihood that a judge will ask the researcher why questions were not included in the survey which asked respondents the extent to which they could be impartial. Research suggests little value in such questions although they are the sort of questions asked in court during a voir dire examination. There is no relationship between a potential juror's claims to be impartial and how much they know about the case and how strong they believe the evidence against the accused to be.

- the defendant or an accomplice made a statement either concerning involvement in crime or lack of involvement in crime;
- the defendant had large numbers of previous convictions (admissible evidence there);
- the defendant was not employed;
- the victim was young;
- it was a less serious rather than a more serious crime.

Juries were not dependent on the following in their decisions:

- eyewitness identification of the defendant;
- expert testimony;
- recovery of stolen property;
- victim's prior criminality and relationship with the defendant;
- past conduct of the victim perhaps warranting the injury.

Interesting as these findings may be, they tend to provide a view of the jury which is rather different from that to be found in the general run of psychological jury research. For example, the lack of influence of things such as eyewitness identification and expert testimony is incongruous considering the great emphasis that researchers have placed on both of these. Furthermore, psychological research into the jury has raised the role of extra-legal or extra-evidential factors on jury decision making – for example, where the defendant is physically attractive or where the racial characteristics of the accused lead to greater or lesser leniency.

What happens behind jury room doors? Gastil, Burkhalter and Black's (2007) study is unusual in that the researchers had cooperation from a Seattle court which allowed them to study accounts by jurors of 60 trials albeit for relatively trivial offences. The researchers were particularly interested in satisfaction with the deliberation process and the outcome of their deliberations. The court typically used six-person juries plus or minus one juror. The gender mix of jurors was about equal though the majority were white. Deliberations generally lasted for about two hours. Data were collected from the juries both before the actual trial and afterwards. Antecedents to the deliberations were measured using a measure called *Trust in the jury system* which included the extent of their confidence in the jury system and the extent to which the criminal jury system is a fair way to determine

guilt and innocence. Other data were also collected at this stage. Having provided these initial data, the jurors participated in a trial and deliberated in the jury room. After the trial, their experiences were measured using five-point scales assessing the extent to which they discussed the relevant facts related to the trials, discussed the judge's instructions thoroughly, listened to each respectfully during the jury's discussions, and the extent to which they were satisfied with the final verdict and the quality of the jury's deliberations. The findings showed that:

- Jurors felt that their jury operated at a 'remarkably' high level of competence.
- The vast majority of jurors rated their experience of jury deliberation as being of a 'remarkably' high quality overall. Very few suggested less than that.
- Almost no juries included a juror who disagreed with the view that the jury listened respectfully to each other, that the relevant facts of the trial were discussed, and that they discussed the judge's instructions.
- Nearly all (98 per cent) indicated that they had an adequate opportunity to express themselves within the jury room.
- However, relationships between the characteristics of the jurors and the characteristics of the deliberation tended to show fairly complex patterns. It was clear that jurors who had the greatest faith in the jury system were more likely to experience the jury deliberations as mutually respectful; the more the juror was self-confident and interested in the trial, the more they were likely to feel that they had adequate opportunities to speak, the more likely they were to engage in careful analysis during the deliberations, and the more likely they were to perceived the deliberations as mutually respectful. Nevertheless, there was a direct relationship between how satisfied the jury was and the perceived quality of the deliberation.

Quite clearly, all of this is a meta-perspective on jury deliberation processes. It is about how the jury members perceived the deliberation process. As such, it is not truly an investigation of the process of deliberation itself.

The nature of interaction in juries: Just what are the processes involved in jury deliberation? How do these relate to psychological theory? Underlying some models of jury decision making is an assumption that a jury consists of people with different arguing and reasoning styles which impact on the deliberations and may, ultimately,

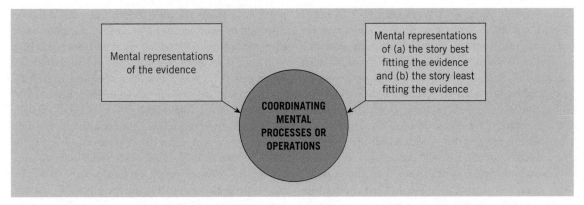

Figure 24.4 Kuhn, Weinstock and Flaton's 1994 theory of juror decision making

influence the verdict. Kuhn, Weinstock and Flaton (1994) suggested that the evidence coordination is the responsibility of each member of the jury (Figure 24.4). They need to construct alternative accounts (or story-verdict constellations) concerning what happened at the scene of the crime which are then evaluated against the available evidence. These accounts may be those supplied by the defence and prosecution lawyers as discussed in Chapter 23. They have to decide between the account which is most consistent with the evidence and the account which is inconsistent with much of the evidence. As can be seen in Figure 24.4, the model involves three components: (a) mental representations of the evidence, (b) representations of each of the accounts or verdict definitions and (c) a set of mental operations coordinating these. Previous research has shown that people whose thinking is the most advanced epistemologically believe that absolute certainty is not possible. These tend to be more highly educated individuals and so are more likely to select moderate verdicts than extreme ones. Skilful performances by jury members during a deliberation tended to involve arguing skills such as discounting, counter-argumentation, and justifying alternative verdicts.

Along similar lines, Warren, Kuhn and Weinstock (2010) suggest that there are three different types of reasoning reflecting different epistemological styles:

- Absolutists: These would tend to say that only one account of the events can be correct and that the other must be wrong. That is, they believe that the absolute and objective truth can be determined.

- Multiplists: Would tend to think that both points of view are accurate from the point of view of the historian involved. They would recognise that accounts of history change at different time periods. That is, they recognise that interpretations are subjective as are judgements and this is given first priority in their thinking.

- Evaluativists: Would also see that both historians are likely to be highly accurate from their own point of view. They would tend to believe that by combining a variety of viewpoints some consensus on what had happened might be achieved. That is, they also recognise the subjectivity of viewpoints though they accept that these can be evaluated and one viewpoint preferred.

It is possible to classify people into the three above thinking styles using the Livia task which involves two different historians' accounts of a war. The task is to answer various questions about what can be known based on these two different viewpoints. In terms of the analysis, the multiplists and the evaluativists were very similar and so they were combined into a single group. Warren and Kuhn (2010) used pairs of about-to-be jurors waiting in a court to be assigned to jury service. They listened to 20-minute, shortened versions of a real homicide trial on audiotape which included many features of the full trial such as the examination, cross-examination and opening and closing statements. There were four alternative verdicts from which the 'juror' could choose – first degree murder, second degree murder, manslaughter and self-defence. The judge in the 'trial' explained the criteria for reaching these different verdicts. Having heard the recording, the juror had to make a verdict choice and justify it. Following this was a interactive phase in which each 'juror' was paired with another juror who had made a different verdict choice. Seventy eight per cent of the jurors managed to reach a joint verdict within the 30 minutes that the researchers allowed them. Their 'deliberations' were then systematically coded by the researchers into units which consisted of either a question or a claim accompanied by supporting justification). Each deliberation included an average of 119 of these units. Generally speaking, each of the jury members contributed substantially – the range of units per member varying within the relatively restricted range of about 40–60 per cent per individual. The 'jurors' made frequent references to the evidence (8 per cent) and nearly as often to the verdict categories (7 per cent) though they rarely mentioned the criteria distinguishing the various verdicts. Jurors were more likely to add to the other juror's statements (9 per cent) than to challenge them (6 per cent). Frequent meta-level statements were made about their own thinking or the other's contribution (18 per cent).

There were some very clear differences between the multiplists/evaluativists (combined) group and the absolutists in terms of how they behaved in the 'jury' deliberations. The multiplists/evaluativists tended to be more persuasive than their partners in the juror dyad and were much more likely to:

- discuss the meta-processes in their deliberation – i.e. talk about aspects of their thinking processes
- critique what the other jury member had said or counter it in some way
- dominate the discussion/deliberation
- refer to the judge's verdict criteria.

In general criticism of the other juror's arguments was relatively less common to add to the other juror's contribution in ways that did nothing to challenge that contribution. Of course, it remains to be seen the extent to which larger juries would show similar trends.

Jurors and the facts of eyewitness evidence: How knowledgeable are jurors about the problems of eye-witness evidence? In some jurisdictions, expert witnesses may provide information about issues related to eye-witness evidence. For example, Loftus (2010) discusses in detail the simple factor of the distance between an eye-witness and something that they believe that they have seen. It is a psychological fact and common sense that the bigger the distance the less detail can be seen, all other things being equal. So imagine an eye-witness claims to have seen a car with a spoiler at the back from a distance of a quarter of a mile (0.4 kilometres). Is it

possible to discern a car's spoiler from this distance? This cannot be answered on the basis of common sense since a specific question of what can be discerned at such a distance is involved. We can make out an aircraft at a much greater height than this but, of course, aircraft are much bigger than cars. So common sense begins to let us down. Loftus explains that it is possible to digitally manipulate (blur) an image to show just how it would appear at different distances. A photo of a car can be made to appear as it would at a quarter-mile distance so that the jury can judge for itself whether a spoiler may indeed be seen at this distance. Just in case you are wondering, this very example was at the centre of an actual Californian road rage case. It is clear that the expert witness can add something over and above what common sense supplies in circumstances like these. Loftus (2010) mentions a number of actual examples of such visual eyewitness issues where the clarity of the view is reduced by distance.

However, many of the issues to do with eyewitness evidence are not so clear cut as we saw in Chapter 13. One question is the extent to which the lay knowledge of jurors about eyewitness evidence is as good as that of expert witnesses. Research suggests that jurors are often poor in terms of their knowledge of factors affecting the quality of eyewitness testimony and, most certainly, their knowledge is somewhat variable and uneven. It can be somewhat frustrating to the psychological profession when judges and prominent lawyers claim that the findings from psychological research into eyewitness testimony are little more than common sense and decisions concerning eyewitness testimony can consequently be left to jurors. Given the problems that researchers have had reaching any sort of consensus about the factors which lead to good eyewitness evidence, the ability of jurors to deal effectively with eyewitness evidence has to be in some doubt. Researchers have some matters on which they agree – these might be termed the important 'facts' of eyewitness testimony. To what extent do jurors agree with the facts as researchers themselves agree on them?

Kassin *et al.* (2001) generated a list of eyewitness testimony 'facts' by carrying out a survey of expert psychologists to identify the research findings which tend to be agreed on by all psychologists. As perfect consensus is rare among researchers, Kassin *et al.* adopted the criterion for a 'fact' that 80 per cent of psychologists agreed that it was true. They divided the research into system variables and estimator variables:

- System variables are things which are in the power of the criminal justice system to alter such as the way in which the line-up is run. Things agreed by 80 per cent of psychologists were:
  - Confidence malleability
  - Line-up instructions
  - Mugshot-induced bias
  - Question wording
- Estimator variables are characteristics of the witness and witnessing situation which the criminal justice system cannot alter such as how drunk the witness was at the time of the crime. These would have to be estimated using whatever methods are possible.
  - Accuracy and confidence
  - Attitudes and expectations
  - Child suggestibility
  - Cross-race bias
  - Exposure time
  - Hypnotic suggestibility
  - Post-event information
  - Unconscious transference
  - Weapon focus

There are doubts about the validity of some of these based on recent developments in eyewitness testimony research (see Chapter 13). Nevertheless they do provide a useful baseline of expert opinion.

To what extent do jurors agree with these 'facts' of eyewitness testimony? Desmarais and Read (2011) carried out a meta-analysis (see Box 4.2) of 23 studies into the public's knowledge of the 'facts' of eyewitness testimony. The majority of the studies were Canadian and used samples of community volunteers (the general public) but student samples were also well represented. Nearly 5,000 participants in total had taken part in the research. Using the criterion of 80 per cent consensus which was applied to researchers, there were very few aspects of eyewitness testimony which the lay public agreed on. These exceptions were:

- alcohol intoxication
- attitudes and expectations
- question wording.

Of course, less stringent criteria for agreement produce greater levels of consensus. Nevertheless, since 80 per cent agreement had been accepted as appropriate for experts then the same criterion is reasonable if the assumption that expert evidence is little more than the common sense

that the general public can provide in equal measure were true! It is important to emphasise that this creates a somewhat misleading impression that the general public is substantially inferior to experts about the 'facts' of eyewitness testimony whereas they did agree with the 'correct' answer based on expert opinion on about two-thirds of occasions. Of course, the extent to which the correct answers are based on knowledge of research findings rather than being the result of a reasoned 'guess' cannot be assessed. Desmarais and Read (2011) believe that their findings indicate that the lay public seem to be increasingly knowledgeable since more recent studies in their meta-analysis tended to produce higher levels of correctness. They take the view that this increased level of awareness can be, in part, attributed to the efforts of researchers in promoting research findings from eyewitness research.

Assessing Credibility in Court: The process of forming judgements about other people and their behaviour is complex and not less so for jurors. One particularly relevant aspect of this in the forensic context is the tendency for some people to blame crime victims for their misfortune. That is, they hold the victim responsible. So the woman who walks home late at night alone is blamed for the sexual assault perpetrated against her or the man who carries large amounts of money in his wallet is blamed when it is stolen from him. Of course, such victim blaming is unjustified but nevertheless it happens – and it is especially important when it happens in court. Bos and Maas (2009) explain the thought processes behind this tendency on the basis of The Just World Theory (Lerner and Goldberg, 1999). According to the Just World Theory, people see the world as a fair, just and equitable place in which we deserve whatever happens to us whether this is a good thing or a bad thing. The idea that people are the architects of their own fortune is built into us through the process of socialisation – for example, we are taught that if we work well at school then we will get a well-paid job. Applied to the victims of crime this encourages the view that the victim is a deserving victim. Closely associated with the Just World Theory is Epstein's Cognitive Experiential Self Theory (Epstein, 1985, 1994; Epstein and Pacini, 1999). This argues that thinking involves two alternative pathways as seen in Figure 24.5. The theory argues that there are two sorts of mindsets which need to be considered in relation to our decision-making processes. These mindsets operate in parallel to each other. They are:

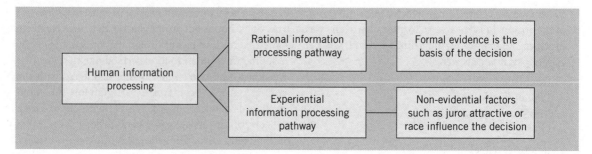

Figure 24.5 When extra-legal or legally irrelevant information may affect jury decisions

- The rational pathway which is a conscious analytic system. It is based on analysis, logic and facts. It requires a lot of cognitive effort to execute rational analyses. The rationalistic mindset is reasoning and based on logic. As such, it is very slow and deliberative in nature with judgements being rational.

- The intuitive-experiential pathway is pre-conscious and intuitive. It essentially depends on what feels good. Little effort is required since it involves emotion and stereotypical thinking based on previous experiences. The processes involved cannot be put into words and it is not amenable to logical analysis. The intuitive-experiential mindset is a quick, straightforward and effortless way of understanding the world.

Bos and Maas use Epstein's Cognitive Experiential Self Theory in order to understand the acceptance and application of the Just World Theory to forensic contexts. If a person bases their judgements of other people on the assumption that the world is a just place, then the logical conclusion is that the victim of a crime deserved what happened to them – for example, they were asking for trouble by dressing provocatively. It is difficult for those who believe in a just world to accept that a victim can be innocent. People who do not have this belief will find less difficulty with the idea of an innocent victim since it is not incongruent with their beliefs. Now Bos and Maas argue that individuals who believe in a just world and adopt the rationalistic way of thinking of Epstein's theory are the most likely to blame the victim for their victimisation. This prediction was supported by two studies carried out by Bos and Maas.

Non-evidential factors and jury decisions: Epstein's Cognitive Experiential Self Theory (Epstein, 2003) discussed above and summarized in Figure 24.6 has been applied to other aspects of the activities of jury members. One of the classic findings of jury research is that physically attractive defendants are treated differently by jurors compared to unattractive ones. This finding is common in psychology textbooks. Studies do not universally reach this conclusion but, nevertheless, it is important to know just how non-evidential (peripheral) factors can affect jury decision making. The range of studies into defendant attractiveness is enormous and there is reasonably clear evidence that physically attractive defendants are treated leniently (the relevant studies

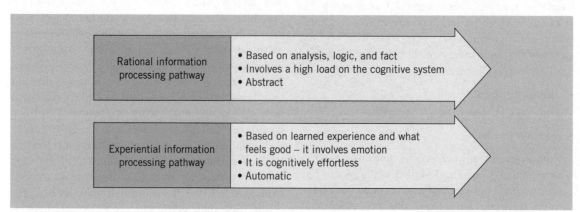

Figure 24.6 Epstein's Cognitive Experiential Self Theory

go back as far as Efran (1974) and Sigall and Ostrove (1975)). Epstein's Cognitive Experiential Self Theory is relevant to jury decision making because it helps us understand some of the circumstances in which such extra-evidential (non-legal) factors as defendant attractiveness may be influential. One suggestion is that legal evidence presented in court will largely be processed through the rational information-processing pathway. The more intuitive and emotion-based extra-evidential information such as the attractiveness of the defendant (and perhaps also the race of the defendant) will be processed through the experiential information-processing pathway which lacks a rational focus. This is the basis of Gunnell and Ceci's (2010) study in which the individual's tendency to use one pathway rather than the other was measured using the Rational Experiential Inventory (REI) (Epstein *et al.*, 1996; Pacini and Epstein, 1999). The basic framework of Gunnell and Ceci's argument is presented in Figure 24.5. Participants in Gunnell and Ceci's research read a criminal trial transcript, a defendant profile and then decided their verdict and appropriate sentencing. Different groups were given different pictures of the defendant – either a more attractive or a less attractive person. Experiential thinkers made more decisions to convict the defendant than did rational thinkers. The findings were a little more complex than expected:

* If the defendant was attractive then the type of thinking made no difference to conviction. That is, experiential and rational thinkers were equally likely to convict.

* If the defendant was unattractive, then the trend was for the experiential thinkers to convict more often than the rational thinkers. Experiential offenders convicted the unattractive offender in 89 per cent of cases whereas the rational thinker convicted on only 67 per cent of occasions.

This is despite the relevant evidence being the same in all cases. Experiential processers were more likely to say that extra-legal factors would influence their verdict.

The credibility of rape victims is, of course, assessed at different levels during a court's proceeding. A study by Lievore (2004) found that Australian Crown Prosecutors unanimously saw the issue of victim credibility in sexual assault trials as being important. The Prosecutors believed that credibility was revealed by the demeanour of the victim. Systematic evidence suggests that rape victims who show high levels of emotionality are viewed as the most credible. Nevertheless, the assumptions of the person

assessing credibility may alter the way in which cues are interpreted in such contexts. Heuristic processing is the way in which particular cues are employed when assessing whether the person is lying or telling the truth. Such heuristics are forms of mental shortcut which speed up the process of making decisions. The heuristics may work fine in many instances but they may result in incorrect judgements in other circumstances because heuristics encourage the individual to neglect important information. In the heuristic-systematic model the assumption is that the least mental effort is applied and that short-cut methods are generally used unless there are good reasons not to use them. Expectance violation theory (Jussim, Coleman and Lerch, 1987) assumes that expectations about another person's behaviour will influence perceptions of their behaviour. So if a rape victim shows a lack of emotional behaviour then that will lead to judgements that the victim lack credibility. That is, if the expectation is that the rape victim is likely to be highly emotional. An experiment by Hackett, Day and Mohr (2008) involved participants watching a video of a rape victim reporting the offence committed against her. The emotional expressiveness of the victim when making this report was varied in terms of (a) non-verbal characteristics such as eye contact and crying and (b) paralinguistic features such as tone of voice. A semi-professional actress played the rape victim in three separate videos in which:

* The victim speaks in a matter-of-fact style looking straight forward.

* The victim is emotionally numbed, nervous and timid.

* The victim is portrayed crying several times with choked, trembling speech.

The offence involved the victim's rape by a neighbour. The 'jurors' rated the woman's credibility on a 24-item credibility scale which including items such as 'Do you believe the woman's story?' Overall, the emotionality of the woman had no effect. Where it did make a difference was when the 'juror' believed that certain emotional behaviours were characteristic of rape victims. In this case, the emotional victim tended to be believed and the unemotional victim tended to be disbelieved.

Perhaps the most contentious of topics in research on juries is the question of racial biases in jury decision making (as well as sentencing). This is not simply a factual question of how the race of the defendant affects jury decisions. It spreads much wider to the idea that black people are treated unfairly by the criminal justice system. This is basically the idea behind the term *anticipatory* injustice – or the belief or expectation that the legal system is basically biased against certain groups of people and will treat them in a biased or prejudicial way. Woolard, Harvell and Graham (2008) employed data from the McArthur Juvenile Competence study which involved nearly 1,400 adolescents/young adults. The research took place in a variety of settings in the USA and involved the young people answering questions about judicial fairness. An example of the sort of question tapping anticipatory injustice would be 'Compared to other people in trouble with the law, are you more likely, less likely, or just as likely to be treated fairly by the legal system' (Woolard et al., 2008, p. 213). Approximately 40 per cent of the young people agreed with at least one of four items asking about anticipatory injustice. Those with greater experience of the legal system and African Americans and Latinos were the most likely to expect unfair treatment by the justice system. The influence of these beliefs ran deep since they were associated with a reduced willingness to confess, incomplete disclosure to their own lawyer, and a reduced likelihood of entering a plea bargaining agreement. These relationships held after other important variables were controlled for such as prior experience of the criminal justice system.

Finally, a classic study in social psychology is Erving Goffman's *The Presentation of Self in Everyday Life* (1959). This contains a framework which can help us to understand the way in which jurors focus on information which is not part of the formal evidence at a trial. This can be referred to as *offstage observation*. Jurors are influenced by the evidence and the formal case presented but, in addition to that, other information obtained by watching people in the courtroom who are not actually part of the evidence presentation or argument. Especially when these people are unaware that they are being observed, they may do things which the juror may regard as informative to the trial. Unusually, Rose, Diamond and Baker (2010) had access to recordings of 50 real jury discussions and deliberations in US civil proceedings largely concerned with motoring offences. During the trials, prior to the jury discussions, the judge explained to the jury that their decisions should be based on the legal instructions and the evidence including testimony, exhibits or other things which they have been instructed to accept. In Goffman's terms, these formal matters take place *frontstage*. However, in a courtroom there are few physical boundaries to separate those performing their roles frontstage and the rest of the people around. Goffman points out that social observers of a social situation – such as the juror

is – take an interest in what people on the periphery of the main social action are doing as well as those more central to the action. One could say that the courtroom is rather like a theatre in the round in which all sorts of people are in full view of the jury; the parties in the action, attorneys and their assistants, those watching in the public gallery of the courtroom, and so forth. Cues from the responses of the secondary parties may well appear to be particularly informative about what is going on in court. Of course impression management will generally characterise the demeanour of professionals working in court as well as others, but this façade may slip at times.

In their study, Rose, Diamond, and Baker (2010) coded any reference to things in the jury deliberations which had not happened front stage in the court. So anything involving members of the public would be offstage as would be anything involving an attorney when they were not directly involved in the formal business of the trial. Some of the behaviours coded as offstage occurred in the courthouse but not in the courtroom. In 80 per cent of trials jurors made at least one offstage remark. The majority of offstage remarks involved courtroom behaviours (74 per cent) and the rest in hallways, elevators or outside the courthouse. The most common observation concerned the plaintiff and the second most common concerned non-witness audience members at the trial. Of course, given the nature of the trials, matters related to the physical health of the plaintiff were common. This included expressions of surprise about how physically mobile the plaintiff was given the nature of their injuries, for example. About half of the comments were positive or negative towards one of the parties in the case. There was evidence that more negative offstage observations were made about the plaintiff during deliberations. However, in this study there was no evidence that this was associated with outcomes (verdicts) favouring the defence. Only one instance was found in which offstage observations related directly to decision making. This particular instance concerned the amount of damages that the plaintiff ought to receive. No factors were found that distinguished jurors making offstage comments from those who didn't in terms of demographic factors. Of course, in this study the offstage observations had to be articulated in the jury room before they were registered by the researchers, so it may be possible that the exchanges between the jurors negated the impact of the observations whatever their effect on the individual making the offstage observation.

Main points

- Research on the jury is considerably affected by legal constraints on studying real juries making real decisions. As a consequence, a great deal of research has simulated trial procedures in psychological laboratories as an alternative means of studying the jury. Sometimes the simulation involves individuals reacting in isolation rather than in interaction as in a real jury. There have been attempts to improve the validity of jury research by using shadow juries which sit and listen to the evidence in court and then 'sit' in parallel to the real jury. Quite clearly great care is needed when generalising from the findings of such 'laboratory' juries to real-life juries.

- Juries differ in many ways, which may have a detrimental effect on the quality of the decision making. For example, in some countries juries are larger and in others they are smaller. The research evidence, such as it is, finds relatively small differences between large and small juries in terms of decisions made but they do not operate identically. The rules that govern how the jury must reach a decision (e.g. is a majority verdict allowed) can affect how the jury operates.

- Psychologists have been involved in providing expert guidance to lawyers about how best to conduct a trial, which potential jurors to reject if possible, and arguments about the effect of pre-trial publicity. Virtually all of the research in this field has been conducted in the United States rather than in other jurisdictions which, for example, may not allow lawyers to challenge jurors in this way. Nevertheless, if there were better evidence on scientific jury selection available and other related activity, it would inform us about some aspects of jury decision making.

Further reading

The classics in this area are getting a little elderly. More modern material is to be found in:

Martin, A.M. and Kaplan, M.F. (ed.) (2006) *Understanding World Jury Systems Through Social Psychological Research* Hove: Psychology Press.

Roesch, R., Carrado, R.R. and Dempster, R. (2001) *Psychology in the Courts: International Advances in Knowledge* London: Routledge.

A useful paper 'What Can the English Legal System Learn From Jury Research Published up to 2001?' can be found at the following address: http://www.kingston.ac.uk/~ku00596/elsres01.pdf

Visit our website at www.pearsoned.co.uk/howitt for self-test and essay questions, annotated further reading, audio interviews with researchers in the field, weblinks and more information on becoming a forensic psychologist.

Chapter 25

Effective prison

Overview

- There are a number of ideologies concerning what prison is for. Retribution holds that prison is for punishment; utilitarianism suggests that prison should produce changes that reduce the risk of reoffending; and humanitarianism suggests that the role should be rehabilitation of casualties of social deprivation and victimisation. Various models of how prisoners should be treated are available according to what views one has on crime's origins. For example, if one believes that there are too many rewards for crime and too little punishment, then the appropriate treatment for prisoners may be harsh and severe in order to make the punishment a deterrent to reoffending and others.

- Prisoners are a population at risk. There is the risk of violence from other prisoners though homicides within the prison environment are relatively infrequent. Additionally, there is a risk of suicide, which is a matter of some considerable concern. There is some evidence that prison itself increases the risk of suicide and this has to be set against the fact that prisoners (largely young males) tend to be a high-risk group for suicide in the community anyway. The period spent in prison before trial is associated with a higher risk of suicide than other time in prison. Action to reduce such imprisonments or increased vigilance on the part of staff have been recommended.

- There is a good deal of evidence based on meta-analyses of numerous studies that prisons and other forms of sentence have some, if limited, effectiveness in terms of criteria such as the reduction of recidivism. Educational programmes for prisoners within prison seems to be the most effective aspect of the prison experience in this regard.

- 'Nothing works' was a dominant view of prison until relatively recently. Increasingly, it is accepted that a lot of the work done within the prison service pays off in terms of reducing future reoffending. In recent years, there has been a more consistent attempt to offer effective treatment programmes to prisoners in an attempt to reduce recidivism. Cognitive behavioural therapies are commonly used by psychologists in prisons for the treatment of various sorts of offender especially sex offenders such as paedophiles and rapists. These are multi-faceted strategies based on groupwork to provide knowledge and insight into the offending process. There is evidence of their immediate effectiveness in terms of treatment goals but also in terms of reducing recidivism, though the latter is based on less extensive research.

Introduction

Well, we have finally got to prison. Although it may seem like the end of the criminal-justice system process, it is actually the start of a new one. For some, prison will contribute something to their rehabilitation and, perhaps, change of lifestyle. For others, prison will be the end of the road – they may spend the rest of their lives there. Others will pass through and return again several times. There is no consensus about the purpose of prison but there is a wide range of different viewpoints. Hollin (2002), along with many others, regards imprisonment as the focus of a current moral debate which has long historical roots. The major views in the debate about prison are:

- Retributionists regard the purpose of prison to deliver punishments.

- Utilitarians see prison as part of a process of bringing about changes which reduce the probability of reoffending.

- Humanitarians see that prisoners often come from backgrounds of deprivation and victimisation, so are deserving of rehabilitation.

This is a complex debate that goes far beyond the work of psychologists in the prison service. It hardly needs pointing out that crime and punishment are at the forefront of the political agenda in many countries. Hollin suggests that sex offenders are a good example where confusion can reign because 'moral beliefs, principles and utility, and effectiveness become fused and can lead to confusion in policies and procedures within the criminal justice system' (Hollin, 2002, pp. 1–2). The repugnance that many feel for sex offenders might encourage lengthy prison sentences in order to make the punishment proportionate to the heinousness of the crime. However, the utilitarian might argue that this in itself has little point unless it reduces the chances of others being victimised in the future and so more than imprisonment is required. The humanitarian might suggest that sex offenders in many instances have been victims of sexual assault themselves such that harsh punishment alone is inappropriate. Humane treatment is required in order to meet the needs of the offender and in order to stop the endless cycle of abuse in which victims become future offenders. The various 'ideologies' associated with imprisonment (retributionism, utilitarianism and humanism) tend to coexist in varying proportions within the criminal justice system. Pure retribution, for example, may be relatively uncommon.

There are many different types of punishment available within the criminal justice system apart from imprisonment. In some systems such as the United Kingdom, relatively minor offences committed by minor offenders might be dealt with by admonitions in the form of a police caution. Generally speaking, monetary fines are the commonest punishment. Sometimes one will find direct compensation of the victim or community associated with the crime. This may involve financial compensation or service to the community through a work programme. Suspended prison sentences are a step up in seriousness. Prison sentences are regarded as being suitable for the most serious offences and more committed or persistent offenders, though it is far from certain that prison is reserved for the worst offenders. For example, those who default on fines may well receive prison sentences eventually.

The utilitarian approach requires that penalties of all sorts should increase the likelihood that the offender (and others seeing the possible outcome of the risk they are taking) will stop offending in the future. The effectiveness of the penal system in reducing crime may be evaluated in various ways. Recidivism in the form of further crimes is very common. There are many offenders who repeatedly offend despite being punished repeatedly. Depending on a large number of factors, about half of criminals reoffend after punishment. These could be regarded in two ways:

- as depressing statistics on the persistence of crime, or

- as evidence of the large numbers who do not reoffend after punishment.

Punishment and rehabilitation are not the only ways in which justice can proceed. For example, there is the concept of restorative justice (*Contemporary Justice Review*, 1998) which is discussed in Chapter 4. A central theme in restorative justice is the righting of the wrong done to victims by helping them to return to their former self as a survivor. The process encourages the offender to reflect upon their harmful behaviours and to accept responsibility for their offending. Restorative justice utilises the methods of reconciliation and mediation in meeting its ends. Sometimes the process operates in parallel with the criminal justice system. (See Table 25.1 for further indications of the functions of prison.)

Some of the more severe consequences of prison can be seen in the evidence of suicide and other forms of death in prison. These are also matters about which the prison service is actively expected to prevent.

Table 25.1 Treatment strategies associated with criminality

Model of criminogenesis	Treatment model
Insufficient deterrent to crime: the rewards for crime are greater than the costs of punishment.	Harsher prison regimes, 'boot camps' for offenders possibly in exchange for reductions in offending.
Emotional distress: deep-seated emotional problems are expressed in criminal behaviour.	Psychodynamic treatments such as psychoanalysis.
Crime is thus seen as a consequence of pathological aspects of the individual.	Client-centred counselling.
Educational deficit: failure to complete schooling leaves the individual with important skill deficits which exclude them from society's mainstream in many instances.	Education programmes such as reading, mathematics, etc. Training in practical job skills.
Learning of criminal behaviour: criminal conduct is learnt.	Institutions organised as token economies in which members are rewarded in tangible ways for improvements and changes in standards of conduct.
Social interaction skills: offenders have difficulty in interacting with others effectively in a social context.	Cognitive behavioural intervention in which the offender's deficits in cognitive and interaction skills are examined and regular group sessions are held involving such things as interpersonal cognitive problem solving and social skills training.
Social/institutional balance: possibly because of early experience of institutions such as children's homes, offenders do not learn a healthy and balanced approach to life and may resolve difficulties inappropriately through the use of violence.	Creating a healthy institutional environment by reducing rigid controls and sanctions, giving the task of controlling the inmates' behaviour to the whole of the community and having forums to discuss problems arising in the institutions.
Labelling individuals as deviant ensures that it is difficult for them to operate effectively in normal contexts, thus forcing them into deviant social systems and crime.	Divert individuals such as young offenders from the prison system into probation, mediation, reparation, community supervision, etc.

Source: Based on Redondo, S., Sanchez-Meca, J. and Garrido, V. (2002) *Offender Rehabilitation and Treatment: Effective Programmes and Policies to Reduce Re-offending*. © John Wiley & Sons, Ltd

Suicide in prison

McHugh (1999) suggested that while not frequent, suicide is a significant issue in the prison context. This is not a surprise since the offenders entering prison have heightened risk due to other risk factors such as low socio-economic status, coming from dysfunctional families and having an involvement with drugs (McHugh, 1998). The extra factors of prison build on these. In the United Kingdom, for instance, the average suicide rate is now just over one per week. This is a decline during the last decade. Nevertheless, the UK prison suicide rate is 12 times higher than in the general population (Safer

Custody Group, 2005) and higher among prisoners with mental health problems (Towl and Crighton, 1996, 2000). Women prisoners are proportionately more common among prison suicide completers (Snow, Paton, Oram and Teers, 2002). Suicide is more likely in prisons housing those on short sentences, the first parts of a long sentence and prisoners awaiting trial. Such prisons are characterised by a rather rapid turnover of inmates.

Suicide sometimes follows quickly after a serious crime which possibly explains some of the suicides in prison among prisoners on remand awaiting trial. However, it has to be stressed that such offence-related suicides are comparatively rare and small in comparison to suicides among prisoners in general. According to Flynn *et al.* (2009), there are only about 30 suicides a year following homicides in England and Wales (these figures exclude suicides after conviction for the killing). Over the nine-year period, 1996–2005, just over 203 cases of suicide following homicide were identified by Flynn *et al.* in their review. Eighty-six per cent were men. The average age of the offender involved was 41 although the range includes virtually all of the adult life span. There were a number of notable trends:

- The suicidal men usually killed their spouse or partner whereas women were more likely to kill their children.
- A wide range of methods of suicide were employed. Sharp instruments were the most common method of homicide but these amounted to only 23 per cent.
- Forty-two per cent died the same day as the homicide and 75 per cent killed themselves within three days.
- Criminal histories were relatively uncommon as were instances of contact with mental health services – only 10 per cent had such histories.

These findings suggest that prison, in itself, is not the primary stimulus to suicide. Nevertheless, it is a potential location for suicide and, consequently, an important matter for the prison service to address.

It may be tempting to explain prison suicides by suggesting that the overcrowding of prisoners, the population density, is responsible. There is plenty of evidence to show that human beings have preferred space requirements and that crowding, at least in some circumstances, is distressing. Nevertheless, one should not jump to conclusions. For example, in the United States it has been noted that about half of prison suicides occur during the first day of confinement. This cannot be explained in terms of the stress of population density. According to Cox, Paulus and McCain (1984), as prison populations increase there is a tendency for rates of death from all causes to increase disproportionately to population increase. Of particular relevance is the finding that single-occupied cells (where clearly crowding is less of an issue) were associated with very few deaths whereas death was much more common in multi-occupied cells (Ruback and Innes, 1988). Nevertheless, prison is a safe place and the overall risk of death in prison is less than in the outside world. Of course, the proper comparison between prison and the outside world needs to compare like with like. Prisoners tend to be younger and disproportionately from a racial minority compared with the

general population. Adjusting for these trends, this leaves the following:

- Deaths due to illness and homicide were significantly *lower* in prison.
- Deaths due to suicide were significantly *higher* in prison.

One can overstate the dangers, since the rate of prison suicide in the United States was 29 per 100,000 of the prison population as opposed to 20 per 100,000 in similar non-prisoner populations.

The possibility of suicide is not an easy one for prison authorities and psychologists working in a prison context to manage effectively. One obvious strategy is to classify prisoners as either suicidal or not at risk. According to Towl, this has its own dangers. If a prisoner has been classified as non-suicidal then this may be a signal for prison officers to lessen their vigilance over them: that is, a great weight is placed on the classifying system, which may be rather less than perfect. There are a number of high-risk-of-suicide situations that may encourage greater vigilance. These include the period immediately after admission, significant clinical improvement and the achievement of some insight, and during periods of leave for offenders in medium secure units for psychiatric difficulties (James, 1996). Towl (1996) suggests a number of strategies that may be helpful in dealing with the potential problem of suicide:

- Reduce the numbers of remand prisoners and those with mental illness.
- Try to avoid the negative consequences for prisoners who report suicidal thoughts to staff. The consequences may be extremely unpleasant such as routine strip searches and the like which may deter reporting.
- Enable staff to identify and assist prisoners with suicidal feelings.

For a time beginning in 1991, the UK prison service's policy on suicide prevention and risk management was referred to as the F2052SH system within the service. This was the reference number of the document recording that the prisoner had been assessed as being at risk of suicide. Historically, the management of suicidal prisoners had been the responsibility of a prison's medical staff. The new policy changed this and gave the responsibility for the management of suicidal prisoners to all members of a prison's staff. Any staff member could initiate the process of assessing whether a prisoner was a suicide risk – a

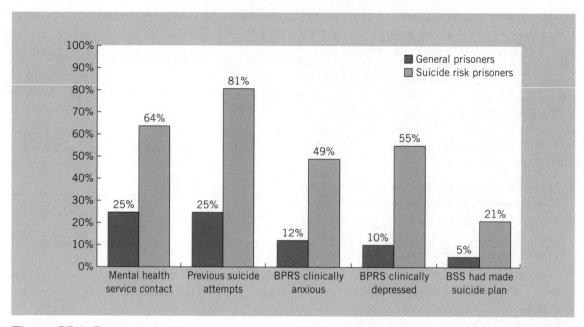

Figure 25.1 Prisoners in general compared with those identified as being a suicide risk on some clinical indicators

decision which involved both medical and other prison staff. If assessed as at risk, then the prisoner had to be observed three times a day, contacts between staff and that prisoner recorded and the case had to be reviewed every two weeks. The records were available to all staff to consult unlike medical records which would be confidential. If the review meeting felt that the prisoner was no longer a suicide risk then the monitoring etc. would be discontinued. This system was replaced by a system known as ACCT (i.e. Assessment, Care in Custody, and Teamwork) which kept the multidisciplinarity which was introduced in F2052SH but introduced new roles of assessor and case manager to ensure accountability in delivering the care plan.

Senior *et al.* (2007) carried out a study of the F2052SH system at four local units housing prisoners – one for adult male prisoners, two for male young offenders, and one for both young and adult female offenders. The researchers compared the prisoners identified as at risk under the system with prisoners in general. Stratified random samples of prisoners were used so that prisoners from all parts of the prison were included (i.e. medical wings, vulnerable prisoner units, remand wings, and sentenced prisoner wings). Each prisoner was interviewed and a number of psychological measures taken. Prisoners in general have significant problems according to the various measures

(see Figure 25.1) such as previous suicide attempts, suicidal thoughts, suicide plans and having the necessary requirements to complete their suicide. This was true of the prisoners assessed as being suicide risks. Remember that these were identified by members of the prison staff. Eighty-one per cent had previously attempted suicide, 53 per cent had levels of suicidal ideation necessitating further clinical assessment, 21 per cent had made a specific suicide plan, and 26 per cent felt that they had the necessary requirements to complete their suicide.

Although the policy has now changed in UK prisons, clearly prison staff can identify successfully many prisoners who pose a significant suicide risk. Unfortunately, despite this, large numbers of prisoners with similar levels of suicide risk according to the assessment instruments used in this study were not identified by the system.

Death from other causes can be a significant factor in deaths in prison. For example, Kullgren, Tengstrom and Gran (1998) found that 7 per cent of Swedish offenders who had been subject to a major forensic psychiatric examination died within a follow-up period of no more than eight years. Less than 3 per cent of these were from suicide in general, although it constituted 6 per cent for those with personality disorders. This is a similar finding to that found in other mentally disordered offender populations.

Violence in prison

Murder is rare in prison in the United Kingdom. For the 15 years between 1972 and 1987, the total of homicides in prison was just 16. Suicide is much more common. There were 300 suicides during the same period. At special hospitals dealing with mentally ill offenders in the United Kingdom, the record is similarly low. Over a 30-year period, in the United Kingdom there were two homicides at Broadmoor, one at Rampton, and the murder of a nurse and a patient at Carstairs State Hospital. Elsewhere, the rate seems to be higher. The rate in the United States is about 10 times higher (Gordon, Oyebode and Minne, 1997). There is evidence that the homicide of prisoners and prison staff has fallen in the USA in recent years although the levels of inmate-on-inmate violence seem to be rising (Stephan and Karberg, 2003). The infamous serial killer Jeffrey Dahmer (Masters, 1993) was killed in prison.

According to Lahm (2008) there are two main theories about violence in the prison context. One is Deprivation Theory and the other is Importation Theory. Both of these are illustrated in Figure 25.2:

- Deprivation theory: Although difficult to attribute to specific authors, *deprivation theory* assumes that prison violence is the consequence of degrading and stigmatising prison conditions (Goffman, 1961; Sykes, 1958). That is, prison violence is the result of the bad prison environment. Some prisoners respond to these oppressive conditions by acting out violently. That is, they are not violent by disposition. In these circumstances they adapt to the brutality of the 'prison code'. This is a purely environmental explanation. It can be considered that there are macro and micro prison-related variables. A micro prison-related variable concerns each individual prisoner such as the length of their prison sentence and the number of outside visits. These are associated with violent behaviour in prison – though negatively for outside visits which are associated with less violence. There are also macro-level variables which have been relatively much less researched in the past than those concerned with the individual inmate. Examples of these include the level of security to be found in each prison, the amount of crowding, and the number of correctional staff to be found.

- In contrast, *importation theory* (e.g. Poole and Regoli, 1980) regards prison as an open system in which adaptation to prison life is shaped by the prisoner's experiences and socialisation prior to imprisonment. What is imported into prison has its origins in attitudes, values and motivations held prior to imprisonment. Thus subcultural values about violent behaviour are

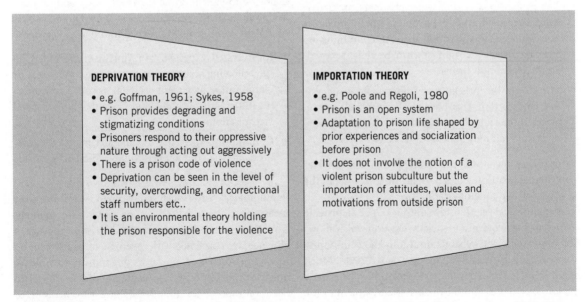

Figure 25.2 A comparison of deprivation theory and importation theory as explanations of prison violence

brought to the prison from outside. So measures such as prior offence types, previous escapes, previous incarceration, and previous violence are all associated with the importation model.

Which of the two theories is best supported by the evidence? Lahm (2008) surveyed inmates at 30 prisons in Kentucky, Ohio and Tennessee. Self-report measures were employed primarily since a lot of prison violence does not get recorded or staff are unaware of it. Serious or deadly assaultive behaviour was somewhat rare in these self-reports and so Lahm excluded them from the study. Thus the violent acts studied were not the most extreme possible. Participants had to have been in the facility for a minimum of six months which gave them a chance to acclimatise to that particular regime. Seventeen per cent had committed at least one assault on another prisoner in the previous year. Being younger and having a higher level of violence in their past were associated with higher levels of involvement in inmate-on-inmate assault. These are good evidence favouring the importation model. However, beliefs and similar violence-related variables did not predict violence in prison. Evidence also emerged supporting the deprivation theory. So, among the micro-level variables, length of time served in prison and sentence length predicted assaultive behaviour in prison as did having fewer prison visitors. In addition, some macro-level variables were predictive of prison violence:

- The proportions of non-white prisoners predictive. Lahm suggests that white prisoners in predominantly non-white prisons may feel that the conditions are more deprived hence more likely to be violent according to deprivation theory.
- The size of the prison population: Lahme suggests that larger prisons may have more contact places and places to be violent than small prisons. Monitoring by prison staff may also be less effective.

In summary, then, both prison and pre-prison variables contributed to prison violence giving support to both the deprivation and the importation theories.

We know that relationships outside of prison provide a level of psychological and social protection which allows for more successful rehabilitation into the community together with less risk of recidivism (Mauer, 2006). Much less interest has been devoted to the relationship between prison experiences and the quality of adjustment to life outside of prison. One exception to this is the interest in the USA concerning the consequences of rape and other non-consensual sexual activity and violence more generally during incarceration in prison. How do prisoners react to their prison experiences? Do they affect their longer-term prospects? Do bad experiences like these influence behaviour on leaving prison? There is little doubt that violent and sexual victimisation can be traumatic and life-changing. However, the majority of this research involves young victims of abuse rather than the population in general. Haden and Scarpa (2008) list the following as consequences of being victimised violently or repeatedly witnessing such episodes:

- interpersonal problems
- depression
- aggression
- post-traumatic stress disorder.

Boxer, Middlemass and DeLorenzo (2009) studied exprisoners from state prison or county jail. On average they had spent 30 months outside of prison and they mostly lived in a very urban metropolitan part of the North East of the United States. Thirty per cent of the sample had violent criminal histories according to their own self-reports and available records. A history of murder, robbery, rape or assault was required for classification into the violent group. There was 87 per cent agreement between the records and self-reports. The remainder of the sample were classified as non-violent. The measure of exposure to violent crime used was based on questions asking about lifetime experiences as observers and victims of violent crime. This was turned into two indicators:

- Incarcerated experience of violent crime based on the following scale: 0 = no witnessing of violence or victimisation by violent crime in prison, 1 = witnessing but no victimisation, and 2 = both witnessing and victimisation.
- Community experience of violent crime used exactly the same scale but applied to the experiences outside of prison.

Psychological and social adjustment variables were measured using a battery of measures. The findings from the research demonstrated that prison exposure to violence was correlated with measures of adjustment on leaving prison. Once indicators of exposure to violence outside of prison as well as demographic variables had been controlled, it was found that those who encountered violence in prison were significantly more likely to be aggressive and to show anti-social tendencies.

The effectiveness of prison

This aim of rehabilitation is explicit to the penal systems of many countries. Examples include the Netherlands, Spain and Germany in Europe. This aim is not explicitly stated in some systems such as France and England and Wales. Nevertheless, rehabilitation may still be seen as an appropriate activity within the latter systems. There are many reasons why rehabilitation might not be a priority in some prison systems. Lack of the needed financial resources to pay for prison psychological, psychiatric, social and educational services might be exacerbated by rapidly expanding prison populations. The growth of offending might lead to a political climate that sees society as soft on crime. Consequently, tougher penalties are needed, not the easy option of training and therapy. Furthermore, only in recent years have effective treatments for, say, sex offenders been developed.

According to Redondo, Sanchez-Meca and Garrido (2002) criminology has demonstrated that punishment may not be effective on all offenders. Crime is not altogether dependent on rationality so sometimes will not be affected by punishment. There are many factors that contribute to crime. Redondo *et al.* list many of the factors already identified in earlier chapters of this book. These should include, among others, social factors such as school failure, ineffective child-rearing, unemployment, illegal drug trafficking, strains between social groups, criminal subcultures and individual psychological factors such as low educational level, aggressive tendencies, occupational incompetence, drug addiction, frustration, beliefs and criminal values, egocentrism, impulsiveness and lack of social perspective. Punishment, as such, is unlikely to have much influence on such criminogenic factors. However, they might be amenable to influence through educational programmes and psychotherapeutic programmes, either in the community or in prison. One would expect psychology to contribute effectively to these.

'Nothing works'

As you now know, 'nothing works' is the idea that interventions to prevent reoffending, especially those of a social or psychological nature, are ineffective. This idea has a long history. It largely developed out of concerns that psychodynamic therapies were ineffective. They simply did not change the behaviour of offenders in relevant ways (Martinson, 1974). Since that time, ideas about how psychological therapy should be conducted have substantially changed. This was a result of the introduction of behaviour therapies around the 1960s but, more importantly, the introduction of cognitive behavioural therapies in the last two decades of the twentieth century. There have been a number of influential analyses of the research into interventions aimed at preventing reoffending. These include, in North America, such reviews as those of Andrews *et al.* (1990). These, and many other similar reviews, employ meta-analysis (see Box 4.2). This involves statistically amalgamating the findings from as many as possible of the relevant studies. The analysis can be refined to examine the effects in subcategories of studies, e.g. those involving say sex offenders, or those involving a particular age group of offender, or those involving a particular type of cognitive behavioural treatment.

It has to be said that at first sight the effect sizes in such studies appear small. A correlation (effect size) of 0.1 or 0.2 between treatment and outcome seems unimpressive. This can be translated into the numbers of treated offenders who will not reoffend. A correlation (effect size) of 0.1 indicates a reduction in recidivism in the treated group of 10 per cent of the rate of recidivism without treatment (i.e. the rate in the control group). Given that recidivism figures tend to be high without treatment, then this may well correspond to a reduction of as much as 5 per cent in recidivism.

Redondo *et al.* (2002) carried out an important meta-analysis of a number of studies of the effectiveness of prison and community treatment programmes in Europe between 1980 and 1998. The same authors had previously published a related study in which they found a global effect size of 0.1, which equates to a reduction in recidivism of 10 per cent (Redondo, Sanchez-Meca and Garrido, 1999). They confined their newer investigation to the prevalence of recidivism involving study designs that included a non-treated control group. Of the studies in their meta-analysis, about two-fifths were British, one-fifth were German and a sixth were Dutch. They found an effect size (correlation) of 0.2 between treatment and outcome. The differential in reoffending was 22 per cent between the treated and untreated offenders. The best outcomes (largest effect sizes) were for educational programmes ($r = 0.49$) followed by cognitive behaviour therapy ($r = 0.3$). Therapeutic communities and diversion programmes were not so effective (effect size = 0.1).

Programmes in the community had the greatest effects. Sex offending had bigger effect sizes than other crimes (such as drug trafficking).

Of course, all of this is evidence that aspects of prison work; it does not indicate that imprisonment, in itself, is a good thing. As might be expected, there has been quite a lot of research into the effects of punishments such as imprisonment and community sanctions on recidivism. Among the most thorough reviews is the work Smith, Goggin and Gendreau (2002) who reviewed over a hundred research studies from the last 40 or so years of the twentieth century into the relationship between (a) the length of prison sentences and (b) receiving a prison sentence rather than a community-based sanction (including greater surveillance and electronic tagging). Meta-analysis was used to assess this plethora of data into the effects of sanctions. Their main findings, which summarise the findings of many different studies, included:

- Recidivism was *not* lower when prison terms were given or when longer prison terms were served.

- This lack of an impact of prison on recidivism applies to juveniles, women and minority groups just as much as men.

- There is a little evidence to suggest that longer periods of incarceration may be associated with small increases in the amount of recidivism.

The researchers suggest that prison sentences should not be assumed to have any influence on criminal recidivism. Gendreau, Goggin and Fulton (2000) found that the only moderator effect found in a large data set was in the case of community sanctions where a small reduction of 10 per cent in recidivism was associated with treatment services.

Recent studies suggest much the same lack of influence of prison on recidivism. The relationship between incarceration and recidivism was studied by Nunes, Firestone, Wexler, Bradford and Jenson (2007) using a sample of 627 adult male sex offenders. The majority were child abusers either inside or outside of the family. Recidivism was based on information gathered from the Canadian Police Information Centre and the researchers concentrated on the first reoffence. Incarceration for a sexual index offence was not related to recidivism for a sexual or violent crime. This was true irrespective of whether a dichotomy of incarcerated versus not or a continuous variable based on length of time in prison was used. Risk was assessed using a modification of the Rapid Risk Assessment for Sexual Offense Recidivism (RRASOR) (Hanson, 1997). The lack of relationship between incarceration and recidivism was unaffected by risk as measured by RRASOR or the length of that incarceration. The authors suggest that incarceration appears to have little or no impact on violent or sexual recidivism following release. Like sexual recidivisim, violent recidivism was not associated with being incarcerated or the length of that incarceration. However RRASOR was correlated with violent recidivism. The researchers suggest that their findings support seeking alternatives to prison for sex offenders whose offending behaviour falls below a certain level of risk.

BOX 25.1 Controversy

What research designs work?

Modern governments frequently engage researchers to carry out evaluation studies relevant to government policy and academics enjoy the benefits of such funding on their research. This is also the case in forensic research where government departments and agencies fund substantial amounts of research into the efficacy of programmes designed to reduce offending. Of course, research findings which support government policy are more likely to be welcomed than those which in some way challenge it. Crime is a major issue on the political agenda and, not surprisingly, the findings of research studies are themselves politically sensitive (e.g. Howitt, 1994). Government departments have research management teams which are actively involved from the start of the commissioning process in decisions about whether research will be publicised. Hollin (2008) reports that the Home Office in the United Kingdom has been reluctant to publish the findings of some research on the effectiveness of certain offending behaviour programmes. Raynor (2008) refers to this as 'sunsetting' which is a graphic way of describing the process by which some research findings disappear into the 'sunset' without being published.

One of the ways in which the impact of some studies is reduced is by evaluating the research against 'gold standard' criteria which stress the scientific worth of some forms of research method and also indicate the diminished scientific value of other forms of research. Indeed, the UK government has used a 'Scientific Methods Scale' (see Hollin, 2008) which gives lower credibility to research that involves merely establishing a correlation between taking part in some crime prevention programme and measures of criminal activity. On the other hand, studies that involve random assignment of participants to experimental and control groups are seen as meeting the necessary criteria of scientifically acceptable evaluation research. This sort of study is often referred to as a randomised control trial (RCT). Anyone familiar with psychological research will know that, historically, this type of research was regarded by many psychologists as the ideal. It is often suggested that such randomised control trials have internal validity which means that strong inferences about causality (what caused the differences between the experimental and control groups) can be made on the basis of the study findings. Unfortunately, often the price of good internal validity is poor external validity in that the study reflects real life very poorly just as laboratory experiments can be very different from real life.

The lack of external validity that is associated with RCTs has meant that many researchers are not totally convinced by claims of the RCT's scientific superiority in the forensic field. Some researchers see advantages in good-quality quasi-experiments in which the participants in the treatment and no-treatment groups are matched (statistically or otherwise) to be as similar as possible on important variables before the treatment is undergone. However, random assignment does not take place in the quasi-experiment.

Do RCTs produce very different findings or better findings than these quasi-experiments?:

- One problem with RCTs in forensic research is that they would require random sentencing to either the treatment or the control conditions. It is easy to see that there might be problems with this. For example, if the sentencing involved a new treatment for paedophilia which seems to work well, then to allocate an offender to the control condition (no treatment) may result in that offender

further offending against children in the future. Consequently, the sentencer may be disinclined to allocate a man to the untreated control group. Furthermore, it might be that not participating in treatment results in the offender being classified as a serious risk and so retained in a high-security prison which itself may have an influence on some outcome measures. Alternatively, an offender who is allocated to the treatment condition but who drops out of treatment might be regarded as a bigger risk because of this non-compliance with treatment and so, once again, may appear different on outcome measures.

- Is there a difference in the findings which are obtained from RCTs and non-randomised studies? Meta-analyses (see Box 4.2) have been used to address this question and consistent results have emerged in a variety of areas of psychological research between good quality RCTs and good quality non-randomised studies (quasi-experiments) (e.g. Heinsman and Shadish, 1996; Lipsey, Chapman and Landenberger, 2001). Such comparability emerges when (1) participants are restricted in their ability to self-select in which condition of the study they partake; (2) there are no major differences between the experimental groups on important variables prior to the treatment programme; and (3) attrition from the different conditions of the study is minimised such as by reducing the number of dropouts from the study.

One overriding danger is that policy-related decisions about how to present the research findings can radically influence just how effective interventions seem to be. For example, if those undergoing the intervention or treatment are presented together as a single group to compare with the control group then this means that those who fail to complete the treatment dilute the data from the treatment completers. That is to say, they reduce the differences between the treatment and non-treatment groups, thus adding to the impression that the intervention did not work – exemplified in the phrase 'nothing works'. This can be justified on the grounds that by combining completers and non-completers then this represents the effectiveness overall of the intervention. However, it completely overlooks the possibility that the problem of non-completion could be targeted and maybe reduced thus increasing the overall effectiveness of the programme.

The many dimensions of psychology in prison

The potential roles for forensic and criminal psychologists in prisons vary widely. By way of illustration of the variety, simply in terms of the work of psychologists with life prisoners in the United Kingdom, the following types of activity have been indicated (Willmot, 1999):

- *Risk assessment*: a prisoner's time in prison needs to be planned and targets set. For example, at what stage may the offender be moved to a less secure environment? When should home leave be permitted and when should the offender be released on licence?

- *Initial risk assessment*: this is dependent on the past history of the offender, including an assessment of the factors that led to their offending. Progress in dealing with these contributory factors needs to be assessed when making future decisions about particular offenders.

- *Individual clinical work*: this might include any of the following – anger and stress management, cognitive behavioural treatments for anxiety or depression and interpersonal skills.

- *Decisions to progress through the prison system possibly to final release*: this is a corporate task rather than for the psychologist alone, although the contribution of the psychologist to the decision may be substantial. Considerations would include attitudes to the offence, insight into offence-related behavioural problems, behaviour in prison and other factors indicating suitability for progression.

- *Discretionary life panels*: in the United Kingdom, once a lifer has completed their basic tariff, a parole board reviews the case every two years. This may include evidence or assessments from psychologists, who may be cross-examined by lawyers for the lifer.

These tasks clearly involve an estimate of the likely future behaviour of the offender. The next chapter considers some of the more objective ways of assessing the potential future risk of offenders.

Main points

- There is little or no role for psychology in the punishment of prisoners. On the other hand, the utilitarian and humanitarian functions of prison can utilise the skills of psychologists effectively in order to produce changes in prisoners that may reduce their likelihood of reoffending in many cases. Psychologists have a part to play in many aspects of prison life from the training of officers to decisions about the release of prisoners. Such activities are rarely carried out solely by psychologists working alone or as part of teams of psychologists only, it is much more likely that psychologists work with other professional groups as part of these activities.

- The range of psychological techniques employed within the prison service is wide. It stretches from assessment using psychological instruments such as intelligence tests to the delivery of therapy to individual prisoners or, more likely, groups of prisoners.

There is every reason to believe that prison, so long as appropriate services are provided, can have a limited but significant impact on future crime. The evidence that prison, as opposed to the services provided in prison, prevents recidivism is weak. It is wrong to believe that this is the consequence of the work of psychologists alone since they are only part of the total package. Meta-analyses seem to suggest that educational services are the most important in terms of allowing prisoners to return to a crime-free life in society. Furthermore, we should not neglect the fact that what happens on release from prison may have an important bearing on an offender's ability not to reoffend. Such services include various forms of supervision as well as housing and employment. The key to all of this is not being too optimistic and not too pessimistic about the value of psychological work within prison.

Further reading

All aspects of psychology in prisons are covered in:

Towl, G. (ed.) (2006) *Psychological Research in Prisons* London: Blackwell.

Towl, G. and Crighton, D. (eds) (2008) *Psychology in Prisons* (2nd edn) London: Wiley-Blackwell.

And for the issue of suicide and self-harm in prison:

Towl, G., Snow, L. and McHugh, M. (2000) *Suicide in Prisons* London: BPS Blackwell.

The American Psychological Association has a version of its publication Monitor covering Psychology and the Prison System online at: http://www.apa.org/topics/law/index.aspx

---

Visit our website at www.pearsoned.co.uk/howitt for self-test and essay questions, annotated further reading, audio interviews with researchers in the field, weblinks and more information on becoming a forensic psychologist.

Chapter 26

Psychological treatments for prisoners and other offenders

Overview

- Psychological treatments for sex offending and violent offending became increasingly common throughout the world in recent years.

- One approach, though, is to employ the entire organisation as a therapeutic environment in which key aspects of the system contribute to change in the offender.

- Nevertheless, treatment programmes are available in most sorts of prison environments especially for longer-term prisoners.

- Sex offender treatment programmes are commonly based on structured group work. Individual therapy is not the norm. Relapse prevention is an integral part of the work to discourage reoffending.

- There is evidence that treatment may reduce reoffending by up to 5 or 10 per cent.

- RNR (risk-need-responsivity) principles seem to lead to better treatment for sex offenders. In this, offenders who pose the greatest risks are assessed in order to understand their criminogenic needs and whatever needs to be done to improve their responsiveness to treatment implemented.

- Programmes are available for violent prisoners such as anger management courses. However, there are important questions about whether anger is fundamental to violent crime.

- Manualisation is an attempt to improve the delivery of psychological treatment which is based on the empirical observation that the effectiveness of treatment varies in different settings. By ensuring that all therapists understand the rationale of the treatment and adopt appropriate therapeutic strategies, the consistency of the delivery of treatment is improved as well as the overall effectiveness of treatment.

Introduction

The perceived value of prisons varies with different political regimes. At the present time, there is some optimism that prison can contribute to crime reduction in some prisoners. The work of psychologists and others within the prison system in terms of therapeutic treatment programmes can be regarded as valuable, to a degree, on the basis of evidence that they reduce the risk of reoffending or produce changes in prisoners that are conducive to them not reoffending. This contrasts with the pessimism of 60 years before in which it was felt that 'nothing works' (see Chapter 25). Studies of the effectiveness of treatment suggest that overall treatments reduced reoffending by about 10 per cent but that some forms of treatment worked better than this. However, some researchers question whether the evidence on which this based is adequate to draw such a conclusion as randomly assignment to treatment and non-treatment groups is rare. As we will see, among the most effective programmes are those based on the psychological principles of cognitive behaviour therapy. Such cognitive skills programmes are regarded by some as an effective means of reducing the recidivism in participants (Blud, 1999). The extent of this reduction is put in the order of 10–30 per cent. Arguably, these treatment programmes are effective because they work to correct a number of cognitive deficits exhibited by offenders. These cognitive deficits are identified as follows:

- *Cognitive style* – lack of empathy with abstract social concepts. Such matters as social harmony and justice may be involved here. Such offenders may be rigid and inflexible in their thinking. They may be poor at tolerating ambiguity, which results in what may be described as rather simplistic, dogmatic thought processes.

- *Critical reasoning* – their thinking is often irrational and illogical. Self-analysis is avoided. They justify what they do by blaming others and, consequently, do not see themselves as to blame.

- *Interpersonal problem solving* – offenders are often socially handicapped without recognising the fact. They are sometimes unaware of the other courses of action available to them. They rarely examine the likely consequences of their actions.

- *Self-control* – to correct impulsiveness and action.

- *Social perspective taking* – prisoners are often egocentric. They fail to understand why they should consider other people. They may lack the skill involved in seeing matters from the perspective of other people. They tend to interpret the actions of others in their own terms and interpret the actions of others wrongly as a consequence.

- *Values* – their moral reasoning skills are poor. They do not recognise the incongruity between their actions and their beliefs.

In the United Kingdom, the prison service has an accreditation system for therapeutic programmes that demonstrates a commitment to research-based therapy. The criteria for evaluation may include:

- a range of targets addressed;

- a structured living environment;

- an aim to change the behaviour of the residents;

- clear and research-based model of change;

- consenting participation in the programme expected from those involved;

- control of behaviour by authorities is not the sole means of changing behaviour;

- effective methods.

Of course, there are alternatives to cognitive therapy within the context of a conventional prison environment. One of these is the therapeutic institutional regime. This has the aim of providing offenders with an institutional environment that will encourage their development as members of an effective community, which may then lead to more effective participation in their community on release. A therapeutic regime has the following characteristics (Woodward, 1999):

- ongoing evaluation;

- ongoing monitoring;

- responsivity;

- skills oriented;

- sufficient 'dosage' or amounts of treatment;

- targeted on criminogenic factors;

- thorough care.

There is some evidence that therapeutic regimes work in some regards. They also appear to reduce recidivism in the residents on release.

Sex offender therapy in prison

The effective treatment of sex offenders originated in the behavioural therapies that began to become common in the 1960s. The most significant previous contribution was Sigmund Freud's belief that sex offenders were untreatable using the psycho-dynamic therapies of the first half of the twentieth century. Not surprisingly, given the dominance of this view, the treatment of sex offenders was not a priority in prison services until recently. For example, in Britain in the 1980s there was clear evidence that sex offenders were more likely to receive custodial sentences (Fisher and Beech, 1999) – a 50 per cent increase in a decade. However, this did not correlate with an increase in determination to help prisoners to avoid reoffending after release. The introduction of therapy for sex offending has, however, slowly become increasingly common. It has to be said that prison is just one of a number of contexts in which sex offenders may receive therapy:

- The probation service has devoted quite a lot of resources to group work with sex offenders in the United Kingdom. Of the 7,000 sex offenders being supervised by the probation service, half are supervised in the community and there is capacity to treat half of these men.
- In England and Wales, some sex offenders receive psychological treatment from psychiatric services in regional secure units and special hospitals. Both of these cater for mentally disordered offenders as inpatients. Others may be treated as outpatients. Generally speaking, sex offenders constitute only a small proportion of the work of these units.

There are numerous accounts of the use of cognitive behavioural therapies in the treatment of sex offenders – both those in prison and those in the community (e.g. Craissati and McClurg, 1997). It is useful to concentrate on a concrete example of what may be typical within the prison service context. As ever, the precise details will differ somewhat from jurisdiction to jurisdiction. The case of the British prison service is well documented and, as it was far from the first of such programmes developed, it adapted features from other programmes. As such, it should be of fairly general interest. It is known as the Sex Offender Treatment Programme (SOTP) and was thoroughly evaluated by the STEP programme (Beech, Fisher and Beckett, 1998).

Fundamental to a treatment programme is a set of decisions about how, when, where, to and by whom therapy is to be delivered. The basic decisions for the prison SOTP included the following:

- *Where*: in a limited number of prison establishments which could be resourced appropriately to deliver the treatment.
- *Who*: priority is given to offenders at the greatest risk of reoffending according to a formal risk-assessment procedure. Some characteristics such as mental illness, lack of English, very low IQ, suicide risk and severe personality disorder effectively debar the individual from the programme.
- *When*: at an appropriate stage in a sentence of two or more years provided that time is available to complete the programme.
- *Whom*: the approach is multi-disciplinary. That is, all sorts of staff besides psychologists may be involved, such as prison officers, teachers and chaplains. Of course, they are given appropriate training in terms of knowledge of cognitive behavioural treatments and relevant skills in working with others in groups.

The therapeutic situation is based on *structured group work*. A group consists of eight offenders and two tutors/therapists. The treatment manual contains a structured series of cognitive behavioural activities and exercises that are explained and described in detail. It concentrates on the thought processes involved in offending as well as attempting to place limits on the behaviour of the offender. The core programme is designed to work on the motivation of the offenders to avoid reoffending and to develop personal skills that enable this. These latter skills are collectively known as *relapse prevention*. According to Beech, Fisher and Beckett (1999), the programme consists of 20 blocks (treatment sessions) that cover a number of areas. These for the purposes of this description may be classified as cognitive modification and relapse prevention. The methods employed in group treatment of this sort are a mixture of methods familiar to those who have engaged in any type of group work, and matters much more specific to sex offending. Some of the techniques involved include the following:

- *Brainstorming and group discussion*: topics discussed by the group are often written down as a list on a board or flip chart. An individual often responds to this collection of ideas in terms of his experiences.

- *Focus on the individual*: the work of one individual is subject to scrutiny and evaluation by the rest of the group.

- *Homework*: activities such as keeping a diary are carried out by members outside the group meeting itself. This is almost always written work.

- *Role-playing*: members of the group (and this may include the tutors or facilitators) may play out a situation. The rest of the group observe and respond to the role-play. The actual participants may also analyse their experiences.

- *Smaller or buzz groups*: some activities are carried out by a pair of offenders, perhaps three or four. This sort of activity helps the offender develop communicative skills with others, assertiveness and a degree of empathy. The experience with the small group can then be combined with that of other groups in a 'plenary' session.

- *Videos*: film is available which deals with various aspects of sex offending. In particular, there may be video available about the experiences of victims. Viewing this is then followed by individual response and group discussion.

The above are the main treatment methods employed. Substantial areas are covered using these methods including the following:

- *Describing the offence*: it is known that sex offenders tend to describe their offences in ways that are self-exculpatory. Often the offender will present himself almost as if he were the victim. Vagueness and being non-committal is characteristic of their responses. The following is a short extract from an interview with an offender (Howitt, 1995a, p. 95):

> Interviewer: Did you kiss her on the breast?
> Bennie: Maybe I did maybe I didn't . . . [when you are arrested] they try to use psychology on you, they make you say you did . . . so I am going to say I did.
> Interviewer: . . . that's no use to me . . . I don't want to know what they say, I want to know what it is.
> Bennie: . . . maybe I probably did . . .

At the end of the exchange, the reader may feel that they still do not know whether or not Bennie accepts that he kissed the girl's breasts sexually despite a clear challenge from the interviewer. Nevertheless, despite

this, Bennie uses the phrase 'maybe I probably did . . .' which leaves him free psychologically to maintain his position that he said things because he, in fact, was the victim of pressure from other people. Therapists may describe this as a 'passive account' since it does not truly describe what the offender did. An active account would be much more direct. For example, in the above example, the offender might have said 'I encouraged the girl to roll about in front of the television with me. We were pretending to play at being animals. I pulled up her clothes and played at biting her stomach. Then I took it further and sucked her breast for a couple of minutes.' In order to encourage the active account, it is necessary for the offender to provide information about the following:

- How the offender actually planned the offence – it did not just happen.
- The offender's sexual or emotional preoccupation with the victim.
- That the offender was responsible for initiating all of the aspects of the abuse.
- That he took measures to try to prevent the victim from disclosing the abuse to others.

- *Challenging distorted thinking*: aspects of the distorted thinking that each offender has about his own offending will be familiar after a while to members of the group. This may be distorted thinking about children's sexual motivations and interest in adults or the adult rape victim's secret desire to be sexually violated, for example. The distorted thinking may be challenged by asking for evidence to support the offender's assumptions that may then be criticised by other members of the group. It has to be stressed that this may occur at any stage of the treatment and not simply during the sessions specifically devoted to distorted thinking.

- *Victim empathy work*: showing a video of victims of abuse talking about the consequences or having outside speakers come and describe these experiences. Given that many offenders will themselves have been victims (see Chapters 6 and 10), this may profoundly influence their response. Their own experiences of vulnerability and being unable to disclose their abuse at the time may contribute to the lessons learnt by the group. Eventually, the offenders will role-play the position of victim in their own offences.

- *Fantasy modification*: it is widely accepted that there is a relationship between sex offending and fantasy (see Box 9.2). Some believe that masturbation to sexual fantasy is the basis for its development through a process of conditioning. *Irrespective* of the actual role of fantasy in sex offending, there would seem to be a compelling case for attempting to reduce this fantasy as part of the treatment programme. Normally this is not included in the work of the therapy group except at the broad level of the role of fantasy in offending behaviour. Otherwise trying to modify sexual fantasy would usually be carried out using one of four or so main behaviour modification techniques on an individual basis with a psychologist:

– *Aversive therapy* – the fantasy would be associated with some negative *consequence*.
– *Masturbatory reconditioning* – new and socially more acceptable fantasies would be associated with masturbation. In other words, the offender masturbates and switches to the new fantasy at the point of orgasm. This is repeated until the new fantasy becomes sexually arousing.
– *Satiation* – the offender repeatedly masturbates to the fantasy until the fantasy is incapable of causing sexual arousal.
– *Covert sensitisation* – the fantasy is extended to the negative consequences. So a fantasy of raping a woman is associated with the negative consequences of arrest, trial and imprisonment, for example.

Details of these techniques can be found in Howitt (1995a), for example.

• *Social skills, assertiveness and anger control*: while a lack of social skills is not a *universal* feature of sex offenders, by any means, the inability to form relationships with adults may be a contributing factor to the offending of some. Anger control problems have to be seen as an issue with rapists for whom issues of anger are common. Social skills including those of knowing how to deal with situations without aggression can contribute to a potentially more social prisoner at the time of release. Issues such as body language, the meaning of social cues and the range of behavioural alternatives available for dealing with situations may be dealt with through analysis and role-play, for example (see Box 26.1).

• *Relapse prevention*: relapse prevention (e.g. Marshall, Hudson and Ward, 1992; Pithers *et al.*, 1988) prepares the offender to deal with the feelings and experiences that he will have on release which are known to be progenitors of offending behaviour. These may be regarded as warning signs that must not go unheeded. It is known, for example, that sex offending patterns in some offenders are preceded by a negative mood state. Thus depression and anxiety might serve as danger signals for imminent offending. Similarly, the return of deviant fantasies may serve a similar function. There are other aspects of offending that a relapse prevention strategy would signal as dangerous: for example, moving into a job involving children, moving to a neighbourhood where there is a school nearby or just offering to babysit for a neighbour. For most people, these may be innocuous life-events; for the paedophile or child molester, they may be a precursor to the offending process.

BOX 26.1 Forensic psychology in action

Does treatment reduce recidivism?

There is a great deal of evidence to suggest that certain types of treatment reduce reoffending (recidivism) in offenders. So, for example, Hanson *et al.* (2002) surveyed the findings of over 30 studies into sex offender reconviction in treated and untreated groups. On average, 17 per cent of non-treated offenders recidivate sexually compared with only 12 per cent of treated offenders. Much the same pattern applied to general recidivism for any type of crime in these two groups.

Among the most effective ways of studying recidivism risk changes following sex offender therapy are meta-analytic studies which systematically review the findings of several studies addressing the question of the effectiveness of treatment. (See Box 4.2 for an explanation of meta-analysis.) Hall (1995) reviewed 12 studies of recidivism involving a total of over 1,300 offenders. The tremendous range of outcomes found in the studies is remarkable. For example, a few found no differences between the treated and untreated groups (or even slight negative relationships) whereas others showed a treatment versus comparison group correlation (effect size) of 0.55. The latter, in one instance, corresponded to a recidivism rate of 15 per cent for the treated group but 68 per cent for the untreated comparison group. The overall recidivism was 19 per cent for all of the treated groups versus 27 per cent for all of the untreated groups. Treatment was not confined to cognitive behavioural methods – behavioural methods and hormonal treatments were also included. There was no statistical difference between the cognitive behavioural treatments and hormonal treatments in terms of their effectiveness. Behavioural modification seems to have a negative effect – that is, it makes matters worse if given alone compared with no treatment at all. There is more or less a consensus from meta-analyses (see Box 4.2) that reoffence rates are between 5 and 10 percentage points lower in treated sex offender groups than untreated controls (Duwe and Goldman, 2009). Furthermore, the indications are that cognitive behaviour therapy involving aspects of relapse prevention is the most effective. Although these positive findings are important, there is always the caveat that the quality of a meta-analysis depends in part on the quality of the studies upon which it is based. So in Lösel and Schmucker's (2005) meta-analysis only 7 per cent of studies employed random allocation to the experimental and control groups. The vast majority of studies (84 per cent) did not use random assignment nor matching techniques to equate treated and untreated control groups. This leaves a distinct gap which would allow one to argue that selection bias may have had an influence. That is to say, the successes apparently due to treatment might be due to the treatment groups being systematically different from the control groups. This lack of random allocation in studies of the effectiveness of therapy has been responsible for some arguing that we cannot confidently assume that therapy works (Hanson, Bourgon, Helmus and Hodgson, 2009). Kenworthy, Adams, Brooks-Gordon and Fenton (2004), for example, questioned whether it was ethical to devote

resources to the treatment of sex offenders when studies involving random allocation produced limited evidence of the success of treatment. However, this study involved a range of different types of therapy and the authors suggest that Cognitive Behaviour Therapies may be superior to, for example, psychodynamic approaches.

This demonstrates, as ever in forensic and criminal psychology, that it is unwise to generalise findings too much. One might glibly suggest that therapy can do no harm even if it does no good. We have already seen that this may not be the case. And there is other evidence that certain sorts of therapy can do harm (Rice, 1997; Rice, Harris and Cormier, 1992). The outcomes for men treated for two or more years (the mean was five years) in a Canadian therapeutic community were compared with those of a control group of men who had spent time in prison but had not received therapy. Most had been admitted to a psychiatric hospital for assessment following a violent offence. The offenders in the treatment and the prison groups were matched man-to-man in terms of age, type of offence and extent of criminal history. The outcome in terms of recidivism after 10 years average time at risk was unimpressive. Some of the recidivism was common assault but there were also cases of multiple homicides and sexual assaults. The men in the treatment programme fared little differently from those sent to prison.

The treatment programme had appeared to be especially suited to the needs of psychopaths (see Chapter 21). Consequently, the researchers studied the outcome of the treatment programme for psychopaths and non-psychopaths separately. The findings were opposite to those expected. For non-psychopaths (as assessed by the Hare Psychopathy Checklist) treatment was associated with much less recidivism. However, the psychopaths fared worse in treatment than in prison. This demonstrates, along with other research on psychopaths in therapeutic communities, that psychopaths may well be a totally different subgroup of offenders. Speculatively, it could be that treatment raised self-esteem in psychopaths, which resulted in a

▶

BOX 26.1 (continued)

greater willingness to use aggression. Alternatively, most prisoners may learn to be empathic with others in treatment whereas manipulatively the psychopath learns how to appear empathic and generally to manipulate the system.

The possibility that treatment can do harm is an important consideration. Jones (2007) discusses the concept of iatrogenic treatment responses, which refers to the fact that some treatments, for some clients, can have an undesirable effect. The concept is more clearly applied to medical interventions (e.g. adverse effects of medicines) than psychological ones. The word literally means outcomes which are the consequence of the healer but it has come to mean adverse consequences due to treatment. Therapies with offenders diagnosed as having personality disorders have long been known to be unsuccessful. Iatrogenic outcomes are difficult to identify from research which concentrates on the success of a treatment in terms of the overall numbers who improve. Such an approach tends to disguise the negative effects if a positive outcome is more likely overall. However, in research where different groups of participants are involved, it may be possible to see that perhaps certain groups tend to respond well to treatment while others seem to worsen.

There are a number of potentially harmful outcomes of therapeutic interventions for offenders according to Jones. It is possible that a treatment may have an impact on an offender's capacity and skills to offend in the future:

- Increased likelihood of reoffending possibly because the offender wishes to demonstrate that they beat the therapy which they felt forced to engage in.
- Increased skills for accessing victims so improved social skills might allow psychopaths to manipulate other people to a greater degree of effectiveness.
- Increased triggering salience such as the sadistic offender who is taught empathy for other people but this greater empathy merely increases the ability of the offender to become aroused by the distress of his victim.

- Increased skills at evading detection which, for example, might emerge as a consequence of hearing how other offenders in the therapy group went about committing their crimes.

While the research in support of most of these processes is fairly fragmentary, the evidence that some types of offenders might become greater risks following therapy should encourage a more systematic approach to researching iatrogenic outcomes.

Another important issue in the effectiveness of treatment is the issue of the offender who does not complete treatment. There is evidence that non-completion of treatment is very high. About a quarter of offenders fail to complete their treatment programme (McMurran and Theodosi, 2007). Non-completion is much commoner for offenders being treated in the community than those treated in prison. It is important to note that non-completion of treatment can be for a number of different reasons, not all of which indicate non-cooperation from the offender. The reasons, according to Wormith and Oliver (2002), include (a) administrative reasons such as where an offender is released from prison or is transferred to another one during treatment, (b) agency-initiated removal from treatment by staff because the offender is unruly or fails to keep to the rules of the treatment, and (c) offender initiated cessation of treatment.

There are numerous studies which consider the fate of those who do not complete treatment compared with those who do. For example, Dutton *et al.* (1997) studied a group of wife-assaulters in Vancouver, Canada. The typical treatment was anger management. The men could be divided into several groups:

- men who did not show up for the assaultive husbands treatment programme;
- men who were assessed but deemed unsuitable for treatment;
- men who were assessed as suitable but did not complete the treatment programme;
- men who completed the treatment programme.

In terms of recidivism ratios (which are the total number of repeat assaults by the group divided by that group's sample size) there were differences. This measure is a better estimate of the amount of recidivism than is the incidence of recidivism:

- no-shows recidivism ratio = 9 per cent;
- unsuitable for treatment = 20 per cent;
- dropouts = 11 per cent;
- completers = 6 per cent.

While these seem small differences, for 1,000 completers this would amount to a total of 320 crimes whereas 1,000 people in the unsuitable for treatment category would generate 810 crimes (these are for all acts of violence). Non-completers would generate 550 and no-shows would generate 400. For violence against women, dropouts would commit 500, no-shows 230, rejects 290 and completers 230. Thus treatment is associated with fewer offences.

Studer and Reddon (1998) in Alberta, Canada, found that treatment may affect the risk prediction for sex offenders. This study looked only at those who completed treatment versus those who failed to complete treatment. The treatment programme included educational components on human sexuality and substance abuse among other things such as relapse therapy. The initial treatment period was up to 12 months followed by a further up to 8 months of outpatient treatment. They used as their predictor of recidivism prior sexual offences. For men who dropped out of the treatment programme the relationship between prior sexual offences and recidivism was statistically significant and positive. That is, previous sex offences predicted recidivism for those who did not complete their treatment. On the other hand, there was virtually a zero correlation between previous offences and recidivism for the men who completed the full treatment. That is, the treatment broke the link between previous offence rates and recidivism. This was true despite the fact that prior recidivism in the two groups was at identical levels. More generally, non-completion of treatment is a good predictor of reoffending (Hanson and Bussière, 1998).

There are problems in terms of how to interpret the common finding from research that those who fail to complete treatment programmes are at greater risk of reoffending than treatment completers. Non-completers may be different in terms of risk of recidivism prior to treatment so that their elevated risk merely reflects this pre-treatment difference. There is growing evidence that this is the case. This raises the question of whether failure to complete treatment actually makes matters worse than not starting treatment at all. McMurran and Theodosi (2007) reviewed research on cognitive behavioural therapy programmes as these are believed to be the most effective at reducing the risk of reoffending. Among the requirements for inclusion in the analysis was that either (a) treatment versus non-treatment was randomly assigned so that there was no systematic bias in the selection process or (b) the treatment versus non-treatment groups were matched by the researchers to be equal on their assessed level of risk prior to treatment. Not many studies existed which met these requirements but data were found for 17 samples. Some of the research was based on prison samples and some on samples living in the community.

There was a small negative relationship between treatment completion and recidivism which led McMurran amd Theodosi to the conclusion that failing to complete cognitive behavioural treatment has an adverse effect. This adverse effect was stronger for the community samples than the prison samples. One reason why failure to complete treatment may be associated with greater risk of reoffending is that an offender who is removed from treatment by staff may feel aggrieved and develop more anti-authority and antisocial attitudes.

Dropouts from treatment programmes are clearly a waste of resources. Is it possible to identify these offenders prior to treatment? Nunes and Corton (2008) studied factors which are associated with non-completion of a sex offender treatment programme in Canada by comparing completers with non-completers. Usually, non-completion was due to the expulsion of the offender from the programme

▶

BOX 26.1 (continued)

because of non-compliance with its requirements. They used the Static-99 measure (see Chapter 27) which can be considered as consisting of items which refer to general criminality as well as those referring to sexual deviance. They found that non-completion of the treatment programme was related to the general criminality component of Static-99 items but it was not associated with the sexual deviance component. The researchers suggest that if one wishes to estimate the likelihood of non-completion of a sexual offender treatment programme then it may be more effective to use general criminality to make one's prediction rather than sexual deviance.

Finally, the research addressed the question of whether RNR (risk-need-responsivity) works with sex offender treatments. RNR is a famous approach to the assessment and treatment of offenders. It was first offered as a formal approach by Andrews, Bonta and Hodge (1990). The basic criteria of RNR are:

- Risk principle: The greater the offender's risk of reoffending the greater should be the services to try to prevent this.
- Need principle: The individual's needs which contributed to their criminal behaviour should be assessed and then targeted during treatment.
- Responsivity principle: Consideration should be given to ways in which the offender's learning from an intervention or treatment is maximised. These considerations include learning style, motivation and strengths and abilities of each offender.

One might expect that these principles might facilitate the effects of treatments for sex offenders. The study by Hanson, Bourgon, Helmus and Hodgson (2009) was a meta-analysis of 23 recidivism outcome studies using the criteria implied by the RNR approach. The treatments involved were coded in terms of the extent to which their aims/objectives addressed a list of criminogenic needs related to sex offence recidivism such as attitudes tolerant of sexual crime, deviant sexual interests, intimacy deficits, and sexual preoccupation. Each of the treatment programmes were assessed in terms of how many of the above three RNR principles were applied (Risk, Need, and Responsivity principles). To be included in the meta-analysis, a study had to involve at a minimum a sex offender treatment group and a sex offender non-treated group. Over all of the studies, the recidivism rates for the treated sex offenders was 11 per cent whereas that for the controls was 19 per cent for sexual recidivism but substantially higher at 32 per cent and 48 per cent for any recidivism in the treated and untreated groups respectively. The RNR-compliant treatments were more likely to be effective. The more recent the study, the more effective RNR-compliant treatments were likely to be, suggesting that RNR principles have been more effectively applied in recent years. Effects were stronger in the weaker designs compared to the stronger designs which is a concern for the validity of the findings. Effects were highest when all three RNR principles were met. Effects were low where no RNR principles were adhered to.

There are many similarities between the contents of this programme and the activities in a medium security unit of the New Zealand prison system (Hudson *et al.*, 1995). Indeed, dissimilarities are few in number. For example:

- The men who volunteer for this treatment are required to undergo phallometric assessment (see Box 9.1) in order to gain information about any potentiality they may have for sexual arousal in response to deviant sexual stimuli.

- One *therapist* is used with a group of 10 offenders compared with the two tutors used in the UK prison service programme.
- The group meets four times a week – rather more frequently than in the United Kingdom – for about the same length of time (24 weeks in New Zealand).

Many of the components of this cognitive behavioural programme were much the same as those of any cognitive behavioural programme. Hughes *et al.* (1997) found evidence of improvements in personality disordered offenders in a high-security setting. They indicate that the cognitive programme in the context of a supportive ward environment (though not a therapeutic community) produced changes in a global measure of various aspects of change which included reduced impulsivity, reduced macho attitudes and better social problem solving.

Particularly pertinent to therapy given in prisons is the question of whether this reduces reoffending. Although evaluation research has been carried out into the cognitive behavioural programme described above, this could be criticised as stopping short of the question of recidivism. Instead, the evaluation concentrated on measures of things such as cognitive distortion, the reduction of which is only a step towards decreasing recidivism (Beech *et al.*, 1998). Box 26.1 contains further pertinent material.

Before moving on to therapy for anger, it might be helpful to point out that almost all therapy for sex offenders occurs in a prison setting or in the community after conviction. This begs the question of the extent to which alternatives to these are neglected. Some potential paedophiles are aware of their potential risk to children. The question is how can these men be found and helped before they begin offending and before a child has been harmed. The Berlin Prevention Project Dunkelfeld (PPD) targets men who freely seek help (Beier *et al.*, 2009). A media campaign was the starting point of recruitment. Those who phoned in were screened over the telephone for 18 months. Of 286 participants who completed the screening (60 per cent completed it), most were interviewed by a clinician; 58 per cent expressed a sexual interest in pre-pubescent minors and pubescent minors (28 per cent). Eleven per cent had a sexual preference for mature adults. The rest were uncategorisable. The majority (70 per cent) had strong or very strong feelings of distress. Many of them (about a half) had previously sought professional help and a similar number had sought helps from their friends etc. The media primarily involved a poster placed into print media but also on billboards in the city. There was a TV spot which was used on various German television stations and in cinemas. Of course, the big problem with such initiatives is that any offences reported to the therapist would have to be passed over to the police.

Treating violent criminals

The need for methods of reducing the violent behaviour of some criminals is self-apparent. For many years, the commonest help for violent criminals was Anger Management courses. Recently, there has been questioning about the value of Anger Management together with the development of newer, wider based methods of treatment. There are many similarities between the different approaches which makes it difficult to differentiate them based merely on descriptions of the procedures involved.

Anger management

Anger management is a classic form of treatment which is employed in a variety of contexts including prison services. In the United Kingdom, the prison service has developed a National Anger Management Package (Towl, 1995) which is used with prisoners with temper control difficulties. It is based on group-work with two facilitators present and a group of six to eight prisoners over, typically, eight sessions. Its main aims are to heighten awareness of the process of becoming angry in the individual, to increase awareness of self-monitoring of one's own behaviour, to learn the benefits of controlling anger, and to enhance their knowledge and skill at managing their anger (Keen, 2000). The components are illustrated in Figure 26.1.

Theoretically, the emphasis of such programmes is on cognitive components of anger and, in particular, the process of appraisal (Howells *et al.*, 1997). The event is appraised and an emotional response is the consequence:

For anger to emerge, the individual must be displeased about the related undesirable event and disapprove of someone's blameworthy action. So, if we hit our finger with a hammer we are unlikely to feel anger. On the other hand, if we hit our finger with a hammer at the moment someone begins talking to us unexpectedly we may well get angry. There is thus an aversive event and a blameable individual. Of course, anger is an inappropriate emotion in these circumstances since the other person almost certainly did not wish to cause harm to you.

Despite the name *Anger Management*, many Anger Management programmes recruit offenders with problems of violence without reference to whether their problem is the management of anger. The difficulty is the sheer variety of the causes of violence in different individuals. Some may be psychopaths who act violently

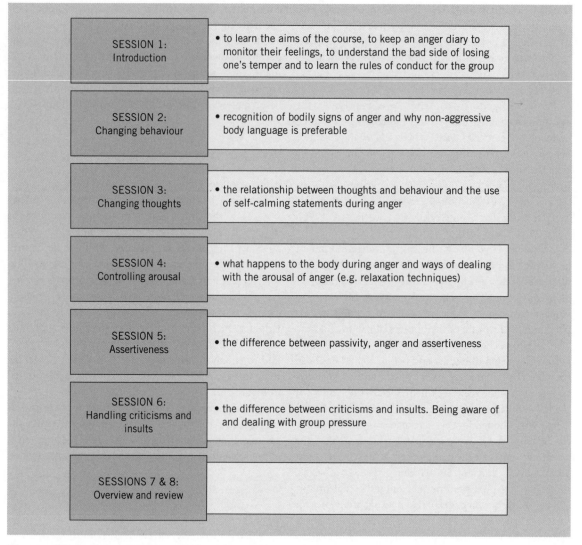

Figure 26.1 Components of the National Anger Management Package

not out of anger but dispassionately in order to achieve their particular goals – perhaps to obtain money. Others may lack self-esteem and be vulnerable to taunts by others. In the first case, a general package of anger reduction may be of no advantage and perhaps even counter-productive since efforts to get such a person to control their temper maybe fail to understand the origins of their violence. Thus Anger Management courses have been criticised for failing to assess the specific factors leading to violent behaviour in individuals. Thus it is a mistake to assume that violence in the context of a theft, say, cannot be helped with anger management – it may or it may not be. The reasons for the violence need to be understood before the relevance of anger management can be addressed.

As to their efficacy, research indicates that their impact on anger is not sufficient to be of clinical significance (Howells, 1998).

Violent offender programmes

More recent attempts to develop programmes to reduce violence have adopted a more in-depth approach to the factors which cause violent behaviour. Special therapeutic programmes for violent offenders are not common in comparison with those for sex offenders. However, this will probably change as special therapeutic programmes for violent offenders are gradually evolving and being introduced into the criminal justice system services. Their effectiveness will be a key to how extensively they are adopted.

According to Attrill (1999), three findings about violent offenders are at the root of treatment:

- Violence is learned behaviour that is adopted as a way of coping with difficult life experiences. Violence, then, works effectively and reliably for them and serves to reinforce their sense of their own power and self-efficiency.

- Patterns of criminal behaviour include a diversity of criminal acts and are rarely confined to violent behaviour. Studies suggest that reoffending by, say, those convicted of crimes against property may well involve violence rather than another property crime.

- Patterns of violent and criminal behaviour are entwined within ways of thinking that support those acts.

Offenders show a sort of antisocial logic, which makes violence seem acceptable and normal, necessary, justified. Attrill indicates that if an offender sees himself as one of society's victims he may regard this as sufficient justification to behave just as he wants. Anyone who interferes with this is being unfair and further victimising the offender. So a prison sentence would be seen as justifying further offending because it was unfair. Furthermore, the offender believes that he is entitled to do what he pleases and should not be told what to do by others. Consequently, if his violent acts in support of these beliefs go unpunished they further reinforce his feelings of entitlement.

The probation service in England and Wales employs the Aggression Replacement Training (ART) Programme to deal with violent offenders. It is a broader programme than Anger Management alone, as we will see. This programme was developed by Goldstein (Goldstein, 2004; Goldstein, Glick and Gibbs, 1998) whose basic assumption was that aggression results from both internal and external *multiple* causes. The internal (personal) factors are threefold. These are listed below together with the ways in which they are dealt with in the ART Programme to reduce violence:

- General deficit of skills of a personal, interpersonal and social-cognitive nature: Skills acquisition exposes the offenders to opportunities to identify, develop,

and then practise pro-social skills. Social learning procedures are used and the core social skills modelled by the group leader. This is followed by group discussion, role-play, and feedback on performance. The participants are encouraged to apply their newly learnt skills to their lives beyond the treatment environment;

- Low levels of anger control accompanied by frequent impulsive and aggressive behaviours: Anger control training essentially follows the founding work of Novaco (1975) – that is Anger Management Training. It seeks to help the individual develop self-control to deal with their anger and aggression. During these sessions the triggers to violence and aggression for the particular individual are identified together with an understanding of the probable consequences of anger and aggression. The offender's consequent improved self-awareness is employed to develop alternative coping strategies to situations. Typical strategies include avoidance of situations which lead to anger and methods of negotiating with others.

- Moral reasoning deficits: Moral reasoning training tackles the very concrete and egocentric thinking typical of those who commit violent crimes. Moral reasoning training seeks to enhance the offenders moral reasoning skills in pro-social ways.

To investigate the effectiveness of this programme, Hatcher, Palmer, McGuire, Housome, Bilby and Hollin (2010) used a quasi-experimental design. The treated group had been allocated to the treatment by probation staff whereas the comparison group were also convicted of a violent offence and had received a community sentence. The two groups were matched by the researchers using the Offender Group Reoffending Scale Version 2 (OGRS2) risk score (National Offender Management Service, 2010). This score is calculated from information on the Offenders Index (a national database of convictions for all offenders in England and Wales) including static offender variables such as gender, custody and breaches of custody, number of previous convictions, offence type, and age amongst other things. Its normal use is to predict the likelihood of reconviction in two years but in this study it was used to ensure that the treated and untreated groups did not differ initially in terms of risk. The findings suggested that the treated group showed a 13 per cent decrease in reconviction compared to their matched controls. The treatment completers were less likely to reoffend than non-completers.

Gilbert and Daffern (2010) review some of the treatments for violent offenders employed within prison services around the world. Most of them claim to be based on social cognition though the extent of this is often far from fully apparent according to Gilbert and Daffern, who are also critical of the lack theoretical guidance involved. Nevertheless, they suggest that many of the social-psychological models of aggression tend to be too broadly conceptualised (that is, too abstract or open-ended for them to be used in comprehensive violence correction programmes). Among those they discuss are:

(a) *Cognitive skills and cognitive self-change programmes*: These focus on the cognitions of violent offenders. Their underlying strategy is to help offenders develop enhanced capabilities in their thinking about and approaches to solving their interpersonal problems in particular. The belief is that skills deficits leave the individual at an increased risk of acting aggressively because they simply do not have the adequate knowledge about how to deal with situations non-violently. The training involves a variety of social skills such as conflict-resolution, critical thinking, impulse control and management, interpersonal skills, and problem solving.

The British prison service has piloted the Cognitive Self-Change Programme which is aimed at reducing the risk of reoffending in men with a record for violent offending. It concentrates on specifically criminogenic types of thinking which are replaced through treatment by an ability by the offenders to recognise and change their criminogenic thought processes. Such criminogenic thought processes include attitudes, assumptions and beliefs which lead to and maintain violent behaviour patterns. The programme assumes that violence is usually intended so that offenders need to do various things to change that behaviour. They need to take control of their lives and become motivated to become skilful at controlling their thoughts and feelings.

The programme is divided into six blocks, each of which consists of sessions totalling 100 hours or so. Group treatment averages four sessions per week:

- Skills are taught which allow offenders to observe and report their thoughts, feelings, attitudes and beliefs.
- Identification of the thinking patterns which have and will result in their offending and violent behaviour in general.

- Offenders try to identify new ways of thinking and ways of stopping these thought patterns.
- A relapse prevention plan is prepared and the strategies are practised.
- The offenders practise the relapse prevention plan in prison.
- The final block has the offender back in the community with structured support and supervision.

Gilbert and Daffern argue that this and similar programmes are based on the social-psychological literature on aggression. Unfortunately they are not specific enough to the individual to change the offenders' well entrenched aggressive patterns. There is evidence that they reduce all sorts of criminal behaviour – not just violence (Polaschek and Collie, 2004).

(b) *Multi-faceted interventions*: Recent innovations in programmes for violent offenders have been much more intense than the original anger management programmes, for example. The cognitive behavioural treatment may involve in excess of 300 hours of group and individual sessions over a 28 week period as in the case of the Violence Prevention Program in New Zealand (Polaschek *et al.*, 2004). Considerable assessment of the offenders is involved such as their social and personal histories, how they are likely to respond to group situations, and details of their offending and its processes in the past and present. The programme consists of different modules such as:

(i)   cognitive restructuring of thinking leading to offending,
(ii) communication/interpersonal skills,
(iii) emotion regulation,
(iv) moral reasoning,
(v)   offence chain identification,
(vi) problem solving,
(vii) planning for relapse prevention, and
(viii) victim empathy.

Research findings suggest that over a two-year follow-up period, twice the number of men in an untreated control group than in the treated group were reconvicted for a violent offence. In contrast to other violence reduction methods, there seemed to be no difference in terms of non-violent offences (Polaschek *et al.*, 2005).

Perhaps the clearest statement that anger is not an essential feature of violence comes from the work of Walker and Bright (2009). They point out a number of problems when applying studies of the effectiveness of anger management training to prison populations since the major meta-analyses of this involve schoolchildren and other non-offender samples. More importantly, there is evidence that anger is not an essential component of violence. For example, although men and women may feel anger equally, men are more violent than woman (Archer, 2004) Violent rapists, non-violent rapists and non-rapist offenders showed no differences in anger (Loza and Loza-Fanous, 1999). Walker and Bright identify humiliation as a missing factor in Anger Management though it features in psychoanalytic traditions. They point to the low level of self-esteem which is apparent in many violent offenders which makes them feel easily humiliated in interactions with others and consequently act violently. Thus the threat to the already low self-esteem coming from others results in a feeling of humiliation. Violence is seen as a justified retaliation which allows the offender to both express and discharge the negative feelings associated with the threat. Furthermore, the violent act of assaulting and injuring the victim serves the social function of restoring a degree of personal pride for the offender.

Walker and Bright refer to three layers of thought which can contribute to violence:

- Layer One: Negative automatic thoughts. These are closely associated with emotions and are fleeting such that they may go unnoticed. Offenders must learn in therapy to be aware of and monitor such thoughts.

- Layer Two: Dysfunctional Assumptions: These are the rules which the individual plays by or applies to their lives. They can be found by simply asking offenders to say what rules they employ in given situations though they may not know their dysfunctional nature. They relate to core beliefs which are deeply held and not consciously accessible.

- Layer Three: Cognitive beliefs or schemas. This is the deepest cognitive level and consists of beliefs about the self, the world, and the future. They are normally somewhat extreme such as 'I am worthless'. The therapist may be required to identify them and understand how they related to a person's psychological state.

Three aims are important for Walker and Bright in therapy for violence and aggression:

- Understanding of the cognitive components specific to a particular individual's violent behaviour and how these impact their behaviour.

- It is the responsibility of the therapist to identify the dysfunctional thoughts which play a role in the individual's violence.

- The modification of the cognitive elements which need to change during therapy and that the individual acknowledges the changes to be their own and that they are for themselves to maintain.

Manualisation

As we have seen, there is sufficient evidence from a variety of sources to indicate that treatment programmes work. Consistency in terms of effectiveness, however, varies in ways which suggest that the quality of the programme's implementation is vital to its effectiveness. Different therapists do differ in terms of their effectiveness, of course, but there is more to it than that. McMurran and Duggan (2005) are among those forensic and criminal psychologists who suggest that effective treatment is 'driven' by theory and is based on research evidence. Adherence to the principles derived from these is termed 'treatment integrity'. A treatment programme that has a high degree of treatment integrity in practice will conform closely to the programme's underlying theory and design. Therapists in programmes demonstrating good treatment integrity will keep on the course determined by the principles of the treatment programme and will not drift away from these. Treatment integrity is dependent on a number of things of which the careful continuing training of personnel is an important component as is their continual monitoring.

Inexperienced therapists, especially, benefit from the use of highly structured materials that provide clear descriptions of the techniques and processes to be used in therapy (Crits-Cristoph et al., 1991). Of course, these highly structured materials are manuals for the treatment programme. Hence, there is a concept – manualisation – which simply means that the structure of the therapeutic programme is enshrined into a formal manual describing the practice of the therapy rather than leaving the programme to the whims of the therapists. Manuals vary in their style. Some are best described as prescriptive in the detail of how and what is to be done. Others stress the concepts underlying the treatment programme and leave more to the individual therapist's discretion in terms of how those principles are implemented. Manualisation is quite simply the process of turning the basic principles of the treatment programme into a detailed, systematic manual describing what must be done in practice.

Manualisation taken at face value may seem a simple, practical step in increasing the effectiveness of therapeutic programmes. However, it actually reverses many of the traditional principles that underlie psychological therapies. Hollin (2002) suggests that the following are among the major criticisms of manualisation although he does not share all of them:

- *Negation of theoretical principles*: rather than tailor cognitive behavioural treatments to the individual needs of offenders, manualisation encourages 'off the peg' treatment which is the same for all. This is particularly evident in the stress of cognitive behavioural programmes on working with groups of offenders rather than individuals. Rapists and child molesters go through identical treatment programmes.

- *Lack of individual case formulation*: the thorough assessment of the individual prior to treatment is a given in traditional cognitive behavioural treatment. So an individually tailored treatment plan would be integral to treatment. Assessment in cognitive behavioural programmes tends to be confined to excluding those

unsuitable for cognitive behaviour therapy by virtue, say, of the low levels of intelligence.

- *Lack of clinical artistry*: the clinician's insights, personal qualities, skill in decision making and judgements in relation to an individual client are seen by some as being integral to good therapy. Treatment is an unfolding process, the precise detail of which is dependent on the therapist's use of these skills. The use of a manual diminishes the opportunity for using such skills. However, it is these very processes in which the therapist makes continuing adjustments on the basis of their clinical skills that actually threaten the integrity of treatment programmes.

- *Emphasis on single schools of therapy*: a treatment manual will almost certainly feature a single theoretical approach to psychotherapeutic intervention. This, most commonly, will be the cognitive behavioural approach. Inevitably, then, this squeezes out eclectic approaches where features of different schools of therapy are used by the therapist depending on circumstances. One consequence of the monopoly of one school of therapy in a treatment programme is that it may stifle the development of new approaches to therapy as it prevents new things from being tried out.

Main points

- Modern prison services are likely to have tailored cognitive behavioural programmes for the treatment of sex offenders and some violent offenders in particular. The important thing is that the demand that such programmes be evaluated for effectiveness has resulted in a number of studies which demonstrate beyond question that such programmes not only produce the changes they intend in some prisoners but that recidivism is also reduced as a consequence. One should not overestimate the effectiveness of such programmes but neither is pessimism appropriate. We have gone a long way from the time when 'nothing works' was the overriding view to today when 'why does it work?' and 'how can we make it work better?' are the more common views. Manualisation refers to the standardisation of treatment such that therapy is effectively used in all locations irrespective of the experience and skills of the particular personnel involved. There are a number of problems in evaluating any programme and

the choice of outcome measures (e.g. psychometric tests versus recidivism rates) is crucial.

- Programmes for sexual offenders tend to be very widely based and tackle a wide variety of aspects of the offender, the offence, and cognitions about the offence. It is not always the case that treatment involves aspects which have been demonstrated empirically to be associated with sexual offending. It would appear that programmes which are based on the RNR principles of risk, need, and responsivity tend to be the most effective.

- The treatment of violent offenders has often involved the methods of anger management. The difficulty with this is the lack of certainty that a great deal of violent offending is due to anger problems. Indeed, there is good reason to believe that it is not. Violence treatment programmes have a more sophisticated theoretical basis and there is some evidence that they are effective.

Further reading

The therapeutic treatment of sex offenders is discussed in depth in the following:

Brown, S. (2005) *Treating Sex Offenders: An Introduction to Sex Offender Treatment Programmes* Cullompton: Willan Publishing.

Marshall, W.L., Fernandez, Y., Marshall, L. and Serran, G. (eds) (2005) *Sexual Offender Treatment: Controversial Issues* Chichester: John Wiley.

For alternative ways of reducing crime:

Hollin, C.R. and Palmer, E.J. (eds) (2006) *Offending Behaviour Programmes: Development, Application and Controversies* Chichester: John Wiley.

Perry, A., McDougall, C. and Farrington, D.P. (eds) (2005) *Reducing Crime: The Effectiveness of Criminal Justice Interventions* Chichester: John Wiley.

The American Psychological Association has a version of its publication Monitor covering Psychology and the Prison System online at: http://www.apa.org/monitor/julaug03/prisontoc.html

---

Visit our website at www.pearsoned.co.uk/howitt for self-test and essay questions, annotated further reading, audio interviews with researchers in the field, weblinks and more information on becoming a forensic psychologist.

Chapter 27

Assessment of risk, dangerousness and recidivism

Overview

- Psychological practitioners have an ethical responsibility and duty of care in relation to those who can be affected by the decisions they make. The decisions that are made by practitioners about the disposal (e.g. early release, to live in the community) of offenders may increase the chances of the public becoming victims. Risk and dangerousness assessments refer to a variety of methods developed to limit the levels of risk and danger to the public while at the same time providing less restrictive arrangements for offenders. The Tarasoff decision in the United States imposed legal requirements pertinent to this. Risk assessment is different from risk management. Risk management is the various techniques that minimise the risk to other people – keeping the potential offender in prison is a form of risk management.

- This is not a precise science though empirical studies have demonstrated that certain variables predict future behaviours reasonably well. These include historical factors such as a background of violent offending. Some psychological measures such as the Psychopathy Checklist are also effective.

- Social and welfare policy can rapidly change the situation in which all psychologists operate. A good example of this has been the process of deinstitutionalisation of the care of the mentally ill such that they participate much more freely in the community. The consequence of this is that decisions have to be made about the treatment of the mentally ill in the community which may, at some level, have an impact on how risk and dangerousness are assessed.

- The factors which need to be taken into account when assessing risk and dangerousness may be to some extent different for a sexual offender than for a violent offender. These in turn may be very different from the predictors of suicide by the offender. Different contexts will influence the risk posed by the offender. For example, a paedophile may not be generally dangerous to children except when he gets the opportunity to work in a setting such as a school when many potential victims are available. Different types of offence require different predictor variables. So the predictors of sexual reoffending are different from those of violent reoffending. The predictors of suicide may also be different. Risk factors are those that predict recidivism, and are different from causal factors that caused the individual to be dangerous to others in the first place.

- Clinical judgement of risk is different from statistical assessment of risk, which is based on empirically established relationships. There are many reasons why clinical judgement may fail, including the lack of available feedback about whether a decision was correct. In recent years, structured clinical methods have been developed which still rely on the judgement of the clinician to some extent but provide a checklist of decisions to be made and means of reaching an assessment. The Psychopathy Checklist Revised (PCL-R) is a very successful example of this approach. One should not confuse sloppy and bad practices with the best clinical work. It should be stressed that some clinicians see things differently.

- The prediction of risk is a prediction of the statistical likelihood of, say, violence in the future. Prediction of dangerousness is different in that it refers to the likely level of, say, violence if it happens. Thus there is a high risk of any of us reacting, say, with a push if angered but the general level of dangerousness would be low – i.e. we could not be provoked to kill.

- Mistakes are inevitable in predictions. It is harder to predict rare events than common events. The numbers of false positives and false negatives are important. False negatives are the offenders who are declared safe but actually reoffend. False positives are those who are declared a risk but do not reoffend.

Introduction

A British forensic psychiatrist once said 'I could let free half of my patients – if I knew which half' (Gretenkord, 1991). The German banker Hermann Josef Abs pointed out 'Prognoses are a difficult matter, especially when regarding future events' (Gretenkord, 1993). The assessment of the risks and dangers posed by offenders is a very serious matter, however. It is of concern to all in forensic work.

Duty to protect

There are a number of responsibilities inherent in decision making in forensic work. These include:

- protecting the general public from dangerous individuals;

- protecting staff of an institution from dangerous individuals;

- protecting other inmates of the institution from dangerous individuals;

- protecting individuals from dangers posed by themselves – including suicide.

These duties include an element of prediction. Individuals within the criminal justice system pass through a number of stages for which assessment of the consequences of particular decisions is required. For example, if a prisoner is to be transferred from a maximum security prison to one more open and free, then this decision implies that some consideration is given to their likely future behaviour: they should be unlikely to abscond from their new prison and constitute little or no danger to the general public, for example. A number of influential societal factors need to be taken into account in understanding assessment of risk and dangerousness.

The *Tarasoff* and other US legal decisions

The spur to research into the prediction of dangerous which occurred in the 1970s was events in American law courts at about this time. The most famous of these was the the *Tarasoff* decision which arose out of a Californian court cases of the early 1970s. The outcome was basically that psychologists and other clinicians began to be under a greater duty to protect the general public from their clients. The basic facts are as follows:

- Tatiana Tarasoff was a young student at the University of California in the late 1960s and early 1970s.

- Another student, Prosenjit Poddar, told a student health therapist that he intended to kill Tatiana.

- These basic facts were reported to the medical authorities at the campus and their response was to get Poddar checked out by the campus police. Apart from this no other action was taken.

- Shortly afterwards, Tatiana was killed by Poddar.

- Tatiana Tarasoff had not been informed about the threat to her life at any stage before her death.

- Her parents pursued the matter through the Californian legal system.

- In a watershed case, *Vitaly Tarasoff v. the Regents of the University of California*, her father won in 1974 a legal ruling that therapists were legally obliged by duty to inform such potential victims of the threat to their safety made by clients of the therapist. This was a duty to inform.

- The judgment was reviewed in 1976 in the light of a number of practical difficulties raised by professional bodies. The 1976 judgment obliged therapists to use reasonable care in order to ensure the public's safety from the therapists' clients. The difficulties inherent in this led to a second judgment in 1976 which revised the obligation to that of using reasonable care to protect potential victims. This is a duty to protect. The new obligation on the therapist involved managing the dangerous individual better, say, with medication, institutionalisation or by whatever means.

One difficulty with the Tarasoff decision lies in the fact that the named potential victim may not be the actual victim: that is, the violence may be against individuals whom the client has not directly threatened. A client who threatens to harm members of his or her own family may actually end up violently assaulting staff supervising him in a psychiatric facility. The threat needs to be evaluated in terms of the potential for attack, which may involve many others apart from those mentioned directly in the threat (McNeil, 1997). Of course, a Californian legal judgment is not US law, let alone international law.

There were a number of lawsuits in the United States during the 1960s and 1970s concerning the civil rights of offenders diverted into institutions for the criminally insane. Two American court cases, in addition to the Tarasoff ones, also led to a new research effort into the prediction of dangerousness starting in the 1970s (Cooper, Griesel and Yuille, 2008). The *Baxstrom v. Herold* (1966) case involved Johnny Baxstrom who had been sentenced in 1958 to up to three years in prison for a second-degree assault. However, in 1961 he was judged to be mentally ill and was relocated from prison into a psychiatric unit and detained there after his original three-year sentence had been completed. A law permitted the detention of mentally ill individuals after their sentence expired. The legal outcome was that the court decided that Johnny's detention beyond his original sentence was not just. This led to about a thousand patients being transferred from maximum security mental hospitals (i.e. hospitals for the criminally insane) to regular psychiatric hospitals for the mentally ill. Some were later released into the community. Psychiatrists had decided implicitly that these patients were dangerous – that, after all, was the reason for them being detained. Researchers realised the need to research thoroughly the adequacy of these psychiatric assessments. Few behavioural problems emerged and the patients were no more violent than any other patients after they had been transferred to the regular hospital. The psychiatrists had simply grossly overestimated the levels of dangerousness of offenders like Johnny Baxstrom (Steadman and Cocozza, 1974). Much the same situation arose in the case of *Dixon v. Attorney General of the Commonwealth of Pennsylvania* (1971) which involved a similar law allowing involuntary and indeterminant commitment based on the opinion of two physicians. A number of patients were detained after the expiry of their sentences for criminal behaviour. No review was required concerning the internment. The legal outcome of this case changed things entirely. Once again, research into these inmates-turned-patients after release revealed that the psychiatrists' assessments of dangerousness were woefully over-pessimistic.

To summarise the current position, two points are important:

- By the 1980s onwards, the ideology had changed to one in which the majority of the mentally ill should be cared for in the community. Institutional care was seen as a temporary respite for use only in acute circumstances when there was no realistic alternative.

- The modern situation balances the right of individuals to their liberty with the inevitability that in some instances the general public and other third parties require protection (Glover, 1999).

Risk assessment

Schwalbe (2007) divides the history of risk assessment into three historical phases though they overlap markedly:

- First-generation risk assessment was based on the impressions or subjective judgements of professionals within the criminal justice system. There were no structured assessment instruments.

- Second-generation risk assessment was dependent on the statistical relationship beween a risk assessment instrument and subsequent offending. The emphasis was on classifying the risk level and predicting reoffending. So long as the assessment method produced the required associations, that was good enough. The content of the assessment was secondary in importance. The risk factors tended to be static in nature such as the number of previous offences for a particular category of crime, etc. (A static predictor is one which is fixed and normally cannot be changed by therapy or another type of intervention.) Schwalbe (2007) describes the actuarial/statistical approach as being the gold-standard for risk assessment.

- Third-generation risk assessment was similarly devoted to the basic statistical association between the predictor instrument and recidivism but introduced dynamic risk factors such as drug use or school problems which may be subject to change through treatment or some other sort of intervention.

Risk assessment is a professional tool in its infancy despite having been part of forensic and criminal psychology for several decades. Traditionally, recidivism has been the crucial topic for psychologists though psychiatry has often concentrated on the prediction of dangerousness. Recidivism is the likelihood that an offender will reoffend after release or some other stage in the future. The study of this dates back to the early twentieth century when researchers used official records or files that held information about the demographic and criminal history of the offender. The earliest manifestation of statistically based methods of risk assessment seems to be the work of Burgess (1928). Conceptually, there is an obvious distinction to be made between the statistical risk of the occurrence of an event in the future and the dangerousness of that event. For example, the likelihood of an offender reoffending in the future by shoplifting may be very high. In terms of the consequences of this reoffending, it poses fairly small consequences for the individual victim (Clark, 1999).

The prediction of dangerousness seems to refer to two distinct professional activities (Hodgins, 1997):

- Deciding which patients or clients or offenders will behave violently or aggressively or criminally in some other way.

- Identifying the particular conditions in which a specific individual is likely to behave violently, aggressively or criminally.

These are very different activities, although clearly interrelated. By knowing more about the conditions encouraging violence, say, in a particular individual, we may be in a position to make more accurate predictions of their dangerousness. If, for example, we know that a particular man is prone to violence only when under stress and challenged by a woman, we are likely to see him as of little danger to other male prisoners in a male-only prison environment. There are no universal predictors of future behaviours and the factors predicting different types of behaviour are different. For example, the predictors of rape are not the same as the predictors of non-violent criminality.

For criminal behaviour and other behaviours, a number of effective but simple predictor variables have been established. These are largely associated with the age of the offender (youthful offenders are more likely to reoffend) and criminal history (those with the most criminal offences are the most likely to reoffend). Such indicators are readily measured and are prime aspects in predicting future behaviour (Clark, 1999). One difficulty is the non-dynamic nature of these predictions. They would give a prisoner the same likelihood of reoffending at the start of a term of imprisonment as when it finishes. Thus if the prisoner has received therapy within the prison context, there perhaps should be some adjustment to the prediction (i.e. successful therapy might reduce reoffending) but much of the data available are not sophisticated enough to allow that to be done.

Care should be taken to distinguish between:

- those factors that predict dangerousness in an individual; and

- the factors that caused that particular individual to be a danger to others (Hodgins, 1997).

This distinction between predictors and causes is important. The predictors of dangerousness are often very simple things such as age and previous history of crime. The causes of crime are multiple and complexly interrelated. For example, assume that studies of twins have established that genetics plays a role in the aetiology of the violence of some offenders. This means that genetic characteristics caused the offending. Just because we know that the cause is genetic does not mean that we have the technology to identify precisely what genes are involved – that is we have no genetic test. Nevertheless, we may still be able to predict dangerousness though not through a genetic test. Research may show that a long history of crime is strongly correlated with future violence. This history of violent crime cannot be said to be the cause of future violent crime – genes are the cause in this example. In these circumstances, we can use history of crime as an indicator of likely future violence but not the explanation of it. Some predictors may turn out to be causes of violence but this is not a requirement.

Risk and dangerousness prediction is at the moment rather inexact and we are unlikely ever to have perfect predictors. In particular, currently we do not know how stable risk factors are across different forensic populations (types of offender, locations of offenders). This sort of uncertainty led Monahan (1993) to argue that *all* organisations dealing therapeutically or otherwise with potentially dangerous client populations (including all forensic settings) should adopt the following principles:

- Experts in assessing client dangerousness should be employed.

- *All* therapists should collect data on the risk demonstrated by their client pool as part of an effort to extend knowledge in the field.

- Data on risk and dangerousness are potentially of value to all practitioners. Consequently, it is incumbent on practitioners to communicate their findings to other practitioners/decision makers working with potentially dangerous client populations.

Box 27.1 Key concept

Risk management

Risk management can be considered to be all of the actions that can be employed by professionals to prevent the risk that they assess to be present in an offender, client or situation materialising. Many of the techniques are not intended to have a lasting effect but merely an immediate one. According to Harris and Rice (1997) these include the following:

- *Static controls* include video monitoring, locked wards and so forth. Situational controls might include, for example, the exclusion of violent partners from the family home or reducing the availability of guns and access to them. Pharmacological controls are common. They involve the use of sedatives and other drugs to reduce aggressive behaviour, for example.
- *Interpersonal controls* include encouraging talking with others as a means of reducing or circumventing the arousal of emotions such as anger. There are procedures available for the use of counselling or therapy in increasing self-control, such as anger management programmes.

Risk management involves the practices and procedures that minimise the risk of clients to others (Monahan, 1993). It is not necessary to know the actual levels of risk posed by a particular individual before they are deployed:

- Hospitalisation or imprisonment may incapacitate (make less risky) potentially dangerous clients effectively compared with, say, releasing them on parole.
- Second opinions from experts in dangerousness are essential in all cases of potentially dangerous clients. A practitioner's sole opinion is insufficient.
- Non-compliance with treatment should not simply be regarded as a stumbling block to effective treatment. It is a major risk indicator for dangerousness and should be responded to in that light.

Some authors stress the positive aspects of risk assessment (e.g. Glover, 1999). If risk had only negative outcomes (such as the general public suffering violent assaults) then there would be no reason to take that risk: just leave the offender behind bars which reduces the risk to the general public to the very minimum. It is because we want the positive benefits of taking the risk that we take that risk. For example, we may feel it more humane to release prisoners into the community wherever possible or we may seek the economic benefit of not having to pay the high financial costs of keeping an offender in prison.

Political context

Risk and dangerousness assessments are subject to political pressures of many sorts. Equally, the management of risk and dangerousness is not solely in the hands of the primary decision makers, including psychologists. In terms of the work of the British Parole Boards, McGeorge (1996) suggests that there is a relation ship between the political climate regarding crime and decisions to allow parole. His index of political influence is the number of life sentence prisoners to whom the Home Secretary (the government minister responsible for law and order matters) refused parole out of those recommended by the Parole Board. As the number rejected increased so

did the number recommended for release by the Parole Board decrease. This suggests that the parole recommendations were influenced by the toughness of the Home Secretary.

Clinical judgement versus statistical assessment

There is a common consensus that there are two types of risk and dangerousness assessment. The first, perhaps the traditional form, as we saw earlier, is based on *clinical judgement*. It is generally held not to be successful. The second type is *statistical or actuarial assessment* and is held to be more successful by modern psychologists. The debate follows the pattern of Meehle's (1954) critique of the efficacy of purely clinical methods such as the interview. One needs to review the evidence with care before any final conclusions can be drawn on the best form of risk and dangerousness assessment. Figure 27.1 is a chart illustrating the complexity of risk and dangerousness assessment. Many factors need to be taken into account. The clear lesson is that the context and intentions of the assessment are a vital consideration in planning that assessment.

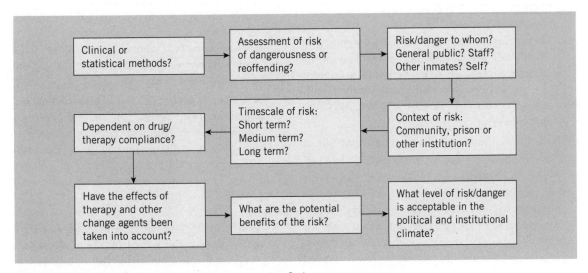

Figure 27.1 Aspects of the assessment of dangerousness

Clinical approaches in risk and dangerousness assessment

There are a number of distinct clinical approaches to the assessment of risk and dangerousness (Limbandari and Sheridan, 1995). They differ in their tactics and scope as much as anything. Some of these approaches are described as clinically based prediction models. This means that they rely on the experience and skilled judgement of the psychiatrist, psychologist or therapist involved rather than empirical evidence favouring the prediction:

- *Linear model*: this is the simplest sort of model. It is based on a limited number of decision choices that can be represented as a flow diagram or a decision tree. The simplicity means that relatively inexpert personnel may use it. An example of this comes from the work of Gross *et al.* (1987). In the event of a threat to the safety of other persons made by the client, the therapist or other decision maker should go through the steps of the decision tree to decide the appropriate action or whether action is appropriate. One route through the decision tree under consideration would be:

  - Is there a clear (as opposed to a vague) threat?
  - Is there serious danger (as opposed to marginal danger)?
  - Is there a specific victim (as opposed to a non-identifiable victim)?
  - Is there an imminent danger (as opposed to no imminent danger)?
  - Is the threat to a public official (as opposed to family member/acquaintances or other person)?
  - The therapist should contact the police (as opposed to, say, warning the person, warning the family, or going through involuntary hospitalisation procedures).

  Had the choices been different, then some clients might be recommended for family therapy.

- *Hypothetico-deductive model*: knowledge about the previous behaviour of the client allows a clinician to formulate hypotheses about the client's likely future behaviour. The hypotheses are integrated with, for example, theories of violence or other relevant theory. This inferential process becomes clearer when expressed with a concrete example:

While tightly clenching his fists, a young man tells his high school counselor that his grades plummeted because his girlfriend, whom he refers to in sexually derogatory terms, broke off their relationship. The counselor knows that this student has a history of frequent alcohol abuse and fighting on school grounds. The young man's father is in the Navy on an extended overseas assignment. The mother reports that her son refuses to accept her authority and that he has become difficult to manage in the absence of the father.

(Gross *et al.*, 1987, p. 7)

In this method, the clinician initially focuses on cues to the individual's behaviour to be found in the case history. Such possible clues include anger, rage, rejection and alcohol abuse. The combination of clinical theory and experience of similar clients might lead to the hypothesis that the client is depressed, full of feelings associated with being abandoned and out of control. Other important factors might include the observation that the location of the school is in an area noted for its high levels of violence. Say if this were confirmed by complaints by other students at the school, the indications are that there is a systematic problem with violence in the community which may lead to extra risk of the client's acting violently. In this example, the counsellor recommended:

- the therapeutic confrontation of the young man's anger;
- that the boy is not to take the same lessons or classes as the individuals against which he had previously aggressed in order to minimise the risk of contact;
- a counsellor–client contract in which the young man would agree to stay away from the girl and not to harm her in any way.

- *Risk assessment model*. This model (Gottfredson and Gottfredson, 1988) accepts the multi-dimensional nature of violence. Thus it is regarded not solely as a characteristic of the personality of an individual but also as the product of certain social and political climates. The following case study illustrates this approach:

Convicted of felony assault on his former girlfriend, a 28-year-old male with a history of alcoholism is up for parole after serving half of a 12-month sentence. While in prison, he completed extensive alcohol treatment and anger management programs. On release from jail he intends to live with his mother. As the clinician, it would be imperative to know that his mother lives less than a block from the former girlfriend and that living in the mother's home are several alcoholic siblings.

(p. 8)

In this case, to release the man to live in the home of his mother is tantamount to encouraging him back towards alcohol and its attendant risks. After all, several of his alcohol-dependent siblings still live at home. Equally, the former girlfriend's residence was close to that of his mother so enhancing the likelihood of future violence.

There is a general consensus in the literature that clinical inference based on case files and interviews is not a very powerful tool for assessing the probability of reoffending or the level of risk. Clark (1999) and Blackburn (1984) suggest on reviewing studies of this sort that clinical prediction is at best weak, at worst totally ineffective. Particularly important is the research that found that even experienced clinicians failed to predict future violence in cases which would have readily been predicted from simple indicators such as previous recidivism. Not all evidence against clinical methods constitutes a fair test. In particular, studies requiring clinicians to predict outside of their domain of expertise (i.e. clinical matters) are unfair. For example, we should not expect a clinician to be able to predict educational achievement accurately since this stretches beyond their normal clinical experience.

Structured clinical methods

Clinical assessments are not necessarily confined to the sorts of subjective impression implied by the critics of the clinical method. Blackburn (2000) stresses that the provision of guidelines to focus the clinician on crucial aspects of prediction can serve to improve matters. Along these lines, Hollin and Palmer (1995; Palmer, 2001) point out that the research indicating the success of actuarial or statistical methods of prediction and the apparent failure of clinical prediction may mean several things. One possibility is that we need better clinical measures of clinical variables to equal the statistical approaches.

If clinical variables do not matter then this suggests that there are no individual differences among offenders that might affect their likelihood of reoffending. This seems most unlikely. Furthermore, it is difficult to believe also that situational factors such as stress are not important in predicting violence in specific circumstances and these are not easily incorporated into future predictions. The distinction is between the role of clinical variables and clinical judgement.

The following are some of the main predictive tools (see Figure 27.2):

(a) **Static-99** is a well-regarded, short, 10-item assessment tool which is simple to score and is cost effective. It essentially combined two earlier scales – RRASOR and Structured Anchored Clinical Judgement (SACJ – min). Its 10 items involve static, historical factors such as age and prior offences which are not generally alterable or manipulable or changed by therapy, for example. An improved version of this is Static-2002 (Hanson and Thornton, 2003) which consists of 14 items organised into five subscales:

- Age at time of release
- Persistence of sexual offending (e.g. measured by things such as number of occasions sentenced for sexual offences
- Relationship to victims (e.g. any stranger victims)
- Deviant sexual interests (e.g. any male victim, any young victim)
- General criminality (e.g. any prior involvement with the criminal justice system)

Based on the total score on the full 14 items, offenders are placed into five categories of risk ranging from low, through low-moderate, to moderate, to moderate-high, and high. Hanson, Helmus and Thornton (2010) present an analysis of the data from a range of studies into the validity of Static-2002 as a predictor of 5- and 10-year recidivism rates. It was found that Static-2002 was successful at predicting sexual, violent and any recidivism. These predictions were marginally better than those based on Static-99. However, it was not possible to predict absolutely the level of risk from a Static-2002 score. Different samples varied in the scores needed to predict recidivism.

(b) **Psychopathy Checklist PCL-R.** Good clinical measures seem capable of predicting reoffending: for example, the Psychopathy Checklist (PCL and PCL-R) (Hare, 1980, 1991) consists of 20 items.

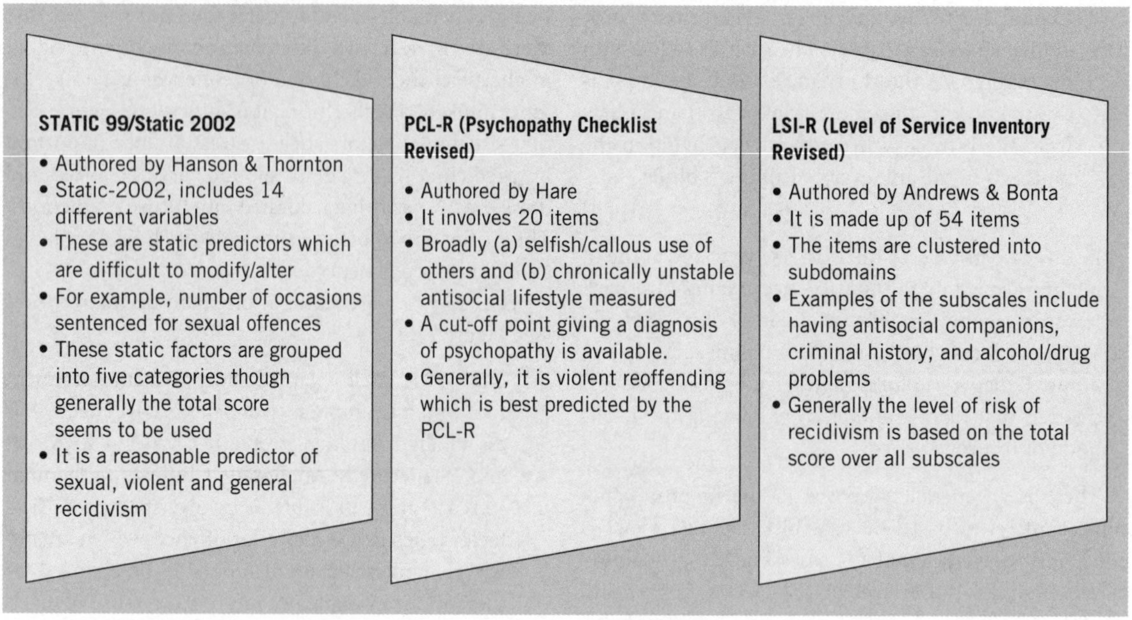

STATIC 99/Static 2002

- Authored by Hanson & Thornton
- Static-2002, includes 14 different variables
- These are static predictors which are difficult to modify/alter
- For example, number of occasions sentenced for sexual offences
- These static factors are grouped into five categories though generally the total score seems to be used
- It is a reasonable predictor of sexual, violent and general recidivism

PCL-R (Psychopathy Checklist Revised)

- Authored by Hare
- It involves 20 items
- Broadly (a) selfish/callous use of others and (b) chronically unstable antisocial lifestyle measured
- A cut-off point giving a diagnosis of psychopathy is available.
- Generally, it is violent reoffending which is best predicted by the PCL-R

LSI-R (Level of Service Inventory Revised)

- Authored by Andrews & Bonta
- It is made up of 54 items
- The items are clustered into subdomains
- Examples of the subscales include having antisocial companions, criminal history, and alcohol/drug problems
- Generally the level of risk of recidivism is based on the total score over all subscales

Figure 27.2 Some well-known structured risk assessment methods

These include a component that may be described as 'selfish, callous and remorseless use of others'. Items reflecting this tap aspects such as superficial charm or glibness, grandiose sense of self-worth, pathological lying, manipulativeness and failure to accept responsibility for one's actions. In many ways, this reflects the psychopath – a type of offender known to be highly involved in persistent offending and reoffending. The other dimension is of a 'chronically unstable and antisocial lifestyle' which includes a need for stimulation, a parasitic lifestyle, poor behavioural controls, early behaviour problems, impulsivity and juvenile delinquency. The Psychopathy Checklist is a good predictor of recidivistic tendencies in some areas. It may be as good as many purely actuarial measures of risk at predicting recidivism (Palmer, 2001), which is not surprising given that the Checklist measures a wide range of criminogenic factors. There is a range of studies demonstrating that the Psychopathy Checklist is a robust indicator of recidivism. Sloore, Rossi and Hauben (2004), for example, found that 36 per cent of their sample of Belgian recidivists had a score on this measure, which defined them as psychopaths. It should also be stressed that the measure requires training before it can be used effectively by the clinician. Generally the Psychopathy

Checklist is used in the prediction of violence for which it has a good track record.

(c) **Level of Service Inventory (LSI)**. The Level of Service Inventory Revised (LSI–R) consists of 54 items in 10 categories. Its purpose is both to help understand and predict criminality (Andrews, 1982; Andrews and Bonta, 1995, 2006). LSI-R assesses rule violation or deviant behaviours in an everyday context. The ten categories or subscales are:

- (Antisocial) companions
- Attitude/Orientations
- Accommodation
- Alcohol/drug problems
- Criminal history
- Education/Employment
- Emotional/Personal Problems
- Finance
- Family/Marital
- Leisure/Recreation

Not only are there individual subscales as defined by the above categories but they are combined into a total score which is relevant to the level of risk of recidivism. According to Andrews and Bonta, it is not possible to understand deviant behaviour unless one considers it alongside common, routine everyday behaviours. It has become clear that this

Inventory has the capacity to identify the heterogeneous patterns of specific needs for particular groups of offender. The different components of the LSI-R score are due to the offenders' special characteristics and the characteristics of the penal setting in question. Useful research findings on LSI-R come from research by Hsu, Caputi and Byrne (2009) involving a sample of nearly 80,000 Australian (New South Wales) offenders. Overall scores on the Inventory were not related to gender but the scores of females exceeded those of males on average for the Finance subscale and the Family/Marital subscale of the Inventory. The total score on the inventory was predictive of reoffending though the largest correlation was for custodial female offenders and was only 0.2. Subscales such as criminal history, education/employment, and antisocial companions were predictive of reoffending for males whereas for female offenders the important subscales were education/employment, alcohol/drug problems, accommodations, antisocial companions and attitudes/orientations. It has to be pointed out, as do the authors, that these correlations indicate very moderate predictive power.

One intriguing question is the extent to which psychiatrists and psychologists can use their knowledge and expertise to compensate for any shortcomings that structured questionnaires like these may have. In other words, can clinical judgement complement the more objective strengths of structured questionnaires? Elkovitch, Viljoen, Scalora and Ullman (2008) studied this issue in terms of the judgements of graduate psychologists of the likelihood of reoffending by young offenders built on the data from structured risk assessment instruments. In this case, the SAVRY (Structured Assessment of Violence Risk in Youth) and J-SOAP-II (Junior Sex offender Assessment Protocol) scales were completed by young offenders. The graduate raters who made the assessments of risk tended to agree strongly in their assessments. The male adolescent offenders who took part in the study were followed up for a minimum of 250 days in order to see whether they reoffended. Eighty per cent of them had sexually offended against another young person three years younger than themselves. Their recidivism was measured in terms of charges rather than convictions against them. The clinical judgements drawing on the assessment instruments were not predictive of sexual recividism but neither were

the structured questionnaires themselves. The measuring instruments did predict non-sexually violent offending but the clinical assessment based on these did not! Whatever clinical judgement was adding to the structured measures did not compensate in any way for their inadequacy at predicting sexual violence. Clinical judgement undermined the scales when predicting non-sexual violent recidivism. Even the confidence of the clinical assessor did not predict more accurate instrument-informed clinical judgements of risk.

Predictors may be specific rather than general

It is important to stress that predictors that are good for one sort of offence may be relatively poor at predicting recidivism for another sort of offence or using a different sort of prisoner group. Sjostedt and Langstrom (2000) carried out a study of *two* well-established measures associated with recidivism (the *Psychopathy Checklist Revised* and the *Violence Risk Appraisal Guide*). Their sample was a group of Swedish rapists diagnosed as having personality disorders. Follow-up was for an average of 92 months after release or discharge from prison or forensic treatment:

- The Psychopathy Checklist Revised (PCL-R), as we have seen, is highly regarded in predicting violent recidivism, and performed moderately well at predicting violent recidivism (of a non-sexual nature) in this sample. It predicted sexual recidivism badly. Similarly, the Violence Risk Appraisal Guide (VRAG) could predict violent recidivism (of a non-sexual nature). The VRAG includes additional assessment on a number of factors, such as:

  - alcohol abuse history
  - evidence on record at the time of the index offence of schizophrenia or personality disorder
  - female victim of the index offence
  - maladjustment at elementary school
  - non-violent criminal offences before the index offence
  - previous failures of conditional release
  - separation from either parent under age 16 (except through death)

- victim injury on a scale from no injury to death with mutilation.

- On the other hand, the PCL-R and the VRAG measures (see Harris, Rice and Quinsey, 1993; Rice and Harris, 1997) both failed to predict sexual reoffending.

- It was possible to predict sexual reoffending from another measure – the *Rapid Risk Assessment for Sexual Offender Recidivism* (RRASOR)(on which Static-2002 is partly based). This consists of just four variables:

  - any male victim of a sex offence
  - extrafamilial victim of a sex offence
  - offender is under 25 years old
  - previous sexual offences.

The more of these characteristics the offender possesses, the greater the risk of sexual reoffending. Despite being good at predicting sexual reoffending, this measure fared poorly at predicting violent recidivism of a sexual nature.

Statistical or actuarial prediction

The statistical prediction of dangerousness attempts to replace the subjectivity of clinical methods with empirically based prediction methods. The essential feature of this method is the availability of a database demonstrating the relationship between predictor variables and reoffending variables in a large group of offenders. To this ought to be added the use of a validation sample for use after the scale has been fine-tuned (see Figure 27.3). These predictor characteristics would include demographic variables such as age, criminal history, personality and similar factors. Reoffending would involve appropriate measures of recidivism such as reconviction for a similar offence in a 5-year period on release. The stronger the relationship between these predictor variables and recidivism, the more useful will be the characteristics in predicting recidivism in other similar offenders. The theory is fairly simple but, in practice, things are a little more complicated.

So basically, statistical prediction is founded on the assumption that a particular offender can be considered in the light of how other, similar offenders behaved. In this sense, the approach can deal only with the characteristics of recidivists that are common to a number of, if not all, offenders. At the same time, it does not take into account totally individual factors which might lead to recidivism in an individual case.

Table 27.1 gives a breakdown, which should help. It is similar to Table 16.1, the diagnosticity table. In predicting recidivism, particular signs are being used to identify the recidivists. So in terms of Table 27.1, the assessment of recidivism should maximise true positives (accurate predictions of recidivism) and minimise false positives (inaccurate predictions of recidivism). The best predictions of (say) recidivism occur when that behaviour is to be found in half (50 per cent) of the group in question (Milner and Campbell, 1995).

This can be elaborated. Imagine that a researcher has developed a test of recidivism that is very accurate – say that it correctly classifies 90 per cent of recidivists as recidivists and 90 per cent of non-recidivists as non-recidivists. Imagine also that half of the sample of 400 offenders is recidivist:

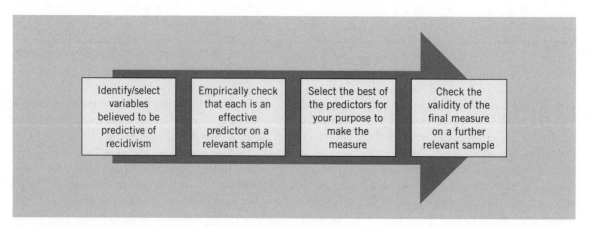

Figure 27.3 The key stages in constructing a recidivism prediction instrument

BOX 27.2 Controversy

Why is clinical judgement bad at risk assessment?

The first major critique of clinical judgement in the prediction of behaviour was Meehle's (1954) examination of clinical versus statistical prediction methods. Assuming for the moment that this is the case, just why are clinicians so poor? Dernevik *et al.* (2000) list some of the reasons:

- The diagnostic categories on which much clinical judgement is based (e.g. schizophrenia, affective disorder) are extremely broad. So allocating offenders to these categories does not say too much about their likely behaviour since, for example, schizophrenics are such a heterogeneous group.
- The ecological validity of the clinical judgement is important. One would not expect clinicians to make an accurate judgement of violent behaviours on which their experience and training are not great. For example, they might be better at making predictions about the mentally ill (the usual location of psychiatry and clinical psychology) than the run of the mill offender with no particular or marked psychiatric characteristics.
- Human information processing, because of the limited capacity of short-term memory, means that

we process information serially rather than in parallel. Thus very simple cues may be dwelt upon when we form our judgements.
- Biases: when making judgements we tend to stick with our initial assessments and do not make full use of new information. Furthermore, there is the issue of illusory correlation in which we assume that there is a correlation between two things if they appear to coexist. Thus, if we notice that children who are sexually abused turn up early for school, we may assume a relationship between the two which comparison with other children who have not been abused would show.
- The sheer amount of information available for clinicians to review when making their judgements may be counterproductive.
- Experience does not necessarily increase the validity of clinical predictions. For example, the true positives in risk prediction may never come to the attention of the clinician again. Their feedback is more likely from the false negatives who are released but reoffend. In other words, the feedback loop is poor with no certainty of useful information coming to the clinician's attention.

- Then the recidivism test will correctly classify 90 per cent of the 200 recidivists (i.e. it will find 180 recidivists).
- By the same token, it will also classify 10 per cent of the non-recidivists as recidivists (i.e. 20 of the non-recidivists).
- In other words, 180 of the recidivists are correctly identified at the cost of 20 of the non-recidivists being

wrongly identified as recidivists (see Table 27.2). This is an impressive 'hit' rate.

But what, say, if recidivism were much lower – 10 per cent rather than 50 per cent?:

- The test remains 90 per cent accurate but because there are only 40 reoffenders then it will classify 36 of them as reoffenders and 4 of them as non-recidivists.

Table 27.1 Predicting recidivism

	Reoffends	Does not reoffend
Shows predictive characteristics	True positive	False positive
Does not show predictive characteristics	False negative	True negative

Table 27.2 Theoretical accuracy in a sample of 200 recidivists and 200 non-recidivists using a 90 per cent accurate test

	Reoffends *N* = 200	Does not reoffend *N* = 200
Shows predictive characteristics	True positive 180	False positive 20
Does not show predictive characteristics	False negative 20	True negative 180

Table 27.3 Theoretical accuracy in a sample of 40 recidivists and 360 non-recidivists using a 90 per cent accurate test

	Reoffends *N* = 40	Does not reoffend *N* = 360
Shows predictive characteristics	True positive 36	False positive 36
Does not show predictive characteristics	False negative 4	True negative 324

- It is just as accurate with the non-recidivists. Out of the 360 non-recidivists the test will select 36 as recidivists and 324 as non-recidivists.

- In this case, the ratio of true positives to false positives is much poorer than in the previous example where the criterion of recidivism was to be found in half of the participants. In fact, as many non-recidivists as recidivists are identified as recidivists in these circumstances (Table 27.3).

Thus, unless recidivism is common, even the best tests are likely to make many mistakes. The general principle is that it is easier to predict relatively frequent events than uncommon events. Thus one is more likely to be able to predict cases of domestic violence than murder simply because the rates of domestic violence are nearer the optimum 50 per cent for accurate prediction.

Of course, one has to consider the costs involved. From the point of view of an offender, the possibility that he or she will not be put on parole is a major cost; from the point of view of the public, the issue may only be keeping in prison those likely to reoffend. If some prisoners are not given parole as a consequence then this is not a problem if this point of view is accepted.

Gretenkord (2000) demonstrates some of the advantages of preparing simple tables for assessing the likely rates of recidivism in a study of mentally disordered offenders. He carried out a study of men hospitalised in a forensic unit. Using complex statistical techniques (logistic regression) he was able to reduce his original list of predictors down to just four predictors of recidivism with a violent offence. These were:

- personality disorder (yes or no);
- violent pre-offence not included in the crime leading to present institutionalisation (yes or no);
- physical aggression during stay at the forensic hospital at least two times (yes or no);
- age at the time of discharge in years.

The worst prognosis by these criteria was for:

- the younger inmates – the group in their 20s;
- who also manifested a personality disorder;
- who had a violent previous offence in their records;
- who manifested physical aggression during the course of their treatment in the institution.

Sixty-five per cent of these reoffended violently after release. In contrast, the likelihood of a 60-year-old who did not have a personality disorder, did not have a violent pre-offence and did not show physical aggression during treatment, reoffending was only 1 per cent. Gretenkord argues for simple contingency tables that allow the clinician access to data on probabilities. (See Table 27.4.) So, given the four contingencies known to predict violent reoffending, it is possible to predict the likelihood of this.

It should be noted that even Gretenkord's simple approach leaves a considerable margin for discretion (i.e. further decisions). It tells us only what groups are likely to reoffend, not which inmates should be released and which should not. That is a further matter for our judgement. Very rarely do researchers actually stipulate

Table 27.4 A simple prediction table based on Gretenkord's data

	Pattern of predictor variables							
	Has personality disorder				Does not have personality disorder			
	Violent pre-offence		No violent pre-offence		Violent pre-offence		No violent pre-offence	
	Aggression during treatment	No aggression during treatment	Aggression during treatment	No aggression during treatment	Aggression during treatment	No aggression during treatment	Aggression during treatment	No aggression during treatment
20 years	65%	36	39	16	37	15	17	6
30 years	52	25	27	10	25	9	11	4
40 years	38	16	18	6	16	6	6	2
50 years	27	19	11	4	10	3	4	1
60 years	17	6	7	2	6	2	2	1

Source: from Gretenkord, L. (2000) 'How to use empirical findings for the prognosis of mentally disordered offenders'. Paper presented at the Tenth European Conference of Psychology and Law, Limassol, Cyprus.

scores on predictors that can be used as cut-off points for decisions of this sort.

Predictive factors

It is important to note that the more precise the question asked, the more likely is statistical prediction to be effective. Consider the following:

- There may be better prediction if the type of offence is taken into account. For example, predictions of domestic violence against adults based on previous violence against adults may be better than predictions of domestic violence against children based on previous violence against adults.

- The time period of a prediction may affect its accuracy. For example, certain factors may predict the short-term or acute dangers posed by an individual but have little validity for predicting longer-term or chronic risks.

The predictive factors for any sort of criminal activity will vary according to the crime in question, the precise circumstances and numerous other factors.

The best predictors of a crime such as domestic violence have been broadly established. They tend to be relatively mundane for the most part (Milner and Campbell, 1995):

- Mental illness is associated with domestic violence.

- Previous history: a person with a track record for domestic violence is more likely to act violently in the future.

- Substance abuse (drugs and/or alcohol) is predictive.

It is too soon to form an overall picture in order to see if other types of offence can be predicted with similar sets of predictors. Furthermore, it is important to realise that even long-established predictors may only be moderately powerful. For example, Dowden and Brown (2002) surveyed 45 studies into the relationship between substance abuse and general recidivism – that is recidivism for any type of crime. Studies were included in their meta-analysis (see Box 4.2) if substance abuse was measured prior to the recidivism. This cuts down the risk that offenders will blame their recidivism on substance abuse as an easy excuse. In this study, general recidivism included things such as reconvictions, new charges and violations, say, of suspended sentence such that the offender has to serve his or her sentence as a consequence. Studies focusing on violent recidivism separately were excluded from this meta-analysis. The analysis showed that various substance abuse indicators correlated (had an effect size of) between 0.1 and 0.2 in general. Alcohol abuse had the lowest effect size whereas a combined category which essentially assessed whether the offender had abused drugs or alcohol or both produced the largest effect size.

The use of a wider variety of predictors may increase the accuracy of predictions. Gresnigt *et al.* (2000) studied predictors of violent crime recidivism among Dutch prison inmates who were also drug users. The addiction severity index, cultural origin, level of education, duration of detention, diagnostic interval schedule and DSM-III classification were among the predictors.

Classification as to the likelihood of future violent convictions was 82 per cent accurate using cultural origin, history of violent offences and property offences. It increased very moderately to 85 per cent when the diagnostic interview schedule was added. It reached 93 per cent when all these factors plus the addiction severity index were added in.

BOX 27.3 Forensic psychology in action

The prediction of child molestation and other sexual offences

Given the intense public interest in sexual offenders against children – paedophiles and others who molest under-age persons – the factors associated with their reoffending are important. Megan's Law (and similar initiatives outside the United States) is founded on the belief that sexual offenders are dangerous and highly likely to reoffend. Megan Kanka was a 7-year-old who was abducted and murdered in 1994 by a convicted sex offender who was living near her home in New Jersey. Megan's Law is US legislation concerning the provision of information to local communities about the presence of sex offenders in the community. For example, in the United States, sex offenders might have their home address, home telephone number, work address, vehicle description and licence plate number released to the community. Similarly, crimes such as rape may attract very significant sentences including life in some jurisdictions, implying that these men are in need of constant surveillance and review.

There have been numerous studies into the characteristics of sex offenders who are likely to reoffend and those who are less likely to reoffend. In their meta-analysis (Box 4.2) of the relevant studies, Hanson and Morton-Bourgon (2005) found 82 relevant studies which involved sex offender recidivism after release from prison. About half of the studies that they included had not been published. Sex offenders reoffend sometimes with sexual offences but they also reoffend more generally. This was discussed in Chapters 9 and 10. The meta-analysis revealed that the major predictors of sexual recidivism over all of these studies were deviant sexual preferences and

antisocial orientations. Antisocial orientation includes things such as antisocial personality, impulsivity, substance abuse, unemployment and a history of violating rules. Antisocial orientation was also the major predictor of violent recidivism and general recidivism. Some of the good and bad predictors of sexual recidivism are shown in Figure 27.4. As the bottom of the figure is reached, the predictors

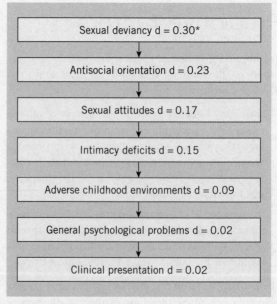

Figure 27.4 Some of the good predictors of sexual recidivism and some of the poorer ones

*A value of d = 0.2 is usually regarded as a small sized effect and a value 0.4 a medium sized effect

such as general psychological problems and clinical presentation have very small effect sizes (indicated by d). An effect size of 0.2 is often described as small, an effect size of 5 is medium, and an effect size of 0.8 is large. At best, the good predictors are small to medium. It is important to note that many of the variables which are commonly focused on in treatment for sex offenders such as denial of sex crime, victim empathy, motivation for treatment and psychological distress do not have any useful association with sexual and violent recidivism. It is worthwhile noting that these are often regarded by clinicians as indicators of a poor prognosis. For example, Freeman, Palk and Davey (2010) chose to investigate the attitudes of forensic psychologists to the effect of denial on risk assessment. A sample of 31 practising Australian psychologists varied considerably about whether denial should affect the assessment of risk for reoffending and whether it should affect suitability for supervised release into the community. That is to say, some forensic psychologists believe that denial is predictive of future behaviour whereas research seems to suggest that it is not.

The research on rates of reoffending in sex offender groups highlights many of the problems of prediction of dangerousness and recidivism. Good examples of this are to be found in the work of Firestone on Canadian sex offenders:

- Firestone *et al.* (1998b) carried out a study of convicted rapists who were followed up for up to 12 years and an average of 7.6 years.
- Because of the constraints of research, such varying lengths of follow-up are typical of studies since the researcher may be limited in the access to offenders and may be constrained to complete the research within a given amount of time.
- About half of these offenders had reoffended by the time they had been out of prison for five years.
- However, one needs to check the type of crime involved. In fact, only 16 per cent reoffended with a sexual crime. Rather more reoffended with a violent crime (26 per cent) though this included sexual crimes and over a half reoffended with any sort of crime (e.g. theft). This sort of figure is

familiar elsewhere in the world for other sex offenders. In Germany, Egg (1999) carried out a 10-year study of recidivism in child molesters. About a half were reconvicted within that period but only about 20 per cent for a sexual offence. In fact, in terms of their previous convictions, only about the same percentage had prior convictions for sexual offences.

- The more important question is whether or not the recidivists can be predicted. According to Firestone *et al.* prediction of recidivism for a sexual offence was not good. Sexual recidivists tended to have been removed from the family home under the age of 16 compared to non-recidivists. The use of the phallometry (see Box 9.1) was not effective in determining the recidivists.
- For a group of child molesters who committed their assaults outside the family, the reoffending figures were slightly lower but with a similar overall pattern.
- Furthermore, the prediction of sexual recidivism in this group was weak. Only men who rated themselves higher on alcohol abuse, men higher on guilt and men who were sexually aroused by assaultive rather than consenting sex stimuli involving children (i.e. the paedophile assault index) showed a greater likelihood of reoffending.
- Incestuous-only (family abuse) offenders showed a different pattern still. They reoffended in any category much less than extrafamily offenders or rapists. Only 6 per cent had reoffended sexually at the end of the up-to-12-year period.
- Finally, Firestone *et al.* (1998a) attempted to differentiate homicidal (actual or attempted) child molesters from non-homicidal ones. Intrafamilial offenders were excluded. In Canada, sexual murders constitute only 3 per cent of killings and of these only 8 per cent involve the deaths of children. In other words, only about a quarter of 1 per cent of murders involve the sexual killing of children. These are rare events not particularly conducive to prediction.
- Many factors did not differentiate between the homicidal and the non-homicidal offenders. Homicidal offenders tended to abuse complete

▶

BOX 27.3 (continued)

strangers whereas non-homicidal ones rarely did. Homicidal offenders rated themselves as having a higher history of violence and having had contact with a forensic psychiatrist. They tended to have higher sexual arousal on the phallometric assault index. The murderers had more extreme sexual involvement with children than the kissing and fondling that was more typical of the non-homicidal offenders.

One of the common criticisms of recidivism statistics is that they deal with reconviction rather than reoffending. That is, offenders may commit crimes which are simply not reported to the criminal justice system, hence the low recidivism. Falshaw, Friendship and Bates (2003) studied 173 offenders' records at a community-based sex offender treatment programme in the United Kingdom. The period at risk of reoffending covered by the study was a minimum of nearly four years. Two different national information sources were examined for information about each of the offenders: the Offender Index had information about reconviction for only about a third of the men for which the Police National Computer had information. This implies that recidivism rates may appear low simply because of problems in recording information on the databases. However, the therapy records of the programme's clientele contained information about offending by clients which was collected in the course of the work of the programme itself. If this information is combined with the national information, then reoffending occurred in the at-risk period in 12 per cent of the clientele. Additional information was available from the project's records about known instances of the sorts of behaviours known to encourage reoffending – for example, waiting around a school gate as children were leaving for home. If this information is added into the measure of recidivism, then 21 per cent exhibited some form of recidivistic behaviour. This figure is between two and seven times higher than the information on the recidivism data on the national databases. Whether or not these figures would apply to offenders leaving

prison cannot be assessed. In themelves, the figures still tend to confirm that recidivism in sex offenders is at relatively low levels.

With sex and violent offenders, especially, we should remember that there is provision for their monitoring in the community after leaving prison or even if there is suspicion about their behaviour. As a consequence, recidivism figures in recent years reflect a situation in which offenders' behaviour is controlled long after they are released from prison. In the United Kingdom, for example, there are two major pieces of legislation which concern the monitoring of sex offenders in the community. Britain does not have a 'Megan's Law' requiring the compulsory notification of communities of sex offenders in their midst (though a version of one is still being trialled). However, it does have a sexual offender register system which requires most sex offenders to keep the police informed about their current address and places severe limits on their foreign travel. Furthermore, there are multi-agency public protection arrangements (MAPPA) in which the police, prison, probation, social and health services are required to work together in order to reduce the risk of reoffending. The evidence seems to suggest that these are effective since the UK figures indicate that 93 per cent of offenders register their whereabouts (Expert Law, 2003). Rates of serious sexual or violent offences for offenders on a MAPPA programme seem low. In a year in which there were 25,000 offenders on the register, only 26 committed a serious sexual or violent offence (*Daily Telegraph*, 2004). In a rare study of offenders' response to community notification laws in the United States where community notification is common, it was found that over two-thirds of offenders believed that this was an incentive for them not to reoffend (Elbogen, Patry and Scalora, 2003). So, in a sense, modern criminal justice system practices will change the meaning of recidivism statistics for the simple reason that sex offenders are not simply released back into the community with little by way of support. Instead, their situation is addressed by a variety of agencies and their activities monitored for signs of possible recidivism.

Sex offender registration is based on the assumption that it promotes public safety and that, if permitted, the accessibility of the information allows the public to protect itself from the predatory offender. The basic question is one of whether sex offender registration actually affects sex offender recidivism. There is a secondary question of whether the other procedures for monitoring sex offenders are effective. As we have just seen, the answer to the second question is quite positive as far as the situation in the United Kingdom is concerned. It is not clear that registration reduces offending. The accuracy of offender registers can be fairly poor in the USA and studies have shown it to be as low as half of registered offenders have their current address accurately recorded. Furthermore, different States have differing rules on whether a sex offender is required to go on a sex offender register and courts have varying amounts of discretion about whether it is required in a particular case. Levenson, D'Amora, and Hern (2007) surveyed 239 sex offenders in Connecticut and Indiana about the negative consequences of sex offender registration They were invited to complete a survey about the influence of sex offender policies on their reintegration into the community. Amongst the findings were:

- 10 per cent said they experienced physical assaults
- 46 per cent said that they were afraid for their own safety because of Megan's Law
- 50 per cent said they had lost friends or a close relationship because of Megan's Law
- 54 per cent said that they felt alone and isolated because of Megan's Law
- 58 per cent said that the shame and embarrassment due to Megan's Law stops them from engaging in activities
- 62 per cent said that recovery was more difficult because Megan's Law causes stress in their lives.

According to Levenson *et al.*, research suggests that job loss, threats and harassment, property damage, and the suffering of other household members were the commonest negative outcomes identified in this sort of research. Fewer experienced housing problems

and physical violence as a consequence of community notification. However, there is generally no difference between sex offenders on the register and sex offenders not on the register in terms of sexual recidivism. In other words, there is a lack of clear evidence that sex offender registration works.

Just what is the implication of a sex offender failing to register on a sex offenders register? Does it indicate that they are at greater risk of reoffending? Is failure to register a predictor of greater risk of recidivism? In Minnesota, failure to register as a predatory offender is the most common form of recidivism for a sexual offence! Duwe and Donnay (2010) studied offenders released from Minnesota prisons between 2000 and 2004 when the first failure to register prisoners were first beginning to be released. They concentrated on whether a failure to register an offence (or a history of failure to register offences) was predictive of sexual, general and failure to register (or FTR) recidivism. A quasi-experimental design was used in which offenders with and without a previous failure to register conviction were compared. The follow up period for recidivism was a minimum of three years.

Failures to Register offenders were different from other non-FTR offenders in a number of ways including (a) longer criminal histories, (b) less likely to have had had treatment in prison, (c) less well educated, (d) less likely to have used force and (e) less likely to have victims from a variety of age groups. The researchers controlled for a number of factors such as prior criminal history, time at risk of recidivism, and so forth. It was found that with such control variables taken into account, a current or prior Failure to Register conviction was *not* predictive of sexual recidivism. In this particular study, neither was there any evidence that Failure to Register was associated with other, non-sexual recidivism. However, there was an elevated risk of a further Failure to Register offence in offenders with a current or past Failure to Register offence.

It might be assumed that men diagnosed as paedophiles might be particularly prone to

BOX 27.3 (continued)

reoffending sexually. One particularly challenging and thought-provoking study (Moulden, Firestone, Kingston and Bradford, 2009) asked the superficially simple question of just how a diagnosis of paedophilia is related to the prediction of recidivism for a child molestation offence. However, just how does one define paedophilia for these purposes? Firestone *et al.* suggested four somewhat different ways of defining paedophilia in practice:

- The formal criteria for a diagnosis of paedophilia to be found in the psychiatric diagnosis manual DSM-IV. Firestone *et al.* used a psychiatrist's diagnoses based on this. In their study, each patient was interviewed by a psychiatrist who offered a DSM diagnosis of some sort. Of course, additional information was available to the psychiatrist about the criminal and psycho-social history of the offender.
- Phallometry can be used to identify a deviant sexual arousal profile (see Chapter 10). In this case, the measure was based on the degree of change in the offender's penis size when presented with sexually deviant stimuli auditorily. Among the sexual stimuli included were (a) child-initiated sexual activity, (b) child–adult mutual sexual activity, (c) non-physical coercion of child into sexual activity, (d) physical coercion of child into sexual activity (e) violent sex with child,

(f) non-sexual assault of child, (g) consenting sex with female adult, and (h) sex with female child relative (incest). Of course, phallometry may not be routinely available for clinicians to use.

- Firestone *et al.* used the non-standard approach of combining the above two measures. That is, one of their measures of paedophilia was a combination of the psychiatrist's diagnosis and a deviant phallometric result. That is, they categorised the offender as paedophilic if both the DSM-IV diagnosis was paedophilia and the phallometric assessment was in the top half of the distribution.
- Use the scale designed to assess sexual interest in children. One notable scale of this sort is the *Screening Scale for Pedophilic Interest* (Seto and Lalumière, 2001) and this was employed by Firestone *et al.*

Participants were a sample of just over 200 adult male Canadians convicted of a contact sexual offence against a non-related child under 16 years of age. Recidivism rates were 23 per cent for sexual crime, 34 per cent for violent crime, and 46 per cent for any crime. Generally speaking the prediction of recidivism controlling for the time at risk was unimpressive. Only the measure based on phallometry had reasonable predictive power for recidivism. However, this has been established in other studies too (Hanson and Bussière, 1998; Hanson and Morton-Bourgon, 2004).

Issues in the assessment of risk and dangerousness

There are a number of issues associated with the assessment of risk and dangerousness that should be highlighted, some of which have already briefly been mentioned (Clark, 1999; Monahan and Steadman, 1994):

- The assessment of risk is different from the assessment of dangerousness. The assessment of risk (of occurrence) involves predicting how *likely* it is that the individual will in the future commit another crime.

Dangerousness is more about the level of the danger or adverse consequences to the victim of such a crime. Thus an offender might be adjudged to be greatly at risk of reoffending but that offence is likely to be no more than getting involved in a modest brawl. On the other hand, a person may have a low risk of reoffending but, if they do, very serious consequences are expected for the victim.

- Along with the assessment of risk and dangerousness should go planning to safeguard others in the light of the level of risk and dangerousness. For example, if there is no option but to release an offender from prison, what is the point of a careful risk and dangerousness assessment? On the other hand, while the individual remains in prison, risk and dangerousness may be helped, say, by placing the offender on an anger management programme.

- Risk and dangerousness are not fixed parameters but will change with context and the passage of time and they should be regarded as such in any assessment.

- There is no single risk factor and consequent likelihood of risk. There are many possible risk factors that need to be understood. Information is also needed on the extent to which these can be found in different contexts of risk. So, for example, a prisoner may be much more at risk of offending violently in prison if sharing his cell with a violent fellow prisoner than if, on release, he goes to live with his mother in isolation.

- Different risk factors have different proven levels of influence on the future behaviour of an offender. Well-established risk factors such as previous recidivism should be given greater weight in decision making than a speculative factor such as that the man has taken up a new hobby or interest.

- There is no evidence that it is possible to predict serious criminal violence by individuals who have not already committed a violent act (Harris and Rice, 1994): in other words, the very group of individuals one needs predictions about the most.

- The criterion to be predicted needs careful consideration as many variants are possible. Gretenkord (2000) illustrates the importance of the criteria for deciding what is reoffending for the rates of reoffending. His was a sample of mentally disordered males in a forensic hospital who had largely committed violent physical or sexual crimes against other people. After discharge from this hospital for the average period of eight years, 44 per cent had reappeared on the German crime register. This would include minor offences such as riding on a bus without paying the fare. Thirty per cent had to return to prison or a forensic hospital. Thirteen per cent committed a violent or sexual offence. Quite clearly, the rate of reoffending is substantially determined by the criteria employed.

It is notable that quite good predictions of reoffending can be obtained from relatively straightforward indicators. A good example of this is the British study that involved a 10-year follow-up of a representative sample of men convicted of sexual offences and sentenced to at least four years in prison (Clark, 1999). This classified higher-risk offenders as the men who had any of these

characteristics: a current or previous conviction for a non-sexual violent assault, four-plus previous convictions for any offence, or a previous conviction for a sexual offence. Lower-risk men were those who showed none of these four features. The high-risk groups showed considerable recidivism in the 10 years after release. A quarter were reconvicted for a sexual offence (but only 1 in 20 of the low-risk group) and nearly a half for a sexual or violent offence (but only 1 in 8 of the low-risk group).

Sometimes offenders approach forensic services about the risk that they will sexually offend against children despite having no history of such offending. Are current risk assessment methods appropriate to evaluate such individuals? Duff and Willis (2006) present a single case study of a man in his early twenties without a previous criminal record who was referred by the probation service which was dealing with him because of a charge of domestic violence. His partner was younger than him and was only 15 years of age when their relationship started – though he denied that there was sexual intercourse before she was 16. Although he had never actually offended against a child, he described sexual fantasies involving children, did a certain amount of grooming, identified locations suitable for offending, and manifested a distrust of women. He also thought that he might sexually offend against a child in the future, though he indicated that as soon as he got to know a young child his sexual interest in them declined. He had a collection of children's television videos and pictures from catalogues. Most forensic risk assessments are based on the assumption that there is a relevant offence history. This leaves us with the unanswerable question of just what risk this man posed.

Types of predictor

There is a distinction between different types of predictor of reoffending (Palmer, 2001). Some of the predictors hardly change and are known as static variables: these would include family background, offence history and others. Another type of variable might in many cases change over time. These are known as dynamic variables and would include social and psychological factors. All variables may change in their correlates with risk but dynamic variables, because they change, are more likely to do so. A static variable such as sex may be a predictor of reoffending, but the association may become less as the individual ages. Dynamic factors such as situational and psychological factors may change. A paedophile who lives close to a school may be less at risk of offending if they move to a child-free location.

Blackburn (2000) offers another useful scheme for classifying risk factors into types:

- Historical factors – especially previous offending/violent patterns.

- Dispositional variables which include cognitive and emotional tendencies. For example, those who are deficient in social problem solving (e.g. for whom aggression is the only response in their repertoire to threat) are more likely to reoffend violently. Nevertheless, the sorts of dispositional variable measured by traditional personality tests (such as the MMPI) have not been shown to be useful in risk and dangerousness assessment.

- Clinical variables: mental disorders, such as schizophrenia, do increase the risk of violence. On the other hand, what they add to the prediction is very small.

- Personality disorder is problematic as criminal activities are both part of the definition of antisocial personality disorder and the effect of having the disorder (Chapter 20).

Gannon *et al.* (2008) schematically consider risk assessment to consist of three distinct components which, taken together, assess these different aspects. The three components are functional assessments, actuarial assessment and dynamic risk assessment. In brief, these can be described as follows:

- Functional assessments are based on interviews with the offender about the events associated with his or her offending. The interview may help identify acute dynamic risk factors which led to the offence. So the interview considers the offender's cognitions, feelings, decisions and actions which led to the heightened risk of offending. The clinician may use this information to help the offender understand his or her offending.

- Actuarial assessments explore the statistical relationship between the characteristics of the offender such as the previous offences, criminality and so forth and the probability of reconviction. Much of this information is readily available on file so is easy to obtain and use. There are problems with such measures especially as they are dependent on official recidivism data which may be an underestimate of offenders' true rates of

reoffending. It also needs to be noted that instruments designed to give these actuarial assessments tend to rely on static or unchanging factors, which may not be very helpful to those interested in understanding the influence of therapy on the likelihood of reoffending.

- Dynamic risk assessments use risk factors which can change as a result of, say, therapy or the experience of prison. Deviant sexual interests and offence-supportive attitudes may be risk factors for future offending but they are also matters which may change as a result of the offender's experiences.

Offence paralleling behaviour

The term Offence Paralleling Behaviour is becoming increasingly familiar in clinical recidivism assessment especially decisions about release. Release from an institution is usually dependent on the following:

- The results of a structured or similar risk assessment measure

- The results of a clinical assessment of progress in therapy and other forms of treatment

- The individual's behaviour within the institution.

Certain changes in the offender's behaviour are regarded positive signs in favour of release such as improvements in pro-social behaviours and attitudes. These are regarded as reducing the likelihood of future violent behaviour. On the other hand, aggressive and violent behaviours against members of staff would be negative signs. Increasingly, it is being accepted that if institutional behaviour patterns are similar to the offender's main offences in the past then this indicates a higher risk of reoffending (Jones, 2004). These matched patterns inside and outside of the institution are called Offence Paralleling Behaviour (OPB). The basic problem is, of course, just how one decides that institutional and pre-institutional behaviours parallel each other. This would require a minimum of two things:

- Criteria to be used to describe the institutional and pre-institutional behaviours

- Ways of saying just what the similarity is between the pre-institutional behaviour (i.e. major offences) and institutional behaviour.

Daffern, Howells, Mannion and Tonki (2009) believe that the criteria of similarity should reflect their functional similarity rather than superficial resemblances. That is, the acts should serve similar purposes. So simple characteristics such as the gender of the target of the pre-institutional and institutional behaviours are probably not useful since, for example, violent/aggressive behaviour is most common between males. Using superficial criteria such as these means that common aspects of violence and aggression are likely to manifest themselves in the institutional setting – and they are unlikely to change. But, despite this, the functions of violent/aggressive behaviour for the individual may have been changed quite considerably under the influence of therapy, for example.

Among the characteristics of the pre-institutional and institutional behaviours that Daffern *et al.* (2009) consider important in a functional analysis of an offender's behaviour are the following:

- Cognitive antecedents to the events such as the belief that one's emotional needs will never be met and the expectation that one will be abused or mistreated by others.

- Distal and proximal environmental triggers for the violence.

- Function of the violent behaviour (e.g. social distance reduction, to observe suffering etc.)

- Psycho-physiological activation such as calm-tense/irritable, passive/tired and active/energetic

- Type of weapon used

- Victim characteristics (e.g. was victim an acquaintance, friend, intimate or stranger).

All of these and others are part of the 'Structured Aggressive Behaviour Analysis Schedule' (SABAS) which the researchers had developed to assess functionally the behaviours of the offender outside and inside the institution.

The Structured Aggressive Behaviour Analysis Schedule provides the criteria by which functional similarity of behaviours could be recorded. So how is this turned into measures of similarity between pre-institutional and institutional behaviours? Daffern *et al.* used several approaches to the data they had collected concerning men in a high-security personality disorder service unit in the UK who were high-risk violent and sexual offenders. These included:

- A clinical psychologist rated the functional similarity measures in terms of their similarity (from not similar, through some similarity, to very similar). Using this, 50 per cent of incidents involving the men in the Unit were rated as not at all similar to the pre-instituralisation index offence, 38 per cent were rated as similar, and 11 per cent were rated as very similar.

- A count of the similarity of features between the index offence and the institutional pattern in terms of the SABAS schedule. The two were considered similar if a certain number of features (four) were found to be shared. Sixty five per cent of the pairs of SABAS schedules met this criterion of similarity.

What is one to make of these findings? Irrespective of the method used to assess similarity, the essential trend seems to be for there to be some association between institutional aggression patterns and pre-institutional (index offence). At the same time, there were some individuals for whom there was a fairly strong relationship and others for whom the relationship was weak or imperceptible. The implication may be that the Offence Paralleling Behaviour may only be relevant to those cases where it is possible to establish that offence characteristics and characteristics shown within the institution are very similar. In these circumstances, a change in pattern may be of considerable clinical importance. For individuals who fail to show stability in their patterns, then the application of Offending Paralleling Behaviour approaches could be very misleading.

Although not couched in the framework of offence paralleling behaviour, the research of Heil, Harrison, English and Ahlmeyer (2009) is of more than passing interest in this context. Is it possible, they asked, to predict future sex offending in the community and violent behaviour more generally on the basis of sex offences committed in prison? The researchers formed four groups of male sex offenders from offenders sentenced in Colorado: (a) offenders with community sex crime convictions, (b) community sex offenders convicted under non-sex-crime charges where somewhere on record was information about sex crimes, (c) offenders known only to commit sexually abusive misconduct in prison, and (d) offenders with both community and prison sex offences. Prison sex offenders generally produced the greatest evidence for recidivism a year and five years after release. They were particularly prone to violent offences but also to sexual offences. The prison plus community sex offenders had the highest rates of

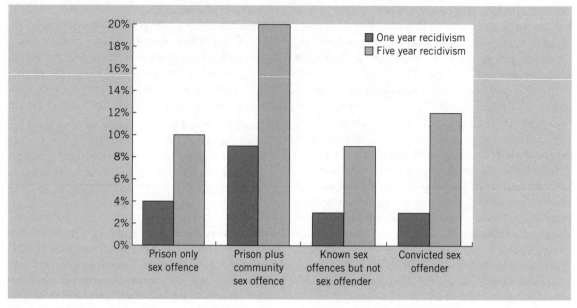

Figure 27.5 One-year and five-year recidivism for sexual offences

hands-on sex offences after release. Prison sex offenders were more likely to be arrested for violent offences on release. Their level of risk was much the same as that for convicted sex offenders in terms of arrests for sex offences but their average time before getting arrested was shorter. After five years from release, the prison-only group still showed the highest levels of violent recidivism (see Figure 27.5).

What stops recidivism?

There is very little research that asks what factors stop some high-risk violent criminals, i.e. men who have many of the signs of dangerousness, getting reconvicted. A Swedish study (Haggård, 2000; Haggård, Gumpert and Grann, 2001) found that the preventative factors included intense social isolation with the exception of a strong family orientation, physical disability and experience of shock such as those due to committing the crime, being arrested or incarcerated.

The idea that sex offenders should not live in close proximity to schools and nurseries is part of relapse prevention programmes but also increasingly part of legal requirements in various parts of the world.

Zandbergen, Levenson and Hart (2010) used a matched sample of recidivists and non-recidivists in Florida over a two-year period. The research question was simply whether offenders who lived close to schools and day-care centres/nurseries are more likely to reoffend than those who live further away. Proximity with other risk factors taken into account does not seem to contribute to sexual recidivism. According to the authors, a minimum of 30 states and many municipalities in the USA require registered sex offenders to live more than certain minimum distances from schools, parks, daycare centres, bus stops and similar places where children are commonly to be found. Sex offenders may intentionally live close to such locations but the financial circumstances of sex offenders due to unemployment means that they are more likely to live in densely populated parts of town where accommodation is cheaper, which also means that schools and other facilities are close together. In Florida, registered sex offenders on probation may be prohibited from living less than 1,000 feet from schools and similar locations. Recidivism in this study was defined in terms of an offender having one conviction for a sex offence and who was rearrested for a new sex offender during the entirety of 2004/5. The offender files were used to obtain a sample of non-recidivists. A number of variables such

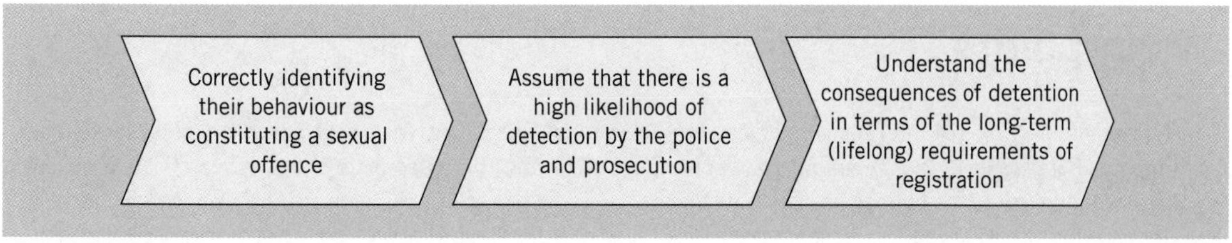

Figure 27.6 The unlikely steps in a juvenile sex offender's thinking which would lead to a deterrent effect of sex offender registration and notification laws

as age, race, marital status, number of prior offences, number of prior sex offences, victim's age category (or previous victim's was used in the case of recidivists), predator/offender status, and residential address were recoded into simple categories which could be used for matching. Only for schools was a recidivist/non-recidivist difference found in terms of numbers of schools within a 1,000-ft buffer zone. There was no difference for the other types of location were children are commonly found.

Juvenile sex offenders are increasingly included in legislation dealing with sex offender registration. In some jurisdictions which have sex offender registration legislation, there is some discretion in whether or not an offender goes on the register. Caldwell and Dickinson (2009) took a group of registered and another group of unregistered juvenile sex offenders. Registered youth had lower risk scores on stardard measures but registered and unregistered youth were charged with new crimes at much the same rates. Some have suggested that registration could be criminogenic by creating barriers to employment and community reintegration, leading to offenders having unstructured time on their hands and possibly new offending. Caldwell and Dickinson (2009) concluded that sex offender registration for juvenile offenders is ineffective as a means of reducing recidivism. Much the same outcome was found in Letourneau, Bandyopadhyay, Armstrong and Singha's (2010) study despite adopting a very different type of methodology. They studied sexual offence registration and juvenile sex crime in South Carolina. They subjected juvenile sex crime data to a trend analysis over the period 1991–2004. Juvenile sex crime registration was introduced in 1995 and online registration was allowed in 1999. Superficially the data seemed to suggest that the policy was having a deterrent effect on first-time juvenile sex crime. However, it emerged that exactly the same trend was appearing for first-time robbery which, of course, does not result in sex offender registration. The researchers interpreted the data as being the result of changes in 1995 which moved the court location for 16-year-old offenders to the adult courts which, of course, reduced the numbers going to juvenile court. These researchers also concluded that sex offender registration for juveniles has no deterrent effect. They suggest that in order for a deterrent effect to happen, juvenile offenders would have to go through several stages in their reasoning as shown in Figure 27.6. These stages seem very unlikely.

Risk of escape

Virtually totally missing from the research on the assessment of dangerousness and risk management is any attempt to understand the phenomenon of escape. Not only does escape from a forensic setting put more people at risk but also it questions the intimate relationship between dangerousness and risk management. There is regrettably little information on this. Gacono et al. (1997) studied patients who escaped from a Texan Maximum Security Forensic Hospital. Because of a pre-existing research programme, there was a great deal of diagnostic and other information available. They matched non-escapee prisoners with the escape group using variables such as age and ethnicity. Characteristically, antisocial personality disorder did not seem to differentiate between the the escapees and the rest but scores on the PCL-R were higher in the escapees who were glib and grandiose, liars and manipulators. Violent crimes against individuals were also more common in the escapees. The authors recommend that a score of 30 or more on the PCL-R should be seen as an indication that the detainee is a likely escapee.

Main points

- The assessment of risk and dangerousness had its impetus from US legislation requiring practitioners to deal with the risk to the public posed by their clients. In part this is achieved by managing the risk in various ways such as keeping the offender physically away from the public and others at risk. However, the decision about how likely an individual is to harm another (risk) and the assessment of how serious the risk is (dangerousness) is a complex one and is a characteristic of the situation as much as the offender in question.

- Risk assessment is an area of psychology in which clinical judgement and empirical research both have a role to play. There is reason to think that it is profitable to use the two methods together in ways that combine the advantages of the two. Empirical methods can demonstrate the broad relationship between risk factors and risk but cannot effectively deal with the

individual instant which needs a careful evaluation within the parameters set by research. As a consequence, measures such as the Psychopathy Checklist Revised have shown themselves to be effective in identifying factors that are strongly predictive of recidivism.

- When we attempt to predict recidivism, we do so with less than perfect predictors, which means that there is always an amount of error. The amount of error that can be tolerated depends on the risk in question. One difficulty with predictions of this sort is that they tend to be the most accurate when the behaviour in question occurs in 50 per cent of the population in question. So predictions of things such as sex offences for which the recidivism rate is actually quite small are likely to be poor. Similarly, predicting which violent mentally ill offenders will kill in future is likely to be fraught with problems simply for statistical reasons.

Further reading

This is a developing field with good recent sources:

Conroy, M.A. and Murrie, D.C. (2007) *Forensic Assessment of Violence Risk: A Guide for Risk Assessment and Risk Management* Chichester: John Wiley.

Craig, L., Browne, K. and Beech, A. (2008) *Assessing Risk in Sex Offenders: A Practitioner's Guide* Chichester: John Wiley.

The following has a variety of materials on recidivism from the Office of Justice Programs: http://www.ojp.usdoj.gov/nij/topics/corrections/recidivism/welcome.htm

Visit our website at www.pearsoned.co.uk/howitt for self-test and essay questions, annotated further reading, audio interviews with researchers in the field, weblinks and more information on becoming a forensic psychologist.

Glossary

A

Absolute judgement: Postulated process by which eyewitness judgements in an identity parade are made by reference to the original sighting of the offender and are not dependent on the characteristics of the members of the line-up.

Absolute liability offences: Offences for which defences of lack of criminal intent are not allowed statutorily.

Accused: The individual(s) charged with an offence or who it has been alleged has committed the offence.

Active listening skills: Methods of being a better listener especially in hostage negotiation. Its main aim is to increase the flow of communication with the hostage taker.

Actuarial assessment: Assessment of clients, etc. based on accumulated statistical information.

Actuarial profiling: Criminal profiling methods based on aggregated statistical data.

Actuary: Someone who is expert with statistical or aggregated information.

Actus reus: The guilty act – the offence which the accused has allegedly committed.

Ad hoc: Decisions or arrangements made to deal with the demands of a particular situation.

Addiction to crime: The theory that criminal behaviour is rather like an addiction and shares many of the characteristics of addiction to drugs.

Admissible evidence: Evidence which conforms to the rules governing the sorts of evidence which may be used in courts of law.

Adolescence: The period from after puberty to adulthood.

Adolescence-limited offender: An offender who offends as an adolescent but at no other stage.

Adoption study: In this context, a study investigating criminality in siblings (especially twins) brought up in a different family.

Adversarial system: The Anglo-American system of court procedure in which two opposing sides take turns to question the accused and witnesses.

Adversarial: Involving conflict or opposition such as cross-examination techniques where the prosecution and defence take turns to question the defendant or a witness.

Advocate: A lawyer representing an individual(s) in court. In the UK this may be a barrister or a solicitor.

Aetiology: The knowledge we have about the causes of phenomena (such as mental illness) and the way that they develop.

Affidavit: A written-down statement made in evidence which is confirmed as truthful in front of an authorised person.

Age of criminal responsibility: The lowest age at which a person can be held to be capable of committing a crime and, hence, charged with that crime. This varies internationally and in terms of the nature of the crime.

Amicus curiae: An independent or neutral individual who provides the court with an independent point of view. The *amicus* does not represent any party in the case.

Amnesia: Memory loss or disturbance.

Anatomical dolls/anatomically correct dolls/anatomically detailed dolls: Toy dolls which have genitals and secondary sexual characteristics sometimes used in sexual abuse interviews with children.

Anchored narratives: 'Stories' linking together a series of events using commonly accepted common-sense notions which are held to be correct.

Anchors: Common-sense assumptions or ideas which are regarded as if they are fact. They underlie our judgements of events. For example, the police make infallible eyewitnesses.

Anger management: A form of counselling which helps individuals deal with anger in a constructive way rather than through aggression.

Antisocial behaviour orders (ASBOs): In the UK, a court order which is tailored to deal with the antisocial behaviour patterns of individuals such as vandalism and graffiti.

Antisocial personality disorder (ADP): A mental disorder appearing in the APA's *Diagnostic and Statistical Manual* which is characterised by persistent disregard for the rights of others and violations of those rights. Sufferers are considered deceitful and manipulative. The term is not applied to persons under 18 years of age.

Appeal: A request or application to a higher court, etc. that the decision of a lower court be reviewed and reversed.

Appellant: A person making an appeal to a higher court.

Arson: Fire-setting or the malicious setting fire to property.

Assertiveness: Assertiveness is strongly differentiated from aggressiveness. It is a manner of communication in which wants wishes are made clear in a respectful manner. Hostility is not involved.

Atavism Theory: a long abandoned theory which claimed that criminals are genetically throwbacks to an earlier stage and their criminal acts simply match those of ancient ancestors.

Attachment theory: The developmental theory which stresses the role of disruptions to children's early relationships with the mother in developing interpersonal relationship problems later in life.

Attention deficit hyperactive disorder (ADHD): A psychological state where a child shows inappropriate levels of hyperactivity and impulsivity combined with a failure to attend appropriately.

Automatism: This is an unconscious act which may be criminal such as a murder when sleepwalking.

Availability heuristic: A cognitive strategy in which assessments and decisions are based on the knowledge that is readily available to the individual. It does not involve examining alternative possibilities or the procedures through which the judgement is made.

Aversion therapy: A form of conditioning therapy in which the 'undesired' behaviour is paired with a punishment (unpleasant experience) in order to reduce its incidence.

B

Bail: When the accused is released from custody until their next court appearance. Sometimes a financial arrangement has to be involved as security and certain conditions may have to be met.

Barrister: This is a member of the bar, a lawyer, who is qualified to represent clients in a court of law.

Behaviour Analysis Interview: This is an interrogation technique developed by Fred Inbau and others. It encourages different responses from liars and truth tellers. This method has been commonly employed by the police in the USA/British Crime Survey.

Behavioural intervention: Any treatment/therapy which is intended to directly change behaviour.

Behavioural therapy: *See* Cognitive behavioural therapy.

Biological determinism: This is the assumption that criminality can be directly inherited in families prone to crime or indirectly inherited in a family the members of which experience insanity or alcoholism.

Biology: The scientific study of living organisms.

Biosocial theory: This assumes that crime is the product of an interaction between biological and social factors.

Bipolar disorder (formerly manic depression): A group of disorders of mood characterised by the presence of one plus periods of abnormally elevated positive mood. This is likely to be followed by a normal mood and then a depressive episode.

Blank line-up: An identification parade in which the suspect is not present.

Blended memories: Memories which are a mixture of what was initially memorised and events that happened later. For example, the original memory of the crime plus suggestions that emerged during a later police interview.

Blind procedure: In eyewitness testimony, this would be a line-up or identity parade in which the identity of the person suspected by the police of committing the crime is unknown to the person conducting the parade, for example.

Bonnie rule: An American test of diminished responsibility.

Borderline personality disorder: A psychiatric term describing a long-standing disturbance of the functioning of personality. Instability and chaos in mood, interpersonal relations, behaviour and sense of identity are among the associated characteristics.

British Crime Survey: A survey of the experiences of victims of crime.

Burglary: Entering a property with the intention of committing theft or damage or to do physical harm to a person.

C

Canteen culture: A term referring to the conservative beliefs and discriminatory attitudes held to characterise the lower ranks of the police.

Catatonic behaviour: This is not a mental disorder in itself but is found in mental disorders such as schizophrenia. The motor skills of the sufferer decline to a significant extent or they may show continuous hyperactive movement. The sufferer shows an extreme.

CCTV: Closed-circuit television.

Chemical restraints: 'chemical straightjackets' or anti-psychotic drugs which are used to treat some violent individuals.

Chicago School: An important movement in criminology which moved the explanation of crime to environment and situational factors.

Child molester: A term used to describe someone who has sexually abused a child. The use of the term avoids the psychological implications of the use of the term paedophile.

Civil: These are legal matters which concern the rights of private individuals and are different from crimes which are offences against the State. Examples include unpaid debts, enforcement of contracts, and so forth. Family matters and employment, for example, are not matters of the civil law in the UK.

Claimant (previously plaintiff in UK law): A person who issues a claim against another person.

Classical conditioning: The conditioning of reflex responses – most famously Pavlov's dogs which learnt to associate a bell with food and salivated to the sound of the bell.

Clear-up rates: The rates of known crimes which lead to prosecution, although they may include offences dealt with by other means such as where an offender admits further offences.

Clinical judgement: Judgements based on the assessment of practitioners in a clinical setting rather than systematic research.

Clinical prediction: Predictions of, for example, recidivism based on clinical judgement.

Clinical psychology: That aspect of the practice of psychology which deals with psychologically based distress or dysfunction.

Clinical samples: Samples of participants obtained from a medical setting.

Closed question: A question worded in such a way that little is required by way of answer other than a yes or no or some other simple, unelaborated response.

Coerced-compliant (false) confession: A confession produced under some form of pressure or coercion but which is not actually believed by the person who confesses.

Coerced-internalised (false) confession: As for coerced-compliant confession but the confessor believes that they had carried out the act confessed.

Cognitive: To do with knowing and perceiving rather than emotion and action.

Cognitive behavioural therapy: Form of psychological therapy directed to altering both behaviour and thoughts usually using procedures based on modifying the way the offender thinks about their behaviours.

Cognitive dissonance: The negative state when there are inconsistencies between an individual's attitudes and their behaviour. It may motivate a change in the individual's cognitions.

Cognitive distortions: A very loose term to describe the unusual, offence-supportive beliefs, attitudes and other cognitions which are conducive to offending behaviour, especially sex offending against children.

Cognitive interview and enhanced cognitive interview: procedures for conducting interviews based on the findings of cognitive psychology and communications psychology in the case of the enhanced cognitive interview.

Cognitive skills training/programmes: Techniques for the improvement of problem solving relevant, especially, to social interaction.

Cognitive-behavioural: Approaches based on behaviourism and cognitive psychology, especially the relationship between the two.

Combat fatigue: Shell shock – the mental and bodily disturbances that result from prolonged involvement in combat. It should be considered in relation to Post-Traumatic Stress Syndrome.

Command hallucinations: A hallucination in which voices instruct the person to do a certain act (possibly a crime).

Common law: The branch of law which is based on precedents such as previous judicial decisions and arrangements well established within the community.

Community sentence: A sentence for a crime based on making direct amends to the community by carrying out relatively menial tasks within that community.

Co-morbidity: The presence of a disease or condition additional to the one of primary interest and the resulting combined effect. For example, alcoholism and schizophrenia may be co-morbid.

Competence to stand trial: A defendant who meets the criteria regarded as sufficient to establish that they can participate in their own defence.

Compliance: Yielding to the wishes or commands of another person.

Compos mentis: Means that the person is of sound mind and legally capable, for example, of being involved in their defence in court.

Conditioning: the learning of behaviour (actions). Includes classical and operant conditioning.

Conduct disorder: a psychological state characterised by repeated, extreme antisocial activities.

Confession culture: the idea that police officers obtain confessions as their primary objective rather than obtain evidence.

Confidence, eyewitness: An eyewitness's belief in the accuracy of their memories and testimony.

Confirmatory factor analysis: A statistical technique which allows the researcher to test the adequacy of a factor structure or a model against new data.

Conformity: Compliance with the behaviours of others.

Confounding factors: Factors which confuse the interpretation of statistical relationships which the researcher may be unaware of.

Context reinstatement: In the cognitive interview, thinking of the context of the original events as part of the process of recall.

Control Question Test: A way of asking questions in a polygraph test.

Conversation management approach: Procedures for conducting interviews which concentrate on managing the flow of the police interview using both verbal and non-verbal techniques.

Correctional psychologist: A psychologist working in a prison or some other organisation devoted to the correction of criminal behaviour.

Correlation coefficient: An index of the degree of association between two variables in which +1 indicates a perfect positive relationship, +0.5 indicates a moderate positive relationship, 0 indicates no relationship and a negative sign (−) indicates a negative relationship.

Corroboration: Supportive information from a second source.

Counselling: The process which takes place between client and counsellor in which a difficulty experienced by the client is explored.

Counselling psychologist: A psychologist who works primarily using counselling techniques in the treatment of clients.

County court: In the UK, these deal with civil law matters, especially those with a financial aspect.

Covert sensitisation: An approach in behaviour modification (conditioning) where an undesired behaviour is associated with a negative image so as to reduce the likelihood of the behaviour reoccurring.

Credible: Believable.

Crime: Actions punishable by the law.

Crime mapping: Research which seeks to place crime in its precise geographical context. It can help identify crime hot spots.

Crime profiling: Usually, but not always, a description of the sorts of person and their characteristics who engage in a particular sort of crime.

Crime reconstruction: Attempts to reproduce the sequence of events which took place during a crime based on the evidence left at the scene.

Crime scene classification: The classification of crime scenes usually into organised and disorganised types.

Criminal Behaviour Profiling: One of a variety of virtually synonymous terms for offender profiling. It is an investigative method which uses information from the crime scene and more to develop a social, behavioural and, possibly, physical description of the offender.

Criminal cases: Concerning cases which are regarded in law as against society (as opposed to the rights of individuals).

Criminal justice system: The governmental organisations and practices which serve to both control crime and maintain control on the population. It includes punishments for violations of the law.

Criminality: this is a personal characteristic or trait of an individual whereas a crime is a particular sort of event.

Criminally insane: To be convicted of a crime the offender has to understand that they were doing wrong at the time of the offence. The mental defects of the criminally insane prevented their understanding that what they were doing was wrong.

Criminogenic: Causing or resulting in crime.

Criminogenic needs: Needs which unless satisfied may lead to or encourage criminal behaviour.

Criminology: The science of crime. It is broader than either forensic or criminal psychology and could be regarded as embracing both of them.

Criterion/criteria-based content analysis (CBCA): Part of statement validity analysis. It is a way of examining, primarily, children's statements for content which is characteristic of truthfulness.

Cross-examination: The questioning of a witness by the other side (e.g. prosecution or defence) in a court hearing.

Cross-race identification: Eyewitness identification of other races.

Crown court: This deals with criminal cases sent to them by a magistrates' court. A judge and a jury are involved. Also deals with certain civil and family isses.

Cycles of abuse: The idea that abuse in one generation leads to abuse by later generations.

D

Dangerous and severe personality disorder: This is a neither a legal nor a psychiatric category but one developed by government. It may be regarded, in the absence of a better definition, as an extreme variant of antisocial personality disorder. It is part of an attempt to protect the public from a small but extremely harmful minority of mentally disordered individuals.

Danish experiment: The liberation of pornography by the Danish government in the late 1960s.

Daubert guidelines: In the USA, rules defining when an expert witness is appropriate.

De facto: In fact.

De jure: Rightful – a matter of right.

Decision rule: The broad principles by which juries reach a verdict. For example, the size of the majority needed.

Deficit model: An explanation based on the lack of certain characteristics.

Deinstitutionalisation: The process by which the mentally ill were transferred to care in the community from care in mental hospitals.

Delusions: a false belief which is relatively fixed or constant.

Dementia praecox: *See* schizophrenia.

Denial: In forensic psychology the refusal to accept aspects of one's offending such as its extent or seriousness.

Desistance: The process of resisting criminal activity in those with a criminogenic profile.

Deviancy Amplification: The process of bringing into focus a particular issue to do with criminal activity by continual reference to it by the media.

Diagnostic and Statistical Manual (DSM): The key published source for definitions of mental illness such as bipolar disorder, schizophrenia, etc.

Diagnostic Interview Schedule: A questionnaire for assessing the presence of various mental illnesses.

Diagnosticity of signs: The extent to which a sign is accurate as an indication of some characteristic. For example, how accurate previous convictions are as a predictor of future offending.

Differential association theory: The idea that criminal ideas are learned through social interaction with others.

Diminished responsibility: Mental and other incapacities which limit the offender's responsibility for a crime and may make them less liable to punishment.

Directed lie test: A way of questioning used for the polygraph.

Disclosure: The requirement in UK law that the sides involved in a civil case must show the other side documentation that they will rely on in court as evidence.

Disinhibition: The removal of factors which inhibit an individual from a course of action. Commonly used as an explanation of sex offending.

Disorganised crime scene: A crime scene which is characterised by chaos. This type of crime scene is seen as being associated with offenders with disorganised lifestyles in some forms of profiling.

Dissociation: The loss of connections between emotions, thoughts, memories, etc. as a defensive reaction to extreme stress.

Distal factors: Things that are more distant (usually in time in psychology) such as early childhood factors in criminality. Opposite = proximal.

Distorted thinking: Patterns of thought which are distortions of reality. Often used to describe the thinking which leads to sex offending.

Divisional court: Courts which have the right to hear appeals from lower courts, etc. They also have their own jurisdiction.

DNA: Deoxyribonucleic acid. This carries a pattern of genetic information unique to each individual.

DNA testing: The process of comparing a suspect's DNA with a sample of DNA from another source to assess whether the two match.

Doli incapax: The incapability of committing a crime because of youth.

Downward comparison process: The idea that we make judgements about ourselves by comparison with those less fortunate than ourselves in some regard.

Drift theory: The idea that criminal activity is the product of the activities of people who drift between a deviant and a non-deviant lifestyle at will.

Drug dependency units: Treatment units for abusers.

DSM: *See Diagnostic and Statistical Manual.*

Dynamic variables: Variables which may be altered by practitioners or researchers as opposed to static variables such as gender which are largely fixed.

E

Early onset: the process by which a criminal career starts early n life (childhood) which leads to persistent crime.

Ecological validity: This is the extent to which behaviours, etc. observed in a research study accurately reflect what occurs in natural settings.

Ectomorphs: Persons with a lean and delicate body build.

EEG activity: Electrical activity of the brain as measured by the electro-encephalogram.

Effect size: A term in statistics for something which indicates the size of the influence of the independent variable in a standardised form which allows comparison of studies. Common examples of effect size measures are Pearson's correlation coefficient and Cohen's *d*.

E-FIT: A method of facial image reconstruction.

Emotional dysregulation: A failure to deal effectively with one's emotions. May result in dysfunctional coping methods.

Encoding: The process by which information is changed into different forms. In psychology, it is the initial process in memory in which the stimulus is transferred into memory.

Endomorph: A body type which is soft and rounded – according to Sheldon's theory.

Enhanced cognitive interview: Interview techniques based on the research findings from memory research and communications psychology.

Erotomania: The deluded belief that another person, e.g. a film or television personality, is in love with him or her.

Escabinato: A system in which a judge sits with lay persons during a trial as opposed to a jury system where a judge conducts the trial and a jury reaches a verdict.

Estimator variable: In eyewitness testimony, an estimator variable is something which affects the accuracy of the eyewitness but is not within the powers of the criminal justice system to influence. So, for example, an estimator variable might be the age of the eyewitness or how close they were to the offender at the crime scene. These are different from system variables which can be controlled by the criminal justice system as they involve the characteristics of the line-up or identity parade, etc.

Evolutionary theory of rape: This argues that males have a propensity to rape because of natural selection – rape is a means by which inadequate males can transmit their genes.

Excitation transfer theory: A theory of aggression which suggests that a person in a state of arousal is more likely to act aggressively irrespective of the source of that arousal.

Exhibitionism: the act of publicly exposing one's genitals for the purpose of personal sexual excitement.

Expert witness: A person qualified in a specific area or otherwise having expertise who is employed to give evidence in court.

Extraversion: A characteristic of personality describing someone who is outgoing and gregarious. According to Hans Eysenck's theory of crime, they condition relatively poorly and consequently do not learn social rules quickly which leaves them more likely to be criminal.

Eyewitness testimony: Evidence provided to a court by a witness who saw the events in question.

F

Facet theory: This is a theory proposed by Louis Guttman which sets out methods of defining observations for multivariate investigations. It has entered forensic psychology through its adoption by David Canter in his approach to criminal profiling.

Facial composites: Representations of faces built up from a set of standard elements.

False allegation: An accusation of committing a crime which the accused party did not commit.

False confession: A confession to a crime which the confessor did not actually commit.

False memory: A memory of something which did not occur or a very distorted memory which is substantially false. *See also* Recovered memories.

False memory induction: The process of developing a false memory for events. It is claimed that this may be the result of the influence of therapists.

False memory syndrome: A description of a state in which an individual has memories which are regarded as being fantasy and this is a central focus of their lives. Usually refers to memories which emerged during or as a consequence of therapy.

Familicide: The killing of one's spouse and children.

Fantasy: Fanciful thoughts and ideas which have little or no basis in real experience.

FBI profiling: The form of crime-scene offender profiling based on largely clinical approaches which was developed by the FBI at their Quantico academy.

Fear of crime: Being afraid of becoming a victim of crime – there is a disproportionality usually in that these fears are not in keeping with the actual risk of victimisation for the particular sort of person in question.

Fear–victimisation paradox: The finding from research that the most likely victims of crime tend not to be afraid of the risk of victimisation and vice versa.

Felony: In the USA this is a significant offence that can lead to one or more years in a state prison.

Feminist movement: A variety of social movements, theories and philosophies which critique gender differences and promote gender equality of women with men.

Feminist theory: Theory which critiques gender differences.

Fetishism: A sexual pathology in which a person is aroused by objects or parts of the body which do not normally serve a sexual function.

Field dependence: The idea that some people are very dependent on peripheral factors in terms of their perceptions and judgements.

Firesetting: *See* Arson.

FIRO: Fundamental Interpersonal Relations Orientation, which is William Schutz's theory of interpersonal relationships. FIRO-B is a measuring instrument to assess components of this theory.

Fitness to plead: In the United Kingdom, to stand trial an accused must be capable of understanding the proceedings. *See also* Competence to stand trial, which is the US equivalent.

Fixated offenders: A sex offender against children whose psychosexual development is held to have been arrested in childhood.

Flashbacks: Intrusive and vivid memories of traumatic episodes.

Flashbulb memory: The photographically detailed memories which occur in response to emotionally and personally significant events.

Flesch index: a measure of the readability of text.

Foils: The non-suspected persons in an identity parade or line-up.

Folie a deux: The co-occurrence of psychosis in two closely associated persons.

Forensic hypnosis: Hypnosis used in the interviewing of witnesses.

Forensic linguistics: Linguistics applied to a forensic setting.

Forensic psychology: Strictly, psychology applied to courts of law but generally used to refer to the forms of psychology used within the criminal justice system.

Forensic validity: The extent to which research findings can be generalised to aspects of the work of courts of law (and the criminal justice system).

Frottage: A perverse sexual act involving obtaining sexual arousal from physical contact with another person in a crowded situation.

Fundamental Interpersonal Relations Orientation: *See* FIRO.

G

Galvanic skin response (GSR): The electrical activity of the skin (electrical resistance) fluctuates over time. Variation in emotional arousal is associated with variations in skin resistance, hence GSR is used in lie detection, for example.

General strain theory (GST): the theory that strain created on the individual by a variety of life's pressures combine with the emotionality of the individual in a way that results in criminality.

Genetic fingerprinting: *See* DNA testing.

Genetic: To do with genes – the basic components of inheritance.

Grooming: The processes by which paedophiles and other sexual offenders against children initiate and maintain social and personal relationships with potential victims prior to offending against them.

Ground truth: The absolute or underlying 'truth' concerning a set of events which may or may not be known to researchers or practitioners.

Guardian: A person who looks after the affairs and interests of a child or someone suffering mental disability.

Guardians (capable): People such as neighbours and the police who act as a deterrent to crime simply because of their presence in the area.

Guilty Knowledge Test: A form of asking questions in a polygraph examination.

H

Habeas corpus: This is a written instruction or command (writ) which instructs that someone held in custody should be brought before the court.

Hallucinations: A perception of something which appears to be real and present but is not.

Halo effect: The process by which a person is perceived to be entirely good on the basis of a small number of positive characteristics.

Hate Crime: Usually a violent crime but based on prejudices against a group such as in homophobia.

Hearsay: Evidence that is anything other than the statement by a witness about things that they witnessed. The rules are complex and varied. For example, evidence confirming that certain things were said out-of-court is not hearsay.

Hedonistic (serial) killer: Someone whose primary motive is some sort of pleasure associated with the killing of another person.

Heuristic: Procedures which reach a solution by a process akin to trial and error in which each stage better approximates the best solution.

Hidden Crime: Crime which does not manifest itself in official statistics.

High court: In the UK this is a civil court which has three divisions dealing with civil disputes, family matters and property (such as fraud and bankruptcy).

Homicide: A killing of another human being, though this is not always an illegal act.

Hostile witness: A non-cooperative witness.

Hung jury: A jury which fails to reach a clear verdict on the basis of legal rules about decision making.

Hypnosis: A trance-like or sleep-like state where the individual responds only to the suggestions of the hypnotist.

Hypothetico-deductive model: A way of proceeding in research whereby the research deduces hypotheses from a theory which are then tested empirically by the researcher.

I

Iatrogenic: Caused by the medical or psychological treatment being given to the individual.

Identification parade: People in a group containing the suspect for a crime who are shown to the witness to see whether the suspect is correctly identified by the witness. Also called identity parade and line-up.

Identikit: A procedure for producing facial composites of suspects based on a set of drawings of different varieties of facial characteristics such as nose shape.

Identity parade: *See* Identification parade.

Imitation: The process of learning by observing another person carry out a task.

Implicit memory: Memories dependent on learning of which the individual is not aware.

In camera: A hearing which takes place in private without details being made public.

In curia: A hearing which takes place in court.

Inadmissible evidence: Evidence which cannot be presented in court because it violates some rule governing evidence.

Incestuous offenders: Sex offenders against children within the biological family and/or the more general social family in some formulations.

Incidence: (From medicine) is the number of people who have a condition on an annual basis.

Indirect aggression: Forms of aggression which do not involve physical attack but verbal attacks and so forth instead.

Individualist culture: A culture in which the individual is the primary unit and in which ties with the family and community are very restricted.

Information-processing theories: Theories of cognition and cognitive development which propose that thought involves strategies which may become more effective with experience or training. The mind has a limited information processing capacity.

Innocence Project: An American organisation which uses evidence from DNA testing technology to seek to deal with cases of wrongful conviction.

Inquisitorial system: The legal system common in Europe and elsewhere where trials are conducted by a judge (and others) seeking to establish the truth of a case. This contrasts with the adversarial Anglo-American system in which opposing sides in the case present their evidence and arguments which are decided between (often by a jury).

Insanity: In legal settings, insanity is the lack of ability of the accused to know that what they did was wrong during the offence. This is a legal judgment and not judged as such by mental health professionals.

Intelligence: A general term to describe a variety of abilities such as problem solving, ability to learn, abstract thinking, comprehension and so forth.

Intentionality: A complex concept with a complex history – however, in a forensic psychology context it generally means purposefulness.

International Classification of Diseases: A systematic categorisation of diseases, including mental health problems.

Interpersonal skills training: Training to improve an individual's ability to interact with others.

Interrogation manuals: Instruction books purportedly giving instruction in how to interview offenders effectively.

Interrogation: Questioning but in a somewhat forceful way which may result in the disclosure of significant information.

Interviewer bias: The process by which the predetermined views of an interviewer may influence the interviewee to answer in ways consistent with that predetermined view.

Intimacy deficits: The idea that sex offenders lack the ability to form close sexual relationships with other adults.

Intra vires: Within the power or jurisdiction of a court.

Investigative interviewing: The term used to describe the interviewing process used by the police during the course of a criminal investigation. Could also be applied, for example, to similar work carried out by psychologists or social workers.

Investigative psychology: A term used by David Canter to describe the application of scientific psychology to the analysis and investigation of crimes.

Irrelevant question technique: A method of questioning in the polygraph lie detector test.

Isomorphism hypothesis: The suggestion that there are marked parallels between the offending behaviour of paedophiles and the sexually abusive/sexualisation experiences of the offender as a child.

J

Joyriding: Taking a vehicle for the enjoyment or thrill of driving it – as opposed to, for example, taking a vehicle for monetary gain.

Judge: An administrator of the law who may hear and try cases in court.

Jurisdiction: The geographical area and the issues over which a court has authority in law.

Jurisprudence: The theory and philosophy of the law and legal systems.

Jury: Usually refers to the group of lay persons sworn to reach an impartial verdict on legal issues presented to them – usually a guilty or not guilty verdict based on the evidence put before them.

Just world: A theoretical notion referring to the tendency of some people to regard life as being based on principles of fairness and justice.

Justice of the Peace (JP): In the UK, a lay magistrate in a magistrates' court. Sometimes found in a Crown court sitting with professional judges in cases of appeals and certain other matters.

K

Kleptomania: A psychiatric term referring to a persistent urge to steal property.

Klinefelter's syndrome: a term used to describe the behaviours, etc. of a person with an XXY-chromosome configuration.

L

Labelling: The idea that being labelled as deviant locks an individual or group of individuals into deviancy.

Larceny: Theft which does not involve violence, threat, or breaking into another person's property.

Law Lords: highest level judges in the House of Lords in the UK. They are known as the Lords of Appeal.

Law: A system of rules established by the highest legislature (parliament in the UK) and by custom which encourages or prohibits certain actions.

Lawyer: A member of the legal profession. In the UK there are barristers who largely operate in the highest courts and solicitors who operate in the lower courts.

Lay person jury: The usual jury in the Anglo-American legal system.

Leading question: A question framed in such a way that it implies a particular answer.

Leakages: This is a term used in lie-detection and refers to behavioural, etc. manifestations of underlying emotions which are aroused by lying.

Learning disabilities: A broad label for various conditions which cause substantial difficulties in skills such as listening, speaking, writing and mathematics. Generally seen as being the consequence of an underlying neurological dysfunction.

Legal psychology: Theoretical and empirical psychology into aspects of the criminal justice system.

Legalese: The argot of members of the legal profession.

Level of Service Inventory – Revised (LSI-R): A questionnaire for the assessment of criminogenic needs.

Lie detector test: Usually refers to the polygraph.

Line-up: *See* Identification parade.

Live links: Video links between a witness and a law court which reduce some of the negative aspects of giving evidence in court.

Long-term memory: Memory after the stage of encoding by the working memory (aka short-term memory). Confusingly, long-term memory may be short lasting or long lasting in the sense that it may last, say, hours or decades.

LSI-R: *See* Level of Service Inventory – Revised.

M

MacArthur Competence Assessment Tool: An assessment procedure dealing with the issue of competence (fitness) to stand trial in North America.

Mad versus bad: A phrase used to capture the difference between psychological and moral explanations of extreme forms of crime.

Madness: *See* Insanity.

Magistrates' court: A lower level court where criminal prosecutions commence. The offence may be dealt with by the magistrates (Justices of the Peace) or sent to a higher court. Some civil matters are also dealt with at the magistrates' court.

Magnetic resonance imaging (MRI): A non-invasive medical technique used in the diagnosis of many diseases, including cancer.

Male rape: Forced/unwanted anal or oral penetration of a male by another male's penis.

Manic depression: *See* Bipolar disorder.

Manslaughter: The killing of another human in a way that is legally less culpable than murder. The intention to kill may not be present, though there may be an element of recklessness.

Manualisation: Defining precisely the procedures which should be employed in psychotherapies: adherence to the theory is known to lead to improved outcomes from therapy.

MAPPA: *See* Multi-agency public protection arrangements.

Masturbatory reconditioning: Techniques used to redirect masturbation to a legal sexual object from an illegal one such as a child (i.e. to substitute fantasies of a legal sex object for fantasies of an illegal one).

Maximisation: A style of questioning in which the strength of the police's evidence is exaggerated in the hope that the suspect will confess.

McNaughten Rule: British rules for determining whether someone is criminally insane and so not legally responsible for the crime.

Megan's Law: A US act which enables the disclosure of information concerning the whereabouts of sex offenders in the community.

Mens rea: Many crimes require that the offender knowingly breaks the law in that they know the law but proceed to ignore it. Thus *mens rea* is criminal intent or a guilty mind.

Mental illness: A variety of psychological conditions in which there is a characteristic disabling and distressing impairment in some aspect of the psychological functioning of the individual.

Mesomorphs: A compact and muscular body type. Appears in Eysenck's Theory of Crime.

Meta-analysis: Statistical methods of synthesising the findings from a variety of different studies on a topic. It is the analysis of analyses.

Methadone: A synthetic version of opium which is used in treatment for addiction.

Microexpressions: These are brief and partial expressions of the face which occur extremely soon after, say, a particular question is put. They are then actively concealed. They might be regarded as informative by the interrogator.

Minimisation: A style of questioning in which the seriousness of an act is underplayed by an interviewer or it is 'justified' in some way. The intention is to encourage a confession.

Minnesota Multiphasic Personality Inventory (MMPI): A long-established personality measure which assesses several aspects of personality.

Miranda rights: US rules governing arrest in which the suspect is explained their legal rights to remain silent, etc.

Miscarriages of justice: This is a failure of the legal system to give the accused a trial which is fair based on the evidence presented to the court. It is not the same thing as wrongful conviction but they do overlap.

Mitigation: Submitted prior to sentencing, mitigation is the reasons submitted on behalf of the accused to provide excuses for the offence in the hope of reducing the sentence awarded.

Mixed crime scene: A crime scene which involves both organised and disorganised characteristics. It may occur, for example, because there are two or more offenders.

MMPI: *See* Minnesota Multiphasic Personality Inventory.

Mock crime: An imitation or pretend crime set up for research purposes.

Mock jury: An imitation or pretend staged jury set up for research purposes.

Monozygotic twins: From the same fertilised egg hence identical twins.

Moral panic: A criminological theory describing situations in which heightened public interest is expressed about groups, people or events which fundamentally challenge dominant values.

Multi-agency public protection arrangements (MAPPA): UK procedures for monitoring sexual and violent offenders in the community.

Multiple killing: Killing several people at the same time.

Munchausen's syndrome by proxy: The condition in which a primary care-giver exaggerates, fabricates, or causes illness or symptoms of illness in a child. The existence of this condition is controversial.

N

Necrophilia: Sexual activity with a dead person.

Neuropsychology: The study of how the structure and functions of the brain relate to behaviour and psychological processes.

Neuroticism: Emotional instability in the sense that neurotic people readily experience negative emotional states and so are vulnerable to anger and depression.

Neutralisation: Mental acts which help protect the criminal from responsibility for their actions.

Next friend: *See* Guardian.

Non compos mentis: A person mentally unfit to take part in legal proceedings.

Norms: Rules describing how members of a group or wider community should behave and should not behave.

Notary public: A person with the authority to perform certain legal procedures – i.e. the swearing of oaths.

Nothing works: The outmoded view that interventions and treatments to reduce offending and reoffending are largely unsuccessful.

O

Offender profiling: *See* Profile analysis.

Open-ended questioning: Questions designed to get the interviewee to respond extensively rather than using a small number of fixed alternatives (such as yes and no).

Operant behaviour (modification): The process of increasing/decreasing the frequency of naturally occurring behaviours through the use of reinforcements or rewards when the targeted behaviour is exhibited.

Optimal foraging theory: An idea from animal ecology which suggests that creatures use foraging strategies which maximise the food they obtain while minimising the risks involved in foraging. Applied to crime, optimal foraging theory suggests that offenders maximise the rewards of burglary while minimising the negative consequences such as getting caught.

Organised crime scene: A crime scene that seems to exhibit methodological rather than chaotic offender behaviours when committing the crime. Is said to reflect certain characteristics of the offender.

Organized Crime: Crime committed by organized criminal groups.

Overkill: Violence beyond what is necessary for an offender to achieve their ends.

P

PACE: *See* Police and Criminal Evidence Act.

Paedophiles: An adult with a sexual interest in children though often used to refer to adults with a sexual interest in young people in general.

Paranoia: An extreme or exaggerated distrust of other people who, often, are seen as persecutors.

Parole: The process by which a prisoner may be let out of prison on a temporary basis subject to certain requirements.

Pathways model of sexual abuse: A theory accounting for the development of sex offending against children which suggests that there are four major routes to offending behaviour.

PCL-R: *See* Psychopathy Checklist–Revised.

PEACE: In the UK this is the best practice approach to investigative interviewing. It is an acronym for preparation and planning, engaging and explaining, accounting, closure and evaluation.

Penology: The study of the management of prisons and punishment for crime.

Peremptory challenge: This refers to the process by which potential jury members may be objected to (at the voir dire phase of the trial) without the requirement to give a valid legal reason for that challenge.

Peripheral route: This is the form of persuasion which involves little cognitive processing. So things such as the credibility of the source of the persuasive message influence attitude change rather than careful cognitive elaboration.

Personality disorder: Mental disorders which involve inflexible thought and behaviour patterns which are somewhat enduring.

Phallometry: *See* Plethysmography.

Phobias: An intense and lasting fear of certain activities, persons, situations and so forth. Phobias are regarded as irrational and are typified by behaviours involving the avoidance of the thing that one is afraid of.

Photofit: A way of constructing a facial composite of a suspect from photographs of different varieties of parts of the face.

Photo-spread: A sort of identification parade or line-up which is based on photographs rather than actual people.

Plaintiff: The person who initiates a case against a defendant in a court of law.

Plethysmography: Measurement of the erection or tumescence of the penis based on its circumference or volume. Regarded by some as an indication of sexual arousal.

Police and Criminal Evidence Act (PACE): An important piece of UK legislation regulating the powers of the police in matters such as interviewing, stopping and searching, arrest.

Police caution: A formal situation in which an offender is addressed by a senior police officer. It is a stern warning about any future misconduct. Sometimes it is treated as the same as a conviction for statistical purposes.

Polygraph: The lie detector which measures physiological responses to certain types of questioning.

Post-event information: Pertinent information which becomes available to the individual at some time after they witnessed a crime.

Post-traumatic anger: One of the possible outcomes of post-traumatic stress.

Post-traumatic stress disorder (PTSD): The psychological defence/coping mechanism which may follow extreme stress.

Power killers: People who kill for the sense of power that this instils in them.

Powerful speech: The type of speech which characterises powerful individuals.

Powerless speech: The type of speech which would be used by powerless individuals.

Preconditions model: A theory (by David Finkelstein) of sex offenders against children which suggests that a number of things must occur or be present before a person will offend sexually against children.

Prejudice: A bias or preconceived view without consideration of the fairness of this.

Pre-trial publicity: Publicity given a crime or offender from the point of a charge being made.

Prevalence: (From medicine) is the number of people who have a particular condition at a particular point in time. *See also* Incidence.

Prima facie: Means first sight and there must be prima facie evidence for a case to be answered and, in itself, is sufficient proof unless disproved at the trial.

Primacy-recency effect: Items at certain serial positions in a list of things to be remembered are more likely to be remembered than those at other positions. Usually items in the middle are the least well remembered.

Probative: Providing proof or evidence.

Profile analysis: One of a number of terms for offender profiling in which elements found at the crime scene are identified and linked with the likely characteristics of the culprit. However, sometimes the term is used to describe research which merely gives the typical characteristics of offenders who commit a particular type of crime.

Profile generation: The process of creating a description of the characteristics of the likely offender from the characteristics of the crime scene.

PRO-fit: A way of generating facial composites based on computer techniques.

Protective factors: Factors which if present tend to protect an otherwise vulnerable person from engaging in a crime.

Proximal factors: Factors which are close (usually in time in psychology) such as peer pressure as a cause of adolescent offending.

Psychiatric disorders: A variety of maladaptive behaviours and psychological functioning problems. They may also be referred to as emotional or mental illness.

Psychiatry: The branch of medical science which deals with mental and emotional conditions.

Psychoanalysis: The approach to the treatment of mental and emotional problems by revealing the unconscious basis for the condition.

Psychodynamic: The study of the interrelations between different aspects of the personality.

Psychological profiling: *See* Crime profiling, Profile analysis.

Psychology: The scientific study of the human mind and behaviour.

Psychopath: A person demonstrating chronic immorality and antisocial behaviours.

Psychopathic disorder (psychopathy): A term describing continual long-term problems associated with lack of morality and antisocial tendencies.

Psychopathy Checklist Revised (PCL-R): A checklist for assessing for psychopathy. It is completed by a psychologist or a psychiatrist.

Psychosis: A general term referring to mental states which involve some degree of loss of contact with reality such as hallucinations or delusional beliefs.

Psychosocial: The way an individual develops through an interaction between the individual's psychology and the social environment.

Psychotherapy: Any form of treatment of mental conditions using psychological techniques.

Psychotic: Various mental states which feature a loss of grasp on reality.

Psychoticism: The state of being psychotic.

PTSD: *See* Post-traumatic stress disorder.

Punishment: The process or act of causing an offender to suffer for their crime.

Pyromania: A psychological impulse to set fire to things as a way of relieving tension which often leads to a sense of relief and euphoria afterwards. It is thus clearly different from arson, although it involves arson.

Q

Quadripartite model: A theory of sex offending against children.

Queen's/King's Counsel: Barristers with a minimum of 10 years' experience can apply for this title. They take on important work.

R

Rape trauma syndrome: The broadly characteristic psychological response to rape and attempted rape (such as shock and denial) which is accompanied by a characteristic accommodation process over a lengthy period of time.

Rape: The precise definition of rape varies from jurisdiction to jurisdiction but is often nowadays defined in terms of the forcible/non-consenting penetration of another person's vagina, anus or mouth by the penis. As such, it is no longer a gender-specific crime.

Rape-Myth Acceptance Scale: A measure of the acceptance of rape myths such as that a woman deserves to be raped if she dresses provocatively.

Rapport: Showing comfortable and harmonious communications or interactions between, usually, an interviewer and interviewee.

Reality monitoring: The process by which people distinguish memories of real events from any other memories.

Recall: The process of memory by which things come back into one's mind. Recall is different from recognition which occurs when the remembered thing is re-presented.

Recidivism: Future reoffending by an offender. Usually measured in terms of reconviction rates or survival rates (the proportions having not reoffended after a particular number of years).

Recovered memories: Memories of traumatic incidents (especially child sexual abuse) which re-emerge in adulthood.

Regressed offenders: Sexual offenders against children who, putatively, in response to stress move their sexual interest from adults to children.

Rehabilitation: The process by which a person is returned to a normal lifestyle.

Relapse prevention: Therapeutic methods for sex offenders that teach ways of avoiding situations and thoughts which will lead to reoffending.

Relative judgement theory: The idea that in identity parades or line-ups the witness tends to choose someone similar to the suspect if the suspect is missing from that line-up.

Relevant question technique: A technique of questioning in a polygraph examination.

Remand prisoners: Prisoners awaiting trial who have not been convicted.

Remand: To order an accused person to be kept in custody or placed on bail pending further court appearance.

Reoffending: *See* Recidivism.

Reparation: Attempts to make good the damage caused to a victim of a crime.

Repressed memory: A memory (usually of child sexual abuse) which is not available at a particular time to conscious experience.

Researcher-practitioners: The term used to indicate that practitioners (e.g. forensic and clinical psychologists) should be active researchers in order that their field may develop in an evidence-based fashion.

Restorative justice: Procedures which, through a mediator, bring offender and victim into direct or indirect contact. The victim may get answers to important questions to them and the offender may learn more about the impact of their offending behaviour and perhaps offer reparation.

Retribution: The idea that the harm done to society by an offender should be counterbalanced by proportionate punishment being given to the offender.

Risk assessment: The methods and procedures by which a judgement is formed about the likely extent of the negative outcomes of a course of action such as releasing a sex offender from prison.

Risk factor: any variable which is predictive of a risk such as the risk of reoffending or the risk of an attempted escape.

Risk management: The procedures and practices employed to limit or prevent the risk materialising that has been perceived to be posed by an offender or client. Incarceration may be one such procedure.

Routine activity theory: A criminological theory which describes offending behaviour in terms of the everyday activities of offenders.

RRASOR (Rapid Risk Assessment for Sexual Offender Recidivism): A questionnaire measure of the likelihood of future recidivism by sex offenders.

Rules of evidence: This refers to the principles governing the presentation of evidence in court. For example, the rules concerning the use of hearsay evidence or previous convictions.

S

Schizophrenia: A complex mental illness in which the sufferer has problems differentiating real experiences from unreal experiences, has problems in thinking logically about issues, and behaving as others do in social situations. No decisive differentiating feature exists and diagnosis calls for a thorough understanding of the condition and other conditions which may have some similar symptoms.

Scientific jury selection: The use of survey and other evidence to identify the characteristics of jurors likely to be sympathetic with one side of a trial which may be used in juror selection.

Scientist-practitioner: A term used to describe the situation in which practitioners (including forensic psychologists) are expected to also be active researchers. *See also* Researcher-practitioner.

Script: Essentially a typical or expected sequence of actions which integrates individual actions in a way which may be regarded as meaningful.

Secondary victimisation: The consequences of being the victim of crime for those who were not directly victimised. Thus the family of a victim of violence may experience secondary victimisation because of the loss of family income while the direct victim is hospitalised.

Sequential line-up/identification parade: Where the eyewitness sees the suspect and the other members of the line-up one at a time.

Serial killers: Where a killer kills three or more people with a clear separation between each of the crimes.

Sexual offender register: A legally required list of most sex offenders who must register many of their movements within defined limits.

Sexual scripts: Much social behaviour follows broad patterns which can be likened to an actor's script. However, the detail of the performance is left to the act. Sexual scripts are the idea that sexual behaviour is similarly broadly structured.

Sexualisation model of paedophilia: The theory that early sexual experiences in childhood in certain circumstances can lead to paedophilia later in life.

Sexually violent predator (SVP) laws: US laws dealing with serious repeat sexual offenders.

Signature: Characteristics of a crime scene which are typical of a particular offender but which have no particular relevance to the crime's perpetration itself.

Simultaneous line-up/identification parade: Where the eyewitness sees the suspect and the other members of the line-up all at the same time.

Smallest space analysis (SSA): A form of complex statistical analysis used to identify underlying patterns in characteristics of a crime scene.

Social learning theory: The idea that much human socialisation takes place through a process of social observation.

Solicitor: A lawyer in the UK who primarily advises clients and may represent clients in some courts.

Somatypes: Body shape types in Sheldon's theory.

Special hospitals: High security units in which mentally disordered offenders are treated.

SSA: *See* Smallest space analysis.

Staging: Altering a crime scene in a way which the offender thinks will divert investigative attention away from them.

Stare decisis: The principle of using previous legal decisions as the standard for making later decisions.

Statement validity (or reality) analysis: A variety of procedures which generate hypotheses about the likely truthfulness or accuracy of a person's (usually a child) evidence. The procedures also allow for the testing of the hypotheses generated.

Statistical profiling: Refers to those forms of offender profiling particularly dependent on aggregated statistical data.

Statute of limitations: the amount of time that the state has in order to bring a prosecution for a crime.

Statutory rape: Sexual intercourse with a person too young to legally give consent.

Statutory: Related to laws produced by the legislature as opposed to common law, for example.

Strain theory: A criminological theory in which it is assumed that social structures may be responsible for crime.

Strategic use of evidence (SUE) technique: A technique for investigative interviewing.

Strict liability: Offences for which there is no requirement of criminal intent (*mens rea*).

Structural equation modelling: A statistical technique which seeks to test different models of the relationships between a number of variables. As such, it can be used in theory development.

Structured interview: A way of describing the typical police interview with a witness (as opposed to the cognitive interview).

Structured trauma writing: *See* Trauma writing.

Sub judice: The matter is under judicial consideration and may not be discussed publicly.

Suggestibility: The characteristic of a person who is easily swayed or influenced by another person such as an interviewer.

Summary offence: In the UK, an offence that can be tried in the lowest courts, i.e. magistrates' courts.

Survival rates: One way of presenting reconviction, recidivism or other data which changes over time. Survival is the rate of persons *not* showing the characteristic in question. So survival rate from reconviction is the number *not* being reconvicted at each point in time.

System variables: Variables over which a researcher or practitioner has control.

T

Tarasoff Decision: An American court decision requiring therapists to deal with threats and risks to third parties from the therapist's clients.

Testosterone: The most common male sex hormone but it is also to be found in females.

Therapeutic community: An organisation for the treatment of mental illness and drug addiction in which the policies and practices of the organisation and the general social atmosphere are part of the curative process.

Tort: This is the law concerned with wrongs and damages caused by one person against another such is libel, slander, negligence and so forth.

Tranquilliser: A drug which has a calming or quietening effect on anxiety.

Trauma: The extreme emotional shock which is the consequence of stressful events.

Trauma writing: Writing about one's own trauma which tends to have therapeutic benefits in itself.

Treatment integrity: This is the extent to which a therapeutic intervention is implemented closely to the original intention or plan.

Trophies: Body parts of or property of a victim sometimes taken by serial killers and others.

U

Ultra vires: The matter is not within a particular court's jurisdiction.

Undeutsch Hypothesis: The idea that language which describes actual experiences has characteristics which are different from those which are imagined. It is the basis for statement validity analysis.

Upward comparison process: The process of making judgements about oneself or one's circumstances by comparison with those more advantaged than oneself.

V

Validity checklist: One of the two components of statement validity analysis.

Validity: Whether something measures what it purports to measure.

Vicarious learning: Learning by observation or imitation of others.

Vicarious reinforcement/learning: Based on observation of other people.

Victim surveys: Surveys of the general population to assess how many have been a victim of crime.

Victimisation: The process of being made a victim.

Victimless crime: A crime with no obvious victims but is more generally perpetrated against society. This might include drug use and graffiti.

Victimology: The branch of criminology devoted to the study of victims.

Video identification: A form of identification parade/line-up in which the witness views video clips of the suspect and others rather than people face to face.

Visionary (serial) killers: Those who kill in response to verbal commands or visions.

Voir dire: In the Anglo-American system, the process of asking questions which help in the decision as to whether the person is suitable to be a member of a jury. The process may be conducted by the judge or by the lawyers or by both in different systems.

Voluntary false confession: A confession made without outside pressures such as the influence of the interviewer.

Voyeurism: The process by which an individual obtains sexual pleasure from observing another person naked, semi-naked or participating in a sexual act.

Vulnerable witness: This refers to a child or any other person suffering a mental, social, intellectual or similar disability which may reduce the quality of their evidence or make the presentation of evidence in court difficult.

W

Weapons effect: In this, an eyewitness focuses dispropor-tionately on the weapons used in a crime in a way which is detrimental to the quality of their memory for other aspects of the crime scene.

Wechsler Adult Intelligence Scale: A well-established measure of intelligence. It is administered to a single person at a time and includes both verbal and non-verbal scales.

White-collar crime: Crimes held to be characteristic of middle-class (white-collar) workers, for example, using the firm's telephone for private calls.

Working memory: A theoretical notion to describe the parts of memory which are actively involved in the processing and putting into storage of things which may pass into long-term memory.

X

XYY chromosome: The outmoded idea that some criminals have an additional male chromosome in their genetic make-up which is partly responsible for their criminality.

Y

Youth Subculture: The idea that there are groups of youngsters who have a somewhat distinct culture which contributes to delinquency.

Z

Zero Tolerance: The policing strategy which requires arrest whenever a crime is committed no matter how trivial an instance it is.

References

A

Aamodt, M.G. (2008) 'Reducing misconceptions and false beliefs in police and criminal psychology' *Criminal Justice and Behavior* **35**, 1231–40.

Aamodt, M.G. and Custer, H. (2006) 'Who can best catch a liar? A meta-analysis of individual differences in detecting deception' *Forensic Examiner* **15** (1), 6–11.

Abdel-Khalek, A. (2004) 'Neither altruistic suicide, nor terrorism but martyrdom: A Muslim perspective' *Archives of Suicide Research* **8**, 99–113.

Abel, G.G., Barlow, D.H., Blanchard, E.B. and Guild, D. (1977) 'The components of rapists' sexual arousal' *Archives of General Psychiatry* **34**, 895–903.

Abel, G.G., Becker, J.V. and Cunningham-Rathner, J. (1984) 'Complications, consent, and cognitions in sex between children and adults' *International Journal of Law and Psychiatry* **7**, 89–103.

Abel, G.G., Becker, J.V., Mittelman, M.S., Cunningham-Rathner, J., Rouleau, J.L. and Murphy, W.D. (1987) 'Self-reported sex crimes on non-incarcerated paraphiliacs'. *Journal of Interpersonal Violence* **2**, 3–25.

Abel, G.G., Mittelman, M., Becker, J.V., Cunningham-Rathner, M.S. and Lucas, L. (1983) 'Characteristics of men who molest young children' Paper presented at the World Congress of Behavior Therapy, Washington, DC.

Abrahams, G. (1954) *The Legal Mind: An Approach to the Dynamics of Advocacy* London: H.F.L. Publishers.

Achenbach, T.M. and Rescorla, L.A. (2003) *Manual for the ASEBA adult forms & profiles* Burlington: University of Vermont, Research Center for Children, Youth, and Families.

Agnew, R. (1992) 'Foundation for a general strain theory of crime and delinquency' *Criminology* **30**, 47–87.

Agnew, R. (1997) 'Stability and change in crime over the life course: A strain theory explanation' in T.P. Thornberry (ed.), *Developmental theories of crime* Brunswick, NJ: Transaction.

Agnew, R. (2001) 'Building on the foundation of general strain theory: Specifying the types of strain most likely to lead to crime and delinquency' *Journal of Research in Crime and Delinquency* **38**, 319–61.

Ainsworth, P.B. (1981) 'Incident perception by British police officers' *Law and Human Behavior*, **5**, 331–6.

Ainsworth, P.B. (1995) *Psychology and Policing in a Changing World* Chichester: John Wiley.

Ainsworth, P.B. (1996) 'Psychological testing and police recruit selection: difficulties and dilemmas' in G. Davies, S. Lloyd-Bostock, M. McMurran and C. Wilson (eds) *Psychology, Law, and Criminal Justice: International Developments in Research and Practice* Berlin: Walter de Gruyter, pp. 579–84.

Ainsworth, P.B. (1998) *Psychology, Law and Eyewitness Testimony* Chichester: Wiley.

Ainsworth, P.B. (2000a) *Psychology and Crime: Myths and Reality* Harlow: Longman.

Ainsworth, P.B. (2000b) 'Psychology and police investigation' in J. McGuire, T. Mason and A. O'Kane (eds) *Behaviour, Crime and Legal Processes* Chichester: John Wiley, pp. 39–63.

Ainsworth, P.B. and Moss, K. (2000) 'Perceptions and misperceptions of crime amongst a sample of British students'. Paper presented at the conference of the European Association of Psychology and Law, Limassol, Cyprus.

Alexy, E., Burgess, A.W., Baker, T. and Smoyak, S. (2005) 'Perceptions of cyberstalking among college students' *Brief Treatment and Crisis Intervention*, 5, 279–89.

Alison, L., Goodwill, A., Almond, L., van den Heuvel, C. and Winter, J. (2010) 'Pragmatic solutions to offender profiling and behavioural investigative advice' *Legal and Criminological Psychology* 15, 115–132.

Alison, L., Smith, M.D. and Morgan, K. (2003) 'Interpreting the accuracy of offender profiles' *Psychology, Crime and Law* 9 (2), 185–95.

Alison, L., Smith, M.D., Eastman, O. and Rainbow, L. (2003) 'Toulmin's philosophy of argument and its relevance to offender profiling' *Psychology, Crime and Law* 9 (2), 173–83.

Allen, J. (2004) 'Worry about crime' in S. Nicholas and A. Walker (eds) *Crime in England and Wales 2002/2003: Supplementary Vol. 2: Crime, Disorder and the Criminal Justice System – Public Attitudes and Perceptions* London: Home Office, pp. 41–54. http://www.homeoffice.gov.uk/rds/pdfs2/hosb0204.pdf

Almerigogna, J., Ost, J., Bull, R. and Akehurst, L. (2008a) 'A state of high anxiety: how non-supportive interviewers can increase the suggestibility of child witnesses' *Applied Cognitive Psychology* 21 (7), 963–74.

Almerigogna, J., Ost, J., Akehurst, L. and Fluck, M. (2008b) 'How interviewers' nonverbal behaviors can affect children's perceptions and susceptibility' *Journal of Experimental Child Psychology* 100 (1), 17–39.

Almond, L., Duggan, L., Shine, J. and Canter, D. (2005) 'Test of the arson action system model in an incarcerated population' *Psychology, Crime and Law* 11 (1), 1–15.

American Psychiatric Association (1987) *Diagnostic and Statistical Manual of Mental Disorders* (3rd edn (revd)) Washington, DC: APA.

American Psychiatric Association (2000) *Diagnostic and Statistical Manual of Mental Disorders* (4th edn) Washington, DC: APA.

Andrews, D.A. (1982) *The level of supervisory inventory (LSI): The first follow-up* Toronto: Ontario Ministry of Correctional Services.

Andrews, D.A. and Bonta, J. (1995) *The Level of Service Inventory – Revised* Toronto: Multi-Health Systems Inc.

Andrews, D.A. and Bonta, J. (2006) *The Psychology of Criminal Conduct* (4th edn) Cincinnati, OH: Anderson Publishing Co.

Andrews, D.A., Bonta, J. and Hoge, R.D. (1990) 'Classification for effective rehabilitation' *Criminal Justice and Behavior* 17 (1), 19–52.

Andrews, D.A., Zinger, I., Hoge, R.D., Bonta, J., Gendreau, P. and Cullen, F.T. (1990) 'Does correctional treatment work? A clinically relevant and psychologically informed meta-analysis' *Criminology* 28, 369–404.

Angermeyer, M.C. and Schulze, B. (2001) 'Reinforcing stereotypes: how the focus on forensic cases in news reporting may influence public attitudes towards the mentally ill' *International Journal of Law and Psychiatry* 24, 469–86.

Appel, A.E. and Holden, G.W. (1998) 'The co-occurrence of spouse and physical child abuse: a review and appraisal' *Journal of Family Psychology* 12 (4), 578–99.

APSAC (1996) 'Practice guidelines: use of anatomical dolls in child sexual abuse assessment' *Pacific Law Review* 28 (1), 78–128.

Araji, S. and Finkelhor, D. (1985) 'Explanations of pedophilia: review of empirical research' *Bulletin of the American Academy of Psychiatry and the Law* 13 (1), 17–37.

Arboleda-Florez, J., Holley, H.L. and Crisanti, A. (1996) *Mental Health and Violence: Proof or Stereotype?* Health Promotion and Programs Branch, Health Canada. http://hwcweb.hwc.ca/hppb/mentalhealth/pubs/mental_illness/index.htm

Arce, R. (1998) 'Empirical studies on jury size' *Expert Evidence* 6, 227–41.

Arce, R., Farina, F., Novo, M. and Seijo, D. (1998) 'In search of causes of hung juries' *Expert Evidence* 6, 1–18.

Arce, R., Farina, F., Vila, C. and Santiago, R. (1996) 'Empirical assessment of the escabinato jury system' *Psychology, Crime and Law* 2, 175–83.

Arce, R., Seijo, D., Farina, F. and Novo, M. (2004) 'Family interaction factor: analysing the effects on personal, social and school inadaptability and delinquent behaviour' Krakow, European Association of Psychology and Law (EAPL) Conference.

Archer, J. (2004) 'Sex differences in aggression in real-world settings: A meta-analytic review' *Review of General Psychology* 8, 291–321.

Arkowitz, S. and Vess, J. (2003) 'An evaluation of the Bumby RAPE and MOLEST scales as measures of cognitive distortions with civilly committed sexual offenders' *Sexual Abuse: A Journal of Research and Treatment* 15 (4), 237–49.

Artz, S. (1998) 'Where have all the school girls gone? Violent girls in the school yard' *Child and Youth Care Forum* **27** (2), 77–109.

Ask, K. and Granhag, P.A. (2005) 'Motivational sources of confirmation bias in criminal investigations: the need for cognitive closure' *Journal of Investigative Psychology and Offender Profiling* **2**, 43–63.

Atran, S. (2003) 'Genesis of suicide terrorism' *Science* **299**, 1534–9.

Attrill, G. (1999) 'Violent offender programmes' in G. Towl, and C. McDougal, (eds), *Issues in Forensic Psychology 1: What do Forensic Psychologists do? Currrent and Future Directions in the Prison and Probation Services*. Leicester: British Psychological Society, pp. 58–61.

Avery-Clark, C.A. and Laws, D.R. (1984) 'Differential erection response patterns of sexual child abusers to stimuli describing activities with children' *Behavior Therapy* **15**, 71–83.

B

Baartman, H.E.M. (1992) 'The credibility of children as witnesses and the social denial of the incestuous abuse of children' in F. Lösel, D. Bender and T. Bliesner (eds) *Psychology and Law: International Perspectives* Berlin: Walter de Gruyter, pp. 345–51.

Bachrach, L.L. (1984) 'Deinstitutionalization and women: assessing the consequences of public policy' *American Psychologist* **39** (10), 1187–92.

Bachrach, L.L. (1989) 'Deinstitutionalization: a semantic analysis' *Journal of Social Issues* **45** (3), 161–72.

Baker, R.R., Lichtenberg, P.A. and Moye, J. (1998) 'A practice guideline for assessment of competence and capacity of the older adult' *Professional Psychology: Research and Practice* **29** (2), 149–54.

Ballard, M.E. and Wiest, J.R. (1996) 'Mortal Kombat™: the effects of violent videogame play on males' hostility and cardiovascular responding' *Journal of Applied Social Psychology* **26** (8), 717–30.

Bandura, A. (1973) *Aggression: A Social Learning Analysis* Englewood Cliffs, NJ: Prentice Hall.

Bandura, A. (1977) *Social Learning Theory* Englewood Cliffs, NJ: Prentice Hall.

Bandura, A. (1983) 'Psychological mechanisms of aggression' in R.G. Green and C.I. Donnerstein (eds) *Aggression, Theoretical and Empirical Reviews Vol. 1: Theoretical and Methodological Issues* New York: Academic Press, pp. 1–40.

Bandura, A. (1986) *Social Foundations of Thought and Action: A Social Cognitive Theory* Englewood Cliffs, NJ: Prentice Hall.

Bandura, A. (1990) 'Mechanisms of moral disengagement' in W. Reich (ed.) *Origins of Terrorism: Psychologies, Ideologies, Theologies, States of Mind* New York: Cambridge University Press, pp. 161–91.

Bandura, A. and Huston, A.C. (1961) 'Identification as a process of incidental learning' *Journal of Abnormal and Social Psychology* **63**, 311–18.

Bandura, A., Ross, D. and Ross, S.A. (1963) 'Imitation of film-mediated aggressive models' *Journal of Abnormal and Social Psychology* **66**, 3–11.

Barbaree, H.E. (1998) 'Denial and minimization among sex offenders: assessment and treatment outcome' *Sex Offender Programming* **3** (4), 1–7.

Barclay, G., Tavares, C. and Siddique, A. (2001) *International Comparisons of Criminal Justice Statistics 1999* London: Home Office Research, Development and Statistics Directorate.

Baron, L. and Straus, M. (1984) 'Sexual stratification, pornography and rape in the United States' in N.M. Malamuth and E. Donnerstein (eds) *Pornography and Sexual Aggression* New York: Academic Press, pp. 185–209.

Baron, L. and Straus, M. (1989) *Four Theories of Rape: A State Level Analysis* New Haven, CT: Yale University Press.

Bartels, J.M., Ryan, J.J., Urban, L.S. and Glass, L.A. (2010) 'Correlations between estimates of state IQ and FBI crime statistics' *Personality and Individual Differences* **48**, 579–83.

Bartlett, D. and Memon, A. (1995) 'Advocacy' in R. Bull and D. Carson (eds) *Handbook of Psychology in Legal Contexts* Chichester: John Wiley, pp. 543–54.

Bartol, C.R. and Bartol, A.M. (1999) 'History of forensic psychology' in A.K. Hess and I.B. Weiner (eds) *Handbook of Forensic Psychology* (2nd edn) London: John Wiley & Sons, pp. 3–23.

Barton, J., Vrij, A. and Bull, R. (2000a) 'High speed driving: police use of lethal force during simulated incidents' *Legal and Criminological Psychology* **5**, 107–21.

Barton, J., Vrij, A. and Bull, R. (2000b) 'The influence of field dependence on excitation transfer by police officers during armed confrontation' in A. Czerederecka, T. Jaskiewicz-Obdzinska and J. Wojcikiewicz (eds) *Forensic Psychology and Law: Traditional Questions and New Ideas* Krakow: Institute of Forensic Research Publishers, pp. 282–6.

Bateman, A.L. and Salfati, C.G. (2007) 'An examination of behavioral consistency using individual behaviors or groups of behaviors in serial homicide' *Behavioral Sciences and the Law* 25 (4), 527–44.

Bates, A. (1996) 'The origins, development and effect on subsequent behaviour of deviant sexual fantasies in sexually violent adult men.' Unpublished manuscript, Thames Valley Project, 17 Park Road, Didcot, OX11 8QL, UK.

Baxter, D.J., Barbaree, H.E. and Marshall, W.L. (1986) 'Sexual responses to consenting and forced sex in a large sample of rapists and non-rapists' *Behavioral Research and Therapy* 24, 513–20.

Baxter, D.J., Marshall, W.L., Barbaree, H.E., Davidson, P.R. and Malcolm, P.B. (1984) 'Deviant sexual behaviour' *Criminal Justice and Behavior* 11, 477–501.

Baxter, J.S. and Bain, S.A. (2002) 'Faking interrogative suggestibility: the truth machine' *Legal and Criminological Psychology* 7 (2), 219–25.

Bazargan, M. (1994) 'The effects of health, environment, and sociopsychological variables on fear of crime and its consequences among urban black elderly individuals' *International Journal of Ageing and Human Development* 38 (2), 99–115.

BBC News (2005) 'Sex offenders may face lie detector tests'. http://news.bbc.co.uk/1/hi/uk/2208779.stm

Beck, A.T. (2002) 'Prisoners of hate' *Behavior Research and Therapy* 40 (3), 209–16.

Beck, A.T., Steer, R.A., & Ranieri, W.F. (1988) 'Scale for Suicidal Ideation: Psychometric properties of a self-report version' *Journal of Clinical Psychology*, 44, 499–505.

Beck, J.C. (1995) 'Forensic psychiatry in Britain' *Bulletin of the American Academy of Psychiatry and the Law* 23 (2), 249–60.

Beech, A., Fisher, D. and Beckett, R. (1998) *Step 3: An Evaluation of the Prison Sex Offender Treatment Programme.* London: Home Office.

Beech, A., Fisher, D. and Beckett, R. (1999) *STEP 3: An Evaluation of the Prison Sex Offender Treatment Programme.* A report for the Home Office by the STEP team, November 1998. London: Home Office Information Publications Group, Research Development Statistics Directorate.

Begic, D., and Begic, N.J. (2001) 'Aggressive behaviour in combat veterans with posttraumatic stress disorder' *Military Medicine* 166, 671–6.

Bègue, L. and Roche, S. (2005) 'Birth order and youth delinquent behaviour testing the differential parental control hypothesis in a French representative sample' *Psychology, Crime & Law* 11 (1), 75–85.

Behrman, B.W. and Davey, S.L. (2001) 'Eyewitness identification in actual criminal cases: An archival analysis' *Law and Human Behavior* 25 (5), 475–91.

Beier, K.M., Ahlers, C.J., Goecker, D., Neutze, J., Mundt, I.A., Hupp, E. and Schaefer, G.A. (2009) 'Can pedophiles be reached for primary prevention of child sexual abuse? First results of the Berlin Prevention Project Dunkelfeld' *Journal of Forensic Psychiatry & Psychology* 20 (6), 851–67.

Bekerian, D. and Dennett, J.L. (1992) 'The truth in content analyses of a child's testimony' in F. Lösel, D. Bender and T. Bliesner (eds) *Psychology and Law: International Perspectives* Berlin: Walter de Gruyter, pp. 335–44.

Bell, S. (1988) *When Salem Came to the Boro.* London: Pan.

Bender, D., Bliesener, T. and Lösel, F. (1996) 'Deviance or resilience? A longitudinal study of adolescents in residential care' in G. Davies, S. Lloyd-Bostock, M. McMurran and C. Wilson (eds) *Psychology, Law and Criminal Justice: International Developments in Research and Practice* Berlin: Walter de Gruyter, pp. 409–23.

Bennell, C. and Canter, D.V. (2002) 'Linking commercial burglaries by *modus operandi*: tests using regression and ROC analysis' *Science & Justice* 42, 153–64.

Bennell, C. and Jones, N. (2005) 'Between a ROC and a hard place: a method for linking serial burglaries by *modus operandi*' *Journal of Investigative Psychology and Offender Profiling* 2, 23–41.

Bennett, T., Holloway, K. and Farrington, D. (2008) 'The statistical association between drug misuse and crime: A meta-analysis' *Aggression and Violent Behavior* 13 (2), 107–18.

Bennett, W.L. and Feldman, M.S. (1981) *Reconstructing Reality in the Courtroom* London: Tavistock Publications.

Ben-Shakhar, G. (2008) 'The case against the use of polygraph examinations to monitor post-conviction sex offenders' *Legal and Criminological Psychology* 13, 191–207.

Benton, T.R., Ross, D.F., Bradshaw, E., Thomas, W.N. and Bradshaw, G.S. (2006) 'Eyewitness memory is still not common sense: comparing jurors, judges and law enforcement to eyewitness experts' *Applied Cognitive Psychology* 20, 115–29.

Berger, M.A. (2008) 'Eyewitness testimony and false confession' in *Beyond Common Sense: Psychological Science in the Courtroom* Oxford: Blackwell, 315–26.

Berkowitz, L. and Rawlings, E. (1963) 'Effects of film violence on inhibitions against sub-sequent aggression' *Journal of Abnormal and Social Psychology* 66, 405–12.

Berkowitz, L., Corwin, R. and Heironimus, M. (1963) 'Film violence and subsequent aggressive tendencies' *Public Opinion Quarterly* 27, 217–29.

Berliner, L. and Conte, J.R. (1993) 'Sexual abuse evaluations: conceptual and empirical obstacles' *Child Abuse and Neglect* 17, 111–25.

Bernasco, W. (2006) 'Co-offending and the choice of target areas in burglary' *Journal of Investigative Psychology and Offender Profiling* 3, 139–55.

Bernet, W. (1997) 'Case study: allegations of abuse created in a single interview' *Journal of the American Academy of Child and Adolescent Psychiatry* 36 (7), 966–70.

Berry, M.J., Robinson, C.A. and Bailey, J. (1999) 'The use of hypnosis to recover evidence from convicted offenders: issues and implications'. Paper presented at International Psychology and Law Conference, University College, Dublin, 6–9 July.

Bibas, S. (2004) 'Plea bargaining outside the shadow of a trial' *Harvard Law Review* 117 (8), 2464–546.

Biro, M., Vuckovic, N. and Duric, V. (1992) 'Towards a typology of homicides on the basis of personality' *British Journal of Criminology*, 32 (3) 361–71.

Bjorkqvist, K. (1994) 'Sex differences in physical, verbal, and indirect aggression: a review of recent research' *Sex Roles* 30 (3/4), 177–88.

Bjorkqvist, K. (1997) 'Learning aggression from models: from a social learning toward a cognitive theory of modeling' in S. Feshbach and J. Zagodzka (eds) *Aggression: Biological, Developmental, and Social Perspectives* New York: Plenum, pp. 69–81.

Bjorkqvist, K. and Niemela, P. (1992) 'New trends in the study of female aggression' in K. Bjorkqvist and P. Niemela (eds) *Of Mice and Women: Aspects of Female Aggression* San Diego: Academic Press, pp. 3–17.

Bjorkqvist, K., Osterman, K. and Kaukiainen, A. (1992) 'The development of direct and indirect aggressive strategies in males and females' in K. Bjorkqvist and P. Niemela (eds) *Of Mice and Women: Aspects of Female Aggression* San Diego: Academic Press, pp. 51–64.

Blaauw, E., Roesch, R. and Kerkhof, A. (2000) 'Mental disorders in European prison systems' *International Journal of Law and Psychiatry* 23 (5–6), 649–63.

Blackburn, R. (1971) 'Personality types among abnormal homicides' *British Journal of Criminology* 11, 14–31.

Blackburn, R. (1984) 'The person and dangerousness' in D.J. Muller, D.E. Blackman and A.J. Chapman (eds) *Psychology and Law* Chichester: John Wiley, pp. 101–11.

Blackburn, R. (1993) *The Psychology of Criminal Conduct* Chichester: John Wiley.

Blackburn, R. (1995a) 'Psychopaths: are they bad or mad?' in N.K. Clark and G.M. Stephenson (eds) *Issues in Criminological and Legal Psychology 22: Criminal Behaviour: Perceptions, Attributions, and Rationality* Leicester: British Psychological Society, pp. 97–103.

Blackburn, R. (1995b) 'Violence' in R. Bull and D. Carson (eds) *Handbook of Psychology in Legal Contexts* Chichester: John Wiley, pp. 357–73.

Blackburn, R. (1996) 'What is forensic psychology?' *Legal and Criminological Psychology*, 1 (1), 3–16.

Blackburn, R. (2000) 'Risk assessment and prediction' in J. McGuire, T. Mason and A. O'Kane (eds) *Behaviour, Crime and Legal Processes: A Guide for Forensic Practitioners* Chichester: John Wiley, pp. 177–204.

Blackburn, R. (2007) 'Personality disorder and psychopathy: conceptual and empirical integration' *Psychology, Crime and Law* 13 (1), 7–18.

Blasi, A. (1980) 'Bridging moral cognition and action: A critical review of the literature' *Psychological Bulletin* 88, 1–45.

Blasi, A. (1983) 'Moral cognition and moral action: a theoretic perspective' *Developmental Review* 3, 179–210.

Blau, J.R. and Blau, P.M. (1982) 'The cost of inequality: Metropolitan structure and violent crime' *American Sociological Review* 47, 114–129.

Blau, T.H. (1994) *Psychological Services for Law Enforcement* New York: John Wiley.

Bliesener, T. and Lösel, F. (1992) 'Resilience in juveniles with high risk of delinquency' in F. Lösel, D. Bender and T. Bliesener (eds) *Psychology and the Law: International Perspectives* Berlin: Walter de Gruyter, pp. 62–75.

Blud, L. (1999) 'Cognitive skills programmes' *Issues in Forensic Psychology* 1, 49–52.

Blumenthal, S., Gudjonsson, G. and Burns, J. (1999) 'Cognitive distortions and blame attribution in sex offenders against adults and children' *Child Abuse and Neglect* 23, 129–48.

Bond, G.D. (2008) 'Deception Detection Expertise' *Law and Human Behavior* 32, 339–51.

Bonnie, R.J. and Grisso, T. (2000) 'Adjudicative competence and youthful offenders' in R.G. Schwartz and T. Grisso (eds) *Youth on Trial: A Developmental Perspective on Juvenile Justice* Chicago, IL: University of Chicago Press, pp. 73–103.

Boon, J. and Baxter, J.S. (2004) 'Minimising extraneous interviewer based interrogative suggestibility' *Legal and Criminological Psychology* **9** (2), 229–38.

Borg, I. and Shye, S. (1995) *Facet Theory: Form and Content* Thousand Oaks, CA: Sage.

Bornstein, B.H., Liebel, L.M. and Scarberry, N.C. (1998) 'Repeating testing in eyewitness memory: A means to improve recall of a negative emotional event'. *Applied Cognitive Psychology*, **12**, 119–31.

Borum, R. (2004) *Psychology of Terrorism* Tampa: University of South Florida.

Bothwell, R.K., Deffenbacher, K.A. and Brigham, J.C. (1987) 'Correlation of eyewitness accuracy and confidence: optimality hypothesis revisited' *Journal of Applied Psychology* **72**, 691–5.

Bowlby, J. (1944) 'Forty-four juvenile thieves: their characteristics and home-life' *International Journal of Psychoanalysis* **25**, 19–53.

Bowlby, J. (1951) *Maternal Care and Mental Health* Geneva: World Health Organization.

Bowlby, J. (1973) *Attachment and Loss: II. Separation Anxiety and Anger* London: Hogarth Press.

Bowlby, J. (1980) *Attachment and Loss: III. Loss, Sadness and Depression* New York: Basic Books.

Box, S. (1981) *Deviance, reality, and society* New York: Holt, Rinehart and Winston.

Boxer, P., Middlemass, K. and Delorenzo, T. (2009) 'Exposure to violent crime during incarceration: Effects on psychological adjustment following release' *Criminal Justice and Behavior* **36** (8), 793–807.

Brace, N.A., Pike, G.E., Allen, P. and Kemp, R.I. (2006) 'Identifying composites of famous faces: investigating memory, language and system issues' *Psychology, Crime and Law* **12** (4), 351–66.

Brace, N.A., Pike, G.E., Kemp, R.I. and Turner, J. (2009) 'Eye-witness identification procedures and stress: a comparison of live and video identification parades' *International Journal of Police Science and Management*, **11** (2), 183–92.

Bradley, A.R. and Wood, J.N. (1996) 'How do children tell? The disclosure process in child sexual abuse' *Child Abuse and Neglect* **9**, 881–91.

Brand, S. and Price, R. (2001) 'The social and economic cost of crime'. Home Office Research Study 217, http://www.homeoffice.gov.uk/rds/pdfs/hors217.pdf

Brennan, M. (1994) 'Cross-examining children in criminal courts: child welfare under attack' in J. Gibbons (ed.) *Language and the Law* London: Longman, pp. 199–216.

Brennan, M. and Brennan, R. (1988) *Stranger Language* Wagga Wagga, New South Wales, Australia: Riverina Murry Institute of Higher Education.

Brewer, N. and Palmer, M.A. (2010) 'Eyewitness identification tests' *Legal and Criminological Psychology* **15**, 77–96.

Brewin, C.R. and Holmes, E.A. (2003) 'Psychological theories of post-traumatic stress disorder' *Clinical Psychology Review* **23**, 339–76.

Brewin, C.R., Andrews, B. and Rose, S. (2000) 'Fear, helplessness and horror in post-traumatic stress disorder: investigating DSM-IV criterion A2 in victims of violent crime' *Journal of Traumatic Stress* **13** (3), 499–509.

Brewin, C.R., Andrews, B. and Valentine, J.D. (2000) 'Meta-analysis of risk factors for post-traumatic stress disorder in trauma-exposed adults' *Journal of Consulting and Clinical Psychology* **68** (5), 748–66.

Brewin, C.R., Dalgleish, T. and Joseph, S. (1996) 'A dual representation theory of post-traumatic stress disorder' *Psychological Review* **103** (4), 670–86.

British Psychological Society (2007/8) Diploma in Forensic Psychology: Candidates Handbook. http://www.bps.org.uk/downloadfile.cfm?file_uuid=984CD7F0-1143-DFD0-7E65-2850080DE7AF&ext=pdf. Accessed 21 April 2011.

British Psychological Society (2010) *Psychologists as Expert Witnesses: Guidelines and Procedures for England and Wales* (3rd edn) http://www.bps.org.uk/document-download-area/document-download$.cfm?file_uuid=FE6DDFB7-D213-5A58-1EA1-F984AF4F7A3B&ext=pdf. Accessed 21 April 2011.

British Psychological Society (2011) *Qualification in Forensic Psychology (Stage 2) Candidate Handbook* http://www.bps.org.uk/document-download-area/document-download$.cfm?file_uuid=5AF45F61-F6D3-3989-C081-642F2A893E9D&ext=pdf. Accessed 21 April 2011.

British Psychological Society Working Party (2004) *A Review of the Current Scientific Status and Fields of Application of Polygraphic Deception Detection: Final Report* (6 October 2004) Leicester: British Psychological Society.

Broken Spirits Network (2004) Post-traumatic stress disorder. http://www.brokenspirits.com/information/ptsd.asp

Brookes, D. (2003) 'Investigating child abuse on-line: the interactive approach' in A. MacVean and P. Spindler (eds) *Policing Paedophiles on the Internet* Bristol: New Police Bookshop, pp. 49–60.

Brown, B. (1995) *CCTV in Town Centres: Three Case Studies* Crime Detection and Prevention Series Paper 68. London: Home Office.

Brown, C.M., Traverso, G. and Fedoroff, J.P. (1996) 'Masturbation prohibition in sex offenders: a crossover study' *Archives of Sexual Behavior* 25 (4), 397–408.

Brown, R. and Kulik, J. (1977) 'Flashbulb memories' *Cognition* 5, 73–99.

Brown, S. (1999) 'Public attitudes to the treatment of sex offenders' *Legal and Criminological Psychology* 4 (2), 239–5.

Browne, D. (1999) 'From the frying pan to the fire: exploring the role of foster care in the development of criminal behaviour'. Paper presented to the Joint International Conference, Dublin.

Browne, D. (2000) 'Foster care and forensic psychology' *Forensic Update* 61, 11–14.

Browne, K.D. (1999) 'Violence in the media causes crime: myth or reality?' Unpublished inaugural lecture, University of Birmingham, 3 June 1999.

Browne, K.D. and Pennell, A.E. (1998) *The Effects of Video Violence on Young Offenders*. Home Office Research and Statistics Directorate, Research Findings No. 65. London: Home Office.

Bruck, M. and Ceci, S.J. (1997) 'The suggestibility of young children' *Current Directions in Psychological Science* 6 (3), 75–9.

Bruck, M., Ceci, S.K., Francoeur, E. and Barr, R. (1995) ' "I hardly cried when I got shot!" Influencing children's reports about a visit to their pediatrician' *Child Development* 66, 193–208.

Brugman, D. and Aleva, E. (2004) 'Developmental delay or regression in moral reasoning by juvenile delinquents?' *Journal of Moral Education* 33, 321–38.

Brusten, C., Stams, G.S. and Gibbs, J.C. (2007) 'Commentary: Missing the mark' *British Journal of Developmental Psychology* 25, 185–9.

Buck, J.A., Warren, A.R., Betman, S.I. and Brigham, J.C. (2002) 'Age differences in criterion-based content analysis scores in typical child sexual abuse interview' *Applied Developmental Psychology* 23, 267–83.

Budd, T., Sharp, C. and Mayhew, P. (2005) 'Offending in England and Wales: first results from the 2003 Crime and Justice Survey' *Findings 244*, Home Office.

Bull, R. (1984) 'Psychology's contribution to policing' in D.J. Muller, D.E. Blackman and A.J. Chapman (eds) *Psychology and Law* Chichester: John Wiley, pp. 409–23.

Bull, R. and Reid, R.L. (1975) 'Police officers' recall of information' *Journal of Occupational Psychology* 48, 73–8.

Bumby, K.T. (1996) 'Assessing the cognitive distortions of child molesters and rapists: Development and validation of the MOLEST and RAPE scales' *Sexual Abuse: A Journal of Research and Treatment* 8 (1), 37–54.

Bureau of Justice (2001a) Characteristics of crime. http://www.ojp.usdoj.gov/bjs/cvict_c.htm#findings/

Bureau of Justice (2001b) The odds of being a crime victim. http://nsi.org/Tips/odds.htm

Bureau of Justice (2001c) Drug and crime facts, 1994. http://www.ojp.usdoj.gov/bjs/abstract/dcfacts.htm

Bureau of Justice (2001d) Intimate homicide. http://www.ojp.usdoj.gov/bjs/homicide/intimates.htm

Bureau of Justice (2004) Criminal offenders statistics. http://www.ojp.usdoj.gov/bjs/crimoff.htm#lifetime

Bureau of Justice (2007) Homicide trends in the U.S.: Long term trends and patterns. http://www.ojp.usdoj.gov/bjs/homicide/hmrt.htm. Accessed 22 January 2008.

Bureau of Justice Statistics (2003) *Reporting Crime to the Police, 1992–2000* Washington, DC: US Department of Justice.

Bureau of Justice Statistics (2011) Violent Crime. http://bjs.ojp.usdoj.gov/index.cfm?ty=tp&tid=31 Accessed 21 February 2011.

Burgess, A.W., Hazelwood, R.R., Rokous, F.E., Hartman, C.R. and Burgess, A.G. (1988) 'Serial rapists and their victims: reenactment and repetition' *Human Sexual Aggression: Current Perspectives* 528, August 12, 277–95.

Burgess, E.W. (ed.) (1928) 'Factors determining success or failure on parole. Springfield: Illinois State Board of Parole' *Law and Human Behavior* (2007) 31: 449–62.

Burt, M. (1980) 'Cultural myths and support for rape' *Journal of Personality and Social Psychology* 38, 217–30.

Burton, A.M., Wilson, S., Cowan, M. and Bruce, V. (1999) 'Face recognition in poor quality video: evidence from security surveillance' *Psychological Science* 10, 243–8.

Busey, T.A. and Loftus, G.R. (2007) 'Cognitive science and the law' *Trends in Cognitive Science* 11 (3), 111–17.

Buss, A.H., and Perry, M. (1992) 'The aggression questionnaire' *Journal of Personality and Social Psychology* 63, 452–9.

Butler-Sloss, E. (1988) *Report of the Inquiry into Child Abuse in Cleveland 1987* London: Her Majesty's Stationery Office, Cm 412.

C

Caldwell, M. (2007) 'Sexual offense adjudication and recidivism among juvenile offenders' *Sexual Abuse: A Journal of Research and Treatment* 19, 107–13.

Caldwell, M.F. and Dickinson, C. (2009) 'Sex offender registration and recidivism risk in juvenile sexual offenders' *Behavioral Sciences and the Law* 27, 941–56.

Calof, D.L. (1993) 'A conversation with Pamela Freyd, Ph.D. Co-Founder and Executive Director, False Memory Syndrome Foundation, Inc., Part I' in *Treating Abuse Today*, Vol. III, No. 3. http://idealist.com/facts/v3n3-pfreyd.shtml. Accessed 12 July 2001.

Candel, I., Merckelbach, H., Loyen, S. and Reyskens, H. (2005) ' "I hit the shift key and then the computer crashed": Children and false admissions' *Personality and Individual Differences* 38, 1381–7.

Cann, J., Friendship, C. and Gozna, L. (2007) 'Assessing crossover in a sample of sexual offenders with multiple victims' *Legal and Criminological Psychology* 12, 149–63.

Canter, D.V. (1983) 'The potential of facet theory for applied social psychology' *Quality and Quantity* 17, 35–67.

Canter, D.V. (1994) *Criminal Shadows* London: HarperCollins.

Canter, D.V. (2004) 'Offender profiling and investigative psychology' *Journal of Investigative Psychology and Offender Profiling* 1, 1–15.

Canter, D.V. and Wentink, N. (2004) 'An empirical test of Holmes and Holmes's serial murder typology' *Criminal Justice and Behavior* 31 (4), 489–515.

Canter, D.V., Bennell, C., Alison, L.J. and Reddy, S. (2003) 'Differentiating sex offences: a behaviorally based thematic classification of stranger rapes' *Behavioral Sciences and the Law* 21, 157–74.

Carter, C.A., Bottom, B.L. and Levine, M. (1996) 'Linguistic and socioemotional influences on the accuracy of children's reports' *Law and Human Behavior* 20, 335–58.

Cauffman, E., Piquero, A.R., Kimonis, E., Steinberg, L., Chassin, L. and Fagan, J. (2007) 'Legal, individual, and environmental predictors of court disposition in a sample of serious adolescent offenders' *Law and Human Behavior* 31, 519–35.

Ceci, S.J. and Bruck, M. (1993) 'Suggestibility and the child witness: a historical review and synthesis' *Psychological Bulletin* 113 (3), 403–39.

Ceci, S.J., Loftus, E.W., Leichtman, M. and Bruck, M. (1994) 'The role of source misattributions in the creation of false beliefs among preschoolers' *International Journal of Clinical and Experimental Hypnosis* 62, 304–20.

Cécile, M. and Born, M. (2009) 'Intervention in juvenile delinquency: Danger of iatrogenic effects?' *Children and Youth Services Review* 31 (2009) 1217–221.

Cederborg, A.-C. (1999) 'The construction of children's credibility in judgements of child sexual abuse' *Acta Sociologica* 42, 147–58.

Centerwall, B.S. (1989) 'Exposure to television as a cause of violence' *Public Communication and Behavior* 2, 1–58.

Centerwall, B.S. (1993) 'Television and violent crime' *Public Interest* 111, 56–71.

Chen, C.-A. and Howitt, D. (2007) 'Different crime types and moral reasoning development in young offenders compared with non-offender controls' *Psychology, Crime and Law* 13 (4), 405–16.

Chermak, S.M. (1995) *Victims in the News: Crime and the American News Media* Boulder, CO: Westview.

Cherryman, J., Bull, R. and Vrij, A. (2000) 'How police officers view confessions: is there still a confession culture?' European Conference on Psychology and Law, Cyprus, March 2000.

Christensen, J., Schmidt, K. and Henderson, J. (1982) 'The selling of the police: media, ideology and crime control' *Contemporary Crises* 6, 227–39.

Christianson, S.-A., Karlsson, I. and Persson, L.G.W. (1998) 'Police personnel as eyewitnesses to a violent crime' *Legal and Criminological Psychology* 3, 59–72.

Clancy, S.A., Schacter, D.L., McNally, R.J. and Pitman, R.K. (2000) 'False recognition in women reporting recovered memories of sexual abuse' *Psychological Science* 11, 26–31.

Clark, D. (1999) 'Risk assessment in prisons and probation' *Forensic Update* 1, 15–18.

Clark, J. (2004) 'Crime, fears and phobias' *Psychiatry, Psychology and Law* 11 (1), 87–95.

Clarke, Ronald V. and Cornish, D.B. (1985) 'Modelling offenders' decisions: a framework for policy and research' in M. Tonry and N. Morris (eds) *Crime and Justice* Vol. 6. Chicago: University of Chicago Press.

Cleary, S. (2004) *Sex offenders and self-control: Explaining sexual violence* New York: LFB Scholarly Publishing LLC.

Cleckley, H. (1976) *The mask of sanity: An attempt to clarify some issues about the so called psychopathic personality* (5th edn) London St. Louis: Mosby.

Clifford, B.R. (1995) 'Psychology's premises, methods and values' in R. Bull and D. Carson (eds) *Handbook* of *Psychology in Legal Contexts* Chichester: John Wiley, pp. 13–28.

Clifford, B.R. and Richards, V.J. (1977) 'Comparison of recall by policemen and civilians under conditions of long and short durations of exposure' *Perceptual and Motor Skills* 45, 503–12.

Clifford, S.R. (1976) 'Police as eyewitnesses' *New Society* 22, 176–7.

Cloninger, C.R., Christiansen, K.O., Reich, T. and Gottesman, I.I. (1978) 'Implications of sex differences in the prevalence of antisocial personality, alcoholism and criminality for familial transmission' *Archives of General Psychiatry* 35, 941–51.

Cloward, R.A. and Ohlin, L.E. (1960) *Delinquency and opportunities. A theory of delinquent gangs* Glencoe, IL: Free Press.

Coates, L., Bavelas, J.B. and Gibson, J. (1994) 'Anomalous language in sexual assault trial judgements' *Discourse and Society* 5 (2), 189–206.

Coates, R.B., Umbreit, M.S. and Vos, B. (2001) 'The impact of victim-offender mediation: Two decades of research' *Federal Probation: A Journal of Correctional Philosophy and Practice* (**December**) 29–35.

Cohen, S. (1972) *Folk Devils and Moral Panics* London: McGibbon and Kee.

Cohen, S. (1980) *Folk Devils and Moral Panics* Oxford: Basil Blackwell.

Cole, S.A. (2009) 'Cultural Consequences of Miscarriages of Justice' *Behavioral Sciences and the Law* 27, 431–49.

Coleman, C. and Norris, C. (2000) *Introducing Criminology* Cullompton, Devon: Willan Publishing.

Coleman, H. (1997) 'Gaps and silences: the culture and adolescent sex offenders' *Journal of Child and Youth Care* 11 (1), 1–13.

Coles, E.M. (2004) 'Psychological support for the concept of psycholegal competencies' *International Journal of Law and Psychiatry* 27, 223–32.

Coles, E.M. and Veiel, H.O.F. (2001) 'Expert testimony and pseudoscience: how mental health professionals are taking over the courtroom' *International Journal of Law and Psychiatry* 24, 607–25.

Collett, M.E. and Kovera, M.B. (2003) 'The effects of British and American trial procedures on the quality of juror decision-making' *Law and Human Behavior* 27 (4), 403–22.

Collins, J.J. and Bailey, S.L. (1990) 'Traumatic stress disorder and violent behaviour' *Journal of Traumatic Stress* 3 (2), 203–20.

Colvin, M. (1993) *Negotiated Justice: A Closer Look at the Implications of Plea Bargains* London: Justice.

Condron, M.K. and Nutter, D.E. (1988) 'A preliminary examination of the pornography experience of sex offenders, paraphiliac sexual dysfunction and controls' *Journal of Sex and Marital Therapy* 14 (4), 285–98.

Connors, E., Lundregan, T., Miller, N. and McEwen, T. (1996) *Convicted by Juries, Exonerated by Science: Case Studies in the Use of DNA Evidence to Establish Innocence after Trial* Washington, DC: National Institute of Justice Research Study.

Cooke, D.J. and Michie, C. (2001) 'Refining the construct of psychopath: Towards a hierarchical model' *Psychological Assessment* 13 (2), 171–88.

Cooke, D.J. and Philip, L. (1998) 'Comprehending the Scottish caution: do offenders understand their right to remain silent?' *Legal and Criminological Psychology* 3, 13–27.

Cooper, B.S., Griesel, D. and Yuille, J.C. (2008) 'Clinical-forensic risk assessment: the past and current state of affairs' *Journal of Forensic Psychology Practice* 7: 4, 1–63.

Cooper, S. (2005) 'Modifying sexual fantasies using behaviour therapy: a case study' *Forensic Update* 80, 17–22.

Cooper, V.G. and Zapf, P.A. (2003) 'Predictor variables in competency to stand trial decisions' *Law and Human Behavior* 27 (4), 423–36.

Cornish, D. and Clarke, R.V.G. (eds) (1986) *The Reasoning Criminal* New York: Springer-Verlag.

Correll, J., Park, B., Judd, C.M. and Wittenbrink, B.W. (2002) 'The police officers dilemma: using ethnicity to disambiguate potentially threatening individuals' *Journal of Personality and Social Psychology* 83, 1314–29.

Corwin, D. and Olafson, E. (1997) 'Videotaped discovery of a reportedly unrecallable memory of child sexual abuse: Comparison with a childhood interview videotaped 11 years before' *Child Maltreatment* 2, 91–112.

Coulthard, M. (1994) 'Powerful evidence for the defence: an exercise in forensic discourse analysis' in J. Gibbons (ed.) *Language and the Law* London: Longman, pp. 414–17.

Coulthard, M. (1999) 'Forensic application of linguistic analysis' in D. Canter and L. Alison (eds) *Interviewing and Deception* Aldershot: Ashgate, pp. 107–25.

Court, J.H. (1977) 'Pornography and sex-crimes: a re-evaluation in the light of recent trends around the world' *International Journal of Criminality and Penology* 5, 129–57.

Court, J.H. (1984) 'Sex and violence: a ripple effect' in N.M. Malamuth and E. Donnerstein (eds) *Pornography and Sexual Aggression* Orlando, FL: Academic Press, 143–72.

Cox, V.C., Paulus, P.B. and McCain, G. (1984) 'Prison crowding research. The relevance for prison housing standards and a general approach regarding crowding phenomena' *American Psychologist* 39 (100), 1148–60.

Craissati, J. and McClurg, G. (1997) 'The Challenge Project: a treatment program evaluation for perpetrators of child sexual abuse' *Child Abuse and Neglect* 21 (7), 637–48.

Cramer, D. and Howitt, D. (1998) 'Romantic love and the psychology of sexual behaviour: open and closed secrets' in V.C. de Munck (ed.) *Romantic Love and Sexual Behaviour: Perspectives from the Social Sciences* Westport, CT: Praeger, pp. 113–32.

Crego, J. and Alison, L. (2004) 'Control and legacy as functions of perceived criticality in major incidents' *Journal of Investigative Psychology and Offender Profiling* 1, 207–25.

Crenshaw, M. (1986) 'The psychology of political terrorism' in M.G. Hermann (ed.) *Political Psychology: Contemporary Problems and Issues* London: Jossey-Bass, pp. 379–413.

Crick, N.R. (1997) 'Engagement in gender normative versus non-normative forms of aggression: links to social-psychological adjustment' *Developmental Psychology* 33 (4), 610–17.

Crick, N.R. and Bigbee, M.A. (1998) 'Relational and overt forms of peer victimization: a multi-informant approach' *Journal of Consulting and Clinical Psychology* 66 (2), 337–47.

Crick, N.R., Casas, J.F. and Mosher, M. (1997) 'Relational and overt aggression in preschool' *Developmental Psychology* 33 (4), 579–88.

Crits-Cristoph, P., Carroll, K., Perry, K., Luborsky, L., McLellan, A.T., Woody, G.E., Thompson, L., Gallagher, D. and Zitrin, C. (1991) 'Meta-analysis of therapist effects in psychotherapy outcome studies' *Psychotherapy Research* 1, 81–91.

Croll, P. (1974) 'The deviant image'. Paper presented at British Sociological Association Mass Communication Study Group.

Crombag, H.F.M., Wagenaar, W.A. and Van Kopen, P.J. (1996) 'Crashing memories and the problem of source monitoring' *Applied Cognitive Psychology* 10, 95–104.

Crown Prosecution Service (2011) The Court Case. http://www.cps.gov.uk/victims_witnesses/going_to_court/court_case.html. Accessed 23 March 2011.

Cullen, F.T., Gendreau, P., Jarjoura, G.R. and Wright, J.P. (1997) 'Crime and the bell curve: lessons from intelligent criminology' *Crime and Delinquency* 3 (4), 387–411.

Cumberbatch, G. and Howitt, D. (1989) *A Measure of Uncertainty* London: Broadcasting Standards Council/John Libbey.

Curtis, G.C. (1963) 'Violence breeds violence – perhaps?' *American Journal of Psychiatry* 120, 386.

Cutler, B.L. and Penrod, S.D. (1989) 'Forensically relevant moderators of the relation between eyewitness identification accuracy and confidence' *Journal of Applied Psychology* 74, 650–3.

Czerederecka, A. and Jaskiewicz-Obydzinska, T. (1996) 'The factors neutralizing developmental disorders in children from broken families' in G. Davies, S. Lloyd-Bostock, M. McMurran and C. Wilson (eds) *Psychology, Law and Criminal Justice: International Developments in Research and Practice* Berlin: Walter de Gruyter, pp. 240–7.

D

Dabbs, J.M., Alford, E.C. and Fielden, J.A. (1998) 'Trial lawyers and testosterone: blue-collar talent in a white-collar world' *Journal of Applied Social Psychology* 28 (1), 84–9.

Dabney, D.A., Dugan, L., Topalli, V. and Hollinger, R.C. (2006) 'The impact of implicit stereotyping on offender profiling: unexpected results from an observational study of shoplifting' *Criminal Justice and Behavior* 33 (5), 646–74.

Daffern, M., Howells, K., Mannion, A. and Tonki, M. (2009) 'A test of methodology intended to assist detection of aggressive offence paralleling behaviour within secure settings' *Legal and Criminological Psychology* 14, 213–26.

Dahle, K.-P. (1999) 'Serious violent crime and offending trajectories in the course of life: an empirical lifespan development of criminal careers'. Paper presented at joint meeting of American Psychology-Law Society and European Association of Psychology and Law, Dublin.

Daily Telegraph (2004) 'Sex offenders register grows by 15 per cent' 28 July 2004. http://www.telegraph.co.uk/news/main.jhtml?xml=/news/2004/07/28/uoffend.xml&sSheet=/portal/2004/07/28/ixportaltop.html

Dale, A., Davies, A. and Wei, L. (1997) 'Developing a typology of rapists' speech' *Journal of Pragmatics* 27, 653–69.

Daleiden, E.L., Kaufman, K.L., Hilliker, D.R. and O'Neil, J.N. (1998) 'The sexual histories and fantasies of youthful males: a comparison of sexual offending, nonsexual offending, and nonoffending groups' *Sexual Abuse: A Journal of Research and Treatment* 10 (3), 19–209.

Daly, K. (2002) 'Restorative justice: The real story' *Punishment and Society* 4, 55–79.

Daly, M. and Wilson, M. (1988) *Homicide* New York: Aldine de Gruyter.

Dando, C., Wilcock, R. and Milne, R. (2008) 'The cognitive interview: Inexperienced police officers' perceptions of their witness/victim interviewing practices' *Legal and Criminological Psychology* 13, 59–70.

Darley, J.M. and Latané, B. (1968) 'Bystander intervention in emergencies: Diffusion of responsibility' *Journal of Personality and Social Psychology* 8, 377–83.

Darwin, C. (1965/1872) *The expression of the emotions in man and animals* Chicago: University of Chicago.

Davies, A. (1997) 'Specific profile analysis: a data-based approach to offender profiling' in J.L. Jackson and D.A. Bekerian (eds) *Offender Profiling* Chichester: Wiley, pp. 191–207.

Davies, F.J. (1952) 'Crime news in Colorado newspapers' *American Journal of Sociology* 57, 325–30.

Davies, G. (2003) 'CCTV: identification in court and in the laboratory' *Forensic Update* 72 (January), 7–10.

Davies, G. and Noon, E. (1993) 'Video links: their impact on child witness trials' in N.K. Clark and G.M. Stephenson (eds) *Issues in Criminological and Legal Psychology 20: Children, Evidence and Procedure* Leicester: Division of Criminological and Legal Psychology, British Psychological Society, pp. 22–6.

Davies, G. and Thasen, S. (2000) 'Closed-circuit television: how effective an identification aid?' *British Journal of Psychology* 91, 411–26.

Davies, G.M., Smith, S. and Blincoe, C. (2008) 'A "weapon focus" effect in children' *Psychology, Crime & Law* 14, 19–28.

Day, D.M. and Page, S. (1986) 'Portrayal of mental illness in Canadian newspapers' *Canadian Journal of Psychiatry* 31, 813–16.

DCLP Training Committee (1994) 'The core knowledge and skills of the Chartered Forensic Psychologists' *Forensic Update* 38, 8–11.

De Fabrique, N., Romano, S.J., Vecchi, G.M. and van Hasselt, V.B. (2007) 'Understanding Stockholm Syndrome' *FBI Law Enforcement Bulletin* 76 (7), 10–15.

de Keijser, J.W. and van Koppen, P.J. (2007) 'Paradoxes of proof and punishment: Psychological pitfalls in judicial decision making' *Legal and Criminological Psychology* 12, 189–205.

De Riviera, J. (1997) 'The construction of false memory syndrome: the experience of retractors' *Psychological Inquiry* 8, 271–92.

Deese, J. (1959) 'On the prediction of occurrence of particular verbal intrusions in immediate recall' *Journal of Experimental Psychology* 58, 17–22.

Deffenbacher, K.A. (1980) 'Eyewitness accuracy and confidence: can we infer anything about the relationship?' *Law and Human Behavior* 4, 243–60.

Degenhardt, L., Conroy, E., Gilmour, S. and Collins, L. (2005) 'The effect of a reduction in heroin supply in Australia upon drug distribution and acquisitive crime' *British Journal of Criminology* 45, 2–24.

Dernevik, M., Johansson, S. and Grann, M. (2000) 'Prediction of violent behaviour in mentally disordered offenders in forensic psychiatric care'. Paper presented at European Association of Psychology and Law (EAPL) Conference, Cyprus.

Dernevik, M., Beck, A., Grann, M., Hogue, T. and McGuire, J. (2009a) 'The use of psychiatric and psychological evidence in the assessment of terrorist offenders' *Journal of Forensic Psychiatry & Psychology* 20 (4), 508–15.

Dernevik, M., Beck, A., Grann, M., Hogue, T. and McGuire, J. (2009b) 'A response to Dr. Gudjonsson's commentary' *Journal of Forensic Psychiatry & Psychology* 20 (4), 520–2.

Desmarais, S.L. and Read, J.D. (2011) 'After 30 years, what do we know about what jurors know? A meta-analytic review of lay knowledge regarding eyewitness factors' *Law and Human Behavior* 35 (3), 200–10.

DeValve, E.Q. (2005) 'A qualitative exploration of the effects of crime victimization for victims of personal crime [Electronic Version]' *Applied Psychology in Criminal Justice* 1 (2), 71–89.

Dhami, M.K. and Ayton, P. (2001) 'Bailing and jailing the fast and frugal way' *Journal of Behavioral Decision Making* 14, 141–68.

Diamond, S.S., Casper, J.D. and Ostergren, L. (1989) 'Blindfolding the jury. Law and Contemporary Problems' 52, 247–67.

DiMaggio, C. and Galea, S. (2006) 'The behavioral consequences of terrorism: a meta-analysis' *Academy of Emergency Medicine* 13, 559–66.

DiMaggio, C., Galea, S. and Richardson, L. (2007) 'Emergency department visits for behavioral and mental health care after a terrorist attack' *Annals of Emergency Medicine* 50 (3), 327–34.

Ditton, J., Chadee, D., Farrall, S., Gilchrist, E. and Bannister, J. (2004) 'From imitation to intimidation: a note on the curious and changing relationship between the media, crime and fear of crime' *British Journal of Criminology* 44, 595–610.

Dobash, R.P. and Dobash, R.E. (2004) 'Women's violence to men in intimate relationships: working on a puzzle' *British Journal of Criminology* 44, 324–49.

Docherty, D. (1990) *Violence in Television Fiction* London: Libbey/Broadcasting Standards Council.

Doerner, W.G. and Ho, T.P. (1994) ' "Shoot/don't shoot": police use of deadly force under simulated field conditions' *Journal of Crime and Justice* 17 (2), 49–68.

Doley, R. (2003) 'Pyromania: fact or fiction?' *British Journal of Criminology* 43, 797–807.

Doob, A.N. and Kirkenbaum, H.M. (1973) 'Bias in police line-ups – partial remembering' *Journal of Police Science and Administration* 1 (3), 287–93.

Douglas, J.E. and Olshaker, M. (1995) *Mind Hunter: Inside the FBI's Elite Serial Crime Unit* New York: Pocket Books.

Douglas, J.E. and Olshaker, M. (1997) *Journey into Darkness* New York: Pocket Star.

Douglas, J.E., Burgess, A.W., Burgess, A.G. and Ressler, R.K. (1992) *Crime Classification Manual* New York: Lexington.

Douglas, K.S., Cox, D.N. and Webster, C.D. (1999) 'Violence risk assessment: science and practice' *Legal and Criminological Psychology* 4, 149–84.

Dowden, C. and Brown, S.L. (2002) 'The role of substance abuse factors in predicting recidivism: a meta-analysis' *Psychology, Crime and Law* 8 (3), 243–64.

Drake, R.D., Ward, T., Nathan, P. and Lee, J.K.P. (2001) 'Challenging the cognitive distortions of child molesters: an implicit theory approach' *Journal of Sexual Aggression* 7 (1), 25–40.

Driver, E. (1989) 'Introduction' in E. Driver and A. Droisen (eds) *Child Sexual Abuse: Feminist Perspectives* London: Macmillan, pp. 1–44.

Dror, I.E. and Charlton, D. (2006) 'Why experts make errors' *Journal of Forensic Identification* 56 (4), 600–16.

Dror, I.E., Champod, C., Langenburg, G., Charlton, D., Hunt, H. and Rosenthal, R. (2011) 'Cognitive issues in finger print analysis: Inter- and intra-expert consistency and the effect of "target" comparison' *Forensic Science* 208, 10–17.

Dror, I.E., Charlton, D. and Peron, A. (2006) 'Contextual information renders experts vulnerable to making erroneous identifications' *Forensic Science International* 156 (1), 74–8.

Dubourg, R., Hamed, J. and Thoms, J. (2005) The economic and social costs of crime against individuals and households 2003/04. Home Office On-Line Report 30/05: June 2005. http://www.crimereduction.homeoffice.gov.uk/statistics/statistics39.htm. Accessed 21 January 2008.

Duff, S. and Willis, A. (2006) 'At the precipice: assessing a non-offending client's potential to sexually offend' *Journal of Sexual Aggression* 12 (1), 43–51.

Dunning, D. and Perretta, S. (2002) 'Automaticity and eyewitness accuracy: A 10- to 12-second rule for distinguishing accurate from inaccurate positive identifications' *Journal of Applied Psychology* 87, 951–62.

Dunning, D. and Stern, L.B. (1994) 'Distinguishing accurate from inaccurate eyewitness identifications via inquiries about decision processes' *Journal of Personality and Social Psychology* 67, 818–35.

Dutton, D.G., Bodnarchuk, M., Kropp, R. and Hart, S.D. (1997) 'Wife assault treatment and criminal recidivism: an 11-year follow-up' *International Journal of Offender Therapy and Comparative Criminology* 4 (1), 9–23.

Duwe, G. and Donnay, W. (2010) 'The effects of failure to register on sex offender recidivism' *Criminal Justice and Behavior* 37, 520–36.

Duwe, G. and Goldman, R.A. (2009) 'The impact of prison-based treatment on sex offender recidivism: Evidence from Minnesota' *Sexual Abuse: A Journal of Research and Treatment* 21 (3), 279–307.

E

East, W.N. and Huber, W.H. de B. (1939) *Report on the Psychological Treatment of Crime* London: HMSO.

Eastman, N. (2000) 'Psycho-legal studies as an interface discipline' in J. McGuire, T. Mason and A. O'Kane (eds) *Behaviour, Crime and Legal Processes: A Guide for Forensic Practitioners* Chichester: John Wiley, pp. 83–110.

Eastwood, C.J. and Snook, B. (2010) 'Comprehending Canadian police cautions: Are the rights to silence and legal counsel understandable?' *Behavioral Science and the Law* 28, 366–77.

Ebberline, J. (2008) 'Geographical offender profiling obscene phone calls: A case study' *Journal of Investigative Psychology & Offender Profiling* 5 (1), 93–105.

Ebbesen, E.B. and Konecni, V.J. (1997) 'Eyewitness memory research: probative v. prejudicial value' *Expert Evidence* 5 (1 and 2), 2–28.

Ebbinghaus, H. (1913) *Grundzüge der psychologie* Leipzig: Von Veit.

Edwards, D.A. (1969) 'Early androgen stimulation and aggressive behavior in male and female mice' *Physiology and Behavior* 4, 333–8.

Edwards, D.A. and Herndon, J. (1970) 'Neonatal estrogen stimulation and aggressive behavior in female mice' *Physiology and Behavior* 4, 993–5.

Edwards, E. (2004) 'An ambiguous participant: the crime victim and criminal justice decision-making' *British Journal of Criminology* 44, 967–82.

Efran, M.G. (1974) 'The effect of physical appearance on the judgment of guilt, interpersonal attraction, and the severity of recommended punishment in a simulated jury task' *Journal of Research in Personality* 8, 45–54.

Egg, R. (1999) 'Criminal careers of sex offenders'. Paper presented at Psychology and Law International Conference, Dublin, 7 July.

Ehrlich, S. (1999) 'Communities of practice, gender, and the representation of sexual assault' *Language in Society* 28 (2), 239–56.

Eigen, J.P. (2004) 'Delusion's odyssey: charting the course of Victorian forensic psychiatry' *International Journal of Law and Psychiatry* 27, 395–412.

Eisen, M.L., Goodman, G.S., Qin, J. and Davis, S. (1998) 'Memory and suggestibility in maltreated children: new research relevant to evaluating allegations of abuse' in S.L. Lynn and K. McConkey (eds) *Truth in Memory* New York: Guilford, pp. 163–89.

Ekman, P. ([1985] 1992) *Telling Lies: Clues to Deceit in the Marketplace, Politics, and Marriage* New York: Norton.

Ekman, P. (1996) 'Why don't we catch liars?' *Social Research* 63 (3), 801–17.

Ekman, P., O'Sullivan, M. and Frank, M.G. (1999) 'A few can catch a liar' *Psychological Science* 10 (3), 263–5.

Elaad, E. (1990) 'Detection of guilty knowledge in real-life criminal invesigations' *Journal of Applied Psychology* 75 (5), 521–9.

Elaad, E., Ginton, A. and Jungman, N. (1992) 'Detection measures in real-life criminal guilty knowledge tests' *Journal of Applied Psychology* 77 (5), 757–67.

Elbogen, E.B., Patry, M. and Scalora, M.J. (2003) 'The impact of community notification laws on sex offender treatment attitudes' *International Journal of Law and Psychiatry* 26, 207–19.

Elkovitch, N., Viljoen, J.L., Scalora, M.J. and Ullman, D. (2008) 'Assessing risk of reoffending in adolescents who have committed a sexual offense: the accuracy of clinical judgments after completion of risk assessment instruments' *Behavioral Sciences and the Law* 26, 511–28.

Ellis, D., Grasmick, H. and Gilman, H. (1974) 'Violence in prison: A sociological analysis' *American Journal of Sociology* 80, 16–43.

Ellis, L. (1989) *Theories of Rape: Inquiries into the Causes of Sexual Aggresssion* New York: Hemisphere.

Emerson, R.M., Ferris, K.O. and Gardner, C.B. (1998) 'On being stalked' *Social Problems* 45 (3), 289–314.

Enzmann, D., Marshall, I.H., Killias, M., Junger-Tas, J., Steketee, M. and Gruszczynska, B. (2010) 'Self-reported youth delinquency in Europe and beyond: First results of the Second International Self-Report Delinquency Study in the context of police and victimization data' *European Journal of Criminology* 7, 159–83.

Epps, K. (1995) 'Sexually abusive behaviour in an adolescent boy with the 48, XXYY syndrome: a case study' in N.K. Clark and G.M. Stephenson (eds) *Investigative and Forensic Decision Making, Issues in Criminological and Legal Psychology No. 26* Leicester: Division of Criminological and Legal Psychology, British Psychological Society, pp. 3–11.

Epstein, S. (1985) 'The implications of cognitive-experiential self-theory for research in social psychology and personality' *Journal for the Theory of Social Behaviour* 15, 283–310.

Epstein, S. (1994) 'Integration of the cognitive and the psychodynamic unconscious' *American Psychologist* 49, 709–24.

Epstein, S. (2003) 'Cognitive-experiential self-theory of personality' in T. Millon and M.J. Lerner (eds) *Handbook of Psychology* Vol. 5 *Personality and social psychology* Hoboken, NJ: Wiley, pp. 159–84.

Epstein, S. and Pacini, R. (1999) 'Some basic issues regarding dual-process theories from the perspective of cognitive-experiential self-theory' in S. Chaiken and Y. Trope (eds) *Dual Process Theories in Social Psychology* New York: Guilford, pp. 462–82.

Ergil, D. (2001) 'Suicide terrorism in Turkey: the Workers' Party of Kurdistan' Herzlia, Israel: Countering Suicide Terrorism, An International Conference, The International Policy Institute for Counter-Terrorism, pp. 105–14, 118–28.

Erikson, M. and Friendship, C. (2002) 'A typology of child abduction events' *Legal and Criminological Psychology* 7, 115–20.

Eron, L.D. (1963) 'Relationship of TV viewing habits and aggressive behavior in children' *Journal of Abnormal and Social Psychology* 67, 193–6.

Eron, L.D., Lefkowitz, M.M., Huesmann, L.R. and Walder, L.O. (1972) 'Does television violence cause aggression?' *American Psychologist* 27, 253–63.

Evans, A.D., Lee, K. and Lyon, T.D. (2009) 'Complex questions asked by defense lawyers but not prosecutors predicts convictions in child abuse trials' *Law and Human Behavior* 33, 258–64.

Evans, J.R. and Claycomb, S. (1998) 'Abnormal QEEG patterns associated with dissociation and violence'. Unpublished manuscript, University of South Carolina. Annual Meeting of the Society for the Study of Neuronal Regulation, Austin, TX.

Everson, M.D. and Boat, B.W. (2002) 'The utility of anatomical dolls and drawings in child forensic interviews' in M.L. Eisen, J.A. Quas and G.S. Goodman (eds) *Memory and Suggestibility in the Forensic Interview* Mahwah, NJ: Lawrence Erlbaum, pp. 383–408.

Expert Law (2003) Megan's Law. http://www.expertlaw.com/library/pubarticles/megans_law.html

Eysenck, H.J. (1947) *Dimensions of Personality* London: Routledge & Kegan Paul.

Eysenck, H.J. (1964) *Crime and Personality* London: Methuen.

Eysenck, H.J. (1970) *Crime and Personality* (2nd edn, rev.) London: Paladin.

Eysenck, H.J. (1977) *Crime and Personality* (3rd edn, rev.) London: Routledge & Kegan Paul.

Eysenck, H.J. (1973) *The Inequality of Man* London: Maurice Temple Smith.

Eysenck, H.J. (1980) *The Causes and Effects of Smoking* London: Sage.

Eysenck, H.J. (1990) *Check Your Own IQ* London: Penguin.

Eysenck, H.J. and Nias, D.K. (1978) *Sex, Violence and the Media* London: Maurice Temple Smith.

F

Faigman, D.L. (2008) 'The limits of science in the courtroom' *Beyond Common Sense: Psychological Science in the Courtroom* Oxford: Blackwell, pp. 303–14.

Falshaw, L., Friendship, C. and Bates, A. (2003) 'Sexual offenders – measuring reconviction, reoffending and recidivism' Findings 183. Home Office, Research, Development and Statistics Directorate. London. http://www.homeoffice.gov.uk/rds/pdf

Farrall, S. and Gadd, D. (2004) 'The frequency of fear of crime' *British Journal of Criminology* 44, 127–32.

Farrell, G. and Bouloukos, A. (2001) 'A cross-national comparative analysis of rates of repeat victimization' in G. Farrell and K. Pease (eds) *Repeat Victimization* Monsey, NY: Criminal Justice Press.

Farrington, D.P. (1979) 'Experiments on deviance with special reference to dishonesty' in L. Berkowitz (ed.) *Advances in Experimental Social Psychology, No. 12* New York: Academic Press, pp. 207–53.

Farrington, D.P. (1987) 'Epidemiology' in H.C. Quay (ed.) *Handbook of Juvenile Delinquency* Chichester: John Wiley, pp. 33–61.

Farrington, D.P. (1990) 'Age, period, cohort, and offending' in D.M. Gottfredson and R.V. Clarke (eds) *Policy and Theory in Criminal Justice: Contributions in Honour of Leslie T. Wilkins* Aldershot: Avebury, pp. 51–75.

Farrington, D.P. (1995) 'The psychology of crime: influences and constraints on offending' in R. Bull and D. Carson (eds) *Handbook of Psychology in Legal Contexts* Chichester: John Wiley, pp. 291–314.

Farrington, D.P. (1996) 'Psychosocial influences on the development of antisocial personality' in G. Davies, S. Lloyd-Bostock, M. McMurran and C. Wilson (eds) *Psychology, Law and Criminal Justice: International Developments in Research and Practice* Berlin: Walter de Gruyter, pp. 424–44.

Farrington, D.P. (1998) 'Developmental crime prevention initiatives in 1997' *Forensic Update* 54, 19–25.

Farrington, D.P. (2010) *Life-Course and Developmental Theories in Criminology. Handbook of Criminological Theory*, E. McLaughlin and T. Newburn (eds) London: Sage, pp. 249–70.

Farrington, D.P. and Kidd, R.F. (1977) 'Is financial dishonesty a rational decision?' *British Journal of Social and Clinical Psychology* 16, 139–46.

Farrington, D.P. and Lambert, S. (1997) 'Predicting offender profiles from victim and witness descriptions' in J.L. Jackson and D.A. Bekerian (eds) *Offender Profiling: Theory, Research and Practice* Chichester: John Wiley, pp. 133–58.

Farrington, D.P., Barnes, G.C. and Lambert, S. (1996) 'The concentration of offending in families' *Legal and Criminological Psychology* 1 (1), 47–63.

Farrington, D.P., Langan, P.A. and Tonry, M. (eds) (2004) *Cross-National Studies in Crime and Justice* Washington: US Department of Justice.

FBI (2009) Crime in the United States. http://www2.fbi.gov/ucr/cius2009/data/table_01.html. Accessed 12 April 2011.

Felson, R., Savolainen, J., Aaltonen, M. and Moustgaard, H. (2008) 'Is the association between alcohol use and delinquency causal or spurious?' *Criminology* 46 (3), 785–808.

Felson, R.B. (1996) 'Mass media effects on violent behavior' *Annual Review of Sociology* 22, 102–28.

Fenichel, O. (1933) 'Outline of clinical psychoanalysis' *Psychoanalytic Quarterly* 2, 562–91.

Ferguson, C.J. (2009) 'Media violence effects: confirmed truth or just another X-file?' *Journal of Forensic Psychology Practice* 9, 103–26.

Ferguson, C.J., Rueda, S.M., Cruz, A.M., Ferguson, D.E., Fritz, S. and Smith, S.M. (2008) 'Violent video games and aggression: Causal relationship or byproduct of family violence and intrinsic violence motivation?' *Criminal Justice and Behavior* 35 (3), 311–32.

Ferguson, C.J., White, D.E., Stacey, C., Lorenz, M. and Bhimani, Z. (2003) 'Defining and classifying serial murder in the context of perpetrator motivation' *Journal of Criminal Justice* 31 (3), 287–92.

Fiedler, K., Schmid, J. and Stahl, T. (2002) 'What is the current truth about polygraph lie detection?' *Basic and Applied Social Psychology* 24 (4), 313–24.

Fine, C. and Kennett, J. (2004) 'Mental impairment, moral understanding and criminal responsibility: psychopathy and the purposes of punishment' *International Journal of Law and Psychiatry* 27, 425–43.

Finkelhor, D. (1984) *Child Sexual Abuse: New Theory and Research* New York: Free Press.

Finlayson, L.M. and Koocher, G.P. (1991) 'Professional judgement and child abuse reporting in sexual abuse cases' *Professional Psychology: Research and Practice* 22, 464–72.

Firestone, P., Bradford, J.M., Greenberg, D.M., Larose, M.R. and Curry, S. (1998a) 'Homicidal and nonhomicidal child molesters: psychological, phallometric and criminal features' *Sexual Abuse: A Journal of Research and Treatment* 10 (4), 305–23.

Firestone, P., Bradford, J.M., McCoy, M., Greenberg, D.M., Curry, S. and Larose, M.R. (1998b) 'Recidivism in convicted rapists' *Journal of American Academy Psychiatry and Law* 26 (2), 185–200.

Fisher, D. and Beech, A.R. (1999) 'Current practice in Britain with sexual offenders' *Journal of Interpersonal Violence* 14 (3), 240–56.

Fisher, D. and Thornton, D. (1993) 'Assessing risk of re-offending in sexual offenders' *Journal of Mental Health* 2, 105–17.

Fisher, R.P. and Geiselman, R.W. (1992) *Memory Enhancing Techniques for Investigative Interviewing: The Cognitive Interview* Springfield: Charles C. Thomas.

Fisher, R.P., Brennan, K.H. and McCauley, M.R. (2002) 'The cognitive interview method to enhance eyewitness recall' in M.L. Eisen, J.A. Quas and G.S. Goodman (eds) *Memory and Suggestibility in the Forensic Interview* Mahwah, NJ: Lawrence Erlbaum, pp. 265–86.

Fitzgerald, P. and Seeman, M.V. (2002) 'Erotomania in women' in J. Boon and L. Sheridan (eds) *Stalking and Psychosexual Obsession: Psychological Perpsectives for Prevention, Policing and Treatment* Chichester: John Wiley, pp. 165–80.

Fitzmaurice, C., Rogers, D. and Stanley, P. (1996) 'Predicting court sentences: a perilous exercise' in G. Davies, S. Lloyd-Bostock, M. McMurran and C. Wilson (eds) *Psychology, Law and Criminal Justice: International Developments in Research and Practice* Berlin: Walter de Gruyter, pp. 305–13.

Flatley, J., Kershaw, C., Smith, K., Chaplin, R. and Moon, D. (eds.) (2010) Home Office Statistical Bulletin. Crime in England and Wales 2009/10. Findings from the British Crime Survey and police recorded crime. http://rds.homeoffice.gov.uk/rds/pdfs10/hosb1210.pdf. Accessed 29 March 2011.

Flood, J.J. (2003) *A report of findings from the Hostage Barricade Database System (HOBAS)* Quantico, VA: Crisis Negotiation Unit, Critical Incident Response Group, FBI Academy.

Flynn, S.M., Swinson, N., While, D., Hunt, I.M., Roscoe, A., Rodway, C., Windfuhr, K., Kapur, N., Appleby, L. and Shaw, J. (2009) 'Homicide followed by suicide: a cross-sectional study' *Journal of Forensic Psychiatry and Psychology* 20 (2), 306–21.

Forrester, A., Ozdural, S., Muthukumaraswamy, A. and Carroll, A. (2008) 'The evolution of mental disorder as a legal category in England and Wales' *Journal of Forensic Psychiatry and Psychology* 19 (4), 543–60.

Fowles, J. (1999) *The Case for Television Violence* Thousand Oaks, CA: Sage.

Fox, C. and Rirke, R. (2002) 'Forecasting trial outcomes: lawyers assign higher probability to possibilities that are described in greater detail' *Law and Human Behavior* 26 (2), 159–73.

Fox, J.A. and Zawitz, M.W. (2004) Homicide trends in the United States. US Bureau of Justice. http://www.ojp.usdoj.gov/bjs/homicide/homtrnd.htm

Fox, J.R.E., Gray, N.S. and Lewis, H. (2004) 'Factors determining compliance with command hallucinations with violent content: The role of social rank, perceived power of the voice and voice malevolence' *Journal of Forensic Psychiatry & Psychology* 15, 511–31.

Freeman, J., Palk, G. and Davey, J. (2010) 'Sex offenders in denial: a study into a group of forensic psychologists' attitudes regarding the corresponding impact upon risk assessment calculations and parole eligibility' *The Journal of Forensic Psychiatry & Psychology* 21 (1), 39–51.

Freyd, J.J. (1996) *Betrayal Trauma: The Logic of Forgetting Childhood Abuse* Cambridge, MA: Harvard University Press.

Friedrich, W.N. (undated) *Psychological Assessment Resources* PO Box 998, Odessa, Florida FL33556.

Friedrich, W.N., Grambach, P., Damon, L., Hewitt, S.K., Koverola, C., Lang, R.A., Wolfe, V. and Broughton, D. (1992) 'Child sexual behavior inventory: normative and clinical comparisons' *Psychological Assessment* 4 (3), 303–11.

Friel, A., White, T. and Hull, A. (2008) 'Posttraumatic stress disorder and criminal Responsibility' *Journal of Forensic Psychiatry & Psychology* 19 (1), 64–85.

Froggio, G. (2007) 'Strain and juvenile delinquency: a critical review of Agnew's General Strain Theory' *Journal of Loss and Trauma* 12 (4), 383–418.

Frowd, C.D., Carson, D., Ness, H., McQuiston-Surrett, D., Richardson, J., Baldwin, H. and Hancock, P. (2004) 'Contemporary composite techniques: the impact of forensically-relevant target delay'. Paper presented at XIV Conference of the European Association of Psychology and Law (EAPL), Krakow, Poland.

Frowd, C.D., Carson, D., Ness, H., Richardson, J., Morrison, L., McLanaghan, S. and Hancock, P.J.B. (2005) 'A forensically valid comparison of facial composite systems' *Psychology, Crime and Law* 11 (1), 35–52.

Fulero, S.M. and Penrod, S. (1990) 'The myths and realities of attorney jury selection and folklore and scientific jury selection: what works?' *Ohio Northern University Law Review* 17, 339–53.

Fullerton, R.A. and Punj, G.N. (2004) 'Shoplifting as moral insanity: historical perspectives on kleptomania' *Journal of Macromarketing* 24 (1), 8–16.

G

Gabriel, R., Ferrando, L., Sainz Corton, E., Mingote, C., Garcia-Camba, E., Fernandez-Liria, A.G. and Galea, S. (2007) 'Psychopathological consequences after a terrorist attack: an epidemiological study among victims, police officers, and the general population' *European Psychiatry* 22 (6), 339–46.

Gacono, C.B., Meloy, J.R., Speth, E. and Roske, A. (1997) 'Above the law: escapees from a maximum security forensic hospital and psychopathy' *Journal of American Academy of Psychiatry and the Law* 25 (4), 547–50.

Gagliardi, G.J., Lovell, D., Peterson, P.D. and Jemelka, R. (2004) 'Forecasting recidivism in mentally ill offenders released from prison' *Law and Human Behavior* 28 (2), 133–55.

Galen, B.R. and Underwood, M.K. (1997) 'A developmental investigation of social aggression among children' *Developmental Psychology* 33 (4), 589–600.

Gannon, T.A. (2006) 'Increasing honest responding on cognitive distortions in child molesters: the bogus pipeline procedure' *Journal of Interpersonal Violence* 21, 358–75.

Gannon, T.A. (2010) 'Female arsonists: Key features, psychopathologies and treatment needs' *Psychiatry: Interpersonal and Biological Processes* 73, 173–89.

Gannon, T.A. and Polaschek, D. (2005) 'Do child molesters deliberately fake good on cognitive distortion questionnaires? An information processing-based investigation' *Sexual Abuse: A Journal of Research and Treatment* 17, 183–200.

Gannon, T.A., Beech, A.R. and Ward, T. (2008) 'Does the polygraph lead to better risk prediction for sexual offenders?' *Aggression and Violent Behavior* 13, 29–44.

Garner, R. (2005) 'Police attitudes: the impact of experience after training' *Applied Psychology in Criminal Justice* 1 (1), 56–70.

Garner, R. (2008) 'Police stress: Effects of criticism management training on health' *Applied Psychology in Criminal Justice* 4 (2), 243–59.

Garrido, E. and Masip, J. (1999) 'How good are police officers at spotting lies?' *Forensic Update* 58, 14–20.

Gastil, J., Burkhalter, S. and Black, L.W. (2007) 'Do juries deliberate? A study of deliberation, individual difference, and group member satisfaction at a municipal courthouse' *Small Group Research* 38 (3), 337–59.

Geberth, V.J. (1996) *Practical Homicide Investigation: Tactics, Procedures and Forensic Techniques* Boca Raton, FL: CRC Press.

Gebhard, P.H., Gagnon, J.H., Pomeroy, W.B. and Christenson, C.V. (1965) *Sex Offenders: An Analysis of Types* New York: Harper & Row.

Geert, J.S., Brugman, D., Deković, M., van Rosmalen, L., van der Laan, P. and Gibbs, J.C. (2006) 'The moral judgment of juvenile delinquents: a meta-analysis' *Journal of Abnormal Child Psychology* **34** (5), 692–708.

Geis, G. and Loftus, E.F. (2009) 'Taus v. Loftus: determining the legal ground rules for scholarly inquiry' *Journal of Forensic Psychology Practice* **9** (2), 147–62.

Geiselman, R.E. and Fisher, R.P. (1997) 'Ten years of cognitive interviewing' in D. Payne and F. Conrad (eds) *Intersections in Basic and Applied Memory Research* New York: Lawrence Erlbaum, pp. 291–310.

Geiselman, R.E., Fisher, R.P., Firstenberg, I., Hutton, L.A., Sullivan, S., Avetissian, I. and Prosk, A. (1984) 'Enhancement of eyewitness memory: an empirical evaluation of the cognitive interview' *Journal of Police Science and Administration* **121**, 74–80.

Gelles, R.J. (1979) *Family Violence* Beverly Hills, CA: Sage.

Gelles, R.J. and Cornell, C. (1985) *Intimate Violence in Families* Beverly Hills, CA: Sage.

Gelles, R.J. and Straus, M.A. (1979) 'Determinants of violence: towards a theoretical integration' in W. Burr, R. Hill, I. Nyer and I. Reiss (eds) *Contemporary Theories About the Family* New York: Free Press, pp. 549–81.

Gendreau, P., Goggin, C. and Fulton, B. (2000) 'Intensive supervision in probation and parole' in C.R. Hollin (ed.) *Handbook of Offender Assessment and Treatment* Chichester: John Wiley, pp. 95–204.

Gendreau, P., Goggin, C., Cullen, F.T. and Paparozzi, M. (2002) 'The common sense revolution and correctional policy' in J. Maguire (ed.) *Offender Rehabilitation and Treatment: Effective Programmes and Policies to Reduce Re-offending* Chichester: John Wiley & Sons, pp. 359–86.

Gentry, C.S. (1991) 'Pornography and rape: an empirical analysis' *Deviant Behaviour* **12** (3), 277–88.

Geraerts, E., Raymaekers, L. and Merckelbach, H. (2008) 'Recovered memories of childhood sexual abuse: Current findings and their legal implications' *Legal and Criminological Psychology* **13**, 165–76.

Gerbner, G. (1972) 'Violence in television drama: trends and symbolic functions' in G.A. Comstock and E.A. Rubenstein (eds) *Television and Social Behaviour, Vol. 1: Media Content and Control* Washington, DC: US Government Printing Office, pp. 28–187.

Gerbner, G., Gross, L., Eley, M.E., Jackson Breek, M., Jeffries-Fox, S. and Signorielli, N. (1977) 'Television violence profile, No. 8' *Journal of Communication* **27**, 171–80.

Gershon, R.M., Barocas, B., Canton, A.N., Li, X. and Vlahov, D. (2009) 'Mental, physical, and behavioral outcomes associated with perceived work stress in police officers' *Criminal Justice and Behavior* **36**, 275–89.

Gibbs, J.C. (2003) *Moral Development and Reality: Beyond the Theories of Kohlberg and Hoffman* Thousand Oaks, CA: Sage Publications.

Gibbs, J.C., Basinger, K.S. and Fuller, D. (1992) *Moral Maturity: Measuring the Development of Sociomoral Reflection* Hillsdale, NJ: Lawrence Erlbaum.

Gierowski, J.F., Jaskiewicz-Obydzinska, T. and Slawik, M. (1998) 'The planning of a criminal act as a fundamental aspect of psychological profiling – its relation to the personality, motivation and modus operandi of a perpetrator'. 8th European Conference on Psychology and Law, Krakow, 2–5 September.

Gierowski, J.F., Jaskiewicz-Obydzinska, T. and Slawik, M. (2000) 'The planning of a criminal act as a fundamental aspect of psychological profiling – its relation to the personality, motivation and modus operandi of a perpetrator' in A. Czerederecka, T. Jaskiewicz-Obdzinska and J. Wojcikiewicz (eds) *Forensic Psychology and Law: Traditional Questions and New Ideas* Krakow: Institute of Forensic Research Publishers, pp. 88–94.

Gilbert, F. and Daffern, M. (2010) 'Integrating contemporary aggression theory with violent offender treatment: How thoroughly do interventions target violent behavior?' *Aggression and Violent Behavior* **15**, 167–80.

Gilchrist, E., Bannister, J., Ditton, J. and Farrall, S. (1998) 'Women and the "fear of crime"' *British Journal of Criminology* **38** (2), 283–98.

Gilligan, C. (1982) *In a Different Voice: Psychological Theory and Women's Development* Cambridge, MA: Harvard University Press.

Glover, N. (1999) *Risk Assessment and Community Care in England and Wales* Liverpool: Faculty of Law, University of Liverpool.

Glueck, S. and Glueck, E. (1962) *Family Environment and Delinquency* London: Routledge and Kegan Paul.

Glueck, S. and Glueck, E. (1968) *Delinquents and Nondelinquents in Perspective* Cambridge, MA: Harvard University Press.

Godfrey, C., Eaton, G., McDougall, C. and Culyer, A. (2002) 'The economic and social costs of Class A drug use in England and Wales, 2000' Home Office Research Study 249. Home Office Research, Development and Statistics Directorate.

Goffman, E. (1959) *The Presentation of the Self in Everyday Life* Garden City, New York: Doubleday/Anchor Books.

Goffman, E. (1961) *Asylums* New York: Anchor Books.

Goldstein, A.P. (2004) 'Evaluations of effectiveness' in A.P. Goldstein, R. Nensen, B. Daleflod and M. Kalt (eds) *New Perspectives on Aggression Replacement Training* Chichester: John Wiley & Sons, pp. 230–44.

Goldstein, A.P., Glick, B. and Gibbs, J.C. (1998) *Aggression Replacement Training* (Rev. ed.). Champaign, IL: Research Press.

Goncalves, R.A. (1998) 'Correctional treatment in Portugal' in J. Boros, I. Munnich and M. Szegedi (eds) *Psychology and Criminal Justice: International Review of Theory and Practice* Berlin: de Gruyter, pp. 327–31.

Goodman, G.S. and Melinder, A. (2007) 'Child witness research and forensic interviews of young children: A review' *Legal and Criminological Psychology* 12, 1–19.

Goodwill, A.M. and Alison, L.J. (2007) 'When is profiling possible? Offense planning and aggression as moderators in predicting offender age from victim age in stranger rape' *Behavioral Sciences and the Law* 25, 823–40.

Goodwill, A.M., Alison, L.J. and Beech, A.R. (2009) 'What works in offender profiling? A comparison of typological, thematic, and multivariate models' *Behavioral Sciences and the Law* 27, 507–29.

Gordon, B.N., Schroeder, C.S. and Abrams, J.M. (1990a) 'Age and social-class differences in children's knowledge of sexuality' *Journal of Clinical Child Psychology* 19, 33–43.

Gordon, B.N., Schroeder, C.S. and Abrams, J.M. (1990b) 'Children's knowledge of sexuality: a comparison of sexually abused and nonabused children' *American Journal of Orthopsychiatry* 60, 250–7.

Gordon, H., Oyebode, O. and Minne, C. (1997) 'Death by homicide in special hospitals' *Journal of Forensic Psychiatry* 8 (3), 602–19.

Gossop, M., Marsden, J., Stewart, D. and Kidd, T. (2003) 'The National Treatment Outcome Research Study (NTORS): 4–5 year follow-up results' *Addiction* 98, 291–303.

Gottfredson, D.M. and Gottfredson, S.D. (1988) 'Stakes and risks in the prediction of violent criminal behavior' *Violence and Victims* 3 (4), 247–62.

Gottfredson, M. and Hirschi, T. (1986) 'The true value of lambda would appear to be zero: an essay on career criminals, criminal careers, selective incapacitation, cohort studies, and related topics' *Criminology* 24, 213–34.

Gottfredson, M.R. and Hirschi, T. (1990) *A General Theory of Crime* Stanford, CA: Stanford University Press.

Graber, D.A. (1980) *Crime News and the Public* New York: Praeger.

Granhag, A. and Vrij, A. (2010) 'Introduction: What works in investigative psychology?' *Legal and Criminological Psychology* 15, 1–3.

Granhag, P.A., Andersson, L.O., Stromwall, L.A. and Hartwig, M. (2004) 'Imprisoned knowledge: criminals beliefs about deception' *Legal and Criminological Psychology* 9, 103–19.

Granhag, P.A., Strömwal, L.A. and Hartwig, M. (2007) 'The SUE technique: the way to interview to detect diction' *Forensic Update* 88, 25–9.

Grant, D. and Williams, D. (2011) 'The importance of perceiving social contexts when predicting crime and anti-social behavior in CCTV images' *Legal and Criminological Psychology* 16 (2), 307–22.

Grant, J.E., Odlaug, B.L., Davis, A.A. and Kim, S.W. (2009) 'Legal consequences of kleptomania' *Psychiatric Quarterly* 80, 251–9.

Graves, R.B., Openshaw, D.K., Ascione, F.R. and Ericksen, S.L. (1996) 'Demographic and parental characteristics of youthful sexual offenders' *International Journal of Offender Therapy and Comparative Criminology* 40 (4), 300–17.

Green, D.P., Glaser, J. and Rich, A. (1998) 'From lynching to gay bashing: the elusive connection between economic conditions and hate crime' *Journal of Personality and Social Psychology* 75 (1), 82–92.

Green, D.P., Strolovitch, D.Z. and Wong, J.S. (1998) 'Defended neighborhoods, integration and racially motivated crime' *American Journal of Sociology* 104 (2), 372–403.

Greenberg, M.S. and Beach, S.R. (2001) 'The role of social influence in crime victim's decision to notify the police' in R. Roesch, R.R. Carrado and R. Dempster (eds), *Psychology in the Courts: International Advances in Knowledge*. London/New York: Routledge, pp. 305–16.

Greenberg, M.S. and Beach, S.R. (2004) 'Property crime victims' decision to notify the police: social, cognitive and affective determinants' *Law and Human Behavior* 28 (2), 177–86.

Gregg, V., Gibbs, J.C. and Basinger, K.S. (1994) Patterns of developmental delay in moral judgement by male and female delinquents. *Merrill-Palmer Quarterly* **40**, 538–53.

Gresnigt, J.A.M., Breteler, M.H.M., Schippers, G.M. and Van den Hurk, A.A. (2000) 'Predicting violent crime among drug-using inmates: the addiction severity index as a prediction instrument' *Legal and Criminological Psychology* **5**, 85–95.

Gresswell, D.M. and Hollin, C.R. (1994) 'Multiple murder: a review' *British Journal of Criminology* **34**, 1–14.

Gresswell, D.M. and Hollin, C.R. (1997) 'Addictions and multiple murder: a behavioural perspective' in J.E. Hodge, M. McMurran and C.R. Hollin (eds) *Addicted to Crime?* Chichester: John Wiley.

Gretenkord, L. (1991) *Prediction of Illegal Behaviour of Mentally Ill Offenders* Proceedings of the 17th International Congress of the International Academy of Law and Mental Health, Leuven, Belgium, May.

Gretenkord, L. (1993) 'Actuarial versus clinical versus political prediction'. Paper presented at XIX International Congress of the International Academy of Law and Mental Health, Lisbon, Portugal, June.

Gretenkord, L. (2000) 'How to use empirical findings for the prognosis of mentally disordered offenders'. Paper presented at the 10th European Conference of Psychology and Law, Limassol, Cyprus.

Greuel, L., Brietzke, S. and Stadle, M.A. (1999) 'Credibility assessment: new research perspectives'. Joint International Conference on Psychology and Law, Dublin, 6–9 July.

Grey, N. (2002) 'The psychological impact of offending on a victim of physical assault: a case of chronic post-traumatic stress disorder' in L. Fanshaw (ed.) *Issues in Forensic Psychology* Leicester: British Psychological Society, pp. 9–19.

Griffith, J.D., Libkuman, T.M. and Poole, D.A. (1998) 'Repressed memories: the effects of expert testimony on mock jurors' decision making' *American Journal of Forensic Psychology* **16** (1), 5–23.

Groscup, J., Penrod, S., Studebaker, C., Huss, M. and O'Neil, K. (2002) 'The effects of *Daubert v. Merrell Dow Pharmaceuticals* on the admissibility of expert testimony in state and federal criminal cases' *Psychology, Public Policy and Law* **8**, 339–72.

Gross, B.H., Southard, M.J., Lamb, R. and Weinberger, L.E. (1987) 'Assessing dangerousness and responding appropriately' *Journal of Clinical Psychiatry* **48** (1), 9–12.

Groth, A.N. and Birnbaum, H.J. (1978) 'Adult sexual orientation and attraction to underage persons' *Archives of Sexual Behavior* **7** (3), 175–81.

Groth, A.N. and Burgess, A.W. (1978) 'Rape: a pseudo-sexual act' *International Journal of Women's Studies* **1** (2), 207–10.

Groth, A.N., Burgess, A.W. and Holmstrom, L.L. (1977) 'Rape, power, anger and sexuality' *American Journal of Psychiatry* **134**, 1239–48.

Grounds, A. (2004) 'Psychological consequences of wrongful conviction and imprisonment' *Canadian Journal of Criminology and Criminal Justice* **46** (2), 165–82.

Grover, C. and Soothill, K. (1999) 'British serial killing: towards a structural explanation' *British Criminology Conferences: Selected Proceedings*, Vol. 2. http://www.lboro.ac.uk/departments/ss/BSC.bccsp/vol02/08GROVE.HTM

Grubin, D. (1996a) *Fitness to Plead in England and Wales* Hove: Psychology Press.

Grubin, D. (1996b) 'Silence in court: psychiatry and the Criminal Justice and Public Order Act 1994' *Journal of Forensic Psychiatry* **7** (3), 647–52.

Grubin, D. (2008) 'The case for polygraph testing of sex offenders' *Legal and Criminological Psychology* **13**, 177–89.

Grubin, D.H. and Kennedy, H.G. (1991) 'The classification of sexual offenders' *Criminal Behaviour and Mental Health* **1**, 123–9.

Grubin, D. and Madsen, L. (2005) 'Lie detection and the polygraph: a historical review' *British Journal of Forensic Psychiatry and Psychology* **16**, 357–69.

Grubin, D., Madsen, L., Parsons, S., Sosnowki, D. and Warberg, B. (2004) 'A prospective study of the impact of polygraphy on high risk behaviors in adult sex offenders' *Sexual Abuse: A Journal of Research and Treatment* **16**, 209–22.

Gudjonsson, G., Sigurdsson, J.F. and Sigfusdottir, I.D. (2009) 'False confessions among 15- and 16-year-olds in compulsory education and the relationship with adverse life events' *Journal of Forensic Psychiatry & Psychology* **20** (6), 950–63.

Gudjonsson, G.H. (1984) 'A new scale of interrogative suggestibility' *Personality and Individual Differences* **5**, 303–14.

Gudjonsson, G.H. (1992) *The Psychology of Interrogations, Confessions and Testimony* Chichester: John Wiley.

Gudjonsson, G.H. (2003) *The Psychology of Interrogations and Confessions: A Handbook* Chichester: John Wiley.

Gudjonsson, G.H. and Copson, G. (1997) 'The role of the expert in criminal investigation' in J.L. Jackson and D.A. Bekerian (eds) *Offender Profiling: Theory, Research and Practice* Chichester: John Wiley, pp. 61–76.

Gudjonsson, G.H. and Haward, L.R.C. (1998) *Forensic Psychology: A Guide to Practice* London: Routledge.

Gudjonsson, G.H. and Sigurdsson, J.F. (1999) 'The Gudjonsson Confession Questionnaire-Revised (GCQ-R): Factor structure and its relationship with personality' *Personality and Individual Differences* 27, 953–68.

Gudjonsson, G.H., Murphy, G.H. and Clare, I.C.H. (2000) 'Assessing the capacity of people with intellectual disabilities to be witnesses in court' *Psychological Medicine* 30 (2), 307–14.

Gudjonsson, G.H., Sigurdsson, J.F., Asgeirsdottir, B.B. and Sigfusdottir, I.D. (2007) 'Custodial interrogation: What are the background factors associated with claims of false confession to police?' *Journal of Forensic Psychiatry and Psychology* 18 (2), 266–75.

Guerette, R.T. and Santana, S.A. (2010) 'Explaining victim self-protective behavior effects on crime incident outcomes: a test of opportunity theory' *Crime and Delinquency* 56 (2) April, 198–226.

Gunn, J. and Buchanan, A. (2006) 'Paranoia in the Criminal Courts' *Behavioural Sciences and the Law* 24, 373–83.

Gunnell, J.J. (2010) 'When emotionality trumps reason: a study of individual processing style and juror bias' *Behavioral Sciences and the Law* 28, 850–77.

Gunnell, J. and Ceci, S.J. (2010) 'When emotionality trumps reason: A study of individual processing style and juror bias' *Behavioral Science and the Law* 28, 850–77.

Gunter, B. (1987) *Television and the Fear of Crime* London: John Libbey.

Guthrie, R.V. (1998) *Even the Rat was White: A Historical View of Psychology* (2nd edn) Boston: Allyn and Bacon.

H

Haapasalo, J. (1999) 'Sons in prison and their mothers: is there a relationship between childhood histories of physical abuse?' Dublin conference, Dublin, Ireland, 6–9 July.

Haapasalo, J. and Kankkonen, M. (1997) 'Self-reported childhood abuse among sex and violent offenders' *Archives of Sexual Behavior* 26 (4), 421–31.

Haapasalo, J. and Pokela, E. (1999) 'Child-rearing and child abuse antecedents of criminality' *Aggression and Violent Behavior* 4 (1), 107–27.

Haapasalo, J. and Tremblay, R.E. (1994) 'Physically aggressive boys from ages 6 to 12: family background, parenting behavior, and prediction of delinquency' *Journal of Consulting and Clinical Psychology* 62 (5), 104–52.

Haapasalo, J., Puupponen, M. and Crittenden, P.M. (1999) 'Victim to victimizer: the psychology of isomorphism in the case of a recidivist pedophile in Finland' *Journal of Child Sexual Abuse* 7 (3), 97–115.

Hackett, L., Day, A. and Mohr, P.L. (2008) 'Expectancy violation and perceptions of rape victim credibility' *Legal and Criminological Psychology* 13, 323–34.

Haden, S.C. and Scarpa, A. (2008) 'Community violence victimization and depressed mood: The moderating effects of coping and social support' *Journal of Interpersonal Violence* 23, 1213–34.

Hagell, A. and Newburn, T. (1994) *Young Offenders and the Media: Viewing Habits and Preferences* London: Policy Studies Institute.

Haggård, U. (2000) 'Against all odds – a qualitative follow-up study of high-risk violent criminals that were not reconvicted'. Paper presented at the European Association of Psychology and Law (EAPL) Conference, Limassol, Cyprus.

Haggård, U., Gumpert, H.C. and Grann, M. (2001) 'Against all odds – a qualitative follow-up study of high-risk violent offenders who were not reconvicted' *Journal of Interpersonal Violence* 16, 1048–65.

Häkkänen, H. and Laajasalo, T. (2006) 'Homicide crime scene actions in a Finnish sample of mentally ill offenders' *Homicide Studies* 10, 33–54.

Häkkänen, H., Lindlof, P. and Santtila, P. (2004) 'Crime scene actions and offender characteristics in a sample of Finnish stranger rapes' *Journal of Investigative Psychology and Offender Profiling* 1, 17–32.

Hall, G.C.N. (1995) 'Sexual offender recidivism revisited: a meta-analysis of recent treatment studies' *Journal of Consulting and Clinical Psychology* 63 (5), 802–9.

Hall, G.C.N. and Barongan, C. (1997) 'Prevention of sexual aggression: sociocultural risk and protective factors' *American Psychologist* 52 (1), 5–14.

Hall, G.C.N. and Hirschman, R. (1991) 'Toward a theory of sexual aggression: a quadri-partite model' *Journal of Consulting and Clinical Psychology* 59, 662–9.

Hall, G.C.N., Hirschman, R. and Oliver, L.L. (1995) 'Sexual arousal and arousability to pedophilic stimuli in a community sample of normal men' *Behavior Therapy* 26, 681–94.

Hall, G.C.N., Shondrick, D.D. and Hirschman, R. (1993) 'The role of sexual arousal in sexually aggressive behavior:

a meta-analysis' *Journal of Consulting and Clinical Psychology* **61** (6), 1091–5.

Hall, J. (2007) 'The emergence of clinical psychology in Britain from 1943 to 1958 Part 1: core tasks and the professionalisation process' *History & Philosophy of Psychology* **9** (1), 29–55.

Hall, S., Crilcher, C., Jefferson, T., Clarke, J. and Roberts, B. (1978) *Policing the Crisis: Mugging, the State and Law and Order* London: Macmillan.

Haller, J.S. and Haller, R.N. (1974) *The Physician and Sexuality in Victorian America* Urbana, IL: University of Illinois Press.

Halloran, J.D., Brown, R.L. and Chaney, D.C. (1970) *Television and Delinquency* Leicester: Leicester University Press.

Halverson, K. (1991) 'Olson on literacy' *Language in Society* **20**, 619–40.

Hamilton, D.L. and Gifford, R.K. (1976) 'Illusory correlation in interpersonal perception: a cognitive basis of stereotypic judgments' *Journal of Experimental Social Psychology* **12**, 392–407.

Hammond, L., Wagstaff, G.F. and Cole, J. (2006) 'Facilitating eyewitness memory in adults and children with context reinstatement and focused meditation' *Journal of Investigative Psychology and Offender Profiling* **3**, 117–30.

Hanks, H., Hobbs, C. and Wynne, J. (1988) 'Early signs and recognition of sexual abuse in the pre-school child' in K. Browne, C. Davies and P. Stratton (eds) *Early Prediction and Prevention of Child Abuse* Chichester: John Wiley, pp. 139–60.

Hanson, R.K. (1997) *The development of a brief actuarial risk scale for sexual offense recidivism*, User Report No. 1997-04. Ottawa: Department of the Solicitor General of Canada.

Hanson, R.K. and Bussière, M.T. (1998) 'Predicting relapse: a meta-analysis of sexual offender recidivism studies' *Journal of Consulting and Clinical Psychology* **66**, 348–64.

Hanson, R.K. and Morton-Bourgon, K. (2004) 'Predictors of sexual recidivism: An updated meta-analysis' Ottawa: Public Safety and Emergency Preparedness Canada.

Hanson, R.K. and Morton-Bourgon, K.E. (2005) 'The characteristics of persistent sexual offenders: a meta-analysis of recidivism studies' *Journal of Consulting and Clinical Psychology* **73** (6), 1154–63.

Hanson, R.K. and Slater, S. (1988) 'Sexual victimization in the history of sexual abusers: a review' *Annals of Sex Research* **1**, 485–99.

Hanson, R.K., Bourgon, G., Helmus, L. and Hodgson, S. (2009) 'The principles of effective correctional treatment also apply to sex offenders: a meta-analysis' *Criminal Justice and Behavior* **36**: 865–91.

Hanson, R.K., Gordon, A., Harris, A.J.R., Marques, J.K., Murphy, W., Quinsey, V.L. and Seto, M.C. (2002) 'First report of the collaborative outcome data project on the effectiveness of psychological treatment for sex offenders' *Sexual Abuse: A Journal of Research and Treatment* **14** (2), 169–94.

Hanson, R.K., Helmus, L. and Thornton, D. (2010) 'Predicting recidivism amongst sexual offenders: a multi-site study of Static-2002' *Law and Human Behavior* **34** (3), 198–211.

Hare, R.D. (1980) 'A research scale for the assessment of psychopathy in criminal populations' *Personality and Individual Differences* **1**, 111–19.

Hare, R.D. (1991) *The Hare Psychopathy Checklist – Revised* Toronto: Multi-Health Systems.

Hare, R.D. (1998) 'The Hare PCL-R: some issues concerning its use and misuse' *Legal and Criminological Psychology* **3**, 99–119.

Hare, R.D. (2003) *Manual for the Revised Psychopathy Checklist* (2nd edn) Toronto, ON: Multi-Health Systems.

Harris, D.A., Mazerolle, P. and Knight, R.A. (2009) 'Understanding male sexual offending: a comparison of general and specialist theories' *Criminal Justice and Behavior* **36**, 1051–69.

Harris, G.T. and Rice, M.E. (1994) 'The violent patient' in R.T. Ammerman and M. Hersen (eds) *Handbook of Prescriptive Treatments for Adults* New York: Plenum, pp. 463–86.

Harris, G.T. and Rice, M.E. (1997) 'Risk appraisal and management of violent behaviour' *Psychiatric Services* **48** (9), 1168–76.

Harris, G.T., Rice, M.E. and Quinsey, V.L. (1993) 'Violent recidivism of mentally disordered offenders: the development of a statistical prediction instrument' *Criminal Justice and Behavior* **20** (4), 315–35.

Harris, S. (1994) 'Ideological exchanges in a British magistrates court' in J. Gibbons (ed.) *Language and the Law* London: Longman, pp. 156–70.

Harrower, J. (1998) *Applying Psychology to Crime* London: Hodder and Stoughton.

Harry, B. (1985) 'Violence and official diagnostic nomenclature' *Bulletin of the American Academy of Psychiatry and the Law* **13**, 385–88.

Hartshorne, H. and May, M.A. (1928) *Studies in the Nature of Character* New York: Macmillan.

Hartwig, M., Granhag, P., Strömwall, L. and Kronkvist, O. (2006) 'Strategic use of evidence during police interviews: when training to detect deception works' *Law and Human Behavior* 30 (5), 603–19.

Hatcher, R.M., Palmer, E.J., McGuire, J., Housome, J.C., Bilby, C.A.L. and Hollin, C.R. (2008) 'Aggression replacement training with adult male offenders within community settings: a reconviction analysis' *Journal of Forensic Psychiatry & Psychology* 19 (4), 517–32.

Hatz, J.L. and Bourgeois, M.J. (2010) 'Anger as a cue to truthfulness' *Journal of Experimental Social Psychology* 46, 680–3.

Hayes, B.K. and Delamothe, K. (1997) 'Cognitive interviewing procedures and suggestibility in children's recall' *Journal of Applied Psychology* 82 (4), 562–77.

Hazelwood, R.R. (1987) 'Analyzing the rape and profiling the offender' in R.R. Hazelwood and A.W. Burgess (eds) *Practical Aspects of Rape Investigation: A Multidisciplinary Approach* New York: Elsevier, pp. 16–24.

Hearold, S. (1986) 'A synthesis of 1,043 effects of television on social behaviour' in G. Comstock (ed.) *Public Communications and Behavior* New York: Academic Press, pp. 65–133.

Heath, W.P. (2009) 'Arresting and convicting the innocent: the potential role of an "inappropriate" emotional display in the accused' *Behavioral Science and the Law* 27, 313–32.

Heil, P., Ahlmeyer, S. and Simons, D. (2003) 'Crossover sexual offenses' *Sexual Abuse: A Journal of Research and Treatment* 15 (4), 221–36.

Heil, P., Harrison, L., English, K. and Ahlmeyer, S. (2009) 'Is prison sexual offending indicative of community risk?' *Criminal Justice and Behavior* 36, 892–908.

Heilbrun, K., Hawk, G. and Tate, D.C. (1996) 'Juvenile competence to stand trial: research issues in practice' *Law and Human Behavior* 20 (5), 573–8.

Heilbrun, K., Leheny, C., Thomas, L. and Huneycutt, D. (1997) 'A national survey of U.S. statutes on juvenile transfer: implications for policy and practice' *Behavioral Sciences and the Law* 15, 125–49.

Heinsman, D.T. and Shadish, W.R. (1996) 'Assignment methods in experimentation: when do nonrandomised experiments approximate answers from randomized experiments?' *Psychological Methods* 1 (2), 154–69.

Henderson, Z., Bruce, V. and Burton, M. (2000a) 'Effects of prior familiarity on video verification'. Paper presented at the European Association of Psychology and Law (EAPL) Conference, Limassol, Cyprus.

Henderson, Z., Bruce, V. and Burton, M. (2000b) 'Identification of faces from CCTV images'. Paper presented at the European Association of Psychology and Law (EAPL) Conference, Limassol, Cyprus.

Henkel, L.A., Coffman, K.A. and Dailey, E.M. (2008) 'A survey of people's attitudes and beliefs about false confessions' *Behavioral Sciences and the Law* 26, 555–84.

Hennigan, K.M., Delrosario, M.L., Heath, L., Cook, T.D., Wharton, J.D. and Calder, B.J. (1982) 'Impact of the introduction of television crime in the United States. Empirical findings and theoretical implications' *Journal of Personality and Social Psychology* 42 (3), 461–77.

Herrnstein, R.R. and Murray, C. (1994) *The Bell Curve: Intelligence and Class Structure in American Life* New York: Free Press.

Hickle, K.E. and Roe-Sepowitz, D.E. (2010) 'Female juvenile arsonists: An exploratory look at characteristics and solo and group arson offences' *Legal and Criminological Psychology* 15 (2), 385–99.

Hiday, V.A., Swanson, J.W., Swartz, M.S., Borum, R. and Wagner, H.R. (2001) 'Victimization: a link between mental illness and violence?' *International Journal of Law and Psychiatry* 24, 559–72.

Hill, C., Memon, A. and McGeorge, P. (2008) 'The role of confirmation bias in suspect interviews: A systematic evaluation' *Legal and Criminological Psychology* 13, 357–71.

Hillbrand, M., Spitz, R.T., Foster, H.G., Krystal, J.H. and Young, J.L. (1998) 'Creatine kinase elevations and aggressive behavior in hospitalized forensic patients' *Psychiatric Quarterly* 69 (1), 69–81.

Hochschild, A. (1983) *The Managed Heart: Commercialization of human feeling* Berkeley: University of California Press.

Hodge, J.E., McMurran, M. and Hollin, C.R. (1997) *Addicted to Crime?* Chichester: John Wiley.

Hodgins, S. (1992) 'Mental disorder, intellectual deficiency and crime: evidence from a birth cohort' *Archives of General Psychiatry* 49, 476–83.

Hodgins, S. (1997) 'An overview of research on the prediction of dangerousness' *Nordic Journal of Psychiatry* 51, Suppl. 39, 33–8.

Hodgins, S. and Cote, G. (1993) 'The criminality of mentally disordered offenders' *Criminal Justice and Behavior* 20, 115–29.

Hodgins, S., Cote, G. and Toupin, J. (1998) 'Major mental disorder and crime: an etiological hypothesis' in D.J. Cooke *et al.* (eds) *Psychopathy: Theory, Research and Implications for Society* (NATO ASI Series. Series D, Behavioural and Social Sciences, No. 88) Dordrecht: Kluwer, pp. 231–56.

Hodgins, S., Mednick, S., Brennan, P.A., Schulsinger, F. and Engberg, M. (1996) 'Mental disorder and crime: evidence from a Danish birth cohort' *Archives of General Psychiatry* **53** (6), 489–96.

Hollin, C.R. (2002) 'An overview of offender rehabilitation: something old, something borrowed, something new' *Australian Psychologist* **37** (3), 1–6.

Hollin, C.R. (2008) 'Evaluating offending behaviour programmes: does only randomization glister?' *Criminology & Criminal Justice* **8** (1), 89–106.

Hollin, C.R. and Palmer, E.J. (1995) *Assessing Prison Regimes: A Review to Inform the Development of Outcome Measures*. Commissioned report for the Planning Group, HM Prison Service.

Hollin, C.R. and Swaffer, T. (1995) 'Mental health: psychology's contribution to diagnosis, assessment and treatment' in R. Bull and D. Carson (eds) *Handbook of Psychology in Legal Contexts* Chichester: John Wiley, pp. 129–44.

Holmes, R.M. and Holmes, S.T. (1996) *Profiling Violent Crimes: An Investigative Tool* Thousand Oaks, CA: Sage.

Holmes, R.M. and Holmes, S.T. (1998) *Serial Murder* (2nd edn) Thousand Oaks, CA: Sage.

Homant, R.J. and Kennedy, D.B. (1998) 'Psychological aspects of crime scene profiling' *Criminal Justice and Behavior* **25** (3), 319–43.

Home Office (2001) The British Crime Survey 2000. http://www.homeoffice.gov.uk/rds/bcs1.html

Home Office (2002) *Tackling drugs to build a better Britain: The Government's 10-year strategy for tackling drug misuse.* London: HMSO.

Home Office (2003) *Criminal statistics: England and Wales 2002. Statistics relating to criminal proceedings for the year 2002* London: The Stationery Office.

Home Office (2004) Reconvictions of prisoners discharged from prison in 1996. Prisons: research development statistics. http://www.homeoffice.gov.uk/rds/prischap9.html

Home Office (2005a) Crime Reduction Toolkit: Arson. http://www.crimereduction.gov.uk/toolkits/an020703.htm

Home Office (2005b) Recorded Crime Statistics 1898–2002/03. http://www.homeoffice.gov.uk/rds/pdfs/100years.xls

Home Office (2007) Recorded Crime Statistics 2002/02–2006/7. http://www.homeoffice.gov.uk/rds/recordedcrime1.html. Accessed 21 January 2008.

Home Office (2008) Home Office crime statistics for England and Wales. http://www.crimestatistics.org.uk/output/Page27.asp. Accessed 10 June 2008.

Home Office (2010) Crime in England and Wales 2009/2010. http://rds.homeoffice.gov.uk/rds/crimeew0910.html. Accessed 8 March 2011.

Home Office Statistical Bulletin (2010) 'Public perceptions of policing, engagement with the police and victimisation: Findings from the 2009/10 British Crime Survey' Supplementary Volume 1 to Matthew Scribbins, John Flatley, Jenny Parfrement-Hopkins and Philip Hall (eds) *Crime in England and Wales 2009/10* http://www.homeoffice.gov.uk/publications/science-research-statistics/research-statistics/police-research/hosb1910/hosb1910?view=Binary

Hood, R., Shute, S., Feilzer, M. and Wilcox, A. (2002) 'Sex offenders emerging from long-term imprisonment' *British Journal of Criminology* **42**, 371–94.

Hopkins, M. (2002) 'Crimes against business: the way forward for future research' *British Journal of Criminology* **42**, 782–97.

Horgan, J. and Braddock, K. (2010) 'Rehabilitating the terrorists?: Challenges in assessing the effectiveness of de-radicalization programs' *Terrorism and Political Violence* **22** (2), 267–91.

Horgan, J. and Taylor, M. (2001) 'The making of a terrorist' *Jane's Intelligence Review*, **13** (12), 16–18.

Horley, J. (2000) 'Cognitions supportive of child molestation' *Aggression and Violent Behaviour* **5**, 551–64.

Horn, R. and Hollin, C.R. (1997) 'Police beliefs about women who offend' *Legal and Criminological Psychology* **2**, 193–204.

Horner, T.M., Guuyer, M.J. and Kalter, N.M. (1993) 'Clinical expertise and the assessment of child sexual abuse' *Journal of the American Academy of Child and Adolescent Psychiatry* **32**, 925–31.

Horowitz, I.A. (1980) 'Juror selection: a comparison of two methods in several criminal cases' *Journal of Applied Social Psychology* **10** (1), 86–99.

Horowitz, M.J. (1986) *Stress Response Syndromes* (2nd edn) Northvale, NJ: Jason Aronson.

Horowitz, S.W. (2009) 'Direct mixed and open questions in child interviewing: An analog study' *Legal and Criminological Psychology* **14**, 135–47.

Horselenberg, R., Merckelbach, H. and Josephs, S. (2003) 'Individual differences and false confessions: a conceptual replication of Kassin and Kiechel (1996)' *Psychology, Crime and Law* 9 (1), 1–8.

Horselenberg, R., Merckelbach, H., Smeets, T., Franssens, D., Peters, G.-J.Y. and Zeles, G. (2006) 'False confessions in the lab: do plausibility and consequences matter?' *Psychology, Crime & Law* 12 (1), 61–75.

Horvath, F. (1977) 'The effect of selected variables on interpretation of polygraph records' *Journal of Applied Psychology* 62, 127–36.

Houran, J. and Porter, S. (2005) 'Statement validity analysis of "The Jim Ragsdale Story": implications for the Roswell incident' http://www.scientificexploration.org/jse/articles/pdf/12.1_houran_porter.pdf. *Journal for Scientific Exploration*, 12 (1), Article 2.

House, J.C. (1997) 'Towards a practical application of offender profiling: the RNC's criminal suspect prioritization system' in J.L. Jackson and D.A. Bekerian (eds) *Offender Profiling: Theory, Research and Practice* Chichester: John Wiley, pp. 177–90.

Hovdestad, W.E. and Kristiansen, C.M. (1996a) 'A field study of "false memory syndrome": construct validity and incidence' *Journal of Psychiatry and Law* **Summer**, 299–338.

Hovdestad, W.E. and Kristiansen, C.M. (1996b) 'Mind meets body: on the nature of recovered memories of trauma' *Women and Therapy* 19 (1), 31–45.

Howells, K., Watt, B., Hall, G. and Baldwin, S. (1997) 'Developing programs for violent offenders' *Legal and Criminological Psychology* 2 (1), 117–28.

Howitt, D. (1991a) 'Britain's "substance abuse policy": realities and regulation in the United Kingdom' *International Journal of the Addictions* 3, 1087–111.

Howitt, D. (1991b) *Concerning Psychology* Milton Keynes: Open University Press.

Howitt, D. (1992) *Child Abuse Errors* Harlow: Harvester Wheatsheaf.

Howitt, D. (1994) 'Pornography's piggy in the middle' in C. Haslam and A. Bryman (eds) *Social Scientists Meet the Media* London: Routledge, pp. 93–107.

Howitt, D. (1995a) *Paedophiles and Sexual Offences Against Children* Chichester: John Wiley.

Howitt, D. (1995b) 'Pornography and the paedophile: is it criminogenic?' *British Journal of Medical Psychology* 68 (1), 15–27.

Howitt, D. (1998a) 'Are causal theories of paedophilia possible? A reconsideration of sexual abuse cycles' in J. Boros, I. Munnich and M. Szegedi (eds) *Psychology and Criminal Justice: International Review of Theory and Practice* Berlin: de Gruyter, pp. 248–53.

Howitt, D. (1998b) *Crime, the Media and the Law* Chichester: John Wiley.

Howitt, D. (1998c) 'Crime news'. Paper presented at the European Association of Psychology and Law (EAPL) Conference, Krakow, Poland.

Howitt, D. (2000) 'Just what is the role of fantasy in sex offending?' Paper presented at the European Association for Psychology and the Law (EAPL) Conference, Limassol, Cyprus, April.

Howitt, D. (2004) 'What is the role of fantasy in sex offending?' *Criminal Behaviour and Mental Health* 14 (3), 182–8.

Howitt, D. (2005) 'Paedophilia prevention and the law' in M. Stevens and K. Moss (eds) *Crime Prevention and the Law* London: Routledge, pp. 113–34.

Howitt, D. and Cramer, D. (2008) *Introduction to Statistics in Psychology* (4th edn) Harlow: Pearson Education.

Howitt, D. and Cramer, D. (2011) *Introduction to SPSS Statistics in Psychology* Harlow: Pearson Education.

Howitt, D. and Cumberbatch, G. (1975) *Mass Media Violence and Society* London: Elek Science.

Howitt, D. and Cumberbatch, G. (1990) *Pornography: Impacts and Influences* London: Home Office Research and Planning Unit.

Howitt, D. and Owusu-Bempah, J. (1994) *The Racism of Psychology* London: Harvester Wheatsheaf.

Hsu, C-I., Caputi, P. and Byrne, M.K. (2009) 'The Level of Service Inventory-Revised (LSI-R): a useful risk assessment measure for Australian offenders?' *Criminal Justice and Behavior* 36, 728–40.

Hudson, R.A. (1999) *The Sociology and Psychology of Terrorism: Who Becomes a Terrorist and Why?* A report prepared under an interagency agreement by the Federal Research Division, Library of Congress.

Hudson, S.M., Marshall, W.L., Ward, T., Johnston, P.W. and Jones, R.L. (1995) 'Kia Marama: a cognitive-behavioural program for incarcerated child molesters' *Behaviour Change* 12 (2), 69–80.

Huesmann, L.R. and Eron, L.D. (eds) (1986) *Television and the Aggressive Child: A Cross-national Comparison* Hillsdale, NJ: Lawrence Erlbaum.

Huffman, M.L., Warren, A.R. and Larson, S.M. (2001) 'Discussing truth and lies in interviews with children: whether, why, and how?' in R. Bull (ed.) *Children and the Law: The Essential Readings* Malden, MA: Blackwell, pp. 225–46.

Hughes, G., Hogue, T., Hollin, C. and Champion, H. (1997) 'First-stage evaluation of a treatment programme for personality disordered offenders' *Journal of Forensic Psychiatry* 8 (3), 515–27.

Hutcheson, G.D., Baxter, J.S., Telfer, K. and Warden, D. (1995) 'Child witness statement quality. Question type and errors of omission' *Law and Human Behavior* 19 (6), 631–48.

I

Iacono, W.G. (2008) 'Polygraph testing' in E. Borgida and S.T. Fiske (eds) *Beyond Common Sense: Psychological Science in the Courtroom* Oxford: Blackwell, pp. 218–35.

Iacono, W.G. and Lykken, D.T. (1997) 'The validity of the lie detector: two surveys of scientific opinion' *Journal of Applied Psychology* 82 (3), 426–33.

Iacono, W.G. and Patrick, C.J. (1997) 'Polygraphy and integrity testing' in R. Rogers (ed.) *Clinical Assessment of Malingering and Deception* New York: Guilford, pp. 252–81.

Inbau, F.E., Reid, J.E. and Buckley, J.P. (1986) *Criminal Interrogation and Confession* Baltimore, MD: Williams and Wilkins.

Inbau, F.E., Reid, J.E., Buckley, J.P. and Jayne, B.P. (2004) *Criminal Interrogations and Confessions* Gaithersburg, MD: Aspen.

Innes, M. (2002) 'The "process structures" of police homicide investigations' *British Journal of Criminology* 42 (4), 669–88.

International Crime Victimisation Survey (2001) http://ruljis.leidenuniv.nl/group/jfcr/www/icvs/Index.htm

Ireland, C.A. and Vecchi, G.M. (2009) 'The Behavioral Influence Stairway Model (BISM): a framework for managing terrorist crisis situations?' *Behavioral Sciences of Terrorism and Political Aggression* 1 (3), 203–18.

Ireland, J.L. (1999) 'Pro-victim attitudes and empathy in relation to bullying behaviour among prisoners' *Legal and Criminological Psychology* 4 (1), 51–66.

Itzin, C. (ed.) (1992) *Pornography: Women, Violence and Civil Liberties* Oxford: Oxford University Press.

J

Jackson, J.L. and Bekerian, D.A. (1997) 'Does offender profiling have a role to play?' in J.L. Jackson and D.A. Bekerian (eds) *Offender Profiling: Theory, Research and Practice* Chichester: John Wiley, pp. 1–7.

Jakob, R. (1992) 'On the development of psychologically oriented legal thinking in German speaking countries' in F. Losel, D. Bender and T. Bliesener (eds) *Psychology and Law: International Perspectives* Berlin: Walter de Gruyter, pp. 519–25.

James, A. (1996) 'Suicide reduction in medium security' *Journal of Forensic Psychiatry* 7 (2), 406–12.

James, D.V., Mullen, P.E., Meloy, J.R., Pathe, M.T., Preston, L., Darnley, B., Farnham, F.R. and Scalora, M.J. (2010) 'Stalkers and harassers of British royalty: an exploration of proxy behaviours for violence' *Behavioral Sciences and the Law* 29 (1), 64–80.

Jamieson, L. and Taylor, P.J. (2004) 'A reconviction study of special (high security) hospital patients' *British Journal of Criminology* 44, 783–802.

Jenkins. P. (1994) *Using Murder: The Social Construction of Serial Homicide* New York: Aldine de Gruyter.

Jespersen, A.F., Lalumière, M.L. and Seto, M.C. (2009) 'Sexual abuse history among adult sex offenders and non-sex offenders: A meta-analysis' *Child Abuse and Neglect* 33, 179–92.

Jhangiani, R. (2010) 'Psychological concomitants of the 11 September 2001 terrorist attacks: A review' *Behavioral Sciences of Terrorism and Political Aggression* 2 (1), 38–69.

Johnson, J.G., Smailes, E., Cohen, P., Kasen, S. and Brook, J.S. (2004) 'Antisocial parental behaviour, problematic parenting and aggressive offspring behaviour during adulthood: a 25-year longitudinal investigation' *British Journal of Criminology* 44, 915–30.

Johnson, S.D. and Bowers, K.J. (2004) 'The stability of space–time clusters of burglary' *British Journal of Criminology* 44, 55–65.

Jones, J.C. and Barlow, D.H. (1990) 'Self-reported frequency of sexual urges: fantasies and masturbatory fantasies in heterosexual males and females' *Archives of Sexual Behavior* 19, 269–79.

Jones, L. (2007) 'Iatrogenic interventions with personality disordered offenders' *Psychology, Crime and Law* 13 (1), 69–79.

Jones, L.F. (2004) 'Offence paralleling behaviour (OPB) as a framework for assessment and interventions with offenders' in A. Needs and G. Towl (eds) *Applying Psychology to Forensic Practice* BPS Blackwell: British Psychological Society, pp. 34–63.

Jones, S. and Cauffman, E. (2008) 'Juvenile psychopathy and judicial decision making: an empirical analysis of an ethical dilemma' *Behavioral Science and the Law* **26**, 151–65.

Jones, S. and Harrison, M. (2009) 'To testify or not to testify – that is the question: Comparing the advantages and disadvantages of testifying across situations' [Electronic Version]. *Applied Psychology in Criminal Justice* **5** (2), 165–81.

Joyce, D. (1993) 'How comprehensible are the Pace Codes of Practice to the majority of persons who might wish to read them?' in N.K. Clark and G.M. Stephenson (eds) *Issues in Criminological and Legal Psychology 20: Children, Evidence and Procedure* Leicester: Division of Criminological and Legal Psychology, British Psychological Society, pp. 70–4.

Jung, J. (1971) *The Experimenter's Dilemma*. New York: Harper and Row.

Junger, M. (1994) 'Accidents' in T. Hirschi and M.R. Gottfredson (eds) *The Generality of Deviance* New Brunswick: Transaction, pp. 81–112.

Junger, M. and Wiegersma, A. (1995) 'The relations between accidents, deviance and leisure time' *Criminal Behaviour and Mental Health* **5**, 144–74.

Junger, M., Terlouw, G.-J. and Van der Haijden, P.G.M. (1995) 'Crime, accidents and social control' *Criminal Behaviour and Mental Health* **5** (4), 386–410.

Jussim, L., Coleman, L.M. and Lerch, L. (1987) 'The nature of stereotypes: A comparison and integration of three theories' *Journal of Personality and Social Psychology* **52**, 536–46.

K

Kamin, L.J. (1977) *The Science and Politics of IQ* Harmondsworth: Penguin.

Kappeler, V., Blumberg, V. and Potter, G. (2000) *The Mythology of Crime and Justice* Prospect Heights, IL: Waveland.

Karlsson, I. and Christianson, S.-A. (1999) 'Memory for traumatic events among police personnel'. Paper presented at the International Conference of Psychology and the Law, Dublin, 6–9 July.

Kassin, S.M. (1997a) 'False memories turned against the self' *Psychological Inquiry* **8** (4), 300–2.

Kassin, S.M. (1997b) 'The psychology of confession evidence' *American Psychologist* **52** (3), 221–33.

Kassin, S.M. (1998) 'Eyewitness identification procedures: the fifth rule' *Law and Human Behavior* **22**, 649–53.

Kassin, S.M. (2008) 'Confession evidence: commonsense myths and misconceptions' *Criminal Justice and Behavior* **35** (10), 1309–22.

Kassin, S.M. and Kiechel, K.L. (1996) 'The social psychology of false confessions: compliance, internalization, and confabulation' *Psychological Science* **7** (3), 125–8.

Kassin, S.M. and McNall, K. (1991) 'Police interrogations and confessions: communicating promises and threats by pragmatic implication' *Law and Human Behavior* **15** (3), 233–51.

Kassin, S.M. and Neumann, K. (1997) 'On the power of confession evidence: an experimental test of the fundamental difference hypothesis' *Law and Human Behavior* **21** (5), 469–84.

Kassin, S.M. and Norwick, R.J. (2004) 'Why people waive their Miranda rights: the power of innocence' *Law and Human Behavior* **28** (2), 211–21.

Kassin, S.M. and Sukel, H. (1997) 'Coerced confessions and the jury: an experimental test of the "harmless error" rule' *Law and Human Behavior* **21** (1), 27–45.

Kassin, S.M., Drizin, S.A., Grisso, T., Gudjonsson, G.H., Leo, R.A. and Redlich, A.D. (2010) 'Police-induced confessions: risk factors and recommendations' *Law and Human Behavior* **34**, 3–38.

Kassin, S.M., Tubb, V.A., Hosch, H.M. and Memon, A. (2001) 'On the "general acceptance" of eyewitness testimony research: A new survey of the experts' *American Psychologist* **56** (5) May, 405–16.

Keane, T.M., Zimering, R.T. and Caddell, R.T. (1985) 'A behavioral formulation of PTSD in Vietnam veterans' *Behavior Therapist* **8**, 9–12.

Kebbell, M.R. and Hatton, C. (1999) 'People with mental retardation as witnesses in court: a review' *Mental Retardation* **37** (3), 179–87.

Kebbell, M.R. and Milne, R. (1998) 'Police officers' perceptions of eyewitness performance in forensic investigations' *Journal of Social Psychology* **138** (3), 323–30.

Kebbell, M.R. and Wagstaff, G.F. (1998) 'Hypnotic interviewing: the best way to interview eyewitnesses?' *Behavioral Sciences and the Law* **16**, 115–29.

Kebbell, M.R., Hatton, C. and Johnson, S.D. (2004) 'Witnesses with intellectual disabilities in court: what questions are asked and what influences do they have?' *Legal and Criminological Psychology* 9, 23–35.

Kebbell, M.R., Milne, R. and Wagstaff, G.F. (1998) 'The cognitive interview: a survey of its forensic effectiveness' *Psychology, Crime and Law* 5, 101–15.

Kebbell, M.R., Wagstaff, G.F. and Covey, J.A. (1996) 'The influence of item difficulty on the relationship between eyewitness confidence and accuracy' *British Journal of Psychology* 87, 653–62.

Keeler, L. (1934) 'Debunking the "lie detector"' *Journal of Civil Law and Criminology* 25, 153–9.

Keen, J. (2000) 'A practitioner's perspective: anger management work with young offenders' *Forensic Update* 60, 20–5.

Kellett, S. and Gross, H. (2006) 'Addicted to joyriding? An exploration of young offenders' accounts of their car crime' *Psychology, Crime and Law* 12 (1), 39–59.

Kelly, L. (1988) *Surviving Sexual Violence* Cambridge: Polity.

Kelly, L. (1989) 'What's in a name? Defining child sexual abuse' *Feminist Review* 28, 65–73.

Kemp, R., Pike, G., Brace, N. and Badal, P. (2000) 'Caught on camera: identification from CCTV footage'. Paper presented at the European Association of Psychology and Law (EAPL) Conference, Limassol, Cyprus.

Kemp, R., Towell, N. and Pike, G. (1997) 'When seeing should not be believing: photographs, credit cards and fraud' *Applied Cognitive Psychology* 11 (3), 211–22.

Kenworthy, T., Adams, C.E., Brooks-Gordon, B. and Fenton, M. (2004) *Psychological interventions for those who have sexually offended or are at risk of offending (CD004858; Cochrane Database of Systematic Reviews, Issue 3)* Chichester: John Wiley & Sons.

Keppel, R.D., Weis, J.G. Brown, K.M. and Welch, K. (2005) 'The Jack the Ripper murders: a modus operandi and signature analysis of the 1888–1891 Whitechapel murders' *Journal of Investigative Psychology and Offender Profiling* 2, 1–21.

Kerby, J. and Rae, J. (1998) 'Moral identity in action: young offenders' reports of encounters with the police' *British Journal of Social Psychology* 37, 439–56.

Kilpatrick, R. (1997) 'Joy-riding: an addictive behaviour' in J.E. Hodge, M. McMurran and C.R. Hollin (eds) *Addicted to Crime?* Chichester: John Wiley, pp. 165–90.

King, L. and Snook, B. (2009) 'Peering inside the Canadian interrogation room: An examination of the Reid model of interrogation, influence tactics, and coercive strategies' *Criminal Justice and Behavior* 36, 674–94.

Kirkendall, L.A. and McBride, L.G. (1990) 'Pre-adolescent and adolescent imagery and sexual fantasies: beliefs and experiences' in M.E. Perry (ed.) *Handbook of Sexology, Vol. 7: Childhood and Adolescent Sexology* Amsterdam: Elsevier, pp. 263–87.

Kitzinger, J. (1988) 'Defending innocence: ideologies of childhood' *Feminist Review* 28, Spring, 77–87.

Kleinmuntz, B. and Szucko, J.J. (1984) 'A field study of the fallibility of polygraphic lie detection' *Nature* 308, 449–550.

Knafo, D. and Jaffe, Y. (1984) 'Sexual fantasizing in males and females' *Journal of Research in Personality* 18, 451–62.

Knight, R.A. and Prentky, R.A. (1990) 'Classifying sexual offenders: The development and corroboration of taxonomic models' in W.L. Marshall, D.R. Laws and H.E. Barbaree (eds) *Handbook of Sexual Assault: Issues, Theories, and Treatment of the Offender* New York: Plenum, pp. 25–32.

Knight, R.A., Prentky, R.A. and Cerce, D.D. (1994) 'The development, reliability, and validity of an inventory for the multidimensional assessment of sex and aggression' *Criminal Justice and Behavior* 21, 72–94.

Kocsis, R.N. (2003a) 'Criminal psychological profiling: Validities and abilities?' *International Journal of Offender Therapy and Comparative Criminology* 47 (2), 126–44.

Kocsis, R.N. (2003b) 'An empirical assessment of content of criminal psychological profiles' *International Journal of Offender Therapy and Comparative Criminology* 47, 37–46.

Kocsis, R.N. (2010) 'Criminal profiling works and everyone agrees' *Journal of Forensic Psychology Practice* 9: 147–62.

Kocsis, R.N., Middledorp, J. and Karpin, A. (2008) 'Taking stock of accuracy in criminal profiling: the theoretical quandary for investigative psychology' *Journal of Forensic Psychology Practice* 8: 3, 244–61.

Kocsis, R.N., Middledorp, J. and Try, A.C. (2005) 'Cognitive processes in criminal profile construction: A preliminary study' *International Journal of Offender Therapy and Comparative Criminology* 49, 662–81.

Kohlberg, L. (1963) 'The development of children's orientations toward a moral order: 1. Sequence in the development of moral thought' *Human Development* 6, 11–33.

Kohlberg, L. (1984) *The Psychology of Moral Development: Essays on Moral Development* (Vol. 2) New York: Harper and Row.

Kohnken, G., Milne, R., Memon, A. and Bull, R. (1999) 'The cognitive interview: a meta-analysis' *Psychology, Crime and Law* 5, 3–27.

Kohnken, G., Thurer, C. and Zoberbeier, D. (1994) 'The cognitive interview: are the interviewers' memories enhanced, too?' *Applied Cognitive Psychology* **8**, 13–24.

Kolton, D.J.C., Boer, A. and Boer, D.P. (2001) 'A revision of the Abel and Becker Cognition Scale for intellectually disabled sexual offenders' *Sexual Abuse: A Journal of Research and Treatment* **13**, 217–19.

Konecni, V.J., Ebbesen, E.B. and Nehrer, E. (2000) 'Retrospective implications for the probative value of psychologists' testimony on eyewitness issues of exonerations by DNA evidence' in A. Czerederecka, T. Jaskiewicz-Obdzinska and J. Wojcikiewicz (eds) *Forensic Psychology and Law: Traditional Questions and New Ideas* Krakow: Institute of Forensic Research Publishers, pp. 41–8.

Korkman, J., Santtila, P., Drzewiecki, T. and Sandnabba, N.K. (2008) 'Failing to keep it simple: language use in child sexual abuse interviews with 3–8 year-old children' *Psychology, Crime & Law* **14** (1), 41–60.

Kovera, M.B., Dickinson, J. and Cutler, B.L. (2002) 'Voir dire and jury selection: practical issues, research findings and directions for future research' in A.M. Goldstein (ed.) *Comprehensive Handbook of Psychology, Vol. 11: Forensic Psychology* New York: John Wiley & Sons, pp. 161–75.

Krackow, E. and Lynn, S.J. (2003) 'Is there touch in the game of twister? The effects of innocuous touch and suggestive questions on children's eyewitness memory' *Law and Human Behavior* **27** (6), 589–604.

Kramer, G.M., Wolbransky, M.S. and Heilbrun, K. (2007) 'Plea bargaining recommendations by criminal defense attorneys: evidence strength, potential sentence, and defendant preference' *Behavioral Sciences and the Law* **25**, 573–85.

Kristiansen, C.M. (1996) 'Recovered memory research and the influence of social attitudes'. Unpublished manuscript, Ottawa, Ontario: Department of Psychology, Carleton University.

Kristiansen, C.M., Felton, K.A. and Hovdestad, W.E. (1996) 'Recovered memories of child abuse: fact, fantasy or fancy?' *Women and Therapy* **19** (1), 47–59.

Krug, K. (2007) 'The relationship between confidence and accuracy: current thoughts of the literature and a new area of research' *Applied Psychology in Criminal Justice* **3** (1), 7–41.

Kruttschnitt, C., Heath, L. and Ward, D.A. (1986) 'Family violence, television viewing habits, and other adolescent experiences related to violent criminal behaviour' *Criminology* **24** (2), 235–65.

Kuhn, D., Weinstock, M. and Flaton, R. (1994) 'How well do jurors reason? Competence dimensions of individual variation in a juror reasoning task' *Psychological Science* **5**, 289–96.

Kulas, J.T., McInnerney, J.E., DeMuth, R.F. and Jadwinski, V. (2007) 'Employee satisfaction and theft: testing climate perceptions as a mediator' *Journal of Psychology* **141** (4), 389–402.

Kullgren, G., Tengstrom, A. and Gran, M. (1998) 'Suicide among personality-disordered offenders: a follow-up study of 1,943 male criminal offenders' *Social Psychiatry and Psychiatric Epidemiology* **33**, 102–6.

Kury, H. (1998) 'Legal psychology in Europe: results of a survey' in J. Boros, I. Munnich and M. Szegedi (eds) *Psychology and Criminal Justice: International Review of Theory and Practice* Berlin: Walter de Gruyter, pp. 428–35.

Kutchinsky, B. (1970) 'The effect of pornography: a pilot experiment on perception, behavior and attitudes' in *Technical Report of the Commission on Obscenity and Pornography*, Vol. VIII, *Erotica and Social Behavior* Washington, DC: US Government Printing Office, pp. 133–70.

Kutchinsky, B. (1973) 'The effect of easy availability of pornography on the incidence of sex crimes: the Danish experience' *Journal of Social Issues* **29** (3), 163–91.

Kutchinsky, B. (1991) 'Pornography and rape: theory and practice?' *International Journal of Law and Psychiatry* **14** (1/2), 145–51.

L

La Fond, J.Q. (1999) 'Clinical, legal and ethical issues in implementing a sexual predator law in the United States'. Paper presented to American Psychology-Law Society/European Association of Psychology and Law, Trinity College, Dublin, Ireland, 6–9 July.

La Fontaine, J. (1990) *Child Sexual Abuse* Cambridge: Polity.

Laajasalo, T. and Häkkänen, H. (2004) 'Background characteristics of mentally ill homicide offenders: a comparison of five diagnostic groups' *Journal of Forensic Psychiatry and Psychology* **15** (3), 451–74.

Lahm, K.F. (2008) 'Inmate-on-inmate assault: a multilevel examination of prison violence' *Criminal Justice and Behavior* **35**, 120–37.

Lamb, M.E., Sternberg, K.J. and Orbach, Y. (1999) 'Forensic interviews of children' in A. Memon and R. Bull (eds) *Handbook of the Psychology of Interviewing* Chichester: John Wiley, pp. 253–77.

Lamb, M.E., Sternberg, K.J., Esplin, P.W., Hershkowitz, I. and Orbach, Y. (1997) 'Assessing the credibility of children's allegations of sexual abuse: a survey of recent research' *Learning and Individual Differences* 9 (2), 175–94.

Lamers-Winkelman, F. (1997) 'The second part of statement validity analysis'. Paper presented at conference on Responding to Child Maltreatment, San Diego.

Lamers-Winkelman, F. and Buffing, F. (1996) 'Children's testimony in the Netherlands: a study of statement validity analysis' *Criminal Justice and Behavior*, 23 (2), 304–21.

Lande, R.G. (1993) 'The video violence debate' *Hospital and Community Psychiatry* 44 (4), 347–51.

Langsdale, A. and Greenberg, M.S. (2006) 'The impact of situational cues and bystander emotion on labeling an event as a robbery' *Applied Psychology in Criminal Justice* 2 (2), 130.

Langstrom, N. (1999) *Young Sex Offenders: Individual Characteristics, Agency Reactions and Criminal Recidivism* Stockholm: Karolinka Instutet, Department of Public Health, Division of Psychosocial Factors and Health, Division of Forensic Psychiatry.

Larissa, K. Barber, Matthew, Grawitch, J. and Trares, Shawn, T. (2009) 'Service-oriented and force-oriented emotion regulation in police officers' *Applied Psychology in Criminal Justice* 5 (2), 182–202.

Larson, B.A. and Brodsky, S.L. (2010) 'When cross-examination offends: how men and women assess intrusive questioning of male and female expert witnesses' *Journal of Applied Social Psychology* 40 (4), 811–30.

Larson, J.A. (1922) 'The cardio-pneumo psychogram and its use in the study of emotions, with practical applications' *Journal of Experimental Psychology* 5, 323–8.

Lassiter, G.D. (2002) 'Illusory causation in the courtroom' *Current Directions in Psychological Science* 11, 204–8.

Lassiter, G.D., Geers, A.L., Munhall, P.J., Handley, I.M. and Beers, M.J. (2001) 'Videotaped confessions: Is guilt is in the eye of the camera?' *Advances in Experimental Social Psychology* 33, 189–254.

Lassiter, G.D., Ware, L.L., Ratcliff, J.J. and Irvin, C.R. (2009) 'Evidence of the camera perspective bias in authentic videotaped interrogations: Implications for emerging reform in the criminal justice system' *Legal and Criminological Psychology* 14, 157–70.

Laws, D.R. (1994) 'How dangerous are rapists to children?' *Journal of Sexual Aggression* 1, 1–14.

Laws, D.R. and Gress, C.L.Z. (2004) 'Seeing things differently: the viewing time alternative to penile plethysmography' *Legal and Criminological Psychology* 9, 183–96.

Laws, D.R. and Marshall, W.L. (1990) 'A conditioning theory of the etiology and maintenance of deviant sexual preference and behaviour' in W.L. Marshall, D.R. Laws and H.E. Barbaree (eds) *Handbook of Sexual Assault. Issues, Theories and Treatment of the Offender* New York: Plenum, pp. 209–230.

Leam, C., Browne, K.D., Stringer, I. and Hogue, T.E. (2008) 'Sexual reconviction rates in the United Kingdom and actuarial risk estimates' *Child Abuse and Neglect* 32, 121–38.

Lecci, L., Snowden, J. and Morris, D. (2004) 'Using social science research to inform and evaluate the contributions of trial consultants in the *voir dire*' *Journal of Forensic Psychology Practice* 4, 67–78.

Lees, S. (1995) 'Media reporting of rape: the 1993 British "date rape" controversy' in D. Kidd-Hewitt and R. Osborne (eds) *Crime and the Media: The Post-modern Spectacle* London: Pluto, pp. 107–30.

Lefkowitz, M.M., Eron, L.D., Walder, L.O. and Huesmann, L.R. (1977) *Growing Up to be Violent: A Longitudinal Study of the Development of Aggression* New York: Pergamon.

Leichtman, M.D. and Ceci, S.J. (1995) 'The effects of stereotypes and suggestions on pre-schoolers' reports' *Developmental Psychology* 31, 568–78.

Leo, R.A. (1996) 'Miranda's revenge: police interrogation as a confidence game' *Law and Society Review* 30 (2), 259–88.

Leo, R.A. and Liu, B. (2009) 'What do potential jurors know about police interrogation techniques and false confessions?' *Behavioral Sciences and the Law* 27, 381–99.

Leo, R.A. and Ofshe, R.J. (1998) 'The consequences of false confessions: deprivations of liberty and miscarriages of justice in the age of psychological interrogation' *Journal of Criminal Law and Criminology* 88 (2), 429–96.

Lerner, M.J. and Goldberg, J.H. (1999) 'When do decent people blame victims? The differing effects of the explicit-rational and implicit-experiential cognitive systems' in S. Chaiken and Y. Trope (eds) *Dual Process Theories in Social Psychology* New York: Guilford Press, pp. 627–40.

Letourneau, E.J., Bandiyioadhyay, K.S., Armstrong, K.S. and Sinha, D. (2010) 'Do sex offender registration and notification requirements deter juvenile sex crimes?' *Criminal Justice and Behavior* 37, 553–69.

Levenson, J.S., D'Amora, D.A. and Hern, A.L. (2007) 'Megan's Law and its impact on community re-entry for sex offenders' *Behavioral Sciences and the Law* 25, 587–602.

Lewis, N. and Yarnell, H. (1951) *Pathological Firesetting (Pyromania)*. Nervous and Mental Disease Monographs, No. 82/437.

Leyton, E. (1986) *Hunting Humans: The Rise of the Modern Multiple Murderer* Toronto: McClelland and Stewart.

Lievore, D. (2004) 'Victim credibility in adult sexual assault cases' *Trends & Issues in Crime and Criminal Justice* no. 288. Available at http://www.aic.gov.au/documents/B/8/3/{7BB8374C06-4C85-4FA7-8BE9-A9361EA23423}tandi288.pdf

Lilienfeld, S.O. and Landfield, K. (2008) 'Science and pseudoscience in law enforcement: a user-friendly primer' *Criminal Justice and Behavior* 35, 1215–30.

Limbandari, B.J. and Sheridan, D.J. (1995) 'Prediction of intentional interpersonal violence: an introduction' in J.C. Campbell (ed.) *Assessing Dangerousness* Thousand Oaks, CA: Sage, pp. 1–19.

Lind, B., Chen, S., Weatherburn, D. and Mattick, R. (2005) 'The effectiveness of methadone maintenance treatment in controlling crime: an Australian aggregate-level analysis' *British Journal of Criminology* 45, 201–11.

Lind, J.E. and Ke, G.Y. (1985) 'Opening and closing statements' in S.M. Kassin and L.S. Wrightsman (eds) *The Psychology of Evidence and Trial Procedure* London: Sage, pp. 229–53.

Lindeman, M., Harakka, T. and Keltikangas-Jarvinen, L. (1997) 'Age and gender differences in adolescents' reactions to conflict situations: aggression, prosociality, and withdrawal' *Journal of Youth and Adolescence* 26 (3), 339–51.

Lindholm, T., Christianson, S.-A. and Karlsson, I. (1997) 'Police officers and civilians as witnesses: intergroup biases and memory performance' *Applied Cognitive Psychology* 11, 431–4.

Link, B.G., Andrews, H. and Cullen, F.T. (1992) 'The violent and illegal behaviour of mental patients reconsidered' *American Sociological Review* 57, 275–92.

Lipian, M.S., Mills, M.J. and Brantman, A. (2004) 'Assessing the verity of children's allegations of abuse: A psychiatric overview' *International Journal of Law and Psychiatry* 27, 249–63.

Lippert, T., Cross, T.P., Jones, L.M. and Walsh, W. (2010) 'Suspect confession of child sexual abuse to investigators' *Child Maltreatment* 15 (2), 161–70.

Lipsey, M. (2009) 'The primary factors that characterize effective interventions with juvenile offenders: a meta-analytic overview' *Victims and Offenders* 4, 124–47.

Lipsey, M.W., Chapman, G.L. and Landenberger, N.A. (2001) 'Cognitive behavioral programs for offenders' *Annals of the American Academy of Political and Social Science* 578 (1), 144–57.

Liska, A.E. and Baccaglini, W. (1990) 'Feeling safe by comparison: crime in the newspapers' *Social Problems* 37 (3), 360–74.

Lloyd, C. and Walmsley, R. (1989) 'Changes in rape offences and sentencing' *Home Office Study No. 105* London: HMSO.

Lloyd-Bostock, S. (1996) 'The jury in the United Kingdom: juries and jury research in context' in G. Davies, S. Lloyd-Bostock, M. McMurran and C. Wilson (eds) *Psychology, Law and Criminal Justice: International Developments in Research and Practice* Berlin: De Gruyter, pp. 349–59.

Loftus, E.F. and Guyer, M.J. (2002) 'Who abused Jane Doe?: The hazards of the single case study' *Skeptical Inquirer* 26 (May–June), 24–32; ibid., 2 (26) (July–August), 37–40, 44.

Loftus, E. and Palmer, J.C. (1974) 'Reconstructions of automobile destruction: an example of the interaction between language and memory' *Journal of Verbal Learning and Verbal Behavior* 13, 585–9.

Loftus, E. and Pickrell, J.E. (1995) 'The formation of false memories' *Psychiatric Annals* 25, 720–5.

Loftus, E., Garry, M. and Hayne, H. (2008) 'Repressed and recovered memories' in E. Borgida and S.T. Fiske (eds) *Beyond Common Sense: Psychological Science in the Courtroom* Oxford: Blackwell, pp. 177–94.

Loftus, E.F., Miller, D.G. and Burns, H.J. (1978) Semantic integration of verbal information into a visual memory *Journal of Experimental Psychology, Human Learning and Memory*, 4 (1), 19–31.

Loftus, G.R. (2010) 'What can a perception–memory expert tell a jury?' *Psychonomic Bulletin and Review* 17 (2), 143–48.

Lombroso, C. (1911) *Crime, Its Causes and Remedies* Boston, MA: Little, Brown.

London, K., Bruck, M. and Melnyk, L. (2009) 'Post-event information affects children's autobiographical memory after one year' *Law and Human Behavior* 33 (4), 344–55.

Looman, J. (1999) 'Mood, conflict and deviant sexual fantasies'. Unpublished manuscript. Ontario: Regional Treatment Centre.

Los, M. (1990) 'Feminism and rape law reform' in L. Gelsthorpe and A. Morris (eds) *Feminist Perspectives in Criminology* Milton Keynes: Open University Press, pp. 164–72.

Los, M. and Chamard, S.E. (1997) 'Selling newspapers or educating the public? Sexual violence in the media' *Canadian Journal of Criminology*, July, 293–328.

Lösel, F., Bender, D. and Bliesener, T. (1999) *Biosocial Risk and Protective Factors for Anti-social Behavior in Juveniles: Heart Rate and Family Characteristics* Nuremberg: Department of Psychology, University of Erlangan-Nuremberg.

Lösel, F. and Schmucker, M. (2005) 'The effectiveness of treatment for sexual offenders: A comprehensive meta-analysis' *Journal of Experimental Criminology* 1, 117–46.

Lowenstein, J.A., Blank, H. and Sauer, J.D. (2010) 'Uniforms affect the accuracy of children's eyewitness identification decisions' *Journal of Investigative Psychology and Offender Profiling* 7, 59–73.

Loza, W. and Loza-Fanous, A. (1999) 'The fallacy of reducing rape and violent recidivism by reducing anger' *International Journal of Offender Therapy and Comparative Criminology* 43, 492–502.

Luckabaugh, R., Fuqua, H.E., Cangemi, J.P. and Kowalski, C.J. (1997) 'Terrorist behavior and United States foreign policy: who is the enemy? Some psychological and political perspectives' *Psychology* 34 (2), 1–15.

Luna, K. and Martin-Luengo, B. (2010) 'New advances in the study of the confidence–accuracy relationship in the memory for events' *The European Journal of Psychology Applied to Legal Context* 2 (1): 55–71.

Lussier, P., Leclerc, B., Calse, J. and Proulx, J. (2007) 'Developmental pathways of deviance in sexual aggressors' *Criminal Justice and Behavior* 34 (11), 1411–62.

Lymburner, J.A. and Roesch, R. (1999) 'The insanity defence: five years of research (1993–97)' *International Journal of Law and Psychiatry* 22 (3–4), 213–40.

Lynn, S.J., Neuschatz, J. and Fite, R. (2002) 'Hypnosis and memory: implications for the courtroom and psychotherapy' in M.L. Eisen, J.A. Quas and G.S. Goodman (eds) *Memory and Suggestibility in the Forensic Interview* Mahwah, NJ: Lawrence Erlbaum, pp. 287–307.

Lyons, P.M., Anthony, C.M., Davis, K.M., Fenandez, K., Torres, A.N. and Marcus, D.K. (2005) 'Police judgements of culpability and homophobia' *Applied Psychology in Criminal Justice* 1 (1), 1–14.

M

MacCulloch, M.J., Snowden, P.R., Wood, P.J.W. and Mills, H.E. (1983) 'Sadistic fantasy, sadistic behaviours and offending' *British Journal of Psychiatry* 143, 20–9.

Mackinnon, A., Copolov, D.L. and Trauer, T. (2004) 'Factors associated with compliance and resistance to command hallucinations' *The Journal Nervous and Mental Disease* 192, 357–62.

MacMartin, C. and Yarmey, A.D. (1998) 'Repression, dissociation and the recovered memory debate: constructing scientific evidence and expertise' *Expert Evidence* 6, 203–26.

Madrigal, D.O., Bowman, D.R. and McClain, B.U. (2009) 'Introducing the Four-Phase Model of Hostage Negotiation' *Journal of Police Crisis Negotiations* 9 (2), 119–33.

Madsen, L., Parsons, S. and Grubin, D. (2004) 'A preliminary study of the contribution of periodic polygraph testing to the treatment and supervision of sex offenders' *British Journal of Forensic Psychiatry and Psychology* 15, 682–95.

Maghan, J. (1998) 'Terrorist mentality' in J. Boros, I. Munnich and M. Szegedi (eds) *Psychology, Law and Criminal Justice: International Review of Theory and Practice* Berlin: Walter de Gruyter, pp. 335–45.

Mair, K.J. (1995) 'Cognitive distortion in the prediction of sexual offending' in N.K. Clark and G.M. Stephenson (eds) *Investigative and Forensic Decision Making, Issues in Criminological and Legal Psychology No. 26.* Leicester: Division of Criminological and Legal Psychology, British Psychological Society, pp. 12–17.

Malamuth, N.M. and Ceniti, J. (1986) 'Repeated exposure to violent and non-violent pornography: likelihood of raping ratings and laboratory aggression against women' *Aggressive Behavior* 12, 129–37.

Malpass, R. and Devine, P. (1981) 'Guided memory in eyewitness identification' *Journal of Applied Psychology* 66 (3), 343–50.

Maniglio, R. (2009) 'Severe mental illness and criminal-victimization: a systematic review' *Acta Psychiatrica Scandinavica* 119, 180–91.

Maniglio, R. (2010) 'The role of deviant sexual fantasy in the etiopathogenesis of sexual homicide: A systematic review' *Aggression and Violent Behavior* 15, 294–302.

Marsh, H.L. (1991) 'A comparative analysis of crime coverage in newspapers in the United States and other countries from 1960 to 1989: a review of the literature' *Journal of Criminal Justice* 19, 67–79.

Marshall, B.C. and Alison, L.J. (2006) 'Structural behavioural analysis as a basis for discrimininating between genuine and simulated rape allegations' *Journal of Investigative Psychology and Offender Profiling* 3, 21–34.

Marshall, W.C. (1988) 'The use of sexually explicit stimuli by rapists, child molesters and non-offenders' *Journal of Sex Research* 25 (2), 267–88.

Marshall, W.L., Hudson, S.M. and Ward, T. (1992) 'Sexual deviance' in P.H. Wilson (ed.) *Principles and Practice of Relapse Prevention* New York: Guilford Press, pp. 235–54.

Marshall, W.L., Marshall, L.E., Sachdev, S. and Kruger, R. (2003) 'Distorted attitudes and perceptions, and their relationship with self-esteem and coping in child molesters' *Sexual Abuse: A Journal of Research and Treatment* 15, 171–81.

Martinson, R. (1974) 'What works? Questions and answers about prison reform' *Public Interest* 10, 22–54.

Maruna, S. and Copes, H. (2005) 'What have we learned in five decades of neutralization research?' *Crime and Justice: A Review of Research* 32, 221–320.

Maruna, S. and Mann, R. (2006) 'Fundamental attribution errors? Re-thinking cognitive distortions' *Legal and Criminological Psychology* 11, 155–77.

Masters, B. (1993) *The Shrine of Jeffrey Dahmer* London: Hodder and Stoughton.

Mathys, C. and Born, M. (2009) '221 Intervention in juvenile delinquency: Danger of iatrogenic effects?' *Children and Youth Services Review* 31, 1217–1.

Matte, J.M. (2002) *Forensic psychophysiology using the polygraph* Williamsville, NY: J.A.M.

Mauer, M. (2006) *Race to Incarcerate* (2nd edn) Washington, DC: The Sentencing Project.

McAdams, D.P. (1990) 'Unity and purpose in human lives: the emergence of identity as a life story' in A.I. Rabin, R.A. Zucker, R.A. Emmons and S. Frank (eds) *Studying Persons and Lives* New York: Springer, pp. 148–200.

McCabe, M.P. and Wauchope, M. (2005) 'Behavioural characteristics of rapists' *Journal of Sexual Aggression* 11 (2), 235–47.

McCabe, S. and Purves, R. (1974) *The Shadow Jury at Work* Oxford: Blackwell.

McCann, J.T. (1998) 'Broadening the typology of false confessions' *American Psychologist* March, 319–20.

McConaghy, N. (1991) 'Validity and ethics of penile circumference measures of sexual arousal: a critical review' *Archives of Sexual Behavior* 19 (4), 357–69.

McConkey, K.M., Roche, S.M. and Sheehan, P.W. (1989) 'Reports of forensic hypnosis: a critical analysis' *Australian Psychologist* 24 (2), 249–72.

McCord, J. (1979) 'Some child-rearing antecedents of criminal behavior in adult men' *Journal of Personality and Social Psychology* 37 (9), 1477–86.

McCoy, S.P. and Aamodt, M.G. (2010) 'A comparison of law enforcement divorce rates with those of other occupations' *Journal of Police and Criminal Psychology* 25, 1–16.

McElvain, J.P. and Kposowa, J. (2008) 'Police officer characteristics and the likelihood of using deadly force' *Criminal Justice and Behavior* 35, 505–21.

McEwan, J. (1995) 'Adversarial and inquisitorial proceedings' in R. Bull and D. Carson (eds) *Handbook of Psychology in Legal Contexts* Chichester: John Wiley, pp. 495–501.

McEwan, T.E., Mullen, P.E. and MacKenzie, R. (2009) 'A study of the predictors of persistence in stalking situations' *Law and Human Behavior* 33, 149–58.

McGeorge, N. (1996) 'Risk assessment and political decision making' *Forensic Update* 45, 21–2.

McGregor, G. and Howells, K. (1997) 'Addiction models of sexual offending' in J.E. Hodge, M. McMurran and C.R. Hollin (eds) *Addicted to Crime?* Chichester: John Wiley, pp. 107–37.

McGuire, J. (1997) '"Irrational" shoplifting and models of addiction' in J.E. Hodge, M. McMurran and C.R. Hollin (eds) *Addicted to Crime?* Chichester: John Wiley, pp. 207–31.

McGuire, J. (2000) 'Explanations of criminal behaviour' in J. McGuire, T. Mason and A. O'Kane (eds) *Behaviour, Crime and Legal Processes: A Guide for Forensic Practitioners* Chichester: John Wiley, pp. 135–59.

McGuire, J. (2004) *Understanding Psychology and Crime: Perspectives on Theory and Action* Maidenhead: Open University Press.

McHugh, M. (1998) 'Strategies for reducing suicides in prison'. Paper presented at Eighth European Conference on Psychology and Law, Krakow, September.

McHugh, M. (1999) 'Suicide and self injury' *Issues in Forensic Psychology* 1, 23–6.

McIntosh, J., Bloor, M. and Robertson, M. (2007) 'The effect of drug treatment upon the commission of acquisitive crime' *Journal of Substance Use* 12 (5), 375–84.

McMurran, M. and Duggan, C. (2005) 'The manualisation of a treatment programme for personality disorder' *Criminal Behaviour and Mental Health* 15 (1), 17–27.

McMurran, M. and Theodosi, E. (2007) 'Is treatment non-completion associated with increased reconviction over no treatment?' *Psychology, Crime and Law* 13 (4), 33–43.

McMurran, M. and Cusens, B. (2005) 'Alcohol and violent and non-violent acquisitive offending' *Addiction Research and Theory* 13 (5), 439–43.

McMurran, M., Hodge, J.E. and Hollin, C.R. (1997) 'Introduction: current issues in the treatment of addictions and crime' in J.E. Hodge, M. McMurran and C.R. Hollin (eds) *Addicted to Crime?* Chichester: John Wiley, pp. 1–9.

McMurran, M., Jinks, M., Howells, K. and Howard, R. (2011) 'Investigation of a typology of alcohol related violence defined by ultimate goals' *Legal and Criminological Psychology* 16 (1), 75–89.

McNeil, D.E. (1997) 'Correlates of violence in psychotic patients' *Psychiatric Annals* 27 (10), 683–90.

McSherry, B. (2004) 'Criminal responsibility, fleeting states of mental impairment, and the power of self-control' *International Journal of Law and Psychiatry* 27, 445–57.

Mednick, S.A., Gabrielli, W.F. and Hutchings, B. (1994) 'Genetic influences in criminal convictions' *Science* 224, 841–94.

Meehle, P.E. (1954) *Clinical Versus Statistical Predictions* Minneapolis: University of Minnesota Press.

Meloy, M.R. (2002) 'Stalking and violence' in J. Boon and L. Sheridan (eds) *Stalking and Psychosexual Obsession: Psychological Perspectives for Prevention, Policing and Treatment* Chichester: John Wiley, pp. 105–24.

Memon, A. and Young, M. (1997) 'Desperately seeking evidence: the recovered memory debate' *Legal and Criminological Psychology* 2, 131–54.

Memon, A., Holley, A., Milne, R., Koehnken, G. and Bull, R. (1994) 'Towards understanding the effects of interviewer training in evaluating the cognitive interview' *Applied Cognitive Psychology* 8, 641–59.

Merari, A. (2007) 'Psychological aspects of suicide terrorism' in B. Bongar, L.M. Brown, L.E. Beutler, J.N. Breckenridge and P.B. Zimbardo (eds) *Psychology of Terrorism* New York: Oxford University Press, pp. 101–15.

Merton, R.K. (1968) *Social theory and social structure* New York: Free Press.

Messner, S.F. (1986) 'Television violence and violent crime: an aggregate analysis' *Social Problems* 33 (3), 218–35.

Miethe, T.D. (1995) 'Fear and withdrawal from urban life' *Annals of the American Association of Political and Social Science* 539, 14–27.

Milavsky, J.R., Kessler, R.C., Stipp, H.H. and Rubins, W.S. (1982) *Television and Aggression: A Panel Study* New York: Academic Press.

Milgram, S. (1974) *Obedience to Authority: An Experimental View* New York: Harper and Row.

Miller, E. (1999a) 'The neuropsychology of offending' *Psychology, Crime and Law* 5, 515–36.

Miller, E. (1999b) 'Head injury and offending' *Journal of Forensic Psychiatry* 10 (1), 157–66.

Miller, M.E., Adya, M., Chamberlain, J. and Jehle, A. (2010) 'The effects of counterfactual thinking on reactions to victimization' *Applied Psychology in Criminal Justice* 6 (1), 17–30.

Miller, N.E. and Dollard, J. (1941) *Social Learning and Imitation* Yale: Yale University Press.

Milne, R. and Bull, R. (1994) 'Improving witness recall: the cognitive interview and the legal profession' *Journal of Child Law* 6 (2), 82–4.

Milne, R. and Bull, R. (1996) 'Interviewing children with mild learning disability with the cognitive interview' in N.K. Clark and G.M. Stephenson (eds) *Issues in Criminological and Legal Psychology 26: Investigative and Forensic Decision Making* Leicester: Division of Criminological and Legal Psychology, British Psychological Society, pp. 44–51.

Milne, R., Bull, R., Koehnken, G. and Memon, A. (1995) 'The cognitive interview and suggestibility' in N.K. Clark and G.M. Stephenson (eds) *Issues in Criminological and Legal Psychology 22: Criminal Behaviour: Perceptions, Attributions and Rationality* Leicester: Division of Criminological and Legal Psychology, British Psychological Society, pp. 21–7.

Milne, R., Clare, I.C.H. and Bull, R. (1999) 'Using the cognitive interview with adults with mild learning disabilities' *Psychology, Crime and Law* 5, 81–99.

Milner, J.S. and Campbell, J.C. (1995) 'Prediction issues for practitioners' in J.C. Campbell (ed.) *Assessing Dangerousness* Thousand Oaks, CA: Sage, pp. 20–40.

Miner, M.H. and Dwyer, S.M. (1997) 'The psychological development of sex offenders: differences between exhibitionists, child molesters and incest offenders' *International Journal of Offender Therapy and Comparative Criminology* 41 (1), 36–44.

Mirrlees-Black, C. (2001) 'Confidence in the criminal justice system'. Home Office Research, Development and Statistics Directorate, Research Findings, 137. http://www.homeoffice.gov.uk/rds/pdfs/r137.pdf

Mischel, W. (1999) 'Personality coherence and dispositions in a cognitive-affective personality system (CAPS) approach' in D. Cervone and Y. Shoda (eds) *The Coherence of Personality: Social-cognitive Bases of Consistency, Variability and Organisation* London: Guilford Press, pp. 37–60.

Mitchell, B. (1997) 'Putting diminished responsibility law into practice: a forensic psychiatric perspective' *Journal of Forensic Psychiatry* 8 (3), 620–34.

Mnookin, R.H. and Kornhauser, L. (1979) 'Bargaining in the shadow of the law: the case of divorce' *Yale Law Journal* **88**, 950.

Moffitt, T.E. (1993) 'Adolescence-limited and life-course-persistent antisocial behavior: A developmental taxonomy' *Psychological Review* **100**, 674–701.

Moffitt, T.E., Caspi, A., Harrington, H. and Milne, B.J. (2002) 'Males on the life-course-persistent and adolescence-limited antisocial pathways: Follow-up at age 26 years' *Development & Psychopathology* **14**, 179–220.

Monahan, J. (1993) 'Mental disorder and violence: another look' in S. Hodgins (ed.) *Mental Disorder and Crime* Newbury Park, CA: Sage, pp. 287–302.

Monahan, J. and Steadman, H. (1994) 'Toward the rejuvenation of risk research in J. Monahan and H. Steadman (eds) *Violence and Mental Disorder: Developments in Risk Assessment* Chicago: University of Chicago Press, pp. 1–17.

Moore, P.J., Ebbesen, E.B. and Konecni, V.J. (1994) *What Does Real Eyewitness Testimony Look Like? An Archival Analysis of Witnesses to Adult Felony Crimes.* Technical Report. San Diego, CA: University of California San Diego, Law and Psychology Program.

Moran, G. and Cutler, B.L. (1991) 'The prejudicial impact of retrial publicity' *Journal of Applied Social Psychology* **21** (5), 345–67.

Mosher, D.L. and Anderson, R.D. (1986) 'Macho personality, sexual aggression and reactions to guided imagery of realistic rape' *Journal of Research in Personality* **20**, 77–94.

Mossman, D. and Kapp, M.B. (1998) ' "Courtroom whores"? – or why do attorneys call us? Findings from a survey on attorneys' use of mental health experts' *Journal of the American Academy of Psychiatry and Law* **26** (1) 27–36.

Motzkau, J.F. (2004) 'Cross-examining suggestibility: memory, childhood, expertise: children's testimony between psychological research and juridical practice'. Paper presented at the 14th European Conference on Psychology and Law, Krakow: Poland.

Moulden, H.M., Firestone, P., Kingston, D. and Bradford, J. (2009) 'Recidivism in pedophiles: an investigation using different diagnostic methods' *Journal of Forensic Psychiatry and Psychology* **20** (5), 680–701.

Mowrer, O.H. (1960) *Learning Theory and Behavior* New York: Wiley.

Muir, G. and Macleod, M.D. (2003) 'The demographic and spatial patterns of recorded rape in a large UK metropolitan area' *Psychology, Crime and Law* **9** (4), 345–55.

Mullen, P.E., James, D.V., Meloy, J.R., Pathé, M.T., Farnham, F.R., Preston, L., Darnley, B. and Berman, J. (2009) 'The fixated and the pursuit of public figures' *Journal of Forensic Psychiatry and Psychology* **20** (1), 33–47.

Murphy, W.D., Haynes, M.R., Stalgaitis, S.J. and Flanagan, B. (1986) 'Differential sexual responding among four groups of sexual offenders against children' *Journal of Psychopathology and Behavioral Assessment* **8** (4), 339–53.

Myers, J.E.B. (1996) 'A decade of international legal reform regarding child abuse investigation and litigation: steps toward a child witness code' *Pacific Law Journal* **28** (1), 169–241.

Myers, J.E.B., Diedrich, S., Lee, D. and Fincher, K.M. (1999) 'Professional writing on child sexual abuse from 1900 to 1975: dominant themes and impact on prosecution' *Child Maltreatment* **4** (3), 201–16.

Myers, J.E.B., Saywitz, K.J. and Goodman, G.S. (1996) 'Psychological research on children as witnesses: practical implications for forensic interviews and courtroom testimony' *Pacific Law Review* **28** (1), 3–92.

Myers, M.A. (1979) 'Rule departures and making law: juries and their verdicts' *Law and Society Review* **13**, 781–97.

Myklebust, T. and Bjøorklund, R.A. (2006) 'The effect of long-term training on police officers' use of open and closed questions in field investigative interviews of children (FIIC)' *Journal of Investigative Psychology and Offender Profiling* **3**, 165–81.

Myklebust, T. and Bjorklund, R.A. (2009) 'The child verbal competence effect in court: a comparative study of field investigative interviews of children in child sexual abuse cases' *Journal of Investigative Psychology and Offender Profiling* **6**, 117–28.

Mythen, G. and Walklate, S. (2005) 'Criminology and terrorism: which thesis? Risk society or governmentality' *British Journal of Criminology* **46**, 379–98.

N

Nash, C.L. and West, D. (1985) 'Sexual molestation of young girls: a retrospective survey' in D. West (ed.) *Sexual Victimization: Two Recent Researches into Sex Problems and their Social Effects* Aldershot: Gower, pp. 1–92.

National Offender Management Service. 2010 Offender Group Reoffending Scale Version 3. http://www.probation.homeoffice.gov.uk/files/pdf/Offender%20Group%20Reconviction%20Scale%20v3%20Guidance%20(Appendix).pdf. Accessed 11 November 2010.

Naughton, M. (2005) 'Redefining miscarriages of justice: a revived human rights approach to unearth subjugated discourses of wrongful criminal conviction' *British Journal of Criminology* 45, 165–82.

Nee, C. (2004) 'Research on burglary at the end of the millennium: a grounded approach to understanding crime' *Security Journal* 16 (3), 37–44.

Nee, C. and Ellis, T. (2005) 'Treating offending children: what works?' *Legal and Criminological Psychology* 10 (1), 133–48.

Nee, C. and Meenaghan, A. (2006) 'Expert decision making in burglars' *British Journal of Criminology* 46, 935–49.

Neisser, U. (1982) *Memory Observed: Remembering in Natural Contexts* San Francisco: W.H. Freeman.

Neisser, U. and Winograd, E. (1988) *Remembering Reconsidered: Ecological and Traditional Approaches to the Study of Memory* Cambridge: Cambridge University Press.

Nelson, J.R., Smith, D.J. and Dodd, J. (1990) 'The moral reasoning of juvenile delinquents: a meta-analysis' *Journal of Abnormal Child Psychology* 18, 231–9.

Nelson, T.O., Gerler, D. and Narens, L. (1984) 'Accuracy of feeling of knowing judgements for predicting perceptual identification and relearning' *Journal of Experimental Psychology: General* 113, 282–300.

Newson, E. (1994a) 'Video violence and the protection of children' *The Psychologist* 7 (6), 272–4.

Newson, E. (1994b) *Video Violence and the Protection of Children.* Report of the Home Affairs Committee. London: HMSO, pp. 45–9.

Nijboer, H. (1995) 'Expert evidence' in R. Bull and D. Carson (eds) *Handbook of Psychology in Legal Contexts* Chichester: John Wiley, pp. 555–64.

Niranjan, S.K. and Steiner, H. (2007) 'Evidence for Interventions for young offenders' *Child and Adolescent Mental Health* 12 (4), 154–9.

Noesner, G.W. and Webster, M. (1997) Crisis intervention: using active listening skills in negotiations. FBI Publications LAW Enforcement Bulletin, http://www.fbi.gov/publications/leb/1997/aug974.htm

Nonnemaker, J.M., McNeely, C.A. and Blum, R.W. (2003) 'Public and private domains of religiosity and adolescent health risk behaviors: evidence from the National Longitudinal Study of Adolescent Health, Social Science and Medicine' *Social Science and Medicine* 57 (11), 2049–54.

Norris, C. and Armstrong, G. (1999a) 'CCTV and the social structuring of surveillance' in K. Painter and N. Tilley (eds) *Surveillance of Public Space: CCTV, Street Lighting and Crime Prevention* Monsey, NY: Criminal Justice Press, 157–78.

Norris, C. and Armstrong, G. (1999b) *The maximum surveillance society: The rise of CCTV* Oxford: Berg.

Novaco, R.W. (1975) *Anger Control: The Development and Evaluation of an Experimental Treatment* Lexington, MA: Lexington Books, D.C. Heath.

Nugent, P.M. and Kroner, D.G. (1996) 'Denial, response styles and admittance of offences among child molesters and rapists' *Journal of Interpersonal Violence* 11 (4), 476–86.

Nunes, K.L. and Corton, F. (2008) 'Dropout from sex-offender treatment and dimensions of risk of sexual recidivism' *Criminal Justice and Behavior* 35, 24.

Nunes, K.L., Firestone, P., Wexler, A.F., Jensen, T.L. and Bradford, J.M. (2007a) 'Incarceration and recidivism among sexual offenders' *Law and Human Behavior* 31, 305–18.

Nunes, K.L., Hanson, K., Firestone, P., Moulden, H.M., Greenberg, D.M. and Bradford, J.M. (2007b) 'Denial predicts recidivism for some sexual offenders' *Sex Abuse* 19, 91–105.

O

O'Donohue, W. and Bowers, A.H. (2006) 'Pathways to false allegations of sexual harassment' *Journal of Investigative Psychology and Offender Profiling* 3, 47–74.

O'Kane, A. and Bentall, R. (2000) 'Psychosis and offending' in J. McGuire, T. Mason and A. O'Kane (eds) *Behaviour, Crime and Legal Processes: A Guide for Forensic Practitioners.* Chichester: John Wiley, pp. 161–76.

O'Kelly, C.M.E., Kebbell, M.R., Hatton, C. and Johnson, S.D. (2003) 'Judicial intervention in court cases involving witnesses with and without learning disabilities' *Legal and Criminological Psychology* 8, 229–40.

O'Sullivan, M. (2008) 'Home runs and humbugs: Comment on Bond and DePaulo' *Psychological Bulletin* 134 (4), 493–7.

O'Sullivan, M. and Ekman, P. (2004) 'The wizards of deception detection' in P.A. Granhag and L. Strömwell (eds) *The Detection of Deception in Forensic Contexts* London: Cambridge University Press.

O'Sullivan, M., Frank, M.G., Hurley, C.M. and Tiwana, J. (2009) 'Police lie detection accuracy: the effect of lie scenario' *Law and Human Behavior* 33, 530–53.

Odlaug, B.L. and Grant, J.E. (2010) 'Impulse control disorders in a college sample' *The Primary Care Companion to the Journal of Clinical Psychiatry* 12 (2), 227–9.

Ofshe, R.J. and Leo, R.A. (1997) 'The decision to confess falsely: rational choice and irrational action' *Denver University Law Review* **74** (4), 979–1122.

Olson, D.R. (1977) 'Oral and written language and the cognitive processes of children' *Journal of Communication* **27** (3), 10–26.

Orth, U., Cahill, S.P., Foa, E.B. and Maercker, A. (2008) 'Anger and posttraumatic stress disorder symptoms in crime victims: a longitudinal analysis' *Journal of Consulting and Clinical Psychology* **76** (2), 208–18.

Ost, J., Costall, A. and Bull, R. (2002) 'A perfect symmetry? Retractors' experiences of recovering then retracting abuse memories' *Psychology, Crime and the Law* **8** (2), 155–81.

Ost, J., Granhag, P.-A., Udell, J. and Roos af Hjelmsäter, E. (2008) 'Familiarity breeds distortion: the effects of media exposure on false reports concerning media coverage of the terrorist attacks in London on 7 July 2005' *Memory* **1**, 76–85.

Osterman, K., Bjorqvist, K. and Lagerspetz, K.M.J. (1998) 'Cross-cultural evidence of female indirect aggression' *Aggressive Behavior* **24**, 1–8.

Otgaar, H., Candel, I., Smeets, T. and Harald Merckelbach (2009) ' "You didn't take Lucy's skirt off": The effect of misleading information on omissions and commissions in children's memory reports' *Legal and Criminological Psychology* **15** (2), 229–41.

Otto, R.K. (2006) 'Competency to stand trial' *Applied Psychology in Criminal Justice* **2** (3), 82–113.

Otto, R.K., Poythress, N.G., Nicholson, R.A., Edens, J.F., Monahan, J., Bonnie, R.J., Hoge, S.K. and Eisenberg, M. (1998) 'Psychometric properties of the MacArthur Competence Assessment Tool – criminal adjudication' *Psychological Assessment* **10** (4), 435–43.

Overholser, J.C. and Beck, S.J. (1988) 'The classification of rapists and child molesters' *Journal of Offender Counseling Services and Rehabilitation* **13**, 1715–25.

Owusu-Bempah, K. and Howitt, D. (2000) *Psychology Beyond Western Perspectives* Leicester: British Psychological Society Books.

Oxburgh, G., Williamson, T. and Ost, J. (2006) 'Police officers' use of emotional language during child sexual abuse investigations' *Journal of Investigative Psychology and Offender Profiling* **3**, 35–45.

P

Paik, H. and Comstock, G. (1994) 'The effects of television violence on antisocial behavior: a meta-analysis' *Communication Research* **21** (4), 516–46.

Paine, C.B., Pike, G.E., Brace, N.A. and Westcott, H.L. (2008) 'Children making faces: the effect of age and prompts on children's facial composites of unfamiliar faces' *Applied Cognitive Psychology* **22** (4), 455–74.

Palmer, E.J. (2001) 'Risk assessment: review of psychometric measures' in D.P. Farrington, C.R. Hollin and M. McMurran (eds) *Sex and Violence: The Psychology of Crimes and Risk Assessment* Reading: Harwood Academic Press, pp. 7–22.

Palmer, E.J. (2003) *Offending Behaviour: Moral Reasoning, Criminal Conduct and the Rehabilitation of Offenders* Cullompton: Willan Publishing.

Palmer, E.J. and Hollin, C.R. (1998) 'A comparison of patterns of moral development in young offenders and non-offenders' *Legal and Criminological Psychology* **3**, 225–35.

Parker, H. and Kirby, P. (1996) *Methadone Maintenance and Crime Reduction on Merseyside* Home Office Police Research Group. Crime Detection and Prevention Series Paper 72, Home Office Police Policy Directorate Police Research Group.

Partridge, G.E. (1930) 'Current conceptions of psychopathic personality' *American Journal of Psychiatry* **10**, 53–99.

Passer, M.W. and Smith, R.E. (2001) *Psychology: Frontiers and Applications* Boston, MA: McGraw-Hill.

Patrick, C.J. and Iacono, W.G. (1991) 'A comparison of field and laboratory polygraphs in the detection of deception' *Psychophysiology* **28**, 632–8.

Payne, J.D., Jackson, E.D., Ryan, L., Hoscheidt, S., Jacobs, W.J. and Nadel, L. (2006) 'The impact of stress on neutral and emotional aspects of episodic memory' *Memory* **14**, 1–16.

Pearse, J. and Gudjonsson, G.H. (1999) 'Measuring influential police interviewing tactics: a factor analytic approach' *Legal and Criminological Psychology* **4**, 221–38.

Pearse, J., Gudjonsson, G.H., Clare, I.C.H. and Rutters, S. (1998) 'Police interviewing and psychological vulnerabilities: predicting the likelihood of a confession' *Journal of Community and Applied Social Psychology* **8**, 1–21.

Pease, K. (2001) 'Rational choice theory' in E. McLaughlin and J. Muncie (eds) *The Sage Dictionary of Criminology* London: Sage, pp. 233–4.

Pease, K. (2007) 'Victims and victimization' in S. Shoham, O. Beck and M. Kent (eds) *International Handbook of Penology and Criminal Justice* Abingdon: Taylor and Francis, 587–611.

Pennebaker, J. (ed.) (1995) *Emotion, Disclosure, and Health* Washington, DC: American Psychological Association.

Pennell, A.E. and Browne, K. (1998a) 'Young offenders' susceptibility to violent media entertainment' *Prison Service Journal* 120, 23–7.

Pennell, A.E. and Browne, K.D. (1998b) 'Film violence and young offenders' *Aggression and Violent Behavior* 4 (1), 13–28.

Pennington, N. and Hastie, R. (1981) 'Juror decision making models: the generalization gap' *Psychological Bulletin* 89, 246–87.

Pennington, N. and Hastie, R. (1986) 'Evidence evaluation in complex decision making' *Journal of Personality and Social Psychology* 51, 242–58.

Pennington, N. and Hastie, R. (1988) 'Explanation-based decision making: the effects of memory structure on judgment' *Journal of Experimental Psychology: Learning, Memory, and Cognition* 14, 521–33.

Pennington, N. and Hastie, R. (1992) 'Explaining the evidence: tests of the story model for juror decision making' *Journal of Personality and Social Psychology* 62, 189–206.

Penrod, S. (2003) 'Eyewitness identification evidence: how well are witnesses and police performing?' *Criminal Justice Magazine* **Spring**, 36–47, 54.

Penrod, S.D. and Heuer, L. (1997) 'Tweaking commonsense: assessing aids to jury decision making' *Psychology, Public Policy and Law* 3 (2/3), 259–84.

Perera, A.L., Van Hasselt, V.B., Baker, M.T., Ramano, S.J., Schlessinger, K.M., Zucker, M. and Dragone, R. (2006) 'Crisis (hostage) negotiation training: a preliminary evaluation of program efficacy' *Criminal Justice and Behavior* 33 (1), 56–69.

Perina, K. (2002) 'Suicide terrorism: suicide bombers have distinctive personality traits' *Psychology Today* 2 October.

Perry, C. (1997) 'Admissibility and per se exclusion of hypnotically elicited recall in American courts of law' *International Journal of Clinical and Experimental Hypnosis* XLV (3), 266–79.

Petty, R.E. and Cacioppo, J.T. (1981) *Attitudes and Persuasion: Classic and contemporary Approaches* Dubuque, IL: Wm. C. Brown.

Philbrick, K. (2002) 'Imprisonment: the impact on children' in L. Falshaw (ed.) *Issues in Forensic Psychology 3* Leicester: British Psychological Society, pp. 72–81.

Piaget, J. (1970) 'Piaget's theory' in P.H. Mussen (ed.) *Carmichael's Manual of Child Psychology* (Vol. 1) New York: Wiley, pp. 703–32.

Pickel, K. (1998) 'The effects of motive information and crime unusualness on jurors' judgments in insanity cases' *Law and Human Behavior* 22 (5), 571–84.

Pickel, K.L., Narter, D.B., Jameson, M.M. and Lenhardt, T.T. (2008) 'The weapon focus effect in child eyewitnesses' *Psychology, Crime & Law* 14, 61–72.

Pike, G., Brace, N. and Kynan, S. (2002) *The Visual Identification of Suspects: Procedures and Practice* Home Office, Briefing Note 2/02.

Pilgrim, D. (2000) 'Psychiatric diagnosis: more questions than answers' *The Psychologist* 19 (6), 303–5.

Pinel, P. (1809) *Traité Medico-philosophique sur l'aliénation mentale, ou la manie* (2nd edn) Paris: Brosson.

Pinizzotto, A.J. and Finkel, N.J. (1990) 'Criminal personality profiling: an outcome and process study' *Law and Human Behavior* 14, 215–33.

Pithers, W.D., Kashima, K.M., Cumming, G.F. and Beal, L.S. (1988) 'Relapse prevention: a method of enhancing maintenance of change in sex offenders' in A.C. Salter (ed.) *Treating Child Sex Offenders and Victims: A Practical Guide* Newbury Park, CA: Sage, pp. 131–70.

Plassmann, R. (1994) 'Munchausen syndromes and factitious diseases' *Psychotherapy and Psychosomatic Medicine* 62, 7–26.

Plotnick, S., Porter, J. and Bagby, M. (1998) 'Is there bias in the evaluation of fitness to stand trial?' *International Journal of Law and Psychiatry* 21 (3), 291–304.

Polaschek, D.L.L. and Collie, R.M. (2004) 'Rehabilitating serious violent adult offenders: an empirical and theoretical stocktake' *Psychology, Crime & Law* 10 (3), 321–34.

Pollock, P.H. (1999) 'When the killer suffers: posttraumatic stress reactions following homicide' *Legal and Criminological Psychology* 4, 185–202.

Poole, D.A. and Lindsay, D.S. (1998) 'Assessing the accuracy of young children's reports: lessons from the investigation of child sexual abuse' *Applied and Preventative Psychology* 7, 1–26.

Poole, D.A. and Lindsay, D.S. (2002) 'Children's suggestibility in the forensic context' in M.L. Eisen, J.A. Quas and G.S. Goodman (eds) *Memory and Suggestibility in the Forensic Interview* Mahwah, NJ: Lawrence Erlbaum, pp. 355–81.

Poole, E. and Regoli, R. (1980) 'Race, institutional rule-breaking, and disciplinary response: A study of discretionary decision making in prison' *Law and Society Review* 14, 931–46.

Porter, S. and ten Brinke, L. (2009) 'A theoretical framework for understanding how judges assess credibility in the courtroom' *Legal and Criminological Psychology* 14, 119–34.

Porter, S. and ten Brinke, L. (2010) 'The truth about lies: What works in detecting high-stakes deception?' *Legal and Criminological Psychology* 15, 57–75.

Porter, S. and Yuille, J.C. (1996) 'The language of deceit: an investigation of the verbal clues to deception in the interrogation context' *Law and Human Behavior* 20 (4), 443–58.

Porter, S., Woodworth, M. and Birt, A.R. (2000) 'Truth, lies and videotape: An investigation of the ability of federal parole officers to detect deception' *Law and Human Behavior* 24, 643–58.

Posey, A.J. and Dahl, L.M. (2002) 'Beyond pre-trial publicity: legal and ethical issues associated with change of venue' *Law and Human Behaviour* 26 (1), 107–25.

Pozgain, I., Mandic, N. and Barkic, J. (1998) 'Homicides in war and peace in Croatia' *Journal of Forensic Sciences* 43 (6), 1124–6.

Price, W.H., Strong, J.A., Whatmore, P.B. and McClemont, W.F. (1966) 'Criminal patients with XYY sex-chromosome complement' *The Lancet* 1, 565–6.

Putkonen, A., Ryynänen, O.P., Eronen, M. and Tiihonen, J. (2007) 'Transmission of violent offending and crime across three generations' *Social Psychiatry and Psychiatric Epidemiology* 42, 94–9.

Q

Quinsey, V.L. (2002) 'Evolutionary theory and criminal behaviour' *Legal and Criminological Psychology* 7 (1), 1–13.

Quinsey, V.L., Steinman, C.M., Bergersen, S.G. and Holmes, T.F. (1975) 'Penile circumference, skin conductance, and ranking responses of child molesters and "normals" to sexual and nonsexual visual stimuli' *Behavior Therapy* 6, 213–19.

R

Radley, L. (2001) 'Attitudes towards sex offenders' *Forensic Update* 66, 5–9.

Rafter, N.H. (2006) 'H.J. Eysenck in Fagin's kitchen: the return to biological theory in 20th-century criminology' *History of the Human Sciences* 19, 37–56.

Rallings, M. (2002) 'The impact of offending on police officers' *Issues in Forensic Psychology* 3, 20–40.

Ramoutar, K. and Farrington, D. (2006) 'Are the same factors related to participation and frequency of offending by male and female prisoners?' *Psychology, Crime and Law* 12 (5), 557–72.

Rappert, B. (2002) 'Constructions of legitimate force: the case of CS sprays' *British Journal of Criminology* 42, 689–708.

Raskin, D.C. and Honts, C.R. (2002) 'The comparison question test' in M. Klener (ed.) *Handbook of Polygraph Testing* San Diego, CA: Academic Press, pp. 1–47.

Rassin, E. (2010) 'Blindness to alternative scenarios in evidence evaluation' *Journal of Investigative Psychology and Offender Profiling* 7, 153–63.

Raynor, P. (2008) 'Community penalties and Home Office research: on the way back to "nothing works"?' *Criminology & Criminal Justice* 8 (1), 73–97.

Redondo, S., Luque, E. and Funes, J. (1996) 'Social beliefs about recidivism in crime' in G. Davies, S. Lloyd-Bostock, M. McMurran and C. Wilson (eds) *Psychology, Law and Criminal Justice: International Developments in Research and Practice* Berlin: Walter de Gruyter, pp. 394–400.

Redondo, S., Sanchez-Meca, J. and Garrido, V. (1999) 'The influence of treatment programmes on the recidivism of juvenile and adult offenders: a European meta-analytic review' *Psychology, Crime and Law* 5, 251–78.

Redondo, S., Sanchez-Meca, J. and Garrido, V. (2002) 'Crime treatment in Europe: a final view of the century and future perspectives' in J. McGuire (ed.) *Offender Rehabilitation and Treatment: Effective Programmes and Policies to Reduce Re-offending* Chichester: John Wiley, pp. 131–41.

Ressler, R.K. and Burgess, A.W. (1985) 'Violent crime' *FBI Law Enforcement Bulletin* **August**, 1–322.

Ressler, R.K. and Shachtman, T. (1997) *I Have Lived in the Monster* New York: St. Martin's Press.

Ressler, R.K., Burgess, A.W. and Douglas, J.E. (1988) *Sexual Homicide: Patterns and Motives* Lexington, MA: Lexington Books.

Reynolds, N. and Scragg, P. (2010) 'Compliance with command hallucinations: the role of power in relation to the voice, and social rank in relation to the voice and Others' *Journal of Forensic Psychiatry & Psychology* 21 (1), 121–38.

Ribeaud, D. and Manzoni, P. (2004) 'The relationship between defendant's social attributes, psychiatric assessment and sentencing – a case study in Switzerland' *International Journal of Law and Psychiatry* 27, 375–86.

Rice, M.E. (1997) 'Violent offender research and implications for the criminal justice system' *American Psychologist* 52 (4), 414–23.

Rice, M.E. and Harris, G.T. (1997) 'Cross-validation and extension of the violence risk appraisal guide for child molesters and rapists' *Law and Human Behavior* 21 (2), 231–41.

Rice, M.E., Harris, G.T. and Cormier, C.A. (1992) 'Evaluation of a maximum security therapeutic community for psychopaths and other mentally disordered offenders' *Law and Human Behavior* 16, 399–412.

Riggs, D.S., Dancu, C.V., Gerhuny, B.S., Greenberg, D. and Foa, E.B. (1992) 'Anger and post-traumatic stress disorder in female crime victims' *Journal of Traumatic Stress* 5 (4), 613–25.

Roach, J. (2010) 'Home is where the heart lies? A study of false address giving to police' *Legal and Criminological Psychology* 15, 209–20.

Robbins, P. and Darlington, R. (2003) 'The role of industry and the Internet Watch Foundation' in A. MacVean and P. Spindler (eds) *Policing Paedophiles on the Internet* Bristol: New Police Bookshop, pp. 79–87.

Roberts, A.D.L. and Coid, J.W. (2007) 'Psychopathy and offending behaviour: Findings from the national survey of prisoners in England and Wales' *Journal of Forensic Psychiatry & Psychology* 18 (1), 23–43.

Roberts, K.A. (2005) 'Associated characteristics of stalking following the termination of romantic relationships' *Applied Psychology in Criminal Justice* 1 (1), 13–35.

Roberts, K.P. and Blades, M. (1995) 'Do children confuse memories of events seen on television and events witnessed in real life?' in N.K. Clark and G.M. Stephenson (eds) *Investigative and Forensic Decision Making, Issues in Criminological and Legal Psychology No. 26* Leicester: Division of Criminological and Legal Psychology, British Psychological Society, pp. 52–7.

Roberts, L. and Wagstaff, G.F. (1996) 'The effects of beliefs and information about hypnosis on the legal defence of automism through hypnosis' *Psychology, Crime and Law* 2, 259–68.

Roberts, Y. (1995) 'Is this modern justice?' *Guardian* 7 October, p. 6.

Robertson, G., Gibb, R. and Pearson, R. (1995) 'Drunkenness among police detainees' *Addiction* 90, 793–803.

Robertson, G., Pearson, R. and Gibb, R. (1996) 'Police interviewing and the use of appropriate adults' *Journal of Forensic Psychiatry* 7 (2), 297–309.

Roesch, R., Ogloff, J.R.P. and Golding, S.L. (1993) 'Competence to stand trial: legal and clinical issues' *Applied and Preventative Psychology* 2, 45–51.

Rose, M.R., Diamond, S.S. and Baker, K.M. (2010) 'Goffman on the Jury: Real Jurors' Attention to the "Offstage" of Trials' *Law and Human Behavior* 34 (4), 310–23.

Rosenthal, R. (1966) *Experimenter Effects in Behavioral Research* New York: Appleton-Century-Crofts.

Roshier, R.J. (1971) 'Crime and the press' *New Society* 468, 502–6.

Roshier, R.J. (1973) 'The selection of crime news by the press' in S. Cohen and J. Young (eds) *The Manufacture of News* London: Constable, pp. 28–39.

Rossmo, D.K. (2000) *Geographic Profiling* Boca Raton, FL: CRC Press.

Royo, J.B. di (1996) 'Legal psychology in Spain: reflections on its short history' in G. Davies, S. Lloyd-Bostock, M. McMurran and C. Wilson (eds) *Psychology, Law and Criminal Justice: International Developments in Research and Practice* Berlin: Walter de Gruyter, pp. 598–601.

Ruback, R.B. and Innes, C.A. (1988) 'The relevance and irrelevance of psychological research' *American Psychologist* 43 (9), 683–93.

Ruby, C.L. (2002) 'The definition of terrorism' *Analyses of Social Issues and Public Policy* 2 (1), 9–14.

Ruchkin, V.V., Eisemann, M. and Cloninger, C.R. (1998a) 'Behaviour/emotional problems in male juvenile delinquents and controls in Russia: the role of personality traits' *Acta Psychiatrica Scandinavica* 98, 231–6.

Ruchkin, V.V., Eisemann, M. and Hagglof, B. (1998b) 'Aggression in delinquent adolescents versus controls: the role of parental rearing' *Children and Society* 12, 275–82.

Ruchkin, V.V., Eisemann, M. and Hagglof, B. (1998c) 'Parental rearing and problem behaviours in male delinquent adolescents versus controls in Northern Russia' *Social Psychiatry and Psychiatric Epidemiology* 33, 477–82.

Rudo, Z.H. and Powell, D.S. (1996) *Family Violence: A Review of the Literature* Tampa, FL: Florida Mental Health Institute, University of South Florida.

Rushton, J.P. (1990) 'Race differences, r/K theory, and a reply to Flynn' *The Psychologist: Bulletin of the British Psychological Society* 5, 195–8.

Russano, M.B., Meissner, C.A., Narchet, F.M. and Kassin, S.M. (2005) 'Investigating true and false confessions within a novel experimental paradigm' *Psychological Science* 16 (6), 481–6.

Russell, C.A. and Miller, B.H. (1977) 'Profile of a terrorist' *Terrorism: An International Journal* 1 (1), 17–34.

Russell, D.E.H. (1988) 'Pornography and rape: a causal model' *Journal of Political Psychology* 9 (1), 41–73.

Russell, D.E.H. (1992) 'Pornography and rape: a causal model' in C. Itzin (ed.) *Pornography: Women, Violence and Civil Liberties* Oxford: Oxford University Press, pp. 310–49.

S

Sacco, V.F. and Fair, B.J. (1988) 'Images of legal control: crime news and the process of organizational legitimation' *Canadian Journal of Communication* 3 (3–4), 114–23.

Safer Custody Group (2005) *Self Inflicted Deaths Trends Report 2005* London: NOMS.

Sageman, M. (2004) *Understanding Terror Networks* Philadelphia: University of Pennsylvania Press.

Sakadi, A., Kristiansson, R., Oberklaid, F. and Bremberg, S. (2007) 'Fathers' involvement and children's developmental outcomes: a systematic review of longitudinal studies' *Acta Pædiatrica* 97, 153–8.

Saks, M.J. (1987) 'Social scientists can't rig juries' in L.S. Wrightsman, S.M. Kassin and C.E. Willis (eds) *In the Jury Box: Controversies in the Courtroom* Thousand Oaks, CA: Sage, pp. 48–61.

Saks, M.J. and Marti, M. (1997) 'A meta-analysis of the effect of jury size' *Law and Human Behavior* 21, 451–67.

Salerno, J.M., Najdowski, C.J., Stevenson, M.C., Wiley, T.R.A., Bottoms, B.L., Vaca, R. and Pimentel, P.S. (2010) 'Psychological mechanisms underlying support for juvenile sex offender registry laws: prototypes, moral outrage, and perceived threat' *Behavioral Sciences and the Law* 28, 58–83.

Salfati, C.G. and Canter, D.V. (1998) 'Differentiating stranger murders: profiling offender characteristics from behavioral styles' *Behavioral Sciences and the Law* 17 (3), 391–406.

Salter, A.C. (1988) *Treating Child Sex Offenders and Victims: A Practical Guide* Newbury Park, CA: Sage.

Sarangi, S. and Alison, L. (2005) 'Life story accounts of left wing terrorists in India' *Journal of Investigative Psychology and Offender Profiling* 2, 69–86.

Sarasalo, E., Bergman, B. and Toth, J. (1997) 'Kleptomania-like behaviour and psychosocial characteristics among shoplifters' *Legal and Criminological Psychology* 2, 1–10.

Sattar, G. and Bull, R. (1996) 'Pre-court preparation for child witnesses' in N.K. Clark and G.M. Stephenson (eds) *Issues in Criminological and Legal Psychology 26, Child Witnesses* Leicester: British Psychological Society, Division of Criminological and Legal Psychology, pp. 67–75.

Savage, J. and Yancey, C. (2008) 'The effects of media violence exposure on criminal aggression: a meta-analysis' *Criminal Justice and Behavior* 35, 772–91.

Saywitz, K.J. (1994) 'Children in court: principles of child development for judicial application' in *A Judicial Primer on Child Sexual Abuse* Chicago: American Bar Association Center on Children and the Law.

Schiffer, B., Peschel, T., Paul, T., Gizwski, E., Forsting, M., Leygraf, N., Schedlowski, M. and Kruege, H.C. (2007) 'Structural brain abnormalities in the frontostriatal system and cerebellum in pedophilia' *Journal of Psychiatric Research* 41 (9), 753–62.

Schlesinger, P., Tumber, H. and Murdock, G. (1991) 'The media politics of crime and criminal justice' *British Journal of Sociology* 42 (3), 397–420.

Schmid, J. and Fiedler, K. (1998) 'The backbone of closing speeches: the impact of prosecution versus defense language on judicial attributions' *Journal of Applied Social Psychology* 28 (13), 1140–72.

Schneider, J.L. (2005) 'Stolen-goods markets: methods of disposal' *British Journal of Criminology* 45, 129–40.

Schulman, J., Shaver, P., Colman, R., Emrich, B. and Christie, R. (1973) 'Recipe for a jury' *Psychology Today* May, 37–44, 77–84.

Schwalbe, C.S. (2007) 'Risk assessment for juvenile justice: a meta-analysis' *Law and Human Behavior* 31 (5), 449–62.

Scott, J.E. and Schwalm, L.A. (1988) 'Pornography and rape: an examination of adult theater rates and rape rates by state' in J.E. Scott and T. Hirschi (eds) *Controversial Issues in Crime and Justice* Beverly Hills: Sage, pp. 40–53.

Scullin, M.H., Kanaya, T. and Ceci, S.J. (2002) 'Measurements of individual differences in children's suggestibility across situations' *Journal of Experimental Psychology: Applied* 8 (4), 233–46.

Scully, D. and Marolla, J. (1984) 'Convicted rapists' vocabulary of motives: excuses and justifications' *Social Problems* 31 (5), 530–44.

Sealy, A.P. and Cornish, W.R. (1973) 'Juries and the rules of evidence' *Criminal Law Review* 208–23.

Sear, L. and Williamson, T. (1999) 'British and American interrogation strategies' in D. Canter and L. Alison (eds) *Interviewing and Deception* Dartmouth: Ashgate, pp. 67–81.

Security Service: MI5 (2007) Counter-terrorism spending increased (10 October 2007 http://www.mi5.gov.uk/output/Page541.html. Accessed 6 December 2007).

Senior, J., Hayes, A.J., Pratti, D., Thomas, S.D., Fahy, T., Leese, M., Bowen, A., Taylor, G., Lever-Green, G., Graham, T., Pearson, A., Ahmed, M. and Shaw, J.J. (2007) 'The identification and management of suicide risk in local prisons' *Journal of Forensic Psychiatry and Psychology* 3, 368–80.

Seto, M.C. and Eke, A.W. (2005) 'The criminal histories and later offending of child pornography offenders' *Sexual Abuse: A Journal of Research and Treatment* 17 (2), 201–10.

Seto, M.C. and Lalumiere, M.L. (2001) 'A brief screening scale to identify pedophilic interests among child molesters' *Sexual Abuse: A Journal of Research and Treatment* 13, 15–25.

Seto, M.C. and Lalumiere, M.L. (2010) 'What is so special about male adolescent sexual offending? A review and test of explanations through meta-analysis' *Psychological Bulletin* 136 (4), 526–75.

Shadish, W.R. (1984) 'Policy research: lessons from the implementation of deinstitutionalization' *American Psychologist* 39 (7), 725–38.

Shaffer, D.R. (1985) 'The defendant's testimony' in S.M. Kassin and L.S. Wrightsman (eds) *The Psychology of Evidence and Trial Procedure* Beverly Hills, CA: Sage, pp. 124–49.

Shaffer, D.R. and Case, T. (1982) 'On the decision to testify in one's own behalf: Effects of withheld evidence, defendant's sexual preferences, and juror dogmatism on juridic decisions' *Journal of Personality and Social Psychology* 42, 335–46.

Shaffer, D.R. and Sadowski, C. (1979) 'Effects of withheld evidence on juridic decision II: Locus of withholding strategy' *Personality and Social Psychology Bulletin* 5, 40–3.

Shapiro, P.N. and Penrod, S. (1986) 'Meta-analysis of facial identification studies' *Psychological Bulletin* 100, 139–56.

Shapland, J., Atkinson, A., Atkinson, H., Dignana, J., Edwards, L., Hibbert, J., Howes, M., Johnstone, J., Robinson, G. and Sorsby, A.L. (2008) *Restorative Justice: Does Restorative Justice affect reconviction? The fourth report from the evaluation of three schemes.* Ministry of Justice Research Series 10/08. http://www.justice.gov.uk/publications/docs/restorative-justice-report_06-08.pdf. Accessed 28 March, 2011.

Shaw, C.R. and McKay, H.D. (1942) *Juvenile Delinquency in Urban Areas* Chicago: University of Chicago Press.

Shaw, J., Appleby, L., Ames, T., McDonnell, R., Harris, C., McCann, K., Kiernan, K., Davies, S., Biddey, H. and Parsons, R. (1999) 'Mental disorder and clinical care in people convicted of homicide: national clinical survey' *British Medical Journal* 318 (8 May), 1240–4.

Shaw, M. and Pease, K. (2002) 'Minor crimes, trivial incidents: the cumulative impact of offending' *Issues in Forensic Psychology* 3, 41–8.

Sheehan, P.W. (1997) 'Recovered memories: towards resolution of some issues across experimental and clinical domains'. Unpublished manuscript, University of Queensland, Australia. Plenary address, 14th International Congress of Hypnosis, San Diego, USA, June.

Sheldon, K. (2004) 'A new type of sex offender? Recent findings on Internet sex offenders: a pilot study' *Forensic Update* 79, 24–31.

Sheldon, K. and Howitt, D. (2007) *Sex Offenders and the Internet* Chichester: John Wiley and Sons.

Sheldon, K. and Howitt, D. (2008) 'Sexual fantasy in paedophile offenders: can any model explain satisfactorily new findings from a study of Internet and contact sexual offenders?' *Legal and Criminological Psychology* 13 (1), 137–58.

Sheldon, W.H. (1940) *The Varieties of Human Physique: An Introduction to Constitutional Psychology* New York: Harper.

Sheldon, W.H. (1942) *The Varieties of Temperament: A Psychology of Constitutional Differences* New York: Harper.

Sheldon, W.H. (1949) *Varieties of Delinquent Youth: An Introduction to Constitutional Psychiatry* New York: Harper.

Shepherd, E. (2007) *Investigative Interviewing: The Conversation Management Approach* Oxford: Oxford University Press.

Shepherd, E. and Milne, R. (1999) 'Full and faithful: ensuring quality practice and integrity of outcome in witness interviews' in A. Heaton-Armstrong, E. Shepherd, D. Wochover and Lord Bingham of Cornhill (eds) *Analysing Eyewitness Testimony: Psychological, Investigative and Evidential Perspectives* London: Blackstone Press, pp. 124–45.

Shepherd, E.W., Mortimer, A.K.O. and Mobaseri, R. (1995) 'The police caution: comprehension and perceptions in the general population' *Expert Evidence* 4, 60–7.

Sheridan, L. and Davies, G.M. (2001) 'What is stalking? The match between legislation and public perception' *Legal and Criminological Psychology* 6, 3–17.

Sheridan, L. and Davies, G.M. (2002) 'Stalking: the elusive crime' *Legal and Criminological Psychology* 6, 133–47.

Sheridan, L.P. and Grant, T. (2007) 'Is cyberstalking different?' *Psychology, Crime and Law* 13 (6), 627–40.

Sherman, L.W., Gartin, P.R. and Buerger, M.E. (1989) 'Hot spots of predatory crime: Routine activities and the criminology of place' *Criminology* 27, 27–55.

Sherman, L.W., Strang, H., Angel, C., Woods, D., Barnes, G., Bennett, S., Inkpen, N. and Rossner, M. (2005) 'Effects of face-to-face restorative justice on victims of crime in four randomized, controlled trials' *Journal of Experimental Criminology* 1 (3), 367–95.

Shrum, L.J. (1996) 'Psychological processes underlying communication effects' *Human Communication Research* 22 (4), 482–509.

Shutz, W. (1994) *The Human Element: Productivity, Self-esteem and the Bottom Line* San Francisco, CA: Jossey-Bass.

Shuy, R.W. (1998) *The Language of Confession, Interrogation and Deception* Thousand Oaks, CA: Sage.

Shye, S. (1985) 'A nonmetric model for behavioral action systems' in D. Canter (ed.) *Facet Theory: Approaches to Social Research* New York: Springer-Verlag, pp. 97–148.

Shye, S. and Elizur, D. (1994) *Introduction to Facet Theory: Content Design and Intrinsic Data Analysis in Behavioural Research* Thousand Oaks, CA: Sage.

Siegelman, C.K., Budd, E.C., Spanhel, C.I. and Schoenrock, C.J. (1981) 'When in doubt say yes: acquiescence in interviews with mentally retarded persons' *Mental Retardation* 19, 53–8.

Sigall, H. and Ostrove, N. (1975) 'Beautiful but dangerous: Effects of offender attractiveness and nature of the crime on juridic judgment' *Journal of Personality and Social Psychology* 31, 410–14.

Sigfusdottir, I.D., Gudjonsson, G.H. and Sigurdsson, J.F. (2010) 'Bullying and delinquency: The mediating role of anger' *Personality and Individual Differences* 48, 391–6.

Signorielli, N. and Gerbner, G. (1988) *Violence and Terror in the Mass Media* New York: Greenwood.

Sigurdsson, J. and Gudjonsson, G. (1997) 'The criminal history of "false confessors" and other prison inmates' *Journal of Forensic Psychiatry* 8 (2), 447–55.

Silas, F.A. (1985) 'Would a kid lie?' *Journal of the American Bar Association* 71, 17.

Silke, A. (1998) 'Cheshire-Catalogic: the recurring theme of terrorist abnormality in psychological research' *Psychology, Crime and Law* 4 (1), 51–69.

Silke, A. (2003) 'Deindividuation, anonymity, and violence: findings from Northern Ireland' *Journal of Social Psychology* 143 (4), 493–9.

Silke, A. (2004) 'Introduction to terrorism research' in A. Silke (ed.) *Research on Terrorism: Trends, Achievements and Failures* London: Frank Cass, pp. 1–29.

Silva, J.A., Derecho, D.V., Leong, G.B., Weinstock, R. and Ferrari, M.M. (2001) 'A classification of psychological factors leading to violent behavior in posttraumatic stress disorder' *Journal of Forensic Sciences* 46, 309–16.

Silvern, L., Karyl, J. and Landis, T. (1995) 'Individual psychotherapy for the traumatized children of abused women' in E. Peled, P. Jaffe and J. Edleson (eds) *Ending the Cycle of Violence: Community Responses to Children of Battered Women* Thousand Oaks, CA: Sage, pp. 43–76.

Simon, L. (2000) 'An examination of the assumptions of specialization, mental disorder, and dangerousness in sex offenders' *Behavioural Sciences and the Law* 18, 275–308.

Simon, R.R. and Eimermann, T. (1971) 'The jury finds not guilty: another look at media influence on the jury' *Journalism Quarterly* 48, 343–4.

Sjogren, L.H. (2000) 'Problems and sources of errors when investigating alleged child sexual abuse' in A. Czerederecka, T. Jaskiewicz-Obdzinska and J. Wojcikiewicz (eds) *Forensic Psychology and Law: Traditional Questions and New Ideas* Krakow: Institute of Forensic Research Publishers, pp. 246–9.

Sjostedt, G. and Langstrom, N. (2000) 'Assessment of risk for criminal recidivism among rapists: a comparison of four different measures'. Unpublished manuscript, Karolinska Institutet, Stockholm, Sweden.

Skeem, J.L. and Cooke, D.J. (2010) 'Criminal behavior a central component of psychopathy? Conceptual directions for resolving the debate' *Psychological Assessment* 22 (2), 433–45.

Skett, S. and Dalkin, A. (1999) 'Working with young offenders' *Issues in Forensic Psychology* 1, 31–5.

Skogan, W.G. (1996) 'The police and public opinion in Britain' *American Behavioral Scientist* 39 (4), 421–32.

Skolnick, J.H. (1966) *Justice Without Trial: Law Enforcement in a Democratic Society* New York: Wiley.

Sloore, H., Rossi, G. and Hauben, C. (2004) 'Are recidivists psychopaths?' Paper presented at the 14th European Conference of Psychology and Law, Krakow, Poland, July.

Slusser, M.M. (1995) 'Manifestations of sexual abuse in pre-school-aged children' *Issues in Mental Health Nursing* 16, 481–91.

Smith, A. (1977) 'Exploiting psychology in the name of the law: what benefits, what dangers?' *Science Forum* 57, 25–7.

Smith, A.D. and Taylor, P.J. (1999) 'Serious sex offending against women by men with schizophrenia' *British Journal of Psychiatry* 174, 233–7.

Smith, C. and Allen, J. (2004) Violent crime in England and Wales. Home Office Online Report 18/04. http://www.homeoffice.gov.uk/rds/pdfs04/rdsolr1804.pdf

Smith, M.R. and Alpert, G.P. (2007) 'A theory of social conditioning and illusory correlation' *Criminal Justice and Behavior* 34 (10), 1262–83.

Smith, P., Goggin, C. and Gendreau, P. (2002) *The Effects of Prison Sentences and Intermediate Sanctions on Recidivism: General Effects and Individual Differences* Ottawa, ON: Correctional Services of Canada.

Smithson, M., Deady, S. and Gracik, L. (2007) 'Guilty, not guilty, or . . . ? Multiple options in jury verdict choices' *Journal of Behavioral Decision Making* 20, 481–498.

Snook, B., Cullen, R.M., Bennell, C., Taylor, P.J. and Gendreau, P. (2008) 'The criminal profiling illusion: What's behind the smoke and mirrors?' *Criminal Justice and Behavior* 35: 1257–76.

Snook, B., Cullen, R.M., Mokros, A. and Harborts, S. (2005) 'Serial murderers' spatial decisions: factors that influence crime location choice' *Journal of Investigative Psychology and Offender Profiling* 2, 147–64.

Snook, B., Dhami, M.K. and Kavanagh, J.M. (2010) 'Simply criminal: predicting burglars' occupancy decisions with a simple heuristic' *Law and Human Behavior.*

Snook, B., Eastwood, J., Gendreau, P., Goggin, C. and Cullen, R.M. (2007) 'Taking stock of criminal profiling: a narrative review and meta-analysis' *Criminal Justice and Behaviour* 34, 437–53.

Snook, B., Eastwood, J., Gendreau, P. and Bennell, C. (2010) 'The importance of knowledge cumulation and the search for hidden agendas: a reply to Kocsis, Middledorp, and Karpin (2008)' *Journal of Forensic Psychology Practice* 10 (3), 214–23.

Snow, L., Paton, J., Oram, C. and Teers, R. (2002) 'Self-inflicted deaths during 2001: An analysis of trends' *The British Journal of Forensic Practice* 4 (4), 3–17.

Snyder, C.J., Lassiter, G.D., Lindberg, M.J. and Pinegar, S.K. (2009) 'Videotaped interrogations and confessions: does a dual-camera approachyield unbiased and accurate evaluations?' *Behavioral Sciences and the Law* 27, 451–66.

Soibelman, M. (2004) 'Palestinian suicide bombers' *Journal of Investigative Psychology and Offender Profiling* 1, 175–90.

Sorochinski, M. and Salfati, C.G. (2010) 'The consistency of inconsistency in serial homicide: Patterns of behavioral change across series' *Journal of Investigative Psychology and Offender Profiling* 7, 109–36.

Spiecker, S.C. and Worthington, D.L. (2003) 'The influence of opening statement/closing argument organization strategy on juror verdict and damage awards' *Law and Human Behavior* 27 (4), 437–56.

Sporer, S.L. (1993) 'Eyewitness identification accuracy, confidence, and decision times in simultaneous and sequential lineups' *Journal of Applied Psychology* 78, 22–33.

Sprott, J.B. (1998) 'Understanding public opposition to a separate youth justice system' *Crime and Delinquency* 44 (3), 399–411.

Stalans, L.J. (1996) 'Family harmony or individual protection? Public recommendation about how police can handle domestic violence situations' *American Behavioral Scientist* 39, 433–48.

Stalenheim, E.G. (1997) *Psychopathy and Biological Markers in a Forensic Psychiatric Population* Uppsala: Acta Universitatis Upsaliensis.

Stams, G.J.M.M., Brugman, D., Dekovic, M., Van Rosmalen, L., Laan, P. van der *et al.* (2006) 'The moral judgment of juvenile delinquents: A meta-analysis' *Journal of Abnormal Child Psychology* 34, 697–713.

Stanik, J.M. (1992) 'Psychology and law in Poland' in F. Losel, D. Bender and T. Bliesener (eds) *Psychology and Law: International Perspectives* Berlin: Walter de Gruyter, pp. 546–53.

Stanko, E.A. (1995) 'Women, crime, and fear' *Annals of the American Association for Political and Social Science* 539, 46–58.

Stark, E. (1993) 'The myth of black violence' *Social Work* 38 (4), 485–90.

Steadman, H.J. and Cocozza, J.J. (1974) 'Some refinements in the measurement and prediction of dangerous behaviour' *American Journal of Psychiatry* 131 (9), 1012–14.

Steblay, N., Dysart, J., Fulero, S. and Lindsay, R.C.L. (2003) 'Eyewitness accuracy rates in police show-up and line-up presentations: a meta-analytic comparison' *Law and Human Behavior* 27 (5), 523–40.

Steck, P. (1998) 'Deadly ending marital conflicts'. Paper presented at 8th European Conference on Psychology and Law, Krakow, 2–5 September.

Steinberg, L. (2003) 'Juveniles on trial: MacArthur Foundation study calls competency into question' *Criminal Justice*

Magazine **Fall 18** (3), http://www.abanet.org/crimjust/juvjus/cjmag/18-3ls.html

Steinmetz, S. (1977) 'The battered husband syndrome' *Victimology* 2, 499–509.

Stekel, W. (1911) 'The sexual root of kleptomania' *Journal of the American Institute of Criminal Law and Criminology* 2 (2), 239–46.

Stephan, J.J. and Karberg, J. (2003) *Census of State and Federal Correctional Facilities, 2000* Washington, DC: Department of Justice, Office of Justice Programs.

Stephenson, G.M. (1992) *The Psychology of Criminal Justice* Oxford: Blackwell.

Stermac, L.E. and Quinsey, V.L. (1986) 'Social competence among rapists' *Behavioral Assessment* 8, 171–81.

Stern, W. (1904) 'Die Aussage als geistige Leistung und als Verhörsprodukt' *Beiträge zur Psychologie der Aussage* 3, 269–415.

Sternberg, K.J., Lamb, M.E., Hershkowitz, L., Orbach, Y., Esplin, P.W. and Hovav, M. (1997) 'Effects of introductory style on children's abilities to describe experiences of sexual abuse' *Child Abuse and Neglect* 21 (11), 1133–46.

Steward, M. and Steward, D. (1996) 'Interviewing young children about body touch and handling' *Monograph Series for the Society for Research in Child Development* 61 (4–5, Serial No. 248).

Stone, A.A., Smyth, J.M., Kaell, A. and Hurewitz, A. (2000) 'Structured writing about stressful events: exploring possible psychological mediators of positive health effects' *Health Psychology* 19 (6), 619–24.

Storey, J.E., Hart, S.D., Meloy, J. and Reavis, J.A. (2009) 'Psychopathy and stalking' *Law and Human Behavior* 33, 237–46.

Straus, M. (1992) 'Sociological research and social policy: the case of family violence' *Sociological Forum* 7 (2), 211–37.

Straus, M., Hamby, S.L., Boney-McCoy, S. and Sugarman, D.B. (1996) 'The Revised Conflict Tactics Scales (CTS2)' *Journal of Family Issues* 76 (3), 283–316.

Strentz, T. (2006) *Psychological Aspects of Crisis Negotiation* Boca Raton, FL: CRC Press.

Strier, F. (1999) 'Whither trial consulting? Issues and projections' *Law and Human Behavior* 23, 93–115.

Stromwall, L.A. and Granhag, P.A. (2003) 'How to detect deception? Arresting the beliefs of police officers, prosecutors and judges' *Psychology, Crime and Law* 9, 19–36.

Studebaker, C.A. and Penrod, S.D. (1997) 'Pre-trial publicity' *Psychology, Public Policy and Law* 3 (2/3), 428–60.

Studebaker, C.A., Robbennolt, J.K., Pathak-Sharma, M.K. and Penrod, S.D. (2000) 'Assessing pre-trial publicity effects: integrating content analytic results' *Law and Human Behavior* 24, 317–36.

Studer, L.H. and Reddon, J.R. (1998) 'Treatment may change risk prediction for sexual offenders' *Sexual Abuse: A Journal of Research and Treatment* 10 (3), 175–81.

Studer, L.H., Aylwin, A.S., Clelland, S.R., Reddon, J.R. and Frenzel, R.R. (2002) 'Primary erotic preference in a group of child molesters' *International Journal of Law and Psychiatry* 25, 173–80.

Sullivan, J. and Beech, A. (2003) 'Are collectors of child abuse images a risk to children?' in A. MacVean and P. Spindler (eds) *Policing Paedophiles on the Internet* Bristol: New Police Bookshop, pp. 11–20.

Swanson, J.W., Holzer, C.E., Ganju, V.K. and Jono, R.T. (1990) 'Violence and psychiatric disorder in the community: evidence from the epidemiologic catchment area surveys' *Hospital and Community Psychiatry* 41, 761–70.

Sweeney, J. (2004) 'The impact of individualism and collectivism on shoplifting attitudes and behaviour' *The UCI Undergraduate Research Journal*, 61–8. http://www.urop.uci.edu/journal/journal99/08_joanne/Joanne%20Sweeney.pdf

Sykes, G. (1958) *The Society of Captives* Princeton, NJ: Princeton University Press.

Sykes, G.M. and Matza, D. (1957) 'Techniques of neutralization: a theory of delinquency' *American Sociological Review* 22, 664–70.

Szegedi, M. (1998) 'The development of Hungarian forensic psychology' in J. Boros, I. Munnich and M. Szegedi (eds) *Psychology and Criminal Justice: International Review of Theory and Practice* Berlin: Walter de Gruyter, pp. 441–56.

Szumski, J. (1993) 'Fear of crime, social rigorism and mass media in Poland' *International Review of Victimology* 2, 209–15.

T

Tarry, H. and Emler, N. (2007) 'Attitudes, values and moral reasoning as predictors of delinquency' *British Journal of Developmental Psychology* 25 (2), 169–83.

Taub, S. (1996) 'The legal treatment of recovered memories of child sexual abuse' *Journal of Legal Medicine* 17, 183–214.

Taylor, D.M. and Louis, W.R. (2004) 'Terrorism and the quest for identity' in F. Moghaddam and A.J. Marsella (eds) *Understanding Terrorism: Psychosocial Roots, Consequences, and Interventions* Washington, DC: APA Press, pp. 169–185.

Taylor, J. (2005) 'The relationship between violence and psychosis: time for a different approach?' *Forensic Update* 82, 10–14.

Taylor, M. (2010) 'Is terrorism a group phenomenon?' *Aggression and Violent Behavior* 15, 121–9.

Taylor, M. and Quayle, E. (1994) *Terrorist Lives* London: Brassey's Publishers.

Taylor, M. and Quayle, E. (2003) *Child Pornography: An Internet Crime* Hove: Brunner-Routledge.

Taylor, S.E. and Fiske, S.T. (1975) 'Point of view and perception so causality' *Journal of Personality and Social Psychology* 32, 439–45.

Taylor, S.E. and Fiske, S.T. (1978) 'Salience, attention, and attribution: Top of the head phenomenon' in L. Berkowitz (ed.) *Advances in Experimental Social psychology* Vol. 11 New York: Academic Press, pp. 249–88.

Teasdale, B. (2009) 'Mental disorder and violent victimization' *Criminal Justice and Behavior* 36, 513–35.

Thibaut, J. and Walker, L. (1975) *Procedural Justice: A Psychological Analysis* Hillsdale, NJ: Wiley.

Thompson, B. (1994) *Soft Core: Moral Crusades Against Pornography in Britain and America* London: Cassell.

Thompson, W.C. (2010) 'An American psychology–law society scientific review paper on police interrogation and confession' *Law and Human Behavior* 34, 1–2.

Thornhill, R. and Palmer, T. (2000) *A Natural History of Rape: Biological Bases of Sexual Coercion* Cambridge, MA: MIT Press.

Thurstone, L.L. (1922) 'The intelligence of policemen' *Journal of Personnel Research* 1, 67–74.

Tieger, T. (1981) 'Self-rated likelihood of raping and the social perception of rape' *Journal of Research in Personality* 15, 147–58.

Tisak, M. (1995) 'Domains of social reasoning and beyond' in R. Vasta (ed.) *Annals of Child Development* Vol. 11 London: Jessica Kingsley, 95–130.

Tjaden, P. and Thoennes, N. (1998) *Stalking in America: Findings from the National Violence against Women Survey* Washington, DC: US Department of Justice.

Tjaden, P. and Thoennes, N. (2000) *Full Report of the Prevalence, Incidence, and Consequences of Violence Against Women: Findings from the National Violence Against Women Survey*. Research Report. Washington, DC: National Institute of Justice and the Centers for Disease Control and Prevention.

Torpy, D. (1994) 'You must confess' in N.K. Clark and G.M. Stephenson (eds) *Rights and Risks: The Application of Forensic Psychology* Leicester: British Psychological Society, pp. 21–3.

Torres, A.N., Boccaccini, M.T. and Miller, H.A. (2006) 'Perceptions of the validity and utility of criminal profiling among forensic psychologists and psychiatrists' *Professional Psychology: Research and Practice* 37 (1), 51–8.

Towl, G. (1995) 'Anger management groupwork' in G.J. Towl (ed.) *Groupwork in Prisons. Issues in Criminological and Legal Psychology, No. 23* Leicester: British Psychological Society, pp. 31–5.

Towl, G. (1996) 'Homicide and suicide: assessing risk in prisons' *The Psychologist* 9 (9), 398–400.

Towl, G.J. and Crighton, D.A. (1996) *The Handbook of Psychology for Forensic Practitioners* London: Routledge.

Towl, G. and Crighton, D. (2000) 'Risk assessment and management' in G. Towl, L. Snow and M. McHugh (eds) *Suicide in prisons* Leicester: British Psychological Society, 66–92.

Townsend, E. (2007) 'Suicide terrorists: Are they suicidal?' *Suicide and Life Threatening Behavior* 37 (1), 35–49.

Tracy, P.E., Wolfgang, M.E. and Figlio, R.M. (1990) *Delinquency Careers in Two Birth Cohorts* New York: Plenum Press.

Travin, S., Bluestone, H., Coleman, E., Cullen, K. and Melella, M.S.W. (1985) 'Pedophile types and treatment perspectives' *Journal of Forensic Science* 31 (2), 614–20.

Triandis, H.C. (1995) *Individualism and Collectivism* Boulder, CO: Westview Press.

Tseloni, A., Wittebrood, K., Farrell, G. and Pease, K. (2004) 'Burglary victimisation in England and Wales, the United States and the Netherlands: a cross-national comparative test of routine activities and lifestyle theories' *British Journal of Criminology* 44, 66–91.

Tulving, E. (1974) 'Cue-dependent forgetting' *American Scientist* 62, 74–8.

Turiel, E. (1983) *The Development of Social Knowledge: Morality and Convention* Cambridge: Cambridge University Press.

Turiel, E., and Nucci, L. (1978) 'Social interactions and the development of social concepts in preschool children' *Child Development* 49, 400–7.

Tyler, T. and Lind, E.A. (1992) 'A relational model of authority in groups' in M.P. Zanna (ed.) *Advances in Experimental Social Psychology, Vol. 25* San Diego: Academic Press, pp. 115–91.

U

US Census Bureau (2011) The 2011 Statistical Abstract. http://www.census.gov/compendia/statab/cats/law_enforcement_courts_prisons/crimes_and_crime_rates.html. Accessed 28 March 2011.

Undeutsch, U. (1992) 'Highlights of the history of forensic psychology in Germany' in F. Lösel, D. Bender and T. Bliesener (eds) *Psychology and Law: International Perspectives* Berlin: Walter de Gruyter, pp. 509–18.

US Department of Commerce, Economics and Statistics Information (1996) *Statistical Abstract of the United States* Washington, DC: US Government Printing Office.

V

Valier, C. (1998) *Psychoanalysis and Crime in Britain During the Inter-war Years.* The British Criminology Conferences: Selected Proceedings. Volume 1: Emerging Themes in Criminology, http://www.lboro.ac.uk/departments/ss/bccsp/vol101/

Van den Bos, K. and Lind, E.A. (2002) 'Uncertainty management by means of fairness judgments' in M.P. Zanna (ed.) *Advances in Experimental Social Psychology* Vol. 34, San Diego, CA: Academic Press, pp. 1–60.

Van den Bos, K. and Maas, M. (2009) 'On the psychology of the belief in a just world: exploring experiential and rationalistic paths to victim blaming' *Personality and Social Psychology Bulletin* 35, 1567–78.

Van Dijk, J., van Kesteren, J. and Smit, P. (2007) 'Criminal Victimisation in International Perspective: Key findings from the 2004–2005 ICVS and EU' Tilburg University: Wetenschappelijk Onderzoeken Documentatiecentrum. http://rechten.uvt.nl/icvs/pdffiles/ICVS2004_05summary.pdf. Accessed 21 February 2011.

van Hasselt, V.B., Romano, S.J. and Vecchi, G.M. (2008) 'Role playing: Applications in hostage and crisis negotiation skills training' *Behavior Modification* 32 (2), 248–63.

Van Koppen, P.J. (1995) 'Judges' decision-making' in R. Bull and D. Carson (eds) *Handbook of Psychology in Legal Contexts* Chichester: John Wiley, pp. 581–610.

Van Koppen, P.J. and Lochun, S.K. (1997) 'Portraying perpetrators: the validity of offender descriptions by witnesses' *Law and Human Behaviour* 21 (6), 661–85.

van Lier, P.A.C., Vitaro, F., Barker, E.D., Koot, H.M. and Tremblay, R.E. (2009) 'Developmental links between trajectories of physical violence, vandalism, theft, and alcohol–drug use from childhood to adolescence' *Journal of Abnormal Child Psychology* 37, 481–92.

Van Wallendael, L. and Cutler, B. (2004) 'Limitations to empirical approaches to jury selection' *Journal of Forensic Psychology Practice* 4 (2), 79–86.

Vaughn, M.G., DeLisi, M., Beaver, K.M. and Howard, M.O. (2008) 'Toward a quantitative typology of burglars: a latent profile analysis of career offenders' *Journal of Forensic Science* 53 (6), 1387–92.

Vecchi, G.M., Van Hasselt, V.B. and Romano, S.S. (2005) 'Crisis (hostage) negotiation: Current strategies and issues in high-risk conflict resolution' *Aggression and Violent Behaviour* 10, 533–51.

Viemero, V. (1996) 'Factors in childhood that predict later criminal behaviour' *Aggressive Behavior* 22, 87–97.

Vitacco, M.J., Viljoen, J. and Petrila, J. (2009) 'Introduction to this issue: adolescent sexual offending' *Behavioral Sciences and the Law* 27, 857–61.

Vitelli, R. and Endler, N.S. (1993) 'Psychological determinants of fear of crime: a comparison of general and situational prediction models' *Personality and Individual Differences* 145 (1), 77–85.

Vizard, E., Hickey, N., French, L. and McCrory, E. (2007) 'Children and adolescents who present with sexually abusive behaviour: A UK descriptive study' *Journal of Forensic Psychiatry and Psychology* 18 (1), 59–73.

Voumvakis, S.E. and Ericson, R.V. (1982) *New Accounts of Attacks on Women. A Comparison of Three Toronto Newspapers* Toronto: University of Toronto, Centre of Criminology.

Vrij, A. (2000) *Detecting lies and deceit: The psychology of lying and its implications for professional practice* Chichester: John Wiley and Sons.

Vrij, A. (2004) 'Why professionals fail to catch liars and how they can improve' *Legal and Criminological Psychology* 9, 159–81.

Vrij, A. (2005) 'Criteria-based content analysis: a qualitative review of the first 37 studies' *Psychology, Public Policy, and Law* 11, 3–41.

Vrij, A. and Mann, S. (2001) 'Who killed my relative? Police officers' ability to detect real-life high stake lies' *Psychology, Crime and Law* 7, 119–32.

Vrij, A., Mann, S. and Fisher, R.P. (2006) 'An empirical test of the Behaviour Analysis Interview' *Law and Human Behavior* 30, 329–45.

Vrij, A., Mann, S., Kristen, S. and Fisher, R.P. (2007) 'Cues to deception and ability to detect lies as a function of police interview styles' *Law and Human Behavior* 31, 499–518.

Vrij, A., Mann, S.A., Fisher, R.P., Fis Bull, R. (2008) 'Increasing cognitive load to facilitate lie detection: the benefit of recalling an event in reverse' *Law and Human Behavior* 32, 253–65.

W

Wagenaar, W.A., van Koppen, P.J. and Crombag, H.F.N. (1993) *Anchored Narratives: The Psychology of Criminal Evidence* Hemel Hempstead: Harvester Wheatsheaf.

Wagstaff, G.F. (1996) 'Should "hypnotized" witnesses be banned from testifying in court? Hypnosis and the M50 murder case' *Contemporary Hypnosis* 13 (3), 186–90.

Wagstaff, G.F. (1997) 'What is hypnosis?' *Interdisciplinary Science Reviews* 22 (2), 155–63.

Wagstaff, G.F., Green, K. and Somers, E. (1997) 'The effects of the experience of hypnosis, and hypnotic depth, on jurors' decisions regarding the defence of hypnotic automatism' *Legal and Criminological Psychology* 2, 65–74.

Wagstaff, G.F., Macveigh, J., Boston, R., Scott, L., Brunas-Wagstaff, J. and Cole, J. (2003) 'Can laboratory findings on eyewitness testimony be generalized to the real world? An archival analysis of the influence of violence, weapon presence, and age on eyewitness accuracy' *Journal of Psychology: Interdisciplinary and Applied* 137 (1), 17–28.

Wahl, O.F. and Roth, R. (1982) 'Television images of mental illness: results of a metropolitan Washington media watch' *Journal of Broadcasting* 26, 599–605.

Walker, J.S. and Bright, J.A. (2009) 'False inflated self-esteem and violence: a systematic review and cognitive model' *Journal of Forensic Psychiatry and Psychology* 1, 1–32.

Walker, J.S. and Bright, J.A. 'Cognitive therapy for violence: reaching the parts that anger management doesn't reach' *Journal of Forensic Psychiatry and Psychology* 20, 2, April 2009, 174–201.

Walker, L.E. and Meloy, J.R. (1998) 'Stalking and domestic violence' in J.R. Meloy (ed.) *The Psychology of Stalking: Clinical and Forensic Perspectives* San Diego: Academic Press, pp. 139–61.

Walmsley, R., Howard, L. and White, S. (1992) *The National Prison Survey 1991* London: Her Majesty's Stationery Office.

Walsh, A. (1994) 'Homosexual and heterosexual child molestation: case characteristics and sentencing differentials' *International Journal of Offender Therapy and Comparative Criminology* 38, 339–53.

Walter, N. (1996) 'Dead women who suit the news agenda' *Guardian* 18 January, p. 15.

Ward, T. (1997) 'Insanity in summary trials' *Journal of Forensic Psychiatry* 8 (3), 658–61.

Ward, T. (2000) 'Sexual offenders' cognitive distortions as implicit theories' *Aggression and Violent Behavior* 5, 491–507.

Ward, T. and Hudson, S.M. (2001) 'Finkelhor's precondition model of child sexual abuse: a critique' *Psychology, Crime and Law* 7, 291–307.

Ward, T. and Keenan, T. (1999) 'Child molesters' implicit theories' *Journal of Interpersonal Violence* 14, 821–38.

Ward, T. and Siegert, R.J. (2002) 'Towards a comprehensive theory of child sexual abuse: a theory knitting perspective' *Psychology, Crime and Law* 8, 319–51.

Warren, A.R. and Woodhall, C.E. (1999) 'The reliability of hearsay testimony: how well do interviewers recall their interviews with children?' *Psychology, Public Policy and Law* 5 (2), 355–71.

Warren, A.R., Nunez, N., Keeney, J.M., Buck, J.A. and Smith, B. (2002) 'The believability of children and their interviewers' hearsay testimony: when less is more' *Journal of Applied Psychology* 87 (5), 846–57.

Warren, A.R., Woodhall, C.E., Hunt, J.S. and Perry, N.W. (1996) 'It sounds good in theory but . . . : do investigative interviewers follow guidelines based on memory research?' *Child Maltreatment* 1, 231–45.

Warren, J., Kuhn, D. and Weinstock, M. (2010) 'How do jurors argue with one another?' *Judgment and Decision Making* 5 (1), 64–71.

Wason, P.C. (1968) 'Reasoning about a rule' *Quarterly Journal of Experimental Psychology* 20, 273–281.

Waterhouse, L., Dobash, R.P. and Carnie, J. (1994) *Child Sexual Abusers* Edinburgh: Central Research Unit.

Weber, N., Brewer, N. and Wells, G.L. (2004) 'Is there a "magical" decision latency that discriminates correct from incorrect eyewitness identifications?' Paper presented at 14th conference of the European European Association of Psychology and Law, Krakow, Poland.

Weber, N., Brewer, N., Wells, G., Semmler, C. and Keast, A. (2004) 'Eyewitness identification accuracy and response latency: the unruly 10–12 second rule' *Journal of Experimental Psychology: Applied* **10** (3), 139–47.

Webster, M. (2004) 'Do crisis negotiators practice what they preach?' *Canadian Review of Policing Research*, 1. http://crpr.icaap.org/index.php/crpr/article/view/16/15

Weller, M.P. and Weller, B.G. (1988) 'Crime and mental illness' *Medicine, Science, and the Law* **28**, 38–45.

Wells, G.L. (1984) 'The psychology of line-up identifications' *Journal of Applied Social Psychology* **14**, 89–103.

Wells, G.L. (1993) 'What do we know about eyewitness identification?' *American Psychologist* **48**, 553–71.

Wells, G.L. and Quinlivan, D.S. (2009) 'Suggestive eyewitness identification procedures and the Supreme Court's Reliability Test in light of eyewitness science: 30 years later' *Law and Human Behavior* **33**, 1–24.

Wells, G.L., Memon, A., and Penrod, S.D. (2006) 'Eyewitness evidence improving its probative value' *Psychological Science in the Public Interest* **7** (2), 45–75.

Wells, G.L., Small, M., Penrod, S., Malpass, R.S., Fulero, S.M. and Brimacombe, C.A.E. (1998) 'Eyewitness identification procedures: recommendations for line-ups and photospreads' *Law and Human Behavior* **22**, 603–47.

Welsh, B.C., Loerber, R., Stevens, B.R., Stouthamer-Loeber, M., Cohen, M.A. and Farrington, D.P. (2008) 'Costs of juvenile crime in urban areas: a longitudinal perspective' *Youth Violence and Juvenile Justice* **6** (1), 3–27.

Wemmers, J.-A. and Cyr, K. (2006a) 'Victims' perspectives on restorative justice: how much involvement are victims looking for?' *International Review of Victimology* **11** (2–3), 259–74.

Wemmers, J.-A. and Cyr, K. (2006b) 'What fairness means to crime victims: a social psychological perspective on victim-offender mediation' *Applied Psychology in Criminal Justice* **2** (2), 102–28.

Wenzel, M., Okimoto, T.G., Feather, N.T. and Platow, M.J. (2008) 'Retributive and restorative justice' *Law and Human Behavior* **32**, 375–89.

West, D.J. (1982) *Delinquency: Its Roots, Careers and Prospects* London: Heinemann.

West, D.J. (1987) *Sexual Crimes and Confrontations: A Study of Victims and Offenders* Aldershot: Gower.

Westcott, H.L. (1995) 'Children's views on investigative interviews for suspected sexual abuse' *Issues in Criminolo-*gical and Legal Psychology* Leicester: Division of Criminological and Legal Psychology, British Psychological Society.

Western, B. and Pettit, B. (2010) 'Incarceration and social inequality' *Daedalus* **139**, 8–19.

Widom, C.S. (1989) 'The cycle of violence' *Science* **244**, 160–6.

Widom, C.S. and Morris, S. (1997) 'Accuracy of adult recollections of childhood victimization. Part 2 Childhood sexual abuse' *Psychological Assessment* **9** (1), 34–46.

Wiegman, O., Kuttschreuter, M. and Barda, B. (1992) 'A longitudinal study of television viewing on aggressive and prosocial behaviours' *British Journal of Social Psychology* **31**, 147–64.

Williams, D. (2007) 'Effective CCTV and the challenge of constructing legitimate suspicion using remote visual images' *Journal of Investigative Psychology and Offender Profiling* **4**, 97–107.

Williams, J.J. (1995) 'Type of counsel and the outcome of criminal appeals: a research note' *American Journal of Criminal Justice* **9** (2), 275–85.

Williams, K.M., Cooper, B.S., Howell, T.M, Yuille, J.C. and Paulhus, D.L. (2009) 'Inferring sexually deviant behavior from corresponding fantasies: the role of personality and pornography consumption' *Criminal Justice and Behavior* **36**, 198–222.

Williams, M. (1994) 'Murder in mind' *Division of Criminological and Legal Psychology Newsletter* **36**, 9–11.

Williams, W.W. (1991) 'The equality crisis: some reflections on culture, courts and feminism' in K.T. Bartlett and R. Kennedy (eds) *Feminist Legal Theory: Readings in Law and Gender* Boulder, CO: Westview, pp. 15–34.

Willmot, P. (1999) 'Working with life sentence prisoners' *Issues in Forensic Psychology* **1**, 36–8.

Willner, P. (2011) 'Assessment of capacity to participate in court proceedings: a selective critique and some recommendations' *Psychology, Crime and Law* **17** (2), 117–31.

Wilson, H. (1980) 'Parental supervision: a neglected aspect of delinquency' *British Journal of Criminology* **20** (3), 203–35.

Wilson, M. and Smith, A. (2000) 'Rules and roles in terrorist hostage taking' in D. Canter and L. Alison (eds) *The Social Psychology of Crime: Groups, Teams and Networks* Aldershot: Ashgate, pp. 129–51.

Wingrove, T., Korpas, A.L. and Weis, B. (2011) 'Why were millions of people not obeying the law? Motivational influences on non-compliance with the law in the case of music piracy' *Psychology, Crime and Law* 17 (3), 261–76.

Winkel, F.W. (1998) 'Fear of crime and criminal victimisation' *British Journal of Criminology* 38 (3), 473–84.

Winkel, F.W. (2007) *Post Traumatic Anger: Missing Link in the Wheel of Misfortune* Tilburg University: Intervict.

Winkel, F.W. and Blaauw, E. (2001) 'Structured trauma writing (STW) as a victim-supportive intervention: examining the efficacy of emotional ventilation and downward writing' in R. Rosesch, R.R. Carrado and R. Dempster (eds) *Psychology in the Courts: International Advances in Knowledge* London/New York: Routledge, pp. 317–29.

Winkel, F.W. and Vrij, A. (1998) 'Who is in need of victim support? The issue of accountable, empirically validated selection and victim referral' *Expert Evidence* 6, 23–41.

Wissler, R.L. and Saks, M.J. (1985) 'On the inefficiency of limiting instructions: When jurors use prior conviction evidence to decide on guilt' *Law and Human Behavior* 9, 37–48.

Witkin, H.A. and Goodenough, D.R. (1981) 'Cognitive styles: essences and origins, field dependence and field independence' *Psychological Issues Monograph No. 51* New York: International Universities Press.

Witkin, H.A., Mednick, S.A. and Schulsinger, F. (1976) 'Criminality in XY and XYY men' *Science* 193 547–55.

Wogalter, M.S., Malpass, R.S. and McQuiston, D.E. (2004) 'A national survey of US police on preparation and conduct of identification line-ups' *Psychology, Crime and Law* 10 (1), 69–82.

Wojcikiewicz, J., Bialek, I., Desynski, K. and Dawidowicz, A.L. (2000) 'Mock witness paradigm in the casework of the Institute of Forensic Research in Cracow'. Paper presented at the 10th European Conference on Psychology and Law, Limassol, Cyprus.

Wood, J.M. (1996) 'Weighting evidence in sexual abuse evaluations: an introduction to Bayes' theorem' *Child Maltreatment* 1, 25–36.

Wood, W., Wong, F.Y. and Chachere, J.G. (1991) 'Effects of media violence on viewers' aggression in unconstrained social interaction' *Psychological Bulletin* 109 (3), 371–83.

Woodhams, J., Grant, T.D. and Price, A.R.G. (2007) 'From marine ecology to crime analysis: improving the detection of serial sexual offences using a taxonomic similarity measure' *Journal of Investigative Psychology and Offender Profiling* 4, 17–27.

Woodhams, J., Hollin, C.R., and Bull, R. (2007) 'The psychology of linking crimes: A review of the evidence' *Legal and Criminological Psychology* 12, 233–49.

Woodward, R. (1999) 'Therapeutic regimes' *Issues in Forensic Psychology* 1, 39–43.

Woody, W.D. and Forrest, K.D. (2009) 'Effects of false-evidence ploys and expert testimony on jurors' verdicts, recommended sentences, and perceptions of confession evidence' *Behavioral Sciences and the Law* 27, 333–60.

Woolard, J.L., Harvell, S. and Graham, S. (2008) 'Behavioral sciences and the law: anticipatory injustice among adolescents: age and racial/ethnic differences in perceived unfairness of the justice system' *Behavioral Sciences and the Law* 26, 207–26.

Woolley, J.D. (1997) 'Thinking about fantasy: are children fundamentally different thinkers and believers from adults?' *Child Development* 68, 991–1011.

Wootton, I. and Brown, J. (2000) 'Balancing occupational and personal identities: the experience of lesbian and gay police officers' *Newsletter of the BPS Lesbian and Gay Psychology Section* 4 (March), 6–13.

World Health Organization (2011) International Classification of Diseases. http://www.who.int/classifications/icd/en/. Accessed 21 March 2011.

Worling, J.R. (1995) 'Sexual abuse histories of adolescent male sex offenders: differences on the basis of the age and gender of their victims' *Journal of Abnormal Psychology* 104 (4), 610–13.

Wormith, J.A. (1986) 'Assessing deviant sexual arousal: physiological and cognitive aspects' *Advances in Behaviour Research and Therapy* 8 (3), 101–37.

Wormith, J.S. and Oliver, M.E. (2002) 'Offender treatment attrition and its relationship with risk, responsivity, and recidivism' *Criminal Justice and Behavior* 29, 447–71.

Wright, A.M. and Alison, L. (2004) 'Questioning sequences in Canadian police interviews: constructing and confirming the course of events?' *Psychology, Crime and Law* 10 (2), 137–54.

Wright, M. (2002) 'The court as last resort: victim-sensitive, community-based responses to crime' *British Journal of Criminology* 42 (3), 657–67.

Wrightsman, L.S. (2001) *Forensic Psychology* Stamford, CT: Wadsworth.

Wyatt, G.W. (1985) 'The sexual abuse of Afro-American and white American women in childhood' *Child Abuse and Neglect* 9, 507–19.

Wyre, R. (1987) *Working with Sex Offenders* Oxford: Perry.

Wyre, R. (1990) 'Why do men sexually abuse children?' in T. Tate (ed.) *Understanding the Paedophile* London: ISTD/The Portman Clinic, pp. 17–23.

Wyre, R. (1992) 'Pornography and sexual violence: working with sex offenders' in C. Itzin (ed.) *Pornography: Women, Violence and Civil Liberties* Oxford: Oxford University Press, pp. 236–47.

Wyre, R. and Tate, T. (1995) *The Murder of Childhood* Harmondsworth: Penguin.

Y

Yokota, K., Fujita, G., Watanabe, K., Yoshimoto, K. and Wachi, T. (2007) 'Application of the Behavioral Investigative Support System for Profiling Perpetrators of Serial Sexual Assaults' *Behavioral Science and the Law* 25, 841–56.

Yokota, K., Iwami, H., Watanabe, K., Fujita, G. and Watanabe, S. (2004) 'High risk factors of hostage barricade incidents in a Japanese sample' *Journal of Investigative Psychology and Offender Profiling* 1, 139–51.

Yokota, K., Watanabe, K., Wachi, T., Hoshino, A., Sato, A. and Fujita, G. (2007) 'Differentiation of international terrorism: attack as threat, means, and violence' *Journal of Investigative Psychology and Offender Profiling* 4, 131–45.

Yoshikawa, H. (1995) 'Long-term effects of early childhood programs on social outcomes and delinquency' *The Future of Children* 5 (3), 51–75.

Youngs, D. (2004) 'Personality correlates of offence style' *Journal of Investigative Psychology and Offender Profiling* 1, 99–119.

Youngs, D. (2006) 'How does crime pay? The differentiation of criminal specialisms by fundamental incentive' *Journal of Investigative Psychology and Offender Profiling* 3, 1–19.

Yuille, J.C. and Cutshall, J.L. (1986) 'A case study of eyewitness memory of a crime' *Journal of Applied Psychology* 71 (2), 291–301.

Yuille, J.C. and Daylen, J. (1998) 'The impact of traumatic events on eyewitness memory' in C. Thompson, D. Hermann, D. Read, D. Payne and M. Toglia (eds) *Eyewitness memory: Theoretical and applied perspectives* Hillsdale, NJ: Lawrence Erlbaum, pp. 155–78.

Yuille, J.C., Ternes, M. and Cooper, B.S. (2010) 'Expert testimony on laboratory witnesses' *Journal of Forensic Psychology Practice* 10 (3), 238–51.

Z

Zahn, M.A. (2007) 'The causes of girls' delinquency and their program implications' *Family Court Review* 45 (3), 456–65.

Zandbergen, P.A., Levenson, J.S. and Hart, T.C. (2010) 'Residential proximity to schools and daycares: an empirical analysis of sex offense recidivism' *Criminal Justice and Behavior* 37, 482–502.

Zapf, P.A. and Roesch, R. (2001) 'A comparison of American and Canadian conceptualizations of comptence to stand trial' in R. Roesch, R.R. Carrado and R. Dempster (eds) *Psychology in the Courts: International Advances in Knowledge* London: Routledge, pp. 121–32.

Zeisel, H. (1971) 'And then there was none: the diminution of federal jury' *University of Chicago Law Review* 35, 228–41.

Zeisel, H. and Diamond, S.S. (1978) 'The effect of peremptory challenges on jury and verdict: an experiment in a federal district court' *Stanford Law Review* 30, 491–531.

Zillmann, D. (1979) *Hostility and Aggression* Hillsdale, NJ: Lawrence Erlbaum.

Zillmann, D. (1982) 'Television viewing and arousal' in D. Pearl, L. Bouthilet and J. Law (eds) *Television and Behavior: Ten Years of Scientific Progress and Implications for the Eighties* Washington, DC: US Government Printing Office, pp. 53–65.

Name index

Subject index